A Dictionary of Literary Pseudonyms in the English Language

A Dictionary of Literary Pseudonyms

in the English Language

Carty

MANSELL

FITZROY
DEARBORN

PUBLISHERS

First published 1995 by
Mansell Publishing Limited. *A Cassell imprint*
Villiers House, 41/47 Strand, London WC2N 5JE

Published in the United States of America by
Fitzroy Dearborn Publishers
70 East Walton Street, Chicago, Illinois 60611

British Library Cataloguing-in-Publication Data
Carty, Terence John
    Dictionary of Literary Pseudonyms in the English
    Language
    I. Title
    808

    ISBN 0–7201–2221–X

Library of Congress Cataloging-in-Publication Data
A catalog record for this book is available from the Library of Congress.

ISBN 1–884964–13–3 Fitzroy Dearborn

Printed and bound in Great Britain

For Anne and Beth

Contents

Preface

The following work arose from the simple need to discover the true identity of the writer Daniel Chaucer and the apparent absence of any book that would provide the answer. Successive enquiries and note-taking, when looking for other names, produced a dossier of unmanageable proportions and the seeds of the present volume were thus planted. It pretends to no other purpose than to satisfy the curious and to be used as a tool by those fortunate enough to have an interest in books and the book trade.

Given the extent to which most new authors struggle to find a sympathetic publisher, it seems strange that any should disguise their identity. Centuries ago, when an incautious writer might have been rash enough to touch upon some religious or political point of controversy, it probably would have been a prudent precaution and, later on, convention might have dictated that anonymity attach to a learned dissertation on a point of law or religion. Whatever the reasons, many books and pamphlets were published with an impersonal attribution, and we find works by 'A Member of the Church of Scotland', 'A Layman', 'A Barrister-at-Law', 'A Learned Divine' or variants on these themes, all seem to infer reluctant, yet driven and competent authorship. Was it delicacy, modesty or etiquette that led to many women writers assuming the mantle of 'A Lady' or 'A Lady of ...', rather than reveal their real names on their works? Or was it because until comparatively recently there was some insecurity attaching to their income and property rights? Mary Augusta Ward, using her husband's first name, published as Mrs Humphry Ward, achieving astonishing levels of popularity. Many novels by her, and others, appeared originally in serial form in the magazines and journals that blossomed in the nineteenth century.

The subterfuge of pseudonymity continues to be practised, and in the present century the genres of romance, crime and science-fiction have generated so much pseudonymous writing that one can only conclude that the convention is merely playful whimsicality. Here and there a few authors, under their real names, may have carefully nurtured a reputation in some more academic field which they seek to protect from critical obloquy, but, given the respectability attaching to much popular fiction, the camouflage seems to be unnecessary.

The compiler, whose real name appears below, accepts all responsibility for any errors or omissions and, being aware that no work such as this is ever complete, requests the reader's indulgence, if only to avoid future pseudonymity. It is appropriate here to express gratitude to those friends and colleagues who have given support and encouragement in the preparation of this work, in particular to Jack Skinner and his family.

T. J. Carty

Arrangement of the Material

In the manner of a good Ordnance Survey map, a reference work should be easy to follow and in setting out the information a straightforward alphabetical approach has been adopted. The dictionary is in two parts. Part I lists pseudonyms in alphabetical order, against which are set the real names of the writers. Part II lists real names, providing brief details about the author and his or her use of the pseudonym, together with some titles of the books or journals where the false name was used. However, no entries should be assumed to be complete bibliographies, as that task lies outside the scope of the present work. Where possible, the best-known title or titles are given.

An asterisk against a pseudonym in Part II indicates joint, or in some cases triple, authorship.

The use of the definite and indefinite article has been ignored. as have the prefixes Mr and Mrs. Familial titles such as Uncle or Aunt appear under U or A as appropriate, as do more formal titles such as Doctor, General, Countess etc., which appear under D, G and C. Names with prefixes, such as De Vere and Le Fevre, are treated as one word. Different pseudonyms used by one person writing for journals are grouped by journal title.

Select Bibliography

Arnott, J. F. and Robinson, J. W. *English Theatrical Literature, 1559–1900*. London: Society for Theatre Research, 1970.

Ash, B. *Who's Who in Science Fiction*. London: Elm Tree Books, 1976.

Book Auction Records. Folkestone: Dawson, pubd annually.

British Library, Department of Printed Books. *British Library General Catalogue of Printed Books to 1975*. London: 1960, 1966, 1971, 1976.

Burke, W. J. and Howe, D. *American Authors and Books, 1640 to the Present Day*. New York: Crown, 1972.

Cambridge Bibliography of English Literature. Cambridge: Cambridge University Press, 1947–77.

Cushing, W. *Initials and Pseudonyms*. New York: Thomas Crowell, 1885–8.

Daiches, D. *The Penguin Companion to Literature*. Harmondsworth: Penguin Books, 1971.

Dictionary of American Biography. London: Milford; New York: Charles Scribner, 1928– .

Dictionary of Australian Biography. Melbourne: Melbourne University Press, 1966– .

Dictionary of Canadian Biography. Toronto: University of Toronto Press, 1968– .

Dictionary of National Biography. Oxford: Oxford University Press, 1885– .

Doyle, B. *Who's Who of Boys' Writers and Illustrators*. London: the Editor, 1964.

Drabble, Margaret. *Oxford Companion to English Literature*. Oxford: Oxford University Press, 1985.

Eighteenth-Century British Books: an Author Union Catalogue. Folkestone: Dawson, 1981– .

Encyclopedia Britannica. 11th edn, Chicago: Encyclopedia Britannica, 1912.

Fletcher, Ifan Kyrle. *Edward Gordon Craig: a Bibliography*. London: Society for Theatre Research, 1967.

Hagen, Ordean A. *Who Done It? A Guide to Detective, Mystery and Suspense Fiction*. New York: Bowker, 1969.

Halkett, S. and Laing, J. *Dictionary of Anonymous and Pseudonymous English Literature*. Edinburgh: Oliver and Boyd, 1926–62.

Harbage, Alfred. *Annals of English Drama 975–1700*. London: Methuen, 1964.

Hart, James D. *Oxford Companion to American Literature*. Oxford: Oxford University Press, 1956.

Harvey, P. *Oxford Companion to English Literature*. Oxford: Oxford University Press, 1973.

International Authors and Writers Who's Who. Cambridge: Cambridge International Biographical Centre, 1934– .

Knight, Charles. *Cyclopedia of Biography*. London: Bradbury & Evans, 1858.

Longman's Guide to Twentieth-Century Literature. London: Longman, 1970.

Olderr, Steve. *The Mystery Index*. Chicago: American Library Association, 1987.

Schwartz, Dr Jacob. *1100 Obscure Points*. Bristol: Chatford House Press, 1969.

Sturm, Terry. *Oxford Companion to New Zealand Literature*. Oxford: Oxford University Press, 1991.

Todd, Janet. *Dictionary of British Women Writers*. London: Routledge, 1989.

Toye, William. *Oxford Companion to Canadian Literature*. Oxford: Oxford University Press, 1983.

The Wellesley Index to Victorian Periodicals 1824–1900. Toronto: University of Toronto Press, 1966– .

Who Was Who. London: A & C Black, 1929– .

Who's Who. London: A & C Black, 1897– .

Who's Who in America. Chicago: Marquis, 1899– .

Who's Who in American History. Chicago: Marquis, 1963– .

Wilde, William H., Hooton, Joy and Andrews, Barry. *Oxford Companion to Australian Literature*. Oxford: Oxford University Press, 1991.

The Writer's Directory 1992–94. London: St James Press, 1991.

Part I

Pseudonyms

A

A.
Matthew Arnold
Benjamin Brierley
Ann Taylor
Bonnell Thornton

A. A.
George A. A. Willis

A. A. M.
Alan Alexander Milne

A. B.
Aphra Behn
Gilbert Burnet
Abraham Cowley
Edward Gordon Craig
Robert Ferguson
Zachary Grey
George Grote
Simon Harcourt
Nathaniel Lardner
Richard Newton
Samuel Rosewell

A. B. C.
Edward Gordon Craig

A. C.
Anthony Collins

A. E.
George William Russell

A. E. C.
Edward Alexander Crowley

A. F. Y.
Sir Charles Vinicombe Penrose

A. G. O. T. U . C.
Owen Manning

A. K. H. B.
Andrew Kennedy Hutchinson
Boyd

A. K. M.
Alan Alexander Milne

A. L. B.
Anna Letitia Barbauld

A. L. O. E.
Charlotte Maria Tucker

A. M.
Alice Christiana Gertrude
Meynell

A. P. H.
Sir Alan Patrick Herbert

A. R.
Allan Ramsay

A. R. P.-M.
John Galsworthy

A. S., PHILOMATH
Abraham Sharp

A. S. – 'Anthony Shandy'
John Hall Stevenson

ABANYA
Thomas Percy Boyd

ABATI, FRANCESCO
William Winwood Reade

ABBE ROBIN
Philip Freneau

ABBEY, KIERAN
Helen Reilly

ABBOT, ANTHONY
Charles Fulton Oursler

ABBOTT, A. A.
Samuel Spewack

ABBOTT, ALICE
Kathryn Borland

ABBOTT, SARA
Charlotte Zolotow

ABDALLAH
Otway Curry

a' BEAR, HOWARD
Donald Howard Boalch

ABHAVANANDA
Edward Alexander Crowley

AN ABOLITIONIST
Thomas Fisher

AB-O'TH'-YATE
Benjamin Brierley

ABRABANEL, SOLOMON
William Arnall

**ABRAHAM, RECHOBOAM
BEN**
William Edmonstoune Aytoun

ABRICHT, JOHANN, A. M.
Jonathan Birch

AN ABSENT BROTHER
Daniel Wilson

**AN ABSENTEE RESIDING IN
BATH**
Edward Mangin

AN ABSTINENCE MAN
John Usher Parsons

**AN ACADEMIC IN THE
METROPOLIS**
Richard Graves

ACADEMICUS
William Pulteney Alison
John Loveday
Aulay MacAulay
William Nind
Charles Seager

ACALUS
Thomas Mounsey Cunningham

ACANTHUS
H. Frank Hoar

ACER
Henry Glassford Bell

ACHATES
Thomas Pinckney

ACHETA DOMESTICA
M. L. Budgen

ACKLAND, RODNEY
Norman Ackland Bernstein

ACKWORTH, JOHN
Frederick R. Smith

ACRE, STEPHEN
Frank Gruber

ACTAEA
Mrs Elizabeth Agassiz

ACTON, LLEWELLYN
Wynne Edwin Baxter

AN ACTRESS
Mrs Anna Cora Ritchie

ADAIR, ALAN
Mrs Everett Holloway

ADAIR, CECIL
Evelyn Everett-Green

ADAIR, HAZEL
Hazel Iris Addis

ADAIR, JAMES
Sir Richard Phillips

ADAMS, ABRAHAM
Henry Fielding

ADAMS, ANDY
Walter B. Gibson

ADAMS, BART
David Ernest Bingley

ADAMS, CHUCK
Edwin Charles Tubb

ADAMS, DANIEL
Christopher Robin Nicole

ADAMS, HARRISON
St George Henry Rathbone

ADAMS, JUSTIN
Lou Cameron

ADAMS, MRS LEITH
Mrs Bertha Jane Laffan

ADAMS, WILL
John Neal

ADAMS, WILLIAM
Sampson Perry

ADDERTONGUE, ALICE
Benjamin Franklin

ADDIO, E. I.
Barry Fantoni

ADDISCOMBE, JOHN
Alfred John Hunter

ADELBERG, DORIS
Doris Orgel

ADELER, MAX
Charles Heber Clark

ADELINE
Miss Emily Frances Adeline
Sergeant

AN ADEPT
Charles Johnson (or Johnstone)

AN ADEPT IN THE ART OF
TRIFLES
Richard Graves

ADIDNAC
Lily C. Whitaker

ADINA
Joseph Holt Ingraham

ADJUTANT TROWELL
Thomas Dawes

ADJUTOR
Joseph Bretland

ADKINS, M. D.
Ezra Pound

ADLARD, MARK
Peter Marcus Adlard

ADLER, IRENE
Catherine Storr

ADMIRARI, NIL, ESQ.
Frederick William Shelton

AN ADMIRER
Stephen Lucius Gwynn

AN ADMIRER OF GREAT
GENIUS
Stephen Weston

AN ADMIRER OF
MONARCHY AND
EPISCOPACY
Zachary Grey

AN ADMIRER OF WALTER
SCOTT
John Roby

ADMONISH CRIME
James Cook Richmond

ADONEY, FRANCIS
Gladys Ellen Easdale

ADRIAN
James L. Cole

ADRIAN, FRANCES
Madeleine Polland

ADRIAN, LESLIE
Jean Robertson

ADVENA
Digby Pilot Starkey

AN ADVOCATE
James Boswell

AN ADVOCATE OF THE
CHRISTIAN
REVELATION
Caleb Fleming

AN ADVOCATE OF THE
CIVIL LAW IN
SCOTLAND
Sir George Mackenzie

AESCHINES
Francis William Blagdon

AESOP
Lillie Devereux Blake

AFFABLE HAWK
Sir Desmond MacCarthy

AN AFFLICTED HUSBAND
Cuthbert Shaw

AFRICANUS
Sir Malcolm Cotter Cariston
Seton

AFRIKANDER
John C. Higginbotham

AFTEREM, GEORGE
Harold Williams

AFTERWIT, ANTHONY
Benjamin Franklin

AGAPIDO, FRIAR ANTONIO
Washington Irving

AGATE
Whitelaw Reid

AGATE, JUNIPER
Thomas Spencer Baynes

AN AGED MAN
Richard Warner

AN AGED MINISTER
Moses Dickinson

AN AGED PERSON
Sir William Blizard

AN AGED PRIEST
Thomas Thellusson Carter

AN AGENT OF THE
CORPORATION
Caleb Eddy

AGHILL, GORDON
Robert Silverberg with Randall
Garrett

AGLAUS
Henry Timrod

AGNUS, ORME
John C. Higginbotham

AGO, FELIX
Samuel Stehman Haldeman

AGRESTIS
John Alston

AGRICOLA
James Anderson
John Ballantyne
William Elliott
John Galt
Percival Stockdale
John Young

AGUECHEEK
Charles Bullard Fairbanks

AHERN, ANNA
Mrs Frances West Pike

AHIEZER
William Brown

AIKIN, BERKELEY
Miss Fanny Aikin Kortright

AIKMAN, HENRY G.
Harold Hunter Armstrong

AILO, THORNY
John Taylor

AIMWELL, WILLIAM
William Simonds

AINSBURY, RAY
Alpheus Hyatt Verrill

AINSLEIGH, NOEL
Edith Lister

AINSLIE, ARTHUR
Arthur Wellesley Pain

AINSLIE, HERBERT
Edward Maitland

AINSWORTH, HARRIET
Violet Elizabeth Cadell

AINSWORTH, RUTH
Ruth Gilbert

AIRD, CATHERINE
Kinn Hamilton McIntosh

AIRLIE, CATHERINE
Jean Sutherland MacLeod

AIRY, HARRIET
Mary Darwall

AKERS, ALAN BURT
Henry Kenneth Bulmer

AKERS, FLOYD
Lyman Frank Baum

AL SIDDIK
Frederick William Rolfe

AN ALABAMAN
Johnson Jones Hooper

ALADDIN
Jonathan Duncan

ALAN, A. J.
Leslie Harrison Lambert

ALAN, MARJORIE
Doris Marjorie Bumpus

ALAZONOMASTIX PHILALETHES
Henry More

ALB
Richard Whiteing

ALBAN, ANTONY
Antony Thompson

ALBANICUS
David Steuart Erskine

ALBANY, JAMES
Hugh Crawford Rae

ALBERT
John Armstrong

ALBRAND, MARTHA
Heidi Huberta Freybe Loewengard

ALBYN
Andrew Shiels

ALCAEUS
Samuel Boyse

ALCIBIADES
James Anderson
Alfred (Lord) Tennyson

ALCOTT, MAY
Louisa May Alcott

ALCOTT, TEN
Charles Adriel Lewis Totten

ALDEN, SUE
Dorothy Brenner Francis

ALDING, PETER
Roderic Jeffries

ALDINGTON, RICHARD
Edward Godfree Aldington

ALDON, ADAIR
Cornelia Meigs

ALDRICH, DARRAGH
Clara C. Thomas Aldrich

ALDYNE, NATHAN
Michael McEachern McDowell

ALENA
Fanny Parnell

ALEPH
William Harvey

ALETHES
Thomas H. Baird
William Cowper

ALETHITHERAS
Laughton Osborn

ALETHOPHILUS GOTTINGENSIS
George William Alberti

MRS ALEXANDER
Annie French Hector

ALEXANDER, JOHN, A JOYNER
John Taylor

ALEXANDER, KENNETH
Alexander Kennedy

ALEXANDER THE CORRECTOR
Alexander Cruden

ALFRED
Samuel Adams
Sir James Bland Burges

David Alfred Doudney
Philip Withers

ALGOL
Cyril Herbert Emmanuel Bretherton

ALI BEY
Samuel Lorenzo Knapp

ALIDA
Mrs Catharine Ladd

ALIEN
Louisa Alice Baker

ALIQUANTO LATIOR
John Gairdner

ALIQUIS
Richard Marks

ALIST
Francis Foster Barham

ALITOPHILUS
Robert Fludd

ALLAN, DENNIS
Elinore Denniston

ALLAN, SYDNEY
Sadakichi Hartmann

ALLAN, TED
Allan Herman

ALLARDYCE, PAULA
Ursula Torday

ALLEN, ALEX B.
Florence Parry Heide

ALLEN, BETSY
Betty Cavanna

ALLEN, ERIC
Eric Allen Ballard

ALLEN, F. M.
Edmund Downey

ALLEN, GRACE
Grace Allen Hogarth

ALLEN, GRAHAM
George Arnold

ALLEN, GRANT
Charles Grant Blairfindie Allen

ALLEN, HUGH
Charles Morris

ALLEN, JAMES
Paul Ader

ALLEN, JOHN
Oscar Clute

ALLEN, JOHN W., JUN.
Peter Lesley

ALLEN, LUKE
William Lacy Amy

ALLEN, ROLAND
Alan Ayckbourne

ALLEN, WILLIAM
Edward Sexby

ALLENDALE, ALFRED
Theodore Edward Hook

ALLERDYCE
Robert Barclay Allardice

ALLERTON, MARK
William Ernest Cameron

ALLERTON, MARY
Mary Govan

ALLEYNE, ELLEN
Christina Georgina Rossetti

ALLISON, CLAY
Henry John Keevill

ALLMAN, JONATHAN
Robert Arthur Wilson

ALLSPY, TOBY
Mrs Catherine Frances Grace
Gore

ALLYSON, KYNN
John M. Kimbro

ALMAVIVA
Clement William Scott

ALMORE, CASPAR
Frederick Williamson Beasley

ALPHA
William Henry Leatham

ALPHA CRUCIS
Robert Dudley Adams

ALPHA OF THE PLOUGH
Alfred George Gardiner

ALPHONSO
John Nichols

ALTAMOUNT
Charles Jenner

ALTER EGO
Robert Edmund Strahorn

ALTHEA
Althea Braithwaite

ALTISONANT, LORENZO
Samuel Klinefelter Hoshour

AN ALUMNUS
Josiah A. Quincy

ALVA
Maurice Stewart Collis

ALVIDAS
Henry Clay Hodges

ALVORD, BURT
Henry John Keevill

AN AMATEUR
Charles Badham
Bernard Barton
William Cox
John Eagles
Francis Grant
James Kirke Paulding
Charles Kirkpatrick Sharpe
Charles Winston

AMATEUR ANGLER
Edward Marston

AN AMATEUR GARDENER
William Earl Johns

**THE AMATEUR LAMBETH
CASUAL**
James Greenwood

AN AMATEUR OF FASHION
John Roby

AN AMATEUR TRAVELLER
James Watson Webb

AMBER
Martha Everts Holden

AMBER, MILES
Ellen M. Sickert

AMBERLEY, RICHARD
Paul Henry James Bourquin

AMBROSE, G. B.
Edward Gordon Craig

AMBROSE, PAUL
John Pendleton Kennedy

AMELIA
Mrs Amelia B. Welby

AN AMERICAN
Robert Baird
Richard Biddle
Henry M. Brackenridge
Mathias Bruen
George Henry Calvert
Thomas Greaves Cary
Lewis Cass
Mrs Lydia Mary Child
David Christy
Benjamin Church
William Cobbett
Moncure Daniel Conway
James Fenimore Cooper
James Ellsworth De Kay
Charles Wyllys Elliott
William Elliott
David Everett
Stephen Fiske
Joseph Galloway
Duff Green
Alexander Hamilton
Francis Lister Hawks
Joseph Hopkinson
Freeman Hunt
Charles Inglis

Arthur Lee
Charles Edwards Lester
Henry Wadsworth Longfellow
Cotton Mather
Samuel Finley Breese Morse
Sidney Edwards Morse
John Lothrop Motley
Henry Pickering
Benjamin Young Prime
Theodore Sedgwick
Nathan Sheppard
John Lloyd Stephens
Henry Theodore Tuckerman
Noah Webster
Hezekiah Hartley Wright

**AN AMERICAN
ABOLITIONIST**
Moncure Daniel Conway

AN AMERICAN AGNOSTIC
John Lawson Stoddard

**AN AMERICAN AMATEUR IN
EUROPE**
James Jackson Jarves

AN AMERICAN ARTIST
Laughton Osborn

AN AMERICAN CITIZEN
Linus Pierpont Brockett
William Beach Lawrence
Charles Randolph
Orville James Victor
James Barr Walker

AN AMERICAN CLERGYMAN
James Cook Richmond

**THE AMERICAN CONSUL
AT LONDON**
Freeman Harlow Morse

**AN AMERICAN
ENGLISHMAN**
Samuel Mather

AN AMERICAN FARMER
William Cobbett
George Logan
Frederick Law Olmsted

**AN AMERICAN, FORMERLY
A MEMBER OF
CONGRESS**
Fisher Ames

AN AMERICAN GENTLEMAN
Richard Alsop
William Clifton
Calvin Colton
Washington Irving
Benjamin Young Prime

**AN AMERICAN GENTLEMAN
IN PARIS**
John Sanderson

AN AMERICAN IN ENGLAND
Alexander Slidell Mackenzie

AN AMERICAN IN LONDON
Calvin Colton

AN AMERICAN IN THE
SERVICE OF THE
VICEROY
George Bethune English

AN AMERICAN LADY
Mrs Anne Grant
Mary Elizabeth Wormeley
Latimer

AN AMERICAN LONG
RESIDENT AT
CONSTANTINOPLE
David Porter

AN AMERICAN LOYALIST
Jonathan Boucher

THE AMERICAN MINISTER
AT PARIS
Lewis Cass

AN AMERICAN MISSIONARY
IN CHINA
Elihu Doty

AN AMERICAN NAVY
OFFICER
Nathaniel Fanning

AN AMERICAN OFFICER IN
THE SERVICE OF
FRANCE
John Skey Eustace

AN AMERICAN PASTOR
Thomas Bacon

AN AMERICAN RECENTLY
RETURNED FROM
EUROPE
Robert Walsh

AN AMERICAN REPUBLICAN
John Russell Young

AN AMERICAN RESIDENT
Samuel Hawkins Marshall
Byers

AN AMERICAN RESIDENT
IN PARIS
Charles Brooks

AN AMERICAN SHIPMASTER
John Codman

AN AMERICAN STUDENT-
GIRL
Emma Louisa Parry

AN AMERICAN TRAVELLER
Alexander Cluny
Isaac Appleton Jewett

AN AMERICAN WANDERER
Arthur Lee

AN AMERICAN YOUTH
Royall Tyler
John Woodworth

AMERICANUS
Edward James Cattell

AMERUS
Alexander Chalmers

AMES, FELICIA
Jean P. Burden

AMES, JENNIFER
Maysie Greig

AMES, LUCIA TRUE
Lucia Ames Mead

AMGIS
Lucius Manlius Sargent

AMICUS
John Canton
Sir Thomas Fairbairn
Benjamin Kent
Joseph Lancaster
Alexander Michie

AMICUS CURIAE
John Payne Collier

AMICUS PATRIAE
William Burt
John Wise

AMORY, ARTHUR R.
Charles Spenser Sarle

AMOS, ALAN
Kathleen More Knight

AMYAND, ARTHUR
Edward Arthur Haggard

AMYNTOR
Jeremy Belknap

AN CRAO BHIN AOIBHINN
Douglas Hyde

AN GALL FADA (or FADD)
Sean O'Casey

AN PILIBIN
John Hacket Pollock

AN ANALYTICAL TEACHER
John Usher Parsons

ANALYTICUS
James Waterman Wise

ANCHOR
John Watts De Peyster

AN ANCIENT ACTOR
Edward Bellasis

AN ANCIENT BRAHMIN
Robert Dodsley

AN ANCIENT
CONTRIBUTOR
James White

AN ANCIENT DOCTOR OF
PHYSICK
Walter Harris

ANDERS, REX
Geoffrey John Barrett

ANDERSON, ELLA
Ellen MacLeod

ANDERSON, LINDSAY
Alexander Christie

ANDERSON, RALPH
Robert Heron

ANDERSON, W. B.
James Willard Schultz

ANDOM, ROBERT
Alfred Walter Barrett

ANDRE, W. J.
William Jerdan

ANDRESS, LESLEY
Laurence Sanders

ANDREW, JAMES, A. M.
Andrew Mackay

ANDREW, STEPHEN
Frank George Layton

ANDREWS, CORINNE
Cicily Isabel Fairfield

ANDREWS, JOHN
John Malcolm

ANDREWS, WENDY
Marjorie W. Sharmat

ANDREZEL, PIERRE
Karen Blixen

ANGELINA
Thomas Peckett Prest

ANGELL, SIR NORMAN
Ralph Norman Angell Lane

ANGELO, MASTER
MICHAEL
Richard Johnson

ANGELONI, BATTISTA
John Shebbeare

ANGELOU, MAYA
Marguerite Annie Johnson

AN ANGLER
Sir Humphry Davy
Charles Lanman
Thomas Tod Stoddart

AN ANGLICAN LAYMAN
Edward Bellasis

AN ANGLICAN SINCE
BECOME A CATHOLIC
Edward Bellasis

ANGLIPOLOSKI
Daniel Defoe

AN ANGLO-EGYPTIAN CIVIL SERVANT
Charles Robert Ashbee

ANGLO-HIBERNIAN
Zachariah Johnson

AN ANGLO-PARISIAN JOURNALIST
Emily Crawford

ANGLO-PHILE EUTHEO
Anthony Munday

ANGLOMANE
Antonio Carlo Napoleone Gallenga

ANGUS, IAN
James Alexander Mackay

ANICETUS
William Adolphus Clark

AN ANIMAL PAINTER
James Wilson

ANMAR, FRANK
William Francis Nolan

ANN OF SWANSEA
Mrs Julia Ann Curtis

ANNESON, JAMES
James Maxwell

ANNOSUS FIDELIS VERIMENTANUS DRUINUS
John Floyd

ANNOTATOR
John Calder

ANOBIUM PERTINAX
William Hand Browne

ANODOS
Miss Mary Elizabeth Coleridge

ANONYMOUS
Edward Gordon Craig
John Disney

AN ANONYMOUS CLERGYMAN
Charles Owen

ANOTHER GENTLEMAN OF CAMBRIDGE
John Duncombe

ANOTHER HAND
John Twysden

ANOTHER LAWYER
George Chalmers

ANSER-PEN-DRAG-ON ESQ.
William Henry Ireland

ANSKEY, S.
Solomon Rappoport

ANSTEY, F.
Thomas Anstey Guthrie

ANSTRUTHER, GILBERT
Russel S. Clark

ANSTRUTHER, JOHN
Richard Horatio Edgar Wallace

ANTENOR
Thomas James Mathias

ANTHONY, C. L.
Dodie (Dorothy Gladys) Smith

ANTHONY, DAVID
William Dale Smith

ANTHONY, EVELYN
Evelyn Ward Thomas

ANTHONY, JOHN
Ronald Brymer Beckett

ANTHONY, PETER
Peter Levin Shaffer with Anthony Shaffer

ANTHONY, PIERS
Piers Anthony Dillingham Jacob

ANTHROPHILOS
Charles Edward De Coetlogon

ANTHROPOS
George Storrs

ANTI-COTTON
Robert Arthur Talbot Gascoyne Cecil

ANTI-DRACO
John Disney

ANTI-EMPIRICUS
John Wesley Thomas

ANTI-ENTHUSIASTICUS
Charles Chauncy

ANTI-HARMONICUS
Alexander Peterkin

ANTI-INNOVATOR
William Pitt Scargill

ANTI-MONOPOLY
William Duane

ANTI-PASTOR
Matthew Tindal

ANTI-PROFANUS
Abraham Portal

ANTI-SCOT
Joseph Ritson

ANTI-SEJANUS
James Scott

ANTICIPATION
John Dickinson

AN ANTIQUARIAN
Royal Ralph Hinman
Henry Phillips

AN ANTIQUARIAN DOCTOR
Thomas Amory

ANTIQUARIUS
John Bowen
John Loveday

AN ANTIQUARY
Walter De Gray Birch
Philip de la Motte
Samuel Pegge
Richard Thomson
Nathaniel H. J. Westlake
Thomas Wright

THE ANTIQUARY
George Livermore

ANTIQUITATIS CONSERVATOR
Thomas Fisher

ANTISOCINUS
Anselm Bayly
John MacGowan

ANTITYPE
Daniel Isaac Eaton

ANTIWELLSTOP
James Boswell

ANTLER, LILIAN
Edward Gordon Craig

ANTON, C.
Augustus Hoppin

ANTONELLI, GUISEPPE
Humphrey Sandwith

ANTONIO
Denis Florence MacCarthy

ANVIL, CHRISTOPHER
Harry C. Crosby

APE
Carlo Pellegrini

THE APOLOGIST
David Huntington

APPLETON, VICTOR
Mrs Harriet Stratemeyer Adams

AN APPRENTICE OF LINCOLN'S INN
Sir Frederick Pollock

AN APPRENTICE OF THE LAW
Percival Weldon Banks

APRIL, STEVE
Leonard S. Zinberg

APT, J.
Edward Gordon Craig

AQUAE HOMO, A. B.
Jotham Waterman

AQUARIUS
Lowis d'Aquilar Jackson

AQUILA
Samuel Alexander

AQUILIUS
John Eagles
John Wilson

AR. CY. DAE.
Romesh Chunder Dutt

ARACHNOPHILUS
Adam White

ARAMIS
William Dutton Burrard

ARBOR, JANE
Eileen Owbridge

ARCH, E. L.
Rachel Cosgrove Payes

ARCHDEACON CHASUBLE
Thomas William Marshall

AN ARCHAEOLOGIST
Frederick William Fairholt
Henry Noel Humphreys

ARCHAEUS
Michael Aislabie Denham
John Sterling

THE ARCHDEACON OF ST ALBANS
Samuel Horsley

ARCHER, A. A.
Archie Lynn Joscelyn

ARCHER, E. M.
Eleanor Ashworth Towle

ARCHER, FRANK
Richard O'Connor

ARCHER, LANE
Louise Platt Hauck

ARCHER, LEE
Harlan Ellison

ARCHER, RON
Theodore Edward White with
Dave Van Arnam

ARCHETTE, GUY
Chester S. Geier

ARCHIBALD, MRS GEORGE
Anna Campbell Palmer

ARCHIMAGIRUS METAPHORICUS
William Kenrick

ARCHIMEDES
Archibald Pitcairne

AN ARCHITECT
John Carter
Arthur William Hakewill
Charles James Richardson
John Burley Waring
George Wightwick
Joseph Woods

ARCTURUS
Mrs Catharine Ladd

ARD, WILLIAM
John William Jakes

ARDELIA
Anne Finch, Countess of
Winchilsea

ARDEN, CLIVE
Lily Clive Nutt

ARDEN, H. T.
Henry Thomas Arnold

ARDEN, J. E. M.
George Robert Acworth
Conquest

ARDEN, W. H.
Wystan Hugh Auden

ARDEN, WILLIAM
Dennis Lynds

ARDESIER-MACDONALD, CHARLES OLIVER, ESQ.
Andrew Kennedy Hutchinson
Boyd

ARETA, MAVIS
Mavis Winder

ARETINO
George Croly

ARETOPHILUS
Alexander Dalrymple

ARGUS
Irwin Willes

ARIEL
Buckner H. Payne

ARISTARCHUS
Edmund Henry Barker

ARISTEDES
Noah Webster

ARISTIDES
James Anderson
Francis William Blagdon
Thomas Wilson Dorr
Alexander Contee Hanson
Thomas Lorraine McKenny
William Peter Van Ness

ARISTIPPUS
John Gilbert Cooper

ARISTOBULUS
Thomas Woolston

ARISTOCLES
Samuel Johnson

ARKE, SIMON
Clifford Howard

ARKWRIGHT, PELEG
David Law Proudfit

ARLEN, LESLIE
Christopher Robin Nicole

ARLEN, MICHAEL
Dikran Kouyoumdjian

ARLEY
Miles Peter Andrews

ARLINGTON
Robert M. Baxter

AN ARMENIAN IN IRELAND
Edmund Sexton Pery

ARMIG, S. P.
Samuel Pordage

ARMITAGE, HAZEL
John Wheway

ARMSTRONG, ANTHONY
George A. A.Willis

ARMSTRONG, DAVID
Winston Clewes

ARMSTRONG, FYTTON
Terence Ian Fytton Armstrong

ARMSTRONG, GEOFFREY
John Russell Fearn

ARMSTRONG, RAYMOND
Norman Lee

ARMYTAGE, DUDLEY (or ERNEST)
William Edward Armytage
Axon

ARNETT, CAROLINE
Lois Dwight Taylor

ARNEY, JAMES
Martin James Russell

ARNO, PETER
Curtis Arnoux Peters

ARNOLD, BIRCH
Mrs Alicia Elinor Bartlett

ARNOLD, JOSEPH H.
Joseph Hayes

ARNOLD, CAPT. MALCOLM
Andrew Nicholas Murray

ARNOLD, MARGOT
Petronelle Marguerite Mary
Cook

ARNOLD, MARY AUGUSTA
Mrs Humphry Ward

AROUET
Joseph Brown Ladd

ARP, BILL
Charles Henry Smith

ARR, E. H.
Mrs Ellen Chapman Rollins

ARRE, HELEN
Zola Helen Ross

ARROW, WILLIAM
Donald Pfeil
William Rotsler

ARTEMAS
Arthur Telford Mason

ARTHUR, FRANK
Frank Arthur Ebert

ARTHUR, PETER
Arthur Porges

ARTHUR, T. C.
Arthur Travers Crawford

ARTHUR, WILLIAM
William Arthur Neubauer

ARTLOVE, SIR ANDREW
John Dennis

ARUNDEL, MARK
Dr Marie Carmichael Stokes

ARUNDO
John Beever

ARVILL, ROBERT
Robert Edward Boote

AN ARYAN
Forster Fitzgerald Arbuthnot

AS I PLEASE
Eric Arthur Blair

ASCOTT, ADELIE
John William Bobin

ASH, FENTON
Frank Atkins

ASH, PETER
Louise Platt Hauck

ASHDOWN, CLIFFORD
Richard Austin Freeman

ASHE, DOUGLAS
John Franklin Bardin

ASHE, GORDON
John Creasey

ASHE, MARY ANNE
Mary Christianna Brand

ASHFIELD, HELEN
Pamela Bennetts

ASHFORD, JEFFREY
Roderic Jeffries

ASHLEY, ANTHONY, JR.
Frank Gray Griswold

ASHLEY, ELLEN
Elizabeth Seifert

ASHLEY, FRED
Frank Atkins

ASHMORE, RUTH
Mrs Isabella Allerdice Mallon

ASHTON, ANN
John M. Kimbro

ASHTON, HELEN
Helen Rosalie Jordan

ASHTON, SHARON
Helen Van Slyke

ASHTON, TEDDY
Charles Allen Clarke

ASHTON, WARREN T.
William Taylor Adams

AN ASIATIC LIBERAL
George Burges

ASIATICUS
John Scott Waring

ASKARI, HASANI MUHAMMAD
Harold Bertram Pereira with Mabel Yeates

ASMODEO
Richard Brinsley Sheridan

AN ASPIRANT
James Beresford

ASSIAC
Heinrich Fraenkel

ASTARTE
Mrs Ann Olivia Adams

ASTLEY, JULIET
Norah Lofts

ASTOLAT, JOHN
Jack Haigh

ASTON, JAMES
Terence Hanbury White

ASTON, TONY
Anthony Aston

ASTOR, HERBERT
Xavier Herbert

ASTRA CIELO
Milton Goldsmith

ASYNCRITUS
John Eliot Howard

AT THE SIGN OF THE BLUE MOON
Dominic Bevan Wyndham Lewis

ATALL, PETER
Robert Waln

ATHELING, WILLIAM
Ezra Pound

ATHELING, WILLIAM, JR.
James Blish

ATHERTON, HARPER
Frank Fowler

ATKINSON, MARY
Mollie Hardwick

ATLEE, PHILIP
James Atlee Phillips

ATOM
Hubert Edward Henry Jerningham

ATTALUS
William Mudford

ATTERLEY, JOSEPH
George Tucker

ATTICUS
John Buchan
De Witt Clinton
Thomas Cooke
Isaac D'Israeli
Richard Fitzwilliam
Sir Philip Francis

ATTICUS SECUNDUS
John M' Diarmid
Joseph Bolles Manning

AN ATTORNEY
Samuel Warren

AUBEPINE
Nathaniel Hawthorne

AUBERON, REGINALD
Horace Cowley Wyndham

AUBREY, FRANK
Frank Atkins

AUCHTERLONIE, DOROTHY
Dorothy Green

AUDAX
John Geoffrey Tristram

AUDI ALTERAM PARTEM
Thomas Perronet Thompson

AUDITOR
Thomas Gibson Bowles

AUGUR
William Blake
Henry Mort Feist

AUGUST, JOHN
Bernard Augustine de Voto

AUGUSTINUS
William Maginn

AUGUSTUS, ALBERT, JR.
Charles A. Neutzel

AUNT ABBIE
Miss Abby Skinner

AUNT BELINDA
Mrs Mary Elizabeth Maxwell

AUNT CARRIE
Mrs Caroline L. Smith

AUNT CARRY
Caroline Elizabeth Sarah
Norton

AUNT CHARLOTTE
Charlotte Mary Yonge

AUNT DOROTHY
Henrietta Georgiana Lascelles,
Lady Chatterton

AUNT ELLA
Amy Ella Blanchard

AUNT ELMINA
Mrs Elmina D. Slenker

AUNT FANNY
Frances Elizabeth Barrow
Mrs Frances Dana Gage

AUNT FRIENDLY
Mrs Sarah S. Baker

AUNT HATTIE
Mrs Harriette Newell Baker

AUNT JANE
Jane Crewdson
Christian Isobel Johnstone

AUNT JO
Louisa May Alcott

AUNT JUDY
Margaret Gatty

AUNT KITTY
Maria Jane McIntosh

AUNT LILY
Lily F.Wesselhoeft

AUNT LOUISA
Mrs Laura Valentine

AUNT LOUISE
Louisa May Alcott

AUNT LUCY
Lucy Elizabeth Bather

AUNT MARY
Miss Mary A. Lathbury

AUNT PATTY
Mrs Caroline Lee Hentz

AUNT SUSAN
Mrs Elizabeth Prentiss

AUNT WEE
Louisa May Alcott

AUNTIE BEE
Bertha H. Buxton

AURELIUS GRATIANUS
John Mason Neale

**AURELIUS PRUDENTIUS,
AMERICANUS**
Samuel Mather

AURORA
Arthur Gordon Smith

AUSPEX
John Buchan

AUSTIN, BRETT
Lee Floren

AUSTIN, FRANK
Frederick Schiller Faust

AUSTIN, HUGH
Hugh Austin Evans

AN AUSTRALIAN
Anna Maria Murray

AN AUSTRALIAN LADY
Mrs Caroline Louisa Waring
Calvert

**AN AUSTRALIAN
POLITICIAN**
Sir Charles Gavan Duffy

AUSTWICK, JOHN
Austin Lee

AN AUTHOR
William Warburton

AUTODICUS
Laughton Osborn

AUTOLYCUS
Leonard Bacon
Michael Aislabie Denham
Alice Christiana Gertrude
Meynell

AUTOMATHES
Richard Griffith

AUTREMONDE
Aubrey Neville St John
Mildmay

AVALON, ARTHUR
Sir John George Woodroffe

AVELLANO, ALBERT
Dan James Marlowe

AVERY, A. A. (or AL)
Rutherford George
Montgomery

AVERY, RICHARD
Edmund Cooper

AVIA
Arthur S. Way

AVON, W.
William Kenrick

AWAHSOOSE THE BEAR
Rowland Evans Robinson

AXIOLOGUS
William Wordsworth

AXTON, DAVID
Dean R. Koontz

AYDY, CATHERINE
Emma Tennant

AYE, JOHN
John Atkinson

**AYES, ANTHONY (or
WILLIAM)**
William Anthony Sambrot

AYLMER, FELIX
Felix Edward Aylmer Jones

AYMAR, PATTERSON
Charles Knight

AYRE, THORNTON
John Russell Fearn

AYRE, WILLIAM, ESQ.
Edmund Curll

AYRES, ALFRED
Thomas Embly Osmun

AYRES, PAUL
Edward Sidney Aarons

AYRTON, J. CALDER
Mary Frances Chapman

AYRTON, MICHAEL
Michael Ayrton Gould

AYSCOUGH, JOHN
Francis B. D. Bickerstaffe-
Drew

B

B.
Robert Bland
John Buchan
George Canning

B. B.
Benjamin Franklin
Baroness Nairne, Carolina
    Oliphant
Denys James Watkins-Pitchford

B. L.
Ezra Pound

B. M.
Bernard Mandeville

B. V.
James Thomson

BAB
Sir William Schwenk Gilbert

BABBLE, NICHOLAS
Edward Long

THE BABBLER
Hugh Kelly

BACH, SEBASTIAN
John Arthur Andrews

A BACHELOR
Donald Grant Mitchell

A BACHELOR OF ARTS
Phyllis Eleanor Bentley

A BACHELOR OF DIVINITY
William Josiah Irons
Edward Bouverie Pusey

BACHMAN, RICHARD
Stephen King

A BACKPEWMAN
Elihu Burritt

**BACKSIGHT
    FORETHOUGHT**
Sir Ernest Dunlop Swinton

A BACKWOODSMAN
William Dunlop
Thomas D'Arcy M'Gee

BACON, J. SOMERS
Edward Gordon Craig

BAGATELLE
Arthur Greville Bagot

BAGBY, GEORGE
Aaron Marc Stein

BAGWEEL
Joshua Barnes with Benjamin
    Avery, Benjamin Grosvenor,
    Samuel Wright, John Evans,
    W. Eames and Moses
    Lowman

BAILEY, FRANK
Bailey Millard

BAILEY, HILEA
Ruth Leonore Marting

BAINE, JEFF
Geoffrey John Barrett

BAIRD, DOROTHEA
Mrs Dorothea Irving

BAKER, ASA
Davis Dresser

BAKER, FRANK, D. O. M.
Sir Richard Francis Burton

BAKER, J., KNIGHT
Alexander Pope

**BALANCE, A., ESQ. OF THE
    MIDDLE TEMPLE**
Thomas Binney

BALANCE, JOHN
Edward Gordon Craig

BALBUS
Julian Sorell Huxley

BALDWIN, EDWARD
William Godwin

BALFOUR, CLARA
Mrs Felicia Dorothea Hemans

BALFOUR, FAIRFAX
Watts Phillips

BALLARD, K. G.
Holly Roth

BALLASTIR, CAD MAC
Thomas Cooper De Leon

BALLEW, CHARLES
Charles Horace Snow

BALTIMORE, J.
Arthur Catherall

BALWHIDDER, MICAH
John Galt

BAMFYLDE, Walter
Thomas Bevan

BANCROFT, LAURA
Lyman Frank Baum

BANDANA
John Galt

THE BANJO
Andrew Barton Paterson

BANK, W. DANE
William Henry Williamson

**THE BANKRUPT
    BOOKSELLER**
William Young Darling

BANKS, ARCHIBALD
Oswald John Crawfurd

BANNATYNE, COLIN
William Dunlop

BANNATYNE, JACK
William James Gaston

BANNER, ANGELA
Angela Mary Maddison

BANNON, MARK
Albert King

BANNON, PETER
Paul Durst

BANTON, COY
Victor G. C. Norwood

A BAPTIST
Henry Burgess
Thomas Comber

BARAGWENETH, BARZILLAI
Mrs Charlotte Champion
    Pascoe

BARAKA, I. A.
Leroi Jones

BARBARA
Mrs Mabel Osgood Wright

BARBAROSSA
John Scott

BARBELLION, W. N. P.
Bruce Frederick Cummings

BARBER, A.
Joseph Moser

BARBER, ANTONIA
Barbara Anthony

BARBETTE, JAY
Bart Spicer

BARBICAN, GEOFFREY
Richard Thomson

BARCLAY, ANN
Maysie Greig

BARCLAY, BILL
Michael Moorcock

BARCLAY, MARGUERITE
Marguerite Florence Jervis

BARD
George Monck Berkeley

THE BARD
William MItchell Banks
Edward Jerningham

BARD, SAMUEL A.
Ephraim George Squier

BAREACRES, HON. BOTIBOL
John Burley Waring

BAREBONE, ISSACHAR
James Ralph

BAREBONES, CAUSTIC, A BROKEN APOTHECARY
Thomas Bridges

BARFLEUR
Sir Reginald Neville Custance

BARLAY, BENNETT
Kendell Foster Crossen

BARLING, CHARLES
Muriel Barling

BARNABAS, OBADIAH
John Allen

BARNACLE, CAPT. B.
Charles Martin Newell

BARNARD, A. M.
Louisa May Alcott

BARNAVAL, LOUIS
Charles De Kay

BARNES, NANCY
Helen Simmons Adams

BARNIVELT, ESDRAS, APOTH.
Alexander Pope

BARNWELL
Robert Barnwell Roosevelt

BARON, ALEXANDER
Joseph Alexander Bernstein

BARON, ANTHONY
Augustus Baker

BARON DE BOOK-WORM
Sir Henry William Lucy

BARONE, MIKE
Marvin Hubert Albert

THE BARONET
William Maginn

BARR, NAT
Norman Molyneux Goddard

BARRETT, REV. J.
William Maginn

BARRETT, MARY
Mary Olivia Nutting

BARRETT, WALTER, CLERK
Joseph Alfred Scoville

BARRINGTON, E.
Eliza Louisa Moresby Beck

BARRINGTON, GEORGE
George Waldron

BARRINGTON, JOHN
John Henry Harvey

BARRINGTON, MAURICE
Sir Denis William Brogan

BARRINGTON, MICHAEL
Michael Moorcock with
Barrington J. Bayley

BARRINGTON, NICHOLAS
Richard Whittington-Egan

BARRINGTON, PAMELA (or P. V.)
Muriel Barling

BARRINGTON, RUTLAND
George Rutland Barrington-Fleet

A BARRISTER
Edward Lowth Badeley
Thomas Banister
Melville M. Bigelow
Sir John Barnard Byles
Thomas Osborne Davis
Richard Fenton
Barron Field
Henry Coleman Folkard
Frederick Lawrence
John MacGregor
Sir Stafford Henry Northcote

Charles Erdman Petersdorff
John Reeves
William Roberts
James Sedgwick
Sir James Fitzjames Stephen

A BARRISTER-AT-LAW
Wiltshire Stanton Austin
Sir John Eardley Eardley-Wilmot
Sir Benjamin Hobhouse
Sir John Lithiby
Samuel Warren

A BARRISTER-AT-LAW OF LINCOLN'S INN
Thomas Denman

A BARRISTER-AT-LAW OF OSGOODE HALL
Robert Vashon Rogers

A BARRISTER OF LINCOLN'S INN
John Malcolm Ludlow

A BARRISTER OF THE INNER TEMPLE
Leonard MacNally
George Spence
Thomas Edlyne Tomlins

A BARRISTER OF THE TEMPLE
George Wharton Marriott

BARROW, REV. S.
Sir Richard Phillips

BARROWCLIFFE, A. J.
Albert Julius Mott

BARRY, CHARLES
Charles Bryson

BARRY, JOCELYN
Jean Bowden

BARRY, MIKE
Barry N. Malzburg

BARSAC, LOUIS
Ernest James Oldmeadow

BARTHOLOMEW, JEAN
Patricia Beatty

A BARTHOLOMEW-LANE MAN
Alexander Chalmers

BARTIMAEUS
Henry Patterson

BARTIMEUS
Sir Lewis Anselmo Ritchie

BARTLETT, NANCY
Charles Stanley Strong

BARTON, E.
Sir William Cusac Smith

BARTON, ERLE (or LEE)
Robert Lionel Fanthorpe

BARTON, JAMES (or JON)
John B. Harvey

BARTROPP, JOHN
Sir Philip Harold Pilditch

A BASHFUL IRISHMAN
William Frederick Deacon

BASIL
Richard Ashe King

BASILICUS
Lewis Way

BASILISK
Alfred Higgins Burne

BASILLE, THEODORE
Thomas Becon

BASS, T. J.
Thomas J. Bassler

BASSET, ARTHUR WARD
Albert E. Bull

BASSETT, JOHN KEITH
Lawrence Alfred Keating

BATES, JENNY
Maura Seger

BATH, JAMES (or OLIVER)
Edward Gordon Craig

BATHONIENSIS
Jonas Dennis

BATTLE, FELIX
Henry Bernard Levin

MR BAVIUS
John Martyn

BAWDEN, NINA
Nina Mary Kark

BAX, ROGER
Paul Winterton

BAXTER, GEORGE OWEN
Frederick Schiller Faust

BAXTER, GREGORY
Eric De Banzie

BAXTER, OLIVE
Helen Eastwood

BAXTER, SHANE
Victor G. C. Norwood

BAXTER, SIMEON, A LICENTIATE
Samuel Andrew Peters

BAXTER, VALERIE
Laurence Walter Meynell

MR BAYLE
Henry Penneck

BAYLEBRIDGE, WILLIAM
Charles William Blocksidge

BAYLEY, ALPHABET
Frederic W. N. Bayley

BAYONET, BRYAN, OF THE FIRST REGIMENT OF GUARDS
John Henley

BEACHCOMBER
John Bernard Arbuthnot
Dominic Bevan Wyndham Lewis
John Bingham Morton

BEALE, STEPHEN
Sir Edward Brown

BEAN, NORMAN
Edgar Rice Borroughs

BEATON, GEORGE
Edward Fitzgerald (Gerald) Brenan

BEAUCHAMP, PHILIP
George Grote

BEAUCLERK, HELEN
Helen Mary D. Bellingham

BEAUFORT, JOHN
John Thelwall

BEAUJOLAIS
Hans Busk

BEAUJON, PAUL
Mrs Beatrice Warde

BEAUMONT, AVERIL
Mrs Margaret Hunt

BEAUMONT, SIR HARRY
Joseph Spence

BEAUMONT, JOSEPH
James Everett

A BEAUTIFUL AND UNFORTUNATE YOUNG LADY
Thomas Sedgwick Whalley

BEAVER, BARRINGTON
William Henry Giles Kingston

BECCARIA ANGLICUS
Richard Wright

BECK, CHRISTOPHER
Thomas Charles Bridges

BECK, LILY ADAMS
Eliza Louisa Moresby Beck

BECKETT, WALTER
Martin À Beckett Boyd

BECKLES, GORDON
Gordon Beckles Willson

BECKWITH, LILLIAN
Lillian Comber

BEDE, CUTHBERT
Edward Bradley

BEDE, SETH
Samuel Evans

BEDFORD, JOHN
Phyllis Dora Hastings

BEE, JOHN
John Badcock

THE BEE-HUNTER
Thomas Bangs Thorpe

BEEDING, FRANCIS
John Leslie Palmer with Hilary A. St George Saunders

BEETHOVEN, BRONZE, A LOOKER-ON
John Turner Sargent

BEGGARSTAFF, J. and W.
William Newzam Prior Nicholson with James Pryde

A BEGGING LETTER WRITER
Henry Fothergill Chorley

BEKE, X.
George Hammond Hawtayne

BELBIN, HARRY
Henry J. Garrish

BELGIAN HARE
Lord Alfred Douglas

A BELIEVER
Zachary Grey
Thomas Mangey

A BELIEVER IN DREAMS
John Rutter Chorley

A BELIEVER IN THE INTERNAL EVIDENCE OF DIVINE REVELATION
William Horatio Clarke

BELINDA
James Heywood

BELIS, ANDREW
Samuel Beckett

BELL, ACTON
Anne Bronte

BELL, CATHERINE
Rosemary Weir

BELL, CURRER
Charlotte Bronte

BELL, ELLIS
Emily Jane Bronte

BELL, GEORGIANA
Anne Rundle

BELL, JANET
Eleanor Lowenton Clymer

BELL, JOSEPHINE
Doris Bell Ball

BELL, LAURA
Julia May Williamson

BELL, NEIL
Stephen Southwold

BELL, PAUL
Henry Fothergill Chorley

BELL, SOLOMON
William Joseph Snelling

BELL, THORNTON
Robert Lionel Fanthorpe

BELLAIRS, GEORGE
Harold Blundell

BELLOC, MARIA ADELAIDE
Mrs Marie Belloc Lowndes

BELPHEGOR
William Combe

BELVOIR, RICHARD
George Darley

BEN TALLYHO
Henry Alken

BENAULEY
Lyman Abbott with Benjamin
    Vaughan Abbott and Austin
    Abbott

BEND, PALMER
George Palmer Putnam

BENDIGO, BENJAMIN
William Makepeace Thackeray

BENEDICT
Joseph Reed

A BENEFICED CLERGYMAN
Henry Soames

A BENEFICED MINISTER
Edward Pearse

BENENGELI, CID HAMET
Thomas Babington Macaulay

BENEVOLUS
William Duncombe

A BENGAL CIVILIAN
William Edwards
Antony Patrick MacDonnell
John Muir
Charles James O'Donnell

A BENGAL OFFICER
John Jacob
John Scott Waring

BENISON, PAUL
John Walter Sherer

BENJAMIN THE
    FLORENTINE
Benjamin Peirce

BENNET, H.
John Pinkerton

BENNETT, DWIGHT
Dwight Bennett Newton

BENNETT, ELIZABETH
Cynthia Harrod-Eagles

BENNETT, H. O.
Osborne Bennett Hardison

BENNETT, JOHN
John Thomas Lutz

BENSON, CARL
Charles Astor Bristed

BENSON, DANIEL
Colin Symons Cooper

BENSON, EDGEWORTH
John Scott

BENSON, THERESE
Emilie Benson Knipe

BENT, JAMES
John Dunton

BENTLEY, JAMES
James Hanley

BENTLEY, JAYNE
Jayne Ann Krentz

BENTLEY, WALTER
Walter Begg

BENTON, JOHN
Edward Gordon Craig

BENTON, JOHN L.
Norman A. Danberg

BENTON, WILL
Lauren Bosworth Paine

BENVOLIO
Anna Seward

A BEREAN
John Cameron

BEREANUS THEOSEBES
William Hazlitt

A BEREAVED HUSBAND
John Mockett Cramp

BERKELEY, ANTHONY
Anthony Berkeley Cox

THE BERKELEY MEN
Charles Edwards Lester and
    Edwin Williams

BERKLEY, MRS HELEN
Mrs Anna Cora Ritchie

A BERKSHIRE CLERGYMAN
Robert Eldridge Aris Willmott

A BERKSHIRE FARMER
John Osborne Sargent

BERNARD, HENRY
Henry Baerlein

BERNARD, ROBERT
Robert Bernard Martin

BERNARDUS UTOPIENSIS
John Rutty

BERRETTON, GRANDALL
Randall Garrett

BERRINGTON, JOHN
Alan Charles Brownjohn

BERRISFORD, JUDITH M.
Clifford Lewis with Mary
    Lewis

BERRY, ERICK
Allena Best

BERTE, HAL
John Thomas Brown

BERWICK, MARY
Adelaide Anne Procter

BERYLLUS
Joseph Priestley

BESCHTER, REV. JOHN
Anthony Kohlman

BESIEGED RESIDENT
Henry Dupre Labouchere

BESTON, HENRY
Henry Beston Sheahan

BET, U.
Robert William Wright

BETHEL, J.
Bryan Waller Procter

BETTERIDGE, ANNE
Margaret Potter

BETTERIDGE, DON
Bernard Newman

BETTERTON, MR THOMAS
William Oldys

BETTINA
Bettina Ehrlich

BEULAH
Miss Fanny D. Bates

BEVAN, ALISTAIR
Keith Roberts

BEVANS, NEILE
Mrs Nellie B. Van Slingerland

BEWLEY, RICHARD, MD
Robert Harrington

BEYER, SYLVIA
John Glassco

BEYNON, JANE
Jane Lewis Brandt

BEYNON, JOHN
John Beynon Harris

A BIBLE STUDENT
Francis Foster Barham
William Cooke Taylor

BIBLICUS
Joseph Priestley
William Thorn
Alexander Tilloch

BIBLIOPHILE
Samuel Austin Allibone

BIBOLET, R. H.
Tim Kelly

BICKERDYKE, JOHN
Charles Henry Cook

BICKERSTAFF, ISAAC
Sir Richard Steele
Jonathan Swift
Benjamin West

THE BIDEFORD POSTMAN
Edward Capern

BIDULPH, MISS SIDNEY
Frances Sheridan

BIGLOW, HOSEA
James Russell Lowell

BIGLY, CANTELL A.
George Washington Peck

BILBO, JACK
Hugo Cyril K. Baruch

BILDJE, JASPER
John Edgell Rickword

BILLABER, SHE P.
Benjamin Penhallow Shillaber

BIILLINGS, JOSH
Henry Wheeler Shaw

BINDER, EANDO
Otto O. Binder with Earl
Binder

BIOGRAPH TRIGLYPH
Richard Griffith

BION
Robert Southey

BIRCH, REV. BUSBY
Bonnell Thornton

BIRCH, CYRIL
Ko Lien Hua Ying

BIRCHLEY, WILLIAM
John Austin

BIRD, CORDWAINER
Harlan Ellison

BIRD, LEWIS
Cecil Goodenough Hayter

BIRD, WILLIAM
Jack Butler Yeats

BIRD, ZENOBIA
Laura Zenobia Le Fevre

BIRKLEY, DOLAN
Julia Dolores Hitchens

BIRMINGHAM, GEORGE A.
James Owen Hannay

**A BIRMINGHAM
CLERGYMAN**
John Cale Miller

A BIRMINGHAM RESIDENT
William Hamper

BIRO, VAL
Balint Stephen Biro

BISHOP, JOHN
Edward (Ted) Henry Willis

BISHOP, MORCHARD
Oliver Stoner

THE BISHOP OF CLOYNE
George Berkeley

BISSET
William Henry West Betty

BLACK, ERNEST
Ernest Hubert Lewis Schwarz

BLACK, GAVIN
Oswald Wynd

BLACK, ISHI
Walter B. Gibson

BLACK, LAURA
Roger Erskine Lomgrigg

BLACK, LIONEL
Dudley Barker

BLACK, MANSELL
Trevor Dudley-Smith

BLACK, ROBERT
Robert P. Holdstock

BLACK, VERONICA
Maureen Peters

THE BLACK DWARF
Thomas Jonathan Wooler

BLACKBURN, JOHN
J. Molden Mott

BLACKBURNE, E. OWENS
Elizabeth Casey

BLACKLIN, MALCOLM
Aidan Chambers

BLACKMANTLE, BERNARD
Charles Molloy Westmacott

BLACKSHEEP, REV. MR
William Hone

**BLACKSTOCK, CHARITY (or
LEE)**
Ursula Torday

BLAINE, SARA
Diana Morgan

BLAIR
Wallace Wilfrid Blair-Fish

BLAIR, REV. DAVID
Sir Richard Phillips

BLAIR, FRANK
Samuel Buckley

BLAIR, HAMISH
J. F. Andrew Blair

BLAISDELL, ANNE
Elizabeth Linington

BLAKE
Ronald Adam

BLAKE, ANDREA
Anne Weale

BLAKE, CAMERON
Michael Henry Mason

BLAKE, ELEANOR
Eleanor Blake Pratt

BLAKE, JENNIFER
Patricia Anne Maxwell

BLAKE, JUSTIN
John Griffith Bowen

BLAKE, KEN
Kenneth Henry Bulmer

BLAKE, MARGARET
Lila Clara Schem

BLAKE, NICHOLAS
Cecil Day-Lewis

BLAKE, PATRICIA
Clive Egleton

BLAKE, PAUL
Harry Major Paull

BLAKE, SALLY
Jean Saunders

BLAKE, SEXTON
William Arthur Howard Baker

BLAKE, STEPHANIE
Jack Pearl

BLANC BEC
Thomas Gibson Bowles

BLANCHAN, NELTJE
Nellie Blanchan Doubleday

BLANCHE CROIX
Charles Edward Long

BLAND, EDITH
Edith Nesbitt

BLAND, FABIAN
Hubert Bland with Edith
Nesbitt

BLAND, JENNIFER
Jean Bowden

BLASIUS MULTIBIBUS
Richard Brathwaite

BLAYN, HUGO
John Russell Fearn

BLAYNE, DIANA
Susan E. S. Kyle

BLAYRE, CHRISTOPHER
Edward Heron-Allen

BLEDDYN
David Owen

BLEECK, OLIVER
Ross E. Thomas

BLEEKER, SONIA
Sonia Elizabeth Zim

BLENKINSOP, VICESSIMUS
Theodore Edward Hook

BLIGHT, ROSE
Germaine Greer

THE BLIND PREACHER
William Henry Milburn

THE BLIND TRAVELLER
James Holman

BLINKHOOLIE
William Allison

BLISS, ELIOT
Eileen Bliss

BLISS, REGINALD
Herbert George Wells

BLOBBS, PETER
Reginald Brooks

A BLOCKADE RUNNER
John Wilkinson

BLODGETT, LEVI
Theodore Parker

BLOT, THOMAS
William Simpson

BLOWER, AMINADAB
John Taylor

A BLUE
Robert Huish

BLUE JACKET
John Adolphus Bernard
Dahlgren

BLUE WOLF
Joyce Reason

BLUEMANTLE, BRIDGET
Elizabeth Thomas

A BLUENOSE
George E. Fenety

BLUFF, BACHELOR
Oliver Bell Bunce

BLUFF, HARRY
Matthew Fontaine Maury

BLUNDELL, PETER
Frank Nestle Butterworth

BLUNT, BENJAMIN
Andrew Valentine Kirwan

BLUNT, DON
Edwin Booth

BLY, NELLY
Elizabeth Cochrane Seaman

BLYTH, JOHN
John Alfred Blyth Hibbs

BLYTHE, HENRY
Geoffrey Henry Cecil Bing

BLYTHE, J. A. ST JOHN
Sophie Frances Fane Veitch

BOAKE, CAPEL
Doris Boake Kerr

BOB, TOALLT
William Graham

BOBBIN, PAUL
James Butterworth

BOBBIN, TIM
John Collier

BOBSON, G.
James White

BOCCA, AL
Bevis Winter

BOCCALINI, TROJANO
Matthias Earbery

BOCHKOVSKY, ELENA
Lola Marie Therese Granville-
Barker

BODEN, HILDA
Hilda Esther Bodenham

BOEHM, LISE
Elise Williamina Giles

MRS BOGAN OF BOGAN
Baroness Nairne, Carolina
Oliphant

BOGGY, TOM
William King

BOLDREWOOD, ROLPH
Thomas Alexander Browne

BOLITHO, WILLIAM
William Bolitho Ryall

BOLSTER, EVELYN
Sister Mary Angela Bolster

BOLT, BEN
Ottwell Binns

BOLT, JUDSON
Cecil E. Hughes with Bertram
Atkey

BOLTON, EVELYN
Anne Evelyn Bunting

BOLTON, ISABEL
Mary Britton Miller

BOMBARDINIO
John Mitchell

A BOMBAY OFFICER
John Jacob

BON GAULTIER
William Edmonstoune Aytoun
with Sir Theodore Martin

BOND, J. HARVEY
Russell Robert Winterbotham

BONEHILL, CAPT. RALPH
Edward Stratemeyer

BONERTO
Nicholas Breton

BONETT, EMERY
Felicity Winifred Carter

BONETT, JOHN
John Hubert Coulson

BONHORST, V.
Frederick William Rolfe

BONMOT, EGOMET
Thomas Griffiths Wainewright

BONNAMY, FRANCIS
Mrs Audrey Walz

BONNER, PARKER
Willis Todhunter Ballard

BONNER, SHERWOOD
Katherine Sherwood Bonner
MacDowell

BONNER, TERRY NELSON
Chelsea Quinn Yarbro

BONNEY, BILL
Henry John Keevill

BONO-JOHNNY
Alexander Charles Fraser

**BONSTITTLE, ADONIRAM,
alias TINDERBOX**
Thomas Flatman

BOOBY, BILL
George Yellott

BOOKMAN, CHARLOTTE
Charlotte Zolotow

A BOOKSELLER
Henry George Bohn
John Dunton

A BOOKWORM
Walter Besant

BOON, FRANCIS
Edward Bacon

MR BOOT
Thomas Bray

BOOT, WILLIAM
Tom Stoppard

BOOTH, GEOFFREY
Jennifer Tann

BOOTH, IRWIN
Edward D. Hoch

BORAX
James Boswell

BORER, MARY CATHCART
Mary Hortense Myers

A BORN NATURAL
Henry Ellison

BORODIN, GEORGE
George Alexis Milkomanovich
Milkomane

BORROW, CHARLES
Edward Gordon Craig

BORTH, WILLAN G.
Willan G. Bosworth

BOS
Thomas Peckett Prest

BOSCAWEN
Nathaniel Greene

BOSCHER, HERMANN
Andrew Lang

BOSSUT, ABBE
Sir Richard Phillips

BOSTON, CHARLES K.
Frank Gruber

THE BOSTON BARD
Robert Stevenson Coffin

A BOSTON BOY
Andrew Eliot Belknap

A BOSTON MERCHANT
Silas Pinckney Holbrook
Amos W. Stetson

A BOSTONIAN
Samuel Adams
William Bentley Fowle
John Lowell
Edgar Allen Poe
Benjamin Bussey Thatcher

BOSWELL, ROGER
Hugo Reid

BOSWELL REDIVIVUS
William Hazlitt

BOTHERALL, SIR CHARLES
Percival Weldon Banks

BOTHWELL, ADAM
Peter Dunsmore Howard

BOTTOME, PHYLLIS
Mrs Ernan Forbes-Dennis

BOUCHER, ANTHONY
William Anthony Parker White

BOUNCE, BENJAMIN, ESQ.
Henry Carey

BOUNCEYCORE, DION
Francis Cowley Burnand

BOURDON, HILAIRE
George Tyrrell

BOURGEOIS
Lewis B. France

BOURNE, GEORGE
George Sturt

BOURNE, LESLEY
Evelyn Marshall

BOURNE, PETER
Graham Montague Jeffries

BOUSTROPHEDONIDES, JOHANNES
Alexander William Crawford
Lindsay

BOUVERIE, BARTHOLOMEW
William Ewart Gladstone

BOUVERIE, LIONEL
John Humphrey St Aubyn

BOWDEN, JIM
William John Duncan Spence

BOWEN, MARJORIE
Margaret Long

BOWER, BARBARA
Barbara Euphan Todd

BOWER, B. M.
Mrs Bertha Muzzey Sinclair

BOWERS, J. MILTON
Ambrose Bierce

BOWIE, JIM
Victor G. C. Norwood

BOWIE, SAM
Willis Todhunter Ballard

BOWOOD, RICHARD
Albert Scott Daniel

BOWYANG, BILL
Alexander Vindex Vennard

BOWYER, LESLIE C.
Leslie Charles Bowyer Yin

BOWYER, WILLIAM
William Bowyer Honey

BOX, EDGAR
Eugene Luther Vidal

BOXER
William James

A BOY
Charles Nordhoff
Samuel Smiles

BOYD, BELLE
Mrs Belle Hardinge

BOYD, FRANK
Frank Kane

BOYD, JOHN
Boyd Bradfield Upchurch

BOYD, NANCY
Edna St Vincent Millay

BOYD, WALTER, ESQ.
William Combe

BOYLE, HENRY
William Henry Ireland

BOYLSTON, PETER
George Ticknor Curtis

BOYNE, FELIX
William Patrick Ryan

BOZ
Charles Dickens

BRABAZON, JAMES
Leslie James Seth-Smith

BRACE, BENJAMIN
Ben Frederick McCutcheon

BRACE, TIMOTHY
Theodore Pratt

BRACHT, FRANZ WILHELM V.
Frederick William Rolfe

BRACKETT, LEIGH
Mrs Leigh Brackett Hamilton

BRADBURY, EDWARD
Michael Moorcock

BRADDON, GEORGE
George Alexis Milkomanovich
Milkomane

BRADDON, MARY E.
Mrs Mary Elizabeth Maxwell

BRADLEY, JOHN
James Anthony Lawson

BRADLEY, MORETON C.
Alfred Maurice Low

BRADLEY, SHELLAND
Francis Bradley Birt

BRADWELL, JAMES
Arthur William Charles Kent

BRADWOOD, WAT
Walter Bradford Woodgate

BRADY, NICHOLAS
John Victor Turner

BRADY, WILLIAM S.
John B. Harvey

BRAHAM, GEORGE
Lewis George Robinson

BRAHMS, CARYL
Doris Caroline Abrahams

BRAIN-WORKMAN, J.
Joshua Williams

BRAINERD, NORMAN
Samuel Richard Fuller

BRALLAGHAN, BARNEY
Edward Vaughan Hyde
Kenealy

BRAMAH, ERNEST
Ernest Bramah Smith

BRAMBLE, MATTHEW
Andrew MacDonald

BRAMBLE, TABITHA
Mary Robinson

BRAMWELL, CHARLOTTE
John M. KImbro

BRAND, CLAY (or VICTOR)
Victor G. C.Norwood

BRAND, MAX
Frederick Schiller Faust

BRANDANE, JOHN
John MacIntyre

BRANDEL, MARC
Marcus Beresford

BRANDON, FRANK
Henry Kenneth Bulmer

BRANDON, ISAAC
William Combe

BRANDON, JOE
Robert Prunier Davis

BRANDON, SHEILA
Claire Rayner

BRANDT, ELLIS
Peter Bayne

BRANDT, TOM
Thomas Blanchard Dewey

BRAYTON, COULTHART
Charles Harry Moody

BREACHAN
Rev. Robert Stephen Hawker

BREITMANN, HANS
Charles Godfrey Leland

BRENNAN, D.
Eric Lambert

BRENNAN, JOHN
Mrs Sidney Czira

BRENNAND, FRANK
Eric Lambert

BRENNING, L. H.
Alfred John Hunter

BRENT OF BIN BIN
Miles Franklin

BRENT, FRANCIS
Alfred John Hunter

BRENT, LINDA
Mrs Harriet Jacobs

BRENT, LORING
George Frank Worts

BRENT, MADELEINE
Peter O'Donnell

BRENT, NIGEL
Cecil Gordon E. Wimhurst

BRENT-DYER, ELINOR M.
Gladys Eleanor May Dyer

BRERELY, JOHN
Laurence Anderton

BRERETON, FORD
Samuel Rutherford Crockett

BRETT, GEORGE IRA
Oswald John Crawfurd

BRETT, HAWKESLEY
Robert Stanley Warren Bell

BRETT, LEO
Robert Lionel Fanthorpe

BRETT, MICHAEL
Miles Barton Tripp

BRETT, ROSALIND
Kathryn Blair

BREVET MAJOR PINDAR
PUFF
Gulian Crommelin Verplanck

BREWSTER, BENJAMIN (or
FRANKLIN)
Franklin Brewster Folsom

BRIAN, JAMES
Arthur George Street

BRIARTON, GRENDAL
Reginald Bretnor

BRICK, TITUS A.
John Camden Hotten

THE BRICKLAYER
Henry Jones

BRIDGE, ANN
Mary Dolling O'Malley

BRIDGER, ADAM
David Ernest Bingley

BRIDGES, BEN
David Henry Whitehead

BRIDGES, MADELINE
Mary de Vere

BRIDGWATER, BENJAMIN
John Dunton

BRIDIE, JAMES
Osborne Henry Mavor

MR BRIEFLESS
Gilbert Abbott À Beckett

BRIEFLESS, A., JUNIOR
Arthur William À Beckett

BRIEFLESS, BARNABY
Gilbert Abbott À Beckett

BRIEFLESS, GEOFFREY,
BARRISTER-AT-LAW
Thomas Percy Boyd

BRIGHTE, JOHN
John Duncan

BRIGHTLAND, JOHN
Sir Richard Steele

BRIGHTWELL, RICHARD
John Frith

BRINE, BARNABY, ESQ.
William Henry Giles Kingston

BRISCO, P. A. (or PATTY)
Patricia A. Matthews

BRISK, RICHARD
John Duncan

A BRISTOL CHURCH-GOER
Henry Thomas Ellacombe

BRITAIN, DAN
Donald Eugene Pendleton

BRITAIN'S REMEMBRANCER
George Wither

BRITANNICUS
Mark Akenside
George Clement Boase
Henry Boase
Thomas Burgess
Edward Gordon Craig
Thomas Doubleday
Neil Douglas
Sir Philip Francis
William Grant
John Stockdale Hardy
Benjamin Hoadly
Samuel Johnson

William Kirby
Charles Lucas
Allan Ramsay Jr.
Francis Randolph

BRITANNUS
James Boswell
Edmund Curll

A BRITISH AUTHOR
Arthur Helps

A BRITISH CANADIAN
Henry James Morgan

A BRITISH COMMONER
Edward Rupert Humphreys

A BRITISH DIPLOMAT
Lord Frederic Spencer
Hamilton

A BRITISH FIELD-OFFICER
Lt.-Col. Arthur Campbell Yate

A BRITISH FREEHOLDER
George Mason

A BRITISH MERCHANT
Malachy Postlethwayt

THE BRITISH OBSERVER
William Henry Coombes

A BRITISH OFFICER
Capt. William Elliot Cairnes
Sir Andrew Leith Hay
Major John Richardson

**A BRITISH OFFICER IN THE
SERVICE OF THE CZAR**
Daniel Defoe

**A BRITISH OFFICER OF
HUSSARS**
Col. Hugh Owen

A BRITISH RESIDENT
John Scarth

**A BRITISH RESIDENT OF
TWENTY YEARS IN THE
EAST**
James Henry Skene

A BRITISH SAILOR
John Mitford

A BRITISH SETTLER
John Fleming

THE BRITISH SPY
William Wirt

A BRITISH SUBJECT
Thomas Colley Grattan
Sir Francis Bond Head
James Long

THE BRITISH TIMON
Charles Gosling

A BRITISHER
William Bartlett Powlett
Wallop

BRITO
James Boswell

A BRITON
John Cleland
Morris Morris-Robinson

**BRITT, SAPPHO
HENDERSON**
Josiah Pitts Woolfolk

BRITTAN, BELLE
Hiram Fuller

BRITTANICUS
Thomas Brittain

BRITTO-BATAVIUS
John Toland

BRITTON, DOROTHY
Lady Isabella D. G. Bouchier

BRITTON, HERBERT
Reginald T. Eves

BROADAXE, BENJAMIN
John Roy Musick

BROADBOTTOM, JEFFREY
William Guthrie

BROADGRIN, PETER
George Colman

A BROADWAY LOUNGER
George Alfred Townsend

BROCH
Robert Bridges

BROCK, LYNN
Alister McAllister

BROCK, ROSE
Joseph Hansen

BROCK, STUART
Louis Preston Trimble

BROGAN, ELISE
Elizabeth Urch

BROGAN, JAMES
Christopher Hodder-Williams

BROKAW, CLARE BOOTH
Clare Booth Luce

A BROKEN-DOWN CRITIC
Charles Astor Bristed

BROMLEY, HENRY
Anthony Wilson

BRONTE, LOUISA
Janet Louise Roberts

BRONTERRE
James O'Brien

BRONTIUS, ADOLPHUS
Edward Cary

BROOK, BARNABY
William Collin Brooks

BROOK, PETER
Alfred Harold Chovil

BROOK, SARA
Katharine Stephen

BROOKE, ARTHUR
John Chalk Claris
Arthur C. Marshall

BROOKE, GREVILLE
James Augustus St John

BROOKE, WESLEY
George Lunt

BROOKER, CLARK
Kenneth A. Fowler

BROOKLYN
Thomas Kinsella

BROOKS, JONATHAN
John Calvin Mellett

BROOKS, SHIRLEY
Charles William Shirley Brooks

BROOKS, T. TYRWHITT
Henry Vizetelly

BROOKSBY
Edward Pennell Elmhirst

BROOME, ADAM
Godfrey Warden James

BROOME, A. N.
William James Linton

A BROTHER
George Clement Boase

BROTHER ABRAHAM
Richard King

BR. ANGELUS FRANCIS
Richard Angelus Mason

BROTHER ANTONINUS
William Everson

BROTHER AZARIAS
Patrick Francis Mullany

BROTHER IGNATIUS
Rev. Joseph Leycester Lyne

BROTHER LOCKE
George Wightwick

BROTHER PEREGRINE
Octavian Blewitt

BROTHER PETER
John Wolcot

A BROTHER IN CHRIST
Stephen Marshall

A BROTHER OF THE
APOLLO LODGE, 711,
OXFORD
Walter Bishop Mant

A BROTHER OF THE BIRCH
William Cobbett

A BROTHER OF THE
NATURAL MAN
James Denney

THE BROTHERS GRINN
Edward Litt Laman Blanchard
with Thomas Longdon
Greenwood

BROUGHTON, H.
Sir George Otto Trevelyan

BROUGHTON, PHILIP
Aubrey Beardsley

MR BROWN
William Makepeace Thackeray

MRS BROWN
George Rose

BROWN, BARTOLOZZI,
GENT.
Sir Henry Miers Elliot with
Henry Whitelock Torrens

BROWN, CAROLINE
Caroline Virginia Krout

BROWN, CARTER
Alan Geoffrey Yates

BROWN, DOUGLAS
Walter B. Gibson

BROWN, EDWARD, ESQ.
John Campbell

BROWN, IRVING
William Taylor Adams

BROWN, ISAAC
William Motherwell

BROWN, JOHN, ESQ.
Thomas Jefferson Hogg

BROWN, JOHN, A DEESIDE
COACHMAN
Joseph Robertson

BROWN, JONES
Arthur Joseph Munby

BROWN, PETER, POET AND
PERIPATETIC
John Francis Waller

BROWN, POLEMOPHILUS
Alexander Geddes

BROWN, THEOCRITUS
James White

BROWN, THOMAS,
REDIVIVUS
Caroline Frances Cornwallis

BROWN, THOMAS, THE
YOUNGER
Thomas Moore

BROWN, VANDYKE
Marc Cook

BROWN, WILL
William Harrison Ainsworth

BROWNE, DUNN
Samuel Wheelock Fiske

BROWNE, FELICIA
DOROTHEA
Mrs Felicia Dorothea Hemans

BROWNE, HENRY
Henry Ellison

BROWNE, JULIUS HENRI
Albert Deane Richardson

BROWNE, MATTHEW
William Brighty Rands

BROWNE, SAM
Sam Hield Hamer
Ronald Gregor Smith

BROWNE, SEPTIMUS
Herbert George Wells

BROWNING, STERRY
Leonard Reginald Gribble

BROWNJOHN, JOHN
Charles Remington Talbot

BROWNRIGG, HENRY
Douglas William Jerrold

BRUCE, ANN
Esme Ross Langley

BRUCE, ARTHUR LORING
Francis Welsh Crowninshield

BRUCE, CARLTON
George Mogridge

BRUCE, DAVID
Mary Elwyn Patchett

BRUCE, EDMUND
Edward George Earle Lytton
Bulwer-Lytton

BRUCE, LEO
Rupert Croft-Cooke

BRUCE, MOSES
Susan Musgrave

BRUIN, JOHN
Dennis Vincent Brutus

BRUNEFILLE, G. E.
Gertrude E. Campbell

BRUNNER, KILIAN
HOUSTON
John Kilian Houston Brunner

A BRUTE OF A HUSBAND
William Brighty Rands

BRUTUS
Henry Mackenzie
Samuel Finley Breese Morse
Robert James Turnbull

BRUTUS, LUCIUS JUNIUS
Fisher Ames
William Cranch

BRYAN, JOHN
Josephine Delves-Broughton

BRYAN, MICHAEL
Brian Moore

BRYANS, ROBIN
Robert Harbinson Bryans

BRYANT, PETER
Peter George

BRYCE, JAMES
Alexander Anderson

BRYCE, RONALD
Howard Rockey

BRYDGES, HAROLD
James Howard Bridge

BRYHER (WINIFRED)
Annie Winifred Ellerman

BRYSON, LEIGH
Nancy Rutledge

BUCHANAN, MARIE
Eileen-Marie Duell

BUCKINGHAM, JOHN
Harold Harris

BUCKLAND, T.
Edmund Thomas Hill

BUCKLEY, FIONA
Valerie May Florence Anand

BUCKMASTER, HENRIETTA
Henrietta Henkle

BUCKROSE, J. E.
Mrs Annie Edith Jameson

BUDD, JACKSON
William John Budd

BUDDLE, JASPER
Albert Richard Smith

BUDDLE, T.
James White

BUDLONG, PHAROAH
Frederic Beecher Perkins

BUFFKINS, HARRY
Harry Verdon Stopes-Roe

BULL, JANE
Elizabeth Missing Sewell

BULL, JOHN
Edward Gordon Craig
John Gibson Lockhart
Benjamin Parsons

BULL, JOHN, JUNIOR
George Henry Kingsley

BULL, THOMAS
William Jones

BULL, W.
Ann Jebb

BULLCALF, PETER
Joseph Storrs Fry

BULLER, JUN.
George Edward Hughes

BULLER, BOB
William Maginn

BULLER, T. R., OF BRAZENNOSE
John Hughes

BULLUS, HECTOR
James Kirke Paulding

BUMPSTEAD, HELION
Arnold Wall

BUNCLE, JOHN, ESQ.
Thomas Amory

BUNDELCUND
Edmund Burke

BUNKER HILL
Benjamin Franklin De Costa

BUNNY
Carl Emil Schultze

BUNTLINE, NED
Edward Zane Carroll Judson

BUNYAN, JOHN, JUNIOR
Wiliam Arnot

BUPP, WALTER
Randall Garrett

BURCHELL, MARY
Ida Cook

BURDICK, AUSTIN C.
Sylvanus Cobb

BURFIELD, EVA
Frances Eva Ebbett

BURFORD, ELEANOR
Eleanor Alice Hibbert

BURG, DAVID
Alexander Dolberg

BURGEON, G. A. L.
Arthur Owen Barfield

BURGER, JOHN
Leopold Marquand

BURGESS, ANTHONY
John Anthony Burgess Wilson

BURGESS, TREVOR
Trevor Dudley-Smith

BURKE, BARBARA
Oona Howard Ball

BURKE, FIELDING
Olive Tilford Dargan

BURKE, JONATHAN
John Frederick Burke

BURKE, LEDA
David Garnett

BURKE, NOEL
Julia Dolores Hitchens

BURKE, OWEN
John Frederick Burke

BURKE, RALPH
Randall Garrett with Robert Silverberg

BURKE, THOMAS
Sydney Terence Burke

BURKHOLZ, HERBERT
Clifford Irving

BURLEIGH
Matthew Hale Smith

BURLINGTON HAWK-EYE MAN
Robert Jones Burdette

BURNABY, NIGEL
Harold Pincton Ellett

BURNE, EVELYN
Ethel Bourne

BURNEY, FANNY
Frances D'Arblay

BURNS, SHEILA
Ursula Bloom

BURRITT, EDWIN C.
Ethel Claire Brill

BURROUGHS, ELLEN
Sophie Jewett

BURTON, JUNIOR
Charles Lamb

BURTON, ALFRED
John Mitford

BURTON, ANNE
Sara Bowen-Judd

BURTON, H. A.
John Habberton

BURTON, MILES
Cecil John Charles Street

BURTON, RICHARD (or ROBERT)
Nathaniel Crouch

BURTON, THOMAS
Stephen Longstreet

BUSBY, SCRIBLERUS
Gulian Crommelin Verplanck

BUSH, CHRISTOPHER
Charles Christmas Bush

BUSHEY HEATH
William Jerdan

A BUSHMAN
Samuel Sidney

DR BUSHWACKER
Frederic Swartwout Cozzens

A BUSY MAN
Sir William John Lancaster

A BUSY WOMAN
Mrs Mary Bayard Clarke

MRS BUTLER
Frances (Fanny) Anne Kemble

BUTLER, DIANA
Henrietta Euphemia Tindal

BUTLER, JOAN
Robert William Alexander

BUTLER, NATHAN
Gerald Allen Sohl

BUTLER, RICHARD
Theodore E. Allbeury

BUTLER, WALTER C.
Frederick Schiller Faust

BUTT, BOSWELL
Charles Henry Rose

BUTT, NATHAN
John Galt

BUTTERS, DOROTHY GILMAN
Dorothy Gilman

BUTTERWORTH, WILLIAM
Henry Schroeder

BUTTLE, MYRA
Victor W. W. S. Purcell

BYATT, A. S.
Antonia Susan Duffy

BYFIELD, T., MD
John Woodward

BYFIELDE, J.
John Freind

BYLES, GROWLEY
William Makepeace Thackeray

BYRNE, DONN
Brian Oswald Donn-Byrne

BYRNE, E. FAIRFAX
Miss Emma Frances Brooke

BYRNE, JAMES
Edward William Garnett

BYROM, JAMES
James Guy Bramwell

BYRON'S GHOST
George Robert Wythen Baxter

BYSSHE VANOLIS
James Thomson

A BYSTANDER
Martin Madan

Corbyn Morris
David Robinson
Goldwin Smith

BYWATER, SYDNEY
Mark Lemon

C

C.
Joseph Addison
John Wilson Croker
George Mogridge
Sir William Pulteney
Sir Walter Scott

C. 3. 3.
Oscar Wilde

C. A.
Christopher Anstey

C. B. B.
Charles Brockden Brown

C. D.
Thomas Edward Lawrence

C. E.
Charlotte Elizabeth Tonna

C. G. E.
Edward Gordon Craig

C. G. S.
Edward Gordon Craig

C. H. R.
Charles Henry Ross

C. J. G.
Thomas Edward Lawrence

C. AND L.
Henry Fielding

C. L.
Charles Lamb

C. L. M.
Cecil Leonard Morley Brown

C - M -
Charles Macklin

C. S.
Charles Sackville
Charles Shadwell

C. S. C.
Charles Stuart Calverley

C. T. O.
Henry Headley

C. W. H.
Chandos Wren Hoskyns

CABLE, BOYD
Ernest Andrew Ewart

CABOCHON, FRANCIS
Philip Bertram Murray Allan

CABOT
John Galt

CADE, ROBIN
Christopher Robin Nicole

CADENUS
Jonathan Swift

CADMUS AND HARMONIA
John Buchan with his wife
Susan

CADWALLADER, GEORGE
James Ralph

CADWALLADER, GEORGE,
GENT.
George Bubb Dodington

CAESAR
Alexander Hamilton

CAESARIENSIS
James Waddel Alexander

CAGNEY, PETER
Bevis Winter

CAILLOU, ALAN
Alan Lyle-Smith

CAINE, MARK
Frederic Raphael with Tom
Maschler

CAIUS
Mathew Carey
James Currie
William Pinkney

CALCHAS
James Louis Garvin

CALCRAFT, J. W.
John William Cole

CALCUTTA
Walter Roper Lawrence

CALDWELL, TAYLOR
Janet Miriam Taylor Caldwell

CALEDONNICUS
Whitelaw Ainslie

CALHOUN, WES
Geoffrey Willis Sadler

CALIBAN
Robert Williams Buchanan
Hubert Phillips

CALISTHENES
Josiah Quincy

CALLAGHAN, WILLIAM
Raymond Z. Gallun

CALLAS, THEO
Shaun Lloyd McCarthy

CALLENDER, TOM, ESQ.,
CITIZEN OF THE
WORLD
James Thomson Callender

A CALM OBSERVER
Sir David Brewster

CALVERT, JOHN
Wilbur Monro Leaf

CALVERT, MARY
Mary Danby

CALVERTON, V. F.
George Goetz

CALVIN, HENRY
Clifford Leonard Clark Hanley

CALVIN, HENRY GUY
Edward Gordon Craig

CALVINIANUS PRESBYTER
Archibald Bruce

CALVINUS
James Grahame

CALVINUS MINOR, SCOTO
BRITANNUS
Archibald Bruce

CALVUS
Walter Savage Landor

CAM
Samuel Badcock
Waller Lewis

CAMBERG, MURIEL
Muriel Spark

CAMBRENSIS
Arthur James Johnes

CAMBRIDGE, ELIZABETH
Barbara K. Hodges

A CAMBRIDGE GRADUATE
Cornelius Neale Dalton

A CAMBRIDGE MAN
Henry Arthur Bright
Charles Hardwick

A CAMBRIDGE MAN IN THE WEST
Henry Arthur Bright

CAMDEN, CHARLES
Richard Rowe

CAMDEN, RICHARD
L. J. Beeston

CAMERON, DONALD
Robert Harbinson Bryans

CAMERON, D. Y.
Dorothy Mary Cook

CAMERON, IAN
Donald Gordon Payne

CAMERON, JOHN
Archibald Gordon MacDonnell

CAMERON, LEILA
Mrs Catherine A. Du Bose

CAMERON, LORNA
Anthea Mary Fraser

CAMILLA
Elizabeth Carter

CAMILLUS
Fisher Ames
William Duane
Alexander Hamilton with Rufus King
Sir Richard Musgrave

CAMPANA
Frederick Richard Chichester

CAMPBELL, CLYDE CRANE
Horace Leonard Gold

CAMPBELL, DONALD
Stephen Cullen Carpenter

CAMPBELL, G. L.
Edward Kimber

CAMPBELL, JUDITH
Marion Pares

CAMPBELL, KAREN
Betty Beaty

CAMPBELL, KEITH
Keith Campbell West-Watson

CAMPBELL, MARIA
June Stifle

CAMPBELL, ROY
Ignatius Royston Dunnachie Campbell

CAMPBELL, R. T.
Ruthven Todd

CAMPBELL, SCOTT
Frederick W. Davis

CAMPION, SARAH
Mary Rose Coulton

A CANDID CONSERVATIVE
Henry Cecil Raikes

CANDID ENQUIRER
James Anderson

A CANDID ENQUIRER AFTER TRUTH
Hopton Haynes

CANDIDUS
Samuel Adams
George Cornelius Gorham
William Henry Leeds
Henry Mayo
Herbert Sidebotham
Daniel Turner

CANDY, EDWARD
Barbara Neville

CANNAN, DENIS
Dennis Pullein-Thompson

CANNAN, JOANNA
Joanna Pullein-Thompson

CANNELL, CHARLES
Evelyn Charles Vivian

CANNISTER, KIT
James Smith

CANNON, CURT
Salvatore A. Lombino

CANON
Henry William Pullen

CANON BARRY
William Francis Barry

CANONE
John Keats

CANONICUS
Charles Chauncy
William Shedd

A CANTAB
James Payn

CANTABRIGIENSIS
Richard Porson

CANTERBURY, FOLKSTONE
William Makepeace Thackeray

CANUCK, ABE
David Ernest Bingley

CANUCK, JANEY
Mrs Emily Ferguson Murphy

CAPA, ROBERT
Andre E. Friedman

CAPE, JUDITH
Patricia Kathleen Page

A CAPE CODDER
William Evans Burton

CAPELSAY, JOHN
John Saunders Holt

CAPP, AL
Alfred Gerald Caplin

CAPSADELL, LOU
Henrietta Hammond

CAPSICUM
George Charles Smith

CAPSTAN
Rex Hardinge

THE CAPTAIN
Edmund George Harvey

CAPT. CLUTTERBUCK
Sir Walter Scott

CAPTAIN DINGLE
Aylward Edward Dingle

CAPTAIN RINGBOLT
John Codman

CAPTAIN ROCK
Thomas Moore

CAPTAIN SHANDON
Charles Smith Cheltnam

A CAPTAIN IN THE NAVY
Frederick Chamier

CAR, MILES
Miles Pinkney

CARADOS
Henry Chance Newton

CARBERY, ETHNA
Mrs Anna MacManus

CARBONELL, LEWIS
Robert Robinson

CARDER, LEIGH
Eugene Cunningham

A CARDIGANSHIRE LANDLORD
Thomas Johnes

CARDINAL, JANE
Ethel Williamson Veheyne

A CAREFUL HAND
Charles Gildon

CARELESS, FRANCIS
Richard Head

CAREW, BURLEIGH
Fred Gordon Cook

CAREY, CHARLES
Charles Carey Waddell

CARFAX, CATHERINE
Eleanor Fairburn

SIGNOR CARINI
Henry Carey

CARLETON
Charles Carleton Coffin

CARLETON, CAPT. GEORGE
Daniel Defoe

CARLETON, COUSIN MARY
Mrs Mary Agnes Fleming

CARLETON, WILLIAM
Frederick Owen Bartlett

CARLFRIED
Charles Frederick Wingate

CARLILE, RICHARD
George Grote

CARLIN, FRANCIS
James Francis Carlin
MacDonnell

CARLISLE, CLARK
James Holding

CARLISLE, D. M.
Dorothy Mary Cook

CARLONE AND CARLUCCI
Charles Armitage Brown

CARLSEN, CHRIS
Robert P. Holdstock

CARLSON, JOHN ROY
Arthur Derounian

CARLTON
Joseph Caldwell

CARLTON, ROBERT
Baynard Rush Hall

CARLTONIENSIS
Sidney James Mark Low

A CARLYLIAN
James Hannay

CARMARTHEN, K.
Katherine Frances Osborne

CARMEN, FELIX
Frank Dempster Sherman

CARMEN, SYLVA
Elizabeth, Queen of Romania

CARMICHAEL, HARRY
Leopold Horace Ognall

CARNAC, CAROL
Edith Caroline Rivett

CARNEGIE, SACHA
Raymond Alexander Carnegie

CAROL, BILL J.
William Cecil Knott

A CAROLINIAN
Daniel Reeves Goodloe

CARP, AUGUSTUS
Sir Henry Howarth Bashford

CARPUS
Samuel Cox

CARR, CATHARINE
Rosalind Herschel Seymour

CARR, CHRISTOPHER
Arthur Christopher Benson

CARR, GLYNN
Frank Showell Styles

CARR, H. D.
Edward Alexander Crowley

CARR, JOLYON
Edith Mary Pargeter

CARR, KENT
Gertrude Kent Oliver

CARR, PHILIPPA
Eleanor Alice Hibbert

CARR, ROBERTA
Irene Roberts

CARRE, THOMAS
Miles Pinkney

CARREL, MARK
Lauren Bosworth Paine

CARRENO, LUIS
Edward Hutton

CARRIC, ALLEN
Edward Gordon Craig

CARRICK, EDWARD
Edward Anthony Craig

CARRIER BOY
Charles Timothy Brooks

CARROLL, ELIZABETH
Elizabeth James with Carol
Barkin

CARROLL, JOHN D.
Carroll John Daly

CARROLL, LEWIS
Charles Lutwidge Dodgson

CARROLL, MARTIN
Margaret Carr

CARROLL, ROBERT
Hollis Alpert

CARROLL, SUSANNA
Susannah Centlivre

CARROLL, SYDNEY W.
Sydney W. Whiteman

CARRUTHERS, JOHN
John Young Thomson Greig

CARSON, ANTHONY
Peter Brooke

CARTER, ASHLEY
Harry B. Whittington

CARTER, BRUCE
Richard Alexander Hough

CARTER, ELIZABETH ELIOT
Cecelia Holland

CARTER, NICK
Frederick V. R. Day
Dennis Lynds

CARTHILL, AL
Sir John Perronet Thompson

A CARTHUSIAN
William J. J. Duff Roper

CARTON, R. C.
Richard Claude Critchett

CARVER, DAVE
David Ernest Bingley

CARVER, JOHN, ESQ.
Nathaniel Shotswell Dodge

CARY, JUDD
Edwin Charles Tubb

CARYL, VALENTINE
Valentine Hawtrey

CASCA
Albert Pike

CASKODEN, EDWIN
Charles Major

CASPAPINA, TAMOC
Jacob Duche

CASS, ZOE
Lois Dorothea Low

CASSANDER, J.
John Bruckner

CASSANDRA
Sir William Neil Connor
John O'Brien Saunders

CASSELLS, JOHN
William Murdoch Duncan

CASSIUS
Aedanus Burke
Michael Mackintosh Foot

CASTELAR, ISABELLA
Mrs Elizabeth Campbell
Winter

CASTIGATOR
Charles Dibdin

CASTLE, FRANCES
Evelyn Barbara Blackburn

CASTLE, JAYNE
Jayne Ann Krentz

CASTLE, STANLEY
Rilma Marion Browne

CASTLEMON, HARRY
Charles Austin Fosdick

A CASUAL CRITIC
Henry James

CATCALL, SIR CRITIC
Thomas D'Urfey

CATCHPOLE, MARGARET
Richard Cobbold

A CATHOLIC
John Lingard
Myles William Patrick O'Reilly

A CATHOLIC AND A
BURKIST
Theobold Mackenna

A CATHOLIC CHRISTIAN
John Milner

A CATHOLIC CLERGYMAN
John Carroll
William Maire

A CATHOLIC DIVINE
John Lingard
Robert Parsons

A CATHOLIC GENTLEMAN
Edward Scarisbrick

A CATHOLIC LAYMAN
Mathew Carey

A CATHOLIC PRIEST
Joseph Berington
Peter Gandolphy

A CATHOLICK GENTLEMAN
John Austin

A CATHOLICKE PRIEST
Richard Broughton

CATHOLICUS
Henry Cotton
Henry Edward Manning
William Matthews
Joseph Mendham
William Augustus Muhlenberg
John Henry Newman

CATHOLICUS, A
PEACEABLE MEMBER
OF THAT SOCIETY
Henry Portsmouth

CATHOLICUS PROTESTANS
Joseph Mendham

A CATHOLIKE DIVINE
William Crashaw

A CATHOLIQUE GENT.
Thomas White

CATIUS JUNIOR
Elizabeth R. Torrey

MR CATLYNE, QC
Martin Francis Mahony

CATO
James Strachen Barty
George Burges
George Clinton
Michael Mackintosh Foot with
Humphrey Frank Owen and
Peter Dunsmore Howard
Thomas Gordon with John
Trenchard
Stephen Higginson
Robert R. Livingston
William Smith
Ezekiel Webster

A CATTLE HAND
Morley Charles Roberts

CATTO, MAX
Max Finkell

MRS CAUDLE
Douglas William Jerrold

CAUDWELL, CHRISTOPHER
Christopher St John Sprigg

CAULDWELL, FRANK
Francis Henry KIng

CAUSTICK, CHRISTOPHER
Thomas Green Fessenden

A CAUTIOUS MAN
James Boswell

CAVAFY, C. P.
Konstantinos Kavaphes

A CAVALRY OFFICER
Robert Blackall Graham
Capt. Daniel Henry Mackinnon
Frederic Charles Lascelles
Wraxall

A CAVALRYMAN
Francis Colburn Adams

CAVEAT EMPTOR
Sir George Stephen

CAVENDISH
Henry Jones

CAVENDISH, PETER
Sydney Horler

CAVERS, CHARLES
William Young Darling

CAVIARE
John Keats

John Francis O'Donnell

CAXTON
William Henry Rhodes

CAXTON, PISISTRATUS
Edward George Earle Lytton
Bulwer-Lytton

CAXTON, TIMOTHY
John Close

CAYER, D. M.
Maureen Patricia Duffy

CECIL
Sidney George Fisher

CECIL, DAVENANT
Derwent Coleridge

CECIL, ERNEST
Sir Ernest Cecil Cochrane

CECIL, HENRY
Henry Cecil Leon

CECIL, HUGH MORTIMER
John Mackinnon Robertson

CECIL, JOHN
William Hone

CECIL, R. H.
Cecil Rolph Hewitt

CELATUS
Robert Owen

A CELEBRATED AUTHOR IN
IRELAND
Jonathan Swift

A CELEBRATED AUTHOR
OF THAT COUNTRY
Mrs Eliza Haywood

A CELEBRATED LITERARY
AND POLITICAL
CHARACTER
Richard Glover

CELIA
Mrs Celia M. Burleigh

CELLARIUS
Samuel Butler
Thomas Welbank Fowle

A CELT
Thomas Osborne Davis

CELTICUS
Aneurin Bevan

CENDRARS, BLAISE
Frederic Sauser-Hall

CENSOR
James Boswell
Oliver Bell Bunce
William Cooke Taylor

CENTURION
Sir Graham John Bower

John Hartman Morgan
Osbert Sitwell

CEPHAS
Leonard Worcester

CERAM, C. W.
Kurt W. Marek

CEREBUS
MacGregor Laird

CERGIEL
Charles Valentine Le Grice

CERIMON
Dr William Thomson

CERNY, FREDERICK
Frederick Guthrie

A CERTAIN FREE ENQUIRER
Peter Annet

CERVANTES
William Henry Ireland

CERVUS, G. I.
William James Roe

CHABER, M. E.
Kendell Foster Crossen

CHACE, ISOBEL
Elizabeth Hunter

CHAD
Henry Chadwick

CHAFF, GUMBO
Elias Howe

CHALLICE, KENNETH
Kenneth Charles Hutchin

CHALLIS, MARY
Sara Bowen-Judd

CHALLIS, SIMON
Dennis Phillips

CHALON, JON
John Seymour Chaloner

CHAMBERS, CATHARINE E.
Nicole St John

CHAMBERS, DANA
Albert Leffingwell

CHAMBERS, KATE
Nicole St John

CHAMBERS, PETER
Dennis Phillips

CHAMPION
Emanuel Lasker

CHAMPION, R.
James L. Corning

CHAMPLIN, VIRGINIA
Grace Virginia Lord

CHANCE, STEPHEN
Philip William Turner

CHANCELLOR, JOHN
Charles de B. Rideaux

A CHANCERY BARRISTER
Basil Montagu

CHANDLER, FRANK
Terence William Harknett

CHANDLER, MARK
John Michael Sharkey

CHANEL
Arthur Edward Clery

CHANERA
Guy W. Ballard

CHANNEL, A. R.
Arthur Catherall

A CHAPERON
Mrs Arabella Sullivan

CHAPIN, PAUL
Philip Jose Farmer

A CHAPLAIN
Henry Norman Hudson

THE CHAPLAIN OF THE 'DISCOVERY'
Charles E. Hodgson

CHAPLAIN OF THE PENITENTIARY AT SHIPMEADOW
William Edward Scudamore

THE CHAPLAIN TO THE MAYORALTY
Robert Crawford Dillon

CHAPMAN, LEE
Marion Zimmer Bradley

CHAPMAN, MARISTAN
Mary Ilsley Chapman with John Stanton Higham Chapman

CHAPMAN, SHEILA
Sheila Mary Haigh

CHAPMAN, WALKER
Robert Silverberg

CHARBON
Desmond Coke

CHARFY, GUINIAD
George Smeeton

CHARIESSA
Elizabeth Carter

A CHARITABLE AND COMPASSIONATE CONFORMIST
Edward Pearse

CHARIVARIA
Walter Emanuel

CHARLES, ANITA
Susan Barrie

CHARLES, FRANKLIN
Cleve Franklin Adams

CHARLES, GERDA
Edna Lipson

CHARLES, HAMPTON
Roy Peter Martin

CHARLES, JOAN
Charlotte Underwood

CHARLES, NICHOLAS
Karla Kuskin

CHARLES, ROBERT
Robert Charles Smith

CHARLES, THERESA
Irene Maude Swatridge

CHARLEY, CHILLY (or SNARLEY)
Charles Clark

CHARLTON, JOHN
Martin C. Woodhouse

CHARTERIS, LESLIE
Leslie Charles Bowyer Yin

CHARTIST PARSON
Charles Kingsley

CHASE, ADAM
Paul W. Fairman with Milton Lesser

CHASE, BEATRICE
Olive Katharine Parr

CHASE, JAMES HADLEY
Rene Raymond

CHASE, LYNDON
Judy Chard

CHASSERESSE, DIANE
Caroline Creyke

CHASSEUR
Capt. Lionel James

CHATEAUCLAIR, WILFRID
William D. Lighthall

CHATHAM, LARRY
David Ernest Bingley

CHATTERBOX, CHARLES
Wiliam Biglow

A CHATTERER
Samuel Adams

CHATTERTON, THOMAS
Robert Scott

CHAUCER, DANIEL
Ford Hermann Hueffer

CHAUFFEUR
Arthur Jerome Eddy

CHAVERTON, BRUCE
Fred Gordon Cook

CHEEKI, TOMO
Philip Freneau

CHEEM, ALIPH
Walter Yeldham

CHEETHAM, ANN
Anne Pilling

CHEIRO
Louis Hamon

CHELTON, JOHN
Paul Durst

CHERRYMAN, A. E.
Henry Bernard Levin

CHESHAM, HENRY
David Ernest Bingley

CHESNEY, WEATHERBY
Charles John Cutcliffe Hyne

A CHESS-PLAYER
George Walker

CHESTER
William Broome

CHESTER, ELIZA
Harriet Eliza Paine

CHESTER, GILBERT
Harry Hornsby Clifford
Gibbons

CHESTER, JOHN
John Mitchell

CHESTER, MAY
Frederick William Rolfe

CHESTER, PETER
Dennis Phillips

CHESTERTON, DENISE
Denise Naomi Robins

CHEVALIER, H. E.
Edward Sears

CHEYNEY, PETER
Reginald Evelyn Peter
Southouse-Cheyney

CHI LO SA
Edward Gordon Craig

A CHILD OF CANDOUR
Mrs Mary Knowles

**A CHILD OF LARGER
GROWTH**
Mrs Anne Mathews

CHILTON, E.
Ellen Georgiana Clutton-Brock

CHIMAERA
Eleanor Farjeon

CHINAMAN, JOHN
Goldsworthy Lowes Dickinson

A CHINESE PHILOSOPHER
Oliver Goldsmith

CHIP, WILL
Hannah More

**CHIPPERFIELD, ROBERT
ORR**
Isabel Egerton Ostrander

CHIRURGUS
William White Cooper

CHITTENDEN, LARRY
William Laurence Chittenden

CHOKER
Thomas Gibson Bowles

CHOLMONDELEY, ALICE
Countess Elizabeth Mary
Russell

A CHRISTIAN
Andrew Henderson
Benjamin Hoadly
Micaijah Towgood
James Patriot Wilson

CHRISTIAN, FREDERICK H.
Frederick Nolan

CHRISTIAN, JOHN
Roger Dixon

CHRISTIAN, OWEN
Henry Curwen

**CHRISTIAN, THEOPHILUS,
ESQ.**
John Owen

A CHRISTIAN BELIEVER
Alexander Dalrymple

**A CHRISTIAN
FREETHINKER**
Joseph Highmore

**A CHRISTIAN IN A COLD
SEASON**
Cotton Mather

A CHRISTIAN POET
John Holland

A CHRISTIAN WHIG
Richard Watson

CHRISTIANUS
Joseph Cockfield
Thomas F. Dibdin
George D'Oyly

**CHRISTIANUS
PRESBYTEROMASTIX**
Sir Thomas Urquhart

CHRISTICOLA
John Bevans Jr.

CHRISTOPHER
Henry Merritt

CHRISTOPHER, JOHN
Christopher Samuel Youd

**CHRISTOPHERSON,
MICHAEL**
Michael Walpole

CHRISTOPHILUS
John Butterworth
John Fawcett
John Palmer

CHRISTOPHUS
George Essex Evans

CHRONIQUEUSE
Mrs Olive Sykes

**CHRONONHOTONTHOLOG
OS**
David Carey

CHRYSAL
Sir William Scott

**CHRYSANTHEUS AND
CHRYSANTHEA**
Thomas Lake Harris

CHURCH, GRANVILLE
Granville Church People

**A CHURCH OF ENGLAND
CLERGYMAN**
Henry Stuart Fagan

**A CHURCH OF ENGLAND
DIVINE**
Edward Synge

**A CHURCH OF ENGLAND
MAN**
Jonathan Swift

CHURCHILL, ELIZABETH
Richard Alexander Hough

A CHURCHMAN
Edward Berens
Edward Bickersteth
Thomas Tregenna Biddulph
John Bowden
Alexander Chalmers
John Jay
Samuel Roffey Maitland
Arthur Philip Perceval
Edward Smedley
William Francis Wilkinson

**A CHURCHMAN OF THE
DIOCESE OF NEW
YORK**
William Jay

CHURNE, WILLIAM, OF STAFFORDSHIRE
Francis Edward Paget

CHURTON, HENRY
Albion Winegar Tourgee

CIBBER, COLLEY
James Rees

CICERO
Joseph Galloway

CIMON
James Anderson

A CIRCUIT TRAMP
John Alderson Foote

A CITIZEN
Hugo Arnot
James Cleland
James B. Congdon
James Dunwoody Brownson De Bow
William Findley
Timothy Fuller
James Hack Jun.
Francis Hare
Edmund Kimball
Philip Livingston
Josiah A Quincy

CITIZEN MUSKEIN
George Howard

A CITIZEN OF BOSTON
Joshua Pollard Blanchard
Alden Bradford
Elias Hasket Derby
David Henshaw

A CITIZEN OF BRISTOL
Rev. John Eagles

A CITIZEN OF BURLINGTON
Henry Charles Carey

A CITIZEN OF CHESTER
William Cowper, MD

A CITIZEN OF CINCINNATI
Thomas Peirce

A CITIZEN OF EDINBURGH
Thomas Dick

A CITIZEN OF EXETER
William Holmes

A CITIZEN OF MAINE
Edward Payson

A CITIZEN OF MARYLAND
Virgil Maxey

A CITIZEN OF MASSACHUSETTS
James Trecothick Austin
James Bowdoin
George Ticknor Curtis

Salma Hale
Oliver Holden
John Lowell
Hermann Mann
Willard Phillips
Charles Prentiss
James Sullivan

A CITIZEN OF NEW ENGLAND
Isaac Hill

A CITIZEN OF NEW YORK
Nicholas F. Beck
James Cheetham
William Dunlap
Edmond Charles Genet
James Hawkes
Myron Holley
Freeman Hunt
John Jay
John Hiram Lathrop
Clement Clarke Moore

A CITIZEN OF PENNSYLVANIA
Albert Gallatin
Frederick Adolphus Packard
William Bradford Reed

A CITIZEN OF PHILADELPHIA
Paul Beck Jr.
Mathew Carey
Frederick Adolphus Packard
David Rittenhouse
Pelatiah Webster

A CITIZEN OF SOUTH CAROLINA
William Smith

A CITIZEN OF THESE STATES
Uzal Ogden

A CITIZEN OF THE UNITED STATES
Tench Coxe
Alexander Hill Everett
Benjamin Lundy
James McBride
William Vans Murray
Charles Phelps
Royall Tyler
Pelatiah Webster
Silas Wood

A CITIZEN OF THE WORLD
Mathew Carey
Oliver Goldsmith

A CITIZEN OF VIRGINIA
George Bourne
John Taylor
George Tucker

A CITIZEN WHO CONTINUED ALL THE WHILE IN LONDON
Daniel Defoe

A CITY EDITOR
Arthur Ellis

A CITY MAN
Sir Robert Bruce

A CIVIL ENGINEER
Francis Roubiliac Conder
Sir Robert Rawlinson

A CIVIL MAGISTRATE
Hamon L'Estrange

A CIVILIAN
George Buchanan
Sir George Campbell
Matthew James Higgins
Arthur Philip Perceval

A CIVILIAN AND AN OFFICER IN THE BENGAL ESTABLISHMENT
Sir Charles D'Oyly

CIVIS
Robert Alonzo Brock
Sir George Dallas
Alexander Dunlop
Robert Forsyth
Charles Valentine Le Grice
Alexander Peterkin
Sir Henry Russell
Alan Sanders
Sir William Scott
Sir William Hale White

CIVIS OF ABERDEEN
John Ewen

CLADPOLE, TIM
Richard Lower

CLANABOY
Charles Henry O'Neill

CLANDON, HENRIETTA
John George Haslette Vahey

CLARA DORIA
Mrs Clara Kathleen Barnett Rogers

CLARE, ADA
Jane McElheney

CLARE, ELIZABETH
Dorothy Mary Cook

CLARE, ELLEN
Olga Ellen Sinclair

CLARE, HELEN
Pauline Clarke

CLARE, MARGUERITE
Mary Heppell

CLARENCE
James Clarence Mangan

CLARENCE, FITZROY
William Makepeace Thackeray

CLARIBEL
Charlotte Barnard

CLARIDGE, R. T.
Thomas Hood

CLARINDA
Mrs Agnes Maclehose

CLARK, CURT
Donald E. Westlake

CLARK, DAVID
Michael Hardcastle

CLARK, HALSEY
Richard Deming

CLARK, MERLE
Lynne Gessner

CLARK, REV. T.
John Galt

CLARKE, REV. C. C.
Sir Richard Phillips

CLARKE, ELIZA
Elizabeth Cobbold

CLARKE, GEORGE H.
William Brighty Rands

CLARKE, HENRY SCOTT
Millard F. Cox

CLARKE, JEAN
Charles Richmond Tuttle

CLARKE, JOHN
Thomas Hartwell Horne

CLARKSON, HELEN
Helen Worrell C. McCloy

CLARKSON, J. F.
Edwin Charles Tubb

CLAUDERO
James Wilson

CLAUDIUS
Thomas Hewitt Key

CLAVERS, MRS MARY
Caroline Stansbury Kirkland

CLAY, BERTHA M.
Charlotte Monica Brame

CLAY, CHARLES M.
Charlotte M. Clarke

CLAYMORE, TOD
Hugh Desmond Clevely

CLAYTON, JOHN
Henry Bertram Law Webb

CLAYTON, THOMAS
Peter Anthony Motteux

CLEAR, CLAUDIUS
Sir William Robertson Nicoll

CLEARPOINT, COUNSELLOR
Edward Long

CLEAVER, KAY
Mrs Kay Cleaver Strahan

CLEEVE, LUCAS
Mrs Adeline Georgina Isabel Kingscote

CLEISHBOTHAM, JEDEDIAH
Sir Walter Scott

CLEMENS
Joseph Priestley

CLEMENT, HAL
Harry Clement Stubbs

CLEMENTS, ARTHUR
Andrew Clement Baker

CLEMO, JACK
Reginald John Clemo

CLEOFAS
James Edward Neild

CLEON
William Collin Brooks

CLEOPHIL
William Congreve

A CLERGYMAN
John Balguy
John Charlesworth
William Dalgleish
Thomas Elrington
William Goode
Francis Hare
George Horne
Samuel Horsley
John Jackson
Thomas Lewis
Moses Margouliouth
William Marsh
Philip Morant
James Murray
Nathaniel Paterson
Arthur Philip Perceval
John Burnett Pratt
William Sewell
Thomas Vowler Short
Thomas Spencer
Henry Stebbing
Hugh Stowell
Arthur Ashley Sykes
Richard Valpy

A CLERGYMAN IN DEBT
Frederick W. N. Bayley

A CLERGYMAN IN THE COUNTRY
Samuel Bold
Samuel Clarke
Matthew Horbery
John Jackson
Isaac Maddox
Arthur Ashley Sykes

A CLERGYMAN IN THE DIOCESE OF WINCHESTER
Arthur Garfit

A CLERGYMAN IN THE WEST
Samuel Nicholson Kingdon

A CLERGYMAN OF MASSACHUSETTS
Enoch Pond

A CLERGYMAN OF THE CHURCH OF ENGLAND
Charles Bradley
Mathew Carey
John Clowes
Henry Comyn
Benjamin Dawson
Richard Hastings Graves
Thomas Herring
Charles Thomas Longley
Alexander MacCaul
Moses Margouliouth
Frederick Denison Maurice
Zachary Pearce
Francis Peck
John Plumptre
Legh Richmond
Thomas Stackhouse
Hugh Stowell
Arthur Ashley Sykes
Charles Voysey
Henry Walter
Joseph Blanco White

A CLERGYMAN OF THE DIOCESE
Charles Pourtales Golightly

A CLERGYMAN OF THE ESTABLISHED CHURCH
John Clowes
Richard Hastings Graves
Benjamin William Mathias

A CLERGYMAN OF THE ESTABLISHED CHURCH AND NO SAINT
Sir Harcourt Lees

A CLERGYMAN OF THE ISLE OF MAN
Hugh Stowell

A CLERGYMAN OF THE SAME CHURCH
John Kirkby

A CLERGYMAN'S
  DAUGHTER
Maria Louisa Charlesworth
Selina Gaye

A CLERICAL FRIEND
George Huntington

A CLERICAL RECLUSE
Francis Jacox

CLERICUS
Augustus Clissold
Alexander Gunn
Richard Hibbs
Charles Patrick Meehan
Charles Plowden

CLERICUS HAMPDENENSIS
Dorus Clarke

CLERICUS LEICESTRIENSIS
Aulay Macaulay

CLERICUS LYVECANUS
Caesar Otway

CLERIHEW, E.
Edmund Clerihew Bentley

CLERIMONT
Mrs Elizabeth Rowe

CLERK, N. W.
Clive Staples Lewis

CLERKE OF OXENFORDE
John Pendleton Kennedy

CLEROPHILUS ALETHES
John Constable

CLERUS
Augustus Montague Toplady

CLEVE, JOHN
Andrew J. V. Offutt

CLEVELAND, JOHN
Elizabeth Adeline McElfresh

CLIFFORD, CHARLES
William Henry Ireland

CLIFFORD, FRANCIS
Arthur Leonard Bell
  Thompson

CLIFFORD, JOHN
John Clifford Bayliss

CLIFFORD, LILIAN
Eileen Fitzgerald

CLIFFORD, MARTIN
Charles Harold St John
  Hamilton

CLIFTON, OLIVER LEE
St George Henry Rathbone

CLIFTON, TOM
Alfred Farthing Robbins

CLIMAX, CHRISTOPHER,
  ESQ.
Josiah Thomas

CLINKER, HUMPHRY
Tobias George Smollett

CLINTON, F. G.
Robert Wright Campbell

CLINTON, JEFF
Jack Miles Bickham

CLINTON, WALTER
William Henry Davenport
  Adams

CLIO
Richard Gough
Thomas Harwood
Thomas Rickman

CLIONAS
Sir Nicholas Harris Nicolas

CLITUS-ALEXANDRINUS
Richard Brathwaite

CLIVE, ARTHUR
Standish James O'Grady

CLIVE, DENNIS
John Russell Fearn

CLIVE, EVERARD
Edward Shepherd Creasy

CLIVE, WILLIAM
Ronald Bassett

CLOS, CHARLES
Edward George Stoke

CLOSE, UPTON
Josef Washington Hall

CLOUD, RICHARD
Richard Horatio Edgar Wallace

CLOUT, COLIN
Frank Challice Constable
Edmund Spenser

CLUNN, HAROLD PHILIP
Horace Jefferson

MR CLUTTERBUCK OF
  CRIPPLEGATE
William Harrison Ainsworth

COATES, SHEILA
Sheila Holland

COBALT, MARTIN
William Mayne

COBB, BELTON
Geoffrey Belton-Cobb

COBB, JOHN
John Cobb Cooper

COBBLEIGH, UNCLE TOM
Walter Raymond

THE COBBLER OF ALSATIA
John Nichols

COBHAM, Frank
Edward Long

COBURN, L. J.
John B. Harvey

COBWEB
Joseph Tinker Buckingham

COCHRAN, JEFF
Paul Durst

COCHRANE, ANDREW
Robert Caldwell

COCK OF THE STEEPLE
Alexander Birnie

COCKBURN, CATHERINE
Catherine Trotter

COCKIN, JOAN
Edith Joan Burbidge

A COCKNEY
James White

THE COCOA-TREE
Sir Philip Francis

CODLIN
John Latey

CODY, AL
Archie Lynn Joscelyn

CODY, C. S.
Leslie Waller

CODY, JAMES R.
Peter Thomas Rohrbach

CODY, STONE
Thomas Ernest Mount

CODY, WALT
Victor G. C. Norwood

COE, TUCKER
Donald E. Westlake

COELEBS
Edward Augustus Carlyon

COFFEY, BRIAN
Dean R. Koontz

COFFIN, GEOFFREY
Francis Van Wyck Mason

COFFIN, JOSHUA
Henry Wadsworth Longfellow

COFFIN, PETER
Jonathan Latimer
Theophilus Parsons

COFYN, CORNELIUS
John De Vere Loder with
  Hilary A. St George
  Saunders

COIT, DAVIDA
Vida Davida Scudder

COLBERT
Mathew Carey

COLCRAFT, HENRY ROWE
Henry Rowe Schoolcraft

COLDSTREAMER
Harry Jocelyn Clive Graham

COLE, BURT
Thomas Dixon

COLE, FRANCIS
Abraham Cowley

COLERIDGE, JOHN
Earl Andrew Binder with Otto
Oscar Binder

COLES, MANNING
Cyril Henry Coles with
Adelaide F. O. Manning

A COLLECTOR
George Hammond Hawtayne

A COLLEGIAN
William Thomas Moncrieff
William Gilmore Simms

COLLET, STEPHEN
Thomas Byerley

COLLIER, COLEMAN
James Everett

COLLIER, JOEL
John Laurens Bicknell
George Veal

COLLIER, MARGARET
Margaret Stewart Taylor

COLLINGWOOD, HARVEY
William Joseph Cosens
Lancaster

COLLINS, CLARK
Dallas McCord Reynolds

COLLINS, HUNT
Salvatore A. Lombino

COLLINS, MABEL
Mabel Cook

COLLINS, MICHAEL
Dennis Lynds

COLLINS, TOM
John Thomas Lutz

COLLINSON, PETER
Samuel Dashiell Hammett

COLLYER, DORIC
Dorothy A. Hunt

COLMOLYN
Charles Sotheran

COLMORE, GEORGE
Mrs Gertrude Baillie Weaver

COLON
Joseph Dennie

COLONEL SURRY
John Esten Cooke

A COLONEL IN THE
GERMAN SERVICE
George Hanger

A COLONIAL PROFESSOR
Arnold Wall

A COLONIST
Thomas Chandler Haliburton

COLONUS
Sir William À Beckett

COLONUS, JUNIOR
John MacGregor

A COLORED MAN
Lewis H. Putnam

COLT, CLEM
Nelson Coral Nye

COLT, ZANDRA
Florence Stevenson

COLTER, SHAYNE
Victor G. C. Norwood

COLTMAN, WILL
David Ernest Bingley

COLTON, JAMES
Joseph Hansen

COLUMBANOS
Charles O'Conor

COLUMELLA
Clement Clarke Moore

COLVIN, CECIL
Francis Cowley Burnand

COLVIN, JAMES
Michael Moorcock

A COMBATANT
Abraham Hayward

COMBERBACK, SILAS
TOMKYN
Samuel Taylor Coleridge

COMICUS
Harry Parlett

A COMMANDER, R. N.
William Dawson

COMMENT, CUTHBERT,
ESQ.
Abraham Tucker

A COMMISSIONER
John Burton

A COMMITTEE MAN
Joseph Nightingale

A COMMON LAWYER
William Prynne

COMMON SENSE
William Carpenter
John Pendleton Kennedy
Thomas Paine
Sir Richard Phillips

A COMMON SOLDIER
James Franklin Fuller

COMPAGINATOR
George Bush

A COMPANION TRAVELLER
Miss Elizabeth Furlong
Shipton Harris

COMPANY, JOHN
John William Kaye

A COMPETITION WALLAH
Sir George Otto Trevelyan

A COMPOSER
David Everard Ford

COMPTON, FRANCIS SNOW
Henry Brooks Adams

COMPTON, GUY
David Guy Compton

COMUS
Robert Michael Ballantyne

A CONGREGATIONAL
NONCONFORMIST
Thomas Binney

CONINGSBY, CHRISTOPHER
Samuel Smith Harris

CONISTON, ED
David Ernest Bingley

A CONNECTICUT FARMER'S
BOY
Fitz-Greene Halleck

A CONNECTICUT PASTOR
Enoch Fitch Burr

CONNELL, F. NORREYS
Conal Holmes O'Connell
O'Riordan

CONNELL, JOHN
John Henry Robertson

CONNINGTON, J. J.
Alfred Walter Stewart

CONNOLLY, PAUL
Thomas Wicker

CONNOR, KEVIN
Frank O'Rourke

CONNOR, KITTY
James McKowen

CONNOR, MARIE
Mrs Marie C. Leighton

CONNOR, RALPH
Charles William Gordon

CONNY-CATCHER, CUTHBERT
Robert Greene

CONQUEST, OWEN
Charles Harold St John Hamilton

CONRAD
Alfred Bunn

CONRAD, BRENDA
Zenith Brown

CONRAD, CLIVE
Frank King

CONRAD, JOSEPH
Jozef Teodor Konrad Korzeniowski

CONRAD, PAUL
Albert King

CONRAD, STEPHEN
Stephen Conrad Stuntz

CONROY, AL
Marvin Hubert Albert

CONSCIENCE, MISS BLANCHE
Samuel Williams Cooper

A CONSERVATIVE
James Dennistoun
James Ferguson

A CONSERVATIVE MEMBER OF CONVOCATION
William Sewell

CONSIDINE, BOB
Charles James Lever

A CONSISTENT CHRISTIAN
Samuel Bourn

A CONSISTENT PROTESTANT
Richard Watson

A CONSISTENT RESTORATIONIST
Adin Ballou

A CONSISTENT WHIG
Thomas Lewis O'Beirne

A CONSTABULARY OFFICER
Robert Curtis

A CONSTANT CORRESPONDENT
James Boswell

A CONSTANT READER
James Boswell
William Maginn

THE CONSTANT READER
Dorothy Parker

A CONSTANT VISITOR
Patrick Kennedy

CONSTANTIA
Judith Sargent Stevens Murray

CONSTANTIUS
Joseph Cottle

CONSTANTIUS ARCHAEOPHILUS
Edward Hatton

CONSTITUTIO
John Cartwright

CONSTITUTIONALIST
James Brinsley Richards

A CONSTITUTIONAL REFORMER
John Rutter

A CONSUL ABROAD
Luigi Monti

A CONSUMPTIVE
Robert Stevenson Coffin

CONTACT
Alan John Bott

THE CONTRIBUTOR AT PARIS
William Makepeace Thackeray

A CONTRIBUTOR TO 'BLACKWOOD'
Sir George Tomkyns Chesney

A CONVERT
Richard Challoner

A CONVERTED JEW
Paul Isaac Hershon

CONWAY, CELINE
Kathryn Blair

CONWAY, DERWENT
Henry David Inglis

CONWAY, HUGH
Frederick John Fargus

CONWAY, LAURA
Dorothy Phoebe Ansle

CONWAY, OLIVE
Harold Brighouse with John Walton

CONWAY, PETER
George Alexis Milkomanovich Milkomane

CONWAY, TROY
Michael Angelo Avallone Jr.

CONYBEARE, CHARLES AUGUSTUS
Thomas Stearns Eliot

CONYNGHAME, KATE
Joseph Holt Ingraham

COODY, ABIMELECH
Gulian Crommelin Verplanck

COO-EE
William Sylvester Walker

COOKE, HESIOD
Thomas Cooke

COOKE, JOHN ESTES
Lyman Frank Baum

COOKE, MARGARET
John Creasey

COOKE, M. E.
John Creasey

COOLIDGE, SUSAN
Sarah Chauncy Woolsey

COOMBS, MURDO
Frederick Clyde Davis

A COONTRIE ATTURNEY
Charles Sandys

COOPER, CHARLES
Arnold Charles Cooper Lock

COOPER, FRANK
William Gilmore Simms

COOPER, HENRY
Barrington Kaye

COOPER, JEFFERSON
Gardner Francis Fox

COOPER, REV. MR
Richard Johnson

COOPER, WILL
William Cooper Carman

COOPER, WILLIAM
Harry Summerfield Hoff

COOPER, REV. WILLIAM U.
James Glass Bertram

COPELAND, WALTER
Walter Jerrold

COPLAND, JOHN
Walter Copland Perry

COPLEY, WARD
Mildred Emily Carr

THE COPPER-FARTHING DEAN
Jonathan Swift

COPPLESTONE, BENNET
Frederick Harcourt Kitchin

COPYWELL, J. OF
LINCOLN'S INN
William Woty

COQUINA
G. O. Shields

CORA
Annie Keary

CORBETT, CHAN
Nathan Schachner

CORBY, DAN
Arthur Catherall

CORCORAN, PETER
John Hamilton Reynolds

CORDELIER, JOHN
Mrs Stuart Moore

CORDELL, ALEXANDER
George Alexander Graber

A CORDIAL FRIEND TO THE
PROTESTANT
RELIGION
Thomas Barlow

A CORDIAL WELL-WISHER
TO ITS PROCEEDINGS
William Prynne

A CORDIAL WELL-WISHER
TO THE CAUSE OF
UNIVERSAL TRUTH
AND RIGHTEOUSNESS
Miss Priscilla Hannah Gurney

CORDUROY
John Gibson Lockhart

CORELLI, MARIE
Mary Mackay

CORIOLANUS
James McMillan

CORISANDE
Mrs Alice Smith

CORKHARDT, MAJOR
DIONYSIUS
(UNATTACHED)
Laurence William Maxwell
Lockhart

CORLEY, ERNEST
Kenneth Henry Bulmer

THE CORN-LAW RHYMER
Ebenezer Elliott

CORNELIUS, PETER
Hugh Peters

CORNERS, GEORGE F.
George Sylvester Viereck

A CORNET IN THE E. I. CO'S
SERVICE
Thomas Lettsom Pettigrew

A CORNISH MAN
Edward Capel Whitehurst

A CORNISH VICAR
Robert Stephen Hawker

A CORNUBIAN
John Trenhaile

CORNWALL, BARRY
Bryan Waller Procter

CORNWALL, C. M.
Miss Mary Abigail Roe

CORNWALL, HUGO
Peter Sommer

A CORONER'S CLERK
Erskine Neale

A CORPORAL
John Ernest Victor Crofts

CORREN, GRACE
Robert Hoskins

A CORRESPONDENT
Samuel Laman Blanchard

THE CORRESPONDENT
John Trumbull

A CORRESPONDING
MEMBER OF THE
SOCIETY FOR
PROPAGATING
CHRISTIAN
KNOWLEDGE
Elisha Smith

CORREY, LEE
George Harry Stine

CORRIGAN, MARK
Norman Lee

CORSON, GEOFFREY
Anna MacClure Sholl

CORTEEN, CRAIG (or WES)
Victor G. C. Norwood

CORVINUS
Travers Twiss

CORVINUS, VALERIUS
Thomas Blacklock

CORVO, BARON
Frederick William Rolfe

CORWIN, CECIL
C. M. Kornbluth

CORY, CAROLINE
Kathleen Freeman

CORY, DESMOND
Shaun Lloyd McCarthy

CORY, HOWARD L.
Jack Owen Jardine with Julie
Anne Jardine

CORYAT JUNIOR
Samuel Paterson

CORYMBAEUS
Richard Brathwaite

COSMO
John Mathew Gutch

COSMO, MYTHOGELASTICK
PROFESSOR AND F. M.
S.
John Hall Stevenson

A COSMOPOLITAN
John Ross Dix
Frank Fowler

A COSMOPOLITE
Lorenzo Dow
James Lawson
Sir James MacPherson Le
Moine
Alfred Tobias John Martin

COSMOS
Nicholas Murray Butler

COST, MARCH
Margaret Mackie Morrison

COSTLER, DR A.
Arthur Koestler

COTEL, G. L.
George Leslie Calderon

COTES, PETER
Arthur Sydney Boulting

COTTAR, GUY
Willoughby Clive Garsia

COTTERELL, BRIAN
Aylward Edward Dingle

COTTON, JOHN
John Russell Fearn

COTTON, ROBERT TURNER
Edward James Mortimer
Collins

COTTON JUNIOR
Thomas Bridges

A COTTON
MANUFACTURER
Edward Atkinson
William Hoyle

THE COUNT JOANNES
George Jones

COUNT SALLAGUB
Francis Doyne Dwyer

COUNTESS BARCYNSKA
Marguerite Florence Jarvis

A COUNTREY DIVINE
Henry Pendlebury

A COUNTREYMAN
John Anderson

A COUNTRY CLERGYMAN
John Balguy
Edward Berens
John Butler
John William Cunningham
John Disney
William Dodwell
Charles Dunster
William Holmes
Robert Ingram
Robert Charles Jenkins
William Jones
Elisha Smith
William Wake
Samuel Wilberforce
Thomas Zouch

A COUNTRY COUSIN
Mrs Catherine Frances Grace
Gore
John Hepburn Millar

A COUNTRY CURATE
Zachary Grey
John Malham
Erskine Neale
Charles Benjamin Tayler
James White

A COUNTRY DIVINE
William Binckes
Samuel Wesley

A COUNTRY GENTLEMAN
James Boswell
William Combe
William Fletcher
Sir Francis Grant
Zachary Grey
Henry Howard Molyneux
Herbert
Richard Polwhele
Thomas Potter
Abraham Tucker
Sir Thomas Turton
Edward Weston
Isaac Wilkins

A COUNTRY MAGISTRATE
Samuel Glasse
William Nelson

A COUNTRYMAN
Isaac Backus

A COUNTRY MINISTER
Alexander Dunlop
Lewis William Forbes
Edward Pearse

A COUNTRY PARSON
Andrew Kennedy Hutchinson
Boyd
Francis Charles Hingeston-
Randolph

William Holmes
Henry Moule
Francis Wollaston

**A COUNTRY PARSON'S
DAUGHTER**
Mrs Elizabeth Holmes

A COUNTRY PASTOR
Richard Whately

A COUNTRY RECTOR
John Spencer Cobbold

A COUNTRY SCHOLAR
Henry Hickman

**A COUNTRY
SCHOOLMASTER**
William Leggett

A COUNTRY TORY
Sir John Skelton

A COUNTY MAGISTRATE
Hugh Barclay
Francis Orpen Morris

**COUPLET, MORDAUNT,
ESQ.**
John Abraham Heraud

COUPLING, J. J.
John Robinson Pierce

COURAGE, JOHN
Richard Goyne

COURTENAY, PEREGRINE
Winthrop Mackworth Praed

COURTNEY, JOHN
John Cournos

COUSIN ALICE
Mary E. Bradley
Alice Haven

COUSIN CICELY
Sarah Bradford

COUSIN CLARA
Daniel Wise

COUSIN GERMAN
Archibald Bruce

COUSIN KATE
Catharine Douglas Bell

COUSIN SUSAN
Mrs Elizabeth Prentiss

COUSIN TRIBULATION
Louisa May Alcott

COUSIN VIRGINIA
Virginia Wales Johnson

COUTEAU, JAMES BAPTISTE
Robert Jephson

COVENANTER
Konni Zilliacus

COVENTRY
Jonathan Evans

COVENTRY, JOHN
John Williamson Palmer

COVER-POINT
Arthur Lincoln Haydon

COVERACK, GILBERT
John Russell Warren

COWEN, FRANCES
Frances Munthe

COWITCH, GABRIEL
David MacBeth Moir

THE COWKEEPER
Samuel Wilberforce

COWPER, RICHARD
Colin Middleton Murry

COWPER, WILLIAM
James Everett

**COWSLIP, EGBERT
AUGUSTUS, ESQ.**
Benjamin Barker

COX, BARBER
William Makepeace Thackeray

COXON, ETHEL
Mrs Ethel Earl

COYLE, WILLIAM
Thomas Michael Keneally

A CRAB MAID
Frederick William Rolfe

CRABTREE, JANE
Herbert George Wells

CRACKEN, JAEL
Brian Wilson Aldiss

MRS CRACKENTHORPE
Thomas Baker

**CRADDOCK, CHARLES
EGBERT**
Mary Noailles Murfree

CRAIG, ALISA
Charlotte Matilda MacLeod

CRAIG, BRIAN
Brian M. Stableford

CRAIG, DAVID
James Tucker

CRAIG, FINLAY
James Sime

CRAIG, GIBSON
James Hain Friswell

**CRAIG, J. H., OF DOUGLAS,
ESQ.**
James Hogg

CRAIG, JOHN ELAND
Joseph E. Chipperfield

CRAIG, WEBSTER
Eric Frank Russell

CRAIGIE, DOROTHY
Dorothy Glover
Henry Graham Greene

CRAMBO, CORNELIUS
William Barnes Rhodes

CRAMER, JULIAN
Joseph Lemuel Chester

CRAMPTON, HELEN
Marion Chesney

CRANE, ICHABOD
John Daniel Thomas

CRANE, ROBERT
Bernard Glemser
Frank Chester Robertson

CRAOBH NA NDEALG
Sean O'Casey

CRASSUS, LUCIUS
Alexander Hamilton

CRAVEN
John William Carleton

CRAVEN, ARTHUR SCOTT
Arthur Keedwell Harvey-James

CRAVEN, HENRY THORNTON
Henry Thornton

CRAVEN, PRISCILLA
Mrs William Teignmouth Shore

CRAWFORD, ROBERT
Hugh Crawford Rae

CRAWLEY, CAPTAIN RAWDON
George Frederick Pardon

CRAYDER, TERESA
Hila Colman

CRAYON, CHRISTOPHER
James Ewing Ritchie

CRAYON, GEOFFREY, JUN.
George Darley

CRAYON, GEOFFREY, GENT.
Washington Irving

CRAYON, GEOFFREY
John Strang

CRAZY NEWS REEL
Dominic Bevan Wyndham Lewis

THE CREATURE OF AN HOUR
Charles Girdlestone

CRECY, JEANNE
Jeanne Williams

CREDENS
Caleb Fleming

CREIGHTON, DON
Maxine Cole Drury

CREPUSCULUS
James Thomson

CRESSINGHAM, J. H.
Edward Carpenter

CRESTON, DORMER
Dorothy Julia Colston-Baynes

CREYTON, PAUL
John Townsend Trowbridge

CRICHTON, JOHN
Norman Gregor Guthrie

CRINE, GEORGE
John Hill

CRINGLE, THOMAS
Michael Scott

CRINKLE, NYM
Andrew Carpenter Wheeler

CRISPIN, EDMUND
Robert Bruce Montgomery

CRISPIN THE COBLER
William Wagstaffe

CRISPINUS
John Westland Marston

CRITHANNAH, JOB
Jonathan Birch

CRITICUS
Thomas Barnes
James Everett

CRITO
John Duncombe
Charles Lamb
John Millar
Thomas Sanderson
Richard Lalor Sheil

CRITO CANTABRIGIENSIS
Thomas Turton

CROAKER & CO.
Fitz-Greene Halleck with Joseph Rodman Drake

CROCKETT, COLONEL
Sir Theodore Martin with William Edmonstoune Aytoun

CROCKETT, DAVID
Augustus Smith Clayton

CROFT, SUTTON
Arnold Henry Moore Lunn

CROFTANGRY, CHRYSTAL
Sir Walter Scott

CROLY, E.
Janet Farwell

CROM A BOO
Mathias M. Bodkin

CROMPTON, RICHMAL
Richmal Crompton Lamburn

CROMWELL, ELSIE
Elsie Lee

CRONIN, MICHAEL
Brendan Lee Cronin

CROOKLEY, WILLIAM
William Tennant

CROQUIS, ALFRED
Daniel MacLise

CROSBY, LEE
Ware Torrey

CROSS, AMANDA
Carolyn Gold Heilbrun

CROSS, BRENDA
Brenda Colloms

CROSS, DAVID
George Clark Chesbro

CROSS, JAMES
Hugh Jones Parry

CROSS, MARK
Archibald Thomas Pechey

CROSS, POLTON
John Russell Fearn

CROSS, VICTOR
Virginia Coffman

CROSSE, VICTORIA
Vivien Corey

CROSSMAN, P. J. (or P. P.)
William Maginn

CROTCHET
Robert Smythe Hichens

CROUCH, HARRY
George Louis Rosa Wilson

CROWE, JOHN
Dennis Lynds

CROWFIELD, CHRISTOPHER
Harriet Elizabeth Beecher Stowe

CROWLEY, ALEISTER
Edward Alexander Crowley

CROWQUILL, A. (or ALFRED)
Alfred Henry Forrester and Charles Robert Forrester (pseudonym used by both,

jointly and separately, but
after 1843 only by the
younger brother, A. H.
Forrester)

CROXEALL, SIMON
John Henley

CRUCK-A-LEAGHAN
Dugald MacFadyen

CRUISER, BENEDICT
George Augustus Henry Sala

CRUM, PAUL
Roger Pettiward

CRUNDEN, REGINALD
Hylton Reginald Cleaver

CRUSOE, ROBINSON
Daniel Defoe

CRUSTY, TIMOTHY, ESQ.
Chauncey Hare Townshend

CRUX
John Harland

CRYPTONYMUS
Joseph Gurney Bevan

CUACH
William White Cooper

CUILLUIM, SLIABH
John O'Hagan

CULLINGFORD, GUY
Constance Lindsay Taylor

CULOTTA, NINO
John Patrick O'Grady

**CULPEPPER, NED, THE
TOMAHAWK**
William Maginn

CULVER, KATHRYN
Davis Dresser

CULVER, TIMOTHY J.
Donald E. Westlake

**A CUMBERLAND LAND-
OWNER**
Sir James Robert George
Graham

CUMBRIENSIS
John Rooke

CUNNINGHAM, E. V.
Howard Fast

CUORE, LAVINIA BUON
Mrs Lavinia Urbino

**A CURATE FROM
SNOWDON**
Evan Evans

**A CURATE IN THE
COUNTRY**
John Overton

A CURATE OF LONDON
Arthur Ashley Sykes

**THE CURATE OF STOKE
DAMERAL**
William B. Flower

A CURATE OF WILTS
William Fleetwood

CURATOR
Egbert Benson

CURIO
Mark Akenside

CURIOSUS
George Oliver

CURL-PATED
John Hamilton Reynolds

CURLEW
James McKowen

CURRIE, KATY
Susan E. S. Kyle

CURRIER, JAY L.
James Leal Henderson

CURRY, AVON
Jean Bowden

CURTIN, PHILIP
Mrs Marie Belloc Lowndes

CURTIS, PETER
Norah Lofts

CURTIS, PRICE
Harlan Ellison

CURTIS, RICHARD HALE
Richard Deming

CURTIS, WADE
Jerry E. Pournelle

CURTIS, WILL
William Curtis Nunn

CURTISS, PERCY
Nellie I. McMaster Cox

CURTIUS
William J. Grayson
William Jackson
Daniel Webster

CURZON, CLARE
Eileen-Marie Duell

CURZON, LOUIS HENRY
James Glass Bertram

CURZON, LUCIA
Florence Stevenson

CURZON, SAM
Samuel A. Krasney

CUSHING, PAUL
Roland Alexander Wood-Seys

CUSHING, TOM
Charles C. Strong Cushing

CUTTER, TOM
Robert Joseph Randisi

**CUTWATER, SIR JULIUS,
BART., KCB**
Richard Hengist Horne

**CYCLOS, A MEMBER OF
THE GLASGOW
SKATING CLUB**
George Anderson

CYNAN
Albert Evans Jones

A CYNIC
Sir Leslie Stephen

CYNICUS
Martin Anderson

A CYPHER
Percival Leigh

CYPHER, PAUL
Hans Busk

CYPRESS, J., JR.
William Post Hawes

D

D
John Ballantyne
George Darley
Goldsworthy Lowes Dickinson
John Stuart Mill
Dowell O'Reilly

D. B.
Sir David Miller Barbour
Edward Ward

D. C. L.
Alexander James Beresford-
Hope
Charles Lutwidge Dodgson

D-D ' B
Lady Dorothea Du Bois

D. E. D. I.
William Butler Yeats

D. E. F. G.
Harvey Goodwin

D. F.
Daniel Defoe

D. F., GENT.
Daniel Defoe

D. G.
David Garrick

D. H.
Richard Gough

D. J. S. D. D. D. S. P. D.
Jonathan Swift

D. M. S.
Dorothy Margaret Stuart

D. N.
Richard Simpson

D. P.
Herbert George Wells

D. W.
Degory Wheare

DABCHICK
Humphrey Priddis

DAEDALUS, STEPHEN
James Augustine Aloysius Joyce

DAEMER, WILL
Bill Miller with Robert Wade

DAGONET
George Robert Sims

A DAILY ATTENDANT ON
HIS SACRED MAJESTY
Sir Edward Walker

THE DAILY NEWS SPECIAL
CORRESPONDENT
John Frederick Maurice

DALE, ALAN
Alfred J. Cohen

DALE, ANNAN
James Wesley Johnston

DALE, COLIN
Thomas Edward Lawrence

DALE, DARLEY
Miss Francesca M. Steele

DALE, EDWIN
Edward Reginald Home-Gall

DALE, ESTIL
Albert Benjamin Cunningham

DALE, FELIX
Herman Charles Merivale

DALE, GEORGE E.
Isaac Asimov

DALE, ROBIN
Alan Hadfield

DALE, WILLIAM
Norman A. Danberg

DALGETTY, DUGALD
Sir Alexander Murray Tulloch

DALLAS, PAUL
Eric Allen Ballard

DALLAS, RUTH
Ruth Mumford

DALMOCAND
George MacDonald

DALRIAD
Lord Colin Campbell

DALTON
Richard Harris Dalton Barham

DALTON, CLIVE
Frederick Stephen Clark

DALTON, PRISCILLA
Michael Angelo Avallone Jr.

DALY, FREDERICK
Louis Frederick Austin

DALY, RANN
Vance Edward Palmer

DAME SHIRLEY
Louise Amelia Knapp Smith
Clappe

DANA, FREEMAN
Phoebe Atwood Taylor

DANBURY, NEWSMAN
James Montgomery Bailey

DANBY, FRANK
Mrs Julia Frankau

DANCER, J. B.
John B. Harvey

DANE, CLEMENCE
Winifred Ashton

DANE, EVA
Edna Dawes

DANE, JOEL Y.
Joseph Francis Delany

DANE, MARK
Michael Angelo Avallone Jr.

DANE, MARY
Nigel Morland

DANER, PAUL
Edward George Stoke

DANFORTH, PARKE
Miss Hannah Lincoln Talbot

DANFORTH, PAUL M.
John Elliston Allen

DANGERFIELD, CLINT
Victor G. C. Norwood

DANGERFIELD, JOHN
Oswald John Crawfurd

DANGLE
Alexander Mattock Thompson

DANIEL
Alan Ian Percy

DANIEL A JESU
John Floyd

DANIEL THE PROPHET
Daniel Defoe

DANIELL, DAVID SCOTT
Albert Scott Daniel

DANIELS, JOHN S.
Wayne Overholser

DANIELS, MAX
Roberta Gellis

DANIELS, NORMAN
Elsie Lee

DANIELS, NORMAN A.
Norman A. Danberg

DANIELS, OLGA
Olga Ellen Sinclair

DANIELS, PHILIP
Dennis Phillips

DANMONIENSIS
William Burt

DANNING, MELROD
Sinclair Gluck

D'ANOIS, BALZAC
John Oxenford

DANTON, REBECCA
Janet Louise Roberts

D'ANVERS, CALEB
Nicholas Amhurst
Henry St John

D'ANVERS, CALEB, OF GRAY'S INN, ESQ.
William Pulteney

DANVERS, JACK
Camille August Marie Caseleyr

D'ANVERS, NANCY
Nancy R. E. Bell

DARBY, CATHERINE
Maureen Peters

DARBY, J. N.
Mary Govan

DARBY, JOHN
James Edmund Garretson

D'ARCY, HENRY WALTER
Charles Stuart Savile

D'ARCY, PAMELA
Mary Lynn Roby

D'ARCY, WILLARD
William Robert Cox

DARE, ALAN
George Goodchild

DARE, ISHMAEL
Arthur Wilberforce Jose

DARE, SIMON
Marjorie Huxtable

DARING, HOPE
Miss Anna Johnson

DARK, JOHNNY
Victor G. C. Norwood

DARLING
Lady Florence Dixie

DARLTON, CLARK
Walter Ernsting

DARRAGH, THOMAS
Edward Everett Hale

DARRAN, MARK
Norman Molyneux Goddard

DARRELL, ELIZABETH
Edna Dawes

DASHMORE, FRANK
Mrs Frances Murdaugh Downing

DATALLER, ROGER
Arthur Archibald Eaglestone

DAUBIGNY, DELACOUR
George Robert Sims

DAUGE, HENRI
Henrietta Hammond

A DAUGHTER OF THE CHURCH OF ENGLAND
Mary Astell

DAUMLING, HANS
Charles James Lever with Hans Christian Andersen

DAVEY, JOCELYN
Chaim Raphael

DAVID, BEN
John Jones

DAVID, C. G.
David Goodman Croly

DAVIDSON, L. H.
David Herbert Lawrence

DAVIE-MARTIN, HUGH
Hugh Davie-Martin McCutcheon

DAVIES, ELIZA RHYL
William Clark Russell

DAVIES, FREDRIC
Ronald C. Ellick with Steve Tolliver

DAVIES, GEORGE
George Davies Harley

DAVIES, LOUISE
Louise Sarah Golding

DAVIES, P.
Margaret Rumer Godden

DAVIOT, GORDON
Elizabeth Mackintosh

DAVIS, DON
Davis Dresser

DAVIS, GORDON
E. Howard Hunt

DAVIS, JULIA
John Marsh

DAVIS, SCHROEDER
Oscar King Davis with Reginald Schroeder

DAVIS, STRATFORD
Maisie Sharman Bolton

DAVISON, LAWRENCE H.
David Herbert Lawrence

DAVUS, MAC
Herbert Mayo

DAVYS, SARAH
Rosemary Joy Manning

DAWES, J. N.
Richard Porson

DAWLISH, HOPE
Sir Francis Taylor Piggott

DAWLISH, PETER
James Lennox Kerr

DAWNE, DARBY
Edward Baynard

DAWPLUCKER, JONATHAN, ESQ.
John Barclay

DAWSON, ELIZABETH
Christine Geach

DAWSON, FLORENCE
Frances Julia Wedgwood

DAWSON, JANE
Dorothy Critchlow

DAWSON, JENNIFER
Jennifer Hinton

DAWSON, PETER
Frederick Schiller Faust
Jonathan H. Glidden

DAX, ANTHONY
Alfred John Hunter

DAYRELL, VAUGHAN
Wiltshire Stanton Austin

A DEACON
Francis Black

DEACON, RICHARD
Donald McCormick

DEAN, MRS ANDREW
Mrs Cecily Sidgwick

DEAN, GREGORY
Jacob D. Posner

DEAN, RAYMOND
Wilfred Partington

DEAN, SPENCER
Prentice Winchell

DEAN SWIFT OF
    BRAZENNOSE
Benson Earle Hill

THE DEAN OF GLOCESTER
Josiah Tucker

THE DEAN OF GUILD
John Galt

THE DEAN OF PIMLICO
Richard Sinclair Brooke

THE DEAN OF ST
    PATRICK'S
Jonathan Swift

DEANE, NORMAN
John Creasey

DEANE, SONIA
Gwendoline Amy Soutar

A DEAR HEARER
Joseph Hine Rylance

DE BEKKER, JAY
Prentice Winchell

DEBORAH
John David Glennie

DE BRANT, CYR
Joseph Vincent Higginson

A DEBUTANTE
Ada Leverson

DECIMUS
Thomas Chatterton

DECIUS
Thomas Peregrine Courtenay
Samuel Jackson Gardner
Wiliam Pinkney

DECLAN
William Phelan

DE CLERIMOND, B. D.
Joseph Cresswell

DECOLTA, RAMON
Raoul Whitfield

DE COMYN, ALEXANDRE
Charles Thomas Browne

DE COVERLEY, SIR ROGER
Jonathan Mitchell Sewall

DE CRESSERON, CHARLES
Joseph Sheridan Le Fanu

DEE, NICHOLAS
Joan Aiken

DEE, ROGER
Roger Dee Aycock

DEE, SYLVIA
Josephine Moore Proffitt

DEENE, KENNER
Charlotte Smith

DEEPING, WARWICK
George Warwick Deeping

DEER, M. J.
George Henry Smith

A DEERSTALKER
William Black

DE FENIX, COMTE
Edward Alexander Crowley

DEFIANCE
James Boswell

DE GARCON, BOUILLON
Michael Joseph Barry

DE GIEVA, MARY
Mary Roberts

DEHAN, RICHARD
Clotilda Inez Mary Graves

DEIGHTON, CYRIL
Len Deighton

DE KATZLEBEN, BARONESS
Caroline Anne Bowles Southey

DEKKER, CARL
Dennis Lynds

DEKOBRA, MAURICE
Ernest Maurice Tessier

DELAFIELD
Mrs Maria Child

DELAFIELD, E. M.
Edmee De La Pasture

DE LA GUARDE, THEODORE
Nathaniel Ward

DELAMER, EUGENE
    SEBASTIAN
Edmund Saul Dixon

DELANEY, DAN
John Sandes

DELANEY, DENIS
Peter Morris Green

DE LA PLUCHE, CHARLES
    JAMES
William Makepeace Thackeray

DE LA SALLE, J.
John Hall

DE LA TORRE, LILLIAN
Lillian Bueno McCue

DELAVAL, BARCLAY
James M. Share

A DELINQUENT BANKER
Sir John Dean Paul

DELL, BELINDA
Jean Bowden

DELL, ETHEL M.
Ethel Mary Savage

DELLA CRUSCA
Robert Merry

DEL MARTIA, ASTRON
John Russell Fearn

DEL OCCIDENTE, MARIA
Maria Brooks

DE LOGHE, SYDNEY
Frederick Loch

DELTA
Walter Cooper Dendy
Benjamin Disraeli
David MacBeth Moir
George Ranken

DE LUNATICO, F., K. F. M.
George Payne Rainsford James

DEL VAGO, SEIGNIOR
    PERIN
Adrian Beverland

DELVER INTO ANTIQUITY
William Barclay David Donald
Turnbull

DELVING, MICHAEL
Jay Williams

DE MAR, PAUL
Pearl Foley

DEMIJOHN, THOM
John Thomas Sladek with
    Thomas Michael Disch

DEMING, KIRK
Harry Sinclair Drago

A DEMOCRAT OF THE OLD
    SCHOOL
Elizur Wright

A DEMOCRAT TORY
Sir John Skelton

DEMOCRITUS
Henry Hugh Brackenridge
Frederick Raymond Coulson
George Daniel

DEMOCRITUS JUNIOR
Robert Burton

Orlando Witherspoon

**DE MONTE ALTO,
RESIDENT IN MOSCOW**
Aylmer Maude

**DE MONTMERENCY,
FREDERICK
HALTAMOUNT**
William Makepeace Thackeray

DEMOS
William Harbutt Dawson

DEMPSEY, HANK
Harry Harrison

DE MULDOR, CARL
Charles Henry Miller

DENARIUS
Henry Cole

DE NATALE, FRANCINE
Barry N. Malzburg

DENDRON, MISS RHODY
Francis Cowley Burnand

DENHAM, MARY
Gladys May Cox

DENISON, CORRIE
Eric Honeywood Partridge

DENMARK, HARRISON
Roger Zelazny

DENNING, MELITA
Vivian Godfrey

DENNIS, PATRICK
Edward Everett Turner

DENTINGER, STEPHEN
Edward D. Hoch

DENTON, H. B.
Edgar Taylor

DENVER, DRAKE C.
Nelson Coral Nye

DENVER, LEE
Leonard Reginald Gribble

DEPRE, J. A.
Michael Angelo Avallone Jr.

A DEPUTY
Bonnell Thornton

DE QUIR, PETER
John Henley

DERBY, MARK
Harry Wilcox

DERBYSHIRE, JANE
Madge Green

DE REYNA, JORGE
Diane Detzer De Reyna

DERLAX
Richard Simpson

DERMITIUS THADAEUS
Antony Hickey

DERRICK, FRANCIS
Mrs Frances Eliza Notley

DERRY DOWN DERRY
Edward Lear

DE RUPE
Frances Maria Kelly

**DERVISH SERIOSAE
FERISHTAH**
Robert Browning

DE SAINT FOIX, M.
Peter George Patmore

**DE ST LEON, COUNT
REGINALD**
Edward Dubois

DE SAINT-LUC, JEAN
John Glassco

DE SAIX, TYLER
Henry De Vere Stacpoole

**DE SALAMANCA, DON
FELIX**
John H. Ingram

A DESCENDANT
George Chambers

**A DESCENDANT OF THE
FOURTH GENERATION**
Charles Henry Parry

**A DESCENDANT OF ONE OF
THE EARLY PURITAN
GOVERNORS**
Albert Welles

**A DESCENDANT OF THE
PLANTAGENET**
Mrs Frances Mary English

A DESENNUYE
Mrs Catherine Frances Grace
Gore

A DESERTER
Alexander Robert Charles
Dallas

DE SHANE, BRIAN
Catherine Bower Alcock

A DESIGNING DEVIL
Mrs Catherine Frances Grace
Gore

DESMOND
Denis Florence MacCarthy

**DE SORBIERE, MONS.
SAMUEL**
William King

DESPARD, LESLIE
John Leslie Despard Howitt

DESTRY, VINCE
Victor G. C. Norwood

A DESULTORY READER
William Hurrell Mallock

DETACHED BADGER
Frederic Michael Halford

DETECTOR
James Boswell
Samuel Burdy
Henry Gauntlett
Nathaniel Brassey Halhed

A DETENU
James Henry Lawrence

DETERMINATUS
Samuel Adams

DETMOLD, E. J.
Thomas Hardy

DE TOURS, MARCEL
Edward Gordon Craig

**THE DETROIT FREE PRESS
MAN**
Charles Bertrand Lewis

DE VERE, JANE
Julia Watson

DEVOTO, GEORGES
Edward Gordon Craig

DE WALDEN, ATHOLL
Alexander Charles Ewald

DE WARMONT, C.
Charlotte Blennerhassett

DEWDNEY, PETER
Alan St Hill Brock

DEWEESE, JEAN
T. Eugene Deweese

DEWES, SIMON
John Saint Clair Muriel

DEWHIMSEY, Sir ROGER
Charles Gildon

DE WINTON, W. H.
William Henry Wilkins

DEXTER, JOHN
Marion Zimmer Bradley

DEXTER, LYNNE
Gladys Sheila Donisthorpe

DEXTER, ROSS
Edward George Stoke

DEXTER, WILLIAM
William Thomas Pritchard

DIABOLUS
Joseph Howard

DIAMOND, DIONYSIUS
Sir John Skelton

DIANA
Mrs Abigail Adams

DIAS, B. H.
Ezra Pound

DI BASSETTO, CORNO
George Bernard Shaw

DI CASTEL CHIUSI,
BIORGIONE
Peter Bayley

DICAIOPHILUS
CANTABRIGIENSIS
Roger Long

DICK, ALEXANDRA
Mrs Sybil Alexandra Erikson

DICKSON, CARTER (or
CARR)
John Dickson Carr

DICUS, M. E., MD
Charles Gatchell

DIDOCLAVIUS, EDWARDUS
David Calderwood

DIDWIN, ISAAC
William Arthur Sturdy

DIETRICH, ROBERT
E. Howard Hunt

DIGGES, JEREMIAH
Josef Berger

A DIGNIFY'D CLERGY-MAN
OF THE CHURCH OF
ENGLAND
George Hickes

A DILETTANTE
Charles John Darling
William Gardiner

A DILETTANTE IN LAW
AND POLITICS
Allan Ramsay

DIMONT, PENELOPE
Penelope Ruth Mortimer

DIMSDALE, C. D.
Rodolfo Louis Megroz

DINER-OUT
Alfred Edye Manning Foster

DINESEN, ISAK
Karen Blixen

DING, J. N.
Jay Norwood Darling

DINGWALL, PETER
Robin Forsyth

DINKELSPIEL, DIEDRICH
George Vere Hobart

DINKS
Capt. Jonathan Peel

DIOGENES
Sir Max Beerbohm
William John Brown

DIOGENES JR.
John Brougham

DIOGENES PESSIMUS
Pearl Mary Teresa Craigie

DION
John Sheares

DIPLOMAT
John Franklin Carter

DIPLOMATICUS
Hubert Edward Henry
Jerningham
Travers Twiss
Lucien Wolf

A DISCIPLE
Samuel Hulbeart Turner

A DISCIPLE OF BISHOP
BUTLER
Thomas Wimberley Mossman

A DISCIPLE OF CRANMER
Richard Walker

A DISCIPLE OF THE OLD
SCHOOL
James Everett

DISCIPULUS
Sir Walter Peace

A DISSENTER
John Ballantyne
David Bogue
John Holland
Joseph Priestley
Micaijah Towgood
Henry Wansey

A DISSENTER IN THE
COUNTRY
James Peirce

A DISSENTING COUNTRY
GENTLEMAN
Abraham Taylor

THE DISSENTING
GENTLEMAN
Micaijah Towgod

A DISSENTING MINISTER
Jabez Burns
Charles Lloyd
Samuel Rosewall
William Pitt Scargill
John Townsend

DISTICH, DICK
Alexander Pope

A DISTINGUISHED AIDE-DE-
CAMP OF A MOST
DISTINGUISHED
FOREIGN
AMBASSADOR
EXTRAORDINARY
Mrs Catherine Frances Grace
Gore

A DISTINGUISHED ENGLISH
COMMONER
Edmund Burke

A DISTINGUISHED
SOUTHERN
JOURNALIST
Edward Alfred Pollard

A DISTINGUISHED WRITER
Eustace Clare Grenville Murray

A DISTRICT OFFICER
Charles Haukes Todd
Crosthwaite

DITTON, JAMES
Douglas Clark

DIVINE, DAVID
Arthur Durham Divine

A DIVINE OF THE CHURCH
OF ENGLAND
Peter Allix
William Assheton
Thomas Bray
Thomas Burnet
William Fleetwood
Francis Gregory
Denis Grenville
Robert Grove
White Kennett
John King
James MacSparran
Simon Patrick
Thomas Randolph
Glocester Ridley
Robert South
Daniel Whitby

A DIVINE OF THE
UNIVERSITY OF
CAMBRIDGE
George Smith

DIX, DOROTHY
Elizabeth Meriweather Gilmer

DIX QUAEVIDI
Edward North

DIXEY, MARMADUKE
Geoffrey Howard

DIXI
William Maginn

DIXON
Sidney Andrews

DIXON, MACEY
Richard Horatio Edgar Wallace

DIXON, NICHOL
William Emerson

DIXON, PAIGE
Barbara Corcoran

DIZ
Edward Jeffrey Irving
Ardizzone

**D'LEINA, WILL, ESQ., OF
THE OUTER TEMPLE**
Daniel Wilson

DMITRI, IVAN
Levon West

DOBLADO, DON LEUCADIO
Joseph Blanco White

DOBSON, JULIA
Julia Tugendhat

DOBSON, MABLE
Edward Gordon Craig

DOCHERTY, JAMES L.
Rene Raymond

THE DOCTOR
George Henry Kingsley
John Samuel Bewley Monsell

DOCTOR BANTLEY
John Arbuthnot

DR CECIL
Dabney Carr

DR CORNELIUS
William Howitt

**DR DODD AND CHACE
PRICE**
William Combe

DR ELLITS
Alfred Stille

DR ESPERANTO
Lazarus Ludovic Zamenhof

DR HELLEBORE
Charles Lucas

DR HUMBUG
Joseph Reed

DR JANUS
Benjamin Franklin

**DR JEHAN OF THE HALL
RYAL**
John Jamieson

DR MERRYMAN
Henry Playford

DOCTOR PENTAGRAM
Thomas Caulfield Irwin

DR SEUSS
Theodor Seuss Geisel

DR SYNTAX
William Combe

**A DOCTOR OF DIVINITY,
BUT NOT OF OXFORD**
Thomas Raffles

**THE DOCTOR'S PATIENT
EXTRAORDINARY**
James Carkesse

DODD, CHARLES
Hugh Tootel

DODGE, LANGDON
Victor Wolfson

DODGE, STEVE
Stephen David Becker

DODMAN
Charles Henry Bellenden Ker

DODO
William Marcus Thompson

DODS, MARGARET
Mrs Christian Isobel Johnstone

DOE, DOROTHY
Mrs Galusha Anderson

DOE, JOHN
Tiffany Thayer

DOE, RICHARD
Frederick George Brabazon
Ponsonby

**DOESTICKS, P. B., Q. K.
PHILANDER**
Mortimer Neal Thompson

DOGBERRY
Hubert Phillips

DOGBOLT, BARNABY
Herbert Silvette

DOGGREL, SIR ILIAD
Sir Thomas Burnet with
George Duckett

**DOGOOD, MISTRESS
SILENCE**
Benjamin Franklin

D ' OLBERT, GERVAS
Terence White Gervais

DOLEMAN, R.
Robert Parsons

DOLIN, ANTON
Patrick Healey-Kay

DOMENICHINO
John Galt

DOMESTICUS
James Boswell

DOMINIC, R. B.
Martha Hennisart with Mary J.
Latsis

THE DOMINIE
Andrew Picken

DOMINO, JOHN
Esther Averill

DON
Goldsworthy Lowes Dickinson

A DON
Sir Leslie Stephen

DONALDS, GORDON
Gordon Donald Shirreffs

DONNE, MAXIM
Madelaine Elizabeth Duke

DONOVAN, DICK
J. E. Preston Muddock

DONOVAN, JOHN
Nigel Morland

DOOKER
James Moray Brown

MR DOOLEY
Finley Peter Dunne

**DOOLITTLE, DUDLEY
DIGGES**
Andrew Valentine Kirwan

DOONE, JICE
James Vance Marshall

DORMAN, LUKE
David Ernest Bingley

DORMIE, M. A.
Marian Edna Sharrock

DORRIAN, HARRY
Charles Harold St John
Hamilton

DORSET, ST JOHN
Hugo John Belfour

DORSETT, DANIELLE
Dorothy Daniels

DOT
C. Bowyer Vaux

DOUBLE, T.
George Duckett

DOUBLEDAY
Alfred Ainger

DOUBLEDAY, ROMAN
Lily Augusta Long

DOUBLEYOWE, D.
Daniel Wilson

A DOUBTFUL GENTLEMAN
James Kirke Paulding

DOUCE, FRANCIS
Reginald Francis Douce
Palgrave

DOUDNEY, M. A.
William Brighty Rands

A DOUGHTY CHAMPION IN HEAVY ARMOUR
Newcome Cappe

DOUGLAS
Andrew Reed

DOUGLAS, ARTHUR
Gerald Arthur Douglas
Hammond

DOUGLAS, BILLIE
Barbara Delinsky

DOUGLAS, EDITH
Mrs Clara Louise Burnham

DOUGLAS, GEORGE
George Douglas Brown
Lady Gertrude Georgina
Douglas

DOUGLAS, JOHN
Dennis Lynds

DOUGLAS, MARION
Mrs Annie Douglas Robinson

DOUGLAS, MICHAEL
Robert Bright
Michael Crichton with his
brother Douglas

DOUGLAS, OLIVE
Anna Buchan

DOUGLAS, SHOLTO
Joseph Clinton Robertson

DOULYE, GEORGE
William Warneford

DOW JUNIOR
Elbridge Gerry Paige

DOWDER, RICHARD
William Maginn

DOWELL, SAMUEL
John Close

DOWLEY, D. M.
Leslie William Marrison

DOWNES, QUENTIN
Michael Harrison

DOWNING, MAJ. JACK
Seba Smith

DOWNMAN, FRANCIS
Ernest James Oldmeadow

DOYLE, JOHN
Harlan Ellison
Robert Ranke Graves

DOYLE, LYNN C.
Leslie Alexander Montgomery

DOYLE, MARTIN
William Ross Hickey

DOYLE, MIKE
Charles Desmond Doyle

DOZIER, ZOE
Dixie Browning

DRACO, F.
Julia Davis Adams

DRAGONET
Thames Ross Williamson

A DRAGOON ON FURLOUGH
Archibald Forbes

DRAKE, BONNIE
Barbara Delinsky

DRAKE, FRANCIS ESQ.
Benjamin Humphrey Smart

DRAKE, PETER, FISHERMAN OF BRENTFORD
Matthew Green

DRAKLOF
Charles James Folkard

DRALLOC, N.
John Collard

DRAPER, HASTINGS
Roderic Jeffries

DRAPER, JOHN
Frederick Scott Oliver

THE DRAPER
William Webster

A DRAPER OF LONDON
William Webster

THE DRAPIER
Jonathan Swift

DRAPIER, M. B.
Jonathan Swift

DRAWCANSIR, SIR ALEXANDER KNT., CENSOR OF GREAT BRITAIN
Henry Fielding

DRAWCANSIR, ALEXANDER, FENCING MASTER AND PHILOMATH
Tobias George Smollett

DRAX, PETER
Eric Elrington Addis

A DREAMER
John Andre
Samuel Hayman
Amy Lowell

Henry Theodore Tuckerman

DRENNAN, JAMES
William Edward David Allen

DREW, D'ARCY
St George Jackson Mivart

DREW, ELEANOR
Edna Dawes

DREW, NICHOLAS
Robert Harling

DRINAN, ADAM
Joseph Todd Gordon MacLeod

DRINKROW, JOHN
Michael Hardwick

DROCH
Robert Bridges

DROPPER, H.
Louis John Jennings

DRUGGER, ABEL
John Hardham

THE DRUID
Henry Hall Dixon
Henry M. Flint

DRUMMOND, ANTHONY
Alfred John Hunter

DRUMMOND, CHARLES
Kenneth Giles

DRUMMOND, EMMA
Edna Dawes

DRUMMOND, IVOR
Roger Erskine Longrigg

DRUMMOND, JOHN
John Newton Chance

DRURY, C. M.
Clare Hoskyns Abrahall

DRURY, KARL
Edgar Fawcett

DRYASDUST
Edward Heron-Allen

DRYASDUST, REV. DR
Sir Walter Scott

DRYASDUST, DR F. S. A.
Dudley Costello

DRYBLOWER
Edwin Greenslade Murphy

DRYDEN MINOR
Francis Hugh O'Donnell

DRYDEN, LENNOX
Marguerite Steen

DRYDEN, PAMELA
Nicole St John

DRYDOG, DOGGREL
Charles Clark

DUBH, TON
Robert Hunter Gordon

THE DUBLIN APOTHECARY
Charles Lucas

DUBOIS, ALFRED
James Stuart Bowes

DUBOIS, M.
Arthur William Charles Kent

DUCANGE ANGLICUS
Bernard Quaritch

DUCAS, THEODORE
Charles Mills

THE DUCHESS
Mrs Margaret Wolfe
Hungerford

DUCHILLON
Louis Dutens

**DUCKETT, CHARLES
WILLIAM**
Charles Clark

**DUCKWORTH, DR
DODIMUS, A. N. Q.**
Asa Greene

DUDGEON, MATHEW
Alfred Henry Huth

DUDLEY, ARTHUR
Marie Blaze de Bury

DUDLEY, FRANK
Ward Greene

DUDLEY, HELEN
Jacynth Hope-Simpson

DUDU
Julia Constance Fletcher

DUFF, R.
Richard Gifford

MR D'UFFEY
Thomas D'Urfey

DUFFLE, THOMAS
John Galt

DUGGAN, DIONYSIUS
William Maginn

DUKE, WILL
William Campbell Gault

DUM-DUM
John Kaye Kendall

DUMAS, CLAUDINE
Barry N. Malzberg

A DUMPLING-EATER
Thomas Stona

DUNBAR, ALEXANDER
Henry Craik

DUNCAN, ALEX
Madelaine Elizabeth Duke

DUNCAN, DUKE
St George Henry Rathbone

DUNCAN, JANE
Elizabeth Jane Cameron

DUNCAN, SARAH JEANETTE
Mrs Everard (Sarah Jeanette)
Cotes

DUNCAN, TERENCE
William Francis Nolan

DUNCANE, BESSIE
Walter William Sayer

DUNCANNON, ERIC
Frederick Edward Neuflize
Ponsonby

DUNDAS, NORMAN
James Bryce

DUNDAS, R.
Richard Middleton

DUNDEE, ROBERT
Robert Kirsch

**DUNDERHEADIUS,
HABBAKUKIUS**
Thomas Jackson

DUNLAP, WALTER B.
Sylvanus Cobb

DUNN, SAUL
Philip M. Dunn

DUNNE, DESMOND
James Lee-Richardson

DUNNING, CHARLOTTE
Charlotte Dunning Wood

DUNSHUNNER, AUGUSTUS
William Edmonstoune Aytoun

DUNSTAN, ANDREW
Arthur Bertram Chandler

DURAC, JACK
Stanley Jack Rachman

DURESME, THO.
Thomas Morton

DURHAM, DAVID
Roy Vickers

DURRANT, THEO
William Anthony Parker White

DUSENBURY, V. HUGO
Henry Cuyler Bunner

DUSTIN, CHARLES
John Ulrich Giesy

DUTHUS, HUGH
Alexander Taylor Innes

**A DUTIFUL SON OF THE
CHURCH OF ENGLAND**
Edmund Elys

**A DUTIFUL SON OF THIS
CHURCH**
Simon Patrick

**A DUTIFULL SONNE OF
THE CHURCH**
Joseph Hall

DUTT, NICHOLAS
Alan Chalkley

DUVAL, JEANNE
Virginia Coffman

DUVAL, KATHERINE
Elizabeth James

DUVAUL, VIRGINIA C.
Virginia Coffman

DWIG
Clare Victor Dwiggins

DWIGHT, JASPER
William Duane

DWIGHT, OLIVIA
Mary Hazzard

DWYER, DEANNA (or K. R.)
Dean R. Koontz

DYCE, GILBERT
Percy Hetherington Fitzgerald

DYE, CHARLES
Katherine Anne MacLean

DYFED, GWILYM
William Richards

DYKES, JACK
Jack Owen

DYMOKE, JULIET
Juliet Dymoke De Schanschieff

MR DYSON
Sydney Smith

E

E.
John Campbell
Maria Edgeworth
Mary Eliza Fullerton

E. A.
Samuel Adams

E. A. P.
James Whitcomb Riley

E. B.
Edward Bentham
Elizabeth Blower
Elizabeth Boyd

E. B. G.
Edward Burnaby Greene

E. B. P.
Edward Bouverie Pusey

E. C.
Edward Capell
Edmund Curll

E. D. M.
Edward Deering Mansfield

E. E.
Emily Eden

E. F.
Jonathan Swift

E. F. G.
Sir Charles Vinicombe Penrose

E. G. B.
Edward George Ballard

E. G. O.
Edward Alexander Crowley

E. H.
Eliza Haywood

E. K.
Edward Kirke

E. M. S.
Sir Ernest Mason Satow

E. P.
Ezra Pound

E. P. B.
Edward Pleydell-Bouverie

E. P. S.
Evelyn Philip Shirley

E. S. S.
Barre Charles Roberts

E. T.
Jessie Chambers

E. V. L.
Edward Verrall Lucas

E. V. O. E.
Edmund George Valpy Knox

EAGLE, SOLOMON
Sir John Collings Squire

EAGLESFIELD, FRANCIS
Arthur Guirdham

EAMES, DAVID
Denys Val Baker

THE EARL
George Robert Charles Herbert

EARL, JOHN PRESCOTT
Beth Gilchrist

EARLE, JEAN
Doris Burge

EARLE, WILLIAM
William Earl Johns

EARLY, JOHN
William Earl Johns

EARLY, TOM
Elmer Stephen Kelton

AN EARLY RISER
John Wilson

AN EARLY SETTLER
Samuel Strickland

AN EARNEST WELL-WISHER
TO THE TRUTH
Daniel Cawdrey

EARP, VIRGIL
Henry John Keevill

EASEL, JACK
Charles Locke Eastlake

EAST, MICHAEL
Morris West

EAST, RACHEL
Cicily Isabel Fairfield

EAST, ROGER
Roger d'Este Burford

EASTAWAY, EDWARD
Philip Edward Thomas

EASTERMAN, DANIEL
Denis MacEoin

EASTERN HERMIT
William Allingham

AN EASTERN STATESMAN
George Washburn

EASY, JAMES
James Heywood

EASY CHAIR
George William Curtis

EBBARE (or EBBAC), G.
George Crabbe

EBIONITA
Joseph Priestley

EBN OSN
Benjamin Stephenson

ECCLESIASTES
George Edward Biber

ECCLETUS
Luke Howard

ECHARD, L.
Samuel Pegge

ECHION
Edward Chatfield

ECIR
Isaac Leopold Rice

ECLEA-NOBJMONI
Benjamin Coole

ECONOMIST
Sir George Campbell
Sir Robert Giffen

EDAX
Charles Lamb

EDGAR, SIR JOHN
Sir Richard Steele

EDGAR, JOSEPHINE
Mary Mussi

EDGAR, PETER
Peter King-Scott

EDGBASTON
James Fitzmaurice-Kelly

EDGELL, JOHN
John Edgell Rickword

**AN EDINBURGH
CORRESPONDENT**
James Boswell

EDINENSIS-GLASGUENSIS
John Hoppus

AN EDITOR
Lewis Gaylord Clark
Henry Morford
Mowbray Walter Morris
William Gilmore Simms

**THE EDITOR OF A
QUARTERLY REVIEW**
William Frederick Deacon

**THE EDITOR OF 'ONCE A
WEEK'**
Eneas Sweetland Dallas

**THE EDITOR OF THE
EVENING POST**
William Coleman

**THE EDITOR OF THE
'NATIONAL'**
George Jacob Holyoake

**THE EDITOR OF THE
'SPIRITUAL QUIXOTE'**
Richard Graves

EDMONDS, CHARLES
Charles Edmund Carrington

EDMONDS, GEORGE
Elizabeth Avery Meriwether

EDMONDSON, WALLACE
Harlan Ellison

**AN EDUCATIONAL
ADVOCATE**
Edward Granville Eliot

EDWARD
Edward James

**EDWARD OF THE GOLDEN
HEART**
Winifred James

AN EDWARDEAN
Joseph Harvey

EDWARDOVITCH, EDWARD
Edward Gordon Craig

EDWARDS, AGNES
Agnes Rothery

EDWARDS, ALBERT
Arthur Bullard

EDWARDS, CHARMAN
Frederick Anthony Edwards

EDWARDS, F. E.
William Francis Nolan

EDWARDS, HANK
Robert Walter Broomall

EDWARDS, JAMES G.
James William MacQueen

EDWARDS, JOHN MILTON
William Wallace Cook

EDWARDS, NORMAN
Terry Carr with Theodore
Edward White

EDWARDS, OLIVER
Sir William Haley

EDWARDS, SAMUEL
Noel Bertram Gerson

EFFINGHAM, CHAMP
John Esten Cooke

EGAN, FRANK
Francis Henry Knethell Green

EGAN, LESLEY
Elizabeth Linington

EGBERT, H. M.
Victor Rousseau Emanuel

EGERTON, GEORGE
Mary Chevalita Bright

EGERTON, SARAH
Sarah Fyge

EGERTON, WILLIAM
Edmund Curll

EGINARDUS
Mary de la Riviere Manley

EGLINTON, JOHN
William Kirkpatrick Magee

EGOMET
Henry Watson Fowler

AN EGYPTIAN KAFIR
Samuel Bailey

EHA
Edward Hamilton Aitken

**AN EIGHT HUNDRED A
YEAR MAN**
Frederic Charles Lascelles
Wraxall

**EIRENAEUS PHILALETHES
COSMOPOLITA**
George Starkey

EL ATCHBY
Lyman Hotchkiss Bagg

EL COMANCHO
Walter Shelley Phillips

EL MUKATTEM
Howard Crosby

ELAGNITIN, J.
Joseph Nightingale

ELBON, BARBARA
Leonora B. Halstead

ELDER, EVELYN
Milward Rodon Kennedy
Burge

ELDER, JOSEPHINE
Olive Potter

AN ELDER BROTHER
Henry Handley Norris

**AN ELDER OF THE CHURCH
OF SCOTLAND**
Hugh Barclay

**AN ELDER OF THE FREE
CHURCH OF
SCOTLAND**
William Milligan

AN ELDERLY SPINSTER
Margaret Wilson

ELDERSHAW, M. BARNARD
Marjorie Faith Barnard with
Flora S. Eldershaw

ELDON, DR ABRAHAM
Thomas Wyse

AN ELECTOR
Henry Romilly
Henry Llewellyn Williams

AN ELECTOR IN 1771
Samuel Adams

ELHEGOS
Elbridge Henry Goss

ELIA
Charles Lamb

ELIOT, ALICE (or A. C.)
Sarah Orne Jewett

ELIOT, GEORGE
Mary Ann Evans

ELIOT, MAX
Anna M. B. Ellis

ELIS
Edward Payson Hammond

ELIZA
Mrs Elizabeth Carter
Mrs Elizabeth Draper

ELIZABETH
Countess Elizabeth Mary
Russell

ELIZABETH, CHARLOTTE
Charlotte Elizabeth Tonna

ELIZAPHAN OF PARNACH
Benjamin Church

ELLANGOWAN
James Glass Bertram

ELLEN OF EXETER
Mrs Anne Marie Mackenzie

ELLIOTT
Samuel Elliott Coues

ELLIOTT. ARTHUR H.
William Davenport Adams

ELLIOTT, EMILIA
Caroline Emilia Jacobs

ELLIOTT, RUTH
Lillie Peck

ELLIS, ALICE THOMAS
Anna Margaret Haycraft

ELLIS, LANDON
Harlan Ellison

ELLIS, N. A. TEMPLE
Neville Aldridge Holdaway

ELLSWORTH, ELMER, JR.
Tiffany Thayer

ELLSWORTH, PAUL
Paul Ellsworth Triem

ELMWOOD, ELNATHAN, ESQ.
Asa Greene

ELPHINSTONE, MURGATROYD
Hugh McNair Kahler

ELSNA, HEBE
Dorothy Phoebe Ansle

ELTON, JOHN
John Marsh

ELY, BRENT
Peter Dunsmore Howard

ELY, DAVID
David Lilienthal

EMANCIPATUS
Joseph Mendham

EMBEY, PHILIP
Elliot Elias Philipp

AN EMBRYO HARVEST-MAN
Jeremiah Bigg

EMENDATOR
Caleb Whitefoord

EMERITUS
Thomas De Quincy
James Louis Garvin

EMERSON, SIR JAMES
Sir James Emerson Tennent

EMERY, GILBERT
Emery Bemsley Pottle

AN EMIGRANT
Joseph Abbott

AN EMIGRANT FARMER
Joseph Abbott

AN EMIGRANT MECHANIC
Alexander Harris

AN EMINENT AUTHOR
James Howell

AN EMINENT CITIZEN OF VIRGINIA
Benjamin Watkins Leigh

AN EMINENT DIVINE OF THE REFORMED CHURCH
Peter Du Moulin

AN EMINENT EDITOR
Hector MacNeill

AN EMINENT HAND
Alexander Pope

EMINENT HANDS
William Edmonstoune Aytoun
and Sir Theodore Martin

AN EMINENT PERSON
John Lind

AN EMINENT PERSON RESIDING AT THE GREAT CZAR'S COURT
Samuel Collins

AN EMINENT PHYSICIAN
Richard Russell
Peter Shaw

AN EMINENT PROFESSOR
Charles Morton

EMMA JANE
Emma Jane Worboise

EMSH, ED
Edmund Alexander Emshwiller

EMSLEY, CLARE
Clare Plummer

AN ENEMY TO DETRACTION
William Wordsworth

AN ENEMY TO PEACE
Jonathan Swift

ENGINAE SOCIETATIS POETA
Augustus Peirce

ENGLAND, PIERS
Gerald Kersh

ENGLAND, S.
Richard Porson

ENGLISH, CHARLES
Charles A. Neutzel

ENGLISH, GEORGE
Samuel Rosewall

ENGLISH, GOLIAH
John Boyle

AN ENGLISH CATHOLIC
Henry Digby Beste

AN ENGLISH CATHOLIC LAYMAN
Peter Le Page Renouf

AN ENGLISH CATHOLIC OF THE METROPOLITAN DIOCESE
Caleb Fleming

AN ENGLISH CIVILIAN
Francis Roubiliac Conder
William Walton

AN ENGLISH COMPANY OFFICER
Gerald Francis Ellison

AN ENGLISH CONGREGATIONAL MINISTER
George Payne

AN ENGLISH CRITIC
George Henry Townsend

AN ENGLISH DIVINE AT DOWAY
Henry Garnet

AN ENGLISH DOMINICAN
Thomas Worthington

AN ENGLISH FREEHOLDER
David Robinson

AN ENGLISH GENTLEMAN
Daniel Defoe
William Thomson
Col. William Windham

AN ENGLISH GOVERNESS
William Ralston Shedden
Ralston
Alice Muriel Williamson

AN ENGLISH JOURNALIST
William Charles Mark Kent

AN ENGLISH LADY
Helena Maria Williams

AN ENGLISH LADY WHO WAS LATELY IN TURKEY
Lady Mary Wortley Montagu

AN ENGLISH LIBERAL
Allen Upward

AN ENGLISH MERCHANT
John Campbell

AN ENGLISH MINISTER
Cotton Mather

AN ENGLISH NOBLEMAN
Henry John George Herbert

AN ENGLISH OFFICER
John Banks
Henry Charles Fletcher
Alexander Jardine
Maj. John Richardson
Sir Garnet Joseph Wolseley

THE ENGLISH OPIUM
EATER
Thomas de Quincy

AN ENGLISH PLAY-GOER
John Oxenford

AN ENGLISH PREACHER
Joseph Parker

AN ENGLISH PRESBYTER
Nathaniel Dimock

AN ENGLISH PRISONER IN
RUSSIA
William Burckhardt Barker

AN ENGLISH PROTESTANT
Thomas Comber

AN ENGLISH REPUBLICAN
Algernon Charles Swinburne

AN ENGLISH RESIDENT IN
RUSSIA
Emile Joseph Dillon

AN ENGLISH RESIDENT IN
THAT CITY
Henry Wreford

AN ENGLISH RESIDENT IN
THE UNITED STATES
Edmund Ruffin

THE ENGLISH SAPPHO
Mary Robinson

THE ENGLISH SPORTSMAN
George C. G. F. Berkeley

AN ENGLISH SUBJECT
William Stafford

AN ENGLISH TORY
Henry Cecil Raikes

ENGLISH TORY
Sir Richard Steele

AN ENGLISH TRAVELLER
Francis William Blagdon
Orville Dewey
Joseph Hunter
Martin Sherlock

AN ENGLISH TRAVELLER
IN SPAIN
John Talbot Dillon

AN ENGLISHMAN
William Whittaker Barry
John Burton
Philip Burton
Henry Richard Vassall Fox
Douglas Goldring
Sir William George Granville
V. V. Harcourt
William Hone
John Jebb
John Lind
Thomas Paine
Joseph Priestley
Daniel Puseley
Joseph Richardson
Frederick William Robertson
John Horne Tooke
John Wesley
Hubert Wrigley Wilson

AN ENGLISHMAN IN PARIS
Albert Dresden Vandam

AN ENGLISHMAN IN SPAIN
James Hannay

AN ENGLISHMAN OF THE
OLD SCHOOL
Edward Maltby

AN ENGLISHMAN
RESIDENT IN PARIS
John Cam Hobhouse

AN ENGLISHWOMAN
Isabella Lucy Bishop
Frances Darusmont
Mrs Barbara Hoole Hofland
Lady Anna Riggs Miller
Mrs Sophia Poole
Miss Jane Porter

AN ENGLISHWOMAN
RESIDENT AT
BRUSSELS IN JUNE 1815
Mrs Charlotte Ann Eaton

ENID
Elizabeth Banks

ENNUYEE
Mrs Anna Brownell Jameson

ENOS
Cecil Percival Stone

ENSIGN SOPHT
Robert Michael Ballantyne

ENTICKNAPPE, E.
Hannah Lynch

EOGANESIUS, JAMES
JUNIUS
John Toland

EPAMINONDAS
Gideon Granger
Augustus Brevoort Woodward

EPAPHRAS
James Hog

EPERNAY, MARK
John Kenneth Galbraith

EPHEMERA
Edward Fitzgibbon

EPHESIAN
Carl Eric Bechhofer Roberts

AN EPICURE
Frederic Saunders

EPICURUS ROTUNDUS
Charles William Shirley Brooks

AN EPISCOPAL
CLERGYMAN
Caleb Sprague Henry

AN EPISCOPAL DIVINE
White Kennett

AN EPISCOPALIAN
Lucius Manlius Sargent
Richard Whately

EPISCOPUS
James Boswell

EPSILON
John Betjeman
James Baldwin Brown
Richard Edmonds

EQUITAS
John Theodore Dodd

ERANISTES
Robert Charles Jenkins

ERASMUS
John Palmer

ERASMUS, D.
Alfred Edward Housman

EREMUS
John Wilson

ERIKSON, WALTER
Howard Fast

ERITH, LYNN
Edward Fox

ERMINE, WILL
Harry Sinclair Drago

ERNEST
Arthur Cleveland Coxe

ERRATIC ENRIQUE
Henry Clay Lukens

ERRYM, MALCOLM J.
James Malcolm Rymer

ERSKINE, FRANK
George Louis Rosa Wilson

ERSKINE, MARGARET
Margaret Wetherby Williams

ERSKINE, ROSALIND
Roger Erskine Longrigg

ERVIE
Mrs Emily C. Pearson

ESCULAPIUS
Samuel Ferrand Waddington

ESDAILE, DAVID
David Esdaile Walker

ESDRAS PHILOPARTHEN
Sir George Wharton

ESKDALE TAM
Thomas Telford

ESMERALDA, AURORA
Ella Stirling Mighels

ESMOND, HARRIET
John Frederick Burke

ESMOND, HENRY
William Makepeace Thackeray

ESMOND, HENRY VERNON
Henry Vernon Jack

ESPARTERO, BALDOMERO
William Makepeace Thackeray

ESPRIELLA, DON MANUEL
ALVAREZ
Robert Southey

AN ESSAYIST ON THE
PASSIONS
Nicholas Michell

ESSE, JAMES
James Stephens

ESSENUS
John Jones

ESSEX, MARY
Ursula Bloom

ESTEVEN, JOHN
Samuel Shellabarger

ESTIBIUS PSYCHALETHES
William Coward

ESTORIL, JEAN
Mabel Esther Allan

ETHELMER, ELLIS
Elizabeth C. Wolstenholme-
Elmy

ETIENNE
William Stephen Richard King-
Hall

ETON, ROBERT
Laurence Walter Meynell

AN ETON BOY
George Nugent Banks

ETONENSIS
John Hungerford Arkwright
William Ewart Gladstone

AN ETONIAN
Charles Rowcroft

ETONIAN, THE YOUNGER
William Ewart Gladstone

THE ETTRICK SHEPHERD
James Hogg

EUBULUS
Samuel Butler
John Martin

EUCAPNUS NEPENTHIACUS
Richard Brathwaite

EUDE, LOUIS EUSTACHE,
THE YOUNGER
Andrew Valentine Kirwan

EUGENE
Hugo Arnot

EUGENIA
Lady Mary Chudleigh

EUGENIUS
John Hall Stevenson

EUGENIUS, JUNIOR
James Owen

EUGENIUS PHILALETHES
Arthur Ashley Sykes
Thomas Vaughan

EUGENIUS PHILANDER
Thomas Guidott

EUISITOR, FRANCISCUS, OF
PALAEOPOLITE
Henry More

EULALIE
Mrs Mary Eulalie Shannon

EULER, L.
John Hewlett

EUMENES
Jacob Green
William Griffith

EUNOMUS
John James Park

EUPATOR
Joseph Mendham

EUPHAN
Barbara Euphan Todd

EUPHRANOR
James Bolivar Manson

EUPHRASIA
Clara Reeve

EUPISTINUS, THEOPHILUS
Robert Witham

EUSEBIA
Mary Hays

EUSEBIUS
Robert Boucher Nickolls
Edmund Rack

EUSEBIUS, VICAR OF
LILLIPUT
Joseph Robertson

EUSTACE
William Read

EUSTACE, ROBERT
Eustace Robert Barton

EVA
Mary Anne Kelly

EVANGELUS PACIFICUS
Hubbard Winslow

EVANS, ALAN
Alan Stoker

EVANS, AUGUSTA J.
Augusta J. Evans Wilson

EVANS, CARADOC
David Evans

EVANS, EDMUND
Charles Henry Ross

EVANS, EVAN
Frederick Schiller Faust

EVANS, JOHN
Howard Browne

EVANS, JONATHAN
Brian Harry Freemantle

EVANS, MARGIAD
Peggy Eileen Arabella Williams

EVANS, OWEN
William Henry Anderdon

EVANS, TABOR
Harry B. Whittington

EVELYN, CHETWOOD, ESQ.
Robert Conger Pell

EVERPOINT
Joseph M. Field

EVERTON, EVELINE T.
Ernest Tetley Ellis

EVERTON, FRANCIS
Francis William Stokes

EVOE
Edmond George Valpy Knox

AN EX-AIDE-DE-CAMP
Lord William Pitt Lennox

THE EX-BARBER TO HIS
    MAJESTY
Asa Greene

AN EX-CADET
James Dabney McCabe

AN EX-COMPETITION
    WALLAH
Swinton Boult

AN EX-CONSUL
Charles Wheeler Denison

AN EX-DIPLOMAT
William James Stillman

AN EX-DIPLOMATIST
Frederick Marshall

AN EX-EDITOR
Cyrus Redding

EX-INTELLIGENCE OFFICER
Capt. Lionel James

AN EX-MADRAS CIVILIAN
James Dewar Bourdillon

AN EX-MEMBER OF THE
    FENIAN DIRECTORY
Alfred S. Aylward

AN EX-OFFICER OF THE
    ROYAL IRISH
    CONSTABULARY
John Wilson Montgomery

AN EX-PENSION AGENT
Henry Morford

AN EX-POLITICAL
Edward Backhouse Eastwick

AN EX-PRIVATE HUSSAR
William Douglas

EX-PRIVATE-X
Alfred McLelland Burrage

AN EX-PUSEYITE
Charles Maurice Davies

AN EX-SERVICEMAN
Arthur Trystan Edwards

EXAMINER
Sir Isaac Pitman

AN EXAMINER OF THE NEW
    CHURCH DOCTRINES
Sir Isaac Pitman

EXCELLENT, MATILDA
Daniel Negley Farson

EXCELLMANS, BARON
    KARLO
William Henry Ireland

AN EXCHANGED OFFICER
Capt. Malcolm Vivian Hay

EXE, BILL
William Carlos Williams

EXONIENSIS, EUSEBIUS
Richard Polwhele

AN EXPERIENCED
    CHAPERONE
Sybella Wilbraham

AN EXPERIENCED FARMER
Arthur Young

AN EXPERIENCED OCULIST
Georg Joseph Beer

EXPERIENTA
John Southward

EXPERTUS
Rev. Malcolm MacColl

EXPLORABILIS
Mrs Eliza Haywood

EXPOSITOR
Aaron Whitney Leland

AN EXTINGUISHED EXILE
Sir Thomas Wemyss Reid

EXTON, CLIVE
Clive Brooks

EXUL
Richard Le Gallienne

AN EYE-WITNESS
Andrew Burn
George Jackson Eldridge
George Robert Gleig
Richard Hartley Kennedy
Charles Lamb
Sir Thomas Dick Lauder
Thomas Edward Lawrence
Thomas M'Lauchlan
William Alexander Parsons
    Martin
Frederick Apthorpe Paley
Alexander Pope
Karl Postl
William Sancroft
Joseph Stock
Henry Tanner
Philip Thicknesse
Thomas Perronet Thompson
William Walton

AN EYE-WITNESS TO THE
    MOST REMARKABLE
    PASSAGES
George Walter Story

EYLES, MERLE
Kathleen Muriel Eyles

EYRE, ANNETTE
Annette Isobel Worboys

EZEKIEL
Thomas Charles Morgan

EZRA I. Y. H. X.
Ezra Pound

F

F.
Harry Sinclair Lewis

F. B.
Francis Brokesby

F. F.
Edward Verrall Lucas

F. G. H.
Fitz-Greene Halleck

F. O. O.
Cecil John Charles Street

a F. R. G. S.
Sir Richard Francis Burton

FABIAN, WARNER
Samuel Hopkins Adams

FABIUS
John Dickinson
John Ireland

FABRICIUS
Joseph Galloway

FADLADEEN
George Darley

FAG, FREDERICK
James Johnson

FAIR, A. A.
Erle Stanley Gardner

FAIRBAIRN, ROGER
John Dickson Carr

FAIRE, ZABRINA
Florence Stevenson

FAIRFAX, ANN
Marion Chesney

FAIRFAX, BEATRICE
Marie Manning

FAIRFAX, L.
Celia Logan Connelly

FAIRFIELD, CLARENCE
Edwin Ross Champlin

FAIRFIELD, FLORA
Louisa May Alcott

FAIRLAMB, SAMPSON
James Kirke Paulding

FAIRLAY, OLIVER
Benjamin Franklin Bache

FAIRLEIGH, FRANK
Francis Edward Smedley

FAIRLEIGH, RUNA
Larry Alan Morse

FAIRLESS, MICHAEL
Margaret Fairless Barber

FAIRPLAY, OLIVER
Thomas Jefferson

MRS FAIRSTAR
Richard Hengist Horne

FAIRWAY, SIDNEY
Sidney Herbert Daukes

A FAITHFUL SON OF THE
    CHURCH OF ENGLAND
Thomas Traherne

A FAITHFULL LOVER OF
    HIS CHURCH
Sir Thomas Aston

FALCON FEATHER
John Collier

FALCONER, EDMUND
Edmund O'Rourke

FALCONER, KENNETH
C. M. Kornbluth

FALCONER, LANOE
Mary Elizabeth Hawker

FALKIRK, RICHARD
Derek William Lambert

FALKLAND
Nathaniel Chapman
Francis Perceval Eliot

FALL, MARCUS
Richard Dowling

FALLON, GEORGE
David Ernest Bingley

FALLON, MARTIN
Harry Patterson

FALSTAFF, JAKE
Herman Fetzer

A FAMILY PARTY
Ellen Wood

THE FAMOUS WRITER FOR
    YOUNG AMERICANS
Elbridge Streeter Brooks

FANE, BRON
Robert Lionel Fanthorpe

FANE, FLORENCE
Mrs Frances Fuller Victor

FANE, VIOLET
Mary Montgomerie Singleton

FANFARLO
George Walter Stonier

FANT, ELI
Edward Bean Underhill

FARBRICK, JONATHAN
Silas Pinckney Holbrook

FARELY, ALISON
Dorothy Poland

FARGO, DOONE
Victor G. C. Norwood

FARLEY, RALPH MILNE
Roger Sherman Hoar

FARMAN, ELLA
Eliza Pratt

A FARMER
James Anderson
Anthony Benezet
Henry Brooke
Tristram Burges
Francis Douglas
Levi Lincoln
George Logan
Arthur Young

FARMER, A. W.
Samuel Seabury

A FARMER AND A BREEDER
John Lawrence

A FARMER OF NEW JERSEY
William Livingston

FARMER TRUEMAN
Jonas Hanway

THE FARMER'S BOY
Robert Bloomfield

FARNDALE, JOHN
John Wilfred Harvey

FARNEWORTH, ELLIS
Thomas Bedford

FARNINGHAM, MARIANNE
Mary Anne Hearn

FARQUHAR, IAN
David Pae

FARQUHARSON, MARTHA
Martha Farquharson Finley

FARR, DIANA
Diana Pullein-Thompson

FARR, JOHN
Jack Webb

FARR, SEBASTIAN
Eric Walter Blom

FARRAN, RICHARD M.
John Betjeman

FARRELL, BEN
Mel Cebulash

FARRELL, DAVID
Frederick E. Smith

FARRELL, M. J.
Mary Nesta (Molly) Keane

FARROW, JAMES S.
Edwin Charles Tubb

FARTHING POET
Richard Hengist Horne

THE FAT CONTRIBUTOR
William Makepeace Thackeray

A FATHER
Robert Ainslie
Benjamin Coole
John Gregory
David Hale
Hosea Hildreth
William Fordyce Mavor

FATHER ABRAHAM
Benjamin Franklin

FATHER BAPTIST
Richard Baptist O'Brien

FATHER IGNATIUS
Rev. Joseph Leycester Lyne

FATHER JEAN
James Beal

FATHER PROUT
Francis Sylvester Mahony

FATHER THOMAS
Thomas Doyle

A FATHER OF THE SOCIETY OF JESUS
Francis Walsingham

FAULKNER, GEORGE
Robert Jephson

FAVONIUS
George Smalridge

FAWCETT, CATHERINE
Catherine Cookson

FAWKES, FRANCIS
Edward Burnaby Greene

FAY, ERICA
Marie Carmichael Stokes

FAY, NICHOLAS
Wilkinson Sherren

FECAMPS, ELISE
John Creasey

FECHER, CONSTANCE
Constance Heaven

THE FEDERAL FARMER
Richard Henry Lee

A FEDERAL REPUBLICAN
Henry William Desaussure

A FEDERALIST
Noah Webster

FEIKEMA, FEIKE
Frederick Manfred

FELICIA
Mrs Mary Mitchell Collyer

FELIX
Nicholas Wanostrocht

FELIX, MARCUS MINUCIUS
Sir David Dalrymple

A FELLOW
Lionel Smith Beale

A FELLOW M. A.
John Rustat Crowfoot

FELLOW, R.
Horace Elisha Scudder

A FELLOW CITIZEN
Henry Thomas Cockburn

A FELLOW OF A COLLEGE
William Bright
Richard Hurd
Capell Lofft
Peter Shaw

A FELLOW OF A COLLEGE IN CAMBRIDGE
Edward Baines

A FELLOW OF ALL-SOULS
Aaron Hill

A FELLOW OF MERTON COLLEGE
Edmund Charles Blunden

A FELLOW OF SEVERAL LEARNED SOCIETIES
John Murray

A FELLOW OF ST JOHN'S COLLEGE, CAMBRIDGE
Samuel Laing

A FELLOW OF THE ANTIQUARIAN SOCIETY
George Robert Ainslie
Foote Gower

A FELLOW OF THE ANTIQUARIAN SOCIETIES OF LONDON AND SCOTLAND
George Robert Ainslie

A FELLOW OF THE COLLEGE OF PHYSICIANS AND OF THE ROYAL SOCIETY
Nehemiah Grew

A FELLOW OF THE COLLEGE OF PHYSICIANS, DUBLIN
James Henry

A FELLOW OF THE COLLEGE OF PHYSICIANS, LONDON
Thomas Gibson

A FELLOW OF THE GEOLOGICAL SOCIETY
John Murray

A FELLOW OF THE LINNAEAN SOCIETY
Adrian Hardy Haworth
John Murray

A FELLOW OF THE ROYAL AND ANTIQUARIAN SOCIETIES
Josiah Forshall

A FELLOW OF THE ROYAL GEOGRAPHICAL SOCIETY
Sir John Peter Grant

A FELLOW OF THE ROYAL SOCIETY
Robert Boyle
James William Gilbart
James Orchard Halliwell-Phillips
Cotton Mather

A FELLOW OF THE
SOCIETY OF
ANTIQUARIES
William John Loftie

A FELLOW OF UNIVERSITY
COLLEGE, OXFORD
Sir Edward West

A FELLOW OF ***
COLLEGE, CAMBRIDGE
Gerard Francis Cobb

A FELLOW SUFFERER
John Park

FELLOWES, C.
Eveline Camilla Gurdon

FEN, ELISAVETA
Lydia Jackson

FENNER, JAMES R.
Edwin Charles Tubb

FERGUSON, HELEN
Helen Woods Edmonds

FERN, FANNY
Sara Payson Willis

FERRARS, ELIZABETH (or E.
X.)
Morna Doris Brown

FERRARS, RALPH
William Peter

FERREX
Ezra Pound

FFOLKES, MICHAEL
Brian Davis

FIACC, PADRAIC
Patrick Joseph O'Connor

FIAT JUSTITIA
Thomas Binney

FIBB, A.
Alfred Henry Forrester

FICTOR NO GO
Francis Cowley Burnand

FIDELIS
William Brocklehurst
Stonehouse

FIDGET, FERDINANDO
Alexander Chalmers

FIDGIT, WRINKLETON
Henry Thomson

FIDLER, KATHLEEN
Kathleen Annie Goldie

FIELD, D. M.
Neil Grant

FIELD, FRANK CHESTER
Frank Chester Robertson

FIELD, GANS T.
Manley Wade Wellman

FIELD, JOANNA
Nina Marion Milner

FIELD, MICHAEL
Katharine Harris Bradley with
Edith Emma Cooper

FIELD, TEMPLE
Raoul Whitfield

A FIELD OFFICER
Lt.-Col. Arthur Wellesley
Torrens

A FIELD OFFICER OF
CAVALRY
Sir Digby Mackworth

A FIELD OFFICER ON THE
RETIRED LIST OF THE
INDIAN ARMY
Maj. David Price

FIELDFARE
Sir Alexander Balmain Bruce
Valentine

FIELDING, A.
Dorothy Fielding

FIELDING, GABRIEL
Alan Gabriel Barnsley

FIELDING, H., GENT.
James Miller

FIELDING, H. (or HENRY or
HAROLD)
Harold Patrick Fielding-Hall

FIELDING, HOWARD
Charles W. Hooke

FIELDING, THOMAS
John Wade

FIELDING, XAN
Alexander Wallace Fielding

FIELDMOUSE, TIMON
William Brighty Rands

FIFESHIRE FORESTER
John Bethune

FIGARO
Henry Clapp

A FIGHTER PILOT
Hugh Anthony Stephen
Johnston

FIGWOOD, JOHN
Joseph Sheridan Le Fanu

FILIA ECCLESIAE
Sarah Anne Dorsey

FILODEXTER
TRANSYLVANUS
Benjamin Woodbridge

FIN BEC
William Blanchard Jerrold

A FINANCIER
Pelatiah Webster

FINCH, MATTHEW (or
MERTON)
Merton Fink

FINDLATER, RICHARD
Kenneth Bruce Findlater Bain

FINDLEY, FERGUSON
Charles W. Frey

FINLEY, SCOTT
Winifred Clark

FINN, MICKEY
Ernest Jarrold

FINNEGAN, ROBERT
Paul William Ryan

FINNEGAN, TERRY
James McCarroll

FIRBANK, ARTHUR (or
RONALD)
Arthur Annesley Ronald
Firbank

THE FIRST CITIZEN
Charles Carroll

A FIRST CLASS MAN OF
BALLIOL COLLEGE,
OXFORD
Thomas Nash

FISGUILL, RICHARD
Richard Henry Wilson

FISHER, BUD
Harry Conway

FISHER, CLAY
Henry Wilson Allen

FISHER, CYRUS
Darwin Teilhet

FISHER, LAINE
James Arch Howard

FISHER, P. (or PAYNE)
William Andrew Chatto

FISHER, STEVE
Stephen Gould Fisher

FISHER, WADE
Victor G. C. Norwood

A FISHERMAN AND
ZOOLOGIST
Francis Trevelyan Buckland

FISK, COLLENE
Wilbur Fisk Crafts

FISK, NICHOLAS
Diavid Higginbottom

FISKE, SHARON
Pamela Hill

FISKE, TARLETON
Robert Albert Bloch

FITCH, CLARKE
Upton Beall Sinclair

FITT, MARY
Kathleen Freeman

FITZ-ADAM, ADAM
Edward Moore

FITZADAM, ISMAEL
John Macken

FITZALAN, ROGER
Trevor Dudley-Smith

FITZBALL, EDWARD
Edward Ball

FITZ-BOODLE, GEORGE
SAVAGE
William Makepeace Thackeray

FITZGERALD, ELLEN
Florence Stevenson

FITZGERALD, ERIC
Gil Brewer

FITZGERALD, ERROL
Lady Josephine Fitzgerald
Clarke

FITZGERALD, FRANCIS
Charles Taylor

FITZGERALD, HUGH
Lyman Frank Baum

FITZGERALD, JULIA
Julia Watson

FITZHERBERT
Thomas Rothwell

FITZNOODLE
Benjamin Vallentine

FITZOSBORNE, SIR
THOMAS
William Melmoth

FITZPATRICK, NINA
Nina Witoszek

FITZSTEWART
William Blacker

FITZTRAVESTY, BLAISE
William Maginn

FITZVICTOR, JOHN
Percy Bysshe Shelley

FITZWORM, REGINALD
John Boyle

FIVE OF CLUBS
Richard Anthony Proctor

FIVE SMALL BEAGLES
John Lilburne

FLACCUS
Thomas Ward

FLAGELLUM
William Henry Ireland

A FLAG OFFICER
Edward Hawker
Sir William Fanshawe Martin
Sir Charles Vinicombe Penrose

A FLAG OFFICER OF HER
MAJESTY'S FLEET
Edward Hawker

FLAGG, FRANCIS
Henry George Weiss

FLAMBEAU, VIKTOR
Gertrude Richardson Brigham

FLAMBRO (or
FLAMBOROUGH),
GEORGE
George William Lamplugh

THE FLANEUR
John Palgrave Simpson
Edmund Yates

THE FLANEUR IN PARIS
John Palgrave Simpson

FLEETWOOD, EVERARD
Samuel Burroughs

FLEMING, CAROLINE
Anne Mather

FLEMING, GEORGE
Julia Constance Fletcher

FLEMING, OLIVER
Philip MacDonald with Ronald
MacDonald

FLEMING, RHODA
Ronald Fleming

FLEMING, STUART
Damon Knight

FLEMING, WALDO
Thames Ross Williamson

FLEMMING, HARFORD
Mrs Harriet McClellan

FLESTRIN, QUINTUS
Christopher Smart

FLETCHER, GEORGE U.
Fletcher Pratt

A FLIRT
Lady Charlotte Susan Maria
Bury

FLORENCE
William Jermyn Florence

FLORENCE, AMBROSE
Edwin Lees

FLORENTIA
Frances Minto Elliot

FLORENZ
Lady Charlotte Elliott

FLORIAN, FRANCOIS M.
Edward Gordon Craig

FLORIANI, GIULIO
Aubrey Beardsley

FLORIO
James Gordon Brooks

FLORRY
J. Frank Kernan

MR FLOTSAM
Bentley Collingwood Hilliam

FLUVIATULIS PISCATOR
Joseph Seccombe

FLYING OFFICER-X
Herbert Ernest Bates

FLYNN, JACKSON
Gordon Donald Shirreffs

FLYNT, JOSIAH
Josiah Flynt Willard

A FOE TO IGNORANCE
Henry Mudge

FOGARTY, JONATHAN
TITULESCU
James Thomas Farrell

FOGARTY, PAT, OF CORK
Edward Vaughan Hyde
Kenealy

A FOGEY
Andrew Lang

FOGLE, FRANCIS, SEN., ESQ.
George Payson

FOLEY, RAE
Elinore Denniston

A FOLLOWER OF LOCKE
Benjamin Humphrey Smart

A FOLLOWER OF PEACE
AND LOVER OF
SINCERITY
John Humphrey

FONTHILL, ARTHUR
Josiah Clifton Firth

FOOL, TOM
Eleanor Farjeon
Robert Ranke Graves

FOOT, FARDINANDO
Christopher Smart

FOOTE, S. JUN.
Francis Wrangham

A FOOTMAN
Robert Dodsley

FORAGER, PHILIP
William Maginn

FORBES, ALECK
St George Henry Rathbone

FORBES, ALEXANDER
William Anderson Forbes

FORBES, BRYAN
John Clarke

FORBES, COLIN
Raymond H. Sawkins

FORBES, DANIEL
Michael Kenyon

FORBES, KATHRYN
Kathryn Anderson McLean

FORBES, ROBERT ERSTONE
Ralph Straus

FORBES, STANTON
Deloris Stanton Forbes

FORD, DAVID
Terence William Harknett

FORD, ELBUR
Eleanor Alice Hibbert

FORD, ELIZABETH
Marjory Elizabeth Bidwell

FORD, FORD MADOX
Ford Hermann Hueffer

FORD, GARRETT
William L. Crawford

FORD, HILARY
Christopher Samuel Youd

FORD, KIRK
William John Duncan Spence

FORD, LESLIE
Zenith Brown

FORDE, NICHOLAS
Arthur Elliott-Cannon

FORDEN, JAMES
James Henry Stanley Barlow

FORDWICH, JACK
Henry J. Garrish

A FOREIGN RESIDENT
Thomas Hay Sweet Escott

A FOREIGNER
George Watterston

A FOREMAN PATTERN-
MAKER
Joseph Gregory Horner

FORESTER
Thomas Paine

FORESTER, FANNY
Emily Chubbuck Judson

FORESTER, FRANK
Henry William Herbert

FORESTIER, AUBER
Annie Aubertine Woodward

THE FORMER AUTHOR, J.
M.
John Milton

A FORMER MEMBER OF H.
C. S.
Arthur Llewellyn Jones

FORREST, COL. CRIS
William Osborn Stoddard

FORREST, DAVID
David Denholm

FORREST, DIAL
William Campbell Gault

FORREST, FELIX C.
Paul Myron Anthony
Linebarger

FORREST, GEORGE, ESQ.,
MA
John George Wood

FORREST, MARK
Guy Mainwaring Morton

FORREST, MARY
Julia Deane Freeman

FORREST, NORMAN
Nigel Morland

FORRESTER, FRANCIS, ESQ.
Daniel Wise

FORRESTER, GILBERT
Henry Braddon

A FORREYNER
John Dayman

FORSYTHE, ROBERT
Kyle Samuel Crichton

FORTH, GEORGE
Harold Frederic

FORTUNE, DION
Violet Mary Firth

FORTUNE, G. AND W.
Walter Herman Aston and
George Francis Collie

FORTY, OLIVER
Nathan Green

FOSCHTER, ALBERT
Aubrey Beardsley

FOSTER, FRANCIS
Reginald Frank Foster

FOSTER, FRANK
Daniel Puseley

FOSTER, GABRIEL
John Edgell Rickword

FOSTER, GEORGE
Chetwynd John Drake Haswell

FOSTER, IAN
Eric De Banzie

FOSTER, IRIS
Richard Posner

FOSTER, RICHARD
Kendell Foster Crossen

FOSTER, SIMON
Duncan Munro Glen

FOSTER, THOMAS
Richard Anthony Proctor

FOSTER, WILLIAM
Oliver William Foster Lodge

FOUGASSE
Cyril Kenneth Bird

FOULEWEATHER, ADAM
Thomas Nash

FOULIS, HUGH
Neil Munro

FOULIS, OLIVER
David Lloyd

THE FOUNDER OF THE
ESTABLISHMENT
Thomas Joplin

A FOUNDLING
Hannah Sherman Brown

FOUR ANGLO INDIAN
WRITERS
Rudyard Kipling

FOURTH FORM
Guy Kendall

FOWLER, SYDNEY
Sydney Fowler Wright

FOX, ANTHONY
Alexander Fergus Fullerton

FOX, BRIAN
Willis Todhunter Ballard

FOX, CONNIE
Hugh Fox

FOX, DAVID
Isabel Egerton Ostrander

FOX, JAMES M.
Johannes M. W. Knipscheer

FOX, SEBASTIAN
Gerald William Bullett

FOXEAR, NICIAS
Francis Jacox

THE FOXHUNTER ROUGH AND READY
Paul Ourry Treby

A FOX-HUNTING MAN
Siegfried Sassoon

FOXTON, E.
Miss Sarah Hammond Palfrey

FOXX, JACK
Bill Pronzini

FRA. ELBERTUS
Elbert Hubbard

FRAME, ROBERT
Sir James Denham Stewart

FRAMPTON, JOSIAH
William Gilpin

FRANCES
Richard Griffith with Mrs
Elizabeth Griffith

FRANCESCA
Francesca Alexander

FRANCIS, C. D. E.
Patrick John Fielding Howarth

FRANCIS, GEORGE
George Francis Thomas

FRANCIS, M. E.
Mary E. Blundell

FRANCIS, WILLIAM
William Francis Urell

FRANCO, HARRY
Charles Frederick Briggs

FRANK, PAT
Harry Hart

FRANK, THEODORE
Dorothea Frances Gardiner

FRANKLIN
William Foster

FRANKLIN, CHARLES
Frank Hugh Usher

FRANKLIN, EDGAR
Edgar Franklin Stearns

FRANKLIN, JAY
John Franklin Carter

FRANKLIN, MAX
Richard Deming

FRASER, ALEX
Henry Brinton

FRASER, JANE
Rosamunde Pilcher

FRASER, NORMAN
David Cuthbertson

FRATER
Francis Lister Hawks

FRATER PERDURABO
Edward Alexander Crowley

FRAZER, ANDREW
Milton Lesser

FRAZER, RENEE
Ronald Fleming

FRAZER, ROBERT CAINE
John Creasey

FRAZIER, ARTHUR
Kenneth Henry Bulmer

FREDERIC, MIKE
William Robert Cox

FREDERICK, WYKEHAM
Frederick Gale

FREDERICKS, ARNOLD
Frederick Arnold Kummer

FREE, JOHN
John Freeth

A FREE CHURCH LAYMAN
James Ferguson

A FREE CHURCHMAN
Andrew Gray

A FREE ENQUIRER AFTER TRUTH
William Ashdowne

A FREE MAN
William Joseph Snelling

A FREE-MAN, THOUGH A PRISONER
George Wither

A FREE SOILER FROM THE START
John Gorham Palfrey

A FREE-THINKER
John Armstrong
James Usher

FREEBETTER, EDMUND
Nathan Daboll

A FREEHOLDER
Henry Boase
Hugh Boyd
Alexander Carlyle
John Erskine
William Pulteney
William Wagstaffe

A FREEHOLDER AND LANDHOLDER OF SCOTLAND
John Campbell Colquhoun

A FREEHOLDER NORTH OF TRENT
William Hutchinson

A FREEHOLDER OF DEVON
John Pike Jones

A FREEHOLDER OF LEICESTER
Ralph Heathcote

A FREEHOLDER OF SOUTH CAROLINA
John J. Zubly

A FREEHOLDER OF SURREY
John Horne Tooke

A FREEHOLDER OF THE COUNTY OF SURREY
Joseph Grove

A FREEMAN
George Allen
William Henry Drayton
Jacob Bailey Moore

FREEMAN, COUNCILLOR
James Russell Endean

FREEMAN, CYNTHIA
Bea Feinberg

FREEMAN, JAY
James Holding

FREEMAN, JONATHAN
Morris Birkbeck

FREEMAN, JOSHUA
Arthur Ashley Sykes

FREEMAN, RICHARD
Richard Horatio Edgar Wallace

FREEMAN, THEOPHILUS
William Matthews

FREEMAN, THOMAS
Theodore Reed Fehrenbach

A FREEMAN, BARBER AND CITIZEN
Charles Lucas

MR FREETHINKER
Ambrose Philips

FRENCH, ASHLEY
Denise Naomi Robins

FRENCH, PAUL
Isaac Asimov

A FRENCH CLERGYMAN
Stephen Norman Badin

FRENCHMAN, JACK
Jonathan Swift

FREYER, FREDRIC
William Sanborn Ballinger

FRIBBLETON, EX-BARBER
Asa Greene

FRICK, C. H.
Constance Irwin

FRIDOLIN
Francis John Harrison Rankin

A FRIEND
Zachary Grey
Sir Richard Hill
Luke Howard
Edward Mangin
John Oldmixon

FRIEND, ED
Richard E. Wormser

A FRIEND AND BROTHER OFFICER
Sir Henry Yule

A FRIEND IN THE CITY
George Meldrum

A FRIEND IN THE COUNTRY
John Erskine
Lord George Lyttelton

A FRIEND IN THE NORTH
Stephen Colwell

A FRIEND OF AMERICAN LIBERTY
Jacob Green

A FRIEND OF DOMESTIC INDUSTRY
Caleb Cushing

A FRIEND OF INDUSTRY
Benjamin Dearborn

A FRIEND OF MR ST___LE
Jonathan Swift

A FRIEND OF POPULAR EDUCATION
John Relly Beard

A FRIEND OF RELIGIOUS LIBERTY
William Paley

A FRIEND OF THE ARMIES
William Dell

A FRIEND OF THE AUTHOR
Jonathan Swift

A FRIEND OF THE PEOPLE
Henry Peter Brougham

A FRIEND OF THE ROAD
Elizur Wright

A FRIEND OF TRUTH
John Cleaveland
Elisha Scott Williams

A FRIEND OF TRUTH AND PEACE
Wiliam Walton

A FRIEND OF TRUTH AND SOUND POLICY
Henry M. Brackenridge

A FRIEND OF YOUTH
Mary Clark
Samuel Willard

A FRIEND OF YOUTH AND CHILDREN
Frederick William Evans

A FRIEND TO ACCURACY
Thomas Bland

A FRIEND TO AMERICAN ENTERPRISE
George W. Simmons

A FRIEND TO CANDOUR AND TRUTH
Stephen Jones

A FRIEND TO CIVIL AND RELIGIOUS LIBERTY
Henry Peckwell

A FRIEND TO CONSISTENCY
William Wordsworth

A FRIEND TO EDUCATION AND MORAL IMPROVEMENT OF THE LABOURING POOR
Thomas Pole

A FRIEND TO ENGLAND'S COMMONWEALTH
Edward Burrough

A FRIEND TO 'FAIR PLAY'
Randle Jackson

A FRIEND TO FEMALE BEAUTY
Richard Russell

A FRIEND TO HUMANITY
Mary Robinson

A FRIEND TO HUSBANDRY
Sir John Sinclair

A FRIEND TO IMPROVEMENTS
Robert John Thornton

A FRIEND TO LIBERTY AND PROPERTY
John Lewis

A FRIEND TO ORDER IN THE CHURCH
Robert Culbertson

A FRIEND TO PUBLIC CREDIT
Sir Philip Francis

A FRIEND TO RIGHTEOUSNESS
Edward Burrough

A FRIEND TO THAT INTEREST
Gilbert Rule

A FRIEND TO THE CHURCHES
Increase Mather

A FRIEND TO THE CHURCH OF ENGLAND
Francis Maseres

A FRIEND TO THE CONSTITUTION
Benjamin Flower

A FRIEND TO THE GOVERNMENT
William Webster

A FRIEND TO THE LIBERTY OF HIS COUNTRY
Benjamin Church

A FRIEND TO THEM THAT HATE INIQUITY
George Whitehead

A FRIEND TO THE MUSES
Thomas Guidott

A FRIEND TO THE NATION
John Wynn Baker

A FRIEND TO THE NATURAL AND RELIGIOUS RIGHTS OF MANKIND
William Graham

A FRIEND TO THE PARLIAMENT
Nathaniel Ward

A FRIEND TO THE PARLIAMENT, CITY AND KINGDOM
Sir Thomas Adams

A FRIEND TO THE SISTERHOOD
William Hayley

A FRIEND TO THE SOUTH
Mrs Belle Hardinge

A FRIEND TO TRUE LIBERTY
Edmund Rack

A FRIEND TO TRUTH
Joseph Eckley
John Jamieson
William Wordsworth

A FRIEND TO TRUTH AND LIBERTY
Henry Augustus Dillon-Lee
Josiah Owen

A FRIEND TO TRUTH AND PEACE
Nicholas Lockyer

**A FRIEND TO TRUTH AND
THE PRESENT
ESTABLISHMENT**
Caleb Fleming

**A FRIEND TO TRUTH WHO
IS NO RESPECTER OF
PERSONS**
Benjamin Furly

A FRIEND UNKNOWN
John Humphrey

**A FRIEND WHO IS LATELY
DECEASED**
Anne Fry

FRIZIUS, JOACHIM
Robert Fludd

HERR FROEHLICH
Thomas William Marshall

FROEST, FRANK
George Dilnot

FROME, DAVID
Zenith Brown

FROST, FREDERICK
Frederick Schiller Faust

FROY, HERALD
Guy Deghy with Keith
Spencer Waterhouse

FRY, CHRISTOPHER
Christopher Harris

FRY, PETE
James Clifford King

FULLER, ROGER
Donald Fiske Tracy

FUME, JOSEPH
William Andrew Chatto

FUNGUS, BARNABY, ESQ.
Arthur Benoni Evans

FUNNEFELLO, ABEL
Charles Molloy Westmacott

A FUNNYMAN
Edward Bradley

FURBER, DOUGLAS
Michael Sultan Lewin

FUREY, MICHAEL
Arthur Sarsfield Ward

FURNEAUX, ROBIN
Frederick William Robin Smith

FURST, ADOLF
Edward Gordon Craig

FUSBOS
Henry Grattan Plunkett

FUTILOE, RICHARD, SEN.
John Ferguson MacLennan

FUZE
Robert Ranke Graves

FYNES, RANDLE
Sir Randle Fynes Wilson
Holme

G

G.
Terence Ian Fytton Armstrong
William Oldys

G. A. S.
George Augustus Henry Sala

G. B.
George Berkeley
George Borrow

G. D.
George Darley

G. F. B.
William Makepeace Thackeray

G. F. P.
George Frederick Pardon

G. G.
William Cowper

G. H.
John Palmer

G. K.
John Boyle

G. L. B. O. C.
George Berkeley

G. M. T.
George Macaulay Trevelyan

G. S. O.
Sir Frank Fox

GABBLER, GRIDIRON
Joseph Haslewood

GABRIEL
James Friell

GABRIELLI
Mrs Mary Meeke

GAGE, GERVAIS
John Laurence Rentoul

GAGE, WILSON
Mary Q. Steele

GAHAGAN, GOLIAH,
SOMETIMES WITH
TITLES MAJOR AND H.
E. I. C. S.
William Makepeace Thackeray

GAINHAM, SARAH
Rachel Ames

GAIRDNER, THE LATE
WILLIAM, WRITER TO
HER MAJESTY'S
SIGNET
William MacGillivray

GALE, JOHN
Richard Gaze

GALE, MARTIN
Eric Greville Earle

GALE, ZONA
Mrs William Llewellyn Breese

GALLAGHER, GALE
Wilbur Charles Oursler

GALLERYITE
Frederick Thomas Bason

GALLI, ANTONIO
Edward Gordon Craig

A GALLOWAY HERD
Henry M. B. Reid

THE GALLOWAY POET
William Nicholson

GALT, WALTER
William Lancaster Gribbon

GALWAY, ROBERT
CONINGTON
Philip Donald McCutchan

GAMBADO, GEOFFREY
Henry William Bunbury

GAMBIER, KENYON
Lorin Andrews Lathrop

GANCONAGH
William Butler Yeats

GANDER, SIR GREGORY,
KT.
George Ellis

GANPAT
Martin Louis Alan Gompertz

GANT, JONATHAN
Clifton Adams

GANT, RICHARD
Brian Freemantle

GAOL CHAPLAIN
Erskine Neale

GAR., BER.
Bernard Garter

GARD, JANICE
Jean Lee Latham

GARD, JOYCE
Joyce Reeves

GARDEN, BRUCE
James Alexander Mackay

GARDEN, JOHN
Harry Fletcher

GARDNER, JEFFREY
Gardner Francis Fox

GARDNER, MIRIAM
Marion Zimmer Bradley

GARDONS, S. S.
William Dewitt Snodgrass

GARDWELL, GODEK
Edward Kellogg

GARGANTUA PANTAGRUEL
William Rufus Chetwood

GARIOCH, ROBERT
Robert Sutherland

GARLAND, BENNETT
Brian Francis Wynne Garfield

GARLAND, GEORGE
Garland Roark

GARNER, ROLF
Bryan Berry

GARNETT, ROGER
Nigel Morland

GARON
Joseph Bretland

GARRARD, KENNER
Lewis Edward Nolan

GARRETT, EDWARD
Isabella Fyvie Mayo

GARRISON, LIEUTENANT FREDERICK, U. S. A.
Upton Beall Sinclair

GARRULOUS, GEORGE
George Arnold

GARRYOWEN
Edmund Finn

GARSTON, GUY
Bernard John Hurren

GARTH, WILL
Henry Kuttner
Manly Wade Wellman

GARVE, ANDREW
Paul Winterton

GASH, JONATHAN
John Grant

GASKELL, A. P.
A. G. Pickard

A GASTRONOME
Mrs Anne Mathews

GATH
George Alfred Townsend

GATOS, STEPHANIE
Steve Katz

GATTY, J. H.
Mrs Juliana Horatia Ewing

GAULT, MARK
John Cournos

GAUNT, GRAHAM
John Grant

GAUNT, JEFFREY
George Ernest Rochester

GAUNT, M. B.
Richard Henry Horsfield

GAVOTTE, HADRIAN JAZZ
Edward Gordon Craig

GAWSWORTH, JOHN
Terence Ian Fytton Armstrong

GAY, AMELIA
Grace Allen Hogarth

GAY, FRANCIS
Herbert Leslie Gee

GAY, JOSEPH
John Durant Breval

GAY, MR JOSEPH
Alexander Pope

GAY, LADY
George Rutland Barrington-Fleet

GAYLE, EMMA
Eleanor Fairburn

GAYLE, NEWTON
Maurice Guinness

GAYLORD, GLANCE
Warren Ives Bradley

GAYTHORNE, ROSA
Rhoda Haddock

GEARON, JOHN
John Flagg

GEDDES, HUGH
Hugh Atkinson

GEMSEGE, PAUL
Samuel Pegge

GENERAL CHASSE
Henry Hall Dixon

GENERAL PUNTA GORDA
Isaac H. Trabue

A GENERAL OFFICER OF CAVALRY
James Thomas Brudenell

A GENERAL OFFICER OF THE LATE CONFEDERATE ARMY
Roswell Sabine Ripley

A GENERAL OFFICER WHO SERVED SEVERAL CAMPAIGNS IN THE AUSTRIAN ARMY
Henry Lloyd

GENET
Janet Flanner

A GENEVESE TRAVELLER
Matthew L. Davis

A GENIUS
James Boswell

A GENT.
Alexander Anderson

A GENTILE CHRISTIAN
John Goldie

A GENTLEMAN
John Adams
Thomas Baker
William Bromley
Alban Butler
Daniel Defoe
Sir Henry Bate Dudley
Paul Dudley
Francis Eyre
Anthony Hammond
John Hippisley
Denzil Holles
Edmund Hoyle
Thomas Hull
Sir John Leslie
Thomas Salmon
George Sewell
Thomas Sherlock

Edward Spelman
Thomas Skinner Surr
Priscilla Wakefield
Hugh Williamson
Browne Willis
Andrew Wilson

A GENTLEMAN, A DESCENDANT OF DAME QUICKLY
James White

A GENTLEMAN AND NO KNIGHT
Zachary Grey

A GENTLEMAN BRED IN THE FAMILY
John Oldmixon

A GENTLEMAN-COMMONER OF OXFORD
Samuel Croxall

A GENTLEMAN EDUCATED AT YALE COLLEGE
Samuel Johnson

A GENTLEMAN, FORMERLY OF BOSTON
Edward Church

A GENTLEMAN FROM ABERDEEN
Thomas Warton

A GENTLEMAN HERE
John Macky

A GENTLEMAN IN AMERICA
Thomas Cooper

A GENTLEMAN IN BOSTON
Charles Chauncy
Lewis Tappan

A GENTLEMAN IN ENGLAND
Thomas Tickell

A GENTLEMAN IN GLOUCESTERSHIRE
Joseph Butler

A GENTLEMAN IN INDIA
Eyles Irwin

A GENTLEMAN IN LONDON
William Knox
William Smith

A GENTLEMAN IN PHILADELPHIA
John Dickinson

A GENTLEMAN IN SCOTLAND
Francis Douglas
Charles Leslie

A GENTLEMAN IN THE CITY
Benjamin Coole
Charles Leslie

A GENTLEMAN IN THE COUNTRY
Charles Blount
John Brown
Adam Ferguson
Nicholas French
William Penn
John Perceval

A GENTLEMAN IN THE ENGLISH HOUSE OF COMMONS
Edmund Burke

A GENTLEMAN IN THE NORTH OF IRELAND
Alexander Knox

A GENTLEMAN IN THE NORTH OF SCOTLAND
Edward Burt

A GENTLEMAN LATELY RESTORED FROM THREATENING SICKNESS
Cotton Mather

A GENTLEMAN, LATE OF BATH
Sir Edward Harington

A GENTLEMAN NEAR OXFORD
William Law

A GENTLEMAN NOW RESIDING THERE
John Durant Breval

A GENTLEMAN OF BOSTON
Nathan Hale

A GENTLEMAN OF CAMBRIDGE
George Sackville Cotter
Francis Fawkes
Thomas Hearne
William Mason
Corbyn Morris
William Warburton

A GENTLEMAN OF CONNECTICUT
Joseph Huntington

A GENTLEMAN OF FOREIGN EXTRACTION
Jacob Duche

A GENTLEMAN OF GREAT SKILL IN THE SAID ART
John Astley

A GENTLEMAN OF IRELAND
John Monck Mason

A GENTLEMAN OF LINCOLN'S INN
Philip Carteret Webb

A GENTLEMAN OF MANCHESTER
Thomas Percival

A GENTLEMAN OF MARYLAND
Henry Hugh Brackenridge

A GENTLEMAN OF MASSACHUSETTS
Gamaliel Bradford

A GENTLEMAN OF NEW YORK
William Irving

A GENTLEMAN OF ONE OF THE INNS OF COURT
William Dodd

A GENTLEMAN OF OXFORD
Daniel Bellamy
William Collins
George Smith Green
Thomas Maurice
Michael Wodhull

A GENTLEMAN OF OXFORD THAT UNDERSTANDS TRAPP
Gilbert Burnet

A GENTLEMAN OF PORTSMOUTH, N. H.
Jonathan Mitchell Sewall

A GENTLEMAN OF QUALITIE
Dudley Digges

A GENTLEMAN OF QUALITY, A WELL-WISHER BOTH TO KING AND PARLIAMENT
Sir John Spelman

A GENTLEMAN OF SCOTLAND
James Boswell

A GENTLEMAN OF SOUTH CAROLINA
Henry Putnam

A GENTLEMAN OF THAT COUNTRY
Archibald Campbell

A GENTLEMAN OF THE ARMY
David Humphreys
Sir Richard Steele

A GENTLEMAN OF THE BAR
Isaac Daniel Rupp

A GENTLEMAN OF THE COMMISSION
Ralph Heathcote

A GENTLEMAN OF THE FACULTY
Hall Jackson

A GENTLEMAN OF THE FORCE
William Makepeace Thackeray

A GENTLEMAN OF THE INNER TEMPLE
George Monck Berkeley
John Campbell
John Mottley
Sir Bartholomew Shower

A GENTLEMAN OF THE INNS OF COURT
Myles Davies

A GENTLEMAN OF THE MIDDLE TEMPLE
Timothy Cunningham
Thomas Babington Macaulay
James Ralph

A GENTLEMAN OF THE PARTIE
Jonas Hanway

A GENTLEMAN OF THE PROVINCE
Samuel Andrew Peters

A GENTLEMAN OF THE TEMPLE
Richard Bentley
John Kelly
William Oldys
Arthur Ashley Sykes

A GENTLEMAN OF THE UNIVERSITY OF CAMBRIDGE
Sir Richard Bulkeley
Edward Alexander Crowley
Zachary Grey

A GENTLEMAN OF THE UNIVERSITY OF OXFORD
Thomas Dudley Fosbrooke
Sir Richard Hill
Percy Bysshe Shelley

A GENTLEMAN OF TRIED INTEGRITY
Henry Robinson

A GENTLEMAN OF WADHAM COLLEGE
James Miller

A GENTLEMAN ON HALF-
PAY
William Hamilton Maxwell

A GENTLEMAN ON HIS
TRAVELS
Sarah Scott

A GENTLEMAN RESIDENT
THERE
Thomas Rickman

A GENTLEMAN RESIDING
IN THIS CITY
Samuel Latham Mitchill

A GENTLEMAN THAT
LOVES THE PEACE OF
THE ENGLISH NATION
Edmund Waller

A GENTLEMAN WHO HAS
LEFT HIS LODGINGS
John Russell

A GENTLEMAN WHO HAS
MADE IT HIS BUSINESS
TO SEARCH AFTER
SUCH PIECES
John Dunton

A GENTLEMAN WHO HAS
RESIDED IN
PENNSYLVANIA
William Smith

A GENTLEMAN WHO
RESIDED FIVE YEARS
ON THE ISLAND
John Campbell

A GENTLEMAN WHO
RESIDED SOMETIME IN
PHILADELPHIA
Jacob Duche

A GENTLEMAN WHO WAS
IN THE TOWN DURING
THE WHOLE SIEGE
John Michelbourne

A GENTLEMAN WITH A
DUSTER
Harold Begbie

A GENTLEWOMAN
Doris Langley Moore

A GENUINE MEDIUM
John Nevil Maskelyne

A GENUINE YANKEE
John Neal

GEOFFREY, THEODATE
Dorothy Godfrey Wayman

A GEOLOGIST
Hugh Miller
William Pengelly

GEORGE, DANIEL
Daniel George Bunting

GEORGE, ELIOT
Gillian Freeman

GEORGE, JONATHAN
John Frederick Burke

GEORGE, WILMA
Wilma Beryl Crowther

A GEORGIA LAWYER
Robert M. Charlton

GERALD, A. F.
Aubrey Fitzgerald Bell

GERARD, DOROTHEA
Mme Dorothea Longarde De
Longarde

GERARD, EMILY G. (or E. D.)
Mme Emily De Laszowska

GERARD, FRANCES A.
Geraldine Penrose Fitzgerald

GERARD, MORICE
John Jessop Teague

GERMANICUS
James Anderson

A GERMAN NOBLEMAN
Francis Joseph Grund

GERRARE, WIRT
William Oliver Greener

GERTRUDE
Jane Cross Simpson

A GHOST IN A WHITE
SHEET OF PAPER
Peter Chamberlen

THE GHOST OF HARRY THE
EIGHTH'S FOOL
Alfred Henry Forrester

THE GHOST OF
VANDEGRAB
Sir James Mackintosh

THE GHOST OF WILLY
SHAKESPEARE
George Moutard Woodward

GIBB, LEE
Guy Deghy with Keith
Spencer Waterhouse

GIBBARD, T. S. J.
Michael Vinter

GIBBON, LEWIS GRASSIC
James Leslie Mitchell

GIBBS, LEWIS
Joseph Walter Cove

GIBBS, MARY ANN
Marjory Elizabeth Bidwell

GIBE
James Headrick

GIBSON, CHARLES
Charles Garvice

GIBSON, FLOYD
Albert King

GIBSON, JOSEPHINE
Sesyle Joslin

GIDDY, DAVIES
Davies Gilbert

GIFFORD, JOHN
Edward Foss
John Richards Green

GIFFORD, WILLIAM
William Frederick Deacon

GILBERT
William Stevens Robinson

GILBERT, ANNA
Margaret Lazarus

GILBERT, ANTHONY
Lucy Beatrice Malleson

GILBERT, E. JAYNE
Eliza Margaret Humphreys

GILCHRIST, JOHN
Jerome Gardner

GILES
Carl Ronald Giles

GILES, GORDON A.
Otto Oscar Binder

GILES, KRIS
Helen Bernice Nielsen

GILL, BARTHOLOMEW
Mark McGarrity

GILL, B. M.
Barbara Margaret Trimble

GILL, PATRICK
John Creasey

GILLEN, LUCY
Rebecca Stratton

GILMAN, GEORGE E.
Terence William Harknett

GILMAN, MRS MARIA
Charles Francis Barnard

GILMAN, ROBERT CHAM
Alfred Coppel

GILMAN, WENONA
Mrs Florence Schoeffel

GILMORE, ANTHONY
Harry Bates with Desmond W.
Hall

GILROONEY
Robert John Cassidy

GIMEL
Elisha Andrews

GIOUANO, B. DEL M. TEMP.
Bartholomew Young

GIRALDUS
William Allingham
Gerald John O'Driscoll

A GIRL OF THE PERIOD
Mrs Eliza Lynn Linton

GIROUX, E. X.
Doris Shannon

THE GIVER
Reginald Walter Macan

GLADSTONE, MAGGIE
Arthur M. Gladstone

GLADWIN, WILLIAM ZACHARY
Gulielma Zollinger

GLAMIS, WALTER
Nathan Schachner

GLANVILLE, ALEC
Alexander Haig Glanville Grieve

GLANVILLE REDIVIVUS
Samuel O'Sullivan

THE GLASGOW UNFORTUNATE
George Donald

GLASGUENSIS
John Buchanan

GLAUCUS
Edwin Troxell Freedley

GLEANER
Nathaniel Ingersoll Bowditch

GLENEELIN
George Richard Boissier

GLOBETROTTER
Robert McMillan

GLOCKENHAMMER, WALKER
Herbert George Wells

A GLOUCESTER COUNTY GENTLEMAN
Chandos Leigh

GLUM, TABITHA
Catherine Frances Grace Gore

GLYN, SIR ANTHONY
Sir Geoffrey Leo Simon Davson

GLYNDON, HOWARD
Mrs Laura Catherine Searing

GNATHAI GAN TARRAIDH
Darrell Figgis

GOAMAN, MURIEL
Edith Muriel Cox

GOBEMOUCHE
William Makepeace Thackeray

GODEY, JOHN
Morton Freedgood

GODFREY, GEORGE
Thomas Gaspey

GODFREY, HAL
Miss Charlotte O'Connor Eccles

GODFREY, WILLIAM
Christopher Samuel Youd

GODOLPHIN, MARY
Lucy Aikin

GOFORTH, ELLEN
Dorothy Brenner Francis

GOLD, MICHAEL
Irving Granich

GOLDEN HORN
Laurence Oliphant

GOLDEN LIGHT
William Watkin Hicks

GOLDSMITH, CHRISTABEL
Mrs Julie P. Smith

GOLDSMITH, REV. J.
Sir Richard Phillips

GOLDSMITH, PETER
John Boynton Priestley

GON, SAIN
Bayle St John

GOOCH, SILAS M.
John Glassco

A GOOD CONSCIENCE
Benjamin Franklin

GOOD-FELLOW, ROBIN
James Henry Leigh Hunt

A GOOD HAND
Humphrey Wanley

THE GOOD VICAR
Richard de Courcy

GOODMAN, DAVID
David Goodman Croly

GOODWIN, JOHN
Sydney Gowing

GOODWIN, SUZANNE
Suzanne Ebel

GOOSEQUILL, BENJAMIN
James Makittrick Adair

NA GOPALEEN, MYLES
Brian O'Nolan

GORDON, A. M. R.
A. M'Gregor Rose

GORDON, SIR COSMO
Sir Samuel Egerton Brydges

GORDON, DAVID
Randall Garrett

GORDON, DIANA
Lucilla Andrews

GORDON, DONALD
Donald Gordon Payne

GORDON, E.
Edward Gordon Craig

GORDON, H. R.
Edward Sylvester Ellis

GORDON, JANE
Elsie Lee

GORDON, JANET
Cecil Woodham-Smith

GORDON, LEW
Gordon Cortis Baldwin

GORDON, MILLARD VERNE
Donald A. Wollheim

GORDON, NEIL
Archibald Gordon MacDonnell

GORDON, REX
Stanley Bennett Hough

GORDON, RICHARD
Gordon Ostlere

GORDON, SPIKE
John Russell Fearn

GORDON, S. S. (or STANLEY)
Stanley Gordon Shaw

GORDON, STEWART
Gordon Donald Shirreffs

GORDON, WALTER
William Aylmer Gowing

GORE, WILLIAM
Jan Gordon

GORHAM, MICHAEL
Franklin Brewster Fulsom

GORMAN, GINNY
Hugh Zachary

GORONVA CAMLAN
Rowland Williams

GORTSCHAKOV, M. MIKAEL
Henry Llewellyn Williams

GORYAN, SIRAK
William Saroyan

GOSLETT, PAUL
Charles James Lever

GOSSAMER, JACK,
RAILROAD
PHILOSOPHER
William Martin

GOSSIP, GORDON
Lawrence Daniel Fogg

MR GOSSIP
Philip Pryce Page
Noel Henry Broadbent
Thompson

A GOTHAMITE
Thomas Picton

GOUGER, ROBERT
Edward Gibbon Wakefield

GOULD, ALAN
Victor Canning

GOULD, ARTHUR LEE
Arthur Stanley Gould Lee

GOULD, BERNARD
Bernard Partridge

GOULD, STEPHEN
Stephen Gould Fisher

A GOVERNMENT AGENT
Robert Brown

THE GOVERNOR
Henry Morford

GOVI, O.
John Robert Gover

GOWER, ERSKINE
Millicent Fanny Sutherland

GOWER, IRIS
Iris Davies

GOWRIE
William Anderson Smith

GRAAF, PETER
Christopher Samuel Youd

GRABSTEIN, PROFESSOR,
PHIL. D., OF
GOTTINGEN
Richard Hengist Horne

GRACCHUS
Charles Kirkpatrick Sharpe

A GRADUATE
Edward Copleston
Sir John Rose Cormack
James Edwin Thorold Rogers

A GRADUATE IN CIVIL LAW
Jonas Dennis

A GRADUATE OF DUBLIN
UNIVERSITY
Thomas Osborne Davis

A GRADUATE OF MEDICINE
William Dansey

A GRADUATE OF OXFORD
Cuthbert Collingwood
James Pycroft
John Ruskin
John Wood Warter

A GRADUATE OF THE
UNIVERSITY OF
OXFORD
William Charles Townsend

A GRADUATE OF YALE OF
THE CLASS OF 1821
John Mitchell

A GRADUATE SCHOLAR OF
HIS COLLEGE
John Mackenzie Bacon

GRADY, PETER
Norman A. Danberg

GRAEME, BRUCE (or DAVID)
Graham Montague Jeffries

GRAEME, RODERIC
Roderic Jeffries

GRAGG, AGNES
Mrs A. H. Blaisdell

GRAHAM, CHARLES S.
Edwin Charles Tubb

GRAHAM, ENNIS
Mary Louisa Molesworth

GRAHAM, GRACE
Mrs Sophie Bronson
Titterington

GRAHAM, HARVEY
Harvey Flack

GRAHAM, JAMES
Harry Patterson

GRAHAM, JOHN
David Graham Phillips

GRAHAM, NEILL
William Murdoch Duncan

GRAHAM, ROBERT
Joe William Haldeman

GRAHAM, SHEILA
Lily Sheil

GRAHAM, TOM
Harry Sinclair Lewis

GRAHAM, VANESSA
Anthea Mary Fraser

GRAHAM, VIVA
Edith Anna Oenone Somerville

GRAHAM, WINIFRED
Winifred Muriel Cory

GRAHAME, JIM
James William Gordon

GRAHAME, NELLIE
Mrs A. K. Dunning

GRANADOS, PAUL
Arthur William Charles Kent

GRAND, SARAH
Frances Elizabeth McFall

A GRAND NEPHEW OF
NAPOLEON THE
GREAT
William Charles Bonaparte
Wyse

GRANDAD GREY
Charles Allen Clarke

A GRANDFATHER
Joseph Sylvester Clark

GRANDFATHER GREENWAY
Charles James Cannon

GRANDFATHER SMITH
Charles Knight

A GRANDMOTHER
Katie Magnus
Harriet Anne Scott

GRANDOWER, ELISSA
Hillary Baldwin Waugh

GRANGE, PETER
Christopher Robin Nicole

GRANT, ALAN
Gilbert Alan Kennington

GRANT, ALLAN
Arthur Douglas Howden Smith
James Grant Wilson

GRANT, AMBROSE
Rene Raymond

GRANT, ANTHONY
Marion Pares

GRANT, DAVID
Craig Thomas

GRANT, DOUGLAS
Isabel Egerton Ostrander

GRANT, J.
James Ramsay MacDonald

GRANT, LANDON
Leonard Reginald Gribble

GRANT, MARGARET
Rose Dorothy Franken

GRANT, MAXWELL
Walter B. Gibson
Dennis Lynds

GRANT, RICHARD
J. Calvitt Clarke

GRANTORTO
David Herbert Lawrence

GRAPHO
James Alonzo Adams

GRASMERIENSIS TEUTONIZANS
Thomas De Quincy

GRATTON, THOMAS
Thomas Ernest Hulme

A GRAVE AUTHOR OF MIDDLE AND UNPARTY PRINCIPLES
John Humphrey

GRAVELEY, GEORGE
George Graveley Edwards

GRAVES, VALERIE
Marion Zimmer Bradley

GRAVIORA MANENT
James R. Manley

GRAY, ANGELA
Dorothy Daniels

GRAY, ANNABEL
Mrs Anne Cox

GRAY, BARRY
Robert Barry Coffin

GRAY, BERKELEY
Edwy Searles Brooks

GRAY, CAROLINE
Christopher Robin Nicole

GRAY, E. CONDER
Alexander Hay Japp

GRAY, ELIZABETH JANET
Elizabeth Gray Vining

GRAY, ELLINGTON
Naomi Ellington Jacob

GRAY, HARRIET
Denise Naomi Robins

GRAY, JONATHAN
Herbert Adams

GRAY, LEONARD
Cynthia Asquith

GRAY, MAXWELL
Mary Gleed Tuttiett

GRAY, OSWALD
Samuel Rowe Simmons

GRAY, ROBERTSON
Rossiter Worthington Raymond

GRAY, RUSSELL
Bruno Fischer
Eleanor Frances Le Fanu

GRAY, SIMON
Sir Alexander Boswell

GRAYBEARD, GAFFER
Robert Sanders

GRAYSON, DAPHNE
G. C. Graveley

GRAYSON, DAVID
Ray Stannard Baker

GRAYSON, ELDRED
Robert Hare

GRAYSON, R. E. H.
Henry Rogers

GRAYSON, RICHARD
Richard Grindal

A GREAT BIG FOOL
John Burley Waring

THE GREAT MERLINI
Clayton Rawson

A GREAT TINKLARIAN DOCTOR
William Mitchel

GREATLEY, T.
Chauncey Hare Townshend

GREAVES, RICHARD
George Barr McCutcheon

GRECK, E.
Marmaduke William Pickthall

GREEN, CHARLES M.
Erle Stanley Gardner

GREEN, GLINT
Margaret Peterson

GREEN, HENRY
Henry Vincent Yorke

GREEN, INVISIBLE, ESQ.
William G. Crippen

GREEN, JOHN
George Henry Townsend

GREEN, MR JOLLY
Dudley Costello

GREEN, JUDITH
Judith Green Rodriguez

GREEN, OLIVE
Myrtle Reed

GREEN, PADDY
George Henry Townsend

GREENDRAKE, GREGORY
Joseph Coad

GREENE, HANNAH
Joanne Greenberg

GREENE, JEAN
Ward Greene

GREENE, JULIA
Joyce Mary Marlow

GREENE, STEVEN
John Thomas Lutz

GREENHALGH, KATHERINE
John William Bobin

GREENHORN, JOSEPH
John T. Bedford

GREENSWARD
Frederick Law Olmsted with C. Bowyer Vaux

GREENWOOD, GRACE
Mrs Sara Jane Clarke Lippincott

GREENWOOD, JOHN
John Buxton Hilton

GREER, RICHARD
Randall Garrett with Robert Silverberg

GREGORY, JOHN
Robert Hoskins

GREGORY, SACHA
Bettina von Hutten

GREGORY, STEPHAN
Donald Eugene Pendleton

GRENDON, STEPHEN
August William Derleth

GRENVIL, WILLIAM
Wyndham Martyn

(H) GREVILLE
John Hawkesworth

GREW, WILLIAM
William O'Farrell

GREX, LEO
Leonard Reginald Gribble

GREY, OLD ALAN
George Mogridge

GREY, ANTHONY
Henry Carl Schiller

GREY, BARTON
George Herbert Sass

GREY, BELINDA
Maureen Peters

GREY, BRENDA
Leila S. Mackinlay

GREY, CAROL
Robert A. W. Lowndes

GREY, CHARLES
Edwin Charles Tubb

GREY, DONALD
Eugene Thomas

GREY, ELIZABETH
Ethel Winifred Savi

GREY, GEORGINA
Mary Lynn Roby

GREY, JULIAN
C. Gordon Glover

GREY, LOUIS
Leonard Reginald Gribble

GREY, ROBIN
Elizabeth F. Gresham

GREY, ROWLAND
Lilian Kate Rowland Brown

GREY OWL
Archibald Stansfield Belaney

GREYDRAKE, GEOFFREY
Thomas Ettingsall

GREYLOCK, GODFREY
Joseph Edward Adams Smith

GRIDBAN, VOLSTED
John Russell Fearn
Edwin Charles Tubb

GRIER, SYDNEY C.
Hilda Caroline Gregg

GRIEVOUS, PETER
Francis Hopkinson

GRIFF, ALAN
William Donald Suddaby

GRIFFIN, GREGORY
George Canning with John
Hookham Frere

GRIFFINHOOF, ARTHUR
George Colman

GRIFFITH, BILL
Bill Granger

GRIFFITH, CECIL
Mrs S. Beckett

GRILE, DOD
Ambrose Bierce

GRIMBOSH, HERMAN
Charles Mackay

GRIMGIBBER, RICHARD
John Sheehan with Sir Edward
Shepherd Creasy and Robert
Gordon Latham

GRIMSHAW, MARK
Ernest L. McKeag

GRINGO, HARRY
Henry Augustus Wise

GRINNELL, DAVID
Donald A. Wollheim

GRINS AND GRIPES
Ebenezer Bailey

GRISKIN, INGLEBERRY
George Daniel

GRISLET
Ernest Andrew Beha

GRISWOLD, GEORGE
Robert George Dean

GRONOVIUS
Charles Valentine Le Grice

GROTIUS
De Witt Clinton

GROVES, GEORGINA
Dorothy Geraldine Symons

GRUB, STEPHEN
Henry Fielding

GRUMBLER, ANTHONY, ESQ.
David Hoffman

GRUNCHER, BEDELL
Thomas Anstey Guthrie

GRUNDY, JEMIMA
William Makepeace Thackeray

A GUARDIAN
Nassau William Senior

GUATIMOZIN
Frederick Jebb

GUBBINS, NATHANIEL
Edward Spencer Mott

GUERNSEY CORRESPONDENT
Jonathan Duncan

A GUEST
John Edward Jenkins

A GUIDE TO THE INFERIOUR CLERGIE
John Phillips

GUILDFORD, JOHN
Bluebell Matilda Hunter

GUILLAUME, ROBERT
Robert Snedden

GUILLIAME
George Darley

GULICK, BILL
Grover C. Gulick

GULL, RANGER
Cyril A. E. Ranger-Gull

GULLIELMUS PHALERIUS
William White

GULLIVER, LEMUEL
John Adams
Jonathan Swift

GULLIVER, CAPT. LEMUEL
John Arbuthnot

GULLIVER, LEMUEL, JUN.
Mrs Elizabeth Susanna Graham

GULLIVER, LEMUEL, POET LAUREATE TO THE KING OF LILLIPUT
Henry Fielding

GULLIVER, LILLIPUTIUS
Richard Johnson

GUN BUSTER
John Charles Austin

GUNSON, GAMALIEL
Aaron Hill

GUSHINGTON, ANGELINA
Charles Wallwyn Radcliffe
Cooke

GUSHINGTON, HON. IMPULSIA
Helen Selina Sheridan

GUTHRIE, ALAN
Edwin Charles Tubb

GUTHRIE, JOHN
John Brodie

GUTHRIE, RAMSAY
John George Bowran

GWENDOLEN
Enoch Arnold Bennett

GWITMARPSCHELDON
William Wishart

GWYNFRYN
Mrs Harriet Mann Miller

GWYNNE, PAUL
Ernest Slater

GWYNNE, TALBOT
Miss Josepha Heath Gulston

H

H.
Robert Stephen Hawker

MR H*****
Jonas Hanway

H. B.
Joseph Hilaire Pierre R. Belloc
Henry Blackwell
John Doyle

H. C.
Henry Clarke
William Henry Ireland

H. D.
Hilda Doolittle

H. D., RIPENSIS
Heneage Dering

H. D. B.
William Hamper

H. E. O.
Thomas George Fonnereau

H. F. E.
Evelyn Everett-Green

H. K.
Henry Keepe

H. L. G.
Arthur Christopher Benson

SIR H. M.
Sir Humphrey Mackworth

H. R.
Hugo Reid

H. W. L.
Henry Wadsworth Longfellow

HABERDASHER, O. M.
Alexander Carlyle

AN HABITUAL CRIMINAL
Charles John Darling

HACKLE PALMER
Robert Blakey

HACKNEY, ISCARIOT
Richard Savage

HACKSTON, JAMES
Harold Frederick Neville Gye

HADDON, CHRISTOPHER
John Leslie Palmer

HADHAM, JOHN
James William Parkes

HADLEY, FRANKLIN
Russell Robert Winterbotham

HADLEY, JOAN
Joan Hess

HAGAR, JUDITH
Judiith Anne Polley

HAGGARD, PAUL
Stephen Longstreet

HAGGARD, WILLIAM
Richard Henry Michael
Clayton

HAGON, PRISCILLA
Mabel Esther Allan

HAIG, FENIL
Ford Hermann Hueffer

HAIRBRAIN, TIMOTHY
James Anderson

HALAM, ANN
Gwyneth A. Jones

HALDANE, HARRY
Richard Oliver Heslop

HALE, CHRISTOPHER
Mrs Frances Moyer Ross
Stevens

HALE, GARTH
Albert Benjamin Cunningham

HALE, KATHERINE
Amelia Beers Garvin

HALE, MICHAEL
Michael Hale Bullock

HALEVI, ZEV BEN SHIMON
Warren Kenton

A HALF-PAY OFFICER
Henry Robert Addison

HALIBURTON, HUGH
James Logie Robertson

HALIBUT, EDWARD
Richard Wilson

HALIDOM, M. Y.
Edward Heron-Allen

HALL, ADAM
Trevor Dudley-Smith

HALL, AYLMER
Norah Eleanor Lyle Hall

HALL, BRADNOCK
Sir Francis George Newbolt

HALL, CAMERON
Harry Harrison

HALL, ELIZA CALVERT
Mrs Eliza Caroline Obenchain

HALL, EVAN
Eugene Edward Halleran

HALL, HOLWORTHY
Harold Everett Porter

HALL, JAMES
Henry Kuttner

HALL, REV. JAMES
William Thomson

HALL, JOHN
Ezra Pound

HALL, JOHN RYDER
William Rotsler

HALL, JOSEPH
James Everett

HALL, OWEN
James Davis
Hugh Hart Lusk

HALL, ROBERT, GENT.
Peter Heylyn

HALL, RUPERT
Edward Reginald Home-Gall

HALL, WHYTE
Augustus Alfred Rayner

HALLAM, ESTHER
Esther Hallam Meynell

HALLARD, PETER
Arthur Catherall

HALLAS, RICHARD
Eric Mowbray Knight

HALLER, BILL
Peggy Anne Bechko

HALLER, JOSHUA
Henry Nelson Coleridge

HALLIDAY, ANDREW
Andrew Halliday Duff

HALLIDAY, BRETT
Davis Dresser

HALLIDAY, DOROTHY
Dorothy Dunnett

HALLIDAY, JAMES
David Symington

HALLIDAY, MICHAEL
John Creasey

HALLIDAY, SHIRLEY
Donald Bobin

HALLS, GERALDINE
Geraldine Mary Jay

HALLUS, TAK
Stephen Robinett

A HALTER-MAKER
Joseph Reed

HAMDEN
Isaac Orr

HAMILL, ETHEL
Jean Francis Webb

HAMILTON
Mathew Carey

HAMILTON, CLIVE
Clive Staples Lewis

HAMILTON, COSMO
Cosmo Hamilton Gibbs

HAMILTON, EDWARD
Alexander Slidell Mackenzie

HAMILTON, GAIL
Barbara Corcoran
Mary Abigail Dodge

HAMILTON, HERVEY
Denise Naomi Robins

HAMILTON, JOHN
John Hamilton Reynolds

HAMILTON, JULIA
Julia Watson

HAMILTON, MAX
Cicely Mary Hammill

HAMILTON, MOLLIE
Mary Margaret Kaye

HAMILTON, PAMELA
Erica Isobel Dunkerley

HAMILTON, PAUL
Harold Dennis-Jones

HAMILTON, PRISCILLA
Roberta Gellis

HAMILTON, RUFUS
Rufus Hamilton Gillmore

HAMILTON, WADE
Lee Floren

HAMILTON, W. J.
Charles Dunning Clark

HAMLET, EDITH
Mrs Alfred (Edith) Lyttelton

HAMLET, OVA
Richard Allen Lupoff

HAMLIN, P., TINMAN
John Wolcot

HAMLINE, DAVID
Katherine Taylor

HAMMERGAFFERSTEIN,
HANS
Henry Wadsworth Longfellow

HAMMON, WILLIAM
Matthew Turner

HAMMOND, JANE
Dorothy Poland

HAMMOND, KEITH
Henry Kuttner with Catherine
Louise Moore

HAMMOND, RALPH
Ralph Hammond Innes

HAMPDEN
Charles Hammond
Adolphus M. Hart
John B. Jervis
Thomas Lister

HAMPDEN, JOHN
Peter Dunsmore Howard

HAMPDEN, JOHN, JUN.
William Howitt

A HAMPSHIRE FISHERMAN
Richard Clarke Sewell

HAMPTON, MARK
Victor G. C. Norwood

HAMST, OLPHAR
Ralph Thomas

HANCOCK
Franklin Dexter
Jonathan Russell

THE HAND THAT
TRANSLATED
MARTIAL
Henry Killigrew

A HANDLOOM WEAVER
William Thom

HANNIBAL, JULIUS CAESAR
William H. Lewison

HANNON, EZRA
Salvatore A. Lombino

AN HANOVERIAN
Augustus Montague Toplady

HARBINSON, ROBERT
Robert Harbinson Bryans

HARBY, CLIFTON
Clifton Harby Levy

HARD PAN
Geraldine Bonner

HARDCASTLE, DANIEL
Richard Page

HARDCASTLE, EPHRAIM
William Henry Pyne

HARDIE, DAVID
John David Ruari McLean

HARDIN, CLEMENT
Dwight Bennett Newton

HARDIN, J. D.
Alan Riefe

HARDIN, PETER
Louis C. Vaczek

HARDIN, WES
Henry John Keevill

HARDING, MATTHEW
WHITMAN
Lee Floren

HARDING, PETER
Sir Henry Howarth Bashford

HARDINGE, E. M.
Ellen Maud Going

HARDMAN, JOHN
Robert Gradwell

HARDWICK, PELHAM
Charles James Mathews

HARDY, ADAM
Kenneth Henry Bulmer

HARDY, EDMUND
Geoffrey Herbert Moore

HARDY, FRANCIS H.
Edward James Cattell

HARDY, LAURA
Sheila Holland

HARDY, STUART
Oscar Schisgall

HARE, BURNHAM
Edmund Henry Colbeck

HARE, CYRIL
Alfred Alexander Gordon Clark

HARE, EMILY
Laura Winthrop

HARE, MARTIN
Zoe Zajdler

HARE, ROBERT
Robert Hare Hutchinson

HARE COURT
Thomas Edward Kebbell

HARFORD, HENRY
William Henry Hudson

HARGRAVE, LEONIE
Thomas Michael Disch

HARI DHU
William Henry Black

HARLAN, GLEN
Mel Cebulash

HARLAND, MARION
Mary Virginia Terhune

HARLE, ELIZABETH
Irene Roberts

HARLEY
Alfred Peter Hillier

HARLEY, JOHN
John Marsh

HARLEY, ROBERT
Sir Humphrey Mackworth

HARMAN, JANE
Terence William Harknett

HARMER, ANTHONY
Henry Wharton

HAROLD
Bartholomew Simmons

HAROLD, CHILDE
Edward S. Field

HARPER, DANIEL
Chandler Brossard

HARPER, HAROLD
Barrett Harper Clark

HARPOLE, JAMES
James Johnston Abraham

HARRIFORD, DAPHNE
Marion Rose Harris

HARRINGTON, GEORGE F.
Wiliam Mumford Baker

HARRINGTON, RALPH
Ralph Thomas

HARRIS, FRANK
James Thomas Harris

HARRIS, KATHLEEN
Adelaide Humphries

HARRIS, LAVINIA
Nicole St John

HARRISON, BRUCE
Edgar Pangborn

HARRISON, CHIP
Laurence Block

HARRISON, EDWIN
Eric Allen Ballard

HARRISON, JOHANN
John Bale

HARRISON, WHIT
Harry B. Whittington

THE HARROVIAN
Robert Eldridge Aris Willmott

HARROVIENSIS
William Harness

HARRUNEY, LUKE
Henry Walker

HARSON, SLEY
Harlan Ellison

HART, CAROLINE
Charles Garvice

HART, ELLIS
Harlan Ellison

HART, GEORGE HENRY
Holbrook Jackson

HART, JOHN
John B. Harvey

HARTE, BRET
Francis Bret Harte

HARTE, MARJORIE
Marjorie McEvoy

HARTLEY, HOWARD
Leopold Horace Ognall

A HARVARD STUDENT
Henry Dana Ward

HARVESTER, SIMON
Henry St John Clair Rumbold-Gibbs

HARVEY, CAROLINE
Joanna Trollope

HARVEY, COIN
William Hope Harvey

HARVEY, KATHRYN
Barbara Wood

HARVEY, PAUL
Paul Harvey Aurandt

HARVEY, RACHEL
Ursula Bloom

HARVEY, ROSS
H. Clarke Hook

HARWOOD, JOHN
Charles Miner

HASAN, ABD'UL
George Steele Seymour

HASLETTE, JOHN
John George Haslette Vahey

HASOLLE, JAS.
Elias Ashmole

HASTATUS
John Thomas Barber Beaumont

HASTINGS, BEVERLY
Carol Barkin with Elizabeth James

HASTINGS, BROOKE
Deborah Hannes Gordon

HASTINGS, GRAHAM
Roderic Jeffries

HASTINGS, HARRINGTON
Florence Shepherd with John Marsh

HATCH, GERALD
Dave Foley

HATTERAS, OWEN
Henry Louis Mencken with George Jean Nathan

HATTON, G. NOEL
Alice Mona Caird

HAVIL, ANTHONY
Elliott Elias Philipp

HAWES, PYX
William Ainslie Hollis

HAWK, ALEX
Brian Francis Wynne Garfield

HAWKES, ZACHARY
Alan Riefe

HAWKINS, HENRY
Ezra Pound

HAWKINS, TOM
Theodore Alois William Buckley

HAWKWOOD, ALAN
Henry J. O. Bedford-Jones

HAWTHORN, J. R. H.
John Richard Houlding

HAWTHORNE
William Lucas Collins

HAWTHORNE, ALICE
Septimus Winner

HAWTHORNE, EMILY
Mrs Emily Thornton Charles

HAWTHORNE, RAINEY
Charlotte Cowan

HAY, ELZEY
Eliza Andrews

HAY, FRANCES
Mrs Sybil Alexandra Erikson

HAY, IAN
John Hay Beith

HAY, ROY
Robert Edwin Hay

HAY, TIMOTHY
Margaret Wise Brown

HAYES, EVELYN
Mary Ursula Bethell

HAYES, HENRY
Ellen Warner Olney Kirk

HAYES, S.
Standish Hayes O'Grady

HAYGOOD, G. ARNOLD
Frank Gill Slaughter

HAYNES, DOROTHY K.
Dorothy Gray

HAYNES, JOHN ROBERT
Philip Wilding

HAYNES, PAT
Ernest L. McKeag

HAYTER, ADRIAN
Vernon Horace Rendall

HAYVE, O. B.
Charles Wayland Towne

HAYWARD, LINCOLN
Arthur Lincoln Haydon

HAYWARD, RICHARD
Frederick Swartwout Cozzens
Baynard H. Kendrick

HAYWARD, THOMAS
William Oldys

HAZARD, JACK
Edwin Booth

HAZEL, HARRY
Justin Jones

HAZELTINE, HORACE
Charles Stokes Wayne

HEAD, ANN
Anne Christensen Morse

HEAD, MATTHEW
John Edwin Canaday

HEADLEY, ELIZABETH
Betty Cavanna

**THE HEADMASTER OF AN
ENGLISH GRAMMAR
SCHOOL**
Edward Rupert Humphreys

HEARD, G. F. (GERALD)
Henry Fitzgerald Heard

HEARING, DANIEL
E. J. (Ted) Hughes

HEARN, MARIANNE
Mary Anne Hearn

**A HEARTY WELL-WISHER
TO THE ESTABLISHED
CHURCH**
Zachary Grey

HEATH, ROYSTON
George C. Wallis

HEATH, VERONICA
Veronica Blackett

HEATH, W. SHAW
William Henry Williamson

HEATHCOTE, CLAUDE
James Harwood Panting

**HEAVISIDE, MARTIN
DANVERS**
Matthew Davenport Hill

HEBDEN, MARK
John Harris

HEDBROOKE, ANDREW
Edward Rowland Sill

HEDGEHOG, HUMPHREY
John Agg
John Richards Green

HEDGES, JOSEPH
Terence William Harknett

HEDLEY, FRANK
Clarence Hedley Barker

HEFFERMAN, MR MICHAEL
Samuel Ferguson

HEIGHAM, JOHN
Thomas Everard

HEINRICH
John Francis Waller

HELD, PETER
John Holbrook Vance

HELFENSTEIN, ERNEST
Elizabeth Oakes Smith

HELIOSTROPOLIS
Daniel Defoe

HELLER, FRANK
Martin Gunnar Serner

HELVICK, JAMES
Claud Cockburn

HELVIDIUS
James Madison

HENDERSON, JOHN
Thomas Davies

HENDERSON, MARY
Osborne Henry Mavor

HENDERSON, PAUL
Ruth France

HENNESSY, MAX
John Harris

HENRY
Richard Griffith with Mrs
Elizabeth Griffith

HENRY, BERNARD
Sir Bernard Henry Coode

HENRY, D.
Henry Dircks

HENRY, O.
William Sydney Porter

HENRY, ROBERT
Talmage Powell

HENRY, WILL
Henry Wilson Allen

HENSEL, OCTAVIA
Mary Alice Seymour

HEPPLE, ANNE
Anne Hepple Dickinson

HEPWORTH, FANNY
Edward Gordon Craig

**HER MAJESTY'S
HISTORIOGRAPHER
FOR THE KINGDOM OF
SCOTLAND**
David Crawford

HERACLIDES
Edward Daniel Clarke

HERALD, KATHLEEN
Kathleen Wendy Peyton

HERBER, LEWIS
Murray Bookchin

HERBERT, EDWARD
John Hamilton Reynolds

HERBERT, FRANCIS, ESQ.
William Cullen Bryant

HERBERT, J. D.
James Dowling

HERBERT, WILLIAM
Herbert David Croly

HERBLOCK
Herbert L. Block

HERDER
John Moore Capes

AN HEREDITARY HIGH
CHURCHMAN
James Hicks Smith

HEREFORD, JOHN
Harry Fletcher

HERFNER, IRYS
Henry Ferris

HERING, JEANIE
Marion Adams-Acton

HERRIOT, JAMES
James Wight

HERITAGE, A. J.
Hazel Iris Addis

HERITAGE, MARTIN
Sydney Horler

HERMANN, WILLIAM
Ambrose Bierce

HERMAS
Joseph Priestley

HERMES
Isaac Cullimore
Benjamin Lumley

HERMIDES
Edward George Earle Lytton
Bulwer-Lytton

THE HERMIT
Felix M'Donough
Robert Waln

HERMITAGE
Charles Edwards Lester

THE HERMIT OF MARLOW
Percy Bysshe Shelley

HERMODACTYL, NEPHEW
TO ALEXANDER
BEMBO
Philip Horneck

HERMOGENES
Isaac Cullimore

HERNE, HUXLEY
Bertram Brooker

HERODOTUS JUN.
George Webbe Dasent

HERON, E. AND H.
Katie O. H. Prichard with
Hesketh V. H. Prichard

HERON, E. M. A.
Emily Manning

HERON, JACK
Evelyn May Clowes

HERON, ROBERT
John Pinkerton

HERRICK, HULDAH
Sarah Endicott Ober

HERRIES, PAUL
NERTHERTON
Frederick William Lanchester

HERRING, GEILLES
Edith Anna Oenone Somerville

HERTFORDSHIRE
INCUMBENT
Joseph William Blakesley

HERTZMANN, RUDOLPH
Mrs Emma Catherine Embury

HERVEY, EVELYN
Henry Reymond Fitzwalter
Keating

HESDIN, BERI
Isaac Story

HESLOP, F.
Fanny Heslop Park

HETEROSCIAN
Rowland Gibson Hazard

HEVELLYN
Edward Carpenter

HEXT, HARRINGTON
Eden Phillpotts

HEYWOOD, MRS ELIZA
Mrs Eliza Haywood

HIBERNIA
Jonathan Swift

HIBERNICUS
James Arbuckle
De Witt Clinton
William Edward Hartpole
Lecky
Samuel O'Sullivan

HIBERNO-ANGLUS
Sir John Joseph Dillon

HICKLING, WILLIAM
Benjamin Franklin de Costa

HICKS, ELEANOR
Eleanor Beatrice Coerr

HICKSON, MRS MURRAY
Mrs Mabel Kitcat

HID-ALLAN
Allan Cunningham

HIEOVER, HARRY
Charles Bindley

HIERONYMUS
PHILADELPHUS
David Calderwood

HIEROPHILUS
John McHale
John Toland

HIGGINBOTHAM, MARK
Horatio Smith

HIGGINS, JACK
Harry Patterson

A HIGH CHURCHMAN OF
THE OLD SCHOOL
William Edward Jelf

A HIGH PRIVATE
Samuel Miller Quincy

HIGHLAND, MONICA
Carolyn See

A HIGHLAND OFFICER
Lord George Murray

HILARIS BENEVOLUS and
CO.
John Britton

HILL, HEADON
Francis Edward Grainger

HILL, H. HAVERSTOCK
James Morgan Walsh

HILL, JAMES
Margaret Storm Jameson

HILL, JOHN
Dean R. Koontz

A HILL-SIDE PREACHER
Sir Thomas Dick Lauder

HILLIARD, JAN
Hilda Kay Grant

HILLMAN, MARTIN
Douglas Hill

HILLS, ERATO
Arthur Richard Shilleto

HILTON, DAVID
David Hilton Wheeler

HILTON, JOSEPH
Joseph Hilton Smyth

HIM THAT PITIES THEE IN
THIS LANGUISHING
STATE
Francis Howgill

HIMSELF
Walter Humboldt Low

HINCKS, REV. E.
William Maginn

HINDE, THOMAS
Sir Thomas Willes Chitty

A HINDOO RAJAH
Elizabeth Hamilton

HINDS, JOHN
John Badcock

A HINDU
Romesh Chunder Dutt

HINTON, JAMES
George Barlow

HIPPONAX
Thomas Monro

HIS NIECE
Frances Dorothy Cartwright

HISON, WILIAM
William Johns

A HISTORIAN
John Hill Burton

HISTORICUS
Benjamin Franklin
Sir William G. G. V. Vernon
Harcourt
Albert Jay Nock
Richard Barry O'Brien

HISTRIONICUS
Sir John Skelton

HOB
Francis Robinson Gladstone
Duckworth

HOBART, ROBERTSON
Norman Lee

HOBBES, JOHN OLIVER
Pearl Mary Teresa Craigie

HOBSON, POLLY
Julia Evans

HOCKABY, STEPHEN
Gladys Maude Winifred
Mitchell

HOD
Albert Bernard Hollowood

HODEMART, PETER
Pierre Audemars

HODGE, T. SHIRLEY
Roger Sherman Tracy

HODGKIN, L. V.
Lucy Violet Holdsworth

HOFFE, MONCKTON
Reaney Monckton Hoff-Miles

HOFFER, FRANZ
Edward Gordon Craig

HOFFMAN, PROF. LOUIS
Angelo John Lewis

HOGAN, DAVID
Frank Gallagher

HOGARTH, CHARLES
John Creasey

HOGG, CERVANTES, F. S. M.
Eaton Stannard Barrett

HOLBEACH, HENRY
William Brighty Rands

HOLDEN, GENEVIEVE
Genevieve Long Pou

HOLDEN, LARRY
Frederic Lorenz

HOLDENBY, CHRISTOPHER
Ronald George Hatton

HOLDING, EPHRAIM
George Mogridge

HOLDRETH, LIONEL H.
Percy Greg

HOLLAND, CLIVE
Charles J. Hankinson

HOLLAND, KEL
Harry B. Whittington

HOLLIS, JIM
Hollis Spurgeon Summers

HOLM, SAXE
Helen Maria Hunt Jackson

HOLME, K. E.
John Edward Christopher Hill

HOLMES, A. R.
Harry Bates

HOLMES, CHARLES
Charles Nordhoff

HOLMES, GORDON
Matthew P. Shiel
Louis Tracy

HOLMES, GRANT
Johannes M. W. Knipscheer

HOLMES, H. H.
William Anthony Parker White

HOLMES, CAPT. HOWARD
Thomas Chalmers Harbaugh

HOLMES, JOHN
Raymond Holmes Souster

HOLMES, RAYMOND
Raymond Holmes Souster

HOLMES, W. (or WILLIAM) ESQ. MP FOR HASLEMERE
William Maginn

HOLT, CONRAD G.
John Russell Fearn

HOLT, FELIX
Mary Ann Evans

HOLT, GAVIN
Percival Charles Rodda

HOLT, GEORGE
Edwin Charles Tubb

HOLT, VICTORIA
Eleanor Alice Hibbert

HOLT, WM.
William Maginn

HOLTON, LEONARD
Leonard P. O'Connor
Wibberley

HOLYOAKE, HETTY
Mrs Caroline Snowden Guild

HOM
Nicholas Brady

HOME, CECIL
Julia Augusta Webster

HOME, MICHAEL
Charles Christmas Bush

A HOME-RULE MP
Justin McCarthy

HOMEBRED, PHILIP
Philip Yorke

HOMES, GEOFFREY
Daniel Mainwaring

HOMESPUN, HENRY
Solomon Southwick

HOMESPUN, MRS PRUDENTIA
Jane West

HOMO ANTHROPOS
George Storrs

THE HON. MEMBER FOR X
Somerset Struben De Chaire

HON. MRS MURRAY
Sarah Aust

HON. SEC. IRISH CITIZEN ARMY
Sean O'Casey

AN HONEST MAN
John Douglas

AN HONEST SAILOR
Edward Vernon

HONESTUS
Benjamin Austin

HONEYCOMB, HARRY
James Henry Leigh Hunt

HONEYCOMB, WILL, ESQ.
Richard Gardiner

HONEYMAN, BRENDA
Brenda Clarke

HONEYWOOD, RICHARD
Claud Lovat Fraser

HONORIA
Marguerite A. Power

HOOD, EU.
Joseph Haslewood

HOOD, GEORGE
George Douglas Brown

HOOD, ROBIN A.
Ernest Alfred Aris

HOOD, THOMAS, THE
YOUNGER
Charles Clark

HOOKER, RICHARD, OF THE
INNER TEMPLE
William Webster

HOOKER, TIMOTHY
John Hildrop

A HOOSIER
Adolphus Mordecai Hart

HOPE, ANDREE
Annie Jane Harvey

HOPE, ANTHONY
Sir Anthony Hope Hawkins

HOPE, ASCOTT R.
A. R. Hope-Moncrieff

HOPE, BRIAN
John Creasey

HOPE, CAMILLA
Grace Elsie Thompson

HOPE, EDWARD
Edward Hope Coffey

HOPE, EVA
Mary Anne Hearn

HOPE, F. T. L.
Frederic William Farrar

HOPE, LAURENCE
Adela Florence Nicolson

HOPE, MARGARET
Alana Knight

HOPE, STANLEY
Joseph Sydney Willes Hodges

HOPE, STANTON
William Edward Stanton-Hope

HOPE, THOMAS
Jonathan Swift

HOPKINS, A. T.
Annette Turngren

HOPKINS, H. W.
Alexander Geddes

HOPKINS, JOHN
Mrs Jane Marcet

HOPKINS, LYMAN
Franklin Brewster Folsom

HOPKINS, STANLEY
Henry Holt

HOPLEY, GEORGE
Cornell Hopley-Woolrich

HORAM, SON OF ASMAR
James Ridley

HORATIUS
Horace Twiss

HORATIUS FLACCUS
Robert William Wright

HORN, ALFRED ALOYSIUS
(TRADER)
Alfred Aloysius Smith

HORNBOOK, ADAM
Thomas Cooper

HORNBOOK, Obadiah
Alexander Comfort

HORNE, GEORGE, D. D.
Walley Chamberlain Oulton

HORNEM, HORACE
Lord George Gordon Byron

HORSLEY, DAVID
David Ernest Bingley

HORTENSIUS
George Hay
William Livingston

HORTON, FELIX LEE
Lee Floren

HORTON, ROBERT J.
James J. Roberts

HOSIER, PETER
Douglas Clark

HOSKINS, PHILIP
Robert Hoskins

HOSMOT, HYTON
William Deal Baker

HOSPITA
Charles Lamb

HOTSPUR
Bryan Curling
Henry Mort Feist
Charles Greenwood

HOUGHTON, CLAUDE
Claude Houghton Oldfield

A HOUSE HOLDER
Samuel Miles Hopkins

HOUSEHOLD, GEOFFREY
Edward West

HOUSTON, R. B.
Hugh Crawford Rae

A HOWADJI
George William Curtis

HOWARD, ELIZABETH
Elizabeth Howard Mizner

HOWARD, HARTLEY
Leopold H. Ognall

HOWARD, HENRY L.
Charles Jeremiah Wells

HOWARD, JOHN M.
Cyril Malcolm Hincks

HOWARD, KEBLE
John Keble Bell

HOWARD, LINDEN
Audrie Manley-Tucker

HOWARD, MARY
Mary Mussi

HOWARD, PROSPER
Charles Harold St John
Hamilton

HOWARD, ROLAND
William L. Catchpole

HOWARD, VECHEL
Howard Rigsby

HOWE, EDWARD
Richard Rowe

HOWE, MARY
Jonathan Swift

HOWE, MURIEL
Muriel Smithies

HOWELL, SCOTT
Albert King

HOWELL, VIRGINIA T.
Virginia T. H. Ellison

HOWLDIN, J.
Sir John Wildman

HOWLETT, I. (or JOHN)
Robert Parsons

HOWLETT, REV. M. OF
DEVONSHIRE
Richard John KIng

HOY, ELIZABETH
Nina Conarain

HUBBARD, MARGARET ANN
Margaret Priley

HUBERT
Hubert Bland

HUDSON, JAN
George Henry Smith

HUDSON, JEFFERY
Michael Crichton

HUDSON, STEPHEN
Sydney Schiff

HUEFFER, FORD MADOX
Ford Hermann Hueffer

HUGGLESTONE, LEONTIUS
ANDROCLES
William Makepeace Thackeray

HUGHES, BRENDA
Brenda Colloms

HUGHES, COLIN
John Creasey

HUGHES, ELIZABETH
Hugh Zachary

HUGHES, MATILDA
Charlotte Matilda MacLeod

HUGHES, PHILIP
Hugh Phillips

HUGHES, ZACH
Hugh Zachary

HUGI, MAURICE G.
Eric Frank Russell

HUGO, GRANT
Sir James Cable

HUGUENOT
Frederick Cornwallis
Conybeare

HULL, H. BRAXTON
Helen Hull Jacobs

HULL, RICHARD
Richard Henry Sampson

O. HUM and CO.
Frederic Saunders

HUMANITAS
George Miller

**AN HUMBLE EXPECTANT
OF THE PROMISE**
William Burgh

AN HUMBLE MODERATOR
Herbert Croft

A HUMBLE PENITENT
Susanna Hopton

HUME, DAVID
John Victor Turner

HUME, ELINOR
Elinor Huddart

HUME, FERGUS
Ferguson Wright Hume

HUMILIS, CLEMENT
James Tait Plowden-Wardlaw

HUMM, SIR HENRY
George Alexander Stevens

A HUMORIST PHYSICIAN
Richard Cobbold

**HUMPFFENSTRUMPFFEN,
BURGOMASTER**
William Makepeace Thackeray

**A HUNGRY
CORRESPONDENT**
James Boswell

HUNT, CLARENCE
Hugh Holman

HUNT, FRANCESCA
Isabelle Holland

HUNT, GILL
Edwin Charles Tubb

HUNT, HARRISON
Willis Todhunter Ballard

HUNT, KYLE
John Creasey

A HUNTER
William Brighty Rands

HUNTER, BORIS M.
Bluebell Matilda Hunter

HUNTER, CLINGHAM, MD
William Taylor Adams

HUNTER, EVAN
Salvatore A. Lombino

HUNTER, HALL
Edison T. Marshall

HUNTER, JOHN
Willis Todhunter Ballard
Alfred John Hunter

HUNTINGTON, FAYE
Theodosia Maria T. Foster

HUNTINGTON, JOHN
Gerald William Phillips

HUNTLEY, W., ESQ.
William Prynne

HUNTLY, FRANCIS E.
Ethel Colburn Mayne

HUNTSMAN
George C. G. F. Berkeley
Thomas Assheton Smith

**HURBIN, LIONEL,
GENTLEMAN**
John Lilburne

HURD, NATHANIEL
Blomfield Jackson

**HURWITZ, HYMAN, OF
HIGHGATE**
Samuel Taylor Coleridge

HUTCHESON, WALTER
Robert Williams Buchanan

HYDE, ELEANOR
Frances Munthe

HYDE, NED
Edward Vaughan Hyde
Kenealy

HYDE, ROBIN
Iris Guiver Wilkinson

HYNIALL
John O'Neill

HYPERION
Josiah Quincy

HYPOCHONDRIACK
James Boswell

HYPODIDASCULUS
James Boswell

I

I.
Joseph Addison
Edward George Ballard

I. D. I.
Isaac D'Israeli

I. O.
Cecil John Charles Street

I. W.
Isaac Watts

I. W. B.
John Wynn Baker

IANTHE
Mrs Emma Catherine Embury

ICHNERETES
Thomas Carlyle

ICONOCLAST
Charles Bradlaugh
Mary Agnes Hamilton

IDAMORE
Mary Cutts

AN IDLE WOMAN
Frances Minto Elliot

AN IDLER
Marguerite Gardiner
Henry Wikoff

IERNE
Richard Robert Madden

IGNATIUS
Stopford Augustus Brooke

IGNORAMUS
Hartley Coleridge
Frederick York Powell

IGNOTA
Elizabeth C. Wolstenholme-
Elmy

IGNOTO SECONDO
James Beresford

IGNOTUS
John Chater
James Franklin Fuller
Aaron Hill
Alexander Hunter

Arthur Blennerhassett Rowan
Herbert Wrigley Wilson

ILES, BERT
Zola Helen Ross

ILES, FRANCIS
Anthony Berkeley Cox

AN ILLUSED CANDIDATE
John Caley

IMBER, HUGH
Alan Colquhoun Duff

IMMERITO
Moses Browne

AN IMPARTIAL HAND
Thomas Allen
James Anderson
William Ashdowne
Thomas Cox
Thomas Foxcroft
Francis Hare
Andrew Henderson
John Hildrop
John Hill
Samuel Johnson
Isaac Kimber
Peter King
Charles Leslie
John MItchell
James Murray
Richard Rawlinson
John Towne
Aaron Tozer
JosiahTucker
Daniel Turner

AN IMPARTIAL
MODERATOR
Isaac Watts

AN IMPARTIALIST
William Tasker

AN IMPROVISING TORY
Sir Thomas Dick Lauder

INCHFAWN, FAY
Mrs Elizabeth Rebecca Ward

INCHIQUIN
Charles Jared Ingersoll
Robert Southey

INCLEDON, PHILIP
Philip Worner

THE INCOMPARABLE MRS
K. P.
Mrs Katherine Philips

L'INCONNUE
Mrs Lucy Virginia French

INDAGATOR
John Canton
William Cowper

AN INDEPENDENT
Edwin Doak Mead
John Hall Stevenson
Robert John Thornton

AN INDEPENDENT CITIZEN
OF LONDON
Joseph Towers

AN INDEPENDENT
FREEHOLDER
Thomas Thirlwall

AN INDEPENDENT
TEACHER OF THE
TRUTH
John Hall Stevenson

AN INDEPENDENT WHIG
John Almon

INDEX
William Ewart Gladstone

INDEX, Q. P.
William M'Crillis Griswold

AN INDIAN AGENT
Henry Walter De Puy

AN INDIAN CHAPLAIN
John Cave-Brown

AN INDIAN CIVIL SERVANT
Henry Whitelock Torrens

AN INDIAN
CORRESPONDENT
Francis Gordon Cardew

AN INDIAN JOURNALIST
William Knighton

AN INDIAN MISSIONARY
Hargrave Jennings

AN INDIAN OFFICER
Ian Standish Monteith
Hamilton

AN INDIAN OFFICIAL
Sir William Henry Sleeman

AN INDIANAN
James Whitcomb

INDICUS
Thomas Evans Bell

INDIGENA
Ada Isaacs Menken

INDIGNATIO
Henry Taylor

INDIGO, JOHN
Sir George Christopher
Molesworth Birdwood

AN INDIVIDUAL OF THIRTY
YEARS' PRACTICAL
EXPERIENCE IN
BANKING AND
COMMERCIAL AFFAIRS
Thomas Skinner Surr

INDOPHILUS
Sir Charles Edward Trevelyan

INGHAM, DANIEL
Isobel Mary Lambot

INGHAM, COL. FREDERIC
Edward Everett Hale

INGLEBY, LEONARD
CRESSWELL
Cyril A. E. Ranger-Gull

INGOLDSBY
James Hildyard

INGOLDSBY, THOMAS
Richard Harris Barham

INGOT
Richard William Barnes Clarke

INGRAM, MARTIN
Mrs Alice Ormond Campbell

AN INHABITANT
Francis Kildale Robinson

AN INHABITANT OF THE
STATE OF MARYLAND
Charles Henry Wharton

AN INHABITANT THERE
Thomas Weld

THE INJURED LADY
Jonathan Swift

MR INKLE
Christopher Anstey

INNES, EVAN
Hugh Zachary

INNES, JEAN
Jean Saunders

INNES, MICHAEL
John Innes Mackintosh Stewart

AN INQUIRER
James Jackson Jarves

THE INSPECTOR
John Hill

THE INSTRUCTER
Henry Wadsworth Longfellow

AN INTELLIGENCE
OFFICER
Lionel James

AN INTIMATE FRIEND OF
HIS
Richard Graves

AN INVALID
John Galt
Harriet Martineau
Henry Matthews
John Strang

INVESTIGATOR
Jacob Barker
Thomas McCulloch
Daniel Oliver

IOTA
Kathleen Caffyn
John Harland
John Ogilvie
John Francis Waller

IPOLPERROC
Jonathan Couch

IRACUNDUS
William Edmonstoune Aytoun

IRELAND, MICHAEL
Darrell Figgis

IRENAEUS
Samuel Irenaeus Prime

IRENAEUS ELEUTHERIUS
Henry Hickman

IRENAEUS PHILADELPHUS
Lewis Du Moulin

IRENICUS
Joseph Besse

IRISH, WILLIAM
Cornelll Hopley-Woolrich

AN IRISH ARCHIVIST
Sir John Thomas Gilbert

AN IRISH BARRISTER-AT-
LAW
Thomas Crofton Croker

THE IRISH BOHEMIAN
John Augustus O'Shea

AN IRISH CATHOLIC
James Warren Doyle
William James MacNevin

AN IRISH COUNTRY
GENTLEMAN
William Parnell-Hayes

AN IRISH DIGNITARY
Thomas Lewis O'Beirne

AN IRISH GENTLEMAN
David Stewart Erskine
Thomas Moore
Thomas Walford

AN IRISH GENTLEMAN, A
MEMBER OF THE WHIG
CLUB
George Chalmers

AN IRISH GENTLEMAN
LATELY DECEASED
William Maginn

AN IRISH LIBERAL
William O'Connor Morris

AN IRISH MISSIONARY
PRIEST
John O'Hanlon

AN IRISH NATIONAL
JOURNALIST
Richard Pigott

THE IRISH OYSTER EATER
John Fisher Murray

AN IRISH POLICE
MAGISTRATE
Henry Robert Addison

AN IRISH POSITIVIST
Henry Dix Hutton

AN IRISH PROTESTANT
Samuel O'Sullivan

AN IRISH PROTESTANT
BISHOP
Edward Wetenhall

THE IRISH WHISKY
DRINKER
John Sheehan

AN IRISHMAN
Henry Robert Addison
Aubrey Thomas De Vere
Thomas Moore

IRON, RALPH
Olive Emilie Albertina
Schreiner

IRONBARK
George Herbert Gibson

IRONDEQUOIT
Francis Trevelyan Buckland

IRONQUILL
Eugene Fitch Ware

IRONSIDE, CHRISTOPHER
William Cowper

IRONSIDE, JOHN
Euphemia Margaret Tait

IRONSIDE, NESTOR
Samuel Croxall

IRONSIDE, THE VENERABLE NESTOR
Sir Richard Steele

AN IRRECONCILABLE
William Brighty Rands

AN IRRESPONSIBLE TAX-PAYER
Mrs Caroline Elizabeth Sarah Norton

AN IRRITABLE MAN
Robert Barry Coffin

IRVING, ROBERT
Irving Adler

AN IRVINGITE
Francis Albert Marshall

IRWIN, G. H.
Raymond A. Palmer

IRWIN, RUSSELL
Irwin Peter Russell

ISA
Isabella Knox

ISABEL
Anna Cora Ritchie
William Gilmore Simms

AN ISLESMAN
Malcolm MacNeill

ISMAEL
Christopher A. M. Harris

ISOP
Ian S. O. Playfair

IT MATTERS NOT WHO
Edward Nares

AN ITALIAN NUN
William Combe

ITHI KEFALENDE
Charles Blackford Mansfield

AN ITINERANT
Abel Stevens

IVANOVITCH, IVAN
Edward Gordon Craig

IVES, JOHN
Brian Francis Wynne Garfield

IVES, MORGAN
Marion Zimmer Bradley

IZAK
John Isaac Ira Adams

IZAK, ICHABOD
George Stanford Stebbins

J

J 47485
Arthur Trystan Edwards

J. A.
John Allen

J. B.
John Beale
Joseph Besse
James Boswell
John Charles Brooke
Sir James Burrow
James Burgh

J. B. M.
John Bingham Morton

J. C.
John Cleveland
James Cobb
Thomas Edward Lawrence

J. C., MD
Jodocus Crull
John Curry

J. D. B.
John Durant Breval

J. G.
John Gay
John Green

J. H.
Jonas Hanway
James Harris
John Hutchinson
Denis Florence MacCarthy

J. H., FRS
James Hodgson

J. H. N.
John Henry Newman

J. J. B-.
John Jelliand Brundish

J. K., FRS and S. A. Sc.
James Keir

J. K. S.
James Kenneth Stephen

J. M.
Charles Blount

J. M., ESQ. FRS
John Mortimer

J. N. D.
John Nelson Darby

J. O.
Matthew James Higgins

J. P. C.
John Payne Collier

J. R.
James Rice
John Ruskin

J. R. R. T.
John Ronald Reuel Tolkien

J. S.
John Sage
John Sergeant
Jonathan Swift

J. S. OF DALE
Frederic Jesup Stimson

J. S. D. D. D. S. P. D.
Jonathan Swift

J. T.
Arthur Christopher Benson
Jethro Tull

J. V.
Ezra Pound

J. W.
Henry Carey
John Worlidge

JABEZ
Clement Mansfield Ingleby

JACKDAW
Wilfred Whitten

JACKS, OLIVER
Kenneth Royce Gandley

JACKSON, E. F.
Edwin Charles Tubb

JACKSON, ELAINE
Gillian Freeman

JACKSON, EVERATT
Margaret Elizabeth Muggeson

JACKSON, GILES
Albert Leffingwell

JACKSON, NEVILLE
Gerald M. Glaskin

JACKSON, STEPHEN ESQ.,
OF THE FLATTS,
MALHAM MOOR
James Henry Dixon

JACKSON, WALLACE
William John Budd

JACOB OMNIUM'S HOSS
William Makepeace Thackeray

JACOB, VIOLET
Lady Helena M. Carnegie with
Mrs Arthur Jacob

JACOBS, LEAH
Roberta Gellis

JACOBS, T. C. H.
Jacques Pendower

JACQUES
James Edward Neild

A JAMAICA PROPRIETOR
Charles Edward Long

JAMBON, JEAN
John Hay Athole MacDonald

JAMES THE LESS
James Everett

JAMES, ANDREW
James Andrew Strahan

JAMES, BILL
Allan James Tucker

JAMES, BRIAN
John Lawrence Tierney

JAMES, CLIVE
Vivian Leopold James

JAMES, CROAKE
James Paterson

JAMES, DYNELY
William Mayne

JAMES, EDWIN
James Edwin Gunn

JAMES, FRANKLIN
Robert Godley

JAMES, JAMES
Arthur Henry Adams

JAMES, MARGARET
Pamela Bennetts

JAMES, MARTHA
Martha Claire MacGowan
Doyle

JAMES, MARY
Marijane Meaker

JAMES, PAUL
James Paul Warburg

JAMES, PHILIP
James Cawthorn

JAMES, S. T.
Horace Elisha Scudder

JAMES, STEPHANIE
Jayne Ann Krentz

JAMES, WILL
Joseph E. N. Dufault

JAMESON, ERIC
Eric Trimmer

JANETTA
Mrs Janetta Norweb

JANIFER, LAURENCE M.
Larry Mark Harris

JANSEN, JARED
Mel Cebulash

JANSON, HANK
Stephen Daniel Francis
Victor G. C. Norwood

JANUS
Henry Wilson Harris

JANUS, HIRAM
Ezra Pound

JANVIER
Joseph Janvier Woodward

JAPHETH
Theodore Dehon

JAQUES
James Hain Friswell

JARVIS, GEOFFREY
Elizabeth Hamilton

JASON
John Lawrence Le Breton
Hammond

JASON, JERRY
George Henry Smith

JASON, STUART
Lee Floren

JAY, CHARLOTTE
Geraldine Mary Jay

JAY, MARION
Ruth Spalding

JAY, SIMON
Colin James Alexander

JAY, W. L. M.
Julia Louisa Matilda Woodruff

JEAKE, SAMUEL, JR.
Conrad Potter Aiken

JEAMES, G. P. R. ESQ.
William Makepeace Thackeray

JEANS, THOMAS
James Cameron Lees

JEFFERIES, IAN
Peter Hays

JEFFERSON
Mathew Carey

JEFFERY, JEFFERY E.
Jeffrey Eardley Marston

JEFFORD, BAT
David Ernest Bingley

JEFFREYS, J. G.
Benjamin James Healey

JEFFRIES, BUDGELL
John Hamilton Reynolds

JEHU JUNIOR
Thomas Gibson Bowles
(Bowles was the first to use
this pseudonym, but later
writers of biographical
entries in Vanity Fair used it
as well)

JENKINS
Douglas William Jerrold

JENKINS, ELIJAH
John Mottley

JENKINS, PETER
Henry Peter Brougham
George Moir with Charles
Neaves

JENKINS, WILL F.
William Fitzgerald Jenkins

JENKINSON, OLINTHUS
John Hamilton Reynolds

**JENKS, JAQUETTA AGNETA
MARIANA**
William Beckford

JENNER, HEATHER
Heather Potter

JENNIFER, SUSAN
Robert Hoskins

JENNINGS, SARA
Maura Seger

**JENNINGS, THOMAS, SODA
WATER
MANUFACTURER**
William Maginn

JEROME, JOSEPH
Brocard Sewell

JEROME, OWEN FOX
Oscar Jerome Friend

JESSAMINE, JAMES
Bryan Waller Procter

JESSEL, JOHN
Stanley G. Weinbaum

MR JETSAM
Malcolm MacEachern

JINKS, JOSHUA JEDEDIAH
William Brisbane Dick

JO AND MEG
Louisa May Alcott and Anna
Bronson Alcott

A JOBBER
Daniel Defoe

JOBBRY, ARCHIBALD
John Galt

JOCELYN, PEN CLER
Pierce Connelly

JOCELYN, RICHARD
Richard Lewis Clutterbuck

JOHANNES CATHOLICUS
John Rutty

JOHANNESBURG
John Buchan

JOHN
John Perrot
Sampson Sandys

JOHN OF ENON
David Benedict

JOHN THE DIPPER
John Sandys

JOHN, ALIX
Alice Jones

JOHN, DON
Jean Ingelow

JOHN, EVAN
Evan John Simpson

JOHN, GABRIEL
Thomas D'Urfey

JOHNS, AVERY
Margaret Cousins

JOHNS, FOSTER
Gilbert Vivian Seldes

JOHNS, KENNETH
Henry Kenneth Bulmer with
John Newman

JOHNSON, ABRAHAM
John Hill

**JOHNSON, BENJAMIN F., OF
BOONE**
James Whitcomb Riley

JOHNSON, CROCKETT
David Johnson Leisk

JOHNSON, EFFIE
Euphemia J. G. Richmond

JOHNSON, FRANK
Norman A. Danberg

JOHNSON, MEL
Barry N. Malzberg

JOHNSON, MIKE
John Michael Sharkey

**JOHNSON, W.
BOLINGBROKE**
Morris Gilbert Bishop

JOHNSON, WILL
Henry St John

JOHNSON, WILLIAM
William Johnson Cory

JOHNSTOUN, A.
Edmund Curll

JON
William Philpin John Jones

JON, B.
Benjamin Johnson

JON, MONTAGUE
John Montague Dovener

JONATHAN
William Cobbett
Moncure Daniel Conway

JONES, ADDA
John Evans

JONES, ANNABEL
Mary Christianna Brand

**JONES, PROFESSOR
CHAUCER**
William H. Beckett

JONES, EDITH NEWBOLD
Edith Wharton

JONES, EZEKIEL
Horatio Hastings Weld

JONES, FRANK
John Russell Fearn

JONES, G. WAYMAN
Norman A. Danberg

JONES, HELEN
Helen Hinckley

JONES, IGNATIUS
Gorham A. Worth

JONES, JOANNA
John Frederick Burke

JONES, JOHN
Thomas Gaspey

JONES, JOHN FRANKLIN
William S. Cardell

JONES, MAJOR JOSEPH
William Tappan Thompson

JONES, RICHARD
Theodore Edward Hook

JONES, T. PERCY
William Edmonstoune Aytoun

JORDAN, LAURA
Sandra Brown

JORGENSEN, IVAR
Harlan Ellison
Paul W. Fairman
Robert Silverberg

JORROCKS
James Albert Garland

JORROCKS, MR JOHN
Robert Smith Surtees

JOSEPHUS
Joseph Priestley

JOSIAH ALLEN'S WIFE
Marietta Holley

A JOURNALIST
Charles Tabor Congdon
Isaac C. Pray

JOURNEYMAN
Albert Jay Nock

JOURNEYMAN ENGINEER
Thomas Wright

A JOURNEYMAN MASON
Hugh Miller

A JOURNEYMAN PRINTER
Charles Manby Smith

JOYCE, THOMAS
Arthur Joyce Lunel Cary

JOYEUSE, VYVIAN
Winthrop Mackworth Praed

JUBA
Benjamin Allen

JUDD, CYRIL
C. M. Kornbluth with Judith
Merrill

JUDD, HARRISON
Norman A. Danberg

JUDEX
Sir George Campbell
William Ewart Gladstone

**THE JUDICIAL
COMMISSIONER**
John Jardine

A JUDICIOUS DIVINE
William Prynne

JULIUS, CHARLES
Charles Bertram

JULIUS JUNIPER
William Margetson Heald

JUNE, JENNY
Jane Cunningham Croly

JUNIA
Caleb Whitefoord

JUNIOLUS CANADENSIS
Thomas Cary

A JUNIOR FELLOW
Richard Robinson

A JUNIOR SOPHISTER
Samuel Dexter Sr.

JUNIOR SUB
John Hay Beith

JUNIUS
Calvin Colton
Charles Fearne
Sir Philip Francis
Philip Thicknesse

JUNIUS JR.
George T. Denison Jr.

JUNIUS, R.
Richard Younge

JUNIUS AMERICANUS
Charles Endicott
David Everett
Arthur Lee
Charles Lee

JUNIUS BRUTUS
Charles Blount

JUNIUS FLORILEGUS
Richard Younge

JUNIUS HIBERNICUS
John Egan

JUNIUS REDIVIVUS
William Bridges Adams

JUNIUS SECUNDUS
William Fletcher

JURIS CONSULTUS
Alonzo Bowen Chapin

JURISCOLA
Tenche Cox

A JURYMAN
William Creech
William Smellie

JUSTIA, A KNOW NOTHING
Francis Colburn Adams

A JUSTICE OF THE PEACE
John Disney

A JUSTIFIED SINNER
James Hogg

JUSTINIAN
Thomas Law

JUSTINOPHILUS
Samuel Badcock

JUSTITIA
Henry Nutcomb Oxenhan
Charles Joseph Weld-Blundell

JUSTUS
Louis Francis Anderson

JUVENIS SUFFOLCIENSIS
Robert Reeve

K

K. D.
Kenelm Henry Digby

K. L.
Charles Chauncy

KAIN, SAUL
Siegfried Sassoon

KAINS, JOSEPHINE
Ronald Joseph Goulart

KAMIN, NICK
Robert J. Antonick

KANE, JULIA
Denise Naomi Robins

KANTO, PETER
Hugh Zachary

KAPHA, BELSHAZZAR, THE JEW
Robert Dodsley

KAPPA
William Archer
John Ward

KARISHKA, PAUL
David Patterson Hatch

KARN-IDZEK
Robert Stephen Hawker

KAROL, ALEXANDER
Arthur William Charles Kent

KARSHISH
Harry Bulkeley Creswell

KARTA, NAT
Victor G. C. Norwood

KATA PHUSIN
John Ruskin

KATE
Catharine Douglas Bell

KATHARINE
Louise G. Stephens

KAVAN, ANNA
Helen Woods Edmonds

KAVANAGH, CYNTHIA
Dorothy Daniels

KAVANAGH, DAN
Julian Barnes

KAVANAGH, PAUL
Laurence Block

KAVANAUGH, IAN
Jean Francis Webb

KAY, BARBARA
Ethel May Keller

KAY, ELLEN
Nelson R. Demille

KAY, GEORGE
Eric Lambert

KAY, JOHN
James Paterson

KAYE, BARBARA
Barbara Kenrick Muir

KAYE, H. B. (or HAROLD B.)
Harold Bertram Kampf

KAYE, LOUIS
Noel Wilson Norman

KAYE, MOLLIE
Mary Margaret Kaye

KAYE, TOM
Barrington Kaye

KAZARINE, VIOLET
Constance Butler

KEARNEY, JULIAN
Ronald Joseph Goulart

KEAT, O. ELIPHAZ
Philip Bertram Murray Allen

KEEFE, JACK
Ringgold Wilmer

A KEEN HAND
Henry Brougham Farnie

KEENE, CAROLYNE
Harriet Stratemeyer Adams
Leslie McFarlane

KEENE, FARADAY
Cora Hardy Jarrett

KEESE, OLIVE
Caroline Woolmer Leakey

KEGO-E-KAY
Frederick Mather

KEIR, CHRISTINE
Christine Pullein-Thompson

KEITH, CARLTON
Keith Carlton Robertson

KEITH, DAVID
Francis Steegmuller

KEITH, LEIGH
Horace Leonard Gold

KEITH, LESLIE
Grace Leslie Keith Johnston

KEITH, MARIAN
Mary Esther Miller MacGregor

KELL, JOSEPH
John Anthony Burgess Wilson

KELLOW, KATHLEEN
Eleanor Alice Hibbert

KELLY, GUY
Nicholas Moore

KELLY, PATRICK
Theodore E. Allbeury

KELLY, RICHARD
Richard Carl Layman

KEMP, SARAH
Michael Butterworth

KEMPEES, T.
Edward Gordon Craig

KENDALL, JOHN
Margaret Maud Brash

KENDALL, MAY
Mrs Leonora Blanche Lang

KENDRAKE, CARLETON
Erle Stanley Gardner

KENDRICKS, JAMES
Gardner Francis Fox

KENNAWAY, JAMES
James Ewing Peebles

KENNEDY, HOWARD
Josiah Pitts Woolfolk

KENNEDY, MILWARD
Milward Rodon Kennedy
Burge

KENNY, CHARLES J.
Erle Stanley Gardner

KENNY, KATHRYN
Nicolette Meredith Stack

KENT, ALEXANDER
Douglas Reeman

KENT, CROMWELL
Raymond Souster

KENT, DAVID
Hoffman Birney

KENT, KELVIN
Arthur Kelvin Barnes with
Henry Kuttner

KENT, MALLORY
Robert A. W. Lowndes

KENT, PAMELA
Susan Barrie

KENT, PHILIP
Henry Kenneth Bulmer

KENT, SIMON
Max Finkell

A KENTISH CLERGYMAN
Edward Hankin

KENTISH RAG
Bernard Rowland Ward

A KENTISH VICAR
Edward Vesey Bligh

KENTON, MAXWELL
Terry Southern

A KENTUCKIAN
James Chamberlayne Pickett

KENTUCKY, JONATHAN
Henry Matthews

KENWORTHY, HUGH
Rowland Walker

KENYON, ROBERT O.
Henry Kuttner

KEPPEL, CHARLOTTE
Ursula Torday

KERN, GREGORY
Edwin Charles Tubb

KEROUAC, JACK (or JOHN)
Jean Louis Lebris de Kerouac

KERR, BEN
William Thomas Ard

KERR, CAROLE
Margaret Carr

KERR, HOWARD
Alec John Dawson

KERR, LENNOX
James Lennox Kerr

KERR, MICHAEL
Robert Hoskins

KERR, M. E.
Marijane Meaker

KERR, ORPHEUS C.
Robert Henry Newell

KERR, REID
Florence Eveleen Eleanore Bell

KERRY, LOIS
Lois Duncan

KERSEY, JOHN
Thurman Warriner

KERSHAW, PETER
John Edward Lucie-Smith

KESSLER, LEO
Charles Whiting

KETCH, JACK
Thomas Kibble Hervey

KETTNER, A.
Eneas Sweetland Dallas

KEVERNE, RICHARD
Clifford James Wheeler Hosken

KEYBER, MR CONNY
Henry Fielding

KEYES, NOEL
David Noel Keightley

KEYS, JAMES
George Spencer Brown

KHALED KHAN
Edward Alexander Crowley

KHANHOO
Sir William Henry Wilkinson

KHAYYAM, OMAR, JUN.
Wallace Admah Irwin

KIEN LUNG
Stephen Weston

KILBURNE, G. G.
Miss Sarah Doudney

KILGALLEN, MILTON
Kenneth Roberts

KILLIN, GLADYS ELLEN
Gladys Ellen Easdale

KILPATRICK, SARAH
Mavis Eileen Underwood

KIMBRO, JEAN
John M. Kimbro

KIMBROUGH, KATHERYN
John M. Kimbro

KINEJI, MABORUSHI
Walter B. Gibson

KING, CHRISTOPHER
Albert King

KING, KENNEDY
George Douglas Brown

KING, OLIVER
Thomas Ernest Mount

KING, RICHARD
Richard King Huskinson

KING, THOROLD
Charles Gatchell

KING, VINCENT
Rex Thomas Vinson

KING, W. SCOTT
William Kingscote Greenland

KING WILLOW
Thomas Stafford Sidney

A KING'S FRIEND
Thomas Pownall

KINGSBURY, CARL LOUIS
Mrs Caroline Louise Marshall

KINGSFORD, JANE
Charles Francis Barnard

KINGSFORD, NINON (or
MRS ALGERNON)
Mrs Anna Kingsford

KINGSLEY, ANNA
Hazel Phillips Hanshew

KINGSLEY, CHARLOTTE
MAY
Thomas W. Hanshew

KINGSLEY, SIDNEY
Sidney Kieschner

KINGSMILL, HUGH
Hugh Kingsmill Lunn

KINGSTON, BRIAN
Percy William Longhurst

KINGSTON, CHARLES
Charles Kingston O'Mahony

KINGSTON, SYD
David Ernest Bingley

KINK, EMMANUEL
Richard Dowling

KINKAID, MATT
Clifton Adams

MME KINKEL
Elizabeth Sara Sheppard

KINSAYDER, W.
John Marston

KINSEY, ELIZABETH
Eleanor Lowenton Clymer

KINSEY-JONES, BRIAN
Brian Neville Ball

KIRK, ELEANOR
Mrs Eleanor Ames

KIRK, LAURENCE
Eric Andrew Simson

KIRK, ROTHAEL
William L. Low

KIRKE, EDMUND
James Roberts Gilmore

KIRMANSHAHI, HAJI MIRZA ALI ASGHAR
Goldsworthy Lowes Dickinson

KIRTLAND, G. B.
Sesyle Joslin

KIRTON, JAMES
Kenneth Benton

KIRWAN
Nicholas Murray

KIT
Mrs Katherine B. Coleman

KITKAT, DICK
Richard Doyle

KITT, TAMARA
Beatrice S. De Regniers

KLASSEN, JAN
Edward Gordon Craig

KLAXON
John Graham Bower

KLINGENSPORREN
Francis Doyne Dwyer

KNICKERBOCKER
John Austin Stevens

KNICKERBOCKER, DIEDRICH
Washington Irving

KNIGHT, ADAM
Laurence Lariar

KNIGHT, DAVID
Richard Scott Prather

KNIGHT, FRANK
Francis Edgar Knight

KNIGHT, GARETH
Basil Leslie Wilby

A KNIGHT ERRANT
Edward Dubois

THE KNIGHT OF CHILLON
Nehemiah Hawkins

THE KNIGHT OF INNISHOWEN
John Sheehan

THE KNIGHT OF KERRY
Maurice Fitzgerald

THE KNIGHT OF MORAR
Sir William Augustus Fraser

KNISH, ANNE
Arthur Davison Ficke

KNOKES, JOHN
John Frith

KNOT, MAPLE
Ebenezer Clemo

KNOTT, EDWARD
Matthias Wilson

KNOTTS, RAYMOND
Gordon Volk

KNOX, CALVIN M.
Robert Silverberg

KNOX, GILBERT
Madge Hamilton MacBeth

KNOX, JAMES
William Brittain

KODAK
Ernest Francis O'Ferrall

KOIZUMI, YAKUMO
Lafcadio Hearn

KONX OMPAX
Richard Whately

KORESH
Cyrus R. Teed

KRANTZOVIUS, IRENAEUS
Benjamin Stillingfleet

KRAPP, ROBERT MARTIN
Robert Martin Adams

KRAUSS, BRUNO
Kenneth Henry Bulmer

KRAWBRIDGE, MICHAEL
John Boyle

KRIN, SYLVIE
Barry Fantoni with Richard Ingrams

KRISLOV, ALEXANDER
Leon Alexander Lee Howard

KRON, KARL
Lyman Hotchkiss Bagg

KRULL, FELIX
James Dillon White

KRUTZCH, GUS
Thomas Stearns Eliot

KUKLOS
W. Fitzwater Wray

KUNST, HERMANN
Walter Chalmers Smith

KWANG CHANG LING
Alexander Delmar

KYD
Joseph Clayton Clarke

KYD, THOMAS
Alfred Bennett Harbage

KYLE, DUNCAN
John Franklin Broxholme

KYLE, ELIZABETH
Agnes Mary Robertson Dunlop

KYLE, SEFTON
Roy Vickers

L

L.
Joseph Addison
George Frederick Beltz
Charles Lamb
Hannah More

L. E.
Samuel Pegge

L. E. L.
Letitia Elizabeth Landon

L. M.
Daniel Defoe

L. M. H.
Miss Louisa M. Hubbard

RIGHT HON. L. M. W. M.
Lady Mary Wortley Montagu

L. N. R.
Ellen Henrietta Ranyard

A LABORING MAN
Thomas Robinson Hazard

A LABOURER
Thomas Hodgskin
Thomas Row

LACCHIO, CARLO
Edward Gordon Craig

LACKLAND, THOMAS
George Canning Hill

LACON
Charles Caleb Colton
Edmund Henry Lacon Watson

LACTANTIUS
Sir David Dalrymple

LACTILLA
Mrs Ann Yearsley

LACY, ED.
Leonard S. Zinberg

LACY, JOHN
George Darley

LADNER, KURT
Nelson R. Demille

A LADY
Mary Anne Arundell
Jane Austen

George Berkeley
Mrs Elizabeth Bonhote
Margaret Botsford
Margaret Ann Burgoyne
Lady Charlotte Susan Maria
    Bury
Mrs Dorothea Celesia
Mrs Mary Mitchell Collyer
Susan Fenimore Cooper
Mrs Eliza Ware Farrar
Sarah Fielding
Anne Finch
Mrs Eliza Lee Follen
Jane Freshfield
Mrs Hannah Glasse
Mrs Elizabeth Griffith
Mrs Susanna Gunning
Sara Josepha Hale
Lady Anne Halkett
Elizabeth Hamilton
Mrs Eliza Haywood
Mrs Felicia Dorothea Hemans
Mrs Margaret Hodson
Mrs Julia Ward Howe
Mrs Anna Brownell Jameson
William Kenrick
Mrs Ann M'Taggart
Harriet Martineau
Lady Mary Wortley Montagu
Hannah Maynard Pickard
Annabella Plumptre
Anne Pratt
Clara Reeve
Mrs Maria Eliza Rundle
Mrs Elizabeth Sanders
Miss Elizabeth Missing Sewell
Elizabeth Isabella Spence
George Alexander Stevens
Mrs Elizabeth Thomas
Miss Emily Trevenen
Lady Eglantine Wallace
Helena Whitford
Maria Julia Young
Mrs Elizabeth Zornlin

LADY MURASAKI
Arthur David Schloss

LADY NIMROD
William Makepeace Thackeray

A LADY AND HER BROTHER
Elizabeth Sophia Tomlins

A LADY IN THE COUNTRY
Anna Gurney

A LADY LATELY DECEASED
Jane Bowdler

A LADY OF FASHION
William Makepeace Thackeray

A LADY OF GREAT BRITAIN
Susannah Centlivre

A LADY OF MAINE
Sarah Sayward Barrell

A LADY OF
    MASSACHUSETTS
Sarah Sayward Barrell
Mrs Lydia Maria Child
Hannah Webster Foster

A LADY OF NEW-
    HAMPSHIRE
Sarah Josepha Hale

A LADY OF NEW ORLEANS
Marion Southwood

A LADY OF NEW YORK
Mrs Sarah Haight

A LADY OF PHILADELPHIA
Margaret Botsford
Mrs Sarah Hall
Eliza Leslie

A LADY OF QUALITY
Enid Bagnold
Lady Mary Chudleigh
Lady Dorothea Dubois
Miss Frances Williams Wynn

A LADY OF RANK
Lady Charlotte Susan Maria
    Bury
Mary Egerton

A LADY VOLUNTEER
Miss Frances Magdalen Taylor

A LADY WHO PREFERS TO
    BE ANONYMOUS
Miss Emily Jolly

LAERTES
George Alfred Townsend

LAFAYETTE, RENE
Ron L. Hubbard

LAGENIENSIS
James Clarence Mangan
John O'Hanlon

LAICK, WILL
George Ridpath

LAICUS
Lyman Abbott
John Poynder

LAIDLAW, ALICE
Alice Munro

LAING, PATRICIA
Amelia Reynolds Long

LAITH, APPLETON
Caryl James Battersby

LAKE, CLAUDE
Mathilde Blind

LAKER, ROSALIND
Barbara Ovstedal

LAMB, CHARLOTTE
Sheila Holland

LAMB, WILLIAM
Margaret Storm Jameson

LAMBERT, CHRISTINE
Heidi Huberta F. Loewengard

**LAMBERT, STEPHEN (or S.
H.)**
Stephen Southwold

LAMBERT LILLY
Francis Lister Hawks

THE LAMBETH LIBRARIAN
John Richard Green

LAMBOURNE, JOHN
John Battersby Crompton
Lamburn

LA MERI
Russell Meriweather Hughes

LAMIA
Alfred Austin

LAMONT, FRANCIS
Eleanor F. Jourdain

LAMONT, MARIANNE
Anne Rundle

**A LANCASHIRE COTTON
SPINNER**
Henry Ashworth

**A LANCASHIRE
INCUMBENT**
Abraham Hume

LANCASTER, G. B.
Mrs Alfred (Edith) Lyttelton

LANCASTER, SHEILA
Sheila Holland

LANCASTER, VICKY
Dorothy Phoebe Ansle

LANCASTER, WILLIAM
John Byrne Leicester Warren

A LANCASTER IDOLATOR
John Lingard

LANCE, LESLIE
Irene Maude Swatridge

**LANCEWOOD, LAWRENCE,
ESQ.**
Daniel Wise

LAND, JANE
Kathryn Borland

LAND, MILTON
Talmage Powell

A LAND-LUBBER
William Marcus Thompson

LANDELS, D. H.
Donald Landel Henderson

A LANDHOLDER
Benjamin Bell
Elisha Reynolds Potter
Wilkins Updike

LANDON, LOUISE
Louise Platt Hauck

A LANDOWNER
Charles Townshend

A LANDSCAPE PAINTER
Charles Lanman

LANE, EDWARD
Kay Dick

LANE, GRANT
Stephen Gould Fisher

LANE, JANE
Elaine Dakers

LANE, JERRY
Patricia Miles Martin

LANE, ROUMELIA
Kay Green

LANG, ANTHONY
John George Haslette Vahey

LANG, FRANCES
Winifred Langford Mantle

LANG, GRACE
Lee Floren

LANG, KING
George Hay
Edwin Charles Tubb

LANGA LANGA
Harry Baldwin Hermon Hodge

LANGART, DARREL T.
Randall Garrett

LANGDON, MARY
Mrs Mary H. Greene Pike

LANGE, JOHN
Michael Crichton

LANGHOLM, NEIL
Kenneth Henry Bulmer

LANGLEY, LEE
Sarah Langley

LANGLEY, PETER
Ronald Fleming

**LANGSTAFF, LAUNCELOT,
ESQ.**
Washington Irving with
William Irving and James
Kirke Paulding

LANGSTON, LAWRENCE
Reverdy Johnson

LANGTON, LIONEL
Llewellyn Archer Atherley-
Jones

LANGTRY, MIKE
Edwin Charles Tubb

LANIA, LEO
Lazar Herrmann

LANIN, E. B.
Emile Joseph Dillon

LANKSIDES, LORENZO
Thomas Campbell

LARA
George Chetwynd Griffith
Jones

LARDNER, RING
Ringgold Wilmer

LARMINIE, MARGARET
Margaret Rivers Tragett

L'ARTSAU, MRS OGNIBLAT
Miles Franklin

LARWOOD, JACOB
Herman van Schevichaven

LA SALLE, VICTOR
Robert Lionel Fanthorpe

**LASCELLES, LADY
CAROLINE**
Mrs Mary Elizabeth Maxwell

LASH
John Lash Latey

LA TENELLA
Mrs Mary Bayard Clarke

THE LATE ARTHUR AUSTIN
John Wilson

A LATE BARRISTER-AT-LAW
Sir John Strange

THE LATE BEN SMITH
Cornelius Mathews

A LATE CHIEF-SECRETARY
OF IRELAND
George Macartney

THE LATE DR ARCHIBALD
MacLEOD
William Lisle Bowles

A LATE EMINENT
CONGREGATIONAL
DIVINE
Philip Nye

A LATE EMINENT JUDGE
OF THIS NATION
Sir Henry Yelverton

A LATE FELLOW OF ALL
SOUL'S COLLEGE,
OXFORD
Arthur Philip Perceval

A LATE FELLOW OF KING'S
COLLEGE, CAMBRIDGE
Thomas Ashton

A LATE GRADUATE OF
OXFORD
Frederick Naghten

A LATE INHABITANT
Edward Hasted

THE LATE J. BROWN
Alexander Wheelock Thayer

THE LATE JAMES HAMLEY
TREGENNA
Robert Bateman Paul

THE LATE J. H.
ALEXANDER, BA
Alexander Hay Japp

THE LATE JOHN PICKARD
OWEN
Samuel Butler

THE LATE JOHN
SURREBUTTER
John Anstey

A LATE LEARNED HAND
Robert Sanderson

A LATE LEARNED JUDGE
Sir Geoffrey Gilbert

A LATE LEARNED PRELATE
Robert Sanderson

A LATE LORD
CHANCELLOR
Charles Yorke

A LATE LORD CHIEF
BARON
Sir Geoffrey Gilbert

A LATE LORD MAYOR OF
LONDON
Sir John Barnard

A LATE MAGISTRATE OF
THE COLONY
Edward Jerningham Wakefield

THE LATE MAJOR LUTIY
Edward Alexander Crowley

THE LATE MASTER OF THE
TEMPLE
Caleb Fleming

A LATE MEMBER OF THE
UNIVERSITY
Theophilus Lindsey
Peter Le Page Renouf

A LATE MEMBER OF THE
UNIVERSITY OF
OXFORD
John Moore Capes

A LATE MERCHANT
Asa Greene

A LATE MINISTER AND
PREACHER IN
ENGLAND
Robert Parsons

A LATE MINISTER IN THE
CHURCH OF
SCOTLAND
John Glas

A LATE MISSIONARY
BISHOP
Thomas Valpy French

A LATE OFFICER IN THE US
ARMY
Jervase Cutler

THE LATE PAUL
CHATFIELD, MD
Horatio Smith

A LATE PERSON OF
QUALITY
Francis Quarles

A LATE PHYSICIAN
Samuel Warren

A LATE PROFESSOR IN THE
UNIVERSITY OF
OXFORD
Robert Lowth

A LATE RESIDENT
Eaton Stannard Barrett
Mrs Harriet Grote
Andrew Picken

A LATE RESIDENT AT
BHAGULPORE
David Hopkins

A LATE RESIDENT IN THE
EAST
John Hobart Caunter

THE LATE REV. LAURENCE
STERNE
William Combe

THE LATE REV.
WILLIAMSON
JAHNSENYKES
William Jenks

A LATE STUDENT AT
HARVARD COLLEGE
Joseph Willard

THE LATE THOMAS LITTLE
Thomas Moore

A LATE UNDER-SECRETARY
OF STATE
William Knox

A LATE VISITANT
William Jerdan

LATHAM, MAVIS
Mavis Thorpe Clark

LATHAM, PHILIP
Robert Shirley Richardson

LATHEN, EMMA
Martha Hennisart with Mary J.
Latsis

LATIMER, FAITH
Mrs John A. Miller

LATIMER, RUPERT
Algernon Victor Mills

LATOUCHE, JOHN
Oswald John Crawfurd

LATOUCHE, VIVIAN
George Henry Lewes

LATROON, MERITON
Richard Head

A LATTER-DAY
PHILOSOPHER
Lionel James Trotter

LAUDER, AFFERBECK
Alistair Ardoch Morrison

LAUNCELOT, DOM CLAUDE
Mary Anne Schimmelpenninck

LAVERTY, DONALD
James Blish with Damon
Knight

LAVIN, MARY
Mary Walsh

LAVOND, PAUL DENNIS
Robert A. W. Lowndes

LAW, ELIZABETH
Maureen Peters

LAW, JOHN
Margaret Elise Harkness

A LAW-STUDENT
Cuthbert Edward Ellison

LAWLESS, ANTHONY
Philip MacDonald

LAWMIND, JOHN
Sir John Wildman

LAWRENCE, IRENE
John Marsh

LAWRENCE, LOUISE
Elizabeth Rhoda Holden

LAWRENCE, P.
Edwin Charles Tubb

LAWRENNY, H.
Edith Jemima Simcox

LAWSON, CHET
Edwin Charles Tubb

LAWSON, W. B.
George Charles Jenks

LAWTON, CHARLES
Charles Newman Heckelmann

A LAWYER
John Fine
Frederick Hallard
Charles Neaves
John Reeves

A LAY BARONET
Sir Henry Martin

A LAY CHURCHMAN
James Fitzjames Stephen

A LAY GENTLEMAN
Edmund Bohun
Francis Lee

A LAY HAND
Sir Richard Cox
Edmund Curll
William Fleetwood

A LAY MEMBER OF THE BRITISH AND FOREIGN BIBLE SOCIETY
George Stokes

A LAY MEMBER OF THE CHURCH OF ENGLAND
Samuel Hinds
John Mitchell Kemble
John Muir
John Poynder

A LAY MEMBER OF THE CHURCH OF SCOTLAND
Thomas Carlyle

THE LAY PREACHER
Joseph Dennie

A LAY SECEDER
George Wilson Meadley

A LAYMAN
Lyman Abbott
Samuel Adams
Robert Ainslie
Sir Edward Hall Alderson
John Allen
Samuel Austin Allibone
John Lavicount Anderdon
Bailey Bartlett
Sir John Baylley
John Bevans Jr.
James Whatman Bosanquet
John Bowles
Charles Bray
William Burgh
Peleg Whitman Chandler
Thomas Cogan
George Colman
Stephen Colwell
John Watts De Peyster
Michael Dodson
Patrick Duigenan
Alexander Dunlop
Thomas Falconer
William Falconer
John Hay Forbes
Richard Gough
Samuel Greg
George Hardinge
Samuel Heywood
Thomas Hughes
Alexander Taylor Innes
Joseph Jewell
John Lowell
James Heywood Markland
Thomas James Mathias
William Milligan
Richard Monckton Milnes
Frederick John Monson
Mowbray Walter Morris
John Muir
Horatio Nelson
William Nicol
Whitlock Nicoll
William Oldisworth
Thomas Paine
Sir James Alan Park
William Penney
Francis Penrose
William Peter
Basil Montagu Pickering
John Poynder
George Psalmanazar
James Augustus St John
John Osborne Sargent
Sir Walter Scott
Robert Benton Seeley
John Shute
Goldwin Smith
William Stevens
John Edmonds Stock
John Struthers
William Witherby
Ralph Nicholson Wornum

A LAYMAN, A FRIEND TO THE TRUE PRINCIPLES OF THE CONSTITUTION
Augustus Henry Fitzroy

A LAYMAN OF BOSTON
Nathan Appleton

A LAYMAN OF THE CHURCH
William Edmonstoune Aytoun

A LAYMAN OF THE CHURCH OF ENGLAND
George Hickes
William Knox

A LAYMAN OF THE CHURCH OF SCOTLAND
George Ridpath

LAYTON, LILLIE
Mrs Emeline H. Johnson

LAZARUS, EBENEZER
Robert Mason

LEADER, BARBARA
Evelyn Barbara Blackburn

LEADER, CHARLES
Robert Charles Smith

LEAF, A.
Lord Ernest William Hamilton

LEAKE, R. E.
Mollie Skinner

LEAR, PETER
Peter Lovesey

LEAR, P. G. and L. O.
Charles Kenneth Scott-Moncrieff

A LEARNED AND IMPARTIAL HAND
Peter Heylyn

A LEARNED AND JUDICIOUS DIVINE
Henry Ainsworth

A LEARNED AND REVEREND DIVINE
Jeremy Taylor

A LEARNED ANTIQUARY
John Selden

THE LEARNED
BLACKSMITH
Elihu Burritt

A LEARNED DOCTOR
Henry Mayo

A LEARNED, FAITHFUL,
ZEALOUS AND
REVEREND MINISTER
OF THE CHURCH OF
SCOTLAND
Ebenezer Erskine

A LEARNED GORILLA
Richard Grant White

A LEARNED HAND
Zachary Grey
Sir Matthew Hale

A LEARNED JUDGE
Sir Francis Buller

A LEARNED PEN
Thomas Barlow
Peter Mews
Gilbert Rule

A LEARNED PERSON
Lancelot Addison

A LEARNED PRELATE
Jeremy Taylor

LEATHES, EDMUND JOHN
Edmund John Donaldson

LEAVER, RUTH
Ruth Tomalin

LEBARON, ANTHONY
John Keith Laumer

LE BRETON, JOHN
Thomas Murray Ford with
Alice May Harte Potts

LE BRETON, THOMAS
Thomas Murray Ford

LE CARON, HENRI
Thomas Miller Beach

LE CARRE, JOHN
David Cornwell

LE CHEMINANT, LOUIS
James Forbes Dalton

LECKY, WALTER
William A. M'Dermott

LEE, AMBER
Faith Baldwin

LEE, ANDREW
Louis Stanton Auchincloss

LEE, ANNE S.
Mabel Ansley Murphy

LEE, GYPSY ROSE
Rose Louise Hovick

LEE, HOLME
Harriet Parr

LEE, HOWARD
Ronald Joseph Goulart

LEE, JULIAN
Jean Lee Latham

LEE, MATT
W. Samuel Merwin

LEE, MINNIE MARY
Mrs Julia Amanda Wood

LEE, PATTY
Alice Cary

LEE, RANGER
Charles Horace Snow

LEE, RAYMOND
E. Le Breton Martin

LEE, ROSIE
Joan Aiken

LEE, SHEPPARD
Robert Montgomery Bird

LEE, SIR SIDNEY
Solomon Lazarus Levy

LEE, STAN
Stanley Leiber

LEE, VERNON
Violet Paget

LEE, WILLIAM
William S. Burroughs

LEEK, MARGARET
Sara Bowen-Judd

LEES, HANNAH
Elizabeth Pickering Fetter

LEES, IAIN C.
John Lees Carvel

LEES, JOHN MORTON
Ellis Middleton

A LEGAL SON AND SINCERE
CONFORMIST TO THE
CHURCH OF ENGLAND
Edmund Hickeringill

LEGION
Daniel Defoe
Robert Baldwin Sullivan

LEGISLATOR
William Arthur Shaw

LE GRAND
Le Grand Henderson

LE GRAND, MARTIN
James Rice

LEGULEIUS, LECTOR
Charles Neaves

MRS LEICESTER
Miss Mary Anne Lamb

LEIGH, ARBOR
Louisa Sarah Bevington

LEIGH, ARRAN
Katherine Harris Bradley

LEIGH, ISLA
Edith Emma Cooper

LEIGH, JOHANNA
Dorothy Leigh Sayers

LEIGHTON
Jesse Appleton

LEIGHTON, LEE
Wayne Overholser

LEILA
Mrs Emma Barlow

LEINSTER, MURRAY
William Fitzgerald Jenkins

LEISURELY SAUNTERER
Edward Eggleston

LEITH, W. COMPTON
Ormonde Maddock Dalton

LEJEUNE, ANTHONY
Edward Anthony Thompson

LELIUS
James Boswell

LELLAND, FRANK
Alfred McClelland Burrage

LEMOINE
Eugene Lemoine Didier

LEMON, IDA
Ida Jane Hildyard

LENANTON, (LADY) C.
Carola Mary Oman

LEO THE SECOND
Laurence Eusden

LEONARD, A. B.
Earl Augustus Aldrich

LEONARD, BERTHA
Bertha Fry

LEONARD, CHARLES
Mary Violet Heberden

LEONARD, HUGH
John K. Byrne

LEONARD, JASON
Jonathan Escott

LEONARDUS, PAULUS
Paul Sherlock

LEONG, GOR YUN
Virginia T. H. Ellison

LEONID
Willan G. Bosworth

LE PETIT HOMME ROUGE
Ernest Alfred Vizetelly

LEPUS
Charles Lamb

LE SIEG, THEO
Theodor Seuss Geisel

LESLIE, AMY
Lillie West

LESLIE, FRANK
Henry Carter

LESLIE, FRED
Frederick Leslie Hobson

LESLIE, JOHN
John Leslie Despard Howitt

LESLIE, MRS MADELINE
Mrs Harriette Newell Baker

LESLIE, O. H.
Henry Slesar

LESLIE, WARD S.
Elizabeth Honor Ward

LESSER, ANTHONY
Anthony Charles Whitby

LESSER, DERWIN
Charles D. Hornig

LESTER, FRANK
Frank Hugh Usher

LESTER, IRVIN
Fletcher Pratt

LESTER, MARK
Martin James Russell

L'ESTRANGE, ANNA
Rosemary Ellerbeck

L'ESTRANGE, CORINNE
Henry Hartshorne

L'ESTRANGE, DAVID
David Ivor Davies

LEVI
Levi H. Dowling

LEVINREW, WILL
Wiliam Levine

LEWESDON, JOHN
Albert Scott Daniell

LEWIS, AUGUSTIN
Louis Frederick Austin

LEWIS, CAROLINE
Harold Begbie with Stafford
Ransome and M. H. Temple

LEWIS, CHARLES
Roger Dixon

LEWIS, FREDERICK
Frederick Lewis Collins

LEWIS, J. MOSER
Edward Gordon Craig

LEWIS, LANGE
Jane Lewis Brandt

LEWIS, MERVYN
Glyn Mervyn Louis Frewer

LEWIS, MONK
Matthew Gregory Lewis

LEWIS, PAUL
Noel Bertram Gerson

LEWIS, ROY
John Royston Lewis

LEWIS, S. A.
Lewis Austin Storrs

LEWIS, S. ANNA
Estelle Anna Blanche Lewis

LEWIS, SARAH ANN
Estelle Anna Blanche Lewis

LEX
Robert Reid

LEX PUBLICA
Augustus Granville Stapleton

LEYLAND, PETER
Walter Kinnear Pyke-Lees

LEYTON, SOPHIE
Sheila Walsh

A LIBERAL MP
John A. M. MacDonald

LIBERIUS
Joseph Priestley

LIBERTAS
Peter Brown
Charles Mayo Ellis
Mrs Caroline Elizabeth Sarah
Norton

LIBRA
Edward Brotherton
Richard Cobden

THE LIBRARIAN
Bernard Quaritch

LICHFIELD, RICHARD
Gabriel Harvey

LT. FRITH IN NEWGATE
James Boswell

LIEUT. MURRAY
Maturin Murray Ballou

**A LIFE-LONG THINKER
AND WANDERER**
Robert Needham Cust

LIGHT CAST
Sir Randal H. Roberts

LIGHTFOOT
John Isaac Ira Adams

LIGHTFOOT, JULIA
Henry Mackenzie

MR LIMBERTONGUE
James Hain Friswell

LIMNELIUS, GEORGE
Lewis George Robinson

LIMNER, LUKE
John Leighton

LIN, FRANK
Miss Gertrude Franklin
Atherton

LINCOLN, GEOFFREY
John Clifford Mortimer

LINCOLN, LOIS
Edward Gordon Craig

LINCOLN, ROBERT O.
George Champlin Mason

A LINCOLNSHIRE GRAZIER
Thomas Hartwell Horne

A LINCOLNSHIRE RECTOR
Robert D. B. Rawnsley

**THE LINCOLNSHIRE
THRASHER**
Charles Richardson

LINDALL, EDWARD
Edward Ernest Smith

LINDAMOUR
Charles Gildon

LINDEN, OLIVER
Doris Caroline Abrahams

LINDSAY, RACHEL
Roberta Leigh

LINDSEY, JOHN
John Saint Clair Muriel

LINE, DAVID
Lionel Davidson

A LINE OFFICER
George Francis Robert
Henderson

LINESMAN
Maurice Harold Grant

LINKLATER, J. LANE
Alex Watkins

LINNE, ELEANOR G.
Frederick Britten Austin with
Lambert F. Williams

LINTOT, BERNARD
Holbrook Jackson

LIONEL, ROBERT
Robert Lionel Fanthorpe

LIONI (or LEONI)
George Croly

LIPSTICK
Lois Long

LISTENER
Joseph Edgar Chamberlin

THE LISTENER
John MacGowan

LISTER, STEPHEN
Digby George Gerahty

LITERARY ANTIQUITY
Frederick William Fairholt

A LITERARY VAGABOND
Frank Fowler

LITTLE, FRANCES
Fannie Caldwell MacAulay

LITTLE ARTHUR
Lady Maria Callcott

LITTLE JIM
James Stanley Little

LITTLEJOHN
Frederick Guest Tomlins

LITTLEMORE, F.
Frank Frankfort Moore

LITTLEPAGE, CORNELIUS
James Fenimore Cooper

LITTLE TICH
Harry Ralph

LITTLETON, MARK
John Pendleton Kennedy

**LITTLETON, MASTER
TIMOTHY**
Richard Johnson

LITTLEWIT, HUMPHREY
Howard Phillips Lovecraft

A LIVE AMERICAN
Henry Morford

A LIVERPOOL MERCHANT
Henry Arthur Bright

LIVINGSTON, KENNETH
Kenneth Livingston Stewart

**LIVINGSTON-STANLEY,
SERENA**
Joan Lindsay

**A LIVING TRUE WITNESS
TO THAT ONE
ETERNAL WAY OF GOD**
William Penn

LIZARD, JOHN
Edward Young

A LLANBRYNMAIR FARMER
Samuel Roberts

LLEWELLYN
Robert Sanders

LLEWELLYN, E. L.
Mrs Lydia H. Sheppard

LLEWELLYN, RICHARD
Richard D. V. Llewellyn Lloyd

LLEWELLYN THE BARD
Philip Edward Thomas

LLEWMYS, WESTON
Ezra Pound

LLOYD, ELLIS
Charles Ellis Lloyd

LLOYD, GRANT
Dame Elizabeth Wordsworth

LLOYD, HUGH
Percy Keese Fitzhugh

LLOYD, JAMES
Elizabeth James

LLOYD, LEVANAH
Maureen Peters

LLOYD, LUCY VAUGHAN
John Keats

LLUCEN
John Cullen

A LOBBYIST
Michael MacDonagh

**LOBSANG RAMPA,
TUESDAY**
Cyril Henry Hoskins

A LOCAL MINISTER
George Griffith

LOCKE, MARTIN
William Murdoch Duncan

LOCKHARD, LEONARD
Theodore L. Thomas

LODER, VERNON
John George Haslette Vahey

**LODOCHOWSKOWSKI,
STANISLAS**
Edward Gordon Craig

LOEMELIUS, HERMANNUS
John Floyd

LOG, ABEL
Charles Butler Greatrex

LOGAN
John Neal
Thomas Bangs Thorpe

LOGAN, FORD
Dwight Bennett Newton

LOGAN, JAKE
Alan Riefe
Martin Cruz Smith

LOGAN, MARK
Christopher Robin Nicole

LOGISTES
George Glasgow

LOGROLLER
Richard Le Gallienne

LOKI
Karl Pearson

LOMAX, BLISS
Harry Sinclair Drago

LOMBARD, NAP
Pamela Hansford Johnson with
Nick Stewart

LOMBARD, PETER
William Benham

MR LONDON
Hannen Swaffer

LONDON, JACK
John Griffith London

LONDON, THOMAS
Philip Thicknesse

LONDON, W.
Simon Waley Waley

LONDON ANTIQUARY
John Camden Hotten

A LONDON CLERGYMAN
John Hobart Caunter

A LONDON DOG-FANCIER
Thomas Boys

LONDON MA
William Gallatly

A LONDON PHYSICIAN
William Augustus Guy
Edward Smith

A LONDON PLAYGOER
Henry Morley

A LONDON TAILOR
Francis Place

A LONDON ZULU
George Jacob Holyoake

A LONDONER
Charles Lamb
Walter White

THE LONDONER
Arthur Oswald Barron

LONE, JOHN
James John Garth Wilkinson

LONG, SILENT
Thomas Toke Lynch

LONG, WESLEY
George Oliver Smith

LONGBAUGH, HARRY
William Goldman

LONGINUS
Thomas Sheridan

LONGLEY, W. B.
Robert Joseph Randisi

LONGMAN, IRWIN
Ingersoll Lockwood

LONGSHANK, LAURENCE, GENT.
Robert Mudie

LONGSTAFF, LAUNCELOT
George Longmore

LONGWAY, A. HUGE
Andrew Lang

LONSDALE, FREDERICK
Lionel Frederick Leonard

A LOOKER-ON
John Ross Dix
Denis Murphy
Hector Orr

A LOOKER-ON FROM AMERICA
Charles Brandon Boynton

LOOSLEY, WILLIAM ROBERT
David Langford

LORAC, E. C. R.
Edith Caroline Rivett

LORAINE, PHILIP
Robin Estridge

LORD, ALISON (or JEFFREY)
Julie Ellis

LORD, JEREMY
Ben Ray Redman

LORD, NANCY
Eve Titus

LORD DUNDREARY
Charles Kingsley

LORD GILHOOLEY
Frederick Henry Seymour

LORENZ, SARAH
Sarah Winston

LORENZO
Lorenzo Dow

LORGNON
Catherine Frances Grace Gore

LORIMER, ADAM
William Lorimer Watson

LORING, ANDREW
Lorin Andrews Lathrop

LORING, PETER
Samuel Shellabarger

L'ORMEGREGNY, SIEUR
Peter Du Moulin

LORNE, CHARLES
Charles Neville Brand

LORRAINE, ANNE
Lilian Mary Chisholm

LORRAINE, PAUL
John Russell Fearn

LORREQUER, HARRY
Charles James Lever

LORRIMER, CLAIRE
Patricia Denise Clark

LOTHIAN, ROXBURGHE
Elizabeth Kerr Coulson

A LOTHIAN JUSTICE, QUONDAM MP
Robert Andrew MacFie

LOTHROP, AMY
Anna Bartlett Warner

LOUIS, PAT
Dorothy Brenner Francis

LOUISA
Elizabeth Boyd

LOUNDSBERRY, CHARLES
Williston Fish

A LOUNGER
William Bromet
Frank Fowler

THE LOUNGER AT THE CLUBS
Edmund Yates

LOURIE, HELEN
Catherine Storr

LOVE, JAMES
James Dance

LOVECHILD, (MRS) SOLOMON
Lady Eleanor Fenn

LOVEGOOD, JOHN
Elliot Lovegood Grant Watson

LOVELL, INGRAHAM
Mrs Josephine D. D. Bacon

LOVELL, MARC
Mark McShane

LOVEMORE, SIR CHARLES
Mary de la Riviere Manley

A LOVER AND FRIEND OF MANKIND
John Adams

A LOVER OF ALL MANKIND
Daniel Taylor

A LOVER OF ANGLING
James Chetham

A LOVER OF BIRDS
Eleazer Albin

A LOVER OF BOOKS
James Henry Leigh Hunt

A LOVER OF CHARITY AND SINCERITY IN ALL
William Penn

A LOVER OF CHRIST
John Collett Ryland

A LOVER OF CHRISTIAN LIBERTY
William Matthews

A LOVER OF CONSISTENCY
James Paull

A LOVER OF CUDWORTH AND TRUTH
George Barrell Cheever

A LOVER OF DECENCY
James Boswell

A LOVER OF EPISCOPACY
Zachary Grey

A LOVER OF FREE GRACE
John Wesley

A LOVER OF HER SEX
Mary Astell

A LOVER OF HIS COUNTRY
Benjamin Coole
Henry Fielding
Caleb Fleming
Cotton Mather
Samuel Pratt
George Ridpath
William Smith
William Sprigg
Arthur Ashley Sykes

A LOVER OF HIS KING AND COUNTREY
John Cleveland

A LOVER OF HIS KING AND COUNTRY
Slingsby Bethel

A LOVER OF HIS NATIVE
COUNTRY
Thomas Fuller

A LOVER OF HISTORY
Zachary Grey

A LOVER OF LEARNING
Robert Wild

A LOVER OF LITERATURE
Thomas Green

A LOVER OF MANKIND
Anthony Benezet

A LOVER OF MANKIND AND
COMMON SENSE
John Wesley

A LOVER OF
MATHEMATICS
Edward Ward

A LOVER OF OLD ENGLAND
Daniel Defoe

A LOVER OF ORDER
Joseph Bretland
William Godwin
Basil Montagu

A LOVER OF PEACE
Gilbert Burnet
John Wesley

A LOVER OF PEACE AND OF
HIS COUNTRY
John Evelyn

A LOVER OF PEACE AND
THE PUBLIC GOOD
John Humphrey

A LOVER OF PEACE AND
TRUTH
Joseph Priestley
William Prynne

A LOVER OF QUIETNESS
AND LIBERTY OF
CONSCIENCE
John William Fletcher

A LOVER OF SOCIAL
ORDER
Robert John Thornton

A LOVER OF SOULS
George Fox

A LOVER OF THAT
INNOCENT AND
HEALTHFUL
DIVERSION
George Smith

A LOVER OF THAT PEOPLE
John Barclay

A LOVER OF THE CHURCH
AND HIS COUNTRY
John Sage

A LOVER OF THE CHURCH
OF SCOTLAND
John Willison

A LOVER OF THE
ESTABLISHED
GOVERNMENT OF
BOTH CHURCH AND
STATE
George HIckes

A LOVER OF THE FINE
ARTS
Maria Brooks
Vaughan Thomas

A LOVER OF THE GOSPEL
Joseph Priestley

A LOVER OF THE SPORT
Robert Nobbes

A LOVER OF THE TRUTH
Robert Fleming
Richard Hollingworth
Charles Prentiss
Carew Ralegh

A LOVER OF THE WEED
Charles Robert Forrester

A LOVER OF TRAVELS
John Dunton

A LOVER OF TRUE LIBERTY
Alexander Shields

A LOVER OF TRUTH
Zachary Grey
Matthew Griffith

A LOVER OF TRUTH AND
LIBERTY
Samuel Bourn
James Ralph

A LOVER OF TRUTH AND
MANKIND
UNIVERSALLY
Francis Hatt

A LOVER OF TRUTH AND
OF HIS COUNTRY
James Tyrrell

A LOVER OF TRUTH AND
OF THE SOULS OF MEN
John Mapletoft

A LOVER OF TRUTH AND
OF TRUE RELIGION
William Whiston

A LOVER OF TRUTH AND
PEACE
Charles Chauncy
Jeremiah Ives
William Penn
Arthur Ashley Sykes

A LOVER OF TRUTH AND
THE BRITISH
CONSTITUTION
Caleb Evans

A LOVER OF TRUTH,
VERTUE AND JUSTICE
Edward Meredith

A LOVER OF VIRTUE AND
GOODNESS IN
WHOMSOEVER
John Pennyman

LOVINGOOD, SUT
George Washington Harris

LOW, DOROTHY MACKIE
Lois Dorothea Low

LOW, GARDNER
Percival Charles Rodda

LOW, MATT
George Garrett

LOWE, KENNETH
Elma K. Lobaugh

THE LOWE FARMER
William Law Gane

LOWELL, ELIZABETH
Ann Elizabeth Maxwell

LOWING, ANNE
Christine Geach

LOXMITH, JOHN
John Kilian Houston Brunner

A LOYAL SUBJECT
Walter Charleton

LUARD, L.
William Blaine Luard

LUCAS, VICTORIA
Sylvia Plath

LUCERNA
James Carrick Moore

LUCIUS
James Blatch Piggott Dennis
Samuel Parr

LUDLOW, GEOFFREY
Laurence Walter Meynell

LUDLOW, JOHNNY
Mrs Ellen Wood

LUDLOW, PARK
Theron Brown

LUDOVICUS, M.
John Campbell

LUKE, THOMAS
Graham Masterson

LUM, PETER
Bettina Lum Crowe

LUMLEY, BENJAMIN
Benjamin Levy

MR LUN, JUNIOR
Henry Woodward

A LUNAR WRAY
Minot Judson Savage

LUNATIC, SIR HUMPHREY, BART.
Francis Gentleman

LUND, JAMES
John Thomson Stonehouse

LUNETTES, HENRY
Miss Margaret C. Conkling

LURGAN, LESTER
Mabel Winifred Knowles

LUSITANICUS
Sir Philip Francis

LUSKA, SIDNEY
Henry Harland

LYALL, ANDREW, A SCHOOLMASTER IN CAWMELTOUN
Sir John Skelton

LYALL, DAVID
Annie S. Swan

LYALL, EDNA
Ada Ellen Bayly

LYLE, MARIUS
Mrs Waring Smyth

LYMINGTON, JOHN
John Newton Chance

LYNCEUS
Frederick Starr

LYNCH, ERIC
David Ernest Bingley

LYNCH, FRANCES
David Guy Compton

LYNCH, LAWRENCE L.
Emma M. Van Deventer

LYNDON, BARRY
George Lowell Austin

LYNDON, BARRY, ESQ.
William Makepeace Thackeray

LYNN, ETHEL
Ethelinda Beers

LYNN, MARGARET
Gladys Battye

THE LYNN BARD
Alonzo Lewis

LYNTON, ANN
Claire Rayner

LYNX
Cicily Isabel Fairfield

LYON, LYMAN R.
L. Sprague de Camp

LYONS, ELENA
Eleanor Fairburn

LYRE, PINCHBECK
Siegfried Sassoon

LYSANDER
James Cheetham
Thomas Wills

M

M.
Hannah More

M. A.
Dorothy Violet Wellesley

M. A. T.
William Makepeace Thackeray

M. B.
Maurice Baring

M. C.
Matthew Concanen
Catherine Edith MaCauley
Martin

M. D.
Manasseh Dawes

M. D. C.
Moncure Daniel Conway

M. E. W. S.
Mary Elizabeth Wilson
Sherwood

M. P.
Dorothy Kilner

M. V.
Robert Ranke Graves

M___Y, C.
Mary (Lady) Chudleigh

MABON
William Abraham

MAC
William McConnell
Seamus McManus

McALAN, PETER
Peter Berresford

MacALISTER, IAN
Marvin Hubert Albert

MacALLAN, ANDREW
James Leasor

McARONE
George Arnold

McARTHUR, JOHN
Arthur Wise

MacAULAY, ALLAN
Charlotte Stewart

McBAIN, ED.
Salvatore A. Lombino

McCABE, CAMERON
Ernest W. J. Bornemann

McCALL, ANTHONY
Henry Kane

McCALL, J. P.
Peter Dawson

MacCALL, SIDNEY
Mrs Mary M'Neil Fenollosa

McCANN, ARTHUR
John Wood Campbell

McCANN, EDSON
Frederik Pohl with Lester Del
Rey

**MacCARTE, DUNCAN, A
HIGHLANDER**
Rev. Samuel Squire

M'CASKEY, MILO
Charles James Lever

McCLELLAN, WILLIAM
Charles Stanley Strong

McCLOUD, VAN
John Thomas Lutz

McCORD, GUY
Dallas McCord Reynolds

McCORD, WHIP
Victor G. C. Norwood

McCORQUODALE, BARBARA
Barbara Cartland

McCREADY, JACK
Talmage Powell

McCREIGH, JAMES
Frederik Pohl

McCULLOCH, JOHN T.
Edgar Rice Burroughs

McCULLOCH, SARAH
Jean Ure

McDANIEL, DAVID
Ted Johnstone

MacDERMOTT, B.
Robert M. Sillard

MacDIARMID, HUGH
Christopher Murray Grieve

MacDONALD, AENEAS
George Malcolm Thomson

MacDONALD, ANSON
Robert Anson Heinlein

MacDONALD, C. A.
Andrew Kennedy Hutchinson
Boyd

McDONALD, JAMIE
Florence Parry Heide

**MacDONALD, JOHN ROSS
(or JOHN, or ROSS)**
Kenneth Millar

MacDONALD, MARCIA
Grace Livingston Hill

MacDOUGAL, JOHN
James Blish with Robert A. W.
Lowndes

MacDOUGAL, WILLIAM
Edward Gordon Craig

McELROY, LEE
Elmer Stephen Kelton

MacFARLANE, KENNETH
Kenneth MacFarlane Walker

MacFARLANE, STEPHEN
John Keir Cross

**M'FUN, PHEDLIM, ROMAN
CATHOLIC RECTOR OF
BALLYMACSCALTHEEN**
William Carleton

MacGHILMHAOIL, UISDEAN
Hugh MacMillan

MacGILLICUDDY, IRENE
Laurence Oliphant

McGINNIS, P.
Robert Blatchford

McGIRR, EDMUND
Kenneth Giles

MacGREGGOR, ARTHUR, OF
KNIGHTSBRIDGE, ESQ.
William Mason

MacGREGGOR, MALCOLM
William Mason

M'GUINNESS, BYRON
William Ernest Henley

McHUGH, HUGH
George Vere Hobart

MacHUMBUG, LEONARD
Leonard McNally

McINTOSH, J. T.
James Murdoch MacGregor

McKAY, KELVIN
Charles Stanley Strong

McKAY, KENNETH R.
Henry Kane

McKAY, SIMON
Christopher Robin Nicole

MacKENZIE, PIERCE
Alan Riefe

MacKREADY, KELVIN
Edgar Gardner Murphy

MacLAGAN, BRIDGET
Mary Borden

McLAGLEN, JOHN J.
John B. Harvey

MacLANE, JACK
Bill Crider

MacLAREN, IAN
John Watson

MacLAREN-ROSS, JULIAN
John MacLaren Ross

MacLEAN, ARTHUR
Edwin Charles Tubb

M'CLEAVER, MAJ. SAWNEY
Lionel Cranfield Sackville

MacLEOD, MRS ALICK
Catherine Edith MaCauley
Martin

MacLEOD, ALLAN
Henry Lemoine

MacLEOD, FIONA
William Sharp

MacLEOD, ROBERT
Robert Corlett Cowell
William Knox

McLOWERY, FRANK
Henry John Keevill

McMAHON, PAT
Edward D. Hoch

McMULLEN, CATHERINE
Catherine Cookson

MacNAB, FRANCES
Agnes D. Fraser

M'NAB, HUGH
Hugh M'Nab Humphry

McNAB, JED
John Russell Fearn

MacNAMARA, BRINSLEY
John Weldon

MacNEE, PATRICK
Peter Leslie

MacNEIL, DUNCAN
Philip Donald McCutchan

McNEIL, NEIL
Willis Todhunter Ballard

McNEILL, ANGUS
Thomas William Hodgson
Crosland

MacNEILL, ANNE
Maura Seger

McNEILL, JANET
Mrs Janet Alexander

MACONOCHIE, PTE. ALF
Edmund Charles Blunden

MACONOCHIE, DONALD
Oswald Atherton Fleming

M'CORKINDALE, ROBERT
William Edmonstoune Aytoun

MacPACKE, JOSE, A
BRICKLAYER'S
LABOURER
James Peacock

McQUILL, THURSTY
Wallace Bruce

MacRAE, TRAVIS
Anita MacRae Feagles

M'REALSHAM, E. D.
Charles Marsh Mead

MacROBIN, MARK
Allan Cunningham

M'RORY, REV. RORY
James Cameron Lees

MacSARCASM, REV. SIR
ARCHIBALD, BART.
William Shaw

MacSARCONICA, ARCHY,
FRS
Thomas Hastings

M'SQUIREEN, CORNELIUS
John William Cole

MacSTAFF, DONALD, OF
THE NORTH
Robert Hepburn

McTEAGUE, P. ESQ.
Philip Meadows Taylor

MacTYRE, PAUL
Robin J. Adam

McVEAN, JAMES
Nicholas Luard

McVEIGH, SUE
Elizabeth Custer Nearing

MacWHIRTER, THERESA
William Makepeace Thackeray

MACEY, CARR
Geoffrey John Barrett

MACHEN, ARTHUR
Arthur Llewellyn Jones

MACKLIN, CHARLES
Charles McLaughlin

MACULARIA, MARGELINA
SCRIBELINDRA
William Kenrick

MACULARIUS, MARTINUS
Christopher Smart

MADA
Mrs Mary Clarke

MADDISON, CAROL
Carol Kidwell

MADDOCK, LARRY
Jack Owen Jardine

MADDOX, CARL
Edwin Charles Tubb

MADISON, FRANK
Francis Gilman Hutchins

MADISON, VIRGINIA
Mrs Sallie A. Putnam

MADRID, LOUIS
Edward Gordon Craig

MAELOG
Arthur James Johnes

MAGILL, MARCUS
Brian Hill

A MAGISTRATE
Robert Aspland
Patrick Colquhoun

A MAGISTRATE FOR
MIDDLESEX
John Thomas Barber Beaumont

A MAGISTRATE OF THE
COUNTY OF ESSEX
Montagu Burgoyne

MAGLONE, BARNEY
Robert Arthur Wilson

MAGNUS, JOHN
Harlan Ellison

MAGNUS, PHILIP
Sir Philip Magnus-Allcroft

A MAID OF ALL WORK
Horace Mayhew

MRS MAIN
Mrs Elizabeth Alice Frances Le
Blond

MAINE, CHARLES ERIC
David McIlwaine

MAINE, TREVOR
Arthur Catherall

MAIRE
John Fisher Murray

MAITLAND, MARGARET, OF
SUNNYSIDE
Mrs Margaret O. Oliphant

MAITLAND, THOMAS
Robert Williams Buchanan

MAITLAND, THOMAS ST
KILDA
Algernon Charles Swinburne

MAJOR, MARTHA
Florence Wallace Pomeroy

MAJOR MARBLE
Henry Theodor Cheever

MAJOR PENNIMAN
Charles Wheeler Denison

MAJOR WORTHINGTON
Joachim Hayward Stocqueler

MAJORS, E. B.
Alan Riefe

MAJORS, SIMON
Gardner Francis Fox

MALACHY, FRANK
Frank M. McAuliffe

MALACK, MULY
Mordecai Manuel Noah

MALAGROWTHER,
MALACHI
Sir Walter Scott

MALCOLM, CHARLES
Cyril Malcolm Hincks

MALET, LUCAS
Mary Kingsley

MALIN, PETER
Patrick Reardon Connor

MALLECHO, MICHING
Percy Bysshe Shelley

MALLET, DAVID
David Malloch

MALLOCH, DAVID
James Boswell with Andrew
Erskine and George
Dempster

MALLOCH, PETER
William Murdoch Duncan

MALLORY, CLARE
Winifred Hall

MALLORY, DREW
Brian Francis Wynne Garfield

MALLORY, MARK
Dallas McCord Reynolds

MALLOWAN, AGATHA
CHRISTIE
Agatha Mary Clarissa Christie

MALONE, LOUIS
Louis MacNeice

MALONE, TED
Frank Alden Russell

MALORY, SHAUN
Reginald James Kingston
Russell

MALWYN
Sir William A'Beckett

A MAN
Robert Blatchford
Horace Walpole

A MAN ABOUT TOWN
Percival Weldon Banks

A MAN IN BUSINESS
John Hope

THE MAN IN THE CLARET
COLORED COAT
Edward Shuman Gould

THE MAN IN THE CLOAK
James Clarence Mangan

THE MAN IN THE MOON
Daniel Defoe
John Eagles
William Lilly
Laura Elizabeth Richards

A MAN OF GREAT
EMINENCE AND
WORTH
Gervase Markham

A MAN OF LEISURE
Charles Leslie

THE MAN OF THE PEOPLE
William Thomson

A MAN OF THE TIMES
John Pendleton Kennedy

A MAN OF THE WORLD
James Payn

A MAN OF ULSTER
James Porter

A MAN ON THE SHADY SIDE
OF FIFTY
Andrew Valentine Kirwan

THE MAN WHO HEARD
SOMETHING
Allen Upward

A MAN WHO WISHES TO BE
THE GOVERNOR OF
PENNSYLVANIA
George W. Woodward

THE MANAGER OF THE
THEATRE ROYAL IN
DUBLIN
Thomas Sheridan

A MANCHESTER
CONSERVATIVE
Thomas Nash

A MANCHESTER MAN
Robert Lamb

MANCHESTER
MANUFACTURER
Richard Cobden

MANDERS, HARRY
Philip Jose Farmer

MANHATTAN
Joseph Alfred Scoville

MANHATTAN, FRANK
Charles Astor Bristed

MANLY, MARLINE
St George Henry Rathbone

MANN, ABEL
John Creasey

MANN, A. CHESTER
Philip Ilott Roberts

MANN, DEBORAH
Ursula Bloom

MANN, JACK
Evelyn Charles Vivian

MANN, JAMES
John B. Harvey

MANN, JOSEPHINE
Josephine Pullein-Thompson

MANNERING, JULIA
Madeleine Bingham

MANNERING, MAX
Josiah Gilbert Holland

MRS MANNERS
Mrs Cornelia H. Richards

MANNERS, ALEXANDRA
Anne Rundle

MANNERS, MRS HORACE
Algernon Charles Swinburne

MANNERS, MOTLEY
Augustine Joseph Hickey
Duganne

MANNING, MARSHA
Hettie Grimstead

MANNINGHAM, BASIL
Basil Henry Homersham

MANOR, JASON
Oakley Maxwell Hall

MANSERGH, JESSIE
Mrs George de Horne Vaizey

MANSFIELD, KATHERINE
Kathleen Mansfield Beauchamp

MANTON, PETER
John Creasey

A MANUFACTURER
John Hustler

MAORI
James Inglis

MAPES, MARY A.
Virginia T. H. Ellison

MAR, HELEN
Mrs D. M. F. Walker

MARA, BERNARD
Brian Moore

MARA, THALIA
Elizabeth Mahoney

MARAS, KARL
Kenneth Henry Bulmer

MARBOURG, DOLORES
Mrs Mary S. Hoke Bacon

MARC
Charles Mark Edward Boxer

MARCELLUS
John Quincy Adams
Allan Ramsay
Noah Webster

MARCH, ANNE
Constance Fenimore Woolson

MARCH, JERMYN
Dorothy Anna Webb

MARCH, MAXWELL
Margery Louise Allingham

MARCH, STELLA
Marjorie Bell Marshall

MARCH, WALTER (or
MAJOR)
Orlando Bolivar Willcox

MARCH, WILLIAM
William Edward March
Campbell

MARCHANT, CATHERINE
Catherine Cookson

MARCHBANKS, SAMUEL
William Robertson Davies

MARCHPANE, WILLIAM
Edward Gordon Craig

MARCLIFFE, THEOPHILUS
William Godwin

MARCO
Lord Louis Francis Albert
Victor Nicholas Mountbatten

MARCUS
Mark Akenside
Joseph Blunt
Benjamin Franklin Butler
Matthew L. Davis
William Peter Van Ness
William Charles Wells
Oliver Wolcott

MARCUS, JOANNA
Lucilla Andrews

MARGE
Marjorie Henderson Buell

MARIA, CARL GEORG JESUS
Ezra Pound

MARIA, LAURA
Mary Robinson

MARIN, ALFRED
Alfred Coppel

A MARINE OFFICER
Andrew Burn

MARINO, NICK
Richard Deming

MARINO, SUSAN
Julie Ellis

MARIOTTI, LUIGI
Antonio Carlo Napoleone
Gallenga

MARITZBURG, PIETER
Thomas Jackson

MARIUS
Thomas Day

MARJORAM, J.
Ralph Hale Mottram

MARK, F. W.
Edward Verrall Lucas

MARK, JULIAN
Kathleen Mansfield Beauchamp

MARK VII
Max (Mark) Plowman

A MARKET GARDENER
Richard Doddridge Blackmore

MRS MARKHAM
Elizabeth Penrose

MARKHAM, GERVIS
Robert Tofte

MARKHAM, HOWARD
Mary Cecil Hay

MARKHAM, IARIUS
Gervase Markham with Lewis
Machin

MARKHAM, ROBERT
Sir Kingsley Amis

MARLAIS, DYLAN
Dylan Marlais Thomas

MARLBOROUGH
John Geoffrey Tristram

MARLOW, RT. HON. LADY
HARRIET
William Beckford

MARLOW, LOUIS
Louis Umfreville Wilkinson

MARLOW, SIDNEY
Paschal Heston Coggins

MARLOWE, CHARLES
Harriet Jay

MARLOWE, HUGH
Harry Patterson

MARLOWE, KATHERINE
Charlotte Vale Allen

MARLOWE, N.
Joseph Maunsell Hone

MARLOWE, STEPHEN
Milton Lesser

MARMADUKE
Charles Edward Wynne
Jerningham

SIR MARMADUKE
Theodore Tilton

MARPRELATE, MARTIN
John Penry

MARRECO, ANNE
Alice Acland

MARRIC, J. J.
John Creasey

MARRIOTT, THOMAS
Thomas F. R. Barling

MARSDEN, ANTHONY
Graham Sutton

MARSDEN, JAMES
John Creasey

MARSH, JEAN
Evelyn Marshall

MARSH, JOAN
John Marsh

MARSH, RICHARD
Richard Bernard Heldmann

MARSHALL, GARY
Charles Horace Snow

MARSHALL, HAMILTON
John Hutton Balfour Browne

MARSHALL, JAMES VANCE
Donald Gordon Payne

MARSHALL, JOANNE
Anne Rundle

MARSHALL, LOVAT
William Murdoch Duncan

MARSHALL, RAYMOND
Rene Raymond

MARSHALL, WILLIAM , GENT.
Horace Walpole

MARSHMAN
J. M. M. M. B. Durham

MARSTEN, RICHARD
Salvatore A. Lombino

MARSTON, JAY
Jill Spencer

MART, DONOVAN
E. Le Breton Martin

MARTEL, CHARLES
Thomas Delf

MARTELL, JAMES
David Ernest Bingley

MARTELLO TOWER
Francis Martin Norman

MARTENS, PAUL
Stephen Southwold

MARTHOL, JOHN
William T. Manning

MARTIN, CHRISTOPHER
F. Harold Peacock

MARTIN, DOROTHEA
Kathleen Douglas Hewitt

MARTIN, EDWARD WINSLOW
James Dabney McCabe

MARTIN, ELLIS
Mrs Marah Ellis Martyn Ryan

MARTIN, FREDERIC
Matthew F. Christopher

MARTIN, JOHN
Morgan Van Roerbach Shepard

MARTIN, PETER
Peter Martin Leckie

MARTIN, RICHARD
John Creasey

MARTIN, RUTH
Claire Rayner

MARTIN, SHANE
George Henry Johnston

MARTIN, STELLA
Georgette Heyer

MARTINGALE
Charles White

MARTINGALE, HAWSER
John Sleeper

MARTINUS SCRIBLERUS
Dr John Arbuthnot
George Crabbe
Robert Morehead
Alexander Pope
Jonathan Swift

MARTLET
Richard Bingham Davis

MARTYN, MYLES
Arthur Elliott-Cannon

MARTYN, OLIVER
Herbert Martyn Oliver White

MARTYN, WILLIAM FREDERICK
William Fordyce Mavor

MARVEL, IK
Donald Grant Mitchell

MARVELL, ANDREW
Howard Davies

MARVELL, HOLT
Eric Maschwitz

MARVIN, JULIE (or SUSAN)
Julie Ellis

MARY
Mary St John

A MARYLANDER
Reverdy Johnson

MASK
Charles Hooton
George Soane

MASON, ERNST
Frederick Pohl

MASON, FRANK W.
Francis Van Wyck Mason

MASON, HOWARD
Jennifer Ramage

MASON, LEE W.
Barry N. Malzberg

MASON, STUART
Christopher Sclater Millard

MASON, TALLY
August William Derleth

MASSACHUSETTENSIS
Daniel Leonard

A MASSACHUSETT'S CITIZEN
James Freeman Clarke

A MASSACHUSETT'S LAWYER
John Lowell

A MASSACHUSETT'S YANKEE
Lyman Hotchkiss Bagg

MASSINGBERD, GODFREY
Digby Pilot Starkey

MASSON, GEORGINA
Marion Johnson

MASTER SHALLOW
Thomas Ford

MASTER THERION
Edward Alexander Crowley

MASTER TIMOTHY
George William MacArthur Reynolds

A MASTER MASON
Henry Dana Ward

A MASTER OF ARTE OF CAMBRIDGE
Robert Parsons

A MASTER OF ARTS
William King

A MASTER OF ARTS AND SCHOOLMASTER OF TWENTY YEARS' EXPERIENCE
Owen Price

A MASTER OF ARTS, FORMERLY OF BALLIOL COLLEGE
William John Birch

A MASTER OF ARTS OF THE UNIVERSITY OF OXFORD
William Asplin
Sir Richard Hill

THE MASTER OF THE
CLEVELAND HOUNDS
William Henry Anthony
Wharton

THE MASTER OF THE
GRAMMAR SCHOOL AT
ARUNDEL
Charles Caraccioli

MASTERSON, WHIT
Bill Miller with Robert Wade

MATHER, BERKELY
John Evan Weston Davies

MATHER, EDWARD
Edward Arthur Mather Jackson

MATHERS, HELEN
Helen Buckingham Reeves

MATHESON, HUGH
Lewis Hugh Mackay

MATHESON, SYLVIA A.
Sylvia Anne Matheson
Schofield

MATHEWS, ANTHONY
Dudley Barker

MATILDA, ANNA
Hannah Cowley

MATILDA, ROSA
Charlotte Dacre

MATTHESON, RODNEY
John Creasey

MATTHEW, THOMAS
John Rogers

MATTHEWS, BRAD
Nelson R. Demille

MATTHEWS, ELLEN
Ellen Bache

MATTHEWS & CO.
Leicester Silk Buckingham

MATUCE, H. OGRAM
Charles Francis Keary

MAULDSLEY, DANIEL
Montgomery Carmichael

MAURICE, FURNLEY
Frank Leslie Thomson Wilmot

MAURICE, MICHAEL
Conrad Arthur Skinner

MAURICE, WALTER
Walter Besant with James Rice

MAVIN, JOHN
John Edgell Rickword with
Douglas Garman

MAVOR, WILLIAM
Sir Richard Phillips

MR MAW, GARDENER TO
THE DUKE OF LEEDS
John Abercrombie

MAWSON, CHRISTIAN
Christian Barman

MAX
Sir Max Beerbohm
George William MacArthur
Reynolds

MAX, NICHOLAS
Bernard Asbell

MAXILLA
James Arthur Wilson

MAXWELL, C. BEDE
Violet Spoole Maxwell

MAXWELL, CLIFFORD
Henry Cecil Leon

MAXWELL, EDWARD
Allan Herman

MAXWELL, ERICA
Lillian Pyke

MAXWELL, HERBERT
Herbert Lomax

MAXWELL, JACK
Ernest L. McKeag

MAXWELL, JOHN
Brian Harry Freemantle

MAXWELL, MARY
MORTIMER
Elizabeth Banks

MAXWELL, VICKY
Annette Isobel Worboys

MAY, EDITH
Anna Drinker

MAY, SOPHIE
Rebecca Clarke
William Fearing Gill

MAYBURY, ANNE
Anne Buxton

MAYER, AGATHA
Romana Weeks

MAYFIELD, JULIA
Phylis Dora Hastings

MAYFIELD, MILLIE
Mrs Mary Sophie Homes

MAYNARD, WALTER
Thomas Willert Beale

MAYNE, LEGER D.
William Brisbane Dick

MAYNE, RUTHERFORD
Samuel J. Waddell

MAYO, JAMES
Stephen Coulter

ME
Henry Cuyler Bunner

ME, PHIL ARCANOS, GENT.
Joseph Green

ME, THE HON. B. B. ESQ.
Joseph Green

MEAD, SHEPHERD
Edward Mead

MEADE, L. T.
Elizabeth Thomasina Meade
Smith

MEADMORE, SUSAN
Susan Sallis

MEADOWS, LINDEN
Charles Butler Greatrex

MEADOWS, STEPHEN
Raymond Meadows Stephenson

MEANWELL, M.
William Cowper M. D.

MEANWELL, MISS NANCY
Richard Johnson

A MECHANIC
Charles Devonshire

A MEDICAL MAN
John Forbes Watson

THE MEDICAL STUDENT
Robert Douglas

MEDICUS
James Boswell
John Epps
Daniel Denison Slade
Gordon Stables
Forbes Benignus Winslow

MEDICUS
CANTABRIGIENSIS
John Spurgin

MEDICUS MENTIS
James Boswell

MEDIUS
Benjamin Franklin

MEDLEY, MATTHEW
Anthony Aston

MEDWAY, LEWIS
William Paterson

MEEK, JOSEPH
Robert Joseph Randisi

A MELANCHOLY STANDER-
BY
Edward Wetenhall

MELANCTHON
Thomas Lewis O'Beirne

MELANTER
Richard Doddridge Blackmore

MELBOURNE, IDA
L. E. Ransome

MELDRUM, JAMES
John Franklin Broxholme

MELEAGER
Hans William Sotheby

MELISSA
Jane Brereton

MELMOTH, COURTNEY
Samuel Jackson Pratt

MELMOTH, SEBASTIAN
Oscar Wilde

MELONEY, FRANKEN
Rose Dorothy Franken with
William Brown Meloney

MELOPOYN
Charles James Dunphie

MELVILLE, ALAN
William Melville Caverhill

MELVILLE, ANNE
Margaret Potter

MELVILLE, JAMES
Roy Peter Martin

MELVILLE, JENNIE
Gwendoline Butler

MELVILLE, LEWIS
Lewis Samuel Benjamin

A MEMBER
Maria Arthington
Daniel Defoe

THE MEMBER FOR SARK
Sir Henry William Lucy

THE MEMBER FOR
TREORKY
Ernest Brown Bowen Rowlands

THE MEMBER FOR THE
CHILTERN HUNDREDS
Sir Henry William Lucy

A MEMBER OF A LAW
SOCIETY
Francis Blackburne

A MEMBER OF
CONVOCATION
White Kennett
Vaughan Thomas

A MEMBER OF COURT
John Archibald Murray

A MEMBER OF HIS PRIVY
COUNCIL
Charles MacCormick

A MEMBER OF LAURENCE
OLIPHANT'S COLONY
Haskett Smith

A MEMBER OF LINCOLN'S
INN
John Raithby

A MEMBER OF MAGDALEN
COLLEGE, OXFORD
James Bateman

A MEMBER OF
PARLIAMENT
Charles Abbot
James Duff
Davies Gilbert
Thomas Gilbert
Sir Francis Grant
William Hay
Joseph Thomas James Hewlett
Archibald Hutcheson
Sir Humphrey Mackworth
William Pulteney
Sir Robert Walpole
Robert Plumer Ward
Sir Charles Whitworth
John Wilkes

A MEMBER OF THAT
CHURCH
Thomas Bisse

A MEMBER OF THAT
PARLIAMENT
Slingsby Bethel

A MEMBER OF THAT
UNIVERSITY
John Wallis

A MEMBER OF THE
ACADEMY OF ANCIENT
MUSIC
Sir John Hawkins

A MEMBER OF THE
AMERICAN BAR
Simon Greenleaf

A MEMBER OF THE
AMERICAN
PHILOSOPHICAL
SOCIETY
William Henry Furness

A MEMBER OF THE
ARCADIAN SOCIETY AT
ROME
Joseph Cooper Walker

A MEMBER OF THE
ATHENIAN SOCIETY
John Dunton

A MEMBER OF THE BAR
Leonard Kip
George Lunt
Phineas Bacon Wilcox

A MEMBER OF THE
BOSTON BAR
John Augustus Bolles

A MEMBER OF THE
BOSTON SOCIETY OF
THE NEW JERUSALEM
Theophilus Parsons

A MEMBER OF THE
BURTON HUNT
Henry Braddon

A MEMBER OF THE
CAMBRIDGE
UNIVERSITY BOAT-
CLUB
John Frederic La Trobe
Bateman

A MEMBER OF THE
CHURCH AT OXFORD
William Palmer

A MEMBER OF THE
CHURCH OF ENGLAND
Martin Madan
William Palmer

A MEMBER OF THE
CHURCH OF GOD AT
OXFORD
Wiliam Palmer

A MEMBER OF THE
CHURCH OF
SCOTLAND
Thomas Blacklock
James Hog

A MEMBER OF THE
COLLEGE OF
PHYSICIANS
John Moyle

A MEMBER OF THE COMET
CLUB
John Sheehan

A MEMBER OF THE
COMMUNITY AND A
SINCERE FRIEND TO
HIS COUNTRY
John Campbell

A MEMBER OF THE
CORPORATION
Samuel Atkins Eliot

A MEMBER OF THE
COUNCIL OF
NATIONAL UNION
Sir William Thomas Charley

A MEMBER OF THE COURT
Henry Home

A MEMBER OF THE EASY
CLUB IN EDINBURGH
Allan Ramsay

A MEMBER OF THE EMBASSY
John Crawfurd

A MEMBER OF THE ENGLISH BAR
John Hodgkin

A MEMBER OF THE EPISCOPAL CHURCH
Samuel Seabury

A MEMBER OF THE ESTABLISHED CHURCH
Sir John Bayley
George Berkeley
Samuel Parr

A MEMBER OF THE FACULTY OF ADVOCATES
Archibald Alison

A MEMBER OF THE GENERAL SYNOD
James Kirkpatrick

A MEMBER OF THE GUILD
James Augustine Stothert

A MEMBER OF THE HON. SOCIETY OF THE MIDDLE TEMPLE
Francis Scott

A MEMBER OF THE HOUSEHOLD OF HIS LATE MAJESTY, NUSSIR-U-DEEN
William Knighton

A MEMBER OF THE HOUSE OF COMMONS
William Arnall
Daniel Defoe
Archibald Hutcheson
Henry St John
Thomas Sherlock
Philip Carteret Webb

A MEMBER OF THE HOUSE OF COMMONS IN IRELAND
Jonathan Swift

A MEMBER OF THE HOUSES OF SHIRLEY AND HASTINGS
Aaron Crossley Hobart Seymour

A MEMBER OF THE HUMANE SOCIETY
John Davis
Wendell Davis

A MEMBER OF THE INNER TEMPLE
Henry Roscoe

A MEMBER OF THE IRISH PARLIAMENT
Harvey Redmond Morres

A MEMBER OF THE LATE PARLIAMENT
Lord Robert Grosvenor

A MEMBER OF THE LEGISLATURE
William Edward Baxter

A MEMBER OF THE LICHFIELD SOCIETY
Francis Edward Paget

A MEMBER OF THE LONDON COLLEGE OF PHYSICIANS
Richard Pearson

A MEMBER OF THE LOWER HOUSE
Sir Robert Walpole

A MEMBER OF THE LOWER HOUSE OF CONVOCATION
Frances Atterbury

A MEMBER OF THE MARINE SOCIETY
Jonas Hanway

A MEMBER OF THE MASSACHUSETT'S BAR
John Pickering

A MEMBER OF THE MASSACHUSETT'S BIBLE SOCIETY
Abiel Holmes

A MEMBER OF THE MUSOMANIK SOCIETY OF ANSTRUTHER
William Tennant

A MEMBER OF THE NATIONAL HEALTH SOCIETY
Lady Eliza Priestley

A MEMBER OF THE NEW ATHENIAN SOCIETY
John Dunton

A MEMBER OF THE NEW ENGLAND HISTORICAL AND GENEALOGICAL SOCIETY
Timothy Farrar

A MEMBER OF THE NEW ORLEANS BAR
James P. Boyd

A MEMBER OF THE NEW YORK BAR
Abraham Oakey Hall

A MEMBER OF THE NY GENEAL. AND BIOG. SOCIETY
William Imgraham Kip

A MEMBER OF THE OXFORD CONVOCATION
Sir John Coxe Hippisley
Charles Adolphus Row

A MEMBER OF THE PARTY
Sir Thomas Dick Lauder

A MEMBER OF THE PHILOLOGICAL SOCIETY
George Cooke Geldart

A MEMBER OF THE POLITICAL ECONOMY CLUB
Robert Torrens

A MEMBER OF THE PRESS
G. P. Ure

A MEMBER OF THE PROTESTANT CHURCH IN THAT KINGDOM
Henry Brooke

A MEMBER OF THE RED RIVER CONFERENCE
Thomas Osmund Summers

A MEMBER OF THE REVISION COMMITTEE OF THE CHURCH OF IRELAND
Humphrey Lloyd

A MEMBER OF THE REVOLUTION SOCIETY
John Scott Waring

A MEMBER OF THE ROCK COUNTY BAR
Jonas Mills Bundy

A MEMBER OF THE ROXBURGHE CLUB
Thomas Frognall Dibdin

A MEMBER OF THE ROYAL ACADEMY OF BERLIN
John Bevis

A MEMBER OF THE ROYAL COLLEGE OF SURGEONS
John Thomson
William Wadd

A MEMBER OF THE ROYAL SOCIETY
Joseph Glanvill

A MEMBER OF THE ROYAL
SOCIETY AND OF THE
SOCIETY OF
ANTIQUARIES
Sir James Burrow

A MEMBER OF THE SAVE-
ALL CLUB
Isaac Robert Cruikshank

A MEMBER OF THE
SCHOOL BOARD OF
LONDON
Benjamin Waugh

A MEMBER OF THE
SCOTCH BAR
Sir James Wellwood Moncreiff

A MEMBER OF THE
SCOTTISH BAR
James Grahame

A MEMBER OF THE SENATE
William Frend
John Howard Marsden

A MEMBER OF THE SENATE
OF CAMBRIDGE
UNIVERSITY
John Rustat Crowfoot

A MEMBER OF THE SEPT
Nottidge Charles MacNamara

A MEMBER OF THE
SOCIETY
Josiah Pratt

A MEMBER OF THE
SOCIETY FOR
CONSTITUTIONAL
INFORMATION
William Davies Shipley

A MEMBER OF THE
SOCIETY OF
ANTIQUARIES
Philip Carteret Webb

A MEMBER OF THE
SOCIETY OF
ANTIQUARIES,
LONDON
Francis Wise

A MEMBER OF THE
SOCIETY OF ARTISTS
AND MANUFACTURERS
OF PHILADELPHIA
Tenche Coxe

A MEMBER OF THE
SOCIETY OF FRIENDS
Frank Arnee
William Collier
Joseph John Gurney
Thomas Greer Jacob
Philip Thompson

A MEMBER OF THE
SOCIETY OF
PSYCHICAL RESEARCH
John Godfrey Ferdinand
Raupert

A MEMBER OF THE
SUFFOLK BAR
Harrison Gray Otis

A MEMBER OF THE 27TH
CONGRESS
John Pendleton Kennedy

A MEMBER OF THE
UNIVERSITY
Francis Ayscough
Benjamin Blayney
Benjamin Kennicott
Edward Smedley

A MEMBER OF THE
UNIVERSITY OF
CAMBRIDGE
William Burdon
Philip Stanhope Dodd
Richard Duppa
William Stephen Gilly
George Long
Conyers Middleton
Samuel Rowe
Thomas Perronet Thompson

A MEMBER OF THE
UNIVERSITY OF
OXFORD
William Lisle Bowles
Charles Pourtales Golightly
John Keble

A MEMBER OF THE
VERMONT BAR
Daniel Pierce Thompson

A MEMBER OF THE WHIP
CLUB
Hewson Clarke
Francis Grose

MEMBERS, MARK
Roy Broadbent Fuller

MEMBERS OF THE WAR
CABINET AND THEIR
FRIENDS
John Joseph Horgan

MEMORY SHORT-HAND
WRITER TO THE
COURT
Robert Gutch

MENANDER
Charles Morgan
Robert Treat Paine

MENASCO, NORMAN
Wyman W. Guin

MENCIUS PHILALETHES
Peter Annet

MENDAX, GEORGE
FAITHFUL
James Wills

MENDL, GLADYS
Henrietta Leslie

MENENIUS
Digby Pilot Starkey

MENTOR
Isaac Ledyard
Josiah Quincy
Nathan D. Urner

MEPHISTOPHELES
John Pendleton Kennedy

MERCATOR
James Anderson
Edward Ellice
Samuel Smith

MERCER
James Cheetham

A MERCHANT
Daniel Defoe
Jonas Hanway
Frank Henderson
David Henshaw

MR MERCHANT
Thomas John Dibdin

A MERCHANT IN LONDON
Josiah Tucker

A MERCHANT OF BOSTON
Samuel Hooper

A MERCHANT WHO
SUBSCRIBED THE
PETITION
Jonas Hanway

MERCURIUS
ACHERONTICUS
James Howell

MERCURIUS BRITANNICUS
Joseph Hall

MERCURIUS CIVICUS
Samuel Butler

MERCURIUS PRAGMATICUS
Marchamont Needham

MERCURIUS RUSTICUS
Thomas Frognall Dibdin

MERCURIUS SPUR
Cuthbert Shaw

MERCUTIO
James Boswell

MERCURY
Thomas Berington

MERDANT, DANIEL
Robert Wynell Mayow

A MERE DON
Alfred Denis Godley

A MERE MAN
Frederick William Andrewes

MEREDITH, ANNE
Lucy Beatrice Malleson

MEREDITH, DAVID WILLIAM
Earl Schenk Miers

MEREDITH, FRANCES
Mary Frances Chapman

MEREDITH, HAL
Harry Blyth

MEREDITH, ISABEL
Olivia Madox Rossetti with Helen Rossetti

MEREDITH, OWEN
Edward Robert Bulwer Lytton

MEREDITH, PETER
Brian Arthur Worthington-Stuart

MERITON, PETER
Alfred John Hunter

MERLIGOGELS, MESRAT
George Mills

MERLIN
Alfred (Lord) Tennyson

MERLIN, CHRISTINA
Constance Heaven

MERLIN, DAVID
David Merlin Moreau

MERLIN, JOHN
John Milner

MERLINUS ANGLICUS, JUNIOR
William Lilly

MERLYN, ARTHUR
James Blish

MERONES
William Emerson

MERRICK, LEONARD
Leonard Miller

MERRIE-BRAINES, JOCUNDARY
Thomas Dekker

MERRILL, P. J.
Holly Roth

MERRIMAN, CHARLES EUSTACE
Wilder Dwight Quint with George Tilton Richardson

MERRIMAN, HENRY SETON
Hugh Stowell Scott

MERRIMAN, MAURICE
Samuel Clarke Hook

MERRIMAN, PAT
Philip Atkey

MERRIWEATHER, MAGNUS
Charles Remington Talbot

MERRY, ANDREW
John Henry Gordon Freeman

MERRY, FELIX
Evert Augustus Duyckinck

MERRY, ROBERT
Samuel Griswald Goodrich

MERRYFELLOW, DICK
Richard Gardiner

MERTON, AMBROSE
William John Thoms

MERTON, TRISTRAM
Thomas Babington Macaulay

MONS. MESNAGER
Daniel Defoe

MESR
Benjamin Disraeli

META
Peggy Bowen Colthurst

METADOR
William Livingston Alden

METCALF, GEORGE
George Metcalf Johnson

METCALF, SUZANNA
Lyman Frank Baum

A METHODIST
Alexander Chalmers

A METHODIST PREACHER IN CAMBRIDGESHIRE
John Berridge

METRODORUS
John Herman Merivale

MEZZOGIORNO, GIOVANNI
Edward Gordon Craig

MIALL, ROBERT
John Frederick Burke

MICHAELS, BARBARA
Barbara Mertz

MICHAELS, DALE
Shepard Rifkin

MICHAELS, KRISTIN
Jeanne Williams

A MIDDLE-AGED MAN
John Ross Dix
Katharine Thomson

MIDDLESEX
William Stevens Robinson

MIDDLESTITCH, GILES
William Maginn

MIDDLING, THEOPHILUS
Denton Jaques Snider

MIDNIGHT, MARY
William Kenrick
Christopher Smart

MIDNIGHT, MRS MARY
John Newbery

A MIDSHIPMAN OF THE LAST CENTURY
Cdr. Robert Campbell

A MIDSHIPMAN OF THE US NAVY
William Leggett

MIKRON, BETA
William Coutts Keppel

MILBROOK, GEOFFREY
George Milner

MILDMAY, A. MURRAY
Charles Neaves

MILES
John Frederick Maurice
Osbert Sitwell
Stephen Southwold

MILES, DAVID
Brendan Leo Cronin

MILES, JOHN
Jack Miles Bickham

MILES, MISKA
Patricia Miles Martin

THE MILFORD BARD
John Lofland

A MILITARY CONTRIBUTOR
Charles Edward Callwell with William Edward Montagu

THE MILITARY CORRESPONDENT OF 'THE TIMES'
Charles A'Court Repington

A MILITARY COUNTRYMAN
William Heath

A MILITARY CRITIC
Charles Cornwallis Chesney

A MILITARY OFFICER
Peter Henry Bruce

MILLER, JOAQUIN
Cincinnatus Hiner Miller

MILLER, JOE, JR.
Thompson Westcott

MILLER, JOHN
William Lane

MILLER, MARGARET J.
Margaret Dale

MILLER, OLIVE THORN
Mrs Harriet Mann Miller

MILLER, WADE
Bill Miller with Robert Wade

MILLIGAN, SPIKE
Terence Alan Milligan

MILLINGTON, POWELL
Mark Synge

MILLS, CRISP
Christlob Mylius

MILLS, MARTIN
Martin A'Beckett Boyd

MILLS, OSMINGTON
Vivian Collin Brooks

MILNE, LARRY
Trevor Hoyle

MILNER, GEORGE
George Edward Charles
Hardinge

MILNER, REV. J.
Francis William Blagdon

MILTON, MARMADUKE,
ESQ.
Charles Dunster

MILTONICUS
Andrew Henderson

MILTOUN, FRANCIS
Milburg Francisco Mansfield

MISS MINIFIE
Mrs Susanna Gunning

MINIMUS, DIONYSIUS
Mowbray Walter Morris

A MINISTER
John Bold
Samuel Clapham
Edmund Gibson
Thomas Green
John Howard Hinton
Sir James Stonhouse

A MINISTER IN BOSTON
Cotton Mather

A MINISTER IN THE
COUNTRY
Philip Doddridge
Edward Welchman

A MINISTER OF A CHAPEL
OF EASE
Andrew Gray

A MINISTER OF A
COUNTRY PARISH
Peter Hately Waddell

A MINISTER OF BELFAST
Claudius Gilbert

A MINISTER OF BOSTON
William Cooper

A MINISTER OF LONDON
George Hickes

A MINISTER OF THAT
CHURCH
Abednego Seller

A MINISTER OF THE
CHURCH OF ENGLAND
Joshua Basset
Thomas Bray
William Dodd
Benjamin Jenks
John Newton
Edward Wells

A MINISTER OF THE
CHURCH OF
SCOTLAND
James Buchanan
John Cumming
Henry Grey
George Logan
Alexander Moncrieff
Gilbert Rule
Andrew Mitchell Thomson
John Willison
William Wilson

A MINISTER OF THE
ESTABLISHED CHURCH
Henry Duncan
Patrick MacFarlan

A MINISTER OF THE
ESTABLISHMENT
Henry Card

A MINISTER OF THE
GOSPEL
Thomas Boston
Nathanael Clap
Robert Fleming

A MINISTER OF THE
GOSPEL IN THE
CHURCH OF
SCOTLAND
Ralph Erskine

THE MINISTER OF THEIR
PARISH
William Clubbe

A MINISTER OF THE NEW
TESTAMENT
Patrick Gillespie

A MINISTER OF THE TRUE
PRESBYTERIAN
CHURCH OF
SCOTLAND
Thomas Forrester

A MINISTER UNDER THE
APPREHENSION OF
THE STONE
John Humphrey

A MINISTERING FRIEND
Daniel Defoe

MINUTE PHILOSOPHER
Charles Kingsley

MINUTIUS FELIX
George Hardinge

MIRA
Mrs Eliza Haywood

MIRANDA
James Heywood

MISACMOS
Sir John Harington

A MISERABLE SINNER
Richard Kilbye

MISOCROTALUS
James Henry Leigh Hunt

MISODIABOLOS
Sir John Harington

MISODOLOS
Charles Leslie

MISOSARUM, GREGORY
Jonathan Swift

MITCHELL, CLYDE
Randall Garrett with Robert
Silverberg

MITCHELL, EWAN
Greville Ewan Janner

MITCHELL, SCOTT
Lionel Robert Holcombe
Godfrey

MITCHELL, WILLIAM
James Hogg

MITCHUM, HANK
Dwight Bennett Newton

MITIO
Edward George Earle Lytton
Bulwer-Lytton

MIZPAH
Henry Charles Lea

THE MOCK PREACHER
George Whitefield

A MODERATE CLERGYMAN
OF THE SYNOD OF
ABERDEEN
George Skene Keith

A MODERN GENIUS
John Fitzgerald Pennie

A MODERN GREEK
Thomas Hope
Robert Mudie

A MODERN LADY
Jonathan Swift

A MODERN MAID
Miss Charlotte O'Connor
Eccles

A MODERN MINSTREL
Daniel Wilson

MODERN PYTHAGOREAN
Robert MacNish

A MODERN SOLDIER
Charles Booth Brackenbury

MODESTUS
John Cleland

THE MOFUSSILITE
John Lane

MOGGRIDGE, SPENCER
Thomas Hamilton

MOINA
Abram J. Ryan

MOIR, ERSKINE
Felicia Mary Frances Skene

MOLDWARP, NICHOLAS, BA
Miss Anne Manning

MOLIN, CHARLES
William Mayne

MOLYNEUX, C. C.
Charles Claude Molyneux
Plumtre

MON DROIT
Richard Ely Selden

MONAHAN, JOHN
William Riley Burnett

THE MONDAY CLUB
Edwin Cone Bissell

MONICA, MARIA
Mrs H. E. Hamilton-King

MONIG, CHRISTOPHER
Kendell Foster Crossen

MONITOR
Arthur Lee

MONK, GEOFFREY, MA
Joseph Henry Shorthouse

MONKSHOOD
Francis Jacox

MONMOUTH, JACK
William Leonard Pember

MONOS
James Clarence Mangan

MONROE, LYLE
Robert Anson Heinlein

MONTAGU, EDWARD
WORTLEY
Edward Vaughan Hyde
Kenealy

MONTAGUE, CHARLES
Charles Montague Duncan
Stewart

MONTAIGNE THE
YOUNGER
John Wade

MONTCLAIR, JOHN W.
John William Weidemeyer

MONTEFIORE, JOSHUA
William Playfair

MONTEZ, LOLA
Charles Chauncey Burr

MONTGOMERIE, HUGH
James Boswell

MONTGOMERY, MISS
BETTY
William Cullen

MONTGOMERY, CHARLES
MONTAGUE
Sir Thomas Dick Lauder

MONTGOMERY, GERARD
John Moultrie

MONTGOMERY, K. L.
Kathleen Montgomery with
Letitia Montgomery

A MONTHLY NURSE
Mrs Harriet Oliver

MONTPELIER
James Henry L. Archer

MONTROSS, DAVID
Jean L. Backus

MOOR, EMILY
Richard Deming

MOOR, WALLACE
Gerard F. Conway

MOORE, AUSTIN
Charles Augustus Carlow Muir

MOORE, EDWARD
Edwin Muir

MOORE, ELIZABETH
Meg Elizabeth Atkins

MOORE, GWYNETH
Patricia Valeria Bannister

MOORE, OLIVE
Constance Vaughan

MOORE, ROBIN
Robert Lowell Moore

MOORE, ROBERT
Robert Moore Williams

MOORE, WENTWORTH
William Hurrell Mallock

MOORE, WILLIAM V.
John Frost

MOORFIELDS DAISY BROS.
Richard Hengist Horne

MOORMAN
William Carnegie

MORAL, MATTHEW
Mrs Mary Pilkington

A MORAL PHILOSOPHER
Peter Annet

MORAN, MIKE
William Thomas Ard

MORDAUNT, ELINOR
Evelyn May Clowes

MORDAUNT, JOHN
John Moore

MORDECAI, BENJAMIN BEN
Henry Taylor

MORE, ADELYNE
Charles Kay Ogden

MORE, JOHN, APOTHECARY
George Bubb Dodington

MORE, MARGARITA
Miss Anne Manning

MORE, RODERIGO
Henry Brinkelow

MORECAMP, ARTHUR
Thomas Pilgrim

MORELL, SIR CHARLES
James Ridley

MORESBY, LOUIS
Eliza Louisa Moresby Beck

MORETON, ANDREW, ESQ.
Daniel Defoe

MORETON, JOHN
Morton Norton Cohen

MORGAN, BAILEY
Gil Brewer

MORGAN, CLAIRE
Mary Patricia Highsmith

MORGAN, EMANUEL
Harold Witter Bynner

MORGAN, TED
Sanche De Gramont

MORGANWG, IOLO
Edward Williams

MORGENSTERN, S.
William Goldman

MORICH, STANTON
George Chetwynd Griffith
Jones

MORISON, ELIZABETH
Charlotte Anne Elizabeth
Moberly

MORITURUS
Charles Lamb

MORLAND, DICK
Reginald Charles Hill

MORLEY, SUSAN
Sarah Frances Spedding

MORLEY, WILFRED OWEN
Robert A. W. Lowndes

MORRELL, JOHN
Thomas C. M. Olson

MORRIS, G. A.
Katherine Anne MacLean

MORRIS, JAMES HUMPHREY
Jan Morris

MORRIS, JOHN
John Hearne

MORRIS, JULIAN
Morris West

MORRIS, KATHERINE
Mrs Frances West Pike

MORRIS, PETER, THE
ODONTIST
John Gibson Lockhart

MORRIS, ROBERT
James Sloan Gibson

MORRIS, SARA
John Frederick Burke

MORRISON, RICHARD
Robert A. W. Lowndes

MORRISON, ROBERTA
Jean Francis Webb

MORROW, JACOB
Olivia Manning

MORSE, CAROL
Marjorie Hall

MORTALIS
James Boswell

MORTIMER, GEOFFREY
Walter Matthew Gallichan

MORTIMER, LEE
Mortimer Lieberman

MORTON, ANTHONY
John Creasey

MORTON, ELEANOR
Elizabeth Gertrude Stern

MORTON, HUGH
Charles Morton Stewart
McLellan

MORTON, LEE
Dionysius Lardner Boucicault

MORTON, VICTOR
John Godfrey Ferdinand
Raupert

MORTON, WILLIAM
William Blair Morton Ferguson

MOSCHUS
Robert Lovell

MOSSMAN, BURT
Henry John Keevill

A MOST RELUCTANT
DINER-OUT
Sir Arthur Helps

MOSTYN, SYDNEY
William Clark Russell

MOTH
Joseph Tinker Buckingham

A MOTHER
Mrs Harriet Miller Davidson
Mrs Maria Gurney

MOTTE, PETER
Richard Motte Harrison

MOTTLES, J. C.
John Coakley Lettsom

MOUBRAY, BONINGTON
John Lawrence

MOUGHER, AURELIUS
Mowbray Walter Morris

MOUNTAIN, DIDYMUS
Thomas Hill

MOUNTAIN BARD
David Hatch Barlow

THE MOUNTAIN MUSE
John Hunter

MOUNTAINEER
Joseph Alston

MOUNTFIELD, DAVID
Neil Grant

MOUNTJOY, DESMOND
William D. M. Chapman
Houston

MOUNTJOY, GUIDO
Charles James Lever

THE MOURNER
James Clarence Mangan

A MOUSE BORN OF THE
MOUNTAIN
Mrs Catherine Frances Grace
Gore

MOWBRAY, JOHN
John George Haslette Vahey

MOWBRAY, J. P.
Andrew Carpenter Wheeler

MOWSHAY, BEN
Woolfe Summerfield

MOYLAND, MONICA
Amanda McKittrick Ros

MOZANS, H. J.
John Augustine Zahm

MOZIS'ADDUMS
George William Bagby

MUDGETT, HERMAN W.
William Anthony Parker White

MUFF, GOLIAH
William Makepeace Thackeray

MUGGINS, WILLIAM
Charles Selby

MUIR, ALAN
Thomas James Morrison

MUIR, DEXTER
Leonard Reginald Gribble

MUIR, HAMILTON
James Bone with Muirhead
Bone and Archibald
Hamilton Charteris

MUIR, JOHN
Thomas Christopher Morgan

THE MUIRKIRK SHEPHERD
James Hyslop

MULHOLLAND, ROSA
Lady Gilbert

MULLER, J. E.
Robert Lionel Fanthorpe

MULLER, PAUL
Albert King

MULLIGAN, MORTY
MACNAMARA
William Maginn

MULLIGAN OF
KILBALLYMULLIGAN
William Makepeace Thackeray

MR MULLION
William Maginn

MULLION, MORDECAI
John Wilson

MULLION, ROSE
Douglas Brooke Wheelton
Sladen

MUM, NED
Zachary Pearce

MUNDITIIS
James Boswell

MUNDY, MAX
Sylvia Anne Matheson
Schofield

MUNDY, TALBOT
William Lancaster Gribbon

MUNRO, C. K.
Charles Kirkpatrick MacMullan

MUNRO, DUNCAN H.
Eric Frank Russell

MUNRO, JAMES
James W. Mitchell

MUNRO, RONALD EADIE
Duncan Munro Glen

A MUNSTER FARMER
William Cooke Taylor

MURALTO, ONUPHRIO
Horace Walpole

MURGATROYD
James Athearn Jones

MURPHY, DENNIS JASPER
Charles Robert Maturin

MURRAY
Robert Sanders

MURRAY, BEATRICE
Richard Posner

MURRAY, CROMWELL
Murray Cromwell Morgan

MURRAY, FIONA
Gloria Bevan

MURRAY, FRANCES
Rosemary Frances Booth

MURRAY, GILBERT
Richard Newman Wycherley

MURRAY, HAMILTON
Marie Blaze De Bury
Henry Malden

MURRAY, HERBERT
Francis Charles Hingeston-
Randolph

MURRAY, MICHAEL
Moray David Shaw McLaren

MURRAY, RUTH
Lady Gilbert

MURRAY, SINCLAIR
Edward Alan Sullivan

**MURRY, COLIN
MIDDLETON**
John Middleton Murry

MUSAEUS
John Morison

MUSAEUS PALATINUS
Richard Brathwait

MUSAIOS
Charles Arthur Muses

MUSCIPULA SENIOR
John Collier

MUSGRAVE, PHILIP
Joseph Abbott

A MUSICAL CRITIC
Francis Hueffer

A MUSICAL PROFESSOR
Edward Holmes

A MUSICAL STUDENT
Richard Mackenzie Bacon

MUSOPHILUS
Richard Brathwaite

Thomas Rogers

MUSSEY, VIRGINIA T.
Virginia T. H. Ellison

MUSTARD & CRESS
Dominic Bevan Wyndham
Lewis

A MUTE
Henry Fothergill Chorley

A MUTUAL FRIEND
Mrs Harriet Grote

**MY AUNT MARGARET
NICHOLSON**
Percy Bysshe Shelley

MY-HEELE MENDSOALE
John Taylor

MYERS, HARRIET KATHRYN
Harry B. Whittington

MYLES, SYMON
Kenneth Martin Follett

MYRA
Mrs Juliana Horatia Ewing

MYRON, PAUL
Paul Myron Wentworth
Linebarger

MYRTLE, HARRIET
Lydia Falconer Miller

MYRTLE, LEWIS
George Canning Hill

MYRTLE, MARMADUKE
Thomas Dermody
Sir Richard Steele

**MYRTLE, MARMADUKE,
GENT.**
John Nichols

MYRTLE, MINNIE
Mrs Anna Cummings Johnson

MYSTAGOGUS
Thomas Woolston

N

N.
John Gibson Lockhart

N. B.
Nathaniel Bacon
Nathaniel Bailey
Ezra Pound

N. D.
George Norman Douglas

N. E.
John Swete

N. M.
Nicholas Magens

N. S. G.
Lyman Hotchkiss Bagg

N. W.
Clive Staples Lewis

NADA, JOHN
John Langdon-Davies

NADIR, WILLIAM, S. X. Q.
William Douglass

NANTUCKET
John Galt

NAPIER, MARK
John Laffin

NAPIER, MARY
Mary Patricia Wright

NARJENN, THO.
Thomas Tanner

NASBY, PETROLEUM
VESUVIUS
David Ross Lock

NASEBY
Geraldine Penrose Fitzgerald

NASH, CHANDLER
Katherine Chandler Hunt

NASH, SIMON
Raymond Chapman

NATHAN, DANIEL
Frederic Dannay

SIR NATHANIEL
Francis Jacox

A NATIVE
James Long

A NATIVE AMERICAN
Richard Hildreth

A NATIVE AND
INHABITANT OF THE
PLACE
Robert Beverley

A NATIVE AND MEMBER OF
THE HOUSE OF
BURGESSES
Thomas Jefferson

A NATIVE ARTIST
Edward Pugh

NATIVE BORN CITIZEN OF
THE US
Oliver Evans

A NATIVE CANADIAN
George T. Denison Jr.

A NATIVE CITIZEN AND
SERVANT OF THE
STATE
Alexander Contee Hanson

A NATIVE GEORGIAN
Augustus Baldwin Longstreet

A NATIVE OF ALGIERS
Peter Markoe

A NATIVE OF AMERICA
John Parke

A NATIVE OF BRITAIN
James Beattie

A NATIVE OF CRAVEN
William Carr

A NATIVE OF NEW
ENGLAND
Daniel Leonard

A NATIVE OF
PENNSYLVANIA
Hugh Williamson

A NATIVE OF THAT
COLONY
Carter Braxton

A NATIVE OF THE FOREST
William Apes

A NATIVE OF THE SOUTH
Thomas Cooper

A NATIVE OF VIRGINIA
Moncure Daniel Conway
William Branch Giles

A NATIVE ROMAN
CATHOLIC PRELATE
John Milner

A NATURALIST
William John Broderip
George Edwards
Denham Jordan
John Leonard Knapp
Sir John Skelton
James Wilson

NAUTICUS
Sir William Laird Clowes

A NAVAL NOBODY
George Granville Campbell

A NAVAL OFFICER
William Fisher
William Harwar Parker

A NAVAL PEER
Edward Plunket

NAVARRENUS, FRANCIS
MILDAPETTUS
Sir William Temple

NAWORTH, GEORGE
Sir George Wharton

NAYLOR, ELIOT
Pamela Frankau

NAZARAEUS
John Wiche

A NECESSITARIAN
John Allen

NECK, MR VANDER
James Burgh

NEEDHAM, MARCHMONT
Josiah Quincy

NEEDHAM, T. H.
Thomas Burgeland Johnson

THE NEIGHBOR
Nathan Fiske

NEIL, ROSS
Isabella Harwood

NELSON, ALEC
Edward Bibbings Aveling

NELSON, GERTRUDE (or VICTOR)
John William Bobin

NELSON, MARGUERITE
Lee Floren

NELSON, MARK
Ronald Johnston

NELSON, RAY
Radell Faraday Nelson

NEMESIS
James Beal
Alfred Farthing Robbins

NEMO
Edward Walter Hamilton

NEMO, HENRY
Sir Henry John Newbolt

NEMO NOBODY
James Fennell

A NEPHEW OF JOHN MILTON
John Phillips

NEREUS
John Wilson Croker

NERKE
Cyrus Redding

NERVA
Samuel Gale

NESBIT, TROY
Franklin Brewster Folsom

NESSMUK
George W. Sears

NESTOR
Hugh Barclay

NETTLE, HUMPHREY
William Jackson

NEVERS, C. O.
Charles Crozat Converse

NEVILLE, MARGOT
Margot Goyder with Anne Joske

A NEW ENGLAND BRIDE
Mrs Caroline Gilman

A NEW ENGLAND FARMER
John Lowell

A NEW ENGLAND HOUSEKEEPER
Mrs Caroline Gilman

A NEW ENGLAND MAN
James Kirke Paulding

A NEW ENGLAND MINISTER
Bennet Tyler

A NEW ENGLAND MINISTER, A. B.
Edward Everett Hale

A NEW ENGLAND PASTOR
Nathaniel Emmons

A NEW ENGLANDER OVER THE SEA
John Neal

A NEW WRITER
Lewis Morris
Frances Eleanor Trollope

A NEW YORKER
Charles Astor Bristed
William Michell Gillespie
Charles Fenno Hoffman
John McVickar
Henry Wikoff

A NEW YORK PRESBYTER
John Cotton Smith

NEWBURY, P.
Thomas Penrose

NEWCOMB, NORMA
William Arthur Neubauer

A NEWDIGATE PRIZEMAN
William Hurrell Mallock

NEWELL, CROSBY
Crosby Newell Bonsall

A NEWFOUNDLAND MISSIONARY
Edward Wix

NEWLIGHT, REV. ARISTARCHUS
Richard Whately

NEWMAN, ERNEST
Wiliam Roberts

NEWMAN, MARGARET
Margaret Potter

NEWTE, THOMAS
William Thomson

NEWTON, DAVID C.
John Newton Chance

NIBLICK
Charles Stedman Hanks

NICHOLAS
William Jeffrey Prowse

NICHOLAS, T. V.
Theresa Victoria Blundell

NICHOLS, LEIGH
Dean R. Koontz

NICHOLS, PETER
Christopher Samuel Youd

NICHOLSON, CHRISTINA
Christopher Robin Nicole

NICHOLSON, JANE
Marguerite Steen

NICK, GROOME OF THE HOBIE-STABLE REGINOBURGI
Sir Edward Hoby

NICOL, ABIOSEH
Davidson S. H. W. Nicol

NICOLSON, ROBIN
Christopher Robin Nicole

NIGHT WATCHMAN
Percy St George Kirke

NILE, DOROTHEA
Michael Angelo Avallone Jr.

NILLA
Miss Abby Allin

NIMBLECHOPS, AQUILINE, DEMOCRAT
Brockholst Livingston

NIMROD
Charles James Apperley
John Hamilton Reynolds

NINCOME, ELLIOTT BUTT, ESQ.
William George Hamley

NIPCLOSE, SIR NICHOLAS
Francis Gentleman

NITSUA, BENJAMIN
Benjamin Fish Austin

NOAKES, JOHN
Tom Taylor

NOBEL, PHIL
Robert Lionel Fanthorpe

NO BIGOT TO, NOR AGAINST, THE CHURCH OF ENGLAND
Samuel Cooper

NO GENIUS
Alexander Chalmers

A NO-PARTY MAN
Eustace Clare Grenville Murray

NO TITHE GATHERER
Samuel Cooper

NOBLE, CHARLES
Martin Edward Pawley

NOBLE, EMILY
James Noble Gifford

A NOBLE AUTHOR
Lord George Gordon Byron

A NOBLE LORD
Anthony Ashley Cooper

A NOBLEMAN
Oliver Goldsmith
John Hervey
Robert Sanders

A NOBLEMAN ABROAD
George Granville

**A NOBLEMAN OF THE
OTHER KINGDOM**
Sir John Perceval

NOBODY
James Cook Richmond
William Stevens

NOBODY, A.
Gordon Frederick Browne

NOBODY, NATHAN
George Yellott

**NOBODY, S., OF KING'S
COLLEGE, OXFORD**
Henry Kett

**NOBODY MUST KNOW
WHOM**
John Eliot

NOCTROFF, ALETHES
Zachary Crofton

A NODUS
Jonathan Swift

NOEL, L.
Leonard Noel Barker

NOMAD
Joseph Edgar Chamberlin
George Armstrong Custer

A NON-ALARMIST
Thomas Tooke

A NON-COMBATANT
Henry Jeffreys Bushby
George Alfred Townsend

A NON-INTRUSIONIST
George Dunbar

A NON-JUROR
Nathaniel Spinckes

NON-PARTISAN
Dorman Bridgman Eaton

**A NON-RESIDENT
AMERICAN**
George Washburn

A NONAGENARIAN
Mrs Sarah Anna Emery

Richard Graves

NONAME
Luis Philip Senarens

NONCATHONI
John Canton

NONSENCE, SIR GREGORY
John Taylor

NOODLE, MAJOR TOM
William Thomas Carden

NOOLAS, RAB
Philip Arnold Heseltine

NOONE, ED (or EDWINA)
Michael Angelo Avallone Jr.

NORBERT, W.
Norbert Weiner

NORCROSS, LISABET
Arthur M. Gladstone

NORDEN, CHARLES
Lawrence George Durrell

NORK, F.
Friedrich Korn

NORMAN, GEORGE
Edward Gordon Craig

NORMAN, JAMES
James Norman Schmidt

NORMANIDES
Edward Mangin

NORMYX
George Norman Douglas with
Elsa Fitzgibbon

NORTH, ANDREW
Alice Mary Norton

NORTH, ANTHEA
Catherine H. Constable

NORTH, ANTHONY
Dean R. Koontz

NORTH, BARCLAY
William Cadwalader Hudson

NORTH, CHRISTOPHER
John Wilson

NORTH, COLIN
David Ernest Bingley

NORTH, DANBY
Daniel Owen Madden

NORTH, ERIC
Charles Bernard Cronin

NORTH, CAPTAIN GEORGE
Robert Louis Stevenson

NORTH, GIL
Geoffrey Horne

NORTH, HOWARD
Trevor Dudley-Smith

NORTH, IDA
Ida Cook

NORTH, JACK
John Nix Pentelow

NORTH, LEIGH
Mrs Elizabeth Stewart Phelps

NORTH, SARA
Barbara Bonham

A NORTH AMERICAN
Myles Cooper
John Dickinson

**A NORTH COUNTRY
ANGLER**
Thomas Doubleday

NORTHCOTE, PETER
Arthur Sydney Boulting

A NORTHERN MAN
Calvin Colton
Joseph Reed Ingersoll
James Kirke Paulding
William Bradford Reed

**A NORTHERN MAN WITH
AMERICAN PRINCIPLES**
Thomas Robinson Hazard

A NORTHERN PRESBYTER
Nathan Lord

A NORTHERN WHIG
Theobald Wolfe Tone

NORTON, ANDRE
Alice Mary Norton

NORTON, SYBIL
Helen Sybil Norton Kestner
Cournos

A NORWICH WEAVER BOY
William Johnson Fox

NOSTRODAMUS, MERLIN
Miss Frances Power Cobbe

**NOTHUS, CORNELIUS
SCRIBLERUS**
Alexander Crowcher
Schomberg

NOTROFE
Ernest Frederick Orton

NOUREDDIN ALRASCHIN
John Armstrong

NOVAK, JOSEPH
Jerzy Nikodem Kosinski

NOVANGLUS
John Adams

NOVELLO, IVOR
David Ivor Davies

NOVUS HOMO
William John Courthope

NOWALL, A.
William Peppernell Pitt

NOX, OWEN
Charles Barney Cory

A NULLIFIER
Thomas Cooper

NUMA MINIMUS
Sir Stanley Mordaunt Leathes

NUNEZ, MAY
Mrs William Loring Spencer

**NUNNEZ, FABRICIA, A
SPINSTER**
Peter Coxe

NUNQUAM
Robert Blatchford

NYE, BILL
Edgar Wilson Nye

NYE, CASSANDRA
John Thomas Sladek with
Thomas Michael Disch

NYNE, ATEY
Joseph Parker

O.
Joseph Addison

O. P.
James Boswell
Edward Gordon Craig

O. P. Q.
Charles Caleb Colton

O. S.
Osbert Sitwell

O. Y.
William Makepeace Thackeray

OAKES, A. H.
Henry Cuyler Bunner

OAKLEY
David Garrick

OAKWOOD, OLIVER
Stacy Gardner Potts

OBERON
Nathaniel Hawthorne

O'BLUNDER, MRS SHARP-SET
Mrs Elizabeth Franchett

O'BRIAN, FRANK
Brian Francis Wynne Garfield

O'BRIEN, CORNELIUS
Isaac Butt

O'BRIEN, E. G.
Arthur C. Clarke

O'BRIEN, EDWARD STEVENSON
Isaac Butt

O'BRIEN, FLANN
Brian O'Nolan

O'BRIEN, HARRY
John Talbot Smith

O'BRIEN, JOHN
Patrick Joseph Hartigan

O'BRIEN, ROBERT C.
Robert Leslie Conly

AN OBSCURE AND NAMELESS BARD ON THE BRAES OF ANGUS
Joseph Gordon

AN OBSCURE INDIVIDUAL
Aedanus Burke

AN OBSCURE LAYMAN IN TOWN
George Psalmanazar

AN OBSCURE MEDIOCRITY
Frederick Waeir Stevens

OBSERVATOR
Samuel Adams
Samuel Blodget

OBSERVATOR, CHARLES
Elijah Robinson Sabin

AN OBSERVATOR ON THE LONDON BILLS OF MORTALITY
Sir William Petty

AN OBSERVER
Marie Louise de la Ramee
John Emory
Francis Joseph Grund
James Alexander Haldane
Dennis O'Bryen
Guy Cadogan Rothery

OBSERVER, R. F. C.
Gordon Alchin

AN OBSOLETE AUTHOR
James Kirke Paulding

O'BYRNE, DERMOT
Sir Arnold Edward Trevor Bax

O'CASEY, J.
Sean O'Casey

O'CATARACT, JOHN
John Neal

AN OCCASIONAL CONTRIBUTOR
Alfred Porter Putnam

AN OCCASIONAL CORRESPONDENT
Henry James

AN OCCASIONAL WRITER IN THE 'BRITISH CRITIC'
Samuel Parr

OCKSIDE, KNIGHT RUSS
Mortimer Neal Thompson

O'CONNELL, EDMOND
William Haliday

O'CONNER, ELIZABETH
Barbara McNamara

O'CONNOR, FRANK
Michael Francis O'Donovan

O'CONNOR, PATRICK
Leonard P. O'Connor
Wibberley

OCONOMOWOC
James Alexander Henshall

OCTAVIA
Mary Alice Seymour

OCTAVIUS
William Hales

AN OCTOGENARIAN
John Mathew Gutch
Sir Brenton Halliburton
Richard Lower
Charles Marsh
Cyrus Redding
James Roche

AN OCTOGENARIAN ACTOR
John Frederick Brent

AN OCTOGENARIAN ARCHITECT
George Ledwell Taylor

AN OCTOGENARIAN OF PHILADELPHIA
Mathew Carey

OCTOGENARY
Daniel Huntington

OCULUS
Josiah Bushnell Grinnell

ODARD
Thomas Acton Warburton

ODDIE, E. M.
Elinor Mary O'Donoghue

ODDY, J. JEPHSON
William Playfair

O'DOHERTY, SIR MORGAN
William Hay Forbes with John
Gibson Lockhart and
William Maginn

O'DONALD, PEREGRINE
William King

O'DONNELL, DONAT
Conor Cruise O'Brien

O'DONNELL, K. M.
Barry N. Malzberg

O'DONNEVAN, FINN
Robert Sheckley

**O'DONOGHUE, C. (or
CORNELIUS or ENSIGN)**
Thomas Crofton Croker

O'DONOVAN, P. M.
Thomas Love Peacock

O'DOWD, CORNELIUS
Charles James Lever

**O'DRYSCULL, REDDY (or
RORY)**
Francis Sylvester Mahony

ODYSSEUS
Sir Charles Eliot
Donald MacIntosh Johnson
Vincent Clarence Scott
O'Connor

O'FAOLAIN, SEAN
John Whelan

OFELLUS
Francis Squire

AN OFFICER
Thomas Anburey
Samuel Ancell
Henry Seymour Conway
Arent Schuyler De Peyster
George Robert Gleig
James Glenie
Arthur Harness
Richard Harrison
Sir Robert Ker Porter
John Richardson
David Roberts
Moyle Sherer
John Gordon Smith

**AN OFFICER EMPLOYED IN
HIS ARMY**
John Fane

**AN OFFICER EMPLOYED ON
THE EXPEDITION**
William Smith

**AN OFFICER IN A
MARCHING REGIMENT**
William Maginn

**AN OFFICER IN THE ARMY
OF WOLFE**
James Athearn Jones

**AN OFFICER IN THE
GUARDS**
George Edward Ayscough

**AN OFFICER IN THE MIL.
AND CIV. SERVICE OF
THE HON. E. I. CO.**
Sir William Henry Sleeman

AN OFFICER IN THE NAVY
John Toup Nicolas

**AN OFFICER IN THE
SERVICE OF THE INDIA
COMPANY**
Richard Hall Gower

**AN OFFICER OF COLONEL
BAILLIE'S
DETACHMENT**
William Thomson

**AN OFFICER OF HM'S
LAND-FORCES**
John Drinkwater Bethune

**AN OFFICER OF HMS
TOPAZE**
Richard Sainthill

AN OFFICER OF RANK
William Nugent Glascock
Sir John Borlase Warren

**AN OFFICER OF RANK IN
THE SQUADRON**
Sir Edward Berry

AN OFFICER OF THE ARMY
Edwin D. Phillips

**AN OFFICER OF THE ARMY
AT DETROIT**
Henry Whiting

**AN OFFICER OF THE
BENGAL STAFF CORPS**
George Bruce Malleson

**AN OFFICER OF THE
'CAROLINE'**
James Johnson

**AN OFFICER OF THE
COLDSTREAM GUARDS**
Charles William Short

**AN OFFICER OF THE
EXPEDITION**
John Whitelocke

**AN OFFICER OF THE
EXPEDITIONARY
FORCE**
Sir Garnet Joseph Wolseley

AN OFFICER OF THE FLEET
Richard Walter

AN OFFICER OF THE LINE
John Lane Gardner

**AN OFFICER OF THE
ORDER OF ST JOACHIM**
'Sir' Levett Hanson

**AN OFFICER OF THE
REGIMENT**
Joseph Mark Califf

**AN OFFICER OF THE
ROYAL ARTILLERY**
Henry Knollys

**AN OFFICER OF THE
ROYAL ENGINEERS**
Charles Edmund Webber

**AN OFFICER OF THE
ROYAL NAVY**
Hugh Colvill Goldsmith
John Walter Tarleton

**AN OFFICER OF THE
UNITED STATES NAVY**
Horatio Bridge
Walter Colton

**AN OFFICER OF THE US
ARMY**
Richard Bache
George C. Strong

**AN OFFICER OF THIS
ESTABLISHMENT AT
CHARLESTOWN**
Gamaliel Bradford

AN OFFICER ON THE STAFF
Charles Hamilton Smith

**OFFICER SERVING AS
QUARTER-MASTER
GENERAL**
Sir George de Lacy Evans

**AN OFFICER THEN
SERVING IN THE
FLEET**
Thomas Lewis O'Beirne

**AN OFFICER UNDER THAT
GENERAL**
Henry Adams Bullard

**AN OFFICER WHO SERVED
IN THE EXPEDITION**
George Robert Gleig

**AN OFFICER WHO SERVED
THERE**
William Wotherspoon Ireland

**AN OFFICER WHO SERVED
UNDER MARQUIS
CORNWALLIS**
Sir Herbert Taylor

AN OFFICER WHO WAS
THERE
Ernest Gambier Parry

O'FINN, THADDEUS
Joseph Thaddeus McGloin

O'FLAHERTY, WILLIAM
Liam O'Flaherty

O'FLUMMERY, IGNATIUS
RABELAIS
Richard Lalor Sheil

O'GARA, A. P. A.
W. R. MacDermott

OGDEN, RUTH
Mrs Fannie Otis Ide

OGE, ERIN
Robert Arthur Wilson

OGILVY, GAVIN
Sir James Matthew Barrie

O'GRADY, ROHAN
June Margaret Skinner

O'HALLORAN, BRYAN
Thomas Baldwin Woods

O'HARA, ABEL
Michael Banim

O'HARA, BARNES
John Banim

O'HARA, KENNETH
Margaret Jean Morris

O'HARA, KEVIN
Marten Cumberland

THE O'HARA FAMILY
John Banim with Michael
Banim

O'HARRIS, PIXIE
Rona Olive Pratt

OHIYESA
Charles Alexander Eastman

OKE, RICHARD
Nigel Millett

O'KEEFE, CORNELIUS
Thomas Francis Meagher

O'KENNEDY, KEVIN
William Patrick Ryan

OLAND, JOHN
Edith Alice Mary Harper

O'LANUS, CORRY
John Stanton

AN OLD ACQUAINTANCE
OF THE PUBLIC
Mrs Hester Lynch Thrale

AN OLD AMATEUR
Richard Edgcumbe

AN OLD ANTIQUARIAN
Peter Armstrong Whittle

AN OLD APPRENTICE OF
THE LAW
Andrew Valentine Kirwan

AN OLD ARMY SURGEON
Samuel Dickson

AN OLD AUTHOR
Sarah Stickney Ellis
Daniel Puseley

AN OLD BACHELOR
Richard Harris Barham
Hartley Coleridge
George William Curtis

THE OLD BARD
Edward Jerningham

AN OLD BENGALER
John Larkins Cheese
Richardson

THE OLD BLOCK
Alonzo Delano

AN OLD BLUE
Courtenay Edmund Boyle

AN OLD BOHEMIAN
Dr Gustav L. M. Strauss

AN OLD BOOKSELLER
William West

AN OLD BOOKWORM
William John Thoms

AN OLD BOOMERANG
John Richard Houlding

AN OLD BOY
Edward Bellasis
Edward Litt Leman Blanchard
James Franklin Fuller
Thomas Hughes
Talbot Baines Reed

OLD BUFFER
Frederick Gale

OLD BURCHELL
Elihu Burritt

AN OLD BUSHMAN
Horace William Wheelwright

AN OLD CAMPAIGNER
Sir John Skelton

AN OLD CATHOLIC
Arthur Cleveland Coxe

AN OLD CAVALRY OFFICER
Charles Montauban Carmichael

OLD CAYEN
Alexander Chalmers

AN OLD CELT
William Bottrell

OLD CHALK
Henry Chadwick

OLD CHATTY CHEERFUL
William Martin

OLD CHUM
William Alexander Jenyns Boyd

AN OLD COLLEGER
Arthur Duke Coleridge

AN OLD COLONIST
Edmund Finn

AN OLD CONSERVATIVE
John Gorham Palfrey

AN OLD CONTRIBUTOR
Mabel Cook
Samuel Warren

AN OLD CONTRIBUTOR TO
MAGA
Charles Neaves

AN OLD CORNISH BOY
Samuel Woolcock Christophers

AN OLD CORRESPONDENT
James Boswell

AN OLD COURTIER
James Boswell

AN OLD CROWN LAWYER
Saxe Bannister

AN OLD DISSECTOR
James Browne

AN OLD DIVINE
Matthew Henry

THE OLD DOG
Frederick Owen Bartlett

AN OLD EDUCATIONALIST
Simon Somerville Laurie

AN OLD ENGLISHMAN
James Rennell

AN OLD FARMER
John Lowell

AN OLD FASHIONED
ENGLISHMAN
Barbara Hoole Hofland

AN OLD FELSTEDIAN
Thomas Seccombe

AN OLD FOGEY
Alfred Austin

AN OLD FRIEND
William Wilberforce Newton
Miss Jane Louisa Willyams

AN OLD FRIEND AND
SERVANT OF THE
CHURCH
William Jones

AN OLD FRIEND OF THE
SOCIETY FOR
PROMOTING
CHRISTIAN
KNOWLEDGE
William Ward

AN OLD GARDENER
Edward Beck

AN OLD GEORGIA LAWYER
Garnett Andrews

OLD GLORY
Ezra Pound

OLD GREY
Thomas Rossell Potter

AN OLD HAND
Percival Weldon Banks
Charles Dent Bell
Charles James Lever

AN OLD HAND ON BOARD
Arthur Benoni Evans

AN OLD HARROVIAN
Douglas Straight

AN OLD HEREDITARY
BURGESS
Sir James Foulis

AN OLD HIGHLANDER
Emily Sarah MacLeod

OLD HUMPHREY
George Mogridge

AN OLD INDIAN
George Robert Gleig

AN OLD INDIAN
MAGISTRATE
John Walter Sherer

AN OLD INHABITANT OF
BRITISH NORTH
AMERICA
Sir Brenton Halliburton

OLD JONATHAN
David Alfred Doudney

OLD JOWETT
Barry Fantoni with Richard
Ingrams

OLD KNICK
Edward Dubois

AN OLD MAN
Alexander Dalrymple
Sir Francis Bond Head
Richard Malcolm Johnston
Josiah Quincy
Philip Skelton

AN OLD MAN OF BUSINESS
Charles Lloyd

AN OLD MARINER
Mary Victoria Cowden-Clarke

AN OLD MEMBER OF
PARLIAMENT
Richard Glover
Sir Richard Hill
Arthur Lee
Charles Marsh

AN OLD MERCHANT
John Nesmith

OLD MERRY
Edwin Hodder

OLD MOORE
Francis Moore

AN OLD MP
Sir William G. G. V. Vernon
Harcourt

AN OLD NEW YORKER
William Alexander Duer

AN OLD OBSERVER
Rowland Hill

AN OLD OFFICER
George Mogridge
Philip Skelton

AN OLD PARIS MAN
William Makepeace Thackeray

AN OLD PAROCHIAL
CLERGYMAN
John Duncan

AN OLD PENINSULAR
Thomas Boys

AN OLD PERSONAL FRIEND
William Wallace

AN OLD PHYSICIAN
Selina Bunbury

AN OLD PIONEER
John Mason Peck

AN OLD PLAYGOER
Peter Hanley
Samuel Parlby

OLD POSSUM
Thomas Stearns Eliot

OLD PROB
Albert J. Myer

AN OLD PUPIL
William Benham

AN OLD REPORTER
Walter Henry Watts

AN OLD RESIDENT
Albert H. Porter
George Washburn

AN OLD RESIDENT AT
BRUSSELS
Pryse Lockhart Gordon

AN OLD REVIEWER
Abraham Hayward

AN OLD RUGBAEAN
Charles Henry Newmarch

THE OLD SAILOR
Matthew Henry Barker

OLD SALISBURY BRIAR
James Boswell

OLD SCRATCH
Gilbert Abbott A'Beckett

AN OLD SEAMAN
Nicholas Tomlinson

AN OLD SERVANT
Ralph Heathcote

THE OLD SHEKARRY
Henry Astbury Leverson

OLD SIMON
Alexander Chalmers

OLD SLEUTH
Harlan P. Halsey

OLD SLI
Samuel White Small

OLD SLYBOOTS
James Scott

AN OLD SMOKER
James Parton
Percy Bolingbroke St John

AN OLD SOLDIER
John Armstrong
Sir George Bell
William Francis Butler
Edward Moor

OLD SOUTH
Benjamin Austin

AN OLD SPORTSMAN
William Flint

AN OLD STAGER
James Aspinall
William Edmonstoune Aytoun
James Shirley Hodson
John Trusler

AN OLD STATESMAN
David Williams

OLD STINGO
James Boswell

OLD STRAWS
Joseph M. Field

AN OLD STUDENT
John Barling

AN OLD STUDENT IN
DIVINITIE
Richard Broughton

OLD STYLE, OLIVER
James Beattie

AN OLD SUSSEX
CRICKETER
Charles Francis Trower

AN OLD TEACHER
George Barrell Emerson

AN OLD TEMPLAR
Thomas Noon Talfourd

AN OLD TORY
Sir John Skelton

AN OLD TOWN CITIZEN
James Boswell

AN OLD TOWNSMAN
James Bisset

AN OLD TRADESMAN
Thomas Bailey

AN OLD TRAMP
John Hill Burton

AN OLD TRAVELLER
James Silk Buckingham
Henry Llewellyn Williams

AN OLD TRAVELLER
THROUGHOUT
EUROPE
Thomas Brown

THE OLD 'UN
Francis Alexander Durivage

AN OLD VICAR
John Samuel Bewley Monsell
John Wood Warter

AN OLD WIFE OF TWENTY
YEARS
Mrs Elizabeth Thomas

OLDACRE, CEDRIC
John Wood Warter

OLDBUG, JOHN, ESQ.
Leonard Withington

OLDCASTLE, GEOFFREY
William Mudford

OLDCASTLE, HUMPHREY
Nicholas Amhurst
Thomas Charles Morgan
Henry St John

OLDCASTLE, JOHN
Wilfrid Meynell

OLDFELLOW, POLYWARP,
MD
Charles Smart

OLDFIELD, PETER
Charles Vernon Oldfield
Bartlett with Per Jacobsson

OLDFIELD, TRAVERSE
George Whitefield Samson

OLDPATH, OBADIAH
James Robinson Newhall

OLDSCHOOL, OLIVER
Nathan Sargent

OLDSCHOOL, OLIVER, ESQ.
Joseph Dennie

OLDSTYLE, JONATHAN,
GENT.
Washington Irving

OLDSTYLE, ROGER
Martin Farquhar Tupper

OLDYS, FRANCIS, MA
George Chalmers

OLE-LUK-OIE
Sir Ernest Dunlop Swinton

O'LINCOLN, NICK
Richard Horatio Edgar Wallace

OLIVEBRANCH, REV.
SIMEON
William Roberts

OLIVER, JANE
Helen Rees

OLIVER, JULIUS
Edward Gordon Craig

OLIVER, MARK
Michael Tyler-Whittle

OLIVER, NATHAN
Robert Blakey

OLIVER, OWEN
Sir Joshua Albert Flynn

OLIVER, PEN
Sir Henry Thompson

OLIVER, STEPHEN
William Andrew Chatto

OLIVIA
Dorothy Bussy
Olivia Wilmot Serres

OLLAPOD
Willis Gaylord Clark

O'LONDON, JOHN
Wilfred Whitten

OLSEN, D. B.
Julia Dolores Hitchens

O'MALLEY, FRANK (or
PATRICK)
Frank O'Rourke

OMEGA
William Cowper

OMICRON
Hugh Barclay
John Newton

OMNIA VINCAM
Victor Benjamin Neuburg

OMNIUM, JACOB
Matthew James Higgins

O'NAIR, MAIRI
Constance May Evans

ONE CALLED AN HIGH-
CHURCHMAN
Charles Leslie

ONE INTIMATELY
CONNECTED WITH
HIM
Cotton Mather

ONE NOT UNEXERCISED IN
THESE KINDS OF
SPECULATION
Henry More

ONE NOT OF THE
ASSOCIATION
Theodore Parker

ONE OF A LITERARY
FAMILY
Mrs Anna Letitia Le Breton

ONE OF HER ADMIRERS
John Esten Cooke

ONE OF HIS CANDID
NEIGHBOURS
Joseph Bellamy

ONE OF HIS
CONSTITUENTS
Henry Boase
Edward Copleston
Henry Drummond

ONE OF HIS COUNTRYMEN
Caleb Cushing

ONE OF HIS MAJESTY'S
CHAPLAINS
David Jenner
Arthur Philip Perceval

ONE OF HM'S JUSTICES OF
THE PEACE
Robert Owen

ONE OF HIS MAJESTY'S
JUSTICES OF THE
PEACE FOR THE
COUNTY OF
SOMERSET
John Langhorne

ONE OF HM'S JUSTICES OF THE PEACE FOR THE THREE INLAND COUNTIES
John Weyland

ONE OF HIS MAJESTY'S SERVANTS
Arthur Philip Perceval

ONE OF HIS OLDEST LIVING DISCIPLES
William Lockhart

ONE OF HIS OLD PUPILS
William MacGillivray

ONE OF HIS OWNE SERVANTS BEING HIS GENTLEMAN USHER
George Cavendish

ONE OF ITS VICTIMS
Charles Welsh

ONE OF NO ARTS, BUT DOWNRIGHT HONESTY
Arthur Annesley

ONE OF NO PARTY
James Grant

ONE OF THAT SOCIETIE
Dudley Digges

ONE OF THE ADDRESSED
Joseph Aston

ONE OF THE BARCLAYS
Mrs Eliza Henderson Otis

ONE OF THE BOYS
Percy Hetherington Fitzgerald

ONE OF THE BRIEFLESS
William Edmonstoune Aytoun

ONE OF THE BROWNS
Frederic Charles Lascelles Wraxall

ONE OF 'THE CLAN'
Francis Crissey Young

ONE OF THE COMMISSIONERS
Sir Charles Edward Grey

ONE OF THE COMMONS AT CHERBOURG
Samuel Warren

ONE OF THE CROWD
James Greenwood

ONE OF THE DEFEATED
Frederick Hallard

ONE OF THE DEMOCRACY
David Robinson

ONE OF THE EDITORS OF THE NY 'MIRROR'
Theodore Sedgwick Fay

ONE OF THE 'EIGHTEEN MILLIONS OF BORES'
Elizur Wright

ONE OF THE 80,000 INCORRIGIBLE JACOBINS
Sir John Colman Rashleigh

ONE OF THE ELECTORS
John Ormsby

ONE OF THE FACULTY
John Coakley Lettsom

ONE OF THE FAMILY OF BOWLESES
William Lisle Bowles

ONE OF THE FANCY
Pierce Egan
Thomas Moore

ONE OF THE FIRM
Anthony Trollope

ONE OF THE FOOLS
Albion Winegar Tourgee

ONE OF THE FRATERNITY
William Morgan

ONE OF THE GREAT UNPLAYED
Alfred Farthing Robbins

ONE OF THE HUMBLEST AND MOST DUTIFUL OF HIS DISSENTING SUBJECTS
William Penn

ONE OF THE IDLE CLASSES
William Thompson

ONE OF THE INSPECTORS OF THE PRISON
Thomas Eddy

ONE OF THEIR BRETHREN
Richard Mant

ONE OF THEIR CONSTITUENTS
Tenche Coxe

ONE OF THEIR NUMBER
Cotton Mather
George Julius Poulett Scrope

ONE OF THE JURYMEN
Philip Thicknesse

ONE OF THE LAITY
Hannah More

ONE OF THE LAMB'S FOLLOWERS
Francis Howgill

ONE OF THE LAST CENTURY
William Stewart Rose

ONE OF THEM
Charles Joseph Weld-Blundell

ONE OF THE MEDICI
James Arthur Wilson

ONE OF THE MEMBERS OF THE COLLEGE
Charles Coote

ONE OF THE MEMORIALISTS
William Augustus Muhlenberg

ONE OF THE MINISTERS IN BOSTON
Cottton Mather

ONE OF THE MINISTERS IN EDINBURGH
John Inglis

ONE OF THE MINISTERS IN THE NORTH PART OF BOSTON
Cotton Mather

ONE OF THE MODERN PROPHETS
John Lacy

ONE OF THEMSELVES
Robert Michael Ballantyne
John Fielder Mackarness
Mrs Charlotte Montefiore
Henry Mudge
William Makepeace Thackeray
Samuel Warren

ONE OF THE NEW POOR
Mary E. Blundell

ONE OF THE OLD CONSTITUTION
John Eagles

ONE OF THE OLD GUARD
Arthur John Butler

ONE OF THE OLD LIVING POETS OF GREAT BRITAIN
William Lisle Bowles

ONE OF THE OLD PEOPLE
Stephen Paget

ONE OF THE OLD SCHOOL
David Robinson
William West

ONE OF THE OLD STAFF
Thomas Arnold

ONE OF THE PEOPLE
Tristram Burges
Churchill C. Cambreling
George Barrell Cheever
Luke James Hansard

ONE OF THE PEOPLE
CALLED CHRISTIANS
George Horne
Jeremiah Waring

ONE OF THE PEOPLE
CALLED QUAKERS
Joseph Besse
Daniel Defoe

ONE OF THE PROFESSORS
Thomas Clark

ONE OF THE PUBLIC
Frederick Guest Tomlins

ONE OF THE RAIDERS
George Wesley Atkinson

ONE OF THE RAMBLERS
John Bishop Putnam

ONE OF THE RELIGIOUS
SOCIETY OF FRIENDS
Edward Backhouse

ONE OF THE REMNANT
Sir John Skelton

ONE OF THE REVEREND
COMMISSIONERS FOR
THE REVIEW OF THE
LITURGY
Thomas Pierce

ONE OF THE RHODE
ISLAND PEOPLE
John Pitman

ONE OF THE SCOTCH
PEOPLE
Hugh Miller

ONE OF THE 687 FRS
Dr Augustus Granville

ONE OF THE SPECIAL
CONSTABLES IN
LONDON
Sir Arthur Helps

ONE OF THE STUDENTS OF
CHRIST CHURCH
Jasper Mayne

ONE OF THE SUFFERING
CLERGY THERE
Andrew Cant

ONE OF THE TRINITY
UNDERGRADUATES
William Copeland Borlase

ONE OF THE WORKING
CLERGY
Charles James Blomfield

ONE RECENTLY RETURNED
FROM THE ENEMY'S
COUNTRY
Edward Alfred Pollard

ONE THAT DESIRES TO BE
FAITHFUL TO HIS
COUNTRY, THOUGH
UNWORTHY TO BE
NAMED
Nathaniel Ward

ONE THAT HAS HAD
EXPERIENCE OF THEM
Cotton Mather

ONE THAT HATH NO
PROPRIETY IN TITHES
Samuel Clarke

ONE THAT HOLDS
COMMUNION WITH
THE CHURCH
John Humphrey

ONE THAT IS
CONSECRATED TO
THE SACRED
MINISTRY
Richard Baxter

ONE THAT IS CONCERNED
FOR HIS FRIEND, A
LOVER OF TRUTH
John Humphrey

ONE THAT LOVES ALL
PRESBYTERIAN
LOVERS OF TRUTH
Francis Rous

ONE THAT WAS ONCE A
SCHOLAR TO HIM
Cotton Mather

'ONE, TWO, THREE, FOUR'
Daniel Defoe

ONE UNCONCERNED
William Daddo

ONE UNDER A HOOD
John Major

ONE VERY NEAR AKIN TO
THE AUTHOR OF 'TALE
OF A TUB'
John Oldmixon

ONE WELL AFFECTED
Nicholas French

ONE WHO DOES
PASSIONATELY WISH
THE PROSPERITY OF
THE CHURCH, HIS
KING AND COUNTRY
John Nalson

ONE WHO DOTH REJOICE
IN THE LORD HIS
SAVIOUR
William Ames

ONE WHO HAS A GOOD
MEMORY
John Wilks

ONE WHO HAS DONE IT
AND CAN DO IT AGAIN
Francis Cowley Burnand

ONE WHO HAS
IMPERSONATED THEM
Helena Saville Faucit

ONE WHO HAS KEPT A
DIARY
George William Erskine Russell

ONE WHO HAS KNOWN
THEM BOTH
Frederick Hardman

ONE WHO HAS NEVER BEEN
A CANDIDATE
George Harwood

ONE WHO HAS SEEN AND
DESCRIBES
Charles Frederick Henningsen

ONE WHO HAS SERVED
Alfred Wilkes Drayson

ONE WHO HAS SERVED IN
THE RANKS
Archibald Forbes

ONE WHO HAS SERVED
UNDER SIR CHARLES
NAPIER
George Bruce Malleson

ONE WHO 'HAS SOME
THERE'
Almira Seymour

ONE WHO HAS SUFFERED
Frederick Oakeley

ONE WHO HAS TRIED IT
Charles Lutwidge Dodgson

ONE WHO HAS WHISTLED
AT THE PLOUGH
James Crighton

ONE WHO HATH BEEN A
CONSTANT EYE AND
EYE-WITNESSE
John Nye

ONE WHO HATH OBTAINED
MERCY TO BE A
MINISTER OF THE
GOSPEL
Thomas Taylor

ONE WHO IS ALSO AN
ELDER
Richard Mant

ONE WHO IS EXTREMELY DESIROUS TO PROMOTE GOOD LITERATURE IN AMERICA
Samuel Johnson

ONE WHO IS NEITHER A JACOBITE NOR REPUBLICAN, PRESBYTERIAN NOR PAPIST
Zachary Grey

ONE WHO IS NO PHILOSOPHER
William Lucas Collins

ONE WHO KEEPS HIS EYES AND EARS OPEN
Henry Ward Beecher

ONE WHO KNEW HER
Frances Julia Wedgwood

ONE WHO KNEW IT ALL
John Malcolm Forbes Ludlow

ONE WHO KNOWS THEM WELL
Charles Frederick Moberly Bell

ONE WHO LOVES AND HONOURS ENGLISH POETRY
William Allingham

ONE WHO LOVES THE SOULS OF THE LAMBS OF CHRIST'S FLOCK
Richard Marks

ONE WHO NEVER CONTRIBUTED TO THE FORMER SERIES
Alexander Robert Charles Dallas

ONE WHO NEVER TRANSGRESSED BEFORE
Charles Cotton

ONE WHO SAVED IT
Matilda Charlotte Houston

ONE WHO TRAVELLED WITH A GENTLEMAN FROM CONNEMARA
William Hamilton Maxwell

ONE WHO VALUES CHRISTIANITY FOR ITS OWN SAKE
John Nelson Darby

ONE WHO WAS CALLED IN DERISION A QUAKER
James Nayler

ONE WHO WAS THERE IN 1857–58
Walter Coningsby Erskine

ONE WHO WENT TO IT
Warren Burton

O'NEIL, ELIZABETH
Richard Tickell

O'NEIL, KERRY
John Thomas MacIntyre

O'NEILL, EGAN
Elizabeth Linington

O'NEILL, MOIRA
Agnes Higginson Skrine

ONEIROPOLOS
Charles Johnson (Johnstone)

ONESIPHORUS
Henry Charles Sirr

ONIONS, BERTA
Amy Roberta Oliver

ONIONS, OLIVER
George Oliver

ONLOOKER
William Roberts

ONSLOW
John Caldwell Calhoun

ONTOLOGOS
William Kenrick

ONYX
Mrs Elizabeth Stuart Phelps

OPAL, LADY PORSTOCK
Ronald Arbuthnot Knox

AN OPERA GOER
Donald Grant Mitchell

OPIFEX
Richard Hengist Horne

O'PINDAR, SCRIBLERUS MURTOUGH
William Paulet Carey

OPTATUS DUCTOR
James Mumford

OPTIC, OLIVER
William Taylor Adams

AN OPTIMIST
John William Kaye

O'REGAN, MILESIUS
John Francis Waller

O'REID, J. C.
Josiah Conder

O'REILLY, MILES
Charles Graham Halpin

O'REILLY, MONTAGU
Wayne Andrews

O'RELL, MAX
Leon Paul Blouet

ORELLANA
William Drennan

THE ORGANIST TO THE FRATERNITY
John Pyke Hullah

ORIEL
John Sandes

ORIEL, ANTRIM
William Arthur Moore

ORIENT
Frederic Kidder

AN ORIENTAL AUTHOR
Robert MacNish

AN ORIENTAL STUDENT
Andrew Archibald Paton

THE ORIGINAL EDITOR OF THE 'BLACK BOOK'
John Wade

ORINDA
Mrs Katherine Philips

ORME, BENJAMIN
Alexander Hay Japp

ORME, MARY
Mrs Mary Nichols

ORMISTON, MARGARET
Margaret Ormiston Curle

ORMOND, FREDERICK
Frederick V. R. Day

ORMSBEE, DAVID
Stephen Longstreet

ORPHEUS
Harold Nicholas

ORPHEUS JUNIOR
William Vaughan

ORRIS
Jean Ingelow

ORTHOCRATOS
Frederick William Rolfe

ORTHODOX, MOSES
John Boyle

AN ORTHODOX CLERGYMAN OF MASSACHUSETTS
Jacob Norton

AN ORTHODOX MINISTER OF THE GOSPEL
James Morris Whiton

AN ORTHODOX PROTESTANT
George Hickes

ORWELL
Walter Chalmers Smith

ORWELL, GEORGE
Eric Arthur Blair

OSANDER
Benjamin Allen

OSBORNE, DAVID
Robert Silverberg

OSBORNE, HELENA
Mary Moore

OSBORNE, MARK
John William Bobin

OSCEOLA
Karen Blixen

AN OSCOTIAN
William Charles Mark Kent

OSSIAN
James MacPherson

O'SULLIVAN, SEUMAS
James Sullivan Starkey

O'SULLIVAN, TIMOTHY
Timothy Daniel Sullivan

OTHER, A. N.
Sir John Collings Squire

THE OTHER GENTLEMAN
OF LINCOLN'S INN
Thomas Edwards

OTIS, JAMES
James Otis Kaler

O'TOOLE, TERENCE
Caesar Otway

OTREB, RUDOLF
Robert Fludd

O'TRIGGER, SIR LUCIUS
Richard Hengist Horne

OTWAY, SYLVESTER
John Oswald

OUDENARDE, DOMINIE
NICHOLAS AEGIDIUS
James Kirke Paulding

OUIDA
Marie Louise De La Ramee

OUR OWN BASHI-BAZOUK
William Makepeace Thackeray

OUR OWN REPORTER
Allan MacLean Skinner

OUR SPECIAL
CORRESPONDENT IN
AMERICA
Edward James Stephen Dicey

OUSELEY, GIDEON
Oliver St John Gogarty

AN OUT-AND-OUTER
James Clarence Mangan

AN OUT-LANDISH DOCTOR
John Lowin

OUTIDANOS
Sir Richard Francis Burton
William Ewart Gladstone

OUTIS
Sir John Francis Davis
Richard Grant White

OUTIS, U. DONOUGH
Richard Grant White

AN OVERSEER
Sir George Nicholls

MRS OVERTHEWAY
Mrs Julliana Horatia Ewing

OWANDA
Emma Robinson

OWEN
Jesse Appleton

OWEN, ASHFORD
Anne Charlotte Ogle

OWEN, CAROLINE DALE
Caroline Dale Snedeker

OWEN, JOHN
Frank Elias

OWEN, PHILIP
Judson Phillips

OWEN, TOM, THE BEE-
HUNTER
Thomas Bangs Thorpe

OWEN, WILLIAM
BICKERSTETH
Samuel Butler

OWENSON, SYDNEY
Lady Sydney Morgan

O'WILLIAMS, TUMMUS
John Collier

THE OWL
Charles Henry Bennett

OWL, EUGENE
Thomas Pilgrim

OWNER DRIVER
Edward Thomas Brown

OXENHAM, ELSIE
JEANNETTE
Elsie Jeannette Dunkerley

OXENHAM, ERICA
Erica Isobel Dunkerley

OXENHAM, JOHN
William Arthur Dunkerley

AN OXFORD BA
Hugh Chisholm

OXFORD CHIEL
Charles Lutwidge Dodgson

AN OXFORD GRADUATE
Sir Edwin Arnold
Arthur Wollaston Hutton
William Stainton Moses

AN OXFORD MAN AND A
WYKEHAMIST
Robert Blachford

AN OXFORD PUPIL
Alexander Dundas Ogilvy
Wedderburn

AN OXFORD TUTOR
William Warde Fowler
Francis John Jayne

MA OXON
William Stainton Moses

AN OXONIAN
Henry John Wilmot Buxton
Clifton Wilbraham Collins
John Duncombe
Samuel Reynolds Hole
Henry Scott Holland
Frederick Metcalfe
Stephen Weston
James White

OXONIENSIS
William Josiah Irons
Thomas Monro
Felicia Mary Frances Skene
Goldwin Smith
Francis Chenevix Trench

OXYMORE
John Ronald Reuel Tolkien

P

P.
Sir Richard Steele

P. A.
Philip Ayres

P. OF HAWICK
William Fowler

P. B. S.
Percy Bysshe Shelley

P. C. W.
Philip Carteret Webb

P. H.
Paul Hiffernan

P. H. I. Z. C. G. S.
Henry Fielding

P. P.
William Cowper
Peter John Martin

REV. P. P., MA
Richard Graves

P. P., A PARISH CLERK
John Arbuthnot

P___ P___ POET LAUREATE
George Daniel

P. T., ESQ.
Philip Thicknesse

PACIFICATOR
David Murray Hoffman

PACIFICUS
Joshua Reid Giddings
Alexander Hamilton
Frederick Scott Oliver
John Collett Ryland

PACKARD, CLARISSA
Caroline Gilman

PACKER, VIN
Marijane Meaker

PADDY
Henry McCluskey

PADGETT, LEWIS
Henry Kuttner with Catherine
Louise Moore

PAETS, CORNELIUS
Arthur Ashley Sykes

PAGANUS
L. Cranmer-Byng

PAGE, ABRAHAM , ESQ.
John Saunders Holt

PAGE, H. A.
Alexander Hay Japp

PAGE, KENNETH CALVIN
Lancelot Thomas Hogben

PAGE, MARCO
Harry Kurnitz

PAGE, R. EDISON
Ford Hermann Hueffer

PAGE, VICKI
Ruby Doreen Avey

A PAGE OF THE PRESENCE
Philip Withers

PAIGE, RICHARD
Dean R. Koontz

PAIN, BARRY
P. R. Guthrie

PAINSWORTH, W.
HARASSING
William Harrison Ainsworth

A PAINTER
Sir Joseph Noel Paton
Sir Martin Archer Shee

A PAKEHA MAORI
Frederick Edward Maning

PALAEOPHILUS MINOR
James Farquharson

PALATINE, TOM
Thomas Nash

PALEMON
Leonard Welsted

A PALESTINE EXPLORER
Claude Regnier Conder

PALETTE, PETER
Thomas Onwhyn

PALINURUS
Cyril Vernon Connolly

PALLET, PETER PAUL
Richard Warner

PALMER, DIANA
Susan E. S. Kyle

PALMER, LYNDE
Mrs Mary Louise Peebles

PALMER, POT-PIE
Edward Sanford

PAMEACH, RYHEN
Henry Peacham

PAMPHILUS
Joseph Priestley

PAMPHILUS, HESYCHIUS
Richard Brathwaite

MADAME PANACHE
Miss Frances Moore

PANBOURNE, OLIVER
Howard Rockey

PANSMOUZER, GOTLIEB
Theophilus Lindsey

PANSY
Isabella MacDonald Alden
Ida M. Loder Donisthorpe

PANTAGRUEL
Thomas Gibson Bowles

PANTARCH
Stephen Pearl Andrews

PAPINIAN
Charles Inglis

PARADISE, MARY
Dorothy Eden

PARAGRAPH, PETER
James Makittrick Adair

PARENS
Henry Craik

A PARENT
Louisa Mary Barwell

A PARIAH
Caroline Frances Cornwallis

PARIS, JOHN
Frank Trelawney Arthur
Ashton-Gwatkin

A PARISH PRIEST
Frederick William Faber
William Edward Scudamore

A PARISHIONER
John Waddington

A PARISHIONER OF ST
CHADS
Job Orton

A PARISHIONER OF ST
GEORGE'S PARISH,
EDINBURGH
James Bryce

A PARISHIONER OF THE
DOCTOR
Caleb Fleming

PARK, JORDAN
Frederick Pohl with C. M.
Kornbluth

PARKER, LESLIE
Angela Margaret Thirkell

PARKER, SETH
Phillip Haynes Lord

PARKES, LUCAS
John Beynon Harris

PARKHILL, JOHN
William Robert Cox

PARLANTE, PRISCILLA
The Hon. Mary Ann
Cavendish Bradshaw

PARLEY, PETER
Samuel Griswold Goodrich
William Martin
George Mogridge
Thomas Tegg

A PARLIAMENTARY
SECRETARY
Arthur Symonds

PARNELL, FRANCIS
Festus Pragnell

A PAROCHIAL BISHOP
John Willison

PARRESIASTES
Charles Edward De Coetlogon

PARRISH, FRANK
Roger Erskine Longrigg

A PARSON
Robert Herbert Story

PARSON H**NE
John Horne Tooke

PARSON LOT
Charles Kingsley

PARTINGTON, RUTH (or
MRS)
Benjamin Penhallow Shillaber

PARTRIDGE, ANTHONY
Edward Phillips Oppenheim

PARTRIDGE, SYDNEY
Kate Margaret Stone

PARVUS, CATO
Richard Heber

PASCAL THE YOUNGER
Pierce Connelly

PASHA, MOHAMMED
William Wirt Howe

PASQUIN
Paul Allen
Henry Fielding

PASQUIN, ANTHONY
John Williams

PASQUIN, PETER
William Henry Pyne

PASQUINO
James Fairfax McLaughlin

PASQUINUS, PETRUS, C. P.
M.
Thomas Comber

PASSANTE, DOM
John Russell Fearn

PASTEL
George Frederick Pardon

PASTIME
Henry Jones

PASTNOR, PAUL
James Buckham

PASTON, GEORGE
Emily Morse Symonds

A PASTOR
Alexander Robert Charles
Dallas
Joshua Noble Danforth
Thomas Frognall Dibdin
Jason Morse
John Turner Sargent
Ichabod Smith Spencer

PASTOR, TONY
Harlan P. Halsey

PASTOR FELIX
Arthur John Lockhart

PASTORINI, SIGNOR
Charles Walmesley

A PASTOR'S WIFE
Mrs Martha Stone Hubbell

PASTY, CAROLINA PETTY
Elizabeth Cobbold

THE PATENTEE
Oliver Abbott Shaw

PATER
John Benjamin Stone

PATERFAMILIAS
Matthew James Higgins

PATERSON, PETER
James Glass Bertram

THE PATHFINDER OF THE
ROCKY MOUNTAINS
John Charles Fremont

PATRICK, JOHN
John Patrick Goggan

PATRICK, KEATS
Walter Karig

PATRICK, MAXINE
Patricia Anne Maxwell

PATRICK, Q.
Richard Wilson Webb with
Hugh Callingham Wheeler

PATRICK, SUSAN
Patricia Denise Clark

PATRICOLA
John Toland

A PATRIOT
Guy L. B. Du Maurier
Joseph Priestley

PATROL-LEADER
Francis Doyne Dwyer

PATTERSON, HARRY
Henry Patterson

PATTIESON, PETER
Sir Walter Scott

PATTISON, MRS MARK
Lady Emilia Francis Strong
Dilke

PATTON, FRANK
Raymond A. Palmer

PAUL
Sir Walter Scott

PAUL, BARBARA
Barbara Ovstedal

PAUL, JOHN
Charles Henry Webb

PAULINUS
John Jebb
Joseph Priestley
Robert Seagrave

PAULUS PURGANTIUS
PEDASCULUS
George Alexander Stevens

PAX
Mary Cholmondeley

PAXTON, LOIS
Lois Dorothea Low

PAXTON, PHILIP
Samuel Adams Hammett

PAYE, ROBERT
Margaret Long

PAYNE, ALAN (or RACHEL ANN)
John William Jakes

PAYNE, WILLIAM
Matthew Davenport Hill

PEABODY, MRS MARK
Mrs Metta Victoria Victor

PEACOCK, NATHANIEL
Tobias George Smollett

PEARL
Mrs Margaret Wolfe Hungerford

PEARL, IRENE
Irene Guyonvarch

PEARSON, MARTIN
Donald A. Wollheim

THE PEASANT BARD
Josiah D. Canning

PECCATOR MAXIMUS
Henry Elford Luxmoore

PECCAVI
Robert Ranke Graves

PECK, GAVILAN
Henry Pope

THE PEDESTRIAN
Edward Payson Weston

PEEPING TOM
Samuel Kettell
Henry Ryder Knapp

A PEER IN SCOTLAND
Sir George Mackenzie

A PEER OF THE REALM
Patrick Murray

A PEER'S SON
George Douglas Campbell

PEERADEAL, PAUL PUCK
Sir William Cusac Smith

PEERIE, MOSES
Robert Herbert Story

PE-GAS-US
Charles Clark

PELAGIUS
Joseph Priestley

PELHAM, HENRY
Edward George Earle Lytton Bulwer-Lytton

PELHAM, MRS (or Miss) MARGARET
Sir Richard Phillips

PELHAM, MARY
Dorothy Kilner

PELL, FRANKLYN
Frank E. Pellegrini

PEMBERTON, NAN
Nina Pykare

PEN, A., ESQ.
John Leech

PENDENNIS, ARTHUR
William Makepeace Thackeray

PENDENNIS, LAUNCELOT
Duke John Young

PENDRAGON
Henry J. M. Sampson

PENFEATHER, ANNABEL
Susan Fenimore Cooper

PENHOLDER
Edward Eggleston

A PENINSULAR MEDALLIST
Thomas Boys

A PENITENT PERI
George C. Pearson

PENLAKE, RICHARD
Percy R. Salmon

PENMARE, WILLIAM
Mavis Elizabeth Nisot

PENN, ARTHUR
James Brander Matthews

PENN, WILLIAM
Stephen Colwell
Jeremiah Evarts

PENNOT, REV. PETER
William Marshall Fitt Round

A PENNSYLVANIA FARMER
John Dickinson

A PENNSYLVANIAN
Mathew Carey
John Kintzing Kane
Benjamin Rush

PENROSE, LLEWELLYN
Rev. John Eagles

PENSEVAL, GUY
George Darley

THE PENSILVANIAN
William Penn

THE PENSIONER
James Abercromby

PENTECOST, HUGH
Judson Philips

PENTWEAZLE, EBENEZER
Christopher Smart

THE PEOPLE'S FRIEND
Daniel Drake

PEPPER, K. N.
James W. Morris

PEPPER, TOM
Charles Frederick Briggs

PEPPER, THOMAS (or ENSIGN)
Ellen Wood

PEPPERBOX, PETER
Thomas Green Fessenden

PEPPERCORN, H.
Richard Harris Barham

PEPPERCORN, PETER
Thomas Love Peacock

PEPPERGRASS, PAUL
John Boyce

PEPPERPOD, PIP
Charles Warren Stoddard

PEQUOT
Charles March

THE PERAMBULATING PHILOSOPHER
Gilbert Abbott A'Beckett

PERCH, PHILEMON
Richard Malcolm Johnston

PERCIVAL, ANNA
Eleanor Alice Hibbert

PERCIVAL, G.
George Percival Best

PERCY, CHARLES HENRY
Dodie (Dorothy Gladys) Smith

PERCY, EDWARD
Edward Percy Smith

PERCY, FLORENCE
Elizabeth Chase Akers

PERCY, REUBEN
Thomas Byerley

PERCY, SHOLTO
Joseph Clinton Robertson

PERCY, STEPHEN
Joseph Cundall

PERDITUS
G. S. Fisher

PEREGOY, CALVIN
Thomas Calvert McClary

PEREGRINE
Gage Earle Freeman
John Paget

PEREGRINUS
Laurence Oliphant
George Carless Swayne

PERENNIS
James Henry Leigh Hunt

PERIPATETIC PHILOSOPHER
Marcus Andrew Hislop Clarke

PERIWINKLE, PAUL
Percy Bolingbroke St John

PERIWINKLE, PETER
Thomas Green Fessenden

PERK, ABNER
Alexander Stevenson Twombly

PERKINS, ABIGAIL
James Otis Kaler

PERKINS, ELI
Melville de Lancy Landon

PERLEY
Benjamin Perley Poore

PEROWNE, BARRY
Philip Atkey

PERRIN, CLYDE
Howard Vincent O'Brien

PERRY, CLAY
Clair Willard Perry

PERRY, WILL
W. J. Weatherby

PERRY, CAPT. WILLIAM B.
William Perry Brown

A PERSIAN IN ENGLAND
Lord George Lyttelton

PERSIC, PEREGRINE
James Justinian Morier

PERSIUS, PAUL
William Henry Ireland

A PERSON CONCERN'D
John Colbatch

A PERSON FORMERLY CONCERNED IN A PUBLICK BREWHOUSE IN LONDON, BUT FOR TWENTY YEARS PAST HAS RESIDED IN THE COUNTRY
William Ellis

A PERSON OF DISTINCTION
Patrick Murray

A PERSON OF GREAT LEARNING AND JUDGMENT
Sir Matthew Hale

A PERSON OF HONOR
William Cavendish

A PERSON OF HONOUR
Roger Boyle
William Brouncker
Henry Carey
John Gauden
Edward Herbert
Edward Hyde
Daniel Kenrick
Roger North
Roger Palmer
John Robartes
George Savile
Thomas Scott
John Somers
Jonathan Swift
Sir William Temple
George Villiers
Sir William Waller
John Wilmot

A PERSON OF HONOUR AND EMINENT MINISTER OF STATE
Arthur Annesley

A PERSON OF HONOUR AND PIETY
Arthur Capel

A PERSON OF HONOUR IN THE COUNTY OF NORFOLK
Roger North

A PERSON OF LEARNING AND PIETY
Charles Morton

A PERSON OF NOTE WHO RESIDED MANY YEARS THERE
John Robinson

A PERSON OF QUALITIE
John Pordage

A PERSON OF QUALITY
Arthur Annesley
Edmund Bohun
Roger Boyle
Sir Charles Cotterell
Nicholas Cross
John Dennis
George Digby
Sir Kenelm Digby
Richard Hampden
John Hervey
Sir Robert Howard
William Lloyd
Sir John Monson
John Pomfret
James Ralph
William Ramesay
John Rowland
Sarah Scott

Elkanah Settle
John Sheffield
Jonathan Swift
Edward Wetenhall

A PERSON OF SOME TASTE
James Ralph

PERSONNE
Felix Gregory De Fontaine
Theodora Elizabeth Lynch

PERTINAX PARTICULAR
Tobias Watkins

PERTINAX PERIOD & CO.
Joseph Tinker Buckingham

PERVIL, DRURY
Edward Gordon Craig

PETER
George Alexander Stevens

PETER OF PONTEFRACT
Richard Graves

PETERLEY, DAVID
Richard Pennington

PETERS, BILL
William Peter McGivern

PETERS, BRIAN
Edward George Stoke

PETERS, ELIZABETH
Barbara Mertz

PETERS, ELLIS
Edith Mary Pargeter

PETERS, GEOFFREY
Madelyn Palmer

PETERS, LIONEL
Arthur Catherall

PETERS, LUDOVIC
Peter Ludwig Brent

A PETITIONING CLERGYMAN
John Disney

PETRE, OLINTHUS
William Maginn

PETRIE, RHONA
Eileen-Marie Duell

PEUDE-SER, DON DIEGO
James Mabbe

PEYTON, K. M.
Kathleen Wendy Peyton

PFAAL, HANS
Edgar Allan Poe

PHAIR, KUNQUER
Frederick Edward Hulme

PHANTASTES
William Hazlitt

PHANTOM, FELIX
Robert Heron

PHELPS, MRS S. B.
Frances Irene B. Griswold

PHIL. ARCHIMEDES
William Wilkins

PHIL. CHRISTIANUS
William Chappell

PHIL-ELIA
Charles Lamb

PHIL-ICON-ERUS
John Norris

PHILADELPHUS
Saxe Bannister
Joanna Southcott
Samuel Whelpley

PHILAGATHOS
Ezra Stiles

PHILAGATHUS
John Haven Dexter
Samuel Rolle
Daniel Taylor

PHILALETHEIA
Charles Paynter

PHILALETHES
Thomas Kingsmill Abbott
James Beezley
Joseph Besse
Richard Bentley
James Boswell
Whitelocke Bulstrode
John Cameron
Archibald Campbell
Richard Challoner
Edmund Curll
Patrick Delaney
Thomas Delaune
William Abernethy Drummond
Henry Fielding
William Goode
John Hancock
William Hazlitt
Sir Richard Hill
Sir Robert John Wilmot
  Horton
John Jones
Nathaniel Lardner
William Lauder
Charles Leslie
Charles Lloyd
Cotton Mather
John Pomfret
Reuben Sherwood
Thomas Stackhouse
Arthur Ashley Sykes
Daniel Taylor
Thomas Taylor
Thomas Twining
John Wesley

PHILALETHES
  CANTABRIGIENSIS
Zachary Grey
John Jackson
James Jurin
John Kaye
Thomas Turton

PHILALETHES
  LONDINIENSIS
Caleb Flemimg

PHILALETHES MA OXON.
Robert Fellowes

PHILALETHES RUSTICANS
Richard Shepherd

PHILALETHES RUSTICUS
William Asplin

PHILALEUTHEROS
Caleb Fleming

PHILANACTOPHIL
Edmund Bolton

PHILANAGNOSTES
  CRITICUS
Thomas Herne

PHILANAX
John Norris

PHILANDER
John Cameron
David Williams

PHILANDER, THEOPHILUS
John Cameron

PHILANGLIA
James Scott

PHILANGLUS
Sir Frederick Morton Eden
William Penn
John Pennyman
William Petyt

PHILANTHROPOS
John Thomas Barber Beaumont
Richard Carlile
William Ladd
Thomas Mortimer
Richard Pockrich
Morgan John Rhees
Thomas Wakefield

PHILANTHROPUM
Mark Hildesley

PHILANTHROPUS
Joseph Besse
Thomas Bott
John Locke

PHILANTHROPUS
  LONDINENSIS
Daniel Scott

PHILANTHROPUS
  OXONIENSIS
Thomas Morgan

PHILANTROPICOS
  PHILALETHES
Neil Douglas

PHILARCHAISMOS
Thomas Sharp

PHILARENUS
James Howell

PHILARET
John Dunton

PHILARETES
Anthony Collins
John Gilbert Cooper

PHILARETES, PHILIPPUS
Thomas Comber

PHILARETUS
Robert Boyle
Edmund Curll
John Whitehead

PHILARGYRUS
William Rider

PHILARGYRUS CANTAB.
Joshua Barnes

PHILAUTUS
Nathaniel Lancaster

PHILEBUS
John Leslie Barford

PHILELEUTH. BANGOR, V.
  E. B.
Thomas Foxcroft

PHILELEUTHERUS
  ANGLICANUS
John William Donaldson

PHILELEUTHERUS
  BRITANNICUS
John Hildrop

PHILELEUTHERUS
  CANTABRIGIENSIS
Thomas Herne

PHILELEUTHERUS
  CHRISTIANUS
Thomas Broughton

PHILELEUTHERUS
  DEVONIENSIS
Thomas Northmore

PHILELEUTHERUS
  DUBLINIENSIS
Patrick Delany

PHILELUETHERUS
  LIPSIENSIS
Richard Bentley

PHILELEUTHERUS
LONDINENSIS
John Burton

PHILELEUTHERUS
LONDONIENSIS
Zachary Pearce

PHILELEUTHERUS
NORFOLCIENSIS
Samuel Parr

PHILEMON
Henry Coventry

PHILENIA, A LADY OF
BOSTON
Sarah Wentworth Morton

PHILHELLEN ETONENSIS
Lancelot Shadwell

PHILINDUS
Friederich Max Muller
Herbert William Wood

PHILIPPES, MORGAN,
BACHELOR OF
DIVINITIE
John Leslie

PHILIPPICUS
John Warner

PHILIRENES
John Nalson

PHILLIP, ALBAN M.
Philip Bertram Murray Allan

PHILLIPS, FRANK
Philip Rooney

PHILLIPS, MARK
Randall Garrett with Larry
Mark Harris

PHILLIPS, OSBORNE
Leon Barcynski

PHILLIPS, RICHARD
Philip Kendred Dick

PHILLIPS, ROG.
Roger Phillips Graham

PHILLIPS, WARD
Howard Phillips Lovecraft

PHILLIPUS
John Gibson Lockhart

PHILMORE, R.
Herbert Edmund Howard

PHILO
Joseph Proud

PHILO-AFRICANUS
Robert Needham Cust

PHILO-BIBLOS
John Wesley

PHILO-BRITANNIAE
Charles Cotton

PHILO-BRITANNUS
Charles Davenant

PHILO-BUCHANANUS
John Love

PHILO-CALEDON
Andrew Fletcher

PHILO-CATO
Matthew L. Davis

PHILO-CELT
Courtenay Edmund Boyle

PHILO-CHRISTIANUS
William Brough

PHILO CHRISTUS
Edwin Abbott Abbott

PHILO-CRITICUS
Francis Hare

PHILO-DRAMATICUS
William Harness

PHILO HIBERNICUS
Gorges Edmond Howard

PHILO MUSA
James Currie

PHILO-MUSUS
Nicholas Amhurst
Thomas Guidott

PHILO-NAUTICUS
Lawrence Hynes (O')Halloran

PHILO PACIFICUS
Noah Worcester

PHILO-PATRIAE
Eustace Budgell

PHILO-ROSKELYNSIS
Robert Forbes

PHILO-SCOTUS
Duncan Forbes

PHILO-SINENSIS
Walter Henry Medhurst

PHILO-TURK
Arthur Nicholson

PHILO-VERITAS
Thomas D'Arcy M'Gee

PHILOBIBLICUS
CANTABRIGIENSIS
John Chapman

PHILOBIBLIUS
Linus Pierpont Brockett
Richard Watson

PHILOBIBLOS
Thomas Rodd

PHILOBIBLOS, JOHN
James Heywood

PHILOCATHOLICUS
John Wiche

PHILOCEPOS
John Evelyn

PHILOCHELIDON
Thomas Ignatius Maria Forster

PHILOCOSMOS
Hamlet Clark

PHILOCRIN, SAMPFILIUS, Z.
Y. X. W.
William Sampson

PHILOCRITICUS
CANTABRIGIENSIS
John Jackson

PHILOFLUENTIMECHANAL
GEGEOMASTROLONGO
William Emerson

PHILOGENES PALEDONIUS
Richard Brathwaite

PHILOGRANTUS
James Henry Monk

PHILOKALIST
Felix Paul Wierzbicki

PHILOMALUS
James Whitehead

T. M. PHILOMATH
Jonathan Swift

PHILOMATHES
Henoch Clapham

PHILOMELA
Mrs Elizabeth Rowe

PHILOMORUS
John Howard Marsden

PHILOMUSUS, BASILIUS
Robert Waring

PHILOPATRIA
Mrs Rachel Frances A. D. Lee
Thomas Paine
Joshua Parry

PHILOPATRIS
Charles Blount
Thomas Burgess
Sir Josiah Child
John Dunton

PHILOPATRIS VARVICENSIS
Samuel Parr

PHILOPENES
John Huddleston

PHILOPHILUS
PARRESIASTES
Henry More

PHILOPHRASTES
Sir Ralph Freeman

PHILOPOLIS
Thomas Williamson Peile

PHILOPOLITES
Cotton Mather
Benjamin Prescott
William Prynne

PHILOPROPOS
William Duncombe

PHILOPSYCHUS
PHILALETHES
Matthew Poole

PHILORTHOS
William Frederick Poole

PHILOS
James Challen

A PHILOSOPHER
Charles Babbage

PHILOTECHNICUS MISO-
MIMIDES
Paul Hiffernan

PHILOTECHNUS
Sir John Leslie

PHILOTHEORUS
Caleb Fleming
Richard Kempenfelt

PHILOTHEOS
PHYSIOLOGUS
Thomas Tryon

PHILOTHEUS, ABRAHAM
Abraham Wright

PHILOXENUS SECUNDUS
Stephen Weston

PHILOXON
Richard Rawlinson

PHILROYE, HUMPHREY
Sir Richard Steele

PHIPS, HENRY
Edward Gordon Craig

PHIZ
Hablot Knight Browne

PHIZ, FRANCIS
Francis Edward Smedley

PHLOGOBOMBUS,
TERENTIUS
Samuel Benjamin Helbert
Judah

PHOCION
George Ticknor Curtis
Alexander Hamilton
Thomas Hartley

PHOENIX, JOHN
George Horatio Derby

PHOSPHORUS
William Edmonstoune Aytoun

PHOTINUS
Joseph Priestley

A PHYSICIAN
Thomas Foster Barham
James Warburton Begbie
William Cadogan
Robert Couper
Sir Philip Crampton
George Darling
Thomas Ignatius Maria Forster
John Gardner
Marshall Hall
James Henry
Alexander Hunter
James Jurin
James Mackenzie
Charles Lewis Meryon
John Ayrton Paris
Benjamin Rush
John Rutty
Anthony Todd Thomson
Robert Willis
Andrew Wilson

A PHYSICIAN IN THE WEST
INDIES
James Grainger

A PHYSICIAN IN TOWN
Daniel Cox

A PHYSICIAN OF
PHILADELPHIA
William Edmunds Horner

PHYSICUS
George John Romanes

PICKERING, PERCIVAL
Mrs Anna Maria Wilhelmina
Stirling

PICKLE, PEREGRINE
George Putnam Upton

PICKLE-HERRING, PETER
PATRICIUS
George Darley

PICTON, BERNARD
Bernard Knight

PICTOR IGNOTUS
William Blake

PIE, BRIAN
Arthur Reed Ropes

A PIECE OF AN ANTIQUARY
Philip Thicknesse

PIED PIPER
Sir Joseph Percival William
Mallalieu

PIERO, GIULIO
Edward Gordon Craig

PIERROT
George Arnold

PIGGOTT, WILIAM
Hubert Wales

PIKE, MORTON
David Harold Parry

PIKE, ROBERT L.
Robert Lloyd Fish

PILEUS QUADRATUS
Stephen Reay

A PILGRIM
Richard Sinclair Brooke
Edward Brotherton
George Barrell Cheever

A PILGRIM FROM NEW
YORK TO OLD ROME
William Lockhart

THE PILGRIM GOOD-
INTENT
Noah Worcester

THE PILGRIM IN LONDON
John Fisher Murray

A PILGRIM IN THE HOLY
LAND
Edward Falkener

PILGRIM, ANNE
Mabel Esther Allan

PILGRIM, DAVID
John Leslie Palmer with Hilary
A. St George Saunders

PILGRIM, DERRAL
Hugh Zachary

PILGRIM, PETER
Robert Montgomery Bird

PILOT
William Earl Johns

PILPAY JUNIOR
Thomas Carlyle

PINDAR
Edmund George Harvey

PINDAR, JONATHAN, ESQ.
Philip Freneau

PINDAR, PAUL, GENT.
John Yonge Akerman

PINDAR, PETER
C. F. Lawler
John Wolcot

PINDAR, PETER, JUN.
John Agg

PINE, CUYLER
Ellen Peck

PINE, M. S.
Mary Paulina Finn

PINE, WILLIAM
Terence William Harknett

PINNA Y RUIZ, DONNA
TERESA
William Preston

PIOT (or PYOTT), LAZARUS
Anthony Munday (or Mundy)

PIOZZI, HESTER LYNCH
Hester Lynch Thrale

PIPER, EVELYN
Miriam Modell

PIPER, PAUL
Seymour Eaton

PIPER, PETER
Theo Lang

PIPES, THOMAS
William Maginn

MR PIPS
Percival Leigh

PISANUS FRAXI
Henry Spencer Ashbee

PISCATOR
Charles Cotton
Walter Henry
William Hughes
Thomas Pike Lathy
George Philip Rigney Pulman

PISO, LUCIUS MANLIUS
William Ware

PISTOPHILUS
PHILECCLESIA
Benjamin McDowell

PITCAIRN, FRANK
Claud Cockburn

PITCHER
Arthur Morris Binstead

PITT, WILLIAM
Robert Wickliffe

PITTS, THOMAS, GENT.
John Tutchin

PLACE, BENJAMIN
Edward Thring

PLAGUE 'EM, PETER
John Hamilton Reynolds

PLAIDY, JEAN
Eleanor Alice Hibbert

PLAIN, HENRY
James Anderson

PLAIN, TIMOTHY
Moncrieff Threepland

A PLAIN, HONEST LAYMAN
Edward King

PLAIN-DEALER, MANLY
Edward Ward

A PLAIN MAN
William Combe
David Malloch
Henry William Pullen

A PLAIN THINKER
Mortimer O'Sullivan
Samuel O'Sullivan

PLAISTER, GABRIEL
STICKING
Richard Warner

PLANTAGENET
William Bromet

A PLANTER
William Cleland
Edward Long

PLATTS, A. MONMOUTH
Anthony Berkeley Cox

A PLAY-GOER
Joseph Norton Ireland

PLAYER, ROBERT
Robert Furneaux Jordan

PLINY THE YOUNGEST
Stanley Kidder Wilson

PLOMINGO
John Robinson

PLOUGH, PETER
James Strachen Barty

A PLOUGHIST
Samuel Pegge

A PLOUGHMAN
Tristram Burges

PLOUGHMAN, JOHN
Charles Haddon Spurgeon

PLOUGHSHARE, JOHN
John Wolcot

PLOWMAN, PIERS
Patrick Kavanagh

PLUG, PERCIVAL, R. N.
James Hannay

PLUM, JENNIFER
Michael Kurland

PLUM, PATRICK
Michael Anthony McConville

PLUMBLINE, EVERARD
Edward Gordon Craig

PLUMMER, BEN
David Ernest Bingley

PLUNDER
Leonard McNally

PLUNKETT, CHARLES HARE
Arthur Christopher Benson

PLUNKETT, JAMES
James Plunkett Kelly

PLUSH, MR J___S
William Makepeace Thackeray

PLYMLEY, PETER
Sydney Smith

A POET
James Montgomery
Laughton Osborn

POET FERUEAT OF THE
BREIDDEN
John Freeman Milward
Dovaston

THE POET LAUREATE
William Makepeace Thackeray

THE POET OF TITCHFIELD
STREET
Ezra Pound

POET STUTTER
Thomas D'Urfey

POINGDESTRE, E.
Edward Ernest Foxwell

POLESWORTH, SIR
HUMPHREY
Jonathan Swift

POLFREMAN, PHILIP
Edward Gordon Craig

POLIARCHUS
Sir Charles Cotterell

POLICEMAN X 54
William Makepeace Thackeray

A POLITICAL DISSENTER
William Brighty Rands

A POLITICAL ECONOMIST
John Ramsay MacCulloch

POLITICUS
James Cheetham

POLIUTO
Frank B. Wilkie

POLLEX, D.
William Allingham

POLLOCK, MARY
Enid Mary Blyton

POLLUX
Robert Ranke Graves

POLO, MARCO, JUNIOR
Benjamin Disraeli

POLYANTHUS
John Wilson

POLYPUS
Eaton Stannard Barrett

POMEROY, BRICK
Marcus M. Pomeroy

PONDER, PATRICIA
Patricia Anne Maxwell

PONDER, REV. PETER
William Bell

PONSONBY, MONTAGU VERNON
Alexander Kenealy

PONT
Graham Laidler

PONTOOSUC
Ensign Hosmer Kellogg

POOLE, MICHAEL
Reginald Heber Poole

A POOR MAN
Rowland Detrosier

THE POOR MAN'S ADVOCATE
Thomas Spence

POOR OLD TOM OF BEDLAM
Luke Milbourne

POOR RICHARD
Benjamin Franklin

A POOR-RICH MAN
John Berrien Lindsley

POOR ROBERT THE SCRIBE
Charles Miner

POOR ROBIN
William Winstanley

POPLAR, ANTHONY (used by the early editors of Dublin University Magazine)
Isaac Butt
Durham Dunlop
Charles Stuart Stanford

POPLICOLA
Charles Brockden Brown

PORCUPINE, PETER
William Cobbett

PORCUPINE, PROTEUS
C. Torrop

PORCUPINUS PELAGIUS
McNamara Morgan

PORCUSTUS
Henry Swinburne

PORLOCK, MARTIN
Philip MacDonald

PORTAL, ELLIS
Bruce Allen Powe

PORTE CRAYON
David Hunter Strother

PORTER, NINA
Nina Pykare

PORTFIRE
Henry Dunnicliffe

PORTIA
Mrs Abigail Adams

PORTIUS
Samuel Pegge

THE PORTRAIT PAINTER
Mary Anne Browne

POSITIVE, PETER
James Montgomery

POSSUM, PETER
Richard Rowe

POST, MORTIMER
Walter Blair

A POST-OFFICE MAN
Edward Bernard Lewin Hill

POTIPHAR, PAUL
George William Curtis

POTTER, PLATT
John Willard

POWDAVIE
Peter Robert Drummond

POWEL, R., THE PUPPET-SHOW MAN
Sir Thomas Burnet

POWELL, NEIL
Brian Innes

POWELL, RICHARD STILLMAN
Ralph Henry Barbour

POWER, CECIL
Charles Grant Blairfindie Allen

POWER, MICHAEL
David Esdaile Walker

POWERS, M. L.
Edwin Charles Tubb

POWERS, NORA
Nina Pykare

POY
Percy Hutton Fearon

POYNTZ, ALBANY
Mrs Catherine Frances Grace Gore

POYNTZ, LAUNCE
Frederick Whittaker

A PRACTICAL BANKER
James B. Congdon

A PRACTICAL FARMER
John Armstrong
David Henry
John Claudius Loudon

A PRACTICAL FLORICULTURIST
Sydenham Teak Edwards

A PRACTICAL GARDENER
Thomas Green Fessenden

A PRACTICAL HAND
John Hill Burton

A PRACTICAL TEACHER
Benjamin Greenleaf

PRACTITIONER OF MORE THAN FIFTY YEARS EXPERIENCE IN THE ART OF ANGLING
John Bartlett

PRAED, LANDOR
George Jacob Holyoake

A PRAEPOSTER
Sir Francis George Newbolt

PRATTLER
Ambrose Bierce

A PREACHER OF THE GOSPEL
Peter Hately Waddell

A PREBEND OF THE CHURCH OF CANTERBURY
Peter Du Moulin

A PREBENDARY OF YORK
Thomas Sharp

A PRE-DISRUPTION ELDER
Benjamin Bell

PREEDY, GEORGE R.
Margaret Long

PRENDERGAST, PAUL
Douglas William Jerrold
Percival Leigh

PRENTIS, RICHARD
James Evershed Agate

PRESBUTEROS
Richard Warner

A PRESBYTER
James Carlile
Henry Duncan
Edward Edwards
Thomas Haweis

PRESBYTER ACADEMICUS
Thomas Fowler

PRESBYTER CATHOLICUS
William Harness

PRESBYTER CICESTRENSIS
Henry Latham

A PRESBYTER IN THE DIOCESE OF CANTERBURY
Arthur Philip Perceval

A PRESBYTER OF THE CHURCH
Robert Crawford Dillon

A PRESBYTER OF THE CHURCH OF ENGLAND
William Binckes
John Bold
John Boswell
Clement Cruttwell
Samuel Grascome
Zachary Grey
Francis Hare
Thomas Haweis
Matthew Hole
Walter Farquhar Hook
John Jackson
William Jones
Simon Lowth
Nathaniel Marshall
Richard Mayo
Richard Newton
Arthur Philip Perceval
William Robertson
William Sclater
John Sharp
William Sherlock
Augustus Montague Toplady

A PRESBYTER OF THE CHURCH OF SCOTLAND
Alexander Monro

A PRESBYTER OF THE DIOCESE OF ILLINOIS
Hugh Miller Thompson

A PRESBYTER OF THE DIOCESE OF LONDON
William Berriman

A PRESBYTER OF THE DIOCESE OF MASSACHUSETTS
Jonathan Mayhew Wainwright

A PRESBYTERIAN
John Brown
James Porter

A PRESBYTERIAN MINISTER OF LONDON
George Walker

A PRESBYTERIAN SCOT
Alexander Patrick Stewart

PRESBYTERUS
Robert Hussey

PRESCOTT, CALEB
David Ernest Bingley

PRESCOTT, DOROTHY
Agnes Blake Poor

PRESCOTT, E. LIVINGSTONE
Katharine Edith Spicer-Jay

MRS PRESIDENT
Lady Mary Wortley Montagu

THE PRESIDENT OF KENYON COLLEGE
Philander Chase

THE PRESIDENT OF THE BOARD OF AGRICULTURE
Sir John Sinclair

PRESLAND, JOHN
Gladys Bendit

PRESTON, GEORGE F.
John Byrne Leicester Warren with George Fortescue (used jointly for one book, Poems, in 1859, but thereafter used by Warren alone)

PRESTON, JANE
Reginald George Thomas

PRESTON, PAUL
Thomas Picton

PRESTON, RICHARD
Jack Lindsay

PREVOST, FRANCIS
Henry Francis Prevost Battersby

PRIAM
Charles James Collins

PRICE, EVADNE
Helen Zenna Smith

PRICEMAN, JAMES
Winifred Margaretta Kirkland

A PRIEST
Charles Seager

A PRIEST OF THE CATHOLIKE AND ROMAN CHURCH
Lawrence Anderton

A PRIEST OF THE CHURCH OF ENGLAND
John Mackenzie Bacon
Hilkiah Bedford
William Maskell

John Mason Neale

A PRIEST OF THE DIOCESE
John Mason Neale

A PRIEST OF THE DIOCESE OF EXETER
Morris Joseph Fuller

A PRIEST OF THE ENGLISH CHURCH
John Mason Neale

A PRIEST OF THE UNIVERSITY OF CAMBRIDGE
John Chapman

THE PRIG
Thomas Longueville

PRIGGINS, PETER
Joseph Thomas James Hewlett

PRIM, OBADIAH
Frederick Albert Winsor

PRIM, SAMUEL
Edward Gordon Craig

PRIMCOCK, A.
James Ralph

PRINCE OUTISKY
George Bunsen

THE PRINCE OF THE INFERNAL REGIONS
John Campbell

THE PRINCIPAL OF McGILL COLLEGE, MONTREAL
Sir John William Dawson

THE PRINCIPAL OF ST MARY HALL, OXFORD
Drummond Percy Chase

PRINCIPIIS OBSTA
Samuel Adams

PRINTER'S DEVIL
Charles James Lever

PRIOR, J., BUTLER
Thomas Humphrey Ward

PRIOR, JAMES
James Prior Kirk

PRIOR, SAMUEL
John Galt

PRISCILLA
Ann Jebb

PRISCILLA ****
Priscilla Wakefield

A PRISON MATRON
Miss Mary Carpenter
Frederick William Robinson

A PRISON VISITOR
Felicia Mary Frances Skene

PRIVATE
Benjamin Franklin De Costa

PRIVATE 19022
Frederic Manning

A PRIVATE CITIZEN
Noah Webster

A PRIVATE DRAGOON
Archibald Forbes

A PRIVATE GENTLEMAN
Thomas Allan
John Cartwright
Daniel Defoe
Edward Synge

A PRIVATE MAN
Francis Wollaston

A PRIVATE OF THE THIRTY EIGHTH ARTIST'S AND MEMBER OF THE ALPINE CLUB
John Barrow

A PRIVATE SOLDIER
John Ryder

A PRIVATE TUTOR
David James Vaughan

PRIVATEER
Charles James Foster

A PRIVY COUNCILLOR
John Satterfield Sandars

A PROBATIONER OF THE FREE CHURCH OF SCOTLAND
Peter Hately Waddell

PROBUS
Thomas Chatterton
David Lee Child

PROBUS BRITANICUS
Samuel Johnson

PROBYN, ERICSON
Percy Robinson

PROCTOR, EVERITT
Rutherford George Montgomery

PROCUL
Robert Stephen Hawker

A PROFESSED ENEMY TO PERSECUTION
Samuel Bold

A PROFESSIONAL FRIEND
John Abernethy

A PROFESSIONAL MUSICIAN
Miss Meredith Brown

A PROFESSIONAL PAINTER
John Zephaniah Bell

PROFESSOR LUMPWITZ
Henry William Bunbury

PROFESSOR PORSON
Samuel Taylor Coleridge with Robert Southey

PROFESSOR X
Daniel Joseph Boorstin

A PROFESSOR OF CHRISTIANITY
Martin Madan

A PROFESSOR OF MUSIC
Edward Miller

A PROFESSOR OF POLITICAL ECONOMY
Thomas Edward Cliffe Leslie

A PROFESSOR OF SURGERY
John Obadiah Justamond

PROLE, LOZANIA
Ursula Bloom

PROLIX, PEREGRINE
Philip Houlbrooke Nicklin

A PROMINENT LONDON JOURNALIST
Frank Harrison Hill

THE PROMOTER OF THE SUNDAY BAND
Sir William Domville

PROMOTION BY MERIT
William Angus

A PROPRIETOR OF INDIAN STOCK
James Silk Buckingham

A PROSER
Charles James Cannon
Chauncey Hare Townshend

PROSPERO AND CALIBAN
Frederick William Rolfe

A PROTESTANT
John Billingsley
John Bowden
Calvin Colton
George Croly
Robert Daly
Caleb Fleming
Thomas Hartwell Horne
Andrew Marvell
Richard Monckton Milnes
John Owen
Robert Shirra
Edward Smedley

A PROTESTANT, A LOVER OF PEACE AND PROSPERITY OF THE NATION
Sir Charles Wolseley

A PROTESTANT CLERGYMAN
Michael Vicary

A PROTESTANT DISSENTER
Samuel Bourn
William Christie

A PROTESTANT DISSENTER OF OLD ENGLAND
Caleb Fleming

A PROTESTANT DISSENTING MINISTER
Caleb Fleming

A PROTESTANT DIVINE
John Williams

A PROTESTANT EPISCOPALIAN
Francis Lister Hawks
William Jay

A PROTESTANT OF THE CHURCH OF ENGLAND
John Williams

A PROTESTANT OF THE SCHOOL OF THE REFORMATION
James Bryce

A PROTESTANT PEER OF THE REALM OF ENGLAND
Anthony Ashley Cooper

A PROTESTANT PERSON OF QUALITY
Richard Burthogge

A PROTESTING CATHOLIC
Alexander Geddes

PROTEUS
Wilfred Scawen Blunt

PROTHEROE, JOHN K.
Mrs Cecil (Ada Elizabeth) Chesterton

PROUDFOOT, WALTER
John George Haslette Vahey

THE PROWLER
Archibald D. Gordon

MR PRY
Maurice Willson Disher

PRY, PAUL
Sydney Terence Burke
Thomas Hill

PRYDE, ANTHONY
Agnes Russell Weekes with Rose Kirkpatrick Weekes

PRYNNE, ARTHUR
Joel Munsell

PRYNNE, PEREGRINE
J. Cahnac

PRYOR, VANESSA
Chelsea Quinn Yarbro

PSEUDO-AFRICANUS
John Buchan

A PUBLIC SCHOOL BOY
Richard Harrison

PUBLICOLA
John Quincy Adams
Robert Harding Evans
William Johnson Fox
Sir Benjamin Hobhouse
Jonathan Swift

PUBLICUS SEVERUS
Sir John Joseph Dillon

PUBLIUS
Alexander Hamilton with James
Madison and John Jay
Samuel B. Williams

PUMPS, PADDY
Horatio Townshend

PUN-SIBE, TOM
Jonathan Swift

PUNGENT, PIERCE
Thomas Powell

PUNJABEE
William Delafield Arnold

PUNSIBI, TOM
Thomas Sheridan

**A PUPIL OF THE LATE DR
W. HUNTER**
John Trusler

**PUPILS OF THE CITY OF
LONDON SCHOOL**
Ernest Abraham Hart

PURCELL, REV. FRANCIS
Joseph Sheridan Le Fanu

PURSER, SEAN
John W. R. Purser

PUTERSCHIEN, H.
William Addison Dwiggins

PUTNAM, B. L.
Bertram Lenox Simpson

PUTNAM, ELEANOR
Mrs Harriet Leonora Bates

PUTNAM, JOHN
Burnham Putnam Beckwith

PUZZLE, PETER
Joseph Addison

PYGGE, EDWARD
Julian Barnes

PYKE, RAFFORD
Harry Thurston Peck

PYM, ARTHUR GORDON
Edgar Allan Poe

A PYTHAGOREAN
Fitz-Hugh Ludlow

Q

Q.
Marcus Andrew Hislop Clarke
Douglas William Jerrold
Thomas Purnell
Sir Arthur Quiller-Couch
Caroline Anne Bowles Southey
William Moy Thomas

Q. E. D.
Edward Gordon Craig
Mrs Catherine Frances Grace
Gore

Q. Q.
Miss Jane Taylor

Q. Q. Q.
Samuel Warren

QUAD, M.
Charles Bertrand Lewis

A QUADRAGENARIAN
Robert Weaver

A QUAKER
Josiah Forster
Thomas Guidott
Joseph Wyeth

QUARLES
Edgar Allan Poe

QUARRY, NICK
Marvin Hubert Albert

A QUARTERLY REVIEWER
William Francis Barry
Malcolm MacColl
Laurie Magnus

QUARTERMAIN, JAMES
James Broom Lynne

QUEBEC, ADELA
Gerard Hugh Tyrwhitt

QUEEN, ELLERY
Frederic Dannay with Manfred
B. Lee
Richard Deming
Edward D. Hoch
Milton Lesser
Talmage Powell
John Holbrook Vance

QUEEN, ELLERY, JR.
James Holding

QUEERFELLOW, QUINTIN
Charles Clark

QUENTIN, DOROTHY
Madeleine Batten

QUENTIN, PATRICK
Hugh Callingham Wheeler with
Richard Wilson Webb

QUERIST
James Boswell

QUERNO, CAMILLO
Jonathan Odell

QUERY
James Topham Brady

QUERY, PETER
Martin Farquhar Tupper

QUEVEDO REDIVIVUS
Lord George Gordon Byron

QUEVEDO REDIVIVUS JUN.
Robert William Wright

QUEX
George Herbert Fosdike
Nichols

QUID
Robert Alan Fitzgerald

QUIDAM
William Meston

QUIET, CHARLES
Charles Henry Noyes

QUIET GEORGE
George Frederick Pardon

A QUIET LOOKER-ON
John Foster

A QUIET MAN
Theodore Sedgwick Fay

A QUIET OBSERVER
Sir William James Erasmus
Wilson

QUI HI
Christian Isobel Johnstone

QUILIBET
Henry Watson Fowler

QUILIBET, PHILIP
George Edward Pond

QUILL, CHARLES
James Waddel Alexander

QUILLER, ANDREW
Kenneth Henry Bulmer

QUILLET
Henry Watson Fowler

QUIN, DAN
Alfred Henry Lewis

QUINCE, PETER
Isaac Story
John William McWean
Thompson

QUINN, HARLEY
Wilfred Charles Thorley

QUINN, MARTIN (or SIMON)
Martin Cruz Smith

QUINQUAGENARIUS
Thomas Godfrey Fausset

QUINTUS
Alpheus Crosby

QUINTUS HORATIUS
FLACCUS
Sir Theodore Martin

QUIRINUS
John E. Dalberg Acton

QUIROLE, PIERRE
Walter William Sayer

QUISPIAN
Henry Hayman

QUITE A GENTLEMAN
Ernest Milton

QUIZ
Edward Caswall
Charles Dickens
Percival Leigh

QUIZ, ROLAND
Richard Martin Howard
Quittenton

QUIZ, ROLAND, JR.
Bertram Quittenton

QUOD, JOHN
John Treat Irving

QUOD R. SCOT
Allan Ramsay

A QUONDAM CRICKETER
Charles Thomas Studd

A QUONDAM SERVANT OF THE COMPANY
John Zephaniah Holwell

QUORUM PARS FUI
Edward Harper Parker

R

R.
  Sir Richard Steele

MARIA R*****
  Maria Riddell

R. A.
  Robert Anderson

R. A. K.
  Ronald Arbuthnot Knox

R. B.
  Robert Boreman
  Richard Brome
  Nathaniel Crouch

R. C.
  Robert Colvill
  Richard Cumberland

R ... C ...
  Richard Challoner

R. D., FOOTMAN
  Robert Dodsley

R. D. V. A.
  Richard Challoner

R. E. E. B.
  Rowland Eyles Egerton-
    Warburton

R. F.
  Rose Amy Fyleman

R. G.
  Richard Gough

R. H.
  Robert Hayman
  Robert Howlett

R. L. V. M.
  Robert Molesworth

R. M.
  Richard Mallett

R. N. C.
  Robert Needham Cust

R. O.
  William Taylor

R. S. H.
  Robert Stephen Hawker

RABBIT, PETER
  William Joseph Long

RACKHAM, JOHN
  John Thomas Phillifent

RADCLIFFE, JANET
  Janet Louise Roberts

A RADICAL
  Joseph Chamberlain
  Leslie Grove Jones
  William Hale White

A RADICAL MP
  Robert Wallace

A RADICAL REFORMER
  Richard Cobden

A RADICAL TEETOTALER
  Louisa Twining

RADIO DOCTOR
  Charles Hill

RADLEY, SHEILA
  Sheila Mary Robinson

RAEBURN, DAVID
  Paul Herring

RAGGED, HYDER
  Sir Henry Chartres Biron

RAGMAN, SENACHERIB, OF
    ST GILES
  Philip Dormer Stanhope

A RAILER
  Edward Stanley

A RAILROAD DIRECTOR OF
    MASSACHUSETTS
  Elias Hasket Derby

A RAILWAY READER
  James Spedding

A RAILWAY WITNESS
  William Edmonstoune Aytoun

RAIMOND, C. E.
  Elizabeth Robins

RAINE, RICHARD
  Raymond H. Sawkins

RAJAH OF VANEPLYSIA
  Richard Penn

RALEIGH, W.
  Henry St John

RALLENTANDO, H. P.
  Dorothy Leigh Sayers

RALSTON, JAN
  Agnes Mary Robertson Dunlop

RAMACHARAKA, YOGI
  William Walker Atkinson

RAMAL, WALTER
  Walter de la Mare

RAMBLER
  Arthur John Hallam
    Montefiore Brice
  Charles James Dunphie
  Charles Henry Newmarch
  Joseph Palmer
  George Augustus Simcox

THE RAMBLER IN MEXICO
  Charles Josepeh Latrobe

RAMBLER, ROBERT
  John Frost

RAMBLING RICHARD
  Rowland Eyles Egerton-
    Warburton

RAME, DAVID
  Arthur Durham Divine

RAMESES
  Claude Scudamore Jarvis

RAMPAGER
  James Boswell

RAMSAY, DIANA
  Rhoda Brandes

RAMSAY, FAY
  Helen Eastwood

RAMSAY, GRACE
  Kathleen O'Meara

MRS RAMSBOTTOM
  Theodore Edward Hook

RAMSNEB, T.
  Benjamin Smart

RAND, BRETT
  Victor G. C. Norwood

RAND, JAMES S.
Bernard George Attenborough

RANDALL, MRS ANNE
FRANCES
Mary Robinson

RANDALL, CLAY
Clifton Adams

RANDALL, JANET
Janet Randall Young

RANDALL, JEAN
Louise Platt Hauck

RANDALL, JOSHUA
Robert Joseph Randisi

RANDALL, ROBERT
Randall Garrett with Robert
Silverberg

RANDALL, RONA
Rona Shambrook

RANDALL, WILLIAM
William R. Gwinn

RANDOLPH, ELLEN
William Edward Daniel Ross

RANDOLPH, J. THORNTON
Charles Jacobs Peterson

RANDOLPH, MARION
Marie Rodell

RANDOLPH, RICHARD
John Nix Pentelow

RANGER
Luther L. Holden

RANGER, CHARLES, ESQ.
Arthur Murphy

RANGER, KEN
John Creasey

RANGLEY, OLIVIA
Hugh Zachary

RANKIN, CHARLES
Charles Patrick Ranke Graves

RANKIN, JOHN S.
Edward Gordon Craig

RANKINE, JOHN
Douglas Rankine Mason

RANSOME, STEPHEN
Frederick Clyde Davis

RAPIER
Alfred Edward Thomas Watson

RATCLIFFE, ALEXANDER
John Henley

RATCLIFFE, SIR ISAAC, OF
ELBOW LANE
John Henley

A RATIONAL CHRISTIAN
Francis Webb

RATIONALIS
William Hazlitt

THE RATIONALIST
William Baker

RATTLER, MORGAN
Percival Weldon Banks

RATTRAY, SIMON
Trevor Dudley-Smith

RAVEN, RALPH
George Payson

RAWDON, HORACE
Harold John Hastings Russell

RAWLEY, CALLMAN
Carl Rakosi

RAY, CYRIL
Cyril Rotenberg

RAY, THOMAS
Thomas Hay Sweet Escott

RAY, WALTER
Bolton King

RAYMOND, DEREK
Robin Cook

RAYMOND, E. T.
Edward Raymond Thompson

RAYMOND, HENRY
AUGUSTUS
Sarah Scott

RAYMOND, IDA
Mrs Mary T. Tardy

RAYMOND, MARY
Mary Constantine Keegan

RAYNER, ELIZABETH
Mrs Marie Belloc Lowndes

RAYNER, OLIVE PRATT
Charles Grant Blairfindie Allen

RAYTER, JOE
Mary F. McChesney

MISS READ
Dora Jessie Saint

READE, HAMISH
Simon Gray

A READER
Walter Besant
Catherine Cooper Hopley

A READER THEREIN
Andrea Crestadoro

A REAL CATHOLICK OF
THE CHURCH OF
ENGLAND
Thomas Barlow

A REAL FRIEND TO THE
CHURCH OF
SCOTLAND
John Brown

A REBEL WAR CLERK
John Beauchamp Jones

A RECENT CONVERT
Edward Healy Thompson

A RECENT TRAVELLER
Robert James Leslie M'Ghee
Charles Henry Pearson

A RECLUSE
Mrs Anne Charlotte Botta
John Brewster
William Benton Clulow
John Barton Derby
Francis Jacox
Mrs Mary Anne Kelty

THE RECORDER OF THE
CITY OF NEW YORK
Daniel Horsmunden

THE RECTOR
Cameron Mann
Samuel Lewis Southard

THE RECTOR OF CHRIST
CHURCH, VICKSBURG
William W. Lord

THE RECTOR OF LINCOLN
COLLEGE
Edward Tatham

REDEN, KARL
Charles Crozat Converse

REDFERN, JOHN
Edith Mary Pargeter

REDFIELD, MARTIN
Alice Brown

REDGAP
George Frederick Pardon

REDRUTH, E.
Richard Edmonds

REDWAY, RALPH
Charles Harold St John
Hamilton

REED, ARTHUR
Arthur Reed Ropes

REED, DAVID V.
David Vern

REED, ELIOT
Eric Ambler with Percival
Charles Rodda

REED, SIMON
Mary Danby

REES, DILWYN
Glyn Edmund Daniel

REEVE, JOEL
William Robert Cox

REEVES, AMBER
Amber Blanco White

A REFORMER
Frederick Nolan

A REFORMING MEMBER OF
PARLIAMENT
Edward George Earle Lytton
Bulwer-Lytton

A REFUGEE
Frederick Augustus Porter
Barnard

REGAN, BRAD
Victor G. C. Norwood

A REGIMENTAL OFFICER
Peter Hawker
Hugh Wodehouse Pearse

REGINALD, ROBERT
M. R. Burgess

REGISTER, SEELEY
Mrs Metta Victoria Victor

REID, CHRISTIAN
Frances Christine Fisher
Tiernan

REID, DESMOND
Michael Moorcock

REID, FRANK
Alexander Vindex Vennard

REID, MARK
Mowbray Walter Morris

REID, PHILIP
Richard Ingrams

REID, WALLACE Q.
George Goodchild

REILLY, WILLIAM K.
John Creasey

REINER, MAX
Janet Miriam Taylor Caldwell

A RELATIVE
William Thomas Brande

A RELIGIOUS POLITICIAN
Samuel Adams

REMINGTON, MARK
David Ernest Bingley

RENAULT, MARY
Mary Challans

RENIER, ELIZABETH
Betty Doreen Baker

RENTON, CAM
Richard Armstrong

A REPORTER
Joseph O'Leary

THE REPORTER OF THE
NEW ORLEANS
'PICAYUNE'
Dennis Corcoran

A REPRESENTATIVE
Henry Clark Barlow

THE REPRESENTATIVE OF A
CYDER-COUNTY
William Dowdeswell

A RESIDENT
Frederick Marshall

A RESIDENT MA
Frederick Edward Weatherly

A RESIDENT BEYOND THE
FRONTIER
William Joseph Snelling

A RESIDENT CLERGYMAN
Mark Hildesley

A RESIDENT IN CRETE
William James Stillman

A RESIDENT IN PEKING
Joseph Edkins

A RESIDENT MEMBER OF
CONVOCATION
Edward Bouverie Pusey
Archibald Campbell Tait

A RESIDENT OF
CONSTANTINOPLE
David Urquhart

A RETIRED BARRISTER
Charles Ambler

A RETIRED COMMON
COUNCILMAN
James Kirke Paulding

A RETIRED
CONSTABULARY
OFFICER
John Wilson Montgomery

THE RETIRED GOVERNOR
OF THE ISLAND OF
JUAN FERNANDEZ
Thomas Sutcliffe

A RETIRED JUDGE
William Webb Follett Synge

A RETIRED OFFICER
William Combe

A RETIRED PRACTITIONER
John Allen

RETNYW, WERDNA
Andrew Wynter

RETORT, DICK
William Cobbett

RETORT, JACK
William Franklin

A RETURNED SOUTH
AFRICAN
Olive Emilie Albertina
Schreiner

REUBEN
Robert Stephen Hawker

A REVEREND AND
JUDICIOUS DIVINE
John Rainolds

A REVEREND DIVINE NOW
WITH GOD
Richard Sibbes

A REVEREND RELIGIOUS
AND JUDICIOUS
DIVINE
Robert Sanderson

REVERIE, REGINALD
Grenville Mellen

REVERMORT, J. A.
J. A. Cramb

A REVISING BARRISTER
Sir John Eardley Eardley-
Wilmot

REVONS, E. C.
Charles Crozat Converse

REYNARD
Frank Foxcroft

REYNOLDS, ADRIAN
Amelia Reynolds Long

REYNOLDS, BEATRICE
Elizabeth Sara Sheppard

REYNOLDS, DICKSON
Helen Mary Greenwood
Reynolds

REYNOLDS, FRANCIS
Francis Reginald Statham

REYNOLDS, JOHN (or
MADGE)
Ralph Whitlock

REYNOLDS, MACK
Dallas McCord Reynolds

REYNOLDS, PETER
Amelia Reynolds Long

RHADAMANTHUS
Charles Seymour Mullan

RHODE, JOHN
Cecil John Charles Street

A RHODE ISLANDER
Mrs Catherine Read Williams

RHYS, JEAN
Ella Gwendolyn Rees Williams

RICE, CRAIG
Georgiana Randolph Craig

RICE, ELMER
Elmer Reizenstein

RICH, BARBARA
Laura Riding with Robert
Ranke Graves

RICH, CAPTAIN BARNABY
Peter Dunsmore Howard

RICHARD AP WILLIAM
Richard Simpson

RICHARD, SUSAN
Julie Ellis

RICHARDS, ALLEN
Richard A. Rosenthal

RICHARDS, CLAY
Kendell Foster Crossen

RICHARDS, FRANCIS
Richard Lockridge

RICHARDS, FRANK
Charles Harold St John
Hamilton

RICHARDS, HILDA
Charles Harold St John
Hamilton
Reginald S. Kirkham
Horace Phillips
L. E. Ransome
John Wheway

**RICHARDSON, HENRY
HANDEL**
Ethel Florence Richardson

RICHARDSON, HENRY S.
William Brighty Rands

RICHELIEU
William Erigena Robinson

RICHMOND, GRACE
John Marsh

A RICHMOND LADY
Mrs Sallie A. Putnam

RICHMONDIENSIS
Christopher Clarkson
Matthew Dawson Duffield

RICHWORTH, MR WILLIAM
Thomas White

RICKARD, COLE
Geoffrey John Barrett

RIDDELL, MRS J. H.
Charlotte Cowan

RIDDELL, JOHN
Corey Ford

RIDGEWAY, ALGERNON
Anna Cogswell Wood

RIDGWAY, JASON
Milton Lesser

RIEFE, BARBARA
Alan Riefe

**RIGMAROLOVICZ,
DEMETRIUS**
William Makepeace Thackeray

RILEY, TEX
John Creasey

RING, DOUGLAS
Richard Scott Prather

RINGLETUB, JEREMIAH
John Styles

RINGO, JOHNNY
Henry John Keevill

RINGOLD, CLAY
Ray Hogan

RIPLEY, JACK
John W. Wainwright

RIPLEY, OZARK
John Baptiste de Macklot
Thompson

RIPOSTE, A.
Evelyn May Clowes

RIQ
Richard Tupper Atwater

RITA
Eliza Margaret Humphreys

RITER, A. W.
Frederick William Rolfe

RITSON, JOHN
Douglas Gordon Baber

RIVERS, AUGUSTINE
Sacheverell Sitwell

RIVERS, GEORGIA
Marjorie Clark

RIVERS, PEARL
Eliza Jane Nicholson

THE RIVERSIDE VISITOR
Thomas Wright

RIVETUS, ANDREAS, JUN.
Andrew Marvell

ROB ROY
John MacGregor

ROBBINS, KAY
Kay Hooper

ROBBINS, WAYNE
William Robert Cox

ROBERT, THE CITY WAITER
John T. Bedford

ROBERTS, CAPT. A.
Augustus Charles Hobart

ROBERTS, CAPT. GEORGE
Daniel Defoe

ROBERTS, IVOR
Irene Roberts

ROBERTS, JAMES HALL
Robert Lipscomb Duncan

ROBERTS, JOHN
David Ernest Bingley
Thomas Swinnerton

ROBERTS, J. R.
Robert Joseph Randisi

ROBERTS, LAWRENCE
Robert Lloyd Fish

ROBERTS, LEE
Robert Lee Martin

ROBERTS, LIONEL
Robert Lionel Fanthorpe

ROBERTS, MORLEY
George Robert Gissing

ROBERTS, MURRAY
Robert Murray Graydon

ROBERTS, TERENCE
Ivan T. Sanderson

ROBERTS, TREV.
Robert E. Trevathan

ROBERTSON, ELSPETH
Joan Audrey Ellison

ROBERTSON, HELEN
Helen Jean Mary Edmiston

**ROBERTSON, IGNATIUS
LOYOLA, LL. D.**
Samuel Lorenzo Knapp

ROBERTSON, JAMES A.
Robert Lipscomb Duncan

ROBERTSON, JOHN
Sir John Robert Seeley

ROBESON, KENNETH
Lester Dent
Ronald Joseph Goulart

ROBIN
Robert Leighton

ABBE ROBIN
Philip Freneau

ROBINS, PATRICIA
Patricia Denise Clark

ROBINSON, JACK
Archibald Michie

ROBINSON, MARTHA
Martha Kathleen Alexander

**ROBINSON, RALPH, OF
WINDSOR**
King George III

ROCHESTER, MARK
William Charles Mark Kent

A ROCHESTER FELLOW
Samuel Hubbard Scudder

ROCKET
Albert Richard Smith

ROCKFERN, DANIELLE
Frederick Nolan

ROCKMAN, CONSTANT, MA
Nicholas Bowes

ROCKWOOD
Thomas Dykes

RODD, RALPH
William North

RODDY THE ROVER
Aodh De Blacam

RODMAN, ELLA
Mrs Eliza Rodman Church

RODO
Robert Downing

RODOLPHUS
Charles Croke

ROFFMAN, JAN
Margaret Summerton

ROGER, B. F.
George Wightwick

ROGERS, FLOYD
William John Duncan Spence

ROGERS, PAT
Arthur Porges

ROGERS, PHILLIP
Albert Edward Idell

ROGERS, WILLIAM
Nehemiah Hawkins

ROHMER, SAX
Arthur Sarsfield Ward

ROILY, ANTHO.
John Taylor

ROLAND
John Mackinnon Robertson

ROLAND, MARY
Mary Christianna Brand

ROLAND, NICHOLAS
Arnold Robert Walmsley

ROLLICKER, HARRY
William Makepeace Thackeray

ROLLS, ANTHONY
Colwyn Edward Vulliamy

ROLPH, C. H.
Cecil Rolph Hewitt

ROLYAT, JANE
E. Jean McDougall

ROMAINE, LINDON
Albert Lee

ROMAINE, ROBERT DEXTER
George Payson

A ROMAN CATHOLIC
Augustus Welby Pugin

A ROMAN CATHOLIC CLERGYMAN OF BALTIMORE
J. B. David

ROMAN CORRESPONDENT OF THE 'WESTMINSTER REVIEW'
Rachel Harriette Busk

ROMANY
George Bramwell Evans

ROMANY RAI
Tom Taylor

ROME, ANTHONY
Marvin Hubert Albert

ROMER, JONATHAN
William Starbuck Mayo

A ROMISH RECUSANT
Thomas Longueville

ROMNEY, A. B.
Anna Beatrice Rambaut

ROMNEY, STEVE
David Ernest Bingley

ROMULUS THE MONK
Frederick Bligh Bond

RONALD, E. B.
Ronald Ernest Barker

RONALD, MARY
Augusta Foote Arnold

RONNS, EDWARD
Edward Sidney Aarons

ROONEY, PATRICK
Tyrone Power

ROOSEVELT, BLANCHE
Blanche Roosevelt Tucker Macchetta

ROOT, RAOUL
Ezra Pound

ROPER, ABEL
Jonathan Swift

ROSCIO, J. L.
John Lowin

ROSE, A. N. MOUNT
Alexander Hay Japp

ROSE, LAURENCE F.
John Russell Fearn

ROSEHARP
James M. Cawdell

ROSEN, LEW
Lewis Rosenthal

ROSENFELD, MORRIS
Moshe Jacob Alter

ROSET, HIPPONAX
Joseph Rupert Paxton

ROSICRUCIUS
Thomas Frognall Dibdin

ROSICRUX
William Butler Yeats

ROSS, ADRIAN
Arthur Reed Ropes

ROSS, ALBERT
Linn Boyd Porter

ROSS, ANGUS
Kenneth Giggal

ROSS, BARNABY
Frederic Dannay with Manfred B. Lee

ROSS, CATHERINE
Betty Beaty

ROSS, DALLAS
Dallas McCord Reynolds

ROSS, DIANA
Diana Denney

ROSS, HELAINE
Dorothy Daniels

ROSS, IVAN T.
Robert Rossner

ROSS, JEAN
Irene Dale Hewson

ROSS, J. H.
Thomas Edward Lawrence

ROSS, JONATHAN
John Rossiter

ROSS, LEONARD Q.
Leo Calvin Rosten

ROSS, MARILYN (or CLARISSA)
William Edward Daniel Ross

ROSS, MARTIN
Violet Florence Martin

ROSSE, IAN
John Foster Straker

ROSSEN, BENJAMIN
Edward Gordon Craig

ROSSITER, OSCAR
Vernon H. Skeels

ROSTREVOR, GEORGE
Sir George Rostrevor Hamilton

ROTHMAN, JUDITH
Maureen Peters

ROUGH HEWER, JUN.
Abraham Yates

ROUGHHEAD, ROBIN
William Maginn

ROUND ROBIN
William Edmonstoune Aytoun

ROUNDELAY, ROGER
William Biglow

ROUNDROBIN, ROGER
Patrick Gibson

ROUSSEAU, VICTOR
Victor Rousseau Emanuel

THE ROVING EDITOR
James Redpath

THE ROVING ENGLISHMAN
Eustace Clare Grenville Murray

ROW, T.
Samuel Pegge

ROWAN, DEIRDRE
Jeanne Williams

ROWAN, HESTER
Sheila Mary Robinson

ROWANS, VIRGINIA
Edward Everett Tanner

ROWLAND, IRIS
Irene Roberts

**ROWLANDS, EFFIE
ADELAIDE**
E. Maria Albanesi

ROWLEY, THOMAS
Thomas Chatterton

ROY, BRANDON
Mrs Florence Louise Barclay

ROY, JOHN
Sir Henry Mortimer Durand

ROYAL, DAN
Geoffrey John Barrett

ROYAL, RALPH
Jacob Ralph Abarbanell

ROYCE, ASHLEY ALLEN
Nathaniel Hawthorne

ROYCE, KENNETH
Kenneth Royce Gandley

RUBICON
Arnold Henry Moore Lunn

RUCK, BERTA
Amy Roberta Oliver

RUDD, MARGARET
Margaret Rudd Newlin

RUDD, STEELE
Arthur Hoey Davis

RUDE BOREAS
Richard Simpson

RUDE DONATUS
Charles Lutwidge Dodgson

RUELL, PATRICK
Reginald Charles Hill

A RUGBAEAN
Joseph Lloyd Brereton

**A RULING ELDER OF THE
CHURCH OF
SCOTLAND**
Robert Forbes

RUMFUNIDOS, QUIZDOM
George Outram

RUNCIMAN, JOHN
Brian Wilson Aldiss

RUNNYMEDE
Benjamin Disraeli
John Bickford Heard

A RURAL DIVINE
Archibald Bruce

A RURAL PEN
Robert Wild

RURIC, PETER
George Sims

RURICOLA
John Curtis
Henry Howard Molyneux
Herbert

RUSHTON, CHARLES
Charles Rushton Shortt

RUSSELL, ARTHUR
Arthur Russell Goode

RUSSELL, JAMES
Terence William Harknett

RUSSELL, JOHN
John Russell Fearn

RUSSELL, MARGARET
Mrs Eleanora Louisa Hervey

RUSSELL, RAYMOND
Lilian Blanche Fearing

RUSSELL, SARAH
Esther Pearl (Marghanita)
Laski

RUSSELL, SHANE
Victor G. C. Norwood

A RUSSIAN LADY
Olga Novikova

**A RUSSIAN PRISONER'S
WIFE IN JAPAN**
Eliza Ruhamah Scidmore

THE RUSTIC BARD
Robert Dinsmoor

RUSTICUS
John Dickinson
John Duncomb
Caleb Fleming
Norman Rowland Gale
Frederick Denison Maurice
Edward Newman
Charles O'Conor
John Watson

RUSTICUS, GENT.
Gerrit Maspeth Furman

RUSTICUS URBANUS
Thomas Edward Kebbell

**RUSTIFIGIUS,
TRISMEGISTUS, D. D.**
Thomas Moore

RUTH
Sir Max Beerbohm

RUTHERFORD, DOUGLAS
James Douglas R. McConnell

RUTHERFORD, MARK
William Hale White

RUTHIN, MARGARET
Arthur Catherall

RUTLEDGE, BRETT
Elliot Harold Paul

RYALTO
William Taylor

RYAN, CARROLL
William Thomas Ryan

RYAN, ELSIE
Deirdre O'Brien

RYAN, RACHEL
Sandra Brown

RYBOT, DORIS
Doris Almon Ponsonby

RYDELL, FORBES
Deloris Stanton Forbes with
Helen Rydell

RYDER, JONATHAN
Robert Ludlum

RYDER, THOM
John B. Harvey

RYE, ANTHONY
Christopher Samuel Youd

RYLAND, CLIVE
Clive Ryland Priestley

RYLEY, SIR HEISTER
Charles Povey

S

S.
Thomas Edward Lawrence
George Bernard Shaw
John Swete

ST E. A., OF M. AND S.
Edward Alexander Crowley

S. C.
Samuel Colvil

S. E. Y.
Denis Florence MacCarthy

S. G. O.
Sidney Godolphin Osborne

S. H.
Samuel Hartlib

S. H- ELOQUENTIAE
PROFESSOR
Samuel Henley

S. J.
Stephen Jones

S. J____N
Samuel Johnson

S. M.
Baroness Nairne, Carolina
Oliphant

S. O.
Lady Sydney Morgan

S. O. S.
Ezra Pound

S. R.
Samuel Rowley

S. S.
Dorothy Kilner
Siegfried Sassoon
Herbert George Wells

REV. DR S___T
Jonathan Swift

SAAL, JENNIFER (or
JOCELYN)
Judith Sachs

SABER, ROBERT O.
Milton K. Ozaki

SABINO
Edward Ballard

SABRE, DIRKE
John Laffin

SABRETACHE, CAPTAIN
ORLANDO
John Mitchell

SACERDOS
William Henry Eyre

SACKBUT, FUSTIAN
Bonnell Thornton

SACKBUT, SOLOMON
Thomas Oliphant

SADDI, NATHAN BEN
Robert Dodsley

SADIE
Sarah Williams

SADLEIR, MICHAEL
Michael Thomas Harvey
Sadler

SADLER, MARK
Dennis Lynds

SAGADAHOC
Frederic Kidder

SAGITTARIUS
Olga Katzin

SAGOLA, MARIO J.
Henry Kane

A SAILOR
William Falconer
Joshua Larwood
Charles Nordhoff
Edward Thompson

A SAILOR AND A
SELDENITE
Andrew Valentine Kirwan

A SAILOR BOY
Charles Nordhoff

A ST ANDREW'S MAN
Robert Fuller Murray

ST AUBYN, ALAN
Mrs Frances Marshall

ST BARBE
Douglas Brooke Wheelton
Sladen

ST BARBE, REGINALD
Douglas Brooke Wheelton
Sladen

ST CLAIR, DEXTER
Prentice Winchell

ST CLAIR, VERNON
George Waldo Browne

ST CLAIR, WILLIAM
William Ford

ST CLAIRE, ERIN
Sandra Brown

ST DENIS LE CADET
Paul Allen

ST GEORGE, HARRY
St George Henry Rathbone

ST IVES
James Henry Lawrence

ST JAMES, ANDREW
James Stern

ST JOHN, CHRISTOPHER
MARIE
Christabel Marshall

ST JOHN, DAVID
E. Howard Hunt

SAINT JOHN, ERIC
William Eric Saint John Brooks

ST JOHN, HENRY
John Creasey

ST JOHN, J. HECTOR
Michel G. J. de Crevecoeur

ST JOHN, LEONIE
William Bayer

ST JOHN, MABEL (or
HENRY)
Henry St John Cooper

ST JOHN, PHILIP
Lester Del Rey

ST JOHN, THEOPHILUS
Samuel Clapham

ST LAURENCE, ALFRED
Alfred Laurence Felkin

ST VINCENT, PAUL
Edward Archibald Markham

SAKI
Hector Hugh Munro

SALADIN
William Stewart Ross

SALAR, SALMO, ESQ.
George Rooper

SALEM, AHAB
James Murray

SALISBURY, CAROLA
Michael Butterworth

SALISBURY, JOHN
John David Caute

SALOPIENSIS
Job Orton

SALTER, CEDRIC
Francis Edgar Knight

SALTER, MARY D.
Mary Dinsmore Ainsworth

THE SAME FRIEND THAT WROTE TO THOMAS BRADBURY
Daniel Defoe

SAMPLETON, SAMUEL, ESQ.
Luigi Monti

SAMPSON, SHORT AND FAT
Samuel Kettell

SANBORN, B. X.
William Sanborn Ballinger

SANCHO
John William Cunningham

SANDERS, ABEL
Ezra Pound

SANDERS, BRETT
Geoffrey John Barrett

SANDERS, NEWTON
Louise Mears

SANDERS, WINSTON P.
Poul Anderson

SANDISON, JANET
Elizabeth Jane Cameron

SANDON, J. D.
John B. Harvey

SANDS, DAVE
Talmage Powell

SANDS, MARTIN
John Frederick Burke

SANDYS, GEORGE WINDLE
Oswald John Crawfurd

SANDYS, OLIVER
Marguerite Florence Jervis

(LORD) SANGFROID
Alfred Austin

MONSIEUR SANS ESPRIT
Henry Fielding

SANTOS, HELEN
Helen Griffiths

SAPPER
Gerard T. Fairlie
Herman Cyril McNeile

SARAC, ROGER
Roger Andrew Caras

SARASIN, JENNIFER
Judith Sachs

SARASIN, J. G.
Geraldine Gordon Salmon

SARBAN
John W. Wall

SARCELLE
Charles Alfred Payton

SARR, KENNETH
Kenneth Sheils Reddin

SARTO, BEN
Frank Dubrez Fawcett

SASHUN, SIGMA
Siegfried Sassoon

SASS, JOB
George Augustus Foxcroft

SASSENACH
John Bernard Arbuthnot

SATAN
John Eagles

SATANELLA
Jane Cunningham Croly

SATYRANE
Samuel Taylor Coleridge

SAUNDERS, CARL MCK.
Philip Ketchum

SAUNDERS, DAPHNE
Georgiana Randolph Craig

SAUNDERS, DIANA
Virginia Coffman

SAUNDERS, JEANNE
Anne Rundle

SAUNDERS, JEFFERSON
Horatio Smith

SAUNDERS, RICHARD
Benjamin Franklin

SAUNDERS, WES
Sydney Bounds

SAUNTER, SAMUEL
Joseph Dennie

SAUNTERER
Hewson Clarke

SAUZADE, JOHN S.
James Payn

SAVAGE, LAURA
Frederic George Stephens

SAVA, GEORGE
George Alexis Milkomanovich Milkomane

SAVAGE, R. C.
Christabel Marshall

SAVAGE, RICHARD
Ivan Roe

SAVEALL
Lucius Manlius Sargent

SAVONAROLA, JEREMY
Francis Sylvester Mahony

SAWLEY, PETRA
John Marsh

SAWNEY
William Douglass

SAWNEY, SQUIRE
William Biglow

SAXON, ALEX
Bill Pronzini

SAXON, ANTONIA
Judith Sachs

SAXON, JOHN
James Noble Gifford

SAXON, PETER
Wilfred McNeilly

SAXON, RICHARD
Joseph Laurence Morrissey

SAXON, VAN
Mrs Evangeline M. Simpson

SAYRE, GORDON
Josiah Pitts Woolfolk

SCAEVA
John Stubbes
Isaac William Stuart

SCALPEL, AESCULAPIUS
Edward Berdoe

MR SCAMPER
William George Hamley

SCANLON, C. K. M.
Norman A. Danberg

SCANNELL, VERNON
John Vernon Bain

SCARABAEUS
David Badham

SCARLETT, REBECCA
Katherin Newlin Burt

SCARLETT, ROGER
Evelyn Page with Dorothy
Blair

SCARLETT, SUSAN
Mary Noel Streatfeild

SCHEFFER, FREDERICK
William King

SCHIFF, SIDNEY
Stephen Hudson

SCHMERZ, RUDOLF
Edward Gordon Craig

SCHOFIELD, PAUL
Edwin Charles Tubb

A SCHOLLAR
Samuel Wesley

A SCHOLLER IN OXFORD
Abraham Cowley

A SCHOOLMASTER
William Alexander Alcott
D'Arcy Wentworth Thompson

**A SCHOOLMASTER IN THE
EASTERN COUNTRY**
Asa Humphrey

**A SCHOOLMASTER OF
TWENTY YEARS
STANDING**
Charles Alexander Johns

SCHUYLER, ELIZABETH
Edith Robinson

A SCIENTIST
Harrison Hayter

SCIOLUS
Francis Wrangham

**A SCION OF THE OLD
CHURCH**
Robert Rodolph Suffield

SCIPIO
Uriah Tracy

SCISSORS AND PASTE
John Baptist Jackson

**A SCLAVONIAN NOBLEMAN
IN LONDON**
John Hill

SCOFIELD, JONATHAN
Paul R. Rothweiler

SCOLOPAX
Maurice Harold Grant

A SCOT
James Anderson

SCOT, NEIL
Lady Sybil Grant

**A SCOTCH FARMER AND A
LAND AGENT**
John Claudius Loudon

**A SCOTCH FARMER NOW
FARMING IN
MIDDLESEX**
John Claudius Loudon

A SCOTCH GENTLEMAN
James Boswell

A SCOTCH GRADUATE
William Minto

A SCOTCH PHYSICIAN
Francis Adams

SCOTLAND, JAY
John William Jakes

SCOTO-BRITANNICUS
James Anderson

SCOTO-BRITANNUS
James Grant

A SCOTS GENTLEMAN
William Carstares

**A SCOTS GENTLEMAN IN
THE SWEDISH SERVICE**
Daniel Defoe

SCOTT, AGNES NEILL
Wilhelmina (Willa) J. Muir

SCOTT, DAN
S. Omar Barker

SCOTT, DANA
Mrs Constance Noyes
Robertson

SCOTT, JACK S.
Jonathan Escott

SCOTT, JANE
Elizabeth Adeline McElfresh

SCOTT, JANEY
Roberta Leigh

SCOTT, KERRY
Harold Norling Swanson

SCOTT, LEADER
Lucy Baxter

SCOTT, NORMAN
Norman Mackintosh

SCOTT, ROBERT
James Robins

SCOTT, RONEY
William Campbell Gault

SCOTT, R. T.
William Maginn

SCOTT, THOMAS
Robert Smith Surtees

SCOTT, WARWICK
Trevor Dudley-Smith

SCOTT, WM. HENRY
John Lawrence

**A SCOTTISH
CONSERVATIVE**
James Ferguson

A SCOTTISH MP
Sir Mountstuart Elphinstone
Grant Duff

SCOTUS
James Boswell
William Reid

SCOTUS NOVANTICUS
Simon Somerville Laurie

SCOTUS VIATOR
Robert William Seton-Watson

SCOUGAL, FRANCIS
Felicia Mary Frances Skene

SCRANNEL, ORPHEUS
Terence Ian Fytton Armstrong

SCREW, MASSINGER
Charles William Shirley Brooks

SCRIBE, SIMON
Adam Black

SCRIBER, PETER
Charles Augustus Davis

SCRIBLERUS, JOHANNES
William Combe

SCRIBLERUS, MARTIN
Thomas James Mathias

**SCRIBLERUS
FLAGELLARIUS**
William Kenrick

SCRIBLERUS QUARTUS
Thomas Cooke

SCRIBLERUS REDIVIVUS
Edward Caswall

SCRIBLERUS SECUNDUS (H)
Henry Fielding

SCRIBLERUS TERTIUS
Thomas Cooke
Paul Whitehead

SCRIVENER, MARK
Marcus Andrew Hislop Clarke

**SCRUB, TIMOTHY, ESQ. OF
RAG FAIR**
John Kelly

SCRUTATOR
William Robert Ancketill
Sir Robert Charles K. Ensor

Walter Henry
Charles Jerram
Malcolm MacColl
Samuel O'Sullivan
Joseph Priestley
John Godfrey Ferdinand
    Raupert
Herbert Sidebotham
John Tucker

THE SCULLER
John Taylor

SCULPTOR, SATIRICUS
William Henry Ireland

SCUPPER, NELSON
    TATTERSALL LEE ESQ.,
    LATE ENSIGN IN HER
    MAJESTY'S HORSE
    MARINES
William Makepeace Thackeray

SEA COAL
William Cadwalader Hudson

SEA-LION
Geoffrey Martin Bennett

SEABRIGHT, IDRIS
Margaret St Clair

SEAFARER
Clarence Hedley Barker

A SEAFARER
William Clark Russell

SEAFORTH, A. NELSON
George Sydenham Clarke

SEAL, BASIL
Julian Barnes

SEALE, SARA
Mrs A. D. L. MacPherson

SEALSFIELD, CHARLES
Karl Postl

A SEAMAN
Thomas Cochrane

SEAMARK
Austin J. Small

SEARCH, EDWARD
Abraham Tucker

SEARCH, JOHN
Thomas Binney
Richard Whateley

SEARCH, SARAH
Frederick Nolan

SEARCH, WARNER
    CHRISTIAN
Sir William Cusac Smith

A SEARCHER AFTER
    RELIGIOUS TRUTH
Jacob Ilive

SEARE, NICHOLAS
Rodney William Whitaker

SEARLE, JANUARY
George Searle Phillips

SEARS, BALDWIN
Elizabeth Guion Young

MRS SEATON
Edmund Yates

SEBASTIAN, MARGARET
Arthur M. Gladstone

SECOND, HENRY
Henry S. Harrison

SECONDSIGHT, SOLOMON
James McHenry

SECONDTHOUGHTS,
    SOLOMON,
    SCHOOLMASTER
John Pendleton Kennedy

THE SECRETARY OF STATE
Timothy Pickering

THE SECRETARY OF THE
    BOSTON SOCIETY
Seth Bliss

THE SECRETARY OF THE
    SOCIETY FOR
    PROMOTING
    CHRISTIANITY AMONG
    THE JEWS
Alfred Long Stackhouse

THE SECRETARY TO THE
    BOARD OF
    AGRICULTURE
Arthur Young

SECUNDER
Alexander Chalmers

SEDGES, JOHN
Pearl S. Buck

SEDGWICK, MODWENA
Modwena Glover

SEEDY, ALFRED
Charles Rowcroft

A SEEKER AFTER TRUTH
Thomas Herne

SEFTON, CATHERINE
Martin Waddell

SEGRAVE, ADOLPHUS
Philip Gilbert Hamerton

SEHLER, TOM
Rex Burns

SEKON, GEORGE
    AUGUSTUS
George Augustus Nokes

SELBER
James Clarence Mangan

SELBIT
Percy Thomas Tibbles

SELDEN, GEORGE
George Selden Thompson

SELIM
Samuel Woodworth

SELINA
James Sheridan Knowles

SELKIRK, JANE
John Stanton Higham
Chapman with Mary Ilsley
    Chapman

SELKIRK, J. B.
James Buchan Brown

SELLINGS, ARTHUR
Robert Arthur Ley

SELMARK, GEORGE
Leslie Seldon Truss

SEMAJ, SEVRUP
James Purves

SEMAR, JOHN
Edward Gordon Craig

SEMEL-DAMNATUS
Charles Lamb

SEMPLE, GORDON
William Arthur Neubauer

A SENATOR OF THIRTY
    YEARS
Thomas Hart Benson

SENCOURT, ROBERT
Robert Esmond Gordon
    George

SENEX
James Anderson
Alexander Chalmers
John Adams Dix
Samuel Pegge
Robert Reid
Horatio Townshend

SENEX RUSTICANUS
Arthur Ransome

SENEX SCOTUS, AN
    HERITOR
Robert Andrew MacFie

A SENIOR
John Penrose

A SENIOR CLERGYMAN OF
    THE DIOCESE
Charles Pourtales Golightly

THE SENIOR CURATE OF ST
LUKE'S, BERWICK
STREET
Henry Whitehead

A SENIOR FELLOW OF A
COLLEGE IN
CAMBRIDGE
John Colbatch

A SENIOR FELLOW OF A
COLLEGE IN OXFORD
Henry Brooke

SENIOR HARVARD
Henry Dana Ward

A SENIOR MEMBER OF THE
CORPORATION
Hans Busk

THE SENIOR MINISTER OF
THE WEST CHURCH IN
BOSTON
Charles Lowell

THE SENIOR PROCTOR
Drummond Percy Chase

A SENIOR RESIDENT
MEMBER OF THE
UNIVERSITY OF
OXFORD
Charles Pourtales Golightly

SENOR ALGUNO
Nathan Ames

SENSE, P. C., BARRISTER
Bernard J. Sage

SENSITIVE, SAMUEL
James Beresford

A SENTIMENTAL
PHILOSOPHER
Washington Irving

SENTINEL
William Henry Bogart

A SEPTUAGENARIAN
James Booth
John Codman
James Forbes Dalton

A SEPTUAGENARIAN
STUDENT
Robert Charles Jenkins

A SEPTUAGENARY
Horatio Smith

SERAFIN, DAVID
Ian David Lewis Michael

SERGEANT BRADSHAW
Sir James Bland Burges

SERGEANT OATS
J. B. Vawter

A SERGEANT IN THE **
REGIMENT OF
INFANTRY
Joseph Donaldson

A SERIOUS ENQUIRER
Anthony Temple

SERTORIUS, COQUILLA, A
BENEDICTINE ABBOT
OF GLENDALOUGH
William Cooke Taylor

THE SERVANT OF CHRIST
George Fox

A SERVANT OF THE LORD
Richard Farnworth
James Nayler

SERVETUS
Sir Charles Abraham Elton

SERVETUS, MICHAEL, MD
Patrick Blair

SETON, GRAHAM
Graham Seton Hutchison

SETOUN, GABRIEL
Thomas Nicoll Hepburn

A SETTLER
John William Bannister

A SETTLER IN SANTO
DOMINGO
Joseph Warren Fabens

A SEVEN YEARS' RESIDENT
IN GREECE
Felicia Mary Frances Skene

SEVERAL YOUNG PERSONS
Jane Taylor with Ann Taylor

SEVERN, DAVID
David Storr Unwin

SEVERN, DONALD
Frederick Nolan

SEVERN, MARK
Franklin Lushington

SEWARD, W.
William Maginn

A SEXAGENARIAN
William Beloe
Simeon DeWitt Bloodgood
Robert Matthew

A SEXAGENARIAN LAYMAN
George Frederick Stutchbury

SEXAGENARIUS
John Holland
Joshua Hughes

SEXBY, EDWARD
Josiah Quincy

A SEXTON OF THE OLD
SCHOOL
Lucius Manlius Sargent

SEYMAR, WILLIAM,
ESQUIRE
William Ramesay

SEYMOUR, ALAN
Sydney Fowler Wright

SEYMOUR, CHARLES
ALFRED
Thomas James Wise with
Edward Dowden

SEYMOUR, HONOURABLE
JULIANA-SUSANNAH
John Hill

SEYMOUR, ROBERT
John Mottley

SEYMOUR, W.
Cuthbert Shaw

SHACKLETON, C. C.
Brian Wilson Aldiss

SHADOW, JOHN
John Byrom

SHAHCOLEN, A HINDU
PHILOSOPHER
RESIDING IN
PHILADELPHIA
Samuel Lorenzo Knapp

SHALIMAR
Frank Coutts Hendry

SHAMROCK
Richard D'Alton Williams

SHANDY, ANTONY
John Hall Stevenson

SHANDY, TRISTRAM, GENT.
Laurence Sterne

SHANE, JOHN
Paul Durst

SHANE, MARK (or RHONDO,
or VICTOR)
Victor G. C. Norwood

SHANE, SUSANNAH
Harriette Ashbrook

SHANNON, DELL
Elizabeth Linington

SHANNON, STEVE
J. L. Bouma

SHAPCOTT, REUBEN
William Hale White

A SHAREHOLDER
Henry Booth

SHARNOL, THOMAS
Thomas Sharper Knowlson

SHARP
Henry Fothergill Chorley

SHARP, B. A.
Platon G. Brounoff

SHARP, GUSTAVUS, ESQ.
Samuel Warren

SHARP, LUKE
Robert Barr

SHASTIN, VAMADEVA
Sir Alfred Comyn Lyall

SHASTRI, VAMADEO
Sir Alfred Comyn Lyall

SHAVEBLOCK, PASQUIN
John MacGowan

SHAW, BRIAN
John Russell Fearn
Edwin Charles Tubb

SHAW, FELICITY
Ann Morice

SHAW, IRENE
Irene Roberts

SHAW, MARTIN
Thomas Charles Bridges

SHAW, T. E.
Thomas Edward Lawrence

SHAWN, FRANK S.
Ronald Joseph Goulart

SHAYNE, GORDON
Bevis Winter

SHEA, TIMOTHY
Alden Arthur Knipe

SHEARING, JOSEPH
Margaret Long

SHEBAUTICAN
Arthur Granville Bradley

SHEBSA, E. H.
Henry Spencer Ashbee

A SHEEP-HERDER
Morley Charles Roberts

SHELBOURNE, CECILY
Suzanne Ebel

SHELDON, LEE
Wayne Cyril Lee

SHELDON, PHOEBE
Helen Lawrence Davis
Partridge

SHELDON, ROY
Edwin Charles Tubb

SHELLEY, A. FISHE
James Watson Gerard

SHEMAYA, EBN
David Parkes

SHEPARD, WILLIAM
William Shepard Walsh

SHEPHARD, HAZEL
Helen Ainslie Smith

SHEPHERD, DOROTHEA
ALICE
Eliza Pratt

SHEPHERD, JOHN
Willis Todhunter Ballard

SHEPHERD, MICHAEL
Robert Ludlum

SHEPHERD, NEAL
Nigel Morland

SHEPHERD, TOM
Thomas Robinson Hazard

SHEPHERD TONIE
Anthony Munday (or Mundy)

SHEPPARTON, PAUL
John Thomas Lutz

SHERATON, NEIL
Norman Edward Mace Smith

SHERIDAN, JANE
Pauline Glen Winslow

SHERIDAN, LEE
Elsie Lee

SHERIDAN, THOMAS
Walter Gillings

SHERLOCK
Solomon Southwick

SHERMAN, (PETER)
MICHAEL
Robert A. W. Lowndes

SHERRIN, NED
Edward George Sherrin

SHERWOOD, NELSON
Henry Kenneth Bulmer

SHERWOOD FORESTER
Spencer Timothy Hall

SHINGAWN
Harry Quilter

SHIPPEN
Samuel Adams

SHIRLEY (JOHN)
Sir John Skelton

SHIRLEY, PENN
Mrs Sara Jane Clarke
Lippincott

SHIRLEY OF
BALMAWHIPPLE
Sir John Skelton

SHIVAJI, PARAMAHANSA
Edward Alexander Crowley

SHOLTO
Robert Shelton Mackenzie

SHONE, PATRICK
James Hanley

A SHOPKEEPER
John MacGregor

SHORE, NORMAN
Norman Edward Mace Smith

SHORT, BOB
Augustus Baldwin Longstreet
Alexander Pope

SHORT, LUKE
Frederick Dilley Glidden

SHORTCUT, DAISY
David Solis Cohen

SHORTFELLOW, HARRY
WANDSWORTH
Mary Victoria Cowden-Clarke

SHORTFIELD, LUKE
John Beauchamp Jones

THE SHOWMAN
John Latey

A SHROPSHIRE
GENTLEMAN
Daniel Defoe

SHUFFLEBOTTOM, ABEL
Robert Southey

SHUTE, NEVIL
Nevil Shute Norway

SHWE DINGA
James George Scott

SHY, TIMOTHY
Dominic Bevan Wyndham
Lewis

SIDDONS, JAMES H.
Joachim Hayward Stocqueler

SIDEROS
Robert Forester Mushet

SIDNEY, ALGERNON
Salma Hale
John Landseer
Samuel Ferrand Waddington

SIDNEY, EDWARD WILLIAM
Nathan Beverley Tucker

SIDNEY, MARGARET
Harriet Mulford Stone Lothrop

SIDNEY, NEILMA
Neilma Gantner

SIEGVOLK, PAUL
Albert Mathews

SIEUR DU BAUDRIER
Jonathan Swift

SIGMA
John Langton Sanford
Lucius Manlius Sargent

SIGNOR COROLINI
Jonathan Swift

SIGNPOST
Herman Charles Hoskier

SIL AWL
Ralph Wallis

SILCHESTER
Leslie Thomas John Arlott

THE SILENT MEMBER
John Latey
William Mudford

A SILENT POLITICIAN
James Stephens

THE SILKWORM
Aglen A. Dowty

SILLY, E. S.
Robert Kraus

SILLY-BILLY
Eustace Clare Genville Murray

SILURIENSIS
John Wilson

SILURIENSIS, LEOLINUS
Arthur Llewellyn Jones

THE SILURIST
Arthur Llewellyn Jones
Henry Vaughan

SILVER, LONG JOHN
Joan Aiken

SILVER, RICHARD
Kenneth Henry Bulmer

SILVERPEN
Eliza Meteyard

SILVERTONGUE, GABRIEL
James Montgomery

SILVESTER, FRANK
David Ernest Bingley

SIMON
Oswell Blakeston with Roger
D'Este Burford
Henry B. Hooker

SIMON, EDITH
Edith Reeve

SIMON, ROBERT
Barry Musto

SIMON THE TANNER
Thomas Prentice

SIMON THE WAGONER
John Downey

SIMONS, ROGER
Ivor McCauley Punnett

SIMPLE, JOHN
George Hay

SIMPLEX
Legh Richmond
John Young

SIMPLEX MUNDITIIS
James Boswell

SIMPSON, WARWICK
William Pett Ridge

SINBAD
Aylward Edward Dingle

**A SINCERE ADMIRER OF
TRUE LIBERTY**
Zachary Grey

**A SINCERE FRIEND OF
MANKIND**
Francis Eyre

**A SINCERE FRIEND TO
AMERICA**
Alexander Hamilton

**A SINCERE LOVER OF OUR
PROTESTANT
ESTABLISHMENT**
Thomas Bray

**A SINCERE LOVER OF THE
PRESENT
CONSTITUTION**
Zachary Grey

**A SINCERE LOVER OF
TRUTH AND PEACE**
James Kirkpatrick

A SINCERE PROTESTANT
Zachary Grey

**A SINCERE PROTESTANT
AND TRUE SON OF
THE CHURCH**
Samuel Palmer

**A SINCERE WELL-WISHER
TO THE PUBLIC**
Martin Madan

**A SINCERE WELL-WISHER
TO THE TRADE AND
PROSPERITY OF GREAT
BRITAIN**
Josiah Tucker

SINCERUS
Samuel Adams

SINCLAIR, JAMES
Reginald Thomas Staples

SINCLAIR, JO
Ruth Seid

SINGE
Carlo Pellegrini

SINGER, BANT
Charles Shaw

SINGLE, CELIA
Benjamin Franklin

**SINGLE, JOHN, OF GREY'S
INN**
Henry Carey

SINGLETON, ANN
Ruth Benedict

SINGLETON, ARTHUR, ESQ.
Henry Cogswell Knight

**SINGLETON, JEREMIAH,
BACHELOR OF PHYSIC**
Percival Leigh

SINGLETON, MARY
Mrs Francesca Brooke

A SINGULAR MAN
Samuel Ward Francis

SINGULARITY, THOMAS
Henry Junius Knott

SINJOHN, JOHN
John Galsworthy

**SIONARA, A JAPANESE
TRAVELLER**
Laurence Oliphant

SIR ALI BABA
George Robert Aberigh-Mackay

SIR ORACLE, OX. COL.
Gerard Edward Smith

SIRIN, VLADIMIR
Vladimir Nabokov

SIRIUS
Edward Martyn

**SIRRHANIO, AN UTTER
ENEMY OF TYRANNIE**
John Harris

A SISTER OF MERCY
Charlotte M. Brame

**SKALDASPILLIR,
SIGFRIOUR**
Mildred Downey Broxon

SKETCH, JEMMY
James Wathen

THE SKETCHER
John Eagles

SKETCHLEY, ARTHUR
George Rose

SKILLET, JOSEPH
John Russell

SKINNER, AINSLIE
Paula Gosling

SKIPPER JOE
Norman Mackintosh

SKITT
Harden E. Taliaferro

SKORPIOS, ANTARES
Jane Barlow

SLADE, GURNEY
Stephen Bartlett

SLADE, JACK
Willis Todhunter Ballard

SLAGG, GLENDA
Barry Fantoni

SLATE, JOHN
John Russell Fearn

SLATER, PATRICK
John Mitchell

SLENDER, ROBERT
Philip Freneau

SLICK, JONATHAN
Ann Sophia Stephens

SLICK, SAM
Thomas Chandler Haliburton

SLICK, SAM, IN TEXAS
Samuel Adams Hammett

SLIEVEGALLIN
Adam Kidd

SLINGSBY, JONATHAN FREKE
John Francis Waller

SLINGSBY, LAWRENCE
George Henry Lewes

SLINGSBY, PHILIP
Nathaniel Parker Willis

SLOLUCK, J. MILTON
Ambrose Bierce

SLOPER, ALLY
Charles Henry Ross

SLOPER, MACE
Charles Godfrey Leland

SLOTH
Robert Thom

SLY, CHRISTOPHER
Maurice Willson Disher
James Edward Neild

SMALL, ERNEST
Blair Lent

SMALL JOHN
William Makepeace Thackeray

A SMALL COURTIER
Jonathan Swift

SMART, BOB
James Heywood

SMATTERLING, VICESSIMUS, B. L.
John Malcolm Forbes Ludlow

SMECTYMNUUS
Edmund Calamy with Stephen
Marshall, Matthew
Newcomen, William
Spurstowe and Thomas
Young

SMEE, WENTWORTH
George Brown Burgin

SMIFF, PHILANDER, O. P. Q.
Aglen A. Dowty

SMILEY, JIM
Raymond Smiley Spears

SMITH, CAESAR
Trevor Dudley-Smith

SMITH, CARMICHAEL (or CORDWAINER)
Paul Myron Anthony
Linebarger

SMITH, C. BUSBY
John Charles Smith

SMITH, C. G.
Edward Gordon Craig

SMITH, CLARKE ASHTON
Howard Phillips Lovecraft

SMITH, E. GRAHAME
Richard Horatio Edgar Wallace

SMITH, ESSEX
Frances Essex Theodora Hope

SMITH, FORD
Oscar Jerome Friend

SMITH, GAMALIEL
Francis Place

SMITH, HAMILTON
George Ernest Rochester

SMITH, HANNIBAL, ESQ.
James White

SMITH, J., GENTLEMAN
Charles Baring

SMITH, JAMES JARDINE
Kenneth Sylvan Launfal
Guthrie

SMITH, MRS JOHN
Timothy Shay Arthur

SMITH, JOHN, LATE FELLOW OF QUENN'S COLLEGE
Sir David Dalrymple

SMITH, JOHN
Henry Swasey M'Kean

SMITH, COLONEL JOHN
Henry George Keene

SMITH, JOHN, OF SMITH HALL, GENT.
John Delaware Lewis

SMITH, JOHN BROWN
Edward Gordon Craig

SMITH, JOHNSTON
Stephen Crane

SMITH, NICHOLAS, S. J.
Matthias Wilson

MR SMITH
Ralph Ingersoll Lockwood

MRS SMITH
Mrs Martha Savory Yeardley

SMITH, ROSAMUND
Joyce Carol Oates

SMITH, SACHEVERELL
William Young Darling

SMITH, SHELLEY
Nancy Hernione Bodington

SMITH, SHIRLEY
Miss Ella J. Curtis

SMITH, S. S.
Thames Ross Williamson

SMITH, STEVIE
Florence Margaret Smith

SMITH, TENNYSON LONGFELLOW, OF CRIPPLEGATE, WITHIN
John Burley Waring

SMITH, Z. Z.
David Westheimer

SMITHIES, WILLIAM, JUNIOR RECTOR OF ST MICHAEL, MILL END, COLCHESTER
Daniel Defoe

SMITS, DE OUDE HERR
Mark Prager Lindo

SMYTHE, JAMES MOORE
James Moore

SNAFFLES
Charles Johnson Payne

SNAPSHOT
Lewis Clements

SNEKUL, HEINRICH YALE
Henry Clay Lukens

MR SNOB
William Makepeace Thackeray

SNODGRASS, THOMAS
JEFFERSON
Samuel Langhorne Clemens

SNOGBY, GEORGE
HOBDENTHWAITE
Henry Ferris

SNOW, ISABELLA
Margaret Isabella Collier

SNOW, LYNDON
Dorothy Phoebe Ansle

SNOWDEN, KEIGHLEY
James Snowden

SOCIUS, OL.
Thomas Humphrey Ward

A SOLDIER
William Elliot Cairnes
Joseph Donaldson
George Ranken
John Cecil Russell

A SOLDIER OF FORTUNE
William Hamilton Maxwell

A SOLICITOR
Edwin Wilkins Field

A SOLITAIRE
John S. Robb

A SOLITARY WANDERER
Charlotte Smith

SOLO, JAY
Harlan Ellison

SOLOMONS, IKEY, JUNR.
William Makepeace Thackeray

SOME-BODY
Thomas Dekker

SOME WELLWISHERS TO
THE PUBLICK
Samuel Hartlib

SOMEBODY WHO IS NOT A
DOCTOR OF THE
SORBONNE
Jean Louis De Lolme

SOMEBODY, FRANK
Charles Lucas

SOMERS, BART
Gardner Francis Fox

SOMERS, JANE
Doris Lessing

SOMERS III, JONATHAN
SWIFT
Philip Jose Farmer

SOMERS, PAUL
Paul Winterton

SOMERS, SUZANNE
Dorothy Daniels

SOMERSET, PERCY
Maurice Christopher Hollis

A SOMERSETSHIRE
CLERGYMAN
Thomas Spencer

SOMERVILLE & ROSS
Edith Anna Oenone Somerville
with Violet Florence Martin

SOMNAMBULAS
Sir Walter Scott

SOMNO, B. F.
George Wightwick

A SONG-WRITER
William Cox Bennett

A SON-IN-DITTO
Richard Seymour Conway
Chermside

THE SON OF A CATHOLIC
COUNTRY SQUIRE
Roger William Bede Vaughan

THE SON OF A MILITARY
OFFICER
Frederick W. N. Bayley

A SON OF CANDOR
George Grenville

A SON OF LIBERTY
Benjamin Church
Silas Downer

A SON OF THE CHURCH
George Musgrave Musgrave

A SON OF THE MARSHES
Denham Jordan

A SON OF THE SOIL
Joseph Smith Fletcher
Sir Justin Sheil

A SON OF TRUTH AND
DECENCY
Charles Inglis

SOREL, JULIA
Rosalyn Drexler

SOUTH, LT. MICHAEL
Edward Bruce Hamley

SOUTH, SIMEON
John MacGregor

SOUTH, THEOPHILUS
Edward Chitty

A SOUTH AFRICAN
Francis Reginald Statham

A SOUTH AFRICAN
COLONIST
William Charles Scully

A SOUTH CAROLINA
PLANTER
Charles Pinckney

A SOUTH CAROLINIAN
Robert Pleasants Hall
Edwin Clifford Holland
Henry Middleton
Charles Pinckney
Joel Roberts Poinsett
Whitemarsh Benjamin
Seabrook
William Gilmore Simms

SOUTHCOTE, GEORGE
Sir George Aston

A SOUTHERN CITIZEN
Reverdy Johnson

A SOUTHERNER
James Dabney McCabe
Edward Alfred Pollard

A SOUTHERN LADY
Mrs Catharine Ann Warfield

A SOUTHERN MAN
John Pendleton Kennedy

A SOUTHERN MATRON
Mrs Caroline Gilman

A SOUTHERN PLANTER
Nathaniel A. Ware

THE SOUTHERN SPY
Edward Alfred Pollard

A SOUTHRON
William Gilmore Simms

SOUTHWELL, HENRY
Robert Sanders

SOUZA, ERNEST
Evelyn Scott

SOYER, CORYDON
William Makepeace Thackeray

SPADE, MARK
Nigel Marlin Balchin

SPADE, RUPERT
Martin Edward Pawley

SPAIN, JOHN
Cleve Franklin Adams

A SPARKISH PAMPHLETEER
OF BUTTON'S COFFEE-
HOUSE
John Arbuthnot

SPARKS, GODFREY
Charles Dickens

SPARKS, TIMOTHY
Charles Dickens

SPARTACUS
William James Linton

SPAVERY
Samuel Putnam Avery

SPEC, ALONZO, HISTORICAL PAINTER.
William Makepeace Thackeray

THE SPECIAL COMMISSIONER OF THE CAPE ARGUS
Joseph Miller Orpen

A SPECTATOR
David W. Bartlett
Cyrus Augustus Bartol
John Nelson Darby
Arthur Ralph Douglas Elliot
Arthur Penrhyn Stanley
Arthur Bingham Walkley

A SPECTATOR OF THE PAST
Christopher Augustus Memminger

SPECULATOR MORUM
Henry Spencer Ashbee

SPEED, NELL
Emma Speed Sampson

SPELLMAN, ROGER C.
William Robert Cox

SPENCER, CORNELIA
Grace Sydenstricker Yaukey

SPENCER, JOHN
Roy Vickers

SPENCER, NATHANIEL
Robert Sanders

SPENCER, ROLAND
Geoffrey Prout
Francis Warwick

SPENSER, ARTHUR
Samuel Rowe

SPENSER, JAMES
Francis Harold Guest

SPENSER, LEONARD G.
Randall Garrett with Robert Silverberg

SPERANZA
Lady Jane Francesca Wilde

SPES
Evelyn Philip Shirley

SPHINX
Mrs Sarah Fox

SPILLANE, MICKEY
Frank Morrison Spillane

SPINDRIFT
Sir Joseph Noel Paton

SPINIFEX
David Martin

SPINNER, ALICE
Mrs Augusta Zelia Fraser

THE SPIRIT OF HAMPDEN
Robert Fellowes

SPLENE, MEGATHYM, BA, OXON.
John Cockburn Thomson

SPONDEE
Royall Tyler

MR SPONGE
Robert Smith Surtees

SPOOPENDYKE
Stanley Hunter

A SPORTSMAN AND A NATURALIST
Charles George William Saint John

A SPORTSMAN OF BERKSHIRE
Peter Beckford

SPRAGUE, CARTER
W. Samuel Merwin

SPRIGGS
Edward Payson Tenney

SPRINGFIELD, DAVID
John Royston Lewis

SPROULE, ZIBA
George Trask

MR SPROUTS
Richard Whiteing

SPUNKEY, SIMON
Thomas Green Fessenden

SPY
Sir Leslie Ward

THE SPY IN WASHINGTON
Matthew L. Davis

SQUARE, A.
Edwin Abbott Abbott

A SQUATTER
John Beauchamp Jones

SQUIBOB, JOHN P.
George Horatio Derby

STACY, DONALD
Frederick Pohl

STACY, O'CONNOR
William Rollins

A STAFF OFFICER
Francis Duncan
Eric Greville Earle
Sir Somerset John Gough-Calthorpe
John Frederick Maurice
James George Smith Neill

Sir Anthony Coningham Sterling
Sir Garnet Joseph Wolseley

A STAFF SURGEON
Walter Henry

STAFFORD, MARY
F. M. Mayor

STAGGE, JONATHAN
Richard Wilson Webb with Hugh Callingham Wheeler

STAIRS, GORDON
Mrs Mary Hunter Austin

STALBRYDGE, HENRY
John Bale

STAMPER, ALEX
Arthur William Charles Kent

STAN-CHING-QUOT, SIR G.
Sir George Thomas Staunton

STANDBY
Richard Sydney Porteous

STANDFAST, SILAS
George Stillman Hillard

STANDISH, BURT L.
William Gilbert Patten

STANDISH, EVELYN
Richard Goyne

STANDISH, J. O.
Sydney Horler

STANDISH, ROBERT
Digby George Gerahty

STANDISH, WINN
Walter Leon Sawyer

STANFIELD, ANNE
Virginia Coffman

STANHOPE, DOUGLAS
Douglas Valder Duff

STANHOPE, JOHN
John Langdon-Davies

STANLEY, ARTHUR
Arthur Stanley Megaw

STANLEY, BENNETT
Stanley Bennett Hough

STANLEY, CHUCK
Charles Stanley Strong

STANLEY, DAVE
David Dachs

STANLEY, T. LLOYD
Richard Morris Smith

STANSER, ROBERT
Sir Alexander Croke

STANTON, CORALIE
Alice Cecil Seymour Hosken

STANTON, EVAN
Thomas Patrick Hughes

STANTON, MARJORIE
Horace Phillips

STANTON, PAUL
David Beaty

STANTON, VANCE
Michael Angelo Avallone Jr

STAPLES, M. J.
Reginald Thomas Staples

STAPLETON, KATHERINE
Henry Kane

STARK, JOHN
Edward George Stoke

STARK, JOSHUA
Theodore Victor Olsen

STARK, MICHAEL
Laurence Lariar

STARK, RICHARD
Donald E. Westlake

STARR, HENRY
David Ernest Bingley

STARR, H. W.
Harold Ward

STARR, KATE
Joyce Dingwell

STARR, LEONORA
Leonora Dorothy Rivers
Mackesey

STARR, RICHARD
Lewis Essex

A 'STATES'-MAN
Edward Vernon Childe

STATTEN, VARGO
John Russell Fearn

STAUNTON, SCHUYLER
Lyman Frank Baum

STEADFAST, SAMPSON
David Robinson

STEBER, A. R.
Raymond A. Palmer

STEDMAN, CHARLES
William Thomson

STEEL, BYRON
Francis Steegmuller

STEEL, KURT
Rudolf H.Kagey

STEELE, CURTIS
Frederick Clyde Davis

STEELE, DERWEN
Donald Stuart

STEELE, ERSKINE
Archibald Henderson

STEFFANSON, CON
Ronald Joseph Goulart

STEIN, C.
John Cecil Russell

STELLA
Mrs Estelle Anna Blanche
Lewis

STENTOR
William Stanley

STEPHENS, GEORGE
John Lloyd Stephens

STEPSURE, MEPHIBOSHETH
Thomas McCulloch

STEPTOE, LYDIA
Djuna Barnes

STERLING, BRETT
Ray Bradbury
Edmond Moore Hamilton

STERLING, JESSICA
Peggy Coghlan with Hugh
Crawford Rae

STERLING, MARIA SANDRA
Lee Floren

STERLING, STEWART
Prentice Winchell

STERLING, WARD
Harold Ward

STERN, PAUL FREDERICK
Paul Frederick Ernst

STERN, STUART
Hugh Crawford Rae

STERNE, STUART
Victor Gertrude Bloede

STET
T. Earle Welby

STEVENS, ANDY
Mary Danby

STEVENS, BLAINE
Harry B. Whittington

STEVENS, DAN J.
Wayne Overholser

STEVENS, E. S.
Ethel May Stefana Drower

STEVENS, JOHN
Edwin Charles Tubb

STEVENS, K.
Reginald Thomas Staples

STEVENS, MARGARET DEAN
Bess Aldrich

STEVENS, R. L.
Edward D. Hoch

STEVENS, ROBERT TYLER
Reginald Thomas Staples

STEVENS, WILLIAM
CHRISTOPHER
Stephen Valentine Allen

STEVENSON, PEARCE
Caroline Elizabeth Sarah
Norton

STEVINUS
John William Fortescue

STEWARD, ELIZABETH
Brenda Elizabeth Spender

STEWART, FRANCES
James Reginald Wilmot

STEWART, JAY
Charles Stuart Palmer

STEWART, MARJORIE
Marjorie Huxtable

STEWART, WENDALL
Gordon Eklund

STEWART, WILL
John Stewart Williamson

STEWER, JAN
Albert John Coles

STILTON, W., HOROLOGIST
Peter Annet

STIRLING, ARTHUR
Upton Beall Sinclair

STIRLING, PETER
David Stern

STIRLING, STELLA
L. E. Ransome

STITCH, WILHELMINA
Ruth Collie

STOCKLEY, CYNTHIA
Lilian Julia Webb

A STOIC
Arthur O'Connor

STOICUS
Sir George Mackenzie

STOKES, SIMPSON
Frank Dubrez Fawcett

STONE, HAMPTON
Aaron Marc Stein

STONE, ROSETTA
Theodor Seuss Geisel

STONE, SIMON
Howard Barrington

STONE, THOMAS H.
Terence William Harknett

STONE, ZACHARY
Kenneth Martin Follett

STONECASTLE, HENRY, OF
NORTHUMBERLAND,
ESQ.
Henry Baker
John Kelly

STONEHENGE
John Henry Walsh

THE STONEMASON OF
CROMARTIE
Hugh Miller

STOOPNAGLE, LEMUEL Q.
Frederick Chase Taylor

STORER, R. E.
Capell Lofft

STORICUS
William John Blew

STORM, CHRISTOPHER
Theodore Victor Olsen

STORM, LESLEY
Mabel Margaret Clark

STORME, PETER
Philip Van Doren Stern

STORY, SYDNEY A.
Mrs Mary H. Greene Pike

STOTHARD, KEMPE
Mrs Anna Eliza Bray

STOWELL, OLIVER
Roland Fairbairn McWilliams
with Margaret Stovel
McWilliams

STRADA
Thomas Barnes

STRADLING, MATTHEW
Martin Francis Mahony

STRAND, PAUL E.
Simon Palestrant

STRANG, HERBERT
George Herbert Ely with
Charles James L'Estrange

STRANG, WILLIAM
Zulfikar Ghose

STRANGE, ELWIN
John Thomas Lutz

STRANGE, JOHN STEPHEN
Dorothy Stockbridge Tillett

STRANGE, MICHAEL
Blanche Oelrichs

THE STRANGER
Francis Lieber
Isaac Story

STRANGER, JOYCE
Joyce Muriel Wilson

STRATEGICUS
Herbert Charles O'Neill

STRATFORD, PHILIP
Henry Kenneth Bulmer

STRATHEIR
Henry Sullivan Jarrett

STRATHERN, WILLIAM
Hamilton Jobson

STRATTON, THOMAS
Robert Coulson with T.
Eugene Deweese

STRAVAIGER
Harry Mortimer Batten

STRAWS
Joseph M. Field

A STRAY HEARER
Hugh Reginald Haweis

STREAMER, COL. D.
Harry Jocelyn Clive Graham

STREBOR, EIGGAM
Maggie Roberts

STRETTON, HESBA
Sarah Smith

A STRICT EXAMINER OF
THE MEDICAL ART
Everard Maynwaring

STRIKE, JEREMY
Thomas Edward Renn

STRIKE BUT HEAR
John Horne Tooke

STRIX
Robert Peter Fleming

STRODE, RALPH
Ralph Straus

A STROLING PLAYER
John Roberts

STRONG, CHARLES
Samuel Epstein

STRONG, PAT
Richard Alexander Hough

STRONG, PATIENCE
Winifred Emma Cushing

STRONG, SUSAN
Joan Rees

STRUTHER, JAN
Joyce Anstruther

STRYFE, PAUL
James R. Newman

STUART, ALEX R.
Stuart Gordon

STUART, ARTHUR
Arthur William Steuart
Cochrane

STUART, BRIAN
Brian Arthur Worthington-
Stuart

STUART, CHARLES
EDWARD
Charles Stuart Hay Allen

STUART, CLAY
Harry B. Whittington

STUART, DON A.
John Wood Campbell

STUART, ELEANOR
Eleanor Stuart Childs
Eleanor H. Porter

STUART, ESME
Amelie C. Leroy

STUART, IAN
Alistair MacLean

STUART, SIDNEY
Michael Angelo Avallone Jr.

A STUDENT
George William Lyttelton

A STUDENT-AT-LAW
Frederick Knight Hunt

A STUDENT IN DIVINITY
John Floyd
Thomas Rennell

A STUDENT IN PARIS
Augustus Kingsley Gardner

A STUDENT IN THEOLOGIE
William Master

A STUDENT OF HARVARD
UNIVERSITY
Thaddeus Mason Harris

A STUDENT OF HISTORY
Edward Denham

A STUDENT OF IRISH
HISTORY
William Butler Yeats

A STUDENT OF LINCOLN'S
INN
Charles Neate

A STUDENT OF MARISCHAL
COLLEGE
Robert Alves

A STUDENT OF MEDICINE
IN THE UNIVERSITY OF
EDINBURGH
Alexander Campbell

A STUDENT OF OXFORD
John Hippisley

A STUDENT OF PASCAL
Thomas Caulfield Irwin

STUDENT OF POLITICS
Herbert Sidebotham

A STUDENT OF THE
TEMPLE
Charles Leslie

A STUDENT OF THE
UNIVERSITY OF
GLASGOW
William Hamilton Drummond

STUDENT OF WAR
Herbert Sidebotham

STURDY, CARL
Charles Stanley Strong

STURGEON, THEODORE
Edward Hamilton Waldo

STURGES, PRESTON
Edmond Preston Biden

STURROCK, JEREMY
Benjamin James Healey

STURTON, HUGH
Hugh Anthony Stephen
Johnston

STUYVESANT, ALICE
Alice Muriel Williamson

A SUBALTERN
Andrew Alexander Irvine

A SUBURBAN CLERGYMAN
John Owen

SUDBURY, RICHARD
Charles Hammond Gibson

SUE-SAND, ALEXANDRE,
FILS
Edward Bruce Hamley

A SUFFERER
Thomas Wilson

A SUFFERER, AUTHOR OF
'POEMS OF MANY
YEARS'
Robert Needham Cust

A SUFFERER FOR CHRIST
Francis Howgill

A SUFFERING MISTRESS
John Moore Capes

A SUFFOLK MINISTER
Thomas Harmer

A SUFFOLK RECTOR
Erskine Neale

A SUFFOLK YEOMAN
James Bird

SUGARTAIL
George Washington Harris

SUGGS, CAPT. SIMON
Johnson Jones Hooper

SULLIVAN, SEAN MEI
Gerald Allen Sohl

SULPICUS
Augustus Granville Stapleton

SULTO
Sir Max Beerbohm

SUMMERFIELD, CHARLES
Alfred W. Arrington

SUMMERLEY, FELIX
Henry Cole

SUMMERS, CHARLIE
Philip William May

SUMMERS, D. B.
Geoffrey John Barrett

SUMMERS, DIANA
George Henry Smith

SUMMERS, ROWENA
Jean Saunders

SUNAVILL, J. F.
James Frank Sullivan

SUNDAY
Mrs Catherine Talbot

SUNDRY WHEREOF
Richard Porson

A SUPERNUMERARY
John Pring

A SUPPOSED DELINQUENT
James Orchard Halliwell-
Phillips

SURFACEMAN
Alexander Anderson

SURGEN, V.
Edward Gordon Craig

A SURGEON
Henry Mudge

A SURGEON-AURIST
William Wright

SURREY, KATHRYN
Phyllis Matthewman

SURREY, RICHARD
Bertram Brooker

A SURROGATE
George Miller

A SURVIVOR WHO FILLED
AN IMPORTANT POST
AT THE GLORIOUS
SIEGE
Sir Frederick Richard Maunsell

SUSSEX, JASPER
John Wilson

SUTHERLAND, ELIZABETH
Elizabeth Margaret Marshall

SUTHERLAND, HARVEY
Eugene Wood

SUTHERLAND, JOAN
Joan Maisie Collings Kelly

SUTHERLAND, WILLIAM
John Murray Cooper

SUTTON
Sir John Sutton

SUTTON, HENRY
David Ritman Slavitt

SUYIN, HAN
Elizabeth Comber

SVAREFF, COUNT
VLADIMIR
Edward Alexander Crowley

SWAMMERDAM, MARTIN
GRIBALDUS
William Mudford

SWAN, SIR SIMON, BART
Joseph Fawcett

SWANWICK, H. M.
Helena Maria Sickert

SWAYNE, MARTIN
Henry Maurice Dunlop Nicoll

SWEET, SARAH O.
Sarah Orne Jewett

SWELLMORE
William Makepeace Thackeray

SWEVERN, GODFREY
John MacMillan Brown

SWIFT, ANTHONY
Joseph Jefferson Farjeon

SWIFT, AUGUSTUS T.
Howard Phillips Lovecraft

SWIFT, BENJAMIN
William Romaine Paterson

SWIFT, BRYAN
William Cecil Knott

SWIFT, JONADAB
John Henley

SWIFT, JULIAN
Arthur Applin

SWIFT, SOLOMON
Percival Leigh

SWING, LUCIFER
Sir Theodore Martin

SWINTON, ANDREW
William Thomson

SYDENHAM, EDWARD
James Boaden

SYDNEY
James Porter

SYDNEY, GEORGE FREDERIC
Sir Henry Seton Steuart

SYLVAN, URBANUS
Henry Charles Beeching

SYLVANDER
Robert Burns

SYLVANUS THEOPHRASTUS
John Thelwall

SYLVATICUS
John Fitzgerald Pennie

SYLVESTER, ARTHUR
Arthur Lewis Tubbs

SYLVESTER, C.
Emma Caroline Wood

SYLVESTER, JOHN
Hector Hawton

SYLVESTER, PHILIP
Philip Worner

SYLVESTRIS
Jehoiada Brewer

SYLVIN, FRANCIS
Sylvia Sybil Seaman

SYLVIUS
Hugh Williamson

SYMMACHUS
John Palmer

SYMPATHES
Joseph Willard

A SYMPATHISER
Arthur John Story

SYNAN, A.
Arthur Edward Clery

SYNDERCOMBE
Henry Flood

SYPHAX
William Godwin

SYR
Samuel A. Allen

T

T.
William Cowper
Samuel Johnson
Sir Richard Steele
Joseph Peter Thorp

T. A. L. V. J.
Therese Albertina Louise
Robinson

T. B.
Arthur Christopher Benson
Thomas Blount
Thomas Branch

T. C.
Thomas Corbett

T. E.
Thomas Edwards

T. G. F.
Thomas George Fonnereau

T. H.
William Cowper
Thomas Hervey

T. J. V.
Ezra Pound

T. K., DD
Thomas Ken

T. P.
Thomas Power O'Connor

T. T.
William Makepeace Thackeray

T. W.
George Savile

T. Z.
Samuel Adams

TA-SHUN, PAI
Frederick Peterson

TABLE TALK
James Bruce

TACITUS
De Witt Clinton

TAFFRAIL
Capt. Henry Taprell Dorling

**MESSRS TAG, RAG AND
  BOBTAIL**
Isaac D'Israeli

TAHITE
James Edward Neild

TAINE, JOHN
Eric Temple Bell

TALBOT, HUGH
Argentine Francis Alington

**TALIESSEN DE
  MONMOUTH**
Thomas Powell

TALKER, THOMAS
William Brighty Rands

TALLENTYRE, S. G.
Miss Evelyn Beatrice Hall

TALLOW
Thomas Alfred Lowe

TALLY, TOM
George Barham

TALMAGE, ANNE
Talmage Powell

TAM
Thomas Mackellar

**TAN CHAU QUA OF QUANG
  CHEW FU, GENT.**
Sir William Chambers

TANK MAJOR
Stephen Henry Foot

TANNER, WILLIAM
Sir Kingsley Amis

TANTE, DILLY
Stanley Jasspon Kunitz

TANTIVY, THOMAS
Alfred Austin

TANTULUS
James Boswell

TAPER
Henry Bernard Levin

TARN, SHIRLEY
Victor Benjamin Neuburg

TARTINI'S FAMILIAR
Henry Fothergill Chorley

TARRANT, JOHN
Clive Egleton

**TASISTRO, LOUIS
  FITZGERALD**
Thomas Tod Stoddart

TASMA
Jessie Catherine Couvrer

TATE, ELLALICE
Eleanor Alice Hibbert

TAVIS, ALEC
Alastair MacTavish Dunnett

TAYLOR, DOMINI
Roger Erskine Longrigg

TAYLOR, GEORGE
Joseph Archer Crowe
Adolf Hausrath

TAYLOR, H. BALDWIN
Hillary Baldwin Waugh

TAYLOR, JANE
Jayne Ann Krentz

TAYLOR, NORMAN
Noel Wood-Smith

TAYLOUR, CHARLES
Henry Keepe

A TEACHER
Henry Russell Cleveland
George Whitefield Samson
Charles Walton Sanders

A TEACHER IN BOSTON
Nathaniel Peabody

MRS TEACHWELL
Lady Eleanor Fenn

TEL-TROTH, THOMAS
Joseph Swetnam

TELA, JOSEPHUS
Joseph Webb

TELESCOPE, TOM
Oliver Goldsmith

TELFAIR, RICHARD
Richard Jessup

TELL-TRUTH, PAUL
George Saville Carey

TELLER, THOMAS
Thomas Day

TELLET, ROY
Albert Eubule Evans

A TEMPERATE DRINKER
William Gauntley

TEMPEST, EVELYN
Edward William Diram
Cuming

TEMPEST, JAN
Irene Maude Swatridge

TEMPEST, SARAH
Doris Almon Ponsonby

TEMPEST, VICTOR
Elliott Elias Philipp

A TEMPLAR
Alfred Ainger
Abraham Hayward
John Hosack
Edward Vaughan Hyde
Kenealy
William Charles Mark Kent
Richard Robinson

TEMPLAR, CLAUDE
John William Daugars

TEMPLE, REV. ALLAN
Charles Benjamin Tayler

TEMPLE, ANN
Penelope Ruth Mortimer

TEMPLE, DAN
Dwight Bennett Newton

TEMPLE, LANCELOT
John Armstrong

TEMPLE, NEVILLE AND
EDWARD TREVOR
Hon. Julian Henry Charles
Fane with Edward Robert
Bulwer Lytton

TEMPLE, PAUL
Francis Henry Durbridge with
James Douglas R. McConnell

TEMPLE, T. B.
Thomas Banister

TEMPLE, THEODORE
Samuel Lorenzo Knapp

TEMPLEMAN, JAMES
Henry Kirke White

TEMPLETON, HORACE
Charles James Lever

TEMPLETON, JESSE
George Goodchild

TEMPLETON, LAWRENCE
Sir Walter Scott

TEMPLETON, TERENCE
Peter George Patmore

TEMPLETON, TRISTRAM
Nicholas Francis Flood Davin

TENN, WILLIAM
Philip Klass

TENNANT, CATHARINE
Kathleen Muriel Eyles

TENNANT, KYLIE
Mrs Lewis Charles Rodd

TENNEBRA, T.
Alfred Rosling Bennett

A TENNESSEAN
John Haywood

TENNESHAW, S. M.
Randall Garrett with Robert
Silverberg

TERMAGENT, PRISCILLA (or
ROXANA)
Bonnell Thornton

TERRAE FILIUS
Robert Edward Garnham
James Clarence Mangan

TERRAE-FILIUS
PHILAGRICOLA
Stephen Weston

TERRIS, WILLIAM
William Charles James Lewin

TERRY, C. V.
Frank Gill Slaughter

TERRY, MONEY, ESQ.
James B. Congdon

TERRY, WILLIAM
Terence William Harknett

TERSON, PETER
Peter Patterson

TESTIS MUNDUS
CATHOLICUS
Edmund Hall

TESTIS OCULATIS
Richard Treffry

TESTY, TIMOTHY
James Beresford

TEUTHA
William Jerdan

TEVIOTDALE
Thomas Scott Anderson

TEY, JOSEPHINE
Elizabeth Mackintosh

THALER, DR KEIN
George Frederick Collier

THAMES, CHRISTOPHER H.
Milton Lesser

THANE, ELSWYTH
Elswyth Thane Ricker Beebe

THANELIAN
Nathaniel W. Coffin

THANET, NEIL
Robert Lionel Fanthorpe

THANET, OCTAVE
Alice French

THAYER, GERALDINE
Dorothy Daniels

THAYER, JANE
Catherine Woolley

THAYER, LEE
Emma Redington Thayer

THEATRICAL LOUNGER
Thomas William Robertson

THEBERTON, EDWARD
Anthony Daniels

THEIR HUMBLE SERVANT,
THE SHAVER
John MacGowan

THEOBOLD, LEWIS, JUN.
Howard Phillips Lovecraft

THEODORIT
Robert Southey

THEODORUS
James Bass Mullinger

THEODOSIA
Anne Steele

THEOPHANES
CANTABRIGIENSIS
Samuel Squire

THEOPHILUS
Caleb Fleming
Joseph Mottershead
Samuel Spring

THEOPHILUS CHURCHMAN
Peter Heylyn
Henry Hickman

THEOPHILUS
PHILADELPHUS
John Ley

THEOPHILUS
PHILANTHROPOS
David Hall
Robert Poole

THEOPHILUS
  PHILOBASILEUS
Thomas Pierce

THEOPHILUS SENEX ESQ.
Daniel Turner

THEOPHRASTUS
William Creech

THEOPTES
Job Durfee

THETA
William Thorn

THINKER, THEODORE
Francis Channing Woodworth

THINKS-I-TO-MYSELF-WHO
?
Edward Nares

A THIRD PERSON
William Creed

THIRIOLD, CHARLES
Richard Shilleto

THIRLMERE, ROWLAND
John Walker

THE THIRTY-ONE
Leonard Withington

THISTLE, DONALD
Howard Clarke Brown

THISTLETHWAITE, BEL
Agnes Ethelwyn Wetherald

THOMAS, ANTHONY
Reginald Heber Poole

THOMAS, B.
Thomas Burgeland Johnson

THOMAS, CAROLINE
Mrs Julia Caroline Dorr

THOMAS, CAROLYN
Actea Caroline Duncan

THOMAS, EDWARD
Philip Edward Thomas

THOMAS, HENRY
Henry Thomas Schnittkind

THOMAS, JOAN GALE
Joan Mary Gale Robinson

THOMAS, JUDY
Reginald George Thomas

THOMAS, LEE
Lee Floren

THOMAS, LESLIE
Leslie Thomas John Arlott

THOMAS, MURRAY
Thomas Murray Ragg

THOMAS, TOBYAS
Thomas Brown

THOMAS, WALTER
Walter Besant

THOMPSON, A. C.
Alice Christiana Gertrude
  Meynell

THOMPSON, CHINA
Mary Christiana Brand

THOMPSON, LOUISA
James Smith

THOMPSON, SETON
Enest Thompson Seton

THOMPSON, WARWICK
William Pett Ridge

THOMSON, EDWARD
Edwin Charles Tubb

THOMSON, JOSEPH
David Macbeth Moir

THONININCA
John Canton

THORN, GUY
Cyril A. E. Ranger-Gull

THORNE, GILBERT
Gilbert Conrad Longstaff

THORNE, MARION
Miss Ida Treadwell Thurston

THORNE, NICOLA
Rosemary Ellerbeck

THORNE, P.
Mrs Mary Prudence Smith

THORNE, VICTOR
Frederick Jackson

THORNE, WHYTE
Richard Whiteing

THORNET, TERESA A.
Mrs Anna Holloway

THORNTON, FAIRELIE
Florence Rudge

THORPE, KAMBA
Elizabeth Bellamy

THORPE, SYLVIA
June Sylvia Thimblethorpe

THORPE, TREBOR
Robert Lionel Fanthorpe

THRIBB, E. J.
Barry Fantoni with Richard
  Ingrams

THRICE, LUKE
John Russell

THUISEN, ISMAR
John MacNie

THUMB, THOMAS, ESQ.
Benjamin Church

THURCASTLE, E. F. O.
Edward Falkener

THURLAND, BILBERRY
Charles Hooton

THURLOCKE, A. R.
Arthur Locke

THURMAN, STEVE
Frank Castle

THURSTON, HENRY T.
Francis Turner Palgrave

THURSTON, OLIVER
Henry Flanders

TI-TI-OF SIAM
Denis Murphy

TIBBER, ROBERT (or
  ROSEMARY)
Eve Rosemary Friedman

TIBBS
Charles Dickens

TICHEBOURNE, CHEVIOT
William Harrison Ainsworth

MISS TICKLETOBY
William Makepeace Thackeray

TICKLER
George Philip Rigney Pulman

TICKLER, TIMOTHY
John Gibson Lockhart with
  William Maginn

TICKLETOOTH, TABITHA
Charles Selby

TIDY, THERESA
Mrs Elizabeth Susanna Graham

TIERNEY, REGINALD
Thomas O'Neill Russell

TIGER, DERRY
Harlan Ellison

TIGER, JOHN
Walter Herman Wager

TIGER LILY
Lillie Devereux Blake

TILBURY TRAMP
Charles James Lever

TILNEY, H. C.
Constance Alexina Napier
  Trollope

TILTON, ALICE
Phoebe Atwood Taylor

TILTON, DWIGHT
Wilder Dwight Quint with
  George Tilton Richardson

TIMANUS, SARAH J.
Mrs Sarah Jane Crafts

TIMBERTOE, TIMOTHY,
ESQ.
Samuel Foote

THE 'TIMES' BEE-MASTER
John Cumming

'THE TIMES'
CORRESPONDENT AT
BERLIN
Carl Abel

TIMOLEON
Isaac Orr
James Tilton

TIMON
Sir Thomas Burnet

TIMON, JOHN
Donald Grant Mitchell

TIMONICULUS
Walter Harris

TIMORCUS, THEOPHILUS
Thomas Gataker with Richard
Vines and Richard Baxter

TIMOTHY
Sylvester Holmes
Thomas Worcester

TIMS THE YOUNGER
William Frederick Deacon

TIMSOL, ROBERT
Frederick Meyer Bird

TINKER, BEAMISH
F. Tennyson Jesse

TINKER, Tom
Jonathan Swift

TINTO, DICK
Frank Boott Goodrich

A TIPLING PHILOSOPHER
OF THE ROYAL
SOCIETY
William Oldisworth

TIPTREE, JAMES, JR.
Alice Hastings Sheldon

TISDALE, ALICE
Alice Hobart

TISH
Edward George Earle Lytton
Bulwer-Lytton

TITAN, EARL
John Russell Fearn

TITCOMB, TIMOTHY
Josiah Gilbert Holland

TITIAN
Minna T. Antrim

TITMARSH, MICHAEL
ANGELO
William Makepeace Thackeray

TITTERWELL, TIMOTHY
Samuel Kettell

TITUS
Henry Thomson

TITYRUS
James Alfred Henry Catton

TIVERTON, FATHER
WILLIAM
Martin Jarrett-Kerr

TLEPOLEMUS
George Carless Swayne

TO-KA-NI-YA
Howard Clarke Brown

TOBY M. P.
Sir Henry William Lucy

TOBY, ABEL'S KINSMAN
William Wagstaffe

TOBY, UNCLE SIMEON
George Trask

TOCHER, E. W.
William Denis Johnston

TODD, LAWRIE
Grant Thorburn

TODD, PAUL
Richard Posner

TODKILL, ANAS
John Esten Cooke

TOGO, HASHIMURA
Wallace Admah Irwin

TOKLAS, ALICE B.
Gertrude Stein

TOLETUS
David Tappan

TOLLY, COLIN
John Henry Douglas Webster

TOMKINS
John Warner

TOMKINS, ISAAC, GENT.
Henry Peter Brougham

TOMKINSON, DUDLEY
Thomas Brown

TOMLINE, F. (or F. L.)
Sir William Schwenk Gilbert

TOMSON, GRAHAM R.
Rosamund Watson

TONSON, JACOB
Enoch Arnold Bennett

TORQUEMADA
Edward Powys Mathers

TORR, A. C.
Frederick Leslie Hobson

TORRIE, MALCOLM
Gladys Maude Winifred
Mitchell

TORRO, PEL
Robert Lionel Fanthorpe

A TORY
Samuel Adams
Thomas Peregrine Courtenay
Edward H. Knatchbull
Hugessen

A TORY MEMBER OF
PARLIAMENT AND
DISTINGUISHED
OFFICER
Denis Murphy

TOSSOFFACAN,
ASDRYASDUST
Edmund Gayton

TOUCH 'EM, TIMOTHY
Thomas Beck

TOUCHSTONE, TIMOTHY
Robert Oliphant

TOUPIUS, JOHANNES
Jonathan Toup

A TOURIST
Charles Lanman
James Talboys Wheeler

TOWERS, REGINA
Nina Pykare

MR TOWN, CRITIC AND
CENSOR GENERAL
George Colman with Bonnell
Thornton

MR TOWN, JUNIOR CRITIC
AND CENSOR-GENERAL
James Henry Leigh Hunt

TOWNE, PETER
Peter Francis Nabakov

TOWNE, STUART
Clayton Rawson

A TOWNSMAN
James Watson

TOWRY, M. H.
Miss Mary Helen White

TOWRY, PETER
David Towry Piper

TRACEY, ALBERT
Albert Leffingwell

A TRADES UNION OFFICIAL
William John Davis

A TRADESMAN OF OXFORD
George Smith Green

A TRADESMAN OF
PHILADELPHIA
Benjamin Franklin

TRADLEG, NITRAM
Edmund Martin Geldart

TRAFFORD, F. G.
Charlotte Cowan

TRAHERNE, MICHAEL
Denys James Watkins-Pitchford

TRAILL, PETER
Guy Mainwaring Morton

TRANSIT, ROBERT
Isaac Robert Cruikshank

THE TRANSLATOR OF THE
CALEDONIAN BARDS
John Clark

TRAPROCK, DR WALTER E.
George Shepard Chappell

A TRAVELLER
John Banim
William Cullen Bryant
John Francis Campbell
Henry Russell Cleveland
De Witt Clinton
George William Curtis
Sir William Draper
Edmund Flagg
Thomas Jefferson Hogg
Silas Pinckney Holbrook
Andrew Valentine Kirwan
Mrs Sarah Lee
Sir John Malcolm
Mrs Anne Royall
Henry Salt
Thomas Victor

TRAVELLER, T. C.
APPRENTICE IN
POETRIE
Sir John Harington

A TRAVELLER
UNDERGROUND
John R. Leifchild

A TRAVELLING ARTIST
Leitch Ritchie

TRAVELLING BACHELOR
James Fenimore Cooper
Robert Gordon Latham

A TRAVELLING PHYSICIAN
Sir George William Lefevre

TRAVEN, BEN (OR BRUNO)
Hermann A. O. M. Feige

TRAVER, ROBERT
John Donaldson Voelker

TRAVERS, GRAHAM
Margaret Todd

TRAVERS, HUGH
Hugh Travers Mills

TRAVERS, JOHN
Eva Mary Bell

TRAVERS, STEPHEN
Henry Garnett Radcliffe

TRAVIS, WILL
Henry John Keevill

A TREASURER OF A
CORPORATION
Thomas Greaves Cary

TREAT, LAWRENCE
Laurence Arthur Goldstone

TREBOUN, SALCHEIN
Nicholas Breton

TREDGOLD, NYE
Nigel Godwin Tranter

TREE, GREGORY
John Franklin Bardin

TREENOODLE, UNCLE JAN
William Sandys

TREGELLIS, JOHN
Sydney Gowing

TREGENNA, JULIA
Frederick Britten Austin

TREHEARNE, ELIZABETH
Patricia Anne Maxwell

TRELEINIE, P. H., GENT.
Peter Heylyn

TREMAINE, JENNIE
Marion Chesney

TREMAYNE, PETER
Peter Berresford Ellis

TRENCHARD, ASA
Henry Watterson

TRENPOLPEN, P. W.
William Prideaux Courtney

TRENT, A. G.
Richard Garnett

TRENT, OLAF
Robert Lionel Fanthorpe

TRENTON, GAIL
Neil Grant

TREPOFF, IVAN
George Hatfield Dingley
Gossip

TRESILLIAN, RICHARD
Royston Ellis

TRESSALL, ROBERT
Robert Noonan

TREVANIAN
Rodney William Whitaker

TREVELYAN, PERCY
Antony Charles Thomas

TREVENA, JOHN
Ernest George Henham

TREVERT, EDWARD
Edward T. Bubier

TREVES, KATHLEEN
Emily Kathleen Walker

TREVOR, EDWARD AND
NEVILLE TEMPLE
Edward Robert Bulwer Lytton
and Julian Henry Charles
Fane

TREVOR, ELLESTON
Trevor Dudley-Smith

TREVOR, GLEN
James Hilton

TREVOR, RALPH
James Reginald Wilmot

TREVOR, WILLIAM
William Trevor Cox

TREVYLYAN, MRS KITTY
Mrs Elizabeth Charles

TRIFOLIUM
Denis Florence MacCarthy

TRIM
Edward Baldwyn
William Broadley Megson

TRINCULO
Andrew Carpenter Wheeler

TRING, A. STEPHEN
Laurence Walter Meynell

A TRINITARIAN
John Penrose

TRIP, TOM
Giles Jones

TRIPE, DR ANDREW
Jonathan Swift

TRIPE, ANDREW, MD
William Wagstaffe

TRIPTOLEMUS
Philip Skelton

TRISMEGISTUS
William Frederick Deacon

TRIX
Sir John Verney

A TROGLODYTE
Ferdinand Canning Scott
Schiller

TROIS-ETOILES
Eustace Clare Grenville Murray

TROLLOPE, H. C.
Constance Alexina Napier
Trollope

TROOPER GERARDY
Edwin Field Gerard

TROT, JOHN, A YEOMAN
Henry St John

TROTANDOT, JOHN
George Philip Rigney Pulman

TROTCOSEY, THOMAS
Mrs Catherine Frances Grace
Gore

TROTT-PLAID, JOHN
Henry Fielding

TROUT, KILGORE
Philip Jose Farmer

TROY, KATHERINE
Anne Buxton

TROY, SIMON
Thurman Warriner

TRUCK, BILL
John Howell

A TRUE BRITON
Hugh Tootel

A TRUE CATHOLICK OF
THE CHURCH OF
ENGLAND
George Hickes

A TRUE ENGLISHMAN
James Drake
George Gascoigne
Henry Robinson

A TRUE LIBERAL
Francis Reginald Statham

A TRUE LOVER OF HIS
COUNTRY
Sir William Coventry

A TRUE LOVER OF HIS
KING AND COUNTRY
Hugh Reilly

A TRUE LOVER OF THE
MATHEMATICKS
William Leybourn

A TRUE LOVER OF TRUTH
AND PEACE
Joseph Hall

A TRUE PROTESTANT
Charles Owen

A TRUE PROTESTANT AND
A HEARTY LOVER OF
HIS COUNTRY
George Savile

A TRUE PROTESTANT AND
NO DISSENTER
John Northleigh

A TRUE SON OF THE
CHURCH OF ENGLAND
William Asplin
Arthur Bury

A TRUE SON OF THE
PROTESTANT CHURCH
OF ENGLAND
Gilbert Burnet

A TRUE TROJAN
Charles Leslie

TRUEMAN, T.
Robert Paltock

TRUEMAN, THOMAS
Jonas Hanway

TRUMP
William Brisbane Dick

TRUMPETARIUS
James Boswell

TRUNCHEON, J., ESQ.
John Trenchard

TRUSCOTT, BRUCE
Edgar Allison Peers

TRUSTA, H.
Mrs Elizabeth Stuart Phelps

A TRUTH-SEEKER
Sir Isaac Pitman

TUBBY, I. M.
Robert Kraus

TUBERVILL, HUGH
Edmund Gayton

TUCK, B. F.
George Wightwick

TUCKER, LINK
David Ernest Bingley

TUGMUTTON, TIMOTHY,
ESQ.
Charles Chorley

TULKET, MARMADUKE
Peter Armstrong Whittle

TULLY, PAUL
Jerome Gardner

A TURKEY MERCHANT
Lady Mary Wortley Montagu

A TURKISH EFFENDI
Laurence Oliphant

TURNER, CLAY
Willis Todhunter Ballard

TURNER, JUDY
Judith Saxton

TURNER, MATTHEW FREKE
Oswald John Crawfurd

TURNLEY, CHRISTOPHER
Una Mary Ellis-Fermor

A TUTOR
William Jones

A TUTOR AND A FELLOW
OF A COLLEGE IN
OXFORD
Edward Bentham

TWAIN, MARK
Samuel Langhorne Clemens
Isaiah Sellers

TWAMLEY, LOUISA ANNE
Mrs Louisa Meredith

A TWELVE YEARS'
RESIDENT
Stephen Williamson

20-BORE
Basil Tozer

TWENTY-EIGHT YEARS IN
INDIA
Charles James O'Donnell

20/1631
Allen Upward

TWIG, TIMOTHY, ESQ.
Alexander Campbell
Joseph Moser

TWIST, ANANIAS
William Curtis Nunn

TWIST-WIT, CHRISTOPHER
Christopher Anstey

TWO ART CRITICS
Andrew Lang and William
Ernest Henley

TWO BROTHERS
Augustus William Hare and
Julius Charles Hare
Arthur John Lockhart and
Burton Wellesley Lockhart
Alfred, Charles and Frederick
Tennyson

TWO CLERKS
Frederick Brooke Westcott and
Henry Charles Beeching

TWO GENTLEMEN OF
HARVARD
John Tyler Wheelwright and
Frederick Jesup Stimson

TWO IDLE APPRENTICES
Sir Thomas Wemyss Reid and
William Henry Cooke

TWO LADIES OF ENGLAND
June Langley Moore and Doris
Langley Moore

TWO MERRY MEN
Francis Edward Smedley and
Edmund Yates

TWO MOUNTED SENTRIES
John Josiah Hort

**TWO OLD FRIENDS,
BROTHER OFFICERS**
Sir Henry Yule and Robert
MacLagan

TWO OF THEMSELVES
Mrs Elizabeth Charles

**TWO READERS OF
DARWIN'S TREATISE
ON THE ORIGIN OF
SPECIES**
Daniel Treadwell and Asa Gray

**TWO SISTERS OF THE
WEST**
Mrs Catharine Ann Warfield
and Eleanor Percy Lee

TWO WAGS
John Kendrick Bangs and
Frank Dempster Sherman

TWO WRITERS
Rudyard Kipling and Beatrice
Kipling

TWYM
Alexander Stuart Boyd

TYGER
William Dunlop

TYGHE, WHYTE
Lewis Strange Wingfield

TYLER, THEODORE
Edward William Ziegler

A TYPO
John S. Robb

TYRANNO-MASTIX, TOM
Marchamont Needham

TYRO
Herbert George Wells

TYRO-PHILELEUTHERUS
John Duncan

TYRO-PHILOLOGIS
William Livingston

TYRO-THEOLOGUS, MA
Francis Stone

A TYTHING MAN
Rufus Wyman

TYTLER, SARAH
Henrietta Keddie

U

UBIQUE
Sir Frederick Gordon
Guggisberg

UHER, LORNA
Lorna Crozier

ULISSIPO BRITANNICUS
Sir Philip Francis

AN ULSTER LANDLORD
Hugh De F. Montgomery

AN ULSTERMAN
George Sigerson

ULYSSES COSMOPOLITE
George Berkeley

UMBRA OXONIENSIS
William Palmer

UMBRIDGE, SCOTSON
Edward Gordon Craig

UNCLE ADAM
George Mogridge
Carl Anton Wetterburgh

UNCLE BEN
Daniel F. Tyler

UNCLE FRANK
Francis Channing Woodworth

UNCLE GEORGE
Increase Niles Tarbox

UNCLE HARDY
William Senior

UNCLE HARRY
John Habberton

UNCLE HERBERT
Timothy Shay Arthur

UNCLE JESSE
Clement Edwin Babb

UNCLE JOHN
John Aikin
Edwin O. Chapman

UNCLE MAC
Derek Ivor Breashur
McCulloch

UNCLE MARK
Mark Lemon

UNCLE MATT
Mordecai Cubitt Cooke

UNCLE PAUL
Samuel Burnham

UNCLE PHILIP
Francis Lister Hawks

UNCLE REMUS
Joel Chandler Harris

UNCLE SHELBY
Shelby Silverstein

UNCLE TED
Herbert Myrick

UNCLE TOBY
Elisha North

UNCUT CAVENDISH
John Willoughby Meares

UNDER PETTY
William Makepeace Thackeray

AN UNDERGRADUATE
Thomas Agar Holland
George Horne
John Delaware Lewis
William Penn
Richard Polwhele
John Purchas
Thomas Whytehead

AN UNDERGRADUATE OF
THE UNIVERSITY OF
CAMBRIDGE
Thomas Dale

UNDERHILL, CHARLES
Reginald Charles Hill

UNDERHILL, EVELYN
Mrs Stuart Moore

UNDERHILL, DR UPDIKE
Royall Tyler

UNDERWOOD, MICHAEL
John Michael Evelyn

UNDERWOOD, MILES
John Glassco

AN UNEDUCATED MAN
Thomas Flindell

AN UNEDUCATED YOUTH
John Jones

AN UNFEIGNED ADMIRER
OF GENUINE BRITISH
JURISPRUDENCE
Henry Constantine Jennings

AN UNFORTUNATE
NOBLEMAN
Thomas Christopher Banks

AN UNFORTUNATE
SCHOOLMASTER
Samuel Lines

A UNION ARMY OFFICER
Frank Wolford

A UNITARIAN
Lant Carpenter
George Harris
Charles Wentworth Upham

AN UNITARIAN
CLERGYMAN
Henry Ware

A UNITARIAN LAYMAN
Henry Arthur Bright
H. J. Huidekoper

A UNITARIAN OF NEW
YORK
Henry Devereux Sewall

AN UNIVERSITY PEN
Luke Howard

AN UNKNOWN AND
DISINTERESTED
CLERGYMAN
John Dunton

AN UNKNOWN AVIATOR
J. MacDougall Grider

AN UNLETTERED BARD
William Hawkins

THE UNLUCKY MAN
Francis Doyne Dwyer

AN UNMARRIED CYNIC
William Bayne Ranken

UNO
George Melville Baker

THE UNOFFICIAL
OBSERVER
John Franklin Carter

AN UNORTHODOX
BELIEVER
Edmond Gore Alexander
Holmes

UNUS DE MULTUS
William Allingham

UNUS QUORUM
William Wadd

AN UNWORTHY MEMBER
OF THAT COMMUNITY
John Rutty

UPDYKE, JAMES
William Riley Burnett

AN UPPER GRADUATE
Alexander Geddes

AN UPPER SERVANT
John Jones
Jonathan Swift

URBAN, FELIX
Edward Gordon Craig

URBAN, SYLVANUS (first
used by Cave and later by
succeeding editors of
Gentlemen's Magazine)
Edward Cave
Joseph Knight
John Nichols

URBANO AMICIOR
Richard Porson

URQUHART, PAUL
Ladbroke Lionel Day Black

USHER, FREEMAN L.
Noah Worcester

A UTOPIAN
Dorothea Beale

UVEDALE, CHRISTIAN
John Hill

V

V.
Caroline Clive
Adeline Virginia Woolf

V. B.
Vincent Bourne

V. C. V.
Vincent Cartwright Vickers

VACUUS
James Clarence Mangan

VACUUS VIATOR
Thomas Hughes

VADE, R. T.
Edward Gordon Craig

THE VAGABOND
Adam Badeau
John Stanley James

VAINALL, THOMAS
John Boyle

VALDARFER, CHRISTOPHER
Joseph Haslewood

VALDES, EDGAR
Vernon Horace Rendall

VALENTINE
Archibald Thomas Pechey
Joseph Holden Pott

VALENTINE, DOUGLAS
George Valentine Williams

VALENTINE, JANE
Nellie J. Meeker

VALENTINE, JO
Charlotte Armstrong

VALERIUS
William Combe

VAMP, HUGO
Thomas William Robertson

VAN
David W. Bartlett

VANARDY, VARICK
Frederick V. R. Day

VAN ARSDALE, WIRT
Martha Wirt Davis

VAN AVOND, JAN
Francis Carey Slater

VAN BUREN, ABIGAIL
Pauline Friedman Phillips

VANBUSTLE, TIMOTHY
John Woodward

VAN CAMPEN, KARL
John Wood Campbell

VANCE, CLARA
Mrs Mary Denison

VANCE, ETHEL
Grace Zaring Stone

VANCE, GERALD
Randall Garrett with Robert
Silbverberg

VANDEGRIFT, MARGARET
Margaret Thomson Janvier

VANDELLI, DOMINICK
James Cavanah Murphy

VANDERDOORT, ABRAHAM
Peter Cunningham

HERR VANDERHAUSSEN
Thomas Caulfield Irwin

VAN DINE, S. S.
Willard Huntington Wright

VAN DYNE, EDITH
Lyman Frank Baum

VANE, BRETT
Arthur William Charles Kent

VANE, NIGEL
Donald Stuart

VANE, PHILLIPA
Phyllis McVean Hambledon

VAN HOLT, JAN
Edward Gordon Craig

VAN LHIN, ERIK
Lester Del Ray

VAN LOOT, CORNELIUS
OBENCHAIN
Newton Booth Tarkington

VANOC
Arnold White

VANOC II
W. E. Hayter Preston

VAN SCELTER, HELTER
James Ridley

VAN SHERMAIN,
THEODORUS
Jacob Green

VAN TROMP
Lucius Manlius Sargent

VAN TRUESDALE, MAJOR
ROGER SHERMAN
POTTER PHELEG
Francis Colburn Adams

VAN WEST, RUPERT
Daniel Clarke Eddy

VAN WINKLE, RIP
Ian Duncan Colvin

VARA, MADELEINE
Laura Riding

VARDRE, LESLIE
Leslie Purnell Davies

VARLEY, JOHN PHILIP
Langdon Elwyn Mitchell

VARON
Cyrus Redding

VARRO
Isaac D'Israeli

VAUGHAN, RICHARD
Ernest Thomas

VAUGHN, CARTER A.
Noel Bertram Gerson

VAZAHA
Francis Cornwallis Maude

VEDDER, JOHN K.
Frank Gruber

VEDDER, PAUL
Edward Alexander Vidler

VEDETTE
William Henry Fitchett

Frederick Hardman
Howard Hensman

VEDRA, YARMO
Holmes Whittier Merton

VENI VIDI
Jane Cunningham Croly

VENISON, ALF
Ezra Pound

VENNING, HUGH
Claude Hubert Van Zeller

VENNING, MICHAEL
Georgiana Randolph Craig

**THE VENTUROUS HARDIE
AND RENOWNED
PASQUILL OF
ENGLAND**
Thomas Nash

VERA
Mrs Alfred Berlyn

VERAX
Samuel Alexander
Robert Blakey
Henry Dunckley
Francis A. Fleming
Thomas Ignatius Maria Forster
William Godwin
Nathaniel Gould

VERAX, THEODORUS
Clement Walker

**A VERDERER OF WINDSOR
FOREST**
Sir David Erskine

VERIDICUS
Sir Richard Musgrave

VERIFICATOR
Thomas Watts

VERIFIER
John Murray

VERIND
Arthur Tomson

VERITAS
John Close
Ebenezer Elliott
Joshua Hughes
Andrew MacGeorge
John Richardson

VERLAG, CORA
E. Richard Churchill

VERNER, GERALD
Donald Stuart

VERNON, HENRY
George Wightwick

VERNON, MAX
Vernon Lyman Kellogg

A VERSE-MAKER
George Tugwell

VERUS
Sir James Bland Burges
Edward Burton
Timothy Pickering
John Taylor

VERVAL, ALAIN
Laurence Montague Lande

**A VERY LEARNED MAN OF
THE CHURCH OF
ENGLAND**
Henry Dodwell

**A VERY MODERATE
PERSON AND DUTIFUL
SUBJECT TO THE
QUEEN**
Mary Astell

A VERY ODD AUTHOR
John Lund

A VERY PARTICULAR MAN
Andrew Kennedy Hutchinson
Boyd

VERYAN, PATRICIA
Patricia Valeria Bannister

VESEY, PAUL
Samuel Washington Allen

VESTAL, STANLEY
Walter Stanley Campbell

MONS. VESTRIS, SEN.
John Nott

A VETERAN JOURNALIST
Sidney James Mark Low

VETERAN OBSERVER
Edward Deering Mansfield

A VETERAN SOLDIER
John Frost

A VETERAN STAGER
George Grant

A VETERAN TRAVELLER
William Rae Wilson

VETO
Theodore Sedgwick

VETUS
Benjamin Bailey
Edward Sterling

VETUSTUS
James Boswell

VIATOR
William Beckford
Jonathan Huntington Bright
Charles Cotton
Thomas Alexander Lacey
George Lipscombe

Henry Edward Manning
John Godfrey Ferdinand
Raupert
Joseph Bradley Varnum

VIATOR A
Anthony Aufrere

VIATOR, JOHN, ESQ.
Samuel Andrew Peters

VIATOR VERAX, MA
George Musgrave Musgrave

VICAR OF CUDHAM
Samuel Ayscough

**THE VICAR OF FROME-
SELWOOD**
William James Early Bennett

**THE VICAR OF
MORWENSTOW**
Robert Stephen Hawker

**A VICAR OF THE CHURCH
OF ENGLAND**
Joseph Bosworth

**VICARION, COUNT
PALMIRO**
Christopher Logue

VICARIUS CANTIANUS
Samuel Pegge

VICKY
Victor Weisz

A VICTIM
Edward Alexander Crowley

VICTOR AND CAZIRE
Percy Bysshe Shelley and his
sister Elizabeth

VICTOR, CHARLES B.
Ray Puechner

VIDAL, GORE
Eugene Luther Vidal

VIDEO
Jonathan Couch

VIEUX MOUSTACHE
Clarence Gordon

VIG
Denis Florence MacCarthy

VIGGARS, FREKE
William Graily Hewitt

VIGIL
Henry Cole
George Cornelius Gorham
John Newton

VIGILANS
Charles Valentine Le Grice

VIGILANS ET AEQUUS
William Thomas Arnold

VIGILANT
John Corlett

VIGILANTES
Konni Zilliacus

VIGILII FILIUS
William Turner

VIGILII NEPOS
William Turner

VIGILIUS
William Turner

VIGORNIUS
Samuel Melanchton Worcester

VIGORS, N. A., JUN., ESQ.
Frederick Nolan

A VILLAGE APOTHECARY
William Frederick Deacon

VINCENT, CLAIRE
Charlotte Vale Allen

VINCENT, HARL
Harl Vincent Schoepflin

VINCENT, JOHN
Jedediah Vincent Huntington

**VINCENT, WILLIAM, OF
GRAYS INN**
Thomas Holcroft

**VINCENZA, DUCHESS OF
DEIRA**
Frederick William Rolfe

VINCEY, LEO
Edward Alexander Crowley

VINDEX
Samuel Adams
George Allen
Joseph Gurney Bevan
John Poage Campbell
Sir Frederick Morton Eden
John Loveday
Malcolm MacColl
Henry Rogers
George William Rusden
Lorenzo Sabine

VINDEX, JULIUS
Denis Taaffe

VINDICATOR
William Woodis Harvey
Henry Thomas Hopkinson

VINE, BARBARA
Ruth Rendell

**VINEGAR, CAPT.
HERCULES, OF
HOCKLEY IN THE
HOLE**
Henry Fielding

VINEGAR, HERCULES, ESQ.
Edward Ward

HERR VINKBOOMS
Thomas Griffiths Wainewright

MONSIEUR VIOLET
Frederick Marryat

A VIOLINIST
Eric Mackay

**VIPONT, CHARLES (or
ELFRIDA)**
Elfrida Vipont Foulds

VIRAKAM, SOROR
Edward Alexander Crowley

A VIRGINIA FARMER
Fairfax Harrison

A VIRGINIAN
John Esten Cooke
Francis Walker Gilmer
George Tucker
Robert Tyler
Abel Parker Upshur

THE VISIONARY
Sir Walter Scott

A VISITOR
Stephen Weston

VIVE VALEQUE
John Eagles

VIVIAN
George Henry Lewes

VIVIAN, PHILIP
Harry Vivian Majendie Philips

VOCES CATHOLICAE
Emile Joseph Dillon

VOCES POPULI
Thomas Anstey Guthrie

VOGEL, HANS
Norman Austin Lazenby

VOLPI, ODOARDO
Edward N. Shannon

A VOLUNTARY
George Armstrong

A VOLUNTARY ADVOCATE
Adam Thomson

A VOLUNTEER
Anna Letitia Barbauld
Sir George Tomkyns Chesney

**A VOLUNTEER IN THE US
SERVICE**
Henry Howard Brownell

**A VOLUNTEER WHO WAS
NEAR HIS PERSON**
John Douglas

**VON ARNIM, ELIZABETH,
COUNTESS**
Elizabeth Mary Russell

VON ASCHENDORF, IGNATZ
Jozef Korzeniowski with Ford
Madox Hueffer

**VON HELMHOLTZ,
BAPTISTE**
Ezra Pound

VON KOSEWITZ, W. F.
Charles Robert Forrester

VON RACHEN, KURT
L. Ron Hubbard

**VON THUNDERTEN-
TRONCLE, ARMINIUS**
Matthew Arnold

A VOYAGER
George Hill
William Scoresby

VOYAGEUR
Henry Stafford Northcote

VOYLE, MARY
Rosemary Joy Manning

VRATSCH
Richard John Anderson

VREPONT, BRIAN
Benjamin Arthur Truebridge

VYSE, BERTIE
Arthur William A'Beckett

W

W.
William Cowper
John Swete
Wilfrid Whitten

W. A.
Ezra Pound

W. A. C.
William Andrew Chatto

W. B.
William Beresford
Walter Besant
John Gay

W. C.
William Cockin
David Garrick
William Coward

W. C. T.
William Cooke Taylor

W. D., FRS
William Derham

W. & D.
Samuel Denne

W. E.
William Emerson

W. H. I.
William Henry Ireland

W. S.
William Shrubsole
William Stebbing

W. S. L.
Walter Savage Landor

WADE, ALAN
John Holbrook Vance

WADE, BILL
Geoffrey John Barrett

WADE, HENRY
Sir Henry Lancelot Aubrey-
Fletcher

WADE, ROSALIND
Rosalind Herschel Seymour

WAGSTAFF, LANCELOT, ESQ.
William Makepeace Thackeray

WAGSTAFF, SIMON
Jonathan Swift

WAGSTAFF, WALTER
William Oldisworth

WAGSTAFFE, JOHN, ESQ.,
OF WILBY GRANGE
Charles Mackay

WAGSTAFFE, THEOPHILE
William Makepeace Thackeray

WAINER, CORD
Thomas Blanchard Dewey

WALBROOK, LOUISE
Edith Templeton

WALDO, DAVE
David Waldo Clarke

WALES, HUBERT
William Pigott

WALES, NYM
Helen Foster Snow

WALEY, ARTHUR DAVID
Arthur David Schloss

WALKER, HARRY
Hillary Baldwin Waugh

WALKER, J.
John Richard Crawford

WALKER, LUCY
Dorothy Lucy Sanders

WALKER, PATRICIUS
William Allingham

WALKER, W. H.
George Ranken

THE WALKER IN THE PINES
Henry Hastings Sibley

A WALKING GENTLEMAN
Thomas Colley Grattan

A WALL STREET MAN
David Law Proudfit

WALLACE, DOREEN
Dora Eileen Rash

WALLACE, JAMES
Geoffrey John Barrett

WALLACE, JENNY
Mary Whitney Morrison

WALLACE, ROBERT
Norman A. Danberg

WALLINBY, OLIVER
William Leybourn

WALLIS, DOROTHY
Walter Besant

WALLIS, JENNY
Mary Whitney Morrison

WALMSLEY, LEO
Lionel Walmsley

WALNEERG
Thomas Knox

WALSINGHAM, FRANCIS
William Arnall

WALTER, EMILE
Alexander Delmar

WALTERS, GORDON
George Walter Locke

WALTERS, HUGH
Walter Llewellyn Hughes

WALTON, FRANCIS
Alfred Hodder

A WANDERER
Matthew Henry Barker
John Keast Lord
Sir Henry Parkes
William Thomas Ryan
Philip Thicknesse
George Watterston

THE WANDERER IN
NORWAY
Thomas Brown

A WANDERING
ENGLISHMAN
William George Hamley
Charles Gipps Prowett

WANLOCK, ROBERT
Robert Reid

WARBOROUGH, MARTIN
LEACH
Charles Grant Blairfindie Allen

WARBURTON, ELIOT
Bartholomew Elliott George
Warburton

A WARBURTONIAN
Richard Hurd

WARD, A. B.
Mrs Alice Ward Bailey

WARD, ARTEMUS
Charles Farrar Browne

WARD, E.
Evelyn Everett-Green

WARD, E. D.
Edward Verrall Lucas

WARD, MRS H. O.
Mrs Clara Jessup Moore

WARD, ZION
John Ward

WARDDEL, NORA HELEN
Edward Heron-Allen

WARDE, EVELYN B.
William Harrison Woodward

WARDE, MARGARET
Edith Kellogg Dunton

WARDEN, FLORENCE
Florence Alice James

WARE, MONICA
John Marsh

WARE, WALLACE
David Karp

A WAREHOUSEMAN
Daniel Puseley

WARLAND, ALLEN
Donald A. Wollheim

WARLOCK, PETER
Philip Arnold Heseltine

A WARM FRIEND TO THE
BRAVE
James Boswell

A WARM WELL-WISHER TO
THE INTERESTS OF
GENUINE
CHRISTIANITY
Newcome Cappe

WARNER, HANNAH
John Howard Jewett

WARRE, MARY DOUGLAS
Maysie Greig

WARREN
James Cheetham

WARRINGTON
William Stevens Robinson

WARRINGTON, GEORGE
James Evershed Agate

WARSHOFSKY, ISAAC
Isaac Bashevis Singer

WARTH, JULIAN
Mrs Julia Parsons

WARTON, JANE
Lady Constance Lytton

WARUNG, PRICE
William Astley

A WASHINGTONIAN
John Lovett

WASTLE, WILLIAM
John Gibson Lockhart

WATANNA, ONOTO
Mrs Winifred Eaton Babcock

A WATCHER IN PALL MALL
Charles Gipps Prowett

A WATCHMAN
Samuel Vyvian Trerice Adams
James Begg

WATER, SILAS
Noel Loomis

A WATER DRINKER
William Dunlap
Basil Montagu

WATER RAIL
Richard Walker

WATERS, JOHN
Henry Cary

WATERS, THOMAS
William Russell

WATKINS, GERROLD
Barry N. Malzberg

WATKINS, DR J.
William Hone

WATKYN, ARTHUR
Arthur Thomas Levi Watkins

WATSON, FREDERICK
Frederick Porter

WATSON, WILL
Lee Floren

WATTS, EPHRAIM
Richard Hengist Horne

WAUGH, MANSIE
David MacBeth Moir

WAUGHBURTON, RICHARD
Robert Byron with Christopher
Hugh Sykes

WAVERLEY, EDWARD
BRADWARDINE
John Wilson Croker

WAYLAC
William Maginn

WAYLAND, PATRICK
Richard O'Connor

WAYNE, DONALD
Wayne D. Dodd

WAYNE, JOSEPH
Wayne Overholser

WAYNFLETE, ZACHARY
Sir Ian Malcolm

WAYTEMORE, GODFREY
William Basil Worsfield

WEALE, P.
Bertram Lenox Simpson

WEALE, B. L. PUTNAM
Bertram Lenox Simpson

WEARY, OGDRED
Edward Gorey

WEATHERCOCK, JANUS
Thomas Griffiths Wainewright

WEAVER, WARD
Francis Van Wyck Mason

WEBB, CHRISTOPHER
Leonard P. O'Connor
Wibberley

WEBBER, FRANK
William H. Bushnell

MR WEBSTER
Francis Reynardson

WEBSTER, NOAH
William Knox

WEDNESDAY'S CLUB IN
FRIDAY STREET
William Paterson

WEEDER
Francis Cowley Burnand

WEEGEE
Arthur Fellig

WEINER, HENRI
Stephen Longstreet

WEISS, LYNDE
Thomas Bangs Thorpe

WELBY, HORACE
John Timbs

WELCH, RONALD
Ronald Oliver Felton

A WELCH FREEHOLDER
David Jones

WELCOME, JOHN
John N. H. Brennan

WELLAND, COLIN
Colin Williams

WELLER, SAM, JR.
Thomas Onwhyn

WELLES, ELIZABETH
Mary Lynn Roby

WELLINGTON, ANNE
Anita Hewett

WELLS, DAVID
Ernest Milton

WELLS, HONDO
Harry B. Whittington

WELLS, JOHN JAY
Marion Zimmer Bradley with
Juanita Ruth Coulson

WELLS, SUSAN
Doris Siegel

WELLS, TOBIAS
Deloris Stanton Forbes

A WELL-WISHER TO GOD'S
TRUTH
William Prynne

A WELL-WISHER TO
MANKIND
Charles Morton
Joseph Townsend

A WELL-WISHER TO
POSTERITY
Marchamont Needham

A WELL-WISHER TO THE
CHURCH'S PEACE, AND
A LAMENTER OF HER
SAD DIVISIONS
Daniel Whitby

A WELL-WISHER TO THE
GOOD PEOPLE OF
GREAT BRITAIN
Sir Matthew Decker

A WELL-WISHER TO THE
NEW TRANSLATION
William Cowper

A WELL-WISHER TO THE
PEACE OF BRITAIN
Daniel Defoe

A WELL-WISHER TO THE
REFORMED RELIGION
Joseph Hill

A WELL-WISHER TO THE
SAINTS NOW
REIGNING ON EARTH
John Lilburne

A WELL-WISHER TO THE
TRUTH AND MASTER
PRIN
Henry Robinson

A WELL-WISHER TO THE
TRUTH OF GOD, AND
THE CHURCH OF
ENGLAND
William Prynne

A WELL-WISHER TO VERITY
AND UNITY
William Prynne

A WELL-WISHING
PHILOPATER
William Prynne

A WELSH CURATE
Edward Davies

WELSTEDE, A.
John Henley

A WELWISHER TO A
COVENANTED
REFORMATION
James Hog

THE WENSLEYDALE POET
William G. M. J. Barker

WENTWORTH, JOHN
Philip Child

WENTWORTH, PATRICIA
Dora Amy Ellis

WERE, MARY WINTER
Mary Elizabeth Josephine
Hughes

WESLEY, ELIZABETH
Elizabeth Adeline McElfresh

WESLEY, MARY
Mary Siepmann

A WESLEYAN PREACHER
Thomas Jackson

WEST, DOUGLAS
Edwin Charles Tubb

WEST, KEITH
Kenneth Westmacott Lane

WEST, KENYON
Frances Louise Morse
Howland

WEST, MONKTON
John Francis O'Donnell

WEST, NATHANAEL
Nathan Weinstein

WEST, NIGEL
Rupert Allason

WEST, OWEN
Dean R. Koontz

WEST, REBECCA
Cicily Isabel Fairfield

WEST, WARD
Harold Glen Borland

A WEST HIGHLANDER
Sir John Skelton

A WEST INDIA PROPRIETOR
Matthew Gregory Lewis

A WEST INDIAN AND AN
ABOLITIONIST
Wiltshire Stanton Austin

WESTBROOK, RAYMOND
William Henry Bishop

A WESTCHESTER FARMER
Samuel Seabury

WESTCOT, REDMAN
Adam Littleton

WESTERHAM, S. C.
Cyril Argentine Alington

A WESTERN HIGHLANDER
Sir John Skelton

WESTGATE, JOHN
Anthony John Westgate
Bloomfield

WESTLAND, LYNN
Archie Lynn Joscelyn

WESTLAND, R. L.
Robert William Lowe

WESTMACOTT, MARY
Agatha Mary Clarissa Christie

WESTMAN, HAB, K. O.
Thomas Ewbank

A WESTMINSTER ELECTOR
Alexander Patrick Stewart

A WESTMINSTER
MAGISTRATE
Edward Bellasis

WESTON, ALLEN
Grace Allen Hogarth with Alice
Mary Norton

WESTON, COLE
Robert Joseph Randisi

WESTON, HELEN GRAY
Dorothy Daniels

WESTON, JAMES
Edward Step

WESTON, MARY
George Ernest Rochester

WETHERELL, ELIZABETH
Susan Bogert Warner

WEYMOUTH, ANTHONY
Ivo Geikie Cobb

WHACK, PADDY
John Fitzgibbon

WHARTON, ANTHONY P.
Alister McAllister

WHARTON, GRACE
Katharine Thomson

WHARTON, PHILIP
John Cockburn Thomson

WHEATON, CAMPBELL
Mrs Helen Campbell Weeks

WHEELS, H. G.
Herbert George Wells

A WHIG
John Butler
John Scott Waring

A WHIG OF THE OLD SCHOOL
Charles Francis Adams

MR WHIGLOVE
Charles Davenant

WHIMSY, SIR FINICAL
Sir Richard Worsley

WHIPEM, BENEDICK
Richard Harris

WHISTLECRAFT, DEUTEROS, GENT.
Charles Lewis Meryon

WHISTLECRAFT, PAUL
William Fraser

WHISTLECRAFT, WM AND ROBERT
John Hookham Frere

WHITBY, SHARON
Maureen Peters

WHITE, ANTONIA
Eirene Botting

WHITE, BABINGTON
Mrs Mary Elizabeth Maxwell

WHITE, BLYTHE, JR.
Solon Robinson

WHITE, CHARLES ERSKINE
Laughton Osborn

WHITE, HARRY
Harry B. Whittington

WHITE, REV. JAMES
John Hill Burton

WHITE, JAMES
Robert Benton Seeley

WHITE, L. C.
Mrs Lucy Cecil Lillie

WHITE, MATTHEW
William Prynne

WHITE, MATTHEW, JR.
William LIvingston Alden

WHITE, ROLD
Victor Benjamin Neuburg

WHITE, TED
Theodore Edward White

WHITE, THOMAS, JUN.
Thomas Stewart Omond

WHITE, TIMOTHY
Terence Hanbury White

WHITE, T. K.
Thomas Ernest Hulme

WHITE, MR TOM
Charles Wyllys Elliott

THE WHITE REPUBLICAN
Hiram Fuller

WHITEBAIT, WILLIAM
George Walter Stonier

WHITEFEATHER, BARABBAS
Douglas Jerrold

WHITEHOOK
Edward Kellogg

WHITLEY, GEORGE
Arthur Bertram Chandler

WHITMAN, MATTHEW
Lee Floren

WHITMORE, CILLA
Arthur M. Gladstone

WHITNEY, HALLAM
Harry B. Whittington

WHITNEY, HARRY
Patrick Kennedy

WHITNEY, LUCIA
Ethel May Keller

WHITTINGTON, PETER
James Alexander Mackay

WHITTLE, TYLER
Michael Tyler-Whittle

WHITTLEBOT, HERNIA
Noel Coward

WHYTE, ARTHUR HENRY
Frederick William Rolfe

WHYTE, VIOLET
Henrietta Eliza Vaughan Palmer

WIAT, PHILIPPA
Philippa Ferridge

WICK, CARTER
Collin Wilcox

WICK, STUART MARY
Kathleen Freeman

WICKHAM, ANNA
Edith Alice Mary Harper

WICKLIFFE
John Stuart Mill
Samuel Gover Winchester

WIDOW BEDOTT
Frances Miriam Whitcher

WIDOW GOLDSMITH
Mrs Julie P. Smith

THE WIFE OF A BENEFICED CLERGYMAN
Annie Besant

A WIFE WITH HER HUSBAND
Richard Holt Hutton

WIGAN, CHRISTOPHER
David Ernest Bingley

WIGG, T. I. G.
Philip Donald McCutchan

WIGGEN, HENRY W.
Mark Harris

WIGGINS, NAPOLEON PUTNAM, OF PASSIMAQUODDY
William Makepeace Thackeray

WILBUR, HOMER
James Russell Lowell

WILDFOWLER
Lewis Clements

WILDGOOSE, GEOFFREY
Richard Graves

WILDING, GRISELDA
Hugh Davie-Martin McCutcheon

WILDRAKE
George Tattersall

WILDWOOD, WILL
Frederick Eugene Pond

WILHELMINA, CAROLINA
John O'Hagan

MR WILKES
Samuel Derrick

WILKINS, PETER
Cyrus Redding

WILLIAMS, BRONWYN
Dixie Browning

WILLIAMS, F. HARALD
Frederick William Orde Ward

WILLIAMS, FRED BENTON
Herbert Elliott Hamblen

WILLIAMS, HAWLEY
William Heyliger

WILLIAMS, IFOR D.
Frederick William Rolfe

WILLIAMS, JOHN
Samuel Phillips

WILLIAMS, JOHN BARRY
John Thomas Lutz
Barry N. Malzberg

WILLIAMS, J. X.
Andrew J. V. Offutt

WILLIAMS, ROGER
Francis Wayland

WILLIAMS, ROTH
Konni Zilliacus

WILLIAMS, TENNESSEE
Thomas Lanier Williams

WILLIAMS, ZACHARIAH
Samuel Johnson

WILLIAMSON, MRS FLORENCE
William Kirkus

WILLIE, ALBERT FREDERICK
Howard Phillips Lovecraft

WILLINGTON, JAMES
Oliver Goldsmith

WILLIS, CHARLES
Arthur C. Clarke

WILLIS, HAL, STUDENT AT LAW
Charles Robert Forrester

WILLOUGHBY, CASS
Theodore Victor Olsen

WILLOUGHBY, HUGH
Charles NIgel Harvey

WILLOUGHBY, LEE DAVIS
William Louis DeAndrea
Richard Deming

WILLS, RONALD
Ronald Wills Thomas

WILLS, THOMAS
William Thomas Ard

WILMER, DALE
Bill Miller with Robert Wade

WILSON, CHARLES, ESQ.
John Oldmixon

WILSON, CHRISTINE
Christine Geach

WILSON, DAVID
David Wilson MacArthur

WILSON, JAMES, DRUGGIST OF PAISLEY
Andrew Park

WILSON, J. ARBUTHNOT
Charles Grant Blairfindie Allen

WILSON, JASPER
James Currie

WILSON, JUNE
June Badeni

WILSON, MARY
Mary Lynn Roby

WILSON, ROMER
Florence Roma Muir Wilson

WILSON, WILLIAM
William More Adey

A WILTSHIRE CLOTHIER
Henry Wansey

WINCH, JOHN
Margaret Long

WINCHESTER, JACK
Brian Harry Freemantle

WINCHESTER, KAY
Emily Kathleen Walker

WINDHAM, BASIL
Pelham Grenville Wodehouse
with W. Townend

WINE, DICK
Richard Posner

WINFIELD, ARTHUR M.
Edward Stratemeyer

WINGATE, PAUL
John Austin Drury Philips

WINGRAVE, ANTHONY
Sydney Fowler Wright

WINIKI, EPHRAIM
John Russell Fearn

WINSLOW, LAUREL
Maura Seger

WINTER, H. G.
Harry Bates with Desmond W. Hall

WINTER, JOHN STRANGE
Henrietta Eliza Vaughan Palmer

WINTERTON, MARK
Beatrice Ethel Kidd

WINTHROP, CHARLES
Sir Charles Inigo Thomas

WINTON, JOHN
John Pratt

WINWAR, FRANCES
Francesca V. Grebanier

WISE, CLEMENT
John Mackinnon Robertson

WISE, JONATHAN B.
Stephen Colwell

WISEMAN, M. A.
John Mackinnon Robertson

WISGART, WILFRED
George Sexton

MR WISHIT
Thomas Spence

WITHERS, E. L.
George William Potter

WITHERSPOON, EDWIN
Edward Gordon Craig

WITHERSPOON, HALLIDAY
William Herbert Nutter

A WITNESS OF CHRIST
George Whitehead

A WITNESS OF THE WAY OF TRUTH
George Whitehead

A WITNESSE OF JESUS CHRIST
Henry Burton

WITTITTERLY, JOHN ALTRAYD
Elizabeth Catherine Thomas Carne

WIZARD
John Corlett

WODEN, GEORGE
George Wilson Slaney

WOLFE, AARON
Dean R Koontz

WOLFE, CEDRIC
Ernest W. Alais

WOLFE, ELIZABETH
Paul Joseph Lederer

WOLFE, REGINALD
Thomas Frognall Dibdin

A WOMAN
Mrs Mary Clemmer
Mrs Dinah Maria Craik
Frances Darusmont
Emily Frances Adeline Sergeant

A WOMAN OF QUALITY
James Ralph

A WOMAN PHYSICIAN AND SURGEON
Mary Edwards Walker

A WONDERFUL QUIZ
James Russell Lowell

WOOD, ERIC
F. Knowles Campling

WOOD, KERRY
Edgar Allardyce Wood

WOOD, LAURA NEWBOLD
Laura Wood Roper

WOOD, SINJON
Christopher a Beckett Williams

WOOD, WILIAM
Jonathan Swift

WOODBINE WILLIE
Geoffrey Studdert Kennedy

WOODCOTT, KEITH
John Kilian Houston Brunner

WOODENSCONCE,
   PAPERNOSE, ESQ.
Robert Barnabas Brough

WOODFALL, WILFRED
Sir Samuel Egerton Brydges

WOODFIELD, SUTTON
Leslie Clement Haylen

WOODFORD, JACK
Josiah Pitts Woolfolk

WOODHEAD, ABRAHAM
Obadiah Walker

WOODHOUSE, EMMA
Cynthia Harrod-Eagles

WOODRUFF, PHILIP
Philip Mason

WOODS, LAWRENCE
Donald A. Wollheim

WOODS, P. F.
Barrington J. Bayley

WOODS, SARA
Sara Bowen-Judd

WOODS, STOCKTON
Richard Stockton Forrest

WOODVILLE, JENNIE
Jennie Latham Stabler

WOODWARD, LILIAN
John Marsh

WOOL-GATHERER
William Henry Smith

WOOLF, DANIEL
Ben Maddow

WOOLF, F. X.
Howard Engel with Janet
Evelyn Hamilton

WOOLF, VICTORIA
Sheila Holland

WOOLRICH, CORNELL
Cornell Hopley-Woolrich

WOON
George Ralph Howard
Wotherspoon

WORBOYS, ANNE EYRE
Annette Isobel Worboys

A WORKER
Mary Carpenter

A WORKING CLERGYMAN
John Henry Blunt
Erskine Neale

A WORKING MAN
John Lash Latey
Charles Manby Smith
Alexander Somerville
Thomas Wright

A WORKING PARSON
Charles Kingsley

WORTH, MARGARET
Margot Teresa Strickland

WORTH, MAURICE
Willan G. Bosworth

WORTH, NICHOLAS
Walter Hines Page

WORTHY, WILL
Sir William Pulteney

WOUIL, GEORGE
George Wilson Slaney

WRATSCH
Richard John Anderson

WRAY, LEOPOLD
Clara Chatelain

WRAY, REGINALD
William Benjamin Home-Gall

WREN, M. K.
Martha Kay Renfroe

WREY, PEYTON
Alfred Edward Thomas Watson

WRIGHT, ARNOLD
Joseph McCabe

WRIGHT, FRANCESCA
Denise Naomi Robins

WRIGHT, KENNETH
Lester Del Rey

WRIGHT, LAN
Lionel Percy Wright

WRIGHT, ROWLAND
Carolyn Wells

THE WRITER BEHIND THE
   GRILLES
Mrs William Pitt Byrne

A WRITER TO THE SIGNET
Alexander K. Kennedy

WRITEWELL, A. M.
John Close

WU-CH'ENG-EN
Arthur David Schloss

WURDZ, GIDEON
Charles Wayland Towne

WURF, KARL
George Scithers

WYCLIFE, JOHN
Henry J. O. Bedford-Jones

A WYKEHAMIST
George Jennings Davies
Frederick Gale

WYLDE, ATHERTON
Miss Frances Ellen Colenso

WYLDE, KATHERINE
Helen Hester Colville

WYLIE, LAURA
Patricia A. Matthews

WYNDHAM, ESTHER
Mary Lutyens

WYNDHAM , JOHN
John Beynon Harris

WYNMAN, MARGARET
Ella Hepworth Dixon

WYNNE, ANTHONY
Robert McNair Wilson

WYNNE, BRYAN (or FRANK)
Brian Francis Wynne Garfield

WYNNE, ELLIS
George Borrow

WYNNE, MAY
Mabel Winifred Knowles

WYNNE, PAMELA
Winifred Mary Scott

WYTHE
Theodore Dwight Weld

WYVERN
Arthur Herbert Kenney

X

Y

Y.
  Samuel Boyse

Y. Y.
  Robert Wilson Lynd

A YALE GRADUATE OF '69
  Lyman Hotchkiss Bagg

YANCEY, WES
  Norman Austin Lazenby

A YANKEE
  Asa Greene
  Joseph Holt Ingraham
  James Clarence Mangan
  John Kearsley Mitchell
  Henry David Thoreau
  Richard Grant White

A YANKEE FARMER
  John Lowell

YASHIMO, TARO
  Jun Atsushi Iwamatsu

YATES, DORNFORD
  Cecil William Mercer

YECHTON, BARBARA
  Miss Lydia Farrington Krause

YEGOREVITSCH, YEGOR
  Sir George Young

YELLOWPLUSH, C. J.
  William Makepeace Thackeray

YENDYS, SYDNEY
  Sydney Thompson Dobell

A YEOMAN
  William Clubbe
  Sir William Cusac Smith

A YEOMAN OF 1796
  Samuel O'Sullivan

YITTADAIRN
  George William Rusden

YOE SHWAY
  James George Scott

YORICK
  Edwin Austin Abbey
  Michael William Ivens
  Rowley Lascelles

MR YORICK
  Laurence Sterne

YORK, ALISON (or ANDREW)
  Christopher Robin Nicole

YORK, JEREMY
  John Creasey

YORK, ROBERT
  Robin Estridge

YORKE, KATHERINE
  Rosemary Ellerbeck

YORKE, MARGARET
  Margaret Beda Nicholson

YORKE, OLIVER
  Francis Sylvester Mahony

YORKE, ONSLOW
  William Hepworth Dixon

YORKE, ROGER
  David Ernest Bingley

YORKE, SKELTON
  Margaret Plues

YORKE, STEPHEN
  Mary Linskill

YORKEL, HANS
  Abraham Oakey Hall

A YORKSHIRE CLERGYMAN
  Francis Orpen Morris

A YORKSHIRE
    FREEHOLDER
  Samuel Bailey

YOU-NO-HOO
  Edward Gordon Craig

YOUNG, ANNIE
  Eliza Anne DuPuy

YOUNG, CARTER TRAVIS
  Louis Henry Charbonneau

YOUNG, COLLIER
  Robert Albert Bloch

YOUNG, ROBERT
  Pierre Stephen Robert Payne

A YOUNG AMERICAN
  Alexander Slidell Mackenzie

A YOUNG AND HAPPY
    HUSBAND
  Aglen A. Dowty

A YOUNG CLERGYMAN
  Joseph Butler

YOUNG ENGLAND
  Frederick William Orde Ward

A YOUNG ENGLAND PEER
  Alexander D. R. W. Cochrane-
    Baillie

A YOUNG ENGLISH PEER
    OF THE HIGHEST
    RANK
  Francis Russell

A YOUNG GENTLEMAN
  James Norris Brewer
  Benjamin Church
  Thomas Dawes
  Thomas Green
  Fortescue Hitchins
  Thomas Rodd
  Richard Valpy

A YOUNG GENTLEMAN AT
    ROME
  Lord George Lyttelton

A YOUNG GENTLEMAN OF
    NEW YORK
  John Blair Linn

A YOUNG GENTLEMAN OF
    PHILADELPHIA
  Joseph R. Hopkins

A YOUNG GENTLEMAN OF
    SIXTEEN
  Bennet Allen

A YOUNG GENTLEMAN OF
    THE UNIVERSITY
  Thomas Dudley Fosbrooke

A YOUNG GENTLEMAN OF
    TRURO SCHOOL
  Richard Polwhele

A YOUNG GENTLEMAN OF
    WINCHESTER SCHOOL
  Robert Lowth

A YOUNG INVALID
William Jeffrey Prowse

YOUNG IRELAND
Robert Arthur Wilson

A YOUNG LADY
Mrs Jane Barker
William Combe
Sarah Fyge
Charlotte Lennox
Hannah More
Mary Roberts
Miss Helen Maria Williams

A YOUNG LADY, EIGHTEEN YEARS OF AGE
Anna Maria Porter

A YOUNG LADY LATELY DECEASED
Miss Elizabeth Smith

A YOUNG MAN
Henry Revell Reynolds

A YOUNG PHYSICIAN
John Spence

A YOUNG TRAVELLER
George Miller

A YOUNG WOMAN
Susannah Harrison

YOUNGE MARTIN MAR-PRIEST, SON TO OLD MARTIN THE METRAPOLITANE
Richard Overton

YOUNGER, HENRY
Michael Carreras

A YOUNGER BROTHER
Samuel Bailey

A YOUNGER SON
Edward John Trelawney

THE YOUNGEST MEMBER
Annie T. Slosson

THE YOUNGEST OF THE TOMKINSES
Sir Francis Henry Goldsmid

YOUR BEWILDERED CONTRIBUTOR
Sir John Skelton

YOUR OLD CONTRIBUTOR
John Francis Waller

YOURS TROOLY
David Ross Locke

A YOUTH OF THIRTEEN
William Cullen Bryant

YU-NO-WHO
Edward Gordon Craig

YUILL, P. B.
Terry Venables with Gordon Williams

Z

Z.
Samuel Adams
James Boswell
Robert Ranke Graves
John Hawkesworth
John Hughes
Hannah More
Alfred William Pollard
Sir Richard Steele

ZACK
Gwendoline Keats

ZADKIEL
William Lilly
Richard James Morrison

ZADKIEL TAO
Richard James Morrison

ZADKIEL THE SEER
Richard James Morrison

ZANDILE
Miss Frances Ellen Colenso

ZEMIA
Frederic Shoberl

ZERO
Allan Ramsay, Jr.

ZETA
Vincent Zachary Cope
James Anthony Froude

ZETFORD, TULLY
Kenneth Henry Bulmer

ZIEGFRIED, KARL
Robert Lionel Fanthorpe

MR ZIGZAG THE ELDER
John Wykeham Archer

ZONIK, E. D.
Eleanor Dorothy Glaser

ZOILUS
Howard Phillips Lovecraft

ZOOLOGUS
Richard Owen

Part II

Real Names

A

AARONS, Edward Sidney [1916–75, US crime and mystery writer]
Paul Ayres (*Dead Heat*)
Edward Ronns (*Terror in the Town*)

ABARBANELL, Jacob Ralph [1852–1922, US editor, translator and novelist]
Ralph Royal (*Mid the Canon's Roar; Ma; The Model Pair*)

ABBEY, Edward Austin [1852–1911, US artist and illustrator]
Yorick (in *Our Boys and Girls*)

ABBOT, Charles [1757–1829, 1st Baron Colchester, Speaker of the House of Commons]
A Member of Parliament (*Observations on the Importance of Navigation Laws*)

ABBOTT, Austin [1831–96, US lawyer and novelist]
*Benauley (*Conecut Corners; Matthew Carnaby*) – see entries for brothers Benjamin Vaughan Abbott and Lyman Abbott below.

ABBOTT, Benjamin Vaughan [1830–90, US lawyer and novelist]
*Benauley (see entries for brothers Austin Abbott and Lyman Abbott above and below)

ABBOTT, Edwin Abbott [1838–1926, English cleric and headmaster]
Philochristus (*Memoirs of a Disciple of the Lord*)
A. Square (*Flatland*)

ABBOTT, Joseph [1789–1863, English missionary in Canada]
An Emigrant (*Memoranda of a Settler in Lower Canada*)
An Emigrant Farmer (*The Emigrant to North America*)
Philip Musgrave (*Adventures of a Missionary in Canada*)

ABBOTT, Lyman [1835–1922, US cleric, novelist and writer]
*Benauley (see entries for brothers Austin Abbott and Benjamin Vaughan Abbott above)
Laicus (*Experiences of a Layman in a Country Parish*)
A Layman (*A Layman's Story*)

ABBOTT, Thomas Kingsmill [1829–1913, Irish philosopher and biblical scholar]
Philalethes (revision of the Authorised Version of the English Bible)

À BECKETT, Arthur William [1844–1909, English journalist and humorist]
A. Briefless, Junior (in *Punch* and for *Papers from Pump Handle Court*)
Bertie Vyse (*On Strike*)

À BECKETT, Gilbert Abbott [1811–56, English journalist and humorist]
Barnaby Briefless; Old Scratch (both used in *Bentley's Miscellany*)
Mr Briefless (in *Punch*)
The Perambulating Philosopher (in the *Illustrated London News*)

À BECKETT, Sir William [1806–69, English jurist; held important legal posts in Australia]
Colonus (*Does the Discovery of Gold in Victoria ... Deserve to be Considered a National Blessing or a National Curse?*)
Malwyn (in the *Port Phillip Herald*)

ABEL, Carl [1837–1906, German philologist, academic and essayist]
'The Times' Correspondent at Berlin (*Letters on International Relations*)

ABERCROMBIE, John [1726–1806, English horticulturist]
Mr Maw, Gardener to the Duke of Leeds (*Everyman his Own Gardener*)

ABERCROMBY, James [1776–1858, 1st Baron Dunfermline; Speaker of the House of Commons]
The Pensioner (*Extracts ... Showing how a Patriot may Pocket £2,000*)

ABERIGH–MACKAY, George Robert [1848–81, Scottish writer]
Sir Ali Baba (in *Vanity Fair* for *Twenty One Days in India, being the Tour of Sir Ali Baba*)

ABERNETHY, John [1764–1831, English surgeon and writer on medicine]
A Professional Friend (letter to the *London Medical Gazette*)

ABRAHALL, Clare Hoskyns [fl. 1937, English novelist]
C. M. Drury (*Kit Norris, Schoolgirl Pilot*)

ABRAHAM, James Johnston [1876–1963, Irish physician and writer]
James Harpole (*Leaves from a Surgeon's Case-Book*; *Behind the Surgeon's Mask*)

ABRAHAM, William [1842–1922, Welsh trade union pioneer and politician]
Mabon (his Eisteddfod name)

ABRAHAMS, Doris Caroline [1901–82, English novelist]
Caryl Brahms (*A Bullet in the Ballet*; *Footnotes to the Ballet*)
Oliver Linden (*Sung Before Six*)

ACLAND, Alice [1912–, English writer]
Anne Marreco (*The Charmer and the Charmed*)

ACTON, John E. Dalberg [1834–1902, 1st Baron Acton; liberal Catholic layman and historian]
Quirinus (*Letters from Rome on the Council*)

ADAIR, James Makittrick [1728–1802, Scottish physician and medical writer]
Benjamin Goosequill (*Anecdotes of the Life*; *Adventures of Benjamin Goosequill*; *Curious Facts and Anecdotes not Contained in the Memoirs of Philip Thicknesse*)
Peter Paragraph (*Essays on Fashionable Diseases*; *The Methodist and the Mimick*)

ADAM, Robin J. [1924–, Scottish science-fiction writer]
Paul Mactyre (*Midge*; *Bar Sinister*)

ADAM, Ronald [fl. 1947, English writer]
Blake (*To You the Torch*)

ADAMS, Mrs Abigail [1744–1818, wife of John Adams, 2nd President of the USA]
Diana; Portia (both used in correspondence with friends)

ADAMS, Mrs Ann Olivia [fl. 1865, US poet]
Astarte (*Poems*; *Lines on a Japanese Fan*)

ADAMS, Arthur Henry [1872–1936, New Zealand novelist and playwright]
James James (*Honeymoon Dialogues*; *Lola of the Chocolates*)

ADAMS, Charles Francis [1807–86, US diplomat and politician]
A Whig of the Old School (*An Appeal from the New to the Old Whigs*)

ADAMS, Cleve Franklin [1895–1949, English crime writer]
Franklin Charles (*Escape to Death*; *Maid for Murder*)
John Spain (*Death is Like That*; *Dig Me a Grave*)

ADAMS, Clifton [1919–, US western novelist]
Jonathan Gant (*Never Say No to a Killer*; *The Long Vendetta*)

Matt Kinkaid (*Hardcase*; *The Race of Giants*)
Clay Randall (*Six-Gun Boss*; *Amos Flagg Rides Out*)

ADAMS, Francis [1797–1861, Scottish classical scholar and physician]
A Scotch Physician (*Arundines Devae*)

ADAMS, Francis Colburn [fl. 1858, US writer]
A Cavalryman (*Our World or, the Slave-Holder's Daughter*; *A Trooper's Adventures in the War for the Union*)
Justia, a Know Nothing (*Our World or, the Democrat's Rule*)
Major Roger Sherman Potter Pheleg van Truesdale (*Life and Adventures of Major Roger Sherman ...*)

ADAMS, Harriet Stratemeyer [1894–1982, English science-fiction writer]
Victor Appleton (*Tom Swift and his Planet Stone*)
Carolyn Keene (*The Secret of Shadow Ranch*; *The Hidden Stair Case*)

ADAMS, Helen Simmons [1897–, US writer]
Nancy Barnes (*The Wonderful Year*; *Carlota, American Express*)

ADAMS, Henry Brooks [1838–1918, US journalist and historian]
Francis Snow Compton (*Esther*)

ADAMS, Herbert [1874–1958, English surveyor and crime novelist]
Jonathan Gray (*Diamonds are Trumps*; *Death on the First Tee*)

ADAMS, James Alonzo [1842–1925, US cleric]
Grapho (*Victoria*)

ADAMS, John [1735–1826, 2nd President of the USA]
A Gentleman (*Thoughts on Government*)
A Lover and Friend of Mankind (*An Affectionate Address to the Inhabitants of the British Colonies in America*)
Novanglus (in the *Boston Gazette*)

ADAMS, John [1786–1856, English lawyer]
Lemuel Gulliver (in *Blackwood's Magazine*)

ADAMS, John Isaac Ira [1826–57, US journalist]
Izak (in the *Boston Republican*)
Lightfoot (in the *Boston Traveller*)

ADAMS, John Quincy [1767–1848, 6th President of the USA]
Marcellus (letters to the *Boston Centinel*)
Publicola (letters to the *Boston Centinel*, and for *Observations on Paine's 'Rights of Man'*)

ADAMS, Julia Davis [1900–, US mystery writer]
F. Draco (*The Devil's Church*)

ADAMS, Robert Dudley [1829–1912, Australian poet and journalist]
Alpha Crucis (*Songs of the Stars and other Poems*)

ADAMS, Robert Martin [1915–, US writer and translator]
Robert Martin Krapp (*An Historical Essay*)

ADAMS, Samuel [1722–1803, American statesman]
Alfred; A Bostonian; Candidus; A Chatterer; Determinatus; E. A.; An Elector in 1771; A Layman; Observator; Principiis Obsta; Shippen; T. Z.; A Tory; Vindex; Z (all used in the *Boston Gazette*)
A Religious Politican (*An Address to the People in General*)
Sincerus (*An Earnest Appeal to the People*)

ADAMS, Samuel Hopkins [1871–1958, US writer]
Warner Fabian (*The Men in Her Life*; *Summer Bachelors*)

ADAMS, Samuel Vyvian Trerice [1900–51, English political researcher and writer]
Watchman (*Right Honourable Gentleman*; *What of the Night?*)

ADAMS, Sir Thomas [1586–1668, English merchant and Lord Mayor of London]
A Friend to the Parliament, City and Kingdom (*Plain Dealing or, a Fair*

Warning to the Gentlemen of the Committee for Union)

ADAMS, William Bridges [1797–1872, English civil engineer]
Junius Redivivus (*The Political Unionist's Catechism; The Rights of Morality; The Producing Man's Companion; Common Sense*)

ADAMS, William Davenport [1851–1904, English journalist and drama critic]
Arthur H. Elliott (*The Witty and Humorous Side of the English Poets*)

ADAMS, William Henry Davenport [1828–91, English journalist and writer]
Walter Clinton (*Sword and Pen*)

ADAMS, William Taylor [1822–97, US writer for children]
Warren T. Ashton (*Hatchie, the Guardian Slave*)
Irving Brown (used for his romantic novels)
Clingham Hunter MD (used for travel writing)
Oliver Optic (*Oliver Optic's Magazine for Boys and Girls; A Missing Million; The Boat Club*)

ADAMS-ACTON, Marion [1846–1928, Scottish novelist]
Jeanie Hering (*Honour is my Guide; Put to the Test*)

ADDIS, Eric Elrington [fl. 1938, English crime writer]
Peter Drax (*Crime within Crime; Tune to a Corpse*)

ADDIS, Hazel Iris [1900–, English writer for children]
Hazel Adair (*Challenge to Seven*)
A. J. Heritage (*The Happy Years*)

ADDISON, Henry Robert [1805–76, English soldier, novelist and dramatist]
A Half-Pay Officer (*All at Sea, Recollections of a Half-Pay Officer*)
An Irishman (in *Tait's Edinburgh Magazine*)
An Irish Police Magistrate (*Recollections of an Irish Police Magistrate*)

ADDISON, Joseph [1672–1719, English essayist, poet and man of letters]
C; L; I; O (all used in *The Spectator*)
Peter Puzzle (in *The Guardian*)

ADDISON, Lancelot [1632–1703, English cleric – father of Joseph Addison]
A Learned Person (*The Moores Baffled*)

ADER, Paul [1919–, US novelist]
James Allen (*We Always Come Back*)

ADEY, William More [1858–1942, English writer and translator]
William Wilson (*Pastor Sang – being the Norwegian Drama, ... – a Translation*)

ADLARD, Peter Marcus [1932–, English science-fiction writer]
Mark Adlard (*Interface; Volteface*)

ADLER, Irving [1913–, US mathematician]
Robert Irving (*Energy and Power*)

AGASSIZ, Mrs Elizabeth [1822–1907, US writer]
Actaea (*A First Lesson in Natural History*)

AGATE, James Evershed [1877–1947, English theatre critic and diarist]
Richard Prentis (in *John o'London's Weekly*)
George Warrington (in the *Sunday Times* for theatrical reviews and in *Country Life* magazine)

AGG, John [d. 1813, English novelist and poet]
Humphrey Hedgehog (*The General Post-Bag , or, News! Foreign and Domestic; The Pavilion, or, a Month in Brighton*)
Peter Pindar Jun. (*Three R___l Bloods etc.; Turning Out or, St___'s in an Uproar*)

AIKEN, Conrad Potter [1889–1973, US novelist and poet]
Samuel Jeake Jr. (in the *New Yorker*)

AIKEN, Joan [1924–, English novelist, poet and writer for children – daughter of Conrad Aiken above]
Nicholas Dee (used in both *Argosy Magazine* and *Woman's Journal*)

Rosie Lee (used for poetry contributions to *Argosy Magazine*)

Long John Silver (used for editorial writing in *Argosy Magazine*)

AIKIN, John [1747–1822, English physician and writer]
Uncle John (*The Children's Album of Pretty Pictures*)

AIKIN, Lucy [1781–1864, English historical writer and biographer]
Mary Godolphin (*Aesop's Fables in Words of One Syllable*; *Evenings at Home*)

AINGER, Alfred [1837–1904, English cleric and writer]
Doubleday; A Templar (both used in *MacMillan's Magazine*)

AINSLIE, George Robert [1776–1839, Scottish soldier and numismatist]
A Fellow of the Antiquarian Society (*Illustrations of the Anglo-French Coinage, 1830*)
A Fellow of the Antiquarian Societies of London and Scotland (*Illustrations of the Anglo-French Coinage, 1847*)

AINSLIE, Robert [1766–1838, Scottish lawyer and religious writer]
A Father (*A Father's Gift to his Children*)
A Layman (*A Father's Second Present to his Family*)

AINSLIE, Whitelaw [1767–1837, Scottish physician in India]
Caledonnicus (*Fitzraymond or, The Rambler on the Rhine*)

AINSWORTH, Henry [1571–1623, English cleric and orientalist]
A Learned and Judicious Divine (*A Guide unto Sion*)

AINSWORTH, Mary Dinsmore [1913–, Canadian psychologist]
Mary D. Salter (*Doctor in the Making*)

AINSWORTH, William Harrison [1805–82, English novelist and publisher]
Will Brown (*Letters from Cockney Lands*)

Mr Clutterbuck of Cripplegate (in *New Monthly Magazine*)

W. Harassing Painsworth (in *Our Miscellany*, 1856)

Cheviot Tichebourne (*Poems*)

AITKEN, Edward Hamilton [1851–1909, Indian-born academic and civil servant; his parents were Scottish, but he lived all his life in India]
Eha (*Tribes on my Frontier*; *Common Birds of Bombay*; *Behind the Bungalow*)

AKENSIDE, Mark [1721–70, English physician and poet]
Britannicus (*A British Philippic*; *The Voice of Liberty*)
Curio (*Epistle to Curio*)
Marcus (in *Gentleman's Magazine*)

AKERMAN, John Yonge [1806–73, English antiquarian and numismatist]
Paul Pindar, Gent. (in *Bentley's Miscellany* and for *Legends of Old London*)

AKERS, Elizabeth Chase [1832–1911, US poet]
Florence Percy (*Forest Birds from the Woods of Maine*; *Rock Me to Sleep Mother*)

ALAIS, Ernest W. [1864–1922, English writer for boys]
Cedric Wolfe (in *Pluck*)

ALBANESI, E. Maria [1859–1936, English romantic novelist]
Effie Adelaide Rowlands (*The Game of Life*; *A Girl with a Heart*)

ALBERT, Marvin Hubert [1924–, US crime and mystery writer]
Mike Barone (*Crazy Joe*)
Al Conroy (*Murder Mission!*; *Death Grip*)
Ian MacAlister (*Driscoll's Diamonds*; *Valley of the Assassins*)
Nick Quarry (*Trail of a Tramp*; *Till it Hurts*)
Anthony Rome (*Miami Mayhem*; *My Kind of Game*)

ALBERTI, George William [1723–58, Dutch-born cleric and essayist – sometime in England]
Alethophilus Gottingensis (*Some Thoughts on the Essay on Natural Religion*)

ALBIN, Eleazer [fl. 1713–59, British natural historian and art teacher]
A Lover of Birds (*A Natural History of Singing Birds*)

ALCHIN, Gordon [d. 1947, English barrister, poet and short-story writer]
Observer, R. F. C. (*Oxford and Flanders*)

ALCOCK, Catherine Bower [fl. 1929, English writer]
Brian De Shane (*De Sade: Being a Series of Wounds Inflicted with Brush and Pen upon Sadistic Wolves Garlanded in Masochist's Wool*)

ALCOTT, Anna Bronson [fl. 1880, US writer – sister of Louisa May Alcott below]
*Jo and Meg (*Comic Tragedies*)

ALCOTT, Louisa May [1832–88, US poet, essayist and writer for children]
May Alcott (in *The Christian Register*)
A. M. Barnard (in *The Flag of our Union*)
Flora Fairfield (in both *Peterson's Magazine* and *Saturday Evening Gazette*)
Aunt Jo (in *Aunt Jo's Scrap Bag*)
*Jo and Meg (*Comic Tragedies*)
Aunt Louise (in *Merry's Museum*)
Cousin Tribulation (in *Morning Glories and Other Stories*)
Aunt Wee (in *Morning Glories and Other Stories*)

ALCOTT, William Alexander [1798–1859, US writer]
A Schoolmaster (*Confessions of a Schoolmaster*)

ALDEN, Isabella MacDonald [1841–1930, US religious writer]
Pansy (*Four Girls at Chautauqua; Following Heavenward*)

ALDEN, William Livingston [1837–1908, US journalist]
Metador (in the *New York Times*)
Matthew White Jr. (used in various journals)

ALDERSON, Sir Edward Hall [1787–1857, English jurist]
A Layman (*Letter to the Bishop of Exeter*)

ALDINGTON, Edward Godfree [1892–1962, English poet, novelist and biographer]
Richard Aldington (*Death of a Hero; All Men are Enemies*)

ALDISS, Brian Wilson [1925–, English science-fiction writer and critic]
Jael Cracken (in *Science Fantasy* magazine)
John Runciman (in *New Worlds* magazine)
C. C. Shackleton (in *SF Horizons*)

ALDRICH, Bess [1881–1954, US novelist]
Margaret Dean Stevens (in the *American Magazine* and other periodicals)

ALDRICH, Clara C. Thomas [fl. 1948, US playwright and novelist]
Darragh Aldrich (*The Luck of the Irish; Some Trails Never End*)

ALDRICH, Earl Augustus [fl. 1933, US crime writer]
A. B. Leonard (*The Judson Murder Case*)

ALEXANDER, Colin James [1920–, English-born physician and writer in New Zealand]
Simon Jay (*Death of a Skin Diver; Sleepers Can Kill*)

ALEXANDER, Francesca [d. 1917, US artist and writer]
Francesca (*The Story of Ida*)

ALEXANDER, James Waddel [1804–59, US cleric and writer]
Caesariensis (in the *Literary World*)
Charles Quill (*The American Mechanic*)

ALEXANDER, Mrs Janet [1907–, Irish novelist and writer for children]
Janet McNeill (*Just Turn the Key; Prisoner in the Park*)

ALEXANDER, Martha Kathleen [1910–, South African playwright, novelist and writer for children]
Martha Robinson (*Wheaton Book of Animal Stories*; *Just One Thing on Top of Another*)

ALEXANDER, Robert William [1905–80, English whimsical science-fiction writer]
Joan Butler (*Double Figures*; *Something Rich*)

ALEXANDER, Samuel [1749–1824, English Quaker]
Aquila (*Serious Thoughts on the Fall and Restoration of Man*)
Verax (*Remarks on Dr Adam Clarke's Discourse*)

ALINGTON, Argentine Francis [1898–, English writer]
Hugh Talbot (*The China General*; *Laughter from the Lowlands*)

ALINGTON, Cyril Argentine [1872–1955, English cleric, headmaster and crime writer]
S. C. Westerham (*Mixed Bags*)

ALISON, Archibald [1792–1867, Scottish historian and legal writer]
A Member of the Faculty of Advocates (*Remarks on the Administration of Criminal Justice*)

ALISON, William Pulteney [1790–1859, Scottish physician]
Academicus (*Correspondence between Academicus and Consiliorus*)

ALKEN, Henry [fl. 1825, English engraver]
Ben Tallyho (*Qualified Horses and Unqualified Riders*)

ALLAN, Charles Stuart Hay [1799–1880, Scottish pretender to the English throne and writer]
Charles Edward Stuart (*The Costume of the Clans*; *Lays of the Deer Forest*; *The Sobieski Stuarts, their Claim to be Descended from Prince Charlie*; *Tales of the Century*)

ALLAN, Mabel Esther [1915–, English writer for children]
Jean Estoril (*Ballet for Drina*; *Drina Dances Again*)
Priscilla Hagon (*Dancing to Danger*; *Mystery at the Villa Bianca*)
Anne Pilgrim (*Clare goes to Holland*; *A Summer in Provence*)

ALLAN, Philip Bertram Murray [1884–1973, English journalist and writer]
Francis Cabochon (*The Golden Ladies of Pampeluna*)
O. Eliphaz Keat (*Princess Pirlipatine – a Translation*)
Alban M. Phillip (*A Boy's Book of Verse*)

ALLAN, Thomas [1777–1833, Scottish mineralogist and geologist]
A Private Gentleman (*Sketch of Mr Davy's Lectures on Geology*)

ALLARDICE, Robert Barclay [1779–1854, English soldier and eccentric athlete]
Allerdyce (*An Agricultural Tour in the United States*)

ALLASON, Rupert [1951–, English politician and espionage writer]
Nigel West (*MI5: British Security Service Operations 1909–45*; *Spy: Six Stories of Modern Espionage*)

ALLBEURY, Theodore (Ted) E. [1917–, English mystery novelist]
Richard Butler (*Italian Assets*; *Where All Girls Are Sweeter*)
Patrick Kelly (*Codeword Cromwell*; *The Lonely Margins*)

ALLEN, Benjamin [1789–1829, US cleric and poet]
Juba (*United We Stand, Divided We Fall*)
Osander (*The Death of Abdallah*; *Miscellaneous Poems on Moral and Religious Subjects*)

ALLEN, Bennet [fl. 1768, English cleric and writer]
A Young Gentleman of Sixteen (*Modern Chastity*)

ALLEN, Charles Grant Blairfindie
[1848–99, Canadian-born English prolific
contributor to magazines and novelist]
Grant Allen (his usual writing name)
Cecil Power (*Philistia*; *Babylon*)
Olive Pratt Rayner (*Rosalba, The Story of
her Development*)
Martin Leach Warborough (*Tom, Unlimited*)
J. Arbuthnot Wilson (in *Longman's
Magazine* and for *Mr Chung*)

ALLEN, Charlotte Vale [1941–, Canadian
romantic novelist]
Katherine Marlowe (*Hearts' Desires*)
Claire Vincent (*Believing in Giants*)

ALLEN, George [1792–1883, US cleric]
A Freeman (*Address to the Freemen of
Massachusetts*)
Vindex (*A Review of the Rev. Aaron Pickett's
Reply*)

ALLEN, Henry Wilson [1912–, US western
and science-fiction writer]
Clay Fisher (*Yellow Hair*; *The Big Pasture*)
Will Henry (*Mackenna's Gold*; *Summer of
the Gun*)

ALLEN, John [fl. 1762, English Baptist cleric]
Obadiah Barnabas (*A Compendius Descant of
the Autogeneal Works of Christ*)
J. A. (*The Christian Pilgrim or, the Travels of
the Children of Israel*)

ALLEN, John [1770–1843, Scottish physician,
political and historical writer]
A Layman (*Enquiry into the Tripartite
Division*; *The Fathers,The Reformers ...
against the Bishop of Lincoln*)
A Necessitarian (*Illustrations of Mr Hume's
Essay*)
A Retired Practitioner (*Thoughts on Medical
Reform*)

ALLEN, John Elliston [1921–, English writer
on aviation]
Paul M. Danforth (*The Channel Tunnel*)

ALLEN, Paul [1775–1826, US journalist and
writer]
Pasquin; St Denis Le Cadet (both used in
The Portico)

ALLEN, Samuel A. [1805–65, US writer]
Syr (*My Own Home and Fireside*)

ALLEN, Samuel Washington [1917–, US
literary academic and poet]
Paul Vesey (*Paul Vesey's Ledger*)

ALLEN, Stephen Valentine [1921–, US
writer]
William Christopher Stevens (*A Flash of
Swallows*)

ALLEN, Thomas [1681–1755, English cleric
and religious writer]
An Impartial Hand (*A Proposal for a Free
and Unexpensive Election*)

ALLEN, William Edward David [1901–73,
English historian]
James Drennan (*Oswald Mosley and British
Fascism*)

ALLIBONE, Samuel Austin [1816–89, US
bibliographer and essayist]
Bibliophile (in *Norton's Literary Gazette*)
A Layman (review of a work entitled *New
Themes*)

ALLIN, Miss Abby [fl. 1850, US poet and
writer]
Nilla (*Home Ballads*)

ALLINGHAM, Margery Louise [1904–66,
English crime novelist]
Maxwell March (*Other Man's Danger*;
Rogues Holiday; *The Shadow in the House*)

ALLINGHAM, William [1824–89, Irish
writer and poet]
Eastern Hermit; One who Loves and
Honours English Poetry; Unus de
Multus (all used in *Fraser's Magazine*)
Giraldus (*Nightingale Valley*)
D. Pollex (*Blackberries Picked from Many
Bushes*)
Patricius Walker (in *Fraser's Magazine* and
for *Rambles*)

ALLISON, William [1851–1925, English
novelist and writer on horses]
Blinkhoolie (*A Secret of the Sea*; *Turnstile of
Night*)

ALLIX, Peter (Pierre) [1641–1717, French-born cleric and writer; settled in England in 1685]
A Divine of the Church of England (*The Book of Psalms*; *The Judgment of the Ancient Jewish Church*)

ALMON, John [1737–1805, English political pamphleteer, printer and journalist]
An Independent Whig (in the *London Gazette* and for *Address to the Interior Cabinet* and *The Revolution in 1782 Impartially Considered*)

ALPERT, Hollis [1916–, US writer]
Robert Carroll (*A Disappearance*)

ALSOP, Richard [1761–1815, US poet and writer]
An American Gentleman (*Geographical, Natural and Civil History*)

ALSTON, John [fl. 1807, US writer]
Agrestis (*A Short Review of the Late Proceedings at New Orleans*)

ALSTON, Joseph [1778–1816, US politician]
The Mountaineer (in the *Charleston Gazette*)

ALTER, Moshe Jacob [1862–1923, Yiddish poet]
Morris Rosenfeld (*Songs from the Ghetto*)

ALVES, Robert [1745–94, Scottish classical scholar and poet]
A Student of Marischal College (*Time: an Elegy*)

AMBLER, Charles [d. 1794, English barrister]
A Retired Barrister (*Review of the Proceedings between James Fox ... Robert Mackreth*)

AMBLER, Eric [1909–, English crime writer]
*Eliot Reed (*Skytrip*; *Tender to Moonlight*)

AMES, Mrs Eleanor [1831–1908, US writer]
Eleanor Kirk (*Influence of the Zodiac on Human Life*; *Perpetual Youth*; *Up Broadway and its Sequel*)

AMES, Fisher [1758–1808, US statesman and political writer]
An American, Formerly a Member of Congress (*The Influences of Democracy on Liberty*)
Lucius Junius Brutus (in the *Boston Independent Chronicle*)
Camillus (used in various newspapers)

AMES, Nathan [d. 1865, US poet]
Senor Alguno (*Childe Harvarde*)

AMES, Rachel [1922–, English mystery writer]
Sarah Gainham (*The Cold Dark Night*; *Hapsburg Twilight*)

AMES, William [1576–1633, English Puritan cleric and theologian]
One who Doth Rejoice in the Lord his Saviour (*A Sound out of Sion from the Holy Mountain*)

AMHURST, Nicholas [1697–1742, English poet and political writer]
Caleb D'Anvers (in *The Craftsman* and for *The Twickenham Hotch-Potch*, *An Argument against Excises* and *A Collection of Poems*)
Humphrey Oldcastle (*Remarks on the History of England*)
Philo-Musus (*Oculus Britanniae*)

AMIS, Sir Kingsley [1922–, English novelist and poet]
Robert Markham (*The James Bond Dossier*; *Colonel Sun*)
William Tanner (*The Book of Bond or, Everyman his own 007*)

AMORY, Thomas [1691–1788, Irish writer and eccentric]
An Antiquarian Doctor (*An Antiquarian Doctor's Sermon*)
John Buncle Esq. (*The Life and Opinions of John Buncle Esq.*)

AMY, William Lacy [fl. 1936, Canadian crime writer]
Luke Allen (*The Black Opal*; *Murder at Midnight*)

ANAND, Valerie May Florence [1937–, English journalist and writer]
Fiona Buckley (in the *Evening News*)

ANBUREY, Thomas [fl. 1789, English soldier and traveller]
An Officer (*Travels Through the Interior Parts of America*)

ANCELL, Samuel [d. 1802, English soldier and military writer]
An Officer (*A Circumstantial Journal of ... the Siege of Gibraltar*)

ANCKETILL, William Robert [1820–89, Irish writer]
Scrutator (*Ultramontanism versus Education in Ireland*; *The Home-Rule and the Ultramonte Alliance*; *Roman Catholic Schools – a Warning to England*)

ANDERDON, John Lavicount [1792–1874, English merchant and writer]
A Layman (*The Life of Thomas Ken*; *The Messiah and His Kingdom*)

ANDERDON, William Henry [1816–90, English Jesuit and writer]
Owen Evans (*The Adventures of Owen Evans*)

ANDERSEN, Hans Christian [1805–75, Danish essayist and writer of short stories and fables]
*Hans Daumling (in *Dublin University Magazine*)

ANDERSON, Alexander [1845–1909, Scottish railway labourer, poet and librarian]
A Gent (*Joseph the Book-Man*)
Surfaceman (*A Song of Labour, and other Poems*; *Ballads and Sonnets*)

ANDERSON, Alexander [1862–1949, Scottish novelist]
James Bryce (*Story of a Plough Boy*; *Apollo in Exile*)

ANDERSON, Mrs Galusha [d. 1860, US writer]
Dorothy Doe (in the *New York Examiner*)

ANDERSON, George [fl. 1852, Scottish writer]
Cyclos, a Member of the Glasgow Skating Club (*The Art of Skating*)

ANDERSON, James [1739–1808, Scottish agriculturist and economist]
Agricola (in the *Edinburgh Weekly Magazine* and for *Miscellaneous Thoughts on Planting*)
Alcibiades; Aristides; Cimon; Germanicus; Timothy Hairbrain; Impartial Hand; Henry Plain; A Scot; Scoto-Britannicus; Senex (all used in *The Bee*)
Candid Enquirer (in *Gentleman's Magazine*)
A Farmer (*Essays Relating to Agriculture*)
Mercator (*Thoughts on the Privileges and Powers of Juries*)

ANDERSON, John [1668–1721, Scottish Presbyterian theologian]
A Countreyman (*A Letter from a Countreyman*)

ANDERSON, Louis Francis [1861–1950, US classical scholar]
Justus (*Prolegomena to Theism*; *Virtues*; *The Religion of the Soul*)

ANDERSON, Martin [1854–1932, English cartoonist and illustrator]
Cynicus (*Who Shall Rule, Briton or Norman?*)

ANDERSON, Poul [1926–, US science-fiction writer]
Winston P. Sanders (in *Analog Magazine*)

ANDERSON, Richard John [1848–1914, Irish academic and surgeon]
Vratsch (*Ancient Hibernia*; *Physical Degeneration*)
Wratsch (*Prehistoric Geographical and Geological notes*; *Protoza and some other Micro-Organisms*)

ANDERSON, Robert [fl. 1703, Scottish mathematician and silk-weaver]
R. A. (*Solid Geometry*)

ANDERSON, Thomas Scott [1853–1919, Scottish physician and writer on field sports]
Teviotdale (*Holloas from the Hills*)

ANDERTON, Laurence [1577–1643, English Jesuit – used the alias Scroop]
John Brerely (*The Lyturgie of the Masse; Luther's Life; Saint Augustin's Religion; The Protestant's Apologie for the Roman Church; The Reformed Protestant*)
A Priest of the Catholike and Roman Church (*Campian Englished*)

ANDRE, John [1751–80, British soldier – hanged as a spy by the Americans in the War of Independence]
A Dreamer (in *Rivington's Royal Gazette*)

ANDREWES, Frederick William [1859–1932, English physician]
A Mere Man (*Dictionary of Dainty Breakfasts*)

ANDREWS, Elisha [1768–1841, US cleric]
Gimel (in the *Boston Christian Watchman*)

ANDREWS, Eliza [1840–1931, US poet and novelist]
Elzey Hay (*A Family Secret; A Mere Adventurer; The War-Time Journal of a Georgia Girl 1864–65*)

ANDREWS, Garnett [1837–1903, US lawyer and writer]
An Old Georgia Lawyer (*Reminiscences of an Old Georgia Lawyer*)

ANDREWS, John Arthur [1865–1903, Australian journalist and writer]
Sebastian Bach (*Temple Mystic; Poems of Freedom*)

ANDREWS, Lucilla [fl. 1970, English romantic novelist]
Diana Gordon (*A Few Days in Endel*)
Joanna Marcus (*Marsh Blood*)

ANDREWS, Miles Peter [d. 1814, English politician and dramatist]
Arley (in *The World*)

ANDREWS, Sidney [1837–80, US journalist]
Dixon (*The South Since the War*)

ANDREWS, Stephen Pearl [1812–86, US journalist and writer]
Pantarch (*Basic Outline of Universology*)

ANDREWS, Wayne [1913–, US writer on architecture]
Montagu O'Reilly (*Who has been Tampering with these Pianos?*)

ANGUS, William [d. 1912, English Liberal Party activist]
Promotion by Merit (*Purchase in the Church*)

ANNESLEY, Arthur [1614–86, 1st Earl of Anglesey; statesman and historian]
One of No Arts but Downright Honesty (*Reflections*)
A Person of Honour and Eminent Minister of State (*The King's Right of Indulgence*)
A Person of Quality (*The Truth Unveiled*)

ANNET, Peter [1693–1769, English freethinker and philosopher – invented his own system of shorthand]
A Certain Free Enquirer (*A Collection of Tracts*)
Mencius Philalethes (*The History of Joseph Consider'd*)
A Moral Philosopher (*The Conception of Jesus Christ; The Resurrection's Defenders Stript of all Defence*)
W. Stilton, Horologist (*A View of the Life of King David*)

ANSLE, Dorothy Phoebe [fl. 1950, English romantic novelist]
Laura Conway (*The Sun Still Shines; Five Mrs Lorrimers*)
Hebe Elsna (*Women Always Forgive*)
Vicky Lancaster (*Daughter at Home*)
Lyndon Snow (*All in the Day's Work*)

ANSTEY, Christopher [1724–1805, English poet and author]
C. A. (*Britain's Genius, a Song Occasioned by the Late Mutiny at the Nore*)
Mr Inkle (*An Election Ball; Poetical Letters from Mr Inkle*)

Christopher Twist-Wit (*Madge's Addresses to C. W. Esq.*)

ANSTEY, John [d. 1819, English humorous poet]
The Late John Surrebutter (*The Pleaders Guide*)

ANSTRUTHER, Joyce [1901–53, English whimsical verse writer and essayist]
Jan Struther (*Mrs Miniver*)

ANTHONY, Barbara [1932–, English mystery novelist]
Antonia Barber (*Amazing Mr Blunden*; *Ghosts*)

ANTONICK, Robert J. [1939–, US science-fiction writer]
Nick Kamin (*Earthrim*; *The Herod Men*)

ANTRIM, Minna T. [1856–?, US writer]
Titian (*A Book of Toasts*)

APES, William [1798–?, American Indian]
A Native of the Forest (*The Experiences of a Native of the Forest*)

APPERLEY, Charles James [1779–1843, Welsh equine writer]
Nimrod (in the *Sporting Magazine* and for *The Life of a Sportsman* and *The Horse and the Hound*)

APPLETON, Jesse [1772–1819, US cleric]
Leighton; Owen (both used in the Boston Panoplist)

APPLETON, Nathan [1779–1861, US politician and merchant]
A Layman of Boston (*The Doctrines of Original Sin*)

APPLIN, Arthur [d. 1949, English actor, novelist and dramatist]
Julian Swift (*God and Mrs Brown*; *Come with Me a Little Way*; *The Chronicles of a Gigolo*)

ARBUCKLE, James [1700–34, British poet and writer]
Hibernicus (in the *Dublin Weekly Journal*)

ARBUTHNOT, Forster Fitzgerald [1833–1901, English Indian civil servant and orientalist]
An Aryan (*Early Ideas: a Group of Hindoo Stories*)

ARBUTHNOT, John [1667–1735, Scottish physician, pamphleteer, wit and essayist]
Doctor Bantley (*Critical Remarks on Capt. Gulliver's Travels*)
Capt. Lemuel Gulliver (*An Account of the State of Learning in the Empire of Lilliput*)
P. P., a Parish Clerk (*Memoirs Written in Imitation of Dr Burnet's History*)
Martinus Scriblerus (principal writer of *Memoirs of M ... S ...*, which were originally published as part of Alexander Pope's works)
A Sparkish Pamphleteer of Button's Coffee-House (*Letter to the Rev. Mr Dean Swift*)

ARBUTHNOT, John Bernard [1875–1950, English soldier and writer]
Beachcomber (in the *Daily Express* before D. B. W. Lewis)
Sassenach (*Arms and the Irishman*; *Irish Sketches*)

ARCHER, James Henry L. [1823–89, English soldier]
Montpelier (*Mnemosyne and other Pieces*)

ARCHER, John Wykeham [1808–64, English engraver, artist and antiquary]
Mr Zigzag the Elder (*The Recreations of Mr Zigzag the Elder*)

ARCHER, William [1856–1924, Scottish theatre critic and playwright]
Kappa (*Let Youth But Know*)

ARD, William Thomas [1922–60, US crime and mystery writer]
Ben Kerr (*Shakedown*; *I Fear You Not*)
Mike Moran (*Double Cross*)
Thomas Wills (*You'll Get Yours*; *Mine to Avenge*)

ARDIZZONE, Edward Jeffrey Irving [1900–79, English writer and artist]
Diz (in *Punch*)

ARIS, Ernest Alfred [1882–1963, English
painter, illustrator and writer for
children]
Robin A. Hood (*Just a Tiny Mite*; *Mother
Mouse*)

ARKWRIGHT, John Hungerford
[1833–1905, English countryman and
sportsman]
Etonensis (*A Dream*; *A Ballad, etc.*)

ARLOTT, Leslie Thomas John [1914–91,
English writer and broadcaster]
Silchester (for football reports in *The
Guardian*)
Leslie Thomas (in *Landmarks*)

ARMSTRONG, Charlotte [1905–69, US
mystery writer]
Jo Valentine (*The Trouble in Thor*)

ARMSTRONG, George [1792–1857, English
cleric]
A Voluntary (in *Tait's Edinburgh Magazine*)

ARMSTRONG, Harold Hunter [1884–?, US
novelist]
Henry G. Aikman (*The Groper*; *For Richer,
For Poorer*)

ARMSTRONG, John [1709–79, Scottish
physician and writer]
A Free-Thinker (*Conjectures upon the
Mortality of the Human Soul*)
Noureddin Alraschin (*The Muncher's and
Guzzler's Diary*)
Lancelot Temple (*A Short Ramble through
Some Parts of France and Italy*; *Sketches
or Essays on Various Subjects*)

ARMSTRONG, John [1758–1843, US soldier
and physician]
An Old Soldier (*Hints to Young Generals*)
A Practical Farmer (*A Treatise on
Agriculture*)

ARMSTRONG, John [1771–97, British
journalist and poet]
Albert (*Sonnets from Shakespeare*)

ARMSTRONG, Richard [1903–86, English
writer for children]
Cam Renton (*The Ship Stealers*; *Big-Head*)

ARMSTRONG, Terence Ian Fytton
[1912–70, English poet, critic and
bibliographer]
Fytton Armstrong (*Full Score*)
G (in *When Armageddon Came* by W. H. G.
Ewart, and for *Annotations on Some of the
Minor Writings of T. E. Lawrence*)
John Gawsworth (*The Collected Poems*; *The
Dowson Legend*)
Orpheus Scrannel (*Snowballs*; *An
Unterrestrial Pity*)

ARNALL, William [1715–41, English writer
of political tracts]
Solomon Abrabanel (*The Complaint of the
Children of Israel*)
A Member of the House of Commons
(*Animadversions on a Reverend Prelate's
Remarks upon the Bill ... to Prevent Suits
for Tythes*)
Francis Walsingham (in *The Inquisitor* and
the *Free Briton*)

ARNEE, Frank [1767–1858, English Quaker]
A Member of the Society of Friends (*Brief
Remarks on an Important Subject*)

ARNOLD, Augusta Foote [1844–1903, US
writer on cookery]
Mary Ronald (*The Century Cook Book*)

ARNOLD, Sir Edwin [1832–1904, English
poet, journalist and orientalist]
An Oxford Graduate (*Political Poems by
Victor Hugo and Garibaldi*)

ARNOLD, George [1834–65, US journalist
and poet]
Graham Allen; George Garrulous; Pierrot
(all used for journalism)
McArone (in *Vanity Fair*)

ARNOLD, Henry Thomas [1840–76, English
dramatist]
H. T. Arden (*The Belle of Barleymowe*; *The
Armourer's Daughter*)

ARNOLD, Matthew [1822–88, English poet
and man of letters]
A. (*The Strayed Reveller*; *Empedocles on
Aetna*)

Arminius von Thundertentroncle (in the *Pall Mall Gazette*)

ARNOLD, Thomas [1795–1842, English cleric and headmaster of Rugby School]
One of the Old Staff (in The *Dublin Review*)

ARNOLD, William Delafield [1828–59, English soldier and writer]
Punjabee (*Oakfield, or Fellowship in the East*)

ARNOLD, William Thomas [1852–1904, Australian-born English journalist]
Vigilans et Aequus (in *The Spectator*)

ARNOT, Hugo [1749–86, Scottish historian]
A Citizen (*Letter to the Heritors, Farmers and Inhabitants of the County of Edinburgh*)
Eugene (*Letter to the Lord Advocate of Scotland*)

ARNOT, William [1808–75, Scottish cleric and preacher]
John Bunyan, Junior (*The Drunkard's Progress*)

ARRINGTON, Alfred W. [1810–67, US cleric, preacher and lawyer]
Charles Summerfield (*The Rangers and Regulators of The Yanaha*)

ARTHINGTON, Maria [d. 1863, English Quaker]
A Member (*A Few Remarks Addressed to the Society of Friends*)

ARTHUR, Timothy Shay [1809–85, US journalist and novelist]
Uncle Herbert (*True Riches or, Wealth Without Wings; The Budget*)
Mrs John Smith (*Confessions of a House-Keeper*)

ARUNDELL, Mary Anne [1787–1845, English writer]
A Lady (in *The Rambler*)

ASBELL, Bernard [1923–, US writer]
Nicholas Max (*President McGovern's First Term*)

ASHBEE, Charles Robert [1863–1942, English architect, craftsman and publisher]
An Anglo-Egyptian Civil Servant (*Lyrics of the Nile*)

ASHBEE, Henry Spencer [1834–1900, English bibliographer and collector of erotica]
Pisanus Fraxi (*Catena Librorum Tacendorum etc; Centuria Librorum Absconditorum, etc; Index Librorum Prohibitorum*)
E. H. Shebsa (in *The Bibliographer*)
Speculator Morum (*Bibliotheca Arcana etc*)

ASHBROOK, Harriette [1898–1946, US novelist]
Susannah Shane (*Diamonds in the Dumpling*)

ASHDOWNE, William [1723–1810, English Unitarian preacher]
A Free Enquirer After Truth (*A Key to the Scripture Character*)
An Impartial Hand (*The Distinction between the Ordinary and Extraordinary Gifts of the Holy Spirit; The True Character of John the Baptist*)

ASHMOLE, Elias [1617–92, English antiquarian and founder of the Ashmolean Museum]
James Hasolle (*Fasciculus Chemicus or Chymical Collections*)

ASHTON, Thomas [1716–75, English cleric and preacher]
A Late Fellow of King's College, Cambridge (*The Election of Aliens into the Vacancies in Eton College, an Unwarrantable Practice*)

ASHTON, Winifred [1887–1965, English artist, actress, novelist and playwright]
Clemence Dane (*Regiment of Women; A Bill of Divorcement; Tradition and Hugh Walpole*)

ASHTON-GWATKIN, Frank Trelawney Arthur [1889–1976, English diplomat, poet and orientalist]
John Paris (*Matsu; Kimono; Sayonara; Banzai; The Island Beyond Japan*)

ASHWORTH, Henry [1794–1880, English political reformer]
A Lancashire Cotton Spinner (*Letter to the Rt. Hon. Lord Ashley*)

ASIMOV, Isaac [1920–92, Russian-born US science-fiction writer]
George E. Dale (in *Astounding Science Fiction* magazine)
Paul French (*David Starr, Space Ranger; Lucky Starr and the Pirates of the Asteroids*)

ASPINALL, James [d. 1861, English cleric and writer]
An Old Stager (*Liverpool a Few Years Since*)

ASPLAND, Robert [1782–1845, English Unitarian cleric]
A Magistrate (*Public Instruction and Moral Improvement*)

ASPLIN, William [1687–1758, English theologian]
A Master of Arts of the University of Oxford (*Alkiba: a Disquisition*)
Philalethes Rusticus (*The Impertinence and Imposture of Modern Antiquaries Display'd*)
A True Son of the Church of England (*The Anatomy of the Kebla*)

ASQUITH, Cynthia [1887–1960, English novelist and biographer]
Leonard Gray (used in her ghost story anthologies)

ASSHETON, William [1641–1711, English cleric and theologian]
A Divine of the Church of England (*The Possibility of Apparitions; A Seasonable Vindication of the Clergy*)

ASTELL, Mary [1668–1731, English controversial religious writer]
A Daughter of the Church of England (*The Christian Religion as Professed by a Daughter of the Church of England*)
A Lover of her Sex (*A Serious proposal to the Ladies*)
A Very Moderate Person and Dutiful Subject to the Queen (*A Fair Way with Dissenters*)

ASTLEY, John [d. 1595, English servant of Queen Elizabeth I and an expert horseman]
A Gentleman of Great Skill in the Said Art (*The Art of Riding*)

ASTLEY, William [1855–1911, English-born Australian novelist and journalist]
Price Warung (*Tales of the Convict System; Half-Crown Bob and Tales of the Riverine*)

ASTON, Anthony [fl. 1730, English actor and dramatist]
Tony Aston (*A Brief Supplement to Colley Cibber Esq.*)
Matthew Medley (*The Fool's Opera*)

ASTON, Sir George [1861–1938, English soldier and angler]
George Southcote (*Mostly about Trout; Letters to Young Fly-Fishers*)

ASTON, Joseph [1762–1844, English publisher and writer]
One of the Addressed (*A Reply to Mr Niven's etc.*)

ASTON, Sir Thomas [1600–45, English royalist in the Civil War – died of wounds]
A Faithful Lover of his Church (*A Collection of Sundry Petitions*)

ASTON, Walter Herman [1913–, English writer]
*G. and W. Fortune (*Hitler Divided France*)

ATHERLEY-JONES, Llewellyn Archer [1851–1929, English barrister, novelist and writer]
Lionel Langton (*The Fall of Lord Paddockslea*)

ATHERTON, Gertrude Franklin [1857–1948, US novelist and writer]
Frank Lin (*What Dreams May Come; A Whirl Asunder*)

ATKEY, Bertram [fl. 1907, English writer]
*Judson Bolt (*The Prodigal Nephew*)

ATKEY, Philip [1908–85, English crime and mystery writer]
Pat Merriman (*Night Call*)
Barry Perowne (*Raffles of the M. C. C.*; *Arrest These Men!*)

ATKINS, Frank [fl. 1900, English writer for juveniles]
Fenton Ash (*A Trip to Mars*; *The Radium Seekers*)
Fred Ashley (*The Temple of Fire*)
Frank Aubrey (*A Queen of Atlantis*; *Devil-Tree of El Dorado*)

ATKINS, Meg Elizabeth [fl. 1979, English writer]
Elizabeth Moore (*Something to Jump For*; *By the North Door*)

ATKINSON, Edward [1827–1905, US economist]
A Cotton Manufacturer (*Cheap Cotton and Free Labour*)

ATKINSON, George Wesley [1845–1925, US writer]
One of the Raiders (*After the Moonshiners*)

ATKINSON, Hugh [fl. 1978, Australian writer]
Hugh Geddes (*The Pyjama Girl Case*)

ATKINSON, John [1877–1945, English barrister, soldier and humorist]
John Aye (*Humour in the Law*; *Clerical Chuckles*)

ATKINSON, William Walker [1862–1932, US lawyer, editor and writer on psychology]
Yogi Ramacharaka (*Arcane Teaching or, Secret Doctrine of the Ancient Atlantis, Egypt etc.*; *Fourteen Lessons in Yogi Philosophy*)

ATTENBOROUGH, Bernard George [fl. 1970, English, journalist and writer]
James S. Rand (*Run for the Trees*; *Viva Ramirez*)

ATTERBURY, Francis [1662–1732, English cleric, politician and writer; Bishop of Rochester until deprived of office]
A Member of the Lower House of Convocation (*The Case of the Schedule Stated ... Adjournment of the Lower House of Convocation*)

ATWATER, Richard Tupper [1892–?, US writer]
Riq (*Rickety Rimes of Riq*)

AUBREY-FLETCHER, Sir Henry Lancelot [1887–1969, English crime novelist]
Henry Wade (*The Verdict of You All*; *The Missing Partners*)

AUCHINCLOSS, Louis Stanton [1917–, US novelist and short-story writer]
Andrew Lee (*The Indifferent Children*)

AUDEN, Wystan Hugh [1907–73, English poet – adopted US citizenship]
W. H. Arden (in *Public School Verse 1924*)

AUDEMARS, Pierre [1909–, English, crime and mystery novelist]
Peter Hodemart (*Wrath of the Valley*)

AUFRERE, Anthony [1756–1833, English antiquary]
Viator A (in *Gentleman's Magazine*)

AURANDT, Paul Harvey [1918–, US journalist and writer]
Paul Harvey (*Autumn of Liberty*; *The Rest of the Story*)

AUST, Sarah [1744–1811, English writer on topography]
Hon. Mrs Murray (*A Companion and Useful Guide to the Beauties of Scotland*)

AUSTEN, Jane [1775–1817, English novelist and poet]
A Lady (*Sense and Sensibility*)

AUSTIN, Alfred [1835–1913, English Poet Laureate and writer]
Lamia (*The Poet's Diary*)
An Old Fogey (in *Temple Bar*)
Lord Sangfroid; Thomas Tantivy (both used in *National Review*)

AUSTIN, Benjamin [1752–1820, US merchant and political writer]
Honestus (*Observations on the Pernicious Practice of Law*)
Old South (*Constitutional Republicanism*)

AUSTIN, Benjamin Fish [1850–?, Canadian writer on spiritualism and religion]
Benjamin Nitsua (*The Mystery of Ashton Hall*)

AUSTIN, Frederick Britten [1885–1941, English dramatist and writer]
*Eleanor G. Linne (*The Virgin and the Fool*)
Julia Tregenna (*The Pipes of Pan*)

AUSTIN, George Lowell [1849–93, US physician and writer]
Barry Lyndon (*Under the Tide*)

AUSTIN, James Trecothick [1784–1870, US lawyer, journalist and writer]
A Citizen of Massachusetts (*Remarks on Dr Channing's Slavery*)

AUSTIN, John [1613–69, English Catholic writer]
William Birchley (*The Christian Moderator*)
A Catholick Gentleman (*The Catholique's Plea*)

AUSTIN, John Charles [fl. 1941, English writer]
Gun Buster (*Battle Dress*; *Grand Barrage*; *Return via Dunkirk*)

AUSTIN, Louis Frederick [1852–1905, English long-time secretary to Sir Henry Irving]
Frederic Daly (*Henry Irving in England and America*)
Augustin Lewis (in *Dublin University Magazine*)

AUSTIN, Mrs Mary Hunter [d. 1934, US novelist and anthropologist]
Gordon Stairs (*Outland*)

AUSTIN, Wiltshire Stanton [1826–75, English cleric and writer]
A Barrister-at-Law; A West Indian and an Abolitionist (both used in *Bentley's Miscellany*)

Vaughan Dayrell (*Lives of the Poets-Laureate*; *Weeds from the Isis*)

AVALLONE, Michael Angelo Jr. [1924–, US popular novelist]
Troy Conway (*The Man-Eater*; *The Cunning Linguist*)
Priscilla Dalton (*The Silent, Silken Shadows*; *The Darkening Willows*)
Mark Dane (*Felicia*)
J. A. DePre (*The Third Woman*; *Warlock's Woman*)
Dorothea Nile (*The Evil Men Do*; *The Third Shadow*)
Ed (or Edwina) Noone (*The Night Walker*)
Vance Stanton (*The Walking Fingers*)
Sidney Stuart (*The Beast With Red Hands*)

AVELING, Edward Bibbings [1851–98, English political activist]
Alec Nelson (*Comic Cricket*)

AVERILL, Esther [1902–, US writer for children]
John Domino (*Fable of a Proud Poppy*)

AVERY, Benjamin [d. 1764, English Presbyterian cleric and physician]
*Bagweel (*A Collection of Occasional Papers etc*)

AVERY, Samuel Putnam [1822–1904, US artist and humorist]
Spavery (*The Harp of a Thousand Strings*; *Mrs Partington's Carpet-Bag of Fun*)

AVEY, Ruby Doreen [1927–, English romantic novelist]
Vicki Page (*Arabian Love Story*; *Nurse in Deep Water*)

AXON, William Edward Armytage [1846–1913, English bibliographer and writer]
Dudley (or Ernest) Armytage (*Shakespeare's House*)

AYCKBOURNE, Alan [1939–, English playwright]
Roland Allen (*The Square Cat*; *Dad's Tale*)

AYCOCK, Roger Dee [1914–, US science-fiction writer]
Roger Dee (*An Earth Gone Mad*)

AYLWARD, Alfred S. [1841–89, Irish nationalist and traveller]
An Ex-Member of the Fenian Directory (in *Blackwood's Magazine*)

AYRES, Philip [1638–1712, English writer]
P. A. (*The Voyages and Adventures of Capt. Barth Sharp and Others in the South Sea*)

AYSCOUGH, Francis [1700–63, English cleric]
A Member of the University (*A Proper Answer to a Late Abusive Pamphlet*)

AYSCOUGH, George Edward [d. 1779, English traveller and dramatist]
An Officer in the Guards (*Letters from an Officer in the Guards*)

AYSCOUGH, Samuel [1745–1804, English librarian, indexer and cleric]
Vicar of Cudham (in *Gentleman's Magazine*)

AYTOUN, William Edmonstoune [1813–65, Scottish poet and humorist]
Rechoboam Ben Abraham; *Colonel Crockett; *Eminent Hands; One of the Briefless (all used in *Tait's Edinburgh Magazine*)
*Bon Gaultier (*The Book of Ballads*)
Augustus Dunshunner; Iracundus; Robert M'Corkindale; An Old Stager; Phosphorus; A Railway Witness; Round Robin (all used in *Blackwood's Magazine*)
T. Percy Jones (*Firmilian, a Spasmodic Tragedy*)
A Layman of the Church (*The Drummond Schism Examined*)

B

BABB, Clement Edwin [1821–1906, US cleric, lawyer and editor]
Uncle Jesse (*Talks About the War*; *Talks About Jesus*)

BABBAGE, Charles [1792–1871, English mathematician and designer of a mathematical calculating machine]
A Philosopher (*Passages from the Life of a Philosopher*)

BABCOCK, Mrs Winifred Eaton [1879–1954, Japanese-born US writer of novels with a Japanese theme]
Onoto Watanna (*The Daughters of Nojo*; *Thama*; *Sunny San*)

BABER, Douglas Gordon [1918–, Irish writer]
John Ritson (*Beneath the Precipice*; *Death of a Maid*)

BACHE, Benjamin Franklin [1769–98, US journalist in Philadelphia]
Oliver Fairlay (*Proposals by Oliver Fairlay*)

BACHE, Ellen [1942–, US writer]
Ellen Matthews (*Culture Clash*)

BACHE, Richard [1794–1836, US soldier]
An Officer of the US Army (*Notes on Columbia taken in the Years 1822–23*)

BACKHOUSE, Edward [1808–79, English Quaker]
One of the Religious Society of Friends (*Ritualism, a Damage to Vital Church Unity*)

BACKUS, Isaac [1724–1806, US cleric]
A Countryman (*A Letter to a Gentleman*)

BACKUS, Jean L. [1914–, US novelist]
David Montross (*Fellow Traveller*; *Traitor's Wife*; *Troika*)

BACON, Edward [1906–, English writer]
Francis Boon (*A Cat among the Rabbits*)

BACON, John Mackenzie [1846–1904, English scientist and aeronaut]
A Graduate Scholar of his College (*Short Notes on the Gospel of St Luke*)
A Priest of the Church of England (*The Curse of Conventionalism*)

BACON, Mrs Josephine D. D. [1876–?, US writer for girls]
Ingraham Lovell (*Ten to Seventeen – a Boarding House Diary*; *An Idyll of All Fool's Day*)

BACON, Leonard [1887–1954, US poet]
Autolycus (*Ulug Beg: an Epic Poem*)

BACON, Mrs Mary S. Hoke [1870–1934, US novelist]
Dolores Marbourg (*I'll Ne'er Consent*; *The Soul of a Woman*)

BACON, Nathaniel [1593–1660, English Puritan enthusiast in the English Civil War and Protectorate]
N. B. (*A Relation of the fearful Estate of Francis Spira*)

BACON, Richard Mackenzie [1775–1844, English music critic and journalist]
A Musical Student (in *New Monthly Magazine*)

BACON, Thomas [1700–68, American cleric]
An American Pastor (*Two Sermons Preached to a Congregation of Black Slaves*)

BADCOCK, John [fl. 1825, English sporting writer]
Jon Bee (*A Dictionary of the Turf, the Ring, the Chase, etc*; *The Dramatic Works of Samuel Foote*)
John Hinds (*Conversations on Conditioning*)

BADCOCK, Samuel [1747–88, English cleric and literary critic]
Cam (in *Gentleman's Magazine*)
Justinophilus (*A Letter Addressed to Mr Priestley*)

BADEAU, Adam [1831–95, US soldier and diplomat]
The Vagabond (*The Vagabond*)

BADELEY, Edward Lowth [d. 1868, English ecclesiastical lawyer]
A Barrister (*Considerations on Divorce*)

BADENI, June [1925–, English writer]
June Wilson (*One Foolish Heart*; *Green Shadows: a Life of John Clare*)

BADHAM, Charles [1780–1845, English physician and classical scholar]
An Amateur (*Brief Recollections, Chiefly of Italy*)

BADHAM, David [1806–57, English naturalist and traveller]
Scarabaeus (*The Question Concerning the Sensibility ... of Insects*)

BADIN, Stephen Theodore [1768–1853, French-born US cleric]
A French Clergyman (*The Real Principles of the Roman Catholics*)

BAERLEIN, Henry [1875–1960, English travel writer]
Henry Bernard (*In Pursuit of Dulcinae*; *The Shade of the Balkans*)

BAGBY, George William [1828–83, US humorist]
Mozis' Addums (*Meekins's Twinses*)

BAGG, Lyman Hotchkiss [1846–1911, US journalist and writer]
El Atchby (in *The Graphic*)

Karl Kron (*Ten Thousand Miles on a Bicycle*)
A Massachusetts Yankee (in the *Anglo-American Times*)
N. S. G. (in *Oliver Optic's Magazine* and in the *New York Citizen*)
A Yale Graduate of '69 (*Four Years at Yale*)

BAGNOLD, Enid [1889–1981, English novelist and playwright]
A Lady of Quality (*Serena Blandish or, the Difficulty, etc.*)

BAGOT, Arthur Greville [1849–1915, English soldier, journalist and sporting writer]
Bagatelle (in the *Country Gentleman and Sporting Gazette* and for *Shooting and Yachting in the Mediterranean* and *Sporting Sketches at Home and Abroad*)

BAILEY, Mrs Alice Ward [1857–?, US writer]
A. B. Ward (*Roberta and her Brothers*; *The Sage Brush Parson*)

BAILEY, Benjamin [1791–1853, English cleric – spent forty years in India]
Vetus (letters to the *Ceylon Times*)

BAILEY, Ebenezer [1795–1839, US educationalist and writer]
Grins and Gripes (in the *New England Galaxy*)

BAILEY, James Montgomery [1841–94, US journalist and humorist]
Newsman Danbury (*Life in Danbury*)

BAILEY, Nathaniel [d. 1742, English lexicographer]
N. B. (*The Antiquities of London and Westminster*)

BAILEY, Samuel [1791–1870, English philosopher and writer]
An Egyptian Kaffir (in the *New York Graphic*)
A Yorkshire Freeholder (*A Discussion of Parliamentary Reform*)
A Younger Brother (*The Right of Primogeniture Examined*)

BAILEY, Thomas [1785–1856, English silk hosier, poet, topographer and writer]
An Old Tradesman (*Recreations in Retirement*)

BAIN, John Vernon [1922–, English poet and writer]
Vernon Scannell (*Graves and Resurrections*; *Drums and Morning*)

BAIN, Kenneth Bruce Findlater [1921–85, English journalist and writer]
Richard Findlater (*The Unholy Trade*; *The Player Kings*)

BAINES, Edward [1800–90, English newspaper editor and politician]
A Fellow of a College in Cambridge (*The Art of Latin Poetry*)

BAIRD, Robert [1798–1863, US preacher and temperance propagandist]
An American (*A Letter to Lord Brougham*)

BAIRD, Thomas H. [1787–1866, US jurist and writer]
Alethes (in the *Pittsburgh Commercial Journal*)

BAKER, Andrew Clement [1842–1913, English journalist and writer]
Arthur Clements (in the *Illustrated Sporting and Dramatic News*)

BAKER, Augustus [fl. 1925, English writer for boys]
Anthony Baron (in *Union Jack*)

BAKER, Betty Doreen [1916–, English novelist and writer for children]
Elizabeth Renier (*Landscape of the Heart*; *Stone People*)

BAKER, Denys Val [1917–84, Welsh writer and novelist]
David Eames (*Pottery for Profit and Pleasure*; *The Title's my Own*)

BAKER, George Melville [fl. 1877, US playwright]
Uno (*Baby Ballads*)

BAKER, Mrs Harriette Newell [1815–93, US writer for children]
Aunt Hattie (*Art and Artlessness*)
Mrs Madeline Leslie (used for The Woodlawn series of books)

BAKER, Henry [1698–1774, English naturalist – son-in-law of Daniel Defoe]
Henry Stonecastle of Northumberland Esq. (in the *Universal Spectator and Weekly Journal* from 1728 to 1739)

BAKER, John Wynn [d. 1775, English agricultural economist]
A Friend to the Nation (*An Address to the Representatives of the People*)
I. W. B. (*Some Hints on the Improvement of Husbandry*)

BAKER, Louisa Alice [1858–1926, New Zealand romantic novelist]
Alien (*A Daughter of the King*; *Looking-Glass Hours*)

BAKER, Ray Stannard [1870–1946, US journalist and essayist]
David Grayson (*Adventures in Solitude*; *The Countryman's Year*)

BAKER, Mrs Sarah S. [1824–1906, US writer for children]
Aunt Friendly (*Bound Out or, Abby at the Farm*)

BAKER, Thomas [1656–1740, English historian and antiquarian]
A Gentleman (*Reflections upon Learning*)

BAKER, Thomas [1680–1749, English dramatist]
Mrs Crackenthorpe (in the *Female Tatler*)

BAKER, William [1742–85, English painter, linguist and classical scholar]
The Rationalist (*Peregrinations of the Mind*)

BAKER, William Arthur Howard [1925–91, English writer for boys]
Sexton Blake (*The Last Tiger*, published in 1963 as the last of the Sexton Blake stories, No. 526)

BAKER, William Deal [1812–76, US lawyer and writer]
Hyton Hosmot (*The Saturniad*)

BAKER, William Mumford [1825–83, US cleric and novelist]
George F. Harrington (*Inside – a Chronicle of Secession*)

BALCHIN, Nigel Marlin [1908–70, English scientist and novelist]
Mark Spade (in *Punch* and for *How to Run a Bassoon Factory* and *Fun and Games*)

BALDWIN, Faith [1893–1978, US romantic novelist]
Amber Lee (*Proud Revelry*)

BALDWIN, Gordon Cortis [1908–, US western novelist and writer for children]
Lew Gordon (*Ambush Basin*)

BALDWYN, Edward [1746–1817, English cleric and pamphleteer]
Trim (*A Congratulatory Letter to William Atkinson*)

BALE, John [1495–1563, English cleric and controversialist; Bishop of Ossory]
Johann Harrison (*Yet a Course at the Romyshe Fox*)
Henry Stalbrydge (*The Epistel Exhortatorye of an Inglyshe Chrystian*)

BALGUY, John [1686–1748, English cleric and philosopher]
A Clergyman (*The Foundations of Moral Goodness*)
A Country Clergyman (*A Letter to a Deist*)

BALL, Brian Neville [1932–, English writer for children]
Brian Kinsey-Jones (*Sundog*)

BALL, Doris Bell [1897–1987, English crime novelist]
Josephine Bell (*Death on the Reserve*; *Question of Inheritance*)

BALL, Edward [1792–1873, English dramatist and songwriter]
Edward Fitzball (*Floating Beacon*; *Jonathan Bradford or, Murder at the Roadside Inn*)

BALL, Oona Howard [d. 1941, English novelist]
Barbara Burke (*Their Oxford Year*; *Barbara Goes to Oxford*)

BALLANTYNE, John [1774–1821, Scottish merchant and publisher]
Agricola; D. (both used in *The Sale Room*)

BALLANTYNE, John [1778–1830, Scottish cleric and pamphleteer]
A Dissenter (*A Comparison of Established and Dissenting Churches*)

BALLANTYNE, Robert Michael [1825–94, Scottish watercolourist and writer for children]
Comus (*Mister Fox*; *My Mother*; *Three Little Kittens*)
One of Themselves (*How Not to Do it: a Manual for the Awkward Squad*)
Ensign Sopht (*The Volunteer Levee*)

BALLARD, Edward [1805–70, US cleric and writer]
Sabino (in The *Boston Daily Advertiser* and for *The Popham Colony*)

BALLARD, Edward George [1791–1860, English civil servant and writer]
E. G. B. (in both The *Literary Chronicle* and *the* Imperial Magazine)
I. (in The *Literary Magnet* and *World of Fashion*)

BALLARD, Eric Allen [1908–68, English writer for children]
Eric Allen (*Pepe Moreno*; *The Latchkey Children*)
Paul Dallas (*Into my Parlour*)
Edwin Harrison (*Killer's Playground*; *Witness to Murder*)

BALLARD, Guy W. [1878–1939, English writer]
Chanera (*I Am – Adorations and Affirmations*)

BALLARD, Willis Todhunter [1903–80, US western novelist]
Parker Bonner (*Plunder Canyon*; *Outlaw Brand*)

Sam Bowie (*Gunlock*; *The Train Robbers*)
Brian Fox (*A Dollar to Die For*; *The Wild Bunch*)
Harrison Hunt (*Murder Picks the Jury*)
John Hunter (*The Man from Yuma*; *Gambler's Gun*)
Neil McNeil (*Third on a See-Saw*; *Two Guns for Hire*)
John Shepherd (*Lights, Camera, Murder*)
Jack Slade (*Bandido*; *The Man from Cheyenne*)
Clay Turner (*Give a Man a Gun*)

BALLINGER, William Sanborn [1912–80, US crime and mystery writer]
Fredric Freyer (*The Black, Black Hearse*)
B. X. Sanborn (*The Doom-Maker*)

BALLOU, Adin [1803–90, US cleric]
A Consistent Restorationist (*The Touchstone, Exhibiting Universalism and Restorationism as They are Moral Contraries*)

BALLOU, Maturin Murray [1820–95, US journalist and editor]
Lieut. Murray (*Red Rupert, The American Buccaneer*; *The Dog Detective and his Young Master*)

BANGS, John Kendrick [1862–1922, US journalist]
*Two Wags (*New Waggings of Old Tales*)

BANIM, John [1798–1842, Irish novelist and dramatist]
Barnes O'Hara (in *Tait's Edinburgh Magazine*)
*The O'Hara Family (*Tales of the O'Hara Family*)
A Traveller (in The *Limerick Evening Post*)

BANIM, Michael [1796–1874, Irish novelist and village postmaster]
Abel O'Hara (in *Tait's Edinburgh Magazine*)
*The O'Hara Family (*Tales of the O'Hara Family*)

BANISTER, Thomas [fl. 1853, English barrister]
A Barrister (*The Suffrage Nationalized*)
T. B. Temple (*Two Papers on Some of the Popular Discontents*)

BANKS, Elizabeth [d. 1938, US journalist]
Enid; Mary Mortimer Maxwell (both used in *The Referee*)

BANKS, George Nugent [fl. 1877 English writer]
An Eton Boy (*A Day of My Life*; *or Every-Day Experiences at Eton*)

BANKS, John [1709–51, English poet and writer of humble background]
An English Officer (*The History of Francis-Eugene*)

BANKS, Percival Weldon [1806–50, Irish barrister, journalist and writer]
An Apprentice of the Law; Sir Charles Botherall; An Old Hand; Morgan Rattler (all used in *Fraser's Magazine*)
A Man About Town (in *New Monthly Magazine*)

BANKS, Thomas Christopher [1765–1854, English lawyer and genealogist]
An Unfortunate Nobleman (*The Detection of Infamy*)

BANKS, William Mitchell [1842–1904, Scottish surgeon and medical lecturer]
The Bard (*Narrative of the Voyage of the Argonaut in 1880*)

BANNISTER, John William [1794–1829, English jurist and former mariner – lived sometime in Canada]
A Settler (*Sketch of a Plan for Settling in Upper Canada*)

BANNISTER, Patricia Valeria [1923–, English romantic novelist]
Gwyneth Moore (*Men Were Deceivers Ever*; *Love's Lady Lost*)
Patricia Veryan (*Debt of Honour*; *Perfect Match*)

BANNISTER, Saxe [1790–1877, English jurist and legal writer]
An Old Crown Lawyer (*The Privy Council at Common Law*)
Philadelphus (*Remarks on the Indians of North America*)

BARBAULD (née Aikin), Anna Letitia
[1743–1825, English writer and poet; she also published under her maiden name]
A. L. B. (*Hymns in Prose for Children*)
A Volunteer (*Sins of the Government, Sins of the Nation*)

BARBER, Margaret Fairless [1869–1901, English essayist]
Michael Fairless (*The Roadmender; The Gathering of Brother Hilarius*)

BARBOUR, Sir David Miller [1841–1928, Irish-born English civil servant in India]
D. B. (*Our Afghan Policy and the Occupation of Candahar*)

BARBOUR, Ralph Henry [1870–1944, US writer]
Richard Stillman Powell (*Phyllis in Bohemia*)

BARCLAY, Mrs Florence Louisa
[1862–1921, English sentimental novelist]
Brandon Roy (*Guy Mervyn*)

BARCLAY, Hugh [1799–1884, Scottish lawyer and legal writer]
A County Magistrate (*Juvenile Delinquency: its Causes and Cure*)
An Elder of the Church of Scotland (*A Plea for Christian Union*)
Nestor (*Rambling Recollections of Old Glasgow*)
Omicron (*The Fountain of Life*)

BARCLAY, John [1758–1826, Scottish cleric and anatomist]
Jonathan Dawplucker (*Remarks on Mr John Bell's Anatomy of the Heart and Arteries*)
A Lover of that People (*An Affectionate Address to such People called Friends*)

BARCYNSKI, Leon [1949–, English occult writer]
Osborne Phillips (*Voudoun Fire*)

BARDIN, John Franklin [1916–81, US crime and mystery writer]
Douglas Ashe (*A Shroud for Grandmama*)
Gregory Tree (*The Case against Myself; So Young to Die*)

BARFIELD, Arthur Owen [1898–, English writer]
G. A. L. Burgeon (*This Ever Diverse Pair*)

BARFORD, John Leslie [fl. 1990, English writer]
Philebus (*Blue Boys*)

BARHAM, Francis Foster [1808–71, English eccentric theologian and editor of *New Monthly Magazine*]
Alist (*Alist on Autobiography*)
A Bible Student (*Scripture Millenium Nigh*)

BARHAM, George [1836–1913, English expert on dairy farming]
Tom Tally (*The Merry Days of Coaching*)

BARHAM, Richard Harris [1788–1845, English cleric, humorist and writer]
Thomas Ingoldsby (*The Ingoldsby Legends; The Jackdaw of Rheims; The Knight and the Lady; The Lay of St Odille; Some Account of my Cousin Nicholas*)
An Old Bachelor (*Baldwin or, A Miser's Heir*)
H. Peppercorn (in the *London Globe*)

BARHAM, Richard Harris Dalton
[1815–86, English cleric and writer]
Dalton (in *Bentley's Miscellany*)

BARHAM, Thomas Foster [1766–1844, English Unitarian, physician and classical scholar]
A Physician (*Genuine Christianity or, The Unitarian Doctrine Briefly Stated*)

BARING, Charles [1743–1829, English merchant and writer]
J. Smith, Gentleman (*Letters on the Prophecies*)

BARING, Maurice [1874–1945, English journalist, diplomat and writer]
M. B. (*Northcourt Nonsense; Triolets; Damozel and other Faery Tales*)

BARKER, Benjamin [fl. 1845, US writer]
Egbert Augustus Cowslip Esq. (*Zoraida or the Witch of Naumkeag*)

BARKER, Clarence Hedley [fl. 1950, English crime writer]
Frank Hedley (*Cavalier of Crime*)
Seafarer (*Bold Buccaneer; Crooks' Cruise*)

BARKER, Dudley [1910–80, English novelist and writer]
Lionel Black (*Death by Hoax; Penny Murders*)
Anthony Mathews (*Swinging Murder*)

BARKER, Edmund Henry [1788–1839, English classical scholar and lexicographer]
Aristarchus (*Anti-Blomfeldianus Aristarchus*)

BARKER, Jacob [1779–1871, US merchant and financier]
Investigator (*The Rebellion: its Consequences ... and the Reconstruction Committee with their Action*)

BARKER, Jane [1652–1727, English poet and writer]
A Young Lady (*Love Intrigues or, The History of Amours*)

BARKER, Leonard Noel [fl. 1930, English crime writer]
L. Noel (*Mystery Street*)

BARKER, Matthew Henry [1790–1846, English mariner and nautical writer]
The Old Sailor (*Nights at Sea; The Quarter Deck; Stories of Greenwich Hospital; Tough Yarns: a Series of Naval Tales; Jem Bunt*)
The Wanderer (*Walks around Nottingham*)

BARKER, Ronald Ernest [1920–76, English publisher, novelist and crime writer]
E. B. Ronald (*Death by Proxy; Cat and Fiddle Murders*)

BARKER, S. Omar [1894–?, US western novelist]
Dan Scott (*The Phantom of Wolf Creek; The Secret of Fort Pioneer*)

BARKER, William Burckhardt [1810–56, English explorer and orientalist]
An English Prisoner in Russia (*Odessa and its Inhabitants*)

BARKER, William G. M. J. [1817–55, English poet]
The Wensleydale Poet (*The Three Days or, History and Antiquities of Wensleydale*)

BARKIN, Carol [1944–, US writer]
*Elizabeth Carroll (*Summer Love*)
*Beverly Hastings (*Don't Talk to Strangers; Watcher in the Dark*)

BARLING, John [1804–83, English Unitarian theologian]
An Old Student (*Leaves from my Writing Desk*)

BARLING, Muriel [1904–, English crime writer]
Charles Barling (*Afternoon of Violence; Motive for Murder*)
Pamela Barrington (*Account Rendered; Final Judgment*)
P. V. Barrington (*Night of Violence*)

BARLING, Thomas F. R. [1936–, English novelist]
Thomas Marriott (*Pagan Land*)

BARLOW, David Hatch [d. 1864, US cleric and writer]
Mountain Bard (in *New England Galaxy*)

BARLOW, Mrs Emma [1854–83, US writer]
Leila (in *Harper's Magazine*)

BARLOW, George [1847–1913, English writer]
James Hinton (*An English Madonna; Love's Offering*)

BARLOW, Henry Clark [1806–76, British architect, physician and Dante scholar]
A Representative (*The Sixth Centenary Festivals of Dante*)

BARLOW, Jane [1857–1917, Irish novelist and poet]
Antares Skorpios (*History of a World of Immortals without God*)

BARLOW, James Henry Stanley [1921–73, English novelist]
James Forden (*The Love Chase*)

BARLOW, Thomas [1607–91, English cleric, librarian and religious writer; Bishop of Lincoln]
A Cordial Friend to the Protestant Religion (*A Discourse Concerning the Laws of Ecclesiastical and Civil made against Hereticks etc.*)
A Learned Pen (*That the Bishops.in England May and Ought to Vote in Cases of Blood*)
A Real Catholick of the Church of England (*A Few Plain Reasons why a Protestant ... Should not Turn Roman Catholick*)

BARMAN, Christian [1898–1980, English architect and writer]
Christian Mawson (*Ramping Cat; Portrait of England*)

BARNARD, Charles Francis [1808–84, US cleric and writer]
Mrs Maria Gilman (*Bach and Beethoven*)
Jane Kingsford (*The Soprano: a Musical Story; The Pretty Missionary*)

BARNARD, Charlotte [1830–69, English ballad composer]
Claribel (*Fireside Thoughts*)

BARNARD, Frederick Augustus Porter [1809–89, US educationalist and scientist]
A Refugee (*Letter to the President of the United States*)

BARNARD, Sir John [1685–1764, English financier, merchant and politician]
A Late Lord Mayor of London (*A Present for an Apprentice*)

BARNARD, Marjorie Faith [1897–1987, Australian novelist]
*M. Barnard Eldershaw (*Coast to Coast; Essays in Australian Fiction*)

BARNES, Arthur Kelvin [1911–69, US science-fiction writer]
*Kelvin Kent (*Roman Holiday; Science is Golden*)

BARNES, Djuna [1892–1982, US poet, novelist and dramatist]
Lydia Steptoe (used for short-story writing)

BARNES, Joshua [1654–1712, English classical scholar]
Philargyrus Cantab (*Aristarchus ... Curis Horatianis ... Querimonia Epistolaris*)

BARNES, Joshua [fl. 1719, English nonconformist cleric]
*Bagweel (*A Collection of Occasional Papers etc.*)

BARNES, Julian [1946–, English novelist and writer]
Dan Kavanagh (*Duffy; Fiddle City*)
Edward Pygge (in the *New Review*)
Basil Seal (in *The Tatler*)

BARNES, Thomas [1786–1841, English journalist and critic, editor of *The Times*]
Criticus (in *The Examiner* and for *Parliamentary Portraits*)
Strada (in the *London Champion*)

BARNSLEY, Alan Gabriel [1916–86, English physician and novelist]
Gabriel Fielding (*The Frog Prince and other Poems; Brotherly Love*)

BARR, Robert [1850–1912, Scottish novelist and journalist in USA]
Luke Sharp (in the *Detroit Free Press* and for *Strange Happenings* and *The Triumph of Eugene Valmont*)

BARRELL, Sarah Sayward [1759–1855, US novelist]
A Lady of Maine (*Tales of the Night*)
A Lady of Massachusetts (*Julia and the Illuminated Baron; Ferdinand and Elmira*)

BARRETT, Alfred Walter [1869–1920, English humorist]
Robert Andom (*We Three and Troddles; Out and About with Troddles*)

BARRETT, Eaton Stannard [1786–1820, English poet and political satirist]
Cervantes Hogg, F. S. M. (*The Rising Sun; The Setting Sun*)
A Late Resident (*Six Weeks at Longs*)
Polypus (*All the Talents*)

BARRETT, Geoffrey John [1928–, English science-fiction writer and novelist]
Rex Anders (*Rider from the Dead*)
Jeff Baine (*Long Ride to Vengeance*)
Carr Macey (*Guns of Dispute*)
Cole Rickard (*Payment in Lead; Blood on the Golden Spur*)
Dan Royal (*Riders to High Gap*)
Brett Sanders (*Forgotten Trails*)
D. B. Summers (*Escape to Oregon*)
Bill Wade (*Brand of Destiny*)
James Wallace (*The Plague of the Golden Rat*)

BARRIE, Sir James Matthew [1860–1937, Scottish novelist and playwright]
Gavin Ogilvy (in the *British Weekly* and for *An Edinburgh Eleven*)

BARRIE, Susan [fl. 1960, English romantic novelist]
Anita Charles (*One Coin in the Fountain; White Rose of Love*)
Pamela Kent (*Desert Doorway; Flight to the Stars*)

BARRINGTON, Howard [fl. 1945, English crime writer]
Simon Stone (*The Bookmaker's Body; Murder Gone Mad*)

BARRINGTON-FLEET, George Rutland [1853–1922, English playwright]
Rutland Barrington (*Bartonmere Towers*)
Lady Gay (in *Punch*)

BARRON, Arthur Oswald [1868–1939, English antiquary and genealogist]
The Londoner (in the *Evening News* and for *Day In and Day Out*)

BARROW, Frances Elizabeth [1822–94, US writer for children]
Aunt Fanny (*How Little Katie Knocked at the Door of Heaven; Little Night-Cap Letters; New Nightcaps told to Charlie; Old Nightcaps*)

BARROW, John [1808–98, English naval historian and alpinist]
A Private of the Thirty Eighth Artists and Member of the Alpine Club (*Expeditions on the Glaciers*)

BARRY, Michael Joseph [1817–89, Irish poet]
Bouillon de Garcon (*The Kishoge Papers*)

BARRY, William Francis [1849–1930, English Catholic writer]
Canon Barry (in the *Dublin Review*)
A Quarterly Reviewer (in *National Review*)

BARRY, William Whittaker [d. 1875, English barrister]
An Englishman (*A Walking Tour round Ireland in 1865*)

BARTLETT, Mrs Alicia Elinor [1848–1920, US writer]
Birch Arnold (*The Mystery of the Monogram; Until the Day-Break*)

BARTLETT, Bailey [1750–1830, US politician and patriot]
A Layman (*Remarks on the Proceedings of the Episcopal Conventions for Forming an American Constitution*)

BARTLETT, Charles Vernon Oldfield [1894–1983, English novelist and writer]
*Peter Oldfield (*The Death of a Diplomat; The Alchemy Murder*)

BARTLETT, David W. [1828–?, US journalist]
Spectator (in the *Boston Congregationalist*)
Van (in the *Springfield Republican*)

BARTLETT, Frederick Owen [1876–?, US journalist and writer]
William Carleton (*One Way Out; The Red Geranium*)
The Old Dog (in the *Saturday Evening Post*)

BARTLETT, John [1820–1905, US publisher; best known for *Familiar Quotations*]
Practitioner of More than Fifty Years' Experience in the Art of Angling (*A Catalogue of Books on Angling*)

BARTLETT, Stephen [fl. 1930, Australian writer for children]
Gurney Slade (*In Lawrence's Bodyguard*; *Gentlemen o' Fortune*)

BARTOL, Cyrus Augustus [1813–1900, US cleric]
A Spectator (*Influence of the Ministry ... in the City of Boston*)

BARTON, Bernard [1784–1849, English bank clerk and poet]
An Amateur (*Poems*)

BARTON, Eustace Robert [1854–?, English physician and writer]
Robert Eustace (*The Tea Leaf*; *Mr Bovey's Unexpected Will*)

BARTY, James Strachen [1805–75, Scottish cleric and writer]
Cato (in *Blackwood's Magazine*)
Peter Plough (*Peter Plough's letter to Lord Kinnaird*)

BARUCH, Hugo Cyril K. [fl. 1944, English writer]
Jack Bilbo (*Reflections in an Art Gallery*; *Carrying a Gun for Al Capone*)

BARWELL, Louisa Mary [1800–85, English musician and educationalist]
A Parent (*The Elder Brother*; *Letters from Hofwyl*)

BASHFORD, Sir Henry Howarth [1880–1961, English physician and writer]
Augustus Carp (*Augustus Carp Esq. by Himself*)
Peter Harding (*The Corner of Harley Street*)

BASON, Frederick Thomas [1907–73, English bookseller, journalist and diarist]
Galleryite (*Gallery Unreserved*)

BASSET, Joshua [1641–1720, English cleric and religious controversialist]
A Minister of the Church of England (*An Essay towards a Proposal for Catholick Communion*)

BASSETT, Ronald [1924–, English novelist and dramatist]
William Clive (*Dando on Delhi Ridge*; *Blood of an Englishman*)

BASSLER, Thomas J. [1932–, US science-fiction writer]
T. J. Bass (*Half Past Human*; *The Godwhale*)

BATEMAN, James [1811–97, English horticulturist]
A Member of Magdalen College, Oxford (*The Oxford Crisis: a Word to the Wise*)

BATEMAN, John Frederic La Trobe [1810–89, English civil engineer]
A Member of the Cambridge University Boat Club (*Aquatic Notes*)

BATES, Miss Fanny D. [fl. 1881, US writer for children]
Beulah (*My Sister Kitty*; *Tatters*; *Zarailla*)

BATES, Mrs Harriet Leonora [1856–86, US writer]
Eleanor Putnam (*Old Salem*; *Prince Vance*)

BATES, Harry [1900–, US science-fiction writer]
*Anthony Gilmore; A. R. Holmes; *H. G. Winter (all used in *Astounding Science Fiction* magazine)

BATES, Herbert Ernest [1905–74, English novelist and short-story writer]
Flying Oficer-X (*How Sleep the Brave*; *The Greatest People in the World*)

BATHER, Lucy Elizabeth [1836–64, English writer for children]
Aunt Lucy (*My Dear Young Friends*)

BATTEN, Harry Mortimer [1888–1958, English natural historian and traveller]
Stravaiger (*Mountains of the Morning*)

BATTEN, Madeleine [1911–, New Zealand romantic novelist]
Dorothy Quentin (*Bright Horizon*; *The Cottage in the Woods*)

BATTERSBY, Caryl James [1858–1927, English writer]
Appleton Laith (in *Temple Bar*)

BATTERSBY, Henry Francis Prevost [1862–1949, English novelist, poet and sporting writer]
Francis Prevost (*The Avenging Hour*; *The Edge of Doom*)

BATTYE, Gladys [1915–, English mystery writer]
Margaret Lynn (*Whisper of Darkness*; *Sweet Epitaph*)

BAUM, Lyman Frank [1856–1919, US novelist and writer for children]
Floyd Akers (*The Boy Fortune Hunters in Alaska*)
Laura Bancroft (*Twinkle Tales*; *Policeman Bluejay*)
John Estes Cooke (*Tamawaca Folks*)
Hugh Fitzgerald (*Sam Steele's Adventures on Land and Sea*)
Suzanna Metcalf (*Annabel*)
Schuyler Staunton (*The Fate of a Crown*; *Daughters of Destiny*)
Edith Van Dyne (*Mary Louise Adopts a Soldier*)

BAX, Sir Arnold Edward Trevor [1883–1953, English composer and short-story writer]
Dermot O'Byrne (*Children of the Hills*; *Wrack and Other Stories*; *Seafoam and Firelight*; *Red Owen – a Play*)

BAXTER, George Robert Wythen [1815–54, English writer]
Byron's Ghost (*Don Juan, Junior*)

BAXTER, Lucy [1837–1902, English writer on art, daughter of William Barnes, the Dorset Poet]
Leader Scott (in the *Magazine of Art* and for *The Castle of Vincigliata*, *The Cathedral Builders* and *The Renaissance of Art in Italy*)

BAXTER, Richard [1615–91, English Puritan theologian]
One that is Consecrated to the Sacred Ministry (*Sacrilegious Desertion of the Holy Ministry*)
*Theophilus Timorcus (*The Covenanter's Plea against Absolvers*)

BAXTER, Robert M. [1851–?, US journalist]
Arlington (in the *New York Star*)

BAXTER, William Edward [1825–90, Scottish Member of Parliament and traveller]
A Member of the Legislature (*Lay Sermons*)

BAXTER, Wynne Edwin [1844–1920, English solicitor and microscopist]
Llewellyn Acton (*Perseverance*)

BAYER, William [1939–, US writer]
Leonie St John (*Love with a Harvard Accent*)

BAYLEY, Barrington J. [1937–, English science-fiction and juvenile writer]
*Michael Barrington (*Peace on Earth*)
P. F. Woods (in *New Worlds* magazine)

BAYLEY, Frederick W. N. [1808–53, English editor of *Illustrated London News* and writer]
Alphabet Bayley (*The New Tale of a Tub*)
A Clergyman in Debt (in *New Monthly Magazine*)
The Son of a Military Officer (*Four Years Residence in the West Indies*)

BAYLEY, Sir John [1763–1841, English jurist]
A Layman (*The Prophecies of Christ and Christian Times*)
A Member of the Established Church (*The Book of Common Prayer*)

BAYLEY, Peter [1778–1823, English writer]
Giorgione di Castel Chiuso (*Sketches from St George's Fields*)

BAYLISS, John Clifford [1919–, English writer]
John Clifford (*Atlantic Adventure*)

BAYLY, Ada Ellen [1857–1903, English novelist and supporter of women's rights]
Edna Lyall (*We Two*; *The Hinderers*)

BAYLY, Anselm [d. 1794, English cleric and theologian]
Antisocinus (*Remarks on David Levi's Answer to Dr Priestley's Letters to the Jews*)

BAYNARD, Edward [1641–?, English physician]
Darby Dawne (*Health, a Poem Shewing how to Procure and Restore it*)

BAYNE, Peter [1830–96, Scottish essayist and journalist]
Ellis Brandt (*Emme Cheyne*)

BAYNES, Thomas Spencer [1823–87, English philosopher and Shakespeare scholar]
Juniper Agate (in the *Edinburgh Guardian*)

BEACH, Thomas Miller [1841–94, English spy in North America for anti-Fenian activities]
Henri Le Caron (in The *New Review*)

BEAL, James [1829–?, English politician, reformer and pamphleteer]
Father Jean (in *The Echo*)
Nemesis (in the *London Dispatch*)

BEALE, Dorothea [1831–1906, English headmistress of Cheltenham Ladies College]
A Utopian (in *Fraser's Magazine*)

BEALE, John [1603–83, English cleric and scientist]
J. B. (*Herefordshire Orchards: a Pattern for all England*)

BEALE, Lionel Smith [1828–1906, English physician, microscopist and horticulturist]
A Fellow (*Vitality: an Appeal to Fellows of the Royal Society*)

BEALE, Thomas Willert [1828–94, English lawyer, musician and impresario]
Walter Maynard (*The Enterprising Impresario*)

BEARD, John Relly [1800–76, English Unitarian cleric]
A Friend of Popular Education (*The Abuses of the Manchester Free Grammar School Considered*)

BEARDSLEY, Aubrey [1872–98, English artist, illustrator and writer]
Philip Broughton; Guilio Floriani; Albert Foschter (all used in *The Yellow Book*)

BEASLEY, Frederick Williamson [1808–78, US cleric]
Caspar Almore (*Papers from Overlook House*)

BEATTIE, James [1735–1803, Scottish poet and philosopher]
A Native of Britain (*Verses Occasioned by the Death of ... Charles Churchill*)
Oliver Oldstyle (in the *Aberdeen Journal*)

BEATTY, Patricia [1922–91, US writer for children]
Jean Bartholomew (*The Englishman's Mistress*)

BEATY, Betty [1922–, English romantic novelist]
Karen Campbell (*Thunder on Sunday*; *The Bells of St Martin*)
Catherine Ross (*Battle Dress*; *Colours of the Night*)

BEATY, David [1919–, English novelist]
Paul Stanton (*Village of Stars*)

BEAUCHAMP, Kathleen Mansfield [1888–1923, New Zealand-born short-story writer; spent her adult life in Europe]
Katherine Mansfield (*The Garden Party*; *The Dove's Nest*)
Julian Mark (in *The Native Companion*, edited by E. J. Brady in 1907)

BEAUMONT, John Thomas Barber [1774–1841, English insurance pioneer]
Hastatus (*The Arcanum of National Defense*)

A Magistrate for Middlesex (*Letters on Public House Licensing*)

Philanthropos (*Life Insurance*)

BECHKO, Peggy Anne [1950–, US writer]
Bill Haller (*Sidewinder's Trail*)

BECK, Edward [1804–61, English Quaker }
An Old Gardener (*A Packet of Seeds Saved by an Old Gardener*)

BECK, Eliza Louisa Moresby [d. 1931, English novelist and occult writer]
E. Barrington (*The Great Romantic; The Graces*)
Lily Adams Beck (*Dream Tea; The Perfume of the Rainbow*)
Louis Moresby (*Captain Java; The Glory of Egypt*)

BECK, Nicholas F. [d. 1830, US lawyer]
A Citizen of New York (*Considerations in Favour of the Construction of a Great State Road from Lake Erie to the Hudson River*)

BECK, Paul, Jr. [1760–1844, US merchant]
A Citizen of Philadelphia (*A Proposal for Altering the Eastern Front*)

BECK, Thomas [1765–1808, English cleric and poet]
Timothy Touch 'em (*The Age of Frivolity*)

BECKER, Stephen David [1927–, US novelist and editor]
Steve Dodge (*Shanghai Incident*)

BECKETT, Ronald Brymer [1891–1970, English civil servant in India and art historian]
John Anthony (*The Story of Hassan; The Story of Maryam*)

BECKETT, Mrs S. [d. 1891, English novelist]
Cecil Griffith (*Corinthia Marazion*)

BECKETT, Samuel Barclay [1906–89, Irish poet, novelist and playwright]
Andrew Belis (in *The Bookman*, August 1934)

BECKETT, William H. [fl. 1874, US humorist]
Professor Chaucer Jones (*Rhymes of Nonsense, Truth and Fiction*)

BECKFORD, Peter [1740–1811, English sportsman and master of foxhounds]
A Sportsman of Berkshire (*Essays on Hunting*)

BECKFORD, William [1760–1844, English writer and eccentric builder]
Jaquetta Agneta Mariana Jenks (*Azemia*)
Rt. Hon. Lady Harriet Marlow (*Modern Novel Writing or, the Elegant Enthusiast*)
Viator (in the *Literary Gazette* and for *Epitaphs*)

BECKWITH, Burnham Putnam [1904–, US economist]
John Putnam (*Modern Case for Socialism*)

BECON, Thomas [1512–67, English cleric and preacher]
Theodore Basille (*A Christmas Bankette Garnyshed; The New Policy of Warre; The Golde Boke of Christen Matrimonye; A New Pathway unto Praier; David's Harpe Ful of most Delectable Armony Newely Stringed and Set in Tune; A New Yeares Gyfte more Precious than Gold; The Newes out of Heaven; A Pleasaunt Newe Nosegaye; The Pathoway unto Prayer; The Right Pathwaye unto Prayer; The True Defense of Peace*)

BEDFORD, Hilkiah [1663–1724, English nonconformist cleric]
A Priest of the Church of England (*A Vindication of the Church of England*)

BEDFORD, John T. [fl. 1870, English humorist]
Joseph Greenhorn (in *Punch*)
Robert, the City Waiter (in *Punch* and for *The Diary of Robert, the City Waiter*)

BEDFORD, Thomas [d. 1773, English cleric – son of Hilkiah Bedford above]
Ellis Farneworth (*History of the Civil Wars in France – a Translation*)

BEDFORD-JONES, Henry J. O. [1887–1949, Canadian fantasy writer]
Alan Hawkwood (*The Wizard of the Atlas*; *John Solomon – Supercargo*)
John Wyclife (*Son of Cincinnati*; *Drums of Dambala*)

BEEBE, Elswyth Thane Ricker [1900–, US writer]
Elswyth Thane (*Dawn's Early Life*; *Ever After*)

BEECHER, Henry Ward [1813–87, US preacher and reformer – brother of Harriet Beecher Stowe]
One who Keeps his Eyes and Ears Open (in the *New York Ledger*)

BEECHING, Henry Charles [1859–1919, English cleric, poet and writer]
Urbanus Sylvan (*Pages from a Private Diary*)
*Two Clerks (*The Epistle to the Hebrews*)

BEER, Georg Joseph [1763–1821, Austrian physician and optician]
An Experienced Oculist (*The Art of Preserving the Sight*)

BEERBOHM, Sir Max [1872–1956, English novelist and caricaturist]
Diogenes (letter to *The Carthusian*)
Max; Ruth; Sulto (all used in *Vanity Fair*)

BEERS, Ethelinda [1827–79, US poet]
Ethel Lynn (*All Quiet along the Potomac*)

BEESTON, L. J. [fl. 1900, English writer for boys]
Richard Camden (in *Chums*)

BEEVER, John [1795–1859, English writer and angler]
Arundo (*Practical Fly-Fishing*)

BEEZLEY, James [1739–1811, English Quaker]
Philalethes (*A Letter to Dr Formey*)

BEGBIE, Harold [1871–1929, English journalist, novelist and biographer]
A Gentleman with a Duster (*In the Hand of the Potter*; *Broken Earthenware*)

*Caroline Lewis (*Clara in Blunderland*; *Lost in Blunderland*)

BEGBIE, James Warburton [1826–76, Scottish physician and writer]
A Physician (*Handy Book of Medical Information*)

BEGG, James [1808–83, Scottish cleric and preacher]
A Watchman (*A Careful and Strict Enquiry into the Pretensions of Dr Heugh*)

BEGG, Walter [1848–1927, Scottish actor and writer]
Walter Bentley (*Elocution and the Art of Acting*)

BEHA, Ernest Andrew [1908–, English journalist]
Grislet (used for boxing articles in the *Sunday Referee*)

BEHN, Aphra [1640–89, English dramatist and writer]
A. B. (*A Companion for the Ladies-Closets ...*)

BEITH, John Hay [1876–1952, Scottish soldier and novelist]
Ian Hay (*The Middle Watch*; *The Housemaster*)
Junior Sub (*The First Hundred Thousand*)

BELANEY, Archibald Stansfield [1888–1938, English-born emigrant to Canada; adopted an Indian lifestyle and persona]
Grey Owl (*The Men of the Last Frontier*; *Pilgrims of the Wild*)

BELFOUR, Hugo John [1802–27, English poet and cleric – died in the West Indies]
St John Dorset (*The Vampire*)

BELKNAP, Andrew Eliot [1780–1858, US merchant]
A Boston Boy (in various Boston newspapers)

BELKNAP, Jeremy [1744–98, US cleric and lexicographer]
Amyntor (*The Foresters*)

BELL, Aubrey Fitzgerald [1881–1950, English librarian and Iberian scholar]
A. F. Gerald (*The Soul's Journey*)

BELL, Benjamin [1749–1806, Scottish surgeon and agriculturist]
A Landholder (*Observations on the Assessment of Tolls*)

BELL, Benjamin [1845–1930, Scottish cleric and religious writer]
A Pre-Disruption Elder (*Thoughts on the Aberdeen Case*)

BELL, Catharine Douglass [d. 1861, Scottish novelist]
Kate (or Cousin Kate) (*The Miner's Sons; Rest and Unrest; Stories for Children; My First Pennies*)

BELL, Charles Dent [1818–98, Irish cleric and religious writer]
An Old Hand (*Reminiscences of a Boyhood*)

BELL, Charles Frederick Moberly [1847–1911, English journalist and publisher]
One who Knows Them Well (*Khedives and Pashas*)

BELL, Eric Temple [1883–1960, Scottish-born US mathematician and science-fiction writer]
John Taine (*Green Fire; The Purple Sapphire*)

BELL, Eva Mary [d. 1959, English journalist, novelist and worker for women in India]
John Travers (*In the Long Run; The Mortimers*)

BELL, Florence Eveleen Eleanore [1851–1930, English writer]
Reid Kerr (in *Temple Bar*)

BELL, Sir George [1794–1877, British soldier]
An Old Soldier (*Rough Notes by an Old Soldier*)

BELL, Henry Glassford [1803–74, Scottish lawyer and writer]
Acer (in *The Observer*)

BELL, John Keble [1875–1928, English playwright and novelist]
Keble Howard (*The Purleys of Wimbledon*)

BELL, John Zephaniah [1794–1883, English artist]
A Professional Painter (in *Fraser's Magazine*)

BELL, Nancy R. E. [1844–1933, English artist and writer on art]
Nancy D'Anvers (*Elementary History of Art*)

BELL, Robert Stanley Warren [1871–1921, English writer for boys]
Hawkesley Brett (in *British Boys' Magazine*)

BELL, Thomas Evans [1825–87, English soldier and historian]
Indicus (*The Rajah and Principality of Mysore*)

BELL, William [1731–1816, English cleric and theologian]
Rev. Peter Ponder (*Cold Souls; Kirk Cumdoon*)

BELLAMY, Daniel [fl. 1722, English dramatist and writer]
A Gentleman of Oxford (*The Cambro-Britannic Engineer; Taffy's Triumph; Back-Gammon or, the Battle of the Friars*)

BELLAMY, Elizabeth [1837–1900, US writer]
Kamba Thorpe (*Four Oaks; Little Joanna*)

BELLAMY, Joseph [1719–90, US theologian and preacher]
One of his Candid Neighbours (*A Letter to the Reverend Author of the Winter-Evening Conversation on Original Sin*)

BELLASIS, Edward [1800–73, English barrister and religious writer]
An Ancient Actor (*The Latin Play at a Catholic School*)
An Anglican Layman (*Convocations and Synods; The Judicial Committee of the Privy Council*)
An Anglican Since Become a Catholic (*Anglican Orders*)

An Old Boy (*Notes for Boys and their Fathers – on Morals*; *The Phormio at the Oratory School*; *The Pincerna at Oratory School*)

A Westminster Magistrate (*The Archbishop of Westminster: a Remonstrance with the Clergy of Westminster*)

BELLINGHAM, Helen Mary D.
[1892–1969, English journalist and romantic novelist]
Helen Beauclerk (*The Green Lacquer Pavilion*; *Where the Treasure is*)

BELLOC, Joseph Hilaire Pierre R.
[1870–1953, English writer]
H. B. (*Lambkin's Remains*; *The Bad Child's Book of Beasts*; *More Beasts for Worse Children*; *The Modern Traveller*)

BELOE, William [1756–1817, English cleric, librarian and bibliographer]
A Sexagenarian (*The Sexagenarian*)

BELTON-COBB, Geoffrey [1892–1971, English crime novelist]
Belton Cobb (*Early Morning Poison*; *Sergeant Ross in Disguise*)

BELTZ, George Frederick [1777–1842, English genealogist and herald]
L. (in *Gentleman's Magazine*)

BENDIT, Gladys [1889–1975, Australian novelist and writer]
John Presland (*Poems of London*; *Escape Me Never*)

BENEDICT, David [1778–1874, US cleric]
John of Enon (*The Watery War*)

BENEDICT, Ruth [1887–1948, US anthropolgist and poet]
Ann Singleton (used for poetry in various magazines)

BENEZET, Anthony [1713–84, French-born pamphleteer and schoolmaster in America]
A Farmer (*A Serious Address to the Rulers of America*)

A Lover of Mankind (*The Mighty Destroyer Displayed*; *The Potent Enemies of America Laid Open*)

BENHAM, William [1831–1910, English cleric and religious writer]
Peter Lombard (in The *Church Times*)
An Old Pupil (in *MacMillan's Magazine*)

BENJAMIN, Lewis Samuel [1874–1932, English novelist and historical writer]
Lewis Melville (*The Huskisson Papers*; *Famous Duels and Assassinations*)

BENNETT, Alfred Rosling [1850–1928, Scottish engineer and writer on science]
T. Tennebra (*A Saga of Guernsey*)

BENNETT, Charles Henry [1829–67, English wood-engraver – worked for *Punch*]
The Owl (in *The Wonderful Drama of Punch and Judy*)

BENNETT, Enoch Arnold [1867–1931, English novelist, dramatist and critic]
Gwendolen (used for a cookery column in *The Woman* magazine)
Jacob Tonson (in *New Age* magazine)

BENNETT, Geoffrey Martin [1909–83, English nautical writer]
Sea-Lion (*Phantom Fleet*; *Sink Me the Ship*)

BENNETT, William Cox [1820–95, English journalist and songwriter and sometime watchmaker]
A Song-Writer (*Songs*)

BENNETT, William James Early [1804–86, Canadian-born English cleric and controversial theologian]
The Vicar of Frome-Selwood (*Swedenborg's Writings and Catholic Teaching*)

BENNETTS, Pamela [1922–86, English romantic and historical novelist]
Helen Ashfield; Margaret James (her publishing names in the USA)

BENSON, Arthur Christopher [1862–1925, English novelist, critic, biographer and essayist]
Christopher Carr (*Essays*; *Lyrics*; *Memoirs of Arthur Hamilton*)
H. L. G. (*Meanwhile: a Packet of War Letters*)
J. T. (*The House of Quiet*)
Charles Hare Plunkett (*The Letters of One: a Study in Limitations*)
T. B. (*The Upton Letters*)

BENSON, Egbert [1746–1833, US jurist]
Curator (*Vindication of the Captors of Major Andre*)

BENTHAM, Edward [1707–76, English cleric and writer]
E. B. (*De Tumultibus Americanis*)
A Tutor and a Fellow of a College in Oxford (*Letter to a Young Gentleman*)

BENTLEY, Edmund Clerihew [1875–1956, English barrister, journalist, crime writer and whimsical verse writer]
E. Clerihew (*Complete Clerihews*; *Biography for Beginners*)

BENTLEY, Phyllis Eleanor [1894–1977, English novelist and biographer]
A Bachelor of Arts (*Pedagomania*)

BENTLEY, Richard [1662–1742, English scholar and writer]
A Gentleman of the Temple (*The Present State of Trinity College, Cambridge*)
Philalethes (*A Letter to the Master of Trinity College ... Greek ... Latin ... Testament*)
Phileleutherus Lipsiensis (*A Discourse of Free-Thinking*; *Remarks upon a Late Discourse of Free-Thinking*)

BENTON, Kenneth [1909–, English writer]
James Kirton (*Time for Murder*)

BENTON, Thomas Hart [1782–1858, US statesman and politician]
A Senator of Thirty Years (*Thirty Years' View*)

BERDOE, Edward [1836–1916, English physician, medical writer and Browning scholar]
Aesculapius Scalpel (*Dying Scientifically: a Key to St Bernard's*; *St Bernard's, The Romance of a Medical Student*)

BERENS, Edward [1778–1859, English cleric]
A Churchman (*Church Reform*)
A Country Clergyman (*Pastoral Advice to Married Persons*; *Village Sermons*)

BERESFORD, James [1764–1840, English cleric and writer]
An Aspirant (*Bibiosophia*)
Ignoto Secondo (in The *Literary Gazette*)
Samuel Sensitive (*The Miseries of Human Life*)
Timothy Testy (*The Miseries of Human Life*)

BERESFORD, Marcus [1919–, English writer]
Marc Brandel (*The Barriers Between*; *The Time of the Fire*)

BERESFORD, William [fl. 1789, English mariner]
W. B. (*A Voyage round the World ... North-West Coast of America*)

BERESFORD-HOPE, Alexander James [1820–87, English politician and philanthropist]
D. C. L. (letters in The *Morning Chronicle*)

BERGER, Josef [1903–, US writer for children]
Jeremiah Digges (*Cape Cod Pilot*; *Operation Underground*)

BERINGTON, Joseph [1746–1827, English priest, philosopher and historian]
A Catholic Priest (*Puritanism and Popery Illustrated*)

BERINGTON, Thomas [1680–1755, English writer]
Mercury (in *News from the Dead*)

BERKELEY, George [1685–1753, Irish bishop and philosopher]
The Bishop of Cloyne (*A Miscellany Containing Several Tracts on Various Subjects*)
G. B. (*De Motu*)
G. L. B. O. C. (*Siris, a Chain of Philosophical Reflexions and Inquiries Concerning the Virtues of Tar-Water*)
A Lady (*Maxims Concerning Patriotism*)
A Member of the Established Church (*A Word to the Wise*)
Ulysses Cosmopolite (in *The Guardian*)

BERKELEY, George C. G. F. [1800–81, English soldier, duellist and sportsman]
The English Sportsman (*In the Western Prairies*)
Huntsman (*Reminiscences of a Huntsman*)

BERKELEY, George Monck [1763–93, English dramatist, poet and writer]
Bard (in *The World*)
A Gentleman of the Inner Temple (*An Elegy on the Death of Miss M___s*)

BERLYN, Mrs Alfred [d. 1943, English journalist, drama critic and writer]
Vera (*Sunrise Land – Rambles in Eastern England; Vera in Poppyland*)

BERNSTEIN, Joseph Alexander [1917–, English writer]
Alexander Baron (*From the City, From the Plough; With Hope Farewell*)

BERNSTEIN, Norman Ackland [1908–91, English playwright]
Rodney Ackland (*Improper People; The Dark River*)

BERRIDGE, John [1716–93, English cleric and preacher]
A Methodist Preacher in Cambridgeshire (*A Fragment of the True Religion*)

BERRIMAN, William [1688–1750, English cleric and theologian]
A Presbyter of the Diocese of London (*A Seasonable Review of Mr Whistler's Account of Primitive Doxologies*)

BERRY, Bryan [1930–55, English science-fiction writer]
Rolf Garner (*Resurgent Dust; The Indestructible*)

BERRY, Sir Edward [1768–1831, English admiral under Lord Nelson]
An Officer of Rank in the Squadron (*Authentic Narrative of the Proceedings of HM's Squadron under Sir Horatio Nelson ... from Gibraltar to the Battle of the Nile*)

BERTRAM, Charles [1723–65, English literary forger]
Charles Julius (his self-styled name)

BERTRAM, James Glass [1824–92, English writer]
Rev. William U. Cooper (*Flagellation and the Flagellants*)
Louis Henry Curzon (*A Mirror of the Turf*)
Ellangowan (*Out-of-Door Sports in Scotland; Sporting Anecdotes*)
Peter Paterson (*Glimpses of Real Life ... in Bohemia; Behind the Scenes – Confessions of a Strolling Player*)

BESANT, Annie [1847–1933, Irish theosophist and writer]
The Wife of a Beneficed Clergyman (*On the Deity of Jesus Christ*)

BESANT, Walter [1836–1901, English novelist, critic and writer]
A Bookworm; A Reader (both used in *Temple Bar*)
*Walter Maurice (*Ready-Money Mortiboy; Such a Good Man*)
Walter Thomas (*All in a Garden Fair*)
Dorothy Wallis (in *Longman's Magazine*)
W. B. (*The Case of Mr Lucraft; This Son of Vulcan*)

BESSE, Joseph [1683–1757, English Quaker and controversialist]
Irenicus (*The Doctrine of the People Called Quakers*)
J. B. (*A Cloud of Witnesses Proving that the Bishop of London ...*)
One of the People Called Quakers (*An Examination of a Discourse or Sermon*

published by Daniel Dobel; *A Letter to Stephen Clarke*)
Philalethes (*The Clergy's Plea for a Settled and Forced Maintenance from the Quakers*)
Philanthropus (*An Enquiry into the Validity of a Late Discourse entitled 'The Nature and Duty of Self-Defence'*)

BEST, Allena [1892–1974, US writer and illustrator]
Erick Berry (*Black Folk Tales; The Winged Girl of Knossos*)

BEST, George Percival [1872–1953, English civil servant]
G. Percival (*The Civil List and the Hereditary Revenues of the Crown*)

BESTE, Henry Digby [1768–1836, English writer]
An English Catholic (*Transalpine Memoirs*)

BETHEL, Slingsby [1619–97, English merchant, republican and pamphleteer]
A Lover of his King and Country (*The Present Interest of England Stated*)
A Member of that Parliament (*A True and Impartial Narrative of the Most Material Debates ... in the Late Parliament*)

BETHELL, Mary Ursula [1874–1945, New Zealand poet and novelist]
Evelyn Hayes (*The Glad Returning; From a Garden in the Antipodes*)

BETHUNE, John [1812–39, Scottish carver and weaver, poet and writer]
Fifeshire Forester (in the *Scottish Christian Herald*)

BETHUNE, John Drinkwater [1762–1844, English soldier and historian; his original surname was Drinkwater, and Bethune was an assumed name]
An Officer of HM's Land Forces (*Narrative of the Proceedings of the British Fleet ...14th Feb. 1797 off Cape St Vincent*)

BETJEMAN, John [1906–84, English Poet Laureate and writer]
Epsilon (*Sir John Piers*)
Richard M. Farran (*Ground Plan to Skyline*)

BETTY, William Henry West [1791–1874, English actor]
Bisset (*The Young Roscius*)

BEVAN, Aneurin [1897–1960, Welsh orator and politician]
Celticus (*Why Not Trust the Tories?*)

BEVAN, Gloria [fl. 1990, New Zealand romantic novelist]
Fiona Murray (*Gold Coast Affair; A Nice Day for Murder*)

BEVAN, Joseph Gurney [1753–1814, British Quaker]
Cryptonymus (*A Brief Reply to Catholicus's Seasonable Address to Disciplinarian*)
Vindex (*An Examination of ... 'An Appeal to the Society of Friends'*)

BEVAN, Thomas [1868–?, English schoolmaster and writer for boys]
Walter Bamfylde (*Midsummer Magic*)

BEVANS, John Jr. [1733–1836, English Quaker]
Christicola (*Some Tracts Relating to the Controversy between Hannah Barnard and the Society of Friends*)
A Layman (*A Vindication of the Authenticity of the Narratives contained in the First Two Chapters of the Gospels of St Matthew and St Luke*)

BEVERLAND, Adrian [1650–1712, Dutch-born lawyer and scholar – sometime in England]
Seignior Perin Del Vago (*Seignior Perin Del Vago's letter to Mr H. B.*)

BEVERLEY, Robert [d. 1716, American writer]
A Native and Inhabitant of the Place (*History and Present State of Virginia*)

BEVINGTON, Louisa Sarah [1844–95, English poet and journalist]
Arbor Leigh (*Key Notes*)

BEVIS, John [1693–1771, English astronomer and physician]
A Member of the Royal Academy of Berlin (*History and Philosophy of Earthquakes*)

BIBER, George Edward [1801–74, German-born theologian; took British nationality]
Ecclesiastes (*Church Emancipation and Church Reform*)

BICKERSTAFFE-DREW, Francis B. D. [1858–1928, English novelist and Catholic priest]
John Ayscough (*Drumina*; *San Celestino*)

BICKERSTETH, Edward [1786–1850, English Evangelical cleric and religious writer]
A Churchman (*A Help to the Study of the Scriptures*)

BICKHAM, Jack Miles [1930–, US western novelist]
Jeff Clinton (*Range Killer*; *Emerald Canyon*)
John Miles (*The Night Hunters*; *The Blackmailer*)

BICKNELL, John Laurens [fl. 1774, English writer]
Joel Collier (*Musical Travels*)

BIDDLE, Richard [1796–1847, US jurist and politician]
An American (*A Review of Capt. B. Hall's Travels*)

BIDDULPH, Thomas Tregenna [1763–1838, English cleric and theologian]
The Churchman (*Reasons for Bringing his Children to the Baptismal Font*)

BIDEN, Edmond Preston [1898–1959, US screenwriter]
Preston Sturges (his name following his adoption)

BIDWELL, Marjory Elizabeth [1900–85, English romantic novelist]
Elizabeth Ford (*Spring Comes to the Crescent*; *So Deep Suspicion*)
Mary Ann Gibbs (*Young Lady with Red Hair*; *The Sea Urchins*)

BIERCE, Ambrose [1842–1914, US short-story writer and humorist]
J. Milton Bowers (*The Dance of Life*)
Dod Grile (*The Fiend's Delight*; *Fantastic Fables*; *Cobwebs: being the Fables etc.*; *Cobwebs from an Empty Skull*)
William Hermann (*The Dance of Death*)
Prattler (used in the *San Francisco Argonaut*, *The Wasp* and the *San Francisco Examiner*)
J. Milton Sloluck (*Nuggets and Dust Panned Out in California*)

BIGELOW, Melville M. [1846–1921, US jurist]
A Barrister (*Rhymes of a Barrister*)

BIGG, Jeremiah [d. 1839, English Quaker]
An Embryo Harvest-Man (*Quakerieties*)

BIGLOW, William [1773–1844, US poet, humorist and writer]
Charles Chatterbox; Roger Roundelay (both used in the *Federal Orrery*)
Squire Sawney (in the *Colombian Centinel*)

BILLINGSLEY, John [1657–1722, English nonconformist cleric]
A Protestant (*A Brief Discourse of Schism*)

BINCKES, WIlliam [d. 1712, English cleric; Dean of Lichfield]
A Country Divine (*An Expedient Propos'd*)
A Presbyter of the Church of England (*A Prefatory Discourse to an Examination of a Late Book, 'An Exposition of the Thirty-Nine Articles etc.'*)

BINDER, Earl [1904–, US science-fiction writer – brother of Otto Oscar Binder below]
*Eando Binder (*Enslaved Brains*; *Lords of Creation*)
*John Coleridge (*Martian Martyrs*; *The New Life*)

BINDER, Otto Oscar [1911–74, US science-fiction writer – brother of Earl Binder above]
*Eando Binder (see entry above)
*John Coleridge (see entry above)
Gordon A. Giles (in *Thrilling Wonder Stories* magazine)

BINDLEY, Charles [1795–1859, English sporting writer]
Harry Hieover (*A Treatise on the Proper Condition of all Horses*)

BING, Geoffrey Henry Cecil [1909–77, English barrister and politician]
Henry Blythe (*Spain over Britain*; *John Bull's Other Ireland*)

BINGHAM, Madeleine [1912–, English writer]
Julia Mannering (*The Passionate Poet*; *Look to the Rose*)

BINGLEY, David Ernest [1920–, English crime and western novelist]
Bart Adams (*Owlhoot Raiders*; *The Coyote Kids*)
Adam Bridger (*Renegade Range*)
Abe Canuck (*Silvertown Trail*; *Hellion's Hostage*)
Dave Carver (*Gunsmoke Gambler*)
Larry Chatham (*Timberwolve's Trail*; *Smith's Canyon*)
Henry Chesham (*Naples or, Die!*; *A Surfeit of Soldiers*)
Will Coltman (*Ghost Town Killers*; *Killer's Creek*)
Ed Coniston (*The Elusive Renegade*)
Luke Dorman (*Renegade's Blade*; *Red Rock Renegades*)
George Fallon (*Rendezvous in Rio*)
David Horsley (*Johnny Pronto*; *Salt Creek Killing*)
Bat Jefford (*Creek Town Killer*)
Syd Kingston (*The Necktie Trail*; *Boot Hill Bandit*)
Eric Lynch (*South Fork Showdown*)
James Martell (*Little Pecos Trail*; *Cowtown Kidnap*)
Colin North (*The Reluctant Gunman*; *Trail of Tragedy*)
Ben Plummer (*Cow Town Killers*)
Caleb Prescott (*The Ruthless Renegades*; *Pecos River Posse*)
Mark Remington (*Silver City Showdown*)
John Roberts (*Colorado Gun Law*)
Steve Romney (*Gunsmoke Lawyer*; *Showdown City*)
Frank Silvester (*Bullhead's Canyon*; *Settler's Stampede*)
Henry Starr (*Short Trigger Valley*; *Lawman's Lament*)
Link Tucker (*Circle M Showdown*)
Christopher Wigan (*The Trail-Blazer*; *Killer's Canyon*)
Roger Yorke (*Owlhoot Bandits*)

BINNEY, Thomas [1798–1874, English nonconformist cleric and hymn writer]
A. Balance Esq., of the Middle Temple (*Leicester Gaol*)
A Congregational Nonconformist (*Hints Illustrative of the Duty of Dissent*)
Fiat Justitia (*A Letter Addressed to the Hon. and Rev. Baptist W. Noel*)
John Search (*Religion and Her Name*; *Strike but Hear*; *What? and Who Says It?*)

BINNS, Ottwell [fl. 1930, English crime writer]
Ben Bolt (*Flaming Crescent*; *Snapshot Mystery*)

BINSTEAD, Arthur Morris [1861–1914, English humorist and sporting writer]
Pitcher (in the *Sporting Times* and for *Gal's Gossip*)

BIRCH, Jonathan [1783–1847, English merchant and translator of German works]
Johann Abricht A. M. (*Divine Emblems*; *Embellished with Emblems on Copper after … Francis Quarles*)
Job Crithannah (*Fables and Morals*)

BIRCH, Walter de Gray [1842–1924, English archaeologist and antiquarian]
An Antiquary (*The Historical Charters*)

BIRCH, William John [1811–63, English writer]
A Master of Arts, formerly of Balliol College (*Paul, an Idea not a Fact*)

BIRD, Cyril Kenneth [1887–1965, English cartoonist and editor]
Fougasse (*You Have Been Warned*)

BIRD, Frederick Meyer [1838–1908, US cleric and hymnologist]
Robert Timsol (*A Pessimist in Theory and Practice*)

BIRD, James [1788–1839, English shopkeeper and poet]
A Suffolk Yeoman (in *Gentleman's Magazine*)

BIRD, Robert Montgomery [1803–54, US physician, dramatist and novelist]
Sheppard Lee (*Sheppard Lee etc.*)
Peter Pilgrim (*Peter Pilgrim or a Rambler's Recollections*)

BIRDWOOD, Sir George Christopher Molesworth [1832–1917, English physician and civil servant in India]
John Indigo (in the *National Review*)

BIRKBECK, Morris [1764–1825, English-born US abolitionist]
Jonathan Freeman (in the *Illinois Gazette*)

BIRNEY, Hoffman [1891–1958, US writer]
David Kent (*A Knife is Silent; Jason Burr's First Case*)

BIRNIE, Alexander [1826–62, Scottish journalist and poet – died of starvation]
Cock of the Steeple (in the *Falkirk Advertiser*)

BIRO, Balint Stephen [1921–, Hungarian-born English illustrator and designer]
Val Biro (used for illustrations in books and on dust jackets)

BIRON, Sir Henry Chartres [1863–1940, English lawyer and writer]
Hyder Ragged (*King Solomon's Wives or, the Phantom Mines!*)

BIRT, Francis Bradley [1874–1963, English colonial lawyer]
Shelland Bradley (*The Doings of Berengaria; The Sacred Crocodile; An American Girl in India; Adventures of an A. D. C.*)

BISHOP, Isabella Lucy [1831–1904, English traveller and writer]
The Englishwoman (*The Englishwoman in America*)

BISHOP, Morris Gilbert [1893–1973, US writer]
W. Bolingbroke Johnson (*The Widening Stain*)

BISHOP, William Henry [1847–1928, US novelist]
Raymond Westbrook (in the *Atlantic Monthly*)

BISSE, Thomas [d. 1731, English cleric and religious writer]
A Member of that Church (*The Beauty of Holiness in the Common Prayer*)

BISSELL, Edwin Cone [1832–94, US cleric and Hebraist]
The Monday Club (in *Sermons by the Monday Club*)

BISSET, James [1762–1832, Scottish poet, publisher and painter]
An Old Townsman (*Comic Strictures on Birmingham's Fine Arts*)

BLACK, Adam [1784–1874, Scottish publisher – founder of the firm of A. & C. Black]
Simon Scribe (*Maynooth* in *Three Letters to Mrs Hadaway*)

BLACK, Francis [d. 1939, English artist]
A Deacon (*The Holy Supper and its Administering Mediums*)

BLACK, Ladbroke Lionel Day [1877–1940, English journalist and writer]
Paul Urquhart (used for Sexton Blake stories)

BLACK, William [1841–98, Scottish novelist, sportsman and journalist]
A Deerstalker (*Rhymes by a Deerstalker*)

BLACK, Wiliam Henry [1808–72, English historical writer]
Hari Dhu (*The Song of the True Antiquary*)

BLACKBURN, Evelyn Barbara [1898–1981, English novelist and playwright]
Frances Castle (*Tara's Daughter*; *The Thread of Gold*)
Barbara Leader (*Spinners Hall*; *The Little Cousin*)

BLACKBURNE, Francis [1705–87, English cleric and controversial writer]
A Member of a Law Society (*Reflections on the Fate of a Petition*)

BLACKER, William [1777–1855, British soldier]
Fitzstewart (in *Dublin University Magazine*)

BLACKETT, Veronica [1927–, English writer on horse riding]
Veronica Heath (*Let's Own a Pony*; *So You Want to Be a Show Jumper*)

BLACKLOCK, Thomas [1721–91, Scottish poet – blind from infancy]
A Member of the Church of Scotland (*The Right Improvement of Time*)
Valerius Corvinus (*The Protestant Interest Vindicated*; *Remarks on the Nature and Extent of Liberty*)

BLACKMORE, Richard Doddridge [1825–1900, English novelist, barrister and horticulturist]
A Market Gardener (*The Farm and Fruit of Old*)
Melanter (*The Bugle of the Black Sea*; *Poems*)

BLACKWELL, Henry [fl. 1730, English fencing-master}
H. B. (*The Gentleman's Tutor for the Small-Sword*)

BLAGDON, Francis William [1778–1819, English journalist and writer]
Aeschines (*A Few Brief Remarks on a Pamphlet ... Supposed to be Connected with the Late Board of Admiralty*)
Aristides (*Reflections on the Naval ... of Earl St Vincent*)
An English Traveller (*Paris as it Was and as it Is*)

Rev. J. Milner (*An Universal History of Christian Martyrdom*)

BLAIR, Dorothy [1913–, English academic and writer]
*Roger Scarlett (*Murder among the Angells*; *Cat's Paw*)

BLAIR, Eric Arthur [1903–50, English novelist and essayist]
As I Please (an occasional column in *The Tribune*)
George Orwell (*Road to Wigan Pier*; *Animal Farm*; *1984*)

BLAIR, J. F. Andrew [1872–1935, Scottish journalist and novelist]
Hamish Blair (*Governor Hardy*; *The Great Gesture*)

BLAIR, Kathryn [fl. 1960, English romantic novelist]
Rosalind Brett (*Hotel Mirador*; *Tangle in Sunshine*)
Celine Conway (*Rustle of Bamboo*)

BLAIR, Patrick [fl. 1728, Scottish physician and botanist]
Michael Servetus MD (*Thoughts on Nature and Religion*)

BLAIR, Walter [1900–, US novelist and academic]
Mortimer Post (*Candidate for Murder*)

BLAIR-FISH, Wallace Wilfrid [1889–1968, English playwright]
Blair (in *Punch*)

BLAISDELL, Mrs A. H. [fl. 1885, US writer]
Agnes Gragg (*Our Odyssey Club*)

BLAKE, Lillie Devereux [1835–1913, US feminist and writer]
Aesop (in the *New York Telegram*)
Tiger Lily (*Southwold*)

BLAKE, William [1757–1827, English painter, illustrator and poet]
Augur (*America: a Prophecy*; *Europe: a Prophecy*)
Pictor Ignotus (*Selections from Poems*)

BLAKESLEY, Joseph Williams [1808–85, English cleric and writer]
Hertfordshire Incumbent (letters to and reviews for *The Times*)

BLAKESTON, Oswell [fl. 1935, English writer and artist]
*Simon (*Murder among Friends*; *Death on the Swim*; *The Cat with the Moustache*)

BLAKEY, Robert [1795–1878, English writer on philosophy, logic and angling; came from a humble background]
Hackle Palmer (*Hints on Angling*)
Nathan Oliver (*A Few Remarkable Events in the Life of Nathan Oliver*)
Verax (*No Popery*)

BLANCHARD, Amy Ella [d. 1926, US writer for children]
Aunt Ella (*The Wonderful Fan*)

BLANCHARD, Edward Litt Laman [1820–89, English dramatist, journalist and writer]
The Brothers Grinn (*Beauty and the Beast*; *Sindbad the Sailor*)
Old Boy (*A Children's Pantomime*)

BLANCHARD, Joshua Pollard [1782–1868, US philanthropist]
A Citizen of Boston (*Essay on American Slavery*)

BLANCHARD, Samuel Laman [1804–45, English journalist and writer]
A Correspondent (in *New Monthly Magazine*)

BLANCO-WHITE, Amber [1887–1981, New Zealand-born English writer]
Amber Reeves (*The Reward of Virtue*; *A Lady and her Husband*)

BLAND, Hubert [1856–1914, English journalist and writer]
*Fabian Bland (*The Prophet's Mantle*)
Hubert (in the *Sunday Chronicle*)

BLAND, Robert [1779–1825, English cleric and classical scholar]
B. (in *Greek Anthology*)

BLAND, Thomas [1740–1818, English Quaker and businessman]
A Friend to Accuracy (in *Gentleman's Magazine*)

BLATCHFORD, Robert [1851–1943, English radical journalist]
P. McGinnis (*A Bohemian Girl*)
A Man (*Julie: a Study of a Girl*)
Nunquam (in *The Clarion*)

BLAYNEY, Benjamin [1728–1801, English Hebrew scholar]
A Member of the University (*An Espostulatory Letter to Dr Randolph*)

BLENNERHASSETT, Charlotte [1843–1917, German-born English historian, biographer and essayist]
C. De Warmont (in The *Nineteenth Century*)

BLEW, William John [1808–94, English cleric, writer and translator]
Storicus (*English Babes and Irish Bullies*)

BLEWITT, Octavian [1810–84, English physician and topographer]
Brother Peregrine (in *Fraser's Magazine*)

BLIGH, Edward Vesey [1829–1908, English cleric]
A Kentish Vicar (*A Visit to the Waldenses*)

BLIND, Mathilde [1841–96, English poet and writer; née Cohen, but adopted step-father's surname]
Claude Lake (*Poems*; *The Prophecy of St Oran*)

BLISH, James [1921–75, US journalist, novelist and science-fiction writer]
William Atheling Jr. (*More Issues at Hand*; *The Issue at Hand*)
*Donald Laverty (in *Galaxy* magazine)
*John MacDougal (in *Astounding Stories* magazine)
Arthur Merlyn (*Sunken Universe*)

BLISS, Eileen [1903–90, Jamaican-born English novelist]
Eliot Bliss (*Saraband*; *Luminous Isle*; *The Albatross*)

BLISS, Seth [1793–1879, US cleric]
The Secretary of the Boston Society (*Letters to the Members of the American Tract Society*)

BLIXEN, Karen [1885–1962, Danish novelist and short-story writer]
Pierre Andrezel (*The Angelic Avengers*)
Isak Dinesen (*Seven Gothic Tales*; *Out of Africa*)
Osceola (used in various Danish periodicals)

BLIZARD, Sir William [1743–1835, English surgeon and medical writer]
An Aged Person (*A Soliloquy*)

BLOCH, Robert Albert [1917–, US fantasy writer]
Tarleton Fiske (used in the following magazines: *Strange Stories*; *Amazing Stories*; *Fantastic Adventures*)
Collier Young (*The Todd Dossier*)

BLOCK, Herbert L. [1909–, US cartoonist]
Herblock (*Herblock's State of the Union*; *Herblock's Here and Now*)

BLOCK, Laurence [1938–, US mystery writer]
Chip Harrison (*No Score*; *Make Out with Murder*)
Paul Kavanagh (*Such Men are Dangerous*; *The Triumph of Evil*)

BLOCKSIDGE, Charles William [1883–1942, Australian poet and writer]
William Baylebridge (*National Notes*; *Life's Testament*; *The New Life*)

BLODGET, Samuel [1724–1807, American businessman and canal builder]
Observator (*Thoughts on the Increasing Wealth ... United States*)

BLOEDE, Victor Gertrude [1845–1905, German-born US poet]
Stuart Sterne (*Giorgio and Other Poems*)

BLOM, Eric Walter [1888–1959, English music critic and writer]
Sebastian Farr (*Death on the Down Beat*)

BLOMFIELD, Charles James [1786–1857, English cleric and classical scholar; Bishop of London]
One of the Working Clergy (*A Remonstrance addressed to H. Brougham Esq.*)

BLOODGOOD, Simon DeWitt [1799–1866, US politician, merchant and writer]
The Sexagenarian (*The Sexagenarian's Memoirs of a Literary Life*)

BLOOM, Ursula [1893–1984, English journalist, playwright and novelist]
Sheila Burns (*Desire is not Dead*; *The Sweet Impulse*)
Mary Essex (*Doctor's Love*; *Heart Surgeon*)
Rachel Harvey (*Doctor Called Harry*; *Doctor who Fell in Love*)
Deborah Mann (*Now Barabbas was a Robber*; *Pilate's Wife*)
Lozania Prole (*Enchanting Princess*; *Henry's Last Love*)

BLOOMFIELD, Anthony John Westgate [1922–, English journalist, playwright and novelist]
John Westgate (used for TV and cinema screenwriting)

BLOOMFIELD, Robert, [1766–1823, English poet, shoemaker and harp-maker]
The Farmer's Boy (*The Farmer's Boy*)

BLOUET, Leon Paul [1848–1903, French-born writer; lived in England]
Max O'Rell (*John Bull's Womankind*)

BLOUNT, Charles [1654–93, English pamphleteer and writer]
A Gentleman in the Country; J. M. (both used in *Reasons Humbly Offered for the Liberty of Unlicens'd Printing*)
Junius Brutus (*An Appeal from the Country to the City*)
Philopatris (*A Just Vindication of Learning*)

BLOUNT, Thomas [1618–79, English writer]
T. B. (*Glossographia*)

BLOWER, Elizabeth [fl. 1785, English novelist]
E. B. (*Maria*)

BLUNDELL, Harold [1902–, English
novelist]
George Bellairs (*Devious Murder; Murder
Adrift*)

BLUNDELL, Mary E. [1855–1930, Irish
novelist and writer]
M. E. Francis (*The Duenna of a Genius;
Galatea of the Wheat Field*)
One of the New Poor (*Simple Annals*)

BLUNDELL, Theresa Victoria [fl. 1934,
English writer]
T. V. Nicholas (*Gospel Rhymes*)

BLUNDEN, Edmund Charles [1896–1974,
English poet and writer]
A Fellow of Merton College (*On Several
Occasions*)
Pte. Alf Maconochie (in *The Blue –
Horsham College* magazine)

BLUNT, John Henry [1823–84, English
cleric and ecclesiastical historian]
A Working Clergyman (*Our Difficulties and
the Way to Deal with Them*)

BLUNT, Joseph [1792–1860, US lawyer,
politician and writer]
Marcus (*An Examination of the Expediency
... of Prohibiting Slavery in the State of
Missouri*)

BLUNT, Wilfred Scawen [1840–1922,
English writer, poet, traveller and
breeder of Arab horses]
Proteus (*Proteus and Amadeus – a
Correspondence; Sonnets and Songs*)

BLYTH, Harry [1852–98, English writer for
boys]
Hal Meredith (in the *Halfpenny Marvel*
magazine for the first Sexton Blake story)

BLYTON, Enid Mary [1897–1968, English
writer for children]
Mary Pollock (*The Children of Kidillin;
Smuggler Ben*)

BOADEN, James [1762–1839, English
journalist and dramatist]
Edward Sydenham (*The Man of Two Lives*)

BOALCH, Donald Howard [1914–, English
writer and poet]
Howard a' Bear (*That Brave Vibration; Each
Way Free*)

BOASE, George Clement [1829–97, English
bibliographer and financier]
Britannicus (in the *Cornish Magazine*)
A Brother (*To Husbands, Fathers and
Brothers ... being a Warning against
Prevailing Delusions*)

BOASE, Henry [1763–1827, English writer
and banker]
A Freeholder (*A Brief Exposition of the
Agricultural Question*)
Britannicus (in the *Poetical Magazine*)
One of his Constituents (*A Letter to Sir
Richard R. Vyvyan*)

BOBIN, Donald [fl. 1932, English writer for
children]
Shirley Halliday (in *Girl's Crystal*)

BOBIN, John William [d. 1935, English
writer for children]
Adelie Ascott; Katherine Greenhalgh (both
used in *Schoolgirl's Weekly*)
Gertrude Nelson (in *Schoolgirl's Own*)
Victor Nelson (in *Boy's Friend*)
Mark Osborne (in both *Union Jack* and
Detective Weekly)

BODENHAM, Hilda Esther [1901–, English
writer for children]
Hilda Boden (*Boomerang; Joanna's Special
Pony*)

BODINGTON, Nancy Hermione [1912–,
English mystery writer]
Shelley Smith (*Afternoon to Kill; Game of
Consequences*)

BODKIN, Mathias M. [1850–1933, Irish
barrister, novelist and historian]
Crom a Boo (*Pat o'Nine Tails; Poteen Punch,
Strong, Hot and Sweet*)

BOGART, William Henry [1810–88, US
journalist]
Sentinel (in the *New York World* and for
Who Goes There? or, Men and Events)

BOGUE, David [1750–1825, Scottish nonconformist cleric]
A Dissenter (*Reasons for Seeking the Repeal of the Corporation*)

BOHN, Henry George [1796–1884, English publisher and bookseller]
A Bookseller (*Observations on the Plan and Progress of the Catalogue of the Library of the British Museum*)

BOHUN, Edmund [1645–99, English jurist; Chief Justice in South Carolina]
A Lay Gentleman (*The Doctrine of Non-Resistance*)
A Person of Quality (*The History of the Desertion or an Account of Public Affairs in England*)

BOISSIER, George Richard [1791–1858, English cleric and Cambridgeshire historian]
Gleneelin (in *Bentley's Miscellany*)

BOLD, John [1679–1751, English cleric and religious writer]
A Minister (*The Duty of Worthily Communicating Recommended and Explained*)
A Presbyter of the Church of England (*The Sin and Danger of Neglecting the Public Service of the Church*)

BOLD, Samuel [1674–1737, English controversial cleric]
A Clergyman in the Country (*The Duty of Christians*)
A Professed Enemy to Persecution (*A Brief Account of the First Rise of the Name Protestant*)

BOLLES, John Augustus [1809–78, US lawyer and politician]
A Member of the Boston Bar (*The Affairs of Rhode Island*)

BOLSTER, Sister Mary Angela [1925–, Irish historian]
Evelyn Bolster (*History of the Diocese of Cork*)

BOLTON, Edmund [1575–1633, English historian and poet]
Philanactophil (*The Roman Histories of Lucius Julius Florus*)

BOLTON, Maisie Sharman [1915–, Scottish crime writer]
Stratford Davis (*Death in Seven Hours*; *The Troubled Mind*)

BOND, Frederick Bligh [1864–1945, English architect, archaeologist and psychic researcher]
Romulus the Monk (*The Light and the Word*)

BONE, James [1872–1962, Scottish journalist and writer – brother of Muirhead Bone below]
*Hamilton Muir (*Glasgow in 1901*)

BONE, Muirhead [1876–1953, Scottish artist and illustrator]
*Hamilton Muir (see entry for brother James Bone above)

BONHAM, Barbara [1926–, US writer]
Sara North (*Jasmine for my Grave*)

BONHOTE, Mrs Elizabeth [1744–1818, English novelist and essayist]
A Lady (*Feeling or, Sketches from Life*)

BONNER, Geraldine [1870–1930, US journalist, novelist and playwright]
Hard Pan (in *Lippincott's Magazine*)

BONSALL, Crosby Newell [1921–, US writer for children]
Crosby Newell (*The Surprise Party*; *Polar Bear Brothers*)

BOOKCHIN, Murray [1921–, US writer]
Lewis Herber (*Crises in our Cities*; *Our Synthetic Environment*)

BOORSTIN, Daniel Joseph [1914–, US historian]
Professor X (*Sociology of the Absurd*)

BOOTE, Robert Edward [1920–, English conservationist]
Robert Arvill (*Man and Environment*)

BOOTH, Edwin [fl. 1970, US western novelist]
Don Blunt (*Dead Giveaway*; *Short Cut*)
Jack Hazard (*Crooked Spur*)

BOOTH, Henry [1788–1869, English merchant and railway pioneer]
A Shareholder (*The Case of Railways Considered*)

BOOTH, James [1796–1880, English jurist and writer]
A Septuagenarian (*The Problem of the World and Church*)

BOOTH, Rosemary Frances [1928–, Scottish novelist and writer for children]
Frances Murray (*Ponies on the Heather*; *Heroine's Sister*)

BORDEN, Mary [1886–1968, US-born novelist – settled in England]
Bridget MacLagan (*Mistress of Kingdoms*; *Collision*)

BOREMAN, Robert [d. 1675, English royalist cleric]
R. B. (*Sermon at the Funerall of Dr Comber*)

BORLAND, Harold Glen [1900–78, US journalist and writer]
Ward West (*Trouble Valley*; *Rustler's Trail*)

BORLAND, Kathryn [1916–, US writer]
Alice Abbott (*Stranger in the Mirror*)
Jane Land (*Good-Bye Julie Scott*; *To Walk the Night*)

BORLASE, William Copeland [1848–99, English historian]
One of the Trinity Undergraduates (*Leaves from the Lime-Walk*)

BORNEMANN, Ernest W. J. [1915–, German-born US scriptwriter and novelist]
Cameron McCabe (*The Face on the Cutting-Room Floor*)

BORROW, George [1803–81, English traveller, linguist and writer]
G. B. (*The Sleeping Bard*)

Ellis Wynne (*Tales of the Wild and Wonderful*)

BOSANQUET, James Whatman [1803–78, English banker and biblical scholar]
A Layman (*Daniel's Prophecy of the Seventy Weeks*)

BOSTON, Thomas [1677–1732, Scottish cleric and theological writer]
A Minister of the Gospel (*The Mystery of Christ in the Form of a Servant*)

BOSWELL, Sir Alexander [1775–1822, Scottish poet and antiquary – son of James Boswell below; died following a duel]
Simon Gray (*Edinburgh or, the Ancient Royalty*)

BOSWELL, James [1740–95, Scottish writer and biographer of Samuel Johnson]
An Advocate; Episcopus; Hypodidasculus; Lelius; Medicus; Munditiis; An Old Correspondent; An Old Town Citizen; Scotus; Simplex Munditiis; Trumpetarius; Vetustus (all used in the *Caledonian Mercury*)
Antiwellstop; Britannus; Brito; A Cautious Man; Defiance; Detector; Domesticus; Lt. Frith in Newgate; A Hungry Corrspondent; J. B.; A Lover of Decency; Mortalis; Old Stingo; O. P.; Rampager; Tantulus; A Warm Friend to the Brave (all used in the *Public Advertiser*)
Borax; A Country Gentleman; An Edinburgh Correspondent; Old Salisbury Briar (all used in the *London Chronicle*)
Censor (letter in the *Edinburgh Chronicle*)
A Constant Correspondent; A Constant Reader (in both the *London Chronicle* and the *Public Advertiser*)
A Genius (*Observations, Good or Bad, Stupid or Clever*)
A Gentleman of Scotland (*An Ode to Tragedy*)
Hypochondriack; Medicus Mentis (both used in *The London Magazine*)

*David Malloch (*Elegy upon the Death of a Young Lady*)
Mercutio; Philalethes; Querist; Z. (all used in *Gentleman's Magazine*)
Hugh Montgomerie (in the *Edinburgh Advertiser*)
An Old Courtier (letter in *The World*)
A Scotch Gentleman (*A Collection of Original Poems*)

BOSWELL, John [1698–1757, English cleric and writer]
A Presbyter of the Church of England (*Remarks on the 'Candid Disquisitions'*)

BOSWORTH, Joseph [1789–1876, English cleric and Anglo-Saxon scholar]
A Vicar of the Church of England (*The Episcopal Church of Scotland proved to be in Full Communion with the Church of England*)

BOSWORTH, Willan G. [1904–, English crime writer]
Willan G. Borth (*Monk's Bridge Mystery*)
Leonid (*The Stars and your Future*)
Maurice Worth (*Pagoda Mystery*)

BOTSFORD, Margaret [fl. 1820, US writer]
A Lady (*The Reign of Reform or, Yankee Doodle Court*)
A Lady of Philadelphia (*Adelaide*; *Viola or, the Heiress of St Valverde*)

BOTT, Alan John [d. 1952, English journalist and former RFC pilot]
Contact (*An Airman's Outings*; *Eastern Nights – and Flights*)

BOTT, Thomas [1688–1754, English cleric]
Philanthropus (*Remarks upon Dr Butler's Sixth Chapter of the Analogy of Religion*)

BOTTA, Mrs Anne Charlotte [1815–91, US poet]
A Recluse (*Leaves from the Diary of a Recluse*)

BOTTING, Eirene [1899–1980, English novelist and translator]
Antonia White (*Frost in May*; *The Sugar House*)

BOTTRELL, William [1816–81, English traveller, recluse and writer]
An Old Celt (*Traditions ... of West Cornwall*)

BOUCHER, Jonathan [1738–1804, English cleric; sometime in America and friend of George Washington]
An American Loyalist (*Reminiscences of an American Loyalist*)

BOUCHIER, Lady Isabella D. G. [1922–, Japanese-born English writer on Japan]
Dorothy Britton (*Haiku Journey*)

BOUCICAULT, Dionysius Lardner [1820–90, Irish actor and playwright]
Lee Morton (*London Assurance*)

BOULT, Swinton [1809–76, English insurance agent]
An Ex-Competition Wallah (in *MacMillan's Magazine*)

BOULTING, Arthur Sydney [1912–, English journalist and writer on the dramatic arts]
Peter Cotes (*No Star Nonsense*; *Origin of a Thriller*; *Thinking Aloud*)
Peter Northcote (used for journalism)

BOUMA, J. L. [fl. 1975, US writer]
Steve Shannon (*The Hell-Fire Kid*)

BOUNDS, Sydney [1920–, English writer]
Wes Saunders (*Vengeance Valley*)

BOURDILLON, James Dewar [1811–83, English civil servant in India]
An Ex-Madras Civilian (*Short Account of the Measures Proposed by the Late Col. J. T. Smith on Indian Exchanges*)

BOURN, Samuel [1689–1754, English cleric, dissenter and controversialist]
A Consistent Christian (*Dialogue between a Baptist and a Churchman*)

BOURN, Samuel [1714–96, English cleric and dissenter – son of Samuel Bourn above]
A Lover of Truth and Liberty (*Protestant Dissenter's Catechism*)

A Protestant Dissenter (*An Address to the Congregation of Protestant Dissenters who Meet at the Castlegate in Nottingham*)

BOURNE, Ethel [1830–? , English novelist]
Evelyn Burne (*Spectre Stricken; The Storm-Beaten and Weary*)

BOURNE, George [1780–1845, US cleric and writer]
A Citizen of Virginia (*The Condensed Anti-Slavery Bible Argument*)

BOURNE, Vincent [1695–1747, English Latin poet]
V. B. (*Carmina Comitialia*, of which he was the editor)

BOURQUIN, Paul Henry James [1916–, English crime writer]
Richard Amberley (*Dead on the Stone; Incitement to Murder*)

BOWDEN, Jean [1920–, Scottish mystery writer and romantic novelist]
Jocelyn Barry (*The Ceaseless Challenge*)
Jennifer Bland (*Hunt for Danger*)
Avon Curry (*The Cruise of Curacao; Next Stop Gretna*)
Belinda Dell (*Summer in the City; The Dancing Years*)

BOWDEN, John [1751–1817, US cleric]
A Churchman (*Letter from a Churchman to his Friend in New Haven*)
A Protestant (*Observations by a Protestant*)

BOWDITCH, Nathaniel Ingersoll [1805–61, US lawyer and writer]
Gleaner (in the *Boston Transcript*)

BOWDLER, Jane [1743–84, English poet and essayist]
A Lady Lately Deceased (*Poems and Essays*)

BOWDOIN, James [1727–90, American politician and scientist]
A Citizen of Massachusetts (*Opinions Respecting the Commercial Intercourse between the United States ... Great Britain*)

BOWEN, John [1756–1832, English painter and genealogist]
Antiquarius (in *Gentleman's Magazine*)

BOWEN, John Griffith [1924–, English novelist and playwright]
Justin Blake (*Garry Halliday and the Sands of Time*)

BOWEN-JUDD, Sara [1922–85, English crime and mystery writer]
Anne Burton (*The Dear Departed; Where There's a Will*)
Mary Challis (*Burden of Proof; Crimes Past*)
Margaret Leek (*The Healthy Grave; We Must Have a Trial*)
Sara Woods (*Dearest Enemy; This Fatal Writ*)

BOWER, Sir Graham John [1848–1933, Irish mariner and colonial civil servant]
Centurion (*An Essay on Practical Federation*)

BOWER, John Graham [1886–1940, English mariner and nautical writer]
Klaxon (*Songs of the Submarine; On Patrol; H. M. S.___*)

BOWES, James Stuart [1789–1864, English journalist]
Alfred Dubois (*Deeds of Dreadful Note*)

BOWES, Nicholas [d. 1755, American cleric]
Constant Rockman, MA (*A Modest Account concerning the Salutations and Kissings in Ancient Times*)

BOWLES, John [1751–1819, English barrister]
A Layman (*The Claims of the Established Church*)

BOWLES, Thomas Gibson [1842–1922, English politician and journalist; founder of *Vanity Fair*]
Jehu Junior (in *Vanity Fair* and for *Vanity Fair Album* and *Vanity Fair Cartoons*)
Auditor; Blanc Bec; Choker; Pantagruel (all used in *Vanity Fair*)

BOWLES, William Lisle [1762–1850, English poet and critic; chaplain to the Prince Regent]
The late Dr Archibald MacLeod (*Ellen Gray*)

A Member of the University of Oxford (*A Voice fron St Peter's and St Paul's*)
One of the Family of Bowleses (*A Reply to an 'Unsentimental Sort of Critic'*)
One of the Old Living Poets of Great Britain (*John in Patmos*)

BOWRAN, John George [1869–1946, English Methodist cleric and writer]
Ramsay Guthrie (*Brotherhood Stories*; *The Old Folks at Home*)

BOXER, Charles Mark Edward [1931–88, English cartoonist]
Marc (*Trendy Ape*; *Marc Time*)

BOYCE, John [1810–64, Irish-born US novelist and writer]
Paul Peppergrass (*Mary Lee or, the Yankee in Ireland*; *The Spaewife*)

BOYD, Alexander Stuart [1854–1930, Scottish cartoonist and illustrator]
Twym (*One-and-Twenty Pages*)

BOYD, Andrew Kennedy Hutchinson [1825–99, Scottish cleric, preacher and writer]
A. K. H. B. (*The Critical Essays of a Country Parson*)
Charles Oliver Ardesier-MacDonald; C. A. MacDonald; A Very Particular Man (all used in *Fraser's Magazine*)
A Country Parson (*Recreations of a Country Parson*)

BOYD, Elizabeth [fl. 1735, English poet]
E. B. (*A Humorous Miscellany*)
Louisa (*Variety – a Poem in Two Cantos*)

BOYD, Hugh [1746–94, British essayist and journalist in India]
A Freeholder (*Letters Addressed to the Electors of ... Antrim*)

BOYD, James P. [1836–1910, US lawyer, historian and writer]
A Member of the New Orleans Bar (*A Brief Analysis of the Military Bill*)

BOYD, Martin a' Beckett [1893–1972, Australian journalist and novelist]
Walter Beckett (*Dearest Idol*)

Martin Mills (*The Montfords*; *Love Gods*)

BOYD, Thomas Percy [1820–75, Irish writer and translator]
Abanya; Geoffrey Briefless, Barrister-at-Law (both used in *Dublin University Magazine*)

BOYD, William Alexander Jenyns [1842–1928, Australian farmer, teacher and writer]
Old Chum (in *The Queenslander*)

BOYLE, Courtenay Edmund [1845–1901, English civil servant, sportsman and writer]
An Old Blue (in *The Times*)
Philo-Celt (in *MacMillan's Magazine*)

BOYLE, John [1707–62, 5th Earl of Cork and Orrery; writer]
Goliah English; Reginald Fitzworm; G. K.; Michael Krawbridge; Moses Orthodox; Thomas Vainall (all used in *The World*)

BOYLE, Robert [1627–91, Irish natural philosopher; noted for 'Boyles Law' experiment, which proved the relation between elasticity and pressure]
A Fellow of the Royal Society (*A Discourse of Things above Reason*; *Of the High Veneration of Man's Intellect*)
Philaretus (used for his autobiography, which was prefixed to the five-volume edition of his works published by Thomas Birch in 1744)

BOYLE, Roger [1621–79, 1st Earl of Orrery; soldier, dramatist and statesman]
A Person of Honour (*English Adventures*)
A Person of Quality (*Reasons Why a Protestant Should Not Turn Papist*)

BOYNTON, Charles Brandon [1806–83, US cleric and preacher]
A Looker-On from America (*The Russian Empire*; *The Four Great Powers*)

BOYS, Thomas [1792–1880, English cleric, Hebraist and antiquary]
A London Dog-Fancier; An Old Peninsular; A Peninsular Medallist (all used in *Blackwood's Magazine*)

BOYSE, Samuel [1708–49, Irish poet]
Alcaeus; Y. (both used in *Gentleman's Magazine*)

BRACKENBURY, Charles Booth [1831–90, British general and military writer]
A Modern Soldier (in *Contemporary Review*)

BRACKENRIDGE, Henry Hugh [1748–1816, Scottish-born US jurist, novelist and writer]
Democritus (*The Standard of Liberty*)
A Gentleman of Maryland (*The Battle of Bunkers Hill*)

BRACKENRIDGE, Henry M. [1786–1871, US lawyer and politician]
An American (*A Letter on South American Affairs*)
A Friend of Truth and Sound Policy (*Strictures on a Voyage to South America*)

BRADBURY, Ray [1920–, US science-fiction writer]
Brett Sterling (in *Thrilling Wonder Stories* magazine)

BRADDON, Henry [fl. 1840, English solicitor and sportsman]
Gilbert Forrester; A Member of the Burton Hunt (both used in *The Sporting Magazine*)

BRADFORD, Alden [1765–1843, US cleric and writer]
A Citizen of Boston (*A Particular Account of the Battle of Bunker or Breed's Hill on 17th June 1775*)

BRADFORD, Gamaliel [1763–1824, US mariner]
An Officer of this Establishment at Charlestown (*Remarks and Documents ..., Massachusetts State Prison*)

BRADFORD, Gamaliel [1795–1839, US physician]
A Gentleman of Massachusetts (*The Writer: a Series of Original Essays*)

BRADFORD, Sarah [1818–?, US writer]
Cousin Cicely (*Aunt Patty's Mirror*; *The Old Portfolio*)

BRADLAUGH, Charles [1833–91, English freethinker, politician, atheist and republican]
Iconoclast (*The Bible: What is it?*; *Half-Hours with Free-Thinkers*; *Is There a God?*; *Atheism or Theism*; *New Life of Abraham*; *Review of the Life of the Rev. E. Mellor*)

BRADLEY, Arthur Granville [1850–1943, English historian and topographical writer]
Shebautican (in *MacMillan's Magazine*)

BRADLEY, Charles [1789–1871, English cleric and preacher]
A Clergyman of the Church of England (*Original Memorials*)

BRADLEY, Edward [1827–89, English cleric, illustrator and writer]
Cuthbert Bede (*Adventures of Verdant Green*)
A Funnyman (*Funny Figures*)

BRADLEY, Katharine Harris [1848–1914, English poet and verse writer]
*Michael Field (*The Wattlefold*; *Long Ago*)
Arran Leigh (*The New Minnesinger and other Poems*; *Bellerophon and other Poems*)

BRADLEY, Marion Zimmer [1930–, US science-fiction writer]
Lee Chapman (*I am a Lesbian*)
John Dexter (*No Adam for Eve*)
Miriam Gardner (*The Strange Women*; *Twilight Lovers*)
Valerie Graves (*Witch Hill*)
Morgan Ives (*Knives of Desire*; *Spare her Heaven*)
*John Jay Wells (in *The Magazine of Science Fiction*)

BRADLEY, Mary E. { 1835–98, US novelist and poet]
Cousin Alice (*Handsome Is That Handsome Does*)

BRADLEY, Warren Ives [1847–68, US writer]
Glance Gaylord (*The Boy at Dr Murray's*; *Mr Pendleton's Cup*)

BRADSHAW, Hon. Mary Ann Cavendish [1757–1849, Irish novelist and biographer]
Priscilla Parlante (*Ferdinand and Ordella, a Russian Story*; *Memoirs of Maria, Countess D'Alva*)

BRADY, James Topham [1815–69, US lawyer]
Query (in *Knickerbocker Magazine*)

BRADY, Nicholas [1659–1726, English cleric, dramatist and poet]
Hom (*The Rape or, the Innocent Impostors*)

BRAITHWAITE, Althea [1940–, English writer for children]
Althea (*Four Pigs and a Bee*; *Jeremy Mouse*)

BRAME, Charlotte Monica [1836–84, English romantic novelist]
Bertha M. Clay (*A Girl to Love*; *The Begum's Necklace*)
A Sister of Mercy (*Tales from the Diary of a Sister of Mercy*)

BRAMWELL, James Guy [1911–, English crime writer]
James Byrom (*Or Be He Dead*; *Take only as Directed*)

BRANCH, Thomas [fl. 1753, English writer]
T. B. (*Principia Legis et Aequitatis*)

BRAND, Charles Neville [1895–1951, English poet, novelist and writer]
Charles Lorne (*Nocturne in Sunlight*; *Flat to Let*)

BRAND, Mary Christianna [1907–88, English novelist and writer for children]
Mary Anne Ashe (*A Ring of Roses*)
Annabel Jones (*The Radiant Dove*)
Mary Roland (*The Single Pilgrim*)
China Thompson (*Starr Below*)

BRANDE, William Thomas [1788–1866, English chemist and scientific writer]
A Relative (*The Life of the Celebrated Walking Stewart*)

BRANDES, Rhoda [fl. 1975, US crime writer]
Diana Ramsay (*Deadly Discretion*; *No Cause to Kill*)

BRANDT, Jane Lewis [1915–, English mystery writer]
Jane Beynon (*Cypress Man*)
Lange Lewis (*Juliet Dies Twice*; *The Passionate Victims*)

BRASH, Margaret Maud [1880–?, English novelist]
John Kendall (*Unborn Tomorrow*)

BRATHWAITE (or Braithwaite), Richard [1588–1673, English poet and writer]
Blasius Multibibus (*A Solemne Joviall Disputation*)
Clitus-Alexandrinus (*Cater-Character, Throwne out of a Box*; *Whimzies*)
Corymbaeus (*Barnabae Itinerarium*)
Eucapnus Nepenthiacus (*The Smoaking Age*)
Musaeus Palatinus (*Two Lancashire Lovers*)
Musophilus (*A New Spring Shadowed*)
Hesychius Pamphilus (*The History of Moderation*)
Philogenes Paledonius (*Ar't Asleepe Husband?*)

BRAXTON, Carter [1736–97, American patriot]
A Native of that Colony (*An Address to the Convention of the Colony of Virginia on the Subject of Government in General*)

BRAY, Mrs Anna Eliza [1790–1883, English historical novelist and writer]
Kempe Stothard (*De Foix or, Sketches of the Manners and Customs of the XIV Century*)

BRAY, Charles [1811–84, English manufacturer, philosopher and social reformer]
A Layman (*Modern Protestantism*)

BRAY, Thomas [1656–1730, English cleric and philanthropist – sometime in Maryland]
A Divine of the Church of England (*A Preliminary Essay towards Rendring the ... Church Catechism Useful*)

A Minister of the Church of England (*Bibliotheca Catechetica*)

A Sincere Lover of our Protestant Establishment (*Papal Usurpation and Tyranny*)

BRAY, Thomas [1706–85, English cleric; Canon of Windsor]
Mr Boot (*Mr Boot's Apology for the Conduct ... Sh—ff...Black Jokes*)

BREESE, Mrs William Llewellyn [1874–1938, US playwright and novelist]
Zona Gale (*Faint Perfume*; *Yellow Gentians*)

BRENAN, Edward Fitzgerald (Gerald) [1894–1987, Maltese-born traveller and writer; educated in England but lived mostly in Spain]
George Beaton (*Jack Robinson*; *Doctor Partridge's Almanack for 1935*)

BRENNAN, John N. H. [1914–, Irish crime and mystery writer]
John Welcome (*Beware of Midnight*; *Mr Merston's Hounds*)

BRENT, John Frederick [fl. 1897, English actor]
An Octogenarian Actor (*Memories of a Mistaken Life*)

BRENT, Peter Ludwig [1931–, English mystery writer]
Ludovic Peters (*Cry Vengeance*; *Two Sets to Murder*)

BRERETON, Jane [1685–1740, Welsh poet]
Melissa (in *Gentleman's Magazine*)

BRERETON, Joseph Lloyd [1822–1901, English educational reformer and cleric]
A Rugbaean (*Prometheus Britannicus*)

BRETLAND, Joseph [1742–1819, English cleric, dissenter and educator]
Adjutor; A Lover of Order (both used in the *Theological Repository*)
Garon (in the *Monthly Repository*)

BRETHERTON, Cyril Herbert Emmanuel [fl. 1934, English journalist]
Algol (in *Punch*)

BRETNOR, Reginald [1911–92, Russian-born US science-fiction writer]
Grendel Briarton (in the *Magazine of Fantasy and Science Fiction*)

BRETON, Nicholas [1545–1626, English poet and writer]
Bonerto (*The Passionate Shepheard*)
Salchein Treboun (*Pasquil's Mistresse*)

BREVAL, John Durant [1680–1730, English soldier, dramatist and writer]
Joseph Gay (*The Confederates*; *The Hoop-Petticoat*; *Ovid in Masquerade*)
A Gentleman Now Residing There (*Calpe or, Gibraltar*)
J. D. B. (*The Art of Dress*)

BREWER, Gil [d. 1983, US mystery writer]
Eric Fitzgerald (in *Pursuit* magazine)
Bailey Morgan (in *Hunted* magazine)

BREWER, James Norris [fl. 1795, English novelist and topographer]
A Young Gentleman (*The Mansion House*)

BREWER, Jehoiada [1752–1817, English dissenting cleric]
Sylvestris (in *The Gospel* magazine)

BREWSTER, Sir David [1781–1868, Scottish natural philosopher and scientist – invented the kaleidoscope]
A Calm Observer (*An Examination of the Letter addressed to Principal Hill on the Case of Mr Leslie*)

BREWSTER, John [1753–1842, English cleric, historian and religious writer]
A Recluse (*Meditations of a Recluse*)

BRICE, Arthur John Hallam Montefiore [d. 1927, English barrister and traveller]
Rambler (*The Isle of Thanet*)

BRIDGE, Horatio [1806–?, US mariner]
An Officer of the US Navy (*The Journal of an African Cruiser*)

BRIDGE, James Howard [1856–1939, English journalist and literary assistant to Andrew Carnegie]
Harold Brydges (*A Fortnight in Heaven*; *Uncle Sam at Home*)

BRIDGES, Robert [1858–1941, US journalist and literary critic]
Broch (*Overheard in Arcady*)
Droch (*Bramble Brae*; *Demeter – a Mask*; *Suppressed Chapters and other Bookishness*)

BRIDGES, Thomas [fl. 1762, English dramatist and parodist]
Caustic Barebones, a Broken Apothecary (*A New Translation of Homer's Iliad*)
Cotton Junior (*Homer Travestie: being a New Translation*)

BRIDGES, Thomas Charles [1868–1944, English writer for boys]
Christopher Beck (in *The Captain*)
Martin Shaw (in *Boy's Realm*)

BRIERLEY, Benjamin [1825–96, English weaver and dialect writer]
A. (*Goin' to Cyprus*)
Ab-o'th-Yate (*Ab-o'th-Yate and the Cobbler of Alderburn*)

BRIGGS, Charles Frederick [1804–77, US journalist]
Harry Franco (*The Trippings of Tom Pepper*; *The Adventures of Harry Franco*)
Tom Pepper (*Asmodeus or, the Iniquities of New York*)

BRIGHAM, Gertrude Richardson [fl. 1925, US writer]
Viktor Flambeau (*Red Letter days in Europe*)

BRIGHOUSE, Harold [1882–1958, English drama critic and playwright]
*Olive Conway (*The Starlight Widow*; *Costume Plays*)

BRIGHT, Henry Arthur [1830–84, English merchant and writer]
A Cambridge Man (*Free Blacks and Slaves*; *The Public Speaker and How to Make One*)

A Cambridge Man in the West (in *Fraser's Magazine*)
A Liverpool Merchant (*Our Free Trade Policy Examined*)
A Unitarian Layman (in the *Theological Review*)

BRIGHT, Jonathan Huntington [1804–37, US journalist and poet]
Viator (used in various periodocals)

BRIGHT (née Dunne), Mary Chevalita [1860–1945, Australian novelist]
George Egerton (*Keynotes*; *Discords*; *Fantasias*)

BRIGHT, Robert [1902–83, US writer for children]
Michael Douglas (*Round, Round World*)

BRIGHT, William [1824–1901, English cleric and theological historian]
A Fellow of a College (*Athanasius and other Poems*)

BRILL, Ethel Claire [1877–?, US writer]
Edwin C. Burritt (*Cameron Island*; *Boy Scout Crusoes*)

BRINKELOW, Henry [d. 1546, English satirist and writer]
Roderigo More (*Lamentacion of a Christian*)

BRINTON, Henry [1901–, English crime and writer]
Alex Fraser (*Bury Their Day*; *Death is so Final*)

BRISTED, Charles Astor [1820–74, US journalist and writer]
Carl Benson (in *The Spirit of the Times* and for *Letter to Dr Henry Halford Jones* and *Anacreontics*)
A Broken-Down Critic (*Pieces of a Broken-Down Critic Picked up by Himself*)
Frank Manhattan (in *Fraser's Magazine*)
A New Yorker (*The Upper Ten Thousand*)

BRITTAIN, Thomas [1806–84, English natural historian]
Brittanicus (*Half a Dozen Songs*)

BRITTAIN, William [1930–, US crime and mystery novelist]
James Knox (in *Ellery Queen's Mystery Magazine*)

BRITTON, John [1771–1857, English antiquary and topographer]
Hilaris Benevolus & Co. (*The Pleasures of Human Life Investigated*)

BROCK, Alan St Hill [fl. 1950, English crime writer]
Peter Dewdney (*Arising from an Accident*; *On Appeal*)

BROCK, Robert Alonzo [1839–1914, US historian]
Civis (*The Public School in Relation to the Negro*)

BROCKETT, Linus Pierpont [1820–93, US physician, publisher and writer]
An American Citizen (*The Philanthropic Results of the War in America*)
Philobiblius (*History and Progress of Education*)

BRODERIP, William John [1789–1859, English conchologist and co-founder of the Zoological Society of London]
A Naturalist (*Leaves from the Note-Book of a Naturalist*)

BRODIE, John [1905–, New Zealand novelist]
John Guthrie (*Journey by Twilight*; *The Little Country*)

BROGAN, Sir Denis William [1900–74, Scottish academic, historian and crime writer]
Maurice Barrington (*Stop on the Green Light!*)

BROKESBY, Francis [1637–1714, English nonjuring cleric]
F. B. (*Of Education with Respect to Grammar Schools and the Universities*)

BROME, Richard [d. 1652, English dramatist]
R. B. (*Lachrymae Musarum ...*)

BROMET, William [d. 1850, English physician and historian]
A Lounger (*Peregrine in France*)
Plantagenet (in *Gentleman's Magazine*)

BROMLEY, William [1664–1732, English politician; Speaker of the House of Commons]
A Gentleman (*Several Years' Travel Through Portugal, Spain etc.*)

BRONTE, Anne [1820–49, English poet and novelist]
Acton Bell (*Agnes Grey*; *Poems*; *The Tenant of Wildfell Hall*)

BRONTE, Charlotte [1816–55, English poet and novelist]
Currer Bell (in the *Manchester Athenaeum Album* in 1850 for *The Orphans* and for *Jane Eyre*, *Poems* and *The Professor*)

BRONTE, Emily Jane [1818–48, English poet and novelist]
Ellis Bell (*Poems*; *Wuthering Heights*)

BROOKE, Miss Emma Frances [d. 1926, English novelist]
E. Fairfax Byrne (*Millicent*)

BROOKE, Mrs Francesca [1724–89, English novelist and dramatist]
Mary Singleton (used when she edited *The Old Maid*)

BROOKE, Henry [1703–83, Irish novelist, poet and pamphleteer]
A Farmer (*A Farmer's Letters*)
A Member of the Protestant Church in that Kingdom (*The Case of the Roman Catholics in Ireland*)
A Senior Fellow of a College in Oxford (*An Appeal to the Publick*)

BROOKE, John Charles [1748–94, English antiquarian and herald]
J. B. (in *Gentleman's Magazine*)

BROOKE, Peter [1907–, US mystery writer]
Anthony Carson (*Any More for the Gondola?*)

BROOKE, Richard Sinclair [1802–82, Irish cleric }
The Dean of Pimlico; A Pilgrim (both used in *Dublin University Magazine*)

BROOKE, Stopford Augustus [1832–1916, Irish cleric and literary critic]
Ignatius (in *Dublin University Magazine*)

BROOKER, Bertram [1888–1955, English-born Canadian painter and writer]
Huxley Herne (*The Tangled Miracle*)
Richard Surrey (*Subconcious Selling; Copy Technique in Advertising*)

BROOKS, Charles [1795–1872, US cleric]
An American Resident in Paris (*The Parisian Linguist*)

BROOKS, Charles Timothy [1813–83, US cleric and poet]
Carrier Boy (used in various newspapers)

BROOKS, Charles William Shirley [1816–74, English novelist, playwright and editor of *Punch*]
Shirley Brooks; Massinger Screw (both used in *Ainsworth's Magazine*)
Epicurus Rotundus (in *Punch*)

BROOKS, Clive [1930–, English dramatist]
Clive Exton (*No Fixed Abode*)

BROOKS, Edwy Searles [1889–1965, English writer for boys]
Berkeley Gray (*Dare-Devil's Conquest; Vultures Ltd.*)

BROOKS, Elbridge Streeter [1846–1902, US literary editor and writer for children]
The Famous Writer for Young Americans (*True Stories of Geat Americans*)

BROOKS, James Gordon [1801–41, US lawyer, journalist and poet]
Florio (used in various periodicals)

BROOKS, Maria [1795–1845, US poet and writer]
Maria del Occidente (*Zophiel or, The Bride of Seven*)

A Lover of the Fine Arts (*Judith, Esther and other Poems*)

BROOKS, Reginald [fl. 1895, English humorist]
Peter Blobbs (in *The Pink 'un*)

BROOKS, Vivian Collin [1922–, English crime writer]
Osmington Mills (*Stairway to Murder*)

BROOKS, William Collin [1893–1959, English journalist and crime novelist]
Barnaby Brook (*Gay Go Up; The Jug*)
Cleon (*For Hellidor*)

BROOKS, Willian Eric St John [1883–1955, Irish journalist and antiquarian]
Eric St John (*A Stranger Here*)

BROOMALL, Robert Walter [1946–, US western novelist]
Hank Edwards (*Texas Feud*)

BROOME, William [1689–1745, English cleric, poet and classical scholar]
Chester (in *Gentleman's Magazine*)

BROSSARD, Chandler [1922–, US journalist, novelist and essayist]
Daniel Harper (*The Wrong Turn*)

BROTHERTON, Edward [1814–66, English merchant, Swedenborgian and popular educator]
Libra; Pilgrim (both used in various Swedenborgian publications)

BROUGH, Robert Barnabus [1828–60, English burlesque writer and satirist]
Papernose Woodensconce Esq. (*The Wonderful Drama of Punch and Judy*)

BROUGH, William [d. 1671, English cleric and religious writer]
Philo-Christianus (*A Preservative against the Plague of Schisme*)

BROUGHAM, Henry Peter [1778–1868, 1st Baron Brougham and Vaux; Lord Chancellor and energetic writer]
A Friend of the People (*A Letter to the Queen on the State of the Monarchy*)

Peter Jenkins (*A Letter to Isaac Tomkins, Gent.*)

Isaac Tomkins, Gent. (*We Can't Afford It!, Being Thoughts on the Aristocracy of England*)

BROUGHAM, John [1814–80, Irish actor, dramatist and humorist]
Diogenes Jr. (in *The Lantern*)

BROUGHTON, Richard [d. 1634, English Catholic historian]
A Catholicke Priest (*A Demonstration by English Protestant Pretended Bishops ... Against their Owne Pretended Bishops and Mynistry*)
An Old Student in Divinitie (*The Judgment of the Apostles*; *A Defense of Catholikes Persecuted in England*)

BROUGHTON, Thomas [1704–74, English cleric, biographer and writer]
Phileleutherus Christianus (*The Inspiration of the New Testament*)

BROUNCKER, William [1620–84, Irish peer, mathematician and first president of the Royal Society]
A Person of Honour (*Renatus Descarte's Compendium of Musick*)

BROUNOFF, Platon G. [1863–1924, US composer and musician]
B. A. Sharp (*Stolen Correspondence from the Dead Letter Office*)

BROWN, Alice [1857–1948, US dramatist and novelist]
Martin Redfield (*My Love and I*)

BROWN, Cecil Leonard Morley [1895–1955, English air vice-marshal and writer]
C. L. M. (in *Punch*)

BROWN, Charles Armitage [1786–1842, English close friend of Keats]
Carlone and Carlucce (in *The Liberal*)

BROWN, Charles Brockden [1771–1810, US novelist and journalist]
C. B. B. (*Arthur Mervyn or, Memoirs of the year 1793*; *Wieland or, the Transformation*)

Poplicola (*Monroe's Embassy*)

BROWN, Sir Edward [1851–1939, English poultry expert and writer]
Stephen Beale (*Profitable Poultry Keeping*)

BROWN, Edward Thomas [1879–1943, English motoring and agricultural journalist]
Owner Driver (*Road Accidents and Speed Limits*)

BROWN, George Douglas [1869–1902, Scottish novelist and writer]
George Douglas (*The House with Green Shutters*)
George Hood (*Famous Fighting Regiments*)
Kennedy King (*Love and a Sword*)

BROWN, George Spencer [fl. 1970, English mathematician]
James Keys (*Only Two Can Play This Game*; *Twenty Three Degrees of Paradise*)

BROWN, Hannah Sherman [fl. 1928, English writer and artist]
A Foundling (*The Child She Bare*)

BROWN, Howard Clarke [1898–?, US poet and writer]
Donald Thistle (*Appleseed Johnny*; *Songs of the Iowa Prairie*)
To-Ka-Ni-Ya (*Pte-Ska the White Buffalo*)

BROWN, James Baldwin [1820–84, English Congregational cleric]
Epsilon (*The Moral Government of God*)

BROWN, James Buchan [1832–1904, Scottish literary scholar and poet]
J. B. Selkirk (*Bible Truths with Shaksperian Parallels*; *Ethics and Aesthetics of Modern Poetry*; *Poems*)

BROWN, James Moray [fl. 1890, English soldier and sporting writer]
Dooker (in *Blackwood's Magazine*)

BROWN, John [1610–79, Scottish cleric and writer]
A Presbyterian (*The History of Indulgence*)

BROWN, John [1722–87, Scottish cleric of humble origin]
A Gentleman in the Country (*Free Thoughts upon the Late Regulation of the Post*)
A Real Friend to the Church of Scotland (*An Historical Account of the Seceders*)

BROWN, John MacMillan [1846–1935, Scottish-born New Zealand academic]
Godfrey Swevern (*Limanora, the Island of Progress; Riallaro the Archipelago of Exiles*)

BROWN, John Thomas [1861–?, English journalist, zoologist and humorous writer]
Hal Berte (used for humorous journalism)

BROWN, Lilian Kate Rowland [1863–1959, English novelist and journalist]
Rowland Grey (*Jacob's Letter; The Craftsman*)

BROWN, Margaret Wise [1910–52, US writer for children]
Timothy Hay (*Horses*)

BROWN, Miss Meredith [d. 1908, English social reformer]
A Professional Musician (*The Service of Praise*)

BROWN, Morna Doris [1907–, English mystery writer]
Elizabeth (or E. X.) Ferrars (*With Murder in Mind; Give a Corpse a Bad Name*)

BROWN, Peter [1784–1863, Scottish-born Canadian journalist]
Libertas (*The Fame and Glory of England Vindicated*)

BROWN, Robert [1842–95, Scottish botanist, traveller and geographer]
A Government Agent (in *Cornhill Magazine*)

BROWN, Sandra [1948–, US romantic novelist]
Laura Jordan (*Hidden Fires; The Silken Web*)
Rachel Ryan (*Love's Encore; Prime Time*)
Erin St Claire (*A Secret Splendor; Tiger Prince*)

BROWN, Theron [1832–1914, US novelist, poet and writer]
Park Ludlow (*NIck Hardy at College; Stories for Sundays*)

BROWN, Thomas [1663–1704, English satirist, humorist and energetic scurrilous writer]
Tobyas Thomas (*The Life of the Late Famous Ccomedian, Jo Haynes*)
Dudley Tomkinson (*The Reasons of Mr Bays Changing his Religion*)

BROWN, Thomas [1770–1851, English merchant in Russia]
An Old Traveller throughout Europe (*The Reminiscences of an Old Traveller etc.*)

BROWN, Thomas [1778–1820, Scottish philosopher and minor poet]
The Wanderer (*The Wanderer in Norway*)

BROWN, William [1769–1846, English Quaker]
Ahiezer (*A Tender Address to the People of Israel*)

BROWN, William John [1894–1960, English politician and trade unionist]
Diogenes (in *Time and Tide*)

BROWN, William Perry [1847–1923, US writer]
Capt. William B. Perry (*Our Sammies in the Trenches; Our Pilots in the Air*)

BROWN, Zenith [1898–1983, US crime and mystery writer]
Brenda Conrad (*The Stars Give Warning; Girl with a Golden Bar*)
Leslie Ford (*Priority Murder; The Town Cried Murder*)
David Frome (*The By-Pass Murder; The Murder on the Sixth Hole*)

BROWNE, Charles Farrar [1834–67, US humorist]
Artemus Ward (in the *Cleveland Plaindealer* and for *Artemus Ward in London* and *Artemus Ward among the Fenians*)

BROWNE, Charles Thomas [1825–68, English poet and writer]
Alexandre de Comyn (*Irene – a Poem*)

BROWNE, George Waldo [1851–1930, US writer for boys]
Vernon St Clair (*Castaway in the Jungle*)

BROWNE, Gordon Frederick [1858–1932, English illustrator]
A. Nobody (*Nonsense for Somebody; Some More Nonsense*)

BROWNE, Hablot Knight [1815–82, English artist and illustrator of Dickens's novels; two illustrations in *Pickwick* were signed 'Nemo']
Phiz

BROWNE, Howard [1908–, US mystery writer]
John Evans (*Halo for Satan*)

BROWNE, James [1793–1841, Scottish writer and journalist]
An Old Dissector (*The Life of the Ettrick Shepherd*)

BROWNE, John Hutton Balfour [1845–1921, English barrister and writer]
Hamilton Marshall (*Nursery Verses*)

BROWNE, Mary Anne [1812–44, Irish poet]
The Portrait Painter (in *Dublin University Magazine*)

BROWNE, Moses [1704–87, English cleric and writer]
Immerito (*Piscatory Eclogues*)

BROWNE, Rilma Marion [fl. 1920, US writer for children]
Stanley Castle (*Indian Story Hour*)

BROWNE, Thomas Alexander [1826–1915, Australian novelist]
Rolf Boldrewood (in *The Australasian* and for *Robbery Under Arms*)

BROWNE, William Hand [1828–1912, US librarian and bibliographer]
Anobium Pertinax (in *The Nation*)

BROWNELL, Henry Howard [1820–72, US lawyer and poet]
A Volunteer in the US Service (*Lyrics of a Day or, Newspaper Poetry*)

BROWNING, Dixie [1930–, US romantic novelist]
Zoe Dozier (*Warm Side of the Island*)
Bronwyn Williams (*White Witch*)

BROWNING, Robert [1812–89, English poet]
Dervish Seriosae Ferishtah (*Diverse Fancies of Dervish Seriosae Ferishtah*)

BROWNJOHN, Alan Charles [1931–, English poet]
John Berrington (*To Clear the River*)

BROXHOLME, John Franklin [1930–, English crime and mystery writer]
Duncan Kyle (*A Cage of Ice; Black Camelot*)
James Meldrum (*The Semenov Impulse*)

BROXON, Mildred Downey [1944–, US science-fiction writer]
Sigfriour Skaldaspillir (*Eric Brighteyes No. 2*)

BRUCE, Archibald [1746–1816, Scottish cleric and satirical poet]
Calvinianus Presbyter (*Annus Secularis; Queries Addressed to the Gentry, Clergy and People of Scotland*)
Calvinus Minor, Scoto Britannus (*Free Thoughts on the Toleration of Popery*)
Cousin German (*A Full and Particular Account of the Trial and Condemnation of John Presbytery*)
A Rural Divine (*Poems Serious and Amusing*)

BRUCE, James [1808–61, Scottish journalist and writer]
Table Talk (in the *Fifeshire Journal*)

BRUCE, Peter Henry [1692–1757, Scottish military engineer – employed by various continental powers]
A Military Officer (*Memoirs of a Military Officer in the Service of Prussia, Russia etc.*)

BRUCE, Sir Robert [1855–1931, English post office executive]
A City Man (*Greystones – Musings without Dates*)

BRUCE, Wallace [1844–1914, US poet and notable orator]
Thursty McQuill (*The Connecticut by Daylight*)

BRUCKNER, John [1726–1804, Dutch-born Lutheran cleric – sometime in England; committed suicide]
J. Cassander (*Criticisms on the Diversions of Purley*)

BRUDENELL, James Thomas [1797–1868, 7th Earl of Cardigan; led the 'Light Brigade' charge at Balaklava]
A General Officer of Cavalry (*Eight Months on Active Service*)

BRUEN, Mathias, [1793–1829, US cleric and preacher]
An American (*Essays, Descriptive and Moral, on Scenes in Italy, Switzerland and France*)

BRUNDISH, John Jelliand [d. 1786, English poet]
J. J. B-. (*An Elegy on a Family Tomb*)

BRUNNER, John Kilian Houston [1934–, English science-fiction and crime writer]
Kilian Houston Brunner (*The Wanton of Argus*)
John Loxmith (in *Astounding Science Fiction* magazine and for *Thou Good and Faithful*)
Keith Woodcott (*I Speak for Earth*; *The Ladder in the Sky*)

BRUTUS, Dennis Vincent [1924–, Rhodesian-born English poet and writer]
John Bruin (*Thoughts Abroad*)

BRYANS, Robert Harbinson [1928–, Irish novelist and travel writer]
Robin Bryans (*Gateway to the Khyber*)
Donald Cameron (*The Field of Sighing*)
Robert Harbinson (*No Surrender*; *Up Spake the Cabin Boy*)

BRYANT, William Cullen [1794–1880, US poet, writer and journalist]
Francis Herbert Esq. (*The Talisman for 1828*)
A Traveller (*Letters of a Traveller 1857–58*)
A Youth of Thirteen (*The Embargo*)

BRYCE, James [1785–1866, Scottish cleric – spent twenty years in India]
A Parishioner of St George's Parish, Edinburgh (*Letter to the Rev. Robert S. Candlish*)
A Protestant of the School of the Reformation (*Pith and Marrow of the Present Controversy*)

BRYCE, James [fl. 1930, Scottish journalist and writer]
Norman Dundas (*A Romance of the Forty-Five*)

BRYDGES, Sir Samuel Egerton [1762–1837, English poet, bibliographer and writer]
Sir Cosmo Gordon (*Letters on Lord Byron*)
Wilfred Woodfall (*My Note-Book for 1822*; *My Note-Book or, Sketches from the Gallery*)

BRYSON, Charles [1887–1963, Irish crime novelist]
Charles Barry (*The Case for Cressider*; *The Wrong Murder Mystery*)

BUBIER, Edward T. [fl. 1904, US writer]
Edward Trevert (*The ABC of Wireless Telegraphy*)

BUCHAN, Anna [d. 1948, Scottish novelist]
Olive Douglas (*The House That Is Our Own*; *Unforgettable, Unforgotten*)

BUCHAN, John [1875–1940, 1st Baron Tweedsmuir; novelist, historian and writer]
Atticus (in the *Sunday Times, 1930–35*)
Auspex (in *The Spectator*)
B. (in the *Glasgow Herald*)
Cadmus and Harmonia (*The Island of Sheep* – written with his wife Susan)
Johannesburg; Pseudo-Africanus (both used in the *National Review*)

BUCHANAN, George [1827–1906, Scottish surgeon and medical writer]
A Civilian (*Camp Life as Seen by a Civilian*)

BUCHANAN, James [1804–70, Scottish Free Church cleric]
A Minister of the Church of Scotland (*Letter to Thomas Erskine Esq.*)

BUCHANAN, John [1802–78, Scottish lawyer and antiquarian]
Glasguensis (*Banking in Glasgow*)

BUCHANAN, Robert Williams [1841–1901, British poet, novelist and dramatist]
Caliban (in *The Spectator*)
Walter Hutcheson (in *St Paul's Magazine*)
Thomas Maitland (in *Contemporary Review* and for *The Fleshly School*)

BUCK, Pearl S. [1892–1973, US novelist and biographer]
John Sedges (*The Long Love*; *Bright Procession*; *Voices in the House*)

BUCKHAM, James [1858–1908, US religious journalist and poet]
Paul Pastnor (*Lora: a Romance in Verse*)

BUCKINGHAM, James Silk [1786–1855, English traveller, journalist and writer]
An Old Traveller (*A Summer Trip to Weymouth and Dorchester*)
A Proprietor of Indian Stock (*A Second Letter to Sir Charles Fox*)

BUCKINGHAM, Joseph Tinker [1779–1861, US journalist and publisher]
Cobweb; Moth (in the *Boston Courier*)
Pertinax Period and Co. (in the *New England Galaxy*)

BUCKINGHAM, Leicester Silk [1825–67, English playwright – son of J. S. Buckingham above]
Matthews and Co. (*Aggravating Sam*)

BUCKLAND, Francis Trevelyan [1826–80, English physician and zoologist]
A Fisherman and Zoologist (*The Log-Book of a Fisherman and a Zoologist*)
Irondequoit (in *The Examiner*)

BUCKLEY, Samuel [1886–1950, Australian writer and poet]
Frank Blair (*Digger Sea Mates*)

BUCKLEY, Theodore Alois William [1826–56, English cleric, translator and writer]
Tom Hawkins (*The Adventures of Sydenham Greenfinch*)

BUDD, William John [fl. 1937, US crime writer]
Jackson Budd (*The Princely Quartet*; *The Gallows Wait*)
Wallace Jackson (*The Sinister Madonna*; *Two Knocks for Death*)

BUDGELL, Eustace [1686–1737, English pamphleteer – wrote for *The Spectator*, *The Guardian* and *The Tatler*; drowned himself in the River Thames]
Philo-Patriae (*Memoirs of the Family of Boyds*)
X. (in *The Spectator*)

BUDGEN, M. L. [fl. 1851, English lady writer on floriculture]
Acheta Domestica (*Episodes of Insect Life*; *March Winds and April Showers*; *May Flowers*)

BUELL, Marjorie Henderson [1904–93, US cartoonist]
Marge (in the *Saturday Evening Post*)

BULKELEY, Sir Richard [1644–1710, English pamphleteer]
A Gentleman of the University of Cambridge (*Letters to Dr Clarke Concerning Liberty*)

BULL, Albert E. [fl. 1930, English journalist and crime novelist]
Arthur Ward Basset (*The Love Trapeze*; *The Yellow Robe Murders*)

BULLARD, Arthur [1879–1929, US journalist, traveller and diplomat]
Albert Edwards (*Panama*)

BULLARD, Henry Adams [1788–1851, US jurist]
An Officer under That General (*History of Don Francisco De Miranda's Attempt to Effect a Revolution in South America*)

BULLER, Sir Francis [1746–1800, English jurist]
A Learned Judge (*An Introduction to the Law*)

BULLETT, Gerald William [1893–1958, English novelist and poet]
Sebastian Fox (*One Man's Poison*; *Odd Woman Out*)

BULLOCK, Michael Hale [1918–, English-born Canadian poet and writer]
Michael Hale (*Transmutations*; *A Savage Darkness*)

BULMER, Kenneth Henry [1921–, English historical novelist and science-fiction writer]
Alan Burt Akers (*Transit to Scorpio*; *Arena of Antares*)
Ken Blake (*Stake Out*; *Fall Girl*)
Frank Brandon (in *Science Fantasy* magazine)
Ernest Corley (*White Out*)
Arthur Frazier (*A Flame in the Fens*)
Adam Hardy (*Prize Money*; *Powder Monkey*)
*Kenneth Johns (in both *Nebula* magazine and *New Worlds* magazine)
Philip Kent (*Mission to the Stars*; *Vassals of Venus*)
Bruno Krauss (*Shark North*; *Shark Trap*)
Neil Langholm (*The Dark Return*)
Karl Maras (*Zhorani*; *Peril from Space*)
Andrew Quiller (*The Land of Mist*)
Nelson Sherwood; Philip Stratford (both used in *New Worlds* magazine)
Richard Silver (*Jaws of Death*)
Tully Zetford (*Whirlpool of Stars*; *Star City*)

BULSTRODE, Whitelocke [1650–1724, English controversial religious writer and pamphleteer]
Philalethes (*A Letter Touching the Late Rebellion and What Means Led to it*)

BULWER-LYTTON, Edward George Earle Lytton 1803–73, 1st Baron Lytton; novelist, poet and politician]
Edmund Bruce (in *Knight's Magazine*)
Pisistratus Caxton (*The Boatman*; *My Novel*; *What Will He Do With It?*; *The Caxtons*)
Hermides; Tish (both used in *Blackwood's Magazine*)
Mitio; Henry Pelham; A Reforming Member of Parliament (all used in *New Monthly Magazine*)

BUMPUS, Doris Marjorie [1905–, English crime writer]
Marjorie Alan (*Dark Prophecy*; *Murder Next Door*)

BUNBURY, Henry William [1750–1811, English political satirist and cartoonist]
Geoffrey Gambado (*An Acadamy for Grown Horsemen*; *Annals of Horsemanship*)
Professor Lumpwitz (*Tales of the Devil*)

BUNBURY, Selina [1802–82, Irish novelist]
An Old Physician (in *Fraser's Magazine*)

BUNCE, Oliver Bell [1828–90, US journalist and writer]
Bachelor Bluff (*A Romance of the Revolution*)
Censor (*Bachelor Bluff*; *Don't: A Manual of Mistakes*)

BUNDY, Jonas Mills [1835–91, US lawyer]
A Member of the Rock County Bar (*State Rights and the Appellate Jurisdiction*)

BUNN, Alfred [1796–1860, English librettist and theatrical manager]
Conrad (*The Stage, Both Before and Behind the Curtain*)

BUNNER, Henry Cuyler [1855–96, US poet, dramatist, journalist and novelist]
V. Hugo Dusenbury; Me; A. H. Oakes (all used in *Puck*)

BUNSEN, George [1824–96, German politician and writer]
Prince Outisky (in *Fortnightly Review*)

BUNTING, Anne Evelyn [1928–, Irish-born US writer for children]
Evelyn Bolton (*Stable of Fear*; *Dream Dancers*)

BUNTING, Daniel George [1890–1967, English essayist and writer]
Daniel George (*All in a Maze*; *Tomorrow Will Be Different*)

BURBRIDGE, Edith Joan [fl. 1950, English crime writer]
Joan Cockin (*Curiosity Killed the Cat*; *Deadly Earnest*)

BURDEN, Jean P. [1914–, US writer]
Felicia Ames (*The Dog You Care For*)

BURDETTE, Robert Jones [1844–1914, US journalist and editor]
Burlington Hawk-Eye Man (in the *Burlington Daily Hawk-Eye*)

BURDON, William [1764–1818, English pit owner and political pamphleteer]
A Member of the University of Cambridge (*A Few Words of Plain Truth*)

BURDY, Samuel [1760–1820, Irish cleric, poet and historian]
Detector (*A Vindication of Burdy's Life of Skelton*)

BURFORD, Roger d'Este [1904–, English crime writer]
Roger East (*Murder Rehearsal*; *Detectives in Gum Boots*)
*Simon (*Death on the Swim*; *Murder among Friends*; *The Cat with the Moustache*)

BURGE, Doris [1909–, English poet and writer]
Jean Earle (*Trial of Strength*)

BURGE, Milward Rodon Kennedy [1894–1968, English mystery writer]
Evelyn Elder (*Angel in the Case*; *Murder in Black and White*)
Milward Kennedy (*Poison in the Parish*; *Who was Old Willy?*)

BURGES, George [1786–1864, English classical scholar]
An Asiatic Liberal (*Erin or, the Cause of the Greeks*; *The Son of Erin*)
Cato (*Cato to Lord Byron on the Immorality of his Writings*)

BURGES, Sir James Bland [1752–1824, English politican, poet and dramatist – known from 1821 as Sir James Lamb]
Alfred (in *The Sun*, and for *Letters ... Europe*)
Sergeant Bradshaw (*Heroic Epistles from Sergeant Bradshaw to John Dunning*)
Verus (*Letters on the Spanish Aggression at Nootka*)

BURGES, Tristram [1770–1853, US lawyer and politician]
A Farmer (*An Address to Men of all Parties*)
One of the People (*Reasons why the Rt. Hon. Elisha R. Potter Should Not be a Senator in Congress*)
A Ploughman (*What a Ploughman Said*)

BURGESS, Henry [1808–86, Scottish cleric]
A Baptist (*The Bible Translation Society*)

BURGESS, M. R. [1948–, US publisher and editor]
Robert Reginald (*Up Your Asteroid!*, a *Science Fiction Farce*)

BURGESS, Thomas [1756–1837, English cleric and social reformer; Bishop of St Davids, later of Salisbury]
Britannicus (*Letters of Britannicus*)
Philopatris (*Letters of Philopatris to Dr Phillimore*)

BURGH, James [1714–75, Scottish political writer and pamphleteer]
J. B. (*Political Disquisitions*; *Youth's Friendly Monitor*)
Mr Vander Neck (*An Account of the First Settlement*)

BURGH, William [1741–1808, Irish landowner, anti-slave campaigner and controversialist]
An Humble Expectant of the Promise (*The Coming of the Day of God*)

A Layman (*A Scriptural Confutation*)

BURGIN, George Brown [1856–1944,
English novelist and journalist]
Wentworth Smee (used for journalism)

BURGOYNE, Margaret Anne [1823–83,
English writer]
A Lady (in *Bentley's Miscellany*)

BURGOYNE, Montagu [1750–1836, English
politician and pamphleteer]
A Magistrate of the County of Essex (*A
Statistical Account of the Hundred of
Harlow*)

BURKE, Aedanus { 1743–1802, Irish-born
American jurist]
Cassius (*Considerations upon the Society or
Order of Cincinnati*)
An Obscure Individual (*Observations upon a
Late Pamphlet entitled 'Considerations upon
the Society or Order of Cincinna*ti')

BURKE, Edmund [1729–97, Irish politician,
and distinguished political writer]
A Distinguished English Commoner (*A
Letter from a Distinguished English
Commoner to a Peer of Ireland*)
A Gentleman in the English House of
Commons (*A Letter from a Gentleman in
the English House of Commons with Regard
to the Affairs of Ireland*)

BURKE, Edmund [1809–92, US lawyer and
politican]
Bundelcund (in The *Washington Post*)

BURKE, John Frederick [1922–, English
science-fiction writer]
Jonathan (or Owen) Burke (*The Figurehead*;
Deep Freeze)
Harriet Esmond (used for work written with
his wife Jean)
(*The Eye Stones*; *The Florian Signet*)
Jonathan George (*The Kill Dog*; *Dead
Letters*)
Joanna Jones (*Nurse is a Neighbour*; *The
Artless Commuter*)
Robert Miall (*Jason King*; *The Adventurer*)
Sara Morris (*A Widow for the Winter*)
Martin Sands (*Maroc 7*)

BURKE, Sydney Terence [1886–1945,
English writer]
Thomas Burke (*The Streets of London*;
English Night Life)
Paul Pry (*For Your Convenience*)

BURLEIGH, Mrs Celia M. [1823–76, US
journalist, poet and writer]
Celia (used in various newspapers)

BURN, Andrew [d. 1814, Scottish soldier in
India]
An Eye-Witness (*A Second Address ... to
Abstain from the Use of West India Sugar*)
A Marine Officer (*The Christian Officer's
Panoply*; *Who Fares Best? The Christian or
the Man of the World?*)

BURNAND, Francis Cowley [1836–1917,
English humorist, burlesque writer and
editor of *Punch*]
Dion Bounceycore (*Chikkin Hazard*)
Cecil Colvin (*My Time and What I Have
Done With It*)
Miss Rhody Dendron (*Gone Wrong*)
Fictor No Go (*One and Three!*)
One who has Done it, and Can Do it Again
(*How to Get Out of Newgate*)
Weeder (in *Punch*)

BURNE, Alfred Higgins [1886–1959, English
soldier and military historian]
Basilisk (*Talks on Leadership Addressed to
Young Officers*)

BURNET, Gilbert [1643–1715, English cleric
of Scottish descent, preacher and
controversialist in both religion and
politics; Bishop of Salisbury]
A. B. (*Histrio Theologicus ...*)
A Lover of Peace (*A Modest and Free
Conference betwixt a Conformist and a
Non-conformist ... Scotland*)
A True Son of the Protestant Church of
England (*The Protestant's Companion*)

BURNET, Gilbert [1690–1726, English
pamphleteer]
A Gentleman of Oxford that Understands
Trapp (*Reality without Existence*)

BURNET, Thomas [d. 1750, English cleric and theologian]
A Divine of the Church of England (*An Appeal to Common Sense*; *The Scripture Trinity Intelligibly Explained*)

BURNET, Sir Thomas [1694–1753, English jurist and political pamphleteer]
*Sir Iliad Doggrel (*Homerides, or, a Letter to Mr Pope*)
R. Powel the Puppet-Show Man (*A Second Tale of the Tub*)
Timon (*The True Character of an Honest Man in Public Affairs ... Marlborough*)

BURNETT, William Riley [1899–1982, US novelist and screenwriter]
John Monahan (*Big Stan*)
James Updyke (*It's Always Four o'Clock*)

BURNHAM, Mrs Clara Louise [1854–1927, US novelist]
Edith Douglas (*We Von Ardens*)

BURNHAM, Samuel [1833–73, US journalist and editor]
Uncle Paul (*Uncle Paul's Stories for Boys and Girls*)

BURNS, Jabez [1805–76, English Baptist cleric and writer]
A Dissenting Minister (*One Hundred Sketches and Skeletons of Sermons*; *Sketches of Sermons on Christian Missions*)

BURNS, Rex [1935–, US writer]
Tom Sehler (*When Reason Sleeps*)

BURNS, Robert [1759–96, Scottish poet]
Sylvander (used in correspondence with Mrs Maclehose)

BURR, Charles Chauncey [1817–83, US teacher, orator and journalist]
Lola Montez (*Lectures of Lola Montez*)

BURR, Enoch Fitch [1818–1907, US cleric and mathematician]
A Connecticut Pastor (*Ecce Coelum, or, Parish Astronomy*)

BURRAGE, Alfred McLelland [1889–1956, English writer]
Ex-Private-X (*Someone in the Room*; *War is War*)
Frank Lelland (in *Detective Weekly* magazine)

BURRARD, William Dutton [1861–1938, English soldier, poet, translator and songwriter]
Aramis (*Monk Raven*)

BURRITT, Elihu [1810–79, US linguist, pamphleteer and philanthropist]
A Backpewman (*A Voice from the Back Pews to the Pulpit*)
The Learned Blacksmith (*Walks in the Black Country*)
Old Burchell (*Old Burchell's Pocket for the Children*)

BURROUGH, Edward [1634–63, English Quaker and pamphleteer]
A Friend to England's Commonwealth (*A Just and Lawful Trial of the Teachers*)
A Friend to Righteousness (*Satan's Design Defeated*)

BURROUGHS, Edgar Rice [1875–1950, US novelist]
Norman Bean (in *All-Story Magazine*)
John T. McCulloch (*Pirate Blood*)

BURROUGHS, Samuel [d. 1761, English writer on the law]
Everard Fleetwood (*The Reasonablenes ... Fines ...*)

BURROUGHS, William S. [1914–, US novelist and wanderer]
William Lee (*Junkie: Confessions of an Unredeemed Drug Addict*)

BURROW, Sir James [1701–82, English barrister and editor of law reports]
J. B. (*A Few Thoughts upon Pointing*)
A Member of the Royal Society and the Society of Antiquaries (*A Few Anecdotes and Observations*)

BURT, Edward [d. 1755, British soldier]
A Gentleman in the North of Scotland
(*Letters from a Gentleman in the North of Scotland*)

BURT, Katherin Newlin [1882–?, US novelist]
Rebecca Scarlett (*The Monkey's Tail*)

BURT, William [1778–1826, English solicitor and writer]
Amicus Patriae (*Twelve Rambles in London*)
Danmoniensis (*Desultory Reflections on Banks in General*)

BURTHOGGE, Richard [1638–94, English physician, philosopher and theologian]
A Protestant Person of Quality (*Prudential Reasons for Repealing the Penal Laws*)

BURTON, Edward [1794–1836, English cleric and writer]
Verus (*An Address to his Fellow Countrymen*)

BURTON, Henry [1578–1648, English cleric and polemicist]
A Witnesse of Jesus Christ (*Replie to a Relation of the Conference between William Laude and Mr Fisher, Jesuit*)

BURTON, John [1696–1771, English cleric and classical scholar]
A Commissioner (*The Present State of Navigation on the Thames*)
Phileleutherus Londinensis (*Remarks on Dr K ...'s Speech*)

BURTON, John [1710–71, English physician and antiquary]
An Englishman (*A Genuine and True Journal of an Englishman*)

BURTON, John Hill [1809–81, Scottish lawyer, historian and biographer]
Historian; An Old Tramp (both used in *Blackwood's Magazine*)
A Practical Hand (*Convicts*)
Rev. James White (*The Eighteen Christian Centuries*; *A History of England*; *A History of France*)

BURTON, Philip [1746–1806, English writer]
An Englishman (*Speculum Britannicum*)

BURTON, Sir Richard Francis [1821–90, English explorer, orientalist and scholar]
Frank Baker, D. O. M. (*Stone Talk*)
a F. R. G. S. (*Wanderings in West Africa from Liverpool to Fernando Po*)
Outidanos (*Priapeia*)

BURTON, Robert [1577–1640, English cleric]
Democritus Junior (*The Anatomy of Melancholy*)

BURTON, Warren [1800–66, US cleric]
One who Went to it (*The District School as it Was*)

BURTON, William Evans [1804–60, English actor and playwright – lived mostly in USA]
A Cape Codder (in *Bentley's Miscellany*)

BURY, Arthur [1624–1713, English cleric and theologian]
A True Son of the Church of England (*The Naked Gospel*)

BURY, Lady Charlotte Susan Maria [1775–1861, English novelist and poet]
A Flirt (*The History of a Flirt, Related by Herself*)
A Lady (*Poems on Several Occasions*; *Suspiriun Sanctorum*)
A Lady of Rank (*The Murdered Queen or, Caroline of Brunswick*)

BUSH, Charles Christmas [1885–1973, English novelist and crime writer]
Christopher Bush (*The Case of the Careless Thief*; *The Case of the Murdered Major*)
Michael Home (*City of the Soul*; *That Was Yesterday*)

BUSH, George [1796–1859, US cleric and religious writer]
Compaginator (*The Heresy of a Professional One-Man Ministry*; *Priesthood and Clergy Unknown to Christianity*; *The Question of Priesthood and Clergy*)

BUSHBY, Henry Jeffreys [1820–1903, English barrister and writer]
A Non-Combatant (*A Month in the Camp Before Sebastopol*)

BUSHNELL, Wiliam H. [1829–99, US lawyer, poet and writer]
Frank Webber (*Prairie Fire*)

BUSK, Hans [1815–82, English lawyer and writer on military and nautical subjects]
Beaujolais (*Maiden-Hours and Maiden-Wiles*)
Paul Cypher (*History of the Hundred of Rowell*)
A Senior Member of the Corporation (*A Sketch of the Origin ... of the New England Company*)

BUSK, Rachel Harriette [1831–1907, English writer and translator of folk-tales]
Roman Correspondent of the 'Westminster Review' (*Contemporary Annals of Rome*)

BUSSY, Dorothy [d. 1960, English novelist and translator; sister of Lytton Strachey]
Olivia (*Olivia*)

BUTLER, Alban [1710–73, English Catholic priest; compiler of *Lives of the Saints*]
A Gentleman (*Remarks on the First Two Volumes of the Late Lives of the Popes*)

BUTLER, Arthur John [1844–1910, English publisher, Italian scholar and alpinist]
One of the Old Guard (in *Cornhill Magazine*)

BUTLER, Benjamin Franklin [1818–93, US lawyer, soldier and politician]
Marcus (*Remarks on Private Banking*)

BUTLER, Constance [1892–?, English writer]
Violet Kazarine (*Poor Fish*; *Five Sisters*)

BUTLER, Gwendoline [1922–, English mystery novelist]
Jennie Melville (*Axwater*; *Dragon's Eye*)

BUTLER, John [1717–1802, English cleric and writer; Bishop of Hereford]
A Country Clergyman (*The Extent and Limits of the subjection due to Princes*)
A Whig (*An Address to the Cocoa-Tree*; *An Answer to the Cocoa-Tree*)

BUTLER, Joseph [1692–1752, English cleric and theologian; Bishop of Durham]
A Gentleman in Gloucestershire (*Several Letters to the Rev. Dr Clarke*)
A Young Clergyman (*A Letter of Thanks to the Rev. Dr Hare*)

BUTLER, Nicholas Murray [1862–1947, US philosopher and educationalist]
Cosmos (*The Basis of Durable Peace*)

BUTLER, Samuel [1612–80, English poet; author of *Hudibras*]
Mercurius Civicus (*A Letter from Mercurius Civicus to Mercurius Rusticus*)

BUTLER, Samuel [1774–1839, English cleric and classical scholar; Bishop of Lichfield]
Eubulus (*A Letter to Philograntus*; *Thoughts on ... Academic Education*)

BUTLER, Samuel [1835–1902, English writer, painter and musician; author of *Erewhon*]
Cellarius (*Darwin among Machines*)
The late John Pickard Owen; William Bickersteth Owen (both used in *The Fair Haven*)

BUTLER, William Francis [1838–1910, Irish soldier – husband of painter Elizabeth Thompson]
An Old Soldier (*The Invasion of England*)

BUTT, Isaac [1813–79, Irish lawyer and nationalist]
Cornelius O'Brien; Anthony Poplar (both used in *Dublin University Magazine*)
Edward Stevenson O'Brien (in *Dublin University Magazine* and for *Chapters of a College Romance*)

BUTTERWORTH, Frank Nestle [fl. 1930, English writer]
Peter Blundell (*The City of Many Waters*; *The Sin of Godfrey Neil*; *Little Brown Baby*)

BUTTERWORTH, James [1771–1837, English historian and Lancashire dialect poet]
Paul Bobbin (*A Dish of Hodge Podge*; *A Sequel to the Lancashire Dialect*)

BUTTERWORTH, John [1727–1803, English Baptist cleric]
Christophilus (*A Serious Address to Dr Priestley*)

BUTTERWORTH, Michael [1924–, English romance and mystery writer]
Sara Kemp (*No Escape*; *The Lure of Sweet Death*)
Carola Salisbury (*Dark Inheritance*; *Shadowed Spring*)

BUXTON, Anne [fl. 1970, English romantic novelist]
Anne Maybury (*Moonlit Door*; *Walk in the Paradise Garden*)
Katherine Troy (*Whisper in the Dark*; *Falcon's Shadow*)

BUXTON, Bertha H. [1884–81, English writer for children of German parentage]
Auntie Bee (*More Dolls*)

BUXTON, Henry John Wilmot [fl. 1865, English cleric]
An Oxonian (*Poems*; *Rosabella – A Doll's Christmas Story*)

BYERLEY, Thomas [d. 1826, English journalist]
Stephen Collet (*Relics of Literature*)
Reuben Percy (*The Percy Anecdotes*; *London or, Interesting Memorials*)

BYERS, Samuel Hawkins Marshall [1838–1933, US soldier and poet]
An American Resident (*Switzerland*)

BYLES, Sir John Barnard [1801–84, English jurist]
A Barrister (*Sophisms of Free-Trade*)

BYNNER, Harold Witter [1881–1968, US poet, parodist and writer]
Emanuel Morgan (*Pins for Wings*; *Spectra*)

BYRNE, John K. [1926–, Irish playwright]
Hugh Leonard (*Patrick Pearse Motel*; *Stephen D.*)

BYRNE, Mrs William Pitt [fl. 1856, English illustrator and writer – daughter of Hans Busk above]
The Writer Behind the Grilles (*Flemish Interiors*)

BYROM, John [1692–1763, English poet; invented a system of shorthand]
John Shadow (in *The Spectator*)

BYRON, George Gordon [1788–1824, 6th Baron Byron; poet and romantic]
Horace Hornem (*The Waltz, an Apostrophic Poem*)
A Noble Author (*Hours of Idleness*)
Quevedo Redivivus (*The Vision of Judgment*)

BYRON, Robert [1905–41, English journalist and traveller]
*Richard Waughburton (*Innocence and Design*)

C

CABLE, Sir James [1920–, English writer]
Grant Hugo (*Britain in Tomorrow's World*)

CADELL, Violet Elizabeth [1903–, English romantic novelist]
Harriet Ainsworth (*Consider the Lilies*; *Death Among Friends*)

CADOGAN, William [1711–97, English physician & medical writer]
A Physician (*An Essay upon Nursing*)

CAFFYN, Kathleen [1853–1926, Irish novelist]
Iota (*A Yellow Aster*; *Mary Mirrilies*)

CAHNAC, J. [fl. 1819, English writer]
Peregrine Prynne (*Histriomastrix or, The Untrussing of the Drury Lane Squad*)

CAIRD, Alice Mona [1855–1932, English novelist]
G. Noel Hatton (*A Romance of the Moors*; *Beyond the Pale*)

CAIRNES, William Elliot [1862–1902, English writer on military matters]
A British Officer (*An Absent Minded War*; *Social Life in the British Army*)
A Soldier (in *MacMillan's Magazine*)

CALAMY, Edmund [1600–66, English Presbyterian cleric]
*Smectymnuus (*An Answer to a Book etc.*; *Smectymnuus Redivivus*)

CALDER, John [1733–1815, Scottish cleric in London]
Annotator (in *The Tatler*)

CALDERON, George Leslie [1868–1915, English playwright and writer]
G. L. Cotel (in *Temple Bar*)

CALDERWOOD, David [1575–1650, Scottish Presbyterian cleric, historian and controversialist]
Edwardus Didoclavius (*Altare Damascenum*)
Hieronymus Philadelphus (*De Regimine Ecclesiae Scoticanae Brevis Relatio*)

CALDWELL, Janet Miriam Taylor [1900–85, English-born US novelist]
Taylor Caldwell (*Captains and Kings*; *Dynasty of Death*)
Max Reiner (*Time No Longer*)

CALDWELL, Joseph [1773–1835, US academic]
Carlton (*Letters of Carlton*)

CALDWELL, Robert [1843–1909, Scottish-born Australian writer]
Andrew Cochrane (*The Pioneers*; *A Vision of Toil*)

CALEY, John [1763–1834, English public servant and archaeologist]
An Illused Candidate (*Indignant Rhymes*)

CALHOUN, John Caldwell [1782–1850, US politician; Secretary of State 1844/45]
Onslow (*Onslow in Reply to Patrick Henry*)

CALIFF, Joseph Mark [1843–1914, US civil war soldier]
An Officer of the Regiment (*Record of ... Seventh Regiment, United States Colored Troops etc.*)

CALLCOTT, Maria, Lady [1785–1842, English traveller and writer for children]
Little Arthur (*Little Arthur's History of England*)

CALLENDER, James Thomson [d. 1803, English journalist – worked in USA from 1794]
Tom Callender Esq., Citizen of the World (*Letters to Alexander Hamilton, King of the Feds*)

CALLWELL, Charles Edward [1859–1928, British general and military writer]
*A Military Contributor (in *Blackwood's Magazine*)

CALVERLEY, Charles Stuart [1831–84, English poet, humorist and satirist; his original surname was Blayds but he changed it in 1852]
C. S. C. (*Fly Leaves; Verses and Translations*)

CALVERT, Mrs Caroline Louisa Waring [1834–72, Australian botanist and writer]
An Australian Lady (*Gertrude the Emigrant*)

CALVERT, George Henry [1803–89, US writer]
An American (*Scenes and Thoughts in Europe*)

CAMBRELING, Churchill C. [1786–1862, US merchant, diplomat and politician]
One of the People (*An Examination of the New Tariff Proposed by Henry Baldwin a Member of Congress*)

CAMERON, Elizabeth Jane [1910–76, Scottish writer for children]
Jane Duncan (*My Friend Monica; My Friends the MacLeans*)
Janet Sandison (*Jean Towards another Day; Jean at Noon*)

CAMERON, John [1724–99, Scottish Presbyterian cleric]
A Berean (*The Doctrine of Orthodoxy*)
Philalethes (*The Catholic Christian Defended*)
Philander (in the *Theological Repository*)
Theophilus Philander (*The Catholic Christian*)

CAMERON, Lou [1924–, US western novelist]
Justin Adams (*Chains*)

CAMERON, William Ernest [fl. 1918, Scottish barrister and writer]
Mark Allerton (*Let Justice be Done; The Case of Richard Eden*)

CAMPBELL, Alexander [1764–1824, Scottish musician, physician and writer]
A Student of Medicine in the University of Edinburgh (*Odes and Miscellaneous Poems*)
Timothy Twig Esq. (*The Guinea Note*)

CAMPBELL, Mrs Alice Ormond [fl. 1940, English crime writer]
Martin Ingram (*Bloodstained Toy; Veiled Murder*)

CAMPBELL, Archibald [d. 1744, Scottish exiled controversial cleric]
A Gentleman of that Country (*Queries to the Presbyterians of Scotland*)
Philalethes (*A Letter to the Archbishop of Canterbury*)

CAMPBELL, Lord Colin [1853–95, Scottish barrister]
Dalriad (*The Crofter in History*)

CAMPBELL, Sir George [1824–92, Scottish lawyer, civil servant in India and Liberal MP]
A Civilian (letters to *The Times*)
Economist (letters to *The Mofussilite*]
Judex (in *The Times*)

CAMPBELL, George Douglas [1823–1900, 8th Duke of Argyll; Whig politician, writer on religion, science and public affairs]
A Peer's Son (*A Letter to the Peers*)

CAMPBELL, George Grenville [1850–1915, English mariner]
A Naval Nobody (in *MacMillan's Magazine*)

CAMPBELL, Gertrude E. [1861–1911, Irish novelist, art critic and writer]
G. E. Brunefille (*Topo – a Tale*)

CAMPBELL, Ignatius Royston Dunnachie [1901–57, South African poet]
Roy Campbell (*The Flaming Terrapin; The Georgiad*)

CAMPBELL, John [1708–75, Scottish historian and biographer]
Edward Brown Esq. (*The Travels and Adventures of Edward Brown Esq.*)
E; X (both used in *Biographia Britannica*)
An English Merchant (*The Spanish Empire in America*)
A Gentleman of the Inner Temple (*The Case of the Opposition Impartially Stated*)
A Gentleman who Resided Five Years on the Island (*An Account of the White Hering Industry*)
M. Ludovicus (*A Particular but Melancholy Account of the Great Hardships ... the Common Women of the Town are Plunged into*)
A Member of the Community and a Sincere Friend to his Country (*The Nationalization Bill Confuted*)
The Prince of the Infernal Regions (*A Letter to a Spiritual Lord*)

CAMPBELL, John Francis [1822–85, Scottish Gaelic scholar; inventor of the meteorological sunshine recorder]
A Traveller (*Frost and Fire, Natural Engines, Tool Marks and Chips*)

CAMPBELL, John Poage [1767–1814, US cleric]
Vindex (*An Answer to Stone's reply*)

CAMPBELL, John Wood [1910–71, US science-fiction writer]
Arthur McCann (used for scientific journalism)
Don. A. Stuart (*Twilight*)
Karl Van Campen (in *Astounding Science Fiction* magazine)

CAMPBELL, Robert [d. 1832, English mariner]
A Midshipman of the Last Century (in *United Service* magazine)

CAMPBELL, Robert Wright [1927–, US writer]
F. G. Clinton (*The Tin Cop*)

CAMPBELL, Thomas [1777–1844, Scottish poet, editor of *New Monthly Magazine*, 1820–30]
Lorenzo Lanksides (in *New Monthly Magazine*)

CAMPBELL, Walter Stanley [1887–1957, US writer]
Stanley Vestal (*Sitting Bull, Champion of the Sioux; New Sources of Indian History 1850–91*)

CAMPBELL, William Edward March [1893–1954, US businessman and novelist]
William March (*The Looking Glass; The Tallons; Come in at the Door*)

CAMPLING, F. Knowles [d. 1940, English writer for boys]
Eric Wood (in *Chums*)

CANADAY, John Edwin [1907–85, US mystery writer]
Matthew Head (*The Devil in the Bush; Congo Venus*)

CANNING, George [1770–1827, British statesman and prime minister]
B; *Gregory Griffin (both used in *Microcosm*)

CANNING, Josiah D. [1816–92, US poet]
The Peasant Bard (*The Harp and the Plow*)

CANNING, Victor [1911–86, English mystery novelist]
Alan Gould (*Mercy Lane; Atlantic Company*)

CANNON, Charles James [1800–60, US poet and writer]
Grandfather Greenway (*Ravellings from the Web of Life*)
A Proser (*Poems*)

CANT, Andrew [1590–1663, Scottish cleric; Principal of Edinburgh University]
One of the Suffering Clergy There (*A Sermon Preached at Edinburgh*)

CANTON, John [1718–72, English natural philosopher – came from humble origins]
Amicus; Indagator; Noncathoni; Thonininca; X. X. (all used in *Gentleman's Magazine*)

CAPEL, Arthur [1610–49, Baron Capel; royalist in Civil War – beheaded at the Tower of London]
A Person of Honour and Piety (*Daily Observations and Meditations*)

CAPELL, Edward [1713–81, English Shakespearian scholar]
E. C. (*Notes and Various Readings to Shakespeare*; *Notitia Dramatica or, Tables of Ancient Plays*)

CAPERN, Edward [1819–94, English poet and postman]
The Bideford Postman (*Ballads and Songs*; *Poems*)

CAPES, John Moore [1812–89, English journalist]
Herder; A Late Member of the University of Oxford (both used in *The Rambler*)
A Suffering Mistress (in *Cornhill Magazine*)

CAPLIN, Alfred Gerald [1909–79, US cartoonist]
Al Capp (*The Life and Times of the Shmoo*)

CAPPE, Newcome [1733–1800, English Unitarian cleric]
A Doughty Champion in Heavy Armour (in the *York Chronicle*)
A Warm Wellwisher to the Interests of Genuine Christianity (*An Alphabetical Explication of Scripture*; *A Selection of Psalms for Social Worship*)

CARACCIOLI, Charles [fl. 1766, English schoolmaster and topographer]
The Master of the Grammar School at Arundel (*Antiquities of Arundel*)

CARAS, Roger Andrew [1928–, US writer]
Roger Sarac (*The Throwbacks*)

CARD, Henry [1779–1844, English cleric, poet and writer]
A Minister of the Establishment (*A Letter to the Duke of Wellington*)

CARDELL, William S. [d. 1828, US publisher]
John Franklin Jones (*Analytical Spelling Book*)

CARDEN, William Thomas [1888–1924, US lawyer]
Major Tom Noodle (*The Squash Family*)

CARDEW, Francis Gordon [1862–?, English soldier]
An Indian Correspondent (in *Blackwood's Magazine*)

CAREY, David [1782–1824, Scottish journalist, novelist and writer]
Chrononhotonthologos (*Ins and Outs*)

CAREY, George Saville [1743–1807, English dramatist, songwriter and failed actor]
Paul Tell-Truth (*Liberty Chastised or, Patriotism in Chains*)

CAREY, Henry [1596–1661, 2nd Earl of Monmouth]
A Person of Honour (*Maximes of State and Government*)

CAREY, Henry [1685–1743, English poet, dramatist and musician]
Benjamin Bounce Esq. (*The Tragedy of Chrononhotonthologus*)
Signor Carini (*The Dragon of Wantley*)
J. W. (*Pudding and Dumpling Burnt to Pot*)
John Single of Grey's Inn (*Cupid and Hymen, a Voyage to the Islands of Love*)

CAREY, Henry Charles [1793–1879, US political economist]
A Citizen of Burlington (*Beauties of the Monopoly System in New Jersey*)

CAREY, Mathew [1760–1839, Irish bookseller and political pamphleteer – emigrated to USA]
Caius (in the *Public Advertiser*)
A Catholic Layman (*Letters on Religious Persecution*)

A Citizen of Philadelphia (*Common Sense Address to the Citizens of the United States*)

A Citizen of the World (*A Fragment Addressed to the Sons and Daughters of Humanity*)

A Clergyman of the Church of England (*Vindiciae Hibernicae*)

Colbert (*Political Economy*)

Hamilton (*The Dissolution of the Union*)

Jefferson (*Examination of the Charleston Memorial*)

An Octogenarian of Philadelphia (*The Querist*)

A Pennsylvanian (*The Crisis: a Solemn Appeal to the President; Twenty-One Golden Rules to Depress Agriculture; A Warning Voice to the Cotton and Tobacco Planters*)

CAREY, William Paulet [1759–1839, English engraver, art critic and writer]
Scriblerus Murtough O'Pindar (*Both Sides of the Gutter*)

CARKESSE, James [fl. 1769, English rhymester]
The Doctor's Patient Extraordinary (*Lucida Intervalla*)

CARLETON, John William [fl. 1847, English sporting writer]
Craven (in *Bailey's Magazine*)

CARLETON, William [1794–1869, Irish novelist of peasant life and superstitions]
Phedlin M'Fun, Roman Catholic Rector of Ballymacscaltheen (in *Dublin University Magazine*)

CARLILE, James [1784–1854, Scottish cleric and religious writer]
Presbyter (*A Comparative View of the Episcopal ... Forms of Church Government*)

CARLILE, Richard [1790–1843, English radical with republican sympathies]
Philanthropos (*The Character of a Peer; The Character of a Soldier*)

CARLYLE, Alexander [1722–1805, Scottish cleric – minister at Inveresk for 57 years]
A Freeholder (*The Question relating to a Scots Militia*)
O. M. Haberdasher (*Plain Reasons for Removing a Certain Great Man*)

CARLYLE, Thomas [1795–1881, Scottish philosopher, essayist and historian]
Ichneretes (in the *Dumfries and Galloway Courier*)
A Lay-Member of the Church of Scotland (*Letter to the Rev. Robert Burns*)
Pilpay Junior (in *Fraser's Magazine*)

CARLYON, Edward Augustus [1823–74, English-born New Zealand lawyer]
Coelebs (in *MacMillan's Magazine* and for *The Laws and Practice of Whist*)

CARMAN, William Cooper [fl. 1874, US verse writer]
Will Cooper (*Rattling Roaring Rhymes on Mormon Utah*)

CARMICHAEL, Charles Montauban [fl. 1840, English soldier]
An Old Cavalry Officer (*A Rough Sketch of the Irregular Horse of the Bengal Army*)

CARMICHAEL, Montgomery [1857–1936, English diplomat and writer]
Daniel Mauldsley (*The Solitaries of Sambuca*)

CARNE, Elizabeth Catherine Thomas [1817–73, English traveller and author]
John Altrayd Wittitterly (*Three Months' Rest at Pau in 1859*)

CARNEGIE, Lady Helena M. [1865–1943, English writer]
*Violet Jacob (*The Northern Lights*)

CARNEGIE, Raymond Alexander [1920–, Scottish writer]
Sacha Carnegie (*Banners of Courage; Banners of War*)

CARNEGIE, William [fl. 1907, English sporting writer]
Moorman (*Practical Game-Preserving*)

CARPENTER, Edward [1844–1929, English
social reformer]
J. H. Cressingham (in the *University
Magazine and Free Review*)
Hevellyn (in *The Star*)

CARPENTER, Lant [1780–1840, English
Unitarian – lost overboard on
Mediterranean voyage]
The Unitarian (*The Unitarian's Appeal*)

CARPENTER, Miss Mary [1807–77, English
educational and social reformer –
daughter of Lant Carpenter above]
A Prison Matron (*Female Life in Prison*)
A Worker (*Ragged Schools*)

CARPENTER, Stephen Cullen [d. 1820,
Irish-born US journalist]
Donald Campbell (*A Journey Overland to
India*)

CARPENTER, William [1797–1874, English
journalist and political pamphleteer]
Common Sense (*The Earth not a Globe; Sir
Isaac Newton's Astronomy Examined*)

CARR, Dabney [1743–73, American politician
and writer]
Dr Cecil (in the *Old Bachelor* journal in
1812)

CARR, John Dickson [1905–77, US journalist
and crime writer]
Carr (or Carter) Dickson (*The Plague Court
Murders; The Red Widow Murders*)
Roger Fairbairn (*Devil Kinsmere*)

CARR, Margaret [1935–, English crime
writer]
Martin Carroll (*Begotten Murder; Dead
Trouble*)
Carole Kerr (*Not For Sale; A Time to
Surrender*)

CARR, Mildred Emily [1877–?, English
novelist]
Ward Copley (*The Second House; Back from
the Plough; The Man Who Deserted*)

CARR, Terry [1937–87, US science-fiction
writer]
*Norman Edwards (*Invasion from 2500;
Warlord of Kor*)

CARR, William [fl. 1828, English cleric]
A Native of Craven (*The Dialect of Craven,
in the West-Riding of the County of York*)

CARRERAS, Michael [1927–94, English film
producer and scriptwriter]
Henry Younger (*Maniac; The Curse of the
Mummy's Tomb*)

CARRINGTON, Charles Edmund
[1897–1990, English writer]
Charles Edmonds (*A Subaltern's War; T. E.
Lawrence*)

CARROLL, Charles [1737–1832, American
politician – longest surviving signatory to
the Declaration of Independence]
The First Citizen (used for journalism)

CARROLL, John [1735–1815, American
Catholic bishop and federalist]
A Catholic Clergyman (*An Address to Roman
Catholics of USA*)

CARSTARES, William [1649–1715, Scottish
cleric – involved in political intrigue]
A Scots Gentleman (*The Scottish Toleration
Argued*)

CARTER, Elizabeth [1717–1806, English
poet and gifted linguist]
Camilla; Eliza (both used in *Gentleman's
Magazine*)
Chariessa (in *The Rambler*)

CARTER, Felicity Winifred [1906–, English
mystery writer]
Emery Bonett (*Dead Lion; Make Do with
Spring*)

CARTER, Henry [1821–80, English engraver
and newspaper illustrator]
Frank Leslie (in *Ainsworth's Magazine*)

CARTER, John [1748–1817, English
architectural draughtsman]
An Architect (in *Gentleman's Magazine*)

CARTER, John Franklin [1897–1967, US crime writer and novelist]
Diplomat (*The Corpse on the White House Lawn*)
Jay Franklin (*La Guaria – a Biography*; *Death in the Senate*)
'The Unofficial Observer' (*The New Dealers*)

CARTER, Thomas Thellusson [1808–91, English cleric]
An Aged Priest (*The Roman Question*)

CARTLAND, Barbara [1901–, English romantic novelist]
Barbara McCorquodale (*Kiss of Silk*; *Runaway Heart*)

CARTWRIGHT, Frances Dorothy [1780–1863, English poet and translator – niece of John Cartwright below]
His Niece (*Life of Maj. John Cartwright*)

CARTWRIGHT, John [1740–1824, English political reformer, supporter of American independence]
Constitutio (*A Letter to Edmund Burke*)
A Private Gentleman (*The Trident*)

CARVEL, John Lees [1895–1959, Scottish journalist]
Iain C. Lees (*Byways from Tyne to Tay*; *On Foot through Clydesdale*)

CARY, Alice [1820–71, US poet and novelist – collaborated with her sister Phoebe]
Patty Lee (in the *National Era*)

CARY, Arthur Joyce Lunel [1888–1957, Irish poet and novelist]
Thomas Joyce (used for stories in the *Saturday Evening Post*, *Strand Magazine* and *Hutchinson's Magazine*)

CARY, Edward [d. 1711, English Catholic cleric and Jacobite]
Adolphus Brontius (*The Catechist Catechiz'd*)

CARY, Henry [1793–1858, US poet, humorist and writer]
John Waters (in both the *New York American* and *Knickerbocker Magazine*)

CARY, Thomas [1751–1823, Canadian journalist]
Juniolus Canadensis (in the *Quebec Mercury*)

CARY, Thomas Greaves [1791–1859, US lawyer, merchant and writer]
An American (*The Americans Defended*)
A Treasurer of a Corporation (*Profits on Manufactures at Lowell*)

CASELEYR, Camille August Marie [1909–, Belgian academic and writer]
Jack Danvers (*The End of it All*)

CASEY, Elizabeth [1847–94, Irish journalist and novelist]
E. Owens Blackburne (*Illustrious Irishwomen*)

CASS, Lewis [1782–1866, US soldier and statesman]
An American (*France: its King, Court and Government*)
The American Minister at Paris (*An Historical and Statistical History of Candia*)

CASSIDY, Robert John [1880–1948, Australian writer]
Gilrooney (*Chandler of Corralinga*; *The Land of the Starry Cross and other Verses*)

CASTLE, Frank [fl. 1960, US writer]
Steve Thurman (*Night after Night*)

CASWALL, Edward [1814–78, English cleric and hymn writer]
Quiz (*Sketches of Young Ladies*)
Scriblerus Redivivus (*The Art of Pluck*; *The Art of Teaching How to be Plucked*)

CATCHPOLE, William L. [fl. 1930, English crime writer]
Roland Howard (in *Detective Weekly* magazine)

CATHERALL, Arthur [1906–80, English writer for children]
J. Baltimore (*Singapore Sari*)
A. R. Channel (*The Tunnel Busters*; *Jungle Rescue*)
Dan Corby (*Lost off the Grand Banks*; *Thunder Dam*)

Peter Hallard (*Barrier Reef Bandits*; *Lost in Lapland*)
Trevor Maine (*Blue Veil and Black Gold*)
Lionel Peters (*Reindeer Rescue*)
Margaret Ruthin (*Jungle Gypsy*; *Secret of the Shetlands*)

CATTELL, Edward James [1856–1938, US journalist, novelist and statistician]
Americanus (in *Cornhill Magazine*)
Francis H. Hardy (*The Mills of God*; *To The Healing of the Sea*)

CATTON, James Alfred Henry [fl. 1910, English sporting writer]
Tityrus (*The Rise of the Leaguers*)

CAUNTER, John Hobart [1794–1851, English cleric, novelist and poet]
A Late Resident in the East (*The Cadet*)
A London Clergyman (*Posthumous Records of a London Clergyman*)

CAUTE, John David [1936–, English novelist and historian }
John Salisbury (*The Baby-Sitters*; *Moscow Gold*)

CAVANNA, Betty [1909–, US writer for children]
Betsy Allen (*The Riddle in Red*; *The Silver Secret*)
Elizabeth Headley (*Catchpenny Street*; *Toujours Diane*)

CAVE, Edward [1691–1754, English founding-editor of *Gentleman's Magazine*; artist who signed his work 'R. Newton']
Sylvanus Urban (in *Gentleman's Magazine*)

CAVE-BROWN, John [1818–98, English cleric]
An Indian Chaplain (*Plain Words for Soldiers*)

CAVENDISH, George [1500–61, English biographer and friend of Cardinal Wolsey]
One of his Owne Servants being his Gentleman Usher (*The Negotiations of Thomas Woolsey*)

CAVENDISH, William [1592–1676, Duke of Newcastle, poet and expert horseman – a major figure in the English Civil War]
A Person of Honor (*The Country Captaine*)

CAVERHILL, William Melville [1910–83, English dramatist and songwriter]
Alan Melville (*Week-End at Thrackley*; *Myself When Young*; *Gnomes and Gardens*)

CAWDELL, James M. [d. 1842, Canadian journalist]
Roseharp (in *Fothergill's Weekly Register*)

CAWDREY, Daniel [1588–1664, English Presbyterian]
An Earnest Well-Wisher to the Truth (*Vindiciae Clavium*)

CAWTHORN, James [1929–, English illustrator and science-fiction writer]
Philip James (*The Distant Suns*)

CEBULASH, Mel [1937–, US writer for children]
Ben Farrell (*Nancy and Jeff*)
Glen Harlan (*Peter the Pup*)
Jared Jansen (*Penny the Poodle*)

CECIL, Robert Arthur Talbot Gascoyne [1830–1903, 3rd Marquess of Salisbury; statesman and prime minister]
Anti-Cotton (in the *Quarterly Review*)

CELESIA, Mrs Dorothea [1738–90, English poet and writer]
A Lady (*Almida*)

CENTLIVRE, Susannah [1667– 1723, English actress and dramatist]
Susanna Carroll (*The Perjured Husband*)
A Lady of Great Britain (*An Epistle to the King of Sweden*)

CHADWICK, Henry [1824–1908, English-born sportsman in USA and sports journalist]
Chad (*The Baseball Player's Book of Reference*)
Old Chalk (in *The Union*)

CHALKLEY, Alan [1918–93, English journalist]
Nicholas Dutt (in the *Far Eastern Economic Review*)

CHALLANS, Mary [1905–83, English novelist – lived in South Africa]
Mary Renault (*The Last of the Wine*; *The King Must Die*)

CHALLEN, James [1802–78, US cleric]
Philos (used for journalism)

CHALLONER, Richard [1691–1781, English Roman Catholic bishop and writer]
A Convert (*The Grounds of the Old Religion*)
Philalethes (*A Specimen of the Spirit of Dissenting Teachers*)
R ... C ... (*The Catholick Christian instructed in the Sacraments, Sacrifice, Ceremonies etc.*)
R. D. V. A. (*Instructions and Meditations on the Jubilee*)

CHALMERS, Alexander [1759–1834, Scottish journalist and publisher]
Amerus; A Bartholomew-Lane Man; A Churchman; Ferdinando Fidget; A Methodist; No Genius; Old Cayen; Old Simon; Secunder (all used in *Gentleman's Magazine*)
Senex (*in St James Chronicle*)

CHALMERS, George [1742–1825, Scottish historian and writer on politics]
Another Lawyer (*Thoughts on the Present Crisis of our Domestic Affairs*)
An Irish Gentleman, a Member of the Whig Club (*Defense of Opposition ... in Irish Affairs*)
Francis Oldys MA (*The Life of Thomas Paine*)

CHALONER, John Seymour [1924–, English publisher and writer for children]
Jon Chalon (*Flying Steamroller*; *Green Bus*)

CHAMBERLAIN, Joseph [1836–1914, British statesman and social reformer]
A Radical (in *Fortnightly Review*)

CHAMBERLEN, Peter [1601–83, English physician and midwifery pioneer]
A Ghost in a White Sheet of Paper (*A Speech Visibly Spoken*)

CHAMBERLIN, Joseph Edgar [1851–1935, US journalist and editor]
Listener (*John Brown*)
Nomad (in the *Boston Transcript*)

CHAMBERS, Aidan [1934–, English bookseller and writer for children]
Malcolm Blacklin (used when editing)

CHAMBERS, George [1786–1866, US jurist]
A Descendant (*A Tribute to ... Irish and Scotch Early Settlers etc.*)

CHAMBERS, Jessie [d. 1944, English friend of D. H. Lawrence]
E. T. (*D. H. Lawrence: a Personal Record*)

CHAMBERS, Sir William [1726–96, British architect and furniture designer]
Tan Chau Qua of Quang Chew Fu, Gent. (*An Explanatory Discourse*)

CHAMIER, Frederick [1796–1870, English novelist and naval historian]
A Captain in the Navy (*The Life of a Sailor*)

CHAMPLIN, Edwin Ross [1854–1928, US poet, journalist and editor]
Clarence Fairfield (*Lovers Lyrics and Other Songs*; *At the Sign of the Song*)

CHANCE, John Newton [1911–83, English crime writer]
John Drummond (*The House on the River*; *The Town of Shadows*)
John Lymington (*The Night of the Big Heat*; *The Green Drift*)
David C. Newton (*The Black Ghost*; *The Dangerous Road*)

CHANDLER, Arthur Bertram [1912–, English mariner and science-fiction writer]
Andrew Dunstan (for his work published in Australia)
George Whitley (in *Astounding Science Fiction* magazine)

CHANDLER, Peleg Whitman [1816–89, US lawyer]
A Layman (*Observations on the Authenticity of the Gospels*)

CHAPIN, Alonzo Bowen [1808–58, US cleric, lawyer and journalist]
Juris Consultus (in *Knickerbocker Magazine*)

CHAPMAN, Edwin O. [fl. 1879, US journalist and writer for boys]
Uncle John (in *Our Boy's Own Stories*)

CHAPMAN, John [1707–84, English cleric, antiquarian and controversialist]
Philobiblicus Cantabrigiensis (*Remarks on a Letter to Dr Waterland*)
A Priest of the University of Cambridge (*Remarks on a book ... Christianity as Old as the Creation*)

CHAPMAN, John Stanton Higham [1891–1972, English-born US novelist]
*Maristan Chapman (*Flood in Glen Hazard*; *Mystery on the Mississippi*)
*Jane Selkirk (*Treasure Box Mystery*)

CHAPMAN, Mary Frances [1838–84, English novelist]
J. Calder Ayrton (*A Scotch Wooing*; *Gerald Marlowe's Wife*)
Frances Meredith (*Mary Bertrand*)

CHAPMAN, Mary Ilsley [1895–, US novelist]
*Maristan Chapman (see J. S. H. Chapman above)
*Jane Selkirk (*Treasure Box Mystery*)

CHAPMAN, Nathaniel [1780–1853, US physician and medical writer]
Falkland (in the *Philadelphia Portfolio*)

CHAPMAN, Raymond [1924–, Welsh academic and historian]
Simon Nash (*Dead Woman's Ditch*; *Unhallowed Murder*)

CHAPPELL, George Shepard [1878–1946, US writer]
Dr Walter E. Traprock (*The Cruise of the Kawa*; *My Northern Exposure*)

CHAPPELL, William [1582–1649, English cleric – imprisoned during the English Civil War]
Phil. Christianus (*The Preacher: or the Art and Method of Preaching*)

CHARBONNEAU, Louis Henry [1924–, US journalist and science-fiction writer]
Carter Travis Young (*The Savage Plain*; *Winchester Quarantine*)

CHARD, Judy [1916–, English romantic novelist]
Lyndon Chase (*Tormentil*)

CHARLES, Mrs Elizabeth [1828–96, English writer of quasi-religious novels]
Mrs Kitty Trevylyan (*Diary of Mrs Kitty Trevylyan*)
Two of Themselves (*Chronicles of the Schonberg-Cotta Family*)

CHARLES, Emily Thornton [fl. 1876, US poet]
Emily Hawthorne (*Hawthorne Blossoms*)

CHARLESWORTH, John [1782–1864, English cleric in Suffolk and London]
A Clergyman (*Providential Deliverance*)

CHARLESWORTH, Maria Louisa [1819–80, English writer of religious fiction]
A Clergyman's Daughter (*The Female Visitor to the Poor*)

CHARLETON, Walter [1619–1707, English physician, wrote on medical and antiquarian topics]
A Loyal Subject (*An Imperfect Portrait of Charles II*)

CHARLEY, Sir William Thomas [1833–1904, English lawyer and writer]
A Member of the Council of National Union (*Conservative Legislation for the Working Classes*)

CHARLTON, Robert M. [1807–54, US lawyer]
A Georgia Lawyer (in *Knickerbocker Magazine*)

CHARTERIS, Archibald Hamilton
[1835–1908, Scottish theologian]
*Hamilton Muir (*Glasgow in 1901*)

CHASE, Drummond Percy [1820–1902,
English cleric and pamphleteer]
The Principal of St Mary Hall, Oxford
(*University Tests*)
The Senior Proctor (*The University Pulpit*)

CHASE, Philander [1775–1852, US cleric]
The President of Kenyon College (*Facts ...
on the Theological Seminary of Ohio*)

CHATELAIN, Clara [1807–76, English
writer of songs and short stories; of
French parentage]
Leopold Wray (in *Reynold's Miscellany*)

CHATER, John [fl. 1767, English writer]
Ignotus (*Another High Road to Hell*)

CHATFIELD, Edward [1800–39, English
artist and writer]
Echion (in *New Monthly Magazine*)

**CHATTERTON, Lady Henrietta
Georgiana Lascelles** [1806–76, English
poet, traveller and writer]
Aunt Dorothy (*Aunt Dorothy's Tales*)

CHATTERTON, Thomas [1752–70, English
precocious poet and writer]
Decimus (in the *Middlesex Journal*)
Probus (in the *Political Register*)
Thomas Rowley (in *Town and Country
Magazine*)

CHATTO, William Andrew [1799–1864,
English tea merchant and writer]
P. (Payne) Fisher (*The Angler's Souvenir*)
Joseph Fume (*A Paper on Tobacco*)
Stephen Oliver (*The Old English Squire*;
Rambles in Northumberland; *Scenes and
Recollections of Fly-Fishing*)
W. A. C. (*The Fisher's Garland for 1835*)

CHAUNCY, Charles [1705–87, American
cleric and theologian]
Anti-Enthusiasticus (*The Wonderful
Narrative*)
Canonicus (*A Letter to George Whitefield*)

A Gentleman in Boston (*A Letter from a
Gentleman in Boston to Mr George
Wishart*)
K. L. (*Letter to the Rev. Mr George
Whitefield*)
A Lover of Truth and Peace (*The Late
Religious Commotions in New England*)

CHEETHAM, James [1773–1810, US
journalist]
A Citizen of New York (*An Answer to
Alexander Hamilton's Letter concerning the
Public Conduct and Character of John
Adams*; *A Narrative of the Suppression by
Col. Burr of the History of the
Administration of John Adams*)
Lysander (*Annals of the Corporation*)
Mercer (*A Letter Concerning the Ten Pound
Court*)
Politicus (*Observations on the Conduct of
Governor Lewis*)
Warren (*An Antidote to John Wood's Poison*)

CHEEVER, George Barrell [1807–90, US
cleric and religious writer]
A Lover of Cudworth and Truth (*Cudworth
Defended and Unitarianism*)
One of the People (*The Republic or the
Oligarchy?*)
A Pilgrim (*Wanderings of a Pilgrim ... Mont
Blanc and the Jungfrau Alp*)

CHEEVER, Henry Theodore [1814–97, US
cleric]
Major Marble (*The Whale and its Captors*)

CHELTNAM, Charles Smith [1822–?,
English dramatist and writer]
Captain Shandon (in *Belgravia Magazine*)

CHERMSIDE, Richard Seymour Conway
[1823–67, English cleric]
A Son-in-Ditto (in *MacMillan's Magazine*)

CHESBRO, George Clark [1940–, US
writer]
David Cross (*Chant*)

CHESNEY, Charles Cornwallis [1826–76,
Irish soldier and military writer]
A Military Critic (in *MacMillan's Magazine*)

CHESNEY, Sir George Tomkyns [1830–95, British general, engineer, writer and novelist]
A Contributor to 'Blackwood' (*The Fall of England?*)
A Volunteer (*Battle of Dorking – Reminiscences of a Volunteer*)

CHESNEY, Marion [1936–, Scottish romantic novelist]
Helen Crampton (*The Marquis Takes a Bride*)
Ann Fairfax (*My Dear Duchess*)
Jennie Tremaine (*Lady Anne's Deception*)

CHESTER, Joseph Lemuel [1821–82, US journalist and genealogist]
Julian Cramer (used for journalism)

CHESTERTON, Mrs Cecil (Ada Elizabeth) [1870–1962, English journalist and philanthropist]
John K. Protheroe (*Memoir of Cecil Chesterton*; *Diamond Cut Diamond*; *With Links of Steel*)

CHETHAM, James [1640–92, English writer on angling]
A Lover of Angling (*The Angler's Vade-Mecum*)

CHETWOOD, William Rufus [d. 1766, English theatre historian and dramatist]
Gargantua Pantagruel (*The Stock-Jobbers or, the Humours of Exchange Alley*)

CHICHESTER, Frederick Richard [1827–53, Earl of Belfast]
Campana (in the *Northern Magazine*)

CHILD, David Lee [1794–1874, US lawyer and journalist]
Probus (*The Texas Revolution*)

CHILD, Sir Josiah [1630–99, English merchant]
Philopatris (*A Treatise wherein it is Demonstrated that the East India Trade is the Most National of all Foreign Trade*)

CHILD, Mrs Lydia Maria [1802–80, US abolitionist, novelist and editor]
An American (*Hobomok*)

A Lady of Massachusetts (*The First Settlers of New England*)

CHILD, Mrs Maria [1797–1877, US writer]
Delafield (in *Arthur's Magazine*)

CHILD, Philip [1898–1978, Canadian novelist]
John Wentworth (*Blow Wind, Come Rack*)

CHILDE, Edward Vernon [1804–61, US journalist – lived in Paris]
A 'States'-Man (letters to *The Times*)

CHILDS, Eleanor Stuart [1876–?, US writer]
Eleanor Stuart (*Stonepastures*; *The Postscript*)

CHIPPERFIELD, Joseph E. [1912–76, English writer for children]
John Eland Craig (*The Dog of Castle Crag*)

CHISHOLM, Hugh [1866–1924, English journalist and editor of *Encyclopaedia Britannica*]
An Oxford BA (in *Fortnightly Review*)

CHISHOLM, Lilian Mary [1906–, English romantic novelist]
Anne Lorraine (*I Shall Be There*; *I Shall Come Home*)

CHITTENDEN, William Lawrence [1862–1934, US farmer, businessman and poet]
Larry Chittenden (*Bermuda Verses*)

CHITTY, Edward [1804–63, English lawyer and legal writer]
Theophilus South (*The Fly-Fisher's Text Book*)

CHITTY, Sir Thomas Willes [1926–, English novelist]
Thomas Hinde (*Sir Henry and Sons*; *Mr Nicholas*)

CHOLMONDELEY, Mary [1859–1925, English novelist]
Pax (in *Temple Bar* and for *The Danvers Jewels*)

CHORLEY, Charles [1810–74, English translator and journalist]
Timothy Tugmutton Esq. (*A Letter Offered to The Times*)

CHORLEY, Henry Fothergill [1808–72, English music critic, novelist and dramatist]
A Begging-Letter Writer; A Mute; Sharp; Tartini's Familiar (all used in *Bentley's Miscellany*)
Paul Bell (*Pomfret*; *Roccabella*)

CHORLEY, John Rutter [1807–67, English railway clerk and writer]
A Believer in Dreams (in *Tait's Edinburgh Magazine*)

CHOVIL, Alfred Harold [1889–?, English novelist]
Peter Brook (*The Tarbrush*; *Fatal Shadows*)

CHRISTIE, Agatha Mary Clarissa [1891–1976, English crime writer]
Agatha Christie Mallowan (*Star over Bethlehem and other Stories*; *Come Tell Me How You Live*)
Mary Westmacott (*Absent in the Spring*; *The Rose and the Yew Tree*)

CHRISTIE, Alexander [1841–95, Scottish seaman and novelist]
Lindsay Anderson (*A Cruise in an Opium Clipper*; *The Story of Allan Gordon*)

CHRISTIE, William [1748–1823, Scottish merchant and Unitarian – emigrated to the USA]
A Protestant Dissenter (*An Essay on Ecclesiastical Establishment*)

CHRISTOPHER, Matthew F. [1917–, US writer for children]
Frederic Martin (*Mystery at Monkey Run*)

CHRISTOPHERS, Samuel Woolcock [1810–89, English cleric]
An Old Cornish Boy (*From Out of the Deeps*)

CHRISTY, David [1802–68, US writer]
An American (*Cotton is King*)

CHUDLEIGH, Lady Mary [1656–1710, English poet and essayist]
M___y C (*The Ladies' Defence*)
Eugenia (*The Female Advocate*)
A Lady of Quality (*The Female Preacher*)

CHURCH, Benjamin [1734–76, American physician, scholar and writer]
An American (*The Times – a Poem*)
Elizaphan of Parnach (*Liberty and Property Vindicated*)
A Friend to the Liberty of his Country (*Liberty and Property Vindicated*)
A Son of Liberty (*An Address to a Provincial Bashaw*)
Thomas Thumb Esq. (*The Monster of Monsters*; *The History of England*)
A Young Gentleman (*The Choice – a Poem*)

CHURCH, Edward [1779–1845, US merchant and politician]
A Gentleman Formerly of Boston (*The Dangerous Vice*)

CHURCH, Mrs Eliza Rodman [fl. 1851, US writer for children]
Ella Rodman (*The Catanese*; *A Grandmother's Recollections*)

CHURCHILL, E. Richard [1937–, US romantic novelist]
Cora Verlag (*Visions of Terror*)

CLAP, Nathaniel [1668–1745, US cleric]
A Minister of the Gospel (*Zebulon Advised*)

CLAPHAM, Henoch [fl. 1602, English cleric and theologian]
Philomathes (*The Historie of England*)

CLAPHAM, Samuel [1755–1830, English cleric and writer]
A Minister (*An Earnest Exhortation to Attend Public Worship*)
Theophilus St John (*The Charges of Massillon*; *Original Sermons*)

CLAPP, Henry [1814–75, US journalist and writer]
Figaro (used for journalism)

CLAPPE, Louise Amelia Knapp Smith [1819–1906, US writer]
Dame Shirley (*The Shirley Letters from California Mines in 1851–52*)

CLARIS, John Chalk [1797–1866, English journalist and poet]
Arthur Brooke (*Duro Vernum*; *Poems*; *Thoughts and Feelings*; *Retrospection and other Poems*)

CLARK, Alfred Alexander Gordon [1900–58, English barrister and crime novelist]
Cyril Hare (*Tenant for Death*; *Tragedy at Law*)

CLARK, Barrett Harper [1890–1953, Canadian writer on drama and theatre]
Harold Harper (*Fires at Valley Forge*; *The House that Died*)

CLARK, Charles [1806–80, English publisher, farmer and satirist]
Chilly (or Snarley) Charley (*Bills, Ills and Chills*; *Bagging and Bragging*)
Doggrel Drydog (*September or Sport on Sporting*; *Oh No! We'll Never Welcome Them*)
Charles William Duckett (stanzas from *The Lay of the Brokenhearts*)
Thomas Hood the Younger (*Epsom Races*)
Pe-Gas-Us (*The Balloons*)
Quintin Queerfellow (*A Doctor's 'Do' ings*)

CLARK, Charles Dunning [d. 1892, US writer]
W. J. Hamilton (*The Flying Scout*; *Ben Bird, the Cave King*)

CLARK, Charles Heber [1847–1915, US journalist and humorist]
Max Adeler (*Out of the Hurly Burly*; *In Happy Hollow*)

CLARK, Douglas [1919–, English crime and mystery writer]
James Ditton (*Copley's Hunch*; *The Bigger They Are*)
Peter Hosier (*The Miracle Makers*)

CLARK, Frederick Stephen [1908–, English writer]
Clive Dalton (*The Jesting Fates*; *A Child in the Sun*)

CLARK, Hamlet [fl. 1865, English natural historian]
Philocosmos (*A Letter to the British Museum*)

CLARK, John [d. 1807, Scottish Gaelic scholar]
The Translator of the Caledonian Bards (*A Letter to Charles Jenkinson*)

CLARK, Joseph Sylvester [1800–61, US cleric]
A Grandfather (*The History of the Pilgrims*)

CLARK, Lewis Gaylord [1810–73, US journalist]
An Editor (*Knicknacks from an Editor's table*)

CLARK, Mabel Margaret [1903–75, Scottish dramatist and writer]
Lesley Storm (*Tony Draws a Horse*; *White Pagan*)

CLARK, Marjorie [d. 1989, Australian novelist and journalist)
Georgia Rivers (*She Dresses for Dinner*; *The Difficult Art*)

CLARK, Mary [1791–1841, US writer]
A Friend of Youth (*Conversations on the History of Massachusetts*)

CLARK, Mavis Thorpe [fl. 1965, Australian writer for children]
Mavis Latham (*John Batman*)

CLARK, Patricia Denise [1921–, English romantic novelist and writer for children]
Claire Lorrimer (*The Chatelaine*; *Tamarisk*)
Susan Patrick (*Statues of Snow*)
Patricia Robins (*Lady Chatterley's Daughter*; *The Fair Deal*)

CLARK, Russel S. [1900–, Australian writer]
Gilbert Anstruther (*To Hell With Love*; *God Glanced Away*)

CLARK, Thomas [1801–67, Scottish chemist; developed process to soften hard water]
One of the Professors (*The Right of Marischal College Aberdeen to Confer Degrees*)

CLARK, William Adolphus [1825–1906, US poet]
Anicetus (*The Cannonade*; *Our Modern Athens*)

CLARK, Willis Gaylord [1810–41, US journalist and poet]
Ollapod (*in Knickerbocker Magazine*)

CLARK, Winifred [fl. 1950, English writer]
Scott Finley (*The Case of the Black Sheep*)

CLARKE, Arthur Charles [1917–, English science-fiction writer]
E. G. O'Brien; Charles Willis (both used for early magazine writing)

CLARKE, Brenda [1926–, English historian]
Brenda Honeyman (*The Kingmaker*; *Edward the Warrior*)

CLARKE, Charles Allen [1863–1935, English journalist and writer]
Teddy Ashton (*Teddy Ashton's Weekly*; *Teddy Ashton's Annual*; *Teddy Ashton's Lancashire Poems*)
Grandad Grey (*Old Tales for Young Folks*)

CLARKE, Charlotte Moon [1850–1935, US novelist]
Charles M. Clay (*A Daughter of the Gods*; *The Modern Hagar*)

CLARKE, David Waldo [1907–, Welsh academic and western novelist]
Dave Waldo (*Ride on Stranger*; *Ride the High Hills*)

CLARKE, Dorus [1797–1883, US cleric and antiquarian]
Clericus Hampdenensis (*Letters to the Hon. Horace Mann*)

CLARKE, Edward Daniel [1769–1822, English traveller, chemist and mineralogist]
Heraclides (*The Tomb of Alexandra Reviewed*)

CLARKE, George Sydenham [1848–?, English soldier and military writer]
A. Nelson Seaforth (*The Last Great Naval War*)

CLARKE, Henry [1743–1818, English mathematician, land-surveyor and schoolmaster]
H. C. (*Tabulae Linguarum*)

CLARKE, Hewson [1787–1832, English journalist and writer]
A Member of the Whip Club (*Lexicon Balatronicum*)
Saunterer (in *The Tyne Mercury*)

CLARKE, J. Calvitt [fl. 1960, English crime writer]
Richard Grant (*The Circle of Death*; *This is Dynamite*)

CLARKE, James Freeman [1810–88, US religious philosopher and poet]
A Massachusetts Citizen (*Secession, Concession or Self-Possession?*)

CLARKE, John [1926–, English actor and writer]
Bryan Forbes (*Truth Lies Sleeping*; *That Despicable Race*)

CLARKE, Joseph Clayton [1840–71, English artist and illustrator]
Kyd (*The Characters of Charles Dickens*)

CLARKE, Lady Josephine Fitzgerald [d. 1953, Irish novelist and playwright]
Errol Fitzgerald (*A Borrowed Coat*; *The Path of Chance*)

CLARKE, Marcus Andrew Hislop [1846–81, Australian novelist and humorist]
Peripatetic Philosopher (in *The Australian*)
Q (in both *The Australasian* and the *Australian Monthly Magazine*)
Mark Scrivener (in the *Australian Monthly Magazine*)

CLARKE, Mrs Mary [fl. 1869, US writer for children]
Mada (*A Birthday Present*)

CLARKE, Mrs Mary Bayard [1827–86, US journalist and patriotic verse writer]
A Busy Woman (*Mosses from a Rolling Stone*)
La Tenella (*Wood Notes or, Carolina Carols*)

CLARKE, Pauline [1921–, English writer for children]
Helen Clare (*Five Dolls in a House; Seven White Pebbles*)

CLARKE, Rebecca Sophia [1833–1906, US writer for children]
Sophie May (*The Asbury Twins; Little Prudy; Dotty Dimple*)

CLARKE, Richard William Barnes [1910–75, English businessman, civil servant and organist]
Ingot (*The Socialisation of Iron and Steel*)

CLARKE, Samuel [1599–1683, English cleric, poet and biographer]
One that Hath No Propriety Tithes (*A Caution against Sacrilege*)

CLARKE, Samuel [1675–1729, English cleric and philosopher]
A Clergyman in the Country (*A Reply to Dr Waterland's Defence of his Queries*)

CLARKE, William Horatio [1840–1913, US organist]
A Believer in the Internal Evidence of Divine Revelation (*The Face of Jesus*)

CLARKSON, Christopher [1758–1833, English antiquarian]
Richmondiensis (in *Gentleman's Magazine*)

CLAYTON, Augustus Smith [1783–1839, US jurist]
David Crockett (*The Life of Martin Van Buren*)

CLAYTON, Richard Henry Michael [1907–, English mystery novelist]
William Haggard (*The Powder Barrel; The Protectors*)

CLEAVELAND, John [1722–99, American cleric]
A Friend of Truth (*The Chebacco Narrative*)

CLEAVER, Hylton Reginald [1891–1961, English writer for boys]
Reginald Crunden (in *Chums*)

CLELAND, James [1770–1840, Scottish cabinet- maker and historian]
A Citizen (*A Letter to the Lord Provost*)

CLELAND, John [1709–89, English novelist, dramatist and journalist]
A Briton; Modestus (both used in the *Public Advertiser*)

CLELAND, William [1674–1741, English public servant]
A Planter (*Some Observations on Trade of the Sugar Colonies*)

CLEMENS, Samuel Langhorne [1835–1910, US novelist, humorist and essayist – see entry for Isaiah Sellers, the original user of the 'Twain' pseudonym]
Thomas Jefferson Snodgrass (*The Adventures of Thomas Jefferson Snodgrass*)
Mark Twain (in the *New York Sunday Press* and for *Adventures of Tom Sawyer, The Innocent Abroad, Adventures of Huckleberry Finn*, etc.)

CLEMENTS, Lewis [fl. 1878, English sporting writer]
Snapshot (*Shooting Adventures*)
Wildfowler (*Modern Wildfowling; Shooting, Yachting and Sea-Fishing*)

CLEMMER, Mrs Mary [1839–84, US writer]
A Woman (letters in the *New York Independent*)

CLEMO, Ebenezer [fl. 1858, Canadian novelist]
Maple Knot (*The Life of Simon Seek*)

CLEMO, Reginald John [1916–94, English poet and writer]
Jack Clemo (*Echoing Tip; Marriage of a Rebel*)

CLERY, Arthur Edward [d. 1932, Irish barrister, novelist, and legal writer]
Chanel (*The Idea of a Nation*)
A. Synan (*The Coming of the King*)

CLEVELAND, Henry Russell [1808–43, US educationalist and writer]
A Teacher (*Remarks on the Classical Education of Boys*)
A Traveller (*Letter to the Hon. Daniel Webster*)

CLEVELAND, John [1613–58, English satirist and poet; royalist in the English Civil War]
J. C. (*Character of a diurnal-maker; Idol of Clownes*)
A Lover of his King and Country (*The Rebellion of Wat Tyler*)

CLEVELY, Hugh Desmond [fl. 1950, English writer for boys]
Tod Claymore (*What Else Could I Do?; Nest of Vipers*)

CLEWES, Winston [1906–57, English writer]
David Armstrong (*Violent Friends; Peacocks on the Lawn; The Tilting Town*)

CLIFTON, William [1772–99, US poet]
An American Gentleman (*A Poetic Epistle*)

CLINTON, De Witt [1769–1828, US politician; failed presidential candidate in 1812]
Atticus (*Remarks on the Canal ... Lake Erie ... Hudson River*)
Grotius (*A Vindication of Thomas Jefferson*)
Hibernicus (*Letters on the Natural History and Internal Resources of the State of New York*)
Tacitus (*The Canal Policy of the State of New York*)
A Traveller (*An Account of Abimelech Coody*)

CLINTON, George [1739–1812, American soldier and politician; Vice President 1804–12]
Cato (in the *New York Journal*)

CLISSOLD, Augustus [1797–1882, English cleric and Swedenborgian]
Clericus (*A Letter to the Vice Chancellor of the Univ. of Oxford*)

CLIVE, Caroline [1801–73, English novelist and poet]
V (*IX Poems*)

CLOSE, John [1816–91, English pamphleteer and rhymester]
Timothy Caxton (*Adventures of an Author*)
Samuel Dowell (*A Month in London*)
Veritas (*Kirkby-Stephen Railway*)
A. M. Writewell (*A Month in London*)

CLOWES, Evelyn May [1877–1942, English novelist and travel writer]
Jack Heron (*The Kid and the Captain*)
Elinor Mordaunt (*Full Circle*)
A. Riposte (*Gin and Bitters*)

CLOWES, John [1743–1831, English cleric and Swedenborgian]
A Clergyman of the Church of England (*The Golden Wedding-Ring; The Spiritual Sun*)
A Clergyman of the Established Church (*An Affectionate Address to the Clergy*)

CLOWES, Sir William Laird [1856–1905, English linguist and nautical writer]
Nauticus (in the *Daily Telegraph* and *Fortnightly Review*)

CLUBBE, William [1745–1814, English cleric and poet]
The Minister of their Parish (*An Address to the Lower Classes*)
A Yeoman (*A Few Words of the Labourers of Great Britain*)

CLULOW, William Benton [1802–82, English dissenter and essayist]
Recluse (*Essays of a Recluse*)

CLUNY, Alexander [fl. 1769, English writer]
American Traveller (*An American Traveller's Observations on the present state of the Culture and Commerce of the British Colonies in America*)

CLUTE, Oscar [1873–1902, US writer on farming]
John Allen (*The Blessed Bees*)

CLUTTERBUCK, Richard Lewis [1917–, English soldier and writer]
Richard Jocelyn (*Across the River*)

CLUTTON-BROCK, Ellen Georgiana [1845–94, English writer]
E. Chilton (in both *Temple Bar Magazine* and *Longman's Magazine*)

CLYMER, Eleanor Lowenton [1906–, US writer for children]
Janet Bell (*The Monday, Tuesda ... Book*)
Elizabeth Kinsey (*Patch*)

COAD, Joseph [1790–1855, Irish journalist]
Gregory Greendrake (*The Angling Excursion of Gregory Greendrake*)

COBB, Gerard Francis [1838–1904, English musician, cyclist and ecumenist]
A Fellow of *** College,Cambridge (*The Kiss of Peace*)

COBB, Ivo Geikie [1887–1953, English physician and medical writer]
Anthony Weymouth (*Tempt Me Not*; *Who'd be a Doctor?*)

COBB, James [1756–1818, English dramatist and East India Company clerk]
J. C. (*Love in the East*)

COBB, Sylvanus [1823–87, US novelist and journalist]
Austin C. Burdick; Walter B. Dunlap (both used for popular magazine fiction)

COBBE, Miss Frances Power [1822–1904, Irish social reformer, philanthropist and writer]
Merlin Nostrodamus (*The Age of Science*)

COBBETT, William [1762–1835, English energetic writer of radical and independent views; sometime soldier, agriculturist and politician]
An American (*Annals of Blood*)
An American Farmer (*Notes on American Gardening and Fruit*)
A Brother of the Birch (*A Twig of Birch for the Butting Calf*)
Jonathan (*An Address to the Clergy of Massachusetts*)

Peter Porcupine (*Democratic Principles Illustrated*; *Detection of a Conspiracy*; *A Kick for a Bite*; *A Letter to the Infamous Tom Paine*; *The Life and Adventures of Peter P.*; *A Little Plain English addressed to the people of the United States on the treaty etc.*; *A New Year's Gift to the Democrats*; *Observations on the Debates of the American Congress*; *Observations on the emigration of Dr Priestley*; *The Rush-Light*; *The Trial of Republicanism*; *Porcupine Gazette*; *The Political Censor*; *Prospect from the Congress Gallery*)
Dick Retort (*Tit for Tat*)

COBBOLD, Elizabeth [1767–1824, English novelist and poet]
Eliza Clarke (*The Sword*)
Carolina Petty Pasty (*The Mince Pye*)

COBBOLD, John Spencer [1768–1837, English cleric and schoolmaster]
A Country Rector (*The Duty of Acknowledging Jesus Christ*)

COBBOLD, Richard [1797–1877, English cleric and writer – son of Elizabeth Cobbold above]
Margaret Catchpole (*Adventures of Margaret Catchpole*)
A Humorist Physician (*Geoffrey Gambado*)

COBDEN, Richard [1804–65, English radical politician, businessman and free trader]
Libra (letters to the *Manchester Times*)
Manchester Manufacturer (*England, Ireland and Armenia*; *Russia*)
A Radical Reformer (*Incorporate your Borough*)

COCHRANE, Arthur William Steuart [1872–1954, English heraldic officer]
Arthur Stuart (in *Temple Bar*)

COCHRANE, Sir Ernest Cecil [1873–1952, Irish barrister and dramatist]
Ernest Cecil (*A Matter of Fact*; *Monica*)

COCHRANE, Thomas [1775–1860, 10th Earl of Dundonald; British admiral – served in Brazilian and Greek navies]
A Seaman (*Autobiography of a Seaman*)

COCHRANE-BAILLIE, Alexander D. R. W. [1816–90, 1st Baron Lamington; politician, poet and novelist]
A Young England Peer (in *Fortnightly Review*)

COCKBURN, Claud [1904–81, English journalist and writer]
James Helvick (*Beat the Devil*)
Frank Pitcairn (used when diplomatic correspondent for the *Daily Worker*)

COCKBURN, Henry Thomas [1779–1854, Scottish jurist, reviewer and pamphleteer]
A Fellow Citizen (*A Letter to the Inhabitants of Edinburgh*)

COCKFIELD, Joseph [1741–1816, English Quaker and writer]
Christianus (in *The Christian* magazine)

COCKIN, William [1736–1801, English writing master]
W. C. (*Occasional Attempts in Verse*)

CODMAN, John [1814–1900, US novelist and writer]
An American Shipmaster (*A Review of the Report on Navigation Interests*)
Captain Ringbolt (*Sailor's Life and Sailor's Yarns*)
A Septuagenarian (*Winter Sketches from the Saddle*)

COERR, Eleanor Beatrice [1922–, US journalist and writer]
Eleanor Hicks (*The Circus Day in Japan*)

COFFEY, Edward Hope [1896–1958, US writer]
Edward Hope (*Spanish Omelette*; *She Loves Me Not*)

COFFIN, Charles Carleton [1823–96, US journalist and novelist]
Carleton (in the *Boston Journal* and for *Caleb Krinkle*)

COFFIN, Nathaniel W. [1815–69, US poet, politician and writer]
Thanelian (in the *Boston Journal*)

COFFIN, Robert Barry [1826–86, US journalist, poet and writer]
Barry Gray (*My Married Life at Hillside*; *Out of Town – a Rural Episode*)
An Irritable Man (*Matrimonial Infelicities*)

COFFIN, Robert Stevenson [1797–1827, US journalist and poet]
The Boston Bard (*The Miscellaneous Poems of the Boston Bard*; *Oriental Harp*; *The Life of the Boston Bard, written by Himself*)
A Consumptive (*The Eleventh Hour*)

COFFMAN, Virginia [1914–, US romantic and historical novelist]
Victor Cross (*Blood Sport*)
Jeanne Duval (*The Lady Serena*; *Ravishers*)
Virginia C. DuVaul (*Masque by Gaslight*)
Diana Saunders (*Tana Maguire*)
Anne Stanfield (*The Golden Marguerite*; *Doxy Masque*)

COGAN, Thomas [1736–1818, English Presbyterian cleric, novelist, traveller and philosopher]
A Layman (*Letters to William Wilberforce*)

COGGINS, Paschal Heston [1852–1917, US lawyer, novelist and writer]
Sidney Marlow (*Harry Ambler*; *The Moncasket Mystery*)

COGHLAN, Peggy [1920–, Scottish mystery novelist]
*Jessica Sterling (*The Spoiled Earth*; *The Dark Pasture*)

COHEN, Alfred J. [1861–1928, English critic and playwright]
Alan Dale (*A Girl Who Wrote*; *The Madonna of the Future*)

COHEN, David Solis [1852–?, US lawyer and humorist]
Daisy Shortcut (*Our Show: One Hundred Years a Republic*)

COHEN, Morton Norton [1921–, Canadian literary academic and reviewer]
John Moreton (*Punky: Mouse for a Day*)

COKE, Desmond [1879–1931, English soldier and writer]
Charbon (in *Hearth and Home* magazine)

COLBATCH, John [1664–1748, English cleric, philosopher and pamphleteer]
A Person Concer'n'd (*Jus Academicum*)
A Senior Fellow of a College in Cambridge (*Reasons for letting Church and College Leases*)

COLBECK, Edmund Henry [1865–1942, English physician and medical writer]
Burnham Hare (*The Golfing Swing Simplified*)

COLE, Henry [1808–82, English civil servant, author and engraver]
Denarius (*Shall we Keep the Crystal Palace?*)
Felix Summerley (*A Glance at the Temple Church*; *Handbook for the City of Canterbury*; *Traditional Nursery Songs of England*; *An Alphabet of Quadrupeds*)
Vigil (*Railway Eccentrics*)

COLE, James L. [1799–1823, US poet and writer]
Adrian (in the *New York Statesman*)

COLE, John William [1792–1870, Irish actor and theatre manager]
J. W. Calcraft (in *Dublin University Magazine* and for *A Defence of the Stage*, *An Address to the Public on Edinburgh Theatre* and *Memoirs of H. M. De Latude*)
Cornelius M' Squireen (in *Dublin University Magazine*)

COLEMAN, Mrs Katherine B. [1864–?, Irish-born Canadian journalist]
Kit (*To London for the Jubilee*)

COLEMAN, William [fl. 1804, US journalist]
The Editor of the Evening Post (*A Collection of Facts and Documents Relative to the Death of Major-General Alexander Hamilton*)

COLENSO, Miss Frances Ellen [1849–87, English writer – daughter of Bishop Colenso]
Atherton Wylde (*My Chief and I*)
Zandile (*Faithful unto Death*; *Two Heroes*)

COLERIDGE, Arthur Duke [1830–1913, English lawyer and writer]
An Old Colleger (*Eton in the Forties*)

COLERIDGE, Derwent [1800–83, English cleric, biographer and pamphleteer – son of Samuel Taylor Coleridge]
Davenant Cecil (in *Knight's Quarterly Magazine*)

COLERIDGE, Hartley [1796–1849, English poet and writer – son of Samuel Taylor Coleridge]
Ignoramus; The Old Bachelor (both used in *Blackwood's Magazine*)

COLERIDGE, Henry Nelson [1798–1843, English barrister – nephew and executor of Samuel Taylor Coleridge]
Joshua Haller (in *Knight's Quarterly Magazine*)

COLERIDGE, Miss Mary Elizabeth [1861–1907, English novelist and essayist]
Anodos (*Fancy's Following*)

COLERIDGE, Samuel Taylor [1772–1834, English poet and philosopher]
Silas Tomkyn Comberback (name used to enlist in the 15th Dragoons)
Hyman Hurwitz of Highgate (*A Hebrew Dirge*)
*Professor Porson (*The Devil's Walk*)
Satyrane (in *The Friend* for *Satyrane's Letters*)

COLES, Albert John [1876–?, English writer]
Jan Stewer (*In a Devonshire Carrier's Cart*; *A Parcel of ol'crams*)

COLES, Cyril Henry [1901–65, English crime and spy writer; sometime secret agent]
*Manning Coles (*Drink to Yesterday*; *The Fifth Man*)

COLLARD, John [1769–1810, English writer]
N. Dralloc (*An Epitome of Logic*; *The Life of James Molesworthy Hobart*)

COLLIE, George Francis [1909–, Scottish barrister]
*G. and W. Fortune (*Hitler Divided France*)

COLLIE, Ruth [1889–1936, English sentimental verse and prose writer]
Wilhelmina Stitch (*Catching the Gleam*; *Lasting Fragrance*)

COLLIER, George Frederick [1799–1877, English physician]
Dr Kein Thaler (in *Tait's Edinburgh Magazine*)

COLLIER, John [1708–86, English painter and satirist]
Tim Bobbin (*The Lancashire Dialect*; *Human Passions Delineated*; *The Miscellaneous Works of Tim Bobbin*)
Falcon Feather (*Lancashire Dialect and Poems*)
Muscipula Senior (*Curious Remarks on the History of Manchester*)
Tummus O'Williams (*A View of the Lancashire Dialect*)

COLLIER, John Payne [1789–1883, English journalist and forger of Shakespearian documents]
Amicus Curiae (*Criticisms on the Bar*)
J. P. C. (*A Few Odds and Ends for Cheerful Friends*; *The First Parte of Churchyarde's Chippes*)

COLLIER, Margaret Isabella [1846–1928, English writer on Italy]
Isabella Snow (*A School of Art*)

COLLIER, William [1770–1856, English Quaker]
A Member of the Society of Friends (*Quakerism*)

COLLINGWOOD, Cuthbert [1826–1908, Scottish surgeon, naturalist and Swedenborgian]
A Graduate of Oxford (*New Studies in Christian Theology*)

COLLINS, Anthony [1676–1729, English free-thinker]
A. C. (*A Dissertation on Liberty and Necessity*)
Philaretes (*An Essay on Free Thinking*)

COLLINS, Charles James [1820–64, English sporting journalist and novelist]
Priam (*Dick Diminy or, the Life of a Jockey*)

COLLINS, Clifton Wilbraham [1848–1918, English writer]
An Oxonian (in *Blackwood's Magazine*)

COLLINS, Edward James Mortimer [1827–76, English novelist and humorist]
Robert Turner Cotton (*Mr Carington*)

COLLINS, Frederick Lewis [1882–1950, US travel writer]
Frederick Lewis (*The Strange Case of Mary Page*)

COLLINS, Samuel [1619–70, English physician]
An Eminent Person Residing at the Great Czar's Court (*The Present State of Russia*)

COLLINS, William [1721–59, English poet]
A Gentleman of Oxford (*Verses Humbly Addressed to Sir Thomas Hanmer*)

COLLINS, William Lucas [1817–87, English cleric]
Hawthorne; One who is No Philosopher (both used in *Blackwood's Magazine*)

COLLIS, Maurice Stewart [1889–1973, Irish-born English civil servant in India and writer]
Alva (his signature on paintings and drawings)

COLLOMS, Brenda [1919–, English writer for children]
Brenda Cross (*Happy Ever After*; *The Film Hamlet*)
Brenda Hughes (*Folk Tales from Chile*)

COLLYER, Mrs Mary Mitchell [d. 1763, English writer and translator]
Felicia (*Letters from Felicia to Charlotte*)
A Lady (*The Death of Cain*)

COLMAN, George [1732–94, English dramatist and theatre owner]
*Mr Town, Critic and Censor General (*The Connoisseur*)

COLMAN, George [1762–1836, dramatist and humorist – son of George Colman above]
Peter Broadgrin (*The Gewgaw or, Brighton Toy*)
Arthur Griffinhoof (*The Battle of Hexham*; *The Gay Deceiver*; *Love Laughs at Locksmiths*; *The Maskers of Moorfields*; *The Review*; *Broad Grins*)
A Layman (*A Sermon for a General Fast*)

COLMAN, Hila [fl. 1975, US novelist and writer for children)
Teresa Crayder (*Sudden Fame*; *Cleopatra*)

COLQUHOUN, John Campbell [1803–70, Scottish writer]
A Freeholder and Landholder of Scotland (*The Constitutional Principles of Parliamentary Reform*)

COLQUHOUN, Patrick [1745–1820, Scottish merchant in London and social and political pamphleteer]
A Magistrate (*A Treatise on the Police of the Metropolis*; *An Account of Meat and Soup Charity*)

COLSTON-BAYNES, Dorothy Julia [d. 1973, English biographer and writer]
Dormer Creston (*Enter a Child*; *Andromeda in Wimpole Street*)

COLTHURST, Peggy Bowen [1815–80, Irish writer]
Meta (in *Dublin University Magazine*)

COLTON, Calvin [1789–1857, US cleric and academic]
An American Gentleman (*The Americans*; *A Voice from America to England*)
An American in London (*The Americans*)
Junius (*The Crisis of the Country*; *One Presidential Term*; *American Jacobinism*)
A Northern Man (*Abolition a Sedition*)
A Protestant (*Protestant Jesuitism*)

COLTON, Charles Caleb [1780–1832, English cleric, writer, and bankrupt wine merchant]
Lacon (*Lacon or, Many Things in a Few Words*)
O. P. Q. (in the *Morning Chronicle*)

COLTON, Walter [1797–1851, US cleric and journalist]
An Officer of the United States Navy (*Ship and Shore*)

COLVIL, Samuel [fl. 1681, Scottish poet]
S. C. (*The Mock Poem or, Whiggs' Supplication*)

COLVILL, Robert [d. 1788, Scottish writer]
R. C. (*The Caledonian Heroine*)

COLVILLE, Helen Hester [1854–?, English novelist]
Katherine Wylde (*Mr Bryant's Mistake*)

COLVIN, Ian Duncan [1877–1938, Scottish journalist and biographer]
Rip Van Winkle (in the *Cape Times*)

COLWELL, Stephen [1800–71, US lawyer, merchant and economist]
A Friend in the North (*The South: a Letter from a Friend in the North*)
A Layman (*Politics for American Christians*)
William Penn (*A Letter to the Legislature of Pennsylvania*)
Jonathan B. Wise (*The Relative Position in our Industry of Foreign Commerce, Domestic Production and Internal Trade*)

COMBE, William [1741–1823, English pamphleteer, satirist and writer]
Belphegor (*The Diabo-Lady*)
Walter Boyd Esq. (*A Letter to William Pitt*)
Isaac Brandon (*Fragments after Sterne*)
A Country Gentleman (*A Letter from a Country Gentleman to a Member of Parliament*)
Dr Dodd and Chace Price (*A Dialogue in the Shades between Dr Dodd and Chace Price*)
An Italian Nun (*Letters of an Italian Nun*)
A Plain Man (*Plain Thoughts of a Plain Man*)

A Retired Officer (*Letter of a Retired Officer in Defence of Colonel Cawthorne*)

Johannes Scriblerus (in *The Repository of Arts*)

The Late Rev. Laurence Sterne (*Original Letters of the Late Rev. Laurence Sterne*)

Dr Syntax (*The Life of Napoleon*)

Valerius (*The Letters of Valerius*)

A Young Lady (in *The Literary Repository*)

COMBER, Elizabeth [1917–, Chinese novelist and writer]
Han Suyin (*Many Splendoured Thing*; *My House Has Two Doors*)

COMBER, Lillian [1916–, English novelist]
Lillian Beckwith (*About my Father's Business*; *Green Hand*)

COMBER, Thomas [1645–99, English cleric and anti-Catholic pamphleteer]
A Baptist (*Three Considerations Proposed to Mr William Pen*)
An English Protestant (*The Plausible Argument of a Romish Priest*)

COMBER, Thomas [fl. 1810, English cleric]
Petrus Pasquinus, C. P. M. (*A Scourge for Adulterers, Duellists etc.*)
Philippus Philaretes (*Adultery Analyzed*)

COMFORT, Alexander [1920–, English physician, novelist, poet and playwright]
Obadiah Hornbook (used for a series of open letters addressed to George Orwell)

COMPTON, David Guy [1930–, US crime and fantasy novelist]
Guy Compton (*Medium for Murder*; *And Murder Came Too*)
Frances Lynch (*Stranger at the Wedding*; *In the House of Dark Music*)

COMYN, Henry [1775–1851, English cleric]
A Clergyman of the Church of England (*A Parish Lecture on Regeneration*)

CONARAIN, Nina [fl. 1946, Irish romantic novelist]
Elizabeth Hoy (*Dear Stranger*)

CONCANEN, Matthew [1701–49, Irish writer]
M. C. (*A Match at Foot-Ball*)

CONDER, Claude Regnier [1848–1910, English soldier, explorer, surveyor and orientalist]
A Palestine Explorer (in *Blackwood's Magazine*)

CONDER, Francis Roubiliac [1815–89, English civil engineer and writer]
A Civil Engineer (*Personal Recollections of the English Engineers*)
An English Civilian (*The Trinity of Italy*)

CONDER, Josiah [1789–1855, English bookseller, poet and writer]
J. C. O'Reid (*Reviewers Reviewed*)

CONGDON, Charles Tabor [1821–91, US journalist]
A Journalist (*Reminiscences of a Journalist*)

CONGDON, James B. [1802–80, US writer and banker]
A Citizen (*A Letter to the Representatives of the General Court*)
A Practical Banker (*A Defense of the Currency of Massachusetts*)
Money Terry Esq. (*New Bedford Money Matters*)

CONGREVE, William [1670–1729, Irish dramatist and poet]
Cleophil (*Incognita*)

CONKLING, Miss Margaret C. [1814–90, US writer]
Henry Lunettes (*The American Gentleman's Guide to Politeness*)

CONLY, Robert Leslie [1918–73, US journalist and novelist]
Robert C. O'Brien (*The Silver Crown*; *A Report from Group 17*)

CONNELLY, Celia Logan [1837–1904, US journalist and writer]
L. Fairfax (*The Elopement*)

CONNELLY, Pierce [1804–83, US cleric]
Pen Cler Jocelyn (*The Pro-Popery Conspiracy*; *The Pope in England: Who Shall Turn Him Out?*)

Pascal the Younger (*Cases of Conscience*)

CONNOLLY, Cyril Vernon [1903–74, English journalist, novelist and essayist]
Palinurus (*The Unquiet Grave*)

CONNOR, Patrick Reardon [1907–, Irish reviewer, novelist and writer for boys]
Peter Malin (*River, Sing Me a Song*; *Kobo the Brave*)

CONNOR, Sir William Neil [1909–67, English journalist]
Cassandra (in the *Daily Mirror*)

CONQUEST, George Robert Acworth [1917–, English poet and novelist]
J. E. M. Arden (*Where Do the Marxists Go from Here?*)

CONSTABLE, Catherine H. [fl. 1935, English writer]
Anthea North (used for writing children's stories and verses)

CONSTABLE, Frank Challice [1846–1937, English barrister in India; humorist and writer]
Colin Clout (*The Curse of Intellect*; *Norman or, Inherited Fate*)

CONSTABLE, John [1676–1744, English Jesuit and theological controversialist – used the alias 'John Lacey']
Clerophilus Alethes (*The Convocation Controvertist*; *The Doctrine of Antiquity*)

CONVERSE, Charles Crozat [1832–1918, US lawyer and composer]
C. O. Nevers (*Spring and Holiday*)
Karl Reden (*The Voice of Praise*)
E. C. Revons (*Sayings of the Sages*)

CONWAY, Gerard F. [fl. 1973, US science-fiction writer]
Wallace Moor (*The Bloodstone*; *The Lights of Zetar*)

CONWAY, Harry [1885–1954, US cartoonist; created 'Mutt and Jeff']
Bud Fisher (in the *San Francisco Examiner*)

CONWAY, Henry Seymour [1721–95, British soldier and politician]
An Officer (*The Military Arguments Fully Considered*)

CONWAY, Moncure Daniel [1832–1907, US cleric and writer – lived in London for 20 years]
An American; An American Abolitionist; Jonathan (all used in *Fraser's Magazine*)
M. D. C. (*Passages from some Journals*)
A Native of Virginia (*The Rejected Stone*)

CONYBEARE, Frederick Cornwallis [1856–1924, English theologian and Armenian scholar]
Huguenot (in the *National Review*)

COODE, Sir Bernard Henry [1887–1962, English House of Commons official]
Bernard Henry (*This Sliding on Wood*)

COOK, Charles Henry [1858–1933, English writer on angling]
John Bickerdyke (*Angling for a Pike*; *Angling for Game Fish*; *The Book of the All-Round Angler*)

COOK, Dorothy Mary [fl. 1970, English romantic novelist]
D. Y. Cameron (*Chasing Shadows*)
D. M. Carlisle (*Night Scented Air*; *Althea's Falcon*)
Elizabeth Clare (*A Land of Stars*; *Sunlight through the Mist*)

COOK, Fred Gordon [1900–, English writer for boys]
Burleigh Carew (in *Chums*)
Bruce Chaverton (in *Detective Weekly* magazine)

COOK, Ida [d. 1986, English romantic novelist]
Mary Burchell (*Here I Belong*; *Under the Stars of Paris*)
Ida North (in *Mab's Fashions*)

COOK, Mabel [1851–1927, English novelist and occult writer]
Mabel Collins (*Light on the Path*; *The Crucible*)

An Old Contributor (in both *Dublin University Magazine* and the *University Magazine*)

COOK, Marc [1854–82, US journalist]
Vandyke Brown (*The Wilderness Cure*)

COOK, Petronelle Marguerite Mary [1925–, English mystery novelist]
Margot Arnold (*Marie, Voodoo Queen*; *Officer's Woman*)

COOK, Robin [1931–94, English crime novelist]
Derek Raymond (*The Devil's Home on Leave*; *He Died with his Eyes Open*)

COOK, William Wallace [1867–1933, US writer]
John Milton Edwards (*The Fiction Factory*)

COOKE, Charles Wallwyn Radcliffe [1841–1911, English writer]
Angelina Gushington (*Thoughts on Men and Things*)

COOKE, John Esten [1830–86, US journalist, historian and novelist]
Champ Effingham Esq. (*The Virginia Comedians*)
One of her Admirers (*Fanchette*)
Colonel Surry (*Surry of Eagle's Nest*)
Anas Todkill (*My Lady Pokahontas*)
A Virginian (*The Life of Stonewall Jackson*)

COOKE, Mordecai Cubitt [1825–1913, English draper's assistant, educated in USA; became an eminent botanist]
Uncle Matt (*Down the Lane ... in search of Wild Flowers*; *An Introduction to the Study of Fungi*; *Mushrooms – Edible and Poisonous*; *A Stroll on the Marsh in search of Wild Flowers*)

COOKE, Thomas [1703–56, English journalist, poet and controversial pamphleteer]
Atticus (in the *London Journal* and for *Letters of Atticus*)
Hesiod Cooke (sobriquet applied to him)
Scriblerus Quartus (*The Bays Miscellany*)

Scriblerus Tertius (*The Battle of the Poets*; *The Hard Us'd Poet's Complaint*; *Hymn to Liberty*)

COOKE, William Henry [1843–1921, English barrister]
*Two Idle Apprentices (*Briefs and Papers*)

COOKSON, Catherine [1906–, English Northumbrian novelist]
Catherine Fawcett (*The Hawk's Nest*; *Sapphires for Sally*)
Catherine McMullen (maiden name used for publishing in USA)
Catherine Marchant (*Fen Tiger*; *Iron Facade*)

COOLE, Benjamin [d. 1717, English Quaker]
Eclea-Nobjmoni (*A Letter from a Gentleman in the City*)
A Father (*Miscellanies: Trade, Conversation and Religion*)
A Gentleman in the City (*A Letter from a Gentleman in the City concerning the Quakers*)
A Lover of his Country (*Religion and Reason United*)

COOMBES, Wiliam Henry [1767–1850, English Catholic cleric]
The British Observer (in *Cobbett's Register*)

COOPER, Anthony Ashley [1671–1713, 3rd Earl of Shaftesbury; moral philosopher]
A Noble Lord (*Several Letters to a Young Man at the University*)
A Protestant Peer of the Realm of England (*Two Speeches Made in the House of Peers*)

COOPER, Colin Symons [1926–, English journalist]
Daniel Benson (*The Argyll Killings*)

COOPER, Edith Emma [1862–1913, English poet]
*Michael Field (*The Wattlefold*; *Long Ago*)
Isla Leigh (*Bellerephon and other Poems*)

COOPER, Edmund [1926–, English science-fiction writer]
Richard Avery (*Rings of Tantulus*; *War Games of Zelos*)

COOPER, Henry St John [1869–1926, English writer for children]
Mabel (or Henry) St John (in *Boy's Friend*, *Boy's Realm*, *Pluck*, *Marvel* and *Union Jack* and for *Shamed by her Husband* and *The Lass that Loved a Sailor*)

COOPER, James Fenimore { 1789–1851, US novelist and writer]
An American (*Gleanings in Europe*; *Gleanings in Italy*; *Sketches of Switzerland*)
Cornelius Littlepage (*Satanstoe, a Tale of the Colony*)
Travelling Bachelor (*Notions of the Americans*)

COOPER, John Cobb [1887–1967, US lawyer and writer on aviation]
John Cobb (*The Gesture*)

COOPER, John Gilbert [1723–69, English poet and writer]
Aristippus (*Epistles to the Great, from Aristippus in Retirement*)
Philaretes (in *The Museum*)

COOPER, John Murray [fl. 1935, English crime writer]
William Sutherland (*Death Rides in the Air Lines*; *The Proverbial Murder Case*)

COOPER, Myles [1735–85, US cleric]
A North American (*The American Querist*)

COOPER, Samuel [1739–1800, English cleric and writer]
No Bigot to, Nor Against the Church of England (*A Full Refutation for the Abolition of Subscription*)
No Tithe Gatherer (*A Letter to the Clergy of Norfolk*)

COOPER, Samuel Williams [1860–1939, US lawyer]
Miss Blanche Conscience (*The Confessions of a Society Man*)

COOPER, Susan Fenimore [1813–94, US writer – daughter of James Fenimore Cooper above]
A Lady (*Rural Hours*)
Annabel Penfeather (*Eleanor Wyllys*)

COOPER, Thomas [1759–1840, British-born American political economist and philosopher]
A Gentleman in America (*Extract of a Letter from a Gentleman in America to a Friend in England*)
A Native of the South; A Nullifier (both used in *Memoirs of a Nullifier*)

COOPER, Thomas [1805–92, English writer and Chartist]
Adam Hornbook (*The Family Feud*; *Alderman Ralph*)

COOPER, William [1694–1743, US cleric]
A Minister of Boston (*A Reply to the Objections ... against the Small-Pox etc.*)

COOPER, Wiliam White [1816–86, English ophthalmic surgeon and writer]
Chirurgus; Cuach (both used in *Bentley's Miscellany*)

COOTE, Charles [1761–1835, English historian]
One of the Members of the College (*Sketches of Eminent English Civilians*)

COPE, Vincent Zachary [1881–1974, English surgeon and medical writer]
Zeta (*The Diagnosis of the Acute Abdomen in Rhyme*)

COPLESTON, Edward [1776–1849, English cleric and literary critic; Bishop of Llandaff]
A Graduate (*The Examiner Examined*)
One of his Constituents (*A Second Letter to Robert Peel MP*)

COPPEL, Alfred [1921–, US science-fiction and juvenile writer]
Robert Cham Gilman (*The Rebel of Rhada*; *The Navigator of Rhada*)
Alfred Marin (*A Storm of Spears*; *The Clash of Distant Thunder*)

CORBETT, Thomas [d. 1751, English secretary with the Admiralty]
T. C. (*An Account of the Expedition to Sicily*)

CORCORAN, Barbara [1911–, US novelist and writer for children]
Paige Dixon (*Silver Woolf; The Search for Charlie*)
Gail Hamilton (*A Candle to the Devil; Titania's Lodestone*)

CORCORAN, Dennis [d. 1858, Irish-born US journalist]
The Reporter of the New Orleans 'Picayune' (*Pickings from the Portfolio of the Reporter of the New Orleans 'Picayune'*)

COREY, Vivien [fl. 1903, English writer]
Victoria Crosse (*The Woman Who Didn't; Six Chapters of a Man's Life*)

CORLETT, John [1841–1915, English sporting journalist]
Vigilant; Wizard (both used in the *Sporting Times*)

CORMACK, Sir John Rose [1815–82, Scottish physician and medical writer]
A Graduate (*Universities of Scotland Bill*)

CORNING, James L. [1855–1923, US neurologist and medical writer]
R. Champion (*Princess Ahmedee*)

CORNWALLIS, Caroline Frances [1786–1858, English essayist]
Thomas Brown, Redivivus (*An Exposition of the Vulgar and Common Errors adapted to the Year of Grace MDCCCXLV*)
A Pariah (*Philosophical Theories*)

CORNWELL, David John Moore [1931–, English spy and thriller writer]
John Le Carre (*Call for the Dead; The Spy who Came in from the Cold*)

CORY, Charles Barney [1857–1921, US writer]
Owen Nox (*Dr Wandermann; Hunting and Fishing in Florida; How to know the Ducks, Geese and Swans*)

CORY, William Johnson [1823–92, English poet and teacher; his original surname was Johnson, and he assumed the name Cory on inheriting an estate at Halsdon in 1872]
William Johnson (*Ionica; Lucretilis*)

CORY, Winifred Muriel [d. 1950, English novelist]
Winifred Graham (*In Fear of a Woman; Till Divorce Us Do Part; Experimental Child*)

COSTELLO, Dudley [1803–65, Irish novelist and journalist]
Dr F. S. A. Dryasdust ; Mr Jolly Green (both used in *New Monthly Magazine*)

COTES, Mrs Everard (Sarah Jeanette) [d. 1922, Canadian journalist and writer]
Sarah Jeanette Duncan (*A Social Departure*)

COTTER, George Sackville [1755–1831, English poet and translator]
A Gentleman of Cambridge (*A Prospect of Happiness*)

COTTERELL, Sir Charles [1612–1702, English courtier and translator]
A Person of Quality (*Cassandra – The Fam'd Romance*)
Poliarchus (letters from 'Orinda' were addressed to Poliarchus)

COTTLE, Joseph [1770–1853, English poet and writer]
Constantius (*Hymns and Sacred Lyrics*)

COTTON, Charles [1630–87, English poet, burlesque writer, translator and countryman]
One who Never Transgressed Before (*Burlesque upon Burlesque*)
Philo-Britanniae (*The Potent Ally*)
Piscator; Viator (both used in *The Complete Angler*)

COTTON, Henry [1789–1879, English bibliographer and writer]
Catholicus (*Notes on the Rhemish Testament*)

COUCH, Jonathan [1789–1870, English physician and naturalist]
Ipolperroc (in the *Imperial Magazine*)

Video (in *Notes and Queries*)

COUES, Samuel Elliott [d. 1867, US educationalist and pacifist]
Elliott (*Remarks on the Bunker Hill Monument*)

COULSON, Elizabeth Kerr [1818–76, English historical novelist]
Roxburghe Lothian (*Dante and Beatrice*)

COULSON, Frederick Raymond [1864–1922, English journalist and writer]
Democritus (*Darwin on Trial at the Old Bailey*)

COULSON, John Hubert [1906–, English crime writer]
John Bonett (*Dead Lion*)

COULSON, Juanita Ruth [1933–, US science-fiction writer]
*John Jay Wells (in the *Magazine of Science Fiction*)

COULSON, Robert [1928–, US writer]
*Thomas Stratton (*Gates of the Universe*)

COULTER, Stephen [1914–, English mystery and crime writer]
James Mayo (*A Season of Nerves*; *Let Sleeping Girls Lie*)

COULTON, Mary Rose [1906–, English-born New Zealand novelist]
Sarah Campion (*Turn Away No More*; *Cambridge Blue*)

COUPER, Robert [1750–1818, Scottish physician and Gaelic poet]
A Physician (*Speculations on ... Impregnation in the Human Female*)

COURNOS, Helen Sybil Norton Kestner [1893–, US novelist]
Sybil Norton (*The Best World Short Stories 1947*; *The Winthrops*)

COURNOS, John [1881–1966, Russian-born poet, novelist and dramatist; lived sometime in both England and the USA]
John Courtney (*The Mask*; *The New Candide*)

Mark Gault (*The Face of Death*)

COURTENAY, Thomas Peregrine [1782–1841, English politician and writer]
Decius (*Observations on the American Treaty*)
A Tory (in *Blackwood's Magazine*)

COURTHOPE, William John [1842–1917, English writer and poetry historian]
Novus Homo (*Poems*; *The Tercentenary of Corydon*)

COURTNEY, William Prideaux [1845–1913, English local historian]
P. W. Trenpolpen (in *Notes and Queries*)

COUVRER, Jessie Catherine [d. 1897, English novelist and journalist]
Tasma (*A Knight of the White Feather*; *The Penance of Portia James*)

COUSINS, Margaret [1905–, US writer for children]
Avery Johns (*Traffic with Evil*)

COVE, Joseph Walter [1891–?, English novelist]
Lewis Gibbs (*Late Final*)

COVENTRY, Henry [d. 1752, English theologian]
Philemon (*Letters of Philemon to Hydaspes*)

COVENTRY, Sir William [1628–86, English statesman and royalist in the English Civil War]
A True Lover of his Country (*England's Appeale from the Private Caballe at Whitehall to the Great Council of the Nation*)

COWAN, Charlotte [1832–1906, Irish novelist and writer]
Rainey Hawthorne (*The Rich Husband*; *The Ruling Passion*)
Mrs J. H. Riddell (*George Geith of Fen Court*; *The Mystery in Palace Gardens*)
F. G. Trafford (*The Moors and the Fens*; *Too Much Alone*)

COWARD, Noël [1899–1973, English actor, playwright, composer and wit]
Hernia Whittlebot (*Poems*)

COWARD, William [1657–1725, English physician, pamphleteer and writer on medicine]
Estibius Psychalethes (*Second Thoughts concerning the Human Soul*)
W. C., MD (*The Just Scrutiny*)

COWDEN-CLARKE, Mary Victoria [1809–98, English writer and compiler of concordance to Shakespeare's works]
An Old Mariner (*Kit Bam's Adventures*)
Harry Wandsworth Shortfellow (*The Song of Drop o' Wather: a London Legend*)

COWELL, Robert Corlett [1845–1908, English natural historian]
Robert MacLeod (in the *London Quarterly Review*)

COWLEY, Abraham [1618–67, English poet, dramatist and essayist]
A. B. (*Poetical Blossomes*)
Francis Cole (*The Prologue and Epilogue to a Comedie ... by the Schollers of Trinity College in Cambridge*)
A Scholler in Oxford (*A Satyre: the Puritan and the Papist*)

COWLEY, Hannah [1743–1809, English dramatist and poet]
Anna Matilda (in both *The World* and the *British Album* and for *The Poetry of Anna Matilda* and *Poetry of the World*)

COWPER, William [1701–67, English physician and antiquary]
A Citizen of Chester (*A Summary of the Life of St Werburgh*)
M. Meanwell (*Il Penseroso*)

COWPER, William [1731–1800, English poet and hymn writer]
Alethes; Indagator; T. H. (all used in *Gentleman's Magazine*)
G. G.; P. P. (both used in the *Analytical Review*)
Christopher Ironside; T; W (all used in *The Connoisseur*)
Omega (in the *Gospel Magazine*)
A Well-Wisher to the New Translation (letter to the *Public Advertiser*)

COX, Mrs Anne [fl. 1891, English novelist]
Annabel Gray (*Jerome*)

COX, Anthony Berkeley [1893–1971, English crime writer]
Anthony Berkeley (*The Silk Stocking Murders*; *Trial and Error*)
Francis Iles (*Malice Afore Thought*; *Before the Fact*)
A. Monmouth Platts (*Cicely Disappears*)

COX, Daniel [d. 1750, Scottish physician and medical writer]
A Physician in Town (*A Letter from a Physician in Town on the Subject of Inoculation*)

COX, Edith Muriel [fl. 1970, English writer]
Muriel Goaman (*Fun with Chess*; *Old Bideford and District*)

COX, Gladys May [1892–?, English physician]
Mary Denham (*Modern Views on Sex*)

COX, Millard F. [1856–?, US lawyer]
Henry Scott Clarke (*Legionaries – a Story of the Great Raid*)

COX, Nellie I. McMaster [d. 1968, US journalist and writer]
Percy Curtiss (*Amy Garnett, the Almshouse Girl*; *Richard Peters*)

COX, Sir Richard [1650–1733, Irish jurist and Protestant pamphleteer]
A Lay Hand (*An Enquiry into Religion*)

COX, Samuel [1826–93, English nonconformist cleric and theologian]
Carpus (*Expository Essays and Discourses*)

COX, Thomas [d. 1734, English topographer and theologian]
An Impartial Hand (in *The Savoy*)

COX, William [d. 1851, English artist and journalist – sometime in the USA]
An Amateur (*Crayon Sketches*)

COX, William Robert [1901–, US crime and mystery writer]
Willard d'Arcy; John Parkhill; Wayne Robbins (all used in *Dime Mystery Magazine*)
Mike Frederic (*Frank Merriwell,Sports Car Racer*)
Joel Reeve (in *Argosy Magazine* and for *Goal Ahead*)
Roger G. Spellman (*Tall for a Texan*)

COX, William Trevor [1928–, Irish novelist and playwright]
William Trevor (*The Old Boys*; *Fools of Fortune*)

COXE, Arthur Cleveland [1818–96, US cleric and writer of religious verse; Bishop of New York]
Ernest (in *Blackwood's Magazine*)
An Old Catholic (*Catholics and Roman Catholics*)

COXE, Peter [1753–1844, English writer]
Fabricia Nunnez, Spinster (*A Word or Two*; *Another Word or Two*)

COXE, Tench [1755–1824, US civil servant and economist]
A Citizen of the United States (*Observations on the Agriculture of the United States*)
Juriscola (*An Examination of the Conduct of Great Britain respecting Neutrals since the Year 1791*)
A Member of the Society of Artists and Manufacturers of Philadelphia (*An Essay on the Manufacturing Interest of the United States*)
One of their constituents (*Thoughts concerning the Bank*)

COZZENS, Frederic Swartwout [1818–69, US humorist and wine merchant]
Dr Bushwacker (*Sayings of Dr Bushwacker and other Learned Men*)
Richard Hayward (in *Knickerbocker Magazine* and for *Prismatics* and *The Sparrowgrass Papers*)

CRABBE, George [1754–1832, English physician, cleric and poet]
G. Ebbare (or Ebbaac) (in the *Lady's Magazine*)
Martinus Scriblerus (used for some of his earlier poems)

CRAFTS, Wilbur Fisk [1850–1922, US cleric and religious writer]
Collene Fisk (*Through the Eye to the Heart*)

CRAFTS, Mrs Sarah Jane [fl. 1870, US Sunday School teacher]
Sarah J. Timanus (*The Infant Class*)

CRAIG, Edward Anthony [1905–, English artist, illustrator and writer]
Edward Carrick (*Art and Design in the British Film*; *The Theatre of Parma*)

CRAIG, Edward Gordon [1872–1966, English actor, designer, artist and writer]
J. Apt (used for illustrations in The *London Mercury*)
James Bath (in *The Artist*)
Oliver Bath (in *The Book of Bookplates,The Artist*, and *Theatre Arts Monthly*)
Francois M. Florian (in the *Architectural Review*)
The following were all used by Craig in his own magazine *The Mask* between 1908 and 1929: A. B.; A. B. C.; G. B. Ambrose; Anonymous; Lilian Antler; J. Somers Bacon; John Balance; John Benton; Charles Borrow; Britannicus; John Bull; C. G. E.; C. G. S.; Henry Guy Calvin; Allen Carric; Chi lo sa; Marcel de Tours; Georges Devoto; Mable Dobson; Edward Edwardovitch; Adolf Furst; Antonio Galli; Hadrian Jazz Gavotte; E. Gordon; Fanny Hepworth; Franz Hoffer; Ivan Ivanovitch; T. Kempees; Jan Klassen; Carlo Lacchio; J. Moser Lewis; Lois Lincoln; Stanislas Lodochowskowski; William McDougal; Louis Madrid; William Marchpane; Giovanni Mezzogiorno; George Norman; O. P.; Julius Oliver; Drury Pervil; Henry Phips; Giulio Piero; Everard Plumbline; Philip Polfreman; Samuel Prim; Q. E.

D.; John S. Rankin; Benjamin Rossen; Rudolf Schmerz; John Semar; C. G. Smith; John Brown Smith; V. Surgen; Scotson Umbridge; Felix Urban; R. T. Vade; Jan van Holt; Edwin Witherspoon; X. Y. Z.; You-no-hoo; Yu-no-whoo

CRAIG, Georgiana Randolph [1908–57, US crime and mystery writer]
Craig Rice (*The Corpse Steps Out*; *The Thursday Turkey Murders*)
Daphne Saunders (*To Catch a Thief*)
Michael Venning (*Murder Through the Looking-Glass*; *Jethro Hammer*)

CRAIGIE, Pearl Mary Teresa [1867–1906, US novelist and dramatist – lived mainly in London]
Diogenes Pessimus (in *Life Magazine*)
John Oliver Hobbes (*Some Emotions and a Moral*; *Sinners Comedy*)

CRAIK, Mrs Dinah Maria [1826–87, English novelist and short-story writer]
A Woman (*A Woman's Thoughts about Women*)

CRAIK, Henry [1805–66, English cleric and writer]
Alexander Dunbar (in *Blackwood's Magazine*)
Parens (*An Easy Introduction to the Hebrew Language*)

CRAMB, J. A. [1862–1913, English historian]
J. A. Revermort (*Schonbrunn*)

CRAMP, John Mockett [1791–1881, English Baptist cleric in Canada]
A Bereaved Husband (*A Portraiture from Life*)

CRAMPTON, Sir Philip [1777–1858, Irish surgeon and zoologist]
A Physician (*An Attempt to Explain the Cures of Miss Lalor*)

CRANCH, William [1769–1855, US jurist]
Lucius Junius Brutus (*Examination of the President's Reply to the New Haven Remonstrance*)

CRANE, Stephen [1871–1900, US novelist and journalist]
Johnston Smith (*Maggie: a Girl of the Streets*)

CRANMER-BYNG, L. [1872–1945, English oriental scholar]
Paganus (*Poems of Paganism*)

CRASHAW, William [1572–1626, English Puritan cleric, poet and religious writer]
A Catholike Divine (*Fiscul Papalis ...*)

CRAWFORD, Arthur Travers [1835–1911, English civil servant in India]
T. C. Arthur (*Our Troubles in Poona and the Deccan*; *Reminiscences of an Indian Police Official*)

CRAWFORD, David [1665–1726, Scottish historian and writer]
Her Majestie's Historiographer for the Kingdom of Scotland (*Memoirs of the Affairs of Scotland*)

CRAWFORD, Emily [1831–1915, Irish journalist and writer]
An Anglo-Parisian Journalist (in *Fortnightly Review*)

CRAWFORD, John Richard [1932–, US writer]
J. Walker (*Only by Thumb*)

CRAWFORD, William L. [1911–, US fantasy and science-fiction publisher]
Garrett Ford (in *The Fantasy Book* and for *Science and Sorcery*)

CRAWFURD, John [1783–1868, Scottish orientalist; Governor of Singapore]
A Member of the Embassy (*Brief Narrative of an Embassy to ... King of Ava 1826–27*)

CRAWFURD, Oswald John [1834–1909, English diplomat, novelist, dramatist and essayist]
Archibald Banks; Matthew Freke Turner (both used in the *New Quarterly Magazine*)
George Ira Brett (*League of the White Hand*; *Revelations of Inspector Morgan*)

John Dangerfield (used in both *Cornhill Magazine* and *New Quarterly Magazine*)
John Latouche (in *New Quarterly Magazine* and for *Travels in Portugal*; *Country House Essays* and *Portugal Old and New*)
George Windle Sandys (*Don Garcia in London*)

CREASEY, John [1908–73, English crime novelist]
Gordon Ashe (*Death in Flames*; *Terror by Day*)
Margaret Cooke (*False Love or True*; *The Turn of Fate*)
M. E. Cooke (*The Black Heart*; *The Crime Gang*)
Norman Deane (*The Silent House*; *Play for Murder*)
Elise Fecamps (*Love of Hate*; *Love's Triumph*)
Robert Caine Frazer (*Mark Kirby Solves a Murder*)
Patrick Gill (*The Fighting Tramp*; *The Fighting Footballers*)
Michael Halliday (*Murder Comes Home*; *Lame Dog Murder*)
Charles Hogarth (*Murder on Largo Island*)
Brian Hope (*Four Motives for Murder*)
Colin Hughes (*Triple Murder*)
Kyle Hunt (*Kill a Wicked Man*; *To Kill a Killer*)
Abel Mann (*Danger Woman*)
Peter Manton (*Murder Manor*; *Death Looks On*)
J. J. Marric (*Gideon's Day*; *Gideon's Men*)
James Marsden (*Ned Cartwright*)
Richard Martin (*Adrian and Jonathan*; *Vote for Murder*)
Rodney Mattheson (*The Dark Shadow*; *The House of Ferrars*)
Anthony Morton (*The Baron Returns*; *Cry for the Baron*)
Ken Ranger (*Roaring Guns*)
William K. Reilly (*Gun Feud*; *Range Vengeance*)
Tex Riley (*Gun-Smoke Range*; *Outlaw Hollow*)
Henry St John (*Chains of Love*; *The Last Lover*)

Jeremy York (*Murder in the Family*; *Wilful Murder*)

CREASY, Edward Shepherd [1812–78, English lawyer and historian]
Everard Clive; *Richard Grimgibber (both used in *Bentley's Miscellany*)

CREECH, William [1745–1815, Scottish publisher and occasional writer to newspapers]
A Juryman (*An Account of the Trial of William Brodie*)
Theophrastus (in the *Edinburgh Courant*)

CREED, William [1614–63, English cleric]
A Third Person (*The Refuter Refuted*)

CRESSWELL, Joseph [1557–1623, English Jesuit and writer]
B. D. De Clerimond (*A Proclamation Published under the Name of James, King of Great Brittany*)

CRESTADORO, Andrea [1808–79, Italian-born librarian in Manchester]
A Reader Therein (*The Art of Making Catalogues of Libraries*)

CRESWELL, Harry Bulkeley [1869–1960, English architect and writer]
Karshish (in *Punch*)

CREWDSON, Jane [1808–63, English poet and writer]
Aunt Jane (*Aunt Jane's Verses for Children*)

CREYKE, Caroline [1844–1946, English writer]
Diane Chasseresse (*Sporting Sketches*)

CRICHTON, Kyle Samuel [1896–1960, US editor, reviewer and writer]
Robert Forsythe (*Reading from Left to Right*; *Redder than the Rose*)

CRICHTON, Michael [1942–, US science-fiction writer and film director]
*Michael Douglas (*Dealing: or The Berkeley-to-Boston Forty-Brick Lost-Bag Blues*)
Jeffery Hudson (*A Case of Need*)
John Lange (*Drug of Choice*; *Odds On*)

CRIDER, Bill [1941–, US writer]
Jack MacLane (*Goodnight Mommy; Rest in Peace*)

CRIGHTON, James [1811–92, Scottish writer]
One who has Whistled at the Plough (used for rural notes and poems in local Arbroath newspapers)

CRIPPEN, William G. [1820–63, US journalist and humorist]
Invisible Green Esq. (*Green Peas, Picked from the Patch of Invisible Green Esq.*)

CRITCHETT, Richard Claude [1858–1928, English playwright]
R. C. Carton (*Liberty Hall; Lady Huntworth's Experiment*)

CRITCHLOW, Dorothy [1904–, English journalist]
Jane Dawson (in the *Manchester Evening News*)

CROCKETT, Samuel Rutherford [1860–1914, Scottish journalist, cleric and novelist]
Ford Brereton (*Dulce Cor*)

CROFT, Herbert [1603–91, English cleric and royalist; Bishop of Hereford]
An Humble Moderator (*The Naked Truth*)

CROFT-COOKE, Rupert [1903–79, English novelist and writer]
Leo Bruce (*Jack on the Gallow's Tree; Bone and a Hank of Hair*)

CROFTON, Zachary [d. 1672, Irish nonconformist cleric]
Alethes Noctroff (*Perjury the Proof of Forgery*)

CROFTS, John Ernest Victor [1887–1972, English academic and writer]
A Corporal (*Field Ambulance Sketches*)

CROKE, Sir Alexander [1758–1842, English jurist, genealogist and Latin poet]
Robert Stanser (*Examination of the Rev. Mr Burke's Letter*)

CROKE, Charles [d. 1657, English cleric]
Rodolphus (*Fortune's Uncertainty*)

CROKER, John Wilson [1780–1857, Irish barrister, public servant, politician and pamphleteer]
C (in *Notes and Queries*)
Nereus (letters in *The Courier*)
Edward Bradwardine Waverley (*Two Letters on Scottish Affairs*)

CROKER, Thomas Crofton [1798–1854, Irish historian and humorist]
An Irish Barrister-at-Law (*The Queen's Question Queried*)
C. (or Cornelius, or Ensign) O'Donoghue (in *Fraser's Magazine*)

CROLY, David Goodman [1829–89, US journalist and editor]
C. G. David (*A Positivist Primer*)
David Goodman (in *The Modern Thinker*)

CROLY, George [1780–1860, Irish cleric, novelist and writer]
Aretino; Lioni (or Leoni); A Protestant (all used in *Blackwood's Magazine*)

CROLY, Herbert David [1869–1930, US magazine editor and writer]
William Herbert (*Houses for Town and Country*)

CROLY, Jane Cunningham [1829–1901, English-born US journalist and writer]
Jenny June (in both the *Mirror of Fashion* and *Demorest's Monthly Magazine* and for *Talks on Women's Topics*)
Satanella (letters to *The Call*)
Veni Vidi (used in various periodicals)

CRONIN, Brendan Leo [fl. 1965, English crime and mystery writer]
Michael Cronin (*Climb the Wall; The Loose End*)
David Miles (*Over the Edge; Pattern of Chalk*)

CRONIN, Charles Bernard [1884–1968, Australian science-fiction and juvenile writer]
Eric North (*The Ant Men*)

CROSBY, Alpheus [1810–74, US writer]
Quintus (*Conservatives and Reformers*)

CROSBY, Harry C. [fl. 1970, US science-fiction writer]
Christopher Anvil (*Warlord's World*; *The Day the Machines Stopped*)

CROSBY, Howard [1826–91, US cleric and religious writer]
El Mukattem (*The Lands of the Moslem*)

CROSLAND, Thomas William Hodgson [1865–1924, English journalist and poet]
Angus McNeill (*The Egregious English*)
X (*War Poems*)

CROSS, John Keir [1914–67, Scottish novelist and writer for children]
Stephen MacFarlane (*Detectives in Greasepaint*; *Mr Bosanko and other Stories*)

CROSS, Nicholas [1616–98, English Franciscan priest]
A Person of Quality (*The Cynosura*)

CROSSEN, Kendell Foster [1910–81, US crime and science-fiction writer]
Bennett Barlay (*Satan Comes Across*)
M. E. Chaber (*The Gallows Garden*; *The Flaming Man*)
Richard Foster (*The Rest Must Die*; *The Girl from Easy Street*)
Christopher Monig (*Abra-Cadaver*; *Once Upon a Crime*)
Clay Richards (*Death of an Angel*; *The Gentle Assassin*)

CROSTHWAITE, Charles Haukes Todd [1835–1915, English civil servant in India and writer]
A District Officer (*Notes on the North-Western Provinces of India*)

CROUCH, Nathaniel [1632–1725, English writer]
Richard (or Robert) Burton (*History of the Lives of English Divines*; *Martyrs in Flames*; *The English Acquisitions in Guinea and East India*)

R. B. (*The English Empire in America*; *The English Hero ... Francis Drake*; *Historical Remarks on London and Westminster*; *Wonderful Prodigies of Judgment and Mercy*; *Extraordinary Adventures and Discoveries of Several famous Men*; *A View of the English Acquisitions in Guinea and the East Indies*; *A History of Scotland and Ireland*; *The Vanity of the Life of Man*; *History of Oliver Cromwell*; *A General History of Earthquakes*; *Surprizing Miracles of Nature and Art*)

CROWE, Bettina Lum [1911–, US travel writer]
Peter Lum (*Italian Fairy Tales*)

CROWE, Joseph Archer [1825–96, English art historian, war correspondent and writer]
George Taylor (*Antinous*)

CROWFOOT, John Rustat [1817–75, English cleric, pamphleteer and traveller]
A Fellow MA (*College Tuition Considered*)
A Member of the Senate of Cambridge University (*The Interpretation of the Composition between the University and King's College*)

CROWLEY, Edward Alexander [1875–1947, English writer on and practitioner of black magic and occult arts]
Abhavananda (*Berashith: an Essay on Ontology*)
A. E. C. (*The Honourable Adulterers*)
H. D. Carr (*Rosa Coeli*; *Rosa Inferni*; *Rosa Mundi*)
Aleister Crowley (*Temperance – a Tract for the Times*; *The Fun of the Fair*; *The City of God*; *Olla*; *Songs for Italy*; *Thumbs Up*)
Comte de Fenix (*The Scientific Solution to the Problem of Government*)
E. G. O. (*The Writing on the Ground*)
A Gentleman of the University of Cambridge (*Aceldam – a Place to Bury Strangers in*; *The Tale of Archais*; *Jepthan*)
Khaled Khan (*The Heart of the Master*)
The late Major Lutiy (*The Secret Garden of Abdullah the Satirist of Shiraz*)

Frater Perdurabo (*The Book of Lies*)
St E. A. of M. and S. (*Carmen Saeculare*)
Paramahansa Shivaji (*Eight Lectures on Yoga*)
Count Vladimir Svareff (*Jezebel and other Tragic Poems*)
Master Therion (*Magick in Theory and Practice*)
A Victim (in *The English Review* for '*Morphia*')
Leo Vincey (*The Rosicrucian Scandal*)
Soror Virakam (*The Equinox*)

CROWNINSHIELD, Francis Welsh [1872–1947, US editor and writer]
Arthur Loring Bruce (*Manners for the Metropolis*; *The Bridge Fiend*)

CROWTHER, Wilma Beryl [1918–, English natural historian]
Wilma George (*Animal Geography*; *Elementary Genetics*)

CROXALL, Samuel [1690–1752, English cleric and writer]
A Gentleman-Commoner of Oxford (*The Fair Circassian*)
Nestor Ironside (*Another Original Canto of Spencer*)

CROZIER, Lorna [1948–, Canadian poet and writer]
Lorna Uher (*Inside Is the Sky*)

CRUDEN, Alexander [1701–70, Scottish compiler of a concordance to the Bible; an eccentric writer given to self-delusion]
Alexander the Corrector (*The Adventures of Alexander the Corrector*; *An Appendix to the Adventures of Alexander the Corrector*)

CRUIKSHANK, Isaac Robert [1789–1856, English caricaturist and miniature painter – brother of George Cruikshank]
A Member of the Save-All Club (*Lessons of Thrift*)
Robert Transit (used for his illustrations in *The English Spy* by 'Bernard Blackmantle')

CRULL, Jodocus [d. 1713, German-born writer – sometime in London]
J. C., MD (*Antiquities of St Peters ... Westminster*)

CRUTTWELL, Clement [1743–1808, English physician, cleric and compiler of gazetteers]
A Presbyter of the Church of England (*The Four Gospels with a Comment*)

CULBERTSON, Robert [1765–1823, Scottish cleric and writer]
A Friend to Order in the Church (*Hints on the Ordinance of a Gospel Ministry*)

CULLEN, John [1836–1914, English cleric and writer]
Llucen (*Sunny Scenes in Europe*; *Sunny Scenes in the British Isles*; *The Atonement*)

CULLEN, William [1710–90, Scottish physician and medical lecturer]
Miss Betty Montgomery (*A Funeral Oration in Honour of Miss Jeany Muir*)

CULLIMORE, Isaac [1791–1852, English orientalist]
Hermes; Hermogenes (both used in *Fraser's Magazine*)

CUMBERLAND, Marten [1892–1972, English crime and mystery writer]
Kevin O'Hara (*The Customer's Always Wrong*; *Exit and Curtain*)

CUMBERLAND, Richard [1732–1811, English dramatist and novelist]
R. C. (*Arundel*)

CUMING, Edward William Diram [1862–1941, English journalist, novelist and sporting writer]
Evelyn Tempest (*The Dawnland Experiment*; *The McArdle Peerage*; *British Sport, Past and Present*)

CUMMING, John [1807–81, Scottish cleric, religious writer and naturalist]
A Minister of the Church of Scotland (*A Short Statement of the origin ... Divisions in the Church of Scotland*)
The 'Times' Bee-Master (*Bee-Keeping*)

CUMMINGS, Bruce Frederick [1889–1919, English biologist and diarist]
W. N. P. Barbellion (*Journal of a Disappointed Man*)

CUNDALL, Joseph [1818–95, English publisher and writer]
Stephen Percy (*Robin Hood and his Merry Forresters*)

CUNNINGHAM, Albert Benjamin [1888–1962, US educationalist]
Estil Dale (*The Last Survivor*)
Garth Hale (*Substance of a Dream*)

CUNNINGHAM, Allan [1784–1842, Scottish writer, poet and songwriter]
Hid-Allan (in *The Star*)
Mark MacRobin (in *Blackwood's Magazine*)

CUNNINGHAM, Eugene [1896–1957, US travel writer and western novelist]
Leigh Carder (*Outlaw Justice*; *Bravo Trail*)

CUNNINGHAM, John William [1780–1861, English cleric, editor and writer]
A Country Clergyman (*Morning Thoughts in Prose and Verse*)
Sancho (*Sancho or, the Proverbialist*)

CUNNINGHAM, Peter [1816–69, Scottish topographer and biographer]
Abraham Vanderdoort (in *Bentley's Miscellany*)

CUNNINGHAM, Timothy [d. 1789, English antiquarian and legal writer]
A Gentleman of the Middle Temple (*The Merchant's Lawyer*)

CUNNINGHAM, Thomas Mounsey [1776–1834, Scottish poet]
Acalus (in *Blackwood's Magazine*)

CURLE, Margaret Ormiston [1889–?, Scottish poet]
Margaret Ormiston (*Tancred the Hero*; *The Dryad and other Poems*)

CURLING, Bryan [1911–, English horse-racing journalist]
Hotspur (in the *Daily Telegraph*, 1946–65)

CURLL, Edmund [1675–1747, English bookseller and publisher of obscene books that attracted the synonym 'Curlicisms']
William Ayre Esq. (*Memoirs of ... Alexander Pope*)
Britannus (*An Answer to Mr Mist's Journal*)
E. C. (*The Life of John Gay*; *The Rarities of Richmond*; *Memoirs of the Life and Writings of Matthew Tindal*)
William Egerton Esq. (*Faithful Memoirs of Mrs Anne Oldfield*)
A. Johnstoun (*Doom's Day or, The Last Judgment*)
A Lay Hand (*Some Considerations Humbly Offered to the Bishop of Salisbury*)
Philalethes (*Some Private Passages of the Life of Sir Thomas Pengelly*; *The Impartial History of the Life, Character ... Mr John Barber ...*)
Philaretus (*Atterburyana*)

CURRIE, James [1756–1805, Scottish physician and medical writer; editor of Robert Burns]
Caius (*An Address to the President of the United States*)
Philo Musa (in the *Liverpool Weekly Herald*)
Jasper Wilson (*A Letter to William Pitt*)

CURRY, John [d. 1780, English physician and writer]
J. C., MD (*Historical and Critical Review of the Civil Wars in Ireland*)

CURRY, Otway [1804–55, US carpenter, poet and journalist]
Abdallah (used for journalism)

CURTIS, Miss Ella J. [1840–?, Irish novelist]
Shirley Smith (*All for Herself*; *Redeemed*)

CURTIS, George Ticknor [1812–94, US lawyer, historian and biographer]
Peter Boylston (*A Constitutional History of the United States*; *A Plea for Religious Liberty*; *The Life of Gen. G. B. M'Clellan*; *John Charaxes: a Tale of the Civil War*)
A Citizen of Massachusetts (*The Merits of Thomas W. Durr and George Bancroft*)

Phocion (in the *Boston Daily Advertiser and Courier*)

CURTIS, George William [1824–92, US journalist, essayist and public servant]
Easy Chair (in *Harper's Magazine*)
A Howadji (*The Nile Notes of a Howadji*; *The Howadji in India*)
Old Bachelor (in *Harper's Bazaar*)
Paul Potiphar (*The Potiphar Papers*)
A Traveller (*Nile Notes*)

CURTIS, John [1791–1862, English engraver and entomologist]
Ruricola (in the *Gardener's Chronicle*)

CURTIS, Mrs Julia Ann [1764–1838, English novelist]
Ann of Swansea (*Cambrian Pictures or, Every One has Errors*; *Chronicles of an Illustrious House or, the Peer, the Lawyer and the Hunchback*)

CURTIS, Robert [1801–75, Irish policeman]
A Constabulary Officer (in *Dublin University Magazine*)

CURWEN, Henry [1845–92, English journalist and novelist; editor of the *Times of India*]
Owen Christian (*Poems*)

CUSHING, Caleb [1800–79, US lawyer and politician]
A Friend of Domestic Industry (*A Summary of Political Economy*)
One of his Countrymen (*A Reply to James Fenimore Cooper*)

CUSHING, Charles C. Strong [1879–1941, US playwright]
Tom Cushing (*Sari*; *Barely Proper*)

CUSHING, Winifred Emma [1907–90, English poet]
Patience Strong (*Friendship*; *Nursery Versery*)

CUST, Robert Needham [1821–1909, English civil servant in India and orientalist]
A Life-Long Thinker and Wanderer (*Poems of Many Years and Many Places*)
Philo-Africanus (*Uganda*)
R. N. C. (*Life of Rama, the son of Dasaratha, King of Ajodya*)
A Sufferer, Author of 'Poems of Many Years' (*Sorrows of Anglo-Indian Life*)

CUSTANCE, Sir Reginald Neville [1847–1935, Irish mariner and nautical writer]
Barfleur (*Naval Policy*; *War at Sea*)

CUSTER, George Armstrong [1839–76, US soldier – killed at the battle of Little Big Horn]
Nomad (used for a series of sporting articles in *Turf, Field and Farm Journal*)

CUTHBERTSON, David [1856–1935, Scottish librarian, poet and writer for children]
Norman Fraser (*Student Life at Edinburgh*; *Student's Pilgrimage*)

CUTLER, Jervase [1768–1844, US pioneer]
A Late Officer in the US Army (*A Topographical Description of Ohio*)

CUTTS, Mary [1801–82, US poet]
Idamore (*Grondalla*)

CZIRA, Mrs Sidney [1889–1974, Irish journalist and broadcaster]
John Brennan (in *Sinn Fein*)

D

DABOLL, Nathan [1750–1818, US educationalist and almanac publisher]
Edmund Freebetter (*New England Almanack*)

DACHS, David [1922–, US writer]
Dave Stanley (*A Treasury of Sports Humor*)

DACRE, Charlotte [1782–1841, English poet and writer]
Rosa Matilda (*The Passions; The Confessions of the Nun of St Omer*)

DADDO, William [1707–65, English cleric and headmaster]
One Unconcerned (*The Tiverton's Woolcombers Defence*)

DAHLGREN, John Adolphus Bernard [1809–70, US admiral – expert on ordinance]
Blue Jacket (in the *Philadelphia National Gazette*)

DAKERS, Elaine [d. 1978, English novelist, biographer and writer for children]
Jane Lane (*His Fight is Ours; Gin and Bitters; Titus Oates*)

DALE, Margaret [1911–, Scottish journalist, scriptwriter and novelist]
Margaret J. Miller (*Far Castles; Fearsome Tide*)

DALE, Thomas [1797–1870, English cleric, poet and theologian]
An Undergraduate of the University of Cambridge (*The Widow of the City of Nain*)

DALGLEISH, William [1733–1807, Scottish theologian]
A Clergyman (*The True Sonship of Christ Investigated*)

DALLAS, Alexander Robert Charles [1791–1869, English cleric and theologian]
A Deserter (*The World*)
One who Never Contributed to the Former Series (*Number Ninety One – a Tract*)
A Pastor (*My Church-Yard*)

DALLAS, Eneas Sweetland [1828–79, Jamaican-born Scottish writer and journalist]
The Editor of 'Once a Week' (*The Stowe–Byron Controversy*)
A. Kettner (*Kettner's Book of the Table, a Manual of Cookery*)

DALLAS, Sir George [1758–1833, English civil servant in India and political pamphleteer]
Civis (in *Anti-Jacobin* and for *A Letter to the Earl of Moira*)

DALRYMPLE, Alexander [1737–1808, Scottish civil servant in India and hydrographer]
Aretophilos (in *Extracts from Juvenila* by G.Withers)
A Christian Believer (*A Letter to a Friend on the Test Act*)
An Old Man (*Thoughts of an Old Man of Independent Mind*)

DALRYMPLE, Sir David [1726–92, Lord Hailes; Scottish jurist]
Marcus Minucius Felix (*Octavius*)

Lactantius (*Of the Manner in which Persecutors Died*)
John Smith, Late Fellow of Queen's College (*Select Discourses by ...*)

DALTON, Cornelius Neale [1842–1920, English barrister and civil servant]
A Cambridge Graduate (*Poems, Original and Translated*)

DALTON, James Forbes [1785–1862, English writer]
Louis Le Cheminant (in *Blackwood's Magazine*)
A Septuagenarian (*Some of my Contributions in Rhyme*)

DALTON, Ormonde Maddock [1866–1945, English archaeologist]
W. Compton Leith (*Apologie Diffidentis*; *Domus Doloris*; *Sirenica*)

DALY, Carroll John [1889–1958, US crime and mystery writer]
John D. Carroll (in *Famous Detective* magazine)

DALY, Robert [1783–1872, Irish cleric; Bishop of Cashel and Waterford]
A Protestant (*A Correspondence which Arose out of the Discussion at Carlow etc.*)

DANBERG, Norman A. [fl. 1960, US mystery writer]
John L. Benton; Frank Johnson (both used in *Detective Novels* magazine)
William Dale (*John Doe – Murderer*)
Norman A. Daniels; C. K. M. Scanlon (both used in *G-Men* detective magazine)
Peter Grady (*Two Trails to Bannack*; *The Marshal of Winter Gap*)
G. Wayman Jones (in the *Black Book* detective magazine)
Harison Judd (*Shadow of a Doubt*)
Robert Wallace (*Murder under the Big Top*)

DANBY, Mary [1941–, English writer for children]
Mary Calvert (*Turnip Tom and Big Fat Rosy*)
Simon Reed (*Quick Quiz*)
Andy Stevens (*World of Stars*)

DANCE, James [1722–74, English actor, poet and pantomimist]
James Love (*Poems on Several Occasions*; *Pamela*)

DANFORTH, Joshua Noble { 1792–1861, US cleric]
A Pastor (*Gleanings and Groupings from a Pastor's Folio*)

DANIEL, George [1789–1864, English bibliophile and writer]
Democritus (*Democritus in London*)
Ingleberry Griskin (*in Bentley's Miscellany*)
P____ P____ Poet Laureate (*The R. First Born*; *R-Y-L Stripes*; *Suppressed Evidence or R. Intriguing*)

DANIEL, Glyn Edmund [1914–86, Welsh archaeologist and bon viveur]
Dilwyn Rees (*The Cambridge Murders*)

DANIELL, Albert Scott [1906–65, English writer for children]
Richard Bowood (*Great Inventions*; *Red Gaskell's Gold*)
David Scott Daniell (*The Time of the Singing*; *By Jiminy Ahoy*)
John Lewesdon (*Ladybird Book of London*)

DANIELS, Anthony [fl. 1985, English physician and writer]
Edward Theberton (in *The Spectator*)

DANIELS, Dorothy [1915–, US romantic novelist]
Danielle Dorsett (*Dueling Oaks*)
Angela Gray (*The Lattimore Arch*; *The Warlock's Daughter*)
Cynthia Kavanagh (*The Deception*)
Helaine Ross (*No Tears Tomorrow*)
Suzanne Somers (*Image of Truth*; *Until Death*)
Geraldine Thayer (*The Dark Rider*)
Helen Gray Weston (*Mystic Manor*; *House of False Faces*)

DANNAY, Frederic [1905–82, US crime writer]
Daniel Nathan (*Golden Summer*)
*Ellery Queen (*The Greek Coffin Mystery*; *The Black Dog Mystery*)

*Barnaby Ross (*The Tragedy of X; The Tragedy of Y*)

DANSEY, William [1792–1856, English cleric, physician and writer on rural sports]
A Graduate of Medicine (*Arrian on Coursing*)

D'ARBLAY, Frances [1752–1840, English novelist, diarist and writer]
Fanny Burney (her maiden name until 1793)

DARBY, John Nelson [1800–82, English theologian and founder of Plymouth Brethren sect]
J. N. D. (*Food for the Desert*)
One Who Values Christianity for its Own Sake (*Dialogues*)
A Spectator (*New Opinions of the Brethren Examined*)

DARGAN, Olive Tilford [1869–1968, US novelist and poet]
Fielding Burke (*A Stone Came Rolling; Call Home the Heart*)

DARLEY, George [1795–1846, Irish poet, mathematician and writer]
Richard Belvoir (in the *Literary Gazette*)
Geoffrey Crayon Jun. (*The New Sketch-Book*)
D (in the *Literary Chronicle and Weekly Review*)
G. D.; Fadladeen (both used in *The Athenaeum*)
Guilliame; John Lacy; Peter Patricius Pickle-Herring (all used in the *London Magazine*)
Guy Penseval (*The Labours of Idleness*)

DARLING, Charles John [1849–1936, English jurist and writer]
A Dilettante (*Seria Ludo*)
An Habitual Criminal (*The Criminal Code Bill*)

DARLING, George [1782–1862, Scottish physician and medical writer]
A Physician (*Instructions for Making Unfermented Bread*)

DARLING, Jay Norwood [1876–1962, US illustrator and cartoonist]
J. N. Ding (*Ding Goes to Russia; A Cartoonist's Catalogue*)

DARLING, William Young [1885–1962, Scottish businessman and writer]
The Bankrupt Bookseller (*Memoirs of a Bankrupt Bookseller*)
Charles Cavers; Sacheverell Smith (both used in *Hades! The Ladies!*)

DARUSMONT, Frances [1795–1852, English philanthropist, social reformer and suffragist]
An Englishwoman (*Views of Society and Manners in America*)
A Woman (*England the Civilizer*)

DARWALL, Mary [1738–1825, English poet]
Harriet Airy (in *Gentleman's Magazine*)

DASENT, George Webbe [1817–96, English diplomat; Icelandic and Norse scholar]
Herodotus Jun. (in *Fraser's Magazine*)

DAUGARS, John William [1849–85, English barrister]
Claude Templar (in *Temple Bar*)

DAUKES, Sidney Herbert [1879–1947, English physician, novelist and writer]
Sidney Fairway (*Doctor Severin's Secret; Reluctant Sinners*)

DAVENANT, Charles [1656–1714, English economist, lawyer and public servant]
Philo-Britannus (*Reflections upon Management of the Trade to Africa*)
Mr Whiglove (*The Old and Modern Whig truly Represented*)

DAVID, J. B. [1761–1841, French-born US cleric]
A Roman Catholic Clergyman of Baltimore (*True Piety or the Day Well Spent*)

DAVIDSON, Mrs Harriet Miller [1839–83, Scottish writer – lived in Australia]
A Mother (*The Two Babies*)

DAVIDSON, Lionel [1922–, English mystery novelist and writer for children]
David Line (*Mike and Me; Run for your life*)

DAVIES, Charles Maurice [1828–1910, English cleric and religious writer]
An Ex-Puseyite (*Philip Paternoster*)

DAVIES, David Ivor [1893–1951, Welsh actor, playwright and songwriter]
David L'Estrange (for the plays *The Rat* and *Down Hill*, both performed but unpublished)
Ivor Novello (*Glamorous Night*; *The Dancing Years*)

DAVIES, Edward [1756–1831, Welsh cleric, schoolmaster and antiquary]
A Welsh Curate (*Eliza Powell*)

DAVIES, George Jennings [1826–84, English cleric]
A Wykehamist (*Papers on Preaching and Public Speaking*)

DAVIES, Howard [fl. 1938, English novelist]
Andrew Marvell (*Three Men Make a World*; *Congratulate the Devil*)

DAVIES, Iris [1939–, Welsh romantic novelist]
Iris Gower (*Beloved Captive*; *Beloved Rebel*)

DAVIES, John Evan Weston [fl. 1970, English mystery writer]
Berkeley Mather (*Midnight Fun*; *The Terminators*)

DAVIES, Leslie Purnell [1914–, English mystery and fantasy writer]
Leslie Vardre (*Tell it to the Dead*; *The Nameless Ones*)

DAVIES, Myles [1662–1715, English cleric, writer and bibliographer]
A Gentleman of the Inns of Court (*Icon Libellorum or A Critical History of Pamphlets*)

DAVIES, Thomas [1712–85, English actor and writer]
John Henderson (*Genuine Narrative of the Life of John Henderson*)

DAVIES, William Robertson [1913–, Canadian journalist, actor, novelist and dramatist]
Samuel Marchbanks (*The Diary of Samuel Marchbanks*; *The Table Talk of Samuel Marchbanks*)

DAVIN, Nicholas Francis Flood [1843–1901, Irish barrister, journalist and politician in Canada]
Tristram Templeton (in the *London Monthly Journal* and for *Charles Kavanah, a story of Modern Life*)

DAVIS, Arthur Hoey [1868–1935, Australian dramatist and novelist]
Steele Rudd (*On Our Selection!*; *The Rudd Family*)

DAVIS, Brian [1925–88, English artist and cartoonist]
Michael ffolkes (in *Punch* and the *New Yorker* and for *ffanfare*; *ffolkes ffauna* and *ffundamental ffolkes*)

DAVIS, Charles Augustus [1795–1867, US merchant and writer on current affairs]
Peter Scriber (in the *New York Commercial Advertiser*)

DAVIS, Frederick Clyde [1902–77, US crime and mystery novelist]
Murdo Coombs (*A Moment of Need*)
Stephen Ransome (*False Bounty*; *Whose Corpse?*)
Curtis Steele (*The Army of the Dead*; *The Masked Invasion*)

DAVIS, Frederick W. [1858–1933, US thriller writer]
Scott Campbell (*A Battle of Wits*)

DAVIS, James [1848–1907, Irish solicitor, journalist and playwright]
Owen Hall (*A Gaiety Girl*; *The Girl from Kay's*; *The Medal and the Maid*; *The Track of a Storm*; *The Geisha*)

DAVIS, John [1761–1847, US jurist]
A Member of the Humane Society (*The Life Boat*)

DAVIS, Sir John Francis [1795–1890, British diplomat and expert on China]
Outis (*Poetry and Criticism*)

DAVIS, Martha Wirt [1905–52, US writer]
Wirt van Arsdale (*The Professor Knits a Shroud*)

DAVIS, Matthew L. [1766–1850, US printer and journalist]
A Genevese Traveller (in *The Times*)
Marcus (*The Plot Discovered!*)
Philo-Cato (*The Celebrated Letters of Philo-Cato*)
The Spy in Washington (in the *New York Courier*)

DAVIS, Oscar King [1866–1932, US newspaper correspondent]
*Schroeder Davis (*Storm Birds*)

DAVIS, Richard Bingham [1771–99, US journalist and poet]
Martlet (in the *New York Magazine*)

DAVIS, Robert Prunier [1929–, US playwright and writer]
Joe Brandon (*Cock-a-Doodle-Dew*; *Paradise in Flames*)

DAVIS, Thomas Osborne [1814–45, Irish journalist, poet and nationalist]
A Barrister (*Speeches of the Rt. Hon. J. P. Curran*)
The Celt (in the *Dublin Nation*)
A Graduate of Dublin University (*The Reform of the Lords*)

DAVIS, Wendell [1776–1830, US lawyer]
A Member of the Humane Society (*A Description of the Eastern Coast of the County of Barnstaple, Massachusetts ... to Cape Malebarre*)

DAVIS, William John [1848–1934, English trade union leader]
A Trades Union Official (in *Fortnightly Review*)

DAVSON, Sir Geoffrey Leo Simon [1922–, English writer; changed his name by deed poll]
Sir Anthony Glyn (*Elinor Glyn*; *Romanza*; *The Jungle of Eden*)

DAVY, Sir Humphrey [1778–1829, English scientist]
An Angler (*Salmonia – or Days of Fly-Fishing*)

DAWES, Edna [fl. 1980, English romantic novelist]
Eva Dane (*A Lion by the Mane*; *Shadows in the Fire*)
Elizabeth Darrell (*Gathering Wolves*; *Jade Alliance*)
Eleanor Drew (*Burn all your Bridges*)
Emma Drummond (*Rice Dragon*; *Scarlet Shadows*)

DAWES, Manasseh [d. 1829, English barrister and writer]
M. D. (*A Letter to Lord Chatham on American Affairs*)

DAWES, Thomas [1757–1825, US jurist and poet]
Adjutant Trowell (*Proposals for Printing by Subscription the History of Adj. Trowell and Bluster*)
A Young Gentleman (*The Law Given at Sinai*)

DAWSON, Alec John [1872–1951, English journalist and novelist]
Howard Kerr (*Leeway*)

DAWSON, Benjamin [1729–1814, English cleric and theologian]
A Clergyman of the Church of England (*An Examination of Dr Rutherford's Argument*)

DAWSON, Sir John William [1820–99, Canadian geologist and natural historian]
The Principal of McGill College, Montreal (*On the Course of Collegiate Education*)

DAWSON, Peter [1882–1961, Australian baritone]
J. P. McCall (used for songwriting)

DAWSON, William [1831–1911, English mariner and writer]
A Commander R. N. (in *Fraser's Magazine*)

DAWSON, William Harbutt [1860–1948, English German scholar and social scientist]
Demos (*Peers or People – Which Shall Rule?*)

DAY, Frederick V. R. [1865–1922, US mystery writer]
Nick Carter (*Not on the Record*; *In Suspicion's Shadow*)
Frederick Ormond (*The Three Keys*)
Varick Vanardy (*The Girl by the Roadside*; *The Two-Faced Man*)

DAY, Thomas [1748–89, English philanthropist and writer]
Marius (*The Letters of Marius*)
Thomas Teller (*Sandford and Merton*)

DAY-LEWIS, Cecil [1904–72, Irish-born British Poet Laureate, critic and crime writer]
Nicholas Blake (*The Beast Must Die*; *Malice in Wonderland*)

DAYMAN, John [1778–1859, English writer]
A Forreyner (*Letter by a Forreyner*)

DEACON, William Frederick [1799–1845, British journalist and writer]
A Bashful Irishman (*The Exile of Erin*)
The Editor of a Quarterly Review (*Warreniana with Notes*)
William Gifford (*Warreniana*)
Tims the Younger; Trismegistus (both used in *Blackwood's Magazine*)
A Village Apothecary (*Murder Will Out or, Confessions of a Village Apothecary*)

DEAN, Robert George [fl. 1950, US writer]
George Griswold (*The Pinned Man*; *Red Pawns*)

DeANDREA, William Louis [1952–, US mystery writer]
Lee Davis Willoughby (*The Voyageurs*)

DEARBORN, Benjamin [1755–1838, US schoolteacher]
A Friend of Industry (in the *New Hampshire Gazette*)

DE BANZIE, Eric [fl. 1930, Scottish journalist and crime novelist]
Gregory Baxter (*Blue Lightning*; *Murder Could Not Kill*)
Ian Foster (used for short-story writing)

DE BLACAM, Aodh [1890–1951, English-born Irish journalist and nationalist]
Roddy the Rover (in the *Irish Press* and for *Roddy the Rover and his Aunt Louisa*)

DE BOW, James Dunwoody Brownson [1820–67, US lawyer and journalist]
A Citizen (*The Political Annals of South Carolina*)

DE BURY, Marie Blaze [1814–94, French-born English critic and writer]
Arthur Dudley; Hamilton Murray (both used in *Bentley's Miscellany*)

DE CAMP, L. Sprague [1907–, US science-fiction writer]
Lyman R. Lyon (in *Astounding Science Fiction* magazine)

DE CHAIRE, Somerset Struben [1911–, English novelist, writer and sometime politician]
The Hon. Member for X (*Peter Public*)

DECKER, Sir Matthew [1679–1749, Dutch-born English merchant and writer]
A Well–Wisher to the Good People of Great Britain (*Serious Considerations on the Several High Duties which the Nation Labours Under*)

DE COETLOGON, Charles Edward [1746–1820, English cleric and theologian]
Anthrophilos (*Strictures of Eternal Import and Universal Concern*)
Parresiastes (*Studies, Sacred and Philosophic*)

DE COSTA, Benjamin Franklin
[1831–1904, US cleric, historian and
novelist]
Bunker Hill; Private (both used in letters to
the *Boston Advertiser*)
William Hickling (*The Rector of Roxburgh*)

DE COURCY, Richard [1743–1803, Irish
cleric and hymn writer]
The Good Vicar (*The Salopian Zealot*)

DE CREVECOEUR, Michel G. J.
[1735–1813, French-born writer – lived
sometime in USA]
J. Hector St John (*Letters from an American
Farmer*)

DEEPING, George Warwick [1877–1950,
English physician and novelist]
Warwick Deeping (*The Sword and the Cross*;
The King behind the King)

DEFOE, Daniel [1661–1731, English writer
and journalist, involved in much political
intrigue; his original surname was Foe
and he added the 'De' later]
Anglipoloski (*The Dyet of Poland*)
A British Officer in the Service of the Czar
(*An Impartial History of Peter Alexovitz*)
Capt. George Carleton (*The Memoirs of
Capt. George Carleton*)
A Citizen who Continued all the While in
London (*A Journal of the Plague Year*)
Robinson Crusoe (*The Life and Strange
Surprizing Adventures of Robinson Crusoe*)
Daniel the Prophet (*Daniel the Prophet no
Conjuror*)
D. F. (*The Poor Man's Plea to all
Proclamations*; *The Present State of
Jacobitism Considered*; *An Inquiry into the
Occasional Conformity of Dissenters in
Cases of Preferment*; *A Letter to Mr How*;
*The Original Power of the Collective Body
of the People of England, Examined and
Asserted*; *Jure Divino: a Satyr in Twelve
Books*)
D. F.,Gent. (*The Compleat Art of Painting –
a Translation*)
An English Gentleman (*An Answer to my
Lord Beilhaven's Speech*)

A Gentleman (*A Tour Thro' the Whole
Island of Great Britain*)
Heliostropolis (*The Comical History of the
Life and Death of Mumper, Generalissimo
of King Charles II's Dogs*)
A Jobber (*The Anatomy of Exchange Alley*)
L. M. (*A Short Narrative of the Life and
Death of John Rhinholdt*)
Legion (*Legion's New Paper being a Second
Memorial to the Gentlemen of a Late
House of Commons*; *Legion's Humble
Address to the Lords*)
A Lover of Old England (*Mercurius
Politicus*)
The Man in the Moon (*A Letter to a True
Born Englishman*)
A Member (*The Secret History of the October
Club*)
A Member of the House of Commons (*A
Letter Relating to a Bill of Commerce*)
A Merchant (*The Case Fairly Stated between
the Turk Company and the Italian
Merchants*)
Mons. Mesnager (*Minutes of the Negotiations
of ... at the Court of England*)
A Ministering Friend (*A Declaration of
Truth to Benjamin Hoadley*)
Andrew Moreton Esq. (*Parochial Tyranny*;
The Protestant Monastery; *Second
Thoughts are Best*; *The Secrets of the
Invisible World*)
One of the People called Quakers (*A
Friendly Rebuke to one Parson Benjamin*)
'One, Two, Three, Four' (*An Enquiry into
Conformity of Dissenters*)
A Private Gentleman (*Christian
Conversation*)
Capt. George Roberts (*The Four Voyages of
Capt. George Roberts*)
The Same Friend that Wrote to Thomas
Bradbury (*A Sharp Rebuke to Henry
Sacheverell*)
A Scots Gentleman in the Swedish Service
(*History of the Wars of Charles XII*)
A Shropshire Gentleman (*The History of the
Civil Wars in Germany*)

William Smithies, Junior Rector of St Michael, Mill End, Colchester (*The Coffee-House Preachers*)

A Well-Wisher to the Peace of Britain (*A Modest Vindication of the Present Ministry*)

DE FONTAINE, Felix Gregory [1834–96, US journalist]

Personne (*Gleanings from a Confederate Army Note-Book*)

DEGHY, Guy [1912–, Hungarian-born English playwright and writer]

*Herald Froy (*How to Avoid Matrimony*)

*Lee Gibb (*The Joneses: How to Keep up with Them*)

DE GRAMONT, Sanche [1932–, US journalist and writer]

Ted Morgan (*On Becoming American*; *Somerset Maugham*)

DEHON, Theodore [1776–1817, US cleric]

Japheth (*Cause and Cure*)

DEIGHTON, Len [1929–, English novelist and writer]

Cyril Deighton (*The Orient Flight L. Z. 127*)

DE KAY, Charles [1848–1935, US novelist and poet]

Louis Barnaval (*Poems*)

DE KAY, James Ellsworth [1792–1851, US physician]

An American (*Sketches of Turkey in 1831 and 1832*)

DE KEROUAC, Jean Louis Lebris [1922–69, US cult writer of the 1960s]

Jack (or John) Kerouac (*Lonesome Traveller*; *On the Road*)

DEKKER, Thomas [1570–1641, English dramatist and pamphleteer]

Jocundary Merrie-Braines (*The Owles Almanack*)

Some-Body (*Newes from Gravesend – Sent to Nobody*)

DE LA MARE, Walter [1873–1956, English poet, essayist, novelist and writer for children]

Walter Ramal (*Songs of Childhood*)

DE LA MOTTE, Philip [d. 1805, British soldier and authority on heraldry]

An Antiquary (*The Principal Arms borne by Families*)

DELANO, Alonzo [1802–74, US playwright]

The Old Block (*A Live Woman in the Mines*; *Penknife Sketches or, Chips off the Old Block*; *Life in the Plains and among the Diggings*)

DELANY, Joseph Francis [1905–, US crime writer]

Joel Y. Dane (*The Christmas Tree Murders*; *Grasp at Straws*)

DELANY, Patrick [1685–1768, Irish cleric and writer]

Philalethes (*A Vindication of the Convocation*)

Phileleutherus Dubliniensis (*Reflections upon Polygamy*)

DE LA PASTURE, Edmee E. M. [1890–1943, English novelist and playwright]

E. M. Delafield (*The Diary of a Provincial Lady*; *The Provincial Lady Goes Further*)

DE LA RAMEE, Marie Louise [1839–1908, English novelist and anti-suffragist!]

An Observer (in *Fortnightly Review*)

Ouida (*Dashwood's Drag*; *Under Two Flags*)

DE LASZOWSKA, Mme Emily [1849–1905, Scottish novelist and critic]

Emily G. (or E. D.) Gerard (*Examination of Love*; *The Waters of Hercules*; *The Voice of a Flower*)

DELAUNE, Thomas [d. 1685, English nonconformist]

Philalethes (*A Plea for the Non-Conformists*)

DE LEON, Thomas Cooper [1839–1914, US journalist and writer]

Cad Mac Ballastir (*Society As I Have Foundered It*)

DELF, Thomas [1812–66, English writer]
Charles Martel (*The Principles of Colouring in Painting*; *The Principles of Form in Ornamental Art*)

DELINSKY, Barbara [1945–, US romantic novelist]
Billie Douglas (*Flip Side of Yesterday*; *Variations on a Theme*)
Bonnie Drake (*Lilac Awakening*; *Lover from the Sea*)

DELL, William [d. 1664, English cleric and academic]
A Friend of the Armies (*The City Ministers Unmasked*)

DELMAR, Alexander [1836–1926, US mining engineer and writer]
Kwang Chang Ling (*Why Should the Chinese Go?*)
Emile Walter (*What Is Free Trade?*)

DE LOLME, Jean Louis [1740–1807, Swiss Jurist; refugee in England from 1769]
Somebody who is not a Doctor of the Sorbonne (*The History of the Flagellants, or The Advantages of Discipline*)

DE LONGARDE, Mme Dorothea Longarde [1855–1915, Scottish novelist]
Dorothea Gerard (*Things that Have Happened*; *The Three Essentials*)

DEL REY, Lester [1915–, US science-fiction writer]
*Edson McCann (*Preferred Risk*)
Philip St John (*Rocket Jockey*; *Rockets to Nowhere*)
Erik van Lhin (*Police your Planet*; *Battle on Mercury*)
Kenneth Wright (in *Rocket Stories* magazine)

DELVES-BROUGHTON, Josephine [1916–, English writer]
John Bryan (*The Difference To Me*; *Man Who Came Back*)

DEMILLE, Nelson R. [1943–, US crime writer]
Ellen Kay (*The Five Million Dollar Woman*)

Kurt Ladner (*Hitler's Children*)
Brad Matthews (*Killer Sharks*)

DEMING, Richard [1915–83, US crime and mystery novelist]
Halsey Clark (*Grand Finale*)
Richard Hale Curtis (*The Barnstormers*)
Max Franklin (*The Last of the Cowboys*; *Hell Street*)
Nick Marino (*City Limits*)
Emily Moor (*The Shadowed Porch*)
Ellery Queen (*Wife or Death*; *How Goes the Murder?*)
Lee Davis Willoughby (*The Smugglers*; *The Bounty Hunters*)

DEMPSTER, George [1732–1818, Scottish agriculturist]
*David Malloch (*Elegy upon the Death of a Young Lady*)

DENDY, Walter Cooper [1794–1871, English surgeon and writer]
Delta (*Wonders Displayed by the Human Body*)

DENHAM, Edward [1849–1925, US bibliographer]
A Student of History (*Why is History Read so Little?*)

DENHAM, Michael Aislabie [d. 1859, English merchant and folklorist]
Archaeus (*Antiquarian Discoveries at Carlebury*; *Roman Imperial Gold Coin*)
Autolycus (*Odd Names and Places in the North of England*)

DENHOLM, David [1924–, Australian writer]
David Forrest (*The Last Blue Sea*; *The Hollow Woodheap*)

DENISON, Charles Wheeler [1809–81, US journalist and poet]
An Ex-Consul (*Antonio, the Italian Boy*)
Major Penniman (*The Tanner Boy*; *Winfield, the Lawyer's Son*)

DENISON, George T., Jr. [1839–1925, Canadian soldier and politician]
Junius Jr. (*A Review of the Militia Policy*)

A Native Canadian (*Canada, is she Prepared for War?*)

DENISON, Mrs Mary [1826–1911, US writer]
Clara Vance (*Andy Luttrell*; *Old Hepsey, a Tale of the South*)

DENMAN, Thomas [1779–1854, English jurist, pamphleteer and anti-slaver]
A Barrister-at-Law of Lincoln's Inn (*A Legal Argument on the Statute 1st William and Mary etc.*)

DENNE, Samuel [1730–99, English cleric and antiquary]
W. & D. (in *Gentleman's Magazine*)

DENNEY, Diana [1910–, English writer for children]
Diana Ross (*The Story of Louisa*; *The Golden Hen and Other Stories*)

DENNEY, James [1856–1917, Scottish cleric and theologian]
A Brother of Natural Man (*On Natural Law in the Spiritual World*)

DENNIE, Joseph [1768–1812, US lawyer and essayist]
Colon; The Lay Preacher (both used in the *Farmer's Weekly Museum*)
Oliver Oldschool Esq. (in *The Portfolio*, which he edited)
Samuel Saunter (in the *American Lounger*)

DENNIS, James Blatch Piggott [1816–61, English cleric and geologist]
Lucius (*A Letter to Lord John Russell*)

DENNIS, John [1657–1734, English dramatist and pamphleteer]
Sir Andrew Artlove (*A Free Consideration of Sir John Egar*)
The Person of Quality (*The Person of Quality's Answer to Mr Collier Containing a Defence of a Regular Stage*)

DENNIS, Jonas [1775–1846, English cleric]
Bathoniensis (*A Challenge to the Pope*; *The Pope's Claim to Universal Supremacy*)
A Graduate in Civil Law (*Observations on the Bill for Precluding Ecclesiastics*)

DENNIS-JONES, Harold [1915–, English travel writer]
Paul Hamilton (used for editing Fodor's Modern Guides)

DENNISTON, Elinore [1900–78, US mystery writer]
Dennis Allan (*Brandon is Missing*; *Dead to Rights*)
Rae Foley (*No Tears for the Dead*; *Death and Mr Potter*)

DENNISTOUN, James [1803–55, Scottish historian and writer]
A Conservative (*A Letter to the Lord Advocate*)

DENT, Lester [1904–59, US crime and science-fiction writer]
Kenneth Robeson (in *Doc Savage Magazine*)

DE PEYSTER, Arent Schuyler [1736–1832, Canadian-born soldier in the American War of Independence]
An Officer (*Miscellanies*)

DE PEYSTER, John Watts [1821–1907, US soldier, novelist, biographer and historian]
Anchor (*Mary, Queen of Scots*)
A Layman (*A Discourse on High Church Doctrines*)

DE PUY, Henry Walter [1820–76, US journalist and lawyer]
An Indian Agent (*Mishaps of an Indian Agent*)

DE QUINCY, Thomas [1785–1859, English writer and essayist]
Emeritus; The English Opium Eater (both used in *Blackwood's Magazine*)
Grasmeriensis Teutonizans (in the *London Magazine*)

DERBY, Elias Hasket [1803–80, US lawyer]
A Citizen of Boston (*Reality versus Fiction*)
A Railroad Director of Massachusetts (*Two Months Abroad*)

DERBY, George Horatio [1823–61, US soldier and humorist]
John Phoenix (*Phoenixiana*)

John P. Squibob (*The Squibob Papers*)

DERBY, John Barton [1793–1867, US lawyer]
A Recluse (*Musings of a Recluse*)

DE REGNIERS, Beatrice S. [1914–, US writer for children]
Tamara Kitt (*Billy Brown the Baby Sitter*; *Sam and the Impossible Thing*)

DE REYNA, Diane Detzer [1930–, US science-fiction writer]
Jorge De Reyna (*The Return of the Starship*)

DERHAM, William [1657–1735, English cleric]
W. D., FRS (*The Artificial Clock-Maker, a Treatise of Watch and Clock Work*)

DERING, Heneage [1665–1750, English cleric and antiquary]
H. D., Ripensis (*De Senectute*; *Reliquiae Eboracensis*)

DERLETH, August William [1909–71, US editor and writer]
Stephen Grendon (in *Weird Tales* magazine and for *Mr George and other Odd Persons*)
Tally Mason (in *Strange Stories* magazine)

DERMODY, Thomas [1775–1803, Irish poet and soldier]
Marmaduke Myrtle (*The Histrionade or, Theatrical Journal*)

DEROUNIAN, Arthur [1909–, Armenian-born US novelist]
John Roy Carlson (*The Plotters*; *Under Cover*; *Cairo to Damascus*)

DERRICK, Samuel [1724–69, English translator and writer]
Mr Wilkes (*A General View of the Stage*)

DESAUSSURE, Henry William [1764–1839, US jurist]
A Federal Republican (*Address to the Citizens of South Carolina*)

DE SCHANSCHIEFF, Juliet Dymoke [1919–, English novelist and writer for children]
Juliet Dymoke (*Born for Victory*; *Prisoner of Rome*)

DETROSIER, Rowland [1800–34, English political philosopher and reformer]
A Poor Man (*Address to the Working Classes of England*)

DE VERE, Aubrey Thomas [1814–1902, Irish poet, critic and Celtic scholar]
An Irishman (in *Fraser's Magazine*)

DE VERE, Mary [1854–1934, US poet]
Madeline Bridges (*The Wind-Swept Wheat*; *The Open Book*)

DEVONSHIRE, Charles [1783–1851, English dramatist]
A Mechanic (*Clara or, the Marriage Feast*)

DE VOTO, Bernard Augustine [1897–1955, US editor, essayist and writer]
John August (*Troubled Star*; *Rain Before Seven*)

DeWEESE, T. Eugene [1934–, US science-fiction writer]
Jean DeWeese (*Web of Guilt*; *The Moonstone Spirit*)
*Thomas Stratton (*Gates of the Universe*)

DEWEY, Orville [1794–1882, US cleric]
An English Traveller (*Letters of an English Traveller*)

DEWEY, Thomas Blanchard [1915–, US crime and mystery writer]
Tom Brandt (*Kiss Me Hard*; *Run Brother,Run!*)
Cord Wainer (*Mountain Girl*)

DEXTER, Franklin [1793–1857, US lawyer]
Hancock (*A Letter to the Hon. Samuel Eliot*)

DEXTER, John Haven [1791–1876, US merchant and antiquarian]
Philagathus (*Waltzing*)

DEXTER, Samuel, Sr. [1761–1816, US jurist]
A Junior Sophister (*The Progress of Science*)

DIBDIN, Charles [1745–1814, English novelist, stage historian, dramatist and songwriter]
Castigator (*The Lion and the Water-Wagtail*)

DIBDIN, Thomas Frognall [1776–1847, English bibliographer]
Christianus (*A Letter to the Editor of The Times*)
A Member of the Roxburghe Club (*Cranmer*)
Mercurius Rusticus (*Bibliophobia*)
A Pastor (*A Word of Caution and Comfort*)
Rosicrucius (*Bibliomania*)
Reginald Wolfe (*Judgment and Mercy for Afflicted Souls*)

DIBDIN, Thomas John 1771–1841, English actor, dramatist and songwriter]
Mr Merchant (*The Mad Guardian*)

DICEY, Edward James Stephen [1832–1911, English journalist]
Our Special Correspondent in America (in *MacMillan's Magazine*)

DICK, Kay [1915–, English journalist, novelist and critic]
Edward Lane (in *The Windmill*)

DICK, Philip Kendred [1928–82, US science-fiction writer]
Richard Phillips (in *Fantastic Universe* magazine)

DICK, Thomas [1774–1857, Scottish astronomer and philosopher]
A Citizen of Edinburgh (*The Curse Removed*; *The Trade of the Future*)

DICK, William Brisbane [1828–93, US publisher and writer]
Joshua Jedediah Jinks (*Uncle Josh's Trunk Full of Fun*)
Leger D. Mayne (*What Shall We Do To-Night?*)
Trump (*Trump's New Card Games*; *The Game of Whist*; *Game of Cinch and Draw Pedro*; *The Modern Pocket Hoyle*; *Modern Whist*)

DICKENS, Charles John Huffam [1812–70, English novelist]
Boz (in *Bentley's Miscellany* and for *Sketches by Boz*)
Quiz (*Sketches of Young Couples*)
Godfrey Sparks (*The Bloomsbury Christening*)
Timothy Sparks (*Sunday Under Three Heads*)
Tibbs (in *Bell's Life in London*)

DICKINSON, Anne Hepple [1877–1959, English novelist and writer]
Anne Hepple (*Annals of a Little Shop*; *Sigh No More*)

DICKINSON, Goldsworthy Lowes [1862–1932, English academic, historian and essayist]
John Chinaman (*Letters of John Chinaman*)
D (in both *The Spectator* and *Cambridge Fortnightly*)
Don (in the *Manchester Guardian*)
Haji Mirza Ali Asghar Kirmanshahi (in *Cambridge Review*)

DICKINSON, John [1732–1808, American politician and pamphleteer]
Anticipation (*An Address on Relations of the US to France*)
Fabius (*The Letters of Fabius in 1788*)
A Gentleman in Philadelphia (*The Late Regulations respecting the British Colonies*)
A North American (*An Address to the Committee in Barbados*)
Pennsylvania Farmer (*Letters to the Inhabitants of the British Colonies*)
Rusticus (*Remarks on a Late Pamphlet ... Plain Truth*)

DICKINSON, Moses [1696–1778, US cleric]
An Aged Minister (*An Answer to a Letter from an Aged Layman*)

DICKSON, Samuel [1802–69, Scottish physician]
An Old Army Surgeon (*What Killed Mr Drummond?*)

DIDIER, Eugene Lemoine [1838–?, US journalist and biographer]
Lemoine (*The Life and Letters of Mme Bonaparte*)

DIGBY, George [1612–77, 2nd Earl of Bristol; writer and royalist]
A Person of Quality (*Elvira*)

DIGBY, Sir Kenelm [1603–65, English Catholic philosopher, politician and medical experimenter]
A Person of Quality (*A Discourse Concerning Infallibility*)

DIGBY, Kenelm Henry [1800–80, English writer]
K. D. (*Momentory Musings*)

DIGGES, Dudley [1613–43, English writer]
A Gentleman of Qualitie (*A Review of the Observations upon Some of His Majesties Late Answers and Expresses*)
One of That Societie (*The Defence of Trade*)

DILKE, Lady Emilia Francis Strong [1840–1904, English art historian and social reformer]
Mrs Mark Pattison (*The Shrine of Death*)

DILLON, Emile Joseph [1854–1933, Irish journalist, biographer and writer]
An English Resident in Russia; Voces Catholicae (both used in *Contemporary Review*)
E. B. Lanin (*Russian Characteristics*)

DILLON, Sir John Joseph [d. 1837, English barrister]
Hiberno-Anglus (*Letters of Hiberno-Anglus*)
Publicus Severus (*Horae Icenae*)

DILLON, John Talbot [1740–1805, English historian and traveller]
An English Traveller in Spain (*Letters of an English Traveller in Spain*)

DILLON, Robert Crawford [1795–1847, English cleric; suspended for immorality]
The Chaplain to the Mayoralty (*The Lord Mayor's Visit to Oxford*)
A Presbyter of the Church (*The Book of Common Prayer Revised*)

DILLON-LEE, Henry Augustus [1777–1832, Viscount Dillon; soldier, politican and writer]
A Friend to Truth and Liberty (*A Discourse upon the Theory of Legitimate Government*)

DILNOT, George [1883–?, English journalist and mystery writer]
Frank Froest (*The Grell Mystery; The Maelstrom*)

DIMOCK, Nathaniel [1825–1909, English cleric and theologian]
An English Presbyter (*The Doctrine of the Sacraments; The Romish Mass and the English Church*)

DINGLE, Aylward Edward [1874–1947, English mariner, novelist and writer]
Brian Cotterell (*Sinister Eden*)
Captain Dingle (*Fathomless; The Flying Kestrel; The Silver Ship; The Pirate Woman*)
Sinbad (*Seaworthy; The Silver Ship; Spin a Yarn Sailor; Red Saunders*)

DINGWELL, Joyce [fl. 1975, Australian novelist]
Kate Starr (*The Enchanted Trapp; Dalton's Daughter*)

DINSMOOR, Robert [1759–1836, American farmer and poet]
The Rustic Bard (*Incidental Poems*)

DIRCKS, Henry [1806–73, English civil engineer]
D. Henry (*Joseph Anstey*)

DISCH, Thomas Michael [1940–, US science-fiction writer]
*Thom Demijohn (*Black Alice*)
Leonie Hargrave (*Clara Reeve*)
*Cassandra Nye (*The House that Fear Built*)

DISHER, Maurice Willson [1893–1969, English theatre critic and stage historian]
Mr Pry (in the *Sunday Herald*)
Christopher Sly (in the *Weekly Scotsman*)

DISNEY, John [1746–1816, English Unitarian cleric and theologian]
Anonymous (*A Short Memoir of Edmund Law*)
Anti-Draco (*Five Letters to Sir Samuel Romilly*)
A Country Clergyman (*Remarks on Bishop Hurd's Charge*)
A Justice of the Peace (*Thoughts on Licensing Public Alehouses*)
A Petitioning Clergyman (*Remarks on Dr Balguy's Sermon*)

DISRAELI, Benjamin [1804–81, 1st Earl of Beaconsfield; novelist and prime minister]
Delta (*Venetia*; *The Tragedy of Count Alarcos*)
Mesr; Marco Polo, Junior (both used in *New Monthly Magazine*)
Runnymede (*Letters of Runnymede*)

D'ISRAELI, Isaac [1766–1848, English man of letters and historian – father of Benjamin Disraeli above]
Atticus; Varro (both used in *New Monthly Magazine*)
I. D. I. (in *Gentleman's Magazine*)
Messrs Tag, Rag and Bobtail (*Flim-Flams!*)

DIVINE, Arthur Durham [1904–87, South African journalist and historical writer]
David Divine (*The King of Fasserai*; *Boy on a Dolphin*)
David Rame (*The Sun Shall Get Them*; *Wine of Good Hope*)

DIX, John Adams [1798–1879, US soldier and politician]
Senex (*On the Mode of Constituting Presidential Electors*)

DIX, John Ross [1800–65, US artist and writer]
A Cosmopolitan (*Pen-and-Ink Sketches*)
A Looker-On (*Local Loitering and Visits in Boston*)
A Middle-Aged Man (*Passages from the History of a Wasted Life*)

DIXIE, Lady Florence [1857–1905, English poet, novelist, explorer and champion of women's rights]
Darling (*The Songs of a Child and other Poems*)

DIXON, Edmund Saul [1809–93, English cleric and writer]
Eugene Sebastian Delamer (*Pigeon Keeper*; *The Flower Garden*; *The Kitchen Garden*; *Rabbit Keeping*; *Flax and Hemp – their Culture*)

DIXON, Ella Hepworth [d. 1932, English journalist, novelist and dramatist]
Margaret Wynman (*My Flirtations*; *The Story of a Modern Woman*)

DIXON, Henry Hall [1822–70, English novelist and sporting writer]
General Chasse (in the *Sporting Magazine*)
The Druid (in the *Sporting Magazine* and for *The Post and the Paddock*, *Field and Fern*, *Saddle and Sirloin* and *Silk and Scarlet*)

DIXON, James Henry [1803–76, English writer]
Stephen Jackson Esq. of The Flatts, Malham Moor (*Chronicles of Craven Dales*)

DIXON, Roger [1930–, English novelist and playwright]
John Christian (*Five Gates to Armageddon*)
Charles Lewis (*The Cain Factor*)

DIXON, Thomas [1930–, US science-fiction writer]
Burt Cole (*The Funco File*)

DIXON, William Hepworth [1821–79, English journalist, biographer and traveller]
Onslow Yorke (*The Secret History of the International*)

DOBELL, Sydney Thompson [1824–74, English poet and critic]
Sydney Yendys (*The Roman*)

DODD, John Theodore [1843–1934, English social reformer]
Equitas (*The Local Rights of Farm Labourers*)

DODD, Philip Stanhope [1775–1852, English cleric]
A Member of the University of Cambridge (*Hints to Freshmen*)

DODD, Wayne D. [1930–, US writer]
Donald Wayne (*The Adventures of Little White Possum*)

DODD, William [1729–77, English cleric and writer – executed for fraud]
A Gentleman of One of the Inns of Court (*A New Book of The Dunciad*)
A Minister of the Church of England (in *Gentleman's Magazine*)

DODDRIDGE, Philip [1702–51, English nonconformist cleric and preacher]
A Minister in the Country (*Free Thoughts on the Dissenting Interest*)

DODGE, Mary Abigail [1833–96, US teacher poet and writer]
Gail Hamilton (*Gala Days; Wool-Gathering*)

DODGE, Nathaniel Shotswell [1810–74, US educationalist]
John Carver Esq. (*Sketches of New England*)

DODGSON, Charles Lutwidge [1832–98, English mathematician and academic]
Lewis Carroll (*Alice's Adventures in Wonderland*)
D. C. L. (*The New Belfry of Christ Church, Oxford*)
One who Has Tried it (*Twelve Months in a Curatorship*)
Oxford Chiel (*Notes by an Oxford Chiel*)
Rude Donatus (*Curiosissima Curatoria*)

DODINGTON, George Bubb [1691–1762, Baron Melcombe; politician and pamphleteer]
George Cadwallader, Gent. (*The Remembrancer*)
John More, Apothecary (*An Epistle from John More, Apothecary*)

DODSLEY, Robert [1703–64, English poet, writer and bookseller]
An Ancient Brahmin (*The Economy of Human Life*)
A Footman (*Servitude – a Poem by a Footman*)
Belshazzar Kapha, the Jew (*The Book of the Chronicle of James the Nephew*)
R. D., Footman (*The Footman's Advice to his Brethren of the Livery*)
Nathan Ben Saddi (*The Second Book of the Chronicles of the Kings*)

DODSON, Michael [1732–99, English barrister and writer]
A Layman (*A New Translation of Isaiah*)

DODWELL, Henry [1641–1711, Irish scholar and controversialist]
A Very Learned Man of the Church of England (*An Abstract of Common Principles*)

DODWELL, William [1709–85, English cleric and writer]
A Country Clergyman (*A Letter to the Author of 'Some considerations on the Act to Prevent Clandestine Marriages'*)

DOLBERG, Alexander [1933–, Russian-born English writer]
David Burg (*Solzhenitsyn*)

DOMVILLE, Sir William [1774–1860, English writer and businessman]
The Promoter of the Sunday Band (*The Sunday Band at Eastbourne*)

DONALD, George [1801–52, Scottish weaver and poet]
The Glasgow Unfortunate (*Autobiography of the Glasgow Unfortunate*)

DONALDSON, Edmund John [1847–91, English actor]
Edmund John Leathes (*An Actor Abroad or, Gossip Dramatic*)

DONALDSON, John William [1811–61, English philologist and biblical scholar]
Phileleutherus Anglicanus (*A Vindication of Protestant Principles*)

DONALDSON, Joseph [1794–1830, Scottish soldier in Peninsular War and in India]
A Sergeant in the ** Regiment of Infantry (*The Eventful Life of a Soldier*)
A Soldier (*Recollections of a Soldier*)

DONISTHORPE, Gladys Sheila [fl. 1942, English writer]
Lynne Dexter (*Other People's Houses*)

DONISTHORPE, Ida Margaret Loder [1873–, English poet and songwriter]
Pansy (*Fireside Poems*)

DONN-BYRNE, Brian Oswald [1889–1928, US journalist and novelist]
Donn Byrne (*A Daughter of the Medici*; *The Island of Youth*)

DOOLITTLE, Hilda [1886–1961, US-born English poet and novelist]
H. D. (*Heliodora and other Poems*; *Flowering of the Rod*)

DORLING, Henry Taprell [1883–1968, English mariner and nautical writer]
Taffrail (*The Navy in Action*; *Western Mediterranean 1942–45*)

DORR, Mrs Julia Caroline [1825–1913, US poet and essayist]
Caroline Thomas (*Farmingdale*)

DORR, Thomas Wilson [1805–54, US lawyer and politician]
Aristides (*Political Frauds Exposed*)

DORSEY, Sarah Anne [1829–79, US writer]
Filia Ecclesiae (*Agnes Graham*; *Athalie*; *Panola, a Tale of Louisiana*)

DOTY, Elihu [1809–64, US cleric]
An American Missionary in China (*Some Thoughts on the Chinese*)

DOUBLEDAY, Nellie Blanchan [1865–1918, US writer on natural history]
Neltje Blanchan (*How to Attract the Birds*; *Nature's Garden*; *Our Wild Flowers*; *The Bird Book*)

DOUBLEDAY, Thomas [1790–1870, English soap manufacturer, dramatist and radical writer]
Britannicus (in the *Newcastle Daily Chronicle*)
A North Country Angler (*The Coquet-Dale Fishing Songs*)

DOUDNEY, David Alfred [1811–94, English cleric, theologian and educational pioneer]
Alfred (*Sympathy or, Words for the Weak*)
Old Jonathan (*Old Jonathan's Jottings*; *Try and Try Again*; *Old Jonathan's Walks and Talks*)

DOUDNEY, Sarah [1843–1926, English novelist]
G. G. Kilburne (*Under False Colours*)

DOUGLAS, Lord Alfred [1870–1945, English poet; 'friend' of Oscar Wilde]
Belgian Hare (*The Duke of Berwick, a Nonsense Rhyme*; *Tails with a Twist*)

DOUGLAS, Francis [1710–90, Scottish Jacobite and farmer]
A Farmer (*The Birthday*)
A Gentleman in Scotland (*Observations on the Douglas Cause*)

DOUGLAS, George Norman [1868–1952, Austrian-born Scottish novelist and writer]
N. D. (*The Blue Grotto and its Literature*)
Normyx (used for *Unprofessional Tales*, written with his wife Elsa Fitzgerald)

DOUGLAS, Lady Gertrude Georgina [1842–93, English novelist]
George Douglas (*Linked Lives*; *Brown as a Berry*)

DOUGLAS, John [1721–1807, Scottish cleric; became Bishop of Salisbury, but literary and other interests took precedence over theological concerns]
An Honest Man (*Seasonable Hints from an Honest Man*)
A Volunteer who was Near his Person (*The Conduct of a Noble Lord etc.* –Referring to George Sackville.)

DOUGLAS, Neil [1750–1823, Scottish poet and preacher]
Britannicus (*A Monitory Address to Great Britain*)
Philantropicos Philalethes (*A Defense of Restoration*)

DOUGLAS, Robert [1820–44, Scottish physician in the Royal Navy]
The Medical Student (in *New Monthly Magazine*)

DOUGLAS, William [1826–95, English soldier]
An Ex-Private Hussar (in *Dark Blue* magazine)

DOUGLASS, William [1690–1752, Scottish-born physician in America]
William Nadir, S. X. Q. (*Mercurius Novanglicanus*)
Sawney (*A Friendly Debate*)

DOVASTON, John Freeman Milward [1782–1864, English barrister and writer]
Poet Ferueat of the Breidden (*The Cambrian and Salopian Minstrel*)

DOVENER, John Montague [1923–81, English barrister]
Montague Jon (*The Wellington Case: a Question of Law*)

DOW, Lorenzo [1777–1834, US preacher]
Cosmopolite (*History of a Cosmopolite*)
Lorenzo (*Polemical Works of Lorenzo*)

DOWDEN, Edward [1842–1913, Irish literary academic and writer]
*Charles Alfred Seymour (*Poems and Sonnets of Percy Bysshe Shelley*)

DOWDESWELL, William [1721–75, English Whig politician]
The Representative of a Cyder-County (*An Address to such of the Electors of Great Britain as are Not Makers of Cyder and Perry*)

DOWLING, James [fl. 1836, Irish writer]
J. D. Herbert (*Irish Varieties for the Last Fifty Years*)

DOWLING, Levi H. [1844–1911, US physician and preacher]
Levi (*The Aquarian Gospel of Jesus the Christ*)

DOWLING, Richard [1846–98, Irish writer]
Marcus Fall (*London Town; Sketches of London Life and Character*)
Emanuel Kink (*On Babies and Ladders; School-Board Essays*)

DOWNER, Silas [d. 1785, American academic and patriot]
A Son of Liberty (*A Discourse Delivered in Providence ... at the Dedication of the Tree of Liberty*)

DOWNEY, Edmund [1856–1937, Irish novelist]
F. M. Allen (*Anchor Watch Yarns; The Voyage of the Arch*)

DOWNEY, John [1770–1827, US schoolmaster]
Simon the Wagoner (used for journalism)

DOWNING, Mrs Frances Murdaugh [1835–94, US novelist and poet]
Frank Dashmore (*Pluto: being the Sad Story and Lamentable Fate of the Fair Minthe*)

DOWNING, Robert [1914–, English writer on the theatre]
Rodo (in *Variety Magazine*)

DOWTY, Aglen A. [1847–1902?, English journalist and humorist]
The Silkworm (*Jon Duan*)
O. P. Q. Philander Smiff (*The Comic History of France; Figaro's History of England; Reminiscence of a Rascal*)
A Young and Happy Husband (*Connubial Bliss*)

DOYLE, Charles Desmond [1928–, Canadian poet and writer]
Mike Doyle (*Noah*)

DOYLE, James Warren [1786–1834, Irish cleric; Bishop of Kildare]
An Irish Catholic (*An Essay of Education*)

DOYLE, John [1797–1868, English caricaturist]
H. B. (*Political Sketches*)

DOYLE, Martha Claire MacGowan [1869–?, US writer for children]
Martha James (*A Hero of Pigeon Camp*; *Little Miss Dorothy*; *Wide Awake*)

DOYLE, Richard [1824–83, English artist and illustrator – designed the distinctive cover page for *Punch*]
Dick Kitcat (used for book illustrations and cartoons)

DOYLE, Thomas [1793–1879, English Catholic cleric]
Father Thomas (letters to *The Tablet*)

D'OYLY, Sir Charles [1781–1845, English civil servant in India }
A Civilian and an Officer in the Bengal Establishment (*Tom Raw the Griffin*)

D'OYLY, George [1778–1846, English cleric, theologian and writer]
Christianus (*A Letter to the Rt. Hon. Robert Peel*)

DRAGO, Harry Sinclair [1888–1979, US novelist and western writer]
Kirk Deming (*Grass Means Fight*)
Will Ermine (*Boss of the Badlands*)
Bliss Lomax (*Closed Range*)

DRAKE, Daniel [1785–1852, US physician]
The People's Friend (*The Peoples' Doctors*)

DRAKE, James [1667–1707, English political writer]
A True English- Man (*Some Necessary Considerations ... Future Elections etc.*)

DRAKE, Joseph Rodman [1795–1820, US satirist and poet]
*Croaker and Co. (in the *New York Evening Post* and for *Poems*)

DRAPER, Mrs Elizabeth [1744–78; the object of Laurence Sterne's flattery and letters – lived sometime in India]
Eliza (*Journal to Eliza* by Sterne, published in 1775)

DRAPER, Sir William [1721–87, English soldier and colonial governor]
A Traveller (*The Thoughts of a Traveller upon our American Disputes*)

DRAYSON, Alfred Wilkes [1827–1901, English soldier]
One who has Served (*The Young Dragoon*)

DRAYTON, William Henry [1742–99, American politician and patriot]
Freeman (*The Letters of a Freeman*)

DRENNAN, William [1754–1820, Irish poet, nationalist and physician]
Orellana (in the *Belfast News-Letter*)

DRESSER, Davis [1904–77, US crime and mystery writer]
Asa Baker (*Mum's the Word for Murder*)
Kathryn Culver (*Too Smart for Love*)
Don Davis (*Death on the Treasure Trail*)
Brett Halliday (*Michael Shayne Investigates*; *The Body Came Back*)

DREXLER, Rosalyn [1926–, US playwright and novelist]
Julia Sorel (*Unwed Widow*)

DRINKER, Anna [1827–?, US poet]
Edith May (*Poems*; *Tales and Verses for Children*)

DROWER, Ethel May Stefana [1879–1972, English writer and Middle East scholar]
E. S. Stevens (*Folk Tales of Iraq*; *The Veil*; *The Mountain of God*)

DRUMMOND, Henry [1786–1860, English politician and religious writer]
One of his Constituents (*Cheap Corn ... a Letter to G. H. Sumner MP*)

DRUMMOND, Peter Robert [1802–79, Scottish bookseller and writer]
Powdavie (*The Tenants and Landlords versus the Free Traders*)

DRUMMOND, William Abernethy [1719–1809, Scottish cleric; Bishop of Edinburgh]
Philalethes (*A Letter to James Grant*)

DRUMMOND, William Hamilton
[1778–1865, Irish cleric, poet and writer]
A Student of the University of Glasgow
(*Juvenile Poems*)

DRURY, Maxine Cole [1914–, US writer]
Don Creighton (*Little League Giant*)

DUANE, William [1760–1835, US journalist
and politician]
Anti-Monopoly (*Observations on the
Operation of Banking*)
Camillus (*The Mississipi Question*)
Jasper Dwight (*A Letter to George
Washington*)

DUBOIS, Lady Dorothea [1728–74, writer
and poet – daughter of the Earl of
Anglesey]
D – D'B (*Poems on Several Occasions*)
A Lady of Quality (*Poems on Several
Occasions*)

DUBOIS, Edward [1774–1850, English
barrister, satirist, poet and writer]
Count Reginald de St Leon (*St Godwin*)
A Knight Errant (*My Pocket-Book*)
Old Knick (*Old Knick's Pocket-Book*)

DU BOSE, Mrs Catharine A. [1926–,
English-born US writer for children]
Leila Cameron (*The Pastor's Household*)

DUCHE, Jacob [1739–98, American cleric]
Tamoc Caspapina (*Caspapina's Letters*)
A Gentleman of Foreign Extraction
(*Observations on a Variety of Subjects*)
A Gentleman who Resided Sometime in
Philadelphia (*Caspapina's Letters*)

DUCKETT, George [d. 1732, English
politician and writer]
*Sir Iliad Doggerel (*Homerides*)
T. Double (*Dr D___nant's Prophecys*)

**DUCKWORTH, Francis Robinson
Gladstone** [1881–1964, English
schoolmaster and writer]
Hob (*Starlight Stories*)

DUDLEY, Sir Henry Bate [1745–1824,
English cleric, journalist, dramatist and
satirist]
A Gentleman (*A Seasonable Caveat against
Popery*)

DUDLEY, Paul [1675–1751, American jurist]
A Gentleman (*An Essay on the Merchandize
of Slaves*)

DUDLEY-SMITH, Trevor [1920–, English
crime and mystery writer]
Mansell Black (*Dead on Course; Sinister
Cargo*)
Trevor Burgess (*A Spy at Monk's Court*)
Roger Fitzalan (*A Blaze of Arms*)
Adam Hall (*The Quiller Memorandum; The
Warsaw Document*)
Howard North (*Express Way*)
Simon Rattray (*Knight Sinister; Dead
Silence*)
Warwick Scott (*Domesday Storey; Image in
the Dust*)
Caesar Smith (*Heatwave*)
Elleston Trevor (*Now Try the Morgue; Bury
him among Kings*)

DUELL, Eileen- Marie [1922–, English
novelist]
Marie Buchanan (*The Countess of Sedgwick*)
Clare Curzon (*Special Occasion; The Trojan
Hearse*)
Rhona Petrie (*Murder by Precedent; Dead
Loss*)

DUER, William Alexander [1780–1858, US
lawyer and academic]
An Old New Yorker (*Reminiscences of an
Old New Yorker*)

DUFAULT, Joseph E. N. [1892–1942,
Canadian writer for children]
Will James (*Young Cowboy; The Dark
House*)

DUFF, Alan Colquhoun [1896–1973, English
soldier and writer]
Hugh Imber (*The Spine; On Helle's Wave;
The House of the Apricots*)

DUFF, Andrew Halliday [1830–77, English dramatist and writer]
Andrew Halliday (*Comical Fellows or, the History of Pantomime*)

DUFF, Douglas Valder [1901–, English writer for boys]
Douglas Stanhope (*Sea-Urchin's First Charter*; *On Special Service for the Foreign Legion*)

DUFF, James [1729–1809, 2nd Earl of Fife; politician and agriculturalist]
A Member of Parliament (*Hints for a Reform of Gambling Clubs*)

DUFFIELD, Matthew Dawson [1792–1866, English cleric]
Richmondiensis (in *Gentleman's Magazine*)

DUFFY, Antonia Susan [1936–, English novelist and critic]
A. S. Byatt (*Virgin in the Garden*; *Shadow of a Sun*)

DUFFY, Sir Charles Gavan [1816–1903, Irish and Australian politician and historian]
An Australian Politician (*Notes in Europe*)

DUFFY, Maureen Patricia [1933–, English novelist, dramatist and poet]
D. M. Cayer (*Scarborough Fear*)

DUGANNE, Augustine Joseph Hickey [1823–84, US novelist and writer]
Motley Manners (*Parnassus in Pillory*)

DUIGENAN, Patrick [1735–1816, Irish lawyer and unionist]
A Layman (*An Address to the Gentry of the Church of Ireland*)

DUKE, Madelaine Elizabeth [1925–, English mystery writer]
Maxim Donne (*Claret, Sandwiches and Sin*)
Alex Duncan (*It's A Vet's Life*; *Vets in the Belfry*)

DU MAURIER, Guy L. B. { 1865–1915, English soldier]
A Patriot (*An Englishman's Home*)

DU MOULIN, Lewis [1606–80, French-born theologian and historian; lived mostly in England]
Irenaeus Philadelphus (*Vox Populi Expressed in XXXV Motions to this Present Parliament*)

DU MOULIN, Peter [1601–84, French-born English Anglican cleric]
An Eminent Divine of the Reformed Church (*The History of the English and Scotch Presbytery*)
Sieur L'Ormegregny (*The Politicks of France*)
A Prebend of the Church of Canterbury (*A Letter to a Person of Quality*)

DUNBAR, George [1774–1851, English gardener, classical scholar and lexicographer]
A Non-Intrusionist (*The Non-Intrusionist*)

DUNCAN, Actea Caroline [1913–, US crime writer]
Carolyn Thomas (*Narrow Gauge to Murder*; *The Cactus Shroud*)

DUNCAN, Francis [1836–88, Scottish soldier]
A Staff Officer (*The Universities and the Scientific Corps*)

DUNCAN, Henry [1774–1846, Scottish cleric, theologian and savings bank pioneer]
A Minister of the Established Church (*A Statement Respecting Parochial Schoolmasters*)
A Presbyter (*Letters on the West India Question*)

DUNCAN, John [1721–1808, English cleric, poet and writer]
John Brighte (*The Book to Keep the Spirits Up*; *Witty Sayings*)
Richard Brisk (*A Railway Book*)
An Old Parochial Clergyman (*The Libertine led to Reflection*)
Tyro-Phileleutherus (*An Address to Rational Advocates*)

DUNCAN, Jonathan [1799–1865, English financial writer]
Aladdin (in *Jerrold's Weekly News*)
Guernsey Correspondent (in *Tait's Edinburgh Magazine*)

DUNCAN, Lois [1934–, US writer for children]
Lois Kerry (*A Promise for Joyce*)

DUNCAN, Robert Lipscomb [1927–, US crime and mystery writer]
James Hall Roberts (*The Q. Document*; *The February Plan*)
James A. Robertson (*The Day the Sun Fell*)

DUNCAN, William Murdoch [1909–76, Scottish crime and mystery writer]
John Cassells (*Council of the Rat*; *Presenting Inspector Flagg*)
Neill Graham (*Hit Me Hard*; *Make Mine Murder*)
Martin Locke (*The Brothers of Judgment*)
Peter Malloch (*Cop Lover*; *Walk In Death*)
Lovat Marshall (*Murder in Triplicate*)

DUNCKLEY, Henry [1823–96, English journalist, editor and writer]
Verax (in the *Manchester Weekly Times* and the *Manchester Guardian*, and for *The Crown and the Cabinet*, *The Crown and the Constitution* and *Politia or, an Analysis of Government*)

DUNCOMBE, John [1729–86, English cleric, archaeologist and writer]
Another Gentleman of Cambridge (*Evening Contemplations in a College*)
Crito; Rusticus (both used in *Gentleman's Magazine*)
An Oxonian (*Parody on Gray's Elegy*)

DUNCOMBE, William [1690–1769, English journalist and writer]
Benevolus; Philopropos (both used in the *London Journal*)

DUNKERLEY, Elsie Jeannette [d. 1960, English writer for girls]
Elsie Jeannette Oxenham (*Secrets of the Abbey*; *Two Joans at the Abbey*)

DUNKERLEY, Erica Isobel [fl. 1925, English writer for girls]
Pamela Hamilton (*Out of the Strong*; *Southern Wood*)
Erica Oxenham (*Lake of Dreams*; *Out of the Body*)

DUNKERLEY, William Arthur [1852–1941, English journalist and novelist]
John Oxenham (*A Saint in the Making*; *God's Candle*)

DUNLAP, William [1766–1839, US painter and dramatist]
A Citizen of New York (*The Father or, American Shandyism*)
A Water Drinker (*Memoirs of a Water Drinker*)

DUNLOP, Agnes Mary Robertson [1910–82, Scottish novelist and writer for children]
Elizabeth Kyle (*Douce*; *Through the Wall*)
Jan Ralston (*Mystery of the Good Adventurer*)

DUNLOP, Alexander [1798–1870, Scottish barrister]
Civis (*Emerson's Orations to the Modern Athenians*)
A Country Minister (*The Law of the Sabbath*)
A Layman (*The Sabbath at Home and Abroad*)

DUNLOP, Durham [1812–82, Irish journalist and writer]
Anthony Poplar (in *Dublin University Magazine*)

DUNLOP, William [1795–1848, Scottish writer – emigrated to Canada]
A Backwoodsman (*Statistical Sketches of Upper Canada*)
Colin Bannatyne (in *Blackwood's Magazine*)
Tyger (in *Fraser's Magazine*)

DUNN, Philip M. [1946–, English science-fiction writer]
Saul Dunn (*Black Moon*; *Tha Cabal*)

DUNNE, Finley Peter [1867–1936, US journalist and humorist]
Mr Dooley (*Mr Dooley in Peace and War*)

DUNNETT, Alastair MacTavish [1908–, Scottish writer]
Alec Tavis (*The Duke's Day*)

DUNNETT, Dorothy [1923–, Scottish novelist]
Dorothy Halliday (*Dolly and the Singing Bird*; *Dolly and the Starry Bird*)

DUNNICLIFFE, Henry [d. 1866, English soldier]
Portfire (in *Bentley's Miscellany*)

DUNNING, Mrs A. K. [fl. 1876, US novelist]
Nellie Grahame (*A First Glass of Wine*)

DUNPHIE, Charles James [1820–1908, Irish essayist and drama and art critic]
Melopoyn (in the *Patriotic Fund Journal*)
Rambler (in *The Observer*)

DUNSTER, Charles [1750–1816, English cleric and writer]
A Country Clergyman (*A Letter to Granville Sharp*)
Marmaduke Milton Esq. (*St James's Street*)

DUNTON, Edith Kellogg [1875–1944, US novelist]
Margaret Warde (*Betty Wales,Junior*; *Joan Jordan's Job*)

DUNTON, John [1659–1733, English bookseller and writer]
James Bent (*The Bloody Assizes*)
A Bookseller (*Religio Bibliopolae*)
Benjamin Bridgwater (*Religio Bibliopolae*)
A Gentleman who has Made it his Business to Search after Such Pieces (*The Phenix*)
John the Hermit (*Stinking Fish*)
A Lover of Travels (*A Voyage Around the World*)
A Member of the Athenian Society (*The Athenian Oracle*; *A Supplement to the Athenian Oracle*; *The Visions of the Soul*)
A Member of the New Athenian Society (*The New Practice of Piety*)

Philaret (*The Conventicle*; *Athenian Sport*)
Philopatris (*Mordecai's Memorial*)
An Unknown and Disinterested Clergyman (*Mordecai's Memorial*)

DUPPA, Richard [1770–1831, English lawyer, artist and writer]
A Member of the University of Cambridge (*An Address to the Parliament on Copywright*)

DUPUY, Eliza Ann [1814–82, US novelist]
Annie Young (in the *New York Ledger*)

DURAND, Sir Henry Mortimer [1850–1924, English diplomat and civil servant in India]
John Roy (*Helen Treveryan*)

DURBRIDGE, Francis Henry [1912–, English crime and mystery writer]
*Paul Temple (*The Tyler Mystery*; *East of Algiers*)

DURFEE, Job [1790–1847, US jurist]
Theoptes (*The Panidea*)

D'URFEY, Thomas [1653–1723, English dramatist and songwriter]
Sir Critic Catcall (used in the preface to his play *The Banditti*)
Mr D'Uffey (*The Houble Bubble*)
Gabriel John (*An Essay on the Theory of the Intelligible World*)
Poet Stutter (*Wit for Money*)

DURHAM, J. M. M. M. B. [fl. 1910, English sporting writer]
Marshman (*A Medley of Sport*)

DURIVAGE, Francis Alexander [1814–81, US writer]
The Old 'Un (*Stray Subjects Arrested and Bound Over*)

DURRELL, Lawrence George [1912–90, English poet and novelist; he signed his paintings and sketches 'Oscar Epfs']
Charles Norden (*Panic Spring*)

DURST, Paul [1921–, US crime and western novelist]
Peter Bannon (*If I Should Die*; *Whisper Murder Softly*)
John Chelton (*My Deadly Angel*)
Jeff Cochran (*Guns of Circle 8*)
John Shane (*Sundown in Sundance*; *Gunsmoke Dawn*)

DUTENS, Louis [1730–1812, Huguenot refugee, diplomat and writer]
Duchillon (*Memoirs of a Traveller, now in Retirement*)

DUTT, Romesh Chunder [1848–1909, Indian civil servant, historian and writer]
Ar. Cy. Dae. (*The Literature of Bengal*)
A Hindu (in *Dark Blue* magazine and for *Three Years in Europe*)

DUYKINCK, Evert Augustus [1816–78, US literary critic, editor and writer]
Felix Merry (in the *New York Literary World*)

DWIGGINS, Clare Victor [1873–1958, US cartoonist and illustrator]
Dwig (used for book illustrations and cartoons)

DWIGGINS, William Addison [1880–1956, US artist and designer]
H. Puterschien (*Paraphs*)

DWYER, Francis Doyne [1809–80, Irish soldier, writer and adventurer]
Klingensporren; Count Sallagub (both used in *Dublin University Magazine*)
Patrol-Leader (in *Dark Blue* magazine)
The Unlucky Man (in *Ainsworth's Magazine*)

DYER, Gladys Eleanor May [1894–1969, English writer for girls]
Elinor M. Brent-Dyer (*Jo of the Chalet School*; *The Chalet School Reunion*)

DYKES, Thomas [1850–?, English writer on sport and sailing]
Rockwood (*Stories of Scottish Sports*)

E

EAGLES, John [1783–1855, English artist, poet and writer]
An Amateur; Aquilius; A Citizen of Bristol; One of the Old Constitution; Satan; The Sketcher; Vive Valeque (all used in *Blackwood's Magazine*)
The Man in the Moon (*Felix Farley Rhymes in Latin and English*)
Llewellyn Penrose (*Journal of Llewellyn Penrose, a Seaman*)

EAGLESTONE, Arthur Archibald [1892–?, English writer]
Roger Dataller (*Uncouth Swain; Steel Saraband*)

EAMES, W. [fl. 1719, English nonconformist cleric]
*Bagweel (*A Collection of Occasional Papers etc.*)

EARBERY, Matthias [fl. 1716, English writer]
Trojano Boccalini (in *Advice from Parnassus*)

EARDLEY-WILMOT, Sir John Eardley [1810–92, English barrister, jurist and politician]
A Barrister at Law (*An Abridgement of Blackstone's Commentaries*)
A Revising Barrister (*Parliamentary Reform*)

EARL, Mrs Ethel [fl. 1881, English novelist]
Ethel Coxon (*A Basil Plant; Monsieur Love*)

EARLE, Eric Greville [1893–1965, English soldier]
Martin Gale (in the *Royal Artillery Magazine*)
Staff Officer (in *The Bystander*)

EASDALE, Gladys Ellen [1913–, English poet]
Gladys Ellen Killin (*Middle Age 1885–1932*)

EASTLAKE, Charles Locke [1793–1865, English artist and art historian]
Jack Easel (*Our Square and Circle*)

EASTMAN, Charles Alexander [1858–1939, English orientalist, linguist and public servant]
Ohiyesa (*Old Indian Days*)

EASTWICK, Edward Backhouse [1814–83, English barrister, diplomat and orientalist]
An Ex-Political (*Dry Leaves from Young Egypt*)

EASTWOOD, Helen [1892–?, English novelist]
Olive Baxter (*Journey into Danger; The Secret of Blackwater House*)
Fay Ramsay (*Secret Heart*)

EATON, Mrs Charlotte Ann [1788–1859, English novelist and writer]
An Englishwoman Resident at Brussels in June 1815 (*The Days of Battle*)

EATON, Daniel Isaac [d. 1814, English bookseller and fugitive]
Antitype (*The Pernicious Effects of the Art of Printing upon Society*)

EATON, Dorman Bridgman [1823–99, US lawyer and civil service reformer]
Non-Partisan (*The Great City Problem*)

EATON, Seymour [1859–1916, US writer for children]
Paul Piper (*Prince Domino and Muffles*; *Teddy B. and Teddy C., the Roosevelt Bears*)

EBBETT, Frances Eva [1925–, English writer]
Eva Burfield (*Yellow Kowhai*)

EBEL, Suzanne [fl. 1980, English romantic novelist and writer]
Suzanne Goodwin (*Emerald*; *Winter Sisters*)
Cecily Shelbourne (*Stage of Love*)

EBERT, Frank Arthur [1902–84, English crime writer]
Frank Arthur (*Confession to Murder*; *Who Killed Netta Maull?*)

ECCLES, Miss Charlotte O'Connor [1863–1911, Irish novelist and writer]
Hal Godfrey (*The Rejuvenation of Miss Semaphore*)
A Modern Maid (*Modern Man*)

ECKLEY, Joseph [1750–1811, US cleric]
A Friend to Truth (*Divine Glory brought to View*)

EDDY, Arthur Jerome [1859–1920, US lawyer and writer on art]
Chauffeur (*Delight, the Soul of Art*)

EDDY, Caleb [1788–1859, US merchant]
The Agent of the Corporation (*Historical Sketch of the Middlesex Canal*)

EDDY, Daniel Clarke [1823–96, US cleric and writer for children]
Rupert van West (*Rip van Winkle's Travels in Foreign Lands*; *Young Folks' Travels in Europe*)

EDDY, Thomas [1758–1827, US merchant and Quaker]
One of the Inspectors of the Prison (*An Account of the State Prison of New York*)

EDEN, Dorothy [1912–82, New Zealand novelist]
Mary Paradise (*Face of an Angel*; *Shadow of a Witch*)

EDEN, Emily [1797–1869, English novelist and traveller]
E. E. (*The Semi-Attached Couple*)

EDEN, Sir Frederick Morton [1766–1809, English social reformer]
Philanglus (letters to *The Porcupine Newspaper*)
Vindex (*On the Maritime Rights of Great Britain*)

EDGCUMBE, Richard [1764–1839, 2nd Earl of Mount-Edgcumbe; amateur musician]
An Old Amateur (*Musical Reminiscences of an Old Amateur*)

EDGEWORTH, Maria [1768–1849, English novelist and feminist]
E. (in *Monthly Magazine*)

EDKINS, Joseph [1823–1905, English academic – lived sometime in China]
A Resident in Peking (in *Contemporary Review*)

EDMISTON, Helen Jean Mary [1913–, English writer]
Helen Robertson (*The Winged Witness*)

EDMONDS, Helen Woods [1901–68, French-born English fantasy novelist]
Helen Ferguson (*Let Me Alone*; *A Charmed Circle*)
Anna Kavan (*Asylum Piece*; *I am Lazarus*)

EDMONDS, Richard [1801–68, English antiquarian and scientific writer]
Epsilon; E. Redruth (both used in the *Cornish Magazine*)

EDWARDS, Arthur Trystan [1884–1973, English architect]
An Ex-Service Man; J 47485 (both used in *A Hundred New Towns of Britain*)

EDWARDS, Edward [1788–1832, English cleric and writer]
A Presbyter (*Pastoral Recollections*)

EDWARDS, Frederick Anthony [fl. 1935, English mystery writer]
Charman Edwards (*The Blue Macaw*; *Drink No Deeper*)

EDWARDS, George [1694–1773, English natural historian]
A Naturalist (*A Discourse on the Emigration of British Birds*)

EDWARDS, George Graveley [1896–, US writer]
George Graveley (*The Last Hour and other Plays*)

EDWARDS, Sydenham Teak [1769–1819, English botanical artist and editor]
A Practical Floriculturist (*The Ornamental Flower-Garden and Shrubbery*)

EDWARDS, Thomas [1699–1757, English lawyer and literary critic]
The Other Gentleman of Lincoln's Inn (*The Canons of Criticism and Glossary being Supplements to Mr Warburton's Edition of Shakespeare*)
T. E. (*Free and Candid Thoughts on the Doctrine of Predestination ...*)

EDWARDS, William [d. 1890, English civil servant in India]
A Bengal Civilian (*Reminiscences of a Bengal Civilian*)

EGAN, John [1750–1810, Irish lawyer and politician]
Junius Hibernicus (in *Dublin General Evening Post*)

EGAN, Pierce [1772–1849, English journalist and sporting writer]
One of the Fancy (*Boxiana*)

EGERTON, Mary [d. 1858, Countess of Wilton; wrote on cookery]
A Lady of Rank (*Book of Costume or, Annals of Fashion*)

EGERTON-WARBURTON, Rowland Eyles [1804–91, English sporting poet]
R. E. E. B. (*Hunting Songs*)
Rambling Richard (*Epigrams and Humorous Verses*)

EGGLESTON, Edward [1837–1902, US Methodist pastor, novelist and editor]
Leisurely Saunterer (in *Hearth and Home*)
Penholder (in the *New York Independent*)

EGLETON, Clive [1927–, English crime and mystery writer]
Patrick Blake (*Escape to Athena*; *Double Griffin*)
John Tarrant (*Clauberg Trigger*; *Rommel Plot*)

EHRLICH, Bettina [1903–85, Austrian-born English illustrator of books for children]
Bettina (*Foo-Tsee the Water Tortoise*; *Carmello*)

EKLUND, Gordon [1945–, US science-fiction writer]
Wendall Stewart (in *Amazing Stories* magazine)

ELDERSHAW, Flora S. [1897–1956, Australian novelist]
*M. Barnard Eldershaw (*Essays in Australian Fiction*; *Tomorrow and Tomorrow*)

ELDRIDGE, George Jackson [d. 1890, English soldier]
An Eyewitness (in *Blackwood's Magazine*)

ELIAS, Frank [1878–1949, English writer]
John Owen (*Many Captives*)

ELIOT, Sir Charles [1863–1931, English diplomat and traveller]
Odysseus (*Turkey in Europe*)

ELIOT, Edward Granville [1798–1877, 3rd Earl of St Germans; diplomat and Viceroy of Ireland]
An Educational Advocate (*Advice to the Government on Irish Education*)

ELIOT, Francis Perceval [1756–1818, English financial expert]
Falkland (*An Essay on Bigotry*)

ELIOT, John [1604–90, English missionary to the American Indians]
Nobody Must Know Whom (*Poems or, Epigrams, Satyrs ... upon Several Persons and Occasions*)

ELIOT, Samuel Atkins [1798–1862, US merchant]
A Member of the Corporation (*A Letter to the President of Harvard College*)

ELIOT, Thomas Stearns [1888–1965, US poet and critic]
Charles Augustus Conybeare (in *The Egoist*)
Gus Krutzch (in *Tyro Magazine*)
Old Possum (*Old Possum's Book of Practical Cats*)

ELIZABETH, QUEEN OF ROMANIA [1843–1916, writer of sentimental verse and prose]
Sylva Carmen (*Thoughts of a Queen; Shadows on Life's Dial*)

ELLACOMBE, Henry Thomas [1790–1885, English cleric and campanologist]
A Bristol Church-Goer (*Bitton Church*)

ELLERBECK, Rosemary [fl. 1980, South African novelist]
Anna L'Estrange (*Return to Wuthering Heights*)
Nicola Thorne (*The Girls; Woman Like Us*)
Katherine Yorke (*The Enchantress; Falcon Gold*)

ELLERMAN, Annie Winifred [1894–1983, English novelist]
Bryher (*Development; The Fourteenth of October*)
Winifred Bryher (*The Lament for Adonis*)

ELLETT, Harold Pincton [fl. 1935, English crime writer]
Nigel Burnaby (*The Clue of the Green-Eyed Girl; Two Deaths a Penny*)

ELLICE, Edward [1781–1863, English merchant and politician]
Mercator (*The Communications of Mercator*)

ELLICK, Ronald C. [1938–68, US science-fiction writer]
*Fredric Davies (*The Man from UNCLE 14*)

ELLIOT, Arthur Ralph Douglas [1846–1923, English lawyer, politician and editor]
A Spectator (in *MacMillan's Magazine*)

ELLIOT, Frances Minto [1820–98, English writer]
Florentia (in *New Monthly Magazine*)

An Idle Woman (*The Diary of an Idle Woman*)

ELLIOT, Sir Henry Miers [1808–53, English historian and civil servant in India]
*Bartolozzi Brown, Gent (*Polyglot Baby's Own Book*)

ELLIOTT, Charles Wyllys [1817–83, US merchant, novelist and writer]
An American (in *Cornhill Magazine*)
Mr Tom White (*Wind and Whirlwind*)

ELLIOTT, Lady Charlotte [1789–1871, English writer of religious poetry]
Florenz (*Stella and other Poems*)

ELLIOTT, Ebenezer [1781–1849, English peasant poet and radical]
The Corn-Law Rhymer (*More Verses and Prose*)
Veritas (in *Tait's Edinburgh Magazine*)

ELLIOTT, William [1788–1863, US farmer and controversialist]
Agricola (*Carolina Sports by Land and Water*)
An American (*Fiesco – a Tragedy*)

ELLIOTT-CANNON, Arthur [1919–, English writer]
Nicholas Forde (*Cornish Cream; West Country Mysteries*)
Myles Martyn (*Cornish Tales; Somerset Tales*)

ELLIS, Anna M. B. [d. 1911, US journalist, writer and drama critic]
Max Eliot (used for journalism)

ELLIS, Arthur [1850–94, English journalist]
A City Editor (*Rationale of Market Fluctuations*)

ELLIS, Charles Mayo [1818–78, US lawyer]
Libertas (*The Power of the Commander-in-Chief*)

ELLIS, Dora Amy [1878–1961, English crime novelist]
Patricia Wentworth (*The Grey Mask; Miss Silver Deals with Death*)

ELLIS, Edward Sylvester [1840–1916, US historian and writer for children]
H. R. Gordon (*Osceola, Chief of the Seminoles; Pontiac, Chief of the Ottowas; Tecumseh of the Shawanoes*)

ELLIS, Ernest Tetley [1893–1953, English horticulturist]
Eveline T. Everton (used for magazine short-story writing)

ELLIS, George [1753–1815, English satirist, caricaturist and writer]
Sir Gregory Gander Kt. (*Poetry and Tales; Poetical Tales and Trifles*)

ELLIS, Julie [1933–, US romantic novelist]
Alison (or Jeffrey) Lord (*Jeb; Deedee*)
Susan Marino (*Vendetta Castle*)
Julie (or Susan) Marvin (*Revolt of the Second Sex; Summer of Fear*)
Susan Richard (*Intruder at Maison Benedict; Chateau Saxony*)

ELLIS, Peter Berresford [1943–, English fantasy novelist and historical writer]
Peter McAlan (*The Judas Battalion; Kitchener's Gold*)
Peter Tremayne (*Dracula Unborn; The Hound of Frankenstein*)

ELLIS, Royston [1941–, English writer on pop-music]
Richard Tresillian (*The Bondmaster; Fleur*)

ELLIS, Sarah Stickney [d. 1872, English writer and moralist]
An Old Author (*My Brother or, the Man of Many Friends*)

ELLIS, William [1700–58, English agriculturist]
A Person Formerly Concerned in a Publick Brewhouse in London, but for Twenty Years Past has Resided in the Country (*The London and Country Brewer*)

ELLIS-FERMOR, Una Mary [1894–1958, English literary scholar and writer]
Christopher Turnley (*The Sharpness of Death; Twenty Two Poems*)

ELLISON, Cuthbert Edward [1817–83, English barrister]
A Law-Student (in *Bentley's Miscellany*)

ELLISON, Gerald Francis [1861–1947, English soldier and writer]
An English-Company Officer (in *MacMillan's Magazine*)

ELLISON, Harlan [1934–, US science-fiction writer and crime writer]
Lee Archer (*Escape Route*)
Cordwainer Bird (*Portrait of the Artist as a Zilch Writer*)
Price Curtis (*The Girl with the Horizontal Mind*)
John Doyle (*The Girl in the Red Room*)
Wallace Edmondson (*Children's Hour*)
Landon Ellis (*Hit and Run*)
Sley Harson (*He Disappeared*)
Ellis Hart (*Made in Heaven; Buy Me That Blade*)
Ivar Jorgensen (*Children of Chaos*)
John Magnus (*Dead Wives Don't Cheat*)
Jay Solo (*Again the Cat Prowls; A Girl at Gun Point*)
Derry Tiger (*Bayou Sex Cat*)

ELLISON, Henry [1811–80, English poet]
A Born Natural (*Mad Moments or, First Attempts*)
Henry Browne (*Poetry of Real Life; Stones from an Old Quarry*)

ELLISON, Joan Audrey [1928–, English microbiologist and food writer]
Elspeth Robertson (*The Findus Book of Fish Cookery*)

ELLISON, Virginia T. H. [1910–, US author and writer for children]
Virginia T. Howell (*Falla, a President's Dog; Who Likes the Dark*)
Gor Yun Leong (*Chinatown Inside Out*)
Mary A. Mapes (*Fun with your Child; Surprise!*)
Virginia T. Mussey (*The Exploits of George Washington*)

ELMHIRST, Edward Pennell [1845–1916, English soldier, foxhunter and writer]
Brooksby (in *The Field* and for *The Hunting Counties of England*)

ELRINGTON, Thomas [1760–1835, Irish cleric, mathematician and philosopher]
A Clergyman (*A Refutation of the Arguments to Lord Kenmare*)

ELTON, Sir Charles Abraham [1778–1853, English soldier and classical scholar]
Servetus (*A Plea for the Unitarians*)

ELY, George Herbert [1866–1958, English writer for children]
*Herbert Strang (*The Adventures of Harry Rochester*; *Martin of Old London*)

ELYS, Edmund [fl. 1670, English cleric and religious poet]
A Dutiful Son of the Church of England (*An Exclamation to All Those that Love the Lord*)

EMANUEL, Victor Rousseau [1879–1963, English science-fiction writer]
H. M. Egbert (*The Sea-Demons*)
Victor Rousseau (*Derwent's Horse*; *The Messiah of the Cylinder*)

EMANUEL, Walter [1869–1915, English humorist]
Charivaria (in *Punch*)

EMBURY, Mrs Emma Catherine [1806–63, US poet and writer]
Rudolph Hertzmann (*Fugitive Writings*)
Ianthe (*Guido and other Poems*)

EMERSON, George Barrell [1797–1881, US schoolteacher in Boston]
An Old Teacher (in the *Journal of Education*)

EMERSON, William [1701–82, English mathematician]
Nichol Dixon; Merones; Philofluentimechanalgegeomastrolongo (all used in various periodicals)
W. E. (*Navigation ... Tables*; *The Projection of the Sphere*)

EMERY, Mrs Sarah Anna [1821–1907, US novelist]
A Nonagenarian (*Reminiscences of a Nonagenarian*)

EMMONS, Nathaniel [1745–1840, US cleric and theologian]
A New England Pastor (*The Platform of Ecclesiastical Government*)

EMORY, John [1789–1835, US cleric]
An Observer (*The Divinity of Christ Vindicated*)

EMSHWILLER, Edmund Alexander [1925–, US science-fiction illustrator]
Ed Emsh (used for work in *Galaxy* and other science-fiction magazines)

ENDEAN, James Russell [1826–76, English publisher]
Councillor Freeman (*The Political Catechism*)

ENDICOTT, Charles Moses [1793–1863, US mariner and historian]
Junius Americanus (in both the *Boston Gazette* and the *New England Historical and Genealogical Register*)

ENGEL, Howard [1931–, Canadian crime writer]
*F. X. Woolf (*Murder in Space*)

ENGLISH, Mrs Frances Mary [1783–1858, English writer]
A Descendant of the Plantagenet (*Tudors and Stuarts*)

ENGLISH, George Bethune [1789–1828, US writer]
An American in the Service of the Viceroy (*A Narrative of the Expedition to Dongola and Sennaar*)

ENSOR, Sir Robert Charles Kirkwood [1877–1960, English journalist, historian and poet]
Scrutator (in the *Sunday Times* from 1940 to 1953)

EPPS, John [1805–69, English physician and homoeopathist]
Medicus (*Internal Evidences of Christianity*)

EPSTEIN, Samuel [1909–, US novelist]
Charles Strong (*Stranger at the Inlet*)

ERIKSON, Mrs Sybil Alexandra [fl. 1945, English writer]
Alexandra Dick (*The Comet's Tail; A Pack of Cards*)
Frances Hay (*There Was No Moon*)

ERNST, Paul Frederick [1902–, US science-fiction writer]
Paul Frederick Stern (in *Weird Tales* magazine)

ERNSTING, Walter [1920–, German science-fiction editor, writer and publisher]
Clark Darlton (used for the early Perry Rhodan series)

ERSKINE, Andrew [fl. 1763, Scottish writer]
*David Malloch (*Elegy upon the Death of a Young Lady*)

ERSKINE, Sir David [1772–1837, Scottish historian and dramatist]
A Verderer of Windsor Forest (*Favorites, Beauties and Amours of Henry of Windsor*)

ERSKINE, David Steuart [1742–1829, 11th Earl of Buchan; biographer and essayist]
Albanicus (*Letters of Albanicus; Lettters on the Impolicy of a Standing Army*)
An Irish Gentleman (*Irish Chiefs or, The Harp of Erin*)

ERSKINE, Ebenezer [1680–1754, Scottish cleric and preacher]
A Learned, Faithful, Zealous and Reverend Minister of the Church of Scotland (*The Groans of Believers*)

ERSKINE, John [1721–1803, Scottish cleric and pamphleteer]
A Freeholder (*Reflexions on Contentions with the Colonies*)
A Friend in the Country (*Meditations and Letters of a Pious Youth*)

ERSKINE, Ralph [1685–1752, Scottish cleric and poet]
A Minister of the Gospel in the Church of Scotland (*Gospel Canticles*)

ERSKINE, Walter Coningsby [1810–72, Scottish soldier]
One who was There in 1857–58 (*A Chapter of the Bengal Army*)

ESCOTT, Jonathan [1922–, English crime and mystery writer]
Jason Leonard (*Meet Mrs Piercey*)
Jack S. Scott (*The Shallow Grave; A Distant View of Death*)

ESCOTT, Thomas Hay Sweet [1844–1924, English journalist and writer]
A Foreign Resident (*Society in London; Society in the new Reign*)
Thomas Ray (in *Temple Bar*)

ESSEX, Lewis [fl. 1930, English mystery writer]
Richard Starr (*Married to a Spy*)

ESTRIDGE, Robin [fl. 1975, English mystery writer]
Philip Loraine (*Lion's Ransome*)
Robert York (*Swords of December*)

ETTINGSALL, Thomas [fl. 1832, Irish writer on angling]
Geoffrey Greydrake (*The Angling Excursions of Gregory Greendrake*)

EUSDEN, Laurence [1688–1730, English Poet Laureate]
Leo the Second (in *The Guardian*)

EUSTACE, John Skey [1760–1805, American soldier – sometime in France]
An American Officer in the Service of France (*Letters on the Crimes of George III*)

EVANS, Albert Eubule [1839–96, English cleric and authority on Germany]
Roy Tellet (*Pastor and Prelate; Prince Maskiloff; The Outcasts*)

EVANS, Arthur Benoni [1781–1854, English cleric, teacher and writer]
Barnaby Fungus Esq. (*Fungusiana*)
An Old Hand on Board (*Britain's Wreck or, Breakers Ahead*)

EVANS, Caleb [1737–91, English Baptist cleric]
A Lover of Truth and the British Constitution (*A Letter to the Rev. John Wesley*)

EVANS, Constance May [1890–?, Canadian romantic novelist]
Mairi O'Nair (*Some Were Lucky*; *Dangerous Lady*)

EVANS, David [1878–1945, Welsh novelist]
Caradoc Evans (*Wasps*)

EVANS, Evan [1731–89, Welsh poet and historian]
A Curate from Snowdon (*The Love of our Country*)

EVANS, Frederick William [1808–93, US socialist and Shaker]
A Friend of Youth and Children (*Brief and Moral Instruction for the Young*)

EVANS, George Bramwell [1884–1943, English naturalist and broadcaster]
Romany (*The Spirit of Romany*)

EVANS, Sir George De Lacy [1787–1870, Irish-born British soldier]
Officer Serving as Quarter- Master General (*Facts Relating to the Capture of Washington*)

EVANS, George Essex [1863–1909, Australian poet]
Christophus (in *The Queenslander*)

EVANS, Hugh Austin [fl. 1940, US crime writer]
Hugh Austin (*Upside Down Murder*; *Death has Seven Faces*)

EVANS, John [fl. 1719, English Presbyterian cleric]
*Bagweel (*A Collection of Occasional Papers etc.*)

EVANS, John [1814–76, Welsh cleric and poet]
Adda Jones (in *The Baner*)

EVANS, Jonathan [1749–1809, English cleric and preacher]
Coventry (in both *The Gospel* magazine and *The Christian* magazine)

EVANS, Julia [1913–, English mystery novelist]
Polly Hobson (*Brought up in Bloomsbury*; *Venus and her Prey*)

EVANS, Mary Ann [1819–90, English novelist and poet]
George Eliot (*Adam Bede*; *Silas Marner*)
Felix Holt (in *Blackwood's Magazine*)

EVANS, Oliver [1755–1819, US mechanic and inventor]
A Native Born Citizen of the US (*An Exposition of Part of the Patent Laws*)

EVANS, Robert Harding [1778–1857, English bookseller and writer]
Publicola (letters in *The Times*)

EVANS, Samuel [fl. 1859, English preacher – uncle of 'George Eliot']
Seth Bede (*Seth Bede the Methody*)

EVARTS, Jeremiah [1781–1831, US lawyer and journalist]
William Penn (*Essays on American Indians*)

EVELYN, John [1620–1706, English diarist, horticulturist and writer]
A Lover of Peace and of his Country (*An Apology for the Royal Party*)
Philocepos (*The French Gardiner*)

EVELYN, John Michael [1916–92, English barrister and crime writer]
Michael Underwood (*Clear Case of Suicide*; *Murder with Malice*)

EVERARD, Thomas [1560–1633, English Jesuit; used the alias 'Everett']
John Heigham (*The Sum of Christian Doctrine*)

EVERETT, Alexander Hill [1792–1847, US diplomat, essayist and writer]
A Citizen of the United States (*America or, a General Survey etc.*; *Europe or, a General Survey etc.*)

EVERETT, David [1769–1813, US journalist]
An American (*An Essay on the Rights and Duties of Nations*)
Junius Americanus (in the *Boston Gazette*)

EVERETT, James [1784–1872, English Methodist and writer]
Joseph Beaumont (*Wesleyan Takings*)
Coleman Collier (*Gatherings from the Pit-Heaps*)
William Cowper (*An Extraordinary Chace*)
Criticus (*The Visions of Sapience*)
A Disciple of the Old School (*The Disputants*)
Joseph Hall (*The Iron Question*)
James the Less (*The Head-Piece or, Phrenology etc.*)

EVERETT-GREEN, Evelyn [1856–1932, English novelist and writer for children]
Cecil Adair (*A Young Autocrat*)
H. F. E. (*Fast Friends or David and Jonathan*; *Fighting the Good Fight*; *His Mother's Book*; *Lady Temple's Grandchildren*; *Little Freddie or Friends in Need*; *Maud Kinglake's Collect*)
E. Ward (*Patricia Pendragon*)

EVERSON, William [1912–, US poet – one time Dominican]
Brother Antoninus (*The Vision of Felicity*; *The Rose of Solitude'*)

EVES, Reginald T. [fl. 1920, English writer for boys]
Herbert Britton (in *Boy's Friend*)

EWALD, Alexander Charles [1842–91, English historian and civil servant]
Atholl De Walden (*Harry Disney*)

EWART, Ernest Andrew [1878–1943, Indian-born Australian writer]
Boyd Cable (*Action Front*; *The Old Contemptibles*)

EWBANK, Thomas [1792–1870, English manufacturer in New York and scientific writer]
Hab Westman K. O. (*The Spoon*)

EWEN, John [1741–1821, Scottish shop-keeper in Aberdeen]
Civis of Aberdeen (*Observations by Civis of Aberdeen*)

EWING, Mrs Julianna Horatia [1841–85, English writer for children]
J. H. Gatty (her maiden name)
Myra (in *Myra's Journal*)
Mrs Overtheway (*Mrs Overtheway's Remembrances*)

EYLES, Kathleen Muriel [fl. 1945, English novelist]
Merle Eyles (*You and Yourself*)
Catharine Tennant (*Last Orders Please*; *Tomorrow is Free*)

EYRE, Francis [1732–1804, English writer]
A Gentleman (*A Few Remarks on the History of the Roman Empire*)
A Sincere Friend of Mankind (*A Short Essay on the Christian Religion*)

EYRE, William Henry [1823–98, English cleric]
Sacerdos (in *The Rambler*)

F

FABENS, Joseph Warren [1821–75, US pioneer]
A Settler in Santo Domingo (*In the Tropics*)

FABER, Frederick William [1814–63, English Catholic cleric and hymn writer]
A Parish Priest (*The Blessed Sacrament*)

FAGAN, Henry Stuart [1827–90, Irish cleric and writer]
A Church of England Clergyman (in *Fraser's Magazine*)

FAIRBAIRN, Sir Thomas [1823–?, English art connoisseur; wrote on labour relations and social conditions]
Amicus (in *The Times*)

FAIRBANKS, Charles Bullard [1827–59, US writer]
Aguecheek (in the *Boston Saturday Evening Gazette* and for *My Unknown Chum*)

FAIRBURN, Eleanor [1928–, Irish crime writer]
Catherine Carfax (*A Silence with Voices*; *The Locked Tower*)
Emme Gayle (*Cousin Caroline*; *Frenchman's Harvest*)
Elena Lyons (*The Haunting of Abbotsgarth*; *A Scent of Lilacs*)

FAIRFIELD, Cicily Isabel [1892–1983, Irish journalist and novelist]
Corinne Andrews (*The War Nurse*)
Rachel East (in *The Freewoman*)
Lynx (*Lions and Lambs*)
Rebecca West (in *The Freewoman* and for *Henry James, The Return of the Soldiers*, etc.)

FAIRHOLT, Frederick William [1814–66, English engraver and antiquarian]
An Archaeologist (*Rambles of an Archaeologist*)
Literary Antiquity (*Holbein's Dance of Death*)

FAIRLIE, Gerard T. [1899–1983, English journalist, novelist and playwright]
Sapper (after H. C. McNeile's death in 1937 used by Fairlie for some Bulldog Drummond stories published in USA)

FAIRMAN, Paul W. [1916–77, US fantasy and science-fiction writer]
*Adam Chase (*The Golden Ape*)
Ivar Jorgensen (*Ten from Infinity*; *Whom the Gods would Slay*)

FALCONER, Thomas [1738–92, English barrister and classical scholar]
A Layman (*Devotions for the Sacrament*)

FALCONER, William [1732–69, English mariner and poet – died at sea]
A Sailor (*The Shipwreck*)

FALCONER, William [1744–1824, Scottish physician and writer]
A Layman (*Dissertation on St Paul's Voyage*)

FALKENER, Edward [1814–96, English architect]
A Pilgrim in the Holy Land (*David's Vision*)
E. F. O.Thurcastle (*Does the Revised Version effect the Doctrines of the New Testament?*)

FANE, John [1784–1859, 11th Earl of Westmorland; soldier, diplomat and musician]
An Officer Employed in his Aarmy (*Memoirs of the Early Campaigns of the Duke of Wellington*)

FANE, Julian Henry Charles [1827–70, English diplomat and poet]
*Neville Temple (and Edward Trevor) (*Tannhauser or, The Battle of the Bards*)

FANNING, Nathaniel [1755–1805, US mariner]
An American Navy Officer (*Narrative of the Adventures of an American Navy Officer*)

FANTHORPE, Robert Lionel [1935–, English science-fiction writer]
Erle Barton (*The Planet Seekers*)
Lee Barton (*The Unseen; The Shadow Man*)
Thornton Bell (*Space Trap; Chaos*)
Leo Brett (*The Drud; Exit Humanity*)
Bron Fane (*Last Man on Earth; The Crawling Fiend*)
Victor La Salle (*Menace from Mercury*)
Robert Lionel (*Time Echo*)
J. E. Muller (*The Ultimate Man; Perilous Galaxy*)
Phil Nobel (*The Hand from Gehenna*)
Lionel Roberts (*Time Echo; The Incredulist*)
Neil Thanet (*Beyond the Veil; The Man Who Came Back*)
Trebor Thorpe (*The Haunted Pool*)
Pel Torro (*Frozen Planet; The Phantom Ones*)
Olaf Trent (*Roman Twilight*)
Karl Ziegfried (*Atomic Nemesis; Projection Barrier*)

FANTONI, Barry [1940–, English cartoonist, writer and musician]
E. I. Addio; Glenda Slagg (both used in *Private Eye*)
*Sylvie Krin (*Born to be Queen; Love in the Saddle*)
*Old Jowett (*The Bible for Motorists*)
*E. J. Thribb (*So Farewell Then ... and other Poems*)

FARGUS, Frederick John [1847–85, English novelist and auctioneer]
Hugh Conway (*Dark Days; Called Back*)

FARJEON, Eleanor [1881–1965, English writer for children]
Chimaera (in *Time and Tide* magazine)
Tom Fool (in the *Daily Herald*)

FARJEON, Joseph Jefferson [1883–1955, English playwright and crime writer]
Anthony Swift (*Murder at a Police Station*)

FARMER, Philip Jose [1918–, US science-fiction writer]
Paul Chapin; Harry Manders; Jonathan Swift Somers III (all used in the *Magazine of Science Fiction*)
Kilgore Trout (*Venus on the Half-Shell*)

FARNIE, Henry Brougham [d. 1889, Scottish sporting writer]
A Keen Hand (*The Golfer's Manual*)

FARNWORTH, Richard [d. 1666, English Quaker cleric]
A Servant of the Lord (*Antichrists Man of War Apprehended*)

FARQUHARSON, James [1781–1843, Scottish cleric and scientist]
Palaeophilus Minor (*Aberdeen Colleges*)

FARRAR, Mrs Eliza Ware [1791–1870, French-born US writer]
A Lady (*The Children's Robinson Crusoe; The Young Lady's Friend*)

FARRAR, Frederick William [1831–1903, English cleric, academic, novelist and writer]
F. T. L. Hope (in *The Quiver* and for *The Three Homes*)

FARRAR, Timothy [1788–1874, US jurist]
A Member of the New England Historical and Genealogical Society (*A Memoir of the Farrar Family*)

FARRELL, James Thomas [1904–79, US novelist and short-story writer]
Jonathan Titulescu Fogarty (*The Name is Fogarty*)

FARSON, Daniel Negley [1927–, English writer]
Matilda Excellent (*The Dog Who Knew Too Much*)

FARWELL, Janet [1897–, English writer for children]
E. Croly (*The Street That Ran Away*; *A Sailing We Will Go*; *The Lucky Tub*)

FAST, Howard [1914–, US historical novelist]
E. V. Cunningham (*Case of the Russian Diplomat*; *Penelope*)
Walter Erikson (*Fallen Angel*)

FAUCIT, Helena Saville [1817–98, Lady Martin; actress]
One who has Impersonated Them (*On Some of Shakespeare's Female Characters*)

FAUSSET, Thomas Godfrey [1829–77, English barrister and archaeologist]
Quinquagenarius (*A Few Plain Reasons for Retaining our Subscription to the Articles of Matriculation*)

FAUST, Frederic Schiller [1892–1944, US mystery and western novelist; war correspondent killed in Italy]
Frank Austin (*King of the Range*)
George Owen Baxter (*The Gauntlet*; *Call of the Blood*)
Max Brand (*Destry Rides Again*; *The Untamed*)
Walter C. Butler (*The Night Flower*)
Peter Dawson (in *Western Story* magazine)
Evan Evans (*The Border Bandit*; *Outlaw Valley*)
Frederick Frost (*The Bamboo Whistle*; *Secret Agent Number One*)

FAWCETT, Edgar [1847–1904, US novelist, poet and writer]
Karl Drury (in the *Family Star*)

FAWCETT, Frank Dubrez [1891–1968, English thriller and science-fiction writer]
Ben Sarto (*Miss Otis Comes to Piccadilly*)
Simpson Stokes (*Air-Gods' Parade*)

FAWCETT, John [1740–1817, English Baptist theologian]
Christophilus (*The Christian's Humble Plea*)

FAWCETT, Joseph [d. 1804, English cleric and poet]
Sir Simon Swan, Bart. (*The Art of Poetry*)

FAWKES, Francis [1720–77, English cleric, translator and poet]
A Gentleman of Cambridge (*The Works of Anacreon, Sappho etc.*)

FAY, Theodore Sedgwick [1807–98, US journalist and writer]
One of the Editors of the NY 'Mirror' (*Sketch of the Life of John Howard Paine*)
A Quiet Man (*Dreams and Reveries of a Quiet Man*)

FEAGLES, Anita MacRae [1926–, US crime writer]
Travis MacRae (*Death in View*; *Trial by Slander*)

FEARING, Lilian Blanche [1863–1901, US poet and writer]
Raymond Russell (*Asleep and Awake*)

FEARN, John Russell [1908–60, English science-fiction writer]
Geoffrey Armstrong (in *Tales of Wonder* magazine)
Thornton Ayre (used in the following magazines: *Astounding Science Fiction*; *Amazing Stories*; *Fantastic Adventures*; *Super Science Stories*; *Future Fiction*; *Planet Stories*; *Science Fiction*)
Hugo Blayn (*The Five Match Boxes*; *What Happened to Hammond?*)
Dennis Clive (in *Science Fiction* and *Future Fiction* magazines and for *Valley of Pretenders* and *The Voice Commands*)
John Cotton (in *Science Fiction and Future Fiction* magazines)
Polton Cross (*Other Eyes Watching*; also used in the following magazines: *Astounding Stories*; *Amazing Stories*; *Thrilling Wonder Stories*; *Fantastic Adventures*; *Astonishing Stories*; *Future Fiction*; *Science Fiction*; *Marvel Stories*; *Super Science Stories*; *Startling Stories*)
Astron del Martia (*The Trembling World*)
Spike Gordon (*Don't Touch Me*)

Volsted Gridban (*The Dyno-Depressant*; *Moons for Sale*)

Conrad G. Holt (*Cosmic Exodus*)

Frank Jones (in *Amazing Stories* magazine)

Paul Lorraine (*Dark Boundaries*)

Jed McNab (*Injun Canyon*; *Guntoter from Kansas*)

Dom Passante; Ephraim Winiki (both used in *Science Fiction* magazine)

Laurence F. Rose (*The Hell-Fruit*)

John Russell (*Account Settled*)

Brian Shaw (*Z Formations*)

John Slate (*Maria Marches On*; *Death in Silhouette*)

Vargo Statten (*Operation Venus*; *The Micro-Men*)

Earl Titan (*The Gold of Akada*; *Anjani the Mighty*)

FEARNE, Charles [1742–94, English jurist and writer]
Junius (in the *Public Advertiser*)

FEARON, Percy Hutton [1874–1948, English cartoonist]
Poy (in the *Evening News* and for *How to Draw Newspaper Cartoons*)

FEHRENBACH, Theodore Reed [1925–, US military writer]
Thomas Freeman (*Crisis in Cuba*)

FEIGE, Hermann Albert Otto Max [1882–1969, US novelist and writer; enigmatic as to his background]
Ben (or Bruno) Traven (*The Death Ship*; *The Treasure of Sierra Madre*)

FEINBERG, Bea [1915–88, US romantic novelist]
Cynthia Freeeman (*Come Pour the Wine*; *Fairy Tales*)

FEIST, Henry Mort [fl. 1875, English sporting writer]
Augur (*The Racing Prophet*)
Hotspur (in the *Sporting Life*)

FELKIN, Alfred Laurence [1856–1942, English school inspector and writer]
Alfred St Laurence (*My Heart and Lute*)

FELLIG, Arthur [1900–68, US photographer]
Weegee (*Naked City*)

FELLOWES, Robert [1771–1847, English academic benefactor and religious writer of liberal opinions]
Philalethes, MA, Oxon. (*The History of Ceylon*)
The Spirit of Hampden (used for journalism)

FELTON, Ronald Oliver [1909–82, Welsh writer for children]
Ronald Welch (*Captain of Dragoons*; *Knight Crusader*)

FENETY, George E. [1812–99, Canadian journalist]
A Bluenose (*The Lady and the Dressmaker*)

FENN, Lady Eleanor [1743–1813, English writer of educational works for children]
(Mrs) Solomon Lovechild (*The Child's Grammar*; *The Mother's Grammar*; *Mrs Lovechild's Golden Present*)
Mrs Teachwell (*Fables*; *The Juvenile Tatler*)

FENNELL, James [1766–1816, English-born US actor]
Nemo Nobody (*Something, Edited by Nemo Nobody*)

FENOLLOSA, Mrs Mary M'Neil [1879–1954, US poet and writer]
Sidney MacCall (*The Dragon Painter*; *Red Horse Hill*)

FENTON, Richard [1746–1821, Welsh historian, barrister and poet]
A Barrister (*A Tour in Quest of Genealogy*)

FERGUSON, Adam [1723–1816, Scottish cleric and natural philosopher]
A Gentleman in the Country (*Remarks on a Pamphlet by Dr Price*)

FERGUSON, James [1857–1917, Scottish writer]
A Conservative; A Free Church Layman; A Scottish Conservative (all used in the *Scottish Review*)

FERGUSON, Robert [1637–1714, English nonconformist cleric]
A. B. (*A Letter to Secretary Trenchard*)

FERGUSON, Samuel [1810–86, Irish lawyer, antiquarian and poet]
Mr Michael Hefferman (*Father Tom and the Pope*)

FERGUSON, William Blair Morton [1881–1944, Irish-born US mystery novelist]
William Morton (*The Murderer*; *The Case of Caspar Gault*)

FERRIDGE, Philippa [fl. 1980, English romantic novelist]
Philippa Wiat (*Bride in Darkness*; *My Lute be Still*)

FERRIS, Henry [fl. 1840, Irish cleric]
Irys Herfner; George Hobdenthwaite Snogby (both used in *Dublin University Magazine*)

FESSENDEN, Thomas Green [1771–1837, US journalist and satirist]
Christopher Caustick (*Democracy Unveiled, or Tyranny Stripped of the Garb of Patriotism*; *The Modern Philosopher*; *A Poetical Petition*; *Terrible Tractoration*)
Peter Pepperbox (*Pills: Poetical, Political and Philosophical*)
Peter Periwinkle; Simon Spunkey (both used in the *Farmer's Weekly Museum*)
A Practical Gardener (*The American Kitchen Gardener*)

FETTER, Elizabeth Pickering [1904–73, US novelist and writer]
Hannah Lees (*Death in the Doll's House*; *Prescription for Murder*)

FETZER, Herman [1899–1935, US journalist and writer]
Jake Falstaff (*The Book of Rabelais*; *Jacoby's Corners*)

FICKE, Arthur Davison [1883–1945, US poet and writer]
Anne Knish (*Spectre*)

FIELD, Barron [1786–1846, English jurist, poet and critic]
A Barrister (*Hints to Witnesses ... in the Courts of Justice*)

FIELD, Edward S. [1878–1936, US dramatist]
Childe Harold (*The Child's Book of Abridged Wisdom*; *In Pursuit of Priscilla*; *Cupid's Understudy*)

FIELD, Edwin Wilkins [1804–71, English solicitor, writer and amateur artist]
A Solicitor (*Observations by a Solicitor on the Equity Courts*)

FIELD, Joseph M. [1810–56, English-born US actor and journalist]
Everpoint (*The Drama in Pokerville*; *Three Years in Texas*)
Old Straws; Straws (both used in the *New Orleans Picayune*)

FIELDING, Alexander Wallace [1918–, English translator and writer]
Xan Fielding (*Corsair Country*; *The Money Spinner*)

FIELDING, Dorothy [fl. 1924, English crime writer]
A. Fielding (*The Eames-Erskine Case*; *Murder in Suffolk*)

FIELDING, Henry [1707–54, English burlesque writer, novelist and essayist]
Abraham Adams; Stephen Grub (in the *True Patriot*)
C. and L.; Capt. Hercules Vinegar of Hockley in the Hole (both used in *The Champion or British Weekly*)
Sir Alexander Drawcansir Knt, Censor of Great Britain (in the *Covent Garden Journal*)
Lemuel Gulliver, Poet Laureate to the King of Lilliput (*The Masquerade*)
Mr Conny Keyber (*An Apology for the Life of Mrs Shamela Andrews*)
A Lover of his Country (*The Crisis, a Sermon*)

Pasquin (letter in *Common Sense* and for
*Tumble-Down Dick ... a Dramatick
Entertainment*)
Philalethes (letter in the *Daily Post*)
P. H. I. Z. C. G. S. (*The Figure of the
Terrestrial Chrysipus*)
Monsieur Sans Esprit (*Tumble-Down Dick
or, Phaeton in the Suds*)
(H) Scriblerus Secundus (*The Tragedy of
Tragedies; The Grub Street Opera; The
Author's Farce; Tom Thumb; The Letters
Written on a New Way to Keep a Wife at
Home; The Welsh Opera*)
John Trott-Plaid (in *Jacobite's Journal*)

FIELDING, Sarah [1710–68, romantic
novelist – sister of Henry Fielding above]
A Lady (*The Adventures of David Simple*)

FIELDING-HALL, Harold Patrick
[1859–1917, Irish novelist]
H. (or Henry or Harold) Fielding (*The Field
of Honour*)

FIGGIS, Darrell [1882–1925, Irish poet,
novelist and journalist]
Gnathai Gan Tarraidh (*Sinn Fein Catechism;
The Sacred Egoism of Sinn Fein*)
Michael Ireland (*The Return of the Hero;
Children of Earth*)

FINCH, Anne [d. 1720, Countess of
Winchilsea; poet]
Ardelia (*The Spleen, a Pindariqe Ode*)
A Lady (*Miscellany of Poems on Several
Occasions*)

FINDLEY, William [1750–1821, Irish-born
US politician]
A Citizen (*A Review of the Revenue System*)

FINE, John [1797–1867, US attorney and
politician]
A Lawyer (*Lectures on Law from Kent*)

FINK, Merton [1921–, English dentist and
writer]
Matthew (or Merton) Finch (*Snakes and
Ladders; Five as Symbols; Simon Bar
Cochba*)

FINKELL, Max [1909–, English novelist]
Max Catto (*The Flanagan Boy; The Devil at
Four o' Clock*)
Simon Kent (*Lions at the Kill; Fire Down
Below*)

FINLEY, Martha Farquharson [1828–1909,
US writer for children]
Martha Farquharson (*Allan's Fault; Elsie
Dinsmoore*)

FINN, Edmund [1819–98, Irish-born
Australian writer]
Garryowen (*The Chronicles of Early
Melbourne*)
An Old Colonist (*The Garryowen Sketches*)

FINN, Mary Paulina [1842–1935, US poet]
M. S. Pine (*Sacred Poems; John Bannister
Tabb, the Priest Poet*)

FIRBANK, Arthur Annesley Ronald
[1886–1926, English novelist]
Arthur (or Ronald) Firbank (*A Study in
Temperament; Inclinations*)

FIRTH, Josiah Clifton [fl. 1880, New
Zealand writer]
Arthur Fonthill (*Weighed in the Balance: a
Play for the Times*)

FIRTH, Violet Mary [1890–1946, US occult
novelist and writer]
Dion Fortune (*The Mystical Qabalah; The
Esoteric Philosophy of Love and Marriage*)

FISCHER, Bruno [1908–, German-born US
mystery writer]
Russell Gray (*The Lustful Ape*)

FISH, Robert Lloyd [1912–81, US crime
writer]
Robert L. Pike (*Mute Witness; Police Blotter*)
Lawrence Roberts (*The Break In; Alley
Fever*)

FISH, Williston [1858–1939, US lawyer and
railway executive]
Charles Loundsberry (*The Happy Testament*)

FISHER, G. S. [fl. 1845, English sporting
writer]
Perditus (in *Bentley's Miscellany*)

FISHER, Sidney George [1809–71, US lawyer and poet]
Cecil (*Kansas and its Constitution*)

FISHER, Stephen Gould [1912–80, US crime and mystery writer]
Steve Fisher (*The Night Before Murder*; *Winter Kill*)
Stephen Gould (*Homicide Johnny*; *Murder of the Admiral*)
Grant Lane (*Spend the Night*)

FISHER, Thomas [1781–1836, English civil servant and antiquarian]
An Abolitionist (*The Negro's Memorial*)
Antiquitatis Conservator (in *Gentleman's Magazine*)

FISHER, William [1780–1852, English admiral]
A Naval Officer (*The Petrel*)

FISKE, Nathan [1733–99, US cleric and writer]
The Neighbor (in the *Massachusetts Spy*)

FISKE, Samuel Wheelock [1828–64, US humorist]
Dunn Browne (in the *Springfield Republican* and for *Mr Dunn Browne's Experiences in the Army*)

FISKE, Stephen [1840–1916, US drama critic and adventurer]
An American (*English Photographs*)

FITCHETT, William Henry [d. 1928, English cleric and historical writer – sometime in Australia]
Vedette (*Deeds that Won the Empire*; *How England Saved Europe*; *A Tale of the Great Mutiny*)

FITZGERALD, Eileen [fl. 1935, Irish writer]
Lilian Clifford (*A Company of Sinners*; *The New Law*; *The Way of a Fool*)

FITZGERALD, Geraldine Penrose [1870–1903, Irish writer]
Frances A. Gerard (*Picturesque Dublin*; *Some Fair Hibernians*; *The Romance of Ludwig II*; *Some Celebrated Irish Beauties*)

Naseby (*The Silver Whistle*; *Oaks and Birches*)

FITZGERALD, Maurice [1774–1849, Irish statesman and politician]
The Knight of Kerry (*A Letter to Sir Robert Peel*)

FITZGERALD, Percy Hetherington [1834–1925, Irish lawyer, novelist, sculptor and painter]
Gilbert Dyce (*Bella Donna*)
One of the Boys (*School Days at Saxonhurst*)

FITZGERALD, Robert Alan [fl. 1866, English sporting writer]
Quid (*Jerks in from Short-Leg*)

FITZGIBBON, Edward [1803–57, Irish journalist and writer on angling]
Ephemera (*The Book of the Salmon*; *A Handbook of Angling*)

FITZGIBBON, John [1749–1802, Earl of Clare, Lord Chancellor of Ireland]
Paddy Whack (*No Union! But Unite and Fall*)

FITZHUGH, Percy Keese [1876–1950, US writer]
Hugh Lloyd (*Roy Blakeley*; *Pee-Wee Harris*; *Tom Slade*)

FITZMAURICE-KELLY, James [1857–1923, English academic and Spanish scholar]
Edgbaston (in the *New Review*)

FITZROY, Augustus Henry [1735–1811, 3rd Duke of Grafton; politician]
A Layman, a Friend to the True Principles of the Constitution (*Hints Submitted to the Serious Attention of the Clergy, Nobility and Gentry Newly Associated*)

FITZWILLIAM, Richard [1745–1816, 7th Viscount Fitzwiliam; writer and museum founder]
Atticus (*Letters of Atticus*)

FLACK, Harvey [1912–66, English physician and writer]
Harvey Graham (used for contributions to learned and unlearned journals and magazines)

FLAGG, Edmund [1815–90, US lawyer, civil servant and writer]
A Traveller (*The Far West*)

FLAGG, John [fl. 1955, US crime writer]
John Gearon (*Death's Lovely Mask*; *Dear Deadly Beloved*)

FLANDERS, Henry [1826–1911, US lawyer]
Oliver Thurston (*Adventures of a Virginian*)

FLANNER, Janet [1892–1978, US journalist and novelist]
Genet (in the *New Yorker*)

FLATMAN, Thomas [1637–88, English painter and poet]
Adoniram Bonstittle, alias Tinderbox (*Naps upon Parnassus*)

FLEETWOOD, William [1656–1723, English cleric and writer; Bishop of Ely]
A Curate of Wilts (*A Letter to the Rev. Dr Snape*)
A Divine of the Church of England (*A Sermon Against Such as Delight in War*)
A Lay Hand (*An Account of the Life of the Blessed Virgin*)

FLEMING, Caleb [1698–1779, English Presbyterian cleric and pamphleteer]
An Advocate of the Christian Revelation (*Remarks on Mr Tho. Chubb's Short Dissertation*)
Credens (*An Antidote for the Rising of Age*)
An English Catholic of the Metropolitan Diocese (*A Catholic Epistle or Pastoral Letter*)
A Friend to Truth and the Present Establishment (*Remarks upon the Life of John, Duke of Argyle*)
The Late Master of the Temple (*Natural and Revealed Religion at Variance*)
A Lover of his Country (*The Immorality of Profane Swearing*)
A Parishioner of the Doctor (*A Letter to the Rev. Dr Cobden*)
Philalethes Londiniensis (*Civil Establishments in Religion*)
Philaleutheros (*St Paul's Heretic*)
Philotheorus (*Religion Not the Magistrate's Province*)
A Protestant (*The Jesuit Unmasked*)
A Protestant Dissenter of Old England (*The Claims of the Church of England*)
A Protestant Dissenting Minister (*A Letter from a Protestant Dissenting Minister on the Alarming Growth of Popery*)
Rusticus (*The Devout Laugh*)
Theophilus (*Free Thoughts upon a Free Enquiry*)

FLEMING, Francis A. [d. 1793, American Catholic cleric]
Verax (*The Calumnies of Verus*)

FLEMING, John [1786–1832, Scottish-born Canadian merchant]
A British Settler (*The Political Annals of Lower Canada*)

FLEMING, Mrs Mary Agnes [1840–79, Canadian writer]
Cousin Mary Carleton (in the *New York Mercury* and the *Boston Pilot*)

FLEMING, Oswald Atherton [d. 1950, Scottish journalist and writer]
Donald Maconochie (*The Craft of the Short Story*)

FLEMING, Robert [1630–94, Scottish cleric and religious writer]
A Lover of the Truth (*A Survey of Quakerism*)
A Minister of the Gospel (*Scripture Truth Confirmed*; *The True Settlement of a Christian's Faith*)

FLEMING, Robert Peter [1907–71, English journalist and travel writer]
Strix (in *The Spectator*)

FLEMING, Ronald [fl. 1950, English writer for girls]
Rhoda Fleming (in *Girl's Crystal*)

Renee Frazer (in both *School Friend* and
Schoolgirl's Own)

Peter Langley (in *School Friend*)

FLETCHER, Andrew [1655–1716, Scottish
anti-unionist]
Philo-Caledon (*A Short View of the Scots
Colony*)

FLETCHER, Harry [1902–, English novelist
and writer on gardening]
John Garden (*All on a Summer's Day*; *6 to
10*)
John Hereford (*Hay Harvest*; *Shepherd's
Tump*)

FLETCHER, Henry Charles [1832–79,
English soldier]
An English Officer (in the *Cornhill
Magazine*)

FLETCHER, John William [1729–85, Swiss-
born English theologian and cleric]
A Lover of Quietness and Liberty of
Conscience (*A Vindication of Mr Wesley's
Last Minutes*)

FLETCHER, Joseph Smith [1863–1935,
English journalist, novelist and crime
writer]
A Son of the Soil (*Old Lattimer's Legacy*;
Where Highways Cross; *The Winding Way*;
Life in Arcadia; *God's Failures*)

FLETCHER, Julia Constance [1858–1939,
US novelist and dramatist]
Dudu (*Kismet*)
George Fleming (*The Head of Medusa*; *The
Fantasticks*)

FLETCHER, William [d. 1845, Irish writer]
A Country Gentleman (*Lights, Shadows of
Whigs and Tories*)
Junius Secundus (in the *Dublin General
Evening Post*)

FLINDELL, Thomas [1767–1824, English
journalist and printer]
An Uneducated Man (*Prison Recreations*)

FLINT, Henry M. [d. 1868, US journalist]
The Druid (in the *New York World*)

FLINT, William [fl. 1815, English writer on
the turf]
An Old Sportsman (*A Treatise on the
Breeding of Horses*)

FLOOD, Henry [1732–91, Irish politician and
duellist]
Syndercombe (letters to the *Freeman's
Journal*)

FLOREN, Lee [1910–, US western novelist]
Brett Austin (*Gambler's Gun-Lock*)
Wade Hamilton (*Ride Against the Rifles*)
Matthew Whitman Harding (*Edge of
Gunsmoke*)
Felix Lee Horton (*Long Knife and Musket*)
Stuart Jason (*Valley of Death*; *Deadly
Doctor*)
Grace Lang (*Nedra*)
Marguerite Nelson (*Mercy Nurse*; *Hard
Rock Nurse*)
Maria Sandra Sterling (*War Drum*)
Lee Thomas (*The Gringo*)
Will Watson (*Wolf Dog Range*)
Matthew Whitman (*Muskets on the
Mississippi*)

FLORENCE, William Jermyn [1831–91, US
actor; his real name was Bernard Conlin]
Florence (*The Gentleman's Handbook of
Poker*)

FLOWER, Benjamin [1755–1829, English
radical political writer]
A Friend to the Constitution (*The Principles
of the British Constitution*)

FLOWER, William B. [1819–68, English
cleric, poet and writer]
The Curate of Stoke Damerel (*A Revival of
the Old Church of England Principles*)

FLOYD, John [1572–1649, English Jesuit and
controversial writer]
Annosus Fidelis Verimentanus Druinus (*A
Survey of the Apostacy of Marcus*)
Daniel a Jesu (*An Apology of the Holy Sea*)
A Student in Divinity (*A Secure and Prudent
Choice of Belief*)

FLUDD, Robert [1574–1637, English physician and Rosicrucian writer]
Alitophilus (*Religio Exculpata*)
Joachim Frizius (*Summum Bonorum*)
Rudolf Otreb (*Tractatus Theologophilosophicus*)

FLYNN, Sir Joshua Albert [1863–1933, English novelist and short-story writer]
Owen Oliver (*A Knight at Heart*; *An Author's Daughter*)

FOGG, Lawrence Daniel [1879–1914, English-born US journalist]
Gordon Gossip (*The Asbestos Society of Sinners*)

FOLEY, Dave [fl. 1963, US science-fiction writer]
Gerald Hatch (*The Day the Earth Froze*)

FOLEY, Pearl [fl. 1933, Canadian writer]
Paul De Mar (*The Gnome Mine Mystery*)

FOLKARD, Charles James [1878–1963, English writer and illustrator for children]
Draklof (created 'Teddy Tail' in the *Daily Mail*)

FOLKARD, Henry Coleman [d. 1914, English barrister and writer]
A Barrister (*Every Man his Own Lawyer*)

FOLLEN, Mrs Eliza Leee [1787–1860, US writer]
A Lady (*Selections from the Writings of Fenelon*)

FOLLETT, Kenneth Martin [1949–, Welsh crime and mystery novelist]
Symon Myles (*The Big Needle*; *The Big Hit*)
Zachary Stone (*Modigliani Scandal*)

FOLSOM, Franklin Brewster [1907–, US writer for children]
Benjamin (or Franklin) Brewster (*The First Book of Eskimos*)
Michael Gorham (*Cowboys*; *Abraham Lincoln*)
Lyman Hopkins (*Real Book about Baseball*)
Troy Nesbit (*Indian Mummy Mystery*; *The Hidden Ruin*)

FONNEREAU, Thomas George [1789–1850, English lawyer, artist and writer]
H. E. O. (*Diary of a Dutiful Son*)
T. G. F. (*Memoirs of a Tour in Italy*)

FOOT, Michael Mackintosh [1913–, English journalist and politician]
Cassius (in the *Daily Herald*)
*Cato (*Guilty Men*; *The Trial of Mussolini*)

FOOT, Stephen Henry [1887–1966, English schoolmaster]
Tank Major (*Tank Tales*)

FOOTE, John Alderson [1848–1922, English barrister]
A Circuit Tramp (*Pie-Powder*)

FOOTE, Samuel [1720–77, English actor and dramatist]
Timothy Timbertoe Esq. (*A Trip to Calais*)

FORBES, Archibald [1838–1900, Scottish soldier, journalist and biographer]
A Dragoon on Furlough; A Private Dragoon (both used in *St Paul's Magazine*)
One who has Served in the Ranks (in *Cornhill Magazine*)

FORBES, Deloris Stanton [1923–, US mystery novelist]
Stanton Forbes (*Encounter Darkness*; *Relative to Death*)
*Forbes Rydell (*They're Not Home Yet*; *No Questions Answered*)
Tobias Wells (*Dead by the Light of the Moon*; *A Die in the Country*)

FORBES, Duncan [1685–1747, Scottish jurist and theologian]
Philo-Scotus (*A Copy of a Letter from a Gentleman in Edinburgh*)

FORBES, John Hay [1776–1854, Lord Medwyn; Scottish jurist]
A Layman (*An Address to Members of the Episcopal Church in Scotland*)

FORBES, Lewis William [1794–1854, English cleric]
A Country Minister (in *Blackwood's Magazine*)

FORBES, Robert [1708–75, Scottish cleric and Jacobite; Bishop of Ross and Caithness]
Philo-Roskelynsis (*An Account of the Chapel of Roslin*)
Ruling Elder of the Church of Scotland (*An Essay on Christian Burial; An Essay on the Nature of the Human Body; Kirks and Kirk-Yards*)

FORBES, William Anderson [1839–79, Scottish-born Australian writer]
Alexander Forbes (*Voices from the Bush*)

FORBES, William Hay [fl. 1824, English writer]
*Sir Morgan O'Doherty (in *Blackwood's Magazine*)

FORBES-DENNIS, Mrs Ernan [1884–1963, English novelist and writer]
Phyllis Bottome (*Master Hope; A Certain Star*)

FORD, Corey [1902–69, US humorist, novelist and playwright]
John Riddell (*The John Riddell Murder Case; In the Worst Possible Taste*)

FORD, David Everard [1797–1875, English cleric, theologian and hymn writer]
A Composer (*Observations on Psalmody*)

FORD, Thomas [1743–1821, English cleric]
Master Shallow (in *Gentleman's Magazine*)

FORD, Thomas Murray [fl. 1910, English novelist]
*John Le Breton (*Mis'ess Joy*)
Thomas Le Breton (*An Amateur Champion; The Dark Horse*)

FORD, William [1821–1905, English novelist and civil servant in India]
William St Clair (*Prince Babar and his Wives; Zobeir or, Turkish Misrule*)

FORREST, Richard Stockton [1932–, US mystery writer]
Stockton Woods (*The Laughing Man; Game Bet*)

FORRESTER, Alfred Henry [1804–72, English artist, engraver and humorist]
*A. or Alfred Crowquill (*A Few Words about Pipes, Smoking and Tobacco; How He Reigned and How He Mizzled; Seymour's Humorous Sketches; Leaves from my Memorandum Book*)
A. Fibb (in *Bentley's Miscellany*)
The Ghost of Harry the Eighth's Fool (*A Missile for Papists!*)

FORRESTER, Charles Robert [1803–50, English novelist and humorist]
*A. or Alfred Crowquill (see entry for brother above)
A Lover of the Weed (in *Bentley's Miscellany*)
W. F. von Kosewitz (*Eccentric Tales*)
Hal Willis, Student at Law (*Castle Baynard; Sir Roland*)

FORRESTER, Thomas [1635–1706, Scottish cleric and preacher]
A Minister of the True Presbyterian Church of Scotland (*A Counter-Essay or, Assertion of Calvin*)

FORSHALL, Josiah [1797–1863, English antiquarian and librarian]
A Fellow of the Royal and Antiquarian Societies (*The Apology of an Israelite*)

FORSTER, Josiah [1726–90, English draper and Quaker]
A Quaker (*A Quaker's Reasons for Opening his Shop on Christmas Day*)

FORSTER, Thomas Ignatius Maria [1789–1860, English astronomer and natural philosopher]
Philochelidon (*Observations on the Brumal Retreat of the Swallow*)
A Physician (*Medicina Simplex*)
Verax (*Christian Unitarianism Vindicated*)

FORSYTH, Robert [1766–1846, Scottish topographer and writer]
Civis (*A Letter to Henry Erskine*)

FORSYTH, Robin [fl. 1934, US writer]
Peter Dingwall (*The Poison Duel*)

FORTESCUE, George [d. 1859, English writer]
*George F. Preston (*Poems*)

FORTESCUE, John William [1859–1933, English military historian]
Stevinus (in *MacMillan's Magazine*)

FOSBROOKE, Thomas Dudley [1770–1842, English cleric and historian]
A Gentleman of the University of Oxford (*The Cosmopolitan*)
A Young Gentleman of the University (*Poetical Essays*)

FOSDICK, Charles Austin [1842–1915, US novelist and writer for boys]
Harry Castlemon (*Frank and Archie*; *Rebellion in Dixie*; *Sailor Jack, the Trader*)

FOSS, Edward [1787–1870, English jurist and biographer]
John Gifford (*Blackstone's Commentaries – an Abridgement*)

FOSTER, Alfred Edye Manning [d. 1939, English journalist and bridge player]
Diner-Out (*London Restaurants*)

FOSTER, Charles James [1820–83, US journalist and sporting writer]
Privateer (in the *New York Sportsman*)

FOSTER, Hannah Webster [1759–1840, US novelist]
A Lady of Massachusetts (*The Coquette*; *The Boarding School: or Lessons of a Preceptress to her Pupils*)

FOSTER, John [1770–1843, English Baptist cleric and writer]
A Quiet Looker- On (in the *Morning Chronicle*)

FOSTER, Reginald Frank [1896–1975, English cleric and writer for boys]
Francis Foster (*The Lift Murder*; *Joyous Pilgrimage*)

FOSTER, Theodosia Maria T. [1838–?, US writer]
Faye Huntington (*Millerton People*; *Opportunity Circle*)

FOSTER, William [1772–1863, US wine merchant]
Franklin (*Fellow Citizens of Philadelphia*; *An Examination of Mr Bradish's Answer*)

FOULDS, Elfrida Vipont [1902–92, English Quaker writer and children's author]
Elfrida (or Charles) Vipont (*Little Bit of Ivory*; *Elephant and the Bad Baby*; *Blow the Man Down*)

FOULIS, Sir James [1714–91, Scottish antiquarian]
An Old Hereditary Burgess (*Observations on the Bridge Tax*)

FOWLE, Thomas Welbank [1835–1903, English cleric and social reformer]
Cellarius (*A New Analogy of Religion*)

FOWLE, William Bentley [1795–1865, US educationalist and essayist]
A Bostonian (*The Socialist Schooled*)

FOWLER, Frank [1833–63, English journalist]
Harper Atherton (*Adrift or, The Rock in the South Atlantic*)
Cosmopolitan (in the *Sydney Empire*)
A Literary Vagabond (in the *Sydney Morning Herald*)
A Lounger (*Dottings of a Lounger*)

FOWLER, Henry Watson [1858–1933, English essayist and philologist]
Egomet (*Si Mihi*)
Quilibet (*Between Boy and Man*)
Quillet (*More Popular Fallacies*)

FOWLER, Kenneth A. [1900–, US journalist and novelist]
Clark Brooker (*Fight at Sun Mountain*)

FOWLER, Thomas [1832–1904, English academic and historian]
Presbyter Academicus (in *MacMillan's Magazine*)

FOWLER, William [1560–1614, Scottish poet]
P. of Hawick (*Triumphs of Petrarke*)

FOWLER, William Warde [1847–1921, English cleric, ornithologist and writer]
An Oxford Tutor (*A Year with the Birds*)

FOX, Edward [1829–62, English poet]
Lynn Erith (*Poetical Tentatives*)

FOX, Sir Frank [1874–1960, Australian-born journalist and writer; settled in England in 1909]
G. S. O. (*G. H. Q.*)

FOX, Gardner Francis [1911–, US science-fiction writer]
Jefferson Cooper (*The Swordsman*; *This Sword for Hire*)
Jeffrey Gardner (*Barbary Devil*; *Cleopatra*)
James Kendricks (*Beyond our Pleasure*; *Love Me Tonight*)
Simon Majors (*The Druid Stone*)
Bart Somers (*Beyond the Black Enigma*; *Abandon Galaxy!*)

FOX, George [1624–91, English founder of the 'Society of Friends']
A Lover of Souls (*A Warning from the Lord to the Pope*)
The Servant of Christ (*A True Account of the State of God's People*)

FOX, Henry Richard Vassall [1773–1840, 3rd Baron Holland; politician, satirist and writer]
An Englishman (*Letters to a Neopolitan from an Englishman*)

FOX, Hugh [1932–, US writer]
Connie Fox (*Our Lady of Laussel*; *Skull Worship*)

FOX, Mrs Sarah [1800–82, English poet]
Sphinx (*Catch Who Can or, Original Double Acrostics*)

FOX, William Johnson [1786–1864, English Unitarian cleric, preacher, politician and social reformer]
A Norwich Weaver Boy (*Letters of a Norwich Weaver Boy*)
Publicola (in the *London Dispatch*)

FOXCROFT, Frank [1850–1921, US journalist and poet]
Reynard (*Transcript Pieces*)

FOXCROFT, George Augustus [1815–75, US farmer and humorist]
Job Sass (in the *Boston Herald*)

FOXCROFT, Thomas [1697–1769, American cleric]
An Impartial Hand (*The Ruling and Ordaining Power of Bishops*)
Phileleuth Bangor, V. E. B. (*Eusebius Inermatus*)

FOXWELL, Edward Ernest [1851–1922, English railway enthusiast]
E. Poingdestre (in *Temple Bar*)

FRAENKEL, Heinrich [1897–1986, German-born English journalist and writer on chess]
Assiac (in the *New Statesman* and for *Adventure in Chess* and *Delights of Chess*)

FRANCE, Lewis B. [1833–1907, US lawyer and writer]
Bourgeois (*Over the Old Trail*; *Pine Valley*)

FRANCE, Ruth [1913–68, New Zealand novelist and poet]
Paul Henderson (*Unwilling Pilgrim*; *The Halting Place*)

FRANCHETT, Mrs Elizabeth [fl. 1773, English writer]
Mrs Sharp-Set O'Blunder (*Granny's Prediction revealed to Mrs Sharp-Set O'Blunder*)

FRANCIS, Dorothy Brenner [1926–, US romantic novelist]
Sue Alden (*The Magnificent Challenge*; *Nurse of St John*)
Ellen Goforth (*Path of Desire*; *A New Dawn*)
Pat Louis (*Treasure of the Heart*)

FRANCIS, Sir Philip [1740–1818, Irish political secretary in London and in India, Member of Parliament and political pamphleteer and writer]
Atticus; Britannicus; A Friend to Public Credit; Junius; Lusitanicus; Ulissipo

Britannicus (all used in letters to the *Public Advertiser*)

The Cocoa-Tree (*Letter from the Cocoa-Tree to the Country Gentleman*)

FRANCIS, Samuel Ward [1835–86, US physician and writer]
A Singular Man (*Inside Out, a Curious Book*)

FRANCIS, Stephen Daniel [1917–, US crime and thriller writer]
Hank Janson (*When Dames Get Tough; Gun Moll for Hire*)

FRANKAU, Mrs Julia [1864–1916, English novelist]
Frank Danby (*Dr Phillips, a Maida Vale Idyll; The Heart of a Child*)

FRANKAU, Pamela [1906–67, English journalist and novelist]
Eliot Naylor (*The Off-Shore Light*)

FRANKEN, Rose Dorothy [1895–1988, US playwright and novelist]
Margaret Grant (*Call Back Love*)
*Franken Meloney (*Strange Victory; American Bred*)

FRANKLIN, Benjamin [1706–90, American scientist, statesman, printer and free-thinker]
Father Abraham (*Father Abraham's Speech to a Great Number of People etc.*)
Alice Addertongue; Anthony Afterwit (both used in the *Pennsylvania Gazette*)
B. B. (*A Modest Enquiry into the Nature and Necessity of Paper Money*)
Mistress Silence Dogood; Dr Janus; Richard Saunders (all used in the *New England Courant*)
A Good Conscience (*The Art of Procuring Pleasant Dreams*)
Historicus (in the *Federal Gazette*)
Medius (*Remarks Relative to the American Paper Money*)
Poor Richard (*Poor Richard's Almanac*)
Celia Single (letter to the *Pennsylvania Gazette*)
A Tradesman of Philadelphia (*Plain Truth*)

FRANKLIN, Miles [1879–1954, Australian writer]
Brent of Bin Bin (*Up the Country; Prelude to Waking*)
Mrs Ogniblat L'Artsau (*Net of Circumstance*)

FRANKLIN, William [1731–1831, American politician]
Jack Retort (*A Humble Attempt at Scurrility*)

FRASER, Alexander Charles [1815–83, Scottish military chaplain]
Bono-Johnny (in *Blackwood's Magazine*)

FRASER, Agnes D. [1859–1944, English writer]
Frances MacNab (in *Temple Bar*)

FRASER, Anthea Mary [fl. 1985, English crime and mystery writer]
Lorna Cameron (*Summer in France*)
Vanessa Graham (*Time of Trail; The Stand-in*)

FRASER, Mrs Augusta Zelia [d. 1925, English writer]
Alice Spinner (*Lucilla: an Experiment; A Reluctant Evangelist*)

FRASER, Claud Lovat [1890–1921, English artist and theatrical designer; his given names were 'Lovat Claud' but he reversed them]
Richard Honeywood (*Two Wizards and Other Songs*)

FRASER, William [1817–79, Scottish cleric and schoolmaster]
Paul Whistlecraft (in *Bentley's Miscellany*)

FRASER, Sir William Augustus [1826–98, English soldier, politician and writer]
The Knight of Morar (*Coila's Whispers; Poems*)

FREDERIC, Harold [1856–98, US journalist and novelist]
George Forth (*March Hares*)

FREEDGOOD, Morton [1912–, US crime and mystery writer]
John Godey (*The Taking of Pelham One Two Three*)

FREEDLEY, Edwin Troxell [1827–1904, US businessman and writer]
Glaucus (*Opportunities for Industry*)

FREEMAN, Gage Earle [1820–1903, English cleric and expert on falconry]
Peregrine (in *The Field*)

FREEMAN, Gillian [1929–, English novelist and writer]
Eliot George (*The Leather Boys*)
Elaine Jackson (*Lovechild*)

FREEMAN, John Henry Gordon [1903–, English journalist]
Andrew Merry (*Rhymes of Andrew Merry*)

FREEMAN, Julia Deane [fl. 1860, US writer]
Mary Forrest (*The Women of the South*)

FREEMAN, Kathleen [1897–1959, Welsh crime novelist and Greek scholar]
Caroline Cory (*Doctor Underground*)
Mary Fitt (*Sweet Poison*)
Stuart Mary Wick (*And Where's Mr Bellamy?*; *The Statue and the Lady*)

FREEMAN, Sir Ralph [fl. 1635, English dramatist and public servant]
Philophrastes (*Seneca the Philosopher*)

FREEMAN, Richard Austin [1862–1943, English physician, surgeon and crime novelist]
Clifford Ashdown (*The Adventures of Romney Pringle*)

FREEMANTLE, Brian Harry [1936–, English crime and mystery novelist]
Jonathan Evans (*The Midas Men*; *Monopoly*)
Richard Gant (*Sean Connery*)
John Maxwell (*HMS Bounty*; *The Mary Celeste*)
Jack Winchester (*The Solitary Man*; *The Choice of Eddie Franks*)

FREETH, John [1730–1808, English writer]
John Free (*Modern Songs on Various Subjects*; *The Warwickshire Medley*)

FREIND, John [1675–1728, English physician and writer]
J. Byfielde (*A Letter to the Learned Dr Woodward*)

FREMONT, John Charles [1813–90, US explorer, soldier and politician]
The Pathfinder of the Rocky Mountains (*To Oregon and North California*)

FRENCH, Alice [1850–1934, US novelist]
Octave Thanet (*Knitters in the Sun*; *Stories of a Western Town*)

FRENCH, Mrs Lucy Virginia [1820–81, US writer]
L'Inconnue (*Kernwood*; *Wind Whispers*; *Legends of the South*)

FRENCH, Nicholas [1604–78, Irish cleric and religious writer]
A Gentleman in the Country (*A Narrative of the Earl of Clarendon's Settlement*)
One Well Affected (*Querees Propounded by the Protestant Partie concerning the Peace in ... Ireland*)

FRENCH, Thomas Valpy [1825–91, English cleric; Bishop of Lahore]
A Late Missionary Bishop (*Some Notes of Travel*)

FREND, William [1757–1841, English academic, mathematician and reformer]
A Member of the Senate (*Considerations on the Oaths required by the University of Cambridge*)

FRENEAU, Philip [1752–1832, American mariner and poet]
Tomo Cheeki (in *The Time-Piece*)
Jonathan Pindar Esq. (*The Probationary Odes of Jonathan Pindar Esq.*)
Abbe Robin (*New Travels through North America*)
Robert Slender (*A Journey from Philadelphia to New York*; *A Laughable Poem*)

FRERE, John Hookham [1769–1846, English diplomat and writer]
*Gregory Griffin (in *Microcosm*)

Wm and Robert Whistlecraft (*The Monks and the Giants*)

FRESHFIELD, Jane [fl. 1861, English writer]
A Lady (*Alpine Byways*)

FREWER, Glyn Mervyn Louis [1931–, English writer]
Mervyn Lewis (*British Tax Law*; *Death of Gold*)

FREY, Charles W. [fl. 1950, US crime writer]
Ferguson Findley (*Remember That Face*; *A Handful of Murder*)

FRIEDMAN, Andre E. [1913–54, Hungarian-born US photo-journalist – killed in Indo-China]
Robert Capa (used chiefly for his coverage of the Spanish Civil War and WW2)

FRIEDMAN, Eve Rosemary [1929–, English novelist and writer]
Robert (or Rosemary) Tibber (*Practice Makes Perfect*; *We All Fall Down*)

FRIELL, James [fl. 1937, English cartoonist]
Gabriel (in the *Daily Worker*)

FRIEND, Oscar Jerome [1897–1963, US editor and science-fiction writer]
Owen Fox Jerome (*The Hand of Horror*; *The Corpse Awaits*)
Ford Smith (*Action at Powder River*)

FRISWELL, James Hain [1825–78, English novelist and writer]
Gibson Craig (*Half-Length Portraits*)
Jaques (in the *Evening Star*)
Mr Limbertongue (*Twelve Insides and One Out*)

FRITH, John [1503–33, English cleric; burnt as heretic at Smithfield]
Richard Brightwell (*A Pistle to the Christian Reader*)
John Knokes (*An Admonition or Warning that the Faithful Christians in London, Newcastel etc.*)

FROST, John [1800–59, US educationalist and writer]
William V. Moore (*Indian Wars of the United States*)
Robert Rambler (*Robert Rambler's Stories*)
A Veteran Soldier (*The Heroes of the American Revolution*)

FROUDE, James Anthony [1818–94, English historian, essayist and biographer]
Zeta (*Shadows of the Clouds*)

FRY, Anne [1764–1829, English writer]
A Friend who is Lateley Deceased (*An Affectionate Address to the Working Classes*)

FRY, Bertha [1884–?, English writer for girls]
Bertha Leonard (*Daphne the Day Girl*; *The School at Kesteven*; *The Star of St Anne's*)

FRY, Joseph Storrs [1826–1913, English merchant and Quaker]
Peter Bullcalf (*The History of John Bull*)

FULLER, Hiram [1812–80, US journalist]
Belle Brittan (*Transformation Scenes in the United States*)
The White Republican (*North and South*)

FULLER, James Franklin [1835–1924, Irish writer]
A Common Soldier (in the *Fortnightly Review*)
Ignotus (*Culmshire Folk*)
An Old Boy (*Billy, a Sketch*)

FULLER, Morris Joseph [1831–1901, English cleric]
A Priest of the Diocese of Exeter (*Ritualism*)

FULLER, Roy Broadbent [1912–91, English poet, novelist and writer]
Mark Members (*Iron Aspidistra*)

FULLER, Samuel Richard [fl. 1909, US writer]
Norman Brainerd (*The Cadet Sergeant*; *Winning his Shoulder Straps*)

FULLER, Thomas [1608–61, English cleric, historian and religious writer]
A Lover of his Native Country (*An Alarum to the Counties of England and Wales*)

FULLER, Timothy [1778–1835, US lawyer and politician]
A Citizen (*The Election of the President of the United States Considered*)

FULLERTON, Alexander Fergus [1924–, English novelist]
Anthony Fox (*Kingfisher Scream*; *Threat Warning Red*)

FULLERTON, Mary Eliza [1868–1946, Australian writer]
E. (*Moles do So Little with their Privacy*; *The Wonder and the Apple*)

FURLY, Benjamin [1636–1714, English translator and Quaker]
A Friend to Truth who is No Respecter of Persons (*The World's Honour Detected*)

FURMAN, Gerrit Maspeth [1782–1848, US poet and novelist]
Rusticus, Gent. (*Long Island Miscellanies*)

FURNESS, William Henry [1802–96, US cleric]
A Member of the American Philosophical Society (*The Voice in Singing*)

FYGE, Sarah [d. 1723, English poet]
Sarah Egerton (*Poems on Several Occasions*)
A Young Lady (*An Ode on the Death of John Dryden*)

FYLEMAN, Rose Amy [1877–1957, English writer for children]
R. F. (in *Punch*)

G

GAGE, Mrs Frances Dana [1808–84, US writer]
Aunt Fanny (*Poems*; *Steps Upwards*; *Gertie's Sacrifice*)

GAIRDNER, John [1790–1876, Scottish physician and medical writer]
Aliquanto Latior (*Robert Burns and the Ayrshire Moderates*)

GALBRAITH, John Kenneth [1908–, Canadian economist, diplomat and writer]
Mark Epernay (in *Esquire Magazine*)

GALE, Frederick [1823–1904, English cricketer and writer]
Wykeham Frederick (*The History of the English Revolution*)
Old Buffer (used in *Punch*, *The Globe*, *Bailey's Magazine* and *Cornhill Magazine*)
Wykehamist (*Paddy-Land and the Lakes of Killarney*; *Ups and Downs of a Public School*)

GALE, Norman Rowland [1862–1942, English poet and literary critic]
Rusticus (*Thistledown Essays*)

GALE, Samuel [1783–1865, Canadian jurist]
Nerva (in the *Montreal Herald*)

GALLAGHER, Frank [1898–1962, Irish journalist]
David Hogan (*Dark Mountain*)

GALLATIN, Albert [1761–1849, Swiss-born US politician and anthropologist]
A Citizen of Pennsylvania (*An Examination of the Conduct of the Executive*)

GALLATLY, William [1850–1914, English mathematician]
London M. A. (in *National Review*)

GALLENGA, Antonio Carlo Napoleone [1810–95, Italian-born British journalist, historian and academic]
Anglomane (in *Fraser's Magazine*)
Luigi Mariotti (*Italy: General Views of its History and Literature*)

GALLICHAN, Walter Matthew [1861–1946, English journalist]
Geoffrey Mortimer (in *Westminster Review*)

GALLOWAY, Joseph [1730–1803, American lawyer and pamphleteer]
An American (*Political Reflections on the Late Colonial Government*)
Cicero (*Letters from Cicero to Catiline the Second*; *The Claim of the American Loyalists*)
Fabricius (*Fabricius's Letters to the people of Great Britain*)

GALLUN, Rymond Z. [1911–, US science-fiction writer]
William Callaghan (*The Machine that Thought*)

GALSWORTHY, John [1867–1933, English novelist and dramatist]
A. R. P.-M. (*The Burning Spear*)
John Sinjohn (*From the Four Winds*; *Jocelyn*; *Villa Rubein*; *A Man of Devon*)

GALT, John [1779–1839, Scottish novelist, poet and writer]
Agricola; Bandana; Cabot; The Dean of Guild; Domenichino; Nantucket (all used in *Blackwood's Magazine*)

Micah Balwhidder (*Annals of the Parish*)
Nathan Butt (in *Fraser's Magazine*)
Rev. T. Clark (*The Wandering Jew*)
Thomas Duffle (*The Steamboat*)
An Invalid (*Efforts by an Invalid*)
Archibald Jobbry (*The Member – an Autobiography*)
Samuel Prior (*All the Voyages Round the World*)

GANDLEY, Kenneth Royce [1920–, English crime and mystery writer]
Oliver Jacks (*Implant*; *Assassination Day*)
Kenneth Royce (*The Third Arm*; *X. Y. Y. Man*)

GANDOLPHY, Peter [1779–1821, English Jesuit and religious writer]
A Catholic Priest (*Letters Addressed to the Archbishop of Canterbury*)

GANE, William Law [1815–79, English-born Canadian journalist]
The Lowe Farmer (used for journalism)

GANTNER, Neilma [1922–, Australian writer]
Neilma Sidney (*Beyond the Bay*; *Saturday Afternoon*)

GARDINER, Alfred George [1865–1946, English journalist and political writer]
Alpha of the Plough (*Essays*; *Windfalls*; *Leaves in the Wind*)

GARDINER, Dorothea Frances [1879–?,English crime and mystery writer]
Theodore Frank (*The Lifted Latch*)

GARDINER, Marguerite [1789–1849, Countess of Blessington; novelist and writer]
Idler (*The Idler in Italy*; *The Idler in France*)

GARDINER, Richard [1723–81, English soldier and writer]
Will Honeycomb Esq. (*The History of Pudica*)
Dick Merryfellow (*September – a Rural Poem*)

GARDINER, William [1770–1853, English musician and publisher]
A Dilettante (*Music and Friends*)

GARDNER, Augustus Kingsley [1812–76, US physician]
A Student in Paris (*Old Wine in New Bottles*)

GARDNER, Erle Stanley [1889–1970, US travel and crime writer]
A. A. Fair (*Double or Quits*; *Gold Comes in Bricks*)
Charles M. Green (in the *Black Mask* magazine)
Carleton Kendrake (*The Clue of the Forgotten Murder*)
Charles J. Kenny (*This is Murder*)

GARDNER, Jerome [1932–, English novelist]
John Gilchrist (*Lifeline*; *The Engendering*)
Paul Tully (*The Horsing Blacksmith*; *The Jehovah's Jailbreak*)

GARDNER, John [1804–80, Scottish physician and medical writer]
A Physician (*Hymns by a Physician*)

GARDNER, John Lane [1793–1869, US soldier]
An Officer of the Line (*Military Control*)

GARDNER, Samuel Jackson [1788–1864, US journalist]
Decius (used in various periodicals)

GARFIELD, Brian Francis Wynne [1939–, US crime and mystery writer]
Bennett Garland (*Seven Brave Men*; *Rio Chama*)
Alex Hawk (*Savage Guns*)
John Ives (*Fear in a Handful of Dust*)
Drew Mallory (*Target Manhattan*)
Frank O'Brian (*The Rimfire Murders*; *Act of Piracy*)
Bryan (or Frank) Wynne (*The Bravos*; *Arizona Rider*)

GARFIT, Arthur [1825–84, English cleric]
A Clergyman in the Diocese of Winchester (*The Ecclesiastical Commission*)

GARLAND, James Albert [1870–1906, US editor and horseman]
Jorrocks (*The Private Stable*)

GARMAN, Douglas [1902–69, English writer]
*John Mavin (*Charles Baudelaire*)

GARNET, Henry [1555–1606, English Jesuit – executed following the 'Gunpowder Plot']
An English Divine at Doway (*An Apology against the Defence of Schisme*)

GARNETT, David [1892–1981, English publisher, critic and novelist]
Leda Burke (*Dope-Darling*)

GARNETT, Edward William [1868–1937, English publisher and essayist]
James Byrne (*Lords and Masters*)

GARNETT, Richard [1835–1906, English librarian, poet and man of letters]
A. G. Trent (in the *University Magazine* and for *The Soul and the Stars*)

GARNHAM, Robert Edward [1753–1802, English cleric]
Terrae Filius (*A Letter to the Rt. Rev.Lewis*)

GARRETSON, James Edmund [1828–95, US physician and writer]
John Darby (*Brushland*; *A System of Oral Surgery and Dentistry*; *Odd Hours of a Physician*; *Nineteenth Century Sense*)

GARRETT, George [fl. 1935, English seaman and writer]
Matt Low (in *The Adelphi*)

GARRETT, Randall [1927–, US science-fiction writer]
*Gordon Aghill; Grandall Berretton; Leonard G. Spenser; *Gerald Vance (all used in *Amazing Stories* magazine)
Walter Bupp (*The Right Time*; *Modus Vivendi*)
*Ralph Burke; *Richard Greer; *Clyde Mitchell (all used in *Fantastic Adventures* magazine)
David Gordon (in *Analog* magazine)
Darrel T. Langart (*Anything You Can Do*)

*Mark Phillips (in *Astounding Science Fiction* magazine)
*Robert Randall (*The Dawning Light*; *The Shrouded Planet*)
*S. M. Tenneshaw (in *Imaginative Tales* magazine)

GARRICK, David [1717–79, English actor, dramatist and poet]
D. G. (*An Ode upon Dedicating a Bbuilding ... to Shakespeare*)
Oakley (letters to *St James's Chronicle*)
W. C. (*Lilliput, a Dramatic Entertainment*)

GARRISH, Henry J. [d. 1956, English writer for boys]
Harry Belbin (in *Pluck*)
Jack Fordwich (in *Film Fun*)

GARSIA, Willoughby Clive [1881–1961, New Zealand soldier and writer]
Guy Cottar (*Tenacity*; *A Key to Victory*; *Planning the War*)

GARTER, Bernard [fl. 1578, English poet]
Ber. Gar. (*Queen Elizabeth's Progress to Norwich, An. 1578*; *The Tragical History of Two English Lovers*)

GARVICE, Charles [1833–1920, English journalist and romantic novelist]
Charles Gibson (*The Price of Honour*)
Caroline Hart (*Hearts of Fire*; *Strange Marriage*)

GARVIN, Amelia Beers [1878–1956, Canadian poet , historian and writer]
Katherine Hale (*Morning in the West*; *The New Joan*; *The White Comrade*)

GARVIN, James Louis [1868–1947, English journalist]
Calchas; Emeritus (both used in *Fortnightly Review*)

GASCOIGNE, George [1525–77, English poet, tragedian and critic]
A True Englishman (*The Spoyle of Antwerpe*)

GASPEY, Thomas [1788–1871, English journalist, historian and novelist]
George Godfrey (*History of George Godfrey Written by Himself*)
John Jones (in *Bentley's Miscellany*)

GASTON, William James [1927–, Scottish crime and mystery writer]
Jack Bannatyne (*Torpedo Squadron*; *The Mountain Eagles*)

GATAKER, Thomas [1574–1654, English Puritan cleric and religious writer]
*Theophilus Timorcus (*The Covenanter's Plea against Absolvers*)

GATCHELL, Charles [1851–1910, US novelist]
M. E. Dicus, MD (*Bless Thee, Bully, Doctor*)
Thorold King (*Haschisch*)

GATTY, Margaret [1807–73, English author and writer for children]
Aunt Judy (*The Fairy Godmothers*; *Aunt Judy's Tales*; *Aunt Sally's Life*; *The Mother's Book of Poetry*)

GAUDEN, John [1605–62, English cleric and religious writer; Bishop of Worcester]
A Person of Honour (*Cromwell's Bloody Slaughter-House*)

GAULT, William Campbell [1910–, US mystery writer]
Will Duke (*Fair Prey*)
Dial Forrest (in *Saga* magazine)
Roney Scott (in *Dime Mystery* magazine)

GAUNTLETT, Henry [1762–1833, English cleric]
Detector (*Letters to the Stranger in Reading*)

GAUNTLEY, William [1775–1860, English Quaker]
A Temperate Drinker (*Animadversions on Teetotalism*)

GAY, John [1685–1732, English poet]
J. G. (*The Present State of Wit*)
W. B. (*The Mohocks*)

GAYE, Selina [fl. 1816, English writer for children]
A Clergyman's Daughter (*Aunt Agnes*)

GAYTON, Edmund [1608–66, English academic – adopted son of Ben Johnson]
Asdryasdust Tossoffacan (*Wit Revived*)
Hugh Tubervill (*Walk Knaves Walk*)

GAZE, Richard [1917–, English scientist and crime writer]
John Gale (*Spare Time for Murder*; *Death for Short*)

GEACH, Christine [1930–, English romantic novelist]
Elizabeth Dawson (*Isle of Dreams*; *The Bending Reed*)
Anne Lowing (*Branch and the Briar*; *Copper Moon*)
Christine Wilson (*Some Other Spring*; *The Man in the Blue Car*)

GEDDES, Alexander [1737–1802, Scottish cleric and biblical scholar]
Polemophilus Brown (*A New Year's Gift to the Good People of England*)
H. W. Hopkins (*A Sermon Preached before the University of Cambridge*)
A Protesting Catholic (*An Answer to the Bishop of Comana*)
An Upper Graduate (*A Letter to the Archbishop*)

GEE, Herbert Leslie [1901–77, English writer]
Francis Gay (*The Friendship Book*)

GEIER, Chester S. [1921–, US fantasy writer]
Guy Archette (in *Amazing and Fantastic Adventures* magazine)

GEISEL, Theodor Seuss [1904–91, US writer for children]
Theo Le Sieg (*Many Mice of Mr Brice*)
Dr Seuss (*The King's Stilts*)
Rosetta Stone (*Because a Little Bug went Ka-Choo!*)

GELDART, Edmund Martin [1844–85, English Unitarian cleric – lost at sea]
Nitram Tradleg (*A Son of Belial*)

GELDART, George Cooke [1820–78, English cleric]
A Member of the Philological Society (in *MacMillan's Magazine*)

GELLIS, Roberta [1927–, US romantic novelist]
Max Daniels (*Space Guardian*; *Offworld!*)
Priscilla Hamilton (*Love Token*)
Leah Jacobs (*The Psychiatrist's Wife*)

GENET, Edmond Charles [1765–1834, French-born writer – sometime in USA]
A Citizen of New York (*Letters to the Electors of President and Vice- President*)

GENTLEMAN, Francis [1728–84, Irish dramatist and actor]
Sir Humphrey Lunatic, Bart. (*A Trip to the Moon*)
Sir Nicholas Nipclose (*The Theatre – a Poetical Dissection*)

GEORGE III [1738–1820, King of England; gardening and farming enthusiast]
Ralph Robinson of Windsor (in *The Annals of Agriculture*)

GEORGE, Peter [1924–66, Welsh writer]
Peter Bryant (*Two Hours to Doom*)

GEORGE, Robert Esmond Gordon [1890–1969, New Zealand writer and biographer]
Robert Sencourt (*The Life of Newman*; *Spain's Ordeal*)

GERAHTY, Digby George [d. 1981, Canadian writer]
Stephen Lister (*Sainte Monique Limited*; *Smell of Brimstone*)
Robert Standish (*End of the Line*; *Three Bamboos*)

GERARD, Edwin Field [1891–1965, Australian writer]
Trooper Gerardy (*The Road to Palestine and Other Verses*; *Australian Light Horse Ballads and Rhymes*)

GERARD, James Watson [1794–1874, US lawyer and poet]
A. Fishe Shelley (*Ostrea*)

GERSON, Noel Bertram [1914–, US novelist]
Samuel Edwards (*Savage Gentleman*; *Theodora*)
Paul Lewis (*Yankee Admiral: a Biography of David Dixon Porter*)
Carter A. Vaughn (*Fortress Fury*; *The River Devils*)

GERVAIS, Terence White [fl. 1967, English writer]
Gervas D'Olbert (*Chastisement Across the Ages*)

GESSNER, Lynne [1919–, US writer for children]
Merle Clark (*Ramrod*)

GHOSE, Zulfikar [1935–, Pakistani writer and academic]
William Strang (*Britain in World Affairs*; *Texas Inheritance*)

GIBBONS, Harry Hornsby Clifford [1888–1958, English writer for boys]
Gilbert Chester (in both *Union Jack* and *Detective Weekly*)

GIBBONS, James Sloan [1810–92, US writer]
Robert Morris (*Courtship and Matrimony*; *The Organisation of the Public Debt*)

GIBBS, Cosmo Hamilton [1872–1942, English journalist , librettist and playwright]
Cosmo Hamilton (*The Belle of Mayfair*; *The Beauty of Bath*)

GIBSON, Charles Hammond [1874–1954, US writer]
Richard Sudbury (*Two Gentlemen in Touraine*)

GIBSON, Edmund [1669–1748, English cleric and historian; Bishop of London }
A Minister (*Serious Advice to Persons who Have Been Sick*)

GIBSON, George Herbert [1846–1921, Australian writer]
Ironbark (*Southerly Busters*)

GIBSON, Patrick [1782–1829, Scottish artist and writer]
Roger Roundrobin (*A Letter to the Managers of the Royal Institution, Edinburgh*)

GIBSON, Thomas [1647–1722, British physician]
A Fellow of the College of Physicians, London (*The Anatomy of the Humane Bodies Epitomized*)

GIBSON, Walter B. [1897–, US mystery writer]
Andy Adams (*Brazilian Gold Mine Mystery; Egyptian Scarab Mystery*)
Ishi Black (*The Key to Judo and Jiujitso*)
Douglas Brown (*Anne Bonny, Pirate Queen; The Key to Solitaire*)
Maxwell Grant (*Eyes of the Shadow; Return of the Shadow*)
Maborushi Kineji (*Judo: Attack and Defense*)

GIDDINGS, Joshua Reid [1795–1864, US lawyer, politician and abolitionist]
Pacificus (*The Rights and Privileges of States in Regard to Slavery; The Exiles of Florida; History of the Rebellion*)

GIESY, John Ulrich [1877–1947, US physician and writer]
Charles Dustin (*Riders of the Desert Trail*)

GIFFEN, Sir Robert [1837–1910, Scottish journalist and statistician]
Economist (*The Approaching General Election; The Statist on Ireland*)

GIFFORD, James Noble [1896–1957, US novelist]
Emily Noble (*Happy Holiday*)
John Saxon (*The Common Passion*)

GIFFORD, Richard [1725–1807, English cleric, poet and writer]
R. Duff (in *Gentleman's Magazine*)

GIGGAL, Kenneth [1927–, English crime and mystery writer]
Angus Ross (*The London Assignment; A Bad April*)

GILBART, James William [1794–1863, English writer and lecturer on banking]
A Fellow of the Royal Society (*Logic for the Million*)

GILBERT, Claudius [d. 1696, Irish cleric and religious writer]
A Minister of Belfast (*A Preservative Against the Change of Religion*)

GILBERT, Davies [1767–1839, English scientist and politician]
Davies Giddy (*A Plain Statement of the Bullion Question*)
A Member of Parliament (*Cursory Observations on the Importation of Corn*)

GILBERT, Sir Geoffrey [1674–1726, English jurist and legal writer]
A Late Learned Judge (*The Law of Evidence; An Historical View of the Court of Exchequer; An Historical Account of the Law of Devises*)
A Late Lord Chief Baron (*A Treatise on Rents; A Treatise on the Court of the Exchequer*)

GILBERT, Sir John Thomas [1829–98, Irish historian]
An Irish Archivist (*On the History of Public Records in Ireland; Record Revelations; Record Revelations Resumed*)

GILBERT, Lady [1841–1921, Irish novelist]
Rosa Mulholland (*Cousin Sara; Twin Sisters*)
Ruth Murray (*Dunmara*)

GILBERT, Ruth [1918–, English writer for children]
Ruth Ainsworth (*Another Lucky Dip; Phantom Cyclist*)

GILBERT, Thomas [1720–98, English barrister, politician and social reformer]
A Member of Parliament (*A Scheme for the Better Relief of the Poor*)

GILBERT, Sir William Schwenk
[1836–1911, English dramatist, barrister and burlesque writer]
Bab (in *Fun* and for *Bab Ballads*)
F. L. Tomline (*Happy Land*)

GILCHRIST, Beth Bradford [1879–1957, US writer]
John Prescott Earl (*The School Camp*; *On the School Team*)

GILDON, Charles [1665–1724, English deist, dramatist and writer]
A Careful Hand (*The Lives of the English Dramatick Poets*)
Sir Roger Dewhimsey (*The Post-Man Robb'd of his Mail, or the Packet Broke Open*)
Lindamour (*The Miscellaneous Works of Charles Blount*)

GILES, Carl Ronald [1916–, English cartoonist]
Giles (in the *Sunday Express* and the *Daily Express*)

GILES, Elise Williamina [1859–1921, English writer]
Lise Boehm (in *Temple Bar*)

GILES, Kenneth [1922–72, English crime and mystery writer]
Charles Drummond (*A Death at the Bar*; *The Odds on Death*)
Edmund McGirr (*The Hearse with Horses*; *An Entry of Death*)

GILES, William Branch [1762–1830, US politician]
A Native of Virginia (*Public Defaulters brought to Light*; *Letters Addressed to the People of the United States*)

GILL, William Fearing [1844–1917, US poet and dramatist]
Sophie May (in *The Horne of Plenty*)

GILLESPIE, Patrick [1617–75, Scottish cleric, Cromwellian and Principal of Glasgow University]
A Minister of the New Testament (*The Ark of the Covenant Opened*)

GILLESPIE, William Michell [1816–68, US civil engineer]
A New Yorker (*Rome, as Seen by a New Yorker*)

GILLINGS, Walter [1912–, English journalist and writer]
Thomas Sheridan (in *Science Fiction Monthly* and for *The Midget from Mars*)

GILLMORE, Rufus Hamilton [1879–1935, US novelist]
Rufus Hamilton (*The Mystery of the Second Shot*; *The Alster Case*)

GILLY, William Stephen [1789–1855, English cleric and writer]
A Member of the University of Cambridge (*Academic Errors or Recollections of Youth*)

GILMAN, Caroline [1794–1888, US writer]
A New England Bride (*Recollections of a New England Bride*)
A New England Housekeeper (*Recollections of a New England Housekeeper*)
Clarissa Packard (*Recollections of a Housekeeper*)
A Southern Matron (*Recollections of a Southern Matron*)

GILMAN, Dorothy [1923–, US novelist and writer for children]
Dorothy Gilman Butters (*Enchanted Caravan*; *Girl in Buckskin*)

GILMER, Elizabeth Meriweather [1861–1951, US journalist]
Dorothy Dix (*Fables of the Elite*; *Mirandy*)

GILMER, Francis Walker [1790–1826, US lawyer]
A Virginian (*Original and Miscellaneous Essays*)

GILMORE, James Roberts [1822–1903, US journalist and writer]
Edmund Kirke (*Life in Dixie's Land*; *Among the Guerillas*)

GILPIN, William [1724–1804, English cleric, biographer, traveller and philanthropist]
Josiah Frampton (*Three Dialogues between a Dean and a Curate*)

GIRDLESTONE, Charles [1797–1881, English cleric and biblical scholar]
The Creature of an Hour (*The Questions of the Day*)

GISSING, George Robert [1857–1903, English novelist and literary critic]
Morley Roberts (*The Private Life of Henry Maitland*; *The Flying Cloud*)

GLADSTONE, Arthur M. [1921–, US romantic novelist]
Maggie Gladstone (*The Lady's Masquerade*)
Lisabet Norcross (*Reluctant Heiress*)
Margaret Sebastian (*Meg Miller*; *Dilemma in Duet*)
Cilla Whitmore (*Mansion for a Lady*)

GLADSTONE, William Ewart [1809–98, English politician and writer]
Bartholomew Bouverie; Etonian, the Younger (both used in *An Eton Miscellany*)
Etonensis; Outidanos (both used in *Contemporary Review*)
Index (in *Fortnightly Review*)
Judex (in *Pall Mall Gazette*)

GLANVILL, Joseph [1636–80, English cleric and religious writer]
A Member of the Royal Society (*A Blow at Modern Sadducism*; *A Philosophical Endeavour towards ... Witches and Apparitions*)

GLAS, John [1695–1773, Scottish cleric and writer]
A Late Minister of the Church of Scotland (*Remarks on Modern Religious Divisions*)

GLASCOCK, William Nugent [1787–1847, British naval captain]
An Officer of Rank (*Naval Sketch Book*)

GLASER, Eleanor Dorothy [1918–, English dramatist]
E. D. Zonik (*Mulligan's Sheebeen*; *We're All Equal, Aren't We?*)

GLASGOW, George [1891–1958, English journalist and writer]
Logistes (*The Dupe as Hero*)

GLASKIN, Gerald M. [1923–, Australian writer]
Neville Jackson (*No End to the Way*)

GLASSCO, John [1909–81, Canadian writer and poet]
Sylvia Beyer (*Fetish Girl*)
Jean De Saint-Luc (*Contes en Crinoline*)
Silas M. Gooch (in the *Tamarack Review*)
Miles Underwood (*The English Governess*)

GLASSE, Mrs Hannah [1708–70, English writer on domestic economy]
A Lady (*The Art of Cookery made Plain and Easy*)

GLASSE, Samuel [1735–1812, English cleric and theologian]
A Country Magistrate (*A Narrative of Proceedings ... Suppression of Vice*)

GLEIG, George Robert [1796–1888, Scottish cleric and military writer – served as a soldier in the Peninsular War]
An Eyewitness (*The Subaltern or, Sketches of the Peninsular War*)
An Officer (*The Campaigns of the British Army at Washington*)
An Officer who served in the Expedition (*A Narrative of the British Army at Washington*)
An Old Indian (in *Blackwood's Magazine*)

GLEMSER, Bernard [1908–, English science-fiction writer]
Robert Crane (*Hero's Walk*)

GLEN, Duncan Munro [1933–, Scottish poet and writer on Scottish literature]
Simon Foster (*Scottish Poetry Now*)
Ronald Eadie Munro (*Kythings and Other Poems*)

GLENIE, James [1750–1817, Scottish mathematician, soldier and writer]
An Officer (*A Short Essay on the Modes of Defence of this Island*)

GLENNIE, John David [1925–, English cleric and educationalist]
Deborah (in *British Bee Journal*)

GLIDDEN, Frederick Dilley [1908–75, US western novelist]
Luke Short (*The Barren Land Murders*)

GLIDDEN, Jonathan H. [1907–, US western writer]
Peter Dawson (*The Crimson Horseshoe*; *Trail Boss*)

GLOVER, C. Gordon [1908–74, Scottish writer and broadcaster]
Julian Grey (*Parish Pump*)

GLOVER, Dorothy [d. 1971, English illustrator]
Dorothy Craigie (*The Little Train*) – see also entry for Henry Graham Greene

GLOVER, Modwena [1916–, English actress and writer for children]
Modwena Sedgwick (*Galldora Omnibus*; *New Adventures of Galldora*)

GLOVER, Richard [1712–85, English politican, balladeer, actor and writer]
A Celebrated Literary and Political Character (*Memoirs of a Celebrated Literary and Political Character*)
An Old Member of Parliament (*Considerations on Peace with America*)

GLUCK, Sinclair [fl. 1925, English writer]
Melrod Danning (*The Majesty of the Law*)

GODDARD, Norman Molyneux [1881–1917, English writer for boys]
Nat Barr (in *Gem*)
Mark Darran (in *Union Jack*)

GODDEN, Margaret Rumer [1907–, English novelist]
P. Davies (*Chinese Puzzle*; *The Lady and the Unicorn*; *Rungli-Rungliot*)

GODFREY, Lionel Robert Holcombe [1932–, English crime writer]
Scott Mitchell (*Deadly Persuasion*; *Some Dames Play Rough*)

GODFREY, Vivian [1921–, English fantasy novelist]
Melita Denning (*Voodoo Fire*)

GODLEY, Alfred Denis [1856–1925, Irish humorous poet and classical scholar]
A Mere Don (*Aspects of Modern Oxford*)

GODLEY, Robert [fl. 1947, US writer]
Franklin James (*The Killer in the Kitchen*)

GODWIN, William [1756–1836, English novelist and dramatist – husband of Mary Wollstonecraft]
Edward Baldwin (*Fables Ancient and Modern*; *History of England*; *History of Greece*; *History of Rome*; *Life of Lady Jane Grey*; *Mylius's School Dictionary*; *A New and Improved Grammar*; *Outlines of English History*; *The Pantheon*; *Outlines of English Grammar*; *A New Guide to the English Tongue*)
A Lover of Order (*Considerations on Sedicious Practices*)
Theophilus Marcliffe (*The Looking Glass*)
Verax (*Letters of Verax to the Morning Chronicle*)

GODWIN, William [1803–82, English journalist and novelist – son of William Godwin above]
Syphax (in *Blackwood's Magazine*)

GOETZ, George [1900–40, US social commentator and writer]
V. F. Calverton (*The Newer Spirit*; *The Liberation of American Literature*)

GOGARTY, Oliver St John [1878–1957, Irish physician, wit and poet]
Gideon Ouseley (*M'Cullagh*)

GOGGAN, John Patrick [1905–, US playwright and writer for cinema]
John Patrick (*The Willow and I*; *The Hasty Heart*)

GOING, Ellen Maud [d. 1925, US writer on natural history]
E. M. Hardinge (*With the Trees*; *With the Wild Flowers*)

GOLD, Horace Leonard [1914–, Canadian-born US science-fiction writer]
Clyde Crane Campbell; Leigh Keith (both used in *Astounding Stories* magazine)

GOLDIE, John [1717–1809, English essayist]
A Gentile Christian (*The Gospel Recovered*)

GOLDIE, Kathleen Annie [1915–, English headmistress and writer for children]
Kathleen Fidler (*Boy with a Bronze Axe*; *Railway Runaways*)

GOLDING, Louise Sarah [1923–, English writer on cookery]
Louise Davies (*Easy Cooking for Three or More*)

GOLDMAN, William [1931–, US novelist and screenwriter]
Harry Longbaugh (*No Way to Treat a Lady*)
S. Morgenstern (*The Silent Gondoliers*)

GOLDRING, Douglas [1887–1960, English journalist, traveller and writer]
An Englishman (*A Stranger in Ireland*; *Dublin*; *Explorations and Reflections*)

GOLDSMID, Sir Francis Henry [1808–78, English politician and first Jewish barrister; accidentally killed at Waterloo Station]
The Youngest of the Tomkinses (*A Scheme of Peerage Reform*)

GOLDSMITH, Hugh Colvill [1789–1841, English naval lieutenant]
An Officer of the Royal Navy (*The Golden Chersonese*)

GOLDSMITH, Milton [1861–1957, US dramatist and writer]
Astra Cielo (*Fortunes and Dreams*; *Signs, Omens and Superstitions*)

GOLDSMITH, Oliver [1728–74, Irish cleric, poet, dramatist and writer]
A Chinese Philosopher (in *The Public Ledger*)
The Citizen of the World (*Chinese Letters*)
A Nobleman (*An History of England*)
Tom Telescope (*The Newtonian System of Philosophy*)
James Willington (*The Memoirs of a Protestant*)

GOLDSTONE, Laurence Arthur [1903–, US crime writer]
Lawrence Treat (*P as in Police*; *V as in Victim*)

GOLIGHTLY, Charles Pourtales [1807–85, English cleric and religious writer]
A Clergyman of the Diocese (*A Letter to the Bishop of Oxford*)
A Member of the University of Oxford (*Strictures on No. 90 of the Tracts for the Times*)
A Senior Clergyman of the Diocese (*250 Facts and Documents showing ... Oxford*)
A Senior Resident Member of the University of Oxford (*The Position of Samuel Wilberforce in Reference to Ritualism*)

GOMPERTZ, Martin Louis Alan [1886–1951, English soldier and travel writer]
Ganpat (*The Voice of Dashin*; *Mirror of Dreams*; *Walls Have Ears*)

GOODCHILD, George [1888–1969, English mystery writer]
Alan Dare (*Body and Soul*; *The Guarded Soul*)
Wallace Q. Reid (*Bluewater Landing*; *Red River*)
Jesse Templeton (*The Eternal Conflict*; *The Woman Accused*)

GOODE, Arthur Russell [1889–1937, Australian writer for boys]
Arthur Russell (*Snowy for Luck*; *The Sky Pirates*)

GOODE, William [1801–68, English cleric and religious essayist]
A Clergyman (*An Answer on the Case of Dissenters*)
Philalethes (*The Established Church, a Reply to ... 'A Quiet Looker-On'*)

GOODLOE, Daniel Reeves [1814–1902, US abolitionist]
A Carolinian (*An Inquiry into the Southern States*)

GOODRICH, Frank Boott [1826–94, US journalist and writer]
Dick Tinto (in the *New York Times* and for *The Court of Napoleon* and *Tri-Colored Sketches in Paris*)

GOODRICH, Samuel Griswald [1793–1860, US publisher and writer for children]
Robert Merry (*Wit Bought*)
Peter Parley (*Fireside Education*; *The Life and Adventures of Thomas Titmouse*; *Adventures of Dick Boldhero*; *Peter Parley's Keepsake*; *Peter Parley's Tales*; *Peter Parley's Tales about China and the Chinese*; *Tales about Animals*)

GOODWIN, Harvey [1818–91, English cleric and mathematician]
D. E. F. G. (in *MacMillan's Magazine*)

GORDON, Archibald D. [1835–95, US journalist]
The Prowler (in the *New York Week's Doings*)

GORDON, Charles William [1860–1937, Canadian novelist and missionary]
Ralph Connor (*Black Rock*; *The Man from Glengarry*)

GORDON, Clarence [1835–?, US writer for children]
Vieux Moustache (*Boarding-School Days*)

GORDON, Deborah Hannes [1946–, US romantic novelist]
Brooke Hastings (*Desert Fire*; *Playing for Keeps*)

GORDON, James William [1874–1949, Australian writer]
Jim Grahame (*Call of the Bush*)

GORDON, Jan [1882–1944, English painter, art critic and traveller]
William Gore (*There's Death in the Churchyard*; *Murder Most Artistic*)

GORDON, Joseph [fl. 1825, Scottish poet]
An Obscure and Nameless Bard on the Braes of Angus (*Poetical Trifles*)

GORDON, Pryse Lockhart [1762–1845, English writer]
An Old Resident at Brussels (*A Companion for the Visitor to Brussels*)

GORDON, Robert Hunter [1815–57, Irish physician]
Ton Dubh (in *Dublin University Magazine*)

GORDON, Stuart [1947–, English writer]
Alex R. Stuart (*The Devil's Rider*)

GORDON, Thomas [1680–1750, Scottish classical scholar and writer]
*Cato (*A Discourse on Standing Armies*)

GORE, Mrs Catherine Grace Frances [1799–1861, English novelist, dramatist and composer]
Toby Allspy; A Distinguished Aide-de-Campe of a Most Distinguished Foreign Ambassador; Albany Poyntz; Q. E. D. (all used in *Bentley's Miscellany*)
A Country Cousin (in *Dublin University Magazine*)
A Desennuyee (*The Diary of a Desennuyee*)
A Designing Devil; Tabitha Glum; Lorgnon; A Mouse Born of the Mountain (all used in *Blackwood's Magazine*)
Thomas Trotcosey (in *Tait's Edinburgh Magazine*)

GOREY, Edward [1925–, US writer and illustrator]
Ogdred Weary (*The Beastly Baby*; *The Curious Sofa*)

GORHAM, George Cornelius [1787–1857, English cleric, genealogist and historian]
Candidus (*Errors Respecting Cranmer's Great Bible 1540*)
Vigil (in the *Christian Guardian*)

GOSLING, Charles [1657–1747, English misogynist]
The British Timon (in *Gentleman's Magazine*)

GOSLING, Paula [1939–, US mystery writer]
Ainslie Skinner (*Mind's Eye*)

GOSS, Elbridge Henry [1830–1908, US banker, biographer and writer]
Elhegos (in the *Boston Daily Advertiser*)

GOSSIP, George Hatfield Dingley [1841–1907, English writer]
Ivan Trepoff (*The Jew of Chamant*; *Spiritmist*)

GOUGH, Richard [1735–1809, English topographer and antiquarian]
Clio (in *St James's Chronicle*)
D. H. (in *Gentleman's Magazine*)
A Layman (*A Letter to the Bishop of London*)
R. G. (*A Comparative View of the Antient Monuments of India*)

GOUGH-CALTHORPE, Sir Somerset John [1831–1912, 7th Baron Calthorpe; soldier]
A Staff Officer (*Letters from Headquarters in the Crimea*)

GOULART, Ronald Joseph [1933–, US crime and mystery writer]
Josephine Kains (*The Whispering Cat Mystery*; *The Devil Mask Mystery*)
Julian Kearney (*Agent of Love*)
Howard Lee (*Superstition*)
Kenneth Robeson (*The Man from Atlantis*; *The Black Chariots*)
Frank S. Shawn (*The Hydra Monster*; *The Swamp Rats*)
Con Steffanson (*The Space Circus*; *The Plague of Sound*)

GOULD, Edward Shuman [1808–85, US merchant and writer]
The Man in the Claret Colored Coat (*The Sleep Rider*)

GOULD, Michael Ayrton [1921–75, English painter and illustrator]
Michael Ayrton (*Fabrications*; *Tittivulus*; *The Midas Consequence*; *British Drawings*)

GOULD, Nathaniel [1857–1919, English-born Australian journalist and writer on the turf]
Verax (*Banker and Broker*; *Running it Off or, Hard Hit*)

GOVAN, Mary [1897–, US novelist]
Mary Allerton (*The Shadow and the Web*)
J. N. Darby (*Murder in the House with Blue Eyes*)

GOVER, John Robert [1929–, US journalist and writer]
O. Govi (*Tomorrow Now Occurs Again*; *Getting Pretty on the Table*)

GOWER, Foote [1726–80, English physician and antiquary]
A Fellow of the Antiquarian Society (*A Sketch for a New History of Cheshire*)

GOWER, Richard Hall [1767–1833, English mariner and naval architect]
An Officer in the Service of the India Company (*A Treatise on the Theory and Practice of Seamanship*)

GOWING, Sydney [1878–?, English mystery and juvenile writer]
John Goodwin (*Blood Money*; *When Dead Men Tell Tales*)
John Tregellis (in *Boy's Friend*)

GOWING, William Aylmer [1823–92, English actor and dramatist]
Walter Gordon (*Dearest Mamma*; *Through Fire and Water*)

GOYDER, Margot [1903–, Australian mystery writer]
*Margot Neville (*Murder and Gardenias*; *Murder of Olympia*)

GOYNE, Richard [1902–57, English writer for children]
John Courage (*Nightingales Never Sing*; *Why Murder Mrs Hope?*)
Evelyn Standish (in *Girl's Friend*)

GRABER, George Alexander [1914–, English novelist and writer for children]
Alexander Cordell (*Rape of the Fair Country*; *To Slay the Dreamer*)

GRADWELL, Robert [1777–1833, English Catholic cleric]
John Hardman (in *The Catholicon* and for *A Winter Evening Dialogue*)

GRAHAM, Mrs Elizabeth Susanna
[1763–1844, English writer for children]
Lemuel Gulliver, Jun. (*A Voyage to Locuta*)
Theresa Tidy (*Eighteen Maxims of Neatness and Order*; *A Selection of Fables from Florian*)

GRAHAM, Harry Jocelyn Clive [1874–1936, English soldier, essayist and humorous verse writer]
Coldstreamer (*Ballads of the Boer War*)
Col. D. Streamer (*Deportmental Ditties*; *Perverted Proverbs*; *Misrepresentative Men*; *Ruthless Rhymes for Heartless Homes*; *The Bolster Book*)

GRAHAM, Sir James Robert George
[1792–1861, English politician]
A Cumberland Land-Owner (*Free Trade in Corn, the Real Interest etc.*)

GRAHAM, Robert Blackall [1874–1944, English soldier in the Indian Army]
A Cavalry Officer (*Photographic Illustrations of the Mandalay Expeditionary Force 1886/87*)

GRAHAM, Roger Phillips [1909–65, US science-fiction writer]
Rog. Phillips (*Time Trap*; *Worlds Within*)

GRAHAM, William [1737–1801, English cleric]
Taollt Bob (*Diana, Great at Ephesus*)
A Friend to the Natural and Religious Rights of Mankind (*An Attempt to Prove Patronage is Foreign*)

GRAHAME, James [1765–1811, Scottish lawyer, cleric and poet]
Calvinus (*Another Letter to Thomas M'Crie*; *Postscript to the Letters of Calvinus*; *Two Letters to Dr Thomas M'Crie*; *Two More Letters etc.*)
A Member of the Scottish Bar (*A Vindication of the Scottish Presbyterians*)

GRAINGER, Francis Edward [1857–1924, English romance and mystery writer]
Headon Hill (*Sir Vincent's Patient*; *By a Hair's-Breadth*)

GRAINGER, James [1721–66, Scottish physician, essayist and poet]
A Physician in the West Indies (*An Essay on West India Diseases*)

GRANGER, Bill [1941–, US journalist and writer]
Bill Griffith (*Time for Frank Coolin*)

GRANGER, Gideon [1767–1822, US lawyer and politician]
Epaminondas (*Address of Epaminondas to Citizens of the State of New York*)

GRANICH, Irving [1896–1967, US writer]
Michael Gold (*Jews without Money*; *Change the World*)

GRANT, Mrs Anne [1755–1838, Scottish writer]
An American Lady (*Memoirs of an American Lady Previous to the Revolution*)

GRANT, Sir Francis [1658–1726, Lord Cullen; Scottish jurist]
A Country Gentleman (*A Letter of a Country Gentleman to his Friend in the City*)
A Member of Parliament (*Reasons in Defense of Patronages*)

GRANT, Francis [1803–78, Scottish portrait painter]
An Amateur (in *Blackwood's Magazine*)

GRANT, George [fl. 1828, English actor]
A Veteran Stager (*An Essay on the Science of Acting*)

GRANT, Hilda Kay [fl. 1960, Canadian novelist]
Jan Hilliard (*Morgan's Castle*)

GRANT, James [1743–1835, Scottish lawyer and Gaelic scholar]
Scoto-Britannus (*A Letter Addressed to the Heritors of Scotland*)

GRANT, James [1802–79, Scottish journalist and writer]
One of No Party (*Random Recollections of the House of Commons*)

GRANT, John [1933–, English crime and mystery writer]
Jonathan Gash (*Gold from Gemini*; *Grail Tree*)
Graham Gaunt (*The Incomer*)

GRANT, Sir John Peter [1807–93, British colonial administrator]
A Fellow of the Royal Geographical Society (*Jamaica and its Governor*)

GRANT, Maurice Harold [1872–1962, English soldier and writer]
Linesman (*The Mechanism of War*; *Words by an Eye-Witness, the Struggle in Natal*; *The Makers of Black Basaltes*)
Scolopax (*A Book of the Snipe*)

GRANT, Neil [1938–, English writer]
D. M. Field (*The Nude in Art*; *Great Masterpieces of World Art*)
David Mountfield (*Antique Collectors Dictionary*; *The Coaching Age*)
Gail Trenton (*Whispered Twilight*; *Reflections in the Stream*)

GRANT, Lady Sybil [d. 1955, English poet, novelist, journalist and authority on airships]
Neil Scot (*The Riding Light*)

GRANT, William [1701–64, Lord Prestongrange; Scottish jurist]
Britannicus (*The Occasional Writer*)

GRANT DUFF, Sir Mountstuart Elphinstone [1829–1906, Scottish historian and politician]
A Scottish MP (*A Few Words on France*)

GRANVILLE, Dr Augustus [1783–1872, English physician and writer of Italian extraction]
One of the 687 FRS (*Science without a Head or, The Royal Society Dissected*)

GRANVILLE, George [1667–1735, Baron Lansdowne; dramatist and poet]
A Nobleman Abroad (*A Letter from a Nobleman Abroad to his Friend in England*)

GRANVILLE-BARKER, Lola Marie Therese [fl. 1934, English novelist and playwright]
Elena Bochkovsky (*Yellow River*)

GRASCOME, Samuel [1641–1708, English cleric and controversialist]
A Presbyter of the Church of England (*Concordia Discors*)

GRATTAN, Thomas Colley [1792–1864, English traveller and diplomat]
A British Subject (*The Boundary Question Raised ...*)
A Walking Gentleman (*High-Ways and Bye-Ways*)

GRAVELEY, G. C. [fl. 1950, English writer for girls]
Daphne Grayson (in *Girl's Crystal*)

GRAVES, Charles Patrick Ranke [1899–1971, English travel writer]
Charles Rankin (*The Pope Speaks*)

GRAVES, Clotilda Inez Mary [1863–1932, Irish playwright and novelist]
Richard Dehan (*The Dope Doctor*; *That which Hath Wings*)

GRAVES, Richard Ranke [1715–1804, English cleric, novelist, essayist and poet]
An Academic in the Metropolis (*The Rout or, a Sketch of Modern Life*)
An Adept in the Art of Trifles (*The Triflers*)
The Editor of the 'Spiritual Quixote' (*The Coalition*; *Columella*)
An Intimate Friend of His (*Recollections of William Shenstone*)
A Nonagenarian (*The Invalid*)
Rev. P. P., MA (*The Farmer's Son*)
Peter of Pontefract (*Lucubriatons*)
Geoffrey Wildgoose (*The Summer's Ramble of Geoffrey Wildgoose*)

GRAVES, Richard Hastings [1791–1877, Irish cleric and theologian]
A Clergyman of the Church of England (*Daniel's Great Period of 2,300 Days*)
A Clergyman of the Established Church (*Apostolical Succession Overthrown*)

GRAVES, Robert [1895–1985, English poet and writer]
John Doyle (*The Marmosite's Miscellany*)
Tom Fool (in *The Spectator* in 1922)
Fuze (in *Woman's Leader* in 1922)
M. V. (in *Epilogue* in 1935)
Peccavi (in *The Carthusian* in 1914)
Pollux (in *The Green Chartreuse* in 1913)
*Barbara Rich (*No Decency Left*)
Z (in *The Carthusian* in both 1913 and 1914)

GRAY, Andrew [1805–61, Scottish Presbyterian cleric]
A Free Churchman (*Dr Struthers on the Free Church*)
A Minister of a Chapel of Ease (*The Chapel Question Considered*)

GRAY, Asa [1810–88, US physician and botanist]
*Two Readers of Darwin's Treatise on the Origin of Species (*A Discussion Between Two Readers etc.*)

GRAY, Dorothy [1918–, Scottish writer]
Dorothy K. Haynes (*Peacocks and Pagodas*)

GRAY, Simon [1936–, English dramatist and writer]
Hamish Reade (*Colmaine*; *A Comeback for Stark*)

GRAYDON, Robert Murray [1891–1937, English writer for boys]
Murray Roberts (in *Modern Boy*)

GRAYSON, William J. [1788–1863, US politician and poet]
Curtius (*Letters of Curtius*)

GREATREX, Charles Butler [1832–98, English cleric and humorist]
Abel Log (*Whittlings from the West*)
Linden Meadows (*The Byron Oak*; *Dame Perkins and her Grey Mare*)

GREBANIER, Francesca V. [1900–, Italian-born US novelist]
Frances Winwar (*The Saint and the Devil*; *The Rosettis and their Circle*)

GREEN, Dorothy [1915–, English journalist and poet]
Dorothy Auchterlonie (*Kaleidoscope*; *Something to Someone*)

GREEN, Duff [1794–1875, US newspaper proprietor and politician]
An American (*The United States and England*)

GREEN, Francis Henry Knethell [1900–77, English physician and medical writer]
Frank Egan (*Through the Hollow Oak*; *Mary in Beastie Land*)

GREEN, George Smith [d. 1762, English watchmaker and writer]
A Gentleman of Oxford (*The New Version of Paradise Lost*)
A Tradesman of Oxford (*The Parson's Parlour*)

GREEN, Jacob [1722–90, US cleric and financial writer]
Eumenes (in the *New Jersey Journal*)
A Friend of American Liberty (*Observations on the Reconciliation of Great Britain and the Colonies*)
Theodorus van Shermain (*A Vision of Hell and a Discovery*)

GREEN, John [fl. 1736, English geographer]
J. G. (*A Journey from Aleppo to Damascus in 1725*)

GREEN, John Richard [1837–83, English historian and journalist]
The Lambeth Librarian (in *MacMillan's Magazine*)

GREEN, John Richards [1758–1818, English writer; he used the name 'Gifford' to avoid his creditors]
John Gifford (in the *Anti-Jacobin Review* and for *Blackstone's Commentaries Abridged*)
Humphrey Hedgehog (*A Rod for the Back of the Critics*)

GREEN, Joseph [1706–80, US humorist and writer]
Me, Phil Arcanos Gent. (*The Grand Arcanum Detected*)
Me, the Hon. B. B. Esq. (*Entertainment for a Winter's Evening*)

GREEN, Kay [1927–, English romantic novelist]
Roumelia Lane (*Sea of Zanj*; *House of Winds*)

GREEN, Madge [1927–, English writer]
Jane Derbyshire (*Flower Arranger's Year*)

GREEN, Matthew [1696–1737, English poet]
Peter Drake, Fisherman of Brentford (*The Grotto – a Poem*)

GREEN, Nathan [1827–1919, US jurist]
Oliver Forty (*The Tall Man of Winton and his Wife*)

GREEN, Peter Morris [1924–, English novelist, historian and translator]
Denis Delaney (*Cat in Gloves*)

GREEN, Thomas [1658–1738, English cleric; Bishop of Norwich]
A Minister (*The Sacrament of the Lord's Supper Explained*)

GREEN, Thomas [1769–1825, English poet and pamphleteer]
A Lover of Literature (*Extracts from the Diary of a Lover of Literature*)
A Young Gentleman (*The Micthodion*)

GREENBERG, Joanne [1932–, US novelist]
Hannah Greene (*I Never Promised you a Rose Garden*)

GREENE, Asa [d. 1837, US journalist and writer]
Dr Dodimus Duckworth, A. N. Q. (*The Life and Adventures of Dr Dodimus etc*)
Elnathan Elmwood Esq.; A Yankee (both used in *A Yankee among the Nullifiers*)
The Ex-Barber to His Majesty (*Travels in America*)
Ex-Barber Fribbleton (*The Travels of Ex-Barber Fribbleton in America*)
A Late Merchant (*The Perils of Pearl Street*)

GREENE, Edward Burnaby [d. 1788, English poet and translator]
E. B. G. (*Poetical Essays*)
Francis Fawkes (*The Idylliums of Theocritus*)

GREENE, Henry Graham [1904–91, English novelist, dramatist and writer]
Dorothy Craigie (*The Little Train*, published in 1946, was written by Greene, but the illustrator Dorothy Craigie was shown as the author)

GREENE, Nathaniel [1797–1876, US postal official and journalist]
Boscawen (used for journalism)

GREENE, Robert [1560–92, English writer, poet and pamphleteer]
Cuthbert Conny-Catcher (*The Defence of Conny-Catching*)

GREENE, Ward [1892–1956, US journalist and writer]
Frank Dudley (*King Cobra*; *Route 28*)
Jean Greene (*Forgetful Elephant*)

GREENER, William Oliver [fl. 1905, English writer]
Wirt Gerrare (*The Exploits of Jo Salis*; *A Secret Agent in Port Arthur*)

GREENLAND, William Kingscote [1868–1957, English cleric, journalist and writer]
W. Scott King (*The Master of Dunholme*; *Came as from Camps*)

GREENLEAF, Benjamin [1786–1864, US academic and educationalist]
A Practical Teacher (*Key to the New Practical Arithmetic*)

GREENLEAF, Simon [1783–1853, US jurist]
A Member of the American Bar (*Testamentary Counsels*)

GREENWOOD, Charles [d. 1905, English sporting journalist]
Hotspur (in *The Daily Telegraph*)

GREENWOOD, James [fl. 1866, English journalist]
The Amateur Lambeth Casual (*The Wilds of London*; *The True History of Little Ragamuffin*)
One of the Crowd (*A Strange Tale*)

GREENWOOD, Thomas Longdon [1806–79, English theatrical manager and dramatist]
The Brothers Grinn (*The Beauty and the Beast*; *Sindbad the Sailor*)

GREER, Germaine [1939–, Australian writer and critic]
Rose Blight (*Revolting Garden*)

GREG, Percy [1836–89, English novelist and writer]
Lionel H. Holdreth (*Shadows of the Past*; *The Spirit of Inquiry*)

GREG, Samuel [1804–76, English merchant and philanthropist]
A Layman (*Legacy in Prose and Verse*)

GREGG, Hilda Caroline [1868–1933, English novelist and writer]
Sydney C. Grier (*Flag of Adventure*; *Prince of Captivity*)

GREGORY, Francis [1625–1707, English cleric and headmaster]
A Divine of the Church of England (*Impartial Thoughts upon the Human Soul*)

GREGORY, John [1724–73, Scottish physician and medical writer]
A Father (*A Father's Legacy to his Daughters*)

GREIG, John Young Thomson [1891–1963, Scottish academic, novelist and writer]
John Carruthers (*Scheherazade*; *Adam's Daughters*; *A Man Beset*)

GREIG, Maysie [1901–71, Australian journalist and romantic novelist]
Jennifer Ames (*Danger Wakes my Heart*; *Lips for a Stranger*)
Ann Barclay (*Men as her Stepping Stones*; *Swing High, Swing Low*)
Mary Douglas Warre (*The Wishing Star*)

GRENVILLE, Denis [1637–1703, English cleric and Jacobite sympathiser – died in exile]
A Divine of the Church of England (*Counsels and Directions, Divine and Moral*)

GRENVILLE, George [1712–70, English barrister and politician]
A Son of Candor (letter to the *Public Advertiser*)

GRESHAM, Elizabeth F. [fl. 1945, US mystery writer]
Robin Grey (*Puzzle in Pewter*; *Puzzle in Porcelain*)

GREW, Nehemiah [1641–1712, English botanist and scientific writer]
A Fellow of the College of Physicians and of the Royal Society (*New Experiments and Useful Observations*)

GREY, Sir Charles Edward [1785–1865, English barrister, judge in India and colonial governor]
One of the Commissioners (*Remarks on the Proceedings as to Canada etc.*)

GREY, Henry [1778–1859, Scottish Free Church cleric]
A Minister of the Church of Scotland (*A Catechism on Baptism*)

GREY, Zachary [1688–1766, English cleric, antiquary and controversialist]
A. B.; An Admirer of Monarchy and Episcopacy (both used in *English Presbyterian Eloquence*)
A Believer (*The Spirit of Infidelity Detected*)
A Country Curate (*A Free and Familiar Letter to William Warburton*)
A Country Gentleman (*An Examination of a Late Edition of Shakespeare*)
A Friend (*A Word or Two of Advice to William Warburton*)
A Gentleman and No Knight (*The Knight of Dumbleton Foiled*)
A Gentleman of the University of Cambridge (*A Chronological Account of Earthquakes*; *A Looking-Glass for the Fanaticks*)

A Hearty Well-Wisher to the Established Church (*Presbyterian Prejudice Display'd*)

A Learned Hand (*A Preface to Dean Moss's Sermons*)

A Lover of Episcopacy (*A Century of Eminent Presbyterian Preachers*)

A Lover of History (*A Caveat against Mr Benjamin Bennet*)

A Lover of Truth (*The True Picture of Quakerism*)

One who is Neither a Jacobite, nor Republican, Presbyterian nor Papist (*A Letter of Thanks to Mr Ben Bennet*)

Philalethes Cantabrigiensis (*Schismatics Delineated from Authentic Vouchers*)

A Presbyter of the Church of England (*The Ministry of Dissenters Proved to be Null; A Vindication of the Church of England*)

A Sincere Admirer of True Liberty (*An Examination of Mr Samuel Chandler's etc.*)

A Sincere Lover of the Present Constitution (*A Caveat against the Dissenters*)

A Sincere Protestant (*Popery in its Proper Colours; A Serious Address to Lay-Methodists*)

GRIBBLE, Leonard Reginald [1908–85, English crime and western novelist]
Sterry Browning (*Coastal Commandos; Dangerous Mission*)
Lee Denver (*Guns of Lariat*)
Landon Grant (*Rustler's Gulch; Texas Buckaroo*)
Leo Grex (*Crooked Sixpence; The Lonely Inn Mystery*)
Louis Grey (*The Signet of Death*)
Dexter Muir (*The Speckled Swan*)

GRIBBON, William Lancaster [1879–1940, English fantasy writer]
Walter Galt (used for writing on boxing)
Talbot Mundy (*The Caves of Terror; The Mystery of Kufu's Tomb*)

GRIDER, J. MacDougall [fl. 1920, US writer]
An Unknown Aviator (*War Birds*)

GRIEVE, Alexander Haig Glanville [fl. 1940, English crime writer]
Alec Glanville (*Death Goes Ashore; Out of the Shadows*)

GRIEVE, Christopher Murray [1892–1978, Scottish poet, journalist and nationalist]
Hugh MacDiarmid (*Song of the Seraphim; O Wha's Been Here Afore me, Lass*)

GRIFFITH, Mrs Elizabeth [1720–93, English novelist and playwright]
*Frances (*Delicate Distress; Letters of Henry and Frances*)
*Henry (*The Gordian Knot; Letters of Henry and Frances*)
A Lady (*Amana; The Platonic Wife*)

GRIFFITH, George [1601–66, English cleric; Bishop of St Asaph]
A Local Minister (*A Bold Challenge of an Itinerant Preacher*)

GRIFFITH, Matthew [1599–1665, English cleric and royalist in the English Civil War]
A Lover of Truth (*A Sermon Preached in the Citie of London*)

GRIFFITH, Richard [1714–88, English writer – husband of Elizabeth Griffith above]
Automathes (*Something New*)
*Frances (*Delicate Distress; Letters of Henry and Frances*)
*Henry (*The Gordian Knot; Letters of Henry and Frances*)
Biograph Triglyph (*The Triumvirate or the Authentic Memoirs of A, B and C*)

GRIFFITH, William [1766–1826, US writer on politics]
Eumenes (*Eumenes: a Collection of Papers*)

GRIFFITHS, Helen [1939–, English writer for children]
Helen Santos (*Caleb's Lamb; If Only*)

GRIMSTEAD, Hettie [d. 1986, English romantic novelist]
Marsha Manning (*Magic of the Moon; Dance of Summer*)

GRINDAL, Richard [fl. 1950, English mystery writer]
Richard Grayson (*Death in Melting*; *Secret Agent in Africa*)

GRINNELL, Josiah Bushnell [1821–91, US cleric, politician and agriculturist]
Oculus (*The Home of the Badgers*)

GRISWOLD, Frances Irene B. [1826–1900, US writer]
Mrs S. B. Phelps (*Sister Eleanor's Brood*)

GRISWOLD, Frank Gray [1854–1937, US writer]
Anthony Ashley Jr. (*Plantation Days*)

GRISWOLD, William McCrillis [1853–99, US journalist and bibliographer]
Q. P. Index (*A General Index to the Nation*; *Q. P. Index Annual*)

GROSE, Francis [1731–91, English antiquarian and architectural draughtsman]
A Member of the Whip Club (*Lexicon Balatronicum*)

GROSVENOR, Benjamin [1675–1758, English cleric]
*Bagweel (*A Collection of Occasional Papers*)

GROSVENOR, Robert [1801–93, 1st Baron Ebury; pamphleteer and writer]
A Member of the Late Parliament (*Leaves from my Journal of 1851*)

GROTE, George [1794–1871, English banker, reforming politician and historian]
A. B. (in *The Spectator* for 'Seven Letters on Switzerland')
Philip Beauchamp (*Analysis of the Influence of Natural Religion*)
Richard Carlile (*Analysis of the Influence of Natural Religion*)

GROTE, Mrs Harriet [1792–1878, English writer – wife of George Grote above]
A Late Resident (*Some Account of the Hamlet of East Burnham*)
A Mutual Friend (*The Case of the Poor against the Rich*)

GROVE, Joseph [d. 1764, English lawyer and writer]
A Freeholder of the County of Surrey (*A Reply to the Famous Jew Question*)

GROVE, Robert [1634–96, English cleric and pamphleteer; Bishop of Chichester]
A Divine of the Church of England (*Seasonable Advice to the Citizens of England*)

GRUBER, Frank [1904–69, US crime and mystery writer]
Stephen Acre (*The Yellow Overcoat*)
Charles K. Boston (*The Silver Jackass*)
John K. Vedder (*The Last Doorbell*)

GRUND, Francis Joseph [1798–1863, German-born US writer]
A German Nobleman (*Aristocracy in America*)
An Observer (in the *Philadelphia Ledger*)

GUEST, Francis Harold [fl. 1938, English writer]
James Spenser (*Crime against Society*)

GUGGISBERG, Sir Frederick Gordon [1869–1930, Canadian soldier and colonial administrator]
Ubique (*How Armies Fight*; *Modern Warfare*; *Military Musings*)

GUIDOTT, Thomas [fl. 1698, English physician and medical writer]
Eugenius Philander (*A Quaere Concerning Drinking Bathwater at Bathe Resolved*)
A Friend to the Muses; Philo-Musus (both used in *The Gideon's Fleece*)
A Quaker (*Epitaph on Don Quicksot: or, Don Quicksilver*)

GUILD, Mrs Caroline Snowden [1817–98, US writer]
Hetty Holyoke (*Never Mind the Face*)

GUIN, Wyman W. [1915–, US science-fiction writer]
Norman Menasco (in *Astounding Science Fiction* magazine)

GUINNESS, Maurice [1897–, Irish crime writer]
Newton Gayle (*Death in the Glass*; *Sinister Crag*)

GUIRDHAM, Arthur [1905–92, English novelist and physician]
Francis Eaglesfield (*Silent Union*)

GULICK, Grover C. [1916–, US writer]
Bill Gulick (*The Hallelujah Trail*; *The Moon-Eyed Appaloosa*)

GULSTON, Miss Josepha Heath [fl. 1852, English novelist]
Talbot Gwynne (*The School for Fathers*)

GUNN, Alexander [1784–1829, US cleric]
Clericus (*Two Letters to a Clergyman of the Dutch Reformed Church*)

GUNN, James Edwin [1923–, US science-fiction writer]
Edwin James (in *Startling Stories* magazine)

GUNNING, Mrs Susanna [1740–1800, English novelist]
A Lady (*Family Pictures*)
Miss Minifie (*Family Pictures*; *The Picture*)

GURDON, Eveline Camilla [1858–94, English writer]
C. Fellowes (in *Temple Bar*)

GURNEY, Anna [1795–1857, English archaeologist and Anglo-Saxon scholar]
A Lady in the Country (*A Literal Translation of the Saxon Chronicle*)

GURNEY, Joseph John [1788–1847, English cleric, Quaker and social reformer]
A Member of the Society of Friends (*The Contribution of a Member of the Society of Friends to a Lady's Album*)

GURNEY, Mrs Maria [1802–68, English poet]
A Mother (*Rhymes for my Children*)

GURNEY, Miss Priscilla Hannah [1757–1828, English Quaker]
A Cordial Well-Wisher to the Cause of Universal Truth and Righteousness (*A Comprehensive View of the Nature of Faith*)

GUTCH, John Mathew [1776–1861, English journalist and controversialist]
Cosmo (in the *Bristol Journal*)
An Octogenarian (in *Gentleman's Magazine*)

GUTCH, Robert [1777–1851, English cleric]
Memory Short-Hand Writer to the Court (*Special Pleadings in the Court of Reason*)

GUTHRIE, Frederick [1833–86, English scientist and poet]
Frederick Cerny (*The Jew*; *Logrono*)

GUTHRIE, Kenneth Sylvan Launfal [1871–1940, Scottish-born US physician and cleric]
James Jardine Smith (*The Message of the Master*)

GUTHRIE, Norman Gregor [1877–1929, Canadian poet]
John Crichton (*A Vista*)

GUTHRIE, P. R. [fl. 1910, English writer]
Barry Pain (*Stories in the Dark*; *One Kind and Another*)

GUTHRIE, Thomas Anstey [1856–1934, English novelist, humorist and playwright]
F. Anstey (*Vice Versa*; *Humour and Fantasy*; *The Pocket Ibsen*)
Bedell Gruncher (in *Cornhill Magazine*)
Voces Populi (in *Punch*)

GUTHRIE, William [1708–70, Scottish historian and writer]
Jeffrey Broadbottom (in *Old England or, the Constitutional Journal*)

GUY, William Augustus [1810–85, English physician, forensic specialist and medical statistician]
A London Physician (*The Principles of Forensic Medicine*)

GUYONVARCH, Irene [1915–, English writer]
Irene Pearl (*Anny*)

GWINN, William R. [fl. 1956, US writer]
William Randall (*Deadly the Daring*)

GWYNN, Stephen Lucius [1864–1950, Irish politician, poet and writer]
An Admirer (in *MacMillan's Magazine*)

GYE, Harold (Hal) Frederick Neville [1888–1967, Australian writer and illustrator]
James Hackston (*Father Clears Out*; *The Hole in the Bedroom Floor*)

H

HABBERTON, John [1842–1921, US printer, journalist and writer]
H. A. Burton (*Helen's Babies, by their Latest Victim*)
Uncle Harry (*Helen's Babies*)

HACK, James [1758–1829, English Quaker]
A Citizen (*An Address to the Inhabitants of Chichester*)

HADDOCK, Rhoda [fl. 1859, English novelist]
Rosa Gaythorne (*Kate Hamilton*)

HADFIELD, Alan [1904–, English poet and writer for children]
Robin Dale (*There Came Two Dancing*)

HAGGARD, Edward Arthur [1860–1925, English soldier and military writer]
Arthur Amyand (*Only a Drummer Boy*; *Comrades in Arms*)

HAIGH, Jack [1910–, English journalist and broadcaster]
John Astolat (*Theory of Genius*)

HAIGH, Sheila Mary [1942–, English writer]
Sheila Chapman (*Mystery Pony*)

HAIGHT, Mrs Sarah [fl. 1840, US writer]
A Lady of New York (*Letters from the Old World*)

HAKEWILL, Arthur William [1808–56, English writer]
An Architect (*An Apology for the Architectural Monstrosities in London*)

HALDANE, James Alexander [1768–1851, Scottish mariner and religious writer]
An Observer (*Two Letters to the Rev. Dr Chalmers*)

HALDEMAN, Joe William [1943–, US science-fiction writer]
Robert Graham (*Attar's Revenge*; *War of Nerves*)

HALDEMAN, Samuel Stehman [1812–80, US naturalist]
Felix Ago (*Rhymes of the Poets*)

HALE, David [1791–1849, US journalist]
A Father (*Letters on the New Theatre*)

HALE, Edward Everett [1822–1909, US cleric and social reformer]
Thomas Darragh (*The Skeleton in the Closet*)
Col. Frederic Ingham (*Daily Bread*; *Easter*; *Christmas in Narra Gansett*; *In his Name, a story of the Waldenses*; *The Ingham Papers*; *Life of George Washington*)
A New England Minister A. B. (*Margaret Percival in America*)

HALE, Sir Matthew [1609–76, English jurist, poet and religious writer]
A Learned Hand (*The Analysis of the Law*; *The History of the Common Law in England*)
A Person of Great Learning and Judgment (*Contemplations Moral and Divine*; *A Treatise on the Registring of all Lands*)

HALE, Nathan [1784–1863, US newspaper proprietor]
A Gentleman of Boston (*Notes Made During an Excursion to New Hampshire*)

HALE, Salma [1787–1866, US lawyer]
A Citizen of Massachusetts (*History of the United States of America*)
Algernon Sidney (*The Administration and the Opposition*)

HALE, Sara Josepha [1788–1879, US editor and poet]
A Lady (*Modern Household Cookery*)
A Lady of New-Hampshire (*The Genius of Oblivion*)

HALES, William [1747–1831, Irish cleric, mathematician, linguist and chronologist]
Octavius (*Pursuits of Literature*)

HALEY, Sir William [1901–87, English newspaper editor]
Oliver Edwards (used for literary articles in *The Times*, of which he was the editor)

HALFORD, Frederic Michael [1844–1914, English writer on angling]
Detached Badger (in *The Field* and for *Day-Fly Fishing* and *Floating Flies and How to Dress Them*)

HALHED, Nathaniel Brassey [1751–1830, English orientalist and employee of the East India Company]
Detector (*The Letters of Detector on the India Registration Bill*; *A Letter to all Proprietors of East India Stock*)

HALIBURTON, Thomas Chandler [1796–1865, Canadian jurist and humorist]
A Colonist (*A Reply to the Report of the Earl of Durham*)
Sam Slick (*The Clockmaker*; *The Attache*)

HALIDAY, William [1788–1812, Irish scholar, Gaelic writer and grammarian]
Edmond O'Connell (*Uraicecht na Gaedhilge*)

HALKETT, Lady Anne [1622–99, Scottish royalist, writer and surgeon]
A Lady (*Meditations on the Twenty Fifth Psalm*)

HALL, Abraham Oakey [1826–98, US lawyer and journalist]
A Member of the New York Bar (*A Review of the Webster Case*)
Hans Yorkel (*Ballads by Hans Yorkel*)

HALL, Baynard Rush [1798–1863, US cleric and writer]
Robert Carlton (*The New Purchase*; *Something for Everybody*)

HALL, David [1682–1756, English Quaker]
Theophilus Philanthropos (*An Essay on Intemperance*)

HALL, Desmond W. [fl. 1935, US science-fiction writer]
*Anthony Gilmore; *H. G. Winter (both used in *Astounding Science Fiction* magazine)

HALL, Edmund [1620–87, English cleric, parliamentarian supporter turned royalist]
Testis Mundus Catholicus (*Lingua Testium*)

HALL, Miss Evelyn Beatrice [1868–?, English novelist]
S. G. Tallentyre (used in both *Cornhill Magazine* and *MacMillan's Magazine*)

HALL, John [1627–56, English poet and political pamphleteer]
J. de la Salle (*Lusus Serius*)

HALL, Josef Washington [1894–1960, US journalist and novelist]
Upton Close (*Behind the Face of Japan*; *In the Lands of the Laughing Buddha*)

HALL, Joseph [1574–1656, English cleric, poet and controversial satirist; Bishop of Norwich]
A Dutifull Sonne of the Church (*An Humble Remonstrance to Parliament*)
Mercurius Britannicus (*The Discovery of a New World*)
A True Lover of Truth and Peace (*A Modest Offer of Some Meet Considerations*)

HALL, Marjorie [1908–, US writer]
Carol Morse (*Roundabout Robin*; *Double Trouble*)

HALL, Marshall [1790–1857, English physician and physiologist]
A Physician (*Eupaedia*)

HALL, Norah Eleanor Lyle [1914–, English writer for children]
Aylmer Hall (*The Admiral's Secret*; *The Marked Man*)

HALL, Oakley Maxwell [1920–, US crime writer]
Jason Manor (*The Pawns of Fear*; *Too Dead to Run*)

HALL, Robert Pleasants [1825–54, US lawyer and writer]
A South Carolinian (*Poems by a South Carolinian*)

HALL, Mrs Sarah [1761–1830, US writer]
A Lady of Philadelphia (*Conversations on the Bible*)

HALL, Spencer Timothy [1812–85, English phrenologist, homoeopath and writer]
Sherwood Forester (*Rambles in the Country*; *Biographical Sketches of Remarkable People*)

HALL, Winifred [fl. 1950, New Zealand writer for children]
Clare Mallory (*Merry Begins*; *Juliet Overseas*)

HALLARD, Frederick [1821–62, Scottish lawyer]
A Lawyer (*Thoughts on our System of Judicial Behaviour*)
One of the Defeated (*The Catalogue Question in the Advocate's Library*)

HALLECK, Fitz-Greene [1790–1867, US poet and satirist]
A Connecticut Farmer's Boy (used for journalism)
*Croaker & Co. (in *New York Evening Post* and for *Poems by Croaker & Co.*)
F. G. H. (*Poet Dreams*)

HALLERAN, Eugene Edward [1905–, US western novelist]
Evan Hall (*Logan*)

HALLIBURTON, Sir Brenton [1775–1860, British jurist in Canada]
An Octogenarian (*Reflections on Passing Events*)

An Old Inhabitant of British North America (*Observations upon the Importance of the North American Colonies*)

HALLIWELL-PHILLIPS, James Orchard [1820–89, English Shakespearian scholar, librarian and writer]
A Fellow of the Royal Society (*An Introduction to the Evidence of Christianity*)
A Supposed Delinquent (*The Stratford Records and the Shakespeare Autotypes*)

(O')HALLORAN, Lawrence Hynes [1766–1831, Irish cleric and poet – transported for forgery]
Philo-Nauticus (*The Female Volunteers*; *Odes, Poems and Translations*; *Newgate or, Desultory Sketches in a Prison*)

HALPIN, Charles Graham [1829–68, Irish journalist and soldier; emigrated to USA – died from an overdose of chloroform]
Miles O'Reilly (*Poetical Works of Miles O'Reilly*; *The Life and Adventures of Private Miles O'Reilly*)

HALSEY, Harlan P. [1835–98, US humorist and novelist]
Old Sleuth (*Brant Adams, the Emperor of Detectives*; *Bruce Angelo, the City Detective*)
Tony Pastor (*201 Bowery Songster*)

HALSTEAD, Leonora B. [fl. 1884, US novelist]
Barbara Elbon (*Bethesda*)

HAMBLEDON, Phyllis McVean [fl. 1960, English crime writer]
Phillipa Vane (*Here is the Evidence*; *Priority for Death*)

HAMBLEN, Herbert Elliott [1849–?, US writer]
Fred Benton Williams (*On Many Seas*; *Tom Benton's Luck*)

HAMER, Sam Hield [d. 1941, English editor and writer for children]
Sam Browne (*Stories and Pictures for Sunday*; *Sunlight and Shade*)

HAMERTON, Philip Gilbert [1834–94, English artist, art critic, novelist and writer]
Adolphus Segrave (*Marmorne*)

HAMILTON, Alexander [1757–1804, West Indian-born US economist and statesman]
An American (in the *Gazette of the United States*)
Caesar (in the *Daily Advertiser*)
*Camillus (in *American Minerva*)
Lucius Crassus (*The Examination of the President's Message*)
Pacificus (*Letters of Pacificus*)
Phocion (*A Letter from Phocion*)
*Publius (in *The Federalist*)
A Sincere Friend to America (*The Farmer Refuted*)

HAMILTON, Charles Harold St John [1875–1961, English writer for children]
Martin Clifford (used in both *Pluck* and *Gem* and for *Tom Merry and Co. of St Jim's* and *The Secret of the Study*)
Owen Conquest (in *Boy's Friend* and for *The Rivals of Rookwood*)
Harry Dorrian (in *Pluck*)
Prosper Howard (in *Gem*)
Ralph Redway (in *Boy's Friend*)
Frank Richards (in *The Magnet*)
Hilda Richards (in *School Friend* and for *Bessie Bunter of Cliffs House School*)

HAMILTON, Edmond Moore [1904–77, US science-fiction and fantasy writer]
Brett Sterling (*Danger Planet*; *The Tenth Planet*)

HAMILTON, Edward Walter [1847–1908, English Treasury civil servant]
Nemo (in *Contemporary Review*)

HAMILTON, Elizabeth [1758–1816, Scottish writer and satirist]
A Hindoo Rajah (*Translation of the Letters of a Hindoo Rajah*)
Geoffrey Jarvis (*Memoirs of Modern Philosophers*)
A Lady (*A Friend's Gift*)

HAMILTON, Lord Ernest William Hamilton [1858–1939, English soldier, politician, novelist and historian]
A. Leaf (*A Maid at Large*; *Strawberry Leaves*)

HAMILTON, Lord Frederic Spencer [1856–1928, English diplomat]
A British Diplomat (*The Vanished Pomps of Yesterday*)

HAMILTON, Sir George Rostrevor [1888–1967, English civil servant and writer]
George Rostrevor (*Escape*; *Stars and Fishes*)

HAMILTON, Ian Standish Monteith [1853–1947, Corfu-born Scottish soldier and military writer]
An Indian Officer (in *Fortnightly Review*)

HAMILTON, Janet Evelyn { fl. 1988, Canadian crime writer]
*F. X. Woolf (*Murder in Space*)

HAMILTON, Mrs Leigh Brackett [fl. 1950, US writer]
Leigh Brackett (*An Eye for an Eye*; *The Tiger Among Us*)

HAMILTON, Mary Agnes [1884–1966, English novelist and socialist politician]
Iconoclast (*Fit to Govern*; *The Man of To-Morrow*)

HAMILTON, Thomas [1789–1842, Scottish soldier and writer]
Spencer Moggridge (in *Blackwood's Magazine*)

HAMILTON-KING, Mrs H. E. [1840–1920, English poet]
Maria Monica (*The Desolate Soul*)

HAMLEY, Edward Bruce [1824–93, British soldier, novelist and military writer]
Lt. Michael South (in *Fraser's Magazine*)
Alexandre Sue-Sand, Fils (*The Last French Hero*)

HAMLEY, William George [1815–93, English soldier and essayist]
Elliott Butt Nincome Esq.; Mr Scamper; A Wandering Englishman (all used in *Blackwood's Magazine*)

HAMMETT, Samuel Adams [1816–65, US novelist and humorist]
Philip Paxton (*A Stray Yankee in Texas*)
Sam Slick in Texas (*Piney Woods Tavern*)

HAMMETT, Samuel Dashiell [1894–1961, US crime and mystery writer]
Peter Collinson (in the *Black Mask* magazine)

HAMMILL, Cicely Mary [1872–1952, English playwright, actress and writer for children]
Max Hamilton (in *Boy's Realm, Boy's Herald* and *Union Jack*)

HAMMOND, Anthony [1668–1738, English poet, politician and pamphleteer; died as a debtor in the Fleet prison]
A Gentleman (*A Modest Apology ... with Relation to Public Credit*)

HAMMOND, Charles [1779–1840, US lawyer and journalist]
Hampden (*Reviews of the Opinion of the Supreme Court*)

HAMMOND, Edward Payson [1831–1910, US cleric and evangelist]
Elis (*Good Will to Men*)

HAMMOND, Gerald Arthur Douglas [fl. 1985, Scottish writer]
Arthur Douglas (*Last Rights; A Worm Turns*)

HAMMOND, Henrietta [1854–83, US novelist]
Lou Capsadell (*Her Waiting Heart*)
Henri Dauge (*A Fair Philosopher*)

HAMMOND, John Lawrence Le Breton [1872–1949, English journalist, biographer and social historian]
Jason (*Past and Future*)

HAMON, Louis [1866–1936, French journalist and screenwriter]
Cheiro (*Cheiro's Book of Numbers; You and your Hand*)

HAMPDEN, Richard [1631–95, English politician]
A Person of Quality (*A Critical History of the Old Testament*)

HAMPER, William [1776–1831, English historian and topographer]
A Birmingham Resident (*An Historical Curiosity; One Hundred and Forty-One Ways of Spelling Birmingham*)
H. D. B. (in *Gentleman's Magazine*)

HANCOCK, John [1703–44, US cleric]
Philalethes (*The Examiner or, Gilbert against Tennent*)

HANGER, George [1751–1824, 4th Baron Coleraine; soldier and military writer]
A Colonel in the German Service (*A Plan for the Formation of a Corps etc.*)

HANKIN, Edward [1747–1835, English cleric and pamphleteer]
A Kentish Clergyman (*Thoughts on the Preliminary Articles of Peace; A Letter to Henry Addington; Observations on the Speech of Sir William Scott*)

HANKINSON, Charles J. [1866–1959, English travel writer]
Clive Holland (*Hungary – the Land and its People; Belgium – the Land and its People*)

HANKS, Charles Stedman [1856–1908, US lawyer and writer on outdoor life]
Niblick (*Camp Kits and Camp Life*)

HANLEY, Clifford Leonard Clark [1922–, Scottish journalist and novelist]
Henry Calvin (*It's Different Abroad; The System*)

HANLEY, James [1901–85, Irish novelist and short-story writer]
James Bentley (*Between the Tides; Towards Horizons*)
Patrick Shone (*The House in the Valley*)

HANLEY, Peter [fl. 1833, English writer]
An Old Playgoer (*Random Recollections of the Stage*)

HANNAY, James [1827–73, Scottish journalist, novelist and writer]
A Carlylian (*Blackwood v. Carlyle, a Vindication*)
An Englishman in Spain (in *Pall Mall Gazette*)
Percival Plug, R. N. (*Biscuits and Grog*; *A Claret Cup*)

HANNAY, James Owen [1865–1950, Irish cleric, novelist and playwright]
George A. Birmingham (*Irish Short Stories*; *Mrs Miller's Aunt*; *A Sea Battle*)

HANSARD, Luke James [1752–1828, English printer of the *House of Commons Journal*]
One of the People (*The People's Budget to Produce Millions etc.*)

HANSEN, Joseph [1923–, US mystery writer]
Rose Brock (*Tarn House*; *Longleaf*)
James Colton (*Strange Marriage*; *The Outward Side*)

HANSHEW, Hazel Phillips [fl. 1935, US journalist and novelist]
Anna Kingsley (*The Valiant Pilgrim*)

HANSHEW, Thomas W. [1857–1914, US mystery writer]
Charlotte May Kingsley (*Arrol's Engagement*)

HANSON, Alexander Contee [d. 1819, US lawyer and politician]
Aristides (*Considerations on the Seat of Government*; *Remarks on the Proposed Plan of Federal Government*)
A Native Citizen and Servant of the State (*Political Schemes and Calculations*)

HANSON, 'Sir' Levett [1754–1814, English writer – lived mostly in continental Europe]
An Officer of the Order of St Joachim (*An Accurate Historical Account of Orders of Knighthood*)

HANWAY, Jonas [1712–86, English merchant, traveller and social reformer]
A Gentleman of the Partie (*A Journal of Eight Days Journey*)
Mr H***** (*A Journal of Eight days Journey from Portsmouth to Kingston upon Thames*)
J. H. (*Letters Admonitory and Argumentative*; *The Soldier's Faithful Friend*)
A Member of the Marine Society (*A Letter from a Member of the Marine Society shewing the Piety etc.*)
A Merchant (*Motives for the Establishment of the Marine Society*)
A Merchant who Subscribed the Petition (*A Review of the Proposed Naturalization of the Jews*)
Farmer Trueman (*Advice from Farmer Trueman*)
Thomas Trueman (*The Whole Truth and Nothing but the Truth*)

HARBAGE, Alfred Bennett [1901–76, US mystery writer]
Thomas Kyd (*Blood is a Beggar*; *Blood of Vintage*; *Cover his Face*)

HARBAUGH, Thomas Chalmers [1849–1924, US mystery writer]
Capt. Howard Holmes (*The Pampas Hunters*; *The Silken Lasso*)

HARCOURT, Simon [1661–1727, 1st Viscount Harcourt; politician]
A. B. (*A Letter from Abingdon*)

HARCOURT, Sir William G. G. V. Vernon [1827–1904, English barrister, politician and writer]
The Englishman (*The Morality of Public Men*)
Historicus (in *The Times* and for *American Neutrality, Belligerent Rights of Maritime Capture* and *Letters by Historicus*)
An Old MP (in *Dark Blue* magazine)

HARDCASTLE, Michael [1933–, English writer for children]
David Clark (*Goalie*; *Grab*)

HARDHAM, John [d. 1772, English
tobacconist and snuffseller]
Abel Drugger (*The Fortune Tellers*)

HARDINGE, Mrs Belle [1843–1900, US
adventuress]
Belle Boyd; A Friend to the South (both
used in *Belle Boyd in Camp and Prison*)

HARDINGE, George [1743–1816, English
barrister, politician and writer]
A Layman (*Sermons written by a Layman*;
Three Sermons by a Layman)
Minutius Felix (*The Essence of Malone*)

HARDINGE, George Edward Charles
[1921–, English crime novelist]
George Milner (*Stately Homicide*; *Shark
among Herrings*)

HARDINGE, Rex [1904–, English crime
writer]
Capstan (*The Broadcast Murder*; *Murder on
the Veldt*)

HARDISON, Osborne Bennett [1928–, US
writer]
H. O. Bennett (*The Last Drop*)

HARDMAN, Frederick [1814–74, English
novelist and foreign correspondent]
One who Has Known Them Both (in *New
Monthly Magazine*)
Vedette (in *Blackwood's Magazine*)

HARDWICK, Charles [1821–59, English
cleric and historian – died when he fell
over a precipice in France]
A Cambridge Man (*The Universities and the
Church of England*)

HARDWICK, Michael [1924–, English
writer]
John Drinkrow (*The Vintage Operetta Book*;
The Vintage Musical Comedy Book)

HARDWICK, Mollie { fl. 1975, English
dramatist and novelist]
Mary Atkinson (*The Thames-Side Book*)

HARDY, John Stockdale [1793–1849,
English lawyer and historian]
Britannicus (*A Series of Letters upon the
Roman Catholic Question*)

HARDY, Thomas [1840–1928, English
novelist and poet]
E. J. Detmold (*The Lizard*, published in
1915 with illustrations by Detmold and
prose text by Florence Dugdale and verse
by Hardy that was unacknowledged)

HARE, Augustus William [1792–1834,
English cleric]
*Two Brothers (*Guesses at Truth*)

HARE, Francis [1671–1740, English cleric;
Bishop of Chichester]
A Citizen (*A Letter to Sir R. Brocas, Lord
Mayor of London*)
The Clergyman (*The Clergyman's Thanks in
a Letter to Dr Bentley*)
An Impartial Hand (*A New Defense of the
Bishop of Bangor's Sermons*)
Philo-Criticus (*A Clergyman's Thanks to
Phileleutherus*)
A Presbyter of the Church of England (*The
Difficulties that Attend the Study of
Scripture*)

HARE, Julius Charles [1795–1855, English
cleric and translator of German texts]
*Two Brothers (*Guesses at Truth*)

HARE, Robert [1781–1858, US scientist and
inventor]
Eldred Grayson (*Standish the Puritan*)

HARINGTON, Sir Edward [1753–1807,
English writer]
A Gentleman, Late of Bath (*An Excursion
from Paris to Fontainebleau*)

HARINGTON, Sir John [1561–1612, English
satirist and writer]
Misacmos (*A New Discourse of a Stale
Subject*)
Misodiaboles (*Ulysses upon Ajax*)
T. C. Traveller, Apprentice in Poetrie (*An
Anatomie of the Metamorphosed Ajax*)

HARKNESS, Margaret Elise [d. 1922, English social reformer and novelist]
John Law (used in both *Fortnightly Review* and *New Review*)

HARKNETT, Terence William [1936–, English crime and western novelist]
Frank Chandler (*A Fistful of Dollars*)
David Ford (*Cyprus*)
George E. Gilman (*Vengeance is Black*; *Ashes and Dust*)
Jane Harman (*Promotion Tour*)
Joseph Hedges (*The Chinese Coffin*)
William Pine (*The Softcover Kill*)
James Russell (*The Balearic Islands*)
Thomas H. Stone (*Stopover Murder*)
William Terry (*Once a Copper*; *The Weekend Game*)

HARLAND, Henry [1861–1905, US novelist; moved to London, where he edited *The Yellow Book*]
Sidney Luska (*Mr Sonnenschein's Inheritance*; *As it Was Written, a Jewish Musician's Story*)

HARLAND, John [1806–68, English journalist and Lancashire historian]
Crux (*Ten Days in Paris*)
Iota (*Stray Leaves Collected for the Athenaeum Bazaar*)

HARLEY, George Davies [d. 1812, English actor and writer]
George Davies (*An Authentic Biographical Sketch of William Betty*)

HARLING, Robert [1910–, English crime writer]
Nicholas Drew (*Amateur Sailor*)

HARMER, Thomas [1714–88, English cleric and writer]
A Suffolk Minister (*Remarks on the Churches of Norfolk and Suffolk*)

HARNESS, Arthur [1838–1927, English soldier]
An Officer (in *Temple Bar*)

HARNESS, William [1790–1869, English cleric and writer]
Harroviensis; Philo-Dramaticus (both used in *Blackwood's Magazine*)
Presbyter Catholicus (*A Short Letter to the Rev. W. B. Noel*; *Visiting Societies and Lay Readers*)

HARPER, Edith Alice Mary [1884–1947, English poet]
John Oland (*Songs of John Oland*)
Anna Wickham (*The Contemplative Quarry*; *The Little Old House*)

HARRINGTON, Robert [fl.1791, English natural philosopher]
Richard Bewley, MD (*A Treatise on Air*)

HARRIS, Alexander [1805–74, English-born migrant to Australia; later became a citizen of USA and died in Canada]
An Emigrant Mechanic (*Settlers and Convicts or, Recollections of Sixteen Years' Labour in the Australian Backwoods*)

HARRIS, Christopher [1907–, English verse playwright]
Christopher Fry (*The Boy with a Cart*; *A Phoenix Too Frequent*)

HARRIS, Christopher A. M. [1801–87, English journalist]
Ismael (*Letters on Great Political Questions*)

HARRIS, Miss Elizabeth Furlong Shipton [1822–52, English writer]
A Companion Traveller (*From Oxford to Rome*)

HARRIS, George [1794–1859, Scottish cleric and controversialist]
A Unitarian (*A Statement of Unitarian Christianity*)

HARRIS, George Washington [1814–69, US riverboat captain and humorist]
Sut Lovingood (*The Sut Lovingood Yarns*)
Sugartail (in the *New York Spirit of the Times* for *The Knob Dance – a Tennessee Frolic*)

HARRIS, Harold [1915–93, English editor and writer]
John Buckingham (used for radio drama)

HARRIS, Henry Wilson [1883–1955, English journalist]
Janus (in *Time and Tide*)

HARRIS, James [1709–80, English politician and writer]
J. H. (*Three Treatises on Art, Music, Painting and Poetry*)

HARRIS, James Thomas [1856–1931, Irish journalist and writer]
Frank Harris (*My Life and Loves*; *The Bomb*)

HARRIS, Joel Chandler [1848–1908, US lawyer, journalist and humorist]
Uncle Remus (*Uncle Remus, his Songs and Sayings*; *Uncle Remus and his Friends*)

HARRIS, John [1588–1658, English cleric, biographer and Greek scholar]
Sirrhanio, an Utter Enemy of Tyrannie (*The Royall Quarrell*)

HARRIS, John [1916–91, English mystery writer]
Mark Hebden (*Pel under Pressure*; *Pride of Dolphins*)
Max Hennessy (*Blunted Lance*; *Lion at Sea*)

HARRIS, John Beynon [1903–69, English science-fiction and fantasy writer]
John Beynon (*The Secret People*; *Foul Play Suspected*)
Lucas Parkes (*The Outward Urge*)
John Wyndham (*The Day of the Triffids*; *The Kraken Wakes*)

HARRIS, Larry Mark [1933–, US science-fiction writer]
Laurence M. Janifer (*The Picked Poodles*; *The Protector*)
*Mark Phillips (in *Astounding Science Fiction* magazine)

HARRIS, Marion Rose [1925–, English writer]
Daphne Harriford (*Around the Home*)

HARRIS, Mark [1922–, US writer]
Henry W. Wiggen (*A Journal*)

HARRIS, Richard [1833–1906, English lawyer, poet and novelist]
Benedick Whipem (*New Nobility*)

HARRIS, Samuel Smith [1841–88, US cleric]
Christopher Coningsby (*Sheltern*)

HARRIS, Thaddeus Mason [1768–1842, US cleric]
A Student of Harvard University (*Triumphs of Superstition*)

HARRIS, Thomas Lake [1823–1906, English-born US writer on spiritualism]
Chrysantheus and Chrysanthea (used jointly with his wife Clarissa for *Hymns of the Two-in-One for Bridal Worship*)

HARRIS, Walter [1647–1732, English physician and medical writer]
An Ancient Doctor of Physick (*The Great and Wonderful Works of God*)
Timoniculus (*An Enquiry into the Caledonian Project*)

HARRISON, Fairfax [1869–1938, US lawyer and railway company president]
A Virginia Farmer (*Cato's Farm Management*; *The Catharsis of Husbandry*)

HARRISON, Harry [1925–, US science-fiction writer and illustrator]
Hank Dempsey (in *Analog* magazine)
Cameron Hall (in *Fantasy Fiction* magazine)

HARRISON, Henry S. [1880–1930, US journalist and novelist]
Henry Second (*Captivating Mary Carstairs*)

HARRISON, Michael [1907–, English crime writer]
Quentin Downes (*No Smoke, No Flame*; *Heads I Win*)

HARRISON, Richard [1837–1931, English soldier and writer]
An Officer (*A Practical Scheme for the Reorganization of the Armies*)

A Public School Boy (*The Volunteer, the Militiaman and the Regular Soldier*)

HARRISON, Richard Motte [1901–, English writer]
Peter Motte (*Fall of the Curtain*; *The Village Called Death*)

HARRISON, Susannah [1752–84, English poet and domestic servant]
A Young Woman (*Songs in the Night*)

HARROD-EAGLES, Cynthia [1948–, English romantic novelist]
Elizabeth Bennett (*The Unfinished*; *Last Run*)
Emma Woodhouse (*Never Love a Stranger*; *Love's Perilous Passage*)

HART, Adolphus Mordecai [1813–79, Canadian writer]
Hampden (*Uncle Tom in Paris*; *The Impending Crisis*)
A Hoosier (*Life in the Far West*)

HART, Ernest Abraham [1835–98, English surgeon and medical journalist]
Pupils of the City of London School (*On the Tragedy of King Lear*)

HART, Harry [1907–64, US science-fiction writer]
Pat Frank (*Mr Adam*; *Alas, Babylon*)

HARTE, Francis Bret [1836–1902, US novelist and short-story writer]
Bret Harte (*The Luck of Roaring Camp and Other Sketches*)

HARTIGAN, Patrick Joseph [1878–1952, Australian writer]
John O'Brien (*Around the Boree Log*; *The Parish of St Mel's*)

HARTLEY, Thomas [1748–1809, American lawyer, soldier and politician]
Phocion (*Observations on the Permanent Residence of Congress*)

HARTLIB, Samuel [d. 1670, Polish-born writer on education and husbandry; lived in England from 1628]
S. H. (*London's Charitie Stilling the Poore Mans Cry etc.*)
Some Wellwishers to the Publick (*A Designe for Plentie*)

HARTMANN, Sadakichi [1869–1944, Japanese writer]
Sydney Allan (*Landscape and Figure Composition*; *Schopenhauer in the Air*)

HARTSHORNE, Henry [1823–97, US novelist]
Corinne L'Estrange (*Woman's Witchcraft*; *Summer's Songs*)

HARVEY, Annie Jane [d. 1898, English novelist and writer]
Andree Hope (*The Secret of Wardale Court*; *The Vyvyans*)

HARVEY, Charles Nigel [1916–, English writer on agricultural affairs]
Hugh Willoughby (*Amid the Alien Corn*)

HARVEY, Edmund George [1828–84, English cleric, musician and writer]
The Captain (*Our Cause in the Undine*)
Pindar (*The Tuck-Net Split*)

HARVEY, Gabriel [1545–1630, English academic, satirist and poet]
Richard Lichfield (*The Trimming of Thomas Nashe, Gentleman*)

HARVEY, John B. [1938–, English writer]
James Barton (*Angels*)
Jon Barton (*Forest of Death*)
William S Brady (*Killing Time*)
L. J. Coburn (*The Raiders*)
J. B. Dancer (*Evil Breed*)
John Hart (*High Slaughter*)
James Mann (*Endgame*)
John J. McLaglen (*Shadow of the Vulture*)
Thom Ryder (*Angel Alone*)
J. D. Sandon (*Border Affair*)

HARVEY, John Henry [fl. 1947, English writer]
John Barrington (*Murder in White Pit*)

HARVEY, John Wilfred [1889–1967, English philosopher and writer]
John Farndale (*The Nine Nicks*)

HARVEY, Joseph [1787–1873, US cleric]
An Edwardean (*Letters on Theological Speculation in Connecticut*)

HARVEY, William [1796–1866, English artist and engraver]
Aleph (*London Scenes and London People*; *The Old City: its Highways and Byways*)

HARVEY, William Hope [1851–1936, US eccentric politician and writer on coins and coinage]
Coin Harvey (*The Money of the People*; *A Tale of Two Nations*)

HARVEY, William Woodis [1798–1864, English cleric and writer]
Vindicator (*Clericus and the Independent Dissenters*; *An Impartial View of Religion in Penzance*)

HARVEY-JAMES, Arthur Keedwell [1875–1917, English playwright]
Arthur Scott Craven (*Alarums and Excursions*; *The Fool's Tragedy*)

HARWOOD, George [1845–1912, English merchant, barrister and writer]
One who Has Never Been a Candidate (*A Candidate's Speeches*)

HARWOOD, Isabella [1840–88, English playwright and novelist]
Ross Neil (*Lady Jane Grey*; *Inez*; *Duke for a Day*)

HARWOOD, Thomas [1767–1842, English cleric and writer]
Clio (in *Gentleman's Magazine*)

HASLEWOOD, Joseph [1769–1833, English historian and writer]
Gridiron Gabbler (*Green Room Gossip*)
Eu. Hood (in *Gentleman's Magazine*)
Christopher Valdarfer (*Bibliomaniac Ballad*)

HASTED, Edward [1732–1812, English genealogist and Kentish historian]
A Late Inhabitant (*The Canterbury Guide*)

HASTINGS, Phyllis Dora [fl. 1960, English romantic novelist and writer]
John Bedford (*Talking about Tea-Pots*; *Delft Ware*)
Julia Mayfield (*The Forest of Stone*)

HASTINGS, Thomas [1740–1801, British political pamphleteer and bookseller]
Archy MacSarconica, F.R.S. (*The Book of the Wars of Westminster*)

HASWELL, Chetwynd John Drake [1919–, English soldier and military historian]
George Foster (*Indian File*; *Soldier on Loan*)

HATCH, David Patterson [1846–1912, US writer]
Paul Karishka (*Straight Goods in Philosophy*)

HATT, Francis [1691–1767, English Quaker]
A Lover of Truth and Mankind Universally (*Friendly Advice to Children*)

HATTON, Edward [1701–83, English Dominican monk]
Constantius Archaeophilus (*Memoirs of the Reformation of England*)

HATTON, Ronald George [1886–1965, English horticultural scientist]
Christopher Holdenby (*Folk of the Furrow*)

HAUCK, Louise Platt [1883–1943, US romantic novelist]
Lane Archer (*Mystery Mansion*)
Peter Ash (*Blazing Tumbleweed*; *Untarnished*)
Louise Landon (*The Strange Death of a Doctor*; *The Green Light*)
Jean Randall (*In Lilac Time*; *Bridesmaid*)

HAUSRATH, Adolf [1837–1909, German theologian and writer]
George Taylor (*Antinous*; *Elfreide*; *Jetta*; *Klytia*)

HAVEN, Alice [1828–63, US writer]
Cousin Alice (*All's Not Gold That Glitters*; *Out of Debt, Out of Danger*)

HAWEIS, Hugh Reginald [1838–1901, English cleric, musician and traveller]
A Stray Hearer (in *Temple Bar*)

HAWEIS, Thomas [1734–1820, English cleric and writer]
The Presbyter (*Plain Truths*)
A Presbyter of the Church of England (*The Church of England Vindicated*)

HAWES, William Post [1821–41, US journalist]
J. Cypress Jr. (*Sporting Scenes and Sundry Sketches*)

HAWKER, Edward [1782–1860, British admiral and journalist]
A Flag Officer (in *The Times*)
A Flag Officer of Her Majesty's Fleet (*A Letter to His Grace the Duke of Wellington*)

HAWKER, Mary Elizabeth [1848–1908, English novelist]
Lanoe Falconer (*Mademoiselle Ixe*; *Cecilia de Noel*)

HAWKER, Peter [1786–1853, English soldier and writer]
A Regimental Officer (*Journal of a Regimental Officer in Portugal and Spain*)

HAWKER, Robert Stephen [1803–75, English cleric, antiquary and poet]
Breachan (*Sir Beville*)
A Cornish Vicar (*A Letter to a Friend*)
H. (*The First Mole in Cornwall*)
Karn-Idzek (*Ichabod*)
Procul (in *The British Magazine*)
Reuben (*Poetical First Buds*; *Tendrils*)
R. S. H. (*The Carol of the Pruss*; *A Voice from the place of S. Morwen*)
The Vicar of Morwenstow (*Rural Synods*; *Reeds Shaken by the Wind: the Second Cluster*; *A Voice from the Place of S. Morwena*)

HAWKES, James [1776–1865, US writer]
A Citizen of New York (*A Retrospect of the Boston Tea Party*)

HAWKESWORTH, John [1715–73, English dramatist, journalist and writer on exploration]
(H.) Greville (in *Gentleman's Magazine*)
Z (in *Spendthrift*)

HAWKINS, Sir Anthony Hope [1863–1933, English lawyer and novelist]
Anthony Hope (*The Prisoner of Zenda*; *Rupert of Hentzau*)

HAWKINS, Sir John [1719–89, English magistrate and writer]
A Member of the Academy of Ancient Music (*An Account of the Institution*)

HAWKINS, Nehemiah [1833–1928, US writer]
The Knight of Chillon (*The Mormon of the Little Manitou Island*)
William Rogers (*Erecting and Operating*)

HAWKINS, William [1722–1801, English cleric, poet and theologian]
An Unlettered Bard (*Poems on Several Occasions, Chiefly Pastoral*)

HAWKS, Francis Lister [1798–1866, US cleric, lawyer and ecclesiastical historian]
An American (*Journal of a Voyage up the Nile in 1848–9*)
Frater (*The Qualifications of Lay Delegates*)
Lambert Lilly (*The Early History of the Southern States*)
Uncle Philip (*Uncle Philip's Conversations*)
A Protestant Episcopalian (*Auricular Confession*)

HAWORTH, Adrian Hardy [1767–1833, English entomologist]
A Fellow of the Linnaean Society (*Prodromus Lepidopterorum Britanicorum*)

HAWTAYNE, George Hammond [1832–1902, English colonial law officer and writer]
X. Beke (*West Indian Yarns*)
A Collector (*Taxidermic and other notes*)

HAWTHORNE, Nathaniel [1804–64, US novelist and writer]
Aubepine (in the *Democratic Review*)
Oberon; Ashley Allen Royce (both used in the *New England Magazine*)

HAWTON, Hector [1901–75, English writer for boys]
John Sylvester (in *Chums*)

HAWTREY, Valentina [fl. 1903, English novelist]
Valentine Caryl (*A Ne'er Do Well*)

HAY, Sir Andrew Leith [1785–1862, Scottish soldier]
A British Officer (*Memoirs of General Sir James Leith*)

HAY, George [1729–1811, Scottish Catholic cleric and theologian]
John Simple (in *Weekly Magazine or Edinburgh Amusement*)

HAY, George [1765–1830, US jurist]
Hortensius (*An Essay on the Liberty of the Press*)

HAY, George [1922–, English science-fiction writer]
King Lang (*Terra!*)

HAY, Mary Cecil [1840–86, English novelist]
Howard Markham (*Old Myddleton's Money*)

HAY, Malcolm Vivian [1881–1962, Scottish historian]
An Exchanged Officer (*Wounded and a Prisoner of War*)

HAY, Robert Edwin [1910–89, English horticulturist]
Roy Hay (*Dictionary of Garden Plants in Colour*)

HAY, William [1695–1755, English barrister and politician]
A Member of Parliament (*Remarks on the Laws Relating to the Poor*)

HAYCRAFT, Anna Margaret [1932–, English novelist]
Alice Thomas Ellis (*The Sin-Eater; The Birds of the Air*)

HAYDON, Arthur Lincoln [1872–1954, English writer on cricket]
Cover-Point (*Cricket*)
Lincoln Hayward (in *Boy's Own Paper*)

HAYES, Joseph [1918–, US novelist and playwright]
Joseph H. Arnold (*The Thompsons; Where's Laurie?*)

HAYLEN, Leslie Clement [1899–1977, Australian playwright and novelist]
Sutton Woodfield (*A for Artemis*)

HAYLEY, William [1745–1820, English poet and biographer]
A Friend to the Sisterhood (*A Philosophical and Moral Essay on Old Maids*)

HAYMAN, Henry [1823–1904, English cleric, headmaster and classicist]
Quispian (in *Temple Bar*)

HAYMAN, Robert [d. 1631, English epigrammatist]
R. H. (*Quodlibets Lately Come Over from New Britaniola, Anciently Called Newfoundland, Epigrams and other Small Parcels both Moral and Divine*)

HAYMAN, Samuel [1818–86, Irish historian]
A Dreamer (in *Dublin University Magazine*)

HAYNES, Hopton [1672–1749, English Unitarian writer]
A Candid Enquirer after Truth (*The Scripture Accounts of the Attributes of God*)

HAYS, Mary [1760–1843, English novelist]
Eusebia (*Cursory Remarks on Public or Social Worship*)

HAYS, Peter [fl. 1960, English writer]
Ian Jefferies (*It Wasn't Me*)

HAYTER, Cecil Goodenough [1871–1922, English writer for boys]
Lewis Bird (in *The Gem*)

HAYTER, Harrison [1825–98, English civil engineer]
A Scientist (*Conversion*)

HAYWARD, Abraham [1803–84, English jurist and essayist]
A Combatant (*The Battle of the Translation*)
An Old Reviewer (*Mr Kinglake and the Quarterlys*)
A Templar (*The Ballot for Benchers*)

HAYWOOD (or HEYWOOD), Mrs Eliza
[1693–1756, English novelist and
dramatist]
A Celebrated Author of That Country
(*Memoirs of a Certain Island Adjacent to
Utopia*)
E. H. (*The Mercenary Lover or, the
Unfortunate Heiress*)
Explorabilis (*The Invisible Spy*)
A Lady (*A Spy upon the Conjuror*)
Mira (*The Wife*)

HAYWOOD, John [1762–1826, US jurist and
historian]
A Tennesseean (*The Christian Advocate*)

HAZARD, Rowland Gibson [1801–88, US
merchant and writer]
Heteroscian (*Language*)

HAZARD, Thomas Robinson [1797–1886,
US writer]
A Laboring Man (*Facts for the Laboring
Man*)
A Northern Man with American Principles
(*A Constitutional Manual for the National
American Party*)
Tom Shepherd (*Recollections of Olden Times*)

HAZLITT, William [1778–1830, English
essayist, journalist and drama critic]
Bereanus Theosebes (*A Discourse on the
Apostle Paul's Mystery*)
Boswell Redivivus; Phantastes (both used in
New Monthly Magazine)
Philalethes; Rationalis (both used in *Monthly
Repository*)

HAZZARD, Mary [1928–, US writer]
Olivia Dwight (*Close his Eyes*)

HEAD, Sir Francis Bond [1793–1875,
English soldier, merchant, dilpomat and
traveller]
A British Subject (*Three Letters to Lord
Brougham*)
An Old Man (*Bubbles from the Brunnen of
Nassau*)

HEAD, Richard [1637–86, English writer and
failed gambler – drowned at sea]
Francis Careless (*The Floating Island*)

Meriton Latroon (*News from the Stars*)

HEADLEY, Henry [1765–88, English poet
and critic]
C. T. O. (in *Gentleman's Magazine*)

HEADRICK, James [1759–1841, English
geologist]
Gibe (*A Peep into the Convent of Clutha*)

HEALD, William Margetson [1767–1837,
English cleric and surgeon]
Julius Juniper (*The Brunoniad*)

HEALEY, Benjamin James [1908–, English
crime and mystery writer]
J. G. Jeffreys (his publishing name in USA)
Jeremy Sturrock (*Suicide Most Foul*; *A
Wicked Way to Die*)

HEALEY-KAY, Patrick [1904–83, English
ballet dancer and choreographer]
Anton Dolin (*Divertissement*)

HEARD, Henry Fitzgerald (Gerald)
[1889–1971, English writer on history,
fantasy and ethics]
G. F. Heard (*A Taste for Henry*; *Murder by
Reflection*)

HEARD, John Bickford [1828–1908, Irish
cleric]
Runnymede (in *Dublin University Magazine*)

HEARN, Lafcadio [1850–1904, journalist,
literary critic, essayist and writer on
Japan of Irish and Greek parentage;
adopted Japanese nationality]
Yakumo Koizumi (his adopted Japanese
name)

HEARN, Mary Anne [1834–1909, English
essayist and hymn writer]
Marianne Farningham (in the *Christian
World* and for *A Working Woman's Life*)
Marianne Hearn (*Echos from Darenth Vale*)
Eva Hope (*Grace Darling*)

HEARNE, John [1926–, Jamaican novelist]
John Morris (*Fever Brass*; *The Candywine
Development*)

HEARNE, Thomas [1678–1735, English historian]
A Gentleman of Cambridge (*A Letter to the Rev. The Prolocutor*)

HEATH, William [1737–1814, American soldier in the Revolutionary War]
A Military Countryman (letters to the *Boston Gazette*)

HEATHCOTE, Ralph [1721–95, English cleric and writer]
A Freeholder of Leicester (*Memoirs of the Election of Leicester*)
A Gentleman of the Commission (*Irenarch*)
An Old Servant (*A Letter to the Lord Mayor*)

HEAVEN, Constance [1911–, English actress and romantic novelist]
Constance Fecher (*King's Legacy*; *Lion of Trevarrock*)
Christina Merlin (*Spy Concerto*; *Sword of Mithras*)

HEBER, Richard [1773–1833, English classical scholar and book collector]
Cato Parvus (*Bibliophobia*)

HEBERDEN, Mary Violet [fl. 1945, US mystery writer]
Charles Leonard (*Deadline for Destruction*; *The Secret of the Spa*)

HECKELMANN, Charles Newman [1913–, US writer for children]
Charles Lawton (*The Winning Forward Pass*)

HECTOR, Annie French [1825–1902, Irish novelist – lived in London]
Mrs Alexander (*Her Dearest Foe*; *The Wooing o'T*)

HEIDE, Florence Parry [1919–, US writer for children]
Alex B. Allen (*The Tennis Menace*; *No Place for Baseball*)
Jamie McDonald (*Hannibal*)

HEILBRUN, Carolyn Gold [1926–, US mystery and crime writer]
Amanda Cross (*Poetic Justice*; *In the Last Analysis*)

HEINLEIN, Robert Anson [1907–88, US science-fiction writer]
Anson MacDonald (*Sixth Column*; *Beyond this Horizon*)
Lyle Monroe (in *Astounding Stories* magazine)

HELDMANN, Richard Bernard [1857–1915, English writer]
Richard Marsh (in the *Strand Magazine* and for *The Beetle*, *Curios* and *An Aristocratic Detective*)

HELPS, Sir Arthur [1813–75, English courtier and historical writer]
A British Author (in *MacMillan's Magazine*)
A Most Reluctant Diner-Out (in *Cornhill Magazine*)
One of the Special Constables in London (*A Letter by one of the Special Constables in London being Called out to Keep the Peace*)

HEMANS, Mrs Felicia Dorothea [1793–1835, English poet and essayist]
Clara Balfour (*Modern Greece*)
Felicia Dorothea Browne (*Juvenile Poems*)
A Lady (*The Restoration of the Works of Art to Italy*)

HENDERSON, Andrew [1734–75, Scottish historian and biographer]
A Christian (*The Case of the Jews Considered*)
An Impartial Hand (*Memoirs of John, late Earl of Stair*)
Miltonicus (*Furius*)

HENDERSON, Archibald [1877–1963, US writer]
Erskine Steele (*The Conquest of the Old Southwest*; *Changing Drama*)

HENDERSON, Donald Landel [fl. 1940, US writer]
D. H. Landels (*Announcer*)

HENDERSON, Frank [1836–89, Scottish politician]
A Merchant (in *Temple Bar*)

HENDERSON, George Francis Robert
[1854–1903, English soldier and military historian]
A Line Officer (*The Campaign at Fredericksburg*)

HENDERSON, James Leal [fl. 1947, US writer]
Jay L. Currier (*Cargo of Fear*)

HENDERSON, Le Grand [1901–, US writer]
Le Grand (*Cap'n Dow and the Hole in the Doughnut*; *Mostly about Mutt*)

HENDRY, Frank Coutts [fl. 1944, English nautical and travel writer]
Shalimar (*True Tales of Sail and Steam*; *Around the Horn and Home Again*)

HENHAM, Ernest George [1870–1946, Canadian poet and novelist – settled in England]
John Trevena (*Off the Beaten Track*; *Pixy in Petticoats*)

HENKLE, Henrietta [1909–, US writer]
Henrietta Buckmaster (*Tomorrow is Another Day*; *Bread from Heaven*)

HENLEY, John [1692–1756, English cleric, writer and orator]
Bryan Bayonet of the First Regiment of Guards; Alexander Ratcliffe; Sir Isaac Ratcliffe of Elbow Lane; Jonadab Swift (all used in *The Hyp-Doctor*)
Simon Croxeall (*The Reed of Egypt Piercing the Hand that Leans upon it*)
Peter De Quir (letter in *The Spectator*)
A. Welstede (*Oratory Transactions No. 1*)

HENLEY, Samuel [1740–1815, English-American scholar and philosopher]
S. H- Eloquentiae Professor (*Ad Anglos ... ode Gratulatoria*)

HENLEY, William Ernest [1849–1903, English critic, dramatist, poet and editor]
Byron M'Guinness (*Mephisto*)
*Two Art Critics (*Pictures at Play*)

HENNINGSEN, Charles Frederick
[1815–77, English soldier and traveller of Swedish parentage]
One who Has Seen and Describes (*Revelations of Russia*)

HENNISART, Martha [fl. 1930, US mystery novelist]
*R. B. Dominic (*Murder in High Place*; *Murder out of Commission*)
*Emma Lathen (*Accounting for Murder*; *By Hook or By Crook*)

HENRY, Caleb Sprague [1804–83, US cleric]
An Episcopal Clergyman (*Politics and the Pulpit*)

HENRY, David [1710–92, Scottish writer]
A Practical Farmer (*The Complete English Farmer*)

HENRY, James [1798–1876, Irish physician and classical scholar]
A Fellow of the College of Physicians, Dublin (*A Dialogue between a Bilious Patient and a Fellow of the College of Physicians, Dublin*)
A Physician (*Religion, Worldly-Mindedness and Philosophy*)

HENRY, Matthew [1662–1714, English nonconformist cleric]
An Old Divine (*The Communicant's Companion*)

HENRY, Walter [1791–1860, Irish-born Canadian journalist]
Piscator; Scrutator (both used in the *New York Albion*)
A Staff Surgeon (*Trifles from my Portfolio*)

HENSHALL, James Alexander [1836–1925, US physician and writer on angling]
Oconomowoc (used for journalism)

HENSHAW, David [1791–1852, US politician]
A Citizen of Boston (*Observations on the Character of Napoleon Bonaparte*; *Remarks upon the Rights and Powers of Corporations*)

A Merchant (*Remarks upon the Banks of the United States*)

HENSMAN, Howard [d. 1916, English journalist and writer]
Vedette (*Britain and Armageddon; The Adventures of an Ensign*)

HENTZ, Mrs Caroline Lee [1800–56, US novelist, playwright and writer for children]
Aunt Patty (*Aunt Patty's Scrap Bag*)

HEPBURN, Robert [1690–1712, English writer]
Donald MacStaff of the North (in *The Tatler*)

HEPBURN, Thomas Nicoll [1861–1930, Scottish novelist and biographer]
Gabriel Setoun (*Child World; Robert Burns; Sunshine and Haar*)

HEPPELL, Mary [fl. 1960, English writer]
Marguerite Clare (*Deadline for Loren; Spin a Dark Web*)

HERAUD, John Abraham [1799–1887, English editor, poet and dramatist]
Mordaunt Couplet Esq. (in *Fraser's Magazine*)

HERBERT, Sir Alan Patrick [1890–1971, English essayist, poet, humorist and dramatist]
A. P. H. (in *Punch*)

HERBERT, Edward [1648–98, Earl of Portland, barrister and supporter of James II]
A Person of Honour (*The Character of a Trimmer*)

HERBERT, George Robert Charles [1850–95, 13th Earl of Pembroke]
The Earl (*South Sea Bubbles*)

HERBERT, Henry Howard Molyneux [1831–90, 4th Earl of Carnarvon; statesman and poet]
A Country Gentleman; Ruricola (both used in *National Review*)

HERBERT, Henry John George [1800–49, 3rd Earl of Carnarvon; traveller and writer]
An English Nobleman (*The Policy of England towards Spain*)

HERBERT, Henry William [1807–58, English novelist and sporting writer; worked much in USA – shot himself in New York]
Frank Forester (*The Deerstalker; The Fisherman's Guide*)

HERBERT, Xavier [1901–84, Australian writer]
Herbert Astor (in the *Australian Journal*)

HERMAN, Allan [1916–, Canadian writer]
Ted Allan (*The Scalpel, the Sword: the Story of Doctor Norman Bethune*)
Edward Maxwell (*Quest for Pajaro*)

HERNE, Thomas [d. 1722, English academic and controversialist]
Philanagnostes Criticus (*An Account of all the Considerable Pamphlets that have been Published on Either Side in the Present Controversy etc.*)
Phileleutherus Cantabrigiensis (*Animadversions Especially upon the University Proceedings Against ... Richard Bentley; An Essay on Imposing and Subscribing; The False Notion of a Christian Priesthood; A Letter to the Rev. Dr Mangey; Three Discourses*)
A Seeker after Truth (*A Second Letter to the Rev. Dr Mangey*)

HERON, Robert [1764–1807, Scottish historian, editor and writer]
Ralph Anderson (*A Letter from Ralph Anderson to Sir John Sinclair*)
Felix Phantom (in *The Ghost*)

HERON-ALLEN, Edward [1861–1943, English marine biologist, zoologist, writer and novelist]
Christopher Blayre (*The Purple Sapphire; Some Women of the University*)
Dryasdust (*Tales of the Wonder Club*)

M. Y. Halidom (*The Wizard Mantle; The Poet's Curse*)
Nora Helen Warddel (*The Romance of a Quiet Watering Place*)

HERRING, Paul [fl. 1905, English writer for boys]
David Raeburn (*Hoodman Grey, Christian*)

HERRING, Thomas [1693–1757, English cleric; Archbishop of Canterbury]
A Clergyman of the Church of England (*A New Form of Common Prayer*)

HERRMANN, Lazar [1896–1961, Russian-born US writer]
Leo Lania (*The Darkest Hour; Land of Promise; Today We Are Brothers*)

HERSHON, Paul Isaac [1817–88, Galician-born Palestine pioneer and Hebraist]
A Converted Jew (*Jerusalem as it Is*)

HERVEY, Mrs Eleonora Louisa [1811–?, English poet, novelist and writer]
Margaret Russell (*Margaret Russell: an Autobiography*)

HERVEY, John [1696–1743, Baron Hervey of Ickworth; courtier, politician and pamphleteer]
A Nobleman (*An Epistle from a Nobleman to a Doctor of Divinity*)
A Person of Quality (*A Satire in the Manner of Persius*)

HERVEY, Thomas [1699–1775, English pamphleteer]
T. H. (*An Elegy upon the Death of the Late Earl Granville*)

HERVEY, Thomas Kibble [1799–1859, English poet and writer]
Jack Ketch (*Australia and other Poems*)

HESELTINE, Philip Arnold [1894–1930, English musician and composer]
Rab Noolas (*Merry-Go-Down*)
Peter Warlock (*Orchesography; Thomas Whythorne; The English Ayre; The Metamorphosis of Ajax*)

HESLOP, Richard Oliver [1842–1916, English merchant, philologist and antiquarian]
Harry Haldane (*Geordy's Last-Newcastle Folkspeech*)

HESS, Joan [fl. 1990, US writer]
Joan Hadley (*The Deadly Ackee*)

HEWETT, Anita [1918–91, English writer for children]
Anne Wellington (*Grandfather Gregory; Mr Bingle's Apple Pie*)

HEWITT, Cecil Rolph [1901–94, English journalist and writer]
R. H. Cecil (in *The Spectator*)
C. H. Rolph (in the *New Statesman*)

HEWITT, Kathleen Douglas [fl. 1943, English writer]
Dorothea Martin (*The Mice are Not Amused*)

HEWITT, William Graily [1864–1952, English novelist]
Freke Viggars (in *Longman's Magazine*)

HEWLETT, John [1762–1844, English cleric and theological scholar]
L. Euler (*Elements of Algebra*)

HEWLETT, Joseph Thomas James [1800–47, English novelist]
A Member of Parliament (*Poetry for the Million*)
Peter Priggins (in *New Monthly Magazine*)

HEWSON, Irene Dale [fl. 1944, Scottish novelist and playwright]
Jean Ross (*Flowers without Sun; Strangers under our Roof*)

HEYER, Georgette [1902–74, English historical novelist]
Stella Martin (*The Transformation of Philip Jettan*)

HEYLIGER, William [1884–?, US writer]
Hawley Williams (*The Winning Hit; Johnson of Lancing*)

HEYLYN, Peter [1600–62, English royalist, cleric and writer on religious affairs]
Robert Hall, Gent. (*A Help to English History*; *Historia Anglorum*)
A Learned and Impartial Hand (*France Painted to the Life*)
Theophilus Churchman (*The Historie of Episcopacie*)
P. H. Treleinie, Gent. (*The Undeceiving of the People in the Point of Tithes*)

HEYWOOD, James [1687–1776, English writer and journalist]
Belinda; Miranda; James Philobiblos; Bob Smart (all used in *The Free-Thinker*)
James Easy (letter to *The Spectator*)

HEYWOOD, Samuel [1753–1828, English jurist]
A Layman (*The Right of Protestant Dissenters to Toleration Asserted*)

HIBBERT (née Burford), Eleanor Alice [1906–93, English novelist and mystery writer]
Eleanor Burford (*Passionate Witness*; *Dear Delusion*)
Philippa Carr (*The Miracle at St Bruno's*; *The Witch from the Sea*)
Elbur Ford (*Poison in Pimlico*; *Such Bitter Business*)
Victoria Holt (*The Shadow of the Lynx*; *Bride of Pendorric*)
Kathleen Kellow (*Danse Macabre*; *Lilith*)
Anna Percival (*The Brides of Lanlory*)
Jean Plaidy (*Murder Most Royal*; *Daughter of Satan*)
Ellalice Tate (*The Scarlet Cloak*; *Madame du Barry*)

HIBBS, John Alfred Blyth [1925–, English poet and writer on transport]
John Blyth (*Being a Patient*; *New Found Land*)

HIBBS, Richard [1812–86, English cleric and social reformer]
Clericus (*Remarks on the Italian Opera in Edinburgh*)

HICHENS, Robert Smythe [1864–1950, English journalist and novelist]
Crotchet (in *The Gentlewoman*)

HICKERINGELL, Edmund [1631–1708, English cleric, soldier and forger]
A Legal Son and Sincere Conformist to the Church of England (*The Fourth Part of Naked Truth*)

HICKES, George [1642–1715, English cleric and controversialist]
A Dignify'd Clergy-Man of the Church of England (*The Celebrated Story of the Thebaean Legion*)
A Layman of the Church of England (*The Doctrine of Passive Obedience*)
A Lover of the Established Government of Both Church and State (*A Letter Sent from Beyond the Seas*)
A Minister of London (*Jovian or, an Answer to Julian*)
An Orthodox Protestant (*The Spirit of Popery Speaking out of the Mouths etc.*)
A True Catholick of the Church of England (*Speculum Beatae Virginus*)

HICKEY, Antony [d. 1641, Irish Franciscan friar]
Dermitius Thadaeus (*Nitela Franciscanae Religionis*)

HICKEY, William Ross [1787–1875, Irish cleric, agriculturist and writer]
Martin Doyle (in the *Wexford Herald* and for *Hints to Small Farmers* and *Rural Economy for Cottage Farmers and Gardeners*)

HICKMAN, Henry [d. 1692, English cleric and controversialist]
A Country Scholar (*Bonasus Vadulans*)
Irenaeus Eleutherius (*Apologia pro Ministris in Anglia*)
Theophilus Churchman (*A Review of the Certamen Epistolare*)

HICKS, William Watkin [1837–1915, US writer]
Golden Light (*Angel's Visits to my Farm in Florida*)

HIFFERNAN, Paul [1719–77, Irish farceur and writer]
P. H. (*The Self-Enamoured or, the Ladies' Doctor*)
Phiolotechnicus Miso-Mimides (*Foote's Prologue Detected*; *Appendix to Foote's Prologue*)

HIGGINBOTHAM, John C. [d. 1919, English novelist]
Afrikander (in *Contemporary Review*)
Orme Agnus (*Jan Oxber*; *Nan of Manchester*)

HIGGINBOTTOM, David [1923–, English writer for children]
Nicholas Fisk (*Monster Maker*; *Space Hostages*)

HIGGINS, Matthew James [1810–68, Irish journalist and social reformer]
Civilian (letters to *The Times*)
J. O. (*Jacob Omnium*)
Jacob Omnium (*Is Cheaper Sugar the Triumph of Free Trade?*; *Light Horse*; *A Letter on Administrative Reform*; *A Letter on Army Reform*; *Letters on Military Education*; *Letters on the Purchase System*; *The Story of the Mhow Court Martial*; *A Third Letter to Lord John Russell*; *Three Letters on Military Education*)
Paterfamilias (*Papers on Public School Education*; *Three Letters on Public School Education*)

HIGGINSON, Joseph Vincent [1896–, US musician and composer]
Cyr De Brant (*Lenten Motets and Hymns*)

HIGGINSON, Stephen [1743–1828, US politician]
Cato (*Examination of the Treaty of Amity*)

HIGHMORE, Joseph [1692–1780, English painter and writer]
A Christian Freethinker (*Observations on a Pamphlet Entitled Christianity Not Founded on Argument*)

HIGHSMITH, Mary Patricia [1921–, US crime novelist]
Claire Morgan (*The Price of Salt*)

HILDESLEY, Mark [1698–1772, English cleric; Bishop of Sodor and Man]
Philanthropum (*Religio Juris Prudentis*)
A Resident Clergyman (*Plain Instructions for Young Persons*)

HILDRETH, Hosea [1782–1835, US cleric and mathematician]
A Father (*A Book for Massachusetts Children*)

HILDRETH, Richard [1807–65, US journalist, lawyer and historian]
A Native American (*Native Americanism Detected and Exposed*)

HILDROP, John [d. 1756, English cleric, satirist and writer]
Timothy Hooker (*An Essay on Honour*)
An Impartial Hand (*The Contempt of the Clergy Considered*)
Phileleutherus Britannicus (*Reflections upon Reason*)

HILDYARD, Ida Jane [1867–?, English novelist]
Ida Lemon (*A Pair of Lovers*; *A Divided Duty*)

HILDYARD, James [1809–87, English cleric and classical scholar]
Ingoldsby (*A Reply to the Bishops in Convocation*)

HILL, Aaron [1685–1750, English poet, dramatist and traveller]
A Fellow of All-Souls (*The Progress of Wit*)
Gamaliel Gunson (*The Progress of Wit*)
Ignotus (*The Impartial*)

HILL, Benson Earle [1795–1845, English journalist and writer]
Dean Swift of Brazennose (*The Pinch of Snuff*)

HILL, Brian [1896–, English crime writer and literary critic]
Marcus Magill (*Death-in-the-Box*; *Murder Out of Time*)

HILL, Charles [1904–89, English physician, politican and broadcaster]
Radio Doctor (*Wednesday Morning Early or, a Little of What you Fancy*)

HILL, Douglas [1935–, Canadian writer for children]
Martin Hillman (*Bridging a Continent*)

HILL, Edmund Thomas [1564–1644, English Benedictine monk]
T. Buckland (*A Plaine Pathway to Heaven*)

HILL, Edward Bernard Lewin [1834–1915, English public servant]
A Post-Office Man (in *Cornhill Magazine*)

HILL, Frank Harrison [1830–1910, English journalist, editor and biographer]
A Prominent London Journalist (*Political Portraits*)

HILL, George [1796–1871, US librarian and poet]
A Voyager (*The Ruins in Athens*)

HILL, George Canning [1825–98, US lawyer and writer]
Thomas Lackland (*Home-Spun or, Twenty Five Years Ago*)
Lewis Myrtle (*Our Parish or, Pen Paintings of Village Life*)

HILL, Grace Livingston [1865–1947, US novelist]
Marcia MacDonald (*Out of the Storm; The White Lady*)

HILL, Isaac [1788–1851, US journalist and politician]
A Citizen of New England (*A Brief Sketch of the Life of Andrew Jackson*)

HILL, Sir John [1716–75, English journalist, botanist and apothecary]
George Crine (*The Management of Gout*)
An Impartial Hand (*The History of a Woman of Quality*)
The Inspector (in the *London Daily Advertiser* and for *Letters from an Inspector to a Lady*)
Abraham Johnson (*Lucina Sine Concubitu*)
A Sclavonian Nobleman in London (*A Dissertation on Royal Societies*)
Honourable Julianna-Susannah Seymour (*On the Management and Education of Children; Conduct of a Married Life*)

Christian Uvedale (*The Construction of the Nerves*)

HILL, John Edward Christopher [1912–, English historian]
K. E. Holme (*Two Commonwealths*)

HILL, Joseph [1625–1707, English nonconformist cleric and pamphleteer]
A Wellwisher to the Reformed Religion (*The Interest of these United Provinces being a Defence of the Zeelanders Choice*)

HILL, Matthew Davenport [1792–1872, English barrister and law reformer]
Martin Danvers Heaviside; William Payne (both used in *Quarterly Magazine*)

HILL, Pamela [1920–, English novelist]
Sharon Fiske (*Summer Cypress*)

HILL, Reginald Charles [1936–, English crime and mystery novelist]
Dick Morland (*Heart Clock; Albion! Albion!*)
Patrick Ruell (*Red Christmas; The Long Kill*)
Charles Underhill (*Captain Fantom*)

HILL, Sir Richard [1732–1808, English academic and politician]
A Friend (*Five Letters to the Rev. Mr F... R ...*)
A Gentleman of the University of Oxford (*An Address to Persons of Fashion*)
A Master of Arts of the University of Oxford (*Pietas Oxoniensis*)
An Old Member of Parliament (*Remarks on a Charge delivered by the Bishop of Lincoln*)
Philalethes (*The Admonisher Admonished; A Letter to the Rev. Dr Adams of Shrewsbury*)

HILL, Rowland [1744–1833, English preacher and writer]
An Old Observer (*Spiritual Characteristics Represented*)

HILL, Thomas [fl. 1590, English writer]
Didymus Mountain (*A Brief and Pleasant Treatise Teaching Howe to Dress, Sowe and Set a Garden; The Profitable Arte of Gardening*)

HILL, Thomas [1760–1840, English book collector]
Paul Pry (*Marmion Travestied*)

HILLARD, George Stillman [1808–79, US lawyer and writer]
Silas Standfast (*Letters of Silas Standfast to his friend Jotham*)

HILLIAM, Bentley Collingwood [1890–1968, English composer and entertainer]
Mr Flotsam (*Flotsam and Jetsam – Verses*)

HILLIER, Alfred Peter { 1858–1911, English physician and writer]
Harley (*In the Veldt*)

HILTON, James [1900–54, English novelist and screenwriter]
Glen Trevor (*Murder at School*; published in the USA as *Was it Murder?*)

HILTON, John Buxton [1921–86, English crime and mystery novelist]
John Greenwood (*Mists over Mosley*; *Mosley by Moonlight*)

HINCKLEY, Helen [1903–90?,US writer]
Helen Jones (*Over the Mormon Trail*)

HINCKS, Cyril Malcolm [1881–?, English writer for boys]
John M. Howard; Charles Malcolm (both used in the *Sports Budget*)

HINDS, Samuel [1793–1872, English cleric; Bishop of Norwich]
A Lay Member of the Church of England (*The Christian's Prayer*)

HINGESTON-RANDOLPH, Francis Charles [1833–1910, English cleric and antiquarian]
A Country Parson (*Records of a Rocky Shore*)
Herbert Murray (in *New Monthly Magazine*)

HINMAN, Royal Ralph [1785–1868, US writer]
An Antiquarian (*The Blue Laws of New Haven Colony*)

HINTON, Jennifer [1929–, English novelist]
Jennifer Dawson (*The Ha-Ha*)

HINTON, John Howard [1791–1873, English Baptist cleric and writer]
A Minister (*Hymns*)

HIPPISLEY, John [d. 1748, English dramatist and actor]
A Gentleman (*Flora: an Opera*)
A Student of Oxford (*A Dissertation on Comedy*)

HIPPISLEY, Sir John Coxe [1748–1825, English barrister, diplomat and politician]
A Member of the Oxford Convocation (*The Via Media or Anglican Orthodoxy*)

HITCHENS, Julia Dolores [1907–73, US mystery writer]
Dolan Birkley (*The Blue Geranium*; *The Unloved*)
Noel Burke (*The Shivering Bow*)
D. B. Olsen (*The Cat Saw Murder*; *The Cat Walks*)

HITCHINS, Fortescue [1784–1814, English poet and Cornish historian]
A Young Gentleman (*A Vision of Memory*)

HOADLY, Benjamin [1676–1761, English physician, dramatist and cleric]
Britannicus (in the *London Journal* and for *Four Tracts*)
A Christian (*Queries Recommended to the author of 'Free-Thinking'*)

HOAR, H. Frank [1909–76, English cartoonist]
Acanthus (in *Punch*)

HOAR, Roger Sherman [1887–1963, US science-fiction writer]
Ralph Milne Farley (in *Argosy Magazine* for *The Radio Man*)

HOBART, Alice [1882–1967, US novelist and writer]
Alice Tisdale (*The Cup and the Sword*; *The Cleft Rock*)

HOBART, Augustus Charles [1822–86, English mariner, admiral in the Turkish service; known as 'Hobart Pasha']
Capt. A. Roberts (*Never Caught: Personal Adventures during the American Civil War*)

HOBART, George Vere [1867–1926, US journalist, humorist, dramatist and writer for children]
Diedrich Dinkelspiel (in the *Baltimore News* and for *Gonversationings*)
Hugh McHugh (*John Henry*; *It's up to You*)

HOBHOUSE, Sir Benjamin [1757–1831, English barrister and politician]
A Barrister at Law (*A Treatise on Heresy*)
Publicola (*A Correspondence between the Rev. R. Wells and Publicola*)

HOBHOUSE, John Cam [1786–1869, Baron Broughton de Gyfford; politician – he was Lord Byron's 'best-man']
An Englishman Resident in Paris (*The Substance of Some Letters Written by an Englishman Resident in Paris*)

HOBSON, Frederick Leslie [1855–92, English playwright]
Fred Leslie (his stage name)
A. C. Torr (used for burlesque writing)

HOBY, Sir Edward [1560–1617, English courtier to James I]
Nick, Groom of the Hobie-Stable Reginoburgi (*A Curry-Combe for a Cox-Combe*)

HOCH, Edward D. [1930–, US crime and mystery writer]
Irwin Booth (*Co-Incidence*)
Stephen Dentinger; R. L. Stevens (both used in *Ellery Queen's Mystery Magazine*)
Pat McMahon (in *The Saint* magazine)
Ellery Queen (*The Blue Movie Murders*)

HODDER, Alfred [1866–1907, US lawyer and writer]
Francis Walton (*A Fight for the City*)

HODDER, Edwin [1837–1904, English civil servant, biographer and writer]
Old Merry (*The Bookstall Boy of Batherton*; *The Junior Clerk*; *A Siberian Exile's Children*; *Simon Peter, his Life, Times and Friends*)

HODDER-WILLIAMS, Christopher [1926–, English science-fiction writer and novelist]
James Brogan (*The Cummings Report*)

HODGE, Harry Baldwin Hermon [1872–1947, Scottish composer and writer]
Langa Langa (*Up Against it in Uganda*)

HODGES, Barbara K. [1893–1949, English novelist and short-story writer]
Elizabeth Cambridge (*Hostages to Fortune*; *The Sycamore Tree*)

HODGES, Henry Clay [1831–1917, US soldier]
Alvidas (*The Science and Key of Life*)

HODGES, Joseph Sydney Willes [1829–1900, English artist and writer]
Stanley Hope (*Geoffrey's Wife*; *Godfrey's Wife*)

HODGKIN, John [1800–75, English barrister and Quaker]
A Member of the English Bar (*Incumbered Estates*)

HODGSKIN, Thomas [1787–1869, English economist]
A Labourer (*Labour Defended against the Claims of Capital*)

HODGSON, Charles E. [fl. 1876, English naval chaplain]
The Chaplain of the 'Discovery' (in *Fraser's Magazine*)

HODGSON, James [1672–1755, English mathematician]
J. H., FRS (*A Correct Table of Logarithms*)

HODSON, James Shirley [fl. 1875, English writer on the theatre]
An Old Stager (*A Complete Guide to the Stage*; *Private Theatricals, being a Practical Guide*)

HODSON, Mrs Margaret [1778–1852, English historian and biographer]
A Lady (*Lines to a Boy Pursuing a Butterfly*)

HOFF, Harry Summerfield [1910–, English novelist and critic]
William Cooper (*Scenes from Provincial Life*; *Scenes from Married Life*)

HOFFMAN, Charles Fenno [1806–84, US novelist, poet and travel writer]
A New Yorker (*A Winter in the West*)

HOFFMAN, David [1784–1854, US jurist]
Anthony Grumbler Esq. (*Miscellaneous Thoughts on Men and Manners*; *Viator or, a Peep into my Note-Book*)

HOFFMAN, David Murray [1791–1876, US jurist]
Pacificator (*A Letter to the Clergy in the Diocese of New York*)

HOFF-MILES, Reaney Monckton [1881–1951, Irish actor and dramatist]
Monckton Hoffe (*The Little Damozal*; *Many Waters*)

HOFLAND, Barbara Hoole [1770–1844, English writer]
An Englishwoman (*A Letter of an Englishwoman*)
An Old Fashioned Englishman (*Says She to her Neighbour, What?*)

HOG, James [1658–1734, Scottish cleric and pamphleteer]
Epaphras (*A Conference betwixt Epaphroditus and Epaphras*)
A Member of the Church of Scotland (*An Essay to Vindicate some Scripture Truths*)
A Welwisher to a Covenanted Reformation (*A Letter Wherein the Scriptural Grounds ... for Reformation of Churches ... are Succinctly Considered and Cleared*)

HOGAN, Ray [1918–, US western novelist]
Clay Ringold (*Return to Rio Fuego*; *The Hooded Gun*)

HOGARTH, Grace Allen [1905–, US writer for children]
Grace Allen (*This to Be Love*)
Amelia Gay (*The End of Summer*)
*Allen Weston (*Murders for Sale*)

HOGBEN, Lancelot Thomas [1895–1975, English academic and scientific writer]
Kenneth Calvin Page (*A Journey to Nineveh*)

HOGG, James [1770–1835, Scottish shepherd, poet and writer]
J. H. Craig of Douglas Esq. (*The Hunting of Badlewe*)
The Ettrick Shepherd (*The Altrive Tales*)
A Justified Sinner (*The Private Memoirs and Confessions of a Justified Sinner*)
William Mitchell (in *Blackwood's Magazine*)

HOGG, Thomas Jefferson [1792–1862, English barrister and writer; an intimate of Shelley]
John Brown Esq. (*Memoirs of Prince Alexy Haimatoff*)
A Traveller (*Two Hundred and Nine Days or, the Journal of a Traveller*)

HOLBROOK, Silas Pinckney [1796–1835, US lawyer and writer]
A Boston Merchant; Jonathan Farbrick (both used in the *Boston Courier*)
A Traveller (*Sketches*)

HOLCROFT, Thomas [1745–1809, English journalist, poet, novelist and dramatist]
William Vincent of Grays Inn (*A Plain and Succinct Narrative of the late Riots*)

HOLDAWAY, Neville Aldridge [1894–, English crime writer]
N. A. Temple Ellis (*The Cauldron Bubbles*; *A Case in Hand*)

HOLDEN, Elizabeth Rhoda [1943–, English writer for children]
Louise Lawrence (*Earth Witch*; *The Power of Stars*)

HOLDEN, Luther L. [1815–1905, English surgeon and medical writer]
Ranger (*A Thrilling Balloon Voyage*)

HOLDEN, Martha Everts [1844–96, US writer]
Amber (*A String of Amber Beads; Amber Glints*)

HOLDEN, Oliver [d. 1831, US composer of religious music]
A Citizen of Massachusetts (*Sacred Dirges Commemorative of Washington*)

HOLDING, James [1907–, US crime and mystery writer]
Clark Carlisle (*Bugs Bunny Carrot Machine*)
Jay Freeman (*The Country Cousins*)
Ellery Queen Jr. (*The Purple Bird Mystery*)

HOLDSTOCK, Robert P. [1948–, English fantasy writer]
Robert Black (*Legend of the Werewolf; The Satanists*)
Chris Carlsen (*Shadow of the Wolf; The Horned Warrior*)

HOLDSWORTH, Lucy Violet [1869–1954, English Quaker writer]
L. V. Hodgkin (*A Book of Quaker Saints; Silent Worship; The Romance of Inward Light*)

HOLE, Matthew [d. 1730, English cleric and theologian]
A Presbyter of the Church of England (*An Antidote against Infidelity*)

HOLE, Samuel Reynolds [1819–1904, English cleric, preacher, horticulturist and writer]
An Oxonian (*A Little Tour in Ireland; Thaumaturgia*)

HOLLAND, Cecelia [1943–, US novelist]
Elizabeth Eliot Carter (*Valley of the Kings*)

HOLLAND, Edwin Clifford [1793–1824, US journalist, poet and writer]
A South Carolinian (*A Refutation of the Calumnies against Western States*)

HOLLAND, Henry Scott [1847–1918, English cleric and writer]
An Oxonian (*Impressions of the Ammergau Passion Play*)

HOLLAND, Isabelle [1920–, US novelist and writer for children]
Francesca Hunt (*The Mystery of Castle Renaldi*)

HOLLAND, John [1766–1826, English nonconformist cleric]
A Dissenter (*An Address to the Members ... of Bolton*)

HOLLAND, John [1794–1872, English journalist, historian and poet]
A Christian Poet (*The Bazaar or, Money and the Church*)
Sexagenarius (*The Old Arm-Chair*)

HOLLAND, Josiah Gilbert [1819–91, US physician, novelist, poet and journalist]
Max Mannering (in the *Springfield Republican*)
Timothy Titcomb (in the *Springfield Republican* and for *Letters to the Joneses* and *Titcomb's Letters to Young People*)

HOLLAND, Sheila [1937–, English romantic novelist]
Sheila Coates (*A Crown Usurped; The Bells of the City*)
Laura Hardy (*Playing with Fire; Dark Fantasy*)
Charlotte Lamb (*Storm Centre; Star-Crossed*)
Sheila Lancaster (*Dark Sweet Wanton; The Tithammer*)
Victoria Woolf (*Sweet Compulsion*)

HOLLAND, Thomas Agar [1803–88, English poet]
An Undergraduate (*The Colossal Statue of William Wallace*)

HOLLES, Denzil [1599–1680, 1st Baron Holles of Ifield; royalist]
A Gentleman (*Letter of a Gentleman to his Friend showing that the Bishops etc.*)

HOLLEY, Marietta [1836–1926, US novelist]
Josiah Allen's Wife (*Miss Jones' Quilting*;
Poems; *Samantha among the Brethren*;
Samantha at Saratoga; *Sweet Cicely*)

HOLLEY, Myron [1779–1841, US journalist
and lawyer]
A Citizen of New York (*An Address to the
People of the United States*)

HOLLINGWORTH, Richard [1607–56,
English cleric]
A Lover of the Truth (*The Truth Guide*)

HOLLIS, Miaurice Christopher [1902–77,
English writer]
Percy Somerset (in *Punch*)

HOLLIS, William Ainslie [1839–92, English
physician]
Pyx Hawes (in *National Review*)

HOLLOWAY, Mrs Anna [fl. 1881, US
novelist]
Teresa A. Thornet (*Kate Comerford*)

HOLLOWAY, Mrs Everett [fl. 1890, English
novelist]
Alan Adair (in *Longman's Magazine*)

HOLLOWOOD, Albert Bernard [1910–81,
English journalist, cartoonist and editor
of *Punch*]
Hod (in *Punch*)

HOLMAN, Hugh [1914–, US writer]
Clarence Hunt (*Small Town Corpses*)

HOLMAN, James [1786–1857, English
traveller who was totally blind]
The Blind Traveller (*Travels in Madeira,
Sierra Leone etc.*)

HOLME, Sir Randle Fynes Wilson
[1864–1957, English solicitor and
Wagnerian writer]
Randle Fynes (*Parsifal*; *The Ring of the
Nibelung*)

HOLMES, Abiel [1763–1837, US cleric]
A Member of the Massachusetts Bible
Society (*An Historical Sketch of
Translations of the Bible*)

HOLMES, Edmond Gore Alexander
[1850–1936, English educationalist, poet,
critic and philosopher]
An Unorthodox Believer (*A Confession of
Faith*)

HOLMES, Edward [1797–1959, English
writer and musical composer]
A Musical Professor (*A Ramble among the
Musicians of Germany*)

HOLMES, Mrs Elizabeth [d. 1843, English
writer]
A Country Parson's Daughter (*Lawrence the
Martyr*; *Realities of Life*; *Scenes in our
Parish*)

HOLMES, Sylvester [d. 1866, US writer]
Timothy (*Fifty-Five Reasons for Not being a
Baptist*)

HOLMES, William [1689–1748, English
cleric, academic and historian]
A Citizen of Exeter (*A Translation of a
Charter... City of Exeter*)
A Country Clergyman (*The Country
Clergyman's Advice to his Parishioners*)
A Country Parson (*The Country Parson's
Advice to the Younger Sort*)

HOLT, Henry [fl. 1935, English thriller
writer]
Stanley Hopkins (*Murder by Inches*; *The
Parchment Key*)

HOLT, John Saunders [1826–86, US lawyer
and novelist]
John Capelsay (*Abraham Page Esq.*)
Abraham Page Esq. (*What I Know About
Ben Eccles*)

HOLWELL, John Zephaniah [1711–98, Irish
surgeon, Governor of Bengal and writer
on Indian history]
A Quondam Servant of the Company
(*Thoughts on East India Affairs*)

HOLYOAKE, George Jacob [1817–1906,
English biographer and social reformer]
The Editor of the 'National' (*The Life of
Thomas Paine*)

A London Zulu (*Cumming Wrong: Colenso Right*)

Landor Praed (*Life of the Celebrated Lord Brougham*; *A History of the Progress of Middlesborough*)

HOME, Henry [1696–1782, Lord Kames; Scottish jurist and historian]
A Member of the Court (*Select Decisions of the Court of Session*)

HOME-GALL, Edward Reginald [1898–?, English writer for boys]
Edwin Dale; Rupert Hall (both used in *Champion*)

HOME-GALL, William Benjamin [1871–1936, English writer for boys]
Reginald Wray (*Tales of Empire*; *Where Honour Sits*)

HOMERSHAM, Basil Henry [1902–, English writer]
Basil Manningham (*Motive for Murder*)

HOMES, Mrs Mary Sophie [fl. 1857, US poet and novelist]
Millie Mayfield (*Carrie Harrington or, Scenes in New Orleans*; *A Wreath of Rhymes*)

HONE, Joseph Maunsell [1882–1959, Irish biographer]
N. Marlowe (*The History of the Irish Rebellion in 1916*; *The Irish Convention and Sinn Fein*)

HONE, William [1779–1842, English publisher, bookseller and satirist]
Rev. Mr Blacksheep (*An Anniversary Sermon on Tithes*)
John Cecil (*Sixty Curious, Interesting ... Narratives*)
An Englishman (*A Political Catechism*)
Dr J. Watkins (*The Trial of Elizabeth Fenning for Murder*)

HONEY, William Bowyer [1889–1956, English writer on the fine arts]
William Bowyer (*Brought out in Evidence*)

HOOD, Thomas [1799–1845, English humorist, journalist and writer]
R. T. Claridge (in *New Monthly Magazine*)

HOOK, H. Clarke [fl. 1912, English writer for boys]
Ross Harvey (in *Chums*)

HOOK, Samuel Clarke [fl. 1920, English writer for boys]
Maurice Merriman (in *Gem*)

HOOK, Theodore Edward [1788–1841, English novelist, humorist and satirist]
Alfred Allendale (*The Man of Sorrow*)
Vicesimus Blenkinsop (*Tentamen*)
Richard Jones (*Exchange No Robbery*)
Mrs Ramsbottom (in *John Bull* magazine for the *Ramsbottom Papers*)

HOOK, Walter Farquhar [1798–1875, English cleric and ecclesiastical writer]
A Presbyter of the Church of England (*Presbyterian Rights Asserted*)

HOOKE, Charles W. [fl. 1927, US writer]
Howard Fielding (*Hidden Out*; *Straight Crooks*)

HOOKER, Henry B. [1802–81, US cleric]
Simon (*Put Off and Put On*)

HOOPER, Johnson Jones [1815–62, US lawyer and humorist]
An Alabaman (in *Bentley's Miscellany*)
Capt. Simon Suggs (*Some Adventures of Capt. Simon Suggs*)

HOOPER, Kay [fl. 1985, US romantic novelist]
Kay Robbins (*Taken by Storm*; *On her Doorstep*)

HOOPER, Samuel [1808–75, US politician]
A Merchant of Boston (*Currency or Money: its Nature and Uses*)

HOOTON, Charles [1813–47, US journalist and novelist]
Mask (in *Bentley's Miscellany*)
Bilberry Thurland (*Adventures of Bilberry Thurland*)

HOPE, Frances Essex Theodora [fl. 1948, English writer]
Essex Smith (*The Wye Valley Mystery*)

HOPE, John [1739–85, English merchant and writer]
A Man in Business (*Occasional Attempts at Sentimental Poetry*)

HOPE, Thomas [1770–1831, Dutch-born English writer and collector of sculpture]
A Modern Greek (*Anastasius or, Memoirs of a Modern Greek*)

HOPE-SIMPSON, Jacynth [1930–, English writer for children]
Helen Dudley (*The Hooded Falcon*)

HOPKINS, David [d. 1814, English physician]
A Late Resident at Bhagulpore (*The Dangers of British India from French Invasion*)

HOPKINS, Joseph R. [fl. 1804, US writer]
A Young Gentleman of Philadelphia (*Hamiltoniad: or the Effects of Discord*)

HOPKINS, Samuel Miles [1772–1837, US lawyer]
A House Holder (*Letters Concerning the General Health*)

HOPKINSON, Francis [1737–91, US jurist, satirist and writer]
Peter Grievous (*A Pretty Story, Written in the Year of Our Lord, 1774*; *A Congratulatory Epistle … Peter Porcupine …*)

HOPKINSON, Henry Thomas [1905–90, English journalist and writer]
Vindicator (*A Strong Hand at the Helm*)

HOPKINSON, Joseph [1770–1842, US lawyer and songwriter]
An American (*What is our Situation and What are our Prospects?*)

HOPLEY, Catherine Cooper [1817–1911, English writer]
A Reader (*Our Library*)

HOPLEY-WOOLRICH, Cornell [1903–68, US crime writer]
George Hopley (*Night has a Thousand Eyes*)
William Irish (*The Blue Ribbon*; *Deadline at Dawn*)
Cornell Woolrich (*The Bride Wore Black*; *The Black Angel*)

HOPPIN, Augustus [1828–96, US artist]
C. Anton (*Recollections of Anton House*; *Two Compton Boys*)

HOPPUS, John [1789–1875, Scottish academic and philosopher]
Edinensi-Glasguensis (*Recollections, Juvenile and Miscellaneous*)

HOPTON, Susanna [1627–1709, English devotional writer]
An Humble Penitent (*Daily Devotions*)

HORBERY, Matthew [1707–73, English cleric and writer]
A Clergyman in the Country (*Animadversions upon a Late Pamphlet*)

HORGAN, John Joseph [1881–1967, Irish solicitor and writer]
Members of the War Cabinet and their Friends (*The Complete Grammar of Anarchy*)

HORLER, Sydney [1888–1954, English journalist and mystery novelist]
Peter Cavendish (*Romeo and Julia*)
Martin Heritage (*The House of Wingate*)
J. O. Standish (in *Boy's Realm*)

HORNE, Geoffrey [1916–, English mystery writer]
Gil North (*Sergeant Cluff Rings True*; *More Deaths for Sergeant Cluff*)

HORNE, George [1730–92, English cleric and theologian; Bishop of Norwich]
A Clergyman (*Considerations on the Reformation of the Church of England*)
One of the People called Christians (*A Letter to Adam Smith*)
An Undergraduate (*A Letter to the Rev. Dr Priestley*)

HORNE, Richard Hengist [1803–84, English traveller, editor and poet]
Sir Julius Cutwater Bart., KCB (in *Fraser's Magazine*)
Mrs Fairstar (*Memoirs of a London Doll*)
Farthing Poet (*Orion*)

Prof. Grabstein, Phil. D. of Gottingen (in
Fraser's Magazine)

Moorfields Daisy Bros. (in *St Paul's Magazine*)

Opifex (in *The University Magazine*)

Sir Lucius O'Trigger (in *The History of Duelling in all Countries*)

Ephraim Watts (*The Life of Van Amburgh*)

HORNE, Thomas Hartwell [1780–1862, English cleric, bibliographer and theologian]

John Clarke (*Bibliotheca Legum*)

A Lincolnshire Grazier (*The Complete Grazier*)

A Protestant (*A Sketch of the Persecutions in Hungary*)

HORNECK, Philip [fl. 1715, English writer]

Hermodactyl, Nephew to Alexander Bembo (in the *High German Doctor*)

HORNER, Joseph Gregory [1847–1927, English engineer]

A Foreman Pattern-Maker (*Helical Gears*; *Metal Turning*; *Pattern-Making*; *Practical Iron Founding*; *Toothed Gearing*)

HORNER, William Edmunds [1793–1853, US academic and physician]

A Physician of Philadelphia (*Observations on the Mineral Waters of Virginia*)

HORNIG, Charles D. [1916–, US science-fiction writer]

Derwin Lesser (in *Science Fiction* magazine)

HORSFIELD, Richard Henry [fl. 1937, English writer]

M. B. Gaunt (*The Leases of Death*)

HORSLEY, Samuel [1733–1806, English cleric, theologian and mathematician]

The Archdeacon of St Albans (*Letters from the Archdeacon of St Albans in Reply to Dr Priestley*)

A Clergyman (*An Apology for the Liturgy and Clergy*)

HORSMUNDEN, Daniel [1691–1778, American jurist]

The Recorder of the City of New York (*Journal of the Proceedings of the Conspiracy Formed by Some White People ... for Burning the City of New York*)

HORT, John Josiah [fl. 1850, English military writer]

Two Mounted Sentries (*The Horse Guards*)

HORTON, Sir Robert John Wilmot [1784–1841, English politician and writer]

Philalethes (*Letters on Colonial Policy concerning Ceylon*; *On Colonies*)

HOSACK, John [1809–87, English magistrate and historical writer]

A Templar (in *Tait's Edinburgh Magazine*)

HOSHOUR, Samuel Klinefelter [1803–83, US cleric]

Lorenzo Altisonant (*Letters to Squire Pedant*)

HOSKEN, Alice Cecil Seymour [1877–?, English novelist]

Coralie Stanton (*The Buried Torch*; *The Dog Star*)

HOSKEN, Clifford James Wheeler [1882–1950, English journalist, novelist and short-story writer]

Richard Keverne (*The Man in the Red Hat*; *White Gas*)

HOSKIER, Herman Charles [1864–1938, English-born US banker, antiquarian and soldier in the French Army during WWI]

Signpost (*In Tune with the Universe*)

HOSKINS, Cyril Henry [1910–, English occult writer]

Tuesday Lobsang Rampa (*Beyond the Tenth*; *Tibetan Sage*)

HOSKINS, Robert [1933–, US fantasy and science-fiction writer]

Grace Corren (*Evil in the Family*)

John Gregory (*Legacy of the Stars*)

Philip Hoskins (in *IF* magazine)

Susan Jennifer (*Country of the Kind*)

Michael Kerr (*The Gemini Run*)

HOSKYNS, Chandos Wren [1812–76, English barrister and writer]
C. W. H. (*Talpa: or The Chronicles of a Clay Farm*)

HOTTEN, John Camden [1832–73, English publisher and writer]
Titus A. Brick (*Awful Crammers*)
London Antiquary (*A Dictionary of Modern Slang*)

HOUGH, Richard Alexander [1922–, English writer for children]
Bruce Carter (*Gunpowder Tunnel; The Deadly Freeze*)
Elizabeth Churchill (*Juliet in Publishing*)
Pat Strong (*The Plane Wreckers*)

HOUGH, Stanley Bennett [1917–, English science-fiction writer]
Rex Gordon (*Utopia 239; No Man Friday*)
Bennett Stanley (*Sea Struck; The Primitives*)

HOULDING, John Richard [1822–1918, Australian writer for children]
J. R. H. Hawthorn (*Launching Away; The Pioneer of a Family*)
An Old Boomerang (*Australia, Rural and City Life; A Flood that Led onto a Fortune; In the Depths of the Sea; Investing Uncle Ben's Legacy; Australian Capers: or Christopher Cockle's Colonial Experiences*)

HOUSMAN, Alfred Edward [1859–1936, English classical scholar and poet]
D. Erasmus (in the *Classical Review*, 1916)

HOUSTON, Matilda Charlotte [1816–92, English novelist]
One who Saved it (*Only a Woman's Life*)

HOUSTON, William D. M.Chapman [d. 1952, Irish biographer, dramatist and writer]
Desmond Mountjoy (*A Creel of Peat; The Hills of Hell; The Melody of God and other Papers*)

HOVICK, Rose Louise [1914–70, US performing artiste]
Gypsy Rose Lee (*The G-String Murders; Mother Finds a Body*)

HOWARD, Clifford [1868–1942, US novelist]
Simon Arke (*Graphology*)

HOWARD, Geoffrey [1889–1973, English jurist, poet and writer]
Marmaduke Dixey (*Hell's Bells; Words, Beasts and Fishes*)

HOWARD, George [1773–1848, 6th Earl of Carlisle; public servant and writer]
Citizen Muskein (in *The Anti-Jacobin*)

HOWARD, Gorges Edmond [1715–86, British legal writer]
Philo Hibernicus (*A Third Letter on the Present Posture of Affairs*)

HOWARD, Herbert Edmund [fl. 1940, English writer]
R. Philmore (*Journey Downstairs; Procession of Two*)

HOWARD, James Arch [1922–, US writer]
Laine Fisher (*Murder in Mind*)

HOWARD, John Eliot [1807–83, English botanist]
Asyncritus (*The Inward Light*)

HOWARD, Joseph [1833–1908, US journalist]
Diabolus (*Corry o' Lanus – his Views and Experiences*)

HOWARD, Leon Alexander Lee [1914–78, English journalist and novelist]
Alexander Krislov (*No Man Sings*)

HOWARD, Luke [1772–1864, English Quaker and botanist]
Eccletus (*A Few Notes on a Letter to the Archbishops etc.*)
A Friend (*The Yorkshireman – A Literary Journal*)
An University Pen (*Extracts from the Spiritual Bee*)

HOWARD, Peter Dunsmore [1908–65, English journalist and playwright]
*Cato (*Guilty Men*)
Adam Bothwell; Brent Ely; John Hampden; Captain Barnaby Rich (all used for journalism)

HOWARD, Sir Robert [1626–98, English public servant, historian and dramatist]
A Person of Quality (*The History of Religion*; *The Life and Reign of King Richard the Second*)

HOWARTH, Patrick John Fielding [1916–, English nautical and historical writer]
C. D. E. Francis (*Portrait of a Killer*)

HOWE, Elias [1819–67, US inventor of the sewing machine]
Gumbo Chaff (*Accordion Songster*)

HOWE, Mrs Julia Ward [1819–1910, US writer and social reformer; composer of 'Battle Hymn of the Republic']
A Lady (*Passion Flowers*)

HOWE, William Wirt [1833–1909, US lawyer and writer]
Mohammed Pasha (*The Pasha Papers*)

HOWELL, James [1594–1666, English diplomat, royalist, poet and pamphleteer]
An Eminent Author (*Poems on Several Choice and Various Subjects*)
Mercurius Acheronticus (*A Trance or, Newes from Hell Brought Fresh to Towne*)
Philarenus (*Mercurius Hibernicus*)

HOWELL, John [1788–1863, English inventor and biographer]
Bill Truck (*The Man- o'-War's-Man*)

HOWGILL, Francis [1618–69, English cleric and Quaker writer]
Him that Pities Thee in this Languishing State (*One Warning More unto England*)
One of the Lamb's Followers (*Darkness and Ignorance Expelled*)
A Sufferer for Christ (*Oaths No Gospel Ordinance, but Prohibited by Christ*)

HOWITT, John Leslie Despard [1895–, English writer]
Leslie Despard (*The Crime without a Flaw*; *The Mystery of the Tower Room*)
John Leslie (*The Slender Debt*)

HOWITT, William [1792–1879, English traveller, historian and writer]
Dr Cornelius (*The Student Life in Germany*)
John Hampden Jun. (*The Aristocracy of England*; *Colonisation and Christianity*; *The Country Book*; *German Experiences*; *The Mad War-Planet*; *The Man of the People*)

HOWLAND, Frances Louise Morse [1855–?, US writer]
Kenyon West (*Broken Bonds*; *Cliveden*)

HOWLETT, Robert [fl. 1709, English writer]
R. H. (*The Royal Pastime of Cock-Fighting*; *The Angler's Sure-Guide*)

HOYLE, Edmund [1672–1769, English chess and whist expert]
A Gentleman (*A Short Treatise on the Game of Whist*)

HOYLE, Trevor [1940–, English writer]
Larry Milne (*Ghostbusters*; *Hearts of Fire*)

HOYLE, William [1831–86, English temperance writer]
A Cotton Manufacturer (*An Enquiry into the Depression in the Cotton-Trade*)

HUBBARD, Elbert [1856–1915, US writer and publisher]
Fra. Elbertus (*The Man of Sorrows*)

HUBBARD, L. Ron [1911–86, US eccentric science-fiction writer]
Rene Lafayette; Kurt von Rachen (both used in *Astounding Science Fiction* magazine)

HUBBARD, Miss Louisa M. [1836–1906, Russian-born English pioneer of the women's movement]
L. M. H. (*The Englishwoman's Year Book*)

HUBBELL, Mrs Martha Stone [1814–56, US writer]
A Pastor's Wife (*The Shady Side*)

HUDDART, Elinor [1853–1902, Welsh novelist]
Elinore Hume (*Commonplace Sinners*; *My Heart and I*)

HUDDLESTON, John [1636–1700, English Jesuit; used the alias 'John Dormer']
Philopenes (*Usury Explain'd*)

HUDSON, Henry Norman [1814–86, US literary academic]
A Chaplain (*The Campaign with General Butler*)

HUDSON, Stephen [1869–1944, English novelist]
Sidney Schiff (*Concessions*)

HUDSON, William Cadwalader [1843–1915, US journalist and dramatist]
Barclay North (*Jack Gordon: Knight Errant, Gotham*; *The Diamond Button – Whose Was It?*)
Seacoal (used in various newspapers)

HUDSON, William Henry [1841–1922, Argentine-born English naturalist and writer]
Henry Harford (*Fan – The Story of a Young Girl's Life*)

HUEFFER, Ford Hermann [1873–1939, English poet and novelist; more commonly known under the surname Ford]
Daniel Chaucer (*The Simple Life Limited*; *The New Humpty-Dumpty*)
Fenil Haig (*The Questions at the Well*)
Ford Madox Hueffer–'Ford' (*The Critical Attitude*; *The Pre-Raphaelite Brotherhood*)
R. Edison Page (in *Transatlantic Review*)
*Ignatz von Aschendorf (*The Nature of a Crime*)

HUEFFER, Francis [1845–89, German-born English musical critic and writer]
A Musical Critic (in *Fortnightly Review*)

HUGESSEN, Edward H. Knatchbull [1829–93, 1st Baron Brabourne; politician and writer for children]
A Tory (*Protectionist Parodies*)

HUGHES, Cecil E. [fl. 1907, English writer]
*Judson Bolt (*The Prodigal Nephew*)

HUGHES, E. J. (Ted) [1930–, English Poet Laureate]
Daniel Hearing (in *Granta* magazine)

HUGHES, George Edward [1821–72, English lawyer]
Buller Jun. (in *Bentley's Miscellany*)

HUGHES, John [1677–1720, English poet and writer]
Z. (for letters 210 and 316 in *The Spectator*)

HUGHES, John [1790–1857, English artist, traveller and writer]
T. R. Buller of Brazennose (in *Ainsworth's Magazine*)

HUGHES, Joshua [1807–89, Welsh cleric; Bishop of St Asaph]
Sexagenarius (*Prayer and Religious Tests*; *The Subject of Prayer at Meetings of the Bible Society*)
Veritas (*The University of Brecknock*)

HUGHES, Mary Elizabeth [fl. 1935, English writer]
Mary Winter Were (*The Angel in the Garden*)

HUGHES, Russell Meriweather [1898–, US writer]
La Meri (*Spanish Decency*)

HUGHES, Thomas [1822–96, English barrister, social reformer, biographer and writer for boys]
A Layman (*A Layman's Faith*)
An Old Boy (*Tom Brown's Schooldays*)
Vacuus Viator (in *The Spectator*)

HUGHES, Thomas Patrick [1838–1911, English-born US cleric and orientalist]
Evan Stanton (*Ruhaimah*)

HUGHES, Walter Llewellyn [1910–93, English writer for children]
Hugh Walters (*First Family on the Moon*; *School on the Moon*)

HUGHES, William [1803–61, English lawyer, legal writer and writer on angling]
Piscator (*Fish: How to Choose and How to Dress*; *The Fly-Fisher's Entomology*; *The Practical Angler*; *A Practical Treatise on the Choice and Cookery of Fish*)

HUIDEKOPER, H. J. [1776–1854, Dutch-born US writer]
A Unitarian Layman (*Unitarianism the Doctrine of the Bible*)

HUISH, Robert [1777–1850, English natural historian and bee expert]
A Blue (*Fitz-Allan*)

HULL, Thomas [1728–1808, English dramatist, actor, poet and novelist]
A Gentleman (*Genuine Letters from a Gentleman to a Young Lady, his Pupil*)

HULLAH, John Pyke [1812–84, English musician and musicologist]
The Organist to the Fraternity (in *MacMillan's Magazine*)

HULME, Frederick Edward [1841–1909, English botanist, artist and writer]
Kunquer Phair (*Evening Recreations with Pencil and Paper*)

HULME, Thomas Ernest [1883–1917, English poet, critic, philosopher – killed in France in WWI]
Thomas Gratton (in *The Commentator*)
T. K. White (in the *Saturday Westminster Gazette*)

HUME, Abraham [1815–84, Scottish cleric, antiquary and writer]
A Lancashire Incumbent (letters in *The Times*)

HUME, Ferguson Wright [1859–1932, New Zealand-born English crime novelist]
Fergus Hume (*Hagar of the Pawn-Shop*; *The Mystery of a Hansom Cab*)

HUMPHREY, Asa [1781–1841, US poet]
A Schoolmaster in the Eastern Country (*Personal Satire*)

HUMPHREY, John [1621–1719, English cleric and religious writer]
A Follower of Peace and Lover of Sincerity (*The Healing Paper*; *The Nonconformists Relief Prepared*)
A Friend Unknown (*A Paper to William Penn*)
A Grave Author of Middle and Unparty Principles (*Free Thoughts Continued upon Several Points*)
A Lover of Peace and the Public Good (*Letters to Parliament-Men*)
A Minister under the Apprehension of the Stone (*A Private Psalter or Manual of Devotion*)
One that Holds Communion with the Church (*A Seasonable Caution to this New Parliament*)
One that is Concerned for his Friend, a Lover of Truth (*An Account of the French Prophets*)

HUMPHREYS, David [1753–1818, American soldier, diplomat, poet and merchant]
A Gentleman of the Army (*A Poem Addressed to the Armies of the United States*)

HUMPHREYS, Edward Rupert { 1820–93, English schoolteacher and writer]
A British Commoner (*Letters by a British Commoner*; *The Warnings of the War*)
The Headmaster of an English Grammar School (*England's Educational Crisis*)

HUMPHREYS, Eliza Margaret [1860–1938, Scottish romantic novelist]
E. Jayne Gilbert (*Episodes*)
Rita (*Souls*; *Diana of the Ephesians*)

HUMPHREYS, Henry Noel [1810–79, English naturalist, numismatist and artist]
An Archaeologist (*Stories*)

HUMPHRIES, Adelaide [1898–, US novelist]
Kathleen Harris (*Change of Heart*)

HUMPHRY, Hugh M'Nab [1855–?, English barrister]
Hugh M'Nab (*Athualpa, the Last of the Incas*; *The Viking and other Poems*)

HUNGERFORD, Mrs Margaret Wolfe [1855–97, Irish novelist]
The Duchess (*Phyllis*; *Molly Bawn*)
Pearl (in *Temple Bar*)

HUNT, Dorothy A. [fl. 1926, English novelist]
Doric Collyer (*Ann of the House of Barlow*)

HUNT, E. Howard [1923–, US crime and mystery writer]
Gordon Davis (*I Came to Kill*; *House Dick*)
Robert Dietrich (*One for the Road*; *The Cheat*)
David St John (*On Hazardous Duty*; *The Towers of Silence*)

HUNT, Frederick Knight { 1814–54, English journalist and editor]
Student-at-Law (*Twilight – a Poem*)

HUNT, Freeman [1804–58, US publisher and writer]
An American (*American Anecdotes*)
A Citizen of New York (*Letters About the Hudson River*)

HUNT, James Henry Leigh [1784–1859, English poet, essayist, editor and poet]
Robin Good-Fellow; Harry Honeycomb; Misocrotalus; Perennis (all used in *New Monthly Magazine*)
A Lover of Books (in *Tait's Edinburgh Magazine*)
Mr Town, Junior Critic and Censor-General (in *The Traveller*)

HUNT, Katherine Chandler [fl. 1960, English writer]
Chandler Nash (*Murder is my Shadow*)

HUNT, Mrs Margaret [1831–1912, English novelist]
Averil Beaumont (*Magdalen Wynyard*)

HUNTER, Alexander [1729–1809, Scottish physician and writer]
Ignotus (*Culina Famulatrix Medicinae*; *Georgical Essays*; *Receipts on Modern Cookery*)
A Physician (*A Treatise on Virtues of the Buxton Waters*)

HUNTER, Alfred John [1891–, English writer for boys]
John Addiscombe (*Drums of Death*)
L. H. Brenning (*Boulevard*; *Devil's Laughter*)
Francis Brent (in *Detective Weekly*)
Anthony Dax (*The Man Behind*)
Anthony Drummond (*Blood Money*; *The Scented Death*)
John Hunter (*Dead Man's Gate*; *Three Dice at Midnight*)
Peter Meriton (*Captain Dack*; *Plunder*)

HUNTER, Bluebell Matilda [fl. 1933, English writer]
John Guildford (*Big Ben Looks On*; *Death Dams the Tide*)
Boris M. Hunter (used for magazine writing)

HUNTER, Elizabeth [1934–, English romantic novelist]
Isobel Chace (*Rhythm of Flamenco*; *The Song and the Sea*)

HUNTER, John [1807–85, Scottish mason, teacher and poet]
The Mountain Muse (in the *Dundee Cornucopia* and other newspapers)

HUNTER, Joseph [1783–1861, English Presbyterian cleric and antiquarian]
An English Traveller (*Notes of an English Traveller during Two Days' Sojourn at Ober-Wesel*)

HUNTINGTON, Daniel [1774–1864, US cleric]
Octogenary (*Memories, Counsels and Reflections*)

HUNTINGTON, David [1745–1812, US cleric]
The Apologist (*Infant Baptism Vindicated*)

HUNTINGTON, George [1825–1905, English cleric and religious writer]
A Clerical Friend (*The Autobiography of John Brown, the Cord-Wainer*)

HUNTINGTON, Jedediah Vincent [1815–62, US journalist, novelist and poet]
John Vincent (*The Pretty Plate*)

HUNTINGTON, Joseph [1735–95, US cleric]
A Gentleman of Connecticut (*A Plea Before the Council at Stockbridge*)

HUNTLEY, Stanley [1845–85, US journalist]
Spoopendyke (*Mr and Mrs Spoopendyke*)

HURD, Richard [1720–1808, English cleric and writer; Bishop of Worcester]
A Fellow of a College (*The Opinion of an Eminent Lawyer etc.*)
A Warburtonian (*Tracts by Warburton and a Warburtonian*)

HURREN, Bernard John [1907–, English writer]
Guy Garston (*The Champagne Mystery*)

HUSKINSON, Richard King [1879–1947, English novelist]
Richard King (*At the Close of the Day*; *Soul's Dark Cottage*)

HUSSEY, Robert [1801–56, English ecclesiastical historian and classical scholar]
Presbyterus (*A Help to Young Clergyman*)

HUSTLER, John [1715–90, English wool merchant, Quaker and philanthropist]
A Manufacturer (*The Occasion of the Dearness of Provisions and the Distress of the Poor*)

HUTCHESON, Archibald [d. 1740, English politician]
A Member of Parliament (*Abstracts of the Yearly Pay of Dragoons*)
A Member of the House of Commons (*An Estimate of the Value of South-Sea Stock*; *Some Considerations Relating to Publick Debts*; *Some Considerations for Proprietors of South-Sea Stock*; *Some Calculations Relating to the South-Sea Company*)

HUTCHIN, Kenneth Charles [1908–, English journalist and physician]
Kenneth Challice (*Family Health and First Aid*)

HUTCHINS, Francis Gilman [1939–, US historian]
Frank Madison (*A View from the Floor: Journal of a US Senate Page Boy*)

HUTCHINSON, John [1674–1737, English theologian and inventor]
J. H. (*Mose's Principia*)

HUTCHINSON, Robert Hare [1887–?, US crime novelist]
Robert Hare (*The Hand of the Chimpanzee*; *The Doctor's First Murder*; *Spectral Evidence*)

HUTCHINSON, William [1732–1814, English solicitor and historian]
A Freeholder North of Trent (*Letters Addressed to the Minister*)

HUTCHISON, Graham Seton [1890–1946, Scottish soldier and military writer]
Graham Seton (*The Governor of Kattowitz*; *Life Without End*; *Blood Money*)

HUTH, Alfred Henry [1850–1910, English traveller and bibliophile]
Mathew Dudgeon (*Adventures of Mathew Dudgeon*)

HUTTON, Arthur Wollaston [1848–1912, English cleric and religious writer]
An Oxford Graduate (*My Experience of Compulsory Vaccination*)

HUTTON, Edward [1875–1969, English historian, travel writer and Italophile]
Luis Carreno (in *Stories of the Spanish Artists*)

HUTTON, Henry Dix [1825–1907, Irish academic]
An Irish Positivist (*A Letter on the Irish Crisis*)

HUTTON, Richard Holt [1826–97, English journalist and writer]
A Wife with her Husband (*Holiday Rambles in Ordinary Places*)

HUXLEY, Julian Sorell [1887–1975, English zoologist, humanist and essayist]
Balbus (in *The Spectator* and the *Fortnightly Review* and for *Reconstruction and Peace*)

HUXTABLE, Marjorie [1897–, English novelist]
Simon Dare (*Goblin Green*; *The Locusts have Passed*)
Marjorie Stewart (*Riding School*; *Queue*)

HYDE, Douglas [1860–1949, Irish Gaelic scholar and writer]
An Crao bhin Aoibhinn (*A Literary History of Ireland*)

HYDE, Edward [1609–74, 1st Earl of Clarendon; historian and statesman]
A Person of Honour (*Animadversions upon a Book etc.*)

HYNE, Charles John Cutcliffe [1865–1944, English traveller and novelist]
Weatherby Chesney (*The Claimant*; *Four Red Night-Caps*)

HYSLOP, James [1798–1827, Scottish shepherd, teacher and poet]
The Muirkirk Shepherd (in the *Greenock Advertiser*)

I

IDE, Mrs Fanny Otis [1853–1927, US writer for children]
Ruth Ogden (*A Little Queen of Hearts*; *Loyal Hearts and True*)

IDELL, Albert Edward [1901–58, US novelist]
Phillip Rogers (*Stag Night*)

ILIVE, Jacob [1705–63, English printer and religious writer]
A Searcher after Religious Truth (*Remarks on Discourses by the Bishop of London*)

INGELOW, Jean [1820–97, English poet, novelist and writer for children]
Don John (*Off the Skelligs*)
Orris (*Tales of Orris*; *A Rhyming Chronicle of Incidents and Feelings*)

INGERSOLL, Charles Jared [1782–1862, US lawyer, politician and writer]
Inchiquin (*Inchiquin's Letters*)

INGERSOLL, Joseph Reed [1786–1868, US lawyer and politician }
A Northern Man (*The Diplomatic Year*)

INGLEBY, Clement Mansfield [1823–86, English Shakespeare scholar }
Jabez (in *Notes and Queries*)

INGLIS, Charles [1734–1816, British cleric and evangelist among the Mohawk Indians; Bishop of Nova Scotia]
An American (*The True Interest of America Impartially Stated*)
Papinian (*Letters of Papinian*)
A Son of Truth and Decency (*A Vindication of the Bishop of Landaff's Sermon*)

INGLIS, Henry David [1795–1835, British traveller and writer]
Derwent Conway (*A Personal Narrative of a Journey through Norway*; *Solitary Walks through Many Lands*; *Tales of the Ardennes*)

INGLIS, James [1845–1908, Scottish-born colonial politician and writer; settled in Australia]
Maori (used for contributions to various Australian newspapers and for *Sport and Work on the Nepaul Frontier*)

INGLIS, John [1763–1834, Scottish cleric]
One of the Ministers in Edinburgh (*An Examination of Mr Dugald Stewart's Pamphlet*)

INGRAHAM, Joseph Holt [1809–61, US mariner, cleric and novelist]
Adina (*The Prince of the House of David*)
Kate Conynghame (*The Sunny South*)
A Yankee (*The South-West*)

INGRAM, John H. [1849–1916, English biographer, critic and linguist]
Don Felix de Salamanca (*The Philosophy of Handwriting*)

INGRAM, Robert [1727–1804, English cleric and theological writer]
A Country Clergyman (*An Explanation of the Prophecy of the Seven Vials*)

INGRAMS, Richard Reid [1937–, English journalist]
*Sylvie Krin (*Born to be Queen*; *Love in the Saddle*)
*Old Jowett (*The Bible for Motorists*)
Philip Reid (*Harris in Wonderland*)

*E. J. Thribb (*So Farewell Then and other Poems*)

INNES, Alexander Taylor [1833–1912, Scottish lawyer and writer]
Hugh Duthus (in *Contemporary Review*)
A Layman (*Letters from the Red Beech*)

INNES, Brian [fl. 1975, English publisher and writer]
Neil Powell (*At The Edge*; *Carpenters of Light*)

INNES, Ralph Hammond [1913–, British novelist and historical writer]
Ralph Hammond (*Isle of Strangers*; *Saracen's Tower*)

IRELAND, John [1761–1842, English cleric, academic and pamphleteer]
Fabius (*Letters of Fabius to William Pitt*)

IRELAND, Joseph Norton [1817–98, US writer]
A Play-Goer (*Fifty Years of Annals of the New York Stage*)

IRELAND, William Henry [1777–1835, English poet and writer; forger of Shakespearian manuscripts]
Anser-Pen-Drag-On Esq. (*Scribbleomania*)
Henry Boyle (*The Universal Chronologist*)
Cervantes (*The Death of Bonaparte*)
Charles Clifford (*The Angler – a Didactic Poem*)
Baron Karlo Excellmanns (*The Eventful Life of Napoleon Bonaparte*)
Flagellum (*All the Blocks! or, an Antidote to 'All The Talents'*)
H. C. (*The Cottage Girl*; *The Fisher Boy*; *The Sailor Boy*)
Paul Persius (*Ballads in Imitation of the Antient*)
Satiricus Sculptor (*Chalcographimania*)
W. H. I. (*Bruno or the Sepulchral Summons*)

IRELAND, William Wotherspoon [1832–1909, Scottish physician in East India Company service and medical writer]
An Officer who Served There (*History of the Siege of Delhi*)

IRONS, William Josiah [1812–83, English cleric and religious writer]
A Bachelor of Divinity (*An Answer to Dr Wiseman's Letter*)
Oxoniensis (*Strictures on the Rev. Mr Bulteel's Sermon*)

IRVINE, Andrew Alexander [1871–1939, Scottish soldier in India, dramatist and short-story writer]
The Subaltern (*Damfool Smith Sahib*; *Lays of a Subaltern*)

IRVING, Clifford [1930–, US writer]
Herbert Burkholz (*Death Freak*)

IRVING, Mrs Dorothea [d. 1933, English actress and welfare worker – wife of Sir Henry Irving]
Dorothea Baird (*The Love Affairs of Amaryllus*)

IRVING, John Treat [1812–1906, US lawyer]
John Quod (in the *Knickerbocker Magazine* and for *The Attorney*)

IRVING, Washington [1783–1859, US humorist, novelist and historical writer]
Friar Antonio Agapido (*A Chronicle of the Conquest of Granada*)
An American Gentleman (*A Voyage to the Eastern Part of Terra Firma*)
Geoffrey Crayon Gent. (*The Sketch Book*; *Bracebridge Hall*; *Tales of a Traveller*)
Diedrich Knickerbocker (*A History of New York*)
*Launcelot Langstaff Esq. (*Salmagundi or, The Whim-Whams etc.*)
Jonathan Oldstyle, Gent. (in the *New York Morning Chronicle* for *Letters on the Drama*)
A Sentimental Philosopher (*Fragments of a Journal of a Sentimental Philosopher*)

IRVING, William [1766–1821, US merchant and humorist – brother of Washington Irving above]
A Gentleman of New York (*The Poetical Works of Thomas Campbell*)
*Launcelot Langstaff Esq. (*Salmagundi or, The Whim-Whams etc.*)

IRWIN, Constance [1913–, US writer]
C. H. Frick (*Five Against the Odds*; *The Comeback Guy*)

IRWIN, Eyles [1751–1817, British writer and Eastern traveller]
A Gentleman in India (*St Thomas's Mount*)

IRWIN, Thomas Caulfield [1823–92, Irish poet and writer]
Doctor Pentagram; A Student of Pascal; Herr Vanderhausen (all used in *Dublin University Magazine*)

IRWIN, Wallace Admah [1876–1959, US writer]
Omar Khayam, Junr. (*Extra !! Fairy Tales of up to Now*)

Hashimura Togo (*Letters of a Japanese Schoolboy*)

IVENS, Michael William [1924–, English poet and writer]
Yorick (used for journalism)

IVES, Jeremiah [fl. 1672, English Baptist and religious controversialist]
A Lover of Truth and Peace (*Vindiciae Veritatis*)

IWAMATSU, Jun Atsushi [1908–, Japanese-born US writer and illustrator for children]
Taro Yashimo (*The Village-Tree*; *The Youngest One*)

J

JACK, Henry Vernon [1869–1922, English playwright]
Henry Vernon Esmond (*Eliza Comes to Stay*; *When We Were Twenty-One*)

JACKSON, Blomfield [1839–1905, English cleric and religious writer]
Nathaniel Hurd (*Kaeso*)

JACKSON, Edward Arthur Mather [1899–1956, English soldier and businessman]
Edward Mather (*Nathaniel Hawthorne*)

JACKSON, Frederick [1886–1953, US writer]
Victor Thorne (*The Man Who Married for Money*; *The Bishop Misbehaves*)

JACKSON, Hall [1739–97, US physician]
A Gentleman of the Faculty (*Observations on the Putrid, Malignant Sore Throat*)

JACKSON, Helen Maria Hunt [1831–85, US poet and novelist]
Saxe Holm (in *Scribner's Monthly*)

JACKSON, Holbrook [1874–1948, English editor, biographer and writer]
George Henry Hart (*Great Soldiers*)
Bernard Lintot (*End Papers*)

JACKSON, John [1686–1763, English cleric and religious writer]
A Clergyman (*Memoirs of Dr Waterland*)
A Clergyman in the Country (*Christian Liberty Asserted*; *A Collection of Queries*; *A Reply to Dr Waterland's Defense of his Queries*)
Philalethes Cantabrigiensis (*Further Remarks on Dr Waterland's Vindication etc.*),
(*Remarks on Dr Waterland's Second Defense etc.*)
Philocriticus Cantabrigiensis (*A Treatise on the Improvements in the Art of Criticism*)
A Presbyter of the Church of England (*An Answer to a Book entitled 'Things Divine etc.'*)

JACKSON, John Baptist [1701–80, English engraver]
Scissors and Paste (*A Humorous Melange*)

JACKSON, Lowis d'Aquilar [1840–?, English engineer and card game expert]
Aquarius (in *National Review*)

JACKSON, Lydia [1900–83, English writer]
Elisaveta Fen (*Spring Floods*)

JACKSON, Randle [1757–1837, English barrister]
A Friend to 'Fair Play' (*Letter to Robert Peel*)

JACKSON, Thomas [1783–1873, English religious biographer and writer]
A Wesleyan Preacher (*The Life, Labours and Travels of Rev. Robert Newton*)

JACKSON, Thomas [1812–86, English cleric and writer]
Habbakukius Dunderheadius (*Uniomachia*)
Pieter Maritzburg (*The Narrative of the Fire of London*)

JACKSON, William [1737–95, Irish preacher and revolutionary]
Curtius (letters in the *Public Ledger*)

JACKSON, William [1730–1803, English musician and composer]
Humphrey Nettle (*Sodom and Onan*)

JACOB, Mrs Arthur [d. 1946, Scottish poet and writer]
*Violet Jacob (*The Northern Lights*)

JACOB, John [1812–58, British soldier in India and military writer]
A Bengal Officer (*A Few Remarks on the Bengal Army*)
A Bombay Officer (*Remarks by a Bombay Officer*)

JACOB, Naomi Ellington [1884–1964, English actress and novelist]
Ellington Gray (*Saffroned Bridesails*)

JACOB, Piers Anthony Dillingham [1934–, English-born US fantasy writer]
Piers Anthony (*Castle Roogna; Vicinity Cluster*)

JACOB, Thomas Greeer [1797–1837, Irish Quaker]
A Member of the Society of Friends (*Brief Remarks on the Christian Sabbath*)

JACOBS, Caroline Emilia [1872–1909, US writer for children]
Emilia Elliott (*Joan's Jolly Vacation; A Texas Blue Bonnet*)

JACOBS, Mrs Harriet [1818–96, US negro slave and writer]
Linda Brent (*Incidents in the Life of a Slave Girl*)

JACOBS, Helen Hull [1908–, US tennis champion and writer]
H. Braxton Hull (*Barry Cort*)

JACOBSSON, Per [1894–1963, Swedish economist; Chairman of the International Monetary Fund]
*Peter Oldfield (*The Death of a Diplomat; The Alchemy Murder Case*)

JACOX, Francis [1825–97, English cleric and essayist]
A Clerical Recluse (*Cues from all Quarters*)
Nicias Foxear (*Shakespeare Diversions*)
Monkshood (in *Bentley's Miscellany*)
Sir Nathaniel (in both *New Monthly Magazine* and *Bentley's Miscellany*)
A Recluse (*Recollections of a Recluse*)

JAKES, John William [1932–, US novelist]
William Ard (*And So to Bed; Give Me This Woman*)
Alan (or Rachel Ann) Payne (*Ghostwind; This'll Slay You*)
Jay Scotland (*Veils of Salome; Arena*)

JAMES, Edward [1907–84, English eccentric patron of the arts]
Edward (*Twenty Sonnets to Mary*)

JAMES, Elizabeth [1945–, US writer]
*Elizabeth Carroll (*Summer Love*)
Katherine Duval (*Ziegfeld: the Man and his Women*)
*Beverly Hastings (*Don't Talk to Strangers; Watcher in the Dark*)
James Lloyd (*Loose Change; Born Losers*)

JAMES, Florence Alice [1857–1929, English novelist]
Florence Warden (*The House on the Marsh; The Mystery of Dudley Horne*)

JAMES, George Payne Rainsford [1799–1860, English historian and historical novelist]
F. De Lunatico, K. F. M. (*The Commissioner*)

JAMES, Godfrey Warden [1888–?, English crime writer]
Adam Broome (*The Crocodile Club; The Oxford Murders*)

JAMES, Henry [1843–1916, US novelist, critic and writer]
A Casual Critic (in *Pall Mall Gazette*)
An Occasional Correspondent; X. X. (both used in *The Nation*)

JAMES, John Stanley [1843–96, English-born Australian journalist]
A Vagabond (in *The Argus* and for *The Vagabond Papers*)

JAMES, Lionel [1871–1955, English soldier, journalist and military writer]
Chasseur (*A Study of the Russo-Japanese War*)
Ex-Intelligence Officer (*The German Spy System from Within*)

An Intelligence Officer (*The Boy Galloper*; *A Subaltern of Horse*; *On the Heels of de Wet*)

JAMES, Vivian Leopold [1937–, Australian writer and broadcaster]
Clive James (*Crystal Bucket*; *Unreliable Memoirs*)

JAMES, William [d. 1827, English lawyer and naval historian]
Boxer (letters in the *Naval Chronicle*)

JAMES, Winifred [d. 1941, Australian-born English journalist, novelist and travel writer]
Edward of the Golden Heart (*A Sweeping*)

JAMESON, Mrs Anna Brownell [1794–1860, Irish art critic and writer]
Ennuyee (*Diary of an Ennuyee*)
A Lady (*A Lady's Diary*)

JAMESON, Mrs Annie Edith [1868–1931, English novelist]
J. E. Buckrose (*Silhouette of Mary Ann*; *Out All Night*)

JAMESON, Margaret Storm [1891–1986, English journalist, critic and novelist]
James Hill (*Loving Memory*; *No Victory for the Soldier*)
William Lamb (*The World Ends*)

JAMIESON, John [1759–1838, Scottish antiquary and Gaelic scholar]
A Friend to Truth (*Socinianism Unmasked*)
Dr Jehan of the Hall Ryal (*A New Bannatyne Garland*)

JANNER, Greville Ewan [1928–, Welsh barrister, politician and legal writer]
Ewan Mitchell (*Business and Professional Man's Lawyer*; *Transport Manager's Lawyer*)

JANVIER, Margaret Thomson [1844–1913, US writer]
Margaret Vandegrift (*Doris and Theodora*; *The Dead Doll and Other Verses*)

JAPP, Alexander Hay [1837–1905, Scottish publisher, editor and writer]
The late J. H. Alexander, BA (*Lights on the Way – Some Tales within a Tale*)
E. Conder Gray (*Idle Musings: Essays on Social Mosaic*; *Wise Words and Loving Deeds*)
Benjamin Orme (*The Treasure Book of Consolation*)
H. A. Page (in *Contemporary Review* and for *De Quincy Memorials*)
A. N. Mount Rose (*Facts and Fancies from the Koran*; *Her Part: a Novel of Real Life*)

JARDINE, Alexander [d. 1799, English soldier and traveller]
An English Officer (*Letters from Barbary, France, Spain etc.*; *Letters from Morrocco*)

JARDINE, Jack Owen [1931–, US science-fiction writer]
*Howard L. Cory (*The Mind of Monsters*; *The Sword of Lankor*)
Larry Maddock (*The Flying Saucer Gambit*; *The Time Trap Gambit*)

JARDINE, John [1844–1919, English jurist in India]
The Judicial Commissioner (*Notes on Buddhist Law*)

JARDINE, Julie Anne [1926–, US science-fiction writer]
*Howard L. Cory (*The Mind of Monsters*; *The Sword of Lankor*)

JARRETT, Cora Hardy [1877–?, US writer]
Faraday Keene (*Pattern in Black and Red*)

JARRETT, Henry Sullivan [1839–1919, English soldier and writer]
Stratheir (*The Book of Songs – Translated from Heine*)

JARRETT-KERR, Martin [1912–91, English cleric and scholar]
Father William Tiverton (*D. H. Lawrence and Human Existence*)

JARROLD, Ernest [1850–?, English-born US journalist]
Mickey Finn (*The Boy Squatter*)

JARVES, James Jackson [1818–88, US historian and writer on art]
An American Amateur in Europe (*Art Thoughts*)
An Inquirer (*The Confessions of an Inquirer*)

JARVIS, Claude Scudamore [1879–1953, English soldier and colonial officer]
Rameses (*Oriental Spotlight*)

JAY, Geraldine Mary [1919–, Australian mystery writer]
Geraldine Halls (*Last Summer of the Men Shortage*; *Felling of Thawle*)
Charlotte Jay (*The Knife is Feminine*; *The Yellow Turban*)

JAY, Harriet [1853–1932, Scottish actress, playwright and novelist]
Charles Marlowe (*Tulip Time*)

JAY, John [1745–1829, American statesman and jurist]
A Citizen of New York (*An Address to the People of the State of New York*)
*Publius (in *The Federalist*)

JAY, John [1817–94, US abolitionist, politician and diplomat – son of William Jay below]
A Churchman (*Caste and Slavery in the American Church*; *The Progress of Puseyism*)

JAY, William [1789–1858, US abolitionist – son of John Jay (1745–1829) above]
A Churchman of the Diocese of New York (*A Letter to Bishop Hobart*)
A Protestant Episcopalian (*A Letter to Rev. Levi Silliman Ives*)

JAYNE, Francis John [1845–1921, English cleric and academic; Bishop of Chester]
An Oxford Tutor (*The Universities and the Scientific Corps*)

JEBB, Ann [1735–1812, English writer]
W. Bull (*Two Penny-Worth of Truth for a Penny*)
Priscilla (letters in the *London Chronicle*)

JEBB, Frederick [fl. 1779, English writer]
Guatimozin (*Guatimozin's Letters on the State ... Ireland*)

JEBB, John [1736–86, English cleric and religious writer]
An Englishman (*A Letter to Sir William Meredith*)
Paulinus (letter in the *Whitehall Evening Post*)

JEFFERSON, Horace [1879–?, English writer]
Harold Philip Clunn (*The Face of London*; *The Face of Paris*)

JEFFERSON, Thomas [1743–1826, 3rd President of the USA]
Oliver Fairplay (*Proposals for Publishing a Life of the First Consul*)
A Native and Member of the House of Burgesses (*A Summary View of the Rights of British America*)

JEFFRIES, Graham Montague [1900–82, English crime and mystery writer]
Peter Bourne (*When the Bells Ring*; *Soldiers of Fortune*)
Bruce (or David) Graeme (*Ten Trails to Tyburn*; *Impeached*; *The Imperfect Crime*; *Blackshirt*)

JEFFRIES, Roderic [1926–, English crime and mystery writer]
Peter Alding (*Despite the Evidence*; *The Murder Line*)
Jeffrey Ashford (*Counsel for the Defense*; *The Burden of Proof*)
Hastings Draper (*Wiggery Pokery*; *Brief Help*)
Roderic Graeme (*Salute to Blackshirt*; *Call for Blackshirt*)
Graham Hastings (*Deadly Game*; *Twice Checked*)

JELF, William Edward [1811–75, English cleric and writer]
A High Churchman of the Old School (*Quosque? How Far? How Long?*)

JENKINS, John Edward [1838–1910, English lawyer, novelist and political satirist]
A Guest (*Ben Changes the Motto*; *The Blot on the Queen's Head*)

JENKINS, Robert Charles [1816–96, English cleric and writer]
A Country Clergyman (*The New Ducal Theology*)
Eranistes (*Semper Eadem*)
A Septuagenarian Student (*Stray Thoughts on the New School of Biblical Criticism*)

JENKINS, William Fitzgerald [1896–1975, US science-fiction writer]
Will. F. Jenkins (*The Murder of the USA*)
Murray Leinster (*Murder in the Family*; *Wings of Chance*)

JENKS, Benjamin [1646–1724, English cleric and writer]
A Minister of the Church of England (*The Liberty of Prayer Guarded from Licentiousness*)

JENKS, George Charles [1850–1929, English-born US journalist and novelist]
W. B. Lawson (in *Diamond Dick Jr. the Boy's Best Weekly* and for *Diamond Dick Decoy Duck* and *Out with the Apache Kid*)

JENKS, William [1778–1866, US cleric]
The late Rev. Williamson Jahnsenykes (*Memoir of the Northern Kingdom*)

JENNER, Charles [1736–74, English poet and writer]
Altamount (*Letters from Altamount in the Capital*)

JENNER, David [d. 1691, English cleric and royalist]
One of His Majesty's Chaplains (*Beaufrons: or a New Discovery of Treason*)

JENNINGS, Hargrave [1817–90, English novelist and occult writer]
An Indian Missionary (*The Indian Religions*)

JENNINGS, Henry Constantine [1731–1819, English collector of fine arts]
An Unfeigned Admirer of Genuine British Jurisprudence (*A Free Enquiry into the Increase of Attornies etc.*)

JENNINGS, Louis John [1836–93, English journalist, politician and writer]
H. Dropper (*Eighty Years of Republican Government*)

JEPHSON, Robert [1736–1803, Irish poet and dramatist]
James Baptiste Couteau (*The Confessions of James Baptiste Couteau, Citizen of France*)
George Faulkner (*An Heroic Epistle to George Edmund Howard*)

JERDAN, William [1782–1869, Scottish journalist, editor and writer]
W. J. Andre (*Eclogue*)
Bushey Heath (in *Notes and Queries*)
A Late Visitant (*Six Weeks in Paris*)
Teutha (in *Bentley's Miscellany*)

JERNINGHAM, Charles Edward Wynne [1854–1921, English writer and composer]
Marmaduke (in both *Truth* and *The Graphic*)

JERNINGHAM, Edward [1727–1812, English poet and dramatist]
The Bard (*The British Album*)
The Old Bard (*The Old Bard's Farewell*)

JERNINGHAM, Hubert Edward Henry [1842–1914, English diplomat and writer]
Atom (in *Temple Bar*)
Diplomaticus (in *Blackwood's Magazine*)

JERRAM, Charles [1770–1853, English cleric and theologian]
Scrutator (*Letters to an Universalist*)

JERROLD, Douglas [1893–1964, English civil servant, publisher and writer]
Barabbas Whitefeather (*The Hand-Book of Swindling*)

JERROLD, Douglas William [1803–57, English dramatist, humorist and novelist]
Henry Brownrigg (*Black-Eyed Susan*; *The Rent-Day*)
Mrs Caudle; Jenkins; Q. (all used in *Punch*)
Paul Prendergast (*Heads of the People*)

JERROLD, Walter [1865–1929, English journalist, biographer and writer for children]
Walter Copeland (*The Farm Book for Little Ones*)

JERROLD, William Blanchard [1826–84, English novelist, biographer and epicure]
Fin Bec (*The Book of Menus*; *Cupboard Papers*; *The Dinner Bell*; *The Epicure's Year-Book*)

JERVIS, John B. [1796–1885, US civil engineer]
Hampden (*Letters Addressed to the Friends of the Union*)

JERVIS, Marguerite Florence [1894–1964, Welsh journalist and romantic novelist]
Marguerite Barclay (*Letters from Fleet Street*; *Yesterday is Tomorrow*)
Countess Barcynska (*We Women*; *Decameron Cocktails*)
Oliver Sandys (*The Woman in the Firelight*; *The Pleasure Garden*)

JESSE, F. Tennyson [1888–1958, English journalist and writer]
Beamish Tinker (*The Man who Stayed at Home*)

JESSUP, Richard [1925–82, US mystery writer]
Richard Telfair (*The Corpse that Talked*; *Good Luck, Sucker*)

JEWELL, Joseph [1763–1846, English Quaker]
A Layman (*An Address to Christians*)

JEWETT, Isaac Appleton [1808–53, US lawyer and traveller]
An American Traveller (in *Bentley's Miscellany*)

JEWETT, John Howard [1843–1925, US writer for children]
Hannah Warner (*More Bunny Stories for Young People*)

JEWETT, Sarah Orne [1849–1909, US poet and writer]
Alice (or A. C.) Eliot (in *Riverside Magazine*)
Sarah O. Sweet (used for juvenile stories)

JEWETT, Sophie [1861–1909, US poet]
Ellen Burroughs (*The Pilgrim and Other Poems*)

JOBSON, Hamilton [1914–81, English crime writer]
William Strathern (*Don't Look for Me – I'm Dead*)

JOHNES, Arthur James [1809–71, Welsh barrister and writer]
Cambrensis (*Four Letters to Connop Thirlwall*)
Maelog (*Translations from Davyth ap Gwilym*)

JOHNES, Thomas [1748–1816, Welsh politician and historical writer]
A Cardiganshire Landlord (*A Cardiganshire Landlord's Advice to his Tenants*)

JOHNS, Charles Alexander [1811–74, Irish educationalist and naturalist]
A Schoolmaster of Twenty Years' Standing (*The Governess*)

JOHNS, William [1771–1845, English Unitarian cleric and theologian]
William Hison (*Four Dialogues between Mr Smith etc.*)

JOHNS, William Earl [1893–1968, English writer for boys – notably the 'Biggles' stories]
An Amateur Gardener (*The Passing Show: a Garden Diary*)
William Earle (*Mossyface*)
John Early (*Blue Blood Runs Red*)
Pilot (in *Boy's Own Paper* from 1941)

JOHNSON, Miss Anna [1860–?, US novelist]
Hope Daring (*The Woods in the Home*; *A Virginian Holiday*)

JOHNSON, Mrs Anna Cummings [1818–92, US writer]
Minnie Myrtle (*The Myrtle Wreath*; *The Iroquois*)

JOHNSON (or Johnstone), Charles [1719–1800, English dramatist and writer]
An Adept (*Adventures of Anthony Varnish*; *Chrysal: or The Adventures of a Guinea*)
Oneiropolos (*The Cobbler of Preston*)

JOHNSON, Donald MacIntosh [1903–78, English physician and barrister]
Odysseus (*Safer than a Known Way*)

JOHNSON, Mrs Emeline H. [1826–50, US poet]
Lillie Layton (in the *American Courier*)

JOHNSON, George Metcalf [1885–?, US writer]
George Metcalf (*The Texas Range Rider*; *The Saddle Bum*)

JOHNSON, James [1777–1845, English physician and medical writer]
Frederick Fag (*The Recess or, Autumnal Relaxation*)
An Officer of the 'Caroline' (*Account of a Voyage to India, China etc.*)

JOHNSON, Marguerite Annie [1928–, US poet and writer]
Maya Angelou (*I Know Why the Caged Birds Sing*; *Now Sheba Sings the Song*)

JOHNSON, Marion [1912–, English writer on Italy]
Georgina Masson (*Italian Villas and Palaces*; *Rome*)

JOHNSON, Pamela Hansford [1912–81, English novelist and critic]
*Nap Lombard (*The Grinning Pug*; *Tidy Death*; *Murder's a Swine*)

JOHNSON, Reverdy [1796–1876, US jurist and politician]
Lawrence Langston (*Bastiles of the North*)
A Marylander (*The Dangerous Condition of the Country*)
A Southern Citizen (*Remarks on Popular Sovereignty*)

JOHNSON, Richard [1733–93, English writer]
Master Michael Angelo (*Juvenile Sports and Pastimes*; *The Drawing School for Little Masters and Misses*)
Rev. Mr Cooper (*Poetical Blossoms*)
Lilliputius Gulliver (*The Lilliputian Library*)
Master Tommy Littleton (*Juvenile Trials for Robbing Orchards*)
Miss Nancy Meanwell (*The History of a Doll*)

JOHNSON, Samuel [1696–1772, US academic and missionary]
Aristocles (*Ethices Elementa*)
A Gentleman Educated at Yale College (*An Introduction to the Study of Philosophy*)
One who is Extremely Desirous to Promote Good Literature in America (*The First Easy Rudiments of Grammar*)

JOHNSON, Samuel [1709–84, English lexicographer and man of letters]
Britannicus (in *Gentleman's Magazine*)
An Impartial Hand (*A Compleat Vindication of the Licensers of the Stage*)
Probus Britanicus (*Marmor Norfolciense*)
S. J____n (in *The Student: or the Oxford and Cambridge Monthly MIscellany*)
T (in *The Adventurer* – 29 contributions in all)
Zachariah Williams (*An Account of an Attempt to Ascertain the Longtitude at Sea ...*)

JOHNSON, Thomas Burgeland [d. 1840, English sporting writer]
T. H. Needham (*The Complete Sportsman*)
B. Thomas (*The Shooter's Guide*)

JOHNSON, Virginia Wales [1849–1916, US novelist and writer for children]
Cousin Virginia (*Calderwood Secret*)

JOHNSON, Zachariah [1810–92, Irish physician and poet]
Anglo-Hibernian (in *Dublin University Magazine*)

JOHNSTON, George Henry [1912–70, US writer]
Shane Martin (*The Man Made of Tin*; *Twelve Girls in the Garden*)

JOHNSTON, Grace Leslie Keith [d. 1929, English novelist]
Leslie Keith (*Near of Kin*; *A Pleasant Rogue*)

JOHNSTON, Hugh Anthony Stephen [1913–67, English colonial civil servant and writer]
A Fighter Pilot (*Tattered Battlements*)
Hugh Sturton (*Zomo the Rabbit*)

JOHNSTON, James Wesley { 1850–?, US cleric and writer]
Annan Dale (*Dwellers in Gotham*)

JOHNSTON, Richard Malcolm [1822–98, US educationalist and humorist]
An Old Man (*Georgia Sketches*)
Philemon Perch (*Georgia Sketches*)

JOHNSTON, Ronald [1926–, Scottish writer]
Mark Nelson (*The Crusoe Test*)

JOHNSTON, William Denis [1901–84, Irish theatre director and playwright]
E. W. Tocher (*The Moon in the Yellow River*)

JOHNSTONE, Mrs Christian Isobel [1781–1857, Scottish novelist and writer]
Margaret Dods (*The Cook and Housewife's Manual*)
Aunt Jane (*Stories from the History of the Jews*)
Qui Hi (in *Blackwood's Magazine*)

JOHNSTONE, Ted [1939–77, US science-fiction writer]
David McDaniel (*The Arsenal out of Time*)

JOLLY, Miss Emily [1820–1900, English novelist]
A Lady Who Prefers to be Anonymous (*A Wife's Story and Other Tales*)

JONES, Albert Evans [1895–1970, Welsh cleric and poet]
Cynan (*A Pageant of Good Tidings*)

JONES, Alice [1853–1933, Canadian novelist and writer]
Alix John (*The Night-Hawk*)

JONES, Arthur Llewellyn [1863–1947, Welsh novelist and essayist]
A Former Member of H. C. S. – 'Hereford Cathedral School' (*Eleusinia*)
Arthur Machen (*Three Impostors*; *Far Off Things*)
Leolinus Siluriensis (*The Anatomy of Tobacco*)
The Silurist (*In the Eighties*)

JONES, David [1765–1816, Welsh barrister and writer]
A Welch Freeholder (*A Letter to the Bishop of St David's*)

JONES, Felix Edward Aylmer [1889–1979, English actor]
Felix Aylmer (*Dickens Incognito*; *The Drood Case*)

JONES, George [1810–79, US lawyer and actor]
The Count Joannes (*History of Ancient America*)

JONES, George Chetwynd Griffith [1857–1906, English travel writer and early science-fiction writer]
Lara (*The Dying Faith*; *Poems, General, Secular and Satirical*)
Stanton Morich (*Thou Shalt Not …*)

JONES, Giles [fl. 1765, Welsh writer]
Tom Trip (*The History of Giles Gingerbread*)

JONES, Gwyneth A. [1952–, English writer for children]
Ann Halam (*Alder Tree*; *Ally, Ally Aster*)

JONES, Henry [1721–70, Irish dramatist and poet; killed in St Martin's Lane when drunk]
The Bricklayer (*Philosophy – a Poem Aaddressed to the Ladies*)

JONES, Henry [1831–99, English surgeon and writer and expert on card games]
Cavendish (*Principles of Whist*; *The Pocket Guide to Bezique*)
Pastime (in *The Queen*)

JONES, James Athearn [1791–1854, US writer]
Murgatroyd (*The Refugee*)
An Officer in the Army of Wolfe (*Memoirs of an Officer in the Army of Wolfe*)

JONES, John [1766–1827, Welsh cleric and writer]
Ben David (letters to the *Quarterly Review* and for *A Reply to Two Deistical Works*)
Essenus (*A New Version of Genesis*)
Philalethes (*The Epistles of St Paul to the Colossians*)

JONES, John [fl. 1827, English poet from humble background]
An Uneducated Youth (*Amatory Odes, Epistles and Sonnets*)
An Upper Servant (*Hints to Servants*)

JONES, John Beauchamp [1810–66, US journalist]
A Rebel War Clerk (*1861–65, Diary of a Rebel War Clerk*)
Luke Shortfield (*The Western Merchant*)
A Squatter (*Wild Western Scenes*)

JONES, John Pike [1790–1857, English cleric and antiquary]
A Freeholder of Devon (*A True and Impartial Account of the Parliamentary conduct of Sir T. D. Acland*)

JONES, Justin [fl. 1870, US novelist]
Harry Hazel (*The Flying Artillerist*; *The Flying Yankee*)

JONES, Leroi [1934–, US playwright and novelist]
I. A. Baraka (*It's Nation Time*)

JONES, Leslie Grove [1779–1839, English soldier and politician]
Radical (letters to *The Times*)

JONES, Stephen [1763–1827, British editor and compiler]
A Friend to Candour and Truth (*Hypercriticism Exposed*)
S. J. (*The Natural History of Fishes*; *The Natural History of Birds*; *A New Biographical Dictionary*)

JONES, William [1726–1800, English cleric, theologian and naturalist]
Thomas Bull (*One Penny-Worth of Truth*; *One Penny-Worth More of Truth*; *A Letter to John Bull*)
A Country Clergyman (*A Preservative against the Publications by Socinians*)
An Old Friend and Servant of the Church (*A Letter to the Church of England*)
A Presbyter of the Church of England (*Reflexions on the Growth of Heathenism*)
A Tutor (*Letters of a Tutor to his Pupils*)

JONES, William Philpin John [1913–92, Welsh cartoonist]
Jon (used for work appearing extensively in many UK magazines and newspapers)

JONSON, Benjamin [1573–1637, English dramatist and poet]
B. Jon (*B. J. his part of King James his Royall and Magnificent Entertainment etc.*)

JOPLIN, Thomas [1790–1847, English banker and writer on finance]
The Founder of the Establishment (*An Essay on the National Provincial Bank of England*)

JORDAN, Denham [1836–1920, English naturalist]
A Naturalist (*Woodland, Moor and Stream*)
*A Son of the Marshes (*Drift from Long Shore*; *From Spring to Fall*; *With the Woodlanders and by the Tide*; *On Surrey Hills*)

JORDAN, Helen Rosaline [1891–1958, English novelist]
Helen Ashton (*Bricks and Mortar*)

JORDAN, Robert Furneaux [1905–78, US writer]
Robert Player (*The Ingenious Mr Stone*)

JOSCELYN, Archie Lynn [fl. 1947, US western novelist]
A. A. Archer (*The Week-End Murders*)
Al Cody (*Bitter Creek*; *Empty Saddles*)
Lynn Westland (*Born to the Saddle*; *Long Loop Raiders*)

JOSE, Arthur Wilberforce [1863–1934, English-born Australian writer]
Ishmael Dare (*Sun and Cloud on River and Sea*)

JOSKE, Anne [1893–?, Australian mystery writer]
*Margot Neville (*Murder and Gardenias*; *Murder of Olympia*)

JOSLIN, Sesyle [1929–, US novelist and writer for children]
Josephine Gibson (*Is There a Mouse in the House?*)
G. B. Kirtland (*One Day in Elizabethan England*)

JOURDAIN, Eleanor F. [d. 1924, English academic and Francophile]
Francis Lamont (*An Adventure*)

JOYCE, James Augustine Aloysius [1882–1941, Irish novelist, poet and playwright]
Stephen Daedalus (in *The Irish Homestead*)

JUDAH, Samuel Benjamin Helbert [1799–1876, US humorist]
Terentius Phlogobombus (*Buccaneers*)

JUDSON, Edward Zane Carroll [1821–86, US novelist]
Ned Buntline (*The King of the Sea*; *The Ghouls of New York*)

JUDSON, Emily Chubbuck [1817–54, US writer]
Fanny Forester (in the *New York Mirror* and for *The Great Secret* and *Trippings in Author-Land*)

JURIN, James [1684–1750, English physician and writer]
Philalethes Cantabrigiensis (*An Appendix to The Republic of Letters*; *Geometry, No Friend to Infidelity*; *The Minute Mathematician*)
A Physician (*Expostulatory Address to J. R.*)

JUSTAMOND, John Obadiah [d. 1786, English military physician]
A Professor of Surgery (*Notes on Chirurgical Cases*)

K

KAGEY, Rudolf H. [1904–46, US mystery writer]
Kurt Steel (*Dead of Night*; *The Impostor*)

KAHLER, Hugh McNair [1883–1969, US writer and editor]
Murgatroyd Elphinstone (*The Collector's Whatnot*)

KALER, James Otis [1848–1912, US journalist and writer for children]
James Otis (in *Harper's Young People Magazine* and for *Braganza Diamond* and *Among the Fur Traders*)
Abigail Perkins (in *The Globe*)

KAMPF, Harold Bertram [fl. 1950, English writer]
H. B. Kaye (*Death is a Black Camel*)
Harold B. Kaye (*Grave Can Wait*; *Red Rafferty*)

KANE, Frank [1912–68, US mystery writer]
Frank Boyd (*The Flesh Peddlers*)

KANE, Henry [1918–, US crime and mystery writer]
Anthony McCall (*Operation Delta*; *Holocaust*)
Kenneth R. McKay (*Shadow of the Knife*; *Indecent Relations*)
Mario J. Sagola (*The Manacle*; *The Naked Bishop*)
Katherine Stapleton (*Without Sin Among You*)

KANE, John Kintzing [1795–1858, US jurist]
A Pennsylvanian (*A Candid View of the Presidential Election*)

KARIG, Walter [1898–1956, US writer]
Keats Patrick (*Death Is a Tory*)

KARK, Nina Mary [1925–, English novelist and writer for children]
Nina Bawden (*On the Run*; *White Horse Gang*)

KARP, David [1922–, US novelist and dramatist]
Wallace Ware (*Platoon*)

KATZ, Steve [1935–, US poet and writer]
Stephanie Gatos (*Posh*)

KATZIN, Olga [1896–1987, English satirical journalist and writer]
Sagittarius (*Sagittarius Rhyming*; *Up the Poll*)

KAVANAGH, Patrick [1904–67, Irish journalist and poet]
Piers Plowman (in the *Irish Press*)

KAVAPHES, Konstantinos [1863–1933, Alexandrian Greek poet]
C. P. Cavafy (*Passions and Ancient Days*)

KAYE, Barrington [1924–, English writer]
Henry Cooper (*Upcountry*)
Tom Kaye (*It Had Been a Mild, Delicate Night*; *Tom Kaye's Love Poems*)

KAYE, John [1783–1853, English cleric; Bishop of Lincoln]
Philalethes Cantabrigiensis (*A Reply to the 'Travels of an Irish Gentleman'*)

KAYE, John William [1814–76, English soldier in India and military writer]
John Company (in *Blackwood's Magazine*)
An Optimist (*Essays of an Optimist*)

KAYE, Mary Margaret [1908–, English novelist and writer for children]
Mollie Hamilton (*Later Than You Think*)

Mollie Kaye (*The Ordinary Princess*; *Thistledown*)

KEANE, Mary Nesta (Molly) [1905–, Irish novelist and playwright]
M. J. Farrell (*Taking Chances*; *Spring Meeting*)

KEARY, Annie [1825–79, English novelist and writer for children]
Cora (*Oldbury*)

KEARY, Charles Francis [d. 1917, English novelist, poet and historian]
H. Ogram Matuce (*The Journalist*; *A Wanderer*)

KEATING, Henry Reymond Fitzwalter [1926–, English journalist and crime novelist]
Evelyn Hervey (*The Governess*; *The Man of Gold*; *Into the Valley of Death*)

KEATING, Lawrence Alfred [1903–, US writer]
John Keith Bassett (*Comrades of the Colt*; *Trailers of the Sage*)

KEATS, Gwendoline [d. 1910, English writer]
Zack (*On Trial*; *The White Cottage*; *Tales of Dunstable Weir*; *The Roman Road*)

KEATS, John [1795–1821, English poet]
Canone; Caviare (both used in *The Indicator*)
Lucy Vaughan Lloyd (*The Cap and Bells*)

KEBBELL, Thomas Edward [1827–1917, English journalist and writer]
Hare Court; Rusticus Urbanus (both used in *Blackwood's Magazine*)

KEBLE, John [1792–1866, English cleric, poet and religious writer]
A Member of the University of Oxford (*The Psalter, or Psalms of David in English Verse*)

KEDDIE, Henrietta [1827–1914, English novelist]
Sarah Tytler (*Days of Yore*; *A Garden of Women*)

KEEGAN, Mary Constantine [1914–, English journalist and romantic novelist]
Mary Raymond (*April Promise*; *Pimpernel Project*)

KEENE, Henry George [1781–1864, English soldier in India and Persian scholar]
John Smith,Colonel (*Sketches in Indian Ink*)

KEEPE, Henry [1652–88, English antiquarian]
H. K. (*Monumenta Westmonasteriensia*)
Charles Taylour (*A True ... Narrative ... Unexpected Finding the Crucifix etc.*)

KEEVILL, Henry John [1914–78, English western novelist]
Clay Allison (*Brand of a Cowboy*; *North from Texas*)
Burt Alvord (*Gunfighter Breed*)
Bill Bonney (*Colorado Gunsmoke*)
Virgil Earp (*Hatchet Rides High*)
Wes Hardin (*Gun Law in Toledo*; *Cattle Country*)
Frank McLowery (*Herds North*; *Guns for the Sioux*)
Burt Mossman (*Guns on Eagle Creek*)
Johnny Ringo (*Lonely Gun*; *Action in Abilene*)
Will Travis (*The Hangrope Trail*)

KEIGHTLEY, David Noel [1932–, English anthologist]
Noel Keyes (*Contact*)

KEIR, James [1735–1820, Scottish chemist]
J. K., FRS and S. A. Sc. (*The First Part of a Dictionary of Chemistry*)

KEITH, George Skene [1752–1823, Scottish cleric and writer]
A Moderate Clergyman of the Synod of Aberdeen (*Address to the Ministers of the Church of Scotland*)

KELLER, Ethel May [1878–?, US writer]
Barbara Kay (*Elizabeth and her Friends*)
Lucia Whitney (*Through my Open Door*)

KELLOGG, Edward [1790–1858, US economist]
Godek Gardwell (*Currency: the Evil and the Remedy*)

Whitehook (*Remarks on Usury and its Effects*)

KELLOGG, Ensign Hosmer [1812–82, US lawyer and politician]
Pontoosuc (*The Johnson Protocol*)

KELLOGG, Vernon Lyman [1867–1937, US zoologist]
Max Vernon (*In and Out of Florence; Insect Stories*)

KELLY, Frances Maria [1790–1882, English actress and singer]
De Rupe (*Poems*)

KELLY, Hugh [1739–77, Irish playwright, editor and political writer]
The Babbler (in the *Public Ledger*)

KELLY, James Plunkett [1920–, Irish writer]
James Plunkett (*Strumpet City; Farewell Companions*)

KELLY, Joan Maisie Collings [1890–1947, English novelist]
Joan Sutherland (*One Man's Journey; Dust before the Wind*)

KELLY, John [1680–1751, English dramatist and journalist]
A Gentleman of the Temple (*The Married Philosopher*)
Timothy Scrub of Rag Fair Esq. (*The Fall of Bob*)
Henry Stonecastle of Northumberland Esq. (for editions of the *Universal Spectator* in both 1747 and 1756)

KELLY, Mary Anne [1826–1910, Irish writer of patriotic verse]
Eva (in *The Nation*, the *Irish Tribune* and other journals, and for a separate volume entitled *Poems*)

KELLY, Tim [1937–, US playwright and western novelist]
R. H. Bibolet (*Navajo House; Barrel of Monkeys*)

KELTON, Elmer Stephen [1926–, US novelist and journalist]
Tom Early (*Sons of Texas*)

Lee McElroy (*Long Way to Texas; The Eyes of the Hawk*)

KELTY, Mrs Mary Anne [1789–1873, English novelist and religious writer]
A Recluse (*Visiting my Relations and its Results*)

KEMBLE, Frances (Fanny) Anne [1809–83, English actress, poet and writer]
Mrs Butler (her married name, used up to 1849)

KEMBLE, John Mitchell [1807–57, English archaeologist, Anglo-Saxon scholar and philologist]
A Lay Member of the Church of England (*A Few Historical Remarks upon Church Rates*)

KEMPENFELT, Richard [1718–82, British admiral of Swedish ancestry]
Philotheorus (*Original Hymns and Poems*)

KEN, Thomas [1637–1711, English cleric; Bishop of Bath and Wells]
T. K., D. D. (*The Royal Sufferer, a Manual of Meditations and Devotions*)

KENDALL, Guy [1876–1960, English schoolteacher and writer]
Fourth Form (*The New Schoolmaster*)

KENDALL, John Kaye [1869–1952, English soldier and writer]
Dum-Dum (in the *Times of India*, in *Punch* and for *His Selected Verses*, *His Book of Beasts* and *Rhymes of the East*)

KENDRICK, Baynard H. [1894–1977, US mystery writer]
Richard Hayward (*Trapped; The Soft Arms of Death*)

KENEALLY, Thomas Michael [1935–, Australian novelist]
William Coyle (*Act of Grace; Chief of Staff*)

KENEALY, Alexander [1864–1915, English journalist]
Montagu Vernon Ponsonby (*The Preposterous Yankee*)

KENEALY, Edward Hyde Vaughan
[1819–90, Irish barrister and writer]
Barney Brallaghan (in both *Bentley's
Miscellany* and *Fraser's Magazine*)
Pat Fogarty of Cork; Ned Hyde (both used
in *Ainsworth's Magazine*)
Edward Wortley Montagu (*... an
Autobiography*)
A Templar (in *Fraser's Magazine*)

KENNEDY, Alexander [1909–60, English
psychiatrist, medical writer and radio
dramatist]
Kenneth Alexander (used for radio plays
such as *Life History of a Delusion* and
Dangerous Drugs)

KENNEDY, Alexander K. [1800–68, Scottish
political economist]
A Writer to the Signet (*Sanitary and Social
Reform*; *The High Price of Food*)

KENNEDY, Geoffrey Studdert [d. 1929,
English cleric and writer]
Woodbine Willie (*Rough Rhymes of a Padre*)

KENNEDY, John Pendleton [1795–1870, US
politician, novelist and writer]
Paul Ambrose (*Mr Ambrose's Letters on the
Rebellion*)
Clerke of Oxenforde (*The Blackwater
Chronicle*)
Common Sense (*The Privilege of the Writ of
Habeas Corpus*)
Mark Littleton (*Swallow Barn*)
A Man of the Times (*Letters of a Man of
the Times to the Citizens of Baltimore*)
A Member of the 27th Congress (*A Defence
of the Whigs*)
Mephistopheles (*A Review of Mr
Cambreling's Report*)
Solomon Secondthoughts, Schoolmaster
(*Quodlibet*)
A Southern Man (*Slavery the Mere Pretext
for Rebellion*)

KENNEDY, Patrick [1801–73, Irish
bookseller and Celtic scholar]
A Constant Visitor (in *Dublin University
Magazine*)

Harry Whitney (*Hunting with the Eskimos*;
Legends of Mount Leinster)

KENNEDY, Richard Hartley [d. 1865,
English physician and surgeon]
An Eye-Witness (in *Bentley's Miscellany*)

KENNETT, White [1660–1728, English cleric
and historian; Bishop of Peterborough]
A Divine of the Church of England (*A Visit
ot Saint Saviour's, Southwark*)
An Episcopal Divine (*A Letter from the
Borders of Scotland*)
A Member of Convocation (*Dr Snape
Instructed in Some Matters*)

KENNEY, Arthur Herbert [1855–1923,
English soldier in India]
Wyvern (*Common Sense Cookery for English
Households*; *Culinary Jottings for Madras*;
Fifty Lunches; *Furlough Reminiscences*)

KENNICOTT, Benjamin [1718–83, English
cleric, Hebraist and librarian]
A Member of the University (*A Word to the
Hutchinsonians*)

KENNINGTON, Gilbert Alan [1906–,
English writer]
Alan Grant (*It Walks in the Woods*)

KENRICK, Daniel [fl. 1700, English
physician and poet]
A Person of Honour (*A New Session of the
Poets*)

KENRICK, William [1725–79, English writer
and editor]
Archimagirus Metaphoricus (*The Kapelion
or, Poetical Ordinary*)
W. Avon (*Frank Milward*; *The Legend of
Fair Rosamund*; *A Midsummer Day's
Dream and Other Poems*)
A Lady (*The Whole Duty of Woman*)
Margelina Scribelindra Macularia (*The Old
Woman's Dunciad*)
Mary Midnight (*The Old Woman's Dunciad*)
Ontologos (*A Reply to the Grand Question
Debated Fully Proving that the Soul of
Man is and Must be Immortal*)
Scriblerus Flagellarius (*A Whipping for the
Welch Parson*)

KENT, Arthur William Charles [1925–, English crime and mystery writer]
James Bradwell (*The Mean City*)
M. Dubois (*El Tafile*; *March and Die*)
Paul Granados (*Broadway Contraband*)
Alexander Karol (*Sword of Vengeance*; *Dark Lady*)
Alex Stamper (*Revolt at Zaluig*)
Brett Vane (*Sunny*; *Gardenia*)

KENT, Benjamin [1707–88, American lawyer and cleric]
Amicus (*A Sermon in Marlborough in 1734*)

KENT, William Charles Mark [1823–1902, English journalist, editor and poet]
An English Journalist (*What Shall Be Done with Cardinal Wiseman?*)
An Oscotian (*Catholicity in the Dark Ages*)
Mark Rochester (*The Derby Ministry*)
A Templar (*The Gladstone Government*)

KENTON, Warren [1933–, English writer]
Zev Ben Shimon Halevi (*Tree of LIfe*)

KENYON, Michael [1931–, English mystery writer]
Daniel Forbes (*Mr Big*; *The Rapist*)

KEPPEL, William Coutts [1832–94, 7th Earl of Albermarle; soldier, politician and writer]
Beta Mikron (in *Fraser's Magazine*)

KER, Charles Henry Bellenden [1785–1871, English barrister and legal reformer]
Dodman (in the *Gardener's Chronicle*)

KERNAN, J. Frank [fl. 1885, US writer]
Florry (*Reminiscences of the Old Fire Ladders of New York*)

KERR, Doris Boake [1899–1944, Australian novelist]
Capel Boake (*The Twig is Bent*; *The Dark Thread*)

KERR, James Lennox [1899–1963, Scottish writer for children]
Peter Dawlish (*Aztec Gold*; *Johnno, the Deep-Sea Diver*)
Lennox Kerr (*The Blackspit Smugglers*)

KERSH, Gerald [1911–68, English journalist and writer – became a US citizen in 1959]
Piers England (used when chief feature writer for *The People* newspaper)

KETCHUM, Philip [1902–69, US crime and western writer]
Carl McK. Saunders (*Death in the Library*; *The Stalkers*)

KETT, Henry [1761–1825, English preacher and writer]
S. Nobody of King's College, Oxford (*The Biter Bit*)

KETTELL, Samuel [1800–55, US journalist and humorist]
Peeping Tom (in the *Boston Courier*)
Sampson, Short and Fat (*Quozziana or, a Letter from Great Goslington*; *Daw's Doings or, the History of the Late War in the Plantations*)
Timothy Titterwell (*Yankee Notions – a Medley*)

KEY, Thomas Hewitt { 1799–1875, English classical scholar and philologist]
Claudius (in the *English Journal of Education*)

KIDD, Adam [1802–31, Irish-Canadian poet]
Slievegallin (in the *Irish Vindicator*)

KIDD, Beatrice Ethel [1867–1958, Welsh novelist and anti-vivisectionist]
Mark Winterton (*The Cassowary*)

KIDDER, Frederic [1804–85, US librarian and writer]
Orient (in the *Boston Daily Advertiser* and for *The Popham Colony*)
Sagadahoc (in the *Boston Daily Advertiser*)

KIDWELL, Carol [1923–, Canadian writer]
Carol Maddison (*Marcantonio Flaminio: Poet, Humanist and Philosopher*)

KIESCHNER, Sidney [1906–, US actor and dramatist]
Sidney Kingsley (*Men in White*; *Dead End*)

KILBYE, Richard [1561–1620, English cleric, Hebraist and scholar]
A Miserable Sinner (*The Burthen of a Loaden Conscience*)

KILLIGREW, Henry [1613–1700, English cleric, royalist and writer]
The Hand that Translated Martial (*A Court of Judicature*)

KILNER, Dorothy [1755–1836, English writer]
M. P. – 'Mary Pelham' (*The Histories of More Children than One, or Goodness Better than Beauty; Letters from a Mother to her Children; The Rotchfords or, the Friendly Counsellor*)
S. S. (*Adventures of a Pincushion; Jemima Placid; Memoirs of a Peg-Top*)

KIMBALL, Edmund [1793–1873, US lawyer]
A Citizen (*Reflections upon the Law of Libel*)

KIMBER, Edward [1719–69, English novelist and writer]
G. L. Campbell (*A Relation or Journal of a late Expedition to St Augustine, Florida*)

KIMBER, Isaac [1692–1755, English Baptist cleric, biographer and editor]
An Impartial Hand (*The History of England to George II*)

KIMBRO, John M. [1929–, US romantic novelist]
Kynn Allyson (*The Wounded Dove; The Moon Shadow*)
Ann Ashton (*Three Cries of Terror; Star Eyes*)
Charlotte Bramwell (*Cousin to Terror; Brother Sinister*)
Jean Kimbro (*Twilight Return*)
Katheryn Kimbrough (*The Broken Sphinx; Unseen Torment*)

KING, Albert [1924–, English science-fiction writer]
Mark Bannon (*The Wayward Robot; The Tomorrow Station*)
Paul Conrad (*Last Man on Kluth; The Slave Bug*)

Floyd Gibson (*A Slip in Time; The Manufactured People*)
Scott Howell (*Menace from Magor; Passage to Oblivion*)
Christopher King (*The World of Jonah Klee; Operation Mora*)
Paul Muller (*The Man from Ger; Brother Gib*)

KING, Bolton [1860–1937, English social reformer and writer]
Walter Ray (*Poems of Yesterday and Today*)

KING, Edward [1735–1807, English barrister and antiquarian]
A Plain, Honest Layman (*Honest Apprehensions*)

KING, Francis Henry [1923–, Swiss-born English writer]
Frank Cauldwell (*The Fire-Walkers*)

KING, Frank [fl. 1950, English writer]
Clive Conrad (*Money's Worth of Murder; The Crime of his Life*)

KING, James Clifford [fl. 1960, US writer]
Pete Fry (*The Grey Sombrero; The Red Stockings*)

KING, John [1652–1732, English cleric and pamphleteer]
A Divine of the Church of England (*Animadversions on a Pamphlet Intituled 'A Letter of Advice'*)

KING, Peter [1669–1734, 1st Baron King of Ockham; barrister and Lord Chancellor]
An Impartial Hand (*The Second Part of the Enquiry into the Constitution etc.; An Enquiry into the Constitution of the Primitive Church*)

KING, Richard [1748–1810, English cleric]
Brother Abraham (*An Answer to the Letters of Peter Plymley*)

KING, Richard Ashe [1839–1932, Irish cleric, novelist and biographer]
Basil (*Love the Debt; A Shadowed Life*)

KING, Richard John [1818–79, English West Country historian]
Rev. M. Howlett of Devonshire (in *Fraser's Magazine*)

KING, Rufus [1755–1827, US lawyer and politician]
*Camillus (in the *American Minerva*)

KING, Stephen [1947–, US mystery novelist]
Richard Bachman (*Rage*; *The Running Man*)

KING, William [1663–1712, English lawyer, poet and writer]
Tom Boggy (*A Second Letter from Tom Boggy to the Canon of Windsor*)
Mons. Samuel de Sorbiere (*A Journey to London in the Year 1698*)

KING, William [1685–1763, English academic and satirist]
A Master of Arts (*Elogium Famae Inserviens Jacci Etonensis*)
Peregrine O'Donald; Frederick Scheffer (both used in *The Toast – an Heroic Poem*)

KING-HALL, William Richard Stephen [1893–1966, English mariner, politician and writer]
Etienne (*A Naval Lieutenant 1914–18*; *The Diary of a U-Boat Commander*; *Strange Tales from the Fleet*)

KING-SCOTT, Peter [fl. 1963, English writer]
Peter Edgar (*Cities of the Dead*)

KINGDON, Samuel Nicholson [1805–72, English cleric]
A Clergyman in the West (*Schism and its Results*)

KINGSCOTE, Mrs Adeline Georgina Isabel [d. 1908, English novelist]
Lucas Cleeve (*Tales of the Sun*; *The Secret Church*)

KINGSFORD, Mrs Anna [1846–88, English physician, theosophist and writer]
Ninon (or Mrs Algernon) Kingsford (used in both the *Penny Post* and *Westminster Review*)

KINGSLEY, Charles [1819–75, English novelist, historian and social reformer]
Chartist Parson (used for journalism)
Lord Dundreary (*The Speech of Lord Dundreary on the Great Hippocampus Question*)
Parson Lot (used in both the *Christian Socialist* and *Politics for the People* and for *Cheap Clothes and Nasty*)
A Minute Philosopher (*Hints to Stammerers*)
A Working Parson (used on a placard posted throughout London, 12 April 1848)

KINGSLEY, George Henry [1827–92, English physician and traveller]
John Bull, Junior (in *MacMillan's Magazine*)
The Doctor (in *The Field* and for *South Sea Bubbles*)

KINGSLEY, Mary [1852–1931, English novelist – daughter of Charles Kingsley above]
Lucas Malet (*Colonel Enderby's Wife*; *The Wages of Sin*)

KINGSTON, William Henry Giles [1814–80, English journalist and writer for boys]
Barrington Beaver (*Adventures of Dickons Low among the Redskins*)
Barnaby Brine Esq. (*The Cruise of the 'Frolic'*)

KINSELLA, Thomas [1832–84, US journalist]
Brooklyn (in the *Brooklyn Eagle*)

KIP, Leonard [1826–1906, US lawyer and writer]
A Member of the Bar (*The Volcano Diggings*)

KIP, William Ingraham [1811–93, US cleric]
A Member of the NY Geneal. and Biog. Society (*The Olden Time in New York 1664–1775*)

KIPLING, Rudyard [1865–1936, English
    novelist and poet]
    Four Anglo Indian Writers (*Quartette*,
    published in 1885, a work by R. K., his
    sister and his parents)
    Two Writers (*Echoes*, published in 1884,
    contained work by R. K. and his sister
    Beatrice)

KIRBY, William [1817–1906, English-born
    Canadian writer]
    Britannicus (*Counter Manifesto to the
    Canadian Annexationists*)

KIRK, James Prior [1851–1922, English
    novelist]
    James Prior (*Ripple and Flood*; *A Walking
    Gentleman*)

KIRKBY, John [1705–54, English cleric and
    religious writer]
    A Clergyman of the Same Church (*A
    Demonstration from Christian Principles*)

KIRK, Ellen Warner Olney [1842–?, US
    novelist]
    Henry Hayes (*Sons and Daughters*; *A
    Daughter of Eve*)

KIRKE, Edward [1553–1613, English
    academic]
    E. K. (in the preface to Spenser's
    Shepheard's Calendar)

KIRKE, Percy St George [d. 1966, English
    research engineer]
    Night Watchman (*Deluded Politicians
    Enslaving Britain*)

KIRKHAM, Reginald S. [fl. 1922, English
    writer for children]
    Hilda Richards (in *Schoolfriend*, 1921–4)

KIRKLAND, Caroline Stansbury [1801–64,
    US novelist]
    Mrs Mary Clavers (*A Garland of Poetry for
    the Young*; *Our New Home in the West*)

KIRKLAND, Winifred Margaretta
    [1872–1943, US novelist]
    James Priceman (*Chaos and a Creed*)

KIRKPATRICK, James [d. 1743, Irish cleric,
    physician and writer]
    A Member of the General Synod (*A Defence
    of Christian Liberty*)
    A Sincere Lover of Truth and Peace (*A
    Vindication of the Presbyterian Ministers in
    the North of Ireland*)

KIRKUS, William [1830–1907, US cleric]
    Mrs Florence Williamson (*Frederick Rivers,
    Independent Parson*)

KIRSCH, Robert [1922–, US novelist and
    historian]
    Robert Dundee (*The Restless Lovers*)

KIRWAN, Andrew Valentine [1804–70,
    English barrister and writer]
    Benjamin Blunt, formerly a Bencherman
    and Trencherman in the Inner Temple,
    now a Rentier of the Rue Rivoli in Paris;
    Dudley Digges Doolittle; An Old
    Apprentice of the Law; A Sailor and a
    Seldenite (all used in *Fraser's Magazine*)
    Louis Eustache Eude, the Younger (in *New
    Monthly Magazine*)
    A Man on the Shady Side of Fifty (in
    MacMillan's Magazine)
    A Traveller (*The Ports, Arsenals and
    Dockyards of France*)

KITCAT, Mrs Mabel [d. 1922, English
    sporting writer]
    Mrs Murray Hickson (*Concerning Teddy*)

KITCHIN, Frederick Harcourt [1867–1932,
    English journalist]
    Bennet Copplestone (*The Secret of the Navy*;
    The Lost Naval Papers)

KLASS, Philip [1920–, US science-fiction
    writer]
    William Tenn (*The Human Angle*; *Of All
    Possible Worlds*)

KNAPP, Henry Ryder [d. 1817, English
    cleric and humorist]
    Peeping Tom (in the *Leicester Herald*)

KNAPP, John Leonard [1767–1845, English
    botanist and writer]
    A Naturalist (*Journal of a Naturalist*)

KNAPP, Samuel Lorenzo [1783–1838, US journalist and lawyer]
Ali Bey (*Extracts from a Journal of Travels in North America*)
Ignatius Loyola Robertson, Ll. D. (*Sketches of Public Characters*)
Shahcolen, a Hindu Philosopher Residing in Philadelphia (*Letters of Shahcolen etc.*)
Theodore Temple (*The Secret Discipline in Ecclesiastical History Explained*)

KNIGHT, Alana [fl. 1975, English playwright and romantic novelist]
Margaret Hope (*Hostage Most Royal; Perilous Voyage*)

KNIGHT, Bernard [1931–, Welsh barrister, physician, pathologist and crime writer]
Bernard Picton (*The Lately Deceased; Mistress Murder; The Expert*)

KNIGHT, Charles [1791–1873, English publisher and writer]
Patterson Aymar (in the *Quarterly Magazine*)
Grandfather Smith (in *Town and Country Magazine*)

KNIGHT, Damon [1922–, US science-fiction writer and editor]
Stuart Fleming; *Donald Laverty (used in *Galaxy* and other science-fiction magazines)

KNIGHT, Eric Mowbray [1897–1943, English-born US journalist and novelist]
Richard Hallas (*You Play Black and the Red Comes Up*)

KNIGHT, Francis Edgar [1905–, English nautical and juvenile writer]
Frank Knight (*True Stories of Exploration; Ships*)
Cedric Salter (*Algarve and Southern Portugal*)

KNIGHT, Henry Cogswell [1788–1835, US cleric and poet]
Arthur Singleton Esq. (*Letters from the South and West*)

KNIGHT, Joseph [1829–1907, English drama critic and writer]
Sylvanus Urban (in *Gentleman's Magazine*)

KNIGHT, Kathleen More [fl. 1955, US writer]
Alan Amos (*Fatal Harvest; Borderline Murder*)

KNIGHTON, William [d. 1900, English colonial academic and writer]
An Indian Journalist (*Tropical Sketches*)
A Member of the Household of His late Majesty Nussir-U-Deen (*The Private Life of an Eastern King*)

KNIPE, Alden Arthur [1870–1950, US physician, novelist and writer for children]
Timothy Shea (*The Cowboy and the Duchess*)

KNIPE, Emilie Benson [1870–1958, US novelist, illustrator and writer for children]
Therese Benson (*The Fourth Lovely Lady; A Maid of Old Manhattan*)

KNIPSCHEER, Johannes M. W. [1946–, Dutch-born US mystery writer]
James M. Fox (*Cheese from a Mousetrap; The Lady Regrets*)
Grant Holmes (*Surabaya; Courier to Marlborough*)

KNOLLYS, Henry [1840–1930, English soldier and essayist]
An Officer of the Royal Artillery (*From Sedan to Saarbruck, via Verdun*)

KNOTT, William Cecil [1927–, US western novelist]
Bill J. Carol (*Scatback; Inside the Ten*)
Bryan Swift (*Mission Code: Springboard*)

KNOWLES, James Sheridan [1784–1862, Irish dramatist, novelist and writer]
Selina (*The Senate or, Social Villagers of Kentish Town*)

KNOWLES, Mabel Winifred [1875–1949, English romantic novelist and writer for children]
Lester Lurgan (*The League of the Triangle*; *A Message from Mars*)
May Wynne (*Whither?*; *The Smugglers of Penreen*)

KNOWLES, Mrs Mary [1733–1807, English Quaker]
A Child of Candour (in *Gentleman's Magazine*)

KNOWLSON, Thomas Sharper [1867–1947, English psychologist and writer]
Thomas Sharnol (*Leon Tolstoy*; *Originality*)

KNOX, Alexander [1751–1831, British religious writer]
A Gentleman in the North of Ireland (*Essays on the Political Circumstances of Ireland*)

KNOX, Edmund George Valpy [1881–1971, English humorist and editor of *Punch*]
E. V. O. E. (or Evoe) (used in *Punch* and for *Fancy Now*, *It Occurs to Me*, etc.)

KNOX, Isabella [1831–1903, Scottish poet and novelist]
Isa (in *The Scotsman* and for *Poems* and *Our Summer Home*)

KNOX, Ronald Arbuthnot [1888–1957, English cleric and writer]
Opal, Lady Porstock (*Memories of the Future*)
R. A. K. (*Signa, Severa*)

KNOX, Thomas [1835–96, US journalist and traveller]
Walneerg (*Rhymed Convictions*)

KNOX, William [1732–1810, British colonial civil servant]
A Gentleman in London (*The Claims of the Colonies to an Exemption etc.*)
A Late Under Secretary of State (*Considerations on the Present State of the Nation*; *Extra-Official State Papers Addressed to Lord Rawdon*)

A Layman of the Church of England (*Considerations on the Universality of the Theocracy*; *Observations on the Liturgy*)

KNOX, William [1928–, Scottish journalist and novelist]
Robert MacLeod (*Cargo Risk*; *Path of Ghosts*)
Noah Webster (used in the USA for some of his work)

KOESTLER, Arthur [1905–83, Hungarian-born British novelist and writer]
Dr A. Costler (*Encyclopedie de la Vie Sexuelle*)

KOHLMAN, Anthony [1771–1836, French-born Catholic priest in USA]
Rev. John Beschter (*The Blessed Reformation*)

KOONTZ, Dean R. [1945–, US fantasy and science-fiction writer]
David Axton (*Prison of Ice*)
Brian Coffey (*Surrounded*; *The Face of Fear*)
Deanna Dwyer (*The Demon Child*; *Dance with the Devil*)
K. R. Dwyer (*Shattered*; *Dragonfly*)
John Hill (*The Long Sleep*)
Leigh Nichols (*The Eyes of Darkness*; *Shadowfires*)
Anthony North (*Strike Deep*)
Richard Paige (*The Door to December*)
Owen West (*The Mask*; *The Funhouse*)
Aaron Wolfe (*Invasion*)

KORN, Friedrich [1803–50, German academic]
F. Nork (in *Fraser's Magazine*)

KORNBLUTH, C. M. [1923–58, US science-fiction writer]
Cecil Corwin (*Thirteen o'Clock*)
Kenneth Falconer (*The Words of Guru*)
*Cyril Judd (*Gunner Cade*; *Outpost Mars*)
*Jordan Park (*Sorority House*)

KORTRIGHT, Miss Fanny Aikin [1821–1900, English novelist]
Berkeley Aikin (*The Old, Old Story, Love*; *The Dean or, The Popular Preacher*)

KORZENIOWSKI, Jozef Teodor Konrad
[1857–1924, Polish-born English novelist
and essayist]
Joseph Conrad (*Lord Jim*; *Nostromo*; etc.)
*Ignatz von Aschendorf (*The Nature of a
Crime*)

KOSINSKI, Jerzy Nikodem [1938–91,
Polish-born US novelist]
Joseph Novak (*The Future is Ours Comrade*)

KOUYOUMDJIAN, Dikran [1895–1956,
Bulgarian-born British novelist and
short-story writer]
Michael Arlen (*Green Hat*; *Ghoul of Golders
Green*)

KRASNEY, Samuel A. [1922–, US journalist
and writer]
Sam Curzon (*Design for Dying*; *The Morals
Squad*)

KRAUS, Robert [1925–, US illustrator,
cartoonist and writer for children]
E. S. Silly (*Squeaky's One Man Band*)
I. M. Tubby (*I'm a Little Tug-Boat*)

KRAUSE, Miss Lydia Farrington
[1864–1939, US writer and editor]
Barbara Yechton (*A Lovable Crank*;
Fortune's Boats)

KRENTZ, Jayne Ann [1948–, US romantic
novelist]
Jayne Bentley (*Turning Towards Home*)
Jayne Castle (*Queen of Hearts*; *Spell Bound*)
Stephanie James (*Corporate Affair*; *The
Silver Snare*)
Jayne Taylor (*Whirlwind Courtship*)

KROUT, Caroline Virginia [1853–1931, US
writer]
Caroline Brown (*Bold Robin and his Forest
Rangers*; *Dionis of the White Veil*)

KUMMER, Frederick Arnold [1873–1943,
US playwright and novelist]
Arnold Fredericks (*Design for Murder*; *The
Road to Fortune*)

KUNITZ, Stanley Jasspon [1905–, US poet]
Dilly Tante (*Living Authors*)

KURLAND, Michael [1938–, US writer]
Jennifer Plum (*The Secret of Benjamin
Square*)

KURNITZ, Harry [1909–68, US mystery
writer]
Marco Page (*The Shadowy Third*; *Suspects
All*)

KUSKIN, Karla [1932–, US writer for
children]
Nicholas Charles (*How Do You Get from
Here to There?*)

KUTTNER, Henry [1914–58, US science-
fiction writer]
Will Garth (*Dr Cyclops*)
James Hall (in *Marvel Science Stories*)
*Keith Hammond (*Valley of the Flame*; *Lord
of the Storm*)
*Kelvin Kent (*Roman Holiday*; *Science is
Golden*)
Robert O. Kenyon (in *Marvel Science
Stories*)
*Lewis Padgett (*A Gnome There Was*; *Live
to Tomorrow*)

KYLE, Susan E. S. [1946–, US romantic
novelist]
Diana Blayne (*Dark Surrender*; *Tangled
Destinies*)
Katy Currie (*Blind Promises*)
Diana Palmer (*Dream's End*; *Heart of Ice*)

L

LABOUCHERE, Henry Dupre [1831–1912,
English journalist, diplomat and radical
politician]
Besieged Resident (in the *Daily News* and
for *Diary of a Besieged Resident in Paris*)

LACEY, Thomas Alexander [1853–1931,
English cleric and religious writer]
Viator (in the *Church Times*)

LACY, John [fl. 1723, English prophet –
committed to a mental institution]
One of the Modern Prophets (*The Scene of
Delusions by the Rev. Mr Owen*)

LADD, Mrs Catharine [1808–99, US writer]
Alida; Arcturus (both used for her
journalism)

LADD, Joseph Brown [1764–86, US poet
and writer – killed in a duel]
Arouet (*Poems*)

LADD, William [1778–1841, US journalist
and pacifist]
Philanthropos (*Letters from an American; A
Brief Illustration of Principles of War and
Peace*)

LAFFAN, Mrs Bertha Jane [d. 1912, English
novelist and dramatist]
Mrs Leith Adams (*Madelon Lemoine;
Winstowe*)

LAFFIN, John [1922–, Australian novelist]
Mark Napier (*Doorways to Danger; A Very
Special Agent*)
Dirk Sabre (*Murder by Bamboo*)

LAIDLER, Graham [d. 1945, English
cartoonist]
Pont (in *Punch*)

LAING, Samuel [1812–97, Scottish barrister,
politician and writer]
A Fellow of St John's College, Cambridge
(in *Monthly Chronicle*)

LAIRD, MacGregor [1808–61, Scottish
explorer of the African continent]
Cerebus (in *The Spectator*)

LAMB, Charles [1775–1834, English essayist]
Burton, Junior; Crito; Edax; Hospita; A
Londoner; Moriturus; Semel-Damnatus
(all used in *The Reflector*)
C. L. (in *Poems on Various Subjects* by
Samuel Taylor Coleridge)
Elia (in the *London Magazine* and for *Essays
of Elia*)
An Eye-Witness (*Satan in Search of a Wife*)
L. (in *New Monthly Magazine*)
Lepus (in the *New Times*)
Phil-Elia (in the *London Magazine*)

LAMB, Miss Mary Anne [1764–1847,
English poet and writer for children –
sister of Charles Lamb above]
Mrs Leicester (*Mrs Leicester's School*)

LAMB, Robert [1812–72, English cleric and
writer]
A Manchester Man (*Free Thoughts on Many
Subjects*)

LAMBERT, Derek William [1929–, English
crime writer]
Richard Falkirk (*The Twisted Wire;
Blackstone on Broadway*)

LAMBERT, Eric [1921–66, Australian
novelist and writer]
D. Brennan (*The Twenty Thousand Thieves*)

Frank Brennand (*Sink the Bismarck; North to Alaska*)
George Kay (*The Siege of Pinchgut*)

LAMBERT, Leslie Harrison [1883–1940, English Foreign Office civil servant and broadcaster]
A. J. Alan (*Good Evening, Everyone!*)

LAMBOT, Isobel Mary [1926–, English crime and mystery writer]
Daniel Ingham (*Contract for Death*)

LAMBURN, John Battersby Crompton [1893–, English novelist]
John Lambourne (*The Kingdom That Was; The Unmeasured Place*)

LAMBURN, Richmal Crompton [1890–1969, English writer of the 'William' books for boys]
Richmal Crompton (*William Again; William and the Artist's Model*)

LAMPLUGH, George William [1859–1926, English geologist and writer]
George Flambro (or Flamborough) (in *MacMillan's Magazine*)

LANCASTER, Joseph [1778–1838, English pioneer educational reformer]
Amicus (*Fruits of Christian Love!*)

LANCASTER, Nathaniel [1701–75, English cleric and writer on etiquette]
Philautus (*The Pretty Gentleman*)

LANCASTER, Sir William John [1841–1929, English insurance executive]
A Busy Man (*Some Leisure Lyrics*)

LANCASTER, William Joseph Cosens [1851–1922, English civil engineer and writer of sea stories]
Harvey Collingwood (*The Homeward Voyage; The Pirate Island*)

LANCHESTER, Frederick William [1868–1946, English engineer and motor and aeronautical pioneer]
Paul Netherton Herries (*A King's Prayer and Other Poems; The Centenarian*)

LANDE, Laurence Montague [1906–, Canadian writer]
Alain Verval (*Experience*)

LANDON, Letitia Elizabeth [1802–38, English poet and novelist]
L. E. L. (*The Troubadour; Francesca Carrara*)

LANDON, Melville de Lancy [1839–1910, US humorist]
Eli Perkins (*Wit, Humor and Pathos*)

LANDOR, Walter Savage [1775–1864, English writer; quarrelsome wanderer but much admired stylist]
Calvus (*Letters Addressed to Lord Liverpool*)
W. S. L. (*Dry Sticks Fagoted by W. S. L.; Letters of an American mainly on Russia and Revolution*)

LANDSEER, John [1769–1852, English engraver and writer]
Algernon Sidney (*Algernon Sidney's Letter to T. Wyse*)

LANE, Kenneth Westmacott [1893–?, English journalist and novelist]
Keith West (*Hanging Waters*)

LANE, Ralph Norman Angell [1872–1967, English journalist and writer]
Sir Norman Angell (*La Grande Illusion; The Unseen Assassins*)

LANE, William [1861–1917, English-born Australian writer]
John Miller (*The Workingman's Paradise*)

LANG, Andrew [1844–1912, Scottish poet, journalist, novelist and anthropologist]
Hermann Boscher (*The Mark of Cain*)
A. Fogey (in *Contemporary Review*)
A. Huge Longway (*Much Darker Days*)
*Two Art Critics (*Pictures at Play*)

LANG, John [1817–64, Australian novelist, dramatist and essayist]
The Mofussilite (*Too Clever by Half or The Harroways*)

LANG, Mrs Leonora Blanche [fl. 1888, English writer – wife of Andrew Lang above]
May Kendall (*Such is Life*; *White Poppies*; *Songs from Dreamland*)

LANG, Theo [fl. 1945, English writer]
Peter Piper (*Death Came in Straw*; *Murder after the Blitz*)

LANGDON-DAVIES, John [1897–1971, English writer]
John Nada (*Carlos the Bewitched*)
John Stanhope (*The Cato Street Conspiracy*)

LANGFORD, David [1953–, Welsh physician and science-fiction writer]
William Robert Loosley (*Account of a Meeting with Denizens of Another World*)

LANGHORNE, John [1735–79, English classical scholar and poet]
One of His Majesty's Justices of the Peace for the County of Somerset (*The Country Justice*)

LANGLEY, Esme Ross [1919–92, English writer]
Ann Bruce (*Should I Be Dismayed?*)

LANGLEY, Sarah [1927–, US writer]
Lee Langley (*Dead Center*; *Osiris Died in Autumn*)

LANMAN, Charles [1819–95, US journalist, lexicographer and writer]
An Angler (*Adventures of an Angler in Canada, Nova Scotia etc.*)
A Landscape Painter (*Letters from a Landscape Painter*)
A Tourist (*Hawho-Noo*)

LARDNER, Nathaniel [1684–1768, Scottish cleric and biblical scholar]
A. B. (*A Letter to Jonas Hanway*)
Philalethes (*A Letter Writ in the Year 1730*)

LARIAR, Laurence [1908–, US artist and novelist]
Adam Knight (*You Can't Catch Me*; *Stone Cold Blonde*)
Michael Stark (*Run for your Life*)

LARWOOD, Joshua [d. 1808, English cleric]
A Sailor (*Erratics*)

LASCELLES, Rowley [1771–1841, British barrister and Irish historian]
Yorick (*Letters to Yorick*)

LASKER, Emanuel [1868–1941, German mathematician and chess champion]
Champion (*Common Sense in Chess*)

LASKI, Esther Pearl – 'Marghanita' [1915–88, English novelist, critic and lexicographer]
Sarah Russell (*To Bed with Grand Music*)

LATEY, John [1842–1902, English novelist and journalist]
Codlin (*The Showman's Panorama*)
The Showman (in the *Penny Illustrated News*)
The Silent Member (in the *Illustrated London News*)

LATEY, John Lash [1808–91, English journalist and writer]
Lash (in *Lloyd's News*)
A Working Man (*Letters to Working People on the New Poor Law*)

LATHAM, Henry [1821–1902, English academic and religious writer]
Presbyter Cicestrensis (*Anthologia Davidica*)

LATHAM, Jean Lee [1902–, US dramatist and writer for children]
Janice Gard (*Listen to Leon*)
Julian Lee (*Washington for All*; *Tiny Jim*)

LATHAM, Robert Gordon [1812–88, English philologist, physician and ethnologist]
*Richard Grimgibber; The Travelling Bachelor (both used in *Bentley's Miscellany*)

LATHBURY, Miss Mary A. [1841–1913, US writer and illustrator]
Aunt Mary (*The Peep o' the Morn*)

LATHROP, John Hiram [1799–1866, US academic]
A Citizen of New York (*An Address on Anti-Masonic Excitement etc.*)

LATHROP, Lorin Andrews [d. 1929, US diplomat, novelist and serial writer]
Kenyon Gambier (*The White Horse and the Red-Haired Girl*; *Princess of Paradise Island*)

LATHY, Thomas Pike [fl. 1820, English writer and plagiarist]
Piscator (*The Angler – a Poem*)

LATIMER, Jonathan [1906–83, US mystery writer]
Peter Coffin (*The Search for my Great Uncle's Head*)

LATIMER, Mary Elizabeth Wormeley [1822–1904, US novelist]
An American Lady (in *Bentley's Miscellany*)

LATROBE, Charles Joseph [1801–75, Australian traveller and explorer]
The Rambler in Mexico (*The Rambler in Mexico in 1834*)

LATSIS, Mary J. [1927–, US mystery novelist]
*R. B. Dominic (*Murder in High Place*; *Murder Out of Commission*)
*Emma Lathen (*Accounting for Murder*; *By Hook or by Crook*)

LAUDER, Sir Thomas Dick [1784–1848, Scottish writer]
An Eye-Witness; A Hill-Side Preacher; An Improvising Tory; A Member of the Party (all used in *Tait's Edinburgh Magazine*)
Charles Montague Montgomery (*Lochandhu*)

LAUDER, William [d. 1771, Scottish classical scholar and forger]
Philalethes (*Calumny Display'd*)

LAUMER, John Keith [1925–, US science-fiction writer]
Anthony Lebaron (*The Meteor Men*)

LAURIE, Simon Somerville [1829–1909, Scottish academic and educational reformer]
An Old Educationalist (in *Fraser's Magazine*)
Scotus Novanticus (*Ethica, or the Ethics of Reason*; *Metaphysica Nova et Vetusta*)

LAW, Thomas [1759–1834, English writer on finance – lived sometime in Washington]
Justinian (*Remarks on the Report of the Secretary of the Treasury*)

LAW, William [1686–1761, English cleric, philanthropist and mystic]
A Gentleman Near Oxford (*The Oxford Methodists*)

LAWLER, C. F. [1728–1819, English satirist]
Peter Pindar (*Selim, a Tale*)

LAWRENCE, David Herbert [1885–1930, English novelist, poet and writer]
L. H. Davidson (in *The Adelphi*)
Lawrence H. Davison (*Movements in European History*)
Grantorto (in *The Athenaeum*)

LAWRENCE, Frederick [1821–67, English barrister and biographer]
A Barrister (*Culverwell versus Sidebottom*)

LAWRENCE, James Henry [1773–1840, English novelist and writer]
A Detenu (*A Picture of Verdun*)
St Ives (in *Gentleman's Magazine*)

LAWRENCE, John [1753–1839, English horse expert and writer]
A Farmer and a Breeder (*The New Farmer's Calendar*)
Bonington Moubray (*Every Man his Own Brewer*; *A Practical Treatise on Breeding, Rearing and Fattening all Kinds of Domestic Poultry etc.*)
Wm. Henry Scott (*British Field Sports*)

LAWRENCE, Thomas Edward [1888–1935, English archaeologist, soldier and writer; died after a motor-cycle accident]
C. D. (in *The Spectator*)
C. J. G. (in *Jesus College Magazine*)

Colin Dale (used in both *The Spectator* and the *World Traveller and Rambler*)
An Eye-Witness (in *Current History*)
J. C.; S. (both used in the *Royal Air Force College Journal*)
J. H. Ross (*Two Arabic Folk Tales – a Translation*)
T. E. Shaw (*The Forest Giant – a Translation*)

LAWRENCE, Walter Roper [1857–1940, English civil servant in India]
Calcutta (in *Contemporary Review*)

LAWRENCE, William Beach [1800–80, US jurist]
An American Citizen (*The History of Louisiana*)

LAWSON, James [1799–1880, Scottish-born US poet and writer]
A Cosmopolite (*Tales and Sketches*)

LAWSON, James Anthony [1817–87, Irish jurist and political economist]
John Bradley (*Narrative of Travel and Sport in Burmah, Siam etc.*)

LAYMON, Richard Carl [1947–, US gothic novelist]
Richard Kelly (*Tread Softly*; *Midnight's Lair*)

LAYTON, Frank George [1872–1941, English novelist]
Stephen Andrew (*Sable and Motley*; *The Serpent and the Cross*)

LAZARUS, Margaret [1916–, English romantic novelist]
Anna Gilbert (*Flowers for Lunch*; *Look of Innocence*)

LAZENBY, Norman Austin [1914–, English writer]
Hans Vogel (*Man Trap*; *Mind my Innocence*)
Wes Yancey (*The Hard Faces*; *Easy Gold*)

LEA, Henry Charles [1825–1909, US publisher and historian]
Mizpah (*The Bible View of Polygamy*)

LEAF, Wilbur Munro [1905–76, US writer and illustrator for children]
John Calvert (*Gwendolyn the Goose*)

LEAKEY, Caroline Woolmer [1827–81, Australian devotional writer]
Oliver Keese (*The Broad Arrow*)

LEAR, Edward [1812–88, English humorist, artist and writer]
Derry Down Derry (*A Book of Nonsense*)

LEASOR, James [1923–, English writer]
Andrew MacAllan (*Diamond Hard*; *Fusillade*)

LEATHAM, William Henry [1815–89, English politician and poet]
Alpha (*The Three Poets*)

LEATHES, Sir Stanley Mordaunt [1861–1938, English historian]
Numa Minimus (*Vox Clamantis*)

LE BLOND, Mrs Elizabeth Alice Frances [1860–1934, Irish traveller, alpinist and writer]
Mrs Main (*Adventures on the Roof of the World*)

LE BRETON, Mrs Anna Letitia [1808–85, English writer]
One of a Literary Family (*Memories of Seventy Years*)

LECKIE, Peter Martin [1890–?, US novelist]
Peter Martin (*Summer in 3000*)

LECKY, William Edward Hartpole [1838–1903, Irish poet, historian and politician]
Hibernicus (*Friendship and Other Poems*)

LEDERER, Paul Joseph [1944–, US writer]
Elizabeth Wolfe (*Boudicca*; Ice Castle)

LEDYARD, Isaac [fl. 1784, US writer]
Mentor (*Mentor's reply to Phocion's etc.*)

LEE, Albert [1852–1935, English cleric and archivist]
Lindon Romaine (*The Frown of Majesty*; *Twixt Love and Duty*; *The Queen's Displeasure*)

LEE, Arthur [1740–92, American lawyer, physician and diplomat]
An American (*An Essay in Vindication of the Continental Colonies*)
An American Wanderer (*An American Wanderer in Europe*)
Junius Americanus (*Letters of Junius Americanus*; *The Political Detection*)
Monitor (*Letters of Monitor*)
An Old Member of Parliament (*An Appeal to the People of Great Britain*)

LEE, Arthur Stanley Gould [1894–1975, English airman and biographer]
Arthur Lee Gould (*An Airplane in the Arabian Nights*)

LEE, Austin [1904–, English writer]
John Austwick (*Hubberthwaite Horror*; *Murder in the Borough Library*)

LEE, Charles [1731–82, American physician and soldier in the Revolutionary War]
Junius Americanus (in the *Public Advertiser*)

LEE, Eleanor Percy [fl. 1843, US poet]
*Two Sisters of the West (*Poems*; *The Wife of Leon and other Poems*)

LEE, Elsie [1912–87, US historical novelist]
Elsie Cromwell (*Ivorstone Manor*; *The Governess*)
Norman Daniels (*Sam Benedict*)
Jane Gordon (*Two Hearts Apart*)
Lee Sheridan (*The Bachelor's Cookbook*)

LEE, Francis [1661–1719, English physician and writer]
A Lay Gentleman (*History of Montanism*)

LEE, Manfred B. [1905–71, US crime writer]
*Ellery Queen (*Calamity Town*; *The Chinese Orange Mystery*)
*Barnaby Ross (*The Tragedy of Z*)

LEE, Norman [1905–62, English crime and mystery novelist]
Raymond Armstrong (*The Sinister Widow*; *Dangerous Limelight*)
Mark Corrigan (*Sinner Takes All*; *Dumb as They Come*)

Robertson Hobart (*The Case of the Shaven Blonde*; *Death of a Love*)

LEE, Mrs Rachel Frances A. D. [1774–1829, English writer; she was the plaintiff in a celebrated abduction trial]
Philopatria (*An Essay on Government*)

LEE, Richard Henry [1732–94, American orator and politician]
The Federal Farmer (*Observations Leading to a Fair Examination etc.*)

LEE, Mrs Sarah [1791–1856, English traveller, natural historian and illustrator]
A Traveller (*Stories of Strange Lands*)

LEE, Wayne Cyril [1917–, US writer]
Lee Sheldon (*Doomed Planet*)

LEE-RICHARDSON, James [1913–, Irish writer]
Desmond Dunne (*Yoga Made Easy*)

LEECH, John [1817–64, English humorist, cartoonist and illustrator]
A. Pen Esq. (*Etchings and Sketchings*)

LEEDS, William Henry [1786–1866, English architectural writer]
Candidus (in *Fraser's Magazine*)

LEES, Edwin [1800–87, English botanist and natural historian]
Ambrose Florence (*The Stranger's Guide to Worcester*)

LEES, Sir Harcourt [1776–1852, English cleric and pamphleteer]
A Clergyman of the Established Church and No Saint (*The Antidote*)

LEES, James Cameron [1834–1913, Scottish cleric and antiquarian]
Thomas Jeans (*The Tommiebeg Shootings*)
Rev. Rory M'Rory (*M'Stotties Tour: a Highland Yarn*)

LE FANU, Eleanor Frances [1845–1903, Irish novelist]
Russell Gray (in *Dublin University Magazine* and for *Up and Down the World* and *Never for Ever*)

LE FANU, Joseph Sheridan [1814–73, Irish journalist and novelist]
Charles de Cresseron; Rev. Francis Purcell (both used in *Dublin University Magazine*)
John Figwood (*The Prelude*)

LEFEVRE, Sir George William [1798–1846, Scottish physician and Eastern European traveller]
A Travelling Physician (*Life of a Travelling Physician*)

LE FEVRE, Laura Zenobia [fl. 1944, US writer]
Zenobia Bird (*Willard Crosby, Airman*; *The Return of the Tide*)

LEFFINGWELL, Albert [1845–1917, US physician and writer]
Dana Chambers (*The Frightened Man*; *Rope for an Ape*)
Giles Jackson (*Witch's Moon*; *Court of Shadows*)
Albert Tracey (*Ramble through Japan without a Guide*; *Illegitimacy and the Influence of Seasons upon Conduct*)

LE GALLIENNE, Richard [1866–1947, English journalist, poet and novelist]
Exul (*Twilight and Candle-Shade*)
Logroller (in *The Star*)

LEGGETT, William [1801–39, US journalist]
A Country Schoolmaster (*Tales and Sketches*)
A Midshipman of the US Navy (*Leisure Hours at Sea*)

LE GRICE, Charles Valentine [1773–1858, English cleric and writer]
Cergiel (*The Pauper's Funeral*)
Civis (*Letters on Church Subjects in the West of Cornwall*)
Gronovius (*A General Theorem for a **** Coll.*)
Vigilans (*Letters on Church Questions*)

LEIBER, Stanley [1923–, US writer]
Stan Lee (used for his prolific comic and science-fiction magazine writing)

LEIFCHILD, John R. [1815–?, English mining engineer and writer]
A Traveller Underground (*Our Coal and Our Coal-Pits*)

LEIGH, Benjamin Watkins [1781–1849, US lawyer and politician]
An Eminent Citizen of Virginia (*Letters of Algernon Sydney in Defence of Civil Liberty*)

LEIGH, Chandos [1791–1850, 1st Baron Leigh; poet and writer]
A Gloucestershire County Gentleman (*Three Tracts by a Gloucestershire County Gentleman*)

LEIGH, Percival [1813–89, English surgeon, humorist and satirist]
A Cypher; Quiz; Jeremiah Singleton, Bachelor of Physic; Solomon Swift (all used in *Bentley's Miscellany*)
Mr Pips (in *Punch*)
Paul Prendergast (used in both *Punch* and *Bentley's Miscellany*)

LEIGH, Roberta [fl. 1980, English romantic novelist]
Rachel Lindsay (*Healing Hands*; *Castle in the Trees*)
Janey Scott (*Memory of Love*)

LEIGHTON, John [1822–1912, Scottish artist, satirist and writer on art]
Luke Limner (*London Out of Town*; *Suggestions in Design*; *London Cries and Public Edifices*; *Madre Natura versus the Moloch of Fashion*)

LEIGHTON, Mrs Marie C. [d. 1941, English novelist]
Marie Connor (*Sweet Magdalen*; *Two Black Pearls*)

LEIGHTON, Robert [1822–69, Scottish poet]
Robin (*Poems*)

LEISK, David Johnson [1906–75, US writer and illustrator for children]
Crockett Johnson (*Harold and the Purple Crayon*; *Barnaby and Mr O'Malley*)

LELAND, Aaron Whitney [1787–1871, US cleric and theologian]
Expositor (*A Letter to the Citizens of Charleston*)

LELAND, Charles Godfrey [1824–1903, US lawyer, humorist and writer]
Hans Breitmann (*Hans Breitmann's Ballads*)
Mace Sloper (*Ballads*)

LEMOINE, Henry [1756–1812, English writer and essayist]
Allan MacLeod (*Lackington's Confessions Rendered into Narrative*)

LE MOINE, Sir James Macpherson [1825–1912, Canadian historian and writer]
Cosmopolite (*The Tourists Note-Book for Quebec*)

LEMON, Mark [1809–70, English dramatist, novelist and humorist; first editor of *Punch*]
Sydney Bywater (in *Bentley's Miscellany*)
Uncle Mark (in *Punch*)

LENNOX, Charlotte [1720–1804, American-born biographer and writer – lived mostly in London]
A Young Lady (*Poems on Several Occasions*)

LENNOX, Lord William Pitt [1799–1881, English soldier, novelist and writer]
An Ex-Aide-de-Camp (*Three Years with the Duke*)

LENT, Blair [1930–, US writer for children]
Ernest Small (*Baba Yaga*)

LEON, Henry Cecil [1902–76, English jurist and humorist]
Henry Cecil (*Full Circle*; *Brothers in Law*)
Clifford Maxwell (*I Married the Girl*)

LEONARD, Daniel [1740–1829, American lawyer and loyalist]
Massachusettensis (in the *Massachusett Gazette and Post Boy* and for *The Origin of the American Contest with Great Britain*)
A Native of New England (*The Present Political State of Massachusett-Bay*)

LEONARD, Lionel Frederick [1881–1954, English librettist and dramatist]
Frederick Lonsdale (*The Maid of the Mountains*; *The Last Mrs Cheyney*)

LEROY, Amelie C. [1851–1934, French-born English novelist and writer for children]
Esme Stuart (*A Faire Damzell*; *Muriel's Marriage*; *Harum Scarum*)

LESLEY, Peter [1819–1903, US geologist]
John W. Allen, Jun. (*Paul Dreiffus, his Holiday Abroad*)

LESLIE, Charles [1650–1722, Irish cleric and controversial pamphleteer]
A Gentleman in Scotland (*Letter from a Gentleman in Scotland to his Friend in England*)
A Gentleman in the City (*A Letter from a Gentleman in the City concerning Prosecution of the Rehearsal*)
An Impartial Hand (*Some Seasonable Reflections upon the Quakers*)
A Man of Leisure (*A New Farce*)
Misodolos (*The Good Old-Cause or, Lying in Truth*)
One Called an High-Churchman (*The History of the Church*; *The Wolf Stript of his Shepherd's Cloathing*)
Philalethes (*The Rehearsal*; *A View of the Times, their Principles etc.*)
A Student of the Temple (*The Best Answer Ever Was Made*)
A True Trojan (*Beaucoup de Bruit pour une Aumelette*)

LESLIE, Eliza [1787–1858, US writer]
A Lady of Philadelphia (*Seventy Five Receipts*; *The Young Americans*)

LESLIE, Henrietta [d. 1946, English novelist and dramatist]
Gladys Mendl (*The Roundabout*; *The Straight Road*)

LESLIE, John [1527–96, Scottish cleric; Bishop of Ross; he was an adviser to Mary, Queen of Scots]
Morgan Philippes, Bachelor of Divinitie (*A Treatise Concerning the Honour of Marie, Queen of Scotland*)

LESLIE, Sir John [1766–1832, Scottish scientist and mathematician]
A Gentleman (*The Connoisseur or, Modern Fashions*)
Philotechnus (*Remarks for a Series of Years on Barometrical Scales*)

LESLIE, Peter [1922–, English journalist and writer]
Patrick MacNee (*Deadline; Dead Duck*)

LESLIE, Thomas Edward Cliffe [1826–82, Irish economist and academic]
A Professor of Political Economy (in *MacMillan's Magazine*)

LESSER, Milton [1928–, US science-fiction, crime and mystery writer]
*Adam Chase (*The Golden Ape*)
Andrew Frazer (*The Fall of Manny Moor; Find Ellen Hardin*)
Stephen Marlowe (*Dead on Arrival; Double Trouble*)
Ellery Queen (*Dead Man's Tale*)
Jason Ridgway (*Adam's Fall; Hardly a Man is Now Alive*)
Christopher H. Thames (*Violence is Golden*)

LESSING, Doris [1919–, Persian-born English novelist and writer]
Jane Somers (*The Diary of Jane Somers; The Diary of a Good Neighbour*)

LESTER, Charles Edwards [1815–90, US cleric and writer]
An American (in *Bentley's Miscellany*)
*The Berkeley Men (*The Napoleon Dynasty; From Charles Bonaparte to Napoleon II*)
Hermitage (*Life of Gen. Frank Pierce the Granite Statesman*)

L'ESTRANGE, Charles James [1880–1947, English writer for children]
*Herbert Strang (*The Adventures of Harry Rochester; The Air Patrol; Martin of Old London; The Boyhood of the King; The Long Trail*)

L'ESTRANGE, Hamon [1674–1767, English legal writer]
A Civil Magistrate (*A Legacy to the World*)

LETTSOM, John Coakley [1744–1815, West Indies-born English physician and writer]
J. C. Mottles; One of the Faculty (both used in *Gentleman's Magazine*)

LEVER, Charles James [1806–72, Irish novelist, physician and writer]
Bob Considine; Milo M'Caskey; An Old Hand (all used in *Blackwood's Magazine*)
*Hans Daumling; Guido Mountjoy; Printer's Devil (all used in *Dublin University Magazine*)
Paul Goslett (in *St Paul's Magazine*)
Harry Lorrequer (*Arthur O'Leary*)
Cornelius O'Dowd (*Cornelius O'Dowd upon Men and Women*)
Horace Templeton (*Diary and Notes of Horace Templeton*)
Tilbury Tramp (*Tales of the Trains: being Some Chapters of Railroad Romance*)

LEVERSON, Ada [1865–1936, English journalist, parodist and novelist]
A Debutante (in *Punch* for *Letters of a Debutante*)

LEVERSON, Henry Astbury [fl. 1875, Irish sporting writer]
The Old Shekarry (*The Camp Fire; The Forest and the Field*)

LEVIN, Henry Bernard [1928–, English journalist and writer]
Felix Battle (used for journalism)
A. E. Cherryman (in *Truth Magazine*)
Taper (in *The Spectator*)

LEVINE, William [1881–?, US writer]
Will Levinrew (*The Wheelchair Corpse; Murder from the Grave*)

LEVY, Benjamin [1811–75, English lawyer, theatre manager and early science-fiction writer]
Benjamin Lumley (*Reminiscences of the Opera*)

LEVY, Clifton Harby [1867–?, US rabbi and religious writer]
Clifton Harby (*The Bible in Art*)

LEVY, Solomon Lazarus [1859–1926, English Shakespearian scholar and founder of the *Dictionary of National Biography*]
Sir Sidney Lee (name change by deed-poll)

LEWES, George Henry [1817–78, English journalist and writer – companion of George Eliot]
Vivian Latouche (in *Fraser's Magazine*)
Lawrence Slingsby (*Sunshine through the Clouds*)
Vivian (in *The Leader*)

LEWIN, Michael Sultan [fl. 1950, English writer]
Douglas Furber (*Just Another Murder*)

LEWIN, William Charles James [1852–97, English actor]
William Terris (*Ruy Blas – a Translation*)

LEWIS, Alfred Henry [1858–1914, US novelist]
Dan Quin (*Wolfville; Confessions of a Detective*)

LEWIS, Alonzo [1794–1861, US poet and antiquarian]
The Lynn Bard (*Forest Flowers and Sea-Shells; Poems*)

LEWIS, Angelo John [1839–1919, English barrister and writer]
Prof. Louis Hoffman (*Tricks with Cards; Conjuror Dick; Modern Magic*)

LEWIS, Charles Bertrand [1842–1924, US journalist and humorist]
The Detroit Free Press Man (*Quads Odds*)
M. Quad (*Field, Fort and Fleet, the late War 1861–1863; Under Fire; The Life and Troubles of Mr Bowser; The Lime-Kiln Club; Mr and Mrs Bowser; Sawed-Off Sketches*)

LEWIS, Clifford [1912–, English writer for children]
*Judith M. Berrisford (*Jackie Won a Pony*)

LEWIS, Clive Staples [1898–1963, Irish novelist, poet, critic and writer for children]
N. W. Clerk (*A Grief Observed*)
Clive Hamilton (*Dymer; Spirits in Bondage*)
N. W. (used for poetry contributions to *Punch* between 1946 and 1958)

LEWIS, Dominic Bevan Wyndham [1894–1969, Welsh journalist, biographer and humorist]
At the Sign of the Blue Moon (in the *Daily Mail*, 1925–30)
Crazy News Reel (in the *Daily Mail* from 1933)
Beachcomber (in the *Daily Express*, 1919–24)
Mustard and Cress (in the *Sunday Referee*, 1931–3)
Timothy Shy (in the *News Chronicle* from 1934 and for *The Terror of St Trinian's* and *Beyond the Headlines*)

LEWIS, Mrs Estelle Anna Blanche [1824–80, US poet, essayist and writer]
S. Anna Lewis (*Child of the Sea and Other Poems*)
Sarah Ann Lewis (*Records of the Heart*)
Stella (*Leaves of my Diary; The King's Stratagem*)

LEWIS, Harry Sinclair [1885–1951, US novelist]
F. (in the *San Francisco Bulletin* in 1909 for *Talks with a Typist*)
Tom Graham (*Hike and the Aeroplane*)

LEWIS, John [1675–1746, English cleric, biographer and antiquarian]
A Friend to Liberty and Property (*Advice to Posterity*)

LEWIS, John Delaware [1828–84, Russian-born English barrister and writer]
John Smith of Smith Hall, Gent. (*Sketches of Cantabs*)
An Undergraduate (*Our College, Leaves from an Undergraduate*)

LEWIS, John Royston [1933–, Welsh crime writer]
Roy Lewis (*A Question of Degree; Double Take*)

David Springfield (*The Company Executive and the Law*)

LEWIS, Mary [1921–, English writer for children]
*Judith M. Berrisford (*Jackie and the Pony*)

LEWIS, Matthew Gregory [1775–1818, English dramatist and novelist – died at sea when returning from the West Indies]
Monk Lewis (his sobriquet)
A West India Proprietor (*Journal of a Proprietor*)

LEWIS, Thomas [1689–1749, English cleric and controversialist]
A Clergyman (*Churches No Charnel-Houses*)

LEWIS, Waller [1711–81, English writer on card games]
Cam (*Whist, What to Lead*)

LEWISON, William H. [1822–57, US journalist]
Julius Caesar Hannibal (*Scientific Discourses*)

LEY, John [1583–1662, English Puritan cleric and religious writer]
Theophilus Philadelphus (*Exceptions Against Two Injurious Petitions*)

LEY, Robert Arthur [1921–68, English science-fiction writer]
Arthur Sellings (*Junk Day; Telepath*)

LEYBOURN, William [1626–1700, English astronomer, mathematician and compiler of the first ready-reckoner]
A True Lover of the Mathematicks (*The Description and Use of Gunter's Quadrant*)
Oliver Wallinby (*Planometria*)

LIEBER, Francis [1800–72, German-born US historian]
The Stranger (*The Stranger in America*)

LIEBERMAN, Mortimer [1905–63, US journalist]
Lee Mortimer (*USA: Confidential; Woman: Confidential*)

LIGHTHALL, William D. [1857–1954, Canadian barrister, poet, critic and historian]
Wilfrid Chateauclair (*The Young Seigneur*)

LILBURNE, John [1614–57, English Quaker and political controversialist]
Five Small Beagles (*The Hunting of the Foxes from Newmarket to Whitehall*)
Lionel Hurbin, Gentleman (*A Plea or Protest made by William Prynne*)
A Well-Wisher to the Saints Now Reigning on Earth (*An Hue and Cry after the Fundamental Lawes*)

LILIENTHAL, David [1899–1981, US lawyer and writer]
David Ely (*Seconds; The Tour*)

LILLIE, Mrs Lucy Cecil [1855–?, US novelist]
L. C. White (*The Story of English Literature for Young Readers*)

LILLY, William [1602–81, English historian and astrologer]
The Man in the Moon (*Some Further Remarks on Mr Gladstone's Defence of Scorpio*)
Merlinus Anglicus, Junior (*The English Merlin Revived: an Almanac*)
Zadkiel (*Astrology and a Grammar of Astrology*)

LINCOLN, Levi [1749–1820, US lawyer and politician]
A Farmer (*A Farmer's Letter to the People*)

LIND, John [1737–81, English barrister and expert on Poland]
An Eminent Person (*The Declaration of Independence – with Notes*)
An Englishman (*An Englishman's Answer to the People of Great Britain*)

LINDO, Mark Prager [1819–77, English-born Dutch journalist and writer]
De Oude Herr Smits (*Dutch Stories; Letters and Confessions*)

LINDSAY, Alexander William Crawford [1812–80, 25th Earl of Crawford; traveller, historian and genealogist]
Johannes Boustrophedonides (in *Blackwood's Magazine*)

LINDSAY, Jack [1900–90, Australian poet and writer]
Richard Preston (*Shadow and Flame*)

LINDSAY, Joan [1896–1984, Australian writer]
Serena Livingstone-Stanley (*Through Darkest Pondelayo*)

LINDSEY, Theophilus [1723–1808, English Unitarian cleric and religious writer]
A Late Member of the University (*Vindiciae Priestleyanae*)
Gotlieb Pansmouzer (*The Polish Partition Illustrated*)

LINDSLEY, John Berrien [1822–97, US physician and journalist]
A Poor-Rich Man (*Our Ruin: its Causes and Cure*)

LINEBARGER, Paul Myron Anthony [1913–66, US orientalist and science-fiction writer]
Felix C. Forrest (*Ria; Carola*)
Carmichael Smith (*Atomsk, a Novel of Suspense*)
Cordwainer Smith (*You Will Never be the Same; Space Lords*)

LINEBARGER, Paul Myron Wentworth [1871–1939, US lawyer and writer]
Paul Myron (*Bugle Rhymes from France; Chinese Interpretive Lyrics*)

LINES, Samuel [1778–1863, English designer and art teacher]
An Unfortunate Schoolmaster (*Stanzas*)

LINGARD, John [1771–1851, English Catholic cleric and historian]
A Catholic (*A New Version of the Four Gospels*)
A Catholic Divine (*A General Vindication of the Catholic's Remarks*)

A Lancaster Idolator (*Is the Bible the Only Rule?*)

LININGTON, Elizabeth [1921–88, US mystery writer]
Anne Blaisdell (*Consequence of Crime; No Villain Need Be*)
Lesley Egan (*Look Back on Death; Scenes of Crime*)
Egan O'Neill (*The Anglophile*)
Dell Shannon (*Ace of Spades; Felony File*)

LINN, John Blair [1777–1804, US cleric]
A Young Gentleman of New York (*Miscellaneous Works*)

LINSKILL, Mary [1840–98, English novelist]
Stephen Yorke (*Tales of the North Riding; Cleveden*)

LINTON, Mrs Eliza Lynn [1822–98, English journalist, biographer and novelist]
The Girl of the Period (in *Saturday Review*)

LINTON, William James [1812–98, English engraver, writer and social and political reformer]
A. N. Broome (*The American Odyssey; Voices of the Dead*)
Spartacus (in *The Nation* and for *Poems*)

LIPPINCOTT, Mrs Sara Jane Clarke [1823–1904, US poet and writer for children]
Grace Greenwood (*History of my Pets; Forest Tragedy*)
Penn Shirley (*Boy Donald; Young Master Kirke*)

LIPSCOMBE, George [1773–1846, English surgeon, antiquarian and writer]
Viator (in *Gentleman's Magazine*)

LIPSON, Edna [1914–, English novelist]
Gerda Charles (*Great Short Stories of the World*, of which she was editor)

LISTER, Edith [1859–1938, English novelist]
Noel Ainsleigh (in *Temple Bar*)

LISTER, Thomas [d. 1828, English writer]
Hampden (*A Mirror for Princes*)

LITHIBY, Sir John [1852–1936, English
barrister]
A Barrister-at-Law (*Shaw's Manual of
Vaccination Law*)

LITTLE, James Stanley [1856–1940, English
journalist and writer]
Little Jim (*What the Boy Thought*)

LITTLETON, Adam [1627–94, English
cleric and lexicographer]
Redman Westcot (*Jani Anglorum Facies
Altera; The Reverse or Back-Face of the
English Janus*)

LIVERMORE, George [1809–65, US
merchant and writer]
The Antiquary (*The Origin of the New
England Primer*)

LIVINGSTON, Brockholst [1757–1823, US
jurist and political pamphleteer]
Aquiline Nimblechops, Democrat
(*Democracy – an Epic Poem*)

LIVINGSTON, Philip [1716–78, American
politician]
A Citizen (*The Other Side of the Question*)

LIVINGSTON, Robert R. [1747–1813, US
lawyer and politician]
Cato (in the *American Remembrancer* and for
Examination of the Treaty of Amity)

LIVINGSTON, William [1723–90, American
lawyer and politician]
A Farmer of New Jersey (*Observations on
Government*)
Hortensius (in the *New Jersey Gazette*)
Tyro-Philologis (letters in the *New York
Weekly Post-Boy*)

LLOYD, Charles [1735–73, English political
secretary and writer]
An Old Man of Business (*Examination of the
Boasted Disinterestedness of a late Rt. Hon.
Gentleman*)

LLOYD, Charles [1766–1829, English cleric]
A Dissenting Minister (*Particulars of the
Life of a Dissenting Minister*)
Philalethes (*The Epistles of St Paul and St
James*)

LLOYD, Charles Ellis [d. 1939, Welsh
barrister, novelist and politician]
Ellis Lloyd (*Scarlet Nest*)

LLOYD, David [1635–92, English cleric and
historical biographer]
Oliver Foulis (*Cabala*)

LLOYD, Henry [1720–83, British soldier and
historian; attached to French, Prussian,
Russian and Austrian armies]
A General Officer who Served Several
Campaigns in the Austrian Army (*The
History of the Late War in Germany; A
History of the War Between the King of
Prussia etc.*)

LLOYD, Humphrey [1800–81, Irish scientist
and academic]
A Member of the Revision Committee of
the Church of Ireland (*The Doctrine of
Absolution*)

LLOYD, Richard D. V. Llewellyn [1907–83,
Welsh novelist and dramatist]
Richard Llewellyn (*How Green Was my
Valley*)

LLOYD, William [1627–1717, English cleric
and controversialist; Bishop of Worcester]
A Person of Quality (*An Answer to the
Bishop of Oxford*)

LOBAUGH, Elma K. [fl. 1955, US writer]
Kenneth Lowe (*Catalyst; No Tears for
Shirley Minton*)

LOCH, Frederick [1889–1954, Australian
writer]
Sydney de Loghe (*The Straits Impregnable;
One Crowded Hour*)

LOCK, Arnold Charles Cooper [fl. 1933,
Australian writer]
Charles Cooper (*The Turkish Spy; The Soul
of Tak-Ming*)

LOCKE, Arthur [1872–1932, English civil
servant]
A. R. Thurlocke (*The Rustic Choir and
Other Poems*)

LOCKE, David Ross [1833–88, US journalist, novelist and humorist]
Petroleum Vesuvius Nasby (*Eastern Fruit and Western Dishes*; *Ekkoes from Kentucky*; *Hannah Jane*; *Morals of Abu Ben Adhem*; *Swingin Round the Cirkle*; *The Nasby Papers*)
Yours Trooly (*Divers Views, Opinions and Prophecies of Yours Trooly*)

LOCKE, George Walter [1936–, English science-fiction writer]
Gordon Walters (in *New Worlds Magazine*)

LOCKE, John [1632–1704, English academic, philosopher and writer]
Philanthropus (*A Second Letter Concerning Toleration*)

LOCKHART, Arthur John [1850–1926, US cleric and writer]
Pastor Felix (*The Papers of Pastor Felix*; *Beside the Narraguagus and Other Poems*)
*Two Brothers (*The Masque of Minstrels*)

LOCKHART, Burton Wellesley [1855–1937, US cleric]
*Two Brothers (*The Masque of Minstrels*)

LOCKHART, John Gibson [1794–1854, Scottish lawyer, novelist and biographer]
John Bull (*Letter to Lord Byron*)
Corduroy; N. (both used in *The Sale Room*)
Peter Morris the Odontist (*Peter's Letters to his Kinsfolk*)
*Sir Morgan O'Doherty; Phillipus; *Timothy Tickler; William Wastle (all used in *Blackwood's Magazine*)

LOCKHART, Laurence William Maxwell [1831–82, Scottish soldier, novelist and journalist]
Major Dionysius Corkhardt-Unattached (in *Blackwood's Magazine*)

LOCKHART, William [1820–92, English Catholic cleric and writer]
One of his Oldest Living Disciples (*Cardinal Newman*)
A Pilgrim from New York to Old Rome (*Saint Etheldreda's and Old London*)

LOCKRIDGE, Richard [1898–1982, US drama critic and writer]
Francis Richards (*A Plate of Red Herrings*)

LOCKWOOD, Ingersoll [1841–1918, US writer and lecturer]
Irwin Longman (*The Travels and Adventures of Little Baron Trump*; *In Varying Mood*)

LOCKWOOD, Ralph Ingersoll [1798–1858, US lawyer, novelist and legal writer]
Mr Smith (*Rosine Laval*; *The Insurgents*)

LOCKYER, Nicholas [1611–85, English cleric and theologian]
A Friend to Truth and Peace (*Some Seasonable Queries upon the Late Act against Conventicles*)

LODER, John de Vere [fl. 1935, English writer]
*Cornelius Cofyn (*The Death-Riders*)

LODGE, Oliver William Foster [1878–1955, English dramatist, poet and writer]
William Foster (*The Candle*)

LOEWENGARD, Heidi Huberta Freybe [1912–81, German-born US mystery novelist]
Martha Albrand (*Intermission*; *No Surrender*)
Christine Lambert (*A Sudden Woman*)

LOFFT, Capell [1806–73, English barrister, poet and writer]
A Fellow of a College (*Self-Formation or the History of an Individual Mind*)
R. E. Storer (*The New Testament: Suggestions for Reformation of the Text*)

LOFLAND, John [1798–1849, US poet]
The Milford Bard (*The Harp of Delaware*; *Poems and Essays*)

LOFTIE, William John [1839–1911, English cleric and antiquarian]
A Fellow of the Society of Antiquaries (*Tourists' Guide Round About London*)

LOFTS, Norah [1904–83, English novelist]
Juliet Astley (*Copsi Castle*; *Fall of Midas*)
Peter Curtis (*Dead March in Three Keys*; *The Devil's Own*)

LOGAN, George [1678–1755, Scottish cleric and writer]
A Minister of the Church of Scotland (*A Continuation of the Humble Inquiry etc.*)

LOGAN, George [1753–1821, US physician and politician]
An American Farmer (*Letters Addressed to the Yeomanry*)
A Farmer (*Five Letters Addressed to the Yeomanry*)

LOGUE, Christopher [1926–, English playwright, poet and writer]
Count Palmiro Vicarion (*Lust, a Pornographic Novel*)

LOMAX, Herbert [fl. 1904, English writer for boys]
Herbert Maxwell (in *Union Jack*)

LOMBINO, Salvatore A. [1926–, US crime and mystery writer]
Curt Cannon (*I Like 'em Tough*; *I'm Cannon – for Hire*)
Hunt Collins (*Cut Me In*; *Tomorrow's World*)
Ezra Hannon (*Doors*)
Evan Hunter (*The Blackboard Jungle*; *Find the Feathered Serpent*)
Ed McBain (*Blood Relatives*; *Hail to the Chief*)
Richard Marsten (*Rocket to Luna*; *Danger: Dinosaurs*)

LONDON, John Griffith [1876–1916, US adventurer and novelist]
Jack London (*The Call of the Wild*; *White Fang*)

LONG, Amelia Reynolds [fl. 1945, English crime writer]
Patricia Laing (*If I Should Murder*; *Stone Dead*)
Adrian Reynolds (*The Round Table Murders*; *Formula for Murder*)
Peter Reynolds (*Behind the Evidence*)

LONG, Charles Edward [1796–1861, English historian]
Blanche Croix (in *Gentleman's Magazine*)

A Jamaica Proprietor (*Negro Emancipation No Philanthropy*)

LONG, Edward [1734–1813, English barrister, historian and writer]
Nicholas Babble (in *The Prater*)
Counsellor Clearpoint (*The Trial of Farmer Carter's Dog*)
Frank Cobham (*The Anti-Gallican or, the History and Adventures of Henry Cobham Esq.*)
A Planter (*Candid Reflections upon the Negro Cause*)

LONG, George [1800–79, English classical scholar and lawyer]
A Member of the University of Cambridge (*Hannibal's Passage of the Alps*)

LONG, James [1814–87, English missionary in India]
A British Subject (*Central Asia and British India*)
A Native (*Nil Darpan*)

LONG, Lily Augusta [d. 1927, US poet and novelist]
Roman Doubleday (*The Saintsbury Affair*; *The Hemlock Avenue Mystery*)

LONG, Lois [1901–74, US journalist]
Lipstick (in the *New Yorker Magazine*)

LONG, Margaret [1888–1952, English playwright and novelist]
Marjorie Bowen (*The Glen o'Weeping*; *I Will Maintain*; *Mr Washington*)
Robert Paye (*The Devil's Jig*; *Julia Roseingrave*)
George R. Preedy (*General Crack*; *The Rocklitz*; *Tumult in the North*)
Joseph Shearing (*Forget Me Not*; *Moss Rose*; *Mignonette*)
John Winch (*Idler's Gate*)

LONG, Roger [1680–1770, English cleric, academic and astronomer]
Dicaiophilus Cantabrigiensis (in *The Rights of Churches and Colleges Defended*)

LONG, William Joseph [1866–1952, US cleric and natural historian]
Peter Rabbit (*The Little Brother to the Bear*; *Northern Trails*; *Brier-Patch Philosophy*)

LONGFELLOW, Henry Wadsworth [1807–82, US poet and writer]
An American (*Outre-Mer or, a Pilgrimage to the Old World*)
Joshua Coffin (*History of Newbury*)
Hans Hammergaffstein (*Nights Revealings from the ancient Sclavonian etc.*)
H. W. L. (*Nights Revealings from the Ancient Sclavonian of Hans Hammergaffstein*)
The Instructer (*French Exercises ... from Wanostrocht*)

LONGHURST, Percy William [fl. 1907, English writer for boys]
Brian Kingston (in *Gem*)

LONGLEY, Charles Thomas [1794–1868, English cleric; Archbishop of Canterbury]
A Clergyman of the Church of England (*The Brothers' Controversy*)

LONGMORE, George [1793–1867, Canadian-born English soldier and writer]
Launcelot Longstaff (*The Charivari or Canadian Poetics*)

LONGRIGG, Roger Erskine [1929–, Scottish crime and mystery writer]
Laura Black (*Castle Raven*; *Wild Cat*)
Ivor Drummond (*Man with a Tiny Head*; *Frog in the Moonflower*)
Rosalind Erskine (*Passion Flower Hotel*)
Frank Parrish (*Fire in the Barley*; *Snare in the Dark*)
Domini Taylor (*Mother Love*; *Suffer Little Children*)

LONGSTAFF, Gilbert Conrad [1884–1964, English traveller and writer]
Gilbert Thorne (*Poems*)

LONGSTREET, Augustus Baldwin [1790–1870, US cleric, judge and humorist]
A Native Georgian (*Georgia Scenes, Characters etc.*)

Bob Short (in the *Georgia Sentinel*)

LONGSTREET, Stephen [1907–, US novelist]
Thomas Burton (*Blond Bird*)
Paul Haggard (*Death Walks on Cat Feet*; *Death Talks Shop*)
David Ormsbee (*The Sound-Fan American*)
Henri Weiner (*Crime on the Cuff*)

LONGUEVILLE, Thomas [1844–1922, Welsh banker and writer]
The Prig (*Egosophy*)
A Romish Recusant (*The Life of Archbishop Laud*)

LOOMIS, Noel [1905–, US science-fiction writer]
Silas Water (*The Man With Absolute Motion*)

LORD, Grace Virginia [d. 1885, US novelist]
Virginia Champlin (*Shadowed by a Detective*)

LORD, John Keast [1818–72, English naturalist and veterinary surgeon]
The Wanderer (*At Home in the Wilderness*)

LORD, Nathan [1793–1870, US cleric]
A Northern Presbyter (*A Letter of Inquiry to Ministers of the Gospel*)

LORD, Phillip Haynes [1902–, US writer]
Seth Parker (*Sunday at Seth Parker's*; *Way Back Home*)

LORD, William W. [1819–1907, US cleric and poet]
The Rector of Christ Church, Vicksburg (*Our Citizenship in the Church*)

LORENZ, Frederic [fl. 1956, US writer]
Larry Holden (*Dead Wrong*; *The Savage Chase*)

LOTHROP, Harriet Mulford Stone [1844–1924, US writer for children]
Margaret Sidney (*A Little Maid of Concord Town*; *So as by Fire*; *Phronsie Pepper*)

LOUDON, John Claudius [1783–1843, Scottish horticulturist and writer]
A Practical Farmer (*A Treatise on the Culture of Wheat*)

A Scotch Farmer and Land Agent (*Utility of Agricultural Knowledge for the Landed Gentry*)

A Scotch Farmer now Farming in Middlesex (*An Immediate and Effectual Mode of Raising the Rental etc.*)

LOVE, John [1695–1750, Scottish educationalist]
Philo-Buchananus (*A Letter to a Gentleman in Edinburgh*)

LOVECRAFT, Howard Phillips [1890–1937, US fantasy and horror novelist]
Humphrey Littlewit (in the *United Amateur* magazine)
Ward Phillips (in *The Philosopher* and in *Pine Cones* magazines)
Clarke Ashton Smith (in *L'Alouette: a Magazine of Verse*)
Augustus T. Swift (letters to *Argosy Magazine*)
Lewis Theobald Jun. (used in the following magazines: the *United Co-Operative*; *The Tryout*; *The Vagrant*; *The Wolverine*; *Marginalia*)
Albert Frederick Willie (in *The Vagrant*)
Zoilus (in *The Wolverine*)

LOVEDAY, John [1742–1809, English scholar and writer]
Academicus; Antiquarius; Vindex (all used in *Gentleman's Magazine*)

LOVELL, Robert [1770–96, English merchant and poet]
Moschus (*Poems by Bion and Moschus*)

LOVER, Samuel [1797–1868, Irish painter, dramatist, balladeer and novelist]
Ben Trovato (*Rival Rhymes in Honour of Burns*)

LOVESEY, Peter [1936–, English crime novelist]
Peter Lear (*Golden Girl*; *Spidergirl*; *The Secret of Spandau*)

LOVETT, John [1768–1818, US poet]
A Washingtonian (*Washington's Birthday – an Historical Poem*)

LOW, Alfred Maurice [1860–1929, English journalist and writer on America]
Moreton C. Bradley (in *National Review*)

LOW, Lois Dorothea [1916–, Scottish crime and romantic novelist]
Zoe Cass (*Island of the Seven Hills*; *The Silver Leopard*)
Dorothy Mackie Low (*Isle for a Stranger*)
Lois Paxton (*Man Who Died Twice*; *Who Goes There?*)

LOW, Sidney James Mark [1857–1932, English journalist and writer]
Carltoniensis; A Veteran Journalist (both used in the *National Review*)

LOW, Walter Humboldt [1864–95, English journalist]
Himself (in *MacMillan's Magazine*)

LOW, William L. [1840–1929, Scottish cleric, novelist and biographer]
Rothael Kirk (*An Address to the Scotch Clergy Society*)

LOWE, Robert William [1853–1902, English dramatist and writer on the theatre]
R. L. Westland (*Whittington and his Cat – a Pantomime*)

LOWE, Thomas Alfred [1888–1967, English soldier, journalist and writer]
Tallow (*Guide to the Duties of an Adjutant*)

LOWELL, Amy [1874–1925, US poet and writer]
A Dreamer (*Dream Drops or Stories from Fairyland*)

LOWELL, Charles [1782–1861, US cleric – father of James Russell Lowell]
The Senior Minister of the West Church in Boston (*Sermons, Chiefly Practical*)

LOWELL, James Russell [1819–91, US poet and essayist]
Hosea Biglow (*The Biglow Papers*)
Homer Wilbur (*Meliboeus-Hipponax*)
A Wonderful Quiz (*Fable for Critics*; *Reader! Walk Up at Once and Buy*)

LOWELL, John [1769–1840, US lawyer, agriculturist and political pamphleteer]
A Bostonian (*The Diplomatic Policy of Mr Madison Unveiled*)
A Citizen of Massachusetts (*The Impartial Enquirer*)
A Layman (*Are You a Christian or a Calvinist?*)
A Massachusett's Lawyer (*Review of a Treatise on Expatriation*)
A New England Farmer (*A Dispassionate Enquiry into the Ruinous War against Great Britain*; *Mr Madison's War*; *Perpetual War, the Policy of Mr Madison*)
An Old Farmer (*The Road to Peace, Commerce, Wealth and Happiness*)
A Yankee Farmer (*Peace Without Dishonour – War Without Hope*)

LOWER, Richard [1782–1865, English poet and pamphleteer]
Tim Cladpole (*Tim Cladpole's Journey to Lunnun*; *Tim Cladpole's Trip to Merricur*)
An Octogenarian (*Stray Leaves from an Old Tree*)

LOWIN, John [1576–1659, English actor and writer]
An Out-Landish Doctor; J. L. Roscio (both used in *Conclusions upon Dances*)

LOWMAN, Moses [1680–1752, English nonconformist cleric and Hebraist]
*Bagweel (*A Collection of Occasional Papers etc.*)

LOWNDES, Mrs Marie Belloc [1868–1947, English novelist, biographer and historian]
Maria Adelaide Belloc (*Edmond and Jules de Goncourt*)
Philip Curtin (*Noted Murder Mysteries*)
Elizabeth Rayner (*Not All Saints*)

LOWNDES, Robert A. W. [1916–, US science-fiction writer]
Carol Grey; Mallory Kent (both used in *Future Fantasy and Science Fiction* magazine)
Paul Dennis Lavond (in *Stirring Science* magazine)

*John MacDougal (in *Astounding Stories* magazine)
Wilfred Owen Morley (used in the following magazines: *Science Fiction*; *Astonishing Stories*; *Stirring Science Stories*; *Super Science Stories*; *Science Fiction Quarterly*; *Future Fantasy and Science Fiction*)
Richard Morrison (in *Science Fiction Quarterly* magazine)
(Peter) Michael Sherman (in both *Future* magazine and *Science Fiction Quarterly*)

LOWTH, Robert [1710–87, English cleric; Bishop of London]
A Late Professor in the University of Oxford (*A Letter to the Author of The Divine Legation of Moses*)
A Young Gentleman of Winchester School (*The Genealogy of Christ*)

LOWTH, Simon [1630–1720, English cleric and nonjuror]
A Presbyter of the Church of England (*Historical Collections Concerning Church Affairs*)

LUARD, Nicholas [1937–, English crime writer]
James McVean (*Blood Spoor*; *Seabird IX*)

LUARD, William Blaine [1897–1979, English mariner, inventor and nautical writer]
L. Luard (*Where the Tides Meet*; *Northern Deeps*)

LUCAS, Charles [1713–71, Irish physician and nationalist]
Britannicus (*A Freeman's Answer to the Freeholder's Address*)
The Dublin Apothecary (*A Letter from the Dublin Apothecary to the Cork Surgeon*)
A Freeman, Barber and Citizen (*A Letter to the Free Citizens of Dublin*)
Dr Hellebore (*The Authentic History of Dr Hellebore*)
Frank Somebody (in *The Censor or Citizen's Journal*)

LUCAS, Edward Verrall [1868–1938, English dramatist and writer]
E. V. L. (*Quoth the Raven*; *Remember Louvain!*)
F. F. (in *Punch*)
F. W. Mark (used for writing theatrical and comic sketches)
E. D. Ward (*Sir Algernon Pulteney*)

LUCE, Clare Booth [1903–87, US novelist, dramatist, politician and diplomat]
Clare Booth Brokaw (*Stuffed Shirts*; *Abide with Me*)

LUCIE-SMITH, John Edward [1933–, English poet and writer on art]
Peter Kershaw (*A Beginner's Guide to Auctions*)

LUCY, Sir Henry William [1843–1924, English journalist and political commentator]
Baron de Book-Worm; Member for Sark; Toby MP (all used in *Punch*)
Member for the Chiltern Hundreds (in *Gentleman's Magazine*)

LUDLOW, Fitz-Hugh [1837–70, US writer]
A Pythagorean (*The Hasheesh-Eater*)

LUDLOW, John Malcolm Forbes [1821–1911, Indian-born English lawyer, Christian Socialist, historian and social reformer]
A Barrister of Lincoln's Inn (*King's College and Mr Maurice*)
One Who Knew it All (in *MacMillan's Magazine*)
Vicessimus Smatterling, B. L. (in *Fraser's Magazine*)

LUDLUM, Robert [1927–, US mystery writer]
Jonathan Ryder (*The Cry of the Halidon*; *Trevayne*)
Michael Shepherd (*The Road to Gandolfo*)

LUKENS, Henry Clay [1838–1900, US journalist and humorist]
Erratic Enrique (*Jets and Flashes*)
Heinrich Yale Snekul (*Lean'nora, a Supernatural though Sub-Pathetic Ballad*)

LUMLEY, Benjamin [1811–75, English lawyer and opera impresario]
Hermes (*Another World or, Fragments from Montalluyah*; *Parliamentary Practice on Passing Private Bills*)

LUND, John [fl. 1779, English humorous poet]
A Very Odd Author (*A Collection of Oddities in Prose and Verse*)

LUNDY, Benjamin [1789–1839, US journalist and abolitionist]
A Citizen of the United States (*The War in Texas*)

LUNN, Arnold Henry Moore [1888–1974, English traveller, sportsman and writer]
Sutton Croft (*Was Switzerland Pro-German?*)
Rubicon (*Auction Piquet*)

LUNN, Hugh Kingsmill [1889–1949, English novelist and writer]
Hugh Kingsmill (*The Fall*; *The Dawn's Delay*)

LUNT, George [1803–85, US lawyer and writer]
Wesley Brooke (*Eastford or, Household Sketches*)
A Member of the Bar (*A Letter upon Law*)

LUPOFF, Richard Allen [1935–, US science-fiction writer and editor]
Ova Hamlet (in *Fantastic Stories* magazine)

LUSHINGTON, Franklin [1892–?, Swiss-born English writer]
Mark Severn (*Back Ground*; *The Gambardier*)

LUSK, Hugh Hart [1837–1926, English barrister – lived mostly in New Zealand]
Owen Hall (*Eureka*; *Hernando*; *In the Track of a Storm*)

LUTYENS, Mary [1908–, English novelist]
Esther Wyndham (used for magazine serial writing)

LUTZ, John Thomas [1939–, US crime and mystery writer]
John Bennett; Van McCloud; Paul Shepparton; Elwin Strange (all used in *The Executioner* magazine)
Tom Collins (in *TV Fact* magazine)
Steven Greene (*Exiled*)
John Barry Williams (in *Alfred Hitchcock's Mystery Magazine*)

LUXMOORE, Henry Elford [d. 1926, English schoolmaster and writer]
Peccator Maximus (*Some Views of Sparrows on House-Tops*)

LYALL, Sir Alfred Comyn [1835–1911, English civil servant in India]
Vamadeva Shastin; Vamadeo Shastri (both used in *Fortnightly Review*)

LYLE-SMITH, Alan [1914–, English mystery writer]
Alan Caillou (*The Plotter; Rogue's Gambit*)

LYNCH, Hannah [1859–1904, English traveller and novelist]
E. Enticknappe (in *MacMillan's Magazine*)

LYNCH, Theodora Elizabeth [1812–85, English writer for children]
Personne (*Lays of the Sea and Other Poems*)

LYNCH, Thomas Toke [1818–71, English hymn writer]
Silent Long (*The Ethics of Quotation; Songs Controversial*)

LYND, Robert Wilson [1879–1949, Irish journalist and essayist]
Y. Y. (in the *New Statesman*)

LYNDS, Dennis [1924–, US crime and mystery writer]
William Arden (*Mystery of the Dancing Devil; Secret of Phantom Lake*)
Nick Carter (*The Green Wolf Connection*)
Michael Collins (*Lukan War; The Planets of Death*)
John Crowe (*Another Way to Die; Crooked Shadows*)
Carl Dekker (*Woman in Marble*)
John Douglas (in *Mike Shayne's Mystery Magazine*)

Maxwell Grant (*Shadow Beware; Cry Shadow*)
Mark Sadler (*Mirror Image; Circle of Fire*)

LYNE, Joseph Leycester [1837–1908, English cleric and preacher; Benedictine monk]
Brother (or Father) Ignatius (*The Catholic Church of England and What She Teaches; The Holy Isle: a Legend of Bardsey Abbey; May a Monk Serve God in the Church of England or Not?*)

LYNNE, James Broom [1920–, English novelist and playwright]
James Quartermain (*The Diamond Hook; Rock of Diamonds*)

LYTTELTON, Mrs Alfred (Edith) [1864–1948, New Zealand dramatist and novelist]
Edith Hamlet (*The Touch of Sorrow*)
G. B. Lancaster (*The Savignys; Grand Parade*)

LYTTELTON, George [1709–73, 1st Baron Lyttelton; politician and writer]
A Friend in the Country (*Considerations upon the Present State of Affairs etc.*)
A Persian in England (*Letters from a Persian in England to a Friend in Ispahan*)
A Young Gentleman at Rome (*An Epistle to Mr Pope from a Young Gentleman at Rome*)

LYTTELTON, George William [1817–76, 4th Baron Lyttelton; scholar and reformer]
A Student (*Contributions towards a Glossary of the Glynne Language*)

LYTTON, Lady Constance [1869–1923, Austrian-born English suffragette who became an invalid following forced feeding while in prison]
Jane Warton (*Prison and Prisoners*)

LYTTON, Edward Robert Bulwer [1831–91, 1st Earl of Lytton; diplomat and poet]
Owen Meredith (*Clytemnestra; The Wanderer*)
*Edward Trevor (*Tannhauser*)

M

MABBE, James [1572–1642, English diplomat and Spanish scholar]
Don Diego Peude-Ser (*The Spanish Bawd – Represented in Celestina*)

McALLISTER, Alister [1877–1943, Irish novelist and playwright]
Lynn Brock (*The Barrington Mystery; The Silver Sickle Case*)
Anthony P. Wharton (*Be Good Sweet Maid; Evil Communications*)

MacARTHUR, David Wilson [1903–81, Scottish journalist and writer]
David Wilson (*The Search for Geoffrey Goring; Murder in Mozambique; Witch's Cauldron*)

MacARTNEY, George [1737–1806, 1st Earl of MacArtney; colonial governor]
A Late Chief-Secretary of Ireland (*An Account of Ireland in 1773*)

MacAULAY, Aulay [1758–1819, Scottish cleric]
Academicus (in *Ruddiman's Magazine*)
Clericus Leicestriensis (in *Gentleman's Magazine* and for *A Tour through South Holland and the Austrian Netherlands*)

MacAULAY, Fannie Caldwell [1863–1941, US novelist]
Frances Little (*Jack and I in Lotus Land; The Lady of the Decoration; Early American Textiles*)

MacAULAY, Thomas Babington [1800–59, 1st Baron MacAulay; historian, barrister and essayist]
Cid Hamet Benengeli (*Fragments of an Ancient Romance*)

A Gentleman of the Middle Temple; Tristram Merton (both used in the *Quarterly Magazine*)

McAULIFFE, Frank M. [1926–, US mystery writer]
Frank Malachy (*Hot Town*)

MacBETH, Madge Hamilton [1880–1965, US novelist and historical writer]
Gilbert Knox (*The Land of Afternoon; The Kinder Bees*)

McBRIDE, James [1789–1859, US writer]
A Citizen of the United States (*Symmes's Theory of Concentric Spheres*)

McCABE, James Dabney [1842–83, US writer]
An Ex-Cadet (*Life of General Thomas J. Jackson*)
Edward Winslow Martin (*A History of the Grange Movement*)
A Southerner (*Fanaticism and its Results*)

McCABE, Joseph [1867–1955, English priest; later a journalist and historian]
Arnold Wright (*In the Shade of the Cloister*)

McCARROLL, James [1814–92, Canadian poet and writer]
Terry Finnegan (*Letters of Terry Finnegan to T. D. M'Gee*)

MacCARTHY, Denis Florence [1817–82, Irish poet, journalist and essayist]
Antonio; Desmond; S. E. Y.; Trifolium; Vig (all used in various journals and periodicals)
J. H. (*Justina – a Translation*)

MacCARTHY, Sir Desmond [1877–1952, English journalist and literary critic]
Affable Hawk (in the *New Statesman*)

McCARTHY, Justin [1830–1912, Irish journalist, novelist and political writer]
A Home-Rule MP (in *New Quarterly Magazine*)

McCARTHY, Shaun Lloyd [1928–, English mystery novelist]
Theo Callas (*City of Kites*)
Desmond Cory (*Secret Ministry*; *Pilgrim at the Gate*)

MacCAUL, Alexander [1799–1863, Irish cleric, missionary and Hebraist]
A Clergyman of the Church of England (*England's Duty to Israel's Sons*)

McCHESNEY, Mary F. [fl. 1954, English writer]
Joe Rayter (*Stab in the Dark*; *The Victim was Important*)

McCLARY, Thomas Calvert [fl. 1935, US science-fiction writer]
Calvin Peregoy (in *Astounding Science Fiction* magazine)

McCLELLAN, Mrs Harriet [1873–1913, US novelist]
Harford Flemming (*Broken Chords Crossed by the Echo of a False Note*)

McCLOY, Helen Worrell C. [1904–, US crime and mystery writer]
Helen Clarkson (*The Last Day*)

McCLUSKEY, Henry [1827–70, US journalist]
Paddy (in the *Brooklyn Eagle*)

MacCOLL, Malcolm [1831–1907, Scottish cleric and controversialist]
Expertus (*Is Liberal Policy a Failure?*)
The Quarterly Reviewer; Vindex (both used in *Fortnightly Review*)
Scrutator (*Is There Not a Cause?*; *Mr Gladstone and Oxford*; *Who is Responsible for the War?*)

McCONNELL, James Douglas R. [1915–, Irish crime and mystery writer]
Douglas Rutherford (*Collision Course*; *Mystery Tour*)
*Paul Temple (*The Tyler Mystery*; *East of Algiers*)

McCONNELL, William [1833–67, English cartoonist and illustrator }
Mac (*Twice Round the Clock*)

McCONVILLE, Michael Anthony [1925–, English diplomat and writer]
Patrick Plum (in *Blackwood's Magazine*)

MacCORMICK, Charles [1755–1807, English historian]
A Member of His Privy Council (*Secret History of the Court and Reign of Charles II*)

McCORMICK, Donald [1911–, Welsh historical writer]
Richard Deacon (*Madoc and the Discovery of America*; *History of the British Secret Service*)

McCUE, Lillian Bueno [1902–, US writer]
Lillian de la Torre (*Elizabeth is Missing*; *The Heir of Douglas*)

MacCULLOCH, Derek Ivor Breashur [1897–1967, English broadcaster and writer for children]
Uncle Mac (*for various BBC publications and annuals*)

MacCULLOCH, John Ramsay [1789–1864, Scottish economist and statistician]
A Political Economist (*Catalogue of Books the Property of a Political Economist*)

McCULLOCH, Thomas [1776–1843, Scottish-born Canadian Presbyterian cleric and educationalist]
Investigator; Mephibosheth Stepsure (both used for letters to the *Acadian Recorder*)

McCUTCHAN, Philip Donald [1920–, English crime and mystery writer]
Robert Conington Galway (*The Negative Man*; *Assignment London*)

Duncan MacNeil (*Lieutenant of the Line*; *Charge of Cowardice*)

T. I. G. Wigg (*A Rum for the Captain*; *For the Sons of Gentleman*)

McCUTCHEON, Ben Frederick [1875–1934, US writer]
Benjamin Brace (*The Seventh Person*)

McCUTCHEON, George Barr [1866–1928, US novelist and journalist]
Richard Greaves (*Beverley of Granstark*; *Castle Craneycrow*)

McCUTCHEON, Hugh Davie-Martin [1909–, Scottish novelist]
Hugh Davie-Martin (*Death's Bright Angel*)
Griselda Wilding (*Promise of Delight*)

M'DERMOTT, William A. [1863–1913, US cleric]
Walter Lecky (*Impressions and Opinions*; *Mr Billy Buttons*)

MacDERMOTT, W. R. [1838–1918, Irish writer]
A. P. A. O'Gara (*The Green Republic*; *Foughilotra: a Forbye Story*)

M'DIARMID, John [1790–1852, Scottish journalist]
Atticus Secundus (*Letters of Junius*)

MacDONAGH, Michael [1860–1946, Irish journalist and historian]
A Lobbyist (in *MacMillan's Magazine*)

MacDONALD, Andrew [1755–90, Scottish dramatist and writer]
Matthew Bramble (*Miscellaneous Works of Matthew Bramble*)

MacDONALD, George [1824–1905, Scottish novelist, poet and writer for childen]
Dalmocand (*Poems and Essays*)

MacDONALD, James Ramsay [1866–1937, Scottish politican and first socialist prime minister]
J. Grant (in the *Scottish Review*)

MacDONALD, John A. M. [1854–1939, Scottish politician]
A Liberal MP (*The Constitutional Crisis*)

MacDONALD, John Hay Athole [1836–1919, Lord Kingsbury; Scottish jurist]
Jean Jambon (*Our Trip to Blunderland*)

MacDONALD, Philip [1899–1981, English mystery writer]
*Oliver Fleming (*Ambrotox and Limping Dick*)
Anthony Lawless (*Harbour*)
Martin Porlock (*X v Rex*; *Mystery at Friar's Pardon*)

MacDONALD, Ronald [1860–1933, English novelist and dramatist, father of Philip MacDonald]
*Oliver Fleming (*Ambrotox and Limping Dick*; *The Spandau Quid*)

MacDONNELL, Antony Patrick [1844–1925, Irish civil servant in India]
A Bengal Civilian (*Agricultural and Administrative Reform in Bengal*)

MacDONNELL, Archibald Gordon [1895–1941, Scottish crime and mystery writer]
John Cameron (*The Seven Stabs*; *Body Found Stabbed*)
Neil Gordon (*The Silent Murderers*; *Murder in Earls Court*)

MacDONNELL, James Francis Carlin [1881–?, US poet and writer]
Francis Carlin (*Reminiscences of an Ex-Detective*)

M'DONOUGH, Felix [d. 1836, English writer]
The Hermit (*The Hermit in the Country*)

McDOUGALL, E. Jean [fl. 1930, Canadian novelist]
Jane Rolyot (*The Lily of Fort Garry*)

McDOWELL, Benjamin [1739–1824, US-Scottish cleric and controversialist]
Pistophilus Philecclesia (*Letters of Importance*)

MacDOWELL, Katherine Sherwood Bonner [1849–83, US writer]
Sherwood Bonner (*Dialect Tales*; *Suwanee River Tales*)

McDOWELL, Michael McEachern [1950–, US writer]
Nathan Aldyne (*Vermilion*)

MacEACHERN, Malcolm [1884–1945, Australian singer and performer]
Mr Jetsam (*Verses*)

McELFRESH, Elizabeth Adeline [1918–, US romantic novelist]
John Cleveland (*Minus One Corpse*)
Jane Scott (*A Nurse for Rebel's Run*)
Elizabeth Wesley (*Doctor Barbara*; *Nurse Judy*)

McELHENEY, Jane [1936–74, US poet and writer]
Ada Clare (*Only a Woman's Heart*)

MacEOIN, Denis [1949–, English writer]
Daniel Easterman (*The Last Assassin*)

McEVOY, Marjorie [d. 1989, English romantic novelist]
Marjorie Harte (*Doctors in Conflict*; *Nurse in the Orient*)

MacFADYEN, Dugald [1867–1936, Scottish cleric, biographer and religious writer]
Cruck- a-Leaghan (*Lays and Legends of the North of Ireland*)

McFALL, Frances Elizabeth [1862–1943, Irish novelist and feminist]
Sarah Grand (*The Heavenly Twins*; *The Winged Victory*; *The Beth Book*)

MacFARLAN, Patrick [1780–1849, Scottish cleric and religious writer]
A Minister of the Established Church (*A Defence of the Ministers of the Church of Scotland*)

McFARLANE, Leslie [1903–77, Canadian journalist and writer]
Carolyn Keene (*The Tower Treasure*)

MacFIE, Robert Andrew [1811–93, Scottish merchant and writer]
A Lothian Justice, quondam MP (*Jubilee and other Rhymings*)
Senex Scotus, an Heritor (*Off-Hand Notes*)

McGARRITY, Mark [1943–, US mystery writer]
Bartholomew Gill (*McGarr at the Dublin Horse Show*; *McGarr on the Cliffs at Moher*)

M'GEE, Thomas D'Arcy [1823–68, Irish-born controversial journalist in USA; became a Canadian politician and was murdered in Ottawa]
A Backwoodsman (*The Crown and the Confederation*)
Philo-Veritas (letters in the *New York Times*)

MacGEORGE, Andrew [1810–91, Scottish lawyer and antiquarian]
Veritas (in the *Glasgow Herald*)

M'GHEE, Robert James Leslie [1789–1872, Irish cleric]
A Recent Traveller (in *Dublin University Magazine*)

MacGILLIVRAY, William [1823–1917, Scottish lawyer and writer]
The late William Gairdner, Writer to Her Majesty's Signet (*Glengoyne: Reminiscences of the Parish*)
One of his Old Pupils (*Rob Lindsay and his School*)

McGIVERN, William Peter [1922–82, US science-fiction writer]
Bill Peters (*Blondes Die Young*)

McGLOIN, Joseph Thaddeus [1917–, US writer]
Thaddeus O'Finn (*Happy Holiday*; *I'll Die Laughing*)

MacGOWAN, John [1726–80, English Baptist cleric and religious writer]
Antisocinus (*The Arians and Socinians Monitor*)

The Listener (*Infernal Conferences or Dialogues of Devils*)
Pasquin Shaveblock (*The Shaver's New Sermon for the Feast Day*)
Their Humble Servant the Shaver (*A Sermon Caused by the Expulsion of Six Young Gentlemen from the University of Oxford*)

MacGREGOR, James Murdoch [1925–, Scottish science-fiction writer]
J. T. McIntosh (*World Out of Mind; One in Three Hundred*)

MacGREGOR, John [1797–1857, Scottish statistician, writer and failed banker]
A Barrister (*Go Out Quickly*)
Junior Colonus (in *Blackwood's Magazine*)
A Shopkeeper (in *Tait's Edinburgh Magazine*)
Simeon South (*Simeon South's Letters to his Kinsfolk*)

MacGREGOR, John [1825–92, English barrister and traveller]
Rob Roy (*A Thousand Miles in the Rob Roy Canoe*)

MacGREGOR, Mary Esther Miller [1876–1961, Canadian novelist]
Marian Keith (*Under the Grey Olives; Little Miss Melody*)

McHALE, John [1791–1881, Irish cleric and religious and Gaelic writer]
Hierophilus (*Catholic Emancipation Proved to be as Necessary for the Peace and Prosperity of Ireland etc.; The Letters of Hierophilus*)

McHENRY, James [1785–1845, Scottish-US poet and novelist]
Solomon Secondsight (*O'Halloran, or the Insurgent Chief; The Spectre of the Forest; The Wilderness; It Would be So*)

McILWAINE, David [1921–, English science-fiction writer]
Charles Eric Maine (*Spaceways; The Mind of Mr Soames*)

McINTOSH, Kinn Hamilton [1930–, English mystery writer]
Catherine Aird (*His Burial Too; Some Die Eloquent*)

McINTOSH, Maria Jane [1803–78, US writer]
Aunt Kitty (*Aunt Kitty's Tales*)

MacINTYRE, John [1869–1947, Scottish playwright]
John Brandane (*The Glen is Mine; The Inn of Adventure*)

MacINTYRE, John Thomas [1875–1951, US writer]
Kerry O'Neil (*Death at Dakar; Mooney Moves Around*)

MACKARNESS, John Fielder [1820–89, English cleric; Bishop of Oxford]
One of Themselves (*A Few Words to the Country Parsons*)

MacKAY, Andrew [1760–1809, Scottish astronomer and mathematician]
James Andrew, A. M. (*Astronomical and Natural Tables*)

MacKAY, Charles [1814–89, Scottish journalist and songwriter]
Herman Grimbosh (*The Whirligig Papers*)
John Wagstaffe Esq., of Wilby Grange (*The Gouty Philosopher*)

MacKAY, Eric [1851–99, Scottish poet]
A Violinist (*Love Letters of a Violinist*)

MacKAY, James Alexander [1936–, Scottish writer]
Ian Angus (*Medals and Decorations*)
Bruce Garden (*Make Money with Stamps*)
Peter Whittington (*Undiscovered Antiques; Kitchen Antiques*)

MacKAY, Lewis Hugh [fl. 1962, Indian-born English writer on international affairs]
Hugh Matheson (*The Third Force*)

MacKAY, Mary [1855–1924, English novelist]
Marie Corelli (*A Romance of Two Worlds; The Sorrows of Satan*)

McKEAG, Ernest L. [1896–?, English writer for children]
Mark Grimshaw; Pat Haynes (both used in *Champion*)
Jack Maxwell (in *Triumph*)

M'KEAN, Henry Swasey [1810–87, US writer]
John Smith (*Lover of Natur' – a Translation*)

MacKELLAR, Thomas [1812–99, US poet and writer]
Tam (*Tam's Fortnight Ramble and Other Poems*)

MACKEN, John [1784–1823, Irish journalist and poet]
Ismael Fitzadam (*Lays on Land*)

MacKENNA, Theobald [d. 1808, Irish political pamphleteer]
A Catholic and a Burkist (*An Argument against Extermination*)

McKENNY, Thomas Lorraine [1784–1858, US Indian agent and writer]
Aristides (*Essays on the Spirit of Jacksonism*)

MacKENZIE, Alexander Slidell [1803–48, US mariner]
An American in England (*The American in England*)
Edward Hamilton (*Life of Paul Jones*)
A Young American (*A Year in Spain*)

MacKENZIE, Mrs Anne Marie [fl. 1796, English novelist]
Ellen of Exeter (*The Neapolitan*)

MacKENZIE, Sir George [1630–1714, 1st Earl of Cromarty; statesman and royalist]
An Advocate of the Civil Law in Scotland (*The Spirit of Fanaticism Exemplified in the trials etc.*)
A Peer in Scotland (*Two Letters Concerning the Present Union*)
Stoicus (*Religio Stoici*)

MacKENZIE, Henry [1745–1831, Scottish lawyer, novelist and essayist]
Brutus (*The Letters of Brutus to Certain Celebrated Political Characters*)

Julia Lightfoot (in *The Sale Room*)

MacKENZIE, James [1680–1761, Scottish physician and medical writer]
A Physician (*Essays on Retirement from Business*; *Essays and Meditations on Various Subjects*)

MacKENZIE, Robert Shelton [1809–80, Irish journalist and writer – settled in USA]
Sholto (in the *Dublin and London Magazine*)

MACKESEY, Leonora Dorothy Rivers [fl. 1945, Scottish novelist]
Leonora Starr (*Colonel's Lady*; *To Keep for Ever*)

MacKINLAY, Leila S. [1910–, English romantic novelist]
Brenda Grey (*How High the Moon*; *Mixed Singles*; *The Pro's Daughter*)

MacKINNON, Daniel Henry [1813–84, Irish soldier and military writer]
A Cavalry Officer (*Military Service and Adventures in the Far East*)

MacKINTOSH, Elizabeth [1897–1952, Scottish novelist and playwright]
Gordon Daviot (*Richard of Bordeaux*; *Kif*)
Josephine Tey (*The Singing Sands*; *The Daughter of Time*)

MacKINTOSH, Sir James [1765–1832, Scottish physician, barrister, philosopher and historian]
The Ghost of Vandegrab (in the *Morning Chronicle*)

MacKINTOSH, Norman [fl. 1935, Scottish-born Canadian journalist]
Norman Scott; Skipper Joe (both used in *The Vancouver Sunset*)

McKOWEN, James [1814–89, Irish poet and rhymester]
Kitty Connor (in the *Northern Whig*)
Curlew (in *The Nation*)

MacLAGAN, Robert [1820–94, British
soldier in India]
*Two Old Friends, Brother Officers
(*Memoir of Gen. Sir William Erskine
Baker*)

McLAREN, Moray David Shaw [1901–71,
Scottish writer]
Michael Murray (*The Noblest Prospect*)

M'LAUCHLAN, Thomas [1816–86, Scottish
cleric and writer]
An Eye-Witness (in *The Witness*)

McLAUGHLIN, Charles [1699–1797, Irish
actor and playwright]
Charles Macklin (*The Man of the World*;
Love in a Maze)

McLAUGHLIN, James Fairfax [1839–1903,
US lawyer and writer]
Pasquino (*The American Cyclops*)

MacLEAN, Alistair [1923–87, Scottish
mystery writer]
Ian Stuart (*The Dark Crusader*; *The Satan
Bug*)

McLEAN, John David Ruari [1917–,
Scottish typographer, printer and writer]
David Hardie (used for the translation of
Late Spring by Joe Lederer and also in
the *Manchester Guardian*, *Men Only* and
London Opinion)

MacLEAN, Katherine Anne [1925–, US
science-fiction writer]
Charles Dye (*Syndrome Johnny*; *The Man
who Staked the Stars*)
G. A. Morris (*The Carnivore*)

McLEAN, Kathryn Anderson [1909–66, US
writer]
Kathryn Forbes (*Transfer Point*)

MacLEHOSE, Mrs Agnes [1759–1841,
Scottish poet]
Clarinda (used in correspondence with
Robert Burns)

McLELLAN, Charles Morton Stewart
[1865–1916, US playwright]
Hugh Morton (*The Belle of New York*; *The
Girl from up There*)

MacLENNAN, John Ferguson [1827–81,
Scottish lawyer and writer]
Richard Futiloe Sen. (in *MacMillan's
Magazine*)

MacLEOD, Charlotte Matilda [1922–,
Canadian mystery and children's writer]
Alisa Craig (*A Pint of Murder*; *The Terrible
Tide*)
Matilda Hughes (*Headlines for Caroline*)

McLEOD, Ellen [1924–, Scottish writer for
children]
Ella Anderson (*The Vanishing Light*; *The
Talking Mountain*)

MacLEOD, Emily Sarah [d. 1896, Scottish
writer]
An Old Highlander (in *Blackwood's
Magazine*)

MacLEOD, Jean Sutherland [1908–,
Scottish romantic novelist]
Catherine Airlie (*Hidden in the Wind*; *The
Unguarded Hour*)

MacLEOD, Joseph Todd Gordon [1903–84,
Scottish writer and broadcaster]
Adam Drinan (*Women in the Happy Island*;
The Men of the Rocks)

MacLISE, Daniel [1806–70, Irish painter and
illustrator]
Alfred Croquis (in *Fraser's Magazine*)

MacMANUS, Mrs Anna [1866–1911, Irish
poet and writer]
Ethna Carbery (*In the Celtic Past*; *The Four
Winds of Eirinn*)

McMANUS, Seaumas [1869–1960, Irish
novelist and short-story writer]
Mac (*Character Sketches*; *Donegal Fairy
Stories*; *In Chimney Corners*)

MacMILLAN, Hugh [1833–1903, Scottish cleric and religious writer]
Uisdean MacGhilmhaoil (in *MacMillan's Magazine*)

McMILLAN, James [1925–, Scottish journalist]
Coriolanus (The Glass Lie)

McMILLAN, Robert [1862–1929, Scottish-born Australian writer]
Globetrotter (*Australian Gossip and Story*)

MacMULLAN, Charles Kirkpatrick [1889–1973, Irish dramatist and essayist]
C. K. Munro (*At Mrs Beam's*; *The True Woman*)

McNALLY, Leonard [1752–1820, Irish barrister, dramatist and government agent]
A Barrister of the Inner Temple (*Acts Passed in Parliament*)
Leonard MacHumbug (*Thespis to Apollo*)
Plunder (*The Apotheosis of Punch*)

McNAMARA, Barbara [1913–, Australian writer]
Elizabeth O'Conner (*The Chinese Bird*; *The Irishman*)

MacNAMARA, Nottidge Charles [d. 1918, British physician and medical writer]
A Member of the Sept. (*The Spectre of the Forest*)

MacNEICE, Louis [1907–63, Irish dramatist, poet and writer]
Louis Malone (*Roundabout Way*)

McNEILE, Herman Cyril [1888–1937, English novelist]
Sapper (*Bulldog Drummond*)

MacNEILL, Hector [1746–1818, Scottish poet]
An Eminent Editor (*Memoirs of the Life of Gilbert Purring*)

MacNEILL, Malcolm [1866–1917, Scottish soldier]
An Islesman (in *Blackwood's Magazine*)

McNEILLY, Wilfred [1921–, Scottish science-fiction and occult writer]
Peter Saxon (*The Disorientated Man*)

MacNEVIN, William James [1763–1841, Irish physician and nationalist – emigrated to USA]
An Irish Catholic (*An Argument for Independence*)

MacNIE, John [1836–1909, US novelist]
Ismar Thuisen (*The Diothas or a Far Look Ahead*)

MacNISH, Robert [1802–37, Scottish physician and writer]
Modern Pythagorean (*The Book of Aphorisms*)
An Oriental Author (in *Fraser's Magazine*)

MacPHERSON, Mrs A. D. L. [d. 1978, English romantic novelist]
Sara Seale (*Reluctant Orphan*; *Truant Bride*)

MacPHERSON, James [1736–96, Scottish poet and Gaelic scholar whose claims for Ossian were widely held to be suspect]
Ossian (*Fingal, an Ancient Epic Poem*)

MacQUEEN, James William [1900–, US writer]
James G. Edwards (*Death Elects a Mayor*; *Murder in the Surgery*)

McSHANE, Mark [1929–, Australian-born English mystery writer]
Marc Lovell (*Hand over Mind*; *Spy Game*)

MacSPARRAN, James [1693–1757, Scottish cleric; missionary in Rhode Island]
A Divine of the Church of England (*America Dissected*)

M'TAGGART, Mrs Ann [1753–1834, English writer]
A Lady (*Memoirs of a Gentleman of the Old School*)

McVICKAR, John [1787–1868, US cleric]
A New Yorker (*Hints on Banking*)

McWILLIAMS, Margaret Stovel [fl. 1931, Canadian writer]
*Oliver Stowell (*If I Were King of Canada*)

McWILLIAMS, Roland Fairbairn
[1874–1957, Canadian barrister and
politician]
*Oliver Stowell (If I Were King of Canada)

MACAN, Reginald Walter [1848–1941, Irish
historian and classical scholar]
The Giver (Hellenikon)

MACCHETTA, Blanche Roosevelt Tucker
[1853–98, US singer and writer]
Blanche Roosevelt (Elisabeth of Roumania;
Hazel Fane)

MACHIN, Lewis [fl. 1610, English dramatist]
*Iarius Markham (The Dumbe Knight)

MACKLIN, Charles [1697–1797, English
actor and stage-manager]
C– M– (The Man of the World)

MACKWORTH, Sir Digby [1789–1852,
English soldier]
A Field Officer of Cavalry (Diary of a Tour
Through Southern India in 1821 and 1822)

MACKWORTH, Sir Humphrey [1657–1727,
English barrister, merchant and writer]
Sir H. M. (Down with the Mug or, Reasons
for Suppressing the Mug-House)
Robert Harley (A Vindication of the Rights of
the Commons in England)
A Member of Parliament (A Letter Giving
an Account of the Tackers)

MACKY, John [d. 1726, English spy and
writer]
A Gentleman Here (A Journey Through
England in Familiar Letters from a
Gentleman Here to His Friend Abroad)

MADAN, Martin [1726–90, English barrister
and Methodist writer]
A Bystander (Remarks on the Answer to
Strictures upon Modern Simony)
A Member of the Church of England
(Seasonable Animadversions upon Mr
Forster's Sermon)
A Professor of Christianity (A Scripture
Account of the Doctrine of Perfection)
A Sincere Well-Wisher to the Public
(Thoughts on Executive Justice)

MADDEN, Daniel Owen [1815–52, Irish
writer]
Danby North (The Mildmayes)

MADDEN, Richard Robert [1798–1886,
Irish physician, historian and colonial
civil servant]
Ierne (in Dublin University Magazine)

MADDOW, Ben [1909–92, US screenwriter
and poet; his family name was
Medvedev]
Daniel Woolf (in the Partisan Review)

MADDOX, Isaac [1697–1759, English cleric;
Bishop of Worcester]
A Clergyman in the Country (The Case of
Dr Rundle's Promotion to the See of
Glocester)

MADISON, Angela Mary [1923–, Indian-
born English writer for children]
Angela Banner (Ant and Bee; Kind Dog on
Monday)

MADISON, James [1751–1836, 4th President
of the USA]
Helvidius (Letters of Helvidius)
*Publius (in The Federalist)

MAGEE, William Kirkpatrick [1868–1961,
Irish essayist]
John Eglinton (Pebbles from a Brook; Anglo-
Irish Essays)

MAGENS, Nicholas [fl. 1756, English writer]
N. M. (Farther Explanations of Some
Particular Subjects relating to Trade, Coin
... Universal Merchant)

MAGINN, William [1793–1842, Irish
journalist, poet and writer]
Augustinus; Rev. J. Barrett; Bob Buller; A
Constant Reader; Richard Dowder; Blaise
Fitztravesty; Philip Forager; Rev. E.
Hincks; William Holmes MP for
Haslemere; Wm. Holt ; An Irish
Gentleman Lately Deceased; Thomas
Jennings, Soda Water Manufacturer;
Giles Middlestitch; Morty MacNamara
Mulligan; Mr Mullion; *Sir Morgan
O'Doherty; Olinthus Petre; Thomas

Pipes; R. T.Scott; W. Seward; *Timothy Tickler (all used in *Blackwood's Magazine*)

The Baronet; Ned Culpepper, the Tomahawk; Dixi; An Officer in a Marching Regiment; Robin Roughhead (all used in *Fraser's Magazine*)

P. J. (or P. P.) Crossman; Dionysius Duggan (both used in the *London Literary Gazette*)

Waylac (in *Bentley's Miscellany*)

MAGNUS, Katie [1844–1924, English writer]
A Grandmother (in *MacMillan's Magazine*)

MAGNUS, Laurie [1872–1933, English publisher, historian and writer]
A Quarterly Reviewer (*Aspects of the Jewish Question*)

MAGNUS-ALLCROFT, Sir Philip [1906–88, English educationalist and writer]
Philip Magnus (*Life of Edmund Burke*; *Sir Walter Raleigh*)

MAHONEY, Elizabeth [1911–, US writer on ballet]
Thalia Mara (*Language of Ballet*; *On your Toes!*)

MAHONY, Francis Sylvester [1804–66, Irish Jesuit, abandoned the cloth, became a journalist, poet and humorist]
Reddy (or Rory) O'Dryscull (in *Bentley's Miscellany*)
Father Prout (in *Fraser's Magazine*)
Jeremy Savonarola (*Facts and Figures from Italy*)
Oliver Yorke (used while editor of *Fraser's Magazine*)

MAHONY, Martin Francis [1831–82, Irish novelist and writer]
Mr Catlyne, QC (in *Fraser's Magazine*)
Matthew Stradling (*The Bar Sinister*)

MAINWARING, Daniel [1902–78, US mystery writer]
Geoffrey Homes (*The Man Who Didn't Exist*; *Then There Were Three*)

MAIRE, William [d. 1769, English Catholic cleric]
A Catholic Clergyman (*Considerations on the Passion of Jesus Christ*)

MAITLAND, Edward [1824–97, English novelist, theosophist and writer]
Herbert Ainslie (*The Pilgrim and the Shrine*)

MAITLAND, Samuel Roffey [1792–1866, English barrister, cleric, historian and essayist]
A Churchman (*The Voluntary System*)

MAJOR, Charles [1856–1913, US historian and novelist]
Edwin Caskoden (*Dorothy Vernon of Haddon Hall*; *The Gentle Knight of Old Brandenberg*)

MAJOR, John [1782–1849, English publisher and writer]
One under a Hood (*A Poetical Description of Bartholomew Fair*)

MALCOLM, Sir Ian [1868–1944, Canadian-born English diplomat, politician and writer]
Zachary Waynflete (*Considerations*)

MALCOLM, Sir John [1769–1833, Scottish historian and civil servant in India]
A Traveller (*Sketches of Persia from the Journals of a Traveller*)

MALCOLM, John [1936–, English crime and mystery writer]
John Andrews (*The Price Guide to Antique Furniture*)

MALDEN, Henry [1800–76, English classical scholar]
Hamilton Murray (*The Origin of Universities and Academical Degrees*)

MALHAM, John [1747–1821, English cleric and writer]
A Country Curate (*Remarks on a Letter to the Bishop of Salisbury*)

MALLALIEU, Sir Joseph Percival William [1908–80, English journalist and politician]
Pied Piper (*Rats!*)

MALLESON, George Bruce (1825–98, English soldier and military historian]
An Officer of the Bengal Staff Corps (*Essays on Indian Historical Subjects*)
One who Has Served under Sir Charles Napier (*The Mutiny of the Bengal Army*)

MALLESON, Lucy Beatrice [1899–1973, English crime writer]
Anthony Gilbert (*Death at Four Corners; Snake in the Grass*)
Anne Meredith (*The Stranger; The Sisters*)

MALLETT, Richard [1910–72, English writer and film critic]
R. M. (in *Punch*)

MALLOCH, David [1700–65, Scottish poet and dramatist]
David Mallet (*Verbal Criticism; Eurydice*)
A Plain Man (*Observations on the Twelfth Article of War*)

MALLOCK, William Hurrell [1849–1923, English novelist, satirist and social reactionary]
A Desultory Reader (in the *National Review*)
Wentworth Moore (*New Poems*)
A Newdigate Prizeman (*Every Man his Own Poet*)

MALLON, Mrs Isabella Allerdice [1857–98, US journalist and writer]
Ruth Ashmore (*Side-Talks with Girls; The Business Girl in Every Phase of her Life*)

MALTBY, Edward [1770–1859, English cleric; Bishop of Durham]
An Englishman of the Old School (*Reflections upon Public Affairs at the Commencement of 1809*)

MALZBERG, Barry N. [1939–, US science-fiction and crime writer]
Mike Barry (*Chicago Slaughter; Harlem Showdown*)
Francine de Natale (*The Circle*)
Claudine Dumas (*Diary of a Parisian Chambermaid*)
Mel Johnson (*Kiss and Run; The Sadist*)

Lee W. Mason (*Lady of a Thousand Sorrows*)
K. M. O'Donnell (*Final War and other Fantasies; Universe Day*)
Gerrold Watkins (*Southern Comfort; A Bed of Money*)
John Barry Williams (in *Alfred Hitchcock's Mystery Magazine*)

MANDEVILLE, Bernard [1670–1733, English philosopher and satirist]
B. M. (*Typhon; The Virgin Unmasked or, Female Dialogues*)

MANFRED, Frederick [1912–, US writer]
Feike Feikema (*This is the Year; The Golden Bowl*)

MANGAN, James Clarence [1803–49, Irish poet and writer]
Clarence; An Out-and-Outer; Selber (all used in *Dublin University Magazine*)
Lageniensis; Monos; The Mourner; A Yankee (all used in *The Nation*)
The Man in the Cloak; Terrae Filius; Vacuus (all used in the *Belfast Vindicator*)

MANGEY, Thomas [1688–1755, English cleric and religious writer]
A Believer (*The Lord Bishop of London's Letter to his Clergy Defended*)

MANGIN, Edward [1772–1852, English cleric and writer]
An Absentee Residing in Bath (*Utopia Found, being an Apology for Irish Absentees*)
A Friend (*Piozziana or, Recollections of the Late Mrs Piozzi*)
Normanides (*Reminiscences for Roman Catholics*)

MANING, Frederick Edward [1812–83, Irish migrant to New Zealand; became a judge]
A Pakeha Maori (*A History of the War against Chief Heke in 1845; Korero Maori; Old New Zealand: a Tale of the Good Old Times*)

MANLEY, James R. [d. 1851, US physician and medical lecturer]
Graviora Manent (*Letters on the College of Physicians and Surgeons*)

MANLEY, Mary de la Riviere [1663–1724, English dramatist, editor and pamphleteer]
Eginardus (*Memoirs of Europe towards the Close of the Eighth Century*)
Sir Charles Lovemore (*The Adventures of Rivella*)

MANLEY-TUCKER, Audrie [1924–83, English romantic novelist]
Linden Howard (*Devil's Lady*; *Foxglove Country*)

MANN, Cameron [1851–1932, US cleric and writer]
The Rector (*Five Discourses on Future Punishment*)

MANN, Hermann [d. 1833, US writer]
A Citizen of Massachusetts (*The Female Review*)

MANNING, Adelaide F. O. [d. 1959, English crime novelist]
*Manning Coles (*Drink to Yesterday*; *The Fifth Man*)

MANNING, Miss Anne [1807–79, English historical novelist]
Nicholas Moldwarp, BA (*Passages in the Life of Mistress Anne Askew*)
Margarita More (*The Household of Sir Thomas More*)

MANNING, Emily [1845–90, Australian writer]
E. M. A. Heron (*The Balance of Pain and Other Poems*)

MANNING, Frederic [1887–1935, Australian-born English essayist and poet]
Private 19022 (*Her Privates We*)

MANNING, Henry Edward [1808–92, English cardinal]
Catholicus (in *The Tablet*)
Viator (*Religio Viatoris*)

MANNING, Joseph Bolles [1787–1854, US lawyer]
Atticus Secundus (*Junius Unmasked*)

MANNING, Marie [d. 1945, US writer]
Beatrice Fairfax (*Judith of the Plains*; *Truce*)

MANNING, Olivia [1908–80, English novelist]
Jacob Morrow (used for her first three published novels)

MANNING, Owen [1721–1801, English cleric and Surrey historian]
A. G. O. T. U. C. (*An Inquiry into Species of Ratiocination*)

MANNING, Rosemary Joy [1911–88, English novelist and writer for children]
Sarah Davys (*Time and a Time*)
Mary Voyle (*Remaining a Stranger*; *A Change of Direction*)

MANNING, William T. [1865–1908, US journalist and political writer]
John Marthol (used when political correspondent for various newspapers)

MANSFIELD, Charles Blackford [1819–55, English chemist and social reformer]
Ithi Kefalende (in *Fraser's Magazine*)

MANSFIELD, Edward Deering [1801–80, US journalist and writer]
E. D. M. (in the *Cincinnati Daily Gazette*)
Veteran Observer (in the *New York Times*)

MANSFIELD, Milburg Francisco [1871–?, US writer and traveller]
Francis Miltoun (*Romantic Ireland*; *Dicken's London*)

MANSFIELD, Robert Blachford [1824–1908, English golfer, rower and writer]
An Oxford Man and a Wykehamist (*The Log of the Water-Lily*)

MANSON, James Bolivar [1879–1945, English writer and art critic]
Euphranor (*Contemporary Scottish Art*)

MANT, Richard [1776–1848, English cleric; Bishop of Down]
One of their Brethren (*Thoughts on the Singing of Unauthorised Hymns*)
One who is Also an Elder (*A Letter to the Rev. Henry Hart Milman*)

MANT, Walter Bishop [1807–69, English cleric and writer]
A Brother of the Apollo Lodge, 711, Oxford (*A Freemason's Pocket Companion*)

MANTLE, Winifred Langford [1911–, English romantic novelist and writer for children]
Frances Lang (*Filigree Bird; To Be a Fine Lady*)

MAPLETOFT, John [1631–1721, English physician and devotional writer]
A Lover of Truth and of the Souls of Men (*Wisdom from Above*)

MARCET, Mrs Jane [1769–1858, Swiss-born English writer for children]
John Hopkins (*Notes on Political Economy*)

MARCH, Charles [1815–64, US journalist and diplomat]
Pequot (in the *Boston Courier*)

MAREK, Kurt W. [1915–72, German writer]
C. W. Ceram (*Gods, Graves and Scholars; Archaeology of the Cinema*)

MARGOLIOUTH, Moses [1820–81, Polish-born Jew who became an English cleric]
A Clergyman (*The Curates of Riversdale*)
A Clergyman of the Church of England (*The Anglo-Hebrews; Sacred Minstrelsy*)

MARKHAM, Edward Archibald [1939–, English poet and writer]
Paul St Vincent (*Philpot in the City*)

MARKHAM, Gervase [1568–1637, English agriculturist, horse-breeder and writer]
A Man of Great Eminence and Worth (*The Inrichment of the Weald of Kent*)
*Iarius Markham (*The Dumbe Knight*)

MARKLAND, James Heywood [1788–1864, English solicitor and antiquary]
A Layman (*Diligence and Sloth*)

MARKOE, Peter [d. 1792, US poet]
A Native of Algiers (*The Patriot Chief*)

MARKS, Richard [1780–1848, English cleric]
Aliquis (*The Retrospect*)
One who Loves the Souls of the Lambs of Christ's Flock (*English History for Children*)

MARLOW, Joyce Mary [1929–, English historian]
Julia Greene (*Flashback*)

MARLOWE, Dan James [1914–, US mystery writer]
Albert Avellano (in *Alfred Hitchcock's Mystery Magazine*)

MARQUAND, Leopold [1897–, South African writer]
John Burger (*Black Man's Burden*)

MARRIOTT, George Wharton [1778–1833, English barrister]
A Barrister of the Temple (*The Toleration Act Explained*)

MARRISON, Leslie William [1901–, Irish chemist and writer on wine]
D. M. Dowley (*Nuttall's Wine Facts*)

MARRYAT, Frederick [1792–1848, English mariner and writer for boys]
Monsieur Violet (*The Narrative of the Travels and Adventures of Monsieur Violet in California, Sonora and Western Texas*)

MARSDEN, John Howard [1803–91, English cleric and antiquary]
A Member of the Senate (*A Letter to the Duke of Devonshire*)
Philomorus (*An Examination of the Poems of Sir Thomas More*)

MARSH, Charles [1774–1835, English barrister, pamphleteer and writer]
An Octogenarian; An Old Member of Parliament (both used in *New Monthly Magazine*)

MARSH, John [1907–, English romantic and mystery novelist]
Julia Davis (*Magic of the Desert*; *Nurse in Arabia*)
John Elton (*The Green Plantations*)
John Harley (*The Four Doctors*)
*Harrington Hastings (*Criminal Square*)
Irene Lawrence (*Hostage of Love*)
Joan Marsh (*Victim of Love*; *The Bride's House*)
Grace Richmond (*The Greater Love*; *That Villa in Spain*)
Petra Sawley (*Love on Ice*)
Monica Ware (*Au Pair Girl*)
Lilian Woodward (*The Tuscan Chalice*; *Out of the Past*)

MARSH, William [1775–1864, English cleric and religious writer]
A Clergyman (*Select Passages from the Sermons of a Clergyman*)

MARSHALL, Arthur C. [d. 1945, English writer for boys]
Arthur Brooke (in *Big Budget*)

MARSHALL, Mrs Caroline Louise [1849–?, US short-story writer]
Carl Louis Kingsbury (*The Girl Ranchers*; *Two Wyoming Girls*)

MARSHALL, Christabel [d. 1960, English novelist, dramatist and writer]
Christopher Marie St John (*Ellen Terry*)
R. C. Savage (in *Temple Bar*)

MARSHALL, Edison T. [1894–1967, US novelist]
Hall Hunter (*The Bengal Tiger*)

MARSHALL, Elizabeth Margaret [1926–, Scottish novelist]
Elizabeth Sutherland (*Eye of God*; *Weeping Rose*)

MARSHALL, Evelyn [1897–, English romantic and mystery novelist]
Lesley Bourne (*Trouble for Tembo*)
Jean Marsh (*Mistress of Tanglewood*; *Unbidden Dream*)

MARSHALL, Mrs Frances [d. 1920, English novelist and archaeologist]
Alan St Aubyn (*Orchard Damorel*)

MARSHALL, Francis Albert [1840–89, English dramatist and writer]
An Irvingite (*Henry Irving, Actor and Manager*)

MARSHALL, Frederick [1839–1910, English writer]
An Ex-Diplomatist; A Resident (both used in *Blackwood's Magazine*)

MARSHALL, James Vance [1887–1964, Australian writer]
Jice Doone (*Timely Tips for New Australians*)

MARSHALL, Marjorie Bell [1916–, English romantic novelist]
Stella March (*Carriage for Fiona*; *Runaway Heiress*)

MARSHALL, Nathaniel [d. 1730, English cleric]
A Presbyter of the Church of England (*The Penitential Discipline of the Primitive Church*)

MARSHALL, Stephen [1594–1655, English Presbyterian cleric and influential controversialist]
A Brother in Christ (*An Expedient to Preserve Peace and Amity*)
*Smectymnuus (*An Answer to a Book etc.*)

MARSHALL, Thomas William [1818–77, English Catholic cleric and religious writer]
Archdeacon Chasuble (*The Comedy of Convocation in the English Church*)
Herr Froehlich (*The Old Catholics at Cologne*)

MARSTON, Edward [1825–1914, English publisher and writer]
Amateur Angler (*By Meadow and Stream*; *After Work: Fragments from the Workshop*; *Days in Clover*; *Dovedale Revisited*; *Easy Chair Memories*; *An Old Man's Holidays*; *On a Sunshine Holiday*)

MARSTON, Jeffrey Eardley [1887–?, English soldier]
Jeffery E. Jeffery (*Longest Shadow*; *Servants of the Guns*)

MARSTON, John [1575–1634, English cleric and dramatist]
W. Kinsayder (*The Scourge of Villanie*; *The Metamorphosis of Pigmalion's Image*)

MARSTON, John Westland [1819–90, English poetic dramatist]
Crispinus (*The Patrician's Daughter*)

MARTIN, Alfred Tobias John [1802–50, English poet – emigrated to Australia]
A Cosmopolite (*The Penzance Library*)

MARTIN, Catherine Edith MaCauley [1847–1937, Scottish-born Australian writer]
M. C. (*The Explorers and Other Poems*)
Mrs Alick MacLeod (*The Silent Sea*)

MARTIN, David [1915–, Hungarian-born Australian journalist]
Spinifex (*Rob the Robber, his Life and Vindication*)

MARTIN, E. Le Breton [1874–1945, English writer for boys]
Raymond Lee (in *Boy's Leader*)
Donovan Mart (in *Big Budget*)

MARTIN, Sir Henry [1801–63, English historian and writer]
A Lay Baronet (*Archbishop Murray's Rhemish Bible*)

MARTIN, John [1741–1820, English cleric and writer]
Eubulus (*A Letter to a Young Gentleman in Prison*)

MARTIN, Patricia Miles [1899–1986, US writer for children]
Jerry Lane (in *The Zoo*)
Miska Miles (*Rabbit Garden*; *Beaver Moon*)

MARTIN, Peter John [1786–1860, English physician and geologist]
P. P. (in the *Gardener's Chronicle*)

MARTIN, Robert Bernard [1918–, US academic and writer]
Robert Bernard (*Death Takes a Sabbatical*; *To Have and to Kill*)

MARTIN, Robert Lee [1908–, US writer]
Lee Roberts (*Little Sister*; *Suspicion*)

MARTIN, Roy Peter [1931–, English mystery writer]
Hampton Charles (*Advantage Miss Seeton*; *Miss Seeton at the Helm*)
James Melville (*Chrysanthemum Chain*; *Sort of Samurai*)

MARTIN, Sir Theodore [1816–1909, Scottish lawyer, humorous poet and drama critic]
*Bon Gaultier (*Bon Gaultier Ballads*)
*Colonel Crockett; *Eminent Hands; Lucifer Swing (all used in *Tait's Edinburgh Magazine*)
Quintus Horatius Flaccus (in *Blackwood's Magazine*)

MARTIN, Violet Florence [1865–1915, Irish novelist]
Martin Ross (see also Somerville and Ross) (*An Irish Cousin*; *Naboth's Vineyard*)

MARTIN, William [1772–1851, English ropemaker, inventor and eccentric philosopher]
Jack Gossamer, Railroad Philosopher (in *Bentley's Miscellany*)

MARTIN, William [1801–67, English schoolmaster and writer for children]
Old Chatty Cheerful (in *The Boy's Own Annual*)
Peter Parley (*The Holiday Keepsake*; *Peter Parley's Tales for Youth*)

MARTIN, William Alexander Parsons [1827–1916, US missionary in China]
An Eye-Witness (*The Siege of Peking*)

MARTIN, Sir William Fanshawe [1801–95, English admiral]
A Flag Officer (*The Admiralty*)

MARTINEAU, Harriet [1802–76, English social reformer and writer]
An Invalid (*Life in the Sick Room*)
A Lady (*Devotional Exercises*)

MARTING, Ruth Leonore [1907–, US writer]
Hilea Bailey (*What Night Will Bring*; *The Smiling Corpse*)

MARTYN, Edward [1859–1923, Irish dramatist]
Sirius (*Morgante the Lesser*)

MARTYN, John [1699–1768, English botanist and writer]
Mr Bavius (in the *Grub Street Journal* and for *Memoirs of the Society of Grub Street*)

MARTYN, Wyndham [1875–?, English writer]
William Grenvil (*Trent Fights Again*; *Murder Island*)

MARVELL, Andrew [1621–78, English poet, pamphleteer and satirist]
A Protestant (*Remarks upon a Late Disingenuous Discourse etc.*)
Andreas Rivetus Jun. (*Mr Smirke or the Divine in Mode*)

MASCHLER, Tom [fl. 1989, English publisher]
*Mark Caine (*The S – Man: a Grammar of Success*)

MASCHWITZ, Eric [1901–69, English librettist and novelist]
Holt Marvell (*Under London*; *Good-Night Vienna*)

MASERES, Francis [1731–1824, English barrister, mathematician and historian]
A Friend to the Church of England (*The Moderate Reformer*)

MASKELL, William [1814–90, English cleric and ecclesiastical historian]
A Priest of the Church of England (*A Letter to the Clergy upon the Speech of the Bishop of Norwich*)

MASKELYNE, John Nevil [1839–1917, English conjuror and magician]
A Genuine Medium (in *Boy's Own Paper*)

MASON, Arthur Telford (fl. 1924, English writer]
Artemas (*The Book of Artemas*; *D'You Know This One?*)

MASON, Douglas Rankine [1918–, Welsh schoolmaster and science-fiction writer]
John Rankine (*The Blockage of Sinitron*; *Interstellar Two-Five*)

MASON, Francis van Wyck [1901–78, US crime, mystery and children's writer]
Geoffrey Coffin (*The Forgotten Fleet Mystery*; *Murder in the Senate*)
Frank W. Mason (*Q-Boat*; *Flight into Danger*)
Ward Weaver (*Hang my Wreath*)

MASON, George [1735–1806, English barrister and writer]
A British Freeholder (*A British Freeholder's Answer to Thomas Paine*)

MASON, George Champlin [1820–94, US journalist and illustrator]
Robert O. Lincoln (*George Ready or How to Live for Others*)

MASON, John Monck [1726–1809, Irish barrister, politician and Shakespearian scholar]
A Gentleman of Ireland (*Remarks upon Poyning's Law*)

MASON, Michael Henry [1909–, Scottish natural historian and writer]
Cameron Blake (*Set Stormy*; *Only Men on Board*)

MASON, Philip [1906–, English writer]
Philip Woodruff (*The Wild Sweet Witch*; *Whatever Dies*)

MASON, Richard Angelus [1601–78, English Franciscan monk and theologian]
Br. Angelus Francis (*The Manuell of the Arch*; *The Rule of Penance of the Seraphicall Father St Francis*)

MASON, Robert [fl. 1789, Scottish writer]
Ebenezer Lazarus (*A Particular Description of the Town of Kelso*)

MASON, William [1724–97, English cleric, lyrical dramatist, musician and political reformer]
A Gentleman of Cambridge (*Mirth*)
Arthur MacGreggor of Knightsbridge Esq. (*An Epistle to Dr Shebbeare*)
Malcolm MacGreggor (*An Heroic Epistle to Sir William Chambers*; *Ode to Mr Pinchbeck*)

MASTER, William [1627–84, English cleric and devotional writer]
A Student in Theologie (*Essays and Observations, Theologicall and Morall*)

MASTERSON, Graham [1946–, Scottish novelist]
Thomas Luke (*Hell Candidate*; *Phobia*)

MATHER, Anne [fl. 1970, English romantic novelist]
Caroline Fleming (*Dark Venetian*)

MATHER, Cotton [1663–1728, American cleric and writer]
An American (*American Tears upon the Ruines of Greek Churches*)
A Christian in a Cold Season (*Christianus Per Ignum*)
An English Minister (*An Epistle to the Christian Indians*)
A Fellow of the Royal Society (*Coheleth*; *The Angel of Bethesda*)
A Gentleman Lately Restored from Threatening Sickness (*Small Offers towards the Service of the Tabernacle*)
A Lover of his Country (*A Brief Account of the Province of Massachusetts Bay*)
A Minister in Boston (*A Letter to a Friend in the Country*)
One Intimately Connected with Him (*Life of His Excellency Sir William Phips*)
One of their Number (*The Minister: a Sermon*)
One of the Ministers in Boston (*Sober Sentiments*)

One of the Ministers in the North part of Boston (*The Soul upon the Wing*)
One that Has Had Experience of Them (*The Nightingale*)
One that Was Once a Scholar to Him (*Corderius Americanus*)
Philalethes (*A Letter of Advice to the Churches of the Nonconformists*)
Philopolites (*A Memorial of the Present Deplorable State of New England*)

MATHER, Frederick [1833–1900, US writer on angling]
Kego-e-Kay (*Men I Have Fished With*)

MATHER, Increase [1639–1723, American cleric and religious writer]
A Friend to the Churches (*A Plea for the Ministers of the Gospel*)

MATHER, Samuel [1706–85, American cleric]
An American Englishman (*An Attempt to Shew the America etc.*)
Aurelius Prudentius, Americanus (*The Sacred Minister*)

MATHERS, Edward Powys [1892–1939, English writer and crossword compiler]
Torquemada (*Cain's Jawbone*)

MATHEWS, Albert [1820–1903, US lawyer and writer]
Paul Siegvolk (*Ruminations*; *Walter Ashwood*)

MATHEWS, Mrs Anne [1782–1869, English actress and writer]
A Child of Larger Growth; A Gastronome (both used in *Bentley's Miscellany*)

MATHEWS, Charles James [1803–78, English actor and dramatist]
Pelham Hardwick (used for an adaptation of *The Bachelor of Arts*)

MATHEWS, Cornelius [1817–89, US journalist and writer]
The late Ben Smith (*The Motley Book*)

MATHIAS, Benjamin Williams [1772–1841, Irish cleric and theologian]
A Clergyman of the Established Church (*Vindiciae Laicae*)

MATHIAS, Thomas James [1754–1835, English publisher, satirist and Italian scholar]
Antenor (*Watsoniana*; *Antenor's Letter to George Chalmers*)
A Layman (*A Letter to the Lord Marquis of Buckingham*)
Martin Scriblerus (*An heroic Epistle to the Rev. Richard Watson*)

MATTHEW, Robert [1825– ?, Scottish writer]
A Sexagenarian (*Reminiscences, Poems, Sketches and Letters*)

MATTHEWMAN, Phyllis [fl. 1945, English writer for girls]
Kathryn Surrey (*Maids A-Waiting*; *Bees at Marlings*)

MATTHEWS, Henry [1789–1828, English jurist]
An Invalid (*The Diary of an Invalid 1817–19*)
Jonathan Kentucky (in *New Monthly Magazine*)

MATTHEWS, James Brander [1852–1929, US playwright and writer]
Arthur Penn (*The Home Library*)

MATTHEWS, Patricia A. [1927–, US romantic novelist]
P. A. (or Patty) Brisco (*The Campus Mystery*; *The Other People*)
Laura Wylie (*The Night Visitor*)

MATTHEWS, William [d. 1816, English Quaker]
Catholicus (*A New and Seasonable Address to Quakers*)
Theophilus Freeman (*A General Epistle of Brotherly Admonition*)
A Lover of Christian Liberty (*Considerations on Public Worship*)

MATURIN, Charles Robert [1782–1824, Irish dramatist and novelist]
Dennis Jasper Murphy (*The Milesian Chief*; *The Fatal Revenge*; *The Wild Irish Boy*)

MAUDE, Aylmer [1858–1938, English merchant in Russia, art critic and translator of Tolstoy]
De Monte Alto, Resident in Moscow (*The Tsar's Coronation as Seen by etc.*)

MAUDE, Francis Cornwallis [1828–1900, English soldier]
Vazaha (in *Fortnightly Review*)

MAUNSELL, Sir Frederick Richard [1828–1916, Irish soldier]
A Survivor who Filled an Important Post at the Glorious Siege (*The Siege of Delhi*)

MAURICE, Frederick Denison [1805–72, English cleric, moral philosopher and writer]
A Clergyman of the Church of England (*The Kingdom of Christ*)
Rusticus (*Subscription No Bondage*)

MAURICE, John Frederick [1841–1912, English soldier and military writer]
The Daily News Special Correspondent (*The Ashantee War*)
Miles (in *Contemporary Review*)
A Staff Officer (in *MacMillan's Magazine*)

MAURICE, Thomas [1754–1824, English cleric and oriental scholar]
A Gentleman of Oxford (*Ode, Sacred to the Genius of Handel*)

MAURY, Matthew Fontaine [1806–73, US mariner, hydrographer and astronomer]
Harry Bluff (in the *Southern Literary Messenger*)

MAVOR, Osborne Henry [1888–1951, Scottish physician and dramatist]
James Bridie (*Tobias and the Angel*; *The Anatomist*)
Mary Henderson (*The Sunlight Sonata*)

MAVOR, William Fordyce [1758–1837, English cleric and educationalist]
A Father (*The Juvenile Olio or, Mental Medley*)
William Frederick Martyn (in the *Geographical Magazine*)

MAXEY, Virgil [1785–1844, US politician]
A Citizen of Maryland (*The Maryland Resolutions*)

MAXWELL, Ann Elizabeth [1944–, US romantic novelist]
Elizabeth Lowell (*Forget Me Not*; *Too Hot to Handle*)

MAXWELL, James [1580–1640, English writer]
James Anneson (*Cardanna*)

MAXWELL (née Braddon), Mrs Mary Elizabeth [1837–1915, English novelist and dramatist]
Aunt Belinda (*The Good Hermione*)
Mary E. Braddon (*Like and Unlike*; *Dead Love Has Chains*)
Lady Caroline Lascelles (*The Black Band*)
Babington White (*Circe*)

MAXWELL, Patricia Anne [1942–, US romantic novelist]
Jennifer Blake (*Love's Wild Desire*; *Tender Betrayal*)
Maxine Patrick (*Snowbound Heart*)
Patricia Ponder (*Haven of Fear*; *Murder for Charity*)
Elizabeth Trehearne (*Storm at Midnight*)

MAXWELL, Violet Spoole [fl. 1948, Australian writer]
C. Bede Maxwell (*Surf: Australians Against the Sea*; *The Cold Nose of the Law*)

MAXWELL, William Hamilton [1792–1850, Irish soldier, cleric and novelist]
A Gentleman on Half-Pay (*Captain O'Sullivan*)
One who Travelled with a Gentleman from Connemara (in *Dublin University Magazine*)
A Soldier of Fortune (*Rambling Recollections of a Soldier of Fortune*)

MAY, Philip William [1864–1903, English cartoonist and illustrator]
Charlie Summers (*The Parson and the Painter*)

MAYHEW, Horace [1816–72, English humorist]
A Maid of All Work (*Letters about Missusses*)

MAYNE, Ethel Colburn [d. 1941, Irish novelist and biographer]
Frances E. Huntley (in both *The Yellow Book* and in *Chapman's Magazine*)

MAYNE, Jasper [1604–72, English cleric, dramatist and pamphleteer]
One of the Students of Christ Church (*A Sermon Concerning Unity and Agreement*)

MAYNE, William [1928–, English writer for children]
Martin Cobalt (*The Swallows*)
Dynely James (*The Gobbling Billy*)
Charles Molin (*Ghosts, Spooks and Spectres*, of which he was the editor; *Dormouse Tales*)

MAYNWARING, Everard [1628–99, English physician and writer]
A Strict Examiner of the Medical Art (*The Catholic Medicine and Soverain Healer*)

MAYO, Henry [1733–93, English dissenting cleric]
Candidus (*The True Scripture Doctrine Regarding Baptism*)
A Learned Doctor (*An Address to Protestant Dissenters*)

MAYO, Herbert [1796–1852, English physician, surgeon and medical writer]
Mac Davus (in *Blackwood's Magazine*)

MAYO, Isabella Fyvie [1843–1914, English novelist and poet]
Edward Garrett (*The Occupations of a Retired Life*; *Premiums Paid to Experience*)

MAYO, Richard [1631–95, English cleric and theologian]
A Presbyter of the Church of England (*Several Hundred Texts of Holy Scripture*)

MAYO, William Starbuck [1811–95, US physician and novelist]
Jonathan Romer (*Kaloolah*)

MAYOR, F. M. [1872–1931, English actress and novelist]
Mary Stafford (*Mrs Hammond's Children*)

MAYOW, Robert Wynell [1777–1817, English cleric]
Daniel Merdant (*Tracts for the Use of the Poor*)

MEAD, Charles Marsh [1836–1911, US cleric and theologian]
E. D. M'Realsham (*Romans Dissected*)

MEAD, Edward [1914–, US writer]
Shepherd Mead (*How to Succeed in Business without Really Trying*)

MEAD, Edwin Doak [1849–1937, US writer]
An Independent (*The Case of Mr Blaine*)

MEAD, Lucia Ames [1856–1936, US writer and lecturer]
Lucia True Ames (*Memoirs of a Millionaire*)

MEADLEY, George Wilson [1774–1818, English merchant and biographer]
A Lay Seceder (*Letter to the Bishop of St David's*)

MEAGHER, Thomas Francis [1823–67, Irish nationalist who was transported to Australia and escaped to the USA; became a journalist]
Cornelius O'Keefe (in *Harper's Magazine*)

MEAKER, Marijane [1932–, US novelist and writer for children]
Mary James (*Shoebag*)
M. E. Kerr (*The Son of Someone Famous; Night Kites*)
Vin Packer (*Intricate Victims; The Evil Friendship*)

MEARES, John Willoughby [1871–1946, English engineer]
Uncut Cavendish (*Contract Bridge Bidding Systems; Golf: Match and Stroke Rules*)

MEARS, Louise [1874–?, US educator and writer]
Newton Sanders (*A Comedy of Three; Concerning Some Fools and their Folly*)

MEDHURST, Walter Henry [1796–1857, English linguist and missionary in China]
Philo-Sinensis (*Notices on Chinese Grammar*)

MEEHAN, Charles Patrick [1812–90, Irish cleric, translator and historian]
Clericus (in *The Nation*)

MEEKE, Mrs Mary [d. 1815, English novelist]
Gabrielli (*Independence; The Mysterious Wife; The Mysterious Husband; Stratagems Defeated*)

MEEKER, Nellie J. [fl. 1901, US novelist]
Jane Valentine (*In the Market-Place; James Brand*)

MEGAW, Arthur Stanley [d. 1961, Irish solicitor and writer]
Arthur Stanley (*The Golden Road; The Out-of-Doors Book*)

MEGROZ, Rodolpho Louis [1891–1968, English journalist, poet, dramatist and biographer]
C. D. Dimsdale (*Come out of Doors; Countryside and Coast*)

MEGSON, William Broadley [fl. 1889, English writer]
Trim (*The Original Story of Old Wilds*)

MEIGS, Cornelia [1884–1973, US novelist and writer for children]
Adair Aldon (*The Island of Appledore; The Hill of Adventure*)

MELDRUM, George [1635–1709, Scottish cleric and religious writer]
A Friend in the City (*A Letter from a Friend in the City to a Member of Parliament*)

MELLEN, Grenville [1799–1841, US poet]
Reginald Reverie (*Glad Tales and Sad Tales*)

MELLETT, John Calvin [1888–?, US writer]
Jonathan Brooks (*Chains of Lightning; High Ground*)

MELMOTH, William [1710–99, English classical scholar and writer]
Sir Thomas Fitzosborne (*Letters on Several Subjects*)

MELONEY, William Brown [1903–71, US novelist]
*Franken Meloney (*Strange Victory*; *American Bred*)

MEMMINGER, Christopher Augustus [1803–88, US lawyer and politician]
A Spectator of the Past (*The Book of Nullification*)

MENCKEN, Henry Louis [1880–1956, US journalist, essayist and critic]
*Owen Hatteras (*Pistols for Two*)

MENDHAM, Joseph [1769–1856, English cleric and religious writer]
Catholicus (*The Episcopal Oath of Allegiance to the Pope*)
Catholicus Protestans (*On the Proposed Papal Cathedral in Birmingham*)
Emancipatus (*The Spiritual Venality of Rome*; *Taxatio Papalis*)
Eupator (*Cardinal Allen's Admonition to the Nobility*; *The Declaration of the Fathers of the Council of Trent*)

MENKEN, Ada Isaacs [1835–68, US actress, teacher and poet]
Indigena (*Memories*)

MERCER, Cecil William [1885–1960, English novelist]
Dornford Yates (*Berry and Co.*; *Jonah and Co.*)

MEREDITH, Edward [1648–89, English Catholic controversialist]
A Lover of Truth, Vertue and Justice (*Some Remarques upon Julian the Apostate*)

MEREDITH (née Twamly), Mrs Louisa Anne [1812–95, English poet and artist – lived sometime in Australia]
Louisa Anne Twamley (*Poems*; *The Romance of Nature*; *Flora's Gems, or The Treasures of Parterre*)

MERIVALE, Herman Charles [1839–1906, English lawyer, novelist and dramatist]
Felix Dale (*He's a Lunatic*; *Six Months Ago*)

MERIVALE, John Herman [1779–1844, English barrister and writer]
Metrodorus (in *Blackwood's Magazine*)

MERIWETHER, Elizabeth Avery [1824–1917, US author]
George Edmonds (*Facts and Falsehoods concerning the War on the South 1861 and 1865*)

MERRIL, Judith [1923–, Canadian science-fiction writer]
*Cyril Judd (*Gunner Cade*; *Outpost Mars*)

MERRITT, Henry [1822–77, English art critic and picture restorer]
Christopher (in *The Reasoner*)

MERRY, Robert [1755–98, English enthusiastic failure ... at Cambridge, in the army, as a gambler and as a dramatist]
Della Crusca (in *The World* and the *British Album* and for *Diversity – a Poem* and *The Poetry of Anna Matilda*)

MERTON, Holmes Whittier [1860–1948, US astrologer]
Yarmo Vedra (*Descriptive Mentality from the Head, Face and Hand*; *Heliocentric Astrology*)

MERTZ, Barbara [1927–, US crime and mystery writer]
Barbara Michaels (*House of Many Shadows*; *Wizard's Daughter*)
Elizabeth Peters (*Devil-May-Care*; *Ghost in Green Velvet*)

MERWIN, W. Samuel [1910–, US science-fiction writer]
Matt Lee (in *Thrilling Wonder Stories* magazine)
Carter Sprague (in *Startling Stories* magazine)

MERYON, Charles Lewis [1783–1877, English physician, traveller and biographer]
A Physician (*Travels of Lady Hester Stanhope*)

Deuteros Whistlecraft, Gent. (*The Origin of Rome and the Papacy*)

MESTON, William [1688–1745, Scottish schoolmaster and poet]
Quidam (*The Knight of the Kirk*)

METCALFE, Frederick [1815–85, English scholar of Scandinavia]
The Oxonian (*The Oxonian in Thelemarken 1856–57*)

METEYARD, Eliza [1816–79, English novelist and essayist]
Silverpen (*Lady Herbert's Gentlewoman*; *Mainstone's Housekeeper*)

MEWS, Peter [1619–1706, English cleric and royalist; Bishop of Winchester]
A Learned Pen (*The Ex-Ale-Tation of Ale*)

MEYNELL, Alice Christiana Gertrude [1847–1922, English poet and essayist]
A. M.; Autolycus (both used in *Pall Mall Gazette*)
A. C. Thompson (*Preludes*)

MEYNELL, Esther Hallam [d. 1955, English biographer and historian]
Esther Hallam (in *Temple Bar*)

MEYNELL, Laurence Walter [1899–1989, English novelist and crime writer]
Valerie Baxter (*Jane: Young Author*)
Robert Eton (*The Corner of Paradise Place*; *The Faithful Years*)
Geoffrey Ludlow (*Inside Out or, Mad as a Hatter*; *Women Had to Do It*)
A. Stephen Tring (*The Old Gang*; *Penny Dreadful*)

MEYNELL, Wilfrid [1852–1948, English journalist, poet and writer]
John Oldcastle (*Journals and Journalism*)

MICHAEL, Ian David Lewis [1936–, English academic]
David Serafin (*Saturday of Glory*)

MICHELBOURNE, John [1647–1721, English Governor of Londonderry]

A Gentleman who Was in the Town during the Whole Siege (*Ireland Preserv'd or the Siege of London-Derry*)

MICHELL, Nicholas [1807–80, Scottish writer]
An Essayist on the Passions (*The Fatalist or the Fortunes of Godolphin*)

MICHIE, Alexander [1833–1902, English merchant in and writer on China]
Amicus (in *Cornhill Magazine*)

MICHIE, Archibald [1810–99, English physician, barrister and legal officer in Australia]
Jack Robinson (*The Hamlet Controversy*)

MIDDLETON, Conyers [1683–1750, English cleric and religious writer]
A Member of the University of Cambridge (*Remarks upon Proposals Lately Published by Richard Bentley*)

MIDDLETON, Ellis [1884–?, English architect and novelist]
John Morton Lees (*Fine Raiment*)

MIDDLETON, Henry [1771–1846, US politician]
A South Carolinian (*The Economical Causes of Slavery in the United States*)

MIDDLETON, Richard [1882–1911, English poet, essayist and short-story writer]
R. Dundas (in *Vanity Fair* for *Blue Blood*)

MIERS, Earl Schenk [1910–72, US writer]
David William Meredith (*The Christmas Card Murders*)

MIGHELS, Ella Stirling [1853–1934, US writer]
Aurora Esmeralda (*Life and Letters of a Forty-Niner's Daughter*)

MILBOURNE, Luke [1649–1720, English cleric and poet]
Poor Old Tom of Bedlam (*The Two Wolves in Lambs' Skins*)

MILBURN, William Henry [1823–1903, US Chaplain to the Congress – blind for most of his adult life]
The Blind Preacher (*Ten Years of a Preacher's Life*)

MILDMAY, Aubrey Neville St John [1865–1955, English cleric, poet and writer]
Autremonde (*Poetical Works of Autremonde*)

MILKOMANE, George Alexis Milkomanovich [1903–, Russian-born physician, novelist and writer; took British nationality in 1938]
George Borodin (*Visions of Contempt; Soviet and Tsarist Siberia*)
George Braddon (*The Dog It Was That Died; Time Off for Death*)
Peter Conway (*The Weather of my Fate*)
George Sava (*The Healing Knife; A Surgeon's Destiny*)

MILL, John Stuart [1806–73, English philosopher and political economist]
D (in *Fraser's Magazine*)
Wickliffe (letters to the *Morning Chronicle*)

MILLAR, John [1735–1801, Scottish jurist and writer]
Crito (*Letters of Crito on the Causes of the Present War*)

MILLAR, John Hepburn [1864–1929, Scottish law professor and essayist]
A Country Cousin (in *Blackwood's Magazine*)

MILLAR, Kenneth [1915–83, US mystery writer]
John MacDonald (*The Moving Target*)
John Ross MacDonald (*Meet Me at the Morgue*)
Ross MacDonald (*Drowning Pool; Underground Man*)

MILLARD, Bailey [1859–1941, US journalist and writer]
Frank Bailey (*Jack Morning's Treasure*)

MILLARD, Christopher Sclater [1872–1927, English bibliographer]
Stuart Mason (*A Bibliography of Oscar Wilde; Oscar Wilde, Art and Morality*)

MILLAY, Edna St Vincent [1892–1950, US poet]
Nancy Boyd (*Distressing Dialogues*)

MILLER, Lady Anna Riggs [1741–81, English poet and writer]
An English Woman (*Letters from Italy in the Years 1770 and 1771*)

MILLER, Bill [1920–61, US mystery writer]
*Will Daemar (*The Case of the Lonely Lovers*)
*Whit Masterson (*Badge of Evil; Hammer in his Hand*)
*Wade Miller (*Devil on Two Sticks; Calamity Fair*)
*Dale Wilmer (*Memo for Murder; Dead Fall*)

MILLER, Charles Henry [1842–1922, US artist and writer]
Carl De Muldor (*The Philosophy of Art in America*)

MILLER, Cincinnatus Hiner [1839–1913, US playwright and poet]
Joaquin Miller (*First Families of the Sierras*)

MILLER, Edward [1731–1807, English organist, musician and local historian]
A Professor of Music (*A Letter to the Country Spectator*)

MILLER, George [1764–1848, Irish cleric, pamphleteer and writer]
Humanitas (*War, a System of Madness and Irreligion*)
A Surrogate (in *Blackwood's Magazine*)
A Young Traveller (*The Traveller's Guide to Madeira and the West Indies*)

MILLER, Mrs Harriet Mann [1831–1918, US ornithologist and writer]
Gwynfryn (*Friends in Fur and Feathers*)
Olive Thorn Miller (*A Bird Lover in the West; Little Folks in Feathers and Fur and others in Neither*)

MILLER, Hugh [1802–56, Scottish stonemason and writer]
A Geologist (*Rambles of a Geologist*)
A Journeyman Mason (*Poems Written in the Leisure Hours of a Journeyman Mason*)
One of the Scotch People (*Letter from One of the Scotch People to Lord Brougham*)
The Stonemason of Cromartie (*Poems*)

MILLER, James [1706–44, English dramatist]
H. Fielding, Gent. (*The Mother-in-Law*)
A Gentleman of Wadham College (*The Humours of Oxford*)

MILLER, Mrs John A. [fl. 1868, US religious writer]
Faith Latimer (*Hidden Talent; In the Temple; The Wedding Feast*)

MILLER, John Cale [1814–80, English cleric and religious writer]
A Birmingham Clergyman (*The Bicentenary Controversy*)

MILLER, Leonard [1864–1939, English novelist and playwright; changed his name to Merrick by deed-poll]
Leonard Merrick (*The Man Who Understood Women; The Little Dog Laughed*)

MILLER, Lydia Falconer [1811–76, Scottish writer for children]
Harriet Myrtle (*Ocean Child*)

MILLER, Mary Britton [1883–1975, US poet and novelist]
Isabel Bolton (*Do I Wake or Sleep?; Many Mansions*)

MILLETT, Nigel [1904–, English writer]
Richard Oke (*Strange Island Story; India's Coral Strand*)

MILLIGAN, Terence Alan [1918–, English-Irish humorist and writer]
Spike Milligan (*Milliganimals; Rommel: Gunner Who?*)

MILLIGAN, William [1821–93, Scottish cleric and theologian]
An Elder of the Free Church of Scotland (*A Scriptural and Historical Catechism*)

A Layman (*New Metrical Readings of the Psalms*)

MILLS, Algernon Victor [fl. 1943, English writer]
Rupert Latimer (*Death in Real Life; Murder After Christmas*)

MILLS, Charles [1788–1826, English historical writer]
Theodore Ducas (*The Travels of Theodore Ducas*)

MILLS, George [1808–81, Scottish shipbuilder, journalist and writer]
Mesrat Merligogels (*Craigclutha*)

MILLS, Hugh Travers [fl. 1967, US crime writer]
Hugh Travers (*Madame Aubrey and the Police; Madame Aubrey Dines with Death*)

MILNE, Alan Alexander [1882–1956, English humorist, essayist and writer for children]
A. A. M. (*The Holiday Round*)
A. K. M. (used for poems written with his brother Kenneth)

MILNER, George [1829–1914, English writer and editor]
Geoffrey Milbrook (*Country Pleasures*)

MILNER, John [1752–1826, English Catholic cleric and theologian]
A Catholic Christian (*The Inquisition: a Letter to Sir John Hippisley*)
John Merlin (*Strictures on the Poet Laureate's Book of the Church*)
A Native Roman Catholic Prelate (*An Humble Remonstrance to the House of Commons*)

MILNER, Nina Marion [1900–, English psychoanalyst and writer]
Joanna Field (*An Experiment in Leisure; A Life of One's Own*)

MILNES, Richard Monckton [1809–85, 1st Baron Houghton; social and political reformer]
A Layman (*One Tract More*)
A Protestant (in *Cornhill Magazine*)

MILTON, Ernest [1890–1974, English actor and writer]
Quite a Gentleman (*Two Novelettes*)
David Wells (*Paganini*)

MILTON, John [1608–74, English poet]
The Former Author J. M. (*Colasterion*)

MINER, Charles [1780–1865, US journalist and humorist]
John Harwood (in the *West Chester Village Record*)
Poor Robert the Scribe (*Essays from the Desk of Poor Robert the Scribe*)

MINTO, William [1845–93, Scottish journalist, critic and novelist]
A Scotch Graduate (*The Claims of Classical Studies*)

MITCHEL, William [1672–1740, Scottish lamplighter and untutored pamphleteer]
A Great Tinklarian Doctor (*The Tinkler's Testament*)

MITCHELL, Donald Grant [1822–1908, US satirist, essayist and writer]
A Bachelor (*Reveries of a Bachelor*)
Ik Marvel (*Fresh Gleanings*; *Fudge Doings: being Tony Fudge's Record of the Same*)
An Opera Goer; John Timon (both used in *The Lorgnette*)

MITCHELL, Gladys Maude Winifred [1901–83, English novelist, crime and children's writer]
Stephen Hockaby (*Outlaws of the Border*; *March Hay*)
Malcolm Torrie (*Heavy as Lead*; *Late and Cold*)

MITCHELL, James Leslie [1901–35, Scottish novelist and archaeologist]
Lewis Grassic Gibbon (*A Scots Quair*; *Grey Granite*; *Niger: the Life of Mungo Park*)

MITCHELL, James W. [1926–, English mystery writer]
James Munro (*The Man Who Sold Death*; *The Innocent Bystanders*)

MITCHELL, John [d. 1772, English-born American physician]
An Impartial Hand (*The Contest in America between Great Britain and France*)

MITCHELL, John [1785–1859, English soldier and biographer]
Bombardinio (in *Fraser's Magazine*)
Captain Orlando Sabretache (*The Art of Conversation*)

MITCHELL, John [1794–1870, US cleric]
John Chester (*Derwent or, Recollections of Young Life in the Country*)
Graduate of Yale of the Class of 1821 (*Reminiscences of Scenes and Characters in College*)

MITCHELL, John [1880–1951, Canadian lawyer and writer]
Patrick Slater (*The Yellow Briar*)

MITCHELL, John Kearsley [1796–1858, US physician]
A Yankee (*Saint Helena*)

MITCHELL, Langdon Elwyn [1862–1935, US dramatist and writer]
John Philip Varley (*The Picture Book of Becky Sharp*; *Poems*; *Love in the Backwoods*; *Sylvian, a Tragedy and Other Poems*)

MITCHILL, Samuel Latham [1764–1831, US academic, scientist and politician]
A Gentleman Residing in this City (*The Picture of New York*)

MITFORD, John [1782–1831, English mariner, journalist and writer]
A British Sailor (*Poems of a British Sailor*)
Alfred Burton (*The Adventures of Johnny Newcome in the Navy*)

MIVART, St George Jackson [1827–1900, English barrister, physician and biologist]
D'Arcy Drew (*Henry Standon*)

MIZNER, Elizabeth Howard [1907–, US novelist]
Elizabeth Howard (*Love Has Two Faces*)

MOBERLY, Charlotte Anne Elizabeth
[1846–1937, English academic and writer]
Elizabeth Morison (*An Adventure*)

MODELL, Miriam [1908–, US mystery writer]
Evelyn Piper (*Bunny Lake is Missing; The Naked Murderer*)

MOGRIDGE, George [1787–1854, English writer for children]
Uncle Adam (*The Chinese*)
Carlton Bruce (*The Boy's Friend; Mirth and Morality*)
C. (*Sarah Martin, the Prison Visitor of Great Yarmouth*)
Ephraim Holding (*Ephraim Holding's Homely Hints to Sunday School Teachers*)
Old Alan Grey (*Cheerful Chapters Adapted to Youth*)
Old Humphrey (*History, Manners and Customs of the North American Indians*)
An Old Officer (*Soldiers and Sailors or Anecdotes etc.*)
Peter Parley (*Tales About Rome and Modern Italy*)

MOIR, David MacBeth [1798–1851, Scottish physician and essayist]
Gabriel Cowitch (in *Fraser's Magazine*)
Delta (in *Blackwood's Magazine* and for *Domestic Verses* and *The Legend of Genevieve*)
Joseph Thomson (in *Blackwood's Magazine*)
Mansie Waugh (*The Life of Mansie Waugh, Tailor in Dalkieth*)

MOIR, George [1800–70, Scottish jurist, academic and writer]
*Peter Jenkins (in *Blackwood's Magazine*)

MOLESWORTH, Mary Louisa [1839–1921, Dutch-born Scottish novelist and writer for children]
Ennis Graham (*Lover and Husband; Cicely*)

MOLESWORTH, Robert [1656–1725, 1st Viscount Molesworth; politician]
R. L. V. M. (*Some Considerations for Promoting Agriculture*)

MONCREIFF, Sir James Wellwood
[1776–1851, Lord Moncreiff; Scottish jurist]
A Member of the Scotch Bar (*Morning and Other Poems*)

MONCRIEFF, Alexander [1695–1761, Scottish Presbyterian writer]
A Minister of the Church of Scotland (*The Proper, True and Supreme Deity*)

MONCRIEFF, Robert Hope [1846–1927, Scottish writer and editor]
Ascott R. Hope (in *Boy's Own Paper* and for *The Adventures of Two Runaways*)

MONCRIEFF, William Thomas
[1794–1857, Scottish dramatist]
A Collegian (*Prison Thoughts*)

MONK, James Henry [1784–1856, English cleric and classical scholar; Bishop of Gloucester]
Philograntus (*A Letter to John, Bishop of Bristol*)

MONRO, Alexander [d. 1715, Scottish cleric and academic]
A Presbyter of the Church of Scotland (*The History of Scotch Presbytery*)

MONRO, Thomas [1764–1815, English cleric and writer]
Hipponax (*Spring in London*)
Oxoniensis (*Philoctetes in Lemnos*)

MONSELL, John Samuel Bewley [1811–75, Irish cleric and hymn writer]
The Doctor (*The Doe Done to Death by the Dog*)
The Old Vicar (*Lights and Shadows*)

MONSON, Frederick John [1809–41, English writer]
A Layman (*Four Sermons*)

MONSON, Sir John [1600–83, English religious writer; royalist in the English Civil War]
A Person of Quality (*A Discourse Concerning Supreme Power and Common Right*)

MONTAGU, Basil [1770–1851, English lawyer and writer]
A Chancery Barrister (*Thoughts on Laughter*)
A Lover of Order (*Some Thoughts upon Liberty and the Rights of Englishmen*)
A Water Drinker (*Inquiries into the Effects of Fermented Liquors*)

MONTAGU, Lady Mary Wortley [1689–1762, English writer, traveller, poet and pioneer for smallpox inoculation]
An English Lady who was Lately in Turkey (*The Genuine Copy of a Letter Written from Constantinople*)
The Right Hon. L. M. W. M. (*Six Town Eclogues*)
A Lady (*Verses Addressed to the Imitator of the Second Book of Horace*)
Mrs President (in *The Spectator*)
A Turkey Merchant (*A Plain Account of the Innoculating of the Small Pox*)

MONTAGUE, William Edward [1838–1906, English soldier]
*A Military Contributor (in *Blackwood's Magazine*)

MONTEFIORE, Mrs Charlotte [d. 1854, English Jewish writer]
One of Themselves (*A Few Words to the Jews*)

MONTGOMERY, Hugh de F. [d. 1924, Irish Ulster politician]
An Ulster Landlord (*Irish Land and Irish Rights*)

MONTGOMERY, James [1771–1854, English journalist, poet and hymn writer]
A Poet (*Prose*)
Peter Positive (*Prison Amusements and Other Trifles*)
Gabriel Silvertongue (*The Whisperer*)

MONTGOMERY, John Wilson [1835–1911, Irish policeman]
An Ex-Officer of the Royal Irish Constabulary; A Retired Constabulary Officer (both used in *Dublin University Magazine*)

MONTGOMERY, Kathleen [d. 1960, Irish novelist and writer]
*K. L. Montgomery (*The Ark of the Curse*; *Tyrol under the Axe of Fascism*)

MONTGOMERY, Leslie Alexander [1873–1961, Irish banker, novelist and humorist]
Lynn C. Doyle (*Ballygullion*; *Lobster Salad*)

MONTGOMERY, Letitia [d. 1930, Irish novelist and writer]
*K. L. Montgomery (*The Ark of the Curse*; *Tyrol under the Axe of Fascism*)

MONTGOMERY, Robert Bruce [1921–78, English musician, crime and science-fiction writer]
Edmund Crispin (*The Case of the Gilded Fly*; *Buried for Pleasure*)

MONTGOMERY, Rutherford George [1894–1985, US novelist and writer for children]
A. A. (or Al) Avery (*A Yankee Flier in Normandy*)
Everitt Proctor (*Thar She Blows*)

MONTI, Luigi [1830–1903, Italian-born US academic and diplomat]
A Consul Abroad (*Adventures of a Consul Abroad*)
Samuel Sampleton Esq. (*Adventures of a Consul Abroad*)

MOODY, Charles Harry [1874–1965, English musicologist]
Coulthart Brayton (used for journalism and musical composition)

MOOR, Edward [1771–1848, English soldier in India and writer on Hinduism]
An Old Soldier (*The Gentle Sponge*)

MOORCOCK, Michael [1939–, English science-fiction and fantasy writer]
Bill Barclay (*Somewhere in the Night*; *Printer's Devil*)
*Michael Barrington (*Peace on Earth*)
Edward Bradbury (*City of the Beast*; *Lord of the Spiders*; *Masters of the Pit*)
James Colvin (*The Deep Fix*)

Desmond Reid (used when writing for the Sexton Blake Library)

MOORE, Brian [1921–, Irish-born Canadian novelist]
Michael Bryan (*Murder in Majorca*; *Intent to Kill*)
Bernard Mara (*French for Murder*; *This Gun for Gloria*; *A Bullet for my Lady*)

MOORE, Catherine Louise [1911–88, US science-fiction writer]
*Keith Hammond (*Valley of the Flame*; *Lord of the Storm*)
*Lewis Padgett (*A Gnome There Was*; *Line to Tomorrow*)

MOORE, Mrs Clara Jessup [1824–99, US poet and writer]
Mrs H. O. Ward (*Keely and his Discoveries*; *Sensible Etiquette of the Best Society*; *Social Ethics and Society Duties*)

MOORE, Clement Clarke [1779–1865, US academic and linguist]
A Citizen of New York (*A Sketch of our Poitical Condition*)
Columella (*Enquiry into our Foreign Carrying Trade*)

MOORE, Doris Langley [1903–89, English novelist and writer]
A Gentlewoman (*The Technique of the Love-Affair*)
*Two Ladies of England (*The Bride's Book*)

MOORE, Edward [1712–57, English dramatist and satirist]
Adam Fitz-Adam (in *The World*)

MOORE, Miss Frances [1788–1880, English novelist and writer]
Madame Panache (*A Year and a Day*)

MOORE, Francis [1657–1715, English physician, astrologer and almanac publisher]
Old Moore (*Vox Stellarum*)

MOORE, Frank Frankfort [1855–1931, Irish novelist, dramatist, poet and journalist]
F. Littlemore (*A Garden of Peace*)

MOORE, Geoffrey Herbert [1920–, English academic and writer]
Edmund Hardy (*Voyage to Chivalry*)

MOORE, Jacob Bailey [1797–1853, US journalist]
A Freeman (*The Principles and Acts of Mr Adams' Administration*)

MOORE, James [1702–34, English playwright and fop]
James Moore Smythe (*The Rival Modes*)

MOORE, James Carrick [1763–1834, Scottish surgeon and medical writer]
Lucerna (in *New Monthly Magazine*)

MOORE, John [1729–1802, Scottish physician and traveller]
John Mordaunt (*Sketches of Life, Characters and Manners in Various Countries*)

MOORE, June Langley [fl. 1932, English writer]
*Two Ladies of England (*The Bride's Book*)

MOORE, Mary [1930–, English writer]
Helena Osborne (*The Joker*)

MOORE, Nicholas [fl. 1945, English writer]
Guy Kelly (*The War of the Little Jersey Cows*)

MOORE, Robert Lowell [1925–, US writer]
Robin Moore (*The Country Team*; *The Green Berets*)

MOORE, Mrs Stuart [1875–1941, English academic, novelist and writer on mysticism]
John Cordelier (*Spiral Way*; *Path of Eternal Wisdom*)
Evelyn Underhill (*Essentials of Mysticism*; *Concerning the Inner Life*)

MOORE, Thomas [1779–1852, Irish poet; friend of Byron, whose manuscript memoirs he destroyed]
Thomas Brown the Younger (*The Two-Penny Post -Bag*; *The World at Westminster*; *Fables for the Holy Alliance*; *Fudge in Ireland*; *Intercepted Letters*; *Rhymes of the Times*; *Rhymes on the Road*;

The Fudge Family in Paris; *The Fudges in England*)

An Irish Gentleman (*Travels of an Irish Gentleman in Search of a Religion*)

An Irishman (*Corruption and Intolerance*)

The Late Thomas Little (*The Poetical Works*)

One of the Fancy (*Tom Crib's Memorial to Congress*)

Captain Rock (*Memoirs of Captain Rock*)

Trismegistus Rustificius, D. D. (*Ode to Nothing*)

MOORE, William Arthur [1880–1962, Irish journalist and writer]
Antrim Oriel (*The Miracle*)

MORANT, Philip [1700–70, English cleric and Essex historian]
A Clergyman (*The Cruelties and Persecutions of the Romish Church*)

MORE, Hannah [1745–1833, English moral and religious writer]
Will Chip (*Village Politics*; *The Country Carpenter's Confession of Faith*)
L. (*A Hymn of Praise for the Abundant Harvest of 1796*)
M. (*The Baker's Dream*; *The Plow-Boy's Dream*)
One of the Laity (*An Estimate of the Religion of the Fashionable World*)
A Young Lady (*A Search after Happiness*)
Z. (*Cheap Repository: the Carpenter or the Danger etc.*; *The Lady and the Pye*; *The Apprentice's Monitor*; *The Gin-Shop*; *The History of Mr Fanton*; *The Market Woman*; *The Shepherd of Salisbury Plain*; *The Roguish Miller*)

MORE, Henry [1614–87, English cleric and theologian]
Alazonomastix Philalethes (*A Free Parliament Proposed to Tender Consciences*; *Observations upon Anthroposophia Theomagica*)
Franciscus Euisitor of Palaeopolite (*Divine Dialogues*)

One Not Unexercised in these Kinds of Speculation (*Annotations upon Lux Orientalis*)
Philophilus Parresiastes (*Enthusiasmus Triumphatus*; *Enthusiasm Explained*)

MOREAU, David Merlin [1927–, English writer]
David Merlin (*The Simple Life*; *The Built-In Urge*)

MOREHEAD, Robert [d. 1840, Scottish cleric]
Martinus Scriblerus (*Explanations in the Text of Shakespeare*)

MORFORD, Henry [1823–81, US novelist and writer]
An Editor (*Rhymes*)
An Ex-Pension Agent (*The Spur of Monmouth*)
The Governor (*Shoulder-Straps*)
A Live American (*Over Sea*)

MORGAN, Charles [1894–1958, English novelist, dramatist and critic]
Menander (in the *Times Literary Supplement* and for *Reflections in a Mirror*)

MORGAN, Diana [1921–, English writer]
Sara Blaine (*Heart of a Doctor*)

MORGAN, Henry James [1842–1913, Canadian politician]
A British Canadian (*The Tour of His Royal Highness etc.*)

MORGAN, John Hartman [1876–1955, English barrister and jurist]
Centurion (*Gentleman at Arms*)

MORGAN, MacNamara [d. 1762, English dramatist]
Porcupinus Pelagius (*The Scandalizade*; *The Triumvirade*; *The Sequel, containing what was Omitted in the Triumvirade*; *The Causidicade*; *The Picopade*; *The Processionade*)

MORGAN, Murray Cromwell [1916–, US novelist]
Cromwell Murray (*Day of the Dead*)

MORGAN, Lady Sydney [1783–1859, Irish novelist and poet]
S. O. (*St Clair or, the Heiress of Desmond*)
Sydney Owenson (*The Wild Irish Girl*; *The Lay of an Irish Harp*)

MORGAN, Thomas [d. 1743, English cleric, physician and religious pamphleteer]
Philanthropus Oxoniensis (*A Letter to the Rev. Dr Waterland*)

MORGAN, Thomas Charles [1783–1843, English physician and philosopher]
Ezekiel (in *New Monthly Magazine*)
Humphrey Oldcastle (*The Royal Progress*)

MORGAN, Thomas Christopher [1914–, English farmer and novelist]
John Muir (*Creatures of Satan*; *Crooks' Turning*)

MORGAN, William [1775–1826, US renegade freemason – thought to have been murdered by outraged members]
One of the Fraternity (*Illustrations of Masonry*)

MORICE, Ann [1918–, English mystery writer]
Felicity Shaw (*Dead on Cue*; *Murder by Proxy*)

MORIER, James Justinian [1780–1849, Turkish-born English traveller and oriental writer]
Peregrine Persic (*Hajji Baba of Ispahan*)

MORISON, John [1750–98, Scottish cleric and writer]
Musaeus (in *Ruddiman's Weekly*)

MORLAND, Nigel [1905–, English crime and mystery writer]
Mary Dane (*Death Traps the Killer*)
John Donovan (*The Case of the Talking Dust*; *The Case of the Plastic Man*)
Norman Forrest (*Death Took a Greek God*; *Death Took a Publisher*)
Roger Garnett (*Eve Finds the Killer*; *The Killing of Paris Norton*)
Neal Shepherd (*Death Flies Low*; *Exit to Music*)

MORLEY, Henry [1822–94, English writer]
A London Playgoer (*Journal of a London Playgoer*)

MORRES, Harvey Redmond [1746–97, 2nd Viscount Mountmorres]
A Member of the Irish Parliament (*Considerations on Modification of Poyning's Law*)

MORRIS, Charles [1833–1922, US historian and writer]
Hugh Allen (*The Detective's Crime*)

MORRIS, Corbyn [d. 1779, English economist and writer]
A Bystander (*Letter from a Bystander to a Member of Parliament*)
A Gentleman of Cambridge (*Letter to the Rev. Thomas Carte*)

MORRIS, Francis Orpen [1810–93, English cleric, ornithologist and naturalist]
A County Magistrate (*In Memoriam – the Burial of the Burials Bill*)
A Yorkshire Clergyman (*Possibilities in a Parish*; *Letter to Archdeacon Wilberforce on Supremacy*)

MORRIS, James W. [fl. 1858, US journalist and humorist]
K. N. Pepper (*The K. N. P... Papers*)

MORRIS, Jan [1926–, Welsh journalist and historian; born male but changed sex]
James Humphrey Morris (*Farewell the Trumpets*; *Pax Britannica*)

MORRIS, Lewis [1833–1907, Welsh lawyer, essayist and poet]
A New Writer (*Songs of Two Worlds*)

MORRIS, Margaret Jean [1924–, English novelist and writer for children]
Kenneth O'Hara (*The Searchers of the Dead*; *Sleeping Dogs Lying*)

MORRIS, Mowbray Walter [1847–1911, English journalist and essayist]
An Editor; A Layman; Dionysius Minimus; Aurelius Mougher; Mark Reid (all used in *MacMillan's Magazine*)

MORRIS, William O'Connor [1824–1904, Irish jurist, biographer and historian]
An Irish Liberal (in *Blackwood's Magazine*)

MORRISON, Alistair Ardoch [1911–, Australian writer]
Afferbeck Lauder (in the *Sydney Morning Herald*)

MORRISON, Margaret Mackie (Peggy) [d. 1973, Scottish writer]
March Cost (*Rachel*; *A Woman of Letters*)

MORRISON, Mary Whitney [1832–1904, US writer for children]
Jenny Wallace (*Songs and Rhymes for the Little Ones*)
Jenny Wallis (*Stories True and Fancies New*)

MORRISON, Richard James [1795–1874, English mariner, astronomer and astrologer]
Zadkiel (*An Essay on Love and Matrimony*; *On the Great First Cause*; *The Horoscope*)
Zadkiel Tao; Zadkiel the Seer (both used in *Zadkiel's Almanac*)

MORRISON, Thomas James [fl. 1963, Scottish mystery and screenwriter]
Alan Muir (*Death Comes on Derby Day*)

MORRISSEY, Joseph Laurence [1905–, English novelist]
Richard Saxon (*The Stars Come Down*; *Future for Sale*)

MORSE, Anne Christenson [1915–, US writer]
Ann Head (*Always in August*; *Everybody Adored Cora*)

MORSE, Freeman Harlow [1807–91, US politician and diplomat]
The American Consul at London (*American Seamen*)

MORSE, Jason [1821–61, US cleric]
The Pastor (*Annals of the Church in Brimfield*)

MORSE, Larry Alan [1945–, US writer]
Runa Fairleigh (*An Old-Fashioned Mystery*)

MORSE, Samuel Finley Breese [1791–1872, US sculptor, scientist and inventor]
An American (*Imminent Dangers to the United States through Foreign Immigrations*)
Brutus (*Foreign Conspiracy against the United States*)

MORSE, Sidney Edwards [1794–1871, US journalist]
An American (*A Letter on American Slavery*)

MORTIMER, John [1656–1736, English agriculturalist]
J. M. Esq., FRS (*The Whole Art of Husbandry ... Countryman's Kalendar*)

MORTIMER, John Clifford [1923–, English barrister, novelist and playwright]
Geoffrey Lincoln (*No Moaning at the Bar*)

MORTIMER, Penelope Ruth [1918–, Welsh journalist and novelist]
Penelope Dimont (*Johanna*; *A Villa in Summer*)
Ann Temple (in the *Daily Mail*)

MORTIMER, Thomas [1730–1810, English diplomat and economist]
Philanthropos (*Every Man his Own Broker*)

MORTON, Charles [1627–98, English Puritan cleric and writer]
An Eminent Professor (*An Enquiry into the Literal Sense of the Scripture*)
A Person of Learning and Piety (*An Essay Towards the Question, Whence Comes the Stork, the Turtle etc.*)
A Well-Wisher to Mankind (*The Gaming-Humor Considered and Reproved*)

MORTON, Guy Mainwaring [1896–1968, English novelist]
Mark Forrest (in the *Saturday Review*)
Peter Traill (*Woman to Woman*; *Golden Oriole*)

MORTON, John Bingham [1893–1979, English journalist, biographer and humorist]
Beachcomber (in the *Daily Express* from 1924)

J. B. M. (*Gorgeous Poetry*)

MORTON, Sarah Wentworth [1759–1846, US poet]
Philenia, a Lady of Boston (in the *Massachusetts Magazine* and for *Ouabi or, the Virtues of Nature*)

MORTON, Thomas [1564–1659, English cleric and religious writer; Bishop of Durham]
Tho. Duresme (*Ezekiel's Wheels*)

MOSER, Joseph [1748–1819, English pamphleteer and dramatist]
A. Barber (*The Meal-Tub Plot*)
Timothy Twig Esq. (*Adventures of Timothy Twig Esq. in a Series of Poetical Epistles*)

MOSES, William Stainton [1840–92, English spiritualist]
M. A. Oxon (*Higher Aspects of Spiritualism; Carpenterian Criticism; Psychography; The Slade Case; Spirit Identity; Spirit Teaching; Ghostly Visitors*)
An Oxford Graduate (*The Mystic Voices of Heaven*)

MOSSMAN, Thomas Wimberley [1826–85, English cleric and controversialist]
A Disciple of Bishop Butler (*A Reply to Dr Tyndall's Lucretian*)

MOTHERWELL, William [1797–1835, Scottish journalist and poet]
Isaac Brown (*Renfrew Characters and Scenery*)

MOTLEY, John Lothrop [1814–77, US diplomat and historian]
An American (*Morton's Hope or, Diary of an American*)

MOTT, Albert Julius [fl. 1860, English novelist]
A. J. Barrowcliffe (*Amberhill*)

MOTT, Edward Spencer [1844–1910, English writer]
Nathaniel Gubbins (*A Roll in the Hay*)

MOTT, J. Molden [fl. 1960, English writer]
John Blackburn (*A Sour Apple Tree; The Gaunt Woman*)

MOTTERSHEAD, Joseph [1688–1771, English cleric and religious writer]
Theophilus (in the *Theological Repository*)

MOTTEUX, Peter Anthony [1660–1718, French-born English journalist, dramatist and merchant]
Thomas Clayton (*Arsinoe, Queen of Cyprus*)

MOTTLEY, John [1692–1750, English dramatist and historical writer]
A Gentleman of the Inner Temple (*History of the Cities of London and Westminster*)
Elijah Jenkins (*Joe Miller's Jests or the Wits Vade-Mecum*)
Robert Seymour (*An Accurate Survey of London and Westminster*)

MOTTRAM, Ralph Hale [1883–1971, English novelist and poet]
J. Marjoram (*Repose and Other Verses; New Poems*)

MOULE, Henry [1801–80, English cleric and writer]
A Country Parson (*My Kitchen Garden, my Cows etc.*)

MOULTRIE, John [1799–1874, English cleric and poet]
Gerard Montgomery (in both *Etonian Magazine* and *Quarterly Magazine*)

MOUNT, Thomas Ernest [1895–, US writer]
Stone Cody (*Dangerous Gold; Five Against the Law*)
Oliver King (*Mustang Trail*)

MOUNTBATTEN, Lord Louis F. A. V. N. [1900–79, English mariner; member of the royal family]
Marco (*An Introduction to Polo*)

MOYLE, John [d. 1714, English naval surgeon and medical writer]
A Member of the College of Physicians (*The Present Ill State of the Practice of Physick*)

MUDDOCK, J. E. Preston [1843–1934, English crime writer]
Dick Donovan (*Eugene Vidocq*; *The Fatal Ring*)

MUDFORD, William [1782–1848, English journalist and essayist]
Attalus (*The Five Nights of St Albans*)
Geoffrey Oldcastle (in the *Canterbury Magazine*)
The Silent Member (in *Blackwood's Magazine*)
Martin Gribaldus Swammerdam (*Life and Adventures of Paul Plaintive Esq.*)

MUDGE, Henry [1806–74, English surgeon and temperance advocate]
A Foe to Ignorance (*Letter to the Rate-Payers of Bodmin*)
One of Themselves (*Alcoholics: a Letter to Practitioners in Medicine*)
A Surgeon (*Dialogues Concerning the Use of Tobacco*)

MUDIE, Robert [1777–1842, Scottish Gaelic scholar, journalist and natural historian]
Laurence Longshank, Gent. (*Things in General*)
A Modern Greek (*The Modern Athens*)

MUGGESON, Margaret Elizabeth [1942–, English writer]
Everatt Jackson (*The Road to Hell*)

MUHLENBERG, William Augustus [1796–1877, US cleric, hymn writer and educationalist]
Catholicus (*Catholic Union Defended*)
One of the Memorialists (*An Exposition of the Memorial of Sundry Presbyters*)

MUIR, Barbara Kenrick [1908–, English novelist]
Barbara Kaye (*Call it Kindness*; *Home Fires Burning*)

MUIR, Charles Augustus Carlow [1892–1989, Canadian-born Scottish novelist and writer]
Austin Moore (*Birds of the Night*; *The House of Lies*)

MUIR, Edwin [1887–1959, Scottish poet, translator and writer]
Edward Moore (*We Moderns*)

MUIR, John [1810–82, Scottish East India Company employee and oriental scholar]
A Bengal Civilian (*An Essay on Conciliation in Matters of Religion*)
A Layman (*Considerations on Religion*)
A Lay Member of the Church of England (*A Brief Examination on the Inspiration of the Scriptures*)

MUIR, Wilhelmina (Willa) J. [1890–1970, Scottish novelist and writer]
Agnes Neill Scott (used for the translation of two books by H. Carossa: *A Roumanian Diary* and *Boyhood and Youth*)

MULLAN, Charles Seymour [1893–1969, Irish-born English colonial civil servant]
Rhadamanthus (*A Scholar in Clive Street*)

MULLANY, Patrick Francis [1847–93, US cleric and academic]
Brother Azarias (*The Development of English Literature*; *Phases of Thought and Criticism*)

MULLER, Friederich Max [1823–1900, German-born philologist and oriental scholar; settled in Oxford in 1848]
Philindus (*Correspondence on an Oriental College in London*; *Controversies of the Day*)

MULLINGER, James Bass [1834–1917, English academic and historian]
Theodorus (*The New Reformation*)

MUMFORD, James [1606–66, English Jesuit and theologian]
Optatus Ductor (*The Question of Questions*)

MUMFORD, Ruth [1919–, New Zealand writer for children]
Ruth Dallas (*Dog Called Wig*; *Shining Rivers*)

MUNBY, Arthur Joseph [1828–1910, English lawyer, poet and civil servant]
Jones Brown (*Vulgar Verses in Dialect and Out of it*)

MUNDAY (or MUNDY), Anthony [1553–1633, English dramatist and balladeer]
Anglo-Phile Eutheo (*A Second and Third Blast of Retrait from Plaies*)
Lazarus Piot (or Pyott) (*The Orator – a Translation*; *The Second Booke of Amadis De Gaul – a Translation*)
Shepherd Tonie (*in England's Helicon*)

MUNRO, Alice [1931–, Canadian writer]
Alice Laidlaw (in *Canadian Forum*)

MUNRO, Hector Hugh [1870–1916, Burmese-born English novelist – killed in France in WWI]
Saki (*Reginald*; *The Unbearable Bassington*)

MUNRO, Neil [1864–1930, Scottish novelist and journalist]
Hugh Foulis (*Erchie, My Droll Friend*; *Jimmy Swan the Joy Traveller*)

MUNSELL, Joel [1809–80, US publisher and writer]
Arthur Prynne (*Prynne's Almanac for 1841*)

MUNTHE, Frances [1915–, English historical novelist and writer for children]
Frances Cowen (*Elusive Lover*; *Wait for the Night*)
Eleanor Hyde (*Tudor Maid*; *Tudor Murder*)

MURFREE, Mary Noailles [1850–1922, US novelist, crippled from infancy]
Charles Egbert Craddock (in *Atlantic Monthly* and for *In the Tennessee Mountains*)

MURIEL, John Saint Clair [1909–, English novelist]
Simon Dewes (*Cul-de-Sac*; *Panic in Pursuit*)
John Lindsey (*A Month in Summer*; *Peacock's Feathers*)

MURPHY, Arthur [1727–1805, Irish lawyer, actor and biographer]
Charles Ranger Esq. (in the *Grays Inn Journal*)

MURPHY, Denis [1805–33, Irish journalist and essayist]
A Looker-On; Ti-Ti-of Siam; A Tory Member of Parliament and Distinguished Officer (all used in *Tait's Edinburgh Magazine*)

MURPHY, Edgar Gardner [1869–1913, US educationalist and reformer]
Kelvin Mackready (*A Beginner's Star-Book*)

MURPHY, Edwin Greenslade [1861–1939, Australian writer]
Dryblower (*Dryblower's Verses 1894–1926*)

MURPHY, Emily Ferguson [1868–1933, Canadian novelist]
Janey Canuck (*Open Trails*; *Seeds of Pine*)

MURPHY, James Cavanah [1760–1814, Irish architect and antiquarian]
Dominick Vandelli (*A General View of the State of Portugal*)

MURPHY, Mabel Ansley [1870–?, US writer]
Anne S. Lee (*When America Was Young*; *The Torchbearers*)

MURRAY, Andrew Nicholas [1880–1928, English writer for boys]
Capt. Malcolm Arnold (in *Boy's Realm*)

MURRAY, Anna Maria [1808–89, Australian writer]
An Australian (*The Guardian*)

MURRAY, Eustace Clare Grenville [1824–81, English journalist, diplomat and satirist]
A Distinguished Writer (*The Press and the Public Services*)
No Party Man (in *Temple Bar*)
The Roving Englishman (*Embassies and Foreign Courts: a History of Diplomacy*; *Pictures from the Battle Fields*; *Turkey, being Sketches from Life*)

Silly-Billy (in *Vanity Fair* and for *Strange Tales*)

Trois-Etoiles (*The Member for Paris*)

MURRAY, Lord George [1700–60, Scottish Jacobite General]
A Highland Officer (*A Particular Account of the Battle of Culloden*)

MURRAY, James [1732–82, Scottish cleric and theologian]
A Clergyman (*History of the Churches in England and Scotland*)
An Impartial hand (*History of Religion*)
Ahab Salem (*The New Maid of the Oaks*)

MURRAY, John [1786–1851, Scottish scientist and lecturer]
A Fellow of Several Learned Societies (*The Truth of Revelation Demonstrated*)
A Fellow of the Geological Society (*A Portrait of Geology*)
A Fellow of the Linnaean Society (*The Economy of Vegetation*)

MURRAY, John [1809–92, Scottish author of travel guides and publisher]
Verifier (*Scepticism in Geology and the Reasons for it*)

MURRAY, John Archibald [1779–1859, Lord Murray; Scottish jurist]
A Member of Court (*A Letter to the Lord Advocate on Jury Trials*)

MURRAY, John Fisher [1811–65, Irish humorist and poet]
The Irish Oyster Eater (*Some Account of Himself*)
Maire (in *The Nation*)
The Pilgrim in London (in *Bentley's Miscellany*)

MURRAY, Judith Sargent Stevens [1751–1820, US playwright and poet]
Constantia (*The Gleaner*)

MURRAY, Nicholas [1802–62, Irish-born US cleric]
Kirwan (*Kirwan's Reply to Dr Cote on Baptism*; *Letters to the Rev. John Hughes Bishop of New York*; *Romanism at Home*)

MURRAY, Patrick [1703–78, 5th Baron Elibank; lawyer and writer]
A Peer of the Realm (*Eight Sets of Queries ... Woolen Manufacturer*)
A Person of Distinction (*Inquiry into the Original Consequences of Public Debt*)

MURRAY, Robert Fuller [1863–94, Scottish poet]
A St Andrew's Man (*The Scarlet Gown*)

MURRAY, William Vans [1760–1803, US political writer]
A Citizen of the United States (*Political Sketches*)

MURRY, John Middleton [1926–, English science-fiction writer]
Richard Cowper (*Breakthrough*; *The Custodians*)
Colin Middleton Murry (*One Hand Clapping*)

MUSES, Charles Arthur [1919–, American mathematician]
Musaios (*The Lion Path*)

MUSGRAVE, George Musgrave [1798–1883, English cleric and travel writer]
A Son of the Church (*Readings for Lent*)
Viator Verax, MA (*Continental Excursions*; *Cautions for the First Tour of Foreign Travel*)

MUSGRAVE, Sir Richard [1757–1818, Irish politician and political writer]
Camillus (*To the Magistrates, the Military and the Yeomanry of Ireland*)
Veridicus (*A Concise Account of the Late Rebellion*)

MUSGRAVE, Susan [1951–, Canadian poet]
Moses Bruce (*Grave Dirt and Selected Strawberries*)

MUSHET, Robert Forester [1811–91, English metallurgist]
Sideros (in the *Mining Journal*)

MUSICK, John Roy [1848–1901, US journalist and writer]
Benjamin Broadaxe (*The Bad Boy and his Sister*)

MUSSI, Mary [1907–91, English romantic novelist]
Josephine Edgar (*Duchess; My Sister Sophie*)
Mary Howard (*Soldiers and Lovers; Young Ones*)

MUSTO, Barry [1930–, English crime writer]
Robert Simon (*The Sunless Land*)

MYER, Albert J. [1828–80, US scientist]
Old Prob (*A Manual of Signals for the US Army and Navy*)

MYERS, Mary Hortense [1913–, US journalist and writer]
Mary Cathcart Borer (*The American Civil War; London Walks and Legends*)

MYLIUS, Christlob [1722–54, Dutch-born writer – sometime in England]
Crisp Mills (*A Letter to Mr Richard Glover*)

MYRICK, Herbert [1860–1927, US publisher, editor and agriculturist]
Uncle Ted (*The Crisis in Agriculture*)

N

NABAKOV, Peter Francis [1940–, US writer]
Peter Towne (*George Washington Carver*)

NABAKOV, Vladimir [1899–1977, Russian-born US novelist, dramatist and lepidopterist]
Vladimir Sirin (in *Esquire* magazine and for *Camera Obscura*)

NAGHTEN, Frederick [1822–45, English poet]
A Late Graduate of Oxford (*A Metrical Version of the Song of Solomon*)

NAIRNE, Baroness (née Oliphant, Carolina) [1766–1845, Scottish poet and songwriter]
B. B.; Mrs Bogan of Bogan; S. M. (all used in *The Scottish Minstrel*)

NALSON, John [1638–86, English historian and pamphleteer]
One who Does Passionately Wish the Prosperity of the Church, his King and Country (*The Countermine*)
Philirenes (*Foxes and Firebrands*)

NARES, Edward [1762–1841, English cleric, novelist and historian]
It Matters Not Who (*Heraldic Anomalies*)
Thinks-I-to-Myself-Who? (*I Says, Says I*)

NASH (or NASHE), Thomas [1567–1601, English satirist and writer]
Adam Fouleweather (*A Wonderful Astrological Prognostication*)
The Venturous Hardie and Renowned Pasquill of England (*A Countercuff Given to Martin Junior*)

NASH, Thomas [1844–85, English barrister and writer]
A First Class Man of Balliol College, Oxford (*The Alcestis of Euripides*; *The Hecuba of Euripides*; *The Medea of Euripides*)
A Manchester Conservative (in *Fortnightly Review*)
Tom Palatine (*A Long Love, a Vacation Idyll*)

NATHAN, George Jean [1882–1956, US journalist and drama critic]
*Owen Hatteras (*Pistols for Two*)

NAYLER, James [1617–60, English Quaker and controversial preacher]
One who Was Called in Derision a Quaker (*Love to the Lost*)
A Servant of the Lord (*A Salutation to the Seed of God*)

NEAL, John [1793–1876, US novelist and poet]
Will Adams (*Errata or, the Work of Will Adams*)
A Genuine Yankee (in *Blackwood's Magazine*)
Logan (*Logan, a Family History*)
A New Englander over the Sea (*Authorship*)
John O'Cataract (*The Battle of Niagara*)

NEALE, Erskine [1804–83, English cleric and religious writer]
A Coroner's Clerk (*The Note-Book of a Coroner's Clerk*)
A Country Curate (*The Living and the Dead*)
Gaol Chaplain (*Recollections of a Gaol Chaplain*)

A Suffolk Rector (*Stray Leaves from a Freemason's Note-Book*)

A Working Clergyman (*The Life-Book of a Labourer*)

NEALE, John Mason [1818–66, English cleric, religious and hymn writer]

Aurelius Gratianus (*The Exiles of the Cevenna*)

A Priest of the Church of England (*Annals of the Virgin Saints; Sermons on the Canticles*)

A Priest of the Diocese (*Pictorial Crucifixes*)

A Priest of the English Church (*The Holy Eastern Church*)

NEARING, Elizabeth Custer [1900–, US novelist]

Sue McVeigh (*Grand Central Murder*)

NEATE, Charles [1806–79, English barrister and political pamphleteer]

A Student of Lincoln's Inn (*Remarks on the Alterations in the Game Laws*)

NEAVES, Charles [1800–76, Lord Neaves; Scottish jurist]

*Peter Jenkins; A Lawyer; Lector Leguleius; A. Murray Mildmay (all used in *Blackwood's Magazine*)

An Old Contributor to Maga (*Legal Songs and Verses; Songs and Verses, Social and Scientific*)

NEEDHAM, Marchamont [1620–78, English lawyer, satirist, journalist and physician]

Mercurius Pragmaticus (*A Plea for the King and Kingdom; An Answer to a Declaration of the Lords and Commons; The Levellers Levell'd*)

Tom Tyranno-Mastix (*The Parliament Arraigned*)

A Well-Wisher to Posterity (*The Excellencies of a Free State above Kingly Government*)

NEILD, James Edward [1824–1906, English-born Australian journalist and physician]

Cleofas (*A Bird in a Golden Cage*)

Jacques; Tahite (both used in *The Australian*)

Christopher Sly (in the *Melbourne Age*)

NEILL, James George Smith [1810–57, English soldier in India – killed at Lucknow]

A Staff-Officer (*Historical Record of the First Madras European Regiment*)

NELSON, Horatio [1823–1913, 3rd Earl Nelson]

A Layman (*Hymns for Saints' Days*)

NELSON, Radell Faraday [1931–, US science-fiction writer]

Ray Nelson (*Ganymede Takeover*)

NELSON, William [1757–1835, 1st Earl Nelson; English cleric – brother of Horatio, Viscount Nelson]

A Country Magistrate (*The Duty of Overseers of the Poor*)

NESBIT, Edith [1858–1924, English poet and writer for children]

Edith Bland (*Flowers I Bring and Songs I Sing*)

*Fabian Bland (*The Prophet's Mantle*)

NESMITH, John [1793–1869, US businessman]

An Old Merchant (*Thoughts on Currency*)

NEUBAUER, William Arthur [1916–, US novelist]

William Arthur (*Marriage Later; Love Business*)

Norma Newcomb (*Maybe it's Love*)

Gordon Semple (*The Price of Passion*)

NEUBERG, Victor Benjamin [1883–1940, English poet and writer]

Omnia Vincam (*The Magical Record of Omnia Vincam*)

Shirley Tarn (*Seven Years*)

Rold White (*Day of Life; Twain One*)

NEUTZEL, Charles A. [1934–, US writer]

Albert Augustus Jr. (*The Slaves of Lamooro*)

Charles English (*Lovers: 2075*)

NEVILLE, Barbara [1925–, English novelist]

Edward Candy (*Bones of Contention; Voices of Children*)

NEWBERY, John [1713–67, English publisher for children]
Mrs Mary Midnight (*An Index to Mankind*)

NEWBOLT, Sir Francis George [1863–1940, English barrister]
Bradnock Hall (*Fish Tales and Some True Ones*)
A Praeposter (*Clifton College Forty Years Ago*)

NEWBOLT, Sir Henry John [1862–1938, English barrister, writer and nautical poet]
Henry Nemo (*Goodchild's Garland*)

NEWCOMEN, Matthew [1610–69, English reforming cleric – died from the plague]
*Smectymnuus (*An Answer to a Book etc.*)

NEWELL, Charles Martin [1821–77, US novelist]
Capt. B. Barnacle (*Leaves from an Old Log; The Fair and the Brave*)

NEWELL, Robert Henry [1836–1901, US poet and novelist]
Orpheus C. Kerr (*Avery Glibun*)

NEWHALL, James Robinson [1809–93, US lawyer and jurist]
Obadiah Oldpath (*The Legacy of an Octogenarian; Lin or, the Jewels of the Third Plantation*)

NEWLIN, Margaret Rudd [1925–, US writer]
Margaret Rudd (*Divided Image: a Study of Yeats and Blake*)

NEWMAN, Bernard [1897–1968, English novelist, travel and spy writer]
Don Betteridge (*The Escape of General Gerard; Cast Iron Alibi*)

NEWMAN, Edward [1801–76, English entomologist and naturalist]
Rusticus (*Letters of Rusticus*)

NEWMAN, James R. [1907–66, US lawyer and academic]
Paul Stryfe (*How to Torture your Friends*)

NEWMAN, John [fl. 1960, English writer on science]
*Kenneth Johns (in *Nebula* and *New Worlds* magazines)

NEWMAN, John Henry [1801–90, English cardinal, poet, theologian and essayist]
Catholicus (in *The Times* and for *The Tamworth Reading Room*)
J. H. N. (*The Dream of Gerontius; Memorials of the Past*)

NEWMARCH, Charles Henry [1824–1903, English cleric and writer]
An Old Rugbaean (*Recollections of Rugby*)
Rambler (in the *Wilts and Gloucester Standard*)

NEWTON, Dwight Bennett [1916–, US western novelist]
Dwight Bennett (*Legend in the Dust; Hangman's Knot*)
Clement Hardin (*The Oxbow Deed*)
Ford Logan (*Fire in the Desert*)
Hank Mitchum (*Station 6: Santa Fe*)
Dan Temple (*Gun and Star*)

NEWTON, Henry Chance [1854–1931, English journalist]
Carados (in *The Referee*)

NEWTON, John [1725–1807, English mariner, cleric and opponent of slavery – friend of William Cowper]
A Minister of the Church of England (*Apologia*)
Omicron (*A Plan of Academical Training for the Ministry*)
Vigil (*Fourteen Letters*)

NEWTON, Richard [1676–1753, English cleric, educationalist and social reformer]
A. B. (*The Expence of University Education*)
A Presbyter of the Church of England (*Pluralities Indefensible*)

NEWTON, William Wilberforce [1843–1914, US cleric and writer]
An Old Friend (*The Child and the Bishop*)

NICHOLAS, Harold [1884–?, English journalist]
Orpheus (used for musical criticism)

NICHOLLS, Sir George [1781–1865, English mariner and social reformer]
An Overseer (in the *Nottingham Journal* and for *Eight Letters on the Management of the Poor Laws*)

NICHOLS, George Herbert Fosdike [d. 1933, English journalist and humorist]
Quex (*Pushed and the Return Push*)

NICHOLS, John [1745–1826, English publisher, printer and editor]
Alphonso (in *Gentleman's Magazine*)
The Cobbler of Alsatia (in the *Westminster Journal*)
Marmaduke Myrtle Gent. (*The Lover*)
Sylvanus Urban (in *Gentleman's Magazine* and for *A Rowland for an Oliver*)

NICHOLS, Mrs Mary [1810–84, US writer]
Mary Orme (*Uncle John*)

NICHOLSON, Eliza Jane [1849–96, US writer and poet]
Pearl Rivers (*Lyrics*)

NICHOLSON, Margaret Beda [1924–, English mystery writer]
Margaret Yorke (*Cost of Silence*; *Death on Account*)

NICHOLSON, William [1782–1849, Scottish pedlar and poet]
The Galloway Poet (*Tales in Verse and Miscellaneous Poems*)

NICHOLSON, William Newzam Prior [1872–1949, English artist and designer]
*J. and W. Beggarstaff (used for poster designs)

NICKLIN, Philip Houlbrooke [1786–1842, US lawyer and writer]
Peregrine Prolix (*Letter Descriptive of the Virginia Springs*; *A Pleasant Peregrination through Pennsylvania*)

NICKOLLS, Robert Boucher [1743–1814, English cleric]
Eusebius (in *The Anti-Jacobin*)

NICOL, Davidson S. H. W. [1924–, Sierra Leone poet and writer]
Abioseh Nicol (*Two African Tales*; *Truly Married Woman and other Stories*)

NICOL, William [1744–97, Scottish physician and theologian – friend of Robert Burns]
A Layman (*Three Letters between a Clergyman and a Layman*)

NICOLAS, John Toup [1788–1851, English admiral]
An Officer in the Navy (*An Enquiry into our Late Naval Disasters*)

NICOLAS, Sir Nicholas Harris [1799–1848, English mariner, barrister and antiquarian]
Clionas (in both *Archaeologia* and *Gentleman's Magazine*)

NICOLE, Christopher Robin [1930–, Guyanese crime and mystery writer]
Daniel Adams (*The Brazilian Series*)
Leslie Arlen (*Love and Honour*; *War and Passion*)
Robin Cade (*The Fear Dealers*)
Peter Grange (*King Creole*; *The Devil's Emissary*)
Caroline Gray (*First Class*; *The Third Life*)
Mark Logan (*Brumaire*)
Simon McKay (*The Anderson Series*)
Christina Nicholson (*Queen of Paris*; *Savage Sands*)
Robin Nicolson (*The Friday Spy*)
Alison York (*Scented Sword*)
Andrew York (*Where the Cavern Ends*; *Dark Passage*)

NICOLL, Henry Maurice Dunlop [1884–1953, English physician, esoteric philosopher and writer]
Martin Swayne (*The Blue Germ*; *In Mesopotamia*)

NICOLL, Whitlock [1786–1838, Scottish physician and religious writer]
A Layman (*An Analysis of Christianity*)

NICOLL, Sir William Robertson [1851–1923, Scottish cleric, journalist and politician]
Claudius Clear (in *British Weekly* and for *Letters on Life*)

NICOLSON, Adela Florence [1865–1904, English writer]
Laurence Hope (*The Garden of Kama; Stars of the Desert*)

NICOLSON, Arthur [1849–1928, English diplomat]
Philo-Turk (in *Fortnightly Review*)

NIELSEN, Helen Bernice [1918–, US crime novelist]
Kris Giles (*Verdict Suspended; The Crime is Murder*)

NIGHTINGALE, Joseph [1775–1824, English religious writer]
A Committee Man (*The Scriptural Deacon*)
J. Elagnitin (*Mock Heroics or, Snuff, Tobacco and Gin*)

NIND, William [1810–56, English cleric and poet]
Academicus (*A Plea for the Triumvirate of Esq. Bedells*)

NISOT, Mavis Elizabeth [1893–?, English novelist]
William Penmare (*The Black Swan; The Scorpion*)

NOAH, Mordecai Manuel [1785–1851, US lawyer and journalist]
Muly Malack (in the *New York Times*)

NOBBES, Robert [1652–1706, English cleric and writer on angling]
A Lover of the Sport (*The Compleat Troller*)

NOCK, Albert Jay [1873–1945, US journalist]
Historicus (*Myth of a Guilty Nation*)
Journeyman (*The Book of Journeyman; Theory of Education in the United States*)

NOKES, George Augustus [1867–1948, English railway and transport historian]
George Augustus Sekon (*The Evolution of the Steam Locomotive 1803–1898; The Railway and Travel Monthly; London and South Western Railway; History of the South Eastern Railway*)

NOLAN, Frederick [1784–1864, Irish cleric, philologist and theologian]
A Reformer (*Fragments of a Civic Feast*)
Sarah Search (*Marriage with a Deceased Wife's Sister*)
N. A. Vigors Jun. Esq. (*Inquiry into the Nature and Extent of Poetick Licence*)

NOLAN, Frederick [1931–, English novelist and writer for children]
Frederick H. Christian (*Find Angel; Sudden Strikes Back*)
Danielle Rockfern (*On the Field of Honour*)
Donald Severn (*Sweet Sister Death*)

NOLAN, Lewis Edward [1820–54, English cavalryman and military writer – killed in the charge of the Light Brigade]
Kenner Garrard (*A System of Training Cavalry Horses*)

NOLAN, William Francis [1928–, US science-fiction and crime writer]
Frank Anmar; F. E. Edwards (both used in *Chase* magazine)
Terence Duncan (*Rio Renegades*)

NOONAN, Robert [1868–1911, Irish artisan and radical author]
Robert Tressell (*The Ragged Trousered Philanthropists*)

NORDHOFF, Charles [1830–1901, US journalist]
A Boy (*Man-of-War Life: a Boy's experience in the United States Navy*)
Charles Holmes (in *Harpers magazine*)
A Sailor (*Nine Years*)
A Sailor Boy (*The Merchant Vessel: a Sailor Boy's Voyage*)

NORMAN, Francis Martin [1833–1918, English mariner]
Martello Tower (*At School and at Sea*)

NORMAN, Noel Wilson [1901–, Australian writer]
Louis Kaye (*Trail of Plunder*; *The Desert Boss*)

NORRIS, Henry Handley [1771–1850, English cleric and devotional writer]
An Elder Brother (*A Manual for the Parish Priest*)

NORRIS, John [1657–1711, English cleric and religious writer]
Philanax (*A Murnival of Knaves*)
Phil-Icon-Erus (*Effigies Amoris – a Translation*)

NORTH, Edward [1820–1903, US classical scholar]
Dix Quaevidi (in *Knickerbocker Magazine*)

NORTH, Elisha [1771–1843, US physician]
Uncle Toby (*The Pilgrim's Progress in Phrenology*)

NORTH, Roger [1653–1734, English barrister and historical writer]
A Person of Honour (*A Discourse of Fish and Fish-Ponds*)
A Person of Honour in the County of Norfolk (*The Gentleman Farmer*)

NORTH, William [fl. 1935, English writer]
Ralph Rodd (*The Claverton Case*; *Without Judge or Jury*)

NORTHCOTE, Henry Stafford [1846–1911, Baron Northcote; colonial governor and traveller]
A Barrister (*A Short Review of the Navigation Laws*)
Voyageur (in *Blackwood's Magazine*)

NORTHLEIGH, John [1657–1705, English physician and writer]
A True Protestant and No Dissenter (*Parliamentum Pacificum*)

NORTHMORE, Thomas [1766–1851, English scientist and local historian]
Phileleutherus Devoniensis (*Letter to 293 Electors of the City of Exeter*; *Memoirs of Planetes*)

NORTON, Alice Mary [1912–, US science-fiction writer and children's author]
Andrew North (*Sargasso of Space*; *Plague Ship*)
Andre Norton (*Voodoo Planet*)
*Allen Weston (*Murders for Sale*)

NORTON, Caroline Elizabeth Sarah [1808–77, English poet, essayist and feminist]
Aunt Carry (*Aunt Carry's Ballads*)
An Irresponsible Tax-Payer (*Taxation*)
Libertas (*Letters to the Mob*)
Pearce Stevenson (*A Plain Letter on the Infant Custody Bill*)

NORTON, Jacob [1764–1858, US cleric]
An Orthodox Clergyman of Massachusetts (*Seasonable and Candid Thoughts on Human Creeds*; *Things Set in a Proper Light*)

NORWAY, Nevil Shute [1899–1960, English engineer and novelist]
Nevil Shute (*A Town Like Alice*; *Trustee from the Toolroom*)

NORWEB, Mrs Janetta [d. 1817, English writer]
Janetta (*The Memoirs of Janetta*)

NORWOOD, Victor G. C. [1920–, English western writer]
Coy Banton (*Gunsmoke Justice*)
Shane Baxter (*Shadow of a Gunhawk*)
Jim Bowie (*Gunshot Grief*)
Clay (or Victor) Brand (*Powdersmoke*)
Walt Cody (*Reap the Wild Wind*)
Shayne Colter (*Halfway to Hell*)
Craig (or Wes) Corteen (*Gun Chore*)
Clint Dangerfield (*Crossfire*)
Johnny Dark (*Fig Leaves for a Lady*)
Vince Destry (*A Badge and a Gun*)
Doone Fargo (*Death Valley*)
Wade Fisher (*Ranger Gun Law*)
Mark Hampton (*Killer Take All*)
Hank Janson (*Drop Dead, Sucker*; *Blood Bath*)
Nat Karta (*Brother Rat*)
Whip McCord (*Hellfire Range*)
Brett Rand (*Code of the Lawless*)

Brad Regan (*Raw Deal for Dames*)
Shane Russell (*Gun Trail to Boot Hill*)
Mark (or Rhondo, or Victor) Shane
(*Vengeance Valley; The Gun Hellion*)

NOTLEY, Mrs Frances Eliza [1820–1912,
English novelist]
Frances Derrick (*Olive Varcoe*)

NOTT, Henry Junius [1797–1837, US lawyer
and academic]
Thomas Singularity (*Novelettes of a
Traveller*)

NOTT, John [1751–1826, English surgeon,
traveller and classical scholar]
Mons. Vestris, Sen. (*An Heroic Epistle to
Mademoiselle Heinel*)

NOVIKOVA, Olga [1848–1925, Russian
writer on politics]
A Russian Lady (*Is Russia Wrong?*)

NOYES, Charles Henry [1849–1909, US
lawyer and poet]
Charles Quiet (*Studies in Verse*)

NUNN, William Curtis [1908–, US Texas
historian]
Will Curtis (*Peace unto You*)
Ananias Twist (*Snide Lights on Texas
History*)

NUTT, Lily Clive [1888–?, English writer]
Clive Arden (*The Veil of Glamour; Sinners in
Heaven*)

NUTTER, William Herbert [1875–1941, US
journalist]
Halliday Witherspoon (*Liverpool Jarge*)

NUTTING, Mary Olivia [1831–1910, US
writer and librarian]
Mary Barrett (*The Story of William the
Silent and the Netherlands War*)

NYE, Edgar Wilson [1850–96, US humorist]
Bill Nye (*The Cadi; Bill Nye and
Boomerang*)

NYE, John [d. 1688, English cleric and
controversialist]
One Who Hath Been a Constant Eye and
Eye-Witnesse (*Mr Sadler Re-Examined*)

NYE, Nelson Coral [1907–, US western
novelist]
Clem Colt (*Guns of Horse Prairie; The Sure-
Fire Kid*)
Drake C. Denver (*Gun Quick; Long Rope*)

NYE, Philip [1596–1672, English
nonconformist cleric and theologian]
A Late Eminent Congregational Divine (*A
Case of Great and Present Use*)

OAKELEY, Frederick [1802–80, English cleric and theologian]
One Who Has Suffered (in *The Rambler*)

OATES, Joyce Carol [1938–, US novelist and writer]
Rosamond Smith (*Lives of the Twins*)

O'BEIRNE, Thomas Lewis [1748–1823, politically controversial Irish cleric; Bishop of Meath]
A Consistent Whig (*Considerations on the Late Disturbances*)
An Irish Dignitary (*Letter on the Subject of Tithes in Ireland*)
Melancthon (*A Letter to Dr Troy*)
An Officer then Serving in the Fleet (*A Candid Narrative of the Fleet under Lord Howe*)

OBENCHAIN, Mrs Eliza Caroline [fl. 1909, US novelist]
Eliza Calvert Hall (*The Land of Long Ago*; *Aunt Jane of Kentucky*)

OBER, Sarah Endicott [fl. 1880, US religious writer]
Huldah Herrick (*Ginsey Krieder*; *Little Tommy*)

O'BRIEN, Conor Cruise [1917–, Irish academic and writer]
Donat O'Donnell (*Maria Cross*)

O'BRIEN, Deirdre [1902–, Irish novelist]
Elsie Ryan (used when editor of the *Irishwoman's Weekly*, 1922–26)

O'BRIEN, Howard Vincent [1888–1947, US journalist and writer]
Clyde Perrin (*The Thunderbolt*)

O'BRIEN, James [1805–64, Irish Chartist and radical writer]
Bronterre (in the *Poor Man's Guardian*)

O'BRIEN, Richard Baptist [1809–85, Irish cleric, poet and novelist]
Father Baptist (in *The Nation*)

O'BRIEN, Richard Barry [1847–1918, Irish barrister, historian and biographer]
Historicus (*The Best Hundred Irish Books*)

O'BRYEN, Dennis [1755–1832, Irish political pamphleteer and writer]
Observer (*View of the Present State of Ireland*)

O'CASEY, Sean [1880–1964, Irish dramatist]
An Gall Fada (used in both the *Peasant and Irish Ireland* and *Sinn Fein*)
An Gall Fadd (in the *Worker's Republic*)
Craobh na nDealg; Hon. Sec. Irish Citizen Army; J. O'Casey (all used in the *Irish Worker*)

O'CONNOR, Arthur [1763–1852, Irish journalist and nationalist – lived sometime in France]
A Stoic (*The Measures of a Ministry*)

O'CONNOR, Patrick Joseph [1924–, Irish poet]
Padraic Fiacc (*Selected Poems*)

O'CONNOR, Richard [1915–75, US writer]
Frank Archer (*The Widow Watchers*; *The Malabang Pearl*)
Patrick Wayland (*The Waiting Game*; *Counter Stroke*)

O'CONNOR, Thomas Power [1848–1929, Irish journalist and politician]
T. P. (in *T. P.'s Weekly*)

O'CONNOR, Vincent Clarence Scott [d. 1945, English civil servant in India, traveller and writer]
Odysseus (*Travels in the Pyrenees*)

O'CONOR, Charles [1710–91, Irish historian and pamphleteer]
Rusticus (*A Counter Appeal to the People of Ireland*)

O'CONOR, Charles [1764–1828, Irish cleric and antiquarian]
Columbanos (*Columbanos ad Hibernos*)

ODELL, Jonathan [1737–1818, English teacher and poet]
Camillo Querno (*The American Times*)

O'DONNELL, Charles James [1850–1934, Irish civil servant in India and writer]
A Bengal Civilian (*The Black Pamphlet of Calcutta*)
Twenty-Eight Years in India (*The Failure of Lord Curzon*)

O'DONNELL, Francis Hugh [1848–1916, Irish nationalist, politician and reformer]
Dryden Minor (*New Paganism*)

O'DONNELL, John Francis [1837–74, Irish journalist and poet]
Caviare (*The Emerald Wreath*)
Monkton West (used for poetic contributions to various Dublin journals)

O'DONNELL, Peter [1920–, English crime writer]
Madeleine Brent (*Tregaron's Daughter*)

O'DONOGHUE, Elinor Mary [fl. 1935, English novelist and biographer]
E. M. Oddie (*April Folly*)

O'DONOVAN, Michael Francis [1903–66, Irish essayist and short-story writer]
Frank O'Connor (*Guests of the Nation; Bones of Contention*)

O'DRISCOLL, Gerald John [1887–?, Irish journalist and humorist]
Giraldus (*Musings of a Merry Matloe; The Kingdom of Jarrabazooka; Awful Disclosures of a Bluejacket*)

OELRICHS, Blanche [d. 1950, US actress and playwright – sometime wife of John Barrymore]
Michael Strange (*Resurrecting Life; Who Tells Me True*)

O'FARRELL, William [fl. 1950, US writer]
William Grew (*Doubles in Death; Murder Has Many Faces*)

O'FERRALL, Ernest Francis [1881–1925, Australian writer]
Kodak (*Stories*)

OFFUTT, Andrew J. V. [1934–, US science-fiction writer]
John Cleve (*Barbarana; Jodinareh*)
J. X. Williams (*The Sex Pill*)

O'FLAHERTY, Liam [1896–1984, Irish novelist and short-story writer]
William O'Flaherty (in *The New Leader for The Sniper*)

OGDEN, Charles Kay [1889–1957, English philologist]
Adelyne More (*Fecundity versus Civilization*)

OGDEN, Uzal [1744–1822, US cleric]
A Citizen of these States (*A Letter to Maj.-Gen. Alexander Hamilton*)

OGILVIE, John [1797–1867, Scottish ploughman and lexicographer]
Iota (in *Aberdeen Magazine*)

OGLE, Anne Charlotte [1832–1918, English novelist]
Ashford Owen (*A Lost Love*)

OGNALL, Leopold Horace [1908–79, Canadian-born English crime writer]
Harry Carmichael (*Candles for the Dead; The Motive*)
Howard Hartley (*Sealed Envelope*)
Hartley Howard (*Department K*)

O'GRADY, John Patrick [1907–81, Australian writer]
Nino Culotta (*They're a Weird Mob*; *Gone Fishin'*)

O'GRADY, Standish Hayes [1832–1915, Irish engineer and Gaelic scholar]
S. Hayes (*Adventures of Donnchadh Ruadh Mac Con-Mara*)

O'GRADY, Standish James [1846–1928, Irish lawyer, historian and novelist]
Arthur Clive (in *Dublin University Magazine*)

O'HAGAN, John [1822–90, Irish jurist and songwriter]
Sliabh Cuilluim; Carolina Wilhelmina (both used in *The Nation*)

O'HANLON, John [1821–1905, Irish cleric and writer]
An Irish Missionary Priest (*Life and Scenery in Missouri*)
Lageniensis (*The Buried Lady*; *Irish Folk-Lore*; *Irish Local Legends*; *Legend Lays of Ireland*)

OLDFIELD, Claude Houghton [1889–1961, English civil servant and novelist]
Claude Houghton (*I Am Jonathan Scrivener*; *Chaos is Come Again*)

OLDISWORTH, William [1680–1734, English poet and writer]
A Layman (*A Dialogue between Timothy and Philatheus*)
A Tipling Philosopher of the Royal Society (*The Delightful Adventures of Honest John Cole*)
Walter Wagstaff (*Annotations on the Tattler – a Translation*)

OLDMEADOW, Ernest James [1867–1949, English journalist and novelist]
Louis Barsac (*Shadows and Fireflies*)
Francis Downman (*In Town Tomorrow*; *Not Claret*)

OLDMIXON, John [1673–1742, English historian, pamphleteer and poet]
A Friend (*A Defence of Mr MacCartney*)

A Gentleman Bred in the Family (*History and Life of Robert Blake*)
One Very Near Akin to the Author of Tale of a Tub (*The History of Addresses*)
Charles Wilson Esq. (*Memoirs of the Life of William Congreve*)

OLDYS, William [1696–1761, English bibliophile and antiquary]
Mr Thomas Betterton (*History of the British Stage*)
G. (*in Biographia Britannica*)
A Gentleman of the Temple (*Celebrated Libraries*)
Thomas Hayward (*The British Muse*)

O'LEARY, Joseph [d. 1845, Irish journalist and songwriter – drowned himself in Regents Canal]
A Reporter (*The Late Election*)

OLIPHANT, Laurence [1829–88, South African-born British journalist, novelist, traveller and eccentric]
Golden Horn (in *MacMillan's Magazine*)
Irene MacGillicuddy; Peregrinus; A Turkish Effendi (all used in *Blackwood's Magazine*)
Sionara, a Japanese Traveller (in the *North American Review*)

OLIPHANT, Mrs Margaret O. [1828–97, English novelist and critic]
Margaret Maitland of Sunnyside (*Passages in the Life of Margaret Maitland etc*)

OLIPHANT, Robert [fl. 1788, English writer]
Timothy Touchstone (in *The Trifler*)

OLIPHANT, Thomas [1799–1873, English musician and composer]
Solomon Sackbut (*Comments of a Chorus Singer in Westminster Abbey in 1834*)

OLIVER, Amy Roberta (Berta) [fl. 1930, English romantic novelist, journalist and illustrator]
Berta Onions (*Missing Girl*; *Wanted on Voyage*)
Berta Ruck (*His Official Fiancé*; *Dancing Star*)

OLIVER, Daniel [1787–1852, US academic]
Investigator (*Remarks on a Pamphlet, Prof. Hale and Dartmouth College*)

OLIVER, Frederick Scott [1864–1934, Scottish barrister and writer]
John Draper (*The Statesman and the Bishop*)
Pacificus (letters to *The Times*)

OLIVER, George [1781–1861, English Jesuit, biographer and local historian]
Curiosus (in the *Exeter and Plymouth Gazette*)

OLIVER, George [1872–1961, English cleric, freemason and writer]
Oliver Onions (*Back of the Moon; The Drakestone*)

OLIVER, Gertrude Kent [fl. 1917, English writer for children]
Kent Carr (in *Boy's Own Paper*)

OLIVER, Mrs Harriet [1778–1845, English writer]
A Monthly Nurse (in *Fraser's Magazine*)

OLMSTED, Frederick Law [1822–1903, US agriculturist, traveller and writer]
An American Farmer (*Walks and Talks of an American Farmer*)
*Greensward (*for the Greensward Plan*)

OLSEN, Theodore Victor [1932–, US western novelist]
Joshua Stark (*The Lockhart Breed; Keno*)
Christopher Storm (*The Young Duke; Campus Motel*)
Cass Willoughby (*Autumn Passion*)

OLSON, Thomas C. M. [1912–, Scottish journalist and wine writer]
John Morrell (*International Guide to Wines of the World*)

O'MAHONY, Charles Kingston [1884–?, English writer]
Charles Kingston (*The Delacott Mystery; Murder in Disguise*)

O'MALLEY, Mary Dolling [1891–1974, English novelist]
Ann Bridge (*Peking Picnic; Ginger Griffin; Illyrian Spring*)

OMAN, Carola Mary [1897–1978, English biographer, novelist and writer for children]
(Lady) C. Lenanton (*Mrs Newdigate's Window; Fair Stood the Wind*)

O'MEARA, Kathleen [1839–88, Irish novelist and biographer]
Grace Ramsay (*A Woman's Trials*)

OMOND, Thomas Stewart [1846–1923, English writer]
Thomas White Jun. (*Poems*)

O'NEILL, Charles Henry [1812–65, Irish barrister]
Clanaboy (in *Dublin University Magazine*)

O'NEILL, Herbert Charles [d. 1953, English journalist, military and historical writer]
Strategicus (in *The Spectator* and for *Foothold in Europe* and *To Stalingrad and Alamein*)

O'NEILL, John [1837–95, English essayist]
Hyniall (in the *Westminster Review*)

O'NOLAN, Brian [1912–66, Irish journalist and novelist]
Myles na Gopaleen (in the *Irish Times*)
Flann O'Brien (*At Swim-Two-Birds*)

ONWHYN, Thomas [d. 1866, English cartoonist and illustrator]
Peter Palette (*Mr and Mrs Brown's Visit to the Exhibition; Peter Palette's Tales and Pictures*)
Sam Weller Jr. (for illustrations in *Pickwick Papers*)

OPPENHEIM, Edward Phillips [1866–1946, English novelist]
Anthony Partridge (*The Ghosts of Society; Passers-By; The Kingdom of Earth*)

O'REILLY, Dowell [1865–1923, Australian writer]
D. (*Australian Poems; A Pedlar's Pack*)

O'REILLY, Myles William Patrick [1825–80, Irish politician and writer]
A Catholic (*Conservatives and Liberals Judged by their Conduct*)

ORGEL, Doris [1929–, US writer for children]
Doris Adelberg (*Grandma's Holidays*; *Lizzie's Twins*)

O'RIORDAN, Conal Holmes O'Connell [1874–1948, Irish actor, dramatist and novelist]
F. Norreys Connell (*In the Green Park*; *Adam of Dublin*)

ORMSBY, John [1829–95, Irish writer and translator of Spanish]
One of the Electors (in *Fraser's Magazine*)

O'ROURKE, Edmund [1814–79, Irish dramatist and actor]
Edmund Falconer (*Extremes or, Men of the Day*; *Memories, the Bequest of my Boyhood*; *Murmurings in the May and Summer of Manhood*; *O'Ruark's Bride*)

ORPEN, Joseph Miller [1828–1923, English colonial civil servant]
The Special Commissioner of the Cape Argus (*History of the Basutus of South Africa*)

O'ROURKE, Frank [1916–, US writer]
Kevin Connor (*New Departure*)
Frank (or Patrick) O'Malley (*The Best Go First*)

ORR, Hector [1769–1855, US physician]
A Looker-On (*A Sketch of Camden City, New Jersey*)

ORR, Isaac [1793–1844, US mathematician and writer]
Hamden; Timoleon (both used in the *Boston Courier*)

ORTON, Ernest Frederick [1874–1960, English soldier in India]
Notrofe (*Cavalry Taught by Experience*)

ORTON, Job [1717–83, English nonconformist cleric and theologian]
A Parishioner of St Chads (*Diotrephes Re-Admonished*)
Salopiensis (*Diatrephes Admonished*)

OSBORN, Laughton [1806–78, US poet and writer]
Alethitheras (*Travels by Sea and Land of Alethitheras*)
An American Artist (*Handbook of Young Artists*)
Autodicus (*The Critique of the Vision of Rubeta*)
A Poet (*The Confessions of a Poet*)
Charles Erskine White (*The Dream of Alla-Ad-Deen*)

OSBORNE, Katherine Frances [1862–1927, English writer]
K. Carmarthen (in *Longman's Magazine*)

OSBORNE, Sidney Godolphin [1808–89, English cleric and philanthropist]
S. G. O. (letters in *The Times* and for *Letters on the Education of Young Children*)

O'SHEA, John Augustus [1839–1905, Irish journalist and writer]
The Irish Bohemian (*Military Mosaics*)

OSMUN, Thomas Embly [1834–1902, US writer and critic]
Alfred Ayres (*Acting and Actors, Elocution and Elocutionists*; *The Essentials of Elocution*; *The Mentor*; *The Orthoepist*; *Some Ill-Used Words*; *The Verbalist*)

OSTLERE, Gordon [1921–, English physician and novelist]
Richard Gordon (*Doctor in the House*; *Doctor at Large*)

OSTRANDER, Isabel Egerton [1885–1924, US novelist]
Robert Orr Chipperfield (*The Doom Dealer*; *The Second Bullet*)
David Fox (*The Man Who Convicted Himself*)
Douglas Grant (*Booty*; *Two-Gun Sue*)

O'SULLIVAN, Mortimer [1791–1859, Irish cleric and religious writer]
A Plain Thinker (in *Dublin University Magazine*)

O'SULLIVAN, Samuel [1790–1851, Irish cleric and writer]
Glanville Redivivus; Hibernicus; An Irish Protestant; Scrutator (all used in *Blackwood's Magazine*)
A Plain Thinker; A Yeoman of 1796 (both used in *Dublin University Magazine*)

OSWALD, John [d. 1793, Scottish soldier, poet and republican pamphleteer]
Sylvester Otway (*Euphrosyne, an Ode to Beauty Addressed to Mrs Crouch*; *Poems to which is Added the Humours of John Bull*)

OTIS, Mrs Eliza Henderson [1796–1873, US novelist]
One of the Barclays (*The Barclays of Boston*)

OTIS, Harrison Gray [1765–1848, US lawyer and politician]
A Member of the Suffolk Bar (*Letter to Josiah Quincy on the Law of Libel*)

OTWAY, Caesar [1780–1842, Irish preacher and writer]
Clericus Lyvecanus (*The Answer of an Unbeneficed Clergyman of Dublin*)
Terence O'Toole (in *Dublin Penny Journal*)

OULTON, Walley Chamberlain [1770–1820, English theatrical historian]
George Horne D. D. (*Occasional Remarks Addressed to N. B. Halhed Esq.*; *Sound Argument Dictated by Common Sense*)

OURSLER, Charles Fulton [1893–1952, US crime and mystery writer]
Anthony Abbot (*The Shadow of the Master*; *About the Murder of Geraldine Foster*)

OURSLER, Wilbur Charles [1913–85, US crime writer]
Gale Gallagher (*I Found Him Dead*; *Chord in Crimson*)

OUTRAM, George [1805–56, Scottish journalist and writer]
Quizdom Rumfunidos (*Legal Lyrics*)

OVERHOLSER, Wayne [1906–, US western novelist]
John S. Daniels (*Gunflame*)

Lee Leighton (*Fight for the Valley*; *You'll Never Hang Me*)
Dan J. Stevens (*Stage to Durango*)
Joseph Wayne (*The Long Wind*; *Land of Promises*)

OVERTON, John [1763–1838, English cleric and religious writer]
A Curate in the Country (*England's Causes for Thankfulness*)

OVERTON, Richard [fl. 1645, English controversial satirist and pamphleteer]
Younge Martin Mar-Priest, Son to Old Martin the Metropolitane (*The Arraignement of Mr Persecution*)

OVSTEDAL, Barbara [fl. 1970, English romantic novelist]
Rosalind Laker (*Claudine's Daughter*; *Smuggler's Bride*)
Barbara Paul (*Curse of Halewood*; *The Frenchwoman*)

OWBRIDGE, Eileen [fl. 1975, English romantic novelist]
Jane Arbor (*Two Pins in a Fountain*; *Where the Wolf Leads*)

OWEN, Charles [d. 1746, English Presbyterian cleric and controversialist]
An Anonymous Clergyman (*Plain Dealing and its Vindication*)
A True Protestant (*Plain Reasons*)

OWEN, David [1794–1866, Welsh journalist and editor]
Bleddyn (*Eliasa, Notes on the Career of John Elias*)

OWEN, Hugh [1784–1861, English soldier; served in the Peninsular War with the Portuguese Army]
A British Officer of Hussars (*The Civil War in Portugal and the Siege of Oporto*)

OWEN, Humphrey Frank [1905–79, Welsh journalist and writer]
*Cato (*Guilty Men*)

OWEN, Jack [1929–, English writer]
Jack Dykes (*Yorkshire Whaling Days*)

OWEN, James [1654–1706, English Presbyterian cleric and controversialist]
Eugenius, Junior (*Church Pageantry Display'd*)

OWEN, John [1616–83, English cleric and theologian]
A Protestant (*Animadversions on a Treatise ... Fiat Lux*; *A Brief Account of the Protestant Religion*)

OWEN, John [1766–1822, English cleric and secretary to the British and Foreign Bible Society]
Theophilus Christian Esq. (*The Fashionable World Displayed*)
A Suburban Clergyman (*A Letter to a Country Clergyman*)

OWEN, Josiah [1711–55, English Presbyterian cleric]
A Friend to Truth and Liberty (*Remarks on Two Charges*)

OWEN, Richard [1804–92, English natural historian]
Zoologus (in *Fraser's Magazine*)

OWEN, Robert [1771–1858, Welsh merchant, philanthropist and social reformer]
Celatus (*The Modern Theme*; *The Public Pearl*)
One of HM's Justices of the Peace (*A New View of Society*)

OXENFORD, John [1812–77, English dramatist and translator]
Balzac D'Anois (in *Bentley's Miscellany*)
An English Play-Goer (*Robin Hood – an Opera*)

OXENHAM, Henry Nutcombe [1829–88, English Catholic cleric, theologian and historian]
Justitia (in *The Rambler*)

OZAKI, Milton K. [fl. 1959, US writer]
Robert O. Saber (*Time for Murder*; *A Dame Called Murder*)

P

PACKARD, Frederick Adolphus
[1794–1867, US lawyer and writer]
A Citizen of Pennsylvania (*Thoughts on Popular Education in the United States*)
A Citizen of Philadelphia (*An Inquiry into Separation of Convicts etc.*)

PAE, David [1864–1948, Scottish journalist and writer]
Ian Farquhar (*The Land Army Girl and the Pickletillie Folk*; *Pickletillie: Stories of Scottish Village Folk*)

PAGE, Evelyn [fl. 1931, English writer]
*Roger Scarlett (*Murder Among the Angels*; *Cat's Paw*)

PAGE, Patricia Kathleen [1916–, Canadian poet and writer]
Judith Cape (*The Sun and the Moon*)

PAGE, Philip Pryce [1887–1968, English journalist]
Mr Gossip (sometime in the *Daily Sketch*)

PAGE, Richard [d. 1841, English writer on finance]
Daniel Hardcastle (*Action of the Corn Laws*; *Banks and Bankers*)

PAGE, Walter Hines [1855–1918, US journalist and writer]
Nicholas Worth (*The Southerner*)

PAGET, Francis Edward [1806–82, English cleric and religious writer]
William Churne of Staffordshire (*The Hope of the Katzekopfs*)
A Member of the Lichfield Society (*A Tract upon Tomb-Stones*)

PAGET, John [1811–98, English barrister and magistrate]
Peregrine (in both *Blackwood's Magazine* and *Tait's Edinburgh Magazine*)

PAGET, Stephen [1855–1926, English surgeon and essayist]
One of the Old People (*The Young People*)

PAGET, Violet [1856–1935, French-born English novelist]
Vernon Lee (*Ariadne in Mantua*; *Hortus Vitae*)

PAIGE, Elbridge Gerry [1816–59, US journalist and humorist]
Dow Junior (*Patent Sermons*)

PAIN, Arthur Wellesley [1841–1920, English-born Australian cleric; Bishop of Gippsland]
Arthur Ainslie (*Water Wizardry*)

PAINE, Harriet Eliza [1845–1910, US teacher and writer]
Eliza Chester (*Girls and Women*)

PAINE, Lauren Bosworth [1916–, US western novelist]
Will Benton (*Bushwhackers Moon*; *The Drifter*)
Mark Carrel (*A Crack in Time*; *The Underground Men*)

PAINE, Robert Treat [1773–1811, US songwriter and poet; his given name was Thomas but he changed it]
Menander (in *American Apollo*)

PAINE, Thomas [1697–1757, American cleric and merchant]
Philopatria (*A Discourse on the Difficulties of the Massachusetts Bay etc.*)

PAINE, Thomas [1737–1809, English radical and author of *The Rights of Man*]
Common Sense (*The American Crisis*)
An Englishman (*Common Sense: Addressed to the Inhabitants of America*)
Forester (in the *Pennsylvania Packet*)
A Layman (*Rational and Revealed Religion Investigated and Compared*)

PALESTRANT, Simon [1907–, US writer and illustrator]
Paul E. Strand (*Mexican Portfolio*)

PALEY, Frederick Apthorp [1815–88, English classical scholar]
An Eye-Witness (in *Longman's Magazine*)

PALEY, William [1743–1805, English cleric, theologian and moral philosopher]
A Friend of Religious Liberty (*A Defence of Subscriptions to Articles of Faith*)

PALFREY, John Gorham [1796–1881, US Unitarian cleric and journalist]
A Free Soiler from the Start (*Remarks upon the Proposed State Constitution*)
An Old Conservative (*A Letter to a Whig Neighbour*)

PALFREY, Miss Sarah Hammond [fl. 1866, US poet]
E. Foxton (*The Chapel and Other Poems; Herman, or, Young Knighthood*)

PALGRAVE, Francis Turner [1824–97, English art critic and poet]
Henry T. Thurston (*The Passionate Pilgrim*)

PALGRAVE, Reginald Francis Douce [1829–1904, English Clerk to the House of Commons]
Francis Douce (in *MacMillan's Magazine*)

PALMER, Anna Campbell [1854–1928, US journalist and librettist]
Mrs George Archibald (*Lady Gray and her Sister; A Dozen Good Times*)

PALMER, Charles Stuart [1905–68, US mystery writer]
Jay Stewart (*Before it's Too Late*)

PALMER, Henrietta Eliza Vaughan [1856–1911, English novelist]
Violet Whyte (in The *Family Herald*)
John Strange Winter (*Cavalry Life; Regimental Legends*)

PALMER, John [1742–86, English Unitarian cleric]
Christophilus; Erasmus; G. H.; Symmachus (all used in the *Theological Repository*)

PALMER, John Leslie [1885–1944, English drama critic, novelist and crime writer]
*Francis Beeding (*The Seven Sleepers; The Six Proud Walkers*)
Christopher Haddon (*Under the Long Barrow*)
*David Pilgrim (*So Great a Man*)

PALMER, John Williamson [1825–1906, US journalist]
John Coventry (*After his Kind*)

PALMER, Joseph [1756–1815, English writer; his original surname was Budworth but he adopted that of his wife]
Rambler (in *Gentleman's Magazine*)

PALMER, Madelyn [1910–, Australian crime writer]
Geoffrey Peters (*Eye of a Serpent; Whirl of a Bird*)

PALMER, Raymond A. [1910–, US science-fiction writer]
G. H. Irwin (in *Amazing Stories* magazine)
Frank Patton (in *Other Worlds* magazine)
A. R. Steber (in *Amazing Stories* magazine)

PALMER, Roger [1634–1705, Earl of Castlemaine; diplomat and pamphleteer]
A Person of Honour (*The Catholique Apology*)

PALMER, Samuel [d. 1724, English cleric and pamphleteer]
A Sincere Protestant and True Son of the Church (*The Plotter's Doom*)

PALMER, Vance Edward [1885–1959, Australian dramatist and novelist]
Rann Daly (*The Outpost*; *The Enchanted Island*)

PALMER, William [1811–79, English cleric and writer]
A Member of the Church at Oxford (*At Him Again or, The Fox without a Tail*)
A Member of the Church of England (*Examination of an Announcement*)
A Member of the Church of God at Oxford (*A Hard Nut to Crack*)
Umbra Oxoniensis (*Results of the Expostulation*)

PALTOCK, Robert [1697–1767, English lawyer and writer]
T. Trueman (*The Unrivalled Adventures of Glum Peter Wilkins*)

PANGBORN, Edgar [1909–76, US science-fiction writer]
Bruce Harrison (*A–100*)

PANTING, James Harwood [fl. 1910, English writer for boys]
Claude Heathcote (in *Boy's Friend*)

PARDON, George Frederick [1824–84, English editor and sporting writer]
Captain Rawdon Crawley (*Whist for all Players*; *Solo-Whist*)
Quiet George (*The Juvenile Museum*)
G. F. P. (*The Further Adventures of the Little Traveller*; *Games for all Seasons*; *Illustrious Women who have distinguished Themselves*)
Pastel (*Dramatic Criticisms*)
Redgap (*The Faces in the Fire*)

PARES, Marion [1914–, English journalist and writer]
Judith Campbell (*Horses and Ponies*)
Anthony Grant (*The Mutant*)

PARGETER, Edith Mary [1913–, English historical novelist and crime writer]
Jolyon Carr (*Murder in the Dispensary*; *Death Comes by Post*)
Ellis Peters (*A Morbid Taste for Bones*; *Death of a Joyful Woman*)

John Redfern (*The Victim Needs a Nurse*)

PARIS, John Ayrton [1785–1856, English physician and medical writer]
A Physician (*A Guide to Mount's Bay and Land's End*)

PARK, Andrew [1807–63, Scottish tradesman and poet]
James Wilson, Druggist of Paisley (*Silent Love*)

PARK, Fanny Heslop [1852–?, English spiritualist]
F. Heslop (*Speaking Across the Border-Line*; *Life Worth Living*)

PARK, Sir James Alan [1763–1838, English jurist]
A Layman (*An Earnest Exhortation to a Frequent Reception of the Holy Sacrament*)

PARK, John [1775–1852, US journalist and teacher]
A Fellow Sufferer (*An Address to the Citizens of Massachusetts*)

PARK, John James [1795–1833, English barrister and jurist]
Eunomus (*Juridical Letters to Robert Peel*)

PARKE, John [1754–89, American poet]
A Native of America (*The Lyric Works of Horace*)

PARKER, Dorothy [1893–1967, US poet, critic and writer]
The Constant Reader (in the *New Yorker*)

PARKER, Edward Harper [1849–1926, English diplomat and orientalist]
Quorum Pars Fui (in *Contemporary Review*)

PARKER, Joseph [1830–1902, English cleric; Minister of the City Temple]
An English Preacher (*Springdale Abbey*)
Atey Nyne (*Wilmot's Child: a Domestic Incident*)

PARKER, Theodore [1810–60, US cleric, abolitionist and religious writer]
Levi Blodgett (*The Previous Question between Andrew Norton etc.*)

One Not of the Association (*Answers to Questions in Mr Parker's Letter*)

PARKER, William Harwar [1826–96, US mariner]
A Naval Officer (*Recollections of a Naval Officer*)

PARKES, David [1763–1833, English schoolmaster and antiquarian]
Ebn Shemaya (*The Star, being a Complete System of Astrology*)

PARKES, Sir Henry [1815–96, English-born Australian politician, historian and poet]
A Wanderer (*The Beauteous Terrorist and Other Poems*)

PARKES, James William [1896–1981, English cleric and Hebraist]
John Hadham (*God in a World at War; Common Sense about Religion*)

PARLBY, Samuel [fl. 1850, English soldier and writer]
An Old Playgoer (*Desultory Thoughts on the National Drama*)

PARLETT, Harry [fl. 1900, English cartoonist and illustrator]
Comicus

PARNELL, Fanny [1854–82, Irish nationalist and poet]
Alena (in the *Irish People*)

PARNELL-HAYES, William [d. 1821, Irish politician and writer]
An Irish Country Gentleman (*An Enquiry into Popular Discontents in Ireland*)

PARR, Harriet [1828–1900, English novelist and biographer]
Holme Lee (*Sylvan Holt's Daughter; Maude Talbot*)

PARR, Olive Katharine [1874–1955, English novelist]
Beatrice Chase (*Lady Agatha; A Dartmoor Galahad*)

PARR, Samuel [1747–1825, English cleric, schoolmaster and controversialist]
Lucius (in the *British Magazine*)

A Member of the Established Church (*A Letter from Irenopolis to the Inhabitants of Eleutheropolis*)
An Occasional Writer in the British Critic (*Remarks on the Statement of Dr Charles Combe*)
Phileleutherus Norfolciensis (*A Discourse on the Late Fast*)
Philopatris Varvicensis (in the *Edinburgh Review* and for *Characters of Charles James Fox*)

PARRY, Charles Henry [1779–1860, English physician and writer]
A Descendant of the Fourth Generation (*Memoir of Peregrine Bertie*)

PARRY, David Harold [1868–1950, English writer for boys]
Morton Pike (in *Chums*)

PARRY, Emma Louisa [fl. 1887, US archaeologist and art historian]
An American Student-Girl (*Life Among the Germans*)

PARRY, Ernest Gambier [1853–1936, English soldier, artist and writer]
An Officer who Was There (*Suakim 1885*)

PARRY, Hugh Jones [1916–, English-born US writer]
James Cross (*Grave of Heroes; To Hell for Half-a-Crown*)

PARRY, Joshua [1719–76, English Presbyterian cleric]
Philopatria (*Political Essays and Satires*)

PARSONS, Benjamin [1797–1855, English Congregational cleric]
John Bull (*Why Have You Become a Paedobaptist?*)

PARSONS, John Usher [1761–1838, US writer]
An Abstinence Man (*The Nazarite*)
An Analytical Teacher (*Analytical Spelling-Book*)

PARSONS, Mrs Julia [fl. 1887, US writer]
Julian Warth (*Dorothy Thorn of Thornton; The Full Stature of Man*)

PARSONS, Robert [1546–1610, English
Jesuit and controversial pamphleteer]
A Catholic Divine (*An Answer to Reports by
Sir Edward Coke*)
R. Doleman (*The Conference on the
Succession to the Crowne of Ingland;
Several Speeches concerning the Power of
Parliament*)
John (or I.) Howlet(t) (*A Brief Discours why
Catholiques Refuse to go to church; A
Discoverie of F.J. Nichols Misreported a
Jesuite*)
A Late Minister and Preacher in England
(*Dutifull Considerations upon Foure
Severall Heads*)
A Master of Arte of Cambridge (*The Copy
of a Letter Written by a Master of Arte of
Cambridge*)

PARSONS, Theophilus [1750–1813,
American jurist]
Peter Coffin (*Result of the Convention of
Delegates Helden at Ipswich*)
A Member of the Boston Society of the
New Jerusalem (*Sunday Lessons*)

PARTINGTON, Wilfred [1888–1955, English
journalist, bibliographer and writer]
Raymond Dean (*A Primer of Book-
Collecting*)

PARTON, James [1822–91, English-born US
journalist and biographer]
An Old Smoker (*Does it Pay to Smoke?*)

PARTRIDGE, Sir Bernard [1861–1945,
English actor, cartoonist and illustrator]
Bernard Gould (in *Punch*)

PARTRIDGE, Eric Honeywood [1894–1979,
New Zealand-born English literary
academic and philologist]
Corrie Denison (*Glimpses*)

PARTRIDGE, Helen Lawrence Davis
[1902–, US writer]
Phoebe Sheldon (*Idle Rainbow*)

PASCOE, Mrs Charlotte Champion
[1781–1874, English dialect writer]
Barzillai Baragweneth (*Wen an'aell, a
Cornish Drawel*)

PATCHETT, Mary Elwyn [1897–,
Australian writer for children]
David Bruce (*Bird of Jove*)

PATERSON, Andrew Barton [1864–1941,
Australian lawyer, journalist and ballad
writer]
The Banjo (in *The Bulletin*)

PATERSON, James [1805–76, Scottish
journalist and antiquary]
Croake James (*Curiosities of Law and
Lawyers; Curiosities of Christian History
prior to the Reformation*)
John Kay (*Kay's Edinburgh Portraits*)

PATERSON, Nathaniel [1787–1871, Scottish
cleric]
A Clergyman (*The Manse Garden*)

PATERSON, Samuel [1728–1802, English
bookseller, publisher and auctioneer]
Coryat Junior (*Another Traveller!; An Appeal
to authors of the Critical Review*)

PATERSON, William [1658–1719, Scottish
merchant; initiator of the Darien Scheme
and of the Bank of England]
Lewis Medway (*An Inquiry into an Union
with Scotland*)
Wednesday's Club in Friday Street
(*Wednesday Club Dialogues upon the
Union*)

PATERSON, William Romaine [1871–1937,
Scottish writer]
Benjamin Swift (*Dartnell: a Bizarre
Incident*)

PATMORE, Peter George [1786–1855,
English writer and editor of *New
Monthly Magazine*]
M. de Saint Foix; Terence Templeton (both
used in *New Monthly Magazine*)

PATON, Andrew Archibald [1811–74,
English diplomat and travel writer]
An Oriental Student (*The Modern Syrians*)

PATON, Sir Joseph Noel [1821–1901,
Scottish painter and writer]
A Painter; Spindrift (both used in *Poems*)

PATRICK, Simon [1626–1707, English cleric and religious writer; Bishop of Ely]
A Divine of the Church of England (*A Sermon Preached upon St Peter's Day*)
A Dutiful Son of this Church (*Angliae Speculum*)

PATTEN, William Gilbert [1866–1945, US novelist]
Burt L. Standish (*Frank Merriwell's Daring*; *Frank Merriwell's Victories*)

PATTERSON, Henry [1867–?, Scottish-born Australian writer]
Bartimaeus (*The King's Chamberlain*; *Armageddon*)

PATTERSON, Henry [1929–, English mystery writer]
Martin Fallon (*The Keys of Hell*; *Year of the Tiger*)
James Graham (*Bloody Passage*; *Khufra Run*)
Jack Higgins (*The Eagle has Landed*; *Storm Warning*)
Hugh Marlowe (*A Candle for the Dead*; *Seven Pillars to Hell*)
Harry Patterson (*Cry of the Hunter*; *Graveyard Shift*)

PATTERSON, Peter [1932–, English playwright]
Peter Terson (*Zigger Zagger*; *Good Lads at Heart*)

PAUL, Elliot Harold [1891–1958, US journalist and novelist]
Brett Rutledge (*The Death of Lord Haw-Haw*)

PAUL, Sir John Dean [1802–68, English failed banker – prosecuted for fraud]
A Delinquent Banker (*Rouge et Noir*)

PAUL, Robert Bateman [1798–1860, English cleric and writer]
The Late James Hamley Tregenna (*The Autobiography of a Cornish Rector*)

PAULDING, James Kirke [1778–1860, US novelist and satirist]
An Amateur (*The New Mirror for Travellers*)
Hector Bullus (*The Diverting History of John Bull and Brother Jonathan*)
A Doubtful Gentleman (*Tales of the Good Woman*)
Sampson Fairlamb (*A Gift from Fairyland*)
*Launcelot Langstaff (*Salma Gundi or, the Whim-Whams*)
A New England Man (*Sketch of Old England*)
A Northern Man (*Letters from the South*)
An Obsolete Author (in the *New York Literary World*)
Dominie Nicholas Aegidius Oudenarde (*The Book of Saint Nicholas*)
A Retired Common Councilman (*Chronicles of the City of Gotham*)

PAULL, Harry Major [1854–1934, Welsh writer and playwright]
Paul Blake (in *Boy's Own Paper*)

PAULL, James [1770–1808, English merchant in India and politician]
A Lover of Consistency (*A Letter to Charles James Fox*)

PAWLEY, Martin Edward [1938–, English architectural writer]
Charles Noble (*Philip Johnson*)
Rupert Spade (*Paul Rudolph*; *Oscar Niemeyer*)

PAXTON, Joseph Rupert [1827–67, US lawyer and writer]
Hipponax Roset (*Jewelry and other Precious Stones*)

PAYES, Rachel Cosgrove [1922–, English novelist]
E. L. Arch (*Bridge to Yesterday*; *Planet of Death*)

PAYN, James [1830–98, English novelist, critic and editor]
A Cantab (in *MacMillan's Magazine*)
A Man of the World (*Maxims*)
John S. Sauzade (*Garret van Horn*)

PAYNE, Buckner H. [1799–1883, US writer]
Ariel (*The Negro, What is his Ethnological Status?*)

PAYNE, Charles Johnson [fl. 1929, English
sporting writer]
Snaffles (*A Half-Century of Memories*; *My
Sketch Book in the Shiny*)

PAYNE, Donald Gordon [1924–, English
novelist]
Ian Cameron (*The Lost Ones*; *The Mountains
at the Bottom of the World*)
Donald Gordon (*Flight of the Bat*; *Leap in
the Dark*)
James Vance Marshall (*My Boy that Went to
Sea*; *Wind at Morning*)

PAYNE, George [1781–1848, Scottish cleric
and metaphysicial writer]
An English Congregational Minister
(*Strictures on Dr Marshall's Late Work on
Atonement*)

PAYNE, Pierre Stephen Robert [1911–,
English novelist]
Robert Young (*The Song of the Peasant*; *The
War in the Marshes*)

PAYNTER, Charles [1791–1873, English
mariner]
Philaletheia (*Instinct and Mind*)

PAYSON, Edward [1783–1827, US cleric and
preacher]
A Citizen of Maine (*The Maine Law in
Balance*)

PAYSON, George [1824–93, US lawyer and
novelist]
Francis Fogle, Sen. Esq. (*A Romance of
California*)
Ralph Raven (*Golden Dreams and Leaden
Realities*)
Robert Dexter Romaine (*The New Age of
Gold*)

PAYTON, Charles Alfred [1843–1926,
English diplomat and angling
correspondent for *The Field*]
Sarcelle (*Moss from a Rolling Stone*)

PEABODY, Nathaniel [1774–1855, US
physician]
A Teacher in Boston (*First Lessons in
Grammar on the Plan of Pestalozzi*)

PEACE, Sir Walter [1840–1917, English
colonial civil servant]
Discipulus (in *National Review*)

PEACHAM, Henry [1576–1643, English artist
and scholar]
Ryhen Pameach (*A Dialogue Between the
Crosse in Cheap and Charing Cross*)

PEACOCK, F. Harold [1904–, English
journalist]
Christopher Martin (in the *Christian Herald*)

PEACOCK, James [1738–1814, English
architect and social reformer]
Jose MacPacke, a Bricklayer's Labourer
(*Nut Shells*)

PEACOCK, Thomas Love [1785–1866,
English merchant, novelist, satirist and
poet]
P. M. O'Donovan (*Sir Proteus*)
Peter Peppercorn (in *The Globe* and for *Rich
and Poor or, Saint and Sinner*)

PEARCE, Zachary [1690–1774, English
cleric, classical scholar and theologian;
Bishop of Rochester]
A Clergyman of the Church of England
(*Letter to the Clergy of the Church of
England*)
Ned Mum (letter to *The Guardian*)
Phileleutherus Londoniensis (*Epistolae Duae
ad ... F. V.*)

PEARL, Jack [fl. 1980, US romantic novelist]
Stephanie Blake (*Daughter of Destiny*;
Flowers of Fire)

PEARSE, Edward [1631–94, English cleric
and controversialist]
A Beneficed Minister (*The Conformists Plea
for the Nonconformist*)
A Charitable and Compassionate Conformist
(*The Conformists Second Plea etc.*)
A Country Minister (*The State of
Northampton from the Beginning of the
Fire etc.*)

PEARSE, Hugh Wodehouse [1855–1919, English soldier]
A Regimental Officer (in *MacMillan's Magazine*)

PEARSON, Charles Henry [1830–94, English historian and educationalist working in Australia]
A Recent Traveller (*The Insurrection in Poland*; *Russia*)

PEARSON, Mrs Emily C. [fl. 1868, US novelist]
Ervie (*Echo-Bank: a Temperance Tale*)

PEARSON, George C. [fl. 1886, US writer]
A Penitent Peri (*Flights Inside and Outside Paradise*)

PEARSON, Karl [1857–1936, English mathematician and scientist]
Loki (*The New Werther*)

PEARSON, Richard [1765–1836, Scottish physician and medical writer]
A Member of the London College of Physicians (*Thesaurus Medicaminum*)

PECHEY, Archibald Thomas [1876–1961, English journalist, novelist and crime writer]
Mark Cross (*The Four Get Going*; *The Shadow of the Four*)
Valentine (*The Adjustors*; *The Blue Pool*)

PECK, Ellen [fl. 1861, US novelist]
Cuyler Pine (*Ecce Femina: or, the Woman Zoe*)

PECK, Francis [1692–1743, English cleric, biographer and antiquarian]
A Clergyman of the Church of England (*Sighs upon the Death of Queen Anne*)

PECK, George Washington [1817–59, US writer]
Cantell A. Bigley (*Aurifodiana or Adventures in the Gold Region*)

PECK, Harry Thurston [1856–1914, US classical scholar and writer]
Rafford Pyke (*The Personal Equation*; *What is Good English?*)

PECK, John Mason [1789–1858, US cleric]
An Old Pioneer (*Father Clark or, the Pioneer Preacher*)

PECK, Lillie [d. 1878, English writer]
Ruth Elliott (*A Voice from the Sea*)

PECKWELL, Henry [1747–87, English cleric and religious writer]
A Friend to Civil and Religious Liberty (*The Account of an Appeal from a Summary Conviction*)

PEEBLES, James Ewing [1928–68, Scottish novelist]
James Kennaway (*Tunes of Glory*; *The Mind Benders*)

PEEBLES, Mrs Mary Louise [1839–1915, US novelist]
Lynde Palmer (*The Good Fight*; *Two Blizzards*)

PEEL, Jonathan [1799–1879, English soldier, politician and patron of the turf]
Dinks (*The Dog*)

PEERS, Edgar Allison [1891–1952, English writer on Spanish religious history]
Bruce Truscott (*First Year at University*; *Redbrick and these Vital Days*)

PEGGE, Samuel [1704–96, English academic and antiquarian]
An Antiquary (*Fitz-Stephen's Description of the City of London*; *The Forme of Cury or, a Roll of Ancient English Cookery*)
L. Echard; Paul Gemsege; L. E.; A Ploughist; Portius; T. Row; Senex; Vicarius Cantianus (all used in *Gentleman's Magazine*)

PEILE, Thomas Williamson [1806–82, English cleric and writer]
Philopolis (*The Christian Temple and its Priesthood*)

PEIRCE, Augustus [1802–49, US physician]
Poeta, Enginae Societatis (*The Rebelliad*)

PEIRCE, Benjamin [1809–80, US mathematician and astronomer]
Benjamin the Florentine (*Ben Yamen's Song of Geometry*)

PEIRCE, James [1674–1726, English Presbyterian cleric]
A Dissenter in the Country (*Enquiry into the Present Duty of a Low Church Man*)

PEIRCE, Thomas [1786–1850, US humorous verse writer]
A Citizen of Cincinnati (*The Muse of Hesperia*)

PELL, Robert Conger [1835–68, US writer]
Chetwood Evelyn Esq. (*The Companion – After Dinner Table-Talk*)

PELLEGRINI, Carlo [1839–89, Italian-born caricaturist and illustrator; in England from 1864]
Ape; Singe (both used in *Vanity Fair*)

PELLEGRINI, Frank E. [fl. 1946, US writer]
Franklyn Pell (*Hangman's Hill*)

PEMBER, William Leonard [fl. 1960, English writer]
Jack Monmouth (*Lightning over Mayfair*; *Not Ready to Die*)

PENDLEBURY, Henry [1626–95, English nonconformist cleric]
A Countrey Divine (*A Plain Representation of Transubstantiation*)

PENDLETON, Donald Eugene [1927–, US mystery writer]
Dan Britain (*Revolt!*)
Stephan Gregory (*Madame Murder*; *All Lovers Accepted*)

PENDOWER, Jacques [1899–1976, English crime and mystery writer]
T. C. H. Jacobs (*Reward for Treason*; *Cavalcade of Murder*)

PENGELLY, William [1812–94, English mathematician and geologist]
A Geologist (in *Once a Week*)

PENN, Richard [1736–1811, American colonist – grandson of William Penn]
The Rajah of Vaneplysia (in *Gentleman's Magazine*)

PENN, William [1644–1718, English Quaker; emigrated to America and founded the state of Pennsylvania]
A Gentleman in the Country (*Second Letter from a Gentleman in the Country to his Friends in London*)
A Living True Witness to that One Eternal Way of God (*The New Witnesses Proved old Heretics*)
A Lover of Charity and Sincerity in All (*Plain-Dealing with a Traducing Anabaptist*)
A Lover of Truth and Peace (*The Counterfeit Christian Detected*)
One of the Humblest and most Dutiful of His Dissenting Subjects (*A Perswasive to Moderation to Church Dissenters*)
The Pensilvanian (*A Defense of the Duke of Buckingham's Book of Religion*)
Phil'Anglus (*England's Concern in the Choice of this New Parliament*; *Our Project for the Good of England*; *The Protestant's Remonstrance against Pope and Presbyter*)

PENN, William [1776–1845, US writer – son of Richard Penn above]
An Undergraduate (*Vindiciae Britannicae*)

PENNECK, Henry [1800–62, English cleric]
Mr Bayle (*Apostolical Succession*)

PENNEY, William [1801–72, Lord Kinloch; Scottish jurist and religious writer]
A Layman (*The Circle of Christian Doctrine*)

PENNIE, John Fitzgerald [1782–1848, English dramatist and poet]
A Modern Genius (*Tale of a Modern Genius or, the Miseries of Parnassus*)
Sylvaticus (Tale of a Modern Genius)

PENNINGTON, Richard [1904–61?, English librarian and writer – sometime in Canada]
David Peterley (*Peterley's Harvest*)

PENNYMAN, John [1628–1706, English royalist and religious writer]
A Lover of Virtue and Goodness in Whomsoever (*Multum in Parvo*)
Phil Anglus (*A Looking-Glass for the Quakers*)

PENROSE, Sir Charles Vinicombe [1759–1830, English admiral]
A. F. Y.; E. F. G. (both used in the *Naval Chronicle*)
A Flag Officer (*Remarks on the Conduct of the Naval Administration since 1815*)

PENROSE, Elizabeth [1780–1837, English writer of educational books for children]
Mrs Markham (*History of England; History of France*)

PENROSE, Francis [1718–98, English physician and medical writer]
A Layman (*Animadversions on a Late Sermon*)

PENROSE, John [1778–1859, English cleric and religious writer]
A Senior (*A Familiar Introduction to the Christian Religion*)
A Trinitarian (*Of God, or the Divine Mind*)

PENROSE, Thomas [1742–79, English cleric, poet and writer]
P. Newbury (in *Gentleman's Magazine*)

PENRY, John [1559–93, Welsh Puritan pamphleteer – hanged for his writings]
Martin Marprelate (for a series of anti-bishop pamphlets issued with Job Throckmorton and John Udall)

PENTELOW, John Nix [1872–1931, English writer on cricket and stories for boys]
Jack North; Richard Randolph (both used in *Pluck*)

PEOPLE, Granville Church [fl. 1941, English writer]
Granville Church (*Bombs Burst Once; Race with the Sun*)

PERCEVAL, Arthur Philip [1799–1853, English cleric and theological writer]
A Churchman (*An Address to Members of the Church of England*)

A Civilian (*Remarks upon the Bill for Church Discipline*)
A Clergyman (*Suggestions for the Relief of British Commerce*)
A Late Fellow of All Souls College, Oxford (*A Letter to the Members of both Houses of Parliament*)
One of His Majesty's Chaplains (*A Claim for Relief on Behalf of the Church of England*)
One of His Majesty's Servants (*A Letter to the Rt. Hon. Earl Grey*)
A Presbyter in the Diocese of Canterbury (*An Address to the Deans of Cathedral Churches*)
A Presbyter of the Church of England (*An Enquiry into the Late Supposed Manifestations*)

PERCEVAL, Sir John [1683–1748, 1st Earl of Egmont; Irish politician]
A Nobleman of the Other Kingdom (*The Question of the Precedency of the Peers of Ireland*)

PERCEVAL, John [1711–70, 2nd Earl of Egmont; Irish politican and political writer]
A Gentleman in the Country (*An Occasional Letter from a Gentleman in the Country*)

PERCIVAL, Thomas [1740–1804, English physician and medical writer]
A Gentleman of Manchester (*Observations and Reflections on the Late Earthquake*)

PERCY, Alan Ian [1880–1930, 8th Duke of Northumberland; soldier, military and political writer]
Daniel (*The Writing on the Wall*)

PEREIRA, Harold Bertram [1890–?, English journalist and writer]
*Hasani Muhammad Askari (*The Food of Kings*)

PERKINS, Frederic Beecher [1828–99, US librarian and bibliographer]
Pharoah Budlong (*President Greeley, President Hoffman etc.*)

PERROT, John [d. 1671, English Quaker and religious writer]
John (*To the Suffering Seed of Royalty*; *To All People upon the Face of the Earth*)

PERRY, Clair Willard [1887–?, US writer]
Clay Perry (*Heart of Hemlock*; *The Two Reds of Travoy*)

PERRY, Sampson [1747–1823, English political journalist – became a refugee in France]
William Adams (*A Disquisition of the Stone and Gravel and other Diseases of the Bladder etc.*)

PERRY, Walter Copland [1814–1911, English barrister, schoolmaster and antiquarian]
John Copland (*Walter Stanhope*)

PERY, Edmund Sexton [1719–1806, Viscount Pery; Irish barrister and politican]
An Armenian in Ireland (*Letters of an Armenian in Ireland to his Friends in Trebisund*)

PETER, William [1788–1853, English barrister and politician]
Ralph Ferrars (*Poems*)
A Layman (*Sacred Songs*)

PETERKIN, Alexander [1780–1846, Scottish lawyer and journalist]
Anti-Harmonicus (*A Poetical Epistel to J ...T ...*)
Civis (*A Letter to Rt. Hon. E. Erskine*)

PETERS, Curtis Arnoux [1906–68, US cartoonist and humorist]
Peter Arno (*Peter Arno's Cartoon Review*; *Whoops Dearie!*)

PETERS, Hugh [1598–1660, English cleric; an early emigrant to America and supporter of the Parliamentarian cause, later executed by Charles II]
Peter Cornelius (*A Way Propounded to Make the Poor Happy*; *The Way to Peace*)

PETERS, Maureen [1935–, Welsh historical novelist]
Veronica Black (*The Wayward Madonna*; *Pilgrim of Desire*)
Catherine Darby (*Falcon for a Witch*; *Moon in Pisces*)
Belinda Grey (*Sweet Wind of Morning*; *Glen of Frost*)
Elizabeth Law (*Regency Morning*)
Levanah Lloyd (*Cauldron of Desire*; *Mail Order Bride*)
Judith Rothman (*With Murder in Mind*; *Dark Gemini*)
Sharon Whitby (*Houseless One*; *Shiver me a Story*)

PETERS, Samuel Andrew [1735–1826, American loyalist and writer]
Simeon Baxter, a Licentiate (*Tyrannicide Proved Lawful*)
A Gentleman of the Province (*A General History of Connecticut*)
John Viator Esq. (*An Answer to Dr Inglis' Defence*)

PETERSDORFF, Charles Erdman [1800–86, English jurist]
A Barrister (*The Law Students Common-Place Book*)

PETERSON, Charles Jacobs [1819–87, US journalist and publisher]
J. Thornton Randolph (*The Cabin and the Parlor*)

PETERSON, Frederick [1859–1938, US physician and poet]
Pai Ta-shun (*Chinese Lyrics*)

PETERSON, Margaret [1883–1933, Indian-born English novelist and poet]
Glint Green (*Poison Death*; *Devil Spider*)

PETTIGREW, Thomas Lettsom [1813–37, English writer]
A Cornet in the E.I. Co's service (*Lucien Greville*)

PETTIWARD, Roger [d. 1941, English cartoonist]
Paul Crum (in *Punch* and for *The Last Cream Bun*)

PETTY, Sir William [1623–87, English political economist]
An Observator on the London Bills of Mortality (*Observations upon the Dublin Bills of Mortality 1681*)

PETYT, William [1636–1707, English barrister and archivist in the Tower of London]
Philanglus (*Britannia Languens*)

PEYTON, Kathleen Wendy [1929–, English writer for children]
Kathleen Herald (*The Mandrake*; *Crab the Roan*)
K. M. Peyton (*Flambards*; *Midsummer Night's Death*)

PFEIL, Donald [fl. 1976, US science-fiction writer]
William Arrow (*Escape from Terror Lagoon*)

PHELAN, William [1789–1830, Irish cleric]
Declan (*The Case of the Church of Ireland Stated*)

PHELPS, Charles [d. 1854, US writer]
A Citizen of the United States (*Vermonters Unmasked*)

PHELPS, Mrs Elizabeth Stewart [d. 1920, US writer]
Leigh North (*The Predecessors of Cleopatra*; *The Bailiff of Tewkesbury*)

PHELPS, Mrs Elizabeth Stuart [1815–52, US novelist]
Onyx (*A Silent Partner*)
H. Trusta (*A Peep at Number Five*; *The Sunny Side*)

PHILIPP, Elliott Elias [1915–, English physician and writer on medicine]
Philip Embey (*Woman's Change of Life*)
Anthony Havil (*Talks on a Vital Subject*)
Victor Tempest (*Near the Sun*)

PHILIPS, Ambrose [1675–1749, English journalist and government clerk in Ireland]
Mr Free-Thinker (in *The Free-Thinker*)

PHILIPS, Harry Vivian Majendie [1860–?, English civil servant in India]
Philip Vivian (*The Churches and Modern Thoughts*)

PHILIPS, John Austin Drury [1875–1947, English post office worker, novelist and short-story writer]
Paul Wingate (*The Heart of a Boy*)

PHILIPS, Judson [1903–89, US crime and mystery writer]
Philip Owen (*Mystery at a Country Inn*)
Hugh Pentecost (*Death Mask*; *Murder in Luxury*)

PHILIPS, Mrs Katherine [1631–64, English poet and translator]
The Incomparable Mrs K. P. (*Poems*)
Orinda (*Letters from Orinda to Poliarchus*)

PHILLIFENT, John Thomas [1916–76, English science-fiction writer]
John Rackham (*Space Puppet*; *The Master Weed*)

PHILLIPS, David Graham [1867–1911, US journalist and novelist – assassinated]
John Graham (*The Great God Success*)

PHILLIPS, Dennis [1924–, English mystery novelist]
Simon Challis (*Death on a Quiet Beach*)
Peter Chambers (*Lady Who Never Was*; *Long Time Dead*)
Peter Chester (*Blueprint for Larceny*; *Murder Forestalled*)
Philip Daniels (*Revenue Incorporated*)

PHILLIPS, Edwin D. [1827–64, US soldier]
An Officer of the Army (*Texas, and its Late Military Occupation*)

PHILLIPS, George Searle [1815–89, English journalist and writer]
January Searle (*The Gypsies of the Dane's Dyke*; *Memoirs of W. Wordsworth*)

PHILLIPS, Gerald William [1884–?, English writer]
John Huntington (*Seven Black Chessmen*)

PHILLIPS, Henry [1838–95, US lawyer and numismatist]
Antiquarian (*Historical Sketches of the Paper Money Issued by Pennsylvania*)

PHILLIPS, Horace [fl. 1921, English writer for children]
Hilda Richards (in *School Friend*, 1919–21, after Charles Hamilton)
Marjorie Stanton (in *Schoolgirl's Own*)

PHILLIPS, Hubert [1891–1964, English journalist, broadcaster and crime writer]
Caliban (in the *New Statesman* from 1930 to 1938 and later in the *Law Journal*)
Dogberry (in the *News Chronicle* from 1931 to 1952)

PHILLIPS, Hugh [fl. 1938, English novelist]
Philip Hughes (*Ragged Robin*; *My Strange Wife*)

PHILLIPS, James Atlee [1915–91, US mystery writer]
Philip Atlee (*The Green Wound*; *The Kiwi Contract*)

PHILLIPS, John [1631–1706, English controversialist]
A Guide to the Inferiour Clergie (*Speculum Crape-Gownorum*)
A Nephew of John Milton (*The Vision of Mons. Chamillard*)

PHILLIPS, Pauline Friedman [1918–, US journalist]
Abigail Van Buren (*Dear Abby*)

PHILLIPS, Sir Richard [1767–1840, English journalist and compiler of educational books for children]
James Adair (*Five Hundred Questions and Answers*)
Rev. S. Barrow (*The Poor Child's Library*; *Sermons for Schools*)
Rev. David Blair (*The Universal Precepter*; *A Million of Facts*; *The Secretary's Companion*)
Abbe Bossut (*The First French and English Grammar*)
Rev. C. C. Clarke (*The Hundred Wonders of the World*)

Common Sense (in *Monthly Magazine*)
Rev. J. Goldsmith (*A Biographical Class-Book*; *The British Empire in 1823*; *The First Step to Knowledge*)
William Mavor (*A Letter to the Livery of London*; *A Morning's Walk from London to Kew*; *Social Philosophy*)
Mrs (or Miss) Margaret Pelham (*The Parent's and Tutor's First Catechism*)

PHILLIPS, Samuel [1814–54, English actor, journalist and critic]
John Williams (in *Blackwood's Magazine*)

PHILLIPS, Walter Shelley [1867–1940, US writer]
El Comancho (*Totem Tales*)

PHILLIPS, Watts [1825–74, English dramatist, novelist and caricaturist]
Fairfax Balfour (*Ida Lee or, The Child of the Wreck*)

PHILLIPS, Willard [1784–1873, US jurist]
A Citizen of Massachusetts (*An Appeal to the Good Sense of the Democrats*)

PHILLPOTTS, Eden [1862–1960, Indian-born English novelist]
Harrington Hext (*Number 87*; *Who Killed Diana?*; *The Thing of Their Heels*)

PICKARD, A. G. [1913–, New Zealand short-story writer]
A. P. Gaskell (*The Big Game and Other Stories*)

PICKARD, Hannah Maynard [1812–44, English writer]
A Lady (*The Widow's Jewels*)

PICKEN, Andrew [1788–1833, Scottish writer]
The Dominie (in *Fraser's Magazine*)
A Late Resident (*The Canadas as They are Now*)

PICKERING, Basil Montagu [1836–78, English publisher and antiquarian bookseller]
A Layman (*Lord Selbourne's Letter ... and an Answer*)

PICKERING, Henry [1781–1838, US merchant and poet]
An American (*Poems*)

PICKERING, John [1777–1846, US lawyer, diplomat and philologist]
A Member of the Massachusetts Bar (*National Rights and State Rights*)

PICKERING, Timothy [1745–1829, American lawyer and politician]
The Secretary of State (*A Letter from the Secretary of State to Charles C. Pinckney Esq.*)
Verus (*Letters of Verus to the Native Americans*)

PICKETT, James Chamberlayne [1793–1872, US diplomat]
A Kentuckian (*The Memory of Pocahontas Vindicated*)

PICKTHALL, Marmaduke William [1875–1936, English journalist in India and orientalist]
E. Greck (in *Temple Bar*)

PICTON, Thomas [1822–91, US journalist]
A Gothamite (*Acrostics from Across the Atlantic*)
Paul Preston (*The Fireside Magician*)

PIERCE, John Robinson [1910–, US scientist and writer]
J. J. Coupling (in *Astounding Science Fiction* magazine)

PIERCE, Thomas [1622–91, English cleric and controversialist]
One of the Reverend Commissioners for the Review of the Liturgy (*Two Letters against Dissenters*)
Theophilus Philobasileus (*A Prophylactick from Disloyalty*)

PIGGOTT, Sir Francis Taylor [1852–1925, English colonial jurist and Japanese expert]
Hope Dawlish (*A Secretary of Legation*)

PIGOTT, Richard [1828–89, Irish journalist and unreliable reporter of events]
An Irish National Journalist (*Personal Recollections*)

PIGOTT, William [1870–1943, English solicitor, novelist and psychic researcher]
Hubert Wales (*The Wife of Colonel Hughes*)

PIKE, Albert [1809–91, US soldier, lawyer and writer]
Casca (*Prose Sketches and Poems, Written in the Western Country*)

PIKE, Mrs Frances West [fl. 1858, US novelist]
Anna Ahern (*Here and Hereafter*)
Katherine Morris (*An Autobiography*)

PIKE, Mrs Mary H. Greene [1827–1908, US novelist]
Mary Langdon (*Ida May*; *Climbing and Sliding – a Book for Boys*)
Sydney A. Storey (*Pearl*; *Caste*)

PILCHER, Rosamunde [1924–, English romantic novelist]
Jane Fraser (*Dangerous Intruder*; *A Family Affair*)

PILDITCH, Sir Philip Harold [1890–1949, English architect and writer]
John Bartropp (*Barbarian: a Tale of the Roman Wall*)

PILGRIM, Thomas [d. 1882, US writer]
Arthur Morecamp (*Live Boys in the Black Hills*)
Eugen Owl (*Old Nick's Camp Meetin'*)

PILKINGTON, Mrs Mary [1766–1839, English novelist]
Matthew Moral (*The Novice or, the Heir of Montgomery Castle*)

PILLING, Anne [1944–, English writer for children]
Ann Cheetham (*Black Harvest*; *The Beggar's Curse*)

PINCKNEY, Charles [1758–1824, US
politician and diplomat]
A South Carolina Planter (*Three Letters on
the Case of Jonathan Robbins*)
A South Carolinian (*Observations to Shew
the Propriety of the Nomination of Colonel
James Monroe to the Presidency etc.*)

PINCKNEY, Thomas [1750–1828, US
lawyer diplomat and politician]
Achates (*Reflections: Late Disturbances in
South Carolina*)

PINKERTON, John [1758–1826, Scottish
historian and numismatist]
H. Bennet (*The Treasury of Wit*)
Robert Heron (*Letters on Literature; An
Essay on Medals*)

PINKNEY, Miles [1599–1674, English
Catholic cleric and religious writer]
Miles Car (*A Treatise of the Love of God – a
Translation*)
Thomas Carre (*The Funeral Sermon of the
Queen of Britanie; Pietas Parisiensis; Pietas
Romana et Parisiensis; A Proper Looking
Glasse for the Daughters of Sion*)

PINKNEY, William [1764–1822, US lawyer
and politician]
Caius (*A Few Remarks on Mr Hamilton's
Late Letter concerning the Public Conduct
and Character of the President*)
Decius (*Decius's Reply to the Republican
Citizens of Maryland*)

PIPER, David Towry [1918–90, English
gallery director and art historian]
Peter Towry (*It's Warm Inside; Trial by
Battle*)

PITCAIRNE, Archibald [1652–1713, Scottish
physician and poet]
Archimedes (*Epistola ... Gelonem*)

PITMAN, Sir Isaac [1813–97, English
publisher]
Examiner (*A Brief Examination of the New
Church*)
An Examiner of the New Church Doctrines
(*A Refutation of Mr Roebuck's Pamphlet*)
A Truth-Seeker (*Cremation Considered*)

PITMAN, John [1784–1864, US jurist]
One of the Rhode Island People (*A Reply to
Marcus Morton*)

PITT, William Peppernell [fl. 1950, English
lawyer, journalist and writer on angling]
A. Nowall (in the *Fly Fisher's Journal*)

PLACE, Francis [1771–1854, English political
radical from humble background]
A London Tailor (*Political Economy*)
Gamaliel Smith (*Not Paul but Jesus*)

PLATH, Sylvia [1932–63, US poet]
Victoria Lucas (*The Bell Jar*)

PLAYFAIR, Ian S. O. [1894–1972, English
soldier and military writer]
Isop (*The Horrors of Peace and Other Trifles*)

PLAYFAIR, William [1759–1823, Scottish
mechanic, pamphleteer and translator]
Joshua Montefiore (*The Spirit of the
Bankrupt Laws*)
J. Jephson Oddy (*European Commerce*)

PLAYFORD, Henry [1657–1706, English
patron and music publisher]
Dr Merryman (*Apollo's Feast or, Wit's
Entertainment*)

PLEYDELL-BOUVERIE, Edward [1818–89,
English barrister and politician]
E. P. B. (letters to *The Times*)

PLOWDEN, Charles [1743–1821, English
Jesuit and religious writer]
Clericus (*Letters of Clericus to Laicus*)

PLOWDEN-WARDLAW, James Tait
[1873–1963, English barrister, cleric and
writer]
Clement Humilis (*Vox Dilecti*)

PLOWMAN, Max (Mark) [1883–1941,
English poet and writer]
Mark VII (*A Subaltern on the Somme in
1916*)

PLUES, Margaret [fl. 1868, English
naturalist, artist and writer]
Skelton Yorke (*Hilda: or the Old Seat of
Council*)

PLUMMER, Clare [1912–80, English romantic novelist]
Clare Emsley (*The Fatal Gift*; *A Time to Heal*)

PLUMPTRE, Annabella [fl. 1810, English linguist, translator and novelist]
A Lady (*Domestic Management or, the Healthful Cook-Book*)

PLUMPTRE, Charles Claude Molyneux [1855–1923, English barrister]
C. C. Molyneux (in *Temple Bar*)

PLUMPTRE, John [1753–1825, English cleric and religious writer]
A Clergyman of the Church of England (*A Plain and Easy Introduction to Revealed Religion*)

PLUNKET, Edward [1808–89, Baron Dunsany; mariner]
A Naval Peer (*Our Naval Position and Policy*)

PLUNKETT, Henry Grattan [fl. 1850, English writer and humorist]
Fusbos (in *Punch*)

POCKRICH, Richard [1690–1759, Irish musician and inventor of musical glasses]
Philanthropos (*The Temple-Oge Ballad*)

POE, Edgar Allan [1809–49, US journalist, poet and short-story writer]
A Bostonian (*Tamerlane and Other Poems*)
Hans Pfaal (*The Unparalleled Adventure of One Hans Pfaal*)
Arthur Gordon Pym (*The Narrative of Arthur Gordon Pym*)
Quarles (in the *American Review*)

POHL, Frederick [1919–, US science-fiction writer]
*Edson McCann (*Preferred Risk*)
James McCreigh (*Danger Moon*)
Ernst Mason (*Tiberius*)
*Jordan Park (*Sorority House*)
Donald Stacy (*The God of Channel 1*)

POINSETT, Joel Roberts [1779–1851, US traveller and politician]
A South Carolinian (*Notes on Mexico*)

POLAND, Dorothy [1937–, Welsh novelist]
Alison Farely (*Archduchess Arrogance*; *Scheming Spanish Queen*)
Jane Hammond (*Fire and Sword*; *The Doomtower*)

POLE, Thomas [1753–1829, Scottish physician, Quaker and medical writer]
A Friend to Education and Moral Improvement of the Labouring Poor (*On the Irreverent Use of Sacred Names*)

POLLAND, Madeleine [1918–, Irish novelist and writer for children]
Frances Adrian (*Double Shadow*)

POLLARD, Alfred William [1859–1944, English writer]
Z. (*Life, Love and Light*)

POLLARD, Edward Alfred [1838–72, US journalist and writer]
A Distinguished Southern Journalist (*The Early Life, Campaigns of Robert E. Lee*)
One Recently Returned from the Enemy's Country (*A Letter on the State of the War*)
A Southerner (*The Southern Spy*)
The Southern Spy (*Letters of the Southern Spy*)

POLLEY, Judith Anne [1938–, English romantic novelist]
Judith Hagar (*Don't Run from Love*; *Shadow of the Eagle*)

POLLOCK, Sir Frederick [1845–1937, English barrister and legal writer]
An Apprentice of Lincoln's Inn (*Leading Cases Done into English*)

POLLOCK, John Hacket [1887–1964, Irish physician, poet, dramatist and novelist]
An Pilibin (*Wild Honey*)

POLWHELE, Richard [1760–1838, English cleric and West Country writer]
A Country Gentleman (*The Family Picture or, Domestic Education*)
Eusebius Exoniensis (*An Essay on the Evidence from Scripture*)
An Undergraduate (*The Follies of Oxford*)

A Young Gentleman of Truro School (*The Fate of Llewellyn*)

POMEROY, Florence Wallace [d. 1911, English writer]
Martha Major (in *MacMillan's Magazine*)

POMEROY, Marcus M. [1833–96, US journalist]
Brick Pomeroy (*Sense or, Saturday Night Musings*)

POMFRET, John [1667–1702, English cleric and poet]
A Person of Quality (*The Choice or Wish*)
Philalethes (*Dies Novissima*)

POND, Enoch [1791–1882, US cleric]
A Clergyman of Massachusetts (*The Eternity of Future Punishment of the Wicked*)

POND, Frederick Eugene [1856–1925, US writer on sporting matters]
Will Wildwood (*The Life and Adventures of Ned Buntline*; *Handbook for Young Sportsmen*)

POND, George Edward [1837–99, US journalist]
Philip Quilibet (in *The Galaxy* magazine)

PONSONBY, Doris Almon [1907–, English historical romance novelist]
Doris Rybot (*Romany Sister*; *A Japanese Doll*)
Sarah Tempest (*A Winter of Fear*)

PONSONBY, Frederick Edward Neuflize [1913–93, 10th Earl of Bessborough]
Eric Duncannon (*Like Stars Appearing*; *The Noon is Night*; *Darker the Sky*)

PONSONBY, Frederick George Brabazon [1815–95, 6th Earl of Bessborough; barrister and sportsman]
Richard Doe (*Barefaced Impostors*)

POOLE, Matthew [1624–79, English cleric and biblical scholar]
Philopsychus Philalethes (*The Blasphemer Slaine with the Sword of the Spirit*)

POOLE, Reginald Heber [1885–?, English writer for boys]
Michael Poole (*Bancroft of the Grammar School*; *Mystery at Merrilees*)
Anthony Thomas (used in both *Magnet* and *Gem*)

POOLE, Robert [1708–52, English physician, traveller, and medical and theological writer]
Theophilus Philanthropos (*Physical Vade Mecum*; *A Token of Christian Love*)

POOLE, Mrs Sophia [1804–91, English traveller and writer]
The Englishwoman (*The Englishwoman in Egypt*)

POOLE, William Frederick [1821–94, US lexicographer and librarian]
Philorthos (*The Orthographical Hobgoblin*)

POOR, Agnes Blake [d. 1922, US novelist]
Dorothy Prescott (*Boston Neighbors*; *Brothers and Strangers*)

POORE, Benjamin Perley [1820–87, US journalist]
Perley (in the *Boston Journal*)

POPE, Alexander [1688–1744, English essayist, poet and satirist]
J. Baker, Knight (*God's Revenge against Punning*)
Esdras Barnivelt, Apoth. (*A Key to the Lock*)
Dick Distich (in *The Guardian*)
An Eminent Hand (*The Impertinent or, a Visit to the Court*)
An Eye-Witness (*A Full and True Account of a Horrid and Barbarous Revenge by Poison on the body of Mr Edmund Curll*)
Mr Joseph Gay (*A Compleat Key to the Non-Juror*)
Martinus Scriblerus (used occasionally)
Bob Short (in *The Guardian*)

POPE, Henry [fl. 1872, US writer]
Gavilan Peck (*The Struggle for Existence*)

PORDAGE, John [1607–83, English cleric and astrologer]
A Person of Qualitie (*Theologia Mystica*)

PORDAGE, Samuel [1633–91, English dramatist and poet]
S. P. Armig (*Mundorum Explicatio*)

PORGES, Arthur [1915–,US science-fiction writer]
Peter Arthur (in *Fantastic Stories* magazine)
Pat Rogers (in *Fear* magazine)

PORSON, Richard [1759–1808, English classical scholar and writer]
Cantabrigiensis; Sundry Whereof (both used in *Gentleman's Magazine*)
J. N. Dawes (in *Monthly Magazine*)
S. England (letter in the *Morning Chronicle*)
Urbano Amicior (letter in *Gentleman's Magazine*)

PORTAL, Abraham [fl. 1760, English dramatist and poet]
Anti-Profanus (*A Letter to David Garrick Esq.*)

PORTEOUS, Richard Sydney [1897–1963, Australian writer]
Standby (*Sailing Orders; Close to the Wind*)

PORTER, Albert H. [fl. 1875, US writer]
An Old Resident (*Niagara Past and Present*)

PORTER, Anna Maria [1780–1832, English novelist]
A Young Lady, Eighteen Years of Age (*Original Poems on Various Subjects*)

PORTER, David [1780–1843, US naval officer, court-martialled in 1824]
An American Long Resident in Constantinople (*Constantinople and its Environs*)

PORTER, Eleanor H. [1868–1920, US novelist and writer for children]
Eleanor Stuart (*The Sunbridge Girls at Six Star Ranch*)

PORTER, Frederick [d. 1949, Scottish physician, medical writer and dramatist]
Frederick Watson (*Strike: a Story in Dialogue*)

PORTER, Harold Everett [1887–1936, US novelist]
Holworthy Hall (*Dormie One and other Golf Stories; Henry of Navarre; Pepper*)

PORTER, James [1753–98, Irish Presbyterian cleric and satirist – hanged as a rebel]
A Man of Ulster; Sydney (both used in the *Northern Star*)
Presbyterian (*Billy Bluff and Squire Firebrand*)

PORTER, Miss Jane [1776–1850, English dramatist and novelist]
An Englishwoman (in *Gentleman's Magazine*)

PORTER, Linn Boyd [1851–1916, US novelist]
Albert Ross (*A Black Adonis; The Garston Bigamy*)

PORTER, Sir Robert Ker [1777–1842, English painter, soldier, traveller and diplomat]
An Officer (*Letters from Portugal and Spain*)

PORTER, William Sydney [1862–1910, US journalist, humorist and writer]
Howard Clark; T. B. Dowd; S. H. Peters (used for some of his early writing)
O. Henry (*Cabbages and Kings; The Four Million*)

PORTSMOUTH, Henry [1703–80, English Quaker]
Catholicus, a Peaceable Member of that Society (*An Essay on the Simplicity of Truth*)

POSNER, Jacob D. [fl. 1937, US writer]
Gregory Dean (*Murder on Stilts; The Case of the Fifth Key*)

POSNER, Richard [1944–, US crime writer]
Iris Foster (*Nightshade; The Crimson Moon*)
Beatrice Murray (*The Dark Sonata*)
Paul Todd (*Blood All Over*)
Dick Wine (*Allegro with Passion*)

POSTL, Karl [1793–1864, German-born novelist – sometime in USA]
An Eye-Witness (*Austria As It Is*)
Charles Sealsfield (his adopted name)

POSTLETHWAYT, Malachy [1707–67, English economist]
A British Merchant (*The African Trade*)

POTT, Joseph Holden [1759–1847, English cleric and writer]
Valentine (*The Tour of Valentine*)

POTTER, Elisha Reynolds [1811–82, US writer]
A Landholder (*An Address to the Freemen of Rhode Island*)

POTTER, George William [1930–, US novelist]
E. L. Withers (*Diminishing Returns*; *Heir Apparent*)

POTTER, Heather [1914–, English writer]
Heather Jenner (*Marriages are Made in Heaven*)

POTTER, Margaret [1926–, English romantic novelist]
Anne Betteridge (*Place for Everyone*)
Anne Melville (*The Lorimer Legacy*)
Margaret Newman (*Murder to Music*)

POTTER, Olive [1895–, English writer for girls]
Josephine Elder (*Erica Wins Through*; *Scholarship Girl*)

POTTER, Thomas [1718–59, English barrister and politician]
A Country Gentleman (*The Expedition against Rochefort*)

POTTER, Thomas Rossell [1799–1873, English historian and writer]
Old Grey (in the *Sporting Magazine*)

POTTLE, Emery Bemsley [1875–1945, US playwright and actor]
Gilbert Emery (*Love-in-a-Mist*; *Persian Poppy*)

POTTS, Alice May Harte [fl. 1905, English novelist]
*John Le Breton (*Mis'ess Joy*)

POTTS, Stacy Gardner [1800–65, US jurist]
Oliver Oakwood (*Village Tales*)

POU, Genevieve Long [1919–, US writer]
Genevieve Holden (*The Velvet Target*; *Deadlier than the Male*)

POUND, Ezra [1885–1972, US poet and critic]
M. D. Adkins (in *Outlook*)
William Atheling; B. H. Dias (both used in *New Age* magazine)
B. L.; T. J. V. (both used in *The Athenaeum*)
E. P. (*Hugh Selwyn Mauberley*)
EZRA I. Y. H. X.; John Hall; Raoul Root; S. O. S.; Abel Sanders (all used in the *Little Review*)
Ferrex; Henry Hawkins; Carl Georg Jesus Maria; Baptiste von Helmholtz (all used in *The Egoist*)
J. V.; N. B.; W. A. (all used in *Edge*)
Hiram Janus (*The Call of the Road* by Edouard Estaunie – a translation)
Weston Llewmys (in *Book News Monthly*)
Old Glory (in the *Transatlantic Review*)
The Poet of Titchfield Street (*Alfred Venison's Poems*)
Alf Venison (in *New English Weekly*)

POURNELLE, Jerry E. [1933–, US scientist and novelist]
Wade Curtis (*Red Heroin*; *Red Dragon*)

POVEY, Charles [1652–1743, English writer and insurance pioneer]
Sir Heister Ryley (*The Visions of Sir Heister Ryley*)

POWE, Bruce Allen [1925–, Canadian writer]
Ellis Portal (*Killing Ground, the Canadian Civil War*)

POWELL, Frederick York [1850–1904, English historian and Scandinavian scholar]
Ignoramus (*Some Words on Allegory in England*)

POWELL, Talmage [1920–, US crime and mystery writer]
Robert Henry (in *The Shadow* magazine)
Milton Land (in *Dime Mystery* magazine)
Jack McCready (*The Smasher*; *The Killer is Mine*)
Ellery Queen (*Murder with a Past*)
Dave Sands (in *Mike Shayne's Mystery Magazine*)
Anne Talmage (*Dark Over Arcadia*)

POWELL, Thomas [d. 1820, Welsh cleric]
Taliessen de Monmouth (*Beauty – an Ode*)

POWELL, Thomas [1809–87, English journalist and writer]
Pierce Pungent (*Chit-Chat of Humor, Wit and Anecdote*)

POWER, Marguerite A. [1815–67, English novelist]
Honoria (*Letters of a Betrothed*)

POWER, Tyrone (William Grattan) [1797–1841, Irish actor and comedian – drowned in the Atlantic]
Patrick Rooney (in *Blackwood's Magazine*)

POWNALL, Thomas [1722–1805, English colonial governor in America]
A King's Friend (*Considerations on the Indignity Suffered by the Crown*)

POYNDER, John [1779–1849, English solicitor and religious writer]
Laicus (letters to *The Times*)
A Layman (*Observations upon Sunday Newspapers*)
A Lay Member of the Church of England (*The Protestant Armory*)

PRAED, Winthrop Mackworth [1802–39, English barrister, politician, poet and essayist]
Peregrine Courtenay; Vyvian Joyeuse (both used in *Knight's Quarterly Magazine*)

PRAGNELL, Festus [1905–, English policeman and science-fiction writer]
Francis Parnell (in *Wonder Stories* magazine)

PRATHER, Richard Scott [1921–, US mystery writer]
David Knight (*Pattern for Murder*)
Douglas Ring (*The Peddler*)

PRATT, Anne [1806–93, English botanist and writer]
A Lady (*The Field, the Garden and the Woodland*)

PRATT, Eleanor Blake [1899–, US writer]
Eleanor Blake (*Seedtime and Harvest*; *Death Down East*)

PRATT, Eliza [1837–1907, US novelist]
Ella Farman (*The Little Cave-Dwellers*)
Dorothea Alice Shepherd (*How Two Girls Tried Farming*)

PRATT, Fletcher [1897–1956, US boxer, journalist, historian and science-fiction writer]
George U. Fletcher (*The Well of the Unicorn*; *The Blue Star*)
Irvin Lester (in *Amazing Stories Magazine*)

PRATT, John [1931–, English nautical writer]
John Winton (*One of Our Warships*; *We Joined the Navy*)

PRATT, John Burnett [1799–1869, Scottish cleric and local historian]
A Clergyman (*The Old Paths Where Is The Good Way*)

PRATT, Josiah [1768–1844, English cleric and secretary to the Church Missionary Society]
A Member of the Society (*Propaganda*)

PRATT, Rona Olive [1903–, Welsh-born Australian writer and illustrator for children]
Pixie O'Harris (*The Pixie O'Harris Fairy Book*)

PRATT, Samuel [1659–1723, English cleric and writer]
A Lover of his Country (*The Regulating of Silver Coin made Practicable*)

PRATT, Samuel Jackson [1750–1814, English cleric, actor and dramatist]
Courtney Melmoth (*The Fair Circassian*; *Shenstone-Green*; *The Shadows of Shakespeare*)

PRATT, Theodore [1901–69, US novelist]
Timothy Brace (*Murder Goes in a Trailer*; *Murder Goes to the Dogs*)

PRAY, Isaac C. [1813–69, US journalist and writer]
A Journalist (*Memoirs of James Gordon Bennett*)

PRENTICE, Thomas [1702–82, American cleric]
Simon the Tanner (*A Letter to the Rev. Andrew Croswell*)

PRENTISS, Charles [1774–1820, US writer]
A Citizen of Massachusetts (*A History of the United States of America*)
A Lover of the Truth (*The Trial: Calvin and Hopkins versus The Bible*)

PRENTISS, Mrs Elizabeth [1823–78, US writer for children]
Aunt (or Cousin) Susan (*Urbane and his Friends*; *Six Little Princesses and What They Turned Into*)

PRESCOTT, Benjamin [1687–1777, US cleric]
Philopolites (*Free and Calm Consideration of the Misunderstandings between the Parliament of Great Britain and the American Colonies*)

PREST, Thomas Peckett [1809–79, English 'penny dreadful' writer]
Angelina (*The Miser of Shoreditch*)
Bos (*The Penny Pickwick*; *The Life and Adventures of Oliver Twiss, the Workhouse Boy*; *Pickwick in America*) – this pseudonym was a collaborative one with William B. Baynard and Morris Barnett

PRESTON, W. E. Hayter [1891–?, English journalist]
Vanoc II (in the *Sunday Referee*)

PRESTON, William [1753–1807, Irish barrister, tragedian and poet]
Donna Teresa Pinna y Ruiz (*An Heroic Epistle to Mr Twiss*; *The Heroic Answer of Mr Twiss*)

PRICE, David [1762–1835, English soldier in India and orientalist]
A Field Officer on the Retired List of the Indian Army (*Autobiographical Memoirs of a Field Officer on the Retired List etc.*)

PRICE, Owen [d. 1671, English headmaster and philologist]
A Master of Arts and Schoolmaster of Twenty Years' Experience (*English Orthography*)

PRICHARD, Hesketh V. H. [1876–1922, English soldier and traveller]
H. Heron (in *Cornhill Magazine*)

PRICHARD, Katie O. H. [fl. 1897, English writer]
E. Heron (in *Cornhill Magazine*)

PRIDDIS, Humphrey [d. 1932, English gamekeeper and writer]
Dabchick (in *The Field*)

PRIESTLEY, Clive Ryland [1892–?, English writer]
Clive Ryland (*The Selminster Murders*; *The Case of the Back Seat Girl*)

PRIESTLEY, Lady Eliza [1836–1909, English writer on health and medicine]
A Member of the National Health Society (*Our Highland Home*)

PRIESTLEY, John Boynton [1894–1984, English novelist, essayist, critic and dramatist]
Peter Goldsmith (*Spring Tide* – in collaboration with George Billam)

PRIESTLEY, Joseph [1733–1804, English scientist and theologian]
Beryllus; Biblicus; Clemens; Ebionita; Hermas; Josephus; Liberius; Pamphilus; Paulinus; Pelagius; Photinus; Scrutator (all used in the *Theological Repository*)

A Dissenter (*A Free Address to Protestant Dissenters as Such*)

An Englishman (*The Present State of Liberty in Great Britain*)

A Lover of Peace and Truth (*A Free Address on the Repeal of the Late Act of Parliament*)

A Lover of the Gospel (*An Appeal to the Professors of Christianity*; *A Familiar Illustration of Passages of Scripture*)

A Patriot (*An Address to the Inhabitants of Birmingham*)

PRILEY, Margaret [1909–, US writer]
Margaret Ann Hubbard (*Murder Takes the Veil*)

PRIME, Benjamin Young [1733–91, US poet and ballad writer]
An American (*Muscipula Sive Cambromyomachia*)
An American Gentleman (*The Patriot Muse*)

PRIME, Samuel Irenaeus [1812–85, US cleric and journalist]
Irenaeus (in the *New York Observer*)

PRING, John [1777–1855, English cleric]
A Supernumerary (*On a Parity of Discipline in Church and State*; *On the Principles of Common or Inceptive Discipline*; *Six Letters to a Brother Curate*)

PRITCHARD, William Thomas [1909–, English science-fiction writer]
William Dexter (*World in Eclipse*; *Children of the Void*)

PROCTER, Adelaide Anne [1825–64, English poet and hymn writer]
Mary Berwick (in *Household Words* and for *Legends and Lyrics*)

PROCTER, Bryan Waller [1787–1874, English solicitor, poet and songwriter]
J. Bethel (in *Fraser's Magazine*)
Barry Cornwall (*A Sicilian Story*; *Memoirs of Charles Lamb*)
James Jessamine (in the *London Literary Gazette*)

PROCTOR, Richard Anthony [1837–88, English mathematician and astronomer]
Five of Clubs (*Chance and Luck*; *Home-Whist, an Easy Guide to Correct Play*; *How to Play Whist*)
Thomas Foster (*Nature Studies*)

PROFFITT, Josephine Moore [1914–, US writer]
Sylvia Dee (*Dear Guest and Ghost*)

PRONZINI, Bill [1943–, US crime writer]
Jack Foxx (*The Jade Figurine*)
Alex Saxon (*A Run in Diamonds*)

PROUD, Joseph [1745–1826, English Swedenborgian cleric and theologian]
Philo (*The Incendiary Corrected or, Injured Virtue and Honesty Defended*)

PROUDFIT, David Law [1842–97, US journalist and poet]
Peleg Arkwright (in the *New York Daily Graphic* and for *Love Among the Gamins*)
A Wall Street Man (*The Man from the West*)

PROUT, Geoffrey [1894–?, English writer for boys]
Roland Spencer (in *Gem*)

PROWETT, Charles Gipps [1818–74, English poet and writer]
A Wandering Englishman; A Watcher in Pall Mall (both used in *Blackwood's Magazine*)

PROWSE, William Jeffrey [1836–70, English humorous verse writer]
Nicholas (in *Fun* and for *The City of Prague*)
A Young Invalid (*My Lost Old Age*)

PRYDE, James [1866–1941, Scottish painter]
*J. and W. Beggarstaff (used for poster designs)

PRYNNE, William [1600–69, English barrister, controversial politician and religious pamphleteer]
A Common Lawyer (*Minors No Senators*)
A Cordial Well-Wisher to its Proceedings (*Twelve Queries of Publick Concernment*)
W. Huntley Esq. (*A Breviate of the Prelates*)

A Judicious Divine (*A Brief, Pithy Discourse upon 1 Corinthians*)

A Lover of Peace and Truth (*Foure Serious Questions of Grand Importance*)

Philopolites (*One Sheet or, if You Will, a Winding Sheet*)

A Well-Wisher to God's Truth (*The Unbishoping of Timothy and Titus*)

A Well-Wisher to the Truth of God and the Church of England (*A Quench-Coale*)

A Well-Wisher to Verity and Unity (*Diotrephes Catechised*)

Well-Wishing Philopater (*A Probable Expedient for Publique Settlement*)

Matthew White (*Newes from Ipswich*)

PSALMANAZAR, George [1679–1763, French-born traveller, impostor and Hebraist; lived in England from 1703]
A Layman (*Essays on Miracles*)
An Obscure Layman in Town (*Essays on – 1. Miracles, 11. Balam, 111. on the Victory Gained by Joshua*)

PUECHNER, Ray [1935–87, US writer]
Charles B. Victor (*The Whole Sky Burned*)

PUGH, Edward [d. 1814, English artist]
A Native Artist (*Cambria Depicta*)

PUGIN, Augustus Welby [1812–52, English architect – became insane]
A Roman Catholic (*The Present State of Public Worship among Roman Catholics*)

PULLEIN-THOMPSON, Christine [1930–, English writer for children]
Christine Keir (*Riding; The Impossible Horse*)

PULLEIN-THOMPSON, Dennis [1919–, English actor and playwright; changed his name from Cannan by deed-poll]
Denis Cannan (*Captain Carvallo; Who's your Father?*)

PULLEIN-THOMPSON, Diana [fl. 1980, English writer]
Diana Farr (*Gilbert Cannan – a Georgian Prodigy; Five at Ten*)

PULLEIN-THOMPSON, Joanna [fl. 1935, English writer]
Joanna Cannan (*Misty Valley; Wild Berry Wine; Snow in Harvest*)

PULLEIN-THOMPSON, Josephine [fl. 1946, English writer for children]
Josephine Mann (*A Place with Two Faces*)

PULLEN, Henry William [1836–1903, English cleric, pamphleteer and travel guide editor]
Canon (*Modern Christianity, a Civilized Heathenism*)
A Plain Man (*Everlasting Punishment*)

PULMAN, George Philip Rigney [1819–80, English antiquarian and topographer]
Piscator (*Rustic Sketches*)
Tickler (*Devonshire Sketches*)
John Trotandot (*Rambles, Roamings and Recollections; Roamings Abroad*)

PULTENEY, Sir William [1684–1764, Earl of Bath; politician and writer]
C. (in *The Craftsman*)
Caleb D'Anvers of Gray's Inn Esq. (*A Proper Reply to Sedition and Defamation Display'd*)
A Freeholder (*An Humble Address to the Knights in the Ensuing Parliament*)
A Member of Parliament (*A Letter Concerning the Sum of £115,000 Civil List*)
Will Worthy (*Bob-Lynn against Franck-Lynn*)

PUNNETT, Ivor McCauley [1927–, English journalist, crime novelist and writer for boys]
Roger Simons (*Murder Joins the Chorus; A Frame for Murder*)

PURCELL, Victor W. W. S. [1896–1965, English colonial civil servant, satirist and orientalist]
Myra Buttle (*The Sweeniad; Toynbee in Elysium*)

PURCHAS, John [1823–72, English cleric]
An Undergraduate (*School-Boy Reminiscences*)

PURNELL, Thomas [1834–89, Irish writer]
Q. (in *The Athenaeum*)

PURSER, John W. R. [fl.1952, Irish writer]
Sean Purser (*A Troth Replighted*)

PURVES, James [1734–95, Scottish cleric and religious writer]
Sevrup Semaj (*A Treatise on Civil Government*)

PUSELEY, Daniel [1814–82, English writer]
An Englishman (*The Rise and Progress of Australia, Tasmania and New Zealand*)
Frank Foster (*The Belgian Volunteer's Visit to England in 1867*)
An Old Author (*Faith, Hope and Charity; New Plays*)
A Warehouseman (*The Saturday Early Closing Movement*)

PUSEY, Edward Bouverie [1800–82, English cleric, Hebraist and Anglican theologian]
E. B. P. (*The Spiritual Combat*)
A Bachelor of Divinity (*Subscription to the Thirty-Nine Articles*)
A Resident Member of Convocation (*Doctor Hampden's Theological Statements*)

PUTNAM, Alfred Porter [1827–1906, US cleric and Unitarian writer]
An Occasional Contributor (*Can Two Walk Together Except They Be Agreed?*)

PUTNAM, George Palmer [1887–1950, US publisher and writer]
Palmer Bend (*The Smiting of the Rock*)

PUTNAM, Henry [d. 1827, US lawyer]
A Gentleman of South Carolina (*A Description of Brunswick in Letters*)

PUTNAM, John Bishop [1848–1915, US publisher and writer]
One of the Ramblers (*A Norwegian Ramble among the Fjords*)

PUTNAM, Lewis H. [fl. 1868, US writer]
A Colored Man (*Review of the Revolutionary Elements of the Rebellion*)

PUTNAM, Mrs Sallie [fl. 1870, US novelist and poet]
Virginia Madison (*Kenneth, my King*)
A Richmond Lady (*Richmond during the War*)

PYCROFT, James [1813–95, English lawyer, cleric, cricketer and writer]
A Graduate of Oxford (*The Student's Guide to a Course of Reading*)

PYKARE, Nina [fl. 1985, US romantic novelist]
Nan Pemberton (*Love's Delusion*)
Nina Porter (*A Daring Dilemma; A Heart in Flight*)
Nora Powers (*This Brief Interlude; A Woman's Wiles*)
Regina Towers (*The Rake's Companion*)

PYKE, Lillian [d. 1927, Australian novelist and writer for children]
Erica Maxwell (*A Wife by Proxy; Clem*)

PYKE-LEES, Walter Kinnear [1909–78, English registrar of the General Medical Council and writer]
Peter Leyland (*The Naked Mountain*)

PYNE, William Henry [1769–1843, English painter and writer]
Ephraim Hardcastle (*Somerset House Gazette and Literary Museum; Wine and Walnuts*)
Peter Pasquin (*A Day's Journal of a Sponge*)

Q

QUARITCH, Bernard [1819–99, German-born English antiquarian bookseller]
Ducange Anglicus (*The Vulgar Tongue*)
The Librarian (*An Ollapodrida of Typographical Curiosities*)

QUARLES, Francis [1592–1644, English royalist, antiquarian and poet]
A Late Person of Quality (*Wisdom's Better than Money*)

QUILLER-COUCH, Sir Arthur [1863–1944, English academic, novelist and poet]
Q. (*Dead Man's Rock*; *The Astonishing History of Troy Town*)

QUILTER, Harry [1851–1907, English art critic and journalist]
Shingawn (*Idle Hours*)

QUINCY, Josiah [1744–75, American lawyer and patriot]
Calisthenes; Hyperion; Mentor; Marchmont Needham; An Old Man; Edward Sexby (all used in the *Boston Gazette*)

QUINCY, Josiah A. [1772–1864, US lawyer and politician]
An Alumnus (*A Plea for Harvard*)

A Citizen (*Remarks on an Act to Establish the Superior Court of Boston*)

QUINCY, Samuel Miller [1833–87, US lawyer and journalist]
A High Private (*The Man who Was Not a Colonel*)

QUINT, Wilder Dwight [1863–1936, US journalist and writer]
*Charles Eustace Merriman (*Letters of a Son to his Self-Made Father*; *A Self-Made Man's Wife*)
*Dwight Tilton (*Miss Petticoats*; *My Lady Laughter*; *On Satan's Mount*)

QUITTENTON, Bertram [fl. 1910, English writer for boys]
Roland Quiz Jr. (in *Young Folks*)

QUITTENTON, Richard Martin Howard [1833–1914, English writer for boys]
Roland Quiz (*Juvenile Rhymes and Little Stories*; *Giant-Land or the Wonderful Adventures of Tim Pippin*)

R

RACHMAN, Stanley Jack [1934–, English academic and writer]
Jack Durac (*A Matter of Taste*)

RACK, Edmund [1735–87, English agriculturist and religious writer]
Eusebius (*Reflections on the Spirit and Essence of Christianity*)
A Friend to True Liberty (*England's True Interest in the Choice of a New Parliament*)

RADCLIFFE, Henry Garnett [1899–, English writer]
Stephen Travers (*The Thirteenth Mummy*; *The Forgotten of Allah*)

RAE, Hugh Crauford [1935–, Scottish crime and mystery writer]
James Albany (*Deacon's Dagger*; *Borneo Story*)
Robert Crawford (*The Shroud Society*; *Whip Hand*)
R. B. Houston (*Two for the Grave*)
Stuart Stern (*The Poison Tree*)
*Jessica Sterling (*The Spoiled Earth*; *The Dark Pasture*)

RAFFLES, Thomas [1788–1863, English cleric and reformer]
A Doctor of Divinity, but Not of Oxford (*Hear the Church! A Word for All*)

RAGG, Thomas Murrray [fl. 1934, English writer]
Murray Thomas (*Inspector Wilkins Reads the Proofs*)

RAIKES, Henry Cecil [1838–91, English barrister and politician]
A Candid Conservative; An English Tory (both used in *Fortnightly Review*)

RAINOLDS, John [1549–1607, English cleric and classical scholar]
A Reverend and Judicious Divine (*The Discovery of a Man of Sinne*)

RAITHBY, John [1766–1826, English barrister and legal writer]
A Member of Lincoln's Inn (*The Study and Practice of the Law Considered*)

RAKOSI, Carl [1903–, German-born US poet; used his real name for writing and his pseudonym for everyday purposes]
Callman Rawley

RALEGH, Carew [1605–66, English politician – son of Sir Walter Ralegh]
A Lover of the Truth (*Observations upon Some Particular Persons*)

RALPH, Harry [1869–1928, English actor and comedian]
Little Tich (*Little Tich's Book of Travels and Wanderings*)

RALPH, James [1705–62, American-born satirist, journalist and historian; in England from 1724]
Issachar Barebone (*The Protester*)
George Cadwallader (in *The Remembrancer*)
A Gentleman of the Middle Temple (*A Critical History of the Administration of Sir Robert Walpole*)
A Lover of Truth and Liberty (*A History of England during the Reigns of King William etc.*)
A Person of Quality (*The Memoirs and History of Prince Titi – a Translation*)
A Person of Some Taste; A. Primcock (both used in *The Touch-Stone*)

A Woman of Quality (*The Other Side of the Question*)

RALSTON, William Ralston Shedden [1828–89, English lawyer and Russian scholar; his original surname was Shedden]
An English Governess (in *Temple Bar*)

RAMAGE, Jennifer [fl. 1951, English writer]
Howard Mason (*The Body Below*; *The Red Bishop*)

RAMBAUT, Anna Beatrice [d. 1944, English painter and writer]
A. B. Romney (*Teddy's Ship*)

RAMESAY, William [fl. 1676, Scottish physician, medical and astrological writer]
A Person of Quality (*The Gentleman's Companion*)
William Seymar Esquire (*Conjugium Conjurgium*)

RAMSAY, Allan [1686–1758, Scottish wig-maker, poet and writer]
A. R. (*An Ode to the Sacred Memory of Her Grace Duchess of Hamilton*)
A Member of the Easy Club in Edinburgh (*A Poem to the Memory of Archibald Pitcairn, MD*)

RAMSAY, Allan [1713–84, Scottish painter and writer]
Britannicus (*Letters on the Present Disturbances in Great Britain and her American Provinces*)
A Dilettante in Law and Politics (*Observations upon the Riot Act*)
Marcellus (in the *Public Advertiser*)
Quod R. Scot (*The Vision*)
Zero (*A Succinct Review of the American Contest*)

RANDISI, Robert Joseph [1951–, US crime and mystery writer]
Tom Cutter (*Lincoln County*; *The Winning Hand*)
W. B. Longley (*China Town Justice*)
Joseph Meek (*Mountain Jack Pike*)
Joshua Randall (*Broadway Bounty*)

J. R. Roberts (*King of the Border*; *Archer's Revenge*)
Cole Weston (*Blood on Staked Plains*)

RANDOLPH, Charles [fl. 1877, US writer]
An American Citizen (*The Future Currency of the United States*)

RANDOLPH, Francis [1752–1831, English cleric and theologian]
Britannicus (*A Letter to William Pitt against the Abolition of the Slave Trade*)

RANDOLPH, Thomas [1701–83, English cleric and theologian]
A Divine of the Church of England (*A Vindication of the Doctrine of the Trinity*)

RANDS, William Brighty [1823–82, English essayist, hymn writer and writer for children]
Matthew Browne (*Verses and Opinions*; *The Chain of Lilies*; *Chaucer's England*)
A Brute of a Husband; A Hunter; An Irreconcilable (all used in *Saint Paul's Magazine*)
George H. Clarke; M. A. Doudney; A Political Dissenter; Henry S. Richardson (all used in *Contemporary Review*)
Timon Fieldmouse (used for journalism)
Henry Holbeach (*Shoemaker's Village*)
Thomas Talker (*Tangled Talk: an Essayist's Holiday*)

RANGER-GULL, Cyril A. E. [1876–1923, English journalist and novelist]
Ranger Gull (*The Air Pirate*; *The City in the Clouds*)
Leonard Cresswell Ingleby (*Oscar Wilde, a Literary Appreciation*)
Guy Thorne (*The Angel*; *Made in his Image*)

RANKEN, George [1827–95, Scottish-born Australian writer and estate agent]
W. H. Walker (*The Invasion*)

RANKEN, George [1828–56, English soldier – killed in the Crimea]
Delta (in the *Morning Post*)
A Soldier (*Canada and the Crimea*)

RANKEN, William Bayne [1829–89, English barrister]
An Unmarried Cynic (in *Temple Bar*)

RANKIN, Francis John Harrison [1806–47, English novelist and writer]
Fridolin (in *Bentley's Miscellany*)

RANSOME, Arthur [1884–1967, English journalist and writer for children]
Senex Rusticanos (*The Rector of St Jacob's*)

RANSOME, L. E. [fl. 1930, English writer for girls]
Ida Melbourne (in *Schoolgirl*)
Hilda Richards (in *School Friend*, 1924–9)
Stella Stirling (in *School Friend*)

RANSOME, Stafford [1860–1931, English journalist, illustrator and writer]
*Caroline Lewis (*Clara in Blunderland*; *Lost in Blunderland*)

RANYARD, Ellen Henrietta [1810–79, English religious writer]
L. N. R. (*Leaves from Life*; *The Missing Link*; *The True Institution of Sisterhood*)

RAPHAEL, Chaim [1908–, English mystery writer]
Jocelyn Davey (*The Undoubted Deed*; *A Killing in Hats*)

RAPHAEL, Frederick [1931–, English novelist and critic]
*Mark Caine (*The S – Man: a Grammar of Success*)

RAPPOPORT, Solomon [1863–1920, English playwright]
S. Anskey (*The Dybbuk*)

RASH, Dora Eileen [1897–89, English novelist]
Doreen Wallace (*Forty Years On*; *The Gentle Heart*)

RASHLEIGH, Sir John Colman [1772–1847, English political writer]
One of the 80,000 Incorrigible Jacobins (*The Case of the People of England*)

RATHBONE, St George Henry [1854–1938, US novelist]
Harrison Adams (*The Pioneer Boys of Ohio*)
Oliver Lee Clifton (*The Camp Fire Boys*)
Duke Duncan (*The Hunted Detective*; *The Head Hunter*)
Aleck Forbes (*The Color Bearer*)
Marline Manly (*Night Riders*; *Leadville Luke*)
Harry St George (*Traps and Trails*; *The Fire Witch*)

RAUPERT, John Godfrey Ferdinand [1858–1929, Irish cleric and writer]
A Member of the Society of Psychical Research (*The Dangers of Spiritualism*)
Victor Morton (*Thoughts on Hell*)
Scrutator (*Back to Rome*)
Viator (in the *Dublin Review* and for *Divorce in its Ecclesiastical Aspect* and *Ten Years in Anglican Orders*)

RAWLINSON, Richard [1690–1755, English cleric, antiquarian and traveller]
An Impartial Hand (*The Conduct of Dr White Kennet*; *The English Topographer*)
Philoxon (*A Full and Impartial Account of the Oxford Riots*)

RAWLINSON, Sir Robert [1810–98, English civil engineer]
A Civil Engineer (*Cosmos*)

RAWNSLEY, Robert D. B. [1818–82, English cleric and writer]
A Lincolnshire Rector (in *MacMillan's Magazine*)

RAWSON, Clayton [1906–71, US mystery writer]
The Great Merlini (*The Golden Book of Magic*)
Stuart Towne (*Death Out of Thin Air*)

RAYMOND, Rene [1906–85, English crime novelist]
James Hadley Chase (*No Orchids for Miss Blandish*; *Tiger by the Tail*)
James L. Docherty (*He Won't Need it Now*)
Ambrose Grant (*More Deadly than the Male*)

Raymond Marshall (*Lady, Here's your Wreath*; *The Sucker Punch*)

RAYMOND, Rossiter Worthington
[1840–1918, US engineer and writer]
Robertson Gray (*Brave Hearts*; *Evolution of Animal Life*)

RAYMOND, Walter [1852–1931, English novelist]
Uncle Tom Cobbleigh (*Gentleman Upcott's Daughter*; *Young Sam*; *Sabina*)

RAYNER, Augustus Alfred [1894–?, English writer]
Whyte Hall (*Crime and a Clock*; *Death of a Doctor's Wife*)

RAYNER, Claire [1931–, English novelist and journalist]
Sheila Brandon (*The Final Year*; *The Lonely One*)
Ann Lynton (*Mothercraft*)
Ruth Martin (as editor of *Before the Baby and After*)

READ, William [1795–1866, Irish poet]
Eustace (in the *Literary Gazette*)

READE, William Winwood [1838–75, English traveller, novelist and religious writer]
Francesco Abati (*See-Saw*)

REASON, Joyce [1894–?, English writer for children]
Blue Wolf (*Dwifa's Curse*)

REAY, Stephen [1782–1861, Scottish librarian and oriental scholar]
Pileus Quadratus (*Observations on the Defense of the Church Missionary Society*)

REDDIN, Kenneth Sheils [1895–1967, Irish lawyer, novelist, playwright and writer for children]
Kenneth Sarr (*The White Bolle-Trie*; *Somewhere to the Sea*)

REDDING, Cyrus [1785–1870, English journalist and writer]
An Ex-Editor (in the *Weekly News*)

Nerke; Varon (both used in *Fraser's Magazine*)
An Octogenarian (in *Dublin University Magazine*)
Peter Wilkins (*A Letter from Peter Wilkins*)

REDMAN, Ben Ray [1896–1961, US journalist and writer]
Jeremy Lord (*The Bannerman Case*; *The Sixty-Nine Diamonds*)

REDPATH, James [1833–91, Scottish-born US journalist]
The Roving Editor (*Talks with Slaves in the Southern States*)

REED, Andrew [1787–1862, English cleric]
Douglas (*A Threatening Letter from Douglas to Lefevre*)

REED, Joseph [1723–87, English ropemaker, dramatist and writer]
Benedict (letters to the *Morning Chronicle*)
A Halter-Maker (*A Sop in the Pan for a Physical Critick*; *A Rope's End for Hempen Monopolists*)
Dr Humbug (*Madrigal and Truletta*)

REED, Myrtle [1874–1911, US writer]
Olive Green (*What to Have for Breakfast*)

REED, Talbot Baines [1852–93, English writer for boys]
An Old Boy (in the first issue of *Boy's Own Paper* for *My First Football Match*)

REED, William Bradford [1806–76, US lawyer and diplomat]
A Citizen of Pennsylvania (*Thoughts on Intervention*)
A Northern Man (*A Review of Mr Seward's Diplomacy*)

REEMAN, Douglas [1925–, English nautical novelist]
Alexander Kent (*Enemy in Sight*; *Inshore Squadron*)

REES, Helen [1903–70, Scottish novelist]
Jane Oliver (*Not Peace but a Sword*; *In No Strange Land*)

REES, James [1802–85, US journalist and writer]
Colley Cibber (*Life of Edwin Forrest*)

REES, Joan [1927–, English romantic novelist]
Susan Strong (*Drama of Love*; *Will to Love*)

REEVE, Clara [1725–1807, English novelist and writer]
Euphrasia (*A Letter to Courtney Melmoth Esq.*)
A Lady (*The Phoenix – a Translation*)

REEVE, Edith [1917–, German-born English novelist and historical writer]
Edith Simon (*Reformation*)

REEVE, Robert [d. 1840, English antiquary]
Juvenis Suffolciensis (in *Gentleman's Magazine*)

REEVES, Helen Buckingham [1853–1921, English novelist]
Helen Mathers (*Pigskin and Petticoat*; *Comin' Through the Rye*; *Cherry Ripe*)

REEVES, John [1752–1829, English barrister, legal writer and pamphleteer]
A Barrister (*Two Tracts Shewing that Americans are not Aliens*)
A Lawyer (*Observations on the Catholic Bill*)

REEVES, Joyce [1911–, English writer for children]
Joyce Gard (*Handysides Shall Not Fall*)

REID, Henry M. B. [1856–1927, Scottish cleric, theological and historical writer]
A Galloway Herd (*About Galloway Folk*)

REID, Hugo [1809–72, Scottish educationalist]
Roger Boswell (*The Art of Conversation*)
H. R. (in *Notes and Queries*)

REID, Robert [1773–1865, Scottish historian and topographer]
Lex (*Remarkable Criminal Trials in Bengal*)
Senex (*An Autobiography*; *Glasgow Past and Present*; *Old Glasgow and its Environs*)
Robert Wanlock (*Moorland Rhymes*; *Poems, Songs and Sonnets*)

REID, Sir Thomas Wemyss [1842–1905, English publisher, biographer and novelist]
An Extinguished Exile (*Charlotte Bronte*)
*Two Idle Apprentices (*Briefs and Papers: Sketches of the Bar and the Press*)

REID, Whitelaw [1837–1912, US journalist, diplomat and writer]
Agate (*Some Newspaper Tendencies*)

REID, William [1764–1831, Scottish dialect poet]
Scotus (*Strictures on the Bank of England Charter*)

REILLY, Helen [1891–1962, US mystery writer]
Kieran Abbey (*Run with the Hare*; *Beyond the Dark*)

REILLY, Hugh [d. 1695, Irish supporter of James II]
A True Lover of his King and Country (*Ireland's Case Briefly Stated*)

REIZENSTEIN, Elmer [1892–1967, US dramatist and novelist]
Elmer Rice (*The Adding Machine*; *Between Two Worlds*)

RENDALL, Vernon Horace [1869–1960, English journalist and writer]
Adrian Hayter (*The Profitable Imbroglio*)
Edgar Valdes (in *Temple Bar*)

RENDELL, Ruth [1930–, English crime novelist]
Barbara Vine (*A Fatal Inversion*; *A Dark-Adapted Eye*)

RENFROE, Martha Kay [1938–, US writer]
M. K. Wren (*Nothing is Certain but Death*; *A Multitude of Sins*)

RENN, Thomas Edward [1939–, US writer]
Jeremy Strike (*A Promising Planet*)

RENNELL, James [1742–1830, English East India Company surveyor and geographer]
An Old Englishman (*War with France, the Only Security of Britain*)

RENNELL, Thomas [1787–1824, English cleric and writer]
A Student in Divinity (*Animadversions on the Unitarian New Testament*)

RENOUF, Peter Le Page [1822–97, English oriental scholar and religious writer]
An English Catholic Layman (*University Education for English Catholics*)
A Late Member of the University (*The Character of the Rev. W. Palmer*)

RENTOUL, John Laurence [1846–1926, Irish cleric in Australia, poet and writer]
Gervais Gage (*From Far Lands: Poems of North and South*)

REPINGTON, Charles A'Court [1858–1925, English soldier, journalist and military writer]
The Military Correspondent of The Times (*Essays and Criticisms; Imperial Strategy; The Foundation of Reform; The War in the Far East 1904–5*)

REYNARDSON, Francis [fl. 1713, English physician and writer]
Mr Webster (*The Stage – a Poem*)

REYNOLDS, Dallas McCord [1917–, US fantasy writer]
Clark Collins; Guy McCord; Mark Mallory; Mack Reynolds; Dallas Ross (all used in *Fantastic Adventures* magazine)

REYNOLDS, George William MacArthur [1814–79, English journalist, radical and novelist]
Max (in *Bentley's Miscellany*)
Master Timothy (*Master Timothy's Bookcase*)

REYNOLDS, Helen Mary Greenwood [fl. 1946, Canadian writer for children]
Dickson Reynolds (*Gold in Mosquito Creek*)

REYNOLDS, Henry Revell [1745–1811, English physician and writer]
A Young Man (*An Address to the Ladies from a Young Man*)

REYNOLDS, John Hamilton [1796–1852, English solicitor and poet]
Peter Corcoran (*The Fancy, a Selection from the Poetical Remains of the Late Peter Corcoran*)
Curl-Pated; Edward Herbert (both used in the *London Magazine*)
John Hamilton (in both *Ainsworth's Magazine* and *New Monthly Magazine*)
Budgell Jeffries; Olinthus Jenkinson (both used in *Bentley's Miscellany*)
Nimrod (*The Oracle of Rural Life*)
Peter Plague'em (*Benjamin the Waggoner*)

RHEES, Morgan John [1760–1804, Welsh cleric – emigrated to the USA]
Philanthropos (*Letters on Liberty and Slavery*)

RHODES, William Barnes [1772–1826, English banker, burlesque writer and dramatist]
Cornelius Crambo (*Eccentric Tales in Verse*)

RHODES, William Henry [1822–76, US lawyer and writer]
Caxton (*The Case of Summerfield; Discovery of the Pacific Ocean*)

RICE, Isaac Leopold [1850–1915, US lawyer, chess player and writer]
Ecir (in the *Philadelphia Bulletin*)

RICE, James [1843–82, English novelist and turf historian]
J. R. (*The Case of Mr Lucraft; This Son of Vulcan*)
Martin Legrand (*The Cambridge Freshman*)
*Walter Maurice (*Ready-Money Mortiboy; Such a Good Man*)

RICHARDS, Mrs Cornelia H. [1822–92, US novelist]
Mrs Manners (*At Home and Abroad or How to Behave; Hester and I*)

RICHARDS, James Brinsley [1846–92, English journalist]
Constitutionalist (in *Temple Bar*)

RICHARDS, Laura Elizabeth [1850–1943, US poet and writer for children]
The Man in the Moon (*Five Miles in a Mouse-Trap*)

RICHARDS, William [1749–1818, Welsh cleric and antiquarian]
Gwilym Dyfed (letters in *Gentleman's Magazine*)

RICHARDSON, Albert Deane [1833–69, US journalist]
Julius Henri Browne (*Four Years in Secessia*)

RICHARDSON, Charles [fl. 1867, English preacher]
The Lincolnshire Thrasher (*Miscellanies*)

RICHARDSON, Charles James [1806–71, English architect and writer]
An Architect (*Studies from Old English Mansions*)

RICHARDSON, Ethel Florence [1870–1946, Australian novelist]
Henry Handel Richardson (*The Getting of Wisdom; The Fortunes of Richard Mahony*)

RICHARDSON, George Tilton [d. 1938, US journalist, editor and novelist]
*Charles Eustace Merriman (*Letters of a Son to his Self-Made Father; A Self-Made Man's Wife*)
*Dwight Tilton (*Miss Petticoats; My Lady Laughter; On Satan's Mount*)

RICHARDSON, John [1755–1831, Canadian businessman]
Veritas (*The Letters of Veritas*)

RICHARDSON, John [1796–1852, English soldier and journalist]
A British Officer (in *New Monthly Magazine*)
An English Officer (*Tecumseh, the Warrior of the West*)
An Officer (*Journal of the Movements of the British Legion*)

RICHARDSON, John Larkins Cheese [1810–78, English soldier in India – migrated to New Zealand]
An Old Bengaler (*A Summer's Excursion in New Zealand*)

RICHARDSON, Joseph [1755–1803, English barrister, journalist and writer]
Englishman (letter in *The Citizen*)

RICHARDSON, Robert Shirley [1902–, US astronomer]
Philip Latham (*Missing Men of Saturn; Five Against Venus*)

RICHMOND, Euphemia J. G. [1825–1905?, US novelist]
Effie Johnson (*Devotional Aspiration; Fact and Fable; In the Fire and Other Fancies*)

RICHMOND, James Cook [1808–66, US cleric]
Admonish Crime (*A Midsummer's Daydream*)
An American Clergyman (*A Visit to Iona*)
Nobody (*Nothing*)

RICHMOND, Legh [1772–1827, English cleric, novelist and writer]
A Clergyman of the Church of England (*The Dairyman's Daughter*)
Simplex (*in The Christian Guardian*)

RICKMAN, Thomas [1761–1834, English radical and writer]
Clio (*Hints upon Hats*)
A Gentleman Resident There (*Emigration to America Candidly Considered*)

RICKWORD, John Edgell [1898–1982, English poet and writer]
Jasper Bildje; Gabriel Foster (both used in *The Calendar*)
John Edgell (in *Our Time*)
*John Mavin (*Charles Baudelaire*)

RIDDELL, Maria [fl. 1792, English writer]
Maria R****** (*Voyages to Madeira and Leeward Caribbean Isles*)

RIDEAUX, Charles de B. [fl. 1935, English writer]
John Chancellor (*Murder Syndicate; Stolen Gold*)

RIDER, William [1723–85, English cleric]
Philargyrus (in *Gentleman's Magazine*)

RIDGE, William Pett [1857–1930, English humorist and novelist]
Warwick Simpson (*Eighteen of Them*)
Warwick Thompson (*A Breaker of Laws*)

RIDING, Laura [1901–91, US novelist, poet and writer; her original surname was Reichenthal but she adopted the name Riding]
*Barbara Rich (*No Decency Left*)
Madeleine Vara (*Convalescent Conversations*)

RIDLEY, Glocester [1702–74, English cleric and writer]
A Divine of the Church of England (*The Christian Passover in Four Sermons*)

RIDLEY, James [1736–65, English cleric and writer]
Horam, Son of Asmar (*Tales of the Genii*)
Sir Charles Morell (*Tales of the Genii*)
Helter van Scelter (in *The Schemer or, Universal Satirist*)

RIDPATH, George [d. 1725, Scottish politicial journalist]
Will Laick (*An Answer to the Scotch Presbyterian Eloquence*; *The Scots Episcopal Innocence*)
A Layman of the Church of Scotland (*The Queries and Protestation of the Scots Episcopal Clergy*)
A Lover of his Country (*A Discourse upon the Union of Scotland and England*)

RIEFE, Alan [1925–, US novelist]
J. D. Hardin (*Blood, Sweat and Gold*; *The Man who Bit Snakes*)
Zachary Hawkes (*Solomon King's Mine*; *Fancy Hatch*)
Jake Logan (*White Hell*; *See Texas and Die*)
Pierce Mackenzie (*Winner Take Nothing*; *The Cockeyed Coyote*)
E. B. Majors (*Slaughter and Son*; *Nightmare Trail*)
Barbara Riefe (*Far Beyond Desire*; *This Ravaged Heart*)

RIFKIN, Shepard [1918–, US writer]
Dale Michaels (*The Warring Breed*)

RIGSBY, Howard [1909–, US writer]
Vechel Howard (*Murder on her Mind*; *Murder with Love*)

RILEY, James Whitcomb [1849–1916, US journalist and dialect poet]
E. A. P. (in the *Kokomo Dispatch*)
Benjamin F. Johnson of Boone (in the *Indianapolis Daily Journal*)

RIPLEY, Roswell Sabine [1822–87, US confederate soldier]
A General Officer of the Late Confederate Army (in *Blackwood's Magazine*)

RITCHIE, Mrs Anna Cora [1819–70, French-born US actress and writer]
An Actress (*Autobiography of an Actress or, Eight Years on the Stage*)
Mrs Helen Berkley (*The Fortune Hunter*)
Isabel (*Pelayo or the Cavern of Covadonga*)

RITCHIE, James Ewing [1826–98, English journalist and writer]
Christopher Crayon (in the *Christian World*)

RITCHIE, Leitch [1800–65, Scottish novelist and writer]
A Travelling Artist (*Head-Pieces and Tail-Pieces*)

RITCHIE, Sir Lewis Anselmo [1886–1967, English sailor and nautical writer; his original surname was Ricci]
Bartimeus (*Naval Occasions*; *Seaways*)

RITSON, Joseph [1752–1803, English literary historian – became insane]
Anti-Scot (in *Gentleman's Magazine*)

RITTENHOUSE, David [1732–96, US mathematician and scientist]
A Citizen of Philadelphia (*Lucy Sampson, or the Unhappy Heiress*)

RIVETT, Edith Caroline [1894–1958, English crime novelist]
Carol Carnac (*Impact of Evidence*; *Policeman at the Door*)
E. C. R. Lorac (*Part for a Poisoner*; *Murder by Matchlight*)

ROARK, Garland [1904–, US writer]
George Garland (*Bugles and Brass*)

ROBARTES, John [1606–85, 1st Earl of Radnor]
A Person of Honour (*A Discourse of the Vanity of the Creature, Grounded on Eccles. 1. 2.*)

ROBB, John S. [fl. 1856, US journalist and humorist]
Solitaire (*Sketches of Squatter Life*)
A Typo (*Western Wanderings of a Typo*)

ROBBINS, Alfred Farthing [1856–1931, English journalist and dramatist]
Tom Clifton (*In Doubt*)
Nemesis (*Abuses of School Board Expenditure*)
One of the Great Unplayed (*Vote by Ballot*)

ROBERTS, Barre Charles [1789–1810, English antiquarian and numismatist]
E. S. S. (in *Gentleman's Magazine*)

ROBERTS, Carl Eric Bechhofer [1894–1949, English barrister, journalist and writer]
Ephesian (*Lord Birkenhead*; *Winston Churchill*)

ROBERTS, David [1757–1819, English soldier and humorist]
An Officer (*The Military Adventures of Johnny Newcome*)

ROBERTS, Irene [1929–, English romantic novelist]
Roberta Carr (*Sea Maiden*; *Golden Interlude*)
Elizabeth Harle (*Spray of Red Roses*; *Buy Me a Dream*)
Ivor Roberts (*Trial by Water*; *Green Hell*)
Iris Rowland (*The Morning Star*; *A Veil of Rushes*)
Irene Shaw (*The Olive Branch*)

ROBERTS, James J. [1947–, US journalist and writer]
Robert J. Horton (*The Crow Flies West*)

ROBERTS, Janet Louise [1925–84, US romantic novelist]
Louisa Bronte (*Greystone Tavern*; *Casino Greystone*)
Rebecca Danton (*Amethyst Love*; *Star Sapphire*)
Janet Radcliffe (*The Gentleman Pirate*; *Scarlet Secrets*)

ROBERTS, John [fl. 1729, English actor and writer]
A Stroling Player (*An Answer to Mr Pope's Preface to Shakespeare*)

ROBERTS, Keith [1935–, English science-fiction writer and illustrator]
Alistair Bevan (in *Science Fantasy* magazine)

ROBERTS, Kenneth [1885–1957, US journalist and novelist]
Milton Kilgallen (*The Collector's Whatnot*)

ROBERTS, Maggie [fl. 1875, US writer]
Eiggam Strebor (*Home Scenes during the Rebellion*)

ROBERTS, Mary [1788–1864, English writer and natural historian]
Mary De Gieva (*An Account of Anne Jackson*)
A Young Lady (*The Royal Exile*)

ROBERTS, Morley Charles [1857–1942, English novelist and traveller]
A Cattle Hand; A Sheep Herder (both used in *Cornhill Magazine*)

ROBERTS, Philip Ilott [1872–1938, US writer]
A. Chester Mann (*Moody, Winner of Souls*)

ROBERTS, Sir Randal H. [1837–99, Irish soldier, journalist and writer on military subjects and the turf]
Light Cast (*The Silver Trout*)

ROBERTS, Samuel [1800–85, Welsh journalist and social reformer]
A Llanbrynmair Farmer (*Diosg Farm, a Sketch of its History*)

ROBERTS, William [1767–1849, English barrister, editor and writer]
A Barrister (*Pourtraiture of a Christian Gentleman*)
Rev. Simeon Olivebranch (in *The Looker-On*)

ROBERTS, William [1868–1959, English journalist, music critic and historian]
Ernest Newman (*Stories of the Great Operas*; *Musical Critic's Holiday*)
Onlooker (in the *Evening Standard*)

ROBERTSON, Mrs Constance Noyes [1897–, Canadian writer]
Dana Scott (*Five Fatal Letters*)

ROBERTSON, Frank Chester [1890–?, US farmer and western novelist]
Robert Crane (*Stormy Range*)
Frank Chester Field (*The Rocky Road to Jericho*)

ROBERTSON, Frederick William [1816–53, English cleric and preacher]
An Englishman (*The Irish Difficulty Addressed to his Countrymen*)

ROBERTSON, James Logie [1846–1922, Scottish poet and writer]
Hugh Haliburton (*Orellana and Other Poems*; *In Scottish Fields*)

ROBERTSON, Jean [1922–90, English journalist and writer]
Leslie Adrian (in *The Spectator*)

ROBERTSON, John Henry [1909–65, English journalist and biographer]
John Connell (*The Fortunate Simpleton*; *The Return of Long John Silver*; *Tomorrow We Shall Be Free*)

ROBERTSON, John Mackinnon [1856–1933, Scottish journalist and politician]
Hugh Mortimer Cecil (*Pseudo-Philosophy*)
Roland (*The Future of Militarism*)
Clement Wise (*Puritanism in Power*)
M. A. Wiseman (*The Dynamics of Religion*)

ROBERTSON, Joseph [1726–1802, English cleric and literary critic]
Eusebius, Vicar of Lilliput (*Observations on the Act for Augmenting the Salaries of Curates*)

ROBERTSON, Joseph [1810–66, Scottish historian and journalist]
John Brown, a Deeside Coachman (*A Guide to Deeside*; *The Book of Bon Accord*)

ROBERTSON, Joseph Clinton [1788–1852, English patent agent and compiler of books]
Sholto Douglas (*London or, Interesting Memorials*)
Sholto Percy (*The Percy Anecdotes*)

ROBERTSON, Keith Carlton [1914–91, US novelist and writer for children]
Carlton Keith (*Missing Presumed Dead*; *The Crayfish Dinner*)

ROBERTSON, Thomas William [1829–71, English actor and dramatist]
Theatrical Lounger (in the *Illustrated Times*)
Hugo Vamp (in *The Welcome Guest*)

ROBERTSON, William [1721–93, Scottish cleric and historian]
A Presbyter of the Church of England (*An Attempt to Explain the Catholic Church*)

ROBINETT, Stephen [fl. 1976, US science-fiction writer]
Tak Hallus (in *Analog* magazine)

ROBINS, Denise Naomi [1897–1985, English romantic novelist]
Denise Chesterton (*Two Loves*; *The Price of Folly*)
Ashley French (*Once is Enough*; *Breaking Point*)
Harriet Gray (*Bride of Doom*; *Dance in the Dust*)
Hervey Hamilton (*Figs in Frost*; *Family Holiday*)
Julia Kane (*The Sin Was Mine*)
Francesca Wright (*The Loves of Lucrezia*)

ROBINS, Elizabeth [1865–1952, US actress, dramatist and novelist]
C. E. Raimond (*George Mandeville's Husband*; *Milley's Story*)

ROBINS, James [d. 1836, English publisher and writer]
Robert Scott (*The Cabinet of Portraits*; *A History of England during the Reign of George the Third*)

ROBINSON, Mrs Annie Douglas [1842–1913, US writer for children]
Marion Douglas (*Picture Poems for Young Folks*)

ROBINSON, David [d. 1849, English essayist]
A Bystander; An English Freeholder; One of the Democracy; One of the Old School; Sampson Steadfast (all used in *Blackwood's Magazine*)

ROBINSON, Edith [1858–?, US writer for children]
Elizabeth Schuyler (*A Loyal Little Maid*)

ROBINSON, Emma [1794–1863, English novelist]
Owanda (*Only a Tramp*)

ROBINSON, Francis Kildale [fl. 1855, English philologist]
An Inhabitant (*A Glossary of Yorkshire Words and Phrases*)

ROBINSON, Frederick William [1830–1901, English novelist]
A Prison Matron (*Female Life in Prison*; *Prison Characters Drawn from Life*; *Memoirs of Jane Cameron, Female Convict*)

ROBINSON, Henry [1605–64, English merchant, economist and writer]
A Gentleman of Tried Integrity (*An Answer to Mr John Drury*)
A True Englishman (*A Short Discourse between Monarchical and Aristocratical Government*)
A Well-Wisher to the Truth and Master Prin (*Certain Brief Observations on Master Prin*)

ROBINSON, Joan Mary Gale [1910–88, English writer and illustrator for children]
Joan Gale Thomas (*My Garden Book*; *The Christmas Angel*)

ROBINSON, John [1650–1723, English cleric; Bishop of London }
A Person of Note who Resided Many Years There (*An Account of Sweden*)

ROBINSON, John [1782–1833, US writer]
Plomingo (*The Savage*)

ROBINSON, Lewis George [1886–?, English writer]
George Braham (*Then a Soldier*)
George Limnelius (*The Medbury Fort Murder*; *...Tell No Tales*)

ROBINSON, Mary [1758–1800, English actress, dramatist and poet]
Tabitha Bramble (used for poems in the *Morning Post*)
The English Sappho (*The Wild Wreath*)
A Friend to Humanity (*Impartial Reflections on the Queen of France*)
Laura Maria (*The Mistletoe*)
Mrs Anne Frances Randall (*A Letter to the Women of England on the Injustice of Mental Subordination*)

ROBINSON, Percy [1829–92, English novelist]
Ericson Probyn (in *Temple Bar*)

ROBINSON, Richard [1844–70, English academic and writer]
A Junior Fellow (in the *Theological Review*)
A Templar (in *MacMillan's Magazine*)

ROBINSON, Robert [1735–90, English Baptist cleric and hymn writer]
Lewis Carbonell (*The History and the Mystery of Good Friday*)

ROBINSON, Rowland Evans [1833–1900, US writer who wrote most of his works after becoming blind]
Awahsoose the Bear (*Forest and Stream Fables*)

ROBINSON, Sheila Mary [1928–, English crime writer]
Sheila Radley (*Death in the Morning*; *Chief Inspector's Daughter*)
Hester Rowan (*Linden Tree*; *Overture in Venice*)

ROBINSON, Solon [1803–80, US journalist]
Blythe White Jr. (*Green Mountain Girls*)

ROBINSON, Therese Albertine Louise [1797–1870, German-born US writer]
Talvj (*Heloise*; *Life's Discipline*)

ROBINSON, William Erigena [1814–92, Irish-born US lawyer and journalist]
Richelieu (in the *Brooklyn Eagle*)

ROBINSON, William Stevens [1818–76, US journalist]
Gilbert (in the *New York Tribune*)
Middlesex (in the *New York Evening Post*)
Warrington (in the *Boston News* and for *A Manual for Officers*)

ROBINSON-MORRIS, Morris [d. 1829, Irish political pamphleteer]
A Briton (*An Essay on Bank-Tokens*)

ROBY, John [1793–1850, English banker, organist and poet]
An Admirer of Walter Scott (*The Lay of the Poor Fiddler*)
An Amateur of Fashion (*Jokeby*)

ROBY, Mary Lynn [1930–, US romantic historical novelist]
Pamela D'Arcy (*Heritage of the Heart*)
Georgina Grey (*Both Sides of the Coin*; *The Queen's Quadrille*)
Elizabeth Welles (*Seagull Crag*)
Mary Wilson (*Wind of Death*; *The Changeling*)

ROCHE, James [1770–1853, Irish wine merchant, banker and writer]
Octogenarian (*Critical and Miscellaneous Essays*)

ROCHESTER, George Ernest [1898–1966, English writer for children]
Jeffrey Gaunt (in *Detective Weekly* and for *The Haunted Man*)

Hamilton Smith (*The S. O. S. Squadron*)
Mary Weston (*Christine – Air Hostess*)

ROCKEY, Howard [1886–1934, US novelist]
Ronald Bryce (*All That I Want*)
Oliver Panbourne (*The Varanoff Tradition*)

RODD, Mrs Lewis Charles [1912–88, Australian writer for children]
Kylie Tennant (*Ride on Stranger*; *Tell Morning This*)

RODD, Thomas [1763–1822, English bookseller and publisher]
Philobiblos (*A Defence of the Veracity of Moses*)
A Young Gentleman (*The Theriad*)

RODDA, Percival Charles [1891–1976, Australian journalist and novelist]
Gavin Holt (*Begonia Walk*; *Ladies in Ermine*)
Gardner Low (*Invitation to Kill*)
*Eliot Reed (used for two novels with Eric Ambler, q. v., and alone for *The Maras Affair*, *Charter to Danger* and *Passport to Panic*)

RODELL, Marie [1912–75, US mystery writer]
Marion Randolph (*Grim Grow the Lilacs*; *Breathe No More*)

RODRIGUEZ, Judith Green [1936–, Australian poet and academic]
Judith Green (*Four Poets*)

ROE, Ivan [1917–, English novelist]
Richard Savage (*When the Moon Died*)

ROE, Miss Mary Abigail [1840–?, US writer]
C. M. Cornwall (*Free, yet Forging their own Chains*)

ROE, William James [fl. 1886, US poet and novelist]
G. I. Cervus (*The Model Wife*; *Cut: a Story of West Point*; *Scarlet Gods*)

ROGERS, Mrs Clara Kathleen Barnett
[1844–1931, English opera singer,
composer and musical educator]
Clara Doria (*My Voice and I*)

ROGERS, Henry [1806–77, English cleric,
theologian and essayist]
R. E. H. Grayson (*Selections from the
Correspondence of R. E. H. Grayson*)
Vindex (*The Eclipse of Faith*)

ROGERS, James Edwin Thorold [1823–90,
English cleric, political economist and
historian]
A Graduate (*Paul of Tarsus*)

ROGERS, John [1500–55, English cleric –
burnt as a heretic]
Thomas Matthew (in *Tyndale's Bible 1537*)

ROGERS, Robert Vashon [1843–1911,
English barrister and writer]
A Barrister-at-Law, of Osgoode Hall
(*Wrongs and Rights of a Traveller*)

ROGERS, Thomas [1660–94, English cleric
and writer]
Musophilus (*A Posie for Lovers*)

ROHRBACH, Peter Thomas [1926–, US
writer]
James R. Cody (*Search and Destroy*)

ROLFE, Frederick William [1860–1913,
English writer and pseudo cleric]
Al Siddik; V. Bonhorst; Franz Wilhelm V.
Bracht; May Chester; A. W.Riter;
Vincenza, Duchess of Deira; Arthur
Henry Whyte; Ifor D. Williams (all used
in the *Holywell Record*)
Baron Corvo (in *The Yellow Book for Stories
Told to Me* and *Chronicles of the House of
Borgia*)
A Crab Maid (in *Gentleman's Magazine*)
Orthocratos (in the *Paternoster Review*)
Prospero and Caliban (*The Weird of the
Wanderer; Hubert's Arthur*)

ROLLE, Samuel [fl. 1669, English cleric,
physician and religious writer]
Philagathus (*A Sober Answer to the Friendly
Debate betwixt a Conformist and a
Nonconformist*)

ROLLINS, Mrs Ellen Chapman [1831–81,
US writer]
E. H. Arr (*New England Bygones; Old-Time
Child Life*)

ROLLINS, William [fl. 1935, US writer]
O'Connor Stacy (*Murder at Cypress Hall;
The Shadow Before*)

ROMANES, George John [1848–94,
Canadian-born English scientist and
academic]
Physicus (*A Candid Examination of Theism*)

ROMILLY, Henry [1805–84, English
merchant and writer]
An Elector (*Public Responsibility and Vote by
Ballot*)

ROOKE, John [1780–1856, English farmer
and political economist]
Cumbriensis (*Remarks on the Nature and
Operation of Money*)

ROONEY, Philip [1907–, Irish journalist]
Frank Phillips (*All Out to Win*)

ROOPER, George [1812–1905, English
sporting writer]
Salmo Salar Esq. (*Autobiography of the late
Salmo Salar Esq.*)

ROOSEVELT, Robert Barnwell [1829–1906,
US banker and natural historian – uncle
of Franklin D. Roosevelt]
Barnwell (*Game Fish of the Northern States
of America*)

ROPER, Laura Wood [1911–, US writer]
Laura Newbold Wood (*Louis Pasteur;
Raymond Ditmars: his Exciting Career*)

ROPER, William J. J. Duff [1830–61,
English writer]
A Carthusian (*Chronicles of Charter-House*)

ROPES, Arthur Reed [1859–1933, Russian-born English librettist and writer]
Brian Pie (in *The Tatler*)
Arthur Reed (*A Double Event*; *Faddimir*)
Adrian Ross (*Joan of Arc*; *The Beloved Vagabond*)

ROS, Amanda McKittrick [1860–1939, Irish novelist and ballad writer]
Monica Moyland (*A Little Belgian Orphan*)

ROSCOE, Henry [1800–36, English barrister and biographer]
A Member of the Inner Temple (*A Discourse on the Study of the Laws*)

ROSE, A. M'Gregor [1846–98, Canadian writer]
A. M. R. Gordon (*Sir Wilfred's Progress through England to France*)

ROSE, George [1817–82, English cleric, dramatist, novelist and humorist]
Mrs Brown (in *Fun*)
Arthur Sketchley (in *Routledge's Annual* and for *A Match in the Dark*)

ROSE, William Stewart [1775–1843, English poet and writer]
One of the Last Century (*Thoughts and Recollections*)

ROSENTHAL, Lewis [1856–1909, US journalist]
Lew Rosen (in *Cornhill Magazine*)

ROSENTHAL, Richard A. [1925–, US writer]
Allen Richards (*The Merchandise Murderers*)

ROSEWELL, Samuel [1679–1722, English cleric and lecturer]
A. B. (*Protestant Dissenters' Hopes from the Present Government Freely Declar'd*)
A Dissenting Minister (*A Confession of Faith*)
George English (*A Letter from a Dissenter to a Member of Parliament*)

ROSS, Charles Henry [1840–97, English humorist]
Boswell Butt (*Hush Money, a Life Drama*)
C. H. R. (*The Wedding and the Twins*)

Edmund Evans (*Merry Conceits and Whimsical Rhymes*)
Ally Sloper (*The Eastern Question Tackled*; *Ally Sloper's Comic Kalendar*)

ROSS, John MacLaren [1912–64, English writer]
Julian MacLaren-Ross (*Of Love and Hunger*; *Memoirs of the Forties*)

ROSS, William Edward Daniel [1912–, Canadian writer]
Ellen Randolph (*The Castle on the Hill*)
Marilyn (or Clarissa) Ross (*China Shadow*; *Satan Whispers*)

ROSS, William Stewart [1844–1906, Scottish publisher and writer]
Saladin (in the *Agnostic Journal and Secular Review*)

ROSS, Zola Helen [fl. 1960, US writer]
Helen Arre (*The Golden Shroud*; *No Tears for the Funeral*)
Bert Iles (*Murder in Mink*)

ROSSETTI, Christina Georgina [1830–94, English poet and devotional writer]
Ellen Alleyne (in *The Germ*)

ROSSETTI, Helen [1879–1969, English writer]
*Isabel Meredith (*A Girl Among the Anarchists*)

ROSSETTI, Olivia Madox [1875–1960, English writer]
*Isabel Meredith (*A Girl Among the Anarchists*)

ROSSITER, John [1916–, English mystery writer]
Jonathan Ross (*Dark Blue and Dangerous*; *Rattling of Old Bones*)

ROSSNER, Robert [1932–, US writer]
Ivan T. Ross (*Murder out of School*; *Requiem for a Schoolgirl*)

ROSTEN, Leo Calvin [1908–, Polish-born US sociologist and humorist]
Leonard Q. Ross (*The Education of H*y*m*a*n K*a*p*l*a*n*; *Rome Wasn't Burned in a Day*)

ROTENBERG, Cyril [1908–91, English journalist and writer on wine]
Cyril Ray (*The Compleat Imbiber*)

ROTH, Holly [1916–64, US crime and mystery writer]
K. G. Ballard (*Trial by Desire*; *The Coast of Fear*)
P. J. Merrill (*The Slender Thread*)

ROTHERY, Agnes [1888–1954, US journalist]
Agnes Edwards (in the *Boston Herald* and for *Cape Cod, Old and New*)

ROTHERY, Guy Cadogan [1863–1940, English journalist and writer on heraldry]
An Observer (*Sanitary and Social Questions of the Day*)

ROTHWEILER, Paul R. [1931–, US writer]
Jonathan Scofield (*The King's Cannon*)

ROTHWELL, Thomas [1814–79, Irish historian]
Fitz-Herbert (in *Bentley's Miscellany*)

ROTSLER, William [1926–, US novelist and illustrator]
William Arrow (*Man, the Hunted Animal*; *Visions from Nowhere*)
John Ryder Hall (*Future World*)

ROUND, William Marshall Fitt [1845–1906, US journalist and social reformer]
Rev. Peter Pennot (*Achsah: a New England Life Study*; *Torn and Mended: a Christmas Story*)

ROUS, Francis [1579–1659, English politician and religious writer]
One that Loves all Presbyterian Lovers of Truth (*The Lawfulness of Obeying the Present Government*)

ROW, Charles Adolphus [1816–96, English cleric]
A Member of the Oxford Convocation (*A Letter to Lord John Russell MP*)

ROW, Thomas [1786–1864, English Baptist cleric]
A Labourer (in the *Gospel Herald*)

ROWAN, Arthur Blennerhassett [1800–61, Irish cleric and antiquarian]
Ignotus (*Letters from Oxford*)

ROWCROFT, Charles [1798–1856, English colonial civil servant]
An Etonian (*Confessions of an Etonian*)
Alfred Seedy (*Chronicles of the Fleet Prison*)

ROWE, Mrs Elizabeth [1674–1737, English poet]
Clerimont (*Friendship in Death*)
Philomela (*Poems on Several Occasions*; *Divine Hymns and Poems*)

ROWE, Richard [1828–79, Scottish journalist and writer for children]
Charles Camden (*The Travelling Menagerie*; *Hoity Toity: the Good Little Fellow*; *When I Was Young*)
Edward Howe (*Roughing it in Van Dieman's Land*)
Peter Possum (*Peter Possum's Portfolio*)

ROWE, Samuel [1793–1853, English cleric and Devon historian]
A Member of the University of Cambridge (*An Epitome of Paley's Evidences*; *An Epitome of Paley's Principles*)
Arthur Spenser (*Iskander or the Hero of Epirus*)

ROWLAND, John [1606–60, English cleric and royalist]
A Person of Quality (*A History of the Wonderful Things of Nature*)

ROWLANDS, Ernest Brown Bowen [1866–1951, Welsh barrister and legal writer]
The Member for Treorky (in the *Welsh Review* and for *The Betrayal of Wales*)

ROWLEY, Samuel [d. 1633, English dramatist]
S. R. (*The Noble Souldier*)

ROYALL, Mrs Anne [1769–1854, US writer]
A Traveller (*Sketches of History, Life and Manners in the United States*)

RUDGE, Florence [1860–?, English-born Australian poet]
Fairelie Thornton (*Heart Cheer for All the Year*)

RUFFIN, Edmund [1794–1865, US agriculturist and publisher]
An English Resident in the United States (*Anticipations of the Future to Serve as Lessons for the Present Time, in the Form of Extracts of Letters from an English Resident of the United States to the London Times from 1864 to 1870*)

RULE, Gilbert [1629–1701, Scottish nonconformist cleric and theologian]
A Friend to That Interest (*A True Representation of Presbyterian Government*)
A Learned Pen (*An Answer to Dr Stillingfleet*)
A Minister of the Church of Scotland (*A Vindication of the Church of Scotland*)

RUMBOLD-GIBBS, Henry St John Clair [1910–75, English crime writer]
Simon Harvester (*Delay in Danger*; *Let Them Prey*)

RUNDLE, Anne [fl. 1970, English romantic novelist]
Georgiana Bell (*Passionate Jade*)
Marianne Lamont (*Horns of the Moon*; *Nine Moons Wasted*)
Alexandra Manners (*The Singing Swans*; *The Stone Maiden*)
Joanne Marshall (*Follow a Shadow*; *Peacock Bed*)
Jeanne Saunders (*Spindrift*)

RUNDLE, Mrs Maria Eliza [1745–1828, English writer on cookery]
A Lady (*A New System of Domestic Cookery*)

RUPP, Isaac Daniel [1803–78, US lawyer and writer]
A Gentleman of the Bar (*The Early History of Western Pennsylvania*)

RUSDEN, George William [1819–1903, English migrant to Australia; historian]
Vindex (*A History of Australia*)
Yittadairn (*Moyarra*)

RUSH, Benjamin [1745–1813, US physician and writer]
A Pennsylvanian (*An Address to British Settlements on the Slavery of etc.*; *A Vindication of the Address on the Slavery of the Negroes of America*)
A Physician (*Sermons to the Rich and Studious*)

RUSKIN, John [1819–1900, English artist, art critic, essayist and social reformer]
A Graduate of Oxford (*Modern Painters, their Superiority etc.*)
J. R. (*Leoni: a Legend of Italy*; *Poems: Collected 1850*)
Kata Phusin (in *Loudon's Magazine*)

RUSSELL, Elizabeth Mary [1866–1941, Countess von Arnim; Australian novelist]
Alice Cholmondeley (*Christine*; *All the Dogs of my Life*)
Elizabeth (*Elizabeth and her German Garden*)

RUSSELL, Eric Frank [1905–78, English science-fiction writer]
Webster Craig; Duncan H. Munro (both used in *Astounding Science Fiction* magazine)
Maurice G. Hugi (in *Tales of Wonder* magazine)

RUSSELL, Francis [1765–1802, 5th Duke of Bedford]
A Young English Peer of the Highest Rank (*A Descriptive Journey through Germany and France*)

RUSSELL, Frank Alden [1908–, US writer]
Ted Malone (*Pack up your Troubles*; *Yankee Doodles*)

RUSSELL, George William [1867–1935, Irish poet, journalist and writer]
AE (*Homeward: Songs by the Way*; *Dark Weeping*)

RUSSELL, George William Erskine [1853–1919, English politician, historical and miscellaneous writer]
One who Has Kept a Diary (*Collections and Recollections*)

RUSSELL, Harold John Hastings [1868–1926, English barrister and natural historian]
Horace Rawdon (in *Cornhill Magazine*)

RUSSELL, Sir Henry [1783–1852, English civil servant in India]
Civis (*Letters of Civis*)

RUSSELL, Irwin Peter [fl. 1944, English writer]
Russell Irwin (*Picnic to the Moon*)

RUSSELL, John [1792–1878, 1st Earl Russell; politician and prime minister]
A Gentleman who Has Left his Lodgings (*Essays and Sketches of Life and Character*)
Joseph Skillet (name he used to sign the preface to the above)

RUSSELL, John [1885–1956, US writer]
Luke Thrice (*The Society Wolf*)

RUSSELL, John Cecil [1839–1909, English soldier]
A Soldier; C. Stein (both used in *Blackwood's Magazine*)

RUSSELL, Jonathan [1771–1832, US politician and diplomat]
Hancock (*The Whole Truth*; *Essex Junta Exposed*)

RUSSELL, Martin James [1934–, English crime and mystery writer]
James Arney (*A View to Ransom*)
Mark Lester (*Terror Trade*)

RUSSELL, Reginald James Kingston [1883–1943, English journalist and novelist]
Shaun Malory (*The Quest of the Golden Spurs*; *Treasure of Tempest*)

RUSSELL, Richard [d. 1771, English physician and medical writer]
An Eminent Physician (*A Dissertation on Sea-Water*)

RUSSELL, Richard [1723–84, English writer]
A Friend to Female Beauty (*War with the Senses*)

RUSSELL, Thomas O'Neill [1828–1908, Irish Gaelic scholar, novelist and dramatist]
Reginald Tierney (*Dick Massey*; *True Heart's Trials*; *The Struggles of Dick Massey*)

RUSSELL, William [fl. 1856, English novelist]
Thomas Waters (*Recollections of a Detective Police-Officer*)

RUSSELL, William Clark [1844–1911, US-born English mariner, journalist and nautical novelist]
Eliza Rhyl Davies (*A Dark Secret*; *The Mystery of Ashleigh Manor*)
Sydney Mostyn (in *Temple Bar*)
A Seafarer (in the *Daily Telegraph* and for *My Watch Below* and *Our Pilots*)

RUTLEDGE, Nancy [fl. 1950, US writer]
Leigh Bryson (*Murder for Millions*; *Blood on the Cat*)

RUTTER, John [1796–1851, English bookseller, Quaker and writer]
A Constitutional Reformer (*History of the Shaftesbury Election, 1830*)

RUTTY, John [1698–1775, Irish physician and natural historian]
Bernardus Utopiensis (*A Second Dissertation on the Liberty of Preaching*)
Johannes Catholicus (*An Essay on a Contract between Quakerism and Methodism*)
A Physician (*A Faithful Narrative of a Remarkable Visitation*)
An Unworthy Member of that Community (*The Liberty of the Spirit and of the Flesh Distinguished*)

RYALL, William Bolitho [1891–1930, South African journalist and writer]
William Bolitho (*Murder for Profit*; *Twelve Against the Gods*)

RYAN, Abram J. [1840–86, US cleric]
Moina (*The Conquered Banner*)

RYAN, Mrs Marah Ellis Martyn [1866–1934, US poet and novelist]
Ellis Martin (*For the Soul of Rafael*; *Indian Love-Letters*)

RYAN, Paul William [1906–47, US crime and mystery writer]
Robert Finnegan (*The Lying Ladies*; *The Bandaged Nude*)

RYAN, William Patrick [1867–1942, Irish journalist, editor and novelist]
Felix Boyne (*Fleet Street in Starlight*)
Kevin O'Kennedy (*Starlight Through the Roof*)

RYAN, William Thomas [1840–1910, Canadian poet and journalist]
Carroll Ryan (*Oscar and Other Poems*; *Picture Poems*)
A Wanderer (*Songs of a Wanderer*)

RYDELL, Helen [fl. 1965, US writer]
*Forbes Rydell (*They're Not Home Yet*; *No Questions Asked*)

RYDER, John [fl. 1853, English soldier – Corporal in 32nd Foot; later a policeman in Leicestershire]
A Private Soldier (*Four Years' Service in India*)

RYLANCE, Joseph Hine [1826–1907, English cleric and writer]
A Dear Hearer (*Preachers and Preaching*)

RYLAND, John Collett [1723–92, English Baptist cleric and schoolmaster]
A Lover of Christ (*Life and Actions of Jesus Christ*)
Pacificus (*A Modest Plea for Free Communion*)

RYMER, James Malcolm [1804–80, Scottish civil engineer and writer of 'penny dreadfuls']
Malcolm J. Errym (*Sea-Drift*)

S

SABIN, Elijah Robinson [1776–1818, US cleric]
Charles Observator (*Life and Reflections of Charles Observator*)

SABINE, Lorenzo [1803–77, US historian and writer]
Vindex (in the *Home Journal*)

SACHS, Judith [1947–, US romantic novelist]
Jennifer Saal (*Honor the Dream*)
Jocelyn Saal (*Dance of Love*; *Running Mates*)
Jennifer Sarasin (*Spring Love*; *The Hidden Room*)
Antonia Saxon (*Paradiso*; *Above the Moon*)

SACKVILLE, Charles [1711–69, 2nd Duke of Dorset; politician]
C. S. (*A Treatise Concerning the Militia in Four Sections*)

SACKVILLE, Lionel Cranfield [1688–1765, 1st Duke of Dorset]
Maj. Sawney M'Cleaver (*Ireland in Tears*)

SADLER, Geoffrey Willis [1943–, English western novelist]
Wes Calhoun (*At Muerto Springs*; *Texas Nighthawks*)

SADLER, Michael Thomas Harvey [1888–1957, English publisher, novelist and biographer]
Michael Sadleir (*Excursions in Victorian Bibliography*; *Fanny by Gaslight*)

SAGE, Bernard J. [1821–1902, US lawyer and politicial writer]
P. C. Sense, Barrister (*A Free Enquiry into the Origin of the Fourth Gospel*)

SAGE, John [1652–1711, Scottish cleric and religious writer]
J. S. (*The Principles of the Cyprianic Age*)
A Lover of the Church and his Country (*The Case of the Afflicted Clergy in Scotland*)

SAINT, Dora Jessie [1913–, English novelist]
Miss Read (*Village School*)

SAINTHILL, Richard [d. 1893, English mariner]
An Officer of HMS Topaze (in *Blackwood's Magazine*)

ST AUBYN, John Humphrey [1790–1857, English cleric]
Lionel Bouverie (*The Elopement or, Deadly Struggle*)

ST CLAIR, Margaret [1911–, US science-fiction writer]
Idris Seabright (in the *Magazine of Fantasy and Science Fiction*)

ST JOHN, Bayle [1822–59, English traveller, journalist and novelist]
Sain Gon (*Gherghis Mahomed*)

SAINT JOHN, Charles George William [1809–56, English sportsman, naturalist and sporting writer]
A Sportsman and a Naturalist (*Field Notes of a Sportsman and a Naturalist, with a Tour in Switzerland*)

ST JOHN, Henry [1678–1751, 1st Viscount Bolingbroke; politician and writer]
Caleb D'Anvers (*The Second Craftsman Extraordinary*)
Will Johnson (in *The Country Gentleman*)

A Member of the House of Commons (*The Case of Dunkirk Faithfully Stated*)
Humphrey Oldcastle (in *The Craftsman*)
W. Raleigh (*The Craftsman Extraordinary*; *Observations on the Public Affairs of Great Britain*)
John Trot, Yeoman (in *The Craftsman* and for *A Letter to Caleb D'Anvers Esq.*)

ST JOHN, James Augustus [1801–75, English traveller and journalist]
Greville Brooke (letter to the *Sunday Times*)
A Layman (*The Reasonableness of Christianity as Delivered*)

ST JOHN, Mary [d. 1830, Irish poet]
Mary (*Ellauna: a Legend of the Thirteenth Century*)

ST JOHN, Nicole [fl. 1980, US writer]
Catharine E. Chambers (*Search for Treasure*)
Kate Chambers (*The Secret of the Singing Strings*)
Pamela Dryden (*Mask my Heart*)
Lavinia Harris (*Dreams and Memories*)

ST JOHN, Percy Bolingbroke [1821–89, English journalist and writer]
An Old Smoker (in *Bentley's Miscellany*)
Paul Periwinkle (*Adventures of Paul Periwinkle*)

SALA, George Augustus Henry [1828–95, English journalist, novelist and illustrator]
Benedict Cruiser (*How I Tamed Mrs Cruiser*)
G. A. S. (for '*Echoes of the Week*' in *Illustrated London News* from 1860 to 1886)

SALLIS, Susan [1929–, English romantic novelist and writer for children]
Susan Meadmore (*Thunder in the Hills*; *An Open Mind*)

SALMON, Geraldine Gordon [1897–, English novelist]
J. G. Sarasin (*Fleur-De-Lys, the Story of a Crime*; *Storm-Bound*)

SALMON, Percy R. [1872–1959, English journalist and writer on photography]
Richard Penlake (*Developers, their Use and Abuse*; *Home Portraiture for Amateur Photographers*)

SALMON, Thomas [1679–1767, English historian and traveller]
A Gentleman (*A Critical Essay Concerning Marriage*)

SALT, Henry [1780–1827, English traveller and Egyptologist]
A Traveller (*Egypt – a Descriptive Poem with Notes*)

SAMBROT, William Anthony [1920–, US science-fiction writer]
William (or Anthony) Ayes (*Island of Fear*)

SAMPSON, Emma Speed [1868–1947, US writer]
Nell Speed (*Miss Minerva's Baby*)

SAMPSON, Henry J. M. [1841–91, English sporting journalist and editor]
Pendragon (in *The Referee* and for *Modern Boxing*)

SAMPSON, Richard Henry [1896–1973, English accountant and crime novelist]
Richard Hull (*The Murder of my Aunt*; *And Death Came Too*)

SAMPSON, William [1764–1836, Irish jurist and nationalist – emigrated to USA]
Sampfilius Philocrin, Z, Y, X, W. (*Beasts at Law or, Zoological Jurisprudence*)

SAMSON, George Whitefield [1819–96, US cleric and educationalist]
Traverse Oldfield (*The Spiritual Medium, its Nature Illustrated*; *Daimonion or, the Spiritual Medium*)
A Teacher (*Outlines of the History of Ethics*)

SANCROFT, William [1617–93, English cleric; Archbishop of Canterbury]
An Eye-Witness (*Modern Politics taken from Machiavel, Borgia etc.*)

SANDARS, John Satterfield [1853–1934, English barrister]
A Privy Councillor (*Studies of Yesterday*)

SANDERS, Alan [1878–1969, English journalist and London historian]
Civis (*A History of Albany*)

SANDERS, Charles Walton [1805–89, US educationalist]
A Teacher (*Metrical Stories in Chemistry and Natural Philosophy*)

SANDERS, Dorothy Lucy [1907–, Australian romantic novelist]
Lucy Walker (*Heaven is Here; Love in a Cloud*)

SANDERS, Mrs Elizabeth [1762–1851, US writer]
A Lady (*The First Settlers of New England*)

SANDERS, Laurence [1920–, US mystery writer]
Lesley Andress (*Caper*)

SANDERS, Robert [1727–83, English topographer and writer]
Gaffer Graybeard (*Lucubrations of Gaffer Graybeard*)
Llewellyn; Murray; Nathaniel Spencer (all used in *The Complete English Traveller*)
A Nobleman (*Roman History*)
Henry Southwell (*New Book of Martyrs*)

SANDERSON, Ivan T. [1911–73, Scottish natural historian]
Terence Roberts (*Report on the Status Quo*)

SANDERSON, John [1783–1844, US classical scholar]
An American Gentleman in Paris (*Sketches of Paris in Familiar Letters to his Friends*)

SANDERSON, Robert [1587–1663, English cleric; Bishop of Lincoln]
A Late Learned Hand (*Five Cases of Conscience*)
A Late Learned Prelate (*Ad Clerum*)
A Reverend Religious and Judicious Divine (*A Soveraigne Antidote against Sabbatarian Errours*)

SANDERSON, Thomas [1759–1829, English schoolmaster and poet]
Crito (in *The Cumberland Packet*)

SANDES, John [1863–1938, Irish-born Australian novelist and writer]
Dan Delaney (*Gentleman Jack, Bushranger; A Rebel of the Bush*)
Oriel (*Ballads of Battle*)

SANDWITH, Humphrey [1822–81, English physician and military surgeon]
Guiseppe Antonelli (*The Hekim Bashi*)

SANDYS, Charles [1786–1859, English solicitor and antiquary]
A Coontrie Atturney (*Vindications of a Coontrie Atturney*)

SANDYS, John [d. 1803, English writer]
John the Dipper (*The Salopian Zealot; The Little Innocent*)

SANDYS, Sampson [1797–1880, English legal functionary and writer]
John (*John's Letters to Dame Europa*)

SANDYS, William [1792–1874, English solicitor and musical historian]
Uncle Jan Treenoodle (*Specimens of the Cornish Provincial Dialect*)

SANFORD, Edward [1805–54, US journalist and poet]
Pot-Pie Palmer (*A Charcoal Sketch of Pot-Pie Palmer*)

SANFORD, John Langton [1824–77, English barrister and historian]
Sigma (in *The Christian Reformer*)

SARGENT, John Osborne [1811–91, US journalist and lawyer]
A Berkshire Farmer (*Chapters for the Times*)
A Layman (*Common Sense versus Judicial Legislation*)

SARGENT, John Turner [d. 1877, US cleric]
Bronze Beethoven, a Looker-On (*The Crisis of Unitarianism*)
A Pastor (*Serious Questions for the New Year from a Pastor*)

SARGENT, Lucius Manlius [1786–1867, US temperance advocate, writer and journalist]
Amgis; Saveall (both used for journalism)
An Episcopalian (*Letters to John H. Hopkins, DD*)
A Sexton of the Old School (in the *Boston Transcript*)
Sigma (*The Ballad of Abolition Blunderbuss*; *Notices of the Histories of Boston*; *Reminiscences of Samuel Dexter*)
Van Tromp (*No. 1 of the New Milk Cheese, or the Comic Heroic Thunderclap*)

SARGENT, Nathan [1794–1875, US journalist and lawyer]
Oliver Oldschool (in the *United States Gazette* and for *A Brief Outline of the Life of Henry Clay* and *Public Men and Events 1817–53*)

SARLE, Charles Spenser [1865–1936, English journalist]
Arthur R. Amory (*The Man from Asia*; *Before the Dawn*; *My Friend in Black*)

SAROYAN, William [1908–81, US playwright and novelist]
Sirak Goryan (*The Daring Young Man on the Flying Trapeze*)

SASS, George Herbert [1825–1908, US poet and writer]
Barton Grey (*The Heart's Quest*)

SASSOON, Siegfried [1886–1967, English writer and poet]
A Fox-Hunting Man (*Memoirs of a Fox-Hunting Man*)
Saul Kain (*The Daffodil Murderer*)
Pinchbeck Lyre (*Poems*)
S. S. (*Early Morning Long Ago*; *An Adjustment*)
Sigma Sashun (*Prehistoric Burials*)

SATOW, Sir Ernest Mason [1843–1929, English diplomat and historian]
E. M. S. (*Japanese Chronological Tables*)

SAUNDERS, Frederic [1807–1902, English-born US librarian and bibliographer]
An Epicure (*Salad for the Solitary and the Social*)
O. Hum & Co. (*Life in New York*)

SAUNDERS, Hilary A. St George [1898–1951, English historian and novelist]
*Francis Beeding (*The Seven Sleepers*; *The Six Proud Walkers*)
*Cornelius Cofyn (*The Death-Riders*)
*David Pilgrim (*So Great a Man*)

SAUNDERS, Jean [1932–, English romantic novelist and writer for children]
Sally Blake (*Devil's Kiss*; *Outback Woman*)
Jean Innes (*Silver Lady*; *White Blooms of Yarrow*)
Rowena Summers (*The Savage Moon*; *Willow Harvest*)

SAUNDERS, John O'Brien [d. 1903, English journalist in India]
Cassandra (*The Bengal Rent Bill*)

SAUSER-HALL, Frederic [1887–1961, French-Swiss traveller, poet and novelist]
Blaise Cendrars (*Nineteen Elastic Poems*; *African Saga*)

SAVAGE, Ethel Mary [1881–1939, English novelist]
Ethel M. Dell (*Keeper of the Door*; *Rosa Mundi*)

SAVAGE, Minot Judson [1841–1918, US cleric]
A Lunar Wray (*At the Back of the Moon*)

SAVAGE, Richard [1697–1743, English dramatist and poet]
Iscariot Hackney (*An Author to be Lett*)

SAVI, Ethel Winifred [1865–1954, Indian-born English romantic novelist]
Elizabeth Grey (*The Law Divine*)

SAVILE, Charles Stuart [1816–70, English diplomat, traveller and novelist]
Henry Walter D'Arcy (in *Bentley's Miscellany*)

SAVILE, George [1633–95, Marquis of Halifax; political pamphleteer]
A Person of Honour (*The Character of a Trimmer Concerning Religion; Historical Observations upon the Reigns of Edward I, II, III, etc.*)
A True Protestant and a Hearty Lover of his Country (*A Seasonable Address to both Houses of Parliament*)
T. W. (*A Letter to a Dissenter*)

SAWKINS, Raymond H. [1923–, English novelist]
Colin Forbes (*Tramp in Armour; The Palermo Affair; The Heights of Zervos*)
Richard Raine (*Bombshell; Night of the Hawk*)

SAWYER, Walter Leon [1862–1915, US editor and journalist]
Winn Standish (*Captain Jack Lorimer; Jack Lorimer's Holidays*)

SAXTON, Judith [1936–, English romantic novelist]
Judy Turner (*My Master Mariner; Follow the Drum*)

SAYER, Walter William [1892–?, English writer for children]
Bessie Duncane (in *Girl's Realm*)
Pierre Quiroule (in *Champion* and for *The Silhouette Symbol* and *The Man with Two Souls*)

SAYERS, Dorothy Leigh [1893–1957, English dramatist and crime writer]
Johanna Leigh (intended for use in an unpublished autobiography)
H. P. Rallentando (in the *Saturday Westminster Gazette* for 'Thomas Angulo's Death')

SCARGILL, William Pitt [1787–1836, English cleric and writer]
Anti-Innovator (in *New Monthly Magazine*)
A Dissenting Minister (*The Autobiography of a Dissenting Minister*)

SCARISBRICK, Edward [1639–1709, English Jesuit; used the alias Neville]
A Catholic Gentleman (*The Life of Lady Warner of Parham in Suffolk*)

SCARTH, John [1826–1909, Scottish cleric and merchant in China]
A British Resident (*Twelve Years in China*)

SCHACHNER, Nathan [1895–1955, US lawyer and biographer]
Chan Corbett; Walter Glamis (both used in *Astounding Stories* magazine)

SCHEM, Lila Clara [1875–1923, US novelist]
Margaret Blake (*Matthew Ferguson; The Voice of the Heart*)

SCHIFF, Sydney [1869–1944, English novelist and translator]
Stephen Hudson (*War-Time Silhouettes; Elinore Cobhouse*)

SCHILLER, Ferdinand Canning Scott [1864–1937, English philosopher]
A Troglodyte (*Riddles of the Sphinx*)

SCHILLER, Henry Carl [1807–71, English writer on the dramatic arts]
Anthony Grey (*Christmas at the Grange*)

SCHIMMELPENNINCK, Mary Anne [1778–1856, English writer]
Dom Claude Launcelot (*Narrative of a Tour in the Year 1667*)

SCHISGALL, Oscar [1901–, US writer]
Stuart Hardy (*Trouble for Texas; The Miracle at Gopher Creek*)

SCHLOSS, Arthur David [1889–1966, English historian and oriental scholar]
Lady Murasaki (*The Tale of a Genji*)
Arthur David Waley (*Chinese Poems; No Plays of Japan*)
Wu-Ch'eng-En (*Monkey*)

SCHMIDT, James Norman [1912–, US writer]
James Norman (*An Inch of Time; The Nightwalkers*)

SCHNITTKIND, Henry Thomas [1888–?, US writer]
Henry Thomas (*Mathematics Made Easy; George Washington Carver*)

SCHOEFFEL, Mrs Florence [1860–1900, US novelist]
Wenona Gilman (*Oni or, the Averted Vengeance; Saddle and Sentiment*)

SCHOEPFLIN, Harl Vincent [1893–1968, US engineer and science-fiction writer]
Harl Vincent (in both *Argosy* and *Astounding Science Fiction* magazines)

SCHOFIELD, Sylvia Anne Matheson [1918–, English crime and mystery writer]
Sylvia A. Matheson (*Tigers of Baluchistan; Persia: an Archaeological Guide*)
Max Mundy (*Pagan Pagoda; Death is a Tiger*)

SCHOMBERG, Alexander Crowcher [1756–92, English academic and poet]
Cornelius Scriblerus Nothus (*Ode on the Present State of English Poetry*)

SCHOOLCRAFT, Henry Rowe [1793–1864, US traveller and anthropologist]
Henry Rowe Colcraft (*Alhalla or, the Land of Talladega*)

SCHREINER, Olive Emilie Albertina [1855–1920, South African novelist and writer]
Ralph Iron (*The Story of an African Farm*)
A Returned South African (in *Fortnightly Review*)

SCHROEDER, Henry [1774–1853, English engraver and topographer]
William Butterworth (*Three Years' Adventures of a Minor in England, Africa etc.*)

SCHROEDER, Reginald [1855–?, US journalist]
*Schroeder Davis (*Storm Birds*)

SCHULTZ, James Willard [fl. 1907, US writer]
W. B. Anderson (*My Life as an Indian*)

SCHULTZE, Carl Emil [1866–1939, US newspaper cartoonist]
Bunny (*The Adventures of Foxy Grandpa; Foxy Grandpa's Mother Goose*)

SCHWARZ, Ernest Hubert Lewis [1873–1928, English geologist and scientific writer]
Ernest Black (*Brendavale*)

SCIDMORE, Eliza Ruhamah [1856–1928, US travel writer]
A Russian Prisoner's Wife in Japan (*As the Hague Ordains*)

SCITHERS, George [1929–, US engineer and science-fiction writer]
Karl Wurf (*To Serve Man*)

SCLATER, William [1638–1717, English cleric and controversialist]
A Presbyter of the Church of England (*An Original Draught of the Primitive Church*)

SCORESBY, William [1760–1829, English Arctic explorer]
A Voyager (*Tales of a Voyager to the Arctic Ocean*)

SCOTT, Clement William [1841–1904, English civil servant, drama critic and writer]
Almaviva (in the *London Figaro* and for *Drawing-Room Plays and Parlour Pantomimes*)

SCOTT, Daniel [1694–1759, English cleric and theologian]
Philanthropus Londinensis (*An Essay Towards Scripture-Trinity*)

SCOTT, Evelyn [1893–1963, US novelist and poet]
Ernest Souza (*Blue Rum*)

SCOTT, Francis [1806–84, English barrister and politician]
A Member of the Hon. Society of the Middle Temple (*Dissection of the Scottish Reform Bill*)

SCOTT, Harriet Anne [1819–94, English novelist]
Grandmother (*Cottager's Comforts and Other Recipes*)

SCOTT, Hugh Stowell [1862–1903, English insurance clerk and novelist]
Henry Seton Merriman (*Barlasch of the Guard*; *The Last Hope*)

SCOTT, James [1733–1814, English cleric, political and religious writer]
Anti-Sejanus; Old Slyboots; Philanglia (all used in the *Public Advertiser*)

SCOTT, James George [1851–1935, English colonial officer]
Shwe Dinga (*The Repentance of Destiny*; *Wholly Without Morals*)
Yoe Shway (*Burma – a Handbook of Information*; *The Burman, his Life and Times*)

SCOTT, John [1783–1821, Scottish journalist and traveller – died following a duel]
Edgeworth Benson (in the *London Magazine*)

SCOTT, John [1820–1907, US politician]
Barbarossa (*The Lost Principle or Sectional Equilibrium*)

SCOTT, Michael [1789–1835, Scottish merchant and writer]
Thomas Cringle (*Tom Cringle's Log*)

SCOTT, Robert [1811–87, English cleric and classical scholar]
Thomas Chatterton (in *MacMillan's Magazine*)

SCOTT, Sarah [d. 1795, English historian and novelist]
A Gentleman on his Travels (*A Description of Millenium Hall and the Country Adjacent* – possibly written with Lady Barbara Montagu, d. 1765)
A Person of Quality (*A Journey Through Every Stage of Life*)
Henry Augustus Raymond (*The History of Gustavus Ericson, King of Sweden*)

SCOTT, Thomas [1580–1626, English cleric, preacher and religious writer; he was assassinated]
A Person of Honour (*A Choice Narrative of Count Gondamor's Transactions*)

SCOTT, Sir Walter [1771–1832, Scottish novelist, essayist and poet]
C. (in *The Sale Room*)
Jedediah Cleishbotham (*Tales of my Landlord*)
Capt. Clutterbuck (*The Fortunes of Nigel*)
Chrystal Croftangry (*Chronicles of the Canongate*)
Rev. Dr Dryasdust (used in the introduction to some of his novels)
A Layman (*Religious Discourses*)
Malachi Malagrowther (letters in the *Edinburgh Weekly Journal*)
Peter Pattieson (*Tales of my Landlord*)
Paul (*Paul's Letters to his Kinsfolk*)
Somnambulas; The Visionary (both used in the *Edinburgh Weekly Journal*)
Lawrence Templeton (*Ivanhoe*)

SCOTT, Sir William [1745–1836, Baron Stowell; English barrister and maritime jurist]
Chrysal (*Letters on the High Price of Bullion*)
Civis (*Some Observations upon the High Price of Bullion*)

SCOTT, Winifred Mary [d. 1959, English novelist]
Pamela Wynne (*Ann's an Idiot*; *The Dream Man*)

SCOTT-MONCRIEFF, Charles Kenneth [1889–1930, Scottish journalist and translator]
P. G. and L. O. Lear (*The Strange and Striking Adventures of Four Authors*)

SCOVILLE, Joseph Alfred [1811–64, US journalist and novelist]
Walter Barrett, Clerk (*The Old Merchants of New York City*; *Vigor*)
Manhattan (in the *London Herald* and for *Marion*)

SCROPE, George Julius Poulett [1797–1876, English geologist and social reformer; his original surname was Thomson but he adopted that of his wife]
One of their Number (*A Letter to the Magistrates of the South and West of England*)

SCUDAMORE, William Edward [1813–81, English cleric and devotional writer]
The Chaplain of the Penitentiary at Shipmeadow (*An Account of the Penitentiary*)
A Parish Priest (*Steps to the Altar*)

SCUDDER, Horace Elisha [1838–1902, US writer and editor of juvenile literature]
R. Fellow (*The Game of Croquet*)
S. T. James (*Stories from my Attic*)

SCUDDER, Samuel Hubbard [1837–1911, US naturalist]
A Rochester Fellow (*The Winnipeg Country*)

SCUDDER, Vida Dutton [1861–1954, US academic and historian]
Davida Coit (*How the Rain-Sprites were Freed*)

SCULLY, William Charles [1855–1943, English colonial legal officer]
A South African Colonist (*Poems*)

SEABROOK, Whitemarsh Benjamin [fl. 1834, US politician and writer]
A South Carolinian (*An Appeal to the People of the Northern and Eastern States*)

SEABURY, Samuel [1729–96, US cleric and loyalist; first Bishop of Connecticut]
A. W. Farmer (*A View of the Controversy between Great Britain and her Colonies*)
A Member of the Episcopal Church (*An Address to the Ministers of the Presbyterian and Independent Persuasions of the United States*)
A Westchester Farmer (*Letters*)

SEAGER, Charles [1808–78, English cleric, Hebraist and biblical scholar]
Academicus (*Auricular Confession*)
A Priest (*The Daily Service of the Anglo-Catholic Church*)

SEAGRAVE, Robert [1693–1760, English cleric and religious writer]
Paulinus (*A Letter to the People of England*)

SEAMAN, Elizabeth Cochrane [1867–1922, US journalist and writer]
Nelly Bly (in the *Pittsburgh Dispatch* and for *Six Months in Mexico*)

SEAMAN, Sylvia Sybil [1910–, US writer]
Francis Sylvin (*Miracle Father*; *Rusty Carousel*)

SEARING, Mrs Laura Catherine [1840–1923, US journalist and poet]
Howard Glyndon (*Sounds from Secret Chambers*; *Idylls of Battle*)

SEARS, Edward [1819–76, Irish-born US writer]
H. E. Chevalier (*Legends of the Sea*)

SEARS, George W. [fl. 1884, US naturalist]
Nessmuk (*Woodcraft*)

SECCOMBE, Joseph [1706–60, American cleric]
Fluviatulis Piscator (*Business and Diversion Inoffensive to God*)

SECCOMBE, Thomas [1866–1923, English biographer and literary critic]
An Old Felstedian (*Felsted School*)

SEDGWICK, James [1775–1851, English barrister, legal and political writer]
A Barrister (*Hints to the Public on Evangelical Preaching*)

SEDGWICK, Theodore [1781–1839, US lawyer]
An American (*Hints to my Countrymen*)

SEDGWICK, Theodore [1811–59, US lawyer and writer]
Veto (in the *New York Evening Post*)

SEE, Carolyn [1934–, US writer]
Monica Highland (*Lotus Land*)

SEELEY, Sir John Robert [1834–95, English historian and academic]
John Robertson (*David and Samuel*)

SEELEY, Robert Benton [1798–1886, English publisher and writer]
A Layman (*Essays on the Church*)
James White (*Is the Bible True?*)

SEGER, Maura [1951–, US romantic novelist]
Jenny Bates (*Gilded Spring; Dazzled*)
Sara Jennings (*Love not the Enemy; Game Plan*)
Anne MacNeill (*A Mind of her Own*)
Laurel Winslow (*Heartsongs; Captured Images*)

SEID, Ruth [1913–, US writer]
Jo Sinclair (*Wasteland; Sing at my Wake*)

SEIFERT, Elizabeth [1897–1983, US romantic novelist]
Ellen Ashley (*Girl in Overalls*)

SELBY, Charles [1802–63, English actor and playwright]
William Muggins (*Maximums and Specimens of William Muggins*)
Tabitha Tickletooth (*The Dinner Question*)

SELDEN, John [1584–1654, English jurist, politician and writer]
A Learned Antiquary (*A Brief Discourse on the Powers of Peers and Commons*)

SELDEN, Richard Ely [1797–1868, US farmer and writer]
Mon Droit (*Criticisms on the Declaration of Independence*)

SELDES, Gilbert Vivian [1893–1970, US journalist, novelist, crime writer and media critic]
Foster Johns (*The Victory Murders*)

SELLER, Abednego [1646–1705, English cleric and religious writer]
A Minister of That Church (*A Plain Answer to a Papish Priest*)

SELLERS, Isaiah [1802–64, US riverboat pilot]
Mark Twain (in the *New Orleans Daily Picayune*)

SENARENS, Luis Philip [1863–1939, US writer for boys]
Noname (used for the Frank Read stories)

SENIOR, Nassau William [1790–1864, English barrister and political economist]
A Guardian (*Remarks on the Opposition to the Poor Law Amendment Bill*)

SENIOR, William [d. 1920, English journalist and writer on angling]
Uncle Hardy (*Notable Shipwrecks*)

SERGEANT, Emily Frances Adeline [1851–1904, English novelist and social worker]
Adeline (*Ernald or, the Martyr of the Alps*)
A Woman (in *Temple Bar*)

SERGEANT, John [1622–1707, English Roman Catholic controversialist]
J. S. (*Transnatural Philosophy or Metaphysicks*)

SERNER, Martin Gunnar [1886–1947, Swedish crime writer]
Frank Heller (*The London Adventures of Mr Collin; The Strange Adventures of Mr Collin*)

SERRES, Olivia Wilmot [1772–1834, English painter, poet and impostor]
Olivia (*Olivia's Letters of Advice to her Daughters*)

SETH-SMITH, Leslie James [1923–, Ugandan-born English writer]
James Brabazon (*Albert Schweitzer; Dorothy L. Sayers*)

SETON, Ernest Thompson [1860–1946, English naturalist – sometime in North America]
Seton Thompson (*The Trail of the Sandhill Stag*)

SETON, Sir Malcolm Cotter Cariston [1872–1940, English writer]
Africanus (*The Transvaal Boers, a Historical Sketch*)

SETON-WATSON, Robert William [1879–1951, English historian and authority on Central Europe and the Balkans]
Scotus Viator (*Corruption and Reform in Hungary; The Future of Austria-Hungary*)

SETTLE, Elkanah [1648–1724, English poet and writer]
A Person of Quality (*The Female Prelate Pope Joan*)

SEWALL, Henry Devereux [fl. 1822, US writer]
A Unitarian of New York (*An Appeal from the Decisions of Rev. Dr Mason*)

SEWALL, Jonathan Mitchell [1748–1808, US poet and writer]
Sir Roger De Coverley (*A Cure for the Spleen: or, Amusements for a Winter's Evening*)
A Gentleman of Portsmouth, NH (*A Versification of Washington's Excellent Farewell Address*)

SEWARD, Anna [1747–1809, English poet and writer]
Benvolio (letters in *Gentleman's Magazine*)

SEWELL, Brocard [1912–, English writer]
Joseph Jerome (*Montague Summers: a Memoir*)

SEWELL, Miss Elizabeth Missing [1815–1906, English novelist and educationalist]
Jane Bull (*Mrs Britton's Letter Touching the Europa Troubles*)
A Lady (*Amy Herbert*)

SEWELL, George [d. 1726, English physician and writer]
A Gentleman (*The Resigners Vindicated*)

SEWELL, Richard Clarke [1803–64, English barrister – practised in Australia]
A Hampshire Fisherman (in *The Field*)

SEWELL, William [1804–74, English cleric and writer]
A Clergyman (*A Clergyman's Recreations or, Sacred Thoughts in Verse*)
A Conservative Member of Convocation (*Misgivings on the Requisition to Lord Derby*)

SEXBY, Edward [d. 1658, English roundhead soldier; imprisoned and died in the Tower of London]
William Allen (*Killing Noe Murder*)

SEXTON, George [fl. 1860, English writer on the theatre]
Wilfred Wisgart (in the *Player's Magazine*)

SEYMOUR, Aaron Crossley Hobart [1789–1870, English hymn writer]
A Member of the Houses of Shirley and Hastings (*Life and Times of Selina, Countess of Huntingdon*)

SEYMOUR, Almira [fl. 1866, US writer]
One who Has Some There (*Our Silent City*)

SEYMOUR, Frederick Henry [1850–1913, US humorist]
Lord Gilhooley (*Dennis Foggarty*)

SEYMOUR, George Steele [1878–1945, US accountant and writer]
Abd'ul Hasan (*Chronicles of Bagdad*)

SEYMOUR, Mary Alice [fl. 1870, US novelist]
Octavia Hensel (*Imperia: a Story from the Court of Austria*; *Life and Letters of Louis Moreau Gottschalk*)
Octavia (*Christmas Holidays at Cedar Grove*)

SEYMOUR, Rosalind Herschel [1909–89, English novelist]
Catharine Carr (*English Summer*; *The Golden City*)
Rosalind Wade (*Children Be Happy*; *Bracelet for Julia*)

SHADWELL, Charles [d. 1726, English dramatist]
C. S. (*The Fair Quaker of Deal or, the Humours of the Navy*)

SHADWELL, Lancelot [1779–1850, English barrister and jurist]
Philhellen Etonensis (*Homer's Iliad in Homeric Verse*; *The Iliad of Homer*)

SHAFFER, Anthony [1926–, English writer –
twin of Peter Levin Shaffer below]
*Peter Anthony (*The Woman in the
Wardrobe*; *How Doth the Little Crocodile?*)

SHAFFER, Peter Levin [1926–, English
dramatist – twin of Anthony Shaffer
above]
*Peter Anthony (see Anthony Shaffer
above)

SHAMBROOK, Rona [fl. 1960, English
actress and novelist]
Rona Randall (*Eagle at the Gate*; *Mating
Dance*)

SHANNON, Doris [1924–, Canadian writer]
E. X. Giroux (*Death for a Darling*; *A Death
for a Doctor*)

SHANNON, Edward N. [1795–1860, Irish
poet]
Odoardo Volpi (*The Comedy of Dante
Alighieri*)

SHANNON, Mrs Mary Eulalie [1824–55,
US poet]
Eulalie (*Buds, Blossoms and Leaves*)

SHARE, James M. [fl. 1878, Irish poet and
writer]
Barclay Delaval (*Shaugh Bridge and Mount
Edgecumbe*)

SHARKEY, John Michael [1931–92, US
playwright and writer]
Mike Chandler (*Doctor Death*)
Mike Johnson (*The Return of the Maniac*;
The Clone People)

SHARMAT, Marjorie W. [1928–, US writer
for children]
Wendy Andrews (*Vacation Fever*; *Are We
There Yet?*)

SHARP, Abraham [1651–1742, English
mathematician]
A. S., Philomath (*Geometry Improv'd*)

SHARP, John [1645–1714, English cleric;
Archbishop of York]
A Presbyter of the Church of England (*An
Appeal of the Clergy to the Bishops*)

SHARP, Thomas [1693–1758, English cleric
and theologian]
A Prebendary of York (*The Enquiry about
the Lawfulness of Eating Blood*; *A Defence
of the Enquiry about Eating Blood*)

SHARP, Thomas [1770–1841, English local
historian and antiquarian]
Philarchaismos (in *Gentleman's Magazine*)

SHARP, William [1855–1905, Scottish poet,
traveller and mystical writer]
Fiona MacLeod (*Pharais*; *The Mountain
Lovers*; *The Immortal Hour*)

SHARPE, Charles Kirkpatrick [1781–1851,
English painter, antiquarian and recluse]
An Amateur (*Portraits*; *Six Portraits*)
Gracchus (*A Friendly Address to the Common
People of Dumfries-Shire*)

SHARROCK, Marian Edna [1897–, US
writer]
M. A. Dormie (*Expatriates*; *Snobs*)

SHAW, Charles [1900–55, Australian writer]
Bant Singer (*You're Wrong Delaney*; *Don't
Slip Delaney*)

SHAW, Cuthbert [1739–71, English poet
from humble background]
An Afflicted Husband (*Monody to the
Memory of a Young Lady*)
Mercurius Spur (*The Race*)
W. Seymour (*Odes on the Four Seasons*)

SHAW, George Bernard [1856–1950, Irish
critic, playwright and essayist]
Corno di Bassetto (in *The Star*)
S (letter in *Public Opinion*, April 1875)

SHAW, Henry Wheeler [1818–85, US
humorist]
Josh Billings (*Josh Billings his Sayings*; *Josh
Billings's Spice-Box*)

SHAW, Oliver Abbott [d. 1855, US cleric]
The Patentee (*A Brief Description of the
Visible Numerator*)

SHAW, Peter [1694–1763, English physician and medical writer]
An Eminent Physician (*A Philosophical and Chymical Analysis of Antimony*)
Fellow of a College (*The Juice of the Grape*)

SHAW, Stanley Gordon [1884–?, English writer for boys]
S. S. (or Stanley) Gordon (in *Chums*)

SHAW, William [1749–1831, Scottish cleric and Gaelic scholar]
Rev. Sir Archibald MacSarcasm, Bart. (*Life of Hannah More*)

SHAW, William Arthur [1865–1943, English civil servant, historical and financial writer]
Legislator (*The Coming Reaction*)

SHEAHAN, Henry Beston [1888–?, US writer for children]
Henry Beston (*Herbs and the Earth*; *The St Lawrence*)

SHEARES, John [1766–98, Irish barrister and nationalist – executed]
Dion (in *The Press*)

SHEBBEARE, John [1709–88, English physician, novelist and satirist]
Battista Angeloni (*Letters to the English Nation*)

SHECKLEY, Robert [1928–, US science-fiction writer]
Finn O'Donnevan (in *Galaxy* magazine)

SHEDD, William [1797–1830, US cleric and academic]
Canonicus (*Letters to W. E. Channing on Fallen Spirits*)

SHEE, Sir Martin Archer [1769–1850, Irish portrait painter]
A Painter (*Rhymes on Art*)

SHEEHAN, John [1812–82, Irish journalist and writer]
*Richard Grimgibber; A Member of the Comet Club (both used in *Bentley's Miscellany*)

The Irish Whisky Drinker; The Knight of Innishowen (both used in *Temple Bar*)

SHEFFIELD, John [1648–1721, 1st Duke of Buckingham; statesman, poet and essayist]
A Person of Quality (*An Ode in Memory of Queen Mary*)

SHEIL, Sir Justin [1803–71, English soldier and diplomat]
A Son of the Soil (*French Thoughts on Irish Evils*)

SHEIL, Lily [1904–88, English-born US Hollywood gossip columnist and writer]
Sheila Graham (*Beloved Infidel*; *College of One*)

SHEIL, Richard Lalor [1791–1851, Irish barrister, dramatist and politician]
Crito; Ignatius Rabelais O'Flummery (both used in *New Monthly Magazine*)

SHELDON, Alice Hastings [1916–, US psychologist and novelist]
James Tiptree Jr. (*Up the Walls of the World*; *Ten Thousand Light-Years from Home*)

SHELLABARGER, Samuel [1888–1954, US mystery novelist]
John Esteven (*The Door of Death*; *While Murder Waits*)
Peter Loring (*He Travels Alone*; *Grief Before Night*)

SHELLEY, Percy Bysshe [1792–1822, English poet and writer]
John Fitzvictor (*Posthumous Fragments of Margaret Nicholson*)
A Gentleman of the University of Oxford (*St Irvyne or, the Rosicrucian*)
The Hermit of Marlow (*An Address to the People on the Death of the Princess Charlotte*; *A Proposal for Putting Reform to the Vote*)
Miching Mallecho (*Peter Bell the Third*)
My Aunt Margaret Nicholson (*Posthumous Fragments of etc.*)
P. B. S. (*Zastrossi*)

Victor and Cazire (used jointly with his sister Elizabeth for *Original Poetry*)

SHELTON, Frederick William [1814–81, US cleric]
Nil Admirari Esq. (*The Trollopiad: or, Travelling Gentlemen in America*)

SHEPARD, Morgan Van Roerbach [1877–?, US writer]
John Martin (*Letters to Children*; *Aesop's Fables in Rhyme*)

SHEPHERD, Florence [fl. 1944, English writer]
*Harrington Hastings (*Criminal Square*)

SHEPHERD, Richard [1732–1809, English cleric, poet and devotional writer]
Philalethes Rusticans (*Reflections on the Doctrine of Materialism*)

SHEPPARD, Elizabeth Sara [1830–62, English novelist]
Mme Kinkel (*Almost a Heroine*)
Beatrice Reynolds (*My First Season*)

SHEPPARD, Mrs Lydia H. [fl. 1867, US writer]
E. L. Llewellyn (*Judge Not, or Hester Power's Girlhood*)

SHEPPARD, Nathan [1834–88, US academic and writer]
An American (in *Fraser's Magazine*)

SHERER, John Walter [1823–1911, English civil servant in India]
Paul Benison (in *Dublin University Magazine* and for *Not to Be*)
An Old Indian Magistrate (in *MacMillan's Magazine*)

SHERER, Moyle [1789–1869, English soldier and traveller]
An Officer (*Sketches of India*)

SHERIDAN, Frances [1724–66, Irish dramatist and writer]
Miss Sidney Bidulph (*Memoirs of Miss Sidney Bidulph*)

SHERIDAN, Helen Selina [1807–67, Countess of Dufferin; playwright and songwriter]
Hon. Impulsia Gushington (*Lispings from Low Latitudes*)

SHERIDAN, Richard Brinsley [1751–1816, Irish dramatist and politician]
Asmodeo (*Clio's Protest or, the Picture Varnished*)

SHERIDAN, Thomas [1687–1738, Irish writer – sometime intimate of Swift and grandfather of Richard Brinsley Sheridan]
Tom Punsibi (*Tom Punsibi's Dream*; *Tom Punsibi's Farewell ... Muses*; *Tom Punsibi's Letter ... Swift*)

SHERIDAN, Thomas [1719–88, Irish actor and lexicographer – father of Richard Brinsley Sheridan]
Longinus (in the *Public Ledger*)
The Manager of the Theatre Royal in Dublin (*A Full Vindication of the Manager of the Theatre Royal, Dublin, Written by Himself*)

SHERLOCK, Martin [d. 1797, Irish cleric and traveller]
An English Traveller (*New Letters from an English Traveller*)

SHERLOCK, Paul [1595–1646, Irish cleric and theologian]
Paulus Leonardus (*Responsio ad Expostulationes Recentium ... Scientam Mediam*)

SHERLOCK, Thomas [1678–1761, English cleric and controversialist; Bishop of London]
A Gentleman (*Remarks upon the Lord Bishop of Bangor's Treatment*)
A Member of the House of Commons (*A Vindication of the Test-Act*)

SHERLOCK, William [1641–1707, English cleric and controversialist]
A Presbyter of the Church of England (*A Discourse about Church Unity*)

SHERMAN, Frank Dempster [1860–1916, US poet and writer]
Felix Carmen (used for writing 'lighter verse')
*Two Wags (*New Waggings of Old Tales*)

SHERREN, Wilkinson [1875–?, English journalist and writer]
Nicholas Fay (*Joy is my Name*)

SHERRIN, Edward George [1931–, English writer and broadcaster]
Ned Sherrin (*Cindy-Ella or, I Gotta Shoe*; *After You Mr Feydeau*)

SHERWOOD, Mary Elizabeth Wilson [1826–1903, US poet and novelist]
M. E. W. S. (*Etiquette*; *The Sarcasm of Destiny*)

SHERWOOD, Reuben [d. 1856, US cleric]
Philalethes (*The Reviewer Reviewed*)

SHIEL, Matthew P. [1865–1947, Irish novelist and futurist writer]
Gordon Holmes (*The Late Tenant*; *An American Emperor*; *The House of Silence*)

SHIELDS, Alexander [1660–1700, Scottish cleric and theologian]
A Lover of True Liberty (*A Hind Let Loose*)

SHIELDS, G. O. [1846–1925, US journalist and natural historian]
Coquina (*The American Book of the Dog*; *Game Fishes*; *The Battle of the Big Hole*)

SHIELS, Andrew [1793–1879, Scottish-Canadian poet]
Albyn (*The Witch of Westcot*; *John Walker's Courtship*)

SHILLABER, Benjamin Penhallow [1814–90, US printer, journalist and humorist]
She P. Billaber (in the *Boston Journal*)
Ruth (or Mrs) Partington (*Life and Sayings of Mrs Partington*; *Knitting Work: a Web of Many Textures*)

SHILLETO, Arthur Richard [1848–94, English classical scholar]
Erato Hills (in *Notes and Queries*)

SHILLETO, Richard [1809–76, English classical scholar]
Charles Thiriold (in *Notes and Queries*)

SHIPLEY, William Davies [1745–1826, English cleric and controversial writer]
A Member of the Society for Constitutional Information (*The Principles of Governement*)

SHIRLEY, Evelyn Philip [1812–82, English politician and antiquarian]
E. P. S. (*Lower Eatington, its Manor House and Church*)
Spes (*The Church in Ireland*; *The Reformation in Ireland*; *Why is the Church in Ireland to be Robbed?*)

SHIRRA, Robert [1724–1803, Scottish cleric]
A Protestant (*Antichrist's Inquest*)

SHIRREFFS, Gordon Donald [1914–, US western novelist]
Gordon Donalds (*Top Gun*; *Arizona Justice*)
Jackson Flynn (*Shootout*)
Stewart Gordon (*Gunswift*)

SHOBERL, Frederic [1775–1853, English editor, translator and writer]
Zemia (in *Bentley's Miscellany*)

SHOLL, Anna MacClure [fl. 1915, US writer]
Geoffrey Corson (*Blue Blood and Red*)

SHORE, Mrs William Teignmouth [fl. 1909, English writer]
Priscilla Craven (*Circe's Daughter*)

SHORT, Charles William [1799–1857, English military writer]
An Officer of the Coldstream Guards (*A Treatise on Swimming*)

SHORT, Thomas Vowler [1790–1872, English cleric; Bishop of St Asaph]
A Clergyman (*Letters to an Aged Mother*)

SHORTHOUSE, Joseph Henry [1834–1903, English novelist]
Geoffrey Monk, MA (*John Inglesant*)

SHORTT, Charles Rushton [fl. 1947, English writer]
Charles Rushton (*Murder in Bavaria; Death in the Wood*)

SHOWER, Sir Bartholomew [1658–1701, English barrister, pamphleteer and writer]
A Gentleman of the Inner Temple (*The Compleat English Copyholder*)

SHRUBSOLE, William [1729–97, English cleric]
W. S. (*A Plea in Favour of the Shipwrights Belonging to the Royal Dockyards*)

SHUTE, John [1678–1734, 1st Viscount Barrington; theologian and lawyer]
A Layman (*The Layman's Letter to the Bishop of Bangor; The Layman's Second Letter to the Bishop of Bangor*)

SIBBES, Richard [1577–1635, English Puritan cleric and religious writer]
A Reverend Divine Now with God (*The Saint's Comforts*)

SIBLEY, Henry Hastings [1811–91, US soldier]
The Walker in the Pines (used for occasional contributions to various periodicals)

SICKERT, Ellen M. [fl. 1907, English romantic novelist]
Miles Amber (*Wistons*)

SICKERT, Helena Maria [1864–1939, English writer and suffragist]
H. M. Swanwick (*Builders of Peace; Women in a Social State*)

SIDEBOTHAM, Herbert [1872–1940, English journalist, barrister and writer]
Candidus (in the *Daily Sketch* and in the *Daily Graphic* in 1923, and for *The Sense of Things*)
Scrutator (in the *Sunday Times*, 1921–3)
Student of Politics (in *The Times* and the *Daily Telegraph*)
Student of War (in the *Manchester Guardian*)

SIDGWICK, Mrs Cecily [d. 1934, English novelist]
Mrs Andrew Dean (*Lesser's Daughter; Cousin Ivo*)

SIDNEY, Samuel [1813–83, English writer; his original surname was Solomons]
A Bushman (*A Voice from the Far Interior of Australia*)

SIDNEY, Thomas Stafford [1863–1917, English barrister and cricket writer]
King Willow (*W. G. up to Date: the Doings of W. G. Grace from 1887 to 1895 Inclusive*)

SIEGEL, Doris [fl. 1943, US crime writer]
Susan Wells (*Death is my Name; Murder is not Enough*)

SIEPMANN, Mary [1912–, English novelist and writer for children]
Mary Wesley (*Camomile Lawn; Speaking Terms; Second Fiddle*)

SIGERSON, George [1836–1925, Irish physician, scientist and political journalist]
An Ulsterman (*Modern Ireland: its Vital Questions*)

SILL, Edward Rowland [1841–87, US poet and essayist]
Andrew Hedbrooke (in *Atlantic Monthly*)

SILLARD, Robert M. [d. 1908, Irish writer on the theatre]
B. MacDermott (*Barry Sullivan and his Contemporaries*)

SILVERBERG, Robert [1934–, US science-fiction writer]
*Gordon Aghill; *Leonard G. Spenser; *Gerald Vance (all used in *Amazing Stories* magazine)
*Ralph Burke; *Richard Greer; * Clyde Mitchell (all used in *Fantastic Adventures* magazine)

Walker Chapman (*The Loneliest Continent*)

Ivar Jorgensen (*Stepsons of Terra*; *Starhaven*)

Calvin M. Knox (*Lest We Forget Thee, Earth*; *The Plot Against Earth*; *One of our Asteroids is Missing*)

David Osborne (*Aliens from Space*; *Invincible Barriers*)

*Robert Randall (*The Dawning Light*; *The Shrouded Planet*)

*S. M. Tenneshaw (in *Imaginative Tales* magazine)

SILVERSTEIN, Shelby [1932–, US writer for children]
Uncle Shelby (*Uncle Shelby's Zoo*; *Uncle Shelby's ABZ Book*)

SILVETTE, Herbert [fl. 1947, US physician and writer]
Barnaby Dogbolt (*Eve's Second Apple*; *The Goose's Tale*)

SIMCOX, Edith Jemima [1844–1901, English essayist and feminist writer]
H. Lawrenny (in *The Academy*)

SIMCOX, George Augustus [1841–1905, English writer]
A Rambler (*Recollections of a Rambler*)

SIME, James [1843–95, Scottish journalist, biographer and writer]
Finlay Craig (*Sunshine and Shade*)

SIMMONS, Bartholomew [1804–50, Irish poet]
Harold (used in various periodicals)

SIMMONS, George W. [1815–82, US businessman]
A Friend to American Enterprise (*Oak Hall Pictorial*)

SIMMONS, Samuel Rowe [1871–1952, Australian writer]
Oswald Gray (*Sonnets and Other Verses*)

SIMMS, William Gilmore [1806–70, US poet and novelist]
A Collegian (*Poems*)
Frank Cooper (*The Lily and the Totem*)
An Editor (*As Good As a Comedy or, The Tennesseean's Story*)

Isabel (*Pelayo or the Cavern of Covadonga*)

A South Carolinian (*Slavery in America*)

A Southron (*Michael Bonham or the Fall of Bexar*; *South Carolina in the Revolutionary War*)

SIMONDS, William [1822–59, US journalist and writer for children]
William Aimwell (*The Aimwell Stories*)

SIMPSON, Bertram Lenox [1877–1930, English linguist, traveller and orientalist]
B. L. Putnam (*The Port of Fragrance*)
B. L. Putnam Weale (*Fight for the Republic of China*; *Indiscreet Letters from Peking*)
P. Weale (*The Eternal Princess*; *The Altar Fire*; *The Temple Bells*)

SIMPSON, Mrs Evangeline M. [fl. 1883, US writer]
Van Saxon (*Marplot Cupid*)

SIMPSON, Evan John [1901–53, English novelist and playwright]
Evan John (*King's Masque*; *Stranger's Gold*)

SIMPSON, Jane Cross [1811–86, Scottish poet and hymn writer]
Gertrude (in the *Greenock Advertiser* and for *The Piety of Daily Life* and *April Hours*)

SIMPSON, John Palgrave [1807–87, English traveller, novelist and dramatist]
The Flaneur; The Flaneur in Paris (both used in *Bentley's Miscellany*)

SIMPSON, Richard [1820–76, English cleric and Shakespearian scholar]
Derlax; D. N.; Richard ap William; Rude Boreas (all used in *The Rambler*)

SIMPSON, William [1823–99, Scottish artist and illustrator]
Thomas Blot (*The Man from Mars*)

SIMS, George [1902–66, US crime and mystery writer]
Peter Ruric (*Fast One*; *Seven Slayers*)

SIMS, George Robert [1847–1922, English journalist, melodramatist and verse writer]
Dagonet (in *The Referee*)

Delacour Daubigny (*The Girl He Left Behind Him*)

SIMSON, Eric Andrew [1895–?, Scottish writer]
Laurence Kirk (*Rings on her Finger*; *The Farm at Santa Fe*)

SINCLAIR, Mrs Bertha Muzzey [1871–1940, US western novelist]
B. M. Bower (*Long Shadow*; *Outlaw Paradise*)

SINCLAIR, Sir John [1754–1835, Scottish barrister, agriculturist and politician]
A Friend to Husbandry (*The Land of Nineveh*)
President of the Board of Agriculture (*An Account of the Origin of the Board of Agriculture*)

SINCLAIR, Olga Ellen [1923–, English historical novelist and writer for children]
Ellen Clare (*Ripening Vine*)
Olga Daniels (*Lord of Leet Castle*; *The Untamed Bride*)

SINCLAIR, Upton Beall [1878–1968, US novelist and writer for children]
Clarke Fitch; Arthur Stirling (both used for writing stories for boys)
Lieutenant Frederick Garrison, USA (in the *Army and Navy Weekly* and for *Songs of our Nation*)

SINGER, Isaac Bashevis [1904–91, Polish-born US journalist and novelist]
Isaac Warshofsky (in the *Daily Forward*)

SINGLETON, Mary Montgomerie [1843–1905, English novelist and poet]
Violet Fane (*Sophy or the Adventures of a Savage*; *Through Love and War*)

SIRR, Henry Charles [1807–72, Irish traveller and writer]
Onesiphorus (in *Dublin University Magazine*)

SITWELL, Osbert [1892–1969, English poet, novelist and essayist]
Centurion (in *The Nation*)

Miles (used in both *The Nation* and *The Spectator*)
O. S. (*C. R. W. Nevinson*)

SITWELL, Sacheverell [1897–1988, English poet and writer]
Augustine Rivers (in *Art and Letters*)

SKEELS, Vernon H. [1918–, US physician and science-fiction writer]
Oscar Rossiter (*Tetrasomy Two*)

SKELTON, Sir John [1831–97, Scottish historian, biographer and writer]
A Country Tory; Dionysius Diamond; A Naturalist; An Old Campaigner (all used in *Fraser's Magazine*)
A Democrat Tory; A Western Highlander (both used in *Contemporary Review*)
Histrionicus; An Old Tory; One of the Remnant; Shirley of Balmawhipple; Your Bewildered Contributor (all used in *Blackwood's Magazine*)
Andrew Lyall Schoolmaster in Cawmeltoun (*Oor New Cawndidate*; *The Sergeant in the Hielans*)
Shirley (*Nugae Criticae*; *Summers and Winters at Balmawhipple*)
John Shirley (in *The Guardian*)
A West-Highlander (*Spring Songs*)

SKELTON, Philip [1707–87, Irish cleric, theologian and philanthropist]
An Old Man (*Senilia or, an Old Man's Miscellany*)
An Old Officer (*A Letter to the Author of Divine Analogy and the Minute Philosopher*)
Triptolemus (*The Necessity of Tillage and Granaries*)

SKENE, Felicia Mary Frances [1821–99, French-born Scottish novelist and poet]
Erskine Moir (*Through the Shadows*)
Oxoniensis (*A Test of the Truth*)
A Prison Visitor (in *Blackwood's Magazine*)
Francis Scougal (*Scenes from a Silent World or, Prisons and their Inmates*)
A Seven Years' Resident in Greece (*Wayfaring Sketches among the Greeks and Turks*)

SKENE, James Henry [1812–86, English colonial civil servant]
A British Resident Twenty Years in the East (*The Danubian Principalities*; *The Frontier Lands of the Christian and the Turk*)

SKINNER, Miss Abby [fl. 1855, US writer for children]
Aunt Abbie (*Carroll Ashton*; *Ida Wilmot*; *Ed Lee and Sailor Dick*)

SKINNER, Allan MacLean [1809–85, English barrister and writer]
Our Own Reporter (in *Bentley's Miscellany*)

SKINNER, Conrad Arthur [1889–?, English cleric and writer]
Michael Maurice (*Not in Our Stars*; *The Final Sentence*; *Frail Ghost*)

SKINNER, June Margaret [1922–, Canadian novelist]
Rohan O'Grady (*Let's Kill Uncle*; *Pippin's Journal*)

SKINNER, Mollie [1876–1955, Australian writer]
R. E. Leake (*Letters of a V. A. D.*)

SKRINE, Mrs Agnes Higginson [fl. 1890, Irish writer – mother of Mary Nesta Keane, q. v.]
Moira O'Neill (in *Blackwood's Magazine* and for *Songs of the Glens of Antrim*)

SLADE, Daniel Denison [1823–96, US physician]
Medicus (*Twelve Days in the Saddle*)

SLADEK, John Thomas [1937–, US engineer and science-fiction writer]
*Thom Demijohn (*Black Alice*)
*Cassandra Nye (*The House that Fear Built*)

SLADEN, Douglas Brooke Wheelton [1856–1947, English traveller, poetry editor and novelist]
Rose Mullion (*Seized by a Shadow*)
St Barbe (in *Pall Mall Budget*)
Reginald St Barbe (*The Princess of Inez*)

SLANEY, George Wilson [1884–1978, English journalist, artist, musician and novelist]
George Woden (*Dusk for Dreams*; *Othersmith*)
George Wouil (*Sowing Clover*; *The New Dawn*; *Paul Moorhouse*)

SLATER, Ernest [d. 1942, English engineer, novelist and lexicographer]
Paul Gwynne (*Marta*; *The Pagan at the Shrine*)

SLATER, Francis Carey [1876–1958, South African banker and poet]
Jan van Avond (*Drought: a South African Parable*)

SLAUGHTER, Frank Gill [1908–, US novelist and medical writer]
G. Arnold Haygood (*Deep is the Shadow*)
C. V. Terry (*Darien Adventure*; *The Golden Ones*)

SLAVITT, David Ritman [1935–, US poet and novelist]
Henry Sutton (*The Exhibitionist*; *Hector*)

SLEEMAN, Sir William Henry [1788–1856, English soldier in India and linguist]
An Indian Official (*An Account of Wolves Nurturing Children in their Dens*; *Rambles and Recollections of an Indian Official*)
An Officer in the Mil. and Civ. Service of the Hon. E. I. Co. (*On Taxes and Public Revenue*)

SLEEPER, John [1794–1878, US journalist and writer]
Hawser Martingale (*Mark Rowland*; *Tales of the Ocean*; *Jack in the Forecastle*)

SLENKER, Mrs Elmina D. [1827–?, US writer on worthy subjects]
Aunt Elmina (*Little Less for Little Folks*)

SLESAR, Henry [1927–, US science-fiction writer]
O. H. Leslie (*A Crime for Mothers and Others*; *Enter Murderers*)

SLOSSON, Annie T. [1838–1926, US natural historian and short-story writer]
The Youngest Member (*The China Hunters' Club*)

SMALL, Austin J. [fl.1928, English writer]
Seamark (*Master Mystery*; *The Man they Couldn't Arrest*)

SMALL, Samuel White [1851–1931, US journalist]
Old Sli (*Old Sli's Savings*)

SMALRIDGE, George [1663–1719, English cleric and writer; Bishop of Bristol]
Favonius (in *The Tatler*)

SMART, Benjamin [1756–1853, English merchant, poet and writer]
T. Ramsneb (in *Gentleman's Magazine*)

SMART, Benjamin Humphrey [1786–1872, English philologist and writer]
Francis Drake Esq. (*Memoir of a Metaphysician*)
A Follower of Locke (*A Letter to Dr Richard Whateley*)

SMART, Charles [1841–1905, Scottish-born US physician and soldier]
Polywarp Oldfellow, MD (*Driven from the Path*)

SMART, Christopher [1722–71, English writer and poet]
Quintus Flestrin (*The Hilliad, an Epic Poem*)
Fardinando Foot; Mary Midnight (both used in *The Midwife or, the Old Woman's Magazine*)
Martinus Macularius (*The Hilliad, an Epic Poem*)
Ebenezer Pentweazle (*The Horatian Canons of Friendship*)

SMEDLEY, Edward [1788–1836, English cleric, historian and poet]
A Churchman (*Religio Clerici*)
A Member of the University (*The Trial of Frederick Kendall*)
A Protestant (*Lux Renata, a Protestant Epistle*)

SMEDLEY, Francis Edward [1818–64, English novelist]
Frank Fairleigh (in *Sharpe's London Magazine*)
Francis Phiz (*Lewis Arundel*)
*Two Merry Men (*Mirth and Metre*)

SMEETON, George [fl. 1820, English printer]
Guiniad Charfy (*The Fisherman or, the Art of Angling Made Easy*)

SMELLIE, William [1740–95, Scottish printer and natural historian]
A Juryman (*An Address to the People of Scotland*)

SMILES, Samuel [1812–1904, Scottish physician, biographer and social reformer]
A Boy (*Round the World*)

SMITH, Albert Richard [1816–60, English physician, novelist, humorist and dramatist]
Jasper Buddle; Rocket (both used in the *Medical Times*)

SMITH, Alfred Aloysius [1851–1931, English merchant and traveller]
Alfred Aloysius (Trader) Horn (*The Ivory Coast in the Earlies*)

SMITH, Mrs Alice [d. 1882, English novelist]
Corisande (in the *London Graphic*)

SMITH, Arthur Douglas Howden [fl. 1925, English writer]
Allan Grant (*Spears of Destiny*; *Grey Maiden*)

SMITH, Arthur Gordon [1873–1953, English mariner and nautical writer]
Aurora (*Jock Scott, Midshipman – his Log*)

SMITH, Mrs Caroline L. [fl. 1870, US writer for children]
Aunt Carrie (*The American Home Book of Games*)

SMITH, Charles Hamilton [1776–1859, English soldier, military writer and natural historian]
An Officer on the Staff (*Costume of the Army of the British Empire 1814*)

SMITH, Charles Henry [1826–1903, US journalist and humorist]
Bill Arp (in the *Atlanta Constitution* and for *A Side-Show of the Southern Side of the War* and *The Farm and the Fireside*)

SMITH, Charles Manby [1804–80, English printer and writer]
A Journeyman Printer (*The Workingman's Way in the World*)
A Working Man (in *Tait's Edinburgh Magazine*)

SMITH, Charlotte [1749–1806, English novelist and poet]
Kenner Deene (*The Dull Stone House*; *The Schoolmaster of Alton*)
A Solitary Wanderer (*Letters of a Solitary Wanderer*)

SMITH, Dorothy Gladys (Dodie) [1896–1990, English actress, novelist and playwright]
C. L. Anthony (*Autumn Crocus*; *Theatre Royal*)
Charles Henry Percy (used for screenwriting, e.g., *Schoolgirl Rebels*)

SMITH, Edward [1818–74, English physician and medical writer]
A London Physician (*How to Get Fat*)

SMITH, Edward Ernest [1915–, Australian novelist]
Edward Lindall (*Lively Form of Death*; *A Kind of Justice*; *No Place to Hide*)

SMITH, Edward Percy [1891–1968, English merchant, politician, novelist and playwright]
Edward Percy (*If Four Walls Told*; *The Shop at Sly Corner*)

SMITH, Elisha [d. 1739, English cleric]
A Corresponding Member of the Society for Propagating Christian Knowledge (*The Law of Laws or, the Golden Rule of the Gospel*)
A Country Clergyman (*The Cure of Deism*)

SMITH, Miss Elizabeth [1776–1806, English linguist and oriental scholar]
A Young Lady lately Deceased (*Fragments in Prose and Verse*)

SMITH, Elizabeth Oakes [1806–93, US writer]
Ernest Helfenstein (*The Salamander*; *The Western Captive*)

SMITH, Elizabeth Thomasina Meade [1854–1914, English mystery novelist and writer for children]
L. T. Meade (*At the Back of the World*; *The Stormy Petrel*)

SMITH, Ernest Bramah [1868–1942, English oriental novelist and mystery writer]
Ernest Bramah (*The Wallet of Kai Lung*; *The Moon of Much Gladness*)

SMITH, Florence Margaret [1902–71, English poet and novelist]
Stevie Smith (*Novel on Yellow Paper*; *Not Waving but Drowning*)

SMITH, Frederick E. [1922–, English playwright and writer]
David Farrell (*Valley of Conflict*; *Mullion Rock*)

SMITH, Frederick R. [1845–1919, English cleric and Lancashire novelist]
John Ackworth (*Beckside Lights*; *The Coming of the Preachers*; *Doxie Dent: a Clogshop Chronicle*; *From Crooked Roots*; *Life's Working Creed*)

SMITH, Frederick William Robin [1936–85, English historian]
Robin Furneaux (*The Amazon*; *William Wilberforce*; *Rudyard Kipling*)

SMITH, George [1693–1756, English cleric and historian]
A Divine of the University of Cambridge (*An Epistolary Dissertation to the Clergy of Middlesex*)

A Lover of that Innocent and Healthful Diversion (*The Anglers Magazine*)

SMITH, George Charles [1782–1863, English mariner, preacher and philanthropist]
Capsicum (*Tarbucket*)

SMITH, George Henry [1922–, US novelist]
M. J. Deer (*A Place Named Hell*)
Jan Hudson (*Love Cult*)
Jerry Jason (*Sexodus*)
Diana Summers (*Fallen Angel*; *Love's Wicked Ways*)

SMITH, George Oliver [1911–, US electronics engineer and science-fiction writer]
Wesley Long (in *Astounding Science Fiction* magazine)

SMITH, Gerard Edward [1804–81, English cleric and botanist]
Sir Oracle, Ox. Coll. (*Stonehenge*)

SMITH, Goldwin [1823–1910, English academic and historian; vigorous commentator on current affairs in the UK and North America)
The Bystander (used in various North American journals)
A Layman (*Concerning Doubt*; *The Suppression of Doubt is not Faith*)
Oxoniensis (in *The Times*)

SMITH, Haskett [1847–1906, English cleric]
A Member of Laurence Oliphant's Colony (in *Blackwood's Magazine*)

SMITH, Helen Ainslie [fl. 1887, US writer]
Hazel Shephard (*A History of Japan in Words of One Syllable*; *A History of Russia in Words of One Syllable*)

SMITH, Helen Zenna [1896–1985, English journalist, dramatist, novelist and writer for children]
Evadne Price (*Probationer*; *Strip Girl*)

SMITH, Horatio [1779–1849, English novelist and parodist]
The late Paul Chatfield, MD (*Echoes from the Tin Trumpet*)

Mark Higginbotham; A Septuagenary (both used in *New Monthly Magazine*)
Jefferson Saunders (*The Tin Trumpet*)

SMITH, James [1775–1839, English solicitor and parodist]
Kit Cannister; Louisa Thompson (both used in *New Monthly Magazine*)

SMITH, James Hicks [1822–81, English barrister and local historian]
An Hereditary High Churchman (*Reminiscences of Forty Years*)

SMITH, John Charles [fl. 1948, English writer]
C. Busby Smith (*Gates of Beauty and Death*)

SMITH, John Cotton [1826–82, US cleric]
A New York Presbyter (*The New Missionary Society*)

SMITH, John Gordon [1792–1833, Scottish physician and jurist]
An Officer (*The English Army in France*)

SMITH, John Talbot [1855–1923, US cleric, novelist and historian]
Harry O'Brien (*The Prairie Boy*; *Saranac*; *The Solitary Island*)

SMITH, Joseph Edward Adams [1822–96, US journalist]
Godfrey Greylock (*Taghconic*)

SMITH, Julie P. [d. 1883, US novelist]
Christabel Goldsmith (*Peace Pelican, Spinster*)
Widow Goldsmith (*The Married Belle*)

SMITH, Martin Cruz [1942–, US crime and mystery writer]
Jake Logan (*Ride for Revenge*)
Martin (or Simon) Quinn (*The Devil in Kansas*; *The Midas Coffin*)

SMITH, Mrs Mary Prudence [1840–1930, US writer for children]
P. Thorne (*Jolly Good Times or, Child Life on a Farm*; *Boys of the Border*)

SMITH, Matthew Hale [1810–79, US
  journalist and preacher]
  Burleigh (*Marvels of Prayer*; *Sunshine and
  Shadow in New York*)

SMITH, Norman Edward Mace [1914–,
  English writer]
  Neil Sheraton (*Cairo Ring*; *The Princess and
  the Pilot*)
  Norman Shore (*The Lonely Russian*; *Russian
  Hi-Jack*)

SMITH, Richard Morris [1827–96, US
  writer]
  T. Lloyd Stanley (*An Outline of the Future
  Religion of the World*)

SMITH, Robert Charles [1938–, English
  crime writer]
  Robert Charles (*The Counter-Terror Mission
  Trilogy*; *Stamboul Intrigue*)
  Charles Leader (*Death of a Marine*)

SMITH, Ronald Gregor [1913–68, Scottish
  cleric and religious writer]
  Sam Browne (*Back from the Front*)

SMITH, Samuel [1836–1906, English
  merchant, politician and reformer]
  Mercator (in the *Liverpool Daily Post*)

SMITH, Sarah [1832–1911, English novelist
  and social reformer]
  Hesba Stretton (*The Doctor's Dilemma*;
  Hester Morley's Promise)

SMITH, Seba [1792–1868, US journalist]
  Maj. Jack Downing (letters in the *Portland
  Courier*)

SMITH, Sydney [1771–1845, English cleric,
  celebrated wit and letter writer]
  Mr Dyson (*Mr Dyson's Speech to the
  Freeholders on Reform*)
  Peter Plymley (*Letters of Peter Plymley*;
  Letters on the Subjects of the Catholics)

SMITH, Thomas Assheton [1776–1858,
  English politican, cricketer and
  sportsman]
  A Huntsman (*Extracts from the Diary of a
  Huntsman*)

SMITH, Walter Chalmers [1824–1908,
  Scottish cleric and poet]
  Hermann Kunst (*Olrig Grange*)
  Orwell (*The Bishop's Walk*)

SMITH, William [1727–1803, Scottish cleric
  – emigrated to America]
  Cato (letters in the *Pennsylvania Gazette*)
  A Gentleman in London (*A Letter from a
  Gentleman in London to his Friend in
  Pennsylvania*)
  A Gentleman who Has Resided in
  Pennsylvania (*A Brief state of the Province
  of Pennsylvania*)
  A Lover of his Country (*An Historical
  Account of the Expedition against the Ohio
  Indians*)
  An Officer Employed on the Expedition (*An
  Impartial Narrative of the Reduction of
  Belle Isle*)

SMITH, William [1762–1840, US lawyer and
  politician]
  A Citizen of South Carolina (*Objections to
  the Treaty of Amity*)

SMITH, William Anderson [1842–1906,
  Scottish topographer and antiquarian]
  Gowrie (*Off the Chain: Notes from the West
  Highlands*)

SMITH, Sir William Cusac [1766–1836,
  Irish jurist and writer]
  E. Barton (*Recent Scenes and Occurrences in
  Ireland*; *Miracles: a Rhapsody*)
  Paul Puck Peeradeal (*The Goblins of
  Neapolis*)
  Warner Christian Search (*Metaphysic
  Rambles*)
  A Yeoman (*A Letter to Hon. William
  Wickham*)

SMITH, William Dale [1929–, US crime
  writer]
  David Anthony (*Blood on a Harvest Moon*;
  *The Midnight Lady and the Mourning
  Man*)

SMITH, William Henry [1808–72, English philosopher, novelist, poet and dramatist]
Wool-Gatherer (used in both the *Literary Gazette* and *The Athenaeum*)

SMITHIES, Muriel [fl. 1945, Irish novelist]
Muriel Howe (*Until the Day*; *Master of Skelgale*)

SMOLLETT, Tobias George [1721–71, Scottish novelist, surgeon and writer]
Humphry Clinker (*The Expedition of Humphry Clinker*)
Alexander Drawcansir, Fencing-Master and Philomath (*A Faithful Narrative of the Base and Inhuman Arts*)
Nathaniel Peacock (*The History and Adventures of an Atom*)

SMYTH, Joseph Hilton [1901–, US publisher and writer]
Joseph Hilton (*The French Girl*)

SMYTH, Mrs Waring [fl. 1938, English writer]
Marius Lyle (*That Child*)

SNEDDEN, Robert [1880–?, Scottish-born US writer]
Robert Guillaume (*Galleon's Gold*)

SNEDEKER, Caroline Dale [1871–1956, US writer for children]
Caroline Dale Owen (*Seth Way: a Romance of the New Harmony Community*)

SNELLING, William Joseph [1804–48, US journalist]
Solomon Bell (*Tales of Travel, West of the Mississippi*)
A Free Man (*A Brief History of Andrew Jackson*)
A Resident Beyond the Frontier (*Tales of the North-West*)

SNIDER, Denton Jaques [1841–1925, US poet and writer]
Theophilus Middling (*Cosmos and Diacosmos*)

SNOW, Charles Horace [fl. 1934, English western novelist]
Charles Ballew (*Bandits of Jupiter Gulch*; *Bloodstain Trails*)

Ranger Lee (*The Sixth Bandit*; *The Silver Train*)
Gary Marshall (*Blood of the Sotone*; *Buffalo Valley*)

SNOW, Helen Foster [1907–, US writer on China]
Nym Wales (*Historical Notes on China*)

SNODGRASS, William DeWitt [1926–, US writer]
S. S. Gardons (*Remains: Poems*)

SNOWDEN, James [1860–1947, English journalist and novelist]
Keighley Snowden (*The Plunder Pit*)

SOAMES, Henry [1785–1860, English cleric and religious historian]
A Beneficed Clergyman (*A Vindication of Church and Clergy*)

SOANE, George [1790–1860, English novelist and writer]
Mask (in *Bentley's Miscellany*)

SOHL, Gerald Allen [1913–, US journalist and science-fiction writer]
Nathan Butler (*Blow-Dry*; *Kaheesh*)
Sean Mei Sullivan (*Supermanchu, Master of Kung Fu*)

SOMERS, John [1651–1716, English barrister – became Lord Chancellor]
A Person of Honour (*The True Secret History of Kings and Queens of England*)

SOMERVILLE, Alexander [1811–85, Scottish radical]
A Working Man (*The Autobiography of a Working Man*)

SOMERVILLE, Edith Anna Oenone [1858–1949, Corfu-born Irish novelist and writer on foxhunting]
Viva Graham; Geilles Herring (both used in *An Irish Cousin*)
Somerville and Ross (*An Irish Cousin*; *Naboth's Vineyard*)

SOMMER, Peter [fl. 1990, English writer on computer studies]
Hugo Cornwall (*The Industrial Espionage Handbook*; *Data Theft*; *The Hacker's Handbook*)

SOTHEBY, Hans William [1826–74, English barrister and classical scholar]
Meleager (in *Temple Bar*)

SOTHERAN, Charles [1847–1902, US journalist and writer]
Colmolyn (*Percy Bysshe Shelley as a Philosopher and Reformer*)

SOUSTER, Raymond Holmes [1921–, Canadian novelist and poet]
John Holmes (*On Target*)
Raymond Holmes (*The Winter of Time*)
Cromwell Kent (*A Book*)

SOUTAR, Gwendoline Amy [1904–, English novelist]
Sonia Deane (*Red Roses from the Doctor*)

SOUTH, Robert [1634–1716, English cleric]
A Divine of the Church of England (*Animadversions on Dr Sherlock's Book*; *Tritheism Charged upon Dr Sherlock's New Notion*)

SOUTHARD, Samuel Lewis [1819–59, US cleric]
The Rector (*A Pastoral from the Rector*)

SOUTHCOTT, Joanna [1750–1814, English eccentric prophet – farmer's daughter]
Philadelphus (*The Holy of Holies Unveiled*)

SOUTHERN, Terry [1924–, US novelist and short-story writer]
Maxwell Kenton (*Candy*)

SOUTHEY, Caroline Anne Bowles [1786–1854, English poet]
Baroness De Katzleben (*The Cat's Tail, being the History of Childe Merlin*)
Q. (in *Blackwood's Magazine*)

SOUTHEY, Robert [1774–1843, English biographer, poet and writer]
Bion (*Poems by Bion and Moschus*)

Don Manuel Alvarez Espriella (*Letters from England by Don Manuel Alvarez Espriella*)
Inchiquin (in the *Quarterly Review*)
*Professor Porson (*The Devil's Walk*)
Abel Shufflebottom (*Poems*; *Minor Poems*)
Theodorit (in the *Annual Anthology*)

SOUTHOUSE-CHEYNEY, Reginald Evelyn Peter [1896–1951, Irish crime novelist and journalist]
Peter Cheyney (*This Man is Dangerous*; *Dames Don't Care*)

SOUTHWARD, John [1840–1902, English typographer and printer]
Experienta (*The Youth's Business Guide*)

SOUTHWICK, Solomon [1773–1839, US journalist and poet]
Henry Homespun (*The Plough-Boy*)
Sherlock (*A Layman's Apology*)

SOUTHWOLD, Stephen [1887–1964, English novelist and writer for children; his original surname was Critten but he changed it by deed-poll]
Neil Bell (*Precious Porcelain*; *Bredon and Sons*)
Stephen (or S. H.) Lambert (*Portrait of Gideon Power*)
Paul Martens (*Death Rocks the Cradle*; *The Truth about my Father*)
Miles (*The Seventh Bowe*; *The Gas War of 1940*)

SOUTHWOOD, Marion [fl. 1867, US writer]
A Lady of New Orleans (*Beauty and Booty*)

SPALDING, Ruth [fl. 1970, English playwright]
Marion Jay (*With this Sword*; *Mistress Bottom's Dream*)

SPARK (née Camberg), Muriel [1918–, Scottish novelist and poet]
Muriel Camberg (*Out of a Book*)

SPEARS, Raymond Smiley [1876–1950, US writer]
Jim Smiley (*The River Prophet*; *Diamond Tolls*)

SPEDDING, James [1808–81, English literary scholar and writer]
A Railway Reader (*Companion to the Railway Edition of the Life of Bacon*)

SPEDDING, Sarah Frances [1836–1921, English novelist]
Susan Morley (*Margaret Chetwynd; Dolly Loraine*)

SPELMAN, Edward [d. 1767, English classical scholar]
A Gentleman (*A Fragment out of the Sixth Book of Polybius*)

SPELMAN, Sir John [1594–1643, English royalist and pamphleteer]
A Gentleman of Quality, a Well-Wisher both to King and Parliament (*Considerations upon the Duties both of Prince and People*)

SPENCE, Elizabeth Isabella [1768–1832, English novelist and writer]
A Lady (*Helen Sinclair*)

SPENCE, George [1787–1850, Scottish reforming jurist]
A Barrister of the Inner Temple (*The Code Napoleon*)

SPENCE, John [1812–82, Scottish physician and medical writer]
A Young Physician (*Ship and Shore ... a Tour in Old England*)

SPENCE, Joseph [1699–1768, English writer and memoirist]
Sir Harry Beaumont (*Moralities, or, Essays Fables etc.; Crito or a Dialogue on Beauty; A Particular Account of the Emperor of China's Gardens*)

SPENCE, Thomas [1750–1814, English bookseller and radical]
The Poor Man's Advocate (*Pig's Meat or Lessons from the Swinish Multitude*)
Mr Wishit (*A Supplement to the History of Robinson Crusoe*)

SPENCE, William John Duncan [1923–, English western novelist]
Jim Bowden (*Two Gun Justice; Black Water Canyon*)
Kirk Ford (*Feud Riders*)
Floyd Rogers (*Revenge Riders; Montana Justice*)

SPENCER, Ichabod Smith [1798–1854, US cleric]
A Pastor (*A Pastor's Sketches*)

SPENCER, Jill [fl. 1935, English writer]
Jay Marston (*Full Moon; Red Lava; Fool's Paradise*)

SPENCER, Thomas [1796–1853, English cleric and social reformer]
A Clergyman (*The Church of England; Clerical Conformity*)
A Somersetshire Clergyman (*The Corn-Laws and the National Debt*)

SPENCER, Mrs William Loring [fl. 1885, US writer]
May Nunez (*The Story of Mary*)

SPENDER, Brenda Elizabeth [1884–?, English journalist and writer]
Elizabeth Steward (*The Unlikely Wooing*)

SPENSER, Edmund [1552–99, English poet]
Colin Clout (*The Shepheardes Calendar; Colin Clouts Come Home Again*)

SPEWACK, Samuel [1898–1971, Russian-born US dramatist]
A. A. Abbott (*Mon Paul: the Private Life of a Privateer; Skyscraper Murder*)

SPICER, Bart [1918–, US novelist]
Jay Barbette (*Final Copy; Look Behind You*)

SPICER-JAY, Katharine Edith [d. 1901, English novelist]
E. Livingstone Prescott (*The Apotheosis of Mr Tyrawley; Helot and Hero*)

SPILLANE, Frank Morrison [1918–, US crime writer]
Mickey Spillane (*Vengeance is Mine!; Kiss Me Deadly*)

SPINCKES, Nathaniel [1653–1727, English cleric and religious writer]
A Non-Juror (*No Just grounds for the New Communion Office*; *No Sufficient Reason for Restoring Prayers*)

SPRIGG, Christopher St John [1907–37, English aviation expert, crime novelist and writer – killed in the Spanish Civil War]
Christopher Caudwell (*Studies in a Dying Culture*; *Illusion and Reality*; *This my Hand*)

SPRIGG, William [fl. 1659, English philosopher and pamphleteer]
A Lover of his Country (*A Modest Plea for an Equal Commonwealth against Monarchy*)

SPRING, Samuel [1746–1819, US cleric]
Theophilus (*An Essay on the Discipline of Christ's House*)

SPURGEON, Charles Haddon [1834–92, English preacher and religious writer]
John Ploughman (*John Plougman's Talk: Plain Advice to Plain People*)

SPURGIN, John [1797–1866, English physician and philosopher]
Medicus Cantabrigiensis (*Wisdom, Intelligence and Science*; *On Division Among the Churches*)

SPURSTOWE, William [1605–66, English Puritan cleric]
*Smectymnuus (*An Answer to a Book etc.*)

SQUIER, Ephraim George [1821–88, US diplomat and archaeologist]
Samuel A. Bard (*Waikna or, Adventures on the Mosquito Shore*)

SQUIRE, Francis [fl. 1845, Irish farmer]
Ofellus (in *Dublin University Magazine* and for *The West Country Farmer*)

SQUIRE, Sir John Collings [1884–1958, English journalist, poet and parodist]
Solomon Eagle (*Essays at Large*; *Books in General*)
A. N. Other (*Pick-Me-Up*)

SQUIRE, Samuel [1713–66, English cleric and historian; Bishop of St David's]
Duncan MacCarte, a Highlander (*A Letter to John Trot-Plaid Esq.*)
Theophanes Cantabrigiensis (*The Ancient History of the Hebrews Vindicated*)

STABLEFORD, Brian M. [1948–93, English science-fiction writer]
Brian Craig (in *Science Fantasy* magazine)

STABLER, Jennie Latham [d. 1882, US novelist]
Jennie Woodville (*Left to Herself*)

STABLES, Gordon [1840–1910, Scottish physician and writer for children]
Medicus (in *Girl's Own Paper*)

STACK, Nicolette Meredith [1899–, US novelist and writer for girls]
Kathryn Kenny (*Blue Jacket Mystery*; *Marshland Mystery*)

STACKHOUSE, Alfred Long [1811–76, English cleric]
The Secretary of the Society for Promoting Christian Knowledge among the Jews (*Darkness Made Light: or The Story of Old Sam*)

STACKHOUSE, Thomas [1677–1752, English cleric, theologian and historian]
A Clergyman of the Church of England (*The Misery and Great Hardship of the Inferiour Clergy*)
Philalethes (*Memoirs of F. Atterbury ... Bishop of Rochester*)

STACPOOLE, Henry De Vere [1863–1951, English physician, poet and writer]
Tyler De Saix (*The Vulture's Prey*)

STAFFORD, William [1593–1684, English Parliamentarian pamphleteer]
An English Subject (*The Question Disputed*; *Reason of the War*)

STANFORD, Charles Stuart [1805–73, Irish cleric and academic]
Anthony Poplar (in *Dublin University Magazine*)

STANHOPE, Philip Dormer [1694–1773, 4th Earl of Chesterfield; politician and essayist]
Senacherib Ragman of St Giles (*The Speech of Senacherib Ragman of St Giles to his Fellow Prisoners*)

STANLEY, Arthur Penrhyn [1815–81, English cleric and ecclesiastical historian]
A Spectator (in *MacMillan's Magazine*)

STANLEY, Edward [1779–1849, English cleric, natural historian and social reformer; Bishop of Norwich]
A Railer (in *Blackwoood's Magazine*)

STANLEY, William [1647–1731, English cleric and religious writer]
Stentor (in *The Tatler*)

STANTON, John [1826–71, US journalist]
Corry O'Lanus (letters to the *Brooklyn Daily Eagle*)

STANTON-HOPE, William Edward [1889–1961, English writer for children]
Stanton Hope (*Rolling Round the World for Fun*)

STAPLES, Reginald Thomas [1911–, English writer]
James Sinclair (*Warrior Queen*; *Canis the Warrior*)
M. J. Staples (*Down Lambeth Way*)
K. Stevens (*Sisters in Arms*)
Robert Tyler Stevens (*Flight from Bucharest*; *Woman of Cordova*)

STAPLETON, Augustus Granville [1800–80, English biographer and political writer]
Lex Publica (in the *Morning Herald*)
Sulpicius (in *The Times*)

STARKEY, Digby Pilot [1806–79, Irish essayist and writer]
Advena; Godfrey Massingberd (both used in *Dublin University Magazine*)
Menenius (*The Game's Up!*; *Ireland: the Political Tracts of Menenius*; *Ode Commemorative of Her Majesty's Visit*)

STARKEY, George [d. 1665, American alchemist and quack doctor]
Eirenaeus Philalethes Cosmopolita (*Three Tracts of the Great Medicine of Philosophers*)

STARKEY, James Sullivan [1879–1958, Irish actor, poet and essayist]
Seumas O'Sullivan (*The Earth Lover*; *Mud and Purple*; *Twilight People*; *The Good Girl*)

STARR, Frederick [1826–67, US cleric]
Lynceus (*Letters for the People*)

STATHAM, Francis Reginald [1844–1908, English journalist, poet and composer]
Francis Reynolds (*Alice Rushton and Other Poems*)
A South African (in *Fortnightly Review*)
A True Liberal (in *Westminster Review*)

STAUNTON, Sir George Thomas [1781–1859, English diplomat, politician and authority on China]
Sir G. Stan-Ching-Quot (*The Lamentation of Sir G. Stan-Ching-Quot, Mandarin of the Celestial Empire*)

STEARNS, Edgar Franklin [fl. 1904, US science-fiction writer]
Edgar Franklin (*Mr Hawkins' Humorous Adventures*)

STEBBING, Henry [1716–87, English cleric and preacher]
A Clergyman (*The Doctrine of Justification by Faith in Jesus Christ*)

STEBBING, William [d. 1926, English writer]
W. S. (*Outlines*)

STEBBINS, George Stanford [fl. 1870, US physician and humorist]
Ichabod Izak (*My Satchel and I*)

STEEGMULLER, Francis [1906–, US crime novelist and writer]
David Keith (*Blue Harpsichord*; *A Matter of Iodine*)
Byron Steel (*O Rare Ben Johnson*)

STEELE, Anne [1717–78, English poet and hymn writer]
Theodosia (*Poems on Subjects Chiefly Devotional; Miscellaneous Pieces in Verse and Prose*)

STEELE, Miss Francesca M. [d. 1931, English novelist and writer for children]
Darley Dale (*Fair Katherine; The Little Doctor*)

STEELE, Mary Q. [1922–, US writer for children]
Wilson Gage (*Mrs Gaddy and the Ghost*)

STEELE, Sir Richard [1672–1729, Irish dramatist, satirist, essayist and politician]
Isaac Bickerstaff (in *The Tatler*)
John Brightland (*A Grammar of the English Tongue*)
Sir John Edgar (in *The Theatre*)
English Tory; The Venerable Nestor Ironside (both used in *The Guardian*)
A Gentleman of the Army (*The Procession*)
Marmaduke Myrtle (*The Lover*)
P.; R.; T.; Z. (all used in *The Spectator*; 'Z' was used for only one letter – no. 286)
Humphrey Philroye (in *Chit-Chat*)

STEEN, Marguerite [1894–1975, English actress and novelist]
Lennox Dryden (*Ancestors*)
Jane Nicholson (*Shelter*)

STEIN, Aaron Marc [1906–, US crime and mystery writer]
George Bagby (*The Corpse with Purple Thighs; Murder at the Piano*)
Hampton Stone (*The Funniest Killer in Town; The Stranger who Couldn't Let Go*)

STEIN, Gertrude [1874–1946, US novelist and poet]
Alice B. Toklas (*The Autobiography of Alice B. Toklas*)

STEP, Edward [1855–1931, English botanist and natural historian]
James Weston (*Dick's Holidays and what He Did with Them; A Night in the Woods and Other Tales*)

STEPHEN, Sir George [1794–1879, English lawyer – emigrated to Australia]
Caveat Emptor (*The Adventures of a Gentleman in Search of a Horse*)

STEPHEN, Sir James Fitzjames [1829–94, English jurist and writer]
A Barrister (in *Saturday Review* and for *Essays*)
A Lay Churchman (in *MacMillan's Magazine*)

STEPHEN, James Kenneth [1859–92, English barrister, journalist and parodist]
J. K. S. (*Lapsus Calami; Quo Musa Tendis*)

STEPHEN, Katharine [1856–1924, English academic, librarian and writer]
Sara Brook (*French History for English Children; Three Sixteenth Century Sketches*)

STEPHEN, Sir Leslie [1832–1904, English journalist, critic and alpinist]
A Cynic (in *Cornhill Magazine*)
A Don (in *Pall Mall Gazette* and for *Sketches from Cambridge*)

STEPHENS, Ann Sophia [1813–86, US novelist]
Jonathan Slick (*High Life in New York*)

STEPHENS, Frederic George [1828–1907, English critic and writer on art]
Laura Savage (in *The Germ*)

STEPHENS, James [1825–1901, Irish civil engineer and republican]
A Silent Politician (*On the Future of Ireland*)

STEPHENS, James [1882–1950, Irish poet and novelist]
James Esse (*Hunger: a Dublin Story*)

STEPHENS, John Lloyd [1805–52, US lawyer and traveller]
An American; George Stephens (both used in *Incidents of Travel in Egypt, Arabia Patraea etc.*)

STEPHENS, Louise G. [fl. 1905, US writer]
Katharine (*Letters from an Oregon Ranch*)

STEPHENSON, Benjamin [1768–1822, English poet]
Ebn Osn (*Attempts at Poetry*)

STEPHENSON, Raymond Meadows [1904–, English engineer and poet]
Stephen Meadows (*Along the Shingle Shore*)

STERLING, Sir Anthony Coningham [1805–71, Scottish soldier and military writer]
A Staff Officer (*Letters from the Army in the Crimea 1854–1856*)

STERLING, Edward [1773–1847, Irish journalist and barrister]
Vetus (in *The Times* and for *The Letters of Vetus 1812*)

STERLING, John [1806–44, Scottish cleric and writer]
Archaeus (in *Blackwood's Magazine*)

STERN, David [1909–, US writer]
Peter Stirling (*Stop Press – Murder!*)

STERN, Elizabeth Gertrude [1889–1954, Polish-born US novelist]
Eleanor Morton (*Josiah White, Prince of Pioneers*)

STERN, James [1904–, Irish writer]
Andrew St James (*The Twins of Nuremberg – a Translation*)

STERN, Philip van Doren [1900–84, US journalist and writer]
Peter Storme (*How to Torture your Friends; The Thing in the Brook*)

STERNE, Laurence [1713–68, Irish cleric, satirist and humorist]
Tristram Shandy Gent. (*The Life and Opinions of Tristram Shandy Gent.*)
Mr Yorick (*Letters from Mr Yorick to Eliza; A Sentimental Journey; The Sermons of Mr Yorick*)

STETSON, Amos W. [fl. 1864, US merchant]
A Boston Merchant (*Our National Debts and Currency*)

STEUART, Sir Henry Seton [1759–1836, Scottish agriculturist]
George Frederic Sydney (*A History of Cataline's Conspiracy*)

STEVENS, Abel [1815–97, US cleric and essayist]
An Itinerant (*Sketches and Incidents*)

STEVENS, Mrs Frances Moyer Ross [fl. 1948, US writer]
Christopher Hale (*Murder in Tour; Exit Screaming*)

STEVENS, Frederick Waeir [1865–1926, US lawyer and businessman]
An Obscure Mediocrity (*Observations by an Obscure Mediocrity*)

STEVENS, George Alexander [1710–84, English actor, humorist and writer]
Sir Henry Humm (*Distress upon Distress*)
A Lady (*The Female Inquisitor*)
Paulus Purgantius Pedasculus (*Stress upon Stress ... a Burlesque*)
Peter (*The Birth-Day Folly*)

STEVENS, John Austin [1827–1910, US historical writer]
Knickerbocker (*Resumption of Specie Payment*)

STEVENS, William [1732–1807, English pamphleteer and biographer]
A Layman (*An Essay on the Nature of the Christian Church*)
Nobody (*The Works of Nobody*)

STEVENSON, Florence [fl. 1980, US romantic novelist]
Zandra Colt (*The Cactus Rose*)
Lucia Curzon (*Queen of Hearts; The Dashing Guardian*)
Zabrina Faire (*Lady Blue; Romany Rebel*)
Ellen Fitzgerald (*A Novel Alliance; The Irish Heiress*)

STEVENSON, John Hall [1718–85, English writer and eccentric]
A. S. (*Crazy Tales*)
Cosmo, Mythogelastick Professor and F. M. S. (*Makarony Fables*)

Eugenius (*Yorick's Sentimental Journey Continued*)
An Independent (*A Pastoral Puke*)
An Independent Teacher of the Truth (*A Pastoral Cordial*)
Antony Shandy (*Two Lyric Epistles*)

STEVENSON, Robert Louis [1850–94, Scottish novelist, poet, dramatist and traveller]
Captain George North (in *Young Folks Magazine for Treasure Island*)

STEWART, Alexander Patrick [1813–83, Scottish physician and medical writer]
A Presbyterian Scot (*Divide and Conquer*)
A Westminster Elector (*Principle is Policy*)

STEWART, Alfred Walter [1880–1947, Scottish scientist and crime writer]
J. J. Connington (*Norden Holt's Million*; *Murder in the Maze*)

STEWART, Charles Montague Duncan [d. 1897, Scottish soldier]
Charles Montague (in *Longman's Magazine*)

STEWART, Charlotte [1863–1918, Scottish writer]
Allan MacCaulay (*Black Mary*)

STEWART, Sir James Denham [1713–80, Scottish lawyer]
Robert Frame (*Considerations on the Interests of Lanark*)

STEWART, John Innes Mackintosh [1906–, Scottish academic and crime writer]
Michael Innes (*Appleby on Ararat*; *The Daffodil Affair*)

STEWART, Kenneth Livingston [1894–?, US writer]
Kenneth Livingston (*The Dodd Cases*)

STEWART, Nick [fl. 1943, English writer]
*Nap Lombard (*The Grinning Pig*; *Tidy Death*; *Murder's a Swine*)

STIFLE, June [1940–, US dramatist and writer for children]
Maria Campbell (*People of the Buffalo*; *Riel's People*)

STILES, Ezra [1727–95, US cleric and educationalist]
Philagathos (*A Poem Commemorative of Goffe, Whalley and Dixwell*)

STILLE, Alfred [1813–1900, US physician]
Dr Ellits (*Othello and Desdemona*)

STILLINGFLEET, Benjamin [1702–71, English librettist, natural historian; acquired the sobriquet 'the blue-stocking']
Irenaeus Krantzovius (*Some Thoughts Concerning Happiness*)

STILLMAN, William James [1828–1901, US painter and journalist]
An Ex-Diplomat (in *Contemporary Review*)
A Resident in Crete (in *MacMillan's Magazine*)

STIMSON, Frederick Jesup [1855–1943, US lawyer and writer]
J. S. of Dale (*The Crime of Henry Vane*; *The Sentimental Calendar*)
*Two Gentlemen of Harvard (*Rollo's Journey to Cambridge*)

STINE, George Harry [1928–, US engineer and science-fiction writer]
Lee Correy (*And a Star to Steer By*; *Contraband Rocket*)

STIRLING, Mrs Anna Maria Wilhelmina [1865–1965, English novelist and biographer]
Percival Pickering (*A Life Awry*; *The Spirit is Willing*; *Toy Gods*; *A Pliable Marriage*)

STOCK, John Edmonds [1774–1835, English physician]
A Layman (*Unitarianism Tried by Scripture and Experience*)

STOCK, Joseph [1740–1813, Irish biographer and historian]
An Eye-Witness (*A Narrative of What Passed at Killala*)

STOCKDALE, Percival [1736–1811, Scottish cleric and writer]
Agricola (letters in the *Public Advertiser*)

STOCQUELER, Joachim Hayward
[1800–85, English historian and military writer]
James H. Siddons (*A Familiar History of British India*; *Norton's Handbook to Europe*)
Major Worthington (*The Old Field Officer or, The History and Sporting Adventures of Major Worthington*)

STODDARD, Charles Warren [1842–1909, US writer and poet]
Pip Pepperpod (in *The Golden Era*)

STODDARD, John Lawson [1850–1931, US traveller and religious writer]
An American Agnostic (*Rebuilding a Lost Faith*)

STODDARD, William Osborn [1835–1925, US writer]
Col. Cris Forrest (*The Crawling Snake*)

STODDART, Thomas Tod [1810–80, Scottish poet and writer on angling]
An Angler (*An Angler's Rambles and Angling Songs*)
Louis Fitzgerald Tasistro (in *Graham's Magazine*)

STOKE, Edward George [1919–, English writer]
Charles Clos (*Call it Experience*)
Paul Daner (*End of the Trail*)
Ross Dexter (*Carson's Killer*)
Brian Peters (*Starbuck*)
John Stark (*Marine Commando*)

STOKER, Alan [1930–, English crime and mystery writer]
Alan Evans (*Escape at Devil's Gate*; *Thunder at Dawn*)

STOKES, Francis William [fl. 1928, English crime writer]
Francis Everton (*Dalehouse Murder*; *The Young Vanish*)

STOKES, George [1789–1847, English writer]
A Lay Member of the British and Foreign Bible Society (*The Bible Society*)

STONA, Thomas [d. 1792, English cleric]
A Dumpling Eater (*A Letter to the Norfolk Militia*)

STONE, Cecil Percival [fl. 1858, English soldier]
Enos (*Philosophy for the Rifle*)

STONE, Francis [1738–1813, English Unitarian cleric and pamphleteer]
Tyro-Theologus, MA (*A Short and Seasonable Application to the Public*)

STONE, Grace Zaring [1891–1991, US novelist]
Ethel Vance (*Escape*; *Reprisal*)

STONE, John Benjamin [1838–1914, English manufacturer, traveller and writer]
Pater (*Children in Norway*)

STONE, Kate Margaret [1871–1953, Australian writer]
Sydney Partridge (*The Lie and Other Lines*; *Rocky Section*)

STONEHOUSE, John Thomson [1925–88, English writer and disgraced politician]
James Lund (*The Ultimate*)

STONEHOUSE, William Brocklehurst [d. 1862, English cleric]
Fidelis (*The Crusade of Fidelis*)

STONER, Oliver [1903–, English biographer and writer]
Morchard Bishop (*James Smetham and Francis Danby*)

STONHOUSE, Sir James [1716–95, English cleric, physician and religious writer]
A Minister (*Hints from a Minister to his Curate for the Management of his Parish*)

STONIER, George Walter [1903–85, Australian-born critic and journalist – sometime in London]
Fanfarlo (in *Penguin New Writing* and for *Shaving Through the Blitz*)
William Whitebait (in the *New Statesman*)

STOPES, Marie Carmichael [1880–1958, English physician, writer and pioneer for women's welfare]
Mark Arundel (*Don't Tell Timothy*)
Erica Fay (*The Road to Fairyland*; *Kings and Heroes*)

STOPES-ROE, Harry Verdon [1924–, English playwright]
Harry Buffkins (*The Story of Buckie's Bear*)

STOPPARD, Tom [1937–, Czech-born English playwright; his original surname was Straussler]
William Boot (used in *Scene* for drama criticism)

STORR, Catherine [1913–, English writer for children]
Irene Adler (*Freud for the Jung*)
Helen Lourie (*A Question of Abortion*)

STORRS, George [1796–1879, US cleric and writer]
Anthropos (*The Unity of Men*)
Homo Anthropos (*The Watch-Tower*)

STORRS, Lewis Austin [1866–1945, US lawyer]
S. A. Lewis (*Koheleth*)

STORY, Arthur John [1864–1938, English teacher of the deaf]
A Sympathiser (*The Freshers Don't*)

STORY, George Walter [d. 1721, Irish cleric and historian]
An Eye-Witness to the Most Remarkable Passages (*A True and Impartial History of Occurrences in the Kingdom of Ireland*)

STORY, Isaac [1774–1803, US journalist and poet]
Beri Hesdin (in the *Farmer's Weekly Museum*)
Peter Quince (*A Parnassian Shop Opened in the Pindaric Style*)
The Stranger (*Liberty, a Poem Delivered on the Fourth of July*)

STORY, Robert Herbert [1835–1907, Scottish cleric and writer]
A Parson (*Poems*)

Moses Peerie (*Nugae Ecclesiasticae*)

STOTHERT, James Augustine [1817–82, Scottish Catholic priest and writer]
A Member of the Guild (*A Short Series of Lectures on the Antiquities of Edinburgh*)

STOWE, Harriet Elizabeth Beecher [1811–96, US novelist and abolitionist]
Christopher Crowfield (*Home and Home Papers*)

STOWELL, Hugh [1799–1865, English cleric, preacher and religious writer]
A Clergyman (*The Day of Rest*)
A Clergyman of the Church of England (*The Peaceful Valley*)
A Clergyman of the Isle of Man (*An Essay on Early Rising*)

STRAHAN, James Andrew [1858–1930, Irish jurist]
Andrew James (*Ninety-Eight and Sixty Years After*)

STRAHAN, Mrs Kay Cleaver [1888–1941, US writer]
Kay Cleaver (*Desert Lake Mystery*; *Hobgoblin Murder*)

STRAHORN, Robert Edmund [1852–1944, US railway pioneer]
Alter Ego (*To the Rockies and Beyond*)

STRAIGHT, Douglas [1844–1914, English writer]
An Old Harrovian (*Harrow Recollections*)

STRAKER, John Foster [1904–87, English mystery writer]
Ian Rosse (*The Droop*)

STRANG, John [1795–1863, Scottish wine merchant, traveller and Glasgow historian]
Geoffrey Crayon (*A Glance at the Exhibition of the Glasgow Dilettante Society*)
An Invalid (*Travelling Notes of an Invalid in Search of Health*)

STRANGE, Sir John [1696–1754, English jurist]
A Late Barrister-at-Law (*A Collection of Select Cases Relating to Evidence*)

STRATEMEYER, Edward [1863–1930, US writer for children]
Capt. Ralph Bonehill (*The Island Camp*; *Off for Hawaii*)
Arthur M. Winfield (*The Rover Boys Winning a Fortune*)

STRATTON, Rebecca [d. 1982, English romantic novelist]
Lucy Gillen (*The Whispering Sea*; *The Pretty Witch*)

STRAUS, Ralph [1882–1950, English novelist and biographer]
Robert Erstone Forbes (*The Transactions of Oliver Prince*)
Ralph Strode (*Heart's Story*)

STRAUSS, Dr Gustav L. M. [1807–87, Canadian novelist and philosopher]
An Old Bohemian (*Dishes and Drinks: or Philosophy in the Kitchen*; *The Reminiscences of an Old Bohemian*; *Stories by an Old Bohemian*)

STREATFEILD, Mary Noel [1895–1986, English actress and writer for children]
Susan Scarlett (*The Man in the Dark*; *Poppies for England*)

STREET, Arthur George [1892–1966, English writer and broadcaster]
James Brian (*Fair Enough*)

STREET, Cecil John Charles [1884–1964, English writer and crime novelist]
Miles Burton (*Tragedy at the Thirteenth Hole*; *To Catch a Thief*; *Death at Low Tide*)
F. O. O. (*With the Guns*; *The Worldly Hope*)
I. O. (*The Administration of Ireland*)
John Rhode (*The Murders in Praed Street*; *Death on the Boat Train*)

STRICKLAND, Margot Teresa [1927–, Spanish-born English writer]
Margaret Worth (*I Want a Hero*; *Fanny's Country Diary*)

STRICKLAND, Samuel [1809–67, English-born emigrant to Canada]
An Early Settler (*Twenty Seven Years in Canada West*)

STRONG, Charles Stanley [1906–62, US novelist]
Nancy Bartlett (*Embassy Ball*)
William McClellan (*Waterfront Waitress*)
Kelvin McKay (*Murder at Barclay House*)
Chuck Stanley (*The Short-Horn Trail*; *Cherokee Fowler*)
Carl Sturdy (*Society Doctor*)

STRONG, George C. [1833–63, US soldier – killed in the American Civil War]
An Officer of the US Army (*Cadet Life at West Point*)

STROTHER, David Hunter [1816–88, US artist and writer]
Porte Crayon (in *Harper's Weekly* and for *The Adventures of Porte Crayon and his Cousins*)

STRUTHERS, John [1776–1853, Scottish cobbler, poet and pamphleteer]
A Layman (*Scripture Grounds for a National Church*)

STUART, Donald [1896–1980, Scottish mystery writer]
Derwen Steele (*The Black Gangster*; *The Avengers*)
Nigel Vane (*The Menace of Li-Sin*; *The Veils of Death*)
Gerald Verner (*The Squealer*; *The Ghost Man*)

STUART, Dorothy Margaret [d. 1963, Scottish historian and poet; her original surname was Browne, but she assumed her mother's maiden name by deed-poll]
D. M. S. (in *Punch*)

STUART, Isaac William [1809–61, US academic and writer]
Scaeva (*Hartford in the Olden Time: its First Thirty Years*)

STUBBES, John [1541–1600, English Puritan and political writer; his right hand was amputated as a punishment for publishing *Discovery of a Gaping Gulf*]
Scaeva (*A Defence of the English Catholics*)

STUBBS, Harry Clement [1922–, US science-fiction writer]
Hal Clement (*Mission of Gravity*; *Close to Critical*)

STUDD, Charles Thomas [1860–1931, English cricketer and missionary in China]
A Quondam Cricketer (*Quaint Rhymes for the Battle-Field*)

STUNTZ, Stephen Conrad [1875–1918, US botanist and bibliographer]
Stephen Conrad (*Mr Jim and Mrs Jimmie*; *The Second Mrs Jim*)

STURDY, William Arthur [1877–1958, English civil servant]
Isaac Didwin (*The Degeneracy of Aristocracy*; *The Open Door*; *Right and Wrong, their Relation to Literal Ethics*; *Shaking the Apple Tree*)

STURT, George [1863–1927, English wheelwright and writer]
George Bourne (*The Bettesworth Book*; *Change in the Village*)

STUTCHBURY, George Frederick [1844–1934, English financial and religious writer]
A Sexagenarian Layman (*Prayer-Book Revision*; *Notes on the Intellectual Condition of the Church of England*)

STYLES, Frank Showell [1908–, English crime writer]
Glyn Carr (*Corpse at Camp Two*; *Lewker in Tirol*)

STYLES, John [1770–1860, English preacher]
Jeremiah Ringletub (*Legend of the Velvet Cushion*)

SUDDABY, William Donald [1901–64, English science-fiction writer and writer for boys]
Alan Griff (*Lost Men in the Grass*)

SUFFIELD, Robert Rodolph [1821–91, English cleric]
A Scion of the Old Church (*Our Churches*)

SULLIVAN, Mrs Arabella [d. 1849, English writer]
A Chaperon (*Recollections of a Chaperon*)

SULLIVAN, Edward Alan [1868–1947, Canadian novelist]
Sinclair Murray (*Cornish Interlude*; *What Fools Men Are!*)

SULLIVAN, James [1744–1808, US politician]
A Citizen of Massachusetts (*The Path to Riches*)

SULLIVAN, James Frank [d. 1936, English writer]
J. F. Sunavill (*The Gnome Hatter!*)

SULLIVAN, Robert Baldwin [d. 1853, Canadian politician and jurist]
Legion (*Letters on Responsible Government*)

SULLIVAN, Timothy Daniel [1827–1914, Irish journalist, poet and writer]
Timothy O'Sullivan (*Dunboy and Other Poems*)

SUMMERFIELD, Woolfe [1897–, English barrister and writer]
Ben Mowshay (*Fraudem Bear*)

SUMMERS, Hollis Spurgeon [1916–, US novelist and poet]
Jim Hollis (*Teach You a Lesson*)

SUMMERS, Thomas Osmund [1812–82, English-born US cleric and theologian]
A Member of the Red River Conference (*Post Oak Circuit*)

SUMMERTON, Margaret [fl. 1960, English writer]
Jan Roffman (*Ashes in an Urn*; *With Murder in Mind*)

SURR, Thomas Skinner [1770–1847, English banker and novelist]
A Gentleman (*Consequences or, Adventures at Braxall Castle*)

An Individual of Thirty Years' Practical
Experience in Banking and Commercial
Affairs (*The Present Critical State of the
Country Developed*)

SURTEES, Robert Smith [1803–64, English
journalist and sporting novelist]
Mr John Jorrocks (*Jorrocks's Jaunts and
Jollities*)
Thomas Scott (in *Bell's Life in London*)
Mr Sponge (*Mr Sponge's Sporting Tour*)

SUTCLIFFE, Thomas [1790–1849, English
mariner, soldier and South American
adventurer]
The Retired Governor of the Island of Juan
Fernandez (*Sixteen Years in Chile and
Peru, 1822–39*)

SUTHERLAND, Millicent Fanny
[1867–1955, Scottish writer]
Erskine Gower (in the *National Review*)

SUTHERLAND, Robert [1909–81, English
poet]
Robert Garioch (*Big Music; Collected Poems;
The Masque of Edinburgh*)

SUTTON, Graham [fl. 1930, English writer]
Anthony Marsden (*The Mycroft Murder
Case; Death Strikes from the Rear*)

SUTTON, Sir John [1820–73, English writer]
Sutton (*A Short Account of Organs built in
England from the reign of Charles II*)

SWAFFER, Hannen [1879–1962, English
journalist]
Mr London (in the *Daily Graphic*)

SWAN, Annie S. [1860–1943, Scottish
novelist and writer for children]
David Lyall (*Married Quarters; The Sign of
the Golden Fleece; The Rise of Philip
Barrett*)

SWANSON, Harold Norling [1899–, US
literary agent and writer]
Kerry Scott (*They Fell in Love*)

SWATRIDGE, Irene Maude [fl. 1975,
English romantic novelist]
Theresa Charles (*Surgeon's Sweetheart; With
Somebody Else*)
Leslie Lance (*Man of the Family*)
Jan Tempest (*Open the Door to Love*)

SWAYNE, George Carless [1818–92, English
cleric and esayist]
Peregrinus; Tlepolemus (both used in
Blackwood's Magazine)

SWETE, John [1752–1821, English cleric and
antiquary; his original surname was
Tripe, but he assumed the name Swete]
N. E. (in *Essays by a Society of Gentleman at
Exeter*)
S. (in *Poems Chiefly by Gentlemen of
Devonshire and Cornwall*)
W. (in *The European Magazine*)

SWETNAM, Joseph [fl. 1615, English writer
and misogynist]
Thomas Tel-Troth (*The Arraignment of
Lewd, Idle, Forward and Unconstant
Women*)

SWIFT, Jonathan [1667–1745, Irish cleric,
poet, essayist, novelist and controversial
pamphleteer]
Isaac Bickerstaff (*Bickerstaff's Almanac –
1710; Predictions for the Year 1708; A
Vindication of Isaac Bickerstaff*)
Cadenus (*Cadenus and Vanessa*)
A Celebrated Author in Ireland (*A Serious
and Useful Scheme to make an Hospital*)
A Church of England Man (*The Sentiments
of a Church of England Man*)
The Copper-Farthing Dean (*The Most
Wonderful Wonder that Ever Appeared*)
Signor Corolini (*A Key: Observations upon
the Travels of Lemuel Gulliver*)
The Dean of St Patrick's (*A Proposal for
giving Badges to Beggars in all the Parishes
of Dublin*)
D. J. S. D. D. D. S. P. D. (*The Mishap*)
The Drapier (*The Hibernian Patriot*)
M. B. Drapier (*The Drapier Letters; A Letter
to the whole People of Ireland; A Letter to*

the Shop-Keepers, Tradesman, Farmers and Common People of Ireland)

Sieur Du Baudrier (*A New Journey to Paris*)

E. F. (*A Letter of Advice to a Young Poet*)

An Enemy to Peace (*A Learned Comment upon Dr Hare's Excellent Sermon*)

Jack Frenchman (*Jack Frenchman's Lamentation*)

A Friend of Mr St__le (*The Importance of the Guardian Considered*)

A Friend of the Author (*Mr C___n's Discourse of Free-Thinking put into Plain English*)

Lemuel Gulliver (*Travels into Several Remote Nations of the World*)

Hibernia (*A Letter from a Lady of Quality against Woods Half-Pence*)

Thomas Hope (*The Swearer's Bank*)

Mary Howe (*A Letter to Miss Susannah Neville*)

The Injured Lady (*The Story of the Injured Lady being a True Picture of Scotch Perfidy*)

J. S. (*Saint Patrick's Purgatory*; *The Beast's Confession to the Priest*)

J. S. D. D. D. S. P. D. (*The Place of the Damn'd*)

Martinus Scriblerus (*The Art of Sinking in Poetry*)

A Member of the House of Commons in Ireland (*A Letter from a Member of the House of Commons in Ireland to a Member of the House of Commons in England*)

Gregory Misosarum (*A Preface to the B___p of S__r__m's Introduction ...*)

A Modern Lady (*The Journal of a Modern Lady*)

A Nodus (*Some Reasons against the Bill ... Hemp, Flax etc.*)

A Person of Honour (*Some Advice Humbly Offer'd to the October Club*)

A Person of Quality (*A Letter to a Young Gentleman ... Holy Orders*; *The Tale of a Nettle*; *An Answer to Bickerstaff*)

T. M. Philomath (*A Famous Prediction of Merlin the British Wizard*)

Sir Humphrey Polesworth (*Law is a Bottomless Pit*)

Publicola (*A Letter to the People of Ireland*)

Tom Pun-Sibe (*The Art of Punning*)

Abel Roper (*Cursory but Curious Observations of Abel Roper*)

A Small Courtier (*The New Way of Selling Places at Court*)

Rev. Dr S___T (*The Lady's Dressing Room*)

Tom Tinker (*Wood's Plot Discover'd*)

Dr Andrew Tripe (*A Letter from the Facetious Dr Andrew Tripe at Bath*)

An Upper Servant (*Advice to Servants by an Upper Servant*)

Simon Wagstaff (*A Complete Collection of Genteel and Ingenious Conversation*)

William Wood (*A Petition to the People of Ireland*)

SWINBURNE, Algernon Charles
[1837–1909, English poet, essayist and critic]

An English Republican (*Notes of an English Republican on the Muscovite Crusade*)

Thomas St Kilda Maitland (letter in *The Examiner*)

Mrs Horace Manners (*A Year's Letters*)

SWINBURNE, Henry [1743–1803, English traveller and writer]

Porcustus (in *Gentleman's Magazine*)

SWINNERTON, Thomas [d. 1554, English Protestant cleric]

John Roberts (*A Mustre of Scismatyke Bysshoppes of Rome*)

SWINTON, Sir Ernest Dunlop [1868–1951, Indian-born English soldier and military writer; invented the word 'tank']

Backsight Forethought (*The Defence of Duffer's Drift*)

Ole-Luk-Oie (*The Green Curve*)

SYKES, Arthur Ashley [1684–1756, English cleric and controversialist]

A Clergyman (*The Safety of the Church under the Present Ministry*)

A Clergyman in the Country (*A Modest Plea for the Baptismal Notion of the Trinity*)

A Clergyman of the Church of England (*An Answer to the Non-Juror's Charge of Schism*)

A Curate of London (*A Letter to the Earl of Nottingham*)

Eugenius Philalethes (*The Innocency of Error*)

Joshua Freeman (*A Letter to Robert Moss and Thomas Gooch*)

A Gentleman of the Temple (*The Reasons Alledged against Dr Rundle's Promotion*)

A Lover of his Country (*A Letter to a Friend*)

A Lover of Truth and Peace (*The Eternal Peace of the Church*)

Cornelius Paets (*An Humble Apology for St Paul*)

Philalethes (*True Grounds of the Expectation of the Messiah*)

SYKES, Christopher Hugh [1907–86, English novelist and biographer]
*Richard Waughburton (*Innocence and Design*)

SYKES, Mrs Olive [1839–1909, US writer, actress and journalist]
Chroniqueuse (*Photographs of Paris Life*)

SYMINGTON, David [1904–84, English writer]
James Halliday (*I Speak of Africa*; *A Special India*)

SYMONDS, Arthur [1806–77, English barrister and essayist]
A Parliamentary Secretary (*Practical Suggestions for Reform of the House of Commons*)

SYMONDS, Emily Morse [d. 1936, English playright and novelist]
George Paston (*A Bread and Butter Miss*; *A Pharisee's Wife*)

SYMONS, Dorothy Geraldine [1909–, English writer for children]
Georgina Groves (*Morning Glory*)

SYNGE, Edward [1659–1741, Irish cleric and religious writer]
A Church of England Divine (*Free Thinking in Matters of Religion*)
A Private Gentleman (*A Gentleman's Religion*)

SYNGE, Mark [1871–1921, English soldier in India]
Powell Millington (*On the Track of the Abor*)

SYNGE, William Webb Follett [1826–91, English diplomat and writer]
A Retired Judge (*Bumblebee Bogo's Budget*)

T

TAAFFE, Dennis [1743–1813, Irish cleric, nationalist, historian and pamphleteer]
Julius Vindex (*Succinct Views of Catholic Affairs*; *Antidotes to Cure the Catholicophobia*; *Goliah Beheaded with his own Sword*; *Vindication of the Irish Nation*)

TAIT, Archibald Campbell [1811–82, Scottish cleric; Archbishop of Canterbury]
A Resident Member of Convocation (*Hints on the Formation of a Professorial System in Oxford*)

TAIT, Euphemia Margaret [fl. 1925, English writer]
John Ironside (*The Marten Mystery*; *The Red Symbol*; *The Call Box Mystery*)

TALBOT, Mrs Catherine [1721–70, English essayist and devotional writer]
Sunday (in *The Rambler*)

TALBOT, Charles Remington [1851–91, US cleric and novelist]
John Brownjohn (*Miltiades Peterkin Paul*; *Don Quixote Jr.*)
Magnus Merriweather (*Royal Lowrie*)

TALBOT, Miss Hannah Lincoln [fl. 1866, US writer]
Parke Danforth (*Not in the Prospectus*)

TALFOURD, Thomas Noon [1795–1854, English lawyer, politican and tragedian]
An Old Templar (in *New Monthly Magazine*)

TALIAFERRO, Harden E. [1818–75, US writer]
Skitt (in the *Southern Literary Messenger* and for *Fisher's River: North Carolina Scenes*)

TANN, Jennifer [1939–, English academic]
Geoffrey Booth (*Industrial Archaeology*)

TANNER, Edward Everett [1921–, US writer]
Patrick Dennis (*Auntie Mame*; *Little Me*)
Virginia Rowans (*House Party*; *Love and Mrs Sargent*)

TANNER, Henry [1849–1935, English architect]
An Eye-Witness (*The Martyrdom of Lovejoy*)

TANNER, Thomas [1674–1735, English cleric and antiquarian; Bishop of St Asaph]
Tho. Narjenn (*A Sober Whisper Concerning the Evils of Things Present*)

TAPPAN, David [1753–1803, US theologian]
Toletus (*Two Friendly Letters from Toletus to Philalethes*)

TAPPAN, Lewis [1788–1873, US merchant]
A Gentleman in Boston (*A Letter from a Gentleman in Boston to a Unitarian Clergyman in that City*)

TARBOX, Increase Niles [1815–88, US cleric and writer for children]
Uncle George (*Uncle George's Stories*)

TARDY, Miss Mary T. [fl. 1870, US biographer]
Ida Raymond (*Southland Writers*)

TARKINGTON, Newton Booth [1869–1946, US novelist and dramatist]
Cornelius Obenchain Van Loot (*The Collector's Whatnot*)

TARLETON, John Walter [1811–80, English mariner]
An Officer of the Royal Navy (in *Blackwood's Magazine*)

TASKER, William [1740–1800, English poet and writer]
An Impartialist (*An Ode to Curiosity*)

TATHAM, Edward [1749–1834, English cleric, pamphleteer and controversialist]
The Rector of Lincoln College (*A New Address to Members of Convocation*)

TATTERSALL, George [1817–49, English artist and sporting illustrator]
Wildrake (*Cracks of the Day*; *The New Sporting Almanac for 1843*; *Pictorial Gallery of English Race-Horses*)

TAYLER, Charles Benjamin [1797–1875, English cleric and writer of religious works for children]
A Country Curate (*May You Like It*)
Rev. Allan Temple (*The Will-Forgers*)

TAYLOR, Abraham [fl. 1725, English cleric and controversialist]
A Dissenting Country Gentleman (*The Scripture Doctrine of the Trinity Vindicated*)

TAYLOR, Ann [1782–1866, English poet and writer for children]
A. (*The Wedding Among the Flowers*)
*Several Young Persons (*Original Poems for Infant Minds*)

TAYLOR, Charles [1756–1823, English engraver and writer]
Francis Fitzgerald (in the *Artist's Repository*)

TAYLOR, Constance Lindsay [1907–, English crime writer]
Guy Cullingford (*Third Party Risk*; *Brink of Disaster*)

TAYLOR, Daniel [1738–1816, English Baptist cleric and religious writer]
A Lover of all Mankind (*Observations on the Rev. Andrew Fuller's Late Pamphlet*)
Philagathus (*Practical Improvement to the Divinity of Christ*)

Philalethes (*Candidus Examined with Candour*)

TAYLOR, Edgar [1793–1839, English lawyer and translator of Grimm's tales]
H. B. Denton (*Lord Brougham's Local Courts Bill Examined*)

TAYLOR, Miss Frances Magdalen [1832–1900, English volunteer nurse in the Crimea]
A Lady Volunteer (*Eastern Hospitals and English Nurses*)

TAYLOR, Frederick Chase [1897–1950, US humorist]
Lemuel Q. Stoopnagle (*You Wouldn't Know Me from Adam*)

TAYLOR, George Ledwell [1788–1873, English architect and archaeologist]
An Octogenarian Architect (*The Auto-Biography of an Octogenarian Architect*)

TAYLOR, Henry [1711–85, English cleric and religious writer]
Indignatio (*Confusion Worse Confounded, Rout on Rout*)
Benjamin Ben Mordecai (*The Apology of Benjamin Ben Mordecai to his Friends for Embracing Christianity*)

TAYLOR, Sir Herbert [1775–1839, English soldier, linguist and political secretary]
An Officer who Served under Marquis Cornwallis (*An Impartial Relation of the Military Operations in Ireland ... August 1798*)

TAYLOR, Jane [1783–1824, English poet and writer for children; wrote *Twinkle, Twinkle, Little Star*]
Q. Q. (in *Youth's Magazine*)
*Several Young Persons (*Original Poems for Infant Minds*)

TAYLOR, Jeremy [1613–67, English cleric, preacher, poet and theologian; Bishop of Down and Connor]
A Learned and Reverend Divine (*Christ's Yoke an Easy Yoke*)

A Learned Prelate (*Christian Consolations Taught*)

TAYLOR, John [1580–1653, English poet and Thames waterman – known as the Water Poet]
Thorny Ailo (*A Full Answer against A Tale in a Tub*)
John Alexander, a Joyner (*Love One Another: a Tub Lecture*)
Aminadab Blower (*Some Small and Simple Reasons Delivered in Waltham Forrest*)
My-Heele Mendsoale (*A Tale in a Tub*)
Sir Gregory Nonsence (*Sir Gregory Nonsence, his Newes from No Place*)
Antho. Roily (*A Brief Relation of the Gleanings of Miles Corbet*)
The Sculler (*Taylor's Water-Works*)

TAYLOR, John [1750–1824, US lawyer and writer on agriculture]
A Citizen of Virginia (*Arator*)

TAYLOR, John [1781–1864, English publisher and writer]
Verus (*Currency Explained*)

TAYLOR, Katherine [1893–?, Australian writer for children]
David Hamline (*Ginger for Pluck*)

TAYLOR, Lois Dwight [1903–79, US novelist and writer for children]
Caroline Arnett (*Clarissa; Theodora*)

TAYLOR, Margaret Stewart [fl. 1978, English writer]
Margaret Collier (*Scars Remained*)

TAYLOR, Philip Meadows [1808–76, English civil servant in India, journalist and novelist]
P. McTeague (in *Dublin University Magazine*)

TAYLOR, Phoebe Atwood [1909–76, US crime and mystery novelist]
Freeman Dana (*Murder at New York's World Fair*)
Alice Tilton (*The Iron Hand; Dead Ernest*)

TAYLOR, Thomas [1618–82, English Quaker and religious writer]
One who Hath Obtained Mercy to be a Minister of the Gospel (*Jacob Wrestling with God and Prevailing*)

TAYLOR, Thomas [1738–1816, English Wesleyan cleric and religious writer]
Philalethes (*An Appeal to the Public, whether a Calvinist etc.*)

TAYLOR, Tom [1817–80, English barrister, dramatist and journalist and editor of *Punch*]
John Noakes (*Barefaced Impostors*)
Romany Rai (in the *Illustrated London News*)

TAYLOR, William [1765–1836, English traveller, translator and writer]
R. O.; Ryalto (both used in the *Annual Anthology*)

TAYLOR, William Cooke [1800–49, Irish writer]
A Bible Student (*Travelling Sketches in Egypt and Sinai – a Translation*)
Censor (*The Quarterly Reviewer Reviewed*)
A Munster Farmer (*Reminiscences of Daniel O'Connell*)
Coquilla Sertorius, Benedictine Abbot of Glendalough (in *Bentley's Miscellany*)
W. C. T. (*Readings in Biography*)

TEAGUE, John Jessop [1856–1929, English cleric]
Morice Gerard (*A Gentleman of London; Under the Red Star*)

TEED, Cyrus R. [1839–1908, US cleric]
Koresh (*The Immortal Manhood; The Mystery of the Two Gentiles*)

TEGG, Thomas [1776–1845, English bookseller and publisher]
Peter Parley (*Peter Parley's Tales about Christmas*)

TEILHET, Darwin [1904–, US writer]
Cyrus Fisher (*The Avion my Uncle Flew; Ab Carmody's Treasure*)

TELFORD, Thomas [1757–1834, Scottish engineer]
Eskdale Tam (in *Ruddiman's Magazine*)

TEMPLE, Anthony [1723–95, English cleric]
A Serious Enquirer (*Objections to Mr Lindsey's Interpretation etc.*)

TEMPLE, M. H. [fl. 1902, English writer]
*Caroline Lewis (*Clara in Blunderland*; *Lost in Blunderland*)

TEMPLE, Sir William [1555–1627, English writer and Provost of Trinity College, Dublin }
Francis Mildapettus Navarrenus (*Admonitio*)

TEMPLE, Sir William [1628–99, English traveller, diplomat and essayist – grandson of above]
A Person of Honour (*Miscellanea*)

TEMPLETON, Edith [1916–, English writer]
Louise Walbrook (*Gordon*)

TENNANT, Emma [1937–, English journalist and novelist]
Catherine Aydy (*The Colour of Rain*)

TENNANT, William [1784–1848, Scottish poet and oriental scholar]
William Crookley (*The Anster Concert*)
A Member of the Musomanik Society of Anstruther (*The Dominie's Disaster*)

TENNENT, Sir James Emerson [1804–69, Irish barrister, politician and traveller; adopted his wife's surname by royal licence in 1831]
Sir James Emerson (*Picture of Greece*; *Letters from the Aegean or Grecian Islands*; *History of Modern Greece*)

TENNEY, Edward Payson [1835–1916, US cleric and writer]
Spriggs (*Jubilee Essays: a Plea for an Unselfish Life*)

TENNYSON, Alfred, Lord [1809–92, English Poet Laureate]
Alcibiades (in *Punch* for 'Literary Squabbles' in the February and March editions of 1846)

Merlin (in *The Examiner*)
Two Brothers (*Poems*, published in 1827, being the joint work of the three Tennyson brothers – Alfred, Charles and Frederick)

TERHUNE, Mary Virginia [1830–1922, US novelist]
Marion Harland (*The Hidden Path*; *Christmas Holly*)

TESSIER, Ernest Maurice [1885–1973, French novelist]
Maurice Dekobra (*Shanghai Honeymoon*; *The Man who Died Twice*)

THACKERAY, William Makepeace [1811–63, Indian-born English novelist, essayist and humorist]
Benjamin Bendigo; Mr Brown; Growley Byles; Folkstone Canterbury; Fitzroy Clarence; The Contributor at Paris; Charles James De La Pluche Esq.; Frederick Haltamount de Montmerency; Baldomero Espartero; The Fat Contributor; A Gentleman of the Force; Gobemouche; Leontius Androcles Hugglestone; Burgomaster Humpffenstrumpffen; G. P. R. Jeames Esq.; A Lady of Fashion; Goliah Muff; Mulligan of Kilballymulligan; Lady Nimrod; An Old Paris Man; Jacob Omnium's Hoss; One of Themselves (and for *The Snobs of England*); Our Own Bashi-Bazouk; Under Petty; Mr J___s Plush; The Poet Laureate; Policeman X 54; Harry Rollicker; Mr Snob; Corydon Soyer; Alonzo Spec, Historical Painter; Swellmore; Miss Tickletoby; Michael Angelo Titmarsh (also in *Fraser's Magazine*) (all used in *Punch*)
Barber Cox (in the *Comic Almanack*)
Henry Esmond (*The History of Henry Esmond*)
George Savage Fitz-Boodle; G. F. B.; Jemimah Grundy; M. A. T.; O. Y.; Demetrius Rigmarolovicz; Nelson Tattersall Lee Scupper Esq., Late Ensign in Her Majestie's Horse-Marines; Small John; Ikey Solomons Junr. (also for

Catherine); Napoleon Putnam Wiggins of Passimaquoddy; C. J. Yellowplush (all used in *Fraser's Magazine*)

Goliah Gahagan, Sometimes with Titles Major and H. E. I. C. S. (in *Ainsworth's Magazine*)

Barry Lyndon Esq. (*Memoirs of Barry Lyndon*)

Theresa McWhirter (in *George Cruikshank's Table Talk*)

Arthur Pendennis (*The Newcomes*)

T. T. (letters to *The Constitutional*, in the *New York Corsair*, 24.8.1839, and also in *Fraser's Magazine*, 18.1.1840)

Lancelot Wagstaff Esq. (in *New Monthly Magazine*)

Theophile Wagstaffe (*Flore et Zephyr*)

THATCHER, Benjamin Bussey [1809–40, US lawyer]
A Bostonian (*Traits of the Tea Party*)

THAYER, Alexander Wheelock [1817–97, US lawyer, diplomat and musical biographer]
The Late J. Brown (*Signor Masoni and the Papers of the Late J. Brown*)

THAYER, Emma Redington [1874–1973, US crime writer]
Lee Thayer (*Dusty Death*; *No Holiday for Death*)

THAYER, Tiffany [1902–, US crime writer]
John Doe (*Eye-Witness!*)
Elmer Ellsworth Jr. (*The Illustrious Corpse*)

THELWALL, John [1764–1834, English poet, elocutionist and controversialist]
John Beaufort (*The Daughter of Adoption*)
Sylvanus Theophrastus (*The Peripatetic*)

THICKNESSE, Philip [1717–92, English colonial governor and writer]
An Eye-Witness (*An Account of Persons in the Prisons in Paris*)
Junius (in *The Crisis*)
Thomas London; A Piece of an Antiquary (both used in *Gentleman's Magazine*)
One of the Jurymen (*An Account of the Four Persons Found Starved to Death etc.*)

P. T. Esq. (*Junius Discovered*)
A Wanderer (in both *Gentleman's Magazine* and *St James Chronicle*)

THIMBLETHORPE, June Sylvia [1926–, English historical novelist]
Sylvia Thorpe (*Devil's Bondsman*; *Tarrington Chase*)

THIRKELL, Angela Margaret [1890–1961, English novelist]
Leslie Parker (*Trooper to the Southern Cross*)

THIRLWALL, Thomas [d. 1827, English cleric]
An Independent Freeholder (*A Calm Address to Sir Francis Burdett*)

THOM, Robert [fl. 1839, English orientalist]
Sloth (*Esop's Fables by Munmooy Seen-Shang*; *The Lasting Resentment of Miss Keasu Lwan Wang*; *Wang Kerou-Lwan Pih Neen Han – a Translation*)

THOM, William [1798–1848, Scottish weaver and poet]
A Handloom Weaver (*Rhymes and Recollections of a Handloom Weaver*)

THOMAS, Antony Charles [1928–, English academic]
Percy Trevelyan (*Mr Holmes in Cornwall*)

THOMAS, Sir Charles Inigo [1846–1929, English naval architect]
Charles Winthrop (*A Petticoat Prince*)

THOMAS, Craig [1942–, English mystery novelist]
David Grant (*Moscow 5,000*; *Emerald Decision*)

THOMAS, Dylan Marlais [1914–53, Welsh poet]
Dylan Marlais (in the February 1927 issue of *Boy's Own Paper*, for a poem, *The Second Best*, which he had plagiarized from an earlier issue of the same magazine)

THOMAS, Mrs Elizabeth [1677–1731, English poet – Dryden's Corinna]
A Lady (*A Dramatic Pastoral*; *Poems on Several Occasions*)

THOMAS, Mrs Elizabeth [1771–?, English poet and novelist]
Bridget Bluemantle (*The Baron of Falconberg*; *The Prison House*)
An Old Wife of Twenty Years (*Purity of Heart*)

THOMAS, Ernest [1904–83, Welsh teacher and novelist]
Richard Vaughan (*Moulded in Earth*; *Son of Justin*; *There is a River*; *Who Rideth So Wild*)

THOMAS, Eugene, [1893–?, US writer]
Donald Grey (*Exiled to Heaven*; *The Morning After*)

THOMAS, Evelyn Ward [1928–, English mystery novelist]
Evelyn Anthony (*Grave of Truth*; *Occupying Power*)

THOMAS, George Francis [fl. 1884, US writer]
George Francis (*Legends of the Land of the Lakes*)

THOMAS, John Daniel [1853–1930, US writer]
Ichabod Crane (*The School-Child*)

THOMAS, John Wesley [1798–1872, English Wesleyan cleric and translator of Dante]
Anti-Empiricus (*The War of the Surplice*)

THOMAS, Josiah [d. 1820, English cleric]
Christopher Climax Esq. (*Riot*)

THOMAS, Philip Edward [1878–1917, English poet of Welsh parentage, biographer and writer – killed at Arras]
Edward Eastaway (in *An Annual of New Poetry* and *This England* and for *Six Poems*)
Llewellyn the Bard (in *Beautiful Wales*)
Edward Thomas (*The Heart of England*; *South Country*)

THOMAS, Ralph [fl. 1880, English bibliographer]
Olphar Hamst (*The Handbook of Fictitious Names*)
Ralph Harrington (*A Few Words on Swimming*)

THOMAS, Reginald George [1899–1960, English writer for children]
Jane Preston; Judy Thomas (both used in *Girl's Crystal*)

THOMAS, Ronald Wills [fl. 1954, US writer]
Ronald Wills (*Food for Fishes*; *Big Fish*)

THOMAS, Ross E. [1926–, US mystery writer]
Oliver Bleeck (*Protocol for a Kidnapping*; *No Questions Asked*)

THOMAS, Theodore L. [1920–, US lawyer and writer]
Leonard Lockhard (in *Astounding Science Fiction* magazine)

THOMAS, Vaughan [1775–1858, English cleric and historian]
A Lover of the Fine arts (*Thoughts on the Cameos and Intaglios of Antiquity*)
A Member of Convocation (*The Legality of the Present Academical System*)

THOMAS, William Moy [1828–1910, US journalist and writer]
Q. (in the *New York Round Table*)

THOMPSON, Alexander Mattock [1861–1948, German-born English journalist and playwright]
Dangle (*Dangle's Mixture*; *Dangle's Rough-Cut*)

THOMPSON, Antony [1939–, English writer]
Antony Alban (*Catharsis Central*)

THOMPSON, Arthur Leonard Bell [1917–75, English crime writer]
Francis Clifford (*Hunting Ground*; *Naked Runner*)

THOMPSON, Daniel Pierce [1795–1868, US lawyer, journalist and novelist]
A Member of the Vermont Bar (*The Adventures of Timothy Peacock Esq.*)

THOMPSON, D'Arcy Wentworth [1829–1902, English classical scholar]
A Schoolmaster (*Day Dreams of a Schoolmaster*)

THOMPSON, Edward [1738–86, English mariner, dramatist, poet and writer of sea-shanties]
Sailor (*A Sailor's Letters from 1754–1759*)

THOMPSON, Edward Anthony [1928–, English crime writer]
Anthony Lejeune (*News of Murder*; *Duel in the Shadows*)

THOMPSON, Edward Healy [1813–91, English journalist and essayist]
A Recent Convert (*A Few Earnest Thoughts on the Catholic Church*)

THOMPSON, Edward Raymond [1872–1928, English journalist and political writer]
E. T. Raymond (*All and Sundry*; *Uncensored Celebrities*)

THOMPSON, George Selden [1929–, US biographer and writer for children]
George Selden (*The Old Meadow*; *The Cricket in Times Square*)

THOMPSON, Grace Elsie [fl. 1935, English writer]
Camilla Hope (*Curiously Planned*)

THOMPSON, Sir Henry [1820–1904, English surgeon, astronomer and medical writer]
Pen Oliver (*Charlie Kingston's Aunt*; *All But: a Chronicle of Laxenford Life*)

THOMPSON, Hugh Miller [1830–1902, Irish-born US cleric and theologian; Bishop of Illinois]
A Presbyter of the Diocese of Illinois (*Unity and its Restoration*)

THOMPSON, John Baptiste de Macklot [fl. 1925, US writer]
Ozark Ripley (*Modern Bait and Fly Casting*; *Sport in Field and Forest*)

THOMPSON, Sir John Perronet [1873–1935, English civil servant in India]
Al Carthill (*False Dawn*; *The Garden of Adonis*; *The Lost Dominion*)

THOMPSON, John William McWean [1920–, English journalist]
Peter Quince (*Country Life*)

THOMPSON, Mortimer Neal [1828–75, US humorist and sometime actor]
Q. K. Philander Doesticks, P. B. (*Doesticks, What He Says*)
Knight Russ Ockside (*The History and Records of the Elephant Club*)

THOMPSON, Noel Henry Broadbent [fl. 1935, English journalist]
Mr Gossip (sometime in the *Daily Sketch*)

THOMPSON, Philip [1785–1848, English Quaker]
A Member of the Society of Friends (*The Remembrancer*)

THOMPSON, Thomas Perronet [1783–1869, English mariner, soldier and reforming politician]
Audi Alteram Partem (*A Catechism on the Currency*)
An Eye Witness (in *Tait's Edinburgh Magazine*)
A Member of the University of Cambridge (*A Catechism of the Corn Laws*)

THOMPSON, William [1785–1833, Irish social reformer and philanthropist]
One of the Idle Classes (*The Claims of Labour and Capital Conciliated*)

THOMPSON, William Marcus [1857–1907, Irish journalist, barrister and radical politician]
Dodo (in *Reynold's Newspaper*)
A Land-Lubber (*Sea-Doggerel*)

THOMPSON, William Tappan [1812–82, US humorist]
Major Joseph Jones (*Major Jones's Courtship*; *Major Jones's Chronicles of Pineville*)

THOMS, William John [1803–85, English historian and writer]
Ambrose Merton (*Gammer Gurton's Pleasant Stories*)
An Old Bookworm (in the *Nineteenth Century*)

THOMSON, Adam [1779–1861, Scottish cleric]
A Voluntary Advocate (*An Appeal from Scotland*)

THOMSON, Andrew Mitchell [1779–1831, Scottish cleric and religious writer]
A Minister of the Church of Scotland (*A Letter to the Rev. Dr Inglis*)

THOMSON, Anthony Todd [1778–1849, Scottish physician and medical writer]
A Physician (in *Bentley's Miscellany*)

THOMSON, George Malcolm [1848–1933, New Zealand botanist and zoologist]
Aeneas MacDonald (*Whisky*)

THOMSON, Henry [1773–1843, English painter]
Wrinkleton Fidgit; Titus (both used in *Blackwood's Magazine*)

THOMSON, James [1834–82, Scottish schoolmaster, poet and writer]
B. V. (in *The Investigator* and for *The City of Dreadful Night*)
Crepusculus (in *Tait's Edinburgh Magazine*)
Bysshe Vanolis (*The Story of a Famous Old Jewish Firm*)

THOMSON, John [1765–1846, Scottish physician and medical writer]
A Member of the Royal College of Surgeons (*A Treatise on Harrogate Mineral Waters*)

THOMSON, John Cockburn [1834–60, English orientalist and Sanskrit scholar]
Megathym Splene, BA, Oxon. (*Almae Matres*)
Philip Wharton (*Wits and Beaux of Society*)

THOMSON, Katharine [1797–1862, English historical novelist and biographer]
A Middle-Aged Man (in *Fraser's Magazine*)
Grace Wharton (*The Queens of Society*; *The Literature of Society*)

THOMSON, Richard [1794–1865, English merchant, librarian and historian]
An Antiquary; Geoffrey Barbican (both used in *Chronicles of London Bridge*)

THOMSON, William [1746–1817, Scottish cleric and writer]
An English Gentleman (*A Tour in England and Scotland in 1785*)
Rev. James Hall (*A Tour Through Ireland*; *Travels in Scotland by an Unusual Route*)
The Man of the People (*The Man in the Moon*)
Thomas Newte (*Prospects ... on a Tour in England and Scotland*)
An Officer of Colonel Baillie's Detachment (*Memoirs of the Late War in Asia*)
Charles Stedman (*The History of the Origin of the American War*)
Andrew Swinton (*Travels into Norway, Denmark and Sweden*)

THOMSON, Dr William [1820–83, English physician in Australia]
Cerimon (*The Political Purpose of Renascence Drama*)

THORBURN, Grant [1773–1863, Scottish writer – emigrated to USA]
Lawrie Todd (*Men and Manners in Great Britain*; *Forty Years' Residence in America*; *Lawrie Todd's Notes on Virginia*)

THOREAU, Henry David [1817–62, US naturalist and recluse]
A Yankee (*A Yankee in Canada*)

THORLEY, Wilfred Charles [1878–1963, English poet and writer for children]
Harley Quinn (*A Caboodle of Beasts*; *Quinn's Quiz*)

THORN, William [1794–1870, English cleric]
Biblicus (*Is Salvation by Water Baptism the Doctrine?*; *The History of Tithes,*

Patriarchal, Levitical etc.; Religious Consistency Enforced)

Theta (*The History of the Thorn Tree and Bush*)

THORNTON, Bonnell [1724–68, English humorist and writer]
A. (in *The Adventurer*)
Rev. Busby Birch (*City Latin: or Critical and Political Remarks on the Latin Inscription ...*)
A Deputy (*Plain English in Answer to City Latin*)
Fustian Sackbut (*Ode on Saint Cecelia's Day*)
Priscilla Termagent (in the *Spring Garden Journal*)
Roxana Termagent (in the *Drury Lane Journal*)
*Mr Town, Critic and Censor General (*The Connoisseur*)

THORNTON, Henry [1818–1905, English actor and dramatist]
Henry Thornton Craven (*Milky White; Meg's Diversion; Too True*)

THORNTON, Robert John [1768–1837, English physician, botanist and writer]
A Friend to Improvements (*The Philosophy of Medicine*)
An Independent (*The Politician's Creed*)
A Lover of Social Order (*The Politician's Creed*)

THORP, Joseph Peter [1873–1962, English typographer – former Jesuit]
T. (in *Punch* for drama criticism)

THORPE, Thomas Bangs [1815–78, US humorist and essayist]
The Bee-Hunter (*Mysteries of the Backwoods*)
Logan (*The Master's House*)
Tom Owen, the Bee-Hunter (*The Hive of Tom Owen, the Bee-Hunter*)
Lynde Weiss (*An Autobiography*)

THRALE (née Salusbury), Hester Lynch [1741–1821, Scottish correspondent and

friend of Samuel Johnson; Piozzi was the name of her second husband]
An Old Acquaintance of the Public (*Three Warnings to John Bull before He Dies*)
Hester Lynch Piozzi (*Anecdotes of the Late Samuel Johnson*)

THREEPLAND, Moncrieff [d. 1838, Scottish lawyer]
Timothy Plain (*Letters Respecting Performances at the Theatre Royal*)

THRING, Edward [1821–87, English educationalist and writer]
Benjamin Place (*Education and School; Thoughts on Life Science*)

THURSTON, Miss Ida Treadwell [1848–1918, US novelist and writer for children]
Marion Thorne (*The Torch Bearer; The Captain of Cadets*)

TIBBLES, Percy Thomas [1879–1938, English magician]
Selbit (*The Magic Art of Entertaining; The Magical Entertainer; The Magician's Handbook*)

TICKELL, Richard [1751–93, English barrister, dramatist and satirist]
Elizabeth O'Neil (*Opposition Mornings*)

TICKELL, Thomas [1686–1740, English poet and translator]
A Gentleman in England (*A Poem in Praise of the Horn-Book*)

TIERNAN, Frances Christine Fisher [1846–1920, US novelist]
Christian Reid (*Valerie Aylmer; The Land of the Sun*)

TIERNEY, John Lawrence [1892–1972, Australian novelist]
Brian James (*First Furrow; Orchards; Cookabundy Bridge; The Advancement of Spencer Button*)

TILLETT, Dorothy Stockbridge [1896–, US crime novelist]
John Stephen Strange (*Come to Judgment; Silent Witness*)

TILLOCH, Alexander [1759–1825, Scottish journalist and writer]
Biblicus (in *The Star*)

TILTON, James [1745–1822, US physician and writer]
Timoleon (*The Biographical History of Dionysius*)

TILTON, Theodore [1835–1907, US journalist, poet and writer]
Sir Marmaduke (*The Sexton's Tale*)

TIMBS, John [1801–75, English journalist and writer]
Horace Welby (*Mysteries of Life, Death and Futurity; Predictions Realised in Modern Times*)

TIMROD, Henry [1829–67, US poet and essayist]
Aglaus (in the *Southern Literary Messenger*)

TINDAL, Henrietta Euphemia [1816–79, English poet]
Diana Butler (*The Heirs of Blackridge Manor*)

TINDAL, Matthew [1657–1733, English controversialist]
Anti-Pastor (*A Second Address to the Inhabitants of London and Westminster*)

TITTERINGTON, Mrs Sophie Bronson [1846–?, Indian-born US writer for children]
Grace Graham (*Everyday Wonders; Mabel Livingstone; A New Endeavour*)

TITUS, Eve [1922–, US writer for children]
Nancy Lord (*My Dog and I*)

TODD, Barbara Euphan [1890–1976, English writer for children]
Barbara Bower (*Miss Ranskill Comes Home*)
Euphan (*The Seventh Daughter; South Country Secrets*)

TODD, Margaret [1859–1918, Scottish physician and novelist]
Graham Travers (*Mona MacLean; The Way of Escape*)

TODD, Ruthven [1914–, Scottish poet, novelist and writer for children – lived in USA]
R. T. Campbell (*Bodies in a Bookshop; Unholy Dying*)

TOFTE, Robert [d. 1620, English traveller, translator and poet]
Gervis Markham (*Ariosto's Satyres – a Translation*)

TOLAND, John [1670–1722, Irish pamphleteer and controversial theologian]
Britto-Batavius (*The Description of Epsom in a Letter to Eudoxa*)
James Junius Eoganesius (*Pantheisticon ... Sodalitatis Socraticae*)
Hierophilus (*A Word to Honest Priests*)
Patricola (*The State Anatomy of Great Britain; The Second Part of the State Anatomy*)

TOLKIEN, John Ronald Reuel [1892–1973, English academic and fantasy writer]
J. R. R. T. (in the *Stapledon Magazine*)
Oxymore (in the *Oxford Magazine*)

TOLLIVER, Steve [fl. 1968, US writer]
*Fredric Davies (*The Man From U. N. C. L. E. 14*)

TOMALIN, Ruth [1916–, Irish journalist, novelist and writer for children]
Ruth Leaver (*Green Ink; The Sound of Pens*)

TOMLINS, Elizabeth Sophia [1763–1828, English writer]
A Lady and her Brother (*Tributes of Affection: With the Slave and Other Poems*)

TOMLINS, Frederick Guest [1804–67, English journalist and drama critic]
Littlejohn (in the *Weekly Times*)
One of the Public (*Major and Minor Theatres*)

TOMLINS, Thomas Edlyne [1762–1841, English barrister and legal writer]
A Barrister of the Inner Temple (*A Familiar Plain Explanation of the Law of Wills*)

TOMLINSON, Nicholas [1765–1847, English mariner and privateer]
An Old Seaman (*Arius Slain and Socinus Mortally Wounded*)

TOMSON, Arthur [1859–1905, English landscape artist]
Verind (in the *Morning Leader*)

TONE, Theobold Wolfe [1763–98, Irish barrister and nationalist – condemned to death but committed suicide]
A Northern Whig (*An Argument on behalf of the Catholics of Ireland*)

TONNA, Charlotte Elizabeth [1790–1846, Irish writer and poet; militant Protestant who composed Orange songs]
C. E. (*Maternal Martyrdom*)
Charlotte Elizabeth (*The Siege of Derry*; *Chapters and Flowers*; *The Maiden City*)

TOOKE, John Horne [1736–1812, English philologist and controversial politician; his original surname was Horne, and he assumed Tooke in 1782]
An Englishman (*The Petition of an Englishman*)
A Freeholder of Surrey; Strike but Hear (both used in the *Public Advertiser*)
Parson H**ne (*Apostate Ecclesiastic*)

TOOKE, Thomas [1774–1858, English pamphleteer and political economist]
A Non-Alarmist (*A Few Words on our Relations with Russia*)

TOOTEL, Hugh [1672–1743, English Catholic theologian]
Charles Dodd (*Certamen Utriusq: Ecclesiae*; *Dodd's Church History of England*)
A True Briton (*Remarks upon Bishop Burnet's History of his Own Time*)

TOPLADY, Augustus Montague [1740–78, English cleric, hymn and theological writer]
Clerus; A Presbyter of the Church of England (both used in *The Church of England Vindicated from the Charge of Arminianism*)

An Hanoverian (*An Old Fox Tarr'd and Feathered*)

TORDAY, Ursula [fl. 1960, English crime and mystery writer]
Paula Allardyce (*Marriage Has Been Arranged*)
Charity Blackstock (*Dream Towers*; *Shirt Front*)
Lee Blackstock (*All Men are Murderers*)
Charlotte Keppel (*Ghosts of Fontenoy*; *Villains*)

TORRENS, Arthur Wellesley [1809–55, English soldier – wounded at Inkerman]
A Field Officer (*Six Familiar Lectures for the Use of Young Military Officers*)

TORRENS, Henry Whitelock [1806–52, English writer and civil servant in India]
*Bartolozzi Brown, Gent. (*Polyglot Baby's Own Book*)
An Indian Civil Servant (*Madame De Malguet*)

TORRENS, Robert [1780–1864, Irish soldier and political economist]
A Member of the Political Economy Club (*The Budget – A Series of Eight Letters*)

TORREY, Elizabeth R. [fl. 1856, US writer]
Catius Junior (*Theognis, a Laugh in the Cavern of Evil*)

TORREY, Ware [fl. 1960, US writer]
Lee Crosby (*Doors to Death*; *Terror by Night*)

TORROP, C. [fl. 1829, English writer]
Proteus Porcupine (*The Dramatic Censor*)

TOTTEN, Charles Adriel Lewis [1851–1908, US soldier, inventor and writer]
Ten Alcott (*Gems, Talismans and Guardians ... Lore of Nativity*)

TOUP, Jonathan [1713–85, English cleric and classical scholar]
Johannes Toupius (*Emendationes in Suidam*)

TOURGEE, Albion Winegar [1838–1905, US lawyer and novelist]
Henry Churton (*A Royal Gentleman*; *Toinette, a Tale of Southern Life*)
One of the Fools (*A Fool's Errand*)

TOWERS, Joseph [1737–99, English cleric and biographer]
An Independent Citizen of London (*Observations on Public Liberty, Patriotism etc.*)

TOWGOOD, Micaijah [1700–92, English cleric and writer]
A Christian (*Serious Thoughts on Church and Religion*)
A Dissenter (*The Dissenter's Apology*; *A Dissent from the Church of England Fully Justified*)
The Dissenting Gentleman (*The Dissenting Gentleman's Answer to the Reverend Mr White's Three Letters*)

TOWLE, Eleanor Ashworth [1847–1912, English novelist]
E. M. Archer (in *MacMillan's Magazine*)

TOWNE, Charles Wayland [1875–?, US journalist and humorist]
O. B. Hayve (*Foolish Etiquette*)
Gideon Wurdz (*Eediotic Etiquette*; *Foolish Finance*; *The Foolish Dictionary*)

TOWNE, John [1711–91, English cleric and controversialist]
An Impartial Hand (*The Argument of the Divine Legation*)

TOWNSEND, George Alfred [1841–1914, US journalist and essayist]
A Broadway Lounger (in the *New York Tribune*)
Gath (*Bohemian Days*; *Katy of Catoctin*; *President Cromwell*)
Laertes (*Washington, Outside and Inside*)
A Non-Combatant (*Campaigns of a Non-Combatant*)

TOWNSEND, George Henry [d. –1869, English editor]
An English Critic (*Shakespeare Not an Impostor*)

John Green (*Evans's Music and Supper Rooms*)
Paddy Green (*Glees and Madrigals*)

TOWNSEND, John [1757–1826, English cleric, founder of deaf and dumb asylum]
A Dissenting Minister (*Remarks on the Charge of the Bishop of St Davids*)

TOWNSEND, Joseph [1739–1816, English physician, cleric and writer]
A Well-Wisher to Mankind (*A Dissertation on the Poor-Laws*)

TOWNSEND, Mary Ashley [1832–1901, US poet and writer]
Xariffa (in the *New Orleans Delta* and for *Poems* and *Down the Bayou*)

TOWNSEND, William Charles [1803–50, English barrister and historian]
A Graduate of the University of Oxford (*The Dawn of Freedom*)

TOWNSHEND, Charles [1725–67, English politician]
A Land-Owner (*National Thoughts*)

TOWNSHEND, Chauncey Hare [1798–1868, English cleric and poet]
Timothy Crusty Esq.; A Proser (both used in *Blackwood's Magazine*)
T. Greatley (*Philosophy in the Fens*)

TOWNSHEND, Horatio [1750–1837, Irish cleric and writer]
Paddy Pumps; Senex (both used in *Blackwood's Magazine*)

TOZER, Aaron [fl. 1749, English journalist and writer]
An Impartial Hand (*A Blow at the Root*)

TOZER, Basil [1896–1949, English journalist]
20-Bore (*Practical Hints on Shooting*)

TRABUE, Isaac H. [1829–1907, US farmer, lawyer, freethinker and socialist]
General Punta Gorda (*The Black Wench*)

TRACY, Donald Fiske [1905–, US journalist and writer]
Roger Fuller (*Second Try*; *Sign of the Pagan*)

TRACY, Louis [1863–1928, English journalist and novelist]
Gordon Holmes (*The Late Tenant*; *By Force of Circumstances*)

TRACY, Roger Sherman [1841–1926, US writer]
T. Shirley Hodge (*The White Man's Burden: a Satirical Forecast*)

TRACY, Uriah [1755–1807, US politician]
Scipio (*Scipio's Reflections on Monroe's View*)

TRAGETT, Margaret Rivers [1855–1964, English sportswoman and novelist]
Margaret Larminie (*Deep Meadows*)

TRAHERNE, Thomas [1637–74, English poet and religious writer]
A Faithful Son of the Church of England (*Roman Forgeries*)

TRANTER, Nigel Godwin [1909–, Scottish romantic and historical novelist]
Nye Tredgold (*Trail Herd*; *Dynamite Trail*)

TRASK, George [1798–1875, US cleric and reformer]
Ziba Sproule (*The Diary of Solomon Spittle*; *A Brief Epistle to Ladies of the Upper Ten Thousand*)
Uncle Simeon Toby (*Thoughts and Stories on Tobacco*)

TREADWELL, Daniel [1791–1872, US inventor and educator]
*Two Readers of Darwin's Treatise on The Origin of Species (*A Discussion between Two Readers etc.*)

TREBY, Paul Ourry [1786–1862, English sporting writer]
The Foxhunter Rough and Ready (in the *Sporting Magazine*)

TREFFRY, Richard [1771–1842, English cleric]
Testis Oculatis (*The Chatham Races*)

TRELAWNEY, Edward John [1792–1881, English adventurer – he was buried alongside Shelley]
A Younger Son (*Adventures of a Younger Son*)

TRENCH, Francis Chenevix [1805–86, English cleric and writer]
Oxoniensis (*A Ride in Sicily*)

TRENCHARD, John [1662–1723, Irish lawyer and political pamphleteer]
*Cato (*A Discourse of Standing Armies*)
J. Truncheon Esq. (*The Secret History of the Trust*)

TRENHAILE, John [1792–1867, English poet]
A Cornubian (*Recreations in Rhyme*)

TREVATHAN, Robert E. [1925–, US western novelist]
Trev. Roberts (*Dead in the Saddle*)

TREVELYAN, Sir Charles Edward [1807–86, English civil servant in India and Governor of Madras]
Indophilus (*The Baropakhya Christians*; *The Letters of Indophilus*)

TREVELYAN, George Macaulay [1876–1962, English historian]
G. M. T. (*The Meredith Pocket Book*)

TREVELYAN, Sir George Otto [1838–1928, English historian and politician]
H. Broughton (*The Dawk Bungalow or, Is His Appointment Pukka?*)
A Competition Wallah (in *MacMillan's Magazine*)

TREVENEN, Miss Emily [1785–1856, English poet]
A Lady (*Little Derwent's Breakfast*)

TRIEM, Paul Ellsworth [fl. 1930, US writer]
Paul Ellsworth (*Alias John Doe*)

TRIMBLE, Barbara Margaret [1921–, Welsh mystery writer]
B. M. Gill (*Death Drop*)

TRIMBLE, Louis Preston [1917–, US scientific writer]
Stuart Brock (*Killer's Choice*; *Death is my Lover*)

TRIMMER, Eric [1923–, English physician and writer]
Eric Jameson (*The National History of Quackery*)

TRIPP, Miles Barton [1923–, English mystery writer]
Michael Brett (*Bridegroom Rose Early*; *Long Shot*)

TRISTRAM, John Geoffrey [1929–, Lord Oaksey; racing journalist]
Audax (in *Horse and Hound*)
Marlborough (in the *Daily Telegraph*)

TROLLOPE, Anthony [1815–82, English novelist]
One of the Firm (in *Cornhill Magazine* and for *The Struggles of Brown, Jones and Robinson*)

TROLLOPE, Constance Alexina Napier [1869–?, English essayist]
H. C. Tilney (in *Temple Bar*)
H. C. Trollope (in *Longman's Magazine*)

TROLLOPE, Frances Eleanor [1830–1913, English traveller and essayist]
A New Writer (*Aunt Margaret's Trouble*)

TROLLOPE, Joanna [1943–, English romantic novelist]
Caroline Harvey (*Legacy of Love*)

TROTTER, Catherine [1679–1749, English dramatist and writer on ethics]
Catherine Cockburn (her married name, used from 1708 for *A Letter to Dr Holdsworth* and *Remarks on Rutherford's Essay on the Nature and Obligation of Virtue*)

TROTTER, Lionel James [1827–1912, English essayist]
A Latter Day Philosopher (in *Dublin University Magazine*)

TROWBRIDGE, John Townsend [1827–1916, US journalist and writer]
Paul Creyton (*Brighthopes*; *Martin Merivale, his Mark*)

TROWER, Charles Francis [1817–91, English barrister and writer]
An Old Sussex Cricketer (*Sussex Cricket, Past and Present*)

TRUEBRIDGE, Benjamin Arthur [1882–1955, Australian, musician, poet and writer]
Brian Vrepont (*Plays and Flower Verses for Youth*; *Beyond the Claw*)

TRUMBULL, John [1750–1831, US poet and satirist]
The Correspondent (in the *Connecticut Journal and New Haven Post Boy*)

TRUSLER, John [1735–1820, English cleric and writer]
An Old Stager (*The Master's Last and Best Gift to his Apprentice*)
A Pupil of the late Dr W. Hunter (*The Practice of Midwifery*)

TRUSS, Leslie Seldon [1892–1990, English novelist]
George Selmark (*Murder in Silence*)

TRYON, Thomas [1634–1703, English philosopher]
Philotheos Physiologus (*The Countryman's Companion*; *Friendly Advice to the Gentleman Planters of the West Indies*; *A Treatise of Dreams and Visions*; *Monthly Observations for the Preserving of Health*; *The Way to Health, Long-Life and Happiness*; *The Way to Make All People Rich*)

TUBB, Edwin Charles [1919–, English science-fiction and western writer]
Chuck Adams (*Trail Blazers*)
Jud Cary (*Sands of Destiny*)
J. F. Clarkson (*Men of the Long Rifle*)
James S. Farrow (*Vengeance Trail*)
James R. Fenner (*Colt Vengeance*)
Charles S. Graham (*Wagon Trail*)
Charles Grey (*The Wall*; *Enterprise 2115*)
Volsted Gridban (*Alien Universe*; *Reverse Universe*)
Alan Guthrie (in *New Worlds* magazine)

George Holt (in the *British Science Fiction* magazine)
Gill Hunt (*Planetfall*)
E. F. Jackson (*Commanche Capture*)
Gregory Kern (*Galaxy of the Lost*; *The Eater of Worlds*)
King Lang (*Saturn Patrol*)
Mike Langtry (*Assignment New York*)
P. Lawrence (*Drums of the Prairie*)
Chet Lawson (*Men of the West*)
Arthur MacLean (*Touch of Evil*)
Carl Maddox (*The Living World*; *Menace from the Past*)
M. L. Powers (*Scourge of the South*)
Paul Schofield (*The Fighting Fury*)
Brian Shaw (*Argentis*)
Roy Sheldon (*The Metal Eater*)
John Stevens (*Quest for Quantrell*)
Edward Thomson (*Atilus the Gladiator*)
Douglas West (in *Authentic Stories* magazine)

TUBBS, Arthur Lewis [1867–1946, US drama critic and playwright]
Arthur Sylvester (*The Finger of Scorn*; *The Village Lawyer*)

TUCKER, Abraham [1705–74, English philosopher and academic]
Cuthbert Comment Esq. (*Man in Quest of Himself*; *Free Will, Foreknowledge and Fate*)
The Country Gentleman (*The Country Gentleman's Advice to his Son on the Subject of Political Conduct*)
Edward Search (*Light of Nature Pursued*; *Vocal Sounds*)

TUCKER, Allan James [1929–, English writer]
Bill James (*You'd Better Believe It*)

TUCKER, Charlotte Maria [1821–93, English missionary in India and writer for children]
A. L. O. E. [cryptically **A Lady of England**] (*The Children's Garland*; *The Wanderer in Africa*; *Zaida's Nursery Note-Book*)

TUCKER, George [1775–1861, US lawyer and academic]
Joseph Atterley (*A Voyage to the Moon*)
A Citizen of Virginia (*Essays on Taste, Morals and Natural Policy*)
A Virginian (*A Defence of the Character of Thomas Jefferson*)

TUCKER, James [1929–, Welsh journalist and crime novelist]
David Craig (*The Alias Man*; *Young Men May Die*)

TUCKER, John [1795–1870, English cleric]
Scrutator (*The Apparition or Ghost of Archbishop Cranmer*)

TUCKER, Josiah [1712–99, English cleric and political economist]
The Dean of Glocester (*A Sequel to Sir William Jones's Pamphlet*)
An Impartial Hand (*The Life of the Rev. Mr George Whitefield*)
A Merchant in London (*A Letter from a Merchant in London to his Nephew in North America*)
A Sincere Well-Wisher to the Trade and Prosperity of Great Britain (*Reflections on Opening the Trade to Turkey*)

TUCKER, Nathan Beverley [1784–1851, US jurist and academic]
Edward William Sidney (in the *Partisan Leader*)

TUCKERMAN, Henry Theodore [1813–71, US writer]
An American (*The Italian Sketch-Book*)
A Dreamer (*Leaves from the Diary of a Dreamer*)

TUGENDHAT, Julia [1941–, English writer for children]
Julia Dobson (*A Crisp Twins Adventure*; *The Wreck Finders*)

TUGWELL, George [1830–1910, English cleric and writer]
A Verse-Maker (*A Book of Verses*)

TULL, Jethro [1674–1741, English agricultural writer and farmer]
J. T. (*The Horse-Hoeing Husbandry*)

TULLOCH, Sir Alexander Murray [1803–64, Scottish lawyer, soldier and controversial military reformer]
Dugald Dalgetty (a name used when writing to various Indian newspapers and journals on the welfare of soldiers)

TUPPER, Martin Farquhar [1810–89, English barrister and proverbial philosopher]
Roger Oldstyle (letters to *The Times*)
Peter Query (*Rides and Reveries of Mr Aesop Smith*)

TURNBULL, Robert James [1775–1833, US physician and politician]
Brutus (*The Crisis or, Essays on Federal Government*)

TURNBULL, William Barclay David Donald [1811–63, Scottish barrister and antiquarian]
Delver into Antiquity (*Fragmenta Scoto-Monastica*; *Historic Memorials of Coldstream Abbey, Berwickshire*)

TURNER, Daniel [1710–98, English cleric and hymn writer]
Candidus (*A Modest Plea for Free Communion*)
An Impartial Hand (*The Fashionable Daughter*)
Theophilus Senex Esq. (*The Monitor or a Friendly Address*)

TURNER, John Victor [fl. 1935, English writer]
Nicholas Brady (*Coupons for Death*; *Ebenezer Investigates*)
David Hume (*Never Say Live*; *Invitation to the Grave*)

TURNER, Matthew [d. 1788, English chemist and philosopher]
William Hammon (*An Answer to Dr Priestley's Letters to a Philosophical Unbeliever*)

TURNER, Philip William [1925–, Canadian-born English playwright and writer for children]
Stephen Chance (*Septimus and the Spy Ring*)

TURNER, Samuel Hulbeart [1790–1861, US cleric and academic]
A Disciple (*Teachings of the Master*)

TURNER, William [1714–94, English cleric and religious writer]
Vigilius (in the *Theological Repository*)

TURNER, William [1761–1859, English cleric and writer]
Vigilii Filius (in the *Monthly Repository*)

TURNER, William [1788–1853, English cleric and biographer]
Vigilii Nepos (used in various periodicals)

TURNGREN, Annette [1902–80, US crime writer]
A. T. Hopkins (*Have a Lovely Funeral*)

TURTON, Thomas [1780–1864, English cleric, mathematician and controversialist; Bishop of Ely]
Crito Cantabrigiensis (*A Vindication of the late Professor Porson*)
Philalethes Cantabrigiensis (*A Letter to Edward Copleston*)

TURTON, Sir Thomas [1764–1844, English soldier]
A Country Gentleman (*An Address to the Candour of the People of England*)

TUTCHIN, John [1661–1707, English controversial pamphleteer; he was a convicted rebel who obtained a pardon by bribery]
Thomas Pitts, Gent. (*A New Martyrology*)

TUTTIETT, Mary Gleed [1847–1923, English novelist]
Maxwell Gray (in the *New Review* and for *The Silence of Dean Maitland*)

TUTTLE, Charles Richmond [fl. 1878, US historical writer]
Jean Clarke (*The Boss Devil of America*)

TWINING, Louisa [1820–1911, English social reformer]
A Radical Teetotaler (in the *National Review*)

TWINING, Thomas [1735–1804, English cleric, musician and classical scholar]
Philalethes (*A Discourse on Baptism*)

TWISS, Horace [1787–1849, English barrister, humorist and politician]
Horatius (*St Stephen's Chapel – a Poem*)

TWISS, Travers [1809–97, English barrister and legal writer]
Corvinus (*Hungary, its Constitution and its Catastrophe*)
Diplomaticus (in *Temple Bar*)

TWOMBLY, Alexander Stevenson [1832–1907, US cleric and writer]
Abner Perk (*Merry Maple Leaves*)

TWYSDEN, John [1607–88, English barrister and physician]
Another Hand (*A Short Discourse of the Religion Delivered by Jesus Christ*)

TYLER, Bennet [1783–1858, US theologian and academic]
A New England Minister (*Letters on the Origin of the New Haven Theology*)

TYLER, Daniel F. [fl. 1872, US writer for children]
Uncle Ben (*How to Get Rich!*)

TYLER, Robert [1816–77, US poet – son of President Tyler]
A Virginian (*Ahasuerus*)

TYLER, Royall [1757–1826, US playwright and novelist]
An American Youth (*The Yankey in London*)
A Citizen of the United States (*The Contrast*)
Spondee (in the *Farmer's Weekly Museum*)
Dr Updike Underhill (*The Algerine Captive*)

TYLER-WHITTLE, Michael [1927–, English writer for children]
Mark Oliver (*A Roll of Thunder; Feet of Bronze*)
Tyler Whittle (*Birth of Greece; Imperial Rome*)

TYRRELL, George [1861–1909, Irish Jesuit and theologian]
Hilaire Bourdon (*The Church and the Future*)

TYRRELL, James [1642–1718, English barrister and historian]
A Lover of Truth and of his Country (*Patriarcha Non Monarcha*)

TYRWHITT, Gerard Hugh [1883–1950, Lord Berners; diplomat, composer, novelist and dramatist]
Adela Quebec (*The Girls of Redcliff Hall*)

U

UNDERHILL, Edward Bean [1813–1901, English grocer and Baptist writer]
Eli Fant (*Struggles and Triumphs of Religious Liberty*)

UNDERWOOD, Charlotte [1914–, US writer]
Joan Charles (*Son and Stranger*; *And the Hunter Home*)

UNDERWOOD, Mavis Eileen [1916–, English writer]
Sarah Kilpatrick (*Fanny Burney*)

UNWIN, David Storr [1918–, English writer for children]
David Severn (*Hermit in the Hills*; *The Cruise of the Maiden Castle*)

UPCHURCH, Boyd Bradfield [1919–, US science-fiction and mystery writer]
John Boyd (*The IQ Merchant*; *The Doomsday Gene*)

UPDIKE, Wilkins [1786–1867, US lawyer]
A Landholder (*An Address to the People of Rhode Island*)

UPHAM, Charles Wentworth [1802–75, US cleric]
Unitarian (*The Salem Controversy*)

UPSHUR, Abel Parker [1791–1844, US jurist and politician]
A Virginian (*A Brief Enquiry into Federal Government*)

UPTON, George Putnam [1834–1919, US journalist and writer on music for children]
Peregrine Pickle (in the *Chicago Tribune* and for *Letters of Peregrine Pickle*)

UPWARD, Allen [1863–1926, English barrister, novelist and dramatist]
An English Liberal (*The Truth About Ireland*)
The Man who Heard Something (*The Slaves of Society*)
20/1631 (*Some Personalities*)

URBINO, Mrs Lavinia [fl. 1854, US writer]
Lavinia Buon Cuore (*Sunshine in the Palace or Cottage*)

URCH, Elizabeth [1921–, Irish writer]
Elise Brogan (*For God's Sake Watch your Language*)

URE, G. P. [d. 1860, Scottish-born Canadian journalist]
A Member of the Press (*The Hand-Book of Toronto*)

URE, Jean [1943–, English novelist and writer for children]
Sarah McCulloch (*Lady for Ludovic*; *Not Quite a Lady*)

URELL, William Francis [fl. 1950, US writer]
William Francis (*Kill or Cure*; *Bury Me Not*)

URNER, Nathan D. [1839–93, US journalist]
Mentor (*Never*)

URQUHART, David [1805–77, Scottish diplomat and politician]
A Resident of Constantinople (*A Statement of Facts*)

URQUHART, Sir Thomas [1611–60, Scottish writer and translator]
Christianus Presbyteromastix (*Discovery of a Most Exquisite Jewel, More Precious than Diamonds ... Worcester-Street*)

USHER, Frank Hugh [1909–, English journalist and writer]
Charles Franklin (*Death on my Shoulder*; *One Night to Kill*)

Frank Lester (*Death in Sunlight*; *Hide my Body*)

USHER, James [1720–72, Irish schoolmaster and philosopher]
A Free Thinker (in the *Public Ledger*)

V

VACZEK, Louis C. [1913–, Hungarian-born English writer]
Peter Hardin (*The Frightened Dove*; *The Hidden Grave*)

VAHEY, John George Haslette [1881–?, English novelist]
Henrietta Clandon (*Rope by Arrangement*; *The Ghost Party*)
John Haslette (*Desmond Rourke*)
Anthony Lang (*The Case with the Three Threads*; *The Crime*)
Vernon Loder (*The Men with Double Faces*; *Kill in the Ring*)
John Mowbray (*Feversham's Brother*; *Call the Yard*)
Walter Proudfoot (*Arrest*; *Conspiracy*)

VAIZEY, Mrs George de Horne [1860–1927, English writer for girls]
Jessie Mansergh (in *Girl's Own Paper*)

VALENTINE, Sir Alexander Balmain Bruce [1899–1977, English railway executive]
Fieldfare (in the *London Evening News* and for *Tramping Round London*)

VALENTINE, Mrs Laura [1814–99, English writer for children]
Aunt Louisa (*Wee Wee Stories*)

VALLENTINE, Benjamin [1843–1926, English dramatist]
Fitznoodle (in *Puck*)

VALPY, Richard [1754–1836, English cleric and educationalist]
A Clergyman (*An Address from a Clergyman*)
A Young Gentleman (*Poetical Blossoms*)

VAN ARNAM, Dave [fl. 1967, US science-fiction writer]
*Ron Archer (*Lost in Space*)

VANCE, John Holbrook [1916–, US science-fiction writer]
Peter Held (*Take my Face*)
Ellery Queen (*A Room to Die In*)
Alan Wade (*Isle of Peril*)

VANDAM, Albert Dresden [1843–1903, French-born English journalist and writer]
An Englishman in Paris (*Notes and Recollections*)

VAN DEVENTER, Emma M. [fl. 1900, US novelist]
Lawrence L. Lynch (*The Last Stroke*; *The Diamond Coterie*)

VAN NESS, William Peter [1778–1826, US jurist]
Aristides (*An Examination of the Various Charges Exhibited against Aaron Burr*)
Marcus (*Letters of Marcus*)

VAN SCHEVICHAVEN, Herman [fl. 1882, Dutch-born English writer]
Jacob Larwood (*Theatrical Anecdotes*)

VAN SLINGERLAND, Mrs Nellie B. [fl. 1905, US writer]
Neile Bevans (*Cupid, the Devil's Stoker*; *Love and Politics*)

VAN SLYKE, Helen [1919–79, US romantic novelist]
Sharon Ashton (*Santa Ana Wind*)

VAN ZELLER, Claude Hubert [1905–,
English cleric and writer]
Hugh Venning (*The End – a Projection Not
a Prophecy*)

VARNUM, Joseph Bradley [1818–74, US
lawyer]
Viator (*The Washington Sketch-Book*)

VAUGHAN, Constance [fl. 1932, English
novelist]
Olive Moore (*Fugue*)

VAUGHAN, David James [1825–1905,
English cleric and social reformer]
A Private Tutor (*A Few Words about Private
Tuition*)

VAUGHAN, Henry [1622–95, Welsh
physician and poet]
Silurist (*Olor Iscanus*; *Silex Scintillans*)

VAUGHAN, Roger William Bede [1834–83,
English Catholic cleric and theologian;
Archbishop of Sydney]
The Son of a Catholic Country Squire
(*What Does it Profit a Man?*)

VAUGHAN, Thomas [1622–66, Welsh cleric,
poet and alchemist]
Eugenius Philalethes (*Anima Magica
Abscondita*; *Anthroposophia Theomagica*;
Lumen de Lumine; *Euphrates, or the
Waters of the East*; *The Fame and
Confession of the Fraternity of R.*; *The
Second Wash or the Moore Scour'd Once
More*; *The Chymists Key to Shut and to
Open*)

VAUGHAN, William [1577–1641, English
colonial patron, poet and writer]
Orpheus Junior (*The Golden Fleece Divided
into Three Parts*)

VAUX, C. Bowyer [1824–95, US writer on
sports]
Dot (*Canoe Handling*)
*Greensward (*The Greensward Plan*)

VAWTER, J. B. [fl. 1880, US soldier]
Sergeant Oats (*Prison Life in Dixie*)

VEAL, George [fl. 1818, English musician
and satirist]
Joel Collier (*Joel Collier Redivivus*)

VEHEYNE, Ethel (Cherry) Williamson [fl.
1935, English novelist]
Jane Cardinal (*Swift Adventure*; *The Living
Idol*; *Taming of the Despot*)

VEITCH, Sophie Frances Fane [fl. 1883,
Scottish novelist and writer]
J. A. St John Blythe (*Wise as a Serpent*)

VENABLES, Terry [1943–, English footballer
and crime writer]
*P. B. Yuill (*Hazel and the Menacing Jester*;
Hazel Plays Solomon)

VENNARD, Alexander Vindex [1884–1947,
Australian writer]
Bill Bowyang (*Australian Bush Recitations*)
Frank Reid (*Toilers of the Reef*)

VERN, David [1924–, US novelist]
David V. Reed (in *Amazing Stories*
magazine)

VERNEY, Sir John [1913–92, English writer]
Trix (in *National Review*)

VERNON, Edward [1684–1757, English
mariner and pamphleteer; he was the
first to issue a grog ration]
An Honest Sailor (*Some Seasonable Advice*)

VERPLANCK, Gulian Crommelin
[1786–1870, US academic and writer]
Scriblerus Busby (*Prolegomena, Notes and
other Scholastic Trimmings*)
Abimelech Coody (*An Account of Abimelech
Coody and other Celebrated Writers*)
Brevet Major Pindar Puff (*Epistles of Brevet
Major Pindar Puff*)

VERRILL, Alpheus Hyatt [1871–1954, US
archaeologist, explorer and novelist]
Ray Ainsbury (*When the Moon Ran Wild*)

VICARY, Michael [1815–?, Irish cleric]
A Protestant Clergyman (*Notes of a
Residence at Rome in 1846*)

VICKERS, Roy [1889–1965, English crime and mystery writer]
David Durham (*The Woman Accused*; *Against the Law*)
Sefton Kyle (*The Vengeance of Mrs Danvers*; *The Notorious Miss Waters*)
John Spencer (*Swell Garrick*; *The Whispering Death*)

VICKERS, Vincent Cartwright [1879–1939, English writer]
V. C. V. (*The Google Book*)

VICTOR, Mrs Frances Fuller [1826–1902, US writer]
Florence Fane (*All Over Oregon and Washington*; *The River of the West*)

VICTOR, Mrs Metta Victoria [1831–86, US journalist and writer]
Mrs Mark Peabody (*A Woman's Heart*)
Seeley Register (*A Dead Letter*; *Figure 8 or the Mystery of Meredete Place*)

VICTOR, Orville James [1827–1910, US journalist, historian and biographer]
An American Citizen (*The American Rebellion*)

VICTOR, Thomas [1828–80, English farmer and poet]
A Traveller (*Sir Humphry Davy's Monument*)

VIDAL, Eugene Luther [1925–, US novelist, playwright and writer]
Edgar Box (*Death in the Fifth Position*; *Death Likes it Hot*; *Death Before Bedtime*)
Gore Vidal (his usual writing name, used for *Myra Breckenridge*, etc.)

VIDLER, Edward Alexander [1863–1942, English-born Australian writer]
Paul Vedder (*Dramatic Year*)

VIERECK, George Sylvester [1884–1962, German-born US poet and writer]
George F. Corners (*Rejuvenation*)

VILLIERS, George [1628–87, 2nd Duke of Buckingham; royalist, statesman, satirist and writer]
A Person of Honour (*The Chances – a Comedy Corrected by a Person of Honour*; *An Epitaph upon Thomas, late Lord Fairfax*; *Poetical Reflections on Absolom and Achitophel*)

VINES, Richard [1600–56, English Puritan cleric, schoolmaster and theologian]
*Theophilus Timorcus (*The Covenanters Plea against Absolvers*)

VINING, Elizabeth Gray [1902–, US writer for children]
Elizabeth Janet Gray (*Jane Hope*; *The Cheerful Heart*)

VINSON, Rex Thomas [1935–, English painter and writer]
Vincent King (*Light a Last Candle*; *Candy Man*)

VINTER, Michael [1927–, English novelist]
T. S. J. Gibbard (*Starseed Mission*; *Torold Core*)

VISGER, Mrs Jean A. [d. 1922, English writer]
*A Son of the Marshes (*Drift from the Long Shore*; *From Spring to Fall*; *With the Woodlanders and by the Tide*; *On Surrey Hills*)

VIVIAN, Evelyn Charles [1882–1947, English novelist and mystery writer]
Charles Cannell (*The Guarded Woman*; *Broken Couplings*)
Jack Mann (*Gees' First Case*; *Nightmare Farm*)

VIZETELLY, Ernest Alfred [1853–1922, French-born English journalist, publisher and translator]
Le Petit Homme Rouge (*The Favourites of Louis XIV*; *The Favourites of Henry of Navarre*; *Republican France 1870–1912*)

VIZETELLY, Henry [1820–94, English artist, publisher and writer]
T. Tyrwhitt Brooks (*Four Months among the Gold-Finders in Alta, California*)

VOELKER, John Donaldson [1903–91, US jurist and novelist]
Robert Traver (*Trouble Shooter*; *Anatomy of a Murder*)

VOLK, Gordon [1885–?, English writer]
Raymond Knotts (*Meeting by Moonlight*)

VON ARNIM, Elizabeth, Countess (see under Russell, Elizabeth Mary)

VON HUTTEN, Bettina [1874–1957, US writer]
Sacha Gregory (*Yellowleaf*)

VOYSEY, Charles [1828–1912, English cleric and preacher]
A Clergyman of the Church of England (*An Examination of Canon Liddon's Lectures*)

VULLIAMY, Colwyn Edward [1886–1971, English writer]
Anthony Rolls (*The Vicar's Experiments*; *Lobelia Grove*)

W

WADD, William [1776–1829, English
surgeon and medical writer]
A Member of the Royal College of Surgeons
(*Cursory Remarks about Corpulence*)
Unus Quorum (*Nugae Canorae*)

WADDELL, Charles Carey [1868–?, US
journalist, novelist and short-story writer]
Charles Carey (*Van Suyden Sapphires*; *Girl
of the Guard Line*)

WADDELL, Martin [1941–, Irish novelist
and writer for children]
Catherine Sefton (*Back House Ghosts*; *Puff
of Smoke*)

WADDELL, Peter Hately [1817–91, Scottish
cleric and literary editor]
A Minister of a Country Parish (*The Gospel
of the Kingdom*)
A Preacher of the Gospel (*A Letter to Ralph
Wardlaw DD*)
A Probationer of the Free Church of
Scotland (*Orthodoxy is Not Evangelism*)

WADDELL, Samuel J. [1879–1967, Japanese-
born Irish dramatist and actor]
Rutherford Mayne (*Turn of the Road*; *Bridge
Head*)

WADDINGTON, John [1810–80, English
cleric and religious historian]
A Parishioner (*The Wolf in the Fold*)

WADDINGTON, Samuel Ferrand [fl. 1810,
English hop merchant and political
pamphleteer]
Esculapius (*A Key to a Delicate
Investigation*)
Algernon Sidney (*An Address to the People of
the United Kingdom*)

WADE, John [1788–1875, English journalist
and writer]
Thomas Fielding (*Select Proverbs of all
Nations*)
Montaigne the Younger (in *New Monthly
Magazine*)
The Original Editor of the Black Book (*The
Black Book, an Exposition of Abuses*; *An
Appendix to the Black Book*)

WADE, Robert [1920–, US crime and
mystery writer]
*Will Daemar (*The Case of the Lonely Lovers*)
*Whit Masterson (*Badge of Evil*; *Hammer in
his Hand*)
*Wade Miller (*Guilty Bystander*; *Deadly
Weapon*)
*Dale Wilmer (*Memo for Murder*; *Dead Fall*)

WAGER, Walter Herman [1924–, US
mystery writer]
John Tiger (*I Spy*; *Mission Impossible*)

WAGSTAFFE, William [1685–1725, English
physician and writer]
Crispin the Cobler (*Crispin the Cobler's
confutation ... Ben Hoadly ...*)
A Freeholder (*The State and Condition of
our Taxes Considered*)
Toby, Abel's Kinsman (*The Character of
Richard St__le Esq.*)
Andrew Tripe MD (*The Small-Pox*)

WAINEWRIGHT, Thomas Griffiths
[1794–1852, English artist and art critic –
poisoned relatives for monetary gain and
was transported to Tasmania]
Egomet Bonmot; Janus Weathercock; Herr
Vinkbooms (all used in the *London
Magazine*)

WAINWRIGHT, John W. [1921–, English mystery writer]
Jack Ripley (*The Pig Got up and Slowly Walked Away*; *My God, How the Money Rolls In*)

WAINWRIGHT, Jonathan Mayhew [1793–1854, US cleric]
A Presbyter of the Diocese of Massachusetts (*Considerations on the Eastern Diocese*)

WAKE, William [1657–1737, English cleric; Archbishop of Canterbury]
A Country Clergyman (*A Letter from a Country Clergyman to his Brother in the Neighbourhood*)

WAKEFIELD, Edward Gibbon [1796–1862, English political pamphleteer and colonial administratror in Australia]
Robert Gouger (*A Letter from Sydney*)

WAKEFIELD, Edward Jerningham [1820–79, English colonist in New Zealand]
A Late Magistrate of the Colony (*The Handbook for New Zealand*)

WAKEFIELD, Priscilla [1751–1832, English Quaker, philanthropist and educational writer for children]
A Gentleman (*Excursions in America Described in Letters from a Gentleman*)
Priscilla **** (*Leisure Hours*)

WAKEFIELD, Thomas [1752–1806, English cleric]
Philanthropos (*Reflections on Faith*)

WALDO, Edward Hamilton [1918–85, US science-fiction witer]
Theodore Sturgeon (*Joyous Invasions*; *Venus Plus X*)

WALDRON, George [1690–1730, English poet and writer]
George Barrington (*The Genuine Life and Trial of George Barrington*; *A Voyage to New South Wales*)

WALES, Hubert [1870–1943, English novelist and writer]
William Piggott (*Mr and Mrs Villiers*; *The Wife of Colonel Hughes*)

WALEY, Simon Waley [1827–75, English stockbroker, musician and writer]
W. London (letters to *The Times*)

WALFORD, Thomas [1752–1833, Irish antiquarian]
An Irish Gentleman (*The Scientific Tourist Through Ireland*)

WALKER, Clement [d. 1651, English independent controversialist – died in the Tower of London]
Theodorus Verax (*Anarchia Anglicana*; *The Triall of Lieut. Colonell John Lilburne*)

WALKER, Mrs D. M. F. [fl. 1877, English novelist]
Helen Mar (*Mary Fairfax*)

WALKER, David Esdaile [1907–68, English journalist and writer]
David Esdaile (*Eat, Drink and Be Merry*)
Michael Power (*Religion in the Reich*)

WALKER, Sir Edward [1612–77, English herald and courtier]
A Daily Attendant on His Sacred Majesty (*Iter Carolinum*)

WALKER, Emily Kathleen [1913–, English journalist]
Kathleen Treves (*I'll Wait Beloved*; *Prior's Holt*)
Kay Winchester (*Love for Doctor Penn*; *Return to Rowanstoke*)

WALKER, George [1581–1651, English cleric and controversial theologian]
A Presbyterian Minister of London (*A Modell of the Government of the Church*)

WALKER, George [1803–79, English stockbroker and chess enthusiast]
A Chess-Player (in *Fraser's Magazine*)

WALKER, Henry [fl. 1650, English controversial journalist]
Luke Harruney (*Perfect Occurrences of Every Dayes Journall*)

WALKER, James Barr [1805–87, US cleric and philanthropist]
An American Citizen (*Philosophy of the Plan of Salvation*; *The Living Questions of the Age*)

WALKER, John [1861–1932, English cotton mill manager and politician]
Rowland Thirlmere (*The Clash of Empires*)

WALKER, Joseph Cooper [1761–1810, Irish historian and scholar]
A Member of the Arcadian Society at Rome (*An Historical Memoir on Italian Tragedy*)

WALKER, Kenneth MacFarlane [1882–1966, English physician and medical writer]
Kenneth MacFarlane (*They Wanted Adventure*)

WALKER, Mary Edwards [1832–1919, US physician and surgeon during the Civil War]
A Woman Physician and Surgeon (*Unmasked or The Science of Immorality*)

WALKER, Obadiah [1616–99, English Catholic cleric and controversialist]
Abraham Woodhead (*Considerations on the Spirit of Martin Luther*)

WALKER, Richard [1679–1764, English cleric and botanist]
A Disciple of Cranmer (*Papistry Defended*)

WALKER, Richard [d. 1985, English writer on angling]
Water Rail (in the *Fishing Gazette*)

WALKER, Rowland [fl. 1935, English writer and journalist]
Hugh Kenworthy (used for journalism)

WALKER, William Sylvester [1846–1926, Australian wanderer and travel writer]
Coo-ee (*From the Land of the Wombat*; *The Silver Queen*)

WALKLEY, Arthur Bingham [1855–1926, English post office employee and drama critic]
Spectator (in *The Star*)

WALL, Arnold [1869–1966, English-born New Zealand writer and academic]
Helion Bumpstead (*King Marchaunt and his Ragamuffin*)
A Colonial Professor (*Blank Verse Lyrics and Other Poems*)

WALL, John W. [1910–89, English diplomat and fantasy writer]
Sarban (*The Sound of his Horn*; *The Doll Maker*; *Ringstones and Other Curious Tales*)

WALLACE, Lady Eglantine [d. 1803, English traveller, poet and dramatist]
A Lady (*A Letter to a Friend, with a Poem, The Ghost of Werter*)

WALLACE, Richard Horatio Edgar [1875–1932, English journalist and crime writer]
John Anstruther; Macey Dixon; E. Grahame Smith (all used in the *Sunday Post*)
Richard Cloud (in *Answers* magazine)
Richard Freeman (in *Ideas* magazine)
Nick O'Lincoln (for racing articles in various newspapers)

WALLACE, Robert [1831–99, Scottish cleric, journalist and radical politician]
A Radical MP (in the *National Review*)

WALLACE, William [1843–1921, Scottish lawyer and legal writer]
An Old Personal Friend (in the *Scottish Review*)

WALLER, Edmund [1606–87, English royalist and politican]
A Gentleman that Loves the Peace of the English Nation (*A Panegyrick to My Lord Protector*)

WALLER, John Francis [1810–94, Irish lawyer, poet and writer]
Peter Brown, Poet and Peripatetic (in *Temple Bar*)

Heinrich; Milesius O'Regan; Jonathan Freke Slingsby (also for *The Dead Bridal, The Revelations of Peter Brown, St Patrick's Day in my Parlour* and *The Slingsby Papers*); Your Old Contributor (all used in *Dublin University Magazine*)
Iota (*The Adventures of a Protestant in Search of a Religion*)

WALLER, Leslie [1923–, US novelist]
C. S. Cody (*Witching Night*)

WALLER, Sir William [1597–1668, English Parliamentarian soldier turned royalist]
A Person of Honour (*Divine Meditations upon Several Occasions*)

WALLIS, George C. [fl. 1900, English fantasy novelist]
Royston Heath (*A Corsair of the Sky*)

WALLIS, John [1616–1703, English cleric and mathematician]
A Member of that University (*An Answer to Dr Sherlock's Modest Examination etc.*)

WALLIS, Ralph [d. 1669, English controversial pamphleteer]
Sil Awl (*More News from Rome*)

WALLOP, William Barton Powlett [1808–86, English soldier]
A Britisher (in *Bentley's Miscellany*)

WALMESLEY, Charles [1722–97, English Catholic cleric, astronomer and mathematician]
Signor Pastorini (*A General History of the Christian Church*)

WALMSLEY, Arnold Robert [1912–, English diplomat and writer]
Nicholas Roland (*The Great One; Who Came by Night*)

WALMSLEY, Lionel [1892–1966, English writer]
Leo Walmsley (*The Silver Blimp; Sound of the Sea*)

WALN, Robert [1797–1825, US poet]
Peter Atall; The Hermit (both used in *The Hermit in America on a Visit to Philadelphia*)

WALPOLE, Horace [1717–97, 4th Earl of Oxford; poet and writer]
A Man (*Reflections on the Different Ideas of the French and English on Cruelty*)
William Marshall, Gent.; Onuphrio Muralto (both used for *The Castle of Otranto*, as translator and author respectively)
Xo-Ho (*A Letter from Xo-Ho, a Chinese Philosopher in London, to his Friend*)

WALPOLE, Michael [1570–1624, English Jesuit and theologian]
Michael Christopherson (*A Treatise of Antichrist; Anti-Christ Extant, against George Downham*)

WALPOLE, Sir Robert [1676–1745, 1st Earl of Orford; politician]
A Member of Parliament (*A Letter from a Member of Parliament to his Friends ... Duties on Wine and Tobacco*)
A Member of the Lower House (*Thoughts of a Member of the Lower House ... Limiting the Power of the Crown in the Future Creation of Peers*)

WALSH, James Morgan [1897–1952, Australian mystery writer]
H. Haverstock Hill (*The Golden Isle; The Secret of the Crater*)

WALSH, John Henry [1810–88, English surgeon and sporting writer]
Stonehenge (*Athletic Sports and Manly Exercise; British Rural Sports; The Dog in Health and Disease; The Dogs of the British Islands; Hints to Sportsmen on Guns and Shooting; A Manual of British Rural Sports; Riding and Driving*)

WALSH, Mary [1912–, US novelist]
Mary Lavin (*The Shrine; Tales from Bective Bridge*)

WALSH, Robert [1784–1859, US journalist]
An American Recently Returned from Europe (*A Letter on the Genius of the French Government*)

WALSH, Sheila [1928–, English historical novelist]
Sophie Leyton (*Lady Cecily's Dilemma*)

WALSH, William Shepard [1854–1919, US writer]
William Shepard (*The Literary Life; Enchiridian of Wit; Paradoxes of a Philistine*)

WALSINGHAM, Francis [1577–1647, English Jesuit and religious writer; used John Fennell as an alias]
A Father of the Society of Jesus (*The Paradise of the Soule*)

WALTER, Henry [1785–1859, English cleric and natural philosopher]
A Clergyman of the Church of England (*A History of England*)

WALTER, Richard [1716–85, English naval cleric – sailed with Anson]
An Officer of the Fleet (*A Voyage to the South Seas in the Year 1740 to June 1744*)

WALTON, John [fl. 1924, English writer]
*Olive Conway (*The Starlight Widow; Costume Plays*)

WALTON, William [1784–1857, English traveller and authority on Spain]
An English Civilian (*A Reply to Two Pamphlets*)
An Eye Witness (*Narrative of the Political Changes in the Island of Terceira*)
A Friend of Truth and Peace (*The True Interests of the European Powers and the Emperor of Brazil*)

WALZ, Mrs Audrey [d. 1983, US writer]
Francis Bonnamy (*Dead Reckoning; The King is Dead on Queen Street*)

WANLEY, Humphrey [1672–1726, English librarian and bibliographer]
A Good Hand (*The Grounds and Principles of the Christian Religion*)

WANOSTROCHT, Nicholas [1804–76, English schoolmaster and cricketer]
Felix (*Felix on the Bat*)

WANSEY, Henry [1752–1827, English merchant and antiquarian]
A Dissenter (*A Letter to the Bishop of Salisbury*)
A Wiltshire Clothier (*Wool Encouraged without Exportation*)

WARBURG, James Paul [1896–1969, German-born US economist]
Paul James (*And Then What?; Shoes and Ships and Sealing Wax*)

WARBURTON, Bartholomew Elliott George [1810–52, Irish barrister, novelist and biographer]
Eliot Warburton (*The Crescent and the Cross; Darien or the Merchant Prince*)

WARBURTON, Thomas Acton [1813–94, English barrister, cleric and writer]
Odard (in *Bentley's Miscellany*)

WARBURTON, William [1698–1779, English cleric and literary enthusiast; Bishop of Gloucester]
An Author (*A Letter from an Author to a Member of Parliament on Literary Property*)
A Gentleman of Cambridge (*Remarks on Mr Hume's Late Essay*)

WARD, Arthur Sarsfield [1886–1959, English mystery writer]
Michael Furey (*Wulfheim*)
Sax Rohmer (*Dr Fu Manchu; The Yellow Claw*)

WARD, Bernard Rowland [1863–1933, English soldier and military writer]
Kentish Rag (*Regimental Rhymes and Other Verses*)

WARD, Edward [1667–1731, English tavern keeper, satirist and poet]
D. B. (*The Insinuating Bawd and the Repenting Harlot*)
A Lover of Mathematics (*Mars Stript of his Armour; The Wooden World Dissected*)

Manly Plain-Dealer (*The Wooden World Dissected in the Character of a Ship of War*)

Hercules Vinegar Esq. (*The Cudgel, or a Crab-Tree Lecture*)

WARD, Elizabeth Honor [1926–, English writer]
Ward S. Leslie (*Touchdown to Adventure*)

WARD, Mrs Elizabeth Rebecca [1881–?, English popular verse writer]
Fay Inchfawn (*Home Lights*; *Poems from a Quiet Room*)

WARD, Frederick William Orde [1843–1922, English cleric and writer]
F. Harald Williams (*A Prisoner of Love*)
Young England (*Pessimus*)

WARD, Harold [fl. 1920, US mystery writer]
H. W. Starr; Ward Sterling (both used in the *Black Mask* magazine)

WARD, Henry Dana [1797–1884, US writer]
A Harvard Student (*Poems*)
A Master Mason (*Freemasonry, its Pretentions Exposed*)
Senior Harvard (*The Gospel of the Kingdom*)

WARD (née Arnold), Mrs Humphry (Mary Augusta) [1851–1920, Australian-born English novelist]
Mary Augusta Arnold (*The Churchman's Companion*)

WARD, John [1781–1837, Irish-born English mystic]
Zion Ward (*The Origin of Evil Discovered*)

WARD, John [1805–90, English diplomat]
Kappa (*Nelson, the Latest Settlement of the New Zealand Company*)

WARD, Sir Leslie [1851–1922, English caricaturist]
Spy (in *Vanity Fair Magazine*)

WARD, Nathaniel [1578–1652, English Puritan cleric and religious writer]
Theodore de la Guarde (*The Simple Cobler of Aggawam*)

A Friend to the Parliament (*A Word to Mr Peters and Two Words for the Parliament*)

One that Desires to be Faithful to his Country though Unworthy to be Named (*A Religious Retreat*)

WARD, Robert Plumer [1765–1846, English barrister, politician and novelist]
A Member of Parliament (*A View of Mr Pitt and Mr Addington etc.*)

WARD, Thomas [1807–73, US poet]
Flaccus (*Passaic, a Group of Poems*)

WARD, Thomas Humphrey [1845–1926, English journalist and writer]
J. Prior, Butler; Ol. Socius (both used in *Brasenose Ale – a Collection of Verses*)

WARD, William [1769–1823, English missionary in and writer on India]
An Old Friend of the Society for Promoting Christian Knowledge (*A Letter on the British and Foreign Bible Society*)

WARDE, Mrs Beatrice Lamberton [1900–69, US writer and lecturer on typography]
Paul Beaujon (in *The Fleuron* and for *XVIIIth Century French Typography* and *Fournier le Jeune*)

WARE, Eugene Fitch [1841–1911, US lawyer and historian]
Ironquill (*The Lyon Campaign in Missouri*; *Rhymes*)

WARE, Henry [1794–1843, US cleric and academic]
An Unitarian Clergyman (*A Letter to the Rev. Nehemiah Adams*)

WARE, Nathaniel A. [1780–1854, US writer]
A Southern Planter (*Notes on Political Economy*)

WARE, William [1797–1852, US cleric and novelist]
Lucius Manlius Piso (*Probus, or Rome in the Third Century*; *Rome and the Early Christians*)

WARFIELD, Mrs Catharine Ann [1816–77, US poet and novelist]
A Southern Lady (*The Household of Bouverie*)
*Two Sisters of the West (*The Wife of Leon and Other Poems*)

WARING, Jeremiah [1757–1829, English Quaker]
One of the People called Christians (*Three Letters Addressed to the Readers of Paine's Age of Reason*)

WARING, John Burley [1823–75, English architect and writer]
An Architect (*Poems*)
Hon. Botibel Bareacres (*Poems Inspired by the Art Treasures Exhibition at Manchester*)
A Great Big Fool (*The English Alphabet Considered Philosophically*)
Tennyson Longfellow Smith of Cripplegate Within (*Poems Inspired by Certain Pictures*)

WARING, John Scott [1747–1819, English soldier in India and agent for Warren Hastings; he assumed the surname Waring in 1798]
Asiaticus (*Letters to the Rt. Hon. Henry Dundas*)
A Bengal Officer (*A Vindication of the Hindoos*)
A Member of the Revolution Society (*A Letter to the Rt. Hon. Edmund Burke*)
A Whig (*Seven Letters to the People of Great Britain*)

WARING, Robert [1614–58, English political pamphleteer and writer]
Basilius Philomusus (*An Account of Mr Pryn's Refutation etc.*)

WARNEFORD, William [1560–1608, English Jesuit and religious writer]
George Doulye (*A Briefe Instruction of Christian Religion; A Briefe Methode for Examination of our Conscience; A Treatise on Penance*)

WARNER, Anna Bartlett [1827–1915, US novelist and writer – sister of Susan Bogert Warner below]
Amy Lothrop (*Dollars and Cents; My Brother's Keeper*)

WARNER, John [1804–77, English barrister and essayist]
Philippicus; Tomkins (both used in *Blackwood's Magazine*)

WARNER, Richard [1763–1857, English cleric, antiquarian and devotional writer]
An Aged Man (*Nugae Poeticae*)
Peter Paul Pallet (*Bath Characters, or Sketches from Life; Rebellion in Bath, or The Battle of the Upper Rooms; The Restoration*)
Gabriel Sticking Plaister (*Thoughts on Duelling*)
Presbuteros (*Practical Religion or Christian Obedience; The Simplicity of Christianity*)

WARNER, Susan Bogert [1819–85, US novelist and religious writer – sister of Anna Bartlett Warner above]
Elizabeth Wetherell (*The Wide, Wide World; Queechy*)

WARREN, Sir John Borlase [1753–1822, English admiral]
An Officer of Rank (*A View of the Naval Force of Great Britain*)

WARREN, John Byrne Leicester [1835–95, 3rd Baron De Tabley; novelist, poet and botanist]
William Lancaster (*Studies in Verse; Praetorita; Eclogues and Monodrames*)
*George F. Preston (*Ballads and Metrical Sketches; Glimpses of Antiquity; Poems; The Threshold of Atrides*)

WARREN, John Russell [1886–?, English crime and mystery novelist]
Gilbert Coverack (*The A. T. S. Murder; Time for Murder*)

WARREN, Samuel [1807–77, Welsh barrister and novelist]
An Attorney (*Adventures of an Attorney in Search of Practice*)

A Barrister-at-Law (*The Opium Question as between Nation and Nation*)

A Late Physician (*Passages from the Diary of a late Physician*)

An Old Contributor; One of the Commons at Cherbourg; One of Themselves; Q. Q. Q. (all used in *Blackwood's Magazine*)

Gustavus Sharp Esq. (*The Confessions of an Attorney*)

WARRINER, Thurmann [fl. 1960, English mystery writer]

John Kersey (*Night of the Wolf*)

Simon Troy (*Drunkard's End*; *Second Cousin Removed*)

WARTER, John Wood [1806–78, English cleric and historian]

A Graduate of Oxford (*The Acharnians, Knights, Wasps and Birds of Aristophanes*)

Cedric Oldacre (*The Last of the Old Squires*)

An Old Vicar (*The Sea-Board and the Down*)

WARTON, Thomas [1728–90, English Poet Laureate and historian of poetry]

A Gentleman from Aberdeen (*The Union: or, Select Scots and English Poems*)

WARWICK, Francis [fl. 1930, English writer for boys]

Roland Spencer (in *Gem*)

WASHBURN, George [1833–1915, US cleric and orientalist]

An Eastern Statesman; A Non-Resident American; An Old Resident (all used in *Contemporary Review*)

WATERHOUSE, Keith Spencer [1929–, English journalist and playwright]

*Herald Froy (*How to Avoid Matrimony*)

*Lee Gibb (*The Jones's: How to Keep up with Them*)

WATERMAN, Jotham [d. 1836, US cleric]

Aquae Homo, A. B. (*The Wren and the Eagle in Contest*)

WATHEN, James [1751–1828, English glover, traveller and walker]

Jemmy Sketch (in *Gentleman's Magazine*)

WATKINS, Alex [fl. 1950, English writer]

J. Lane Linklater (*Black Opal*; *She Had a Little Knife*)

WATKINS, Arthur Thomas Levi [1907–65, Welsh civil servant and playwright]

Arthur Watkyn (*Geese are Getting Fat*)

WATKINS, Tobias [1780–1855, US journalist and writer]

Pertinax Particular (*Tales of the Tripod*)

WATKINS-PITCHFORD, Denys James [1905–90, English artist, writer and illustrator]

B. B. (*Brendon Chase*; *Confessions of a Carp Fisher*)

Michael Traherne (*Be Quiet and Go a-Angling*)

WATSON, Alfred Edward Thomas [1849–1922, English music and drama critic and sporting writer]

Rapier (in the *Illustrated Sporting and Dramatic News* and for *The Turf: A Treatise on Racing and Steeple-Chasing* and *Types of the Turf*)

Peyton Wrey (*The Elfin Tree*)

WATSON, Edmund Henry Lacon [1865–1948, English schoolmaster and novelist]

Lacon (*Lectures to Living Authors*)

WATSON, Elliot Lovegood Grant [1885–1970, English novelist and writer]

John Lovegood (*The Partners*)

WATSON, James [1775–1820, English writer on the theatre]

A Townsman (in the periodical of the same name)

WATSON, John [1850–1907, Scottish cleric and novelist]

Ian MacLaren (*Beside the Bonnie Brier*; *The Days of Auld Lang Syne*)

WATSON, John [d. 1928, English writer on country life]

Rusticus (in the *National Review*)

WATSON, John Forbes [d. 1871, Scottish military physician and writer on India]
A Medical Man (*Flowers and Gardens: Notes on Plant Beauty*)

WATSON, Julia [1943–, Welsh romantic novelist]
Jane de Vere (*The Scarlet Woman*)
Julia Fitzgerald (*Royal Slave*; *Salamander*)
Julia Hamilton (*Snow Queen*)

WATSON, Richard [1737–1816, English cleric, scientist and controversialist; Bishop of Llandaff]
A Christian Whig (*A Letter to the Members of the House of Commons*)
A Consistent Protestant (*Considerations on Revising the Liturgy*)
Philobiblius (*The Sophist Unmasked*)

WATSON, Rosamund [1863–1911, English writer]
Graham R. Tonson (*Vespertilia and Other Verses*; *The Patch-Work Quilt*; *Ballads of the North Countrie*)

WATSON, William Lorimer [d. 1921, English writer on golf]
Adam Lorimer (*Sir Sergeant*)

WATTERSON, Henry [1840–1921, US journalist and historian]
Asa Trenchard (*Comic Sketches*)

WATTERSTON, George [1783–1854, US librarian and writer]
A Foreigner (*Letters from Washington on the Constitution and Laws*)
The Wanderer (*The Wanderer in Washington*)

WATTS, Isaac [1674–1748, English educationalist and hymn writer]
An Impartial Moderator (*The Strength and Weakness of Human Reason*)

WATTS, Thomas [1811–69, English bibliographer and British Museum librarian]
Verificator (letters in *The Athenaeum*)

WATTS, Walter Henry [1776–1842, English miniature painter and journalist]
An Old Reporter (*My Private Note-Book*)

WAUGH, Benjamin [1839–1908, English cleric, philanthropist and social reformer]
A Member of the School Board of London (*The Gaol Cradle: Who Rocks It?*)

WAUGH, Hillary Baldwin [1920–, US crime novelist]
Elissa Grandower (*Blackbourne Hall*; *Rivergate House*)
H. Baldwin Taylor (*The Trouble with Tycoons*; *The Duplicate*)
Harry Walker (*Murder on the Terrace*; *The Case of the Missing Gardener*)

WAY, Arthur S. [1847–1930, English classical scholar]
Avia (*The Odyssey of Homer Done into English Verse*)

WAY, Lewis [1772–1840, English barrister and cleric]
Basilicus (*Thoughts on the Scriptural Expectations of the Christian Church*)

WAYLAND, Francis [1826–1904, US academic and philanthropist]
Roger Williams (*Notes on the Principles of Baptist Churches*)

WAYMAN, Dorothy Godfrey [1893–1975, US writer]
Theodate Geoffrey (*An Immigrant in Japan*; *Powdered Ashes*)

WAYNE, Charles Stokes [1858–?, US writer]
Horace Hazeltine (*The City of Enchantments*)

WEALE, Anne [1929–, English romantic novelist]
Andrea Blake (*Night of the Hurricane*)

WEATHERBY, W. J. [1930–92, English journalist and writer]
Will Perry (*Death of an Informer*)

WEATHERLY, Frederick Edward [1848–1929, English barrister and writer]
A Resident MA (*Oxford Days or How Ross Got his Degree*)

WEAVER, Mrs Gertrude Baillie [d. 1926, English novelist]
George Colmore (*Brother of Shadow*; *Whispers*)

WEAVER, Robert [1773–1852, English cleric and antiquarian]
A Quadragenarian (*The Reconciler*)

WEBB, Charles Henry [1834–1905, US journalist, poet and writer]
John Paul (*Parodies, Prose and Verse*; *Vagrom Verses*; *The Wickedest Woman in New York*)

WEBB, Dorothy Anna [fl. 1927, English writer]
Jermyn March (*Dear Traitor*; *The Scarlet Thumb*)

WEBB, Francis [1735–1815, English cleric, pamphleteer and poet]
A Rational Christian (*The Morality of the New Testament Digested*)

WEBB, Henry Bertram Law [fl. 1936, English schoolmaster – husband of Mary Webb]
John Clayton (*The Silver Swan*; *Dew in April*)

WEBB, Jack [1920–, US actor and writer]
John Farr (*The Deadly Combo*; *The Lady and the Snake*)

WEBB, James Watson [1802–84, US journalist, soldier and diplomat]
An Amateur Traveller (*Altowan*)

WEBB, Jean Francis [1910–, US romantic novelist]
Ethel Hamill (*Bluegrass Doctor*; *Runaway Nurse*)
Ian Kavanaugh (*A Waltz on the Wind*)
Roberta Morrison (*Tree of Evil*)

WEBB, Joseph [1735–87, American writer and mason]
Josephus Tela (*The Philosophical Library*)

WEBB, Lilian Julia [1877–1936, South African actress and novelist]
Cynthia Stockley (*Virginia of the Rhodesians*; *Wild Honey*)

WEBB, Philip Carteret [1700–70, English lawyer, pamphleteer and collector of antiquities]
The Gentleman of Lincoln's Inn (*A Letter to the Rev. William Warburton*; *The Question whether a Jew both within British Dominions etc.*)
A Member of the House of Commons (*Some Observations on ... Discharging Mr Wilkes etc*)
A Member of the Society of Antiquaries (*A Short Account of Danegeld*; *A Short Account of the Domesday Book*)
P. C. W. (*A State of Facts on His Majesty's Right to Certain Fee-Farm Rents ... Norfolk*)

WEBB, Richard Wilson [fl. 1960, US mystery writer]
*Q. Patrick (*Death and the Maiden*; *Death in Bermuda*)
*Patrick Quentin (*Puzzle for Fiends*; *Puzzle for Pilgrims*)
*Jonathan Stagge (*Call a Hearse*; *Light from a Lantern*)

WEBBER, Charles Edmund [1838–1904, English soldier and electrical engineer]
An Officer of the Royal Engineers (*Military Work by Military Labour*)

WEBSTER, Daniel [1782–1852, US jurist, orator and politician]
Curtius (in the *American Minerva*)

WEBSTER, Ezekiel [1780–1829, US lawyer]
Cato (*A Defence of the National Administration*)

WEBSTER, John Henry Douglas [1882–1975, Scottish physician and writer]
Colin Tolly (*Poems*)

WEBSTER, Julia Augusta [1837–94, English poet and novelist]
Cecil Home (*Lesley's Guardians*)

WEBSTER, Noah [1758–1843, US journalist and lexicographer]
An American (*The Revolution in France*)
Aristedes; A Federalist (both used in *A Letter to Alexander Hamilton*)
Marcellus (*A Letter to Daniel Webster*)
A Private Citizen (*Attention! or New Thoughts on a serious Subject*)

WEBSTER, Pelatiah [1725–95, American merchant and patriot]
A Citizen of Philadelphia (*A Plea for the Poor Soldiers; The Weaknesses of Brutus Exposed; An Essay on the Seat of Federal Government; A Fifth Essay on Free Trade and Finance; A Dissertation upon the Political Union; An Essay on Free Trade and Finance*)
A Citizen of the United States (*An Essay on Money as a Medium of Commerce*)
A Financier (*An Essay on the Danger of Too Much Circulating Cash*)

WEBSTER, William [1689–1758, English cleric and religious writer]
The Draper (*The Draper's Reply*)
A Draper of London (*The Consequences of Trade as to Wealth*)
A Friend to the Government (*The Draper Confuted*)
Richard Hooker of the Inner Temple (*The Miscellany*)

WEDDERBURN, Alexander Dundas Ogilvy [1854–1931, Scottish editor and writer]
An Oxford Pupil (in *Contemporary Review*)

WEDGWOOD, Frances Julia [1833–1913, English writer – niece of Charles Darwin]
Florence Dawson (*An Old Debt*)
One who Knew Her (in *Contemporary Review*)

WEEKES, Agnes Russell [1880–?, English novelist – sister of Rose Kirkpatrick Weekes below]
*Anthony Pryde (*Emerald Necklace; The Figure on the Terrace*)

WEEKES, Rose Kirkpatrick [fl. 1930, English writer]
*Anthony Pryde (see entry for her sister above)

WEEKS, Mrs Helen Campbell [1839–1918, US social reformer and writer for children]
Campbell Wheaton (*Six Sinners or, Schooldays in Bantam Valley*)

WEEKS, Romana [1934–, US writer]
Agatha Mayer (*Secret of the Dark Stranger*)

WEIDEMEYER, John William [1819–96, US poet and publisher]
John W. Montclair (*Themes and Translations; Real and Ideal*)

WEINBAUM, Stanley G. [1900–35, US science-fiction writer]
John Jessel (*The Adaptive Ultimate*)

WEINSTEIN, Nathan [1903–40, US novelist and screenwriter]
Nathanael West (*Miss Lonelyhearts; The Day of the Locust*)

WEIR, Rosemary [1905–, South African writer for children]
Catherine Bell (*Devon Venture*)

WEISS, Henry George [1898–1946, US fantasy and science-fiction writer]
Francis Flagg (in both *Weird Tales* and *Amazing Stories* magazines)

WEISZ, Victor [1913–66, German-born political cartoonist in England]
Vicky (in the *News Chronicle* and later in the *Daily Mirror*)

WELBY, Mrs Amelia Ball [1821–52, US poet]
Amelia (*Poems*)

WELBY, T. Earle [1881–1933, Indian-born English journalist and literary critic]
Stet (in *Week-End Review* and for *Back Numbers*)

WELCHMAN, Edward [1665–1739, English cleric and theologian]
A Minister in the Country (*The Husbandman's Manual*)

WELD, Horatio Hastings [1811–88, US cleric and writer]
Ezekiel Jones (*Jonce Smiley*)

WELD, Theodore Dwight [1803–95, US abolitionist and pamphleteer]
Wythe (*The Power of Congress over the District of Columbia*)

WELD, Thomas [1590–1662, English cleric and religious writer]
An Inhabitant There (*A Brief Narration of the Practices in the Churches of New England*)

WELD-BLUNDELL, Charles Joseph [1845–1927, English traveller and journalist]
Justitia (*Tithes and the Church which Owns Them*)
One of Them (*Are We a Stupid People?*)

WELDON, John [1891–1963, Irish actor, novelist and dramatist]
Brinsley MacNamara (*The Rebellion in Ballycullion; The Valley of the Squinting Windows*)

WELLES, Albert [fl. 1845, US writer]
A Descendant of One of the Early Puritan Governors (*Things New and Old*)

WELLESLEY, Dorothy Violet [1889–1956, English poet]
M. A. (*Early Poems*)

WELLMAN, Manley Wade [1903–, African-born US crime and science-fiction writer]
Gans T. Field (in *Weird Tales* magazine)
Will Garth (*Dr Cyclops*)

WELLS, Carolyn [1869–1942, US mystery writer]
Rowland Wright (*The Disappearance of Kimball Webb*)

WELLS, Charles Jeremiah [1799–1879, English solicitor and poet]
Henry L. Howard (*Joseph and his Brethren*)

WELLS, Edward [1667–1727, English cleric, geographer and mathematician]
A Minister of the Church of England (*A Letter from a Minister of the Church of England to Mr Peter Dowley*)

WELLS, Herbert George [1866–1946, English novelist and writer]
Reginald Bliss (*Boon, the Mind of the Race*)
Septimus Browne; Walker Glockenhammer; S. S.; Tyro; H. G. Wheels (all used in *Science Schools Journal*)
Jane Crabtree (in *Pall Mall Budget*)
D. P. (in *The Times*)

WELLS, William Charles [1757–1817, American-born Scottish physician and medical writer]
Marcus (in the *Public Advertiser*)

WELSH, Charles [1850–1914, US journalist and writer for children]
One of its Victims (*Poker: How to Play It*)

WELSTED, Leonard [1688–1747, English satirist and poet]
Palemon (*The Triumvirate or, a Letter in Verse*)

WESLEY, John [1703–91, English Methodist evangelist]
An Englishman (*Thoughts upon Liberty*)
A Lover of Free Grace (*The Question: What is an Armenian?*)
A Love of Mankind and Common Sense (*The Desideratum: or, Electricity made Plain and Useful*)
A Lover of Peace (*A Seasonable Address to the More Serious Inhabitants of Great Britain*)
Philalethes (*A Letter to Dr Priestley*)
Philo-Biblos (*The Scripture Doctrine of Atonement*)

WESLEY, Samuel [1662–1735, English cleric and poet]
A Country Divine (*A Letter from a Country Divine concerning the Education of the Dissenters*)
A Schollar (*Maggots or, Poems on Several Subjects*)

WESSELHOEFT, Lily F. [1840–1919, US writer for children]
Aunt Lily (*Jack the Fire-Dog*)

WEST, Benjamin [1738–1820, American-born painter – settled in London]
Isaac Bickerstaff Esq. (*An Astronomical Diary 1790; The New England Almanack*)

WEST, Sir Edward [1782–1828, English barrister and political economist]
A Fellow of University College, Oxford (*Essay on the Application of Capital to Land*)

WEST, Edward [1900–88, English writer]
Geoffrey Household (*Rogue Male; The Europe That Was*)

WEST, Jane [1758–1852, English novelist, poet and dramatist]
Mrs Prudentia Homespun (*A Gossip's Story; The Advantages of Education*)

WEST, Levon [1900–68, US writer and artist]
Ivan Dmitri (*Making an Etching; Flight to Everywhere*)

WEST, Lillie [1860–1939, US actress and writer]
Amy Leslie (*Plays and Players; Some Players*)

WEST, Morris [1916–, Australian novelist and mystery writer]
Michael East (*McCreary Moves In; The Naked Country*)
Julian Morris (*Moon in my Pocket*)

WEST, William [1770–1854, English bookseller and historian]
An Old Bookseller (*Fifty Years' Recollections of an Old Bookseller*)
One of the Old School (*Tavern Anecdotes and Reminiscences*)

WESTCOTT, Frederick Brooke [1857–1918, English cleric and headmaster]
*Two Clerks (*The Epistle to the Hebrews*)

WESTCOTT, Thompson [1820–88, US journalist and lawyer]
Joe Miller Jr. (in the *St Louis Reveille* and in *Knickerbocker Magazine*)

WESTHEIMER, David [1917–, US writer]
Z. Z. Smith (*A Very Private Island*)

WESTLAKE, Donald E. [1933–, US crime and mystery writer]
Curt Clark (*Anarchaos*)
Tucker Coe (*Murder Among Children; Kinds of Love, Kinds of Death*)
Timothy J. Culver (*Ex-Officio*)
Richard Stark (*The Outfit; The Green Eagle Score*)

WESTLAKE, Nathaniel H. J. [1833–1921, English painter and writer on art]
An Antiquary (*The Dance from 3300 BC to 1911 AD*)

WESTMACOTT, Charles Molloy [1787–1868, English journalist and writer]
Bernard Blackmantle (*The English Spy; Fitzalleyne of Berkeley; The Punster's Pocket-Book*)
Abel Funnefello (*The Blue-Coat Boy*)

WESTON, Edward [1703–70, English journalist and writer]
A Country Gentleman (*The Country Gentleman's Advice to his Neighbours; Family Discourses*)

WESTON, Edward Payson [1839–1929, US journalist and long-distance walker]
The Pedestrian (*Journal of a Walk from Boston to Washington*)

WESTON, Stephen [1747–1830, English cleric, linguist and writer]
An Admirer of Great Genius (*A Short Account of the Late Mr Richard Porson*)
Kien Lung (*The Conquest of the Miao-Toe*)
An Oxonian (*A Trimester in France and Switzerland*)

Philoxenus Secundus (*Persian Recreations*)
Terrae Filius Philagricola (*Werneria*)
A Visitor (*A Slight Sketch of Paris*)

WEST-WATSON, Keith Campbell [fl. 1945, English writer]
Keith Campbell (*That Was No Lady*; *Last Journey*)

WETENHALL, Edward [1636–1713, English cleric, educational and religious writer; Bishop of Kilmore and Ardagh]
An Irish Protestant Bishop (*Hexapla Jacoboea*)
A Melancholy Stander-By (*An Earnest and Compassionate Suit for Forbearance*)
A Person of Quality (*A Judgement of the Comet*)

WETHERALD, Agnes Ethelwyn [1857–1940, Canadian poet and writer]
Bel Thistlethwaite (in the *Toronto Globe*)

WETTERBURGH, Carl Anton [1804–89, Swedish writer]
Uncle Adam (*The Fatal Chain*; *The Serf's Daughter*)

WEYLAND, John [1774–1854, English barrister and writer]
One of HM's Justices of the Peace for the Three Inland Counties (*A Short Enquiry into the Policy of the Poor Laws*)

WHALLEY, Thomas Sedgwick [1746–1828, English cleric and poet]
A Beautiful and Unfortunate Young Lady (*The Fatal Kiss*)

WHARTON, Charles Henry [1748–1833, US cleric]
An Inhabitant of the State of Maryland (*A Poetical Epistle to George Washington*)

WHARTON (née Jones), Edith [1862–1937, US novelist and writer]
Edith Newbold Jones (for *Verses*, published in 1878)

WHARTON, Sir George [1617–81, English mathematician and astronomer]
George Naworth (*Mercurio – Coelico Mastix*; *Naworth 1643, a New Almanacke*)

Esdras Philoparthen (*Poems*)

WHARTON, Henry [1664–95, English cleric and religious writer]
Anthony Harmer (*A Specimen of Some Errors in The History of the Reformation*)

WHARTON, William Henry Anthony [1859–1938, English sportsman]
The Master of the Cleveland Hounds (*Hints for the Hunting Field*)

WHATELY, Richard [1787–1863, English cleric, educationalist and political economist; Archbishop of Dublin]
A Country Pastor (*Lectures on Scripture Revelations*)
An Episcopalian (*Letters on the Church*)
Konx Ompax (*Historic Doubts Relative to Napoleon Bonaparte*)
Rev. Aristarchus Newlight (*Historic Certainties Respecting the Early History of America*)
John Search (*Religion and her Name*)

WHEARE, Degory [1573–1647, English historian]
D. W. (*Relectiones Hyemales*)

WHEELER, Andrew Carpenter [1836–1903, US drama critic and writer]
Nym Crinkle (in the *New York World* and for *The Gentle Savage*)
J. P. Mowbray (*Tangled up in Beulah Land*; *A Journey to Nature*; *The Making of a Country Home*)
Trinculo (in the *New York Leader* for drama criticism)

WHEELER, David Hilton [1829–1902, US cleric and classical scholar]
David Hilton (*Brigandage in South Italy*)

WHEELER, Hugh Callingham [1916–87, US mystery writer]
*Q. Patrick (*Death and the Maiden*; *Death in Bermuda*)
*Patrick Quentin (*Puzzle for Fiends*; *Puzzle for Pilgrims*)
*Jonathan Stagge (*Call a Hearse*; *Light from a Lantern*)

WHEELER, James Talboys [1824–97, English civil servant in India and historian]
A Tourist (*Adventures of a Tourist from Calcutta to Delhi*)

WHEELWRIGHT, Horace William [d. 1867, English traveller and writer]
An Old Bushman (*Bush Wanderings of a Naturalist; Sporting Sketches at Home and Abroad; A Spring and Summer in Lapland; Ten Years in London*)

WHEELWRIGHT, John Tyler [1856–1925, US lawyer and writer]
*Two Gentlemen of Harvard (*Rollo's Journey to Cambridge*)

WHELAN, John [1900–91, Irish novelist, playwright and short-story writer]
Sean O'Faolain (*Come back to Erin; King of the Beggars*)

WHELPLEY, Samuel [1766–1817, US cleric and preacher]
Philadelphus (*A Compend of History*)

WHEWAY, John [fl. 1931, English writer for children]
Hazel Armitage (in both *School Friend* and *Girl's Crystal*)
Hilda Richards (in *School Friend* from 1931)

WHISTON, William [1667–1752, English cleric, scientist, mathematician and theologian]
A Lover of Truth and of True Religion (*Athanasian Forgeries, Impositions etc.*)

WHITAKER, Lily C. [fl. 1880, US writer and poet]
Adidnac (*Donata and Other Poems*)

WHITAKER, Rodney William [1931–, US novelist and writer]
Nicholas Seare (*Rude Tales and Glorious*)
Trevanian (*The Eiger Sanction; The Loo Sanction*)

WHITBY, Anthony Charles [1929–, English playwright]
Anthony Lesser (*The Bedwinner*)

WHITBY, Daniel [1638–1726, English cleric and religious writer]
A Divine of the Church of England (*Obedience Due to the Present King*)
A Well-Wisher to the Church's Peace and a Lamenter of her Sad Divisions (*The Protestant Reconciler*)

WHITCHER, Frances Miriam [1814–52, US humorist]
Widow Bedott (*The Widow Bedott Papers*)

WHITCOMB, James [1795–1852, US writer]
An Indianan (*The Other Side of Facts for the People*)

WHITE, Adam [1817–79, English zoologist and natural historian]
Arachnophilus (*A Contribution Towards an Argument for Scripture*)

WHITE, Arnold [1848–1925, English writer on social and political affairs]
Vanoc (in the *Sunday Referee* and for *The Day of my Life*)

WHITE, Charles [1794–1861, US cleric]
Martingale (*English Country Life; Turf Characters; Sporting Scenes and Country Characters*)

WHITE, Henry Kirke [1785–1806, English poet]
James Templeman (in the *Monthly Preceptor*)

WHITE, Herbert Martyn Oliver [1885–1963, Irish academic and mystery writer]
Oliver Martyn (*The Body in the Pound; The Man They Couldn't Hang*)

WHITE, James [1775–1820, English publicist and Falstaffian writer]
A Gentleman, a Descendant of Dame Quickly (*Original Letters of Sir John Falstaff and his Friends*)

WHITE, James [1803–62, English cleric, historian and writer]
An Ancient Contributor; G. Bobson; Theocritus Brown; T. Buddle; A

Cockney; An Oxonian; Hannibal Smith Esq. (all used in *Blackwood's Magazine*)
A Country Curate (*The Village Poorhouse*)

WHITE, James Dillon [1913–, English writer]
Felix Krull (*The Village Pub Murders*)

WHITE, Joseph Blanco [1775–1841, Spanish-born English cleric and writer]
A Clergyman of the Church of England (*Preparatory Observations on the Study of Religion*)
Don Leucadio Doblado (*Letters from Spain*)

WHITE, Miss Mary Helen [d. 1923, US playwright and writer]
M. H. Towry (*Clanship and the Clans*)

WHITE, Richard Grant [1821–85, US lawyer, journalist and humorist]
A Learned Gorilla (*The Fall of Man*)
Outis (*The Irish Middleman*)
U. Donougn Outis (*The Chronicles of Gotham*)
A Yankee (in *The Spectator* and for *Words and their Uses, Past and Present*)

WHITE, Terence Hanbury [1906–64, Indian-born English novelist, poet and writer for children]
James Aston (*Loved Helen*; *They Winter Abroad*)
Timothy White (in *Cambridge Poetry 1929*)

WHITE, Theodore Edward [1938–, US fantasy and science-fiction writer]
*Ron Archer (*Lost in Space*)
*Norman Edwards (*Invasion from 2500*; *Warlords of Kor*)
Ted White (*Sideslip*)

WHITE, Thomas [1593–1676, English Catholic cleric and controversialist]
A Catholique Gent. (*A Contemplation of Heaven*)
Mr William Richworth (*The Dialogues of Mr William Richworth*)

WHITE, Walter [1811–93, English cabinet-maker, librarian and writer]
A Londoner (*A Londoner's Walk to Land's End*)

WHITE, William [1604–78, English cleric and writer]
Gullielmus Phalerius (*Via Ad Pacem Ecclesiasticum*)

WHITE, William Anthony Parker [1911–68, US science-fiction and crime writer]
Anthony Boucher (*The Case of the Crumpled Knave*; *The Case of the Seven Sneezes*)
Theo Durrant (*The Marble Forest*, reissued as *The Big Fear*)
H. H. Holmes (*Nine Times Nine*; *Rocket to the Morgue*)
Herman W. Mudgett (in the *Magazine of Fantasy and Science Fiction*)

WHITE, Sir William Hale [1857–1949, English physician and medical writer]
Civis (*The State of the Navy in 1907*)

WHITE, William Hale [1831–1913, English civil servant, novelist and writer]
A Radical (in the *Rochdale Observer*)
Mark Rutherford (*Catharine Furze*; *A Dream of Two Dimensions*)
Rueben Shapcott (*The Revolution in Tanner's Lane*)

WHITEFIELD, George [1714–70, English Methodist cleric, writer and missionary in America]
The Mock Preacher (*The Mock Preacher: a Satyric Comical Allegorical Farce*)

WHITEFOORD, Caleb [1734–1810, English diplomat and writer]
Emendator (*Advice to Editors of Newspapers*)
Junia (letter in the *Public Advertiser*)

WHITEHEAD, David Henry [1918–, English western novelist]
Ben Bridges (*Hard as Nails*; *The Deadly Dollars*)

WHITEHEAD, George [1636–1723, English Quaker and controversialist]
A Friend to Them that Hate Iniquity (*The Key of Knowledge Not Found in the University Library*)
A Witness of Christ (*The He-Goat's Horn Broken*)
A Witness of the Way of Truth (*An Unjust Plea Confuted*)

WHITEHEAD, Henry [1825–96, English cleric and social commentator]
The Senior Curate of St Luke's, Berwick St (*The Cholera in Berwick Street*)

WHITEHEAD, James [1812–85, Scottish physician and medical writer]
Philomalos (*The Wife's Domain*)

WHITEHEAD, John [1740–1804, English physician and biographer of John Wesley]
Philaretus (*An Essay on Liberty and Necessity*)

WHITEHEAD, Paul [1710–74, English satirist]
Scriblerus Tertius (*The Hard-Us'd Poet's Complaint*)

WHITEHURST, Edward Capel [1824–87, English barrister, biographer and essayist]
A Cornish Man (*The Falmouth Rectory Scandal*)

WHITEING, Richard [1840–1928, English journalist and novelist]
Alb (in *Living Paris and France*)
Mr Sprouts (in the *Evening Star*)
Whyte Thorne (*The Democracy*)

WHITELOCKE, John [1757–1833, English soldier – court martialled in 1808 after a humiliating defeat in South America]
An Officer of the Expedition (*An Authentic Narrative of the Expedition ... Brig.-Gen. Crawfurd*)

WHITEMAN, Sydney W. [1877–1958, Australian-born English actor and critic]
Sydney W. Carroll (in the *Sunday Times* and the *Daily Telegraph*)

WHITFIELD, Raoul [1898–1945, US mystery writer]
Ramon Decolta (in the *Black Mask* magazine)
Temple Field (*Killer's Carnival*)

WHITFORD, Helena [1762–1824, US novelist]
A Lady (*The Step-Mother*)

WHITING, Charles [1926–, English novelist and historian]
Leo Kessler (*Valley of the Assassins*; *Otto's Phoney War*)

WHITING, Henry [1790–1851, US soldier]
An Officer of the Army at Detroit (*Ontwa, the Son of the Forest*)

WHITLOCK, Ralph [1914–, English writer on rural and farming matters]
John (or Madge) Reynolds (*Bees and Wasps*; *The Farmer's Wife*)

WHITON, James Morris [1833–1920, US cleric and educationalist]
An Orthodox Minister of the Gospel (*Is Eternal Punishment Endless?*)

WHITTAKER, Frederick [1838–89, US writer]
Launce Poyntz (in the *Fireside Companion*)

WHITTEN, Wilfred [d. 1942, English journalist]
Jackdaw (in *John O'London's Weekly*)
John O'London (*Treasure Trove*)
W (*Between the Cupolas*)

WHITTINGTON, Harry B. [1915–89, US crime and mystery novelist]
Ashley Carter (*Master of Blackoaks*; *Panama*)
Tabor Evans (*Longarm and the Hatchet Men*)
Whit Harrison (*Girl on Parole*; *A Woman Possessed*)
Kel Holland (*The Tempted*)
Harriet Kathryn Myers (*Small Town Nurse*; *Prodigal Nurse*)
Blaine Stevens (*The Outlanders*)
Clay Stuart (*His Brother's Wife*)

Hondo Wells (*Prairie Riders*)

Harry White (*Shadow at Noon*)

Hallam Whitney (*Sinners Club*; *The Wild Seed*)

WHITTINGTON-EGAN, Richard [1924–, English journalist and writer]

Nicholas Barrington (*Mendip: the Complete Caves*)

WHITTLE, Peter Armstrong [1789–1866, English bookseller and Lancashire historian]

An Old Antiquarian (*A Topographical History of Stonyhurst*)

Marmaduke Tulket (*A Topographical and Historical Account of Preston*)

WHITWORTH, Sir Charles [1714–78, English politician and writer]

A Member of Parliament (*A Collection of Ways and Means from the Revolution*)

WHYTEHEAD, Thomas [1815–43, English cleric and poet; Bishop of New Zealand]

An Undergraduate (*College Life, Letters by an Undergraduate*)

WIBBERLEY, Leonard P. O'Connor [1915–83, Irish journalist, crime and mystery novelist and writer for children]

Leonard Holton (*Out of the Depths*; *The Saint Maker*)

Patrick O'Connor (*The Water Melon Mystery*; *Seawind from Hawaii*)

Christopher Webb (*The Quest of the Otter*; *Matt Tyler's Chronicle*)

WICHE, John [1718–94, English Baptist cleric and religious writer]

Nazaraeus (in the *Theological Repository*)

Philocatholicus (*A Defence of the Rev. Dr Foster's Sermon*; *An Idea of Christian Communion and Christian Discipline*)

WICKER, Thomas [1926–, US journalist and writer]

Paul Connolly (*Get Out of Town*; *Treasure for Angels*)

WICKLIFFE, Robert [d. 1850, US political writer]

William Pitt (*Letters to the Hon. James T. Morehead*)

WIENER, Norbert [1894–1964, German-born US mathematician and science-fiction writer]

W. Norbert (in the *Magazine of Fantasy and Science Fiction*)

WIERZBICKI, Felix Paul [d. 1861, Polish-born US writer]

Philokalist (*The Ideal Man*)

WIGHT, James [1916–, English writer of veterinary novels]

James Herriot (*If Only They Could Talk*; *All Creatures Great and Small*)

WIGHTWICK, George [1802–72, English architect and dramatist]

An Architect (in *Bentley's Miscellany*)

Brother Locke; Roger B. F.; Somno B. F.; Tuck B. F. (all used in *Fraser's Magazine*)

Henry Vernon (*The Life and Remains of Wilmot Warwick*)

WIKOFF, Henry [1813–84, US traveller and diplomat]

An Idler (*Reminiscences of 1823–40*)

A New Yorker (*A New Yorker in the Foreign Office*)

WILBERFORCE, Samuel [1805–73, English cleric and historian; Bishop of Winchester]

A Country Clergyman (*The Note-Book of a Country Clergyman*)

The Cowkeeper (in *John Bull Magazine*)

WILBRAHAM, Sybella [d. 1871, English writer]

An Experienced Chaperone (in *MacMillan's Magazine*)

WILBY, Basil Leslie [1930–, English occult writer]

Gareth Knight (*Experience of the Inner Worlds*; *The Practice of Ritual Magic*)

WILCOX, Collin [1924–, US mystery writer]
Carter Wick (*The Faceless Man*)

WILCOX, Harry [fl. 1960, English writer]
Mark Derby (*Element of Risk*; *Sun in the Hunter's Eye*)

WILCOX, Phineas Bacon [1796–1863, US lawyer]
A Member of the Bar (*A Few Thoughts*)

WILD, Robert [1609–79, English Puritan cleric, satirist and poet]
A Lover of Learning; A Rural Pen (both used in *Iter Boreale*)

WILDE, Lady Jane Francesca [1826–96, Irish poet and writer – mother of Oscar Wilde below]
Speranza (in *The Nation* and for *Poems* and *Ugo Bassi*)

WILDE, Oscar Fingal O'Flahertie Wills [1854–1900, Irish dramatist, poet and wit]
C. 3. 3. (*The Ballad of Reading Gaol*)
Sebastian Melmoth (*The Satyrican of Petronius*)

WILDING, Philip [fl. 1956, English science-fiction writer]
John Robert Haynes (*The Scream from Outer Space*)

WILDMAN, Sir John [1621–93, English indefatigable plotter and pamphleteer]
J. Howldin (*The Lawes of Subversion, or Sir John Maynard's Case*)
John Lawmind (*Putney Projects, or the Old Serpent in a New Forme*)

WILKES, John [1727–97, English politician and controversial essayist]
A Member of Parliament (*Observations on the Rupture with Spain*)

WILKIE, Frank B. [1832–92, US writer]
Poliuto (*Sketches Beyond the Sea*; *Petrolia. or the Oil Regions of the United States*)

WILKINS, Isaac [1741–1830, US cleric and loyalist]
A Country Gentleman (*Short Advice to the Counties of New York*)

WILKINS, William Henry [1860–1905, English novelist and biographer]
W. H. De Winton (*Forbidden Sacrifice*; *St Michael's Eve*)

WILKINSON, Iris Guiver [1906–39, South African-born New Zealand journalist and novelist]
Robin Hyde (*Dragon Rampant*; *Passport to Hell*)

WILKINSON, James John Garth [1812–99, English Swedenborgian philosopher]
John Lone (*Painting with both Hands*)

WILKINSON, John [1821–91, US confederate sailor]
A Blockade Runner (*Narrative of a Blockade Runner*)

WILKINSON, Louis Umfreville [1881–1966, English biographer and novelist]
Louis Marlow (*The Devil in Crystal*; *The Puppet's Dallying*; *Seven Friends*)

WILKINSON, William Francis [1812–79, English cleric]
A Churchman (*The Rector in Search of a Curate*)

WILKINSON, Sir William Henry [1858–1930, English orientalist and consular official in China]
Khanhoo (*Bridge Maxims*)

WILKS, John [d. 1846, English lawyer, politician and fraudster]
One who Has a Good Memory (in *Fraser's Magazine*)

WILLARD, John [1792–1862, US jurist]
Platt Potter (*A Treatise on Equity Jurisprudence*)

WILLARD, Joseph [1738–1804, American cleric and academic]
A Late Student at Harvard College (*Ames's Almanack Revised and Improved*)
Sympathes (*Poetical Elegy*)

WILLARD, Josiah Flynt [1869–1907, US writer]
Josiah Flynt (*The Little Brother – a Story of Tramp Life*; *My Life*; *Notes of an Itinerant Policeman*; *The Rise of Roderick Clowd*; *Tramping with Tramps*)

WILLARD, Samuel [1775–1859, US cleric]
A Friend of Youth (*The Franklin Family Primer*)

WILLCOX, Orlando Bolivar [1823–1907, US soldier]
Major March (*Faca: an Army Memoir*)
Walter March (*Shoepac Recollections*)

WILLES, Irwin [d. 1871, English sporting writer]
Argus (in the *Morning Post*)

WILLIAMS, Mrs Catherine Read [1787–1872, US writer]
A Rhode Islander (*Might and Right*)

WILLIAMS, Christopher a Beckett [1890–?, English composer and journalist]
Sinjon Wood (used when editor of *Musical Opinion*, 1923–30)

WILLIAMS, Colin [1934–, English actor and playwright]
Colin Welland (*Roomful of Holes*; *Say Goodnight to Grandma*)

WILLIAMS, David [1738–1816, English cleric and religious writer]
An Old Statesman (*Lessons to a Young Prince*)
Philander (*Letters Concerning Education*)

WILLIAMS, Edward [1746–1826, Welsh stonemason, bookseller and bardic poet]
Iolo Morganwg (*Poems, Lyric and Pastoral*)

WILLIAMS, Edwin [1797–1854, US journalist and writer]
*The Berkeley Men (*From Charles Bonaparte to Napoleon II*; *The Napoleon Dynasty*)

WILLIAMS, Elisha Scott [1757–1845, US cleric]
A Friend of Truth (*A Serious and Familiar Dialogue Concerning Baptism*)

WILLIAMS, Ella Gwendolyn Rees [1894–1979, English novelist]
Jean Rhys (*Good Morning Midnight*; *Sleep it off Lady*)

WILLIAMS, George Valentine [1883–1946, English mystery writer]
Douglas Valentine (*The Man with the Club Foot*)

WILLIAMS, Gordon [1939–, Scottish journalist and crime writer]
*P. B. Yuill (*Hazel and the Menacing Jester*; *Hazel Plays Solomon*)

WILLIAMS, Harold [1853–1926, US novelist]
George Afterem (*Mr and Mrs Morton*; *Silken Threads*)

WILLIAMS, Miss Helena Maria [1762–1827, English verse writer and Francophile]
An English Lady (*A Residence in France during the Years 1792 ...1795*)
A Young Lady (*Edwin and Eltruda*)

WILLIAMS, Henry Llewellyn [1842–?, Welsh writer]
An Elector (*Why I Am a Conservative*)
M. Mikael Gortschakov (*The Mysteries of St Petersburg*)
An Old Traveller (*Gay Life in New York!*)

WILLIAMS, Jay [1914–78, US mystery novelist and writer for children]
Michael Delving (*Die Like a Man*; *No Sign of Life*)

WILLIAMS, Jeanne [1930–, US novelist]
Jeanne Crecy (*The Lightning Tree*; *The Evil Among Us*)
Kristin Michaels (*Song of the Heart*; *Enchanted Twilight*)
Deirdre Rowan (*Shadow of the Volcano*)

WILLIAMS, John [1636–1709, English cleric and controversialist; Bishop of Chichester]
A Protestant Divine (*A Sermon Preached upon Fifth November 1678*)
A Protestant of the Church of England (*A Catechism Truly Representing the Doctrines and Practices of the Church of Rome with an Answer Thereunto*)

WILLIAMS, John [1761–1818, English playwright and satirist – worked sometime in New York]
Anthony Pasquin (*The Hamiltoniad; The Children of Thespis; The Eccentricities of John Edwin, Comedian*)

WILLIAMS, Joshua [1813–81, English barrister and legal writer]
J. Brain – Workman (*A Few Words on Reform Addressed to John Handy – Workman*)

WILLIAMS, Lambert F. [fl. 1904, English writer]
*Eleanor G. Linne (*The Virgin and the Fool*)

WILLIAMS, Margaret Wetherby [fl. 1960, Canadian-born English mystery writer]
Margaret Erskine (*Give up the Ghost; Case with Three Husbands*)

WILLIAMS, Peggy Eileen Arabella [1909–58, English novelist and poet]
Margiad Evans (*Country Dance; Ray of Darkness*)

WILLIAMS, Richard D'Alton [1822–62, Irish physician and poet]
Shamrock (in *The Nation*)

WILLIAMS, Robert Moore [1907–78, US science-fiction writer]
Robert Moore (in *Astounding Science Fiction* magazine)

WILLIAMS, Rowland [1817–70, Welsh cleric and Hebraist]
Goronva Camlan (*Lays from the Cimbric Lyre; Orestes and the Avengers*)

WILLIAMS, Samuel B. [fl. 1849, US writer]
Publius (*Publius on Banking; Thoughts on Finance and Colonies*)

WILLIAMS, Sarah [d. 1868, English poet]
Sadie (*Twilight Hours*)

WILLIAMS, Thomas Lanier [1911–83, US playwright]
Tennessee Williams (*Baby Doll; Cat on a Hot Tin Roof; The Glass Menagerie*)

WILLIAMS, William Carlos [1883–1963, US physician and poet]
Bill Exe (in the *Transatlantic Review*)

WILLIAMSON, Alice Muriel [1869–1933, US novelist]
An English Governess (*What I Found Out in the House of a German Prince*)
Alice Stuyvesant (*The Vanity Box*)

WILLIAMSON, Hugh [1735–1819, US writer]
A Gentleman (*A Description of the Genesee Country*)
A Native of Pennsylvania (*The Plea of the Colonies on the Charge Brought Against Them by Lord Mansfield*)
Sylvius (*Letters from Sylvius*)

WILLIAMSON, John Stewart [1908–,US science-fiction writer]
Will Stewart (in *Astounding Science Fiction* magazine and for *Seetee Ship* and *Seetee Shock*)

WILLIAMSON, Julia May [1859–1909, US poet and teacher]
Laura Bell (*Echoes of Time and Tide; The Choir of the Year*)

WILLIAMSON, Stephen [1827–1903, English merchant and writer on economics]
A Twelve Years' Resident (in *MacMillan's Magazine*)

WILLIAMSON, Thames Ross [1894–?, US novelist and writer for children]
Dragonet (*Beyond the Great Wall; Saltar the Mongol*)

Waldo Fleming (*The Island Mystery*; *The Lost Caravan*)

S. S. Smith (*The Falcon Mystery*)

WILLIAMSON, William Henry [fl. 1930, English writer]

W. Dane Bank (*James*; *An Average Woman*)

W. Shaw Heath (*Woman Guides*)

WILLIS, Browne [1682–1760, English lawyer and ecclesiastical historian]

A Gentleman (*The Whole Duty of Man Considered*)

WILLIS, (Lord) Edward Henry [1918–92, English dramatist, crime and mystery writer]

John Bishop (*Sabotage*)

WILLIS, George A. A. [1897–1976, Canadian-born English novelist and humorist]

A. A. (in *Punch*)

Anthony Armstrong (*We Keep Going*; *The Laughter Omnibus*)

WILLIS, Nathaniel Parker [1806–67, US poet , novelist and journalist]

Philip Slingsby (in the *London Magazine*)

WILLIS, Robert [1799–1878, Scottish physician and medical writer]

A Physician (*A Dialogue by way of Catechism*; *The Pentateuch and Book of Joshua*)

WILLIS, Sarah Payson [1811–72, US novelist and writer]

Fanny Fern (*Fern Leaves*; *Ruth Hall*)

WILLISON, John [1680–1750, Scottish cleric and religious writer]

A Lover of the Church of Scotland (*Queries to the Scots Innovators in Divine Service*)

A Minister of the Church of Scotland (*A Defense of National Churches*)

A Parochial Bishop (*A Letter from a Parochial Bishop concerning the Government of the Church*)

WILLMOTT, Robert Eldridge Aris [1809–63, English cleric and writer]

A Berkshire Clergyman; The Harrovian (both used in *Fraser's Magazine*)

WILLS, James [1790–1868, Irish lawyer, cleric and poet]

George Faithful Mendax (in *Dublin University Magazine*)

WILLS, Thomas [fl. 1804, US writer]

Lysander (*A Correct Statement of the Late Melancholy Affair of Honor between General Hamilton and Col. Burr*)

WILLSON, Gordon Beckles [1901–54, English journalist]

Gordon Beckles (*Tankard Travels*; *Dunkirk and After*)

WILLYAMS, Miss Jane Louisa [1786–1878, English poet]

An Old Friend (*The Reason Rendered*)

WILMER, Ringgold [1885–1933, US journalist]

Jack Keefe (in the *Chicago Tribune*)

Ring Lardner (*Gullible's Travels*)

WILMOT, Frank Leslie Thomson [1881–1942, Australian writer and poet]

Furnley Maurice (*Path to Parnassus*; *Melbourne Odes*; *The Gully and Other Verses*)

WILMOT, James Reginald [fl. 1938, English journalist and crime novelist]

Frances Stewart (*Love is a Patient Thing*; *Such Love is Dangerous*)

Ralph Trevor (*Death Burns the Candle*; *Front Page Murder*)

WILMOT, John [1647–80, 2nd Earl of Rochester; profligate libertine and poet]

A Person of Honour (*A Satyr against Mankind*; *Upon Nothing: a Poem*)

WILSON, Andrew [1718–92, Scottish physician, philosopher and medical writer]

A Gentleman (*Human Nature Surveyed by Philosophy and Revelation*)

A Physician (*An Essay on the Autumnal Dysentery*)

WILSON, Anthony [fl. 1793, English lexicographer]
Henry Bromley (*Catalogue of Engraved British Portraits*)

WILSON, Augusta J. Evans [1835–1909, US novelist]
Augusta J. Evans (*St Elmo*)

WILSON, Daniel [1778–1858, English cleric and preacher; Bishop of Calcutta)
An Absent Brother (*Letters from an Absent Brother*)

WILSON, Daniel [1816–92, Scottish educationalist and archaeologist – sometime in Canada]
Wil. D'Leina Esq. of the Outer Temple (*Spring Wild Flowers*)
D. Doubleyowe (*Ane Aulde Prophecie, Bot Doubtebe Merlyne*)
A Modern Minstrel (*Saint Catherine of the Nopes*)

WILSON, Florence Roma Muir [1891–1930, English novelist and writer]
Romer Wilson (*Dragon's Blood*; *The Death of Society*)

WILSON, George Louis Rosa [fl. 1936, Scottish poet]
Harry Crouch (*The Poet Anthology of 1937*)
Frank Erskine (*Dream Pedlary*)

WILSON, Herbert Wrigley [1866–1940, English journalist and essayist]
An Englishman (in *Temple Bar*)
Ignotus; The Man in the Street (both used in *National Review*)

WILSON, James [d. 1787, Scottish poet and writer]
Claudero (*Arts Catchpolaria, or the Art of Destroying Mankind*)

WILSON, James [1795–1856, Scottish natural historian and zoologist]
An Animal Painter (*Photographed Illustrations of Scripture Animals*)
A Naturalist (*Illustrations of Scripture*)

WILSON, James Arthur [1795–1882, English physician and medical writer]
Maxilla (in the *London Gazette*)
One of the Medici (*The Duke of Florence*)

WILSON, James Grant [1832–1914, Scottish-born US editor and biographer]
Allan Grant (*Mr Secretary Pepys*; *Love in Letters*)

WILSON, James Patriot [1769–1830, US cleric]
A Christian (*Moral Agency or Natural Ability*)

WILSON, John [1785–1854, Scottish philosopher and essayist]
Aquilius (in *Gentleman's Magazine*)
The late Arthur Austin (*Lights and Shadows of Scottish Life*)
An Early Riser; Eremus; Polyanthus; Siluriensis; Jasper Sussex (all used in *Blackwood's Magazine*)
Mordecai Mullion (*Some Illustrations of Mr M'Culloch's Principals of Political Economy*)
Christopher North (in *Blackwood's Magazine* and for *The City of the Plague* and *Heart-Break, the Trials of Literary Life*)

WILSON, John Anthony Burgess [1917–93, English novelist and critic; *English Literature for Students: a Survey for Students* was published in 1958 under his real name]
Anthony Burgess (his usual writing name – *The Clockwork Orange*, etc.)
Joseph Kell (*One Hand Clapping*; *Inside Mr Enderby*)

WILSON, Joyce Muriel [1924–, English novelist and writer for children]
Joyce Stranger (*Lakeland Vet*; *Never Tell a Secret*)

WILSON, Margaret [1882–1973, US novelist]
An Elderly Spinster (in the *Atlantic Review*)

WILSON, Matthias [1582–1656, English Jesuit]
Edward Knott (*Infidelity Unmasked; Charity Mistaken*)
Nicholas Smith, S. J. (*A Modest Briefe Discussion of Some Points Taught by M. Doctour Kellison etc.*)

WILSON, Richard [1920–, US science-fiction writer and journalist]
Edward Halibut (in *Astonishing Stories* magazine)

WILSON, Richard Henry [1870–?, US writer]
Richard Fisguill (*Venus of Cadiz*)

WILSON, Robert Arthur [1820–75, Irish journalist and humorist – sometime in USA]
Jonathan Allman; Erin Oge; Young Ireland (all used in the *Ulster Weekly News*)
Barney Maglone (in the *Boston Republic*)

WILSON, Robert McNair [1882–1963, Scottish physician, medical journalist and crime writer]
Anthony Wynne (*The Toll House Murder; Murder in a Church*)

WILSON, Stanley Kidder [1879–1944, US writer]
Pliny the Youngest (*Guess Who?*)

WILSON, Thomas [1703–84, English cleric]
A Sufferer (*A Review of the Building of a New Square at Wesrminster*)

WILSON, William [1690–1741, Scottish cleric and religious writer]
A Minister of the Church of Scotland (*The Douay-Elder Unmasked*)

WILSON, Sir William James Erasmus [1809–84, English surgeon and medical writer]
A Quiet Observer (*Quiet Observations on the Ways of the World*)

WILSON, William Rae [1772–1849, Scottish solicitor and traveller]
A Veteran Traveller (*Notes Abroad and Rhapsodies at Home*)

WIMHURST, Cecil Gordon E. [1905–, English crime novelist and writer on dogs]
Nigel Brent (*No Space for Murder; The Scarlet Lily*)

WINCHELL, Prentice [1895–?, US crime and mystery writer]
Spencer Dean (*The Merchant of Murder; Credit for Murder*)
Jay de Bekker (*Keyhole Peeper*)
Dexter St Clair (*The Lady's Not for Living*)
Stewart Sterling (*Down Among the Dead Men*)

WINCHESTER, Samuel Gover [1805–41, US cleric]
Wickliffe (*The People's Right Defended*)

WINDER, Mavis [fl. 1965, New Zealand romantic novelist]
Mavis Areta (*Shadowed Journey; The Gulf Between*)

WINDHAM, William [1717–61, English soldier in Hungary and writer on military subjects]
An English Gentleman (*An Account of the Glaciers or Ice Alps in the Savoy*)

WINGATE, Charles Frederick [1848–1909, US engineer and journalist]
Carlfried (*Views and Interviews on Journalism*)

WINGFIELD, Lewis Strange [1842–91, Irish actor, journalist and novelist]
Whyte Tyghe (in *The Globe*)

WINNER, Septimus [1827–1902, US songwriter]
Alice Hawthorne (*Hawthorne Ballads*)

WINSLOW, Forbes Benignus [1810–74, English physician and medical writer]
Medicus (*On the Nature of Symptoms and Treatment of Cholera*)

WINSLOW, Hubbard [1800–64, US cleric]
Evangelus Pacificus (*The Evangelical View of Regeneration*)

WINSLOW, Pauline Glen [fl. 1980, English mystery writer]
Jane Sheridan (*Damaris*; *Love at Sunset*)

WINSOR, Frederick Albert [1763–1830, German inventor and pioneer of gas lighting – sometime in England]
Obadiah Prim (*An Address to the Sovereigns of Europe*)

WINSTANLEY, William [1628–98, English barber and writer]
Poor Robin (used for *Poor Robin's Almanac*)

WINSTON, Charles [1814–64, English barrister and authority on glass painting]
An Amateur (*An Inquiry into the Difference of Style Observable in Ancient Glass Paintings, Especially in England*)

WINSTON, Sarah [1912–, US writer]
Sarah Lorenz (*And Always Tomorrow*)

WINTER, Bevis [1918–, English crime writer]
Al Bocca (*Trouble Calling*; *No Room at the Morgue*)
Peter Cagney (*A Grave for Madam*; *Hear the Stripper Scream*)
Gordon Shayne (*Ticket to Eternity*; *And So to Death*)

WINTER, Mrs Elizabeth Campbell [1841–1922, Scottish-born US novelist]
Isabella Castelar (*The Spanish Treasure*)

WINTERBOTHAM, Russell Robert [1904–71, US journalist, science-fiction and western novelist]
J. Harvey Bond (*The Other World*)
Franklin Hadley (*Planet Big Zero*)

WINTERTON, Paul [1911–, English crime and mystery writer]
Roger Bax (*Blueprint for Murder*; *The Trouble with Murder*)
Andrew Garve (*No Mask for Murder*; *A Hole in the Ground*)
Paul Somers (*Operation Piracy*; *Broken Jigsaw*)

WINTHROP, Laura [1825–89, US poet]
Emily Hare (*Poems of Twenty Years*; *Little Blossom's Reward*)

WIRT, William [1772–1834, US lawyer]
The British Spy (*The Letters of the British Spy*)

WISE, Arthur [1923–, English mystery writer]
John McArthur (*Days in the Hay*; *How Now Brown Cow*)

WISE, Daniel [1813–98, English-born US cleric and writer]
Cousin Clara (*The Lindendale Stories*)
Francis Forrester Esq. (*Ben Blinker or, Maggie's Golden Motto*; *Nat and his Chum*; *Florence Baldwin's Picnic*)
Lawrence Lancewood Esq. (*Nellie Warren or, The Last Watch*; *Sydney De Grey or, The Rival School-Boys*)

WISE, Francis [1695–1767, English archaeologist, librarian and cleric]
A Member of the Society of Antiquaries, London (*History and Chronology of the Fabulous Ages Considered*; *Some Enquiries Concerning the First Inhabitants of Europe*)

WISE, Henry Augustus [1819–69, US mariner and novelist]
Harry Gringo (*Los Gringos*; *Captain Brand*)

WISE, James Waterman [1901–, US writer]
Analyticus (*Jews are Like That*)

WISE, John [1652–1725, American cleric and religious writer]
Amicus Patriae (*A Word of Comfort to a Melancholy Country*)

WISE, Thomas James [1859–1937, English bibliophile and forger]
*Charles Alfred Seymour (*Poems and Sonnets of Percy Bysshe Shelley*)

WISHART, William [fl. 1739, Scottish academic]
Gwitmarpscheldon (*The Principles of Liberty and Conscience Defended*)

WITHAM, Robert [d. 1738, English biblical scholar]
Theophilus Eupistinus (*Remarks on the Lives of the Saints*)

WITHER, George [1588–1667, English satirist, poet and hymn writer]
Britain's Remembrancer (*A Suddain Flash Timely Discovering Some Reasons etc.*)
A Free-Man, though a Prisoner (*What Peace to the Wicked?*)

WITHERBY, William [1758–1840, English merchant]
A Layman (*A Review of Scripture*)

WITHERS, Philip [d. 1790, English cleric – imprisoned for libel]
Alfred (*Alfred's Apology*)
A Page of the Presence (*History of the Royal Malady*)

WITHERSPOON, Orlando [fl. 1882, US writer]
Democritus Junior (*Doctor Ben*)

WITHINGTON, Leonard [1789–1885, US cleric]
John Oldbug Esq. (*The Puritan*)
The Thirty-One (*Penitential Tears*)

WITOSZEK, Nina [1959–, Polish-born Irish writer]
Nina Fitzpatrick (*Fables of the Irish Intelligentsia*)

WIX, Edward [1802–66, English cleric]
A Newfoundland Missionary (*Six Months of a Newfoundland Missionary's Journal 1835*)

WODEHOUSE, Pelham Grenville [1881–1975, English writer for boys, playwright and whimsical novelist]
*Basil Windham (used in *Chums* magazine for a story written with his friend William Townend)

WODHULL, Michael [1740–1816, English book collector and translator]
A Gentleman of Oxford (*An Ode to Criticism*)

WOLCOT, John [1738–1819, English physician, cleric, satirist and poet]
P. Hamlin, Tinman (*The Horrors of Bribery*)
Brother Peter (*Brother Peter to Brother Tom*)

Peter Pindar (*Lyric Odes; The Apple Dumplings and a King; Six Picturesque Views from Printings; Tristia: or the Sorrows of Peter*)
John Ploughshare (*The Royal visit to Exeter*)

WOLCOTT, Oliver [1760–1833, US politician]
Marcus (*British Influence in the Affairs of the United States*)

WOLF, Lucien [1857–1930, English writer on Jewish and current affairs]
Diplomaticus (*The Struggle for South African Supremacy*)

WOLFORD, Frank [fl. 1864, US soldier]
A Union Army Officer (*Military Tyranny Denounced*)

WOLFSON, Victor [1910–, US playwright and novelist]
Langdon Dodge (*Midsummer Madness*)

WOLLASTON, Francis [1731–1815, English cleric]
A Country Parson (*A Country Parson's Address to his Flock*)
A Private Man (*The Secret History of a Private Man*)

WOLLHEIM, Donald A. [1914–, US science-fiction writer]
Millard Verne Gordon (used in the following magazines: *Comet Stories; Cosmic Stories; Stirring Science Stories; Science Fiction; Science Fiction Quarterly; Future Fantasy and Science Fiction*)
David Grinnell (*Destiny's Orbit; Across Time*)
Martin Pearson (used in the following magazines: *Science Fiction Quarterly; Astounding Science Fiction; Stirring Science Stories; Astonishing Stories; Super Science Stories; Science Fiction Stories*)
Allen Warland (in the *Science Fiction Quarterly*)
Lawrence Woods (in *Stirring Science Stories* and *Future Fiction* magazines)

WOLSELEY, Sir Charles [1630–1714, English politician and religious pamphleteer]
A Protestant, a Lover of Peace and Prosperity of the Nation (*Liberty of Conscience, the Magistrate's Interest*)

WOLSELEY, Sir Garnet Joseph [1833–1913, Irish-born British soldier and field-marshal]
An English Officer; An Officer of the Expeditionary Force (both used in *Blackwood's Magazine*)
A Staff Officer (in *MacMillan's Magazine*)

WOLSTENHOLME-ELMY, Elizabeth C. [1834–1918, English suffragist, poet and writer]
Ellis Ethelmer (*The Human Flower*; *Woman Free*)
Ignota (in the *Westminster Review*)

WOOD, Anna Cogswell [fl. 1890, US novelist]
Algernon Ridgeway (*Diana Fontaine*; *The Westovers*)

WOOD, Barbara [1947–, English-born US novelist]
Kathryn Harvey (*Butterfly*)

WOOD, Charlotte Dunning [fl. 1886, US writer]
Charlotte Dunning (*A Step Aside*; *Upon a Cast*)

WOOD, Edgar Allardyce [1907–, Canadian journalist and writer for children]
Kerry Wood (*The Boy and the Buffalo*; *The Medicine Man*)

WOOD, Ellen (Mrs Henry) [1814–87, English novelist and short-story writer]
A Family Party (*Letters from the Irish Highlands of Connemara*)
Johnny Ludlow (in *Argosy Magazine*)
Thomas (or Ensign) Pepper (in *New Monthly Magazine*)

WOOD, Emma Caroline (Lady) [1802–79, English novelist]
C. Sylvester (*On Credit*; *Rose Warne*; *Ruling the Roast*)

WOOD, Eugene [1860–1923, US socialist, essayist and pamphleteer]
Harvey Sutherland (*The Book of Bugs*)

WOOD, Herbert William [1837–79, English soldier in India]
Philindus (in *MacMillan's Magazine*)

WOOD, John George [1827–89, English cleric and natural historian]
George Forrest Esq., MA (*Every Boy's Book*; *An Account of the History of St Leonard's, Edinburgh*; *Handbook of Gymnastics*; *The Playground*; *Handbook of Swimming and Skating*)

WOOD, Mrs Julia Amanda [1825–1903, US poet and novelist]
Minnie Mary Lee (*Hubert's Wife*)

WOOD, Silas [1769–1847, US writer]
A Citizen of the United States (*Thoughts on the State of the American Indians*)

WOODBRIDGE, Benjamin [1622–84, English cleric]
Filodexter Transylvanus (*Church Members Set in Joynt*)

WOODGATE, Walter Bradford [1840–1920, English rower and sportsman]
Wat Bradwood (*Ensemble*; *A Hunt Cup or, Loyalty Before All!*; *The O. V. H. or, How Mr Blake became an M. F. H.*; *Reminiscences of an Old Sportsman*)

WOODHAM-SMITH, Cecil [1896–1977, Welsh historian and novelist]
Janet Gordon (*April Sky*; *Tennis Star*; *Just Off Bond Street*)

WOODHOUSE, Martin C. [1932–, English novelist and mystery writer]
John Charlton (*The Remington Set*)

WOODROFFE, Sir John George [1865–1936, English barrister, and jurist in India]
Arthur Avalon (*Hymns to the Goddess, from the Tantra*; *Principles of Tantra*; *Studies of the Mantra Shastra*; *Tantra of the Great Liberation*; *The Wave of Bliss*)

WOODRUFF, Julia Louisa Matilda
[1833–1909, US writer]
W. L. M. Jay (*Holden with Chords; The Daisy Seekers*)

WOODS, Joseph [1776–1864, English architect, traveller and botanist]
An Architect (*Letters of an Architect from France, Italy and Greece*)

WOODS, Thomas Baldwin [1810–70, English journalist]
Bryan O'Halloran (in *Bentley's Miscellany*)

WOOD-SEYS, Roland Alexander [1854–1919, US novelist]
Paul Cushing (in *Blackwood's Magazine*)

WOOD-SMITH, Noel [fl. 1927, English writer for boys]
Norman Taylor (in *Union Jack*)

WOODWARD, Annie Aubertine [fl. 1877, US poet]
Auber Forestier (*Echoes from Mist-Land; The Spell-Bound Fiddler*)

WOODWARD, Augustus Brevoort [1774–1827, US jurist]
Epaminondas (*Considerations on the Government of Columbia*)

WOODWARD, George Moutard [1760–1809, English caricaturist]
The Ghost of Willy Shakespeare (*Familiar Verses from the Ghost of Willy Shakespeare to Sammy Ireland*)

WOODWARD, George W. [1809–75, US jurist]
A Man who Wishes to be the Governor of Pennsylvania (*The Opinions of a Man who Wishes to be the Governor of Pennsylvania*)

WOODWARD, Henry [1714–77, English actor and dramatist]
Mr Lun, Junior (*The Beggar's Pantomime*)

WOODWARD, John [1665–1728, English physician and natural historian]
T. Byfield, MD (*The Two Sosias*)
Timothy Vanbustle (*The Art of Getting into Practice in Physic*)

WOODWARD, Joseph Janvier [1833–84, US writer]
Janvier (*Ada*)

WOODWARD, William Harrison [1855–1941, English educationalist and historian]
Evelyn B. Warde (*Elena*)

WOODWORTH, Francis Channing [1812–59, US printer and writer for children]
Uncle Frank (*Uncle Frank's Pleasant Pages for the Fireside*)
Theodore Thinker (*Jack Mason the Old Sailor; The Balloon and Other Stories*)

WOODWORTH, John [1768–1858, US lawyer]
An American Youth (*The Battle of Plattsburgh*)

WOODWORTH, Samuel [1785–1842, US poet, playwright and writer for children]
Selim (*Quarter Day; New-Haven*)

WOOLER, Thomas Jonathan [1786–1853, English journalist and writer]
The Black Dwarf (*A Political Lecture on Heads; The Kettle Abusing the Pot*)

WOOLF, Adeline Virginia [1882–1941, English novelist and essayist]
V. (in the *New Statesman* in 1923)

WOOLFOLK, Josiah Pitts [1894–?, US writer]
Sappho Henderson Britt (*Love in Virginia*)
Howard Kennedy (*Lady Killer; Lady Mislaid*)
Gordon Sayre (*Assistant Wife; Possessed*)
Jack Woodford (*White Meat; Delinquent*)

WOOLLEY, Catherine [1904–, US writer for children]
Jane Thayer (*Gus and the Baby Ghost; Little Mister Greenthumb*)

WOOLSEY, Sarah Chauncy [1835–1905, US writer for girls]
Susan Coolidge (*What Katy Did; What Katy Did Next*)

WOOLSON, Constance Fenimore
[1840–94, US novelist]
Anne March (*The Old Stone House; Two Women*)

WOOLSTON, Thomas [1670–1733, English cleric and religious controversialist]
Aristobulus (in *The Delphick Oracle* and for *A Letter to the Rev. Dr Bennet, Rector of St Giles*)
Mystagogus (*Dissertatio de Pontii Pilati ad Tiberium Epistola*)

WORBOISE, Emma Jane [1825–87, English novelist]
Emma Jane (*The Autobiography of Maude Bolingbroke*)

WORBOYS, Annette Isobel [fl. 1962, New Zealand romantic novelist]
Annette Eyre (*A Net to Catch the Wind; The House of Five Pines*)
Vicky Maxwell (*Other Side of Summer; Way of the Tamarisk*)
Anne Eyre Worboys (*Bhunda Jewels; Lion of Delos*)

WORCESTER, Leonard [1767–1846, US cleric]
Cephas (*Inquiries on the Doctrine of this Trinity*)

WORCESTER, Noah [1758–1837, US cleric and pacifist]
Philo Pacificus (*A Solemn Review of the Custom of War; The Friend of Peace*)
The Pilgrim Good Intent (*A Parable Occasioned by the late Portentous Phenomenon*)
Freeman L. Usher (*The Signal*)

WORCESTER, Samuel Melanchton [1801–66, US cleric]
Vigornius (*Essays on Slavery*)

WORCESTER, Thomas [1768–1831, US cleric]
Timothy (*A Letter to the Moderator of the New Hampshire Association*)

WORDSWORTH, Dame Elizabeth [1840–1932, English academic]
Grant Lloyd (*Thornwell Abbas; Ebb and Flow or, He Did His Best*)

WORDSWORTH, William [1770–1850, English Poet Laureate]
Axiologus (*Sonnet on Seeing Miss Helen Maria Williams*)
An Enemy to Detraction (letter in the *Westmorland Gazette*)
A Friend to Consistency; A Friend to Truth (both used in letters to the *Kendal Chronicle*)

WORLIDGE, John [fl. 1690, English agricultural writer and merchant]
J. W. (*A Compleat System of Husbandry ... Gardening ...*)

WORMSER, Richard E. [1908–77, US mystery writer]
Ed Friend (*The Scalp Hunters*)

WORNER, Philip [1910–, English poet and playwright]
Philip Incledon (*The Cactus Hedge*)
Philip Sylvester (*All Dreaming Gone; Freedom is my Fame*)

WORNUM, Ralph Nicholson [1812–77, English painter and art critic]
A Layman (*Saul of Tarsus*)

WORSFOLD, William Basil [1858–1939, English traveller and writer]
Godfrey Waytemore (*The Profiteer*)

WORSLEY, Sir Richard [1751–1805, English diplomat and politician]
Sir Finical Whimsy (*Memoirs of Sir Finical Whimsy and his Lady*)

WORTH, Gorham A. [1773–1856, US businessman]
Ignatius Jones (*Random Recollections of Albany from 1800–1808*)

WORTHINGTON, Thomas [1671–1754, Scottish Dominican monk and ecclesiastical historian]
An English Dominican (*An Introduction to the Catholic Faith*)

WORTHINGTON-STUART, Brian Arthur
[fl. 1954, English writer]
Peter Meredith (*The Crocodile Man*; *Sands of the Desert*)
Brian Stuart (*The Serpent's Fangs*; *The Silver Phantom Murder*)

WORTS, George Frank [1892–?, US writer]
Loring Brent (*No More a Corpse*; *The Return of George Washington*)

WOTHERSPOON, George Ralph Howard
[1897–1979, English writer and humorist]
Woon (in *Punch*)

WOTY, William [1731–91, English solicitor's clerk and verse writer]
J. Copywell of Lincoln's Inn (*The Shrubs of Parnassus*)

WRANGHAM, Francis [1769–1842, English cleric and classical scholar]
S. Foote Jun. (*Reform, a Farce Modernised from Aristophanes*)
Sciolus (in the *York Herald*)

WRAXALL, Frederic Charles Lascelles
[1828–65, English novelist and military writer]
A Cavalry Officer; An Eight Hundred a Year Man; One of the Browns (all used in *Bentley's Miscellany*)

WRAY, W. Fitzwater [d. 1938, English journalist and illustrator]
Kuklos (*A Vagabond's Note-Book*)

WREFORD, Henry [1806–92, English journalist]
An English Resident in that City (*Rome, Pagan and Papal*)

WRIGHT, Abraham [1611–90, English cleric, epigramist and writer]
Abraham Philotheus (*Anarchie Reviving*)

WRIGHT, Elizur [1804–85, US journalist and writer]
A Democrat of the Old School (*The Programme of Peace*)
A Friend of the Road (*The Northern Pacific Railroad*)

One of the Eighteen Millions of Bores (*Perforations in the Latter-Day Pamphlets*)

WRIGHT, Hezekiah Hartley [d. 1840, US traveller and writer]
An American (*Desultory Reminiscences of a Tour through Germany*)

WRIGHT, Lionel Percy [1923–, English novelist]
Lan Wright (*Who Speaks of Conquest?*; *The Last Hope of Earth*)

WRIGHT, Mrs Mabel Osgood [1859–1934, US naturalist and novelist]
Barbara (*The Open Window*; *The Woman Errant*)

WRIGHT, Mary Patricia [1932–, English romantic novelist]
Mary Napier (*Blind Chance*; *Forbidden Places*)

WRIGHT, Richard [1764–1836, English cleric, Unitarian and theological writer]
Beccaria Anglicus (*Letters on Capital Punishments*)

WRIGHT, Robert William [1816–65, US lawyer]
U. Bet (*The Pious Chi-Neh*)
Horatius Flaccus (*The Church Knaviad, or Horace in West Haven*)
Quevedo Redivivus Jun. (*The Vision of Judgment*)

WRIGHT, Samuel [1683–1746, English nonconformist cleric]
*Bagweel (*A Collection of Occasional Papers*)

WRIGHT, Sydney Fowler [1874–1965, English accountant, poet and novelist]
Sydney Fowler (*The Island of Captain Sparrow*; *The Bell Street Murders*)
Alan Seymour (*Scenes from Morte D'Arthur*; *Was Murder Done?*; *The Hand-Print Mystery*)
Anthony Wingrave (*The Vengeance of Gwa*)

WRIGHT, Thomas [1810–77, English historian and archaeologist]
An Antiquary (*Wanderings of an Antiquary*)

WRIGHT, Thomas [fl. 1870, English writer]
Journeyman Engineer (*Johnny Robinson*; *Our New Masters*; *Some Habits and Customs of the Working Classes*; *Bill Banks's Day Out*)
The Riverside Visitor (*The Pinch of Poverty*; *The Great Army*)
A Working Man (in *Fraser's Magazine*)

WRIGHT, Willard Huntington [1888–1939, US journalist and crime writer]
S. S. van Dine (*The Benson Murder Case*; *The Scarab Murder Case*)

WRIGHT, William [1773–1860, English surgeon and medical writer]
A Surgeon-Aurist (*A Few Minutes' Advice to Deaf Persons*)

WYCHERLEY, Richard Newman [fl. 1908, English Methodist writer]
Gilbert Murray (*The Methodist Class-Meeting*)

WYETH, Joseph [1663–1731, English Quaker]
A Quaker (*The Athenian Society Unavail'd*)

WYMAN, Rufus [d. 1842, US physician]
A Tything Man (*Remarks on the Observance of the Lord's Day*)

WYND, Oswald, [1913–, Scottish mystery novelist]
Gavin Black (*Bitter Tea*; *Eyes Around Me*)

WYNDHAM, Horace Cowley [1873–1970, English writer]
Reginald Auberon (*The Nineteen Hundreds*)

WYNN, Miss Frances Williams [1780–1857, Welsh writer]
A Lady of Quality (*Diaries of a Lady of Quality*)

WYNTER, Andrew [1819–76, English physician and medical writer]
Werdna Retnyw (*Odds and Ends from an Old Drawer*; *Pictures of Town and Country Life*)

WYSE, Thomas [1791–1862, Irish politician and writer]
Dr Abraham Eldon (*The Continental Traveller's Oracle*)

WYSE, William Charles Bonaparte [1826–92, English poet and writer]
A Grand Nephew of Napoleon the Great (*In Memoriam of the Prince Imperial of France*)

Y

YARBRO, Chelsea Quinn [1942–, US fantasy novelist]
Terry Nelson Bonner (*The Making of Australia – The Outback*)
Vanessa Pryor (*A Taste of Wine*)

YATE, Arthur Campbell [1853–1929, English soldier in India]
A British Field Officer (*The Army and the Press in 1900*)

YATES, Abraham [1724–96, American politician]
Rough Hewer Jun. (*Political Papers*)

YATES, Alan Geoffrey [1923–85, English crime writer]
Carter Brown (*The Rip-Off*; *Strawberry Blonde Jungle*)

YATES, Edmund [1831–94, English journalist, drama critic and novelist]
The Flaneur (in the *Morning Star*)
The Lounger at the Clubs (in the *Illustrated Times*)
Mrs Seaton (in *The Queen*)
*Two Merry Men (*Mirth and Metre*)

YAUKEY, Grace Sydenstricker [1899–, US writer – sister of Pearl S. Buck]
Cornelia Spencer (*China Trader*; *The Missionary*)

YEARDLEY, Mrs Martha Savory [1782–1851, English Quaker]
Mrs Smith (*Pathetic Tales Founded on Facts*)

YEARSLEY, Mrs Ann [1756–1806, English poet and novelist]
Lactilla (*Poems*)

YEATES, Mabel [fl. 1935, English writer]
*Hasani Muhammed Askari (*The Food of Kings*)

YEATS, Jack Butler [1871–1957, London-born Irish artist, novelist and playwright]
William Bird (in *Punch*)

YEATS, William Butler [1865–1939, Irish poet, critic and dramatist]
D. E. D. I. (in the *Irish Theosophist*)
Ganconagh (*John Sherman and Dhoya*)
Rosicrux (in the *Dublin Daily Express*)
A Student of Irish Literature (*letters in United Ireland*)

YELDHAM, Walter [fl. 1865, English writer]
Aliph Cheem (*Lays of Ind*)

YELLOTT, George [fl. 1845, US humorist]
Bill Booby; Nathan Nobody (both used in *The Thompsonian Quack*)

YELVERTON, Sir Henry [1566–1629, English jurist]
A Late Eminent Judge of this Nation (*The Rights of the People Concerning Impositions*)

YIN, Leslie Charles Bowyer [1907–93, Singapore-born English crime novelist]
Leslie C. Bowyer (in *Hutchinson's Sovereign Magazine*)
Leslie Charteris (*Saint on Guard*; *Saint versus Scotland Yard*)

YING, Ko Lien Hua [1883–?, Chinese poet and short-story teller]
Cyril Birch (*Chinese Myths and Fantasies*)

YONGE, Charlotte Mary [1823–1901, English novelist and writer for children]
Aunt Charlotte (*Aunt Charlotte's Evenings at Home with the Poets*)

YONGE, Duke John [1809–46, Scottish cleric]
Launcelot Pendennis (*Cornish Carelessness*)

YORKE, Charles [1722–70, English jurist]
A Late Lord Chancellor (*Two Speeches*)

YORKE, Henry Vincent [1905–73, English engineer and novelist]
Henry Green (*Living; Party Going*)

YORKE, Philip [1690–1764, 1st Earl of Hardwicke; lawyer, statesman and Lord Chancellor]
Philip Homebred (in *The Spectator*)

YOUD, Christopher Samuel [1922–, English science-fiction novelist and writer for children]
John Christopher (*The World in Winter; The Twenty-Second Century*)
Hilary Ford (*Felix Walking; Bella on the Roof*)
William Godfrey (*Malleson at Melbourne; The Friendly Game*)
Peter Graaf (*Daughter Fair; The Gull's Kiss*)
Peter Nichols (*Patchwork as Death*)
Anthony Rye (*The Inn of Birds; Poems from Selbourne*)

YOUNG, Alexander Bell Filson [1876–1938, Irish journalist and writer]
X-Rays (*A Psychic Vigil*)

YOUNG, Arthur [1741–1820, English agriculturist]
An Experienced Farmer (*The Farmer's Kalendar*)
A Farmer (*A Plain and Earnest Address to Britons, Especially Farmers*)
The Secretary to the Board of Agriculture (*A General View of the Agriculture of Hertfordshire; On the Husbandry of Three Celebrated Farmers; A View of the Agriculture of Oxfordshire*)

YOUNG, Bartholomew [fl. 1587, English Spanish scholar]
B. Giouano Del M. Temp (*Amorous Fiametta – a Translation*)

YOUNG, Edward [1683–1765, English satirist, cleric and poet]
John Lizard (in *The Guardian*)

YOUNG, Elizabeth Guion [1876–?, US short-story writer]
Baldwin Sears (*The Circle in the Square*)

YOUNG, Francis Crissey [fl. 1903, US writer]
One of The Clan (*Echoes from Arcadia: the Story of Central City*)

YOUNG, Sir George [1872–1952, English diplomat]
Yegor Yegorevitsch (in *Cornhill Magazine*)

YOUNG, Janet Randall [1919–, US western novelist]
Janet Randall (*Desert Venture; Island Ghost*)

YOUNG, John [d. 1808, Scottish writer]
Simplex (*An Inquiry into the Constitution of the Church of Christ; Letters Addressed to Soame Jenyns Esq.; A Letter to Mr James Baine*)

YOUNG, John [1811–78, Canadian merchant and politician]
Agricola (*Letters of Agricola on the Principle of Vegetation and Tillage*)

YOUNG, John Russell [1840–99, US journalist and diplomat]
An American Republican (in *MacMillan's Magazine*)

YOUNG, Mary Julia [fl. 1792, English writer]
A Lady (*Genius and Fancy, or Dramatic Sketches*)

YOUNG, Thomas [1587–1655, English cleric and controversialist]
*Smectymnuus (*An Answer to a Book etc.*)

YOUNGE, Richard [fl. 1653, English
Calvinist]
  R. Junius (*The Drunkard's Character*; *The
  Cure of Misprison*; *The Pastor's Advocate*;
  Self-Examination; *Sinne Stigmatized*)
  Junius Florilegus (*Philarguromastix*; *Carnal
  Reason or, The Wisdom of the Flesh*)

YULE, Sir Henry [1820–89, Scottish
orientalist and engineer in India]
  A Friend and Brother Officer (*Memorial of
  Maj.-Gen. W. W. H. Greathed*)
  *Two Old Friends, Brother Officers
  (*Memoir of Gen. Sir William Erskine
  Baker*)

Z

ZACHARY, Hugh [1918–, US writer]
Ginny Gorman (*Flames of Joy*)
Elizabeth Hughes (*The Legend of the Deadly Doll*)
Zach Hughes (*The Legend of Miaree*; *The Stork Factor*)
Evan Innes (*City in the Mist*)
Peter Kanto (*A Small Slice of War*; *Angel Baby*)
Derral Pilgrim (*Lolila*)
Olivia Rangley (*The Bashful Lesbian*)

ZAHM, John Augustine [1851–1921, US Catholic cleric and writer]
H. J. Mozans (*Along the Andes and Down the Amazon*; *From Berlin to Bagdad to Babylon*)

ZAJDLER, Zoe [fl. 1934, Irish journalist and writer]
Martin Hare (*If This Be Error*)

ZAMENHOF, Lazarus Ludovic [1859–1917, Polish occulist and inventor of Esperanto]
Dr Esperanto (*An Attempt towards an International Language*)

ZELAZNY, Roger [1937–, US fantasy and science-fiction writer]
Harrison Denmark (in *Amazing Stories* magazine)

ZIEGLER, Edward William [1932–, US science-fiction writer]
Theodore Tyler (*The Man Whose Name Wouldn't Fit*)

ZILLIACUS, Konni [1894–1967, Japanese-born English socialist politician and writer]
Covenanter (*Labour and War Resistance*)
Vigilantes (*Why the League has Failed*; *Inquest on Peace*)
Roth Williams (*The Technique of the League of Nations*)

ZIM, Sonia Elizabeth [1919–, Russian-born US anthropologist]
Sonia Bleeker (*Life and Death*)

ZINBERG, Leonard S. [1911–68, US crime and mystery writer]
Steve April (*Route 13*)
Ed Lacy (*Bugged for Murder*; *Pity the Honest*)

ZOLLINGER, Miss Gulielma [fl. 1897, US writer]
William Zachary Gladwin (used for contributions in serial form to periodicals)

ZOLOTOW, Charlotte [1915–, US writer for children]
Sara Abbott (*Where I Begin*; *The Old Dog*)
Charlotte Bookman (*The City Boy and the Country Horse*)

ZORNLIN, Mrs Elizabeth [1770–1851, English poet]
A Lady (*An Ode Written upon the Victory and Death of Nelson*)

ZOUCH, Thomas [1737–1815, English cleric, biographer and religious writer]
A Country Clergyman (*A Letter to Bishop Horsey*)

ZUBLY, John J. [1724–81, Swiss-born American cleric and writer]
A Freeholder of South Carolina (*An Humble Enquiry into Dependancy of the American Colonies*)